HUNTS' HIGHLIGHTS
of
MICHIGAN

Mary and Don Hunt

Albion, Michigan

Hunts' Highlights of Michigan, Third Edition
Copyright 1996 by Mary and Don Hunt

For information, call Midwestern Guides, (517) 629-4494
or write Box 477, Albion, MI 49224.

Credits for illustrations
Mark J. Arpin 201. Copyright Jerry Berta 429. Binder Park Zoo 112. Wayne Bronner 375. Sharon McInturff Burton 331. Detroit Zoo 281, 303, 304. Dennis DiCello rendering 165. Dossin Great Lakes Museum Archives 206, 286, 691, 768. Pam Duvall 215, 274. First of America Bank 543. Gerald R. Ford Library 456. Henry Ford Museum/Greenfield Village 346, 352. Gregory Fox 328. Courtesy Gwen Frostic 568, 569. Great Lakes Shipwreck Historical Museum 742. Holocaust Memorial Center 327. Pat Juntti 834. Benyas Kaufman 257. Keweenaw Tourism Council 831. Balthazar Korab 221, 301. Balthazar Korab, copyright Korab Hedrich Blessing 321. Debbie Axelrod Kruz 189. Lake Michigan Carferry 557. Paul LaMarre, Jr. drawing 285. Jean Lau drawing 639. Les Cheneaux Historical Society archives 707, 709. B. J. Litsenberger drawing 847. Mackinac State Historic Parks 659, 663, 666, 670, 674. Lyla Messick drawing 696. Michigan State Historic Parks 842. Michigan State Parks, Earl Wolf 523, 549, 562, 594. Michigan Travel Bureau 117, 145, 279, 324, 385, 396, 501, 503, 511, 573, 615, 685, 745, 756, 761, 784, 825, 848. The Music House 610. Muskegon County Museum 528, 530. Muskegon Museum of Art 534. Rick Neumann 645, 651. David Odette 127. R. E. Olds Museum 435. Pewabic Pottery 288, 289. Public Museum of Grand Rapids 458, 459, 460, 475. Bill Pugliano 198. David Rau 316. Ted and Jean Reuther 750, 752. Sue Scheffler drawings 409, 411. Shrine of the Pines 565. State Archives of Michigan 48. Courtesy Steelcase Inc. 467, 468. Dan Urbanski, Silver Image Studio 791. Wayne State University Archives of Labor and Urban Affairs 361. J. Adrian Wylie 266. Irene Young drawing 623.

Library of Congress Cataloging in Publication Data
Hunt, Mary. Hunt, Donald
Hunts' Highlights of Michigan Third Edition.
Includes index.
1. Michigan — Description and travel — Guidebooks
2. Outdoor recreation — Michigan — Guidebooks
917.74

Library of Congress Catalog Card Number 91-062335

ISBN 0-9623499-8-4

To Karl Hoffmann

For all the Saturday trips
to that old textile factory
near the St. Louis riverfront,
and to the old city neighborhoods.
They planted the seeds that give
this book an added dimension.

Special thanks to Maria Sudnykovich
for the countless cheerful phone calls
and for caring about the myriad details
of updating this book.

Thanks too to Celeste Novak
for her help on the Birmingham
art gallery chapter,
and to Patrice and Josh Smith
for putting on paper their years of experiences
at the Detroit Zoo.

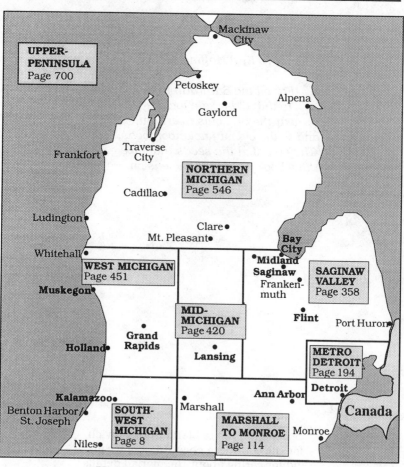

Mackinaw City

Petoskey

Alpena

Gaylord

Traverse City

Frankfort

Cadillac

Ludington

Clare

Mt. Pleasant

Bay City

Whitehall

Midland
Saginaw

Franken-
muth

Muskegon

Flint

Port Huron

Grand Rapids

Holland

Lansing

Detroit

Kalamazoo

Ann Arbor

Benton Harbor /
St. Joseph

Marshall

Canada

Niles

Monroe

Key to contents and regions

CONTENTS

Introduction

THIS GUIDEBOOK is the product of eight years' research and countless miles spent checking out thousands of places. From this vast pool we have selected and assembled 166 highlights of exceptional interest. Most highlights are followed by a section in smaller print that points out other interesting things to see and do in the vicinity — a pleasant beach, noteworthy restaurant, nice picnic spot, good book about the subject, etc.

No one paid to be included in this book, nor are there any commercial tie-ins with editorial content. In every highlight we try to give enough candid information for you to decide if a destination would suit your interests and needs. Some highlights are whole areas, some are a single place, large or small. Our research in discovering these attractions goes well beyond heavily promoted points of interest. For many travellers, it is the more obscure, quirkier destinations that are most fondly remembered.

Some well-known places were left out because we didn't feel they were quite worth a trip. Other places, while pleasant, weren't exceptioinal enough to qualify as highlights. We found many of the most interesting places were created by a person with a dream who made it happen. Many highlights are about old environments, whether natural places with mature trees or man-made like a historic neighborhood.

It all adds up to an 850-page book — and that only after reducing the type size and margins a little for this third edition! This edition adds a lot about the central and western Upper Peninsula. (*Hunts' Highlights of Michigan* actually deals with the entirety of the U. P. more fully than any other single book.)

Our next edition (possibly in two volumes) will have more highlights including the Tawas/Lower Au Sable area; Traverse City; historic Manistee and nearby cross-country skiing and fishing; the Lionel Visitor Center in Mt. Clemens; more varied Ann Arbor destinations; and interesting small-scale sights along the St. Clair River, in the Chelsea area, southern Jackson County, and the route along M-60 between Jackson and Niles.

Now for a few reminders and explanations.

◆ **Everything changes over time.** Please remember that! Our information was fresh as we went to press. It's still a good idea to <u>call</u> <u>ahead</u> if you need to be sure of current prices, hours, etc. before setting out on a trip. We've taken the trouble to include phone numbers for virtually every place mentioned, so please make use of them.

◆ **Travel with kids.** Experienced travelers with kids have good results by focusing on the children's interests. Save your own interests for another trip. Plan interesting pauses along the way. Often the little things turn out to be the most memorable. Dole out little treats judiciously but don't reinforce whining. Build up the drama of the destination.

◆ **About personal safety.** Personal safety has become almost an incapacitating worry for many people. We often avoid cities because of such fears. Bad things can and do happen everywhere. But people who live their lives in fear and don't venture beyond familiar turf miss out on a lot. Every place in this book can be reasonably visited by a single woman, alone, in the daytime, taking ordinary, sensible precautions (lock car doors, be aware of who's around you, avoid places with loiterers, be a considerate driver, have your car in good operating condition, etc.). Night is a different matter, however. Then it's better in many places to have a companion, make sure the car is full of gas, know your route, and use lighted guarded parking when possible.

The really big risks are the ones we take every day driving. Reduce them by not driving when tired, by avoiding high-traffic times (afternoon drive time in metro Detroit is from 3:30 to 6 and later), by studying complicated freeway routes before you drive them, and by trying to stay off the road on Friday and Saturday nights when more drunks are out.

◆ **Ethnic vestiges.** Beyond Michigan's obvious charms — its shoreline on four Great Lakes, its wonderful fruit, its separate ecosystem in the North Woods, its many cities and towns with distinctive personalities, this state is interesting because of its early 20th century immigration, largely connected with auto manufacturing and mining. Furthermore, many parts of western and northern Michigan have substantial populations of Native Americans whose culture, so recently ignored or consigned to the past, has become newly influential. We have made ethnicity a subtheme that pops up in many places: the beautiful Polish basilica of St. Adalbert's on Grand Rapids' west side; the Italian north end of Iron Mountain, home of Bimbo's fabulous porketta sandwich; the Minsk Russian grocery in Oak Park; Saginaw's big Cinco de Mayo parade; the North American tribal radio network heard in the Upper Peninsula; and Detroit's Mexicantown and Polish Hamtramck, port of entry for many Eastern European peoples today.

Michigan stands out as the American heartland of three important ethnic groups: Finns in the western Upper Peninsula, Muslim Arabs in Dearborn, and the conservative 19th-century Dutch separatists in West Michigan, where they have in this century distinctively stamped the region's politics and economy.

Michigan's immigration is recent enough that you can eat in many kinds of ethnic restaurants that satisfy Calvin Trillin's requirement for authenticity: to be in an ethnic community big enough to elect a councilman. (That way a knowledgeable clientele keeps the food honest.) In Missouri, where I grew up, immigration was earlier, less varied, and by now more invisible than in the Great Lakes states. Missouri is unfortunately dull by comparison. To follow these threads, see "Ethnic groups" in the thematic index.

◆ **Where are restaurants, lodgings, and camping?** Because this book has grown so large, we are putting our recommended restaurants and lodgings (a brief feature of the first edition) in a separate book. We've been working on it for years. Look for *Hunts' Compact Guide to Michigan* with lodgings and restaurants in spring, 1998.

— *Mary Hunt*

Helpful sources
for state-wide travel information

Michigan Welcome Centers are located at every major entrance to Michigan except Detroit, and within the state at Clare, Mackinaw City, St. Ignace, and Marquette. They are marked on state highway maps.

Not only is the supply of printed brochures and booklets vast at these welcome centers, but the year-round staff is typically well informed about detailed local information and about distant state-wide attractions, too. It's a bureaucratic agency that belies the common notion that government is inefficient and unresponsive. Welcome Centers will even respond to phone requests by mailing you specific brochures! Some outstanding brochures: *Michigan Herbs Visitor Guide, Arts & Crafts Trails of Northern Michigan, Michigan Golf Guide, Ford History Trails* (about Ford's village industries in southeastern Michigan).

Here are Welcome Center locations and phone numbers, arranged from southwest to north like our book: **New Buffalo** (616) 469-0011; **Coldwater** (517) 238-2670; **Dundee** (313) 856-6980; **Monroe** (313) 242-1768; **Port Huron** (810) 984-2361; **Clare** (517) 386-7634; **Mackinaw City** (616) 436-5566; **St. Ignace** (906) 643-6979; **Sault Ste. Marie** (906) 632-8242; **Marquette** (906) 249-9066; **Menominee** (906) 863-6496; **Iron Mountain** (906) 774-4201; **Ironwood** (906) 932-3330.

MITS: Customized travel information about Michigan

(800) 5432-YES. Weekdays 8 a.m.-11 p.m, Sat. & Sun. 8 a.m.-5 p.m.
An operator, not a voice mail system, answers your call. You can get two kinds of information. *First*, you can request a basic information packet (state map, calendar of seasonal events, glossy annual *Michigan Travel Ideas* magazine published by *Midwest Living*, and optional golf guide. *Second*, you can ask for specific customized information about, for instance, what bed and breakfasts with jacuzzis are in Saugatuck, or which downhill ski areas are within three hours of your home, or where to stay in Metro Detroit, or golf or ski packages in certain areas. The operator then consults the MITS computer database to answer your questions. The results depend on which destinations have responded to MITS' requests for information. The database, begun in 1993, is much better than at first and constantly improving. The basic info packet is

mailed third-class and takes 7 to 10 business days to arrive. The customized computer info is mailed first-class, or faxed or e-mailed.

Recommended books on Michigan travel & recreation

As a service to our readers, we offer a selection of the most useful books. Check out our web site **http;//www.traverse.com/michguides** Or call (517) 629-4494 to receive a critically annotated list to order by mail.

Four park systems with camping, beaches and trails

National Parks and Lakeshores. Michigan has three, Sleeping Bear Dunes (page 571), Pictured Rocks (page 757), and Isle Royale (page 847). It takes unusual scenery or history to become part of the national parks system. National parks have staff from everywhere, who move around a lot. Visitors come from farther away. Campgrounds often are rustic (no showers). Funding problems mean special programs have been cut back or supported by local friends groups.

State Parks. This widely publicized system is so popular, it's hard to get a campsite without reservations, often way in advance, now that the new integrated **reservation system** is in place. Call **1-800-44 PARKS.** Consider off-season camping. Most campgrounds are modern (toilets, showers, etc.), so they fill quickly and campsites are close together.

National Forests. Managed for timber, mineral resources, and for recreation (fishing, hunting, canoeing, hiking, snowmobiling, skiing). Campgrounds can be large or small, but are usually rustic, spacious, more private, and not reservable. They are almost always on lakes or rivers. Public beaches here are less crowded. Offices can supply interesting info sheets on camping and recreational opportunities. The **Huron-Manistee National Forest** (616-775-2421) covers almost a million acres in the northern Lower Peninsula. The **Hiawatha National Forest** (906-786-4062) is in the eastern and central Upper Peninsula, the **Ottawa National Forest** (906-932-1330) in the western U.P.

State Forests. Hidden treasures for people who like privacy and off-the-beaten-path places. Remote beaches. Rustic campgrounds on lakes or rivers are often laid out with an artist's sensibility. Made up of land owners couldn't pay taxes on during the Depression, augmented by land trust purchases from gas and oil drilling proceeds. Call offices for info. *In the Lower Peninsula:* **Mackinaw State Forest** (Gaylord) 517-732-3541. **Pere Marquette State Forest** (Cadillac) 616-775-9727; **AuSable State Forest** (517-826-3211. *In the Upper Peninsula:* **Lake Superior State Forest** (Newberry) 906-293-5131; **Escanaba River State Forest** (Gladstone) 906-786-2351; **Copper Country State Forest** (Baraga) 906-353-6651. Get helpful separate **overview/locator brochures** for state forest campgrounds and pathways in the Upper and Lower Peninsulas from state forest offices or Welcome Centers.

Southwest Michigan

BEACHES AND FRUIT have long drawn visitors to this pleasant region. Lake Michigan's north-south axis, coupled with winds coming from the west, has given Michigan's west coast two distinctive features: enormous stretches of sand beaches and dunes, and a productive fruit belt. Everything from peaches to wine grapes to blueberries thrives here because Lake Michigan moderates the coastal temperatures. Beautiful orchards and fruit stands are common sights along the hilly back roads.

The most popular **beaches** are at **Warren Dunes State Park**, **St. Joseph**, and the **South Haven** area. The Lake Michigan shore is lined with communities developed over the decades as summer resorts for almost the whole spectrum of southside Chicago. The Irish summered at **Grand Beach**, Bohemians in **New Buffalo**, professors and meat packers in **Lakeside**, Swedes in **Harbert**, Jews in **Union**

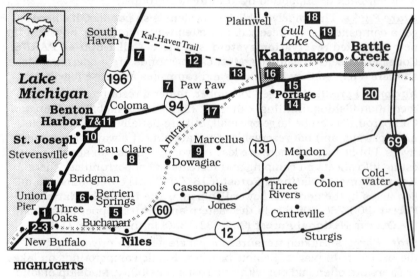

HIGHLIGHTS

Pier and **South Haven**, which was the Catskills of the Midwest. Traces of bygone eras of tourism (summer hotels, motor courts, dance halls, drive-ins) are found, now affectionately renovated, along the **Red Arrow Highway**, the old shoreline highway that starts at New Buffalo, goes north through **St. Joseph** and **Benton Harbor**, and turns east through the fruit belt to **Paw Paw** and **Kalamazoo**.

Michigan's southern tier of counties, mostly linked by the beautiful **St. Joseph River** and its tributaries, remains remarkably agricultural and rural. It's interesting to explore by car or canoe the area's quaint towns and villages. Settlements of Amish farmers are centered around Nottawa and Centreville in **St. Joseph County**. The River Country Tourism Council (below) provides good county biking and canoe guides.

The old industrial and college city of **Kalamazoo** has evolved into the area's center of art, music, and new ideas. By contrast, America's cereal city, **Battle Creek**, has languished as automation has greatly reduced the supply of jobs at Kellogg's, Post, and Ralston, and as other economic mainstays have disappeared. Massive downtown improvements in Battle Creek have been bankrolled largely by the Kellogg Corporation and Kellogg Foundation, one of the nation's largest philanthropic institutions.

Information sources: CONVENTION AND VISITOR BUREAUS

Harbor Country Lodging Assn.
New Buffalo, Harbert, Grand Beach, Union Pier, Lakeside, Sawyer, 3 Oaks
(616) 469-5409, (800) 362-7251

Southwestern Michigan Tourist Council (616) 925-6301
 Berrien, Van Buren, Cass counties

Branch County Tourism Bureau
(517) 278-5985

Lakeshore CVB   South Haven area
(616) 637-5252

Kalamazoo County CVB
(616) 381-4003

River Country Tourism Council
St. Joseph County   (616) 467-4505

Battle Creek Area CVB
Calhoun County
(616) 9622-2240, (800) 397-2240

Information sources: LOCAL CHAMBERS OF COMMERCE

Coloma   (616) 468-3377
Dowagiac   (616) 782-8212
Paw Paw   (616) 657-5395
Plainwell   (616) 685-8877

South Haven   (616) 637-5171
Stevensville   (616) 429-1170
Sturgis   (616) 651-5758
Three Rivers   (616) 278-8193

Harbor Country

*A beguiling mix of roadside nostalgia
and international art, good food and antiques.*

IN THE MID-1980s the sleepy resort area around New Buffalo and Lakeside was discovered by overstressed Chicago media people seeking convenient weekend getaways. Their word-of-mouth has transformed what was once a series of low-key resort communities frequented by many southside Chicagoans: Lithuanians, Bohemians, Jews, meat-packers, and professors. Today "Harbor Country" is home of the largest marina-condo complex on Lake Michigan, in New Buffalo. A recent addition is a large, nouveau Mission-style hotel. *New York Times* lifestyle articles gush over the area's exciting new shops and second homes by famous Chicago architects like Harry Weese and Stanley Tigerman.

All the exposure, plus all the new condos and renovated cottages to be decorated, have provided fertile soil for the galleries and shops strung out along and off the Red Arrow Highway from Grand Beach and New Buffalo to Harbert, eight miles north. The four-lane road, predating interstate highways, now enjoys a growing reputation as a great place to drive, browse, eat, and see art. That is, it's great except on summer weekends. Traffic then can be fierce.

There's some provocative art and offbeat antiques here as well. Harbor Country shops focusing on interior decor can be unusually fresh and witty. Don't be surprised to find folk art like bottle cap figures and popsicle stick lamps. After all, many customers here are not self-conscious members of the middle-class who insist on proper English period looks, but sophisticated urban refugees, high-powered if somewhat burned out, who are attempting to slow down and enjoy life. Lately, however, the area's tone is "slicking up" in a less relaxed direction, in the words of one innkeeper.

The Red Arrow Highway itself is a nostalgic stretch of

Area cottages and resorts span the decades of styles since 1910 or so. Many are simple, a few rather grand. Vignettes on these two pages show details of the Pine Garth Inn and Cottages in Union Pier.

auto-age Americana. It's several blocks
east of the lakeshore road that goes
through the residential heart of resort
communities, beginning with Michiana
and Grand Beach on the Indiana line.
The highway was named after the Red
Arrow World War I army division in
which many local men served. Here
roadhouses and tourist courts of the
1920s and 1930s miraculously live on.
They've been refurbished as monuments to the childhoods of war babies
and aging baby boomers who vaca-
tioned here as kids, before interstate
highways and cheap air fares made
more exotic vacations widely possible.

A shop and gallery tour of Harbor
Country along the Red Arrow Highway seems to work best going
from north (Sawyer or Bridgman) to south (New Buffalo). In that
direction, it builds to a climax with the concentrated activity of New
Buffalo and its busy beach and harbor. Also, more shops are on the
right, avoiding left turns if traffic is heavy.

This tour focuses on established highlights. Of course, each
season brings new shops; retailing is in a constant flux. The concentration of antiques malls and shops is nearing two dozen. It
would be easy to spend a day browsing along these 10 miles.

The Red Arrow Highway bypasses the old cottage areas that
blossomed with the coming of electricity in 1918. Along shady
Lakeshore Road an interesting cross-section of summer homes,
from a few remaining tumble-down old resorts to gracious, sedate
lakefront estates, can be seen. Find it by turning north onto Lakeside Road in Lakeside, near the quaint Elizabethan-style shelter in
the little triangular park. In two blocks, turn left onto Lakeshore and

follow it into Union Pier. A
gate to discourage automobile sightseers eventually
blocks the way to New
Buffalo's public beach, so
turn south onto the Red
Arrow Highway. Lakeshore
is fine for **biking** and **cross-
country skiing** in winter.
It's especially beautiful in
fall and after fresh snowfall.

For a **shopping and eating tour**, start in Sawyer. Take the
I-94 Sawyer Road exit and go west to the Red Arrow Highway.
Incidentally, that improbably elegant and urbane two-story building
on Sawyer Road east of I-94 in the heart of tiny **Sawyer** was built in
the 1920s by a Chicago teamster official to house a tea room, a
soda grill, and his own luxurious second-story apartment. At the
triangle made where the Red Arrow Highway angles across Three
Oaks Road, turn right, then left onto the highway.

Here are some highlights on the short but rich stretch to New
Buffalo. New attractions merit extra stops.

◆ **Tara Hill Antiques Mall.** 17 dealers in 17-room, 3.400-square-
foot mall that's much bigger than it looks. *13832 Red Arrow
Highway in Sawyer. (616) 426-8673. May thru September: daily 11-
5:30. October thru April: Sat & Sun 11-5:30.*

◆ **Dunes Antique Center.** New mall in the old Dunes Furniture
Store is biggest in the area, with some 70 dealers in 20,000 square
feet of space. Strong on period furniture through mid-20th-century,
porcelain, sterling and plate, without many collectibles or artifacts
of recent popular culture. *East side of Red Arrow Highway just
north of Sawyer Rd. (I-94 exit 12.) 616) 426-4043. Open daily 10-6
except closed Tues, Sun hours 11-6. &: call.*

◆ **Harbert Swedish Bakery.** Full-line bakery spotlights traditional
Swedish breads and cakes. It has been here since the days when
Harbert was largely Swedish and Carl Sandburg had his goat farm
nearby. Tables outside and in; coffee, milk, and pop are available.
*Red Arrow Hwy. at Prairie Rd. (616) 469-1777. Open from Easter to
Thanksgiving. Fri & Sat 7:30-6, Sun 7:30-4. From July 4 thru late
Aug also open Wed & Thurs 7:30-6. &: no.*

◆ **Judith Racht Gallery.** Long before the self-taught, naive, visionary, grassroots art known as "outsider art" became prominent it's
been a big part of this gallery's fresh, unpretentious, eclectic mix of
contemporary paintings, furniture, and ceramics with primitive art,
quilts, and furniture. Judith Racht opened her gallery, the area's
most significant, in Harbert's two-room brick schoolhouse in 1987.
Now, after a brief hiatus, she's back in business and is getting more
Chicago and national press and more wherewithal. Changing shows
run May through December. Call for Saturday-night openings.
Don't miss the primitives and quilts in the basement. A recent
annual highlight: late July's **Outsiders Outside: Outsider, Self-
Taught, Folk Art Fair.** Dozens of national dealers set up in the
field behind the school, and many artists (an uncommon mix of
hobbyists, recluses, and self-promoters) show up to socialize. It

benefits Chicago's INTUIT: Center for Intuitive & Outsider Art, 1926 N. Halsted (312-759-1406). *13707 Prairie Rd. just south of the Red Arrow Hwy. in the center of Harbert. (Harbert Rd. makes a little triangle here.) (616) 469-1080. Open Sat & Sun 10-5 and by appointment. From Mem. to Labor Day, also open Fri & Mon 10-5. &: no.*

◆ **Lakeside Antiques.** Two interconnected barns and a turquoise 1950s diner out front are filled with quality pieces, including 1950s; folk art, bamboo, wicker, and painted furniture, plus primitive and country. Dependably interesting browsing, thanks to offbeat pieces, eye-catching displays. Different dealers run **Vintage Cargo**, a shop and mall next door. *(616) 469-4467. 14866 Red Arrow Highway, just north of East Rd in the center of Lakeside. Summer hours: daily except Wednesday 11-6. Winter hours: Fri & Mon noon-4, Sat & Sun 11-6. Call for transition season in spring, fall.*

Contrasting styles, similar enthusiasms: outsider artist Wesley Merritt and a patron at the Judith Racht Gallery's Outsiders Outside Folk Art Fair in Harbert.

◆ **East Road Gallery.** Peaceful shop in a former cottage features generic Mission and related styles, plus copper lamps, etchings, old Arts-and-Crafts books, etc. Turning a 1912 Craftsman-style resort in Lakeside into The Pebble House bed and breakfast introduced Ed Lawrence to the furniture the old place seemed to want. Now he publishes helpful guides to Midwest antiquing. *14906 Red Arrow Highway, between East Road and Lakeside Road in Lakeside. (616) 469-5995. Open at least May-Oct, Sat & Sun 12-5, otherwise by chance or appt. &: call.*

◆ **Old Lakeside general store/post office.** This picturesque half-timber building was part of the quaint, Shakespearean look that took hold in Lakeside when a Chicago replica of Shakespeare's birthplace was dismantled and moved here to become a golf clubhouse. The Silver Crane Gallery (p. 16) was here for years; the coming tenant (a name has not been decided) will sell antiques and furniture and install an outdoors garden center. *14950 Lakeside Road, just west of the Red Arrow Highway in the heart of Lakeside.*

◆ **Flutter the Dovecotes.** A signature picket fence marks the showroom of South Bend furniture-maker Michael O'Shea. He designs and builds custom furniture incorporating architectural themes. For instance, in his English Garden collection, a bed ($1,000) has picket-fence headboards and footboards and a birdhouse on one post. The trellis desk uses a trellis. The Country House collection uses a window motif. He makes accessories, too, like clocks resembling bird houses ($59). The effect is charming but not fussy. This is not painted furniture; the shop's only flowers are real ones in vases. ("Flutter the dovecotes" means making a stir in a quiet rural area.) *14931 Lakeside Rd., west of the Red Arrow Hwy., one door west of the grocery. (616) 469-0200. Open May-Oct Fri-Mon 11-5 and by appointment. &: call.*

◆ **Filoni Vestimenti.** Owner Shari Filoni used to rep for Chicago clothes designers. Here she has assembled sophisticated but laid-back clothing for men and women, in natural fibers plus recycled Polarfleece. Organic dyes and unbleached fabrics with lots of texture result in an earth-toned palette with lots of beige. *In "Wilkinson Village" complex, 15300 Red Arrow Highway, Lakeside. (616) 469-4944. Open daily 10-6 year-round. &: call.*

◆ **Lakeside Gallery.** Here in the sales gallery of the nearby Lakeside Center for the Arts, art comes alive as an exciting process of exploration and experiment. Both the center and gallery were started by John Wilson, the ceramist and print dealer who, in 1980, organized Chicago's influential Art Expo at Navy Pier. The center is a working artists' retreat that furthers artistic and cultural exchange among artists from around the world, mainly the U.S., Poland, Latvia, Lithuania, England, and France. It's in studios behind an old Lakeside summer hotel,

Artists donate half the work they create there to support the center; it's sold in this gallery. Works are produced under conditions of unusual freedom. Artists are selected after submitting proposals for projects. Sales from their works help support the center. Current works are likely to include lots of ceramics, sculpture, jewelry, paintings, fibers, and original prints in many printmaking media. *15486 Red Arrow Highway at Warren Woods Road in Lakeside. (616) 469-3022. Open Fri-Sun noon-6. Closed January & February except by appointment.*

◆ **Lakeside Center for the Arts.** Visitors are welcome to tour the studios at this international artists' retreat. Artists stay on the eight-acre property here and use the studios (painting, printmaking, ceramics, and sculpture). It's sort of a sharecropping arrangement, in which artists give half the work made here to the center. It is sold in the Lakeside Gallery (see above). *15251 Lakeshore Road in Lakeside. From the Red Arrow Highway, take Warren Woods Road west to Lakeshore, turn right. Center is in a few blocks. Call first. (616) 469-1377.*

◆ **Rabbit Run Antiques & Interiors.** Vivid mix of Mission, rustic, and English pine antiques, Amish quilts, upholstered furniture, folk art, and more, assembled with a decorator's eye for area second homes. Established by early émigrés to Harbor Country. *15460 Red Arrow Highway at the south end of Lakeside. (616) 496-0468. Year-round, daily 10-6.*

◆ **Riviera Gardens** and **Heart of the Vineyard** tasting room. Drink excellent wines in a Monet garden setting, either indoors or on a screened patio at this large garden center. Ornamental grasses are a specialty. *16024 Red Arrow Hwy. north but within sight of blinker at Union Pier Rd. (800) 716-WINE. Open daily from Mem. to Labor Day 12-6, otherwise Fri-Sun 12-6.* ♿.

◆ **Downtown Union Pier** is along Union Pier/Elm Valley Road at the Red Arrow Highway, easily accessible by going west from I-94 exit 6. It has most requirements of a small town center, including a post office and pharmacy. **Ramberg's Bakery** is a favorite with bicyclists. The **Harbert Auction House** has antique auctions, usually the third Monday of the month. Buyers may view items on Sunday and leave sealed bids. Call (616) 426-8673 for particulars.

◆ **Antique Mall and Village.** A fanciful "village" in the woods, with interesting dealers, largely from Chicago. A metal chapel in the back has a re-creation of Michelangelo's Sistine Chapel ceiling, and a log cabin has rustic and Native American things. The general store serves coffees and refreshments and sells candies and gifts. *9300 Union Pier Rd at I-94 exit 6, almost a mile east of the Red Arrow Highway and downtown Union Pier. (616) 469-2555. April thru Dec: open Mon-Sat 10-6, Sun noon-6. Jan-March February: closed Tues & Wed.* ♿.

◆ **St. Julian Winery Tasting Room.** *Union Pier Road at I-94 exit.* A good chance to sample the interesting, constantly improving array of inexpensive to mid-priced wines and sparkling juices made from Michigan grapes at Michigan's largest winery. No charge for tasting. *(616) 469-3150. From mid-June thru Labor Day open 10-7 Mon-Sat, noon-7 Sun. Otherwise closes at 6 p.m.*

◆ **Local Color.** Works in many media by some 90 artists and crafts-people from the area are attractively displayed in this consignment gallery. Some are whimsical, some serious, and all are contemporary in style. There's a good deal of painted furniture and hand-decorated wearable art. *16187 Red Arrow Highway south of the light at Union Pier; east/side of highway. (616) 469-5332. Open year-round daily 12-5. &: one step.*

◆ **Kite's Kitchen.** Takeout bakery/restaurant that's the dream project of Chicago caterer/meeting planner Judy Kite. Known for breads, dinners, with everything prepared from scratch with fresh, seasonal ingredients. Entrees from $4-$8, dinners (with appetizer and sides) $8-$15 per person. *In The Shops at Union Pier, 16170 Red Arrow Highway, 1 block south of flasher light at Union Pier Road. (616) 469-1800. From Mem. to Labor Day open daily except Tues. Otherwise open Thurs-Sun. Always opens at 9 a.m. &.*

◆ **Catherine & Co.** Catherine Cuttleback makes custom-finished lampshades in many fabrics and papers to play up aspects of home decor. Artful display of many striking lamps, new and old. Unusual finials. *In The Shops at Union Pier (see Kite's, above). (616) 469-2742. Open Fri-Mon 11-5. (&.*

◆ **Downtown New Buffalo.** Whittaker Street, until recently a fairly humble place, now has some tony shops for home accessories and women's clothing in the old retail district, between the Red Arrow Highway and the lake. New stores, cleverly aimed at second home-owners, continue to open, like **Michigan Thyme**, a coffee bar/gourmet shop down from the drugstore.

The **Whittaker House** at 26 North Whittaker stands out on account of its relaxed, contemporary classic clothing for women, in beautiful fabrics of excellent quality. It also carries fashion and home accessories. *It's open daily, year-round. (616) 469-0220.*

The **Silver Crane Gallery** has moved next door to 24. It claims to have one of the Midwest's largest collections of sterling silver — mostly jewelry. Prices range from $20-$40 for many pins and earrings imported direct from Mexico to $800 and up for turquoise and sterling necklaces by Navajos. *(616) 469-4000. May-Oct: daily 11-6. Nov-April: 1-4 weekdays, 11-6 weekends.*

The developer of the new Prairie-style Harbor Grand Hotel in New Buffalo is Jack Kennedy, Chicago Board of Trade member and yet another Chicago baby boomer reworking childhood memories of Michigan summers. A long-time Frank Lloyd Wright fan, he wanted the hotel to make a strong statement of regional identity, in contrast to its neighbor, the New England-inspired South Cove condos designed by famed architect Harry Weese.

Years ago, **Hearthwoods** owner Andy Brown became fascinated with rustic furniture made of tree trunks, branches, and twigs. He followed utility crews to get his materials, that often played off chunky trunks with the delicate tracery of twig branches. Now that he has been lionized by Chicago interior designers, his place is much bigger, busier, and less quirkily interesting. What's next? An Andrew Brown designer label? *116 North Whittaker, downtown. (616) 469-5551. Mem.-Labor Day: Mon-Sat 10-6, Sun 12-5. Labor Day-Mem. Day: Mon-Sat 10-5, Sun 12-5, closed Tuesdays.*

Across the street at the corner, **Buffalo Drugs** (also called V&S Variety) functions as a community hub, with out-of-town papers, beach gear, videos, etc. A few doors down on North Whittaker, **Sweetwater Boating Supply** (616-469-5660) has enough interesting gadgets, books, and T shirts to appeal even to non-boaters. Down a ways at 125 North Whittaker, **Anchors** (616-469-6800) made its mark by offering virtually all of the popular Nautica menswear line, now with other men's and women's clothing. No wonder — the first owner's husband was Nautica's Chicago rep. *Open 10-6, Fri & Sat to 9. Closed Tues in off-season.*

On U.S. 12 a block west of Whittaker, **Country Mates** is the rambling, 7,000-square-foot home of the country look. Now it's being repositioned to "the more elegant and cosmopolitan Country Living style." So says the new owner, part of the local Oselka family involved in construction and marinas. Its patio and Christmas shops are extensive. *(616) 469-2890. Open 7 days year-round, daily 10-6, Sunday 12-6. In July & August, Saturdays open 'til 9.*

More shops are scattered on South Whittaker, between the old downtown and I-94. In the two-story brick building by the train tracks, **La Grand Trunk** offers fashion-forward, contemporary women's clothes — everything from socks to black-tie formal wear. The look seems quintessentially big-city; actually, the store is a branch of a popular shop in nearby Valparaiso, Indiana, home to more and more Chicago commuters. *447 S. Whittaker. (616) 469-2122. Summer hours: 11-7, except Sunday to 6. Winter: 11-5 daily.*

AN EXCELLENT SMALL RAILROAD MUSEUM . . . . . occupies the meticulously reconstructed New Buffalo depot and commemorates the central role the railroad played in the town's history. Volunteers at the New Buffalo Railroad Museum work at expanding the big working **model train display** of New Buffalo in its 1920s railroad heyday. At that time the Pere Marquette Railroad, which went up Lake Michigan's eastern shore, had its shops here and employed much of the town. There's lots of information about the Pere Marquette and its successor, the Chesapeake & Ohio. A photograph shows the original Chessie, C & O chairman's pet cat and inspiration for the railroad's feline mascot. Visitors can also see a remaining part of the railroad roundhouse next door at **The Round House**, an ambitious shopping complex now occupied by a successful gym. *Museum is at 530 South Whittaker. (616) 469-3166. Open April thru Halloween, weekends noon to 5. Also open Fridays in summer.*

HARBOR COUNTRY'S MAIN PUBLIC BEACH . . . . . south of the spectacular, huge Warren Dunes State Park (page 27) is the **New Buffalo Beach**. It's within walking distance of downtown New Buffalo and right at the busy outlet of the Galien River near the harbor. The swimming area here is more protected from the boating traffic than it at first seems, and the public beach is longer and more natural than first impressions suggest. There are **restrooms**, a **refreshment stand**, a small **play area** for children, and a dune **stairway** and longish **overlook and boardwalk** atop the dunes.

FRESH-PICKED FRUIT . . . . . In Sawyer, blueberries are in season from mid-July into September at **The Blueberry Patch**, 1/2 mile west of the Red Arrow Highway on Sawyer Road. Shaded picnic area. U-pick or picked berries and preserves also for sale. *Open 10-6. Always call first; (616) 426-4521 or evenings (616) 545-8125.* . . . . Picked fruits from cherries (July) and peaches, melons, and plums (August) to fall grapes, pears, and apples are for sale at the **Phillippi Fruit and Cider Mill** (616-422-1700). It's on Cleveland Avenue 1/4 mile south of Glendora and 5 miles east of Sawyer. Cleveland runs north-south between Sawyer Road and U.S. 12 at Galien. Many fresh vegetables, from asparagus through tomatoes to pumpkins. . . . . See also: **Lemon Creek Winery and Fruit Farm**, page 41, 5 miles east of Bridgman.

Warren Woods Natural Area

*A primeval virgin woodland
an hour and a half from Chicago's Loop*

THESE 311 ACRES comprise one of Michigan's few remaining virgin beech-maple climax forests. The woods you see from the car off Elm Valley Road don't look different from a hundred other places. But if you take the foot trail across the Galien River (pronounced "Ga-leen") to the loop along the river, you'll come to some enormous, majestic beech trees, along with maples and hemlocks — the kind of woods the pioneers encountered. The damp soil here makes for a jungly, humid environment that's sunnier and quite unlike the stand of virgin oaks and hickories on the drier upland of Russ Forest, another piece of southwest Michigan virgin forest not too far from here (page 59). Warren Woods is an outstanding place to watch birds, thanks to its location on the main Lake Michigan shoreline flyway and the abundance of dead wood for woodpeckers and for nesting.

"This natural area has long been considered one of the best birding spots in the state, especially for warblers — including Hooded, Cerulean, and Kentucky Warblers — and songbirds such as Acadian Flycatchers and Louisiana Waterthrushes," says Tom Powers in his helpful *Natural Michigan* guide to natural areas. "Other birds spotted here include many that are usually only found farther south." Look for warblers from early to mid spring. The May **wildflower display** in this rich, damp woods is also outstanding as is the fall color. You will find morels here, but visitors are not allowed to pick them. This is a protected area and nothing, not even a fallen tree, can be removed. To gather morels, mushroom-hunters should go to Warren Dunes. An **interpretive sign** tells about the beech-maple climax forest visible across the river, one of the very few remaining vir-

Warren Woods is a prime birding site. It attracts many warblers and some birds like the Acadian flycatcher (above) that are uncommon in Michigan and usually seen only much farther south.

gin beech forests in Michigan that have never been logged. A section of foot trail begins at the **Elm Valley Road entrance** and pullover, near the Galien River. A drive leads to parking, a picnic table, and restrooms. The trail includes a suspension bridge over the river.

That this Natural National Landmark was preserved at all is due to the foresight of E. K. Warren, the Three Oaks storekeeper who made a fortune by inventing a better, cheaper corset stay made of turkey feathers. Over a hundred years ago, when most business-men were figuring out how to exploit natural resources, he decided to buy this virgin timberland in order to preserve it.

Entrances on Elm Valley Rd. and Warren Woods Rd. (both roads go east from the Red Arrow Highway) about a mile west of Three Oaks Rd. (which is the north-south extension of Three Oaks' main street between U.S. 12 and the Red Arrow Hwy.). Parking lot is off Elm Valley Rd. (616) 426-4013. Always open. ♿*: only the picnic area off the gravel parking lot. State park sticker required $4/day, $20/year.*

ANOTHER FAVORITE WOODLAND WALK . . . . . close to Harbor Country resort communities is the **Robinson Preserve** along the Galien River. When you leave the road and walk down into the valley, it's hard to believe you're just a mile from the Red Arrow Highway and Lakeside's shops and galleries. *Take East Rd. east from the center of Lakeside. Preserve is on the north side of the road just past Basswood Rd*

A RARE REMNANT OF A FLOWERING WET PRAIRIE . . . . . may be seen near Dayton, between Three Oaks and Buchanan. The Michigan Nature Conservancy owns 47 acres of what was once 15,000 acres of prairie in Michigan and Indiana. Curran Road and the turnoff alongside it provide a dry viewing platform from which to see prairie grasses and rare plants like rosin weed, spotted phlox, and Jacob's ladder. *From U.S. 12 at Dayton, take Dayton Rd. south a little over a mile, turn left (east) onto Curran. In about 2 miles, look for a pullover. Or, from the east, take Red Bud Trail south from U.S. 12 at Buchanan, and turn right (west) onto Curran Rd. in about 2 miles,.*

Three Oaks

A destination for food-lovers, bicyclists and film buffs, thanks to the energy and flair of local entrepreneurs.

THREE OAKS, population 1,786, five miles from Lake Michigan and less to Indiana, has become quite a remarkable little place in recent years. It's the kind of place city people would think they had "discovered" and tell all their friends about. It has a famous sausage shop loaded with atmosphere, a bike museum with unusual old bikes and bikes to rent for a series of marked Backroads Bikeways, a sleek, European-style bakery-deli with homegrown jams and sauces, and now a spiffy renovation of the old movie theater, used for live music, plays, and classic films.

None of this happened because of a flood of gentrifiers and urban refugees. Local people supplied the vision, the imaginative details, and the sweat. All Chicago did was to provide a huge market. Every small town is different, contrary to city people's stereotypes. Towns are not only products of different economic and social forces, past and present, but in small places the influence of a few exceptional leaders and inspirational models can be great, often greater than in a larger place.

Here's a look at four unusual institutions.

DRIER'S MEAT MARKET

They used to hold Chicago-bound trains at the Three Oaks depot so passengers could walk across to Drier's to buy some of its famous ring bologna and ham. Trains don't stop here any more, but people still go out of their way to shop at Drier's. This exceptional butcher shop continues to make sausage and cure hams and bacon the old, careful, German way. The ancient frame building is an operating antique, listed on the prestigious National Register of Historic Places. Old tools and a fancy Victorian meat rack have been here over a hundred years. The four-paned windows predate the introduction of plate glass in the 1880s.

Despite the many old-fashioned touches — the sawdust on the floor, the corny signs like "This baloney cuts the mustard" — Drier's is actually one astute man's business response to changing times. The late Ed Drier cleverly crafted his business to preserve quality of life — his own, and his employees'

Three Oaks' handsome depot now is home to the Bicycle Museum & Information Center. Proceeds from the nation's largest one-day 100-mile bicycle ride enabled the local bike club to buy it. From the station, marked bike routes radiate into the countryside and to Lake Michigan.

and customers.' Drier's today offers a few choice items: hot dogs; Polish sausage; ring bologna at about $4 a pound ("all beef, less fat, no belching," a sign points out); smoked hams, bacon, and bologna (done on the premises); and liver sausage. The cheese has been made elsewhere. Choice meat justifies the premium prices.

Back in the 1930s, at the University of Michigan, a professor told Ed Drier he'd be better off making baloney than pursuing a medical degree. After getting out of the service in 1945, he did decide to go back to work with his dad. "We always enjoyed our work," he once told me. Drier also enjoyed living two minutes from his shop, playing tennis with old Kalamazoo College chums, and taking a vacation from January 1 to shortly before Easter.

Antiques and art make Drier's today a lot more interesting than the plain place it once was. Three massive marble butcher's tables from France were picked up on midwinter travels. There's a deer head, family memorabilia, signs like *"Nicht auf den Boden spucken"* ("no spitting on the floor" in German, a reminder that this place is quintessentially German in its earthy, unassuming style), and caricatures — frequently of Ed Drier. The portrait of him as a grumpy-looking knight was done in magazine-cover style by a *Time* cover artist and customer.

All this stuff launched conversations with customers. "That's part of the deal — the dog and pony show," said Drier, who relished the personal side of the business and the nice letters that come with orders for holiday hams. For help Drier relied on his family, especially his daughter, Carolyn, and about a dozen young men from the area. Even after they've gone out into the work world to become teachers, dentists, engineers, and the like, some came back to help out on vacations.

Ed Drier died on the tennis court in1994, having filled the Christmas orders and gone on vacation. His daughter Carolyn, her daughter Susan, nephews David and Scott Wooley, and Gary Lange continue to operate the business the way he did.

14 S. Elm in downtown Three Oaks, about a block north of the intersection with U.S. 12. (616) 756-3101. Closed Jan. 1 until 3 weeks before Easter. Mon-Sat 9-5:30, Sun 11-5:30. The comical branch store on U.S. 12 east of town is open Sat 9-5:30 & Sun 11-5:30, but closed in winter. &.

THREE OAKS BICYCLE MUSEUM & INFORMATION CENTER

Three Oaks' handsome 1899 depot, home of the nonprofit Three Oaks Spokes bicycle club, is an ideal spot for visitors to become acquainted with the slower, subtler attractions of this rural area. Here are **bicycle rentals** (mostly $5 an hour or $10 a day), statewide bike maps, and loads of general visitor information about southwest Michigan. Cyclists can rent single-speed Schwinns or try an unusual quadricycle (a four-wheeled bike for two people) , a Cannondale bike trailer for little ones, or a combination adult-child tandem. The club's **Backroad Bikeways** are bike routes, from 5 to 60 miles, radiating out from Three Oaks to many attractions in this book, as far north as Grand Mere State Park. Some are easy, others challenging..

The **museum** consists of historical displays on bicycling and a growing collection of local history and local railroad memorabilia plus unusual bicycles. The newest addition: an Toledo-made 1896 tandem Tally-Ho. An interesting gift shop focuses on bikes, trains, and Three Oaks' fascinating history. (See below.)

The club's **Apple Cider Century** regularly attracts 7,000 riders to Three Oaks in September. It's the nation's largest one-day 100-mile ride. Register well in advance. The Apple Cider Century funds the museum and supports its enthusiastic and resourceful creator, Brian Volstorf. A quietly gung-ho kind of guy, he started the bicycle club when he took up bicycling, and started the ride in 1974. Characteristically, he did better than average job of mar keting the event and found he had tapped into the huge Chicago market. After he and hundreds of other area residents lost their jobs when Clark Equipment left Buchanan, he discovered that a small percentage of the entry fee was able to pay him a living salary. Now mayor of Three Oaks, he's a one-man grassroots economic development whirlwind.

The bike club purchased this brick depot. It was built for President McKinley's visit to present Three Oaks citizens with the first cannon captured by Admiral George Dewey in the jingoistically popular Spanish-American War. (Ask to hear the story.) *From U.S. 12, go north on Oak one street east of Elm (the main street). It's in two blocks. From Elm, turn east just south of the tracks. (616) 756-3361. Open daily 9-5 year-round. Call to confirm in winter.* ♿ *Free.*

FROEHLICH'S

This dazzling little deli in downtown Three Oaks looks like the result of a long love affair with the earthy, life-loving Italian approach to food. Bare brick walls and a crisp, black-and-white tile floor set off the sensuous food. Big, crusty loaves of bread like potato-rosemary bread or fresh-ground cracked corn bread sit atop the deli case where the likes of spicy peanut noodles, olive salad relish, Mediterranean romaine salad, and roasted eggplant soup are artfully arranged. Salsas and jams shimmer like jewels in simple, elegant glass jars. All this is prepared right here, often

Colleen Froehlich in front of her deli, where much of the food is home-grown and the breads home-baked. She and her husband, a graphic artist, spent two years renovating the downtown storefront into a sunny place that visually bursts with the harvest's bounty.

with vegetables grown in the owner's huge garden and with cilantro. basil, and other herbs from the back-door garden here, Everything tastes as good as it looks and costs less than you'd expect. Fat is kept to a minimum.

Not Italy but her grandparents' grocery in St. Joseph was Colleen Froehlich's inspiration. She spent a happy chunk of her childhood working there, learning to garden and can from her mom and digging up her first garden in the store's side yard when she was 12. "From the day the store closed in 1986," she says, "I knew I'd open a store named Froehlich's."

The original Froehlich's sign is behind the counter. The other creatively retro signs, like the big smoked chili and the coffee, are by Froehlich's husband, Bruce Hawkins, whose Three Oaks Signs is down the street across from Drier's. It's open by appointment: (616) 756-3225. They moved to town from Chicago in 1992 and plunged into renovating their respective downtown buildings — massively hard work, done without help. An artist's eye, a cook's palate, a big heart, and a tremendous amount of energy have created this remarkable place. Locals regarded them as "Chicago people" with fancy ideas and deep pockets. Nothing irritates Froehlich more.

Froehlich's has three indoor tables and more on the sidewalk in good weather. For picnics, Dewey Cannon Park is a block east by the tracks, and there's a picnic area in Warren Woods a few miles west. (See p. 19.) Order bread early; it does sell out. And don't overlook the chance to buy elegant, unusual gifts like sweet-hot pineapple chutney, smoked jalapeños in BBQ sauce, strawberry-rhubarb marmalade, and the like. Mail-order is available.
Downtown at 26 N. Elm, about a block north of the tracks. (616) 756-6002. Closed Jan-March. Open at least Thurs & Fri 8 a.m.-6 p.m., Sat & Sun 10-5. &: no.

VICKERS THEATRE

This stunningly rebuilt little movie theater downtown is a true anomaly: a small-town art house. Jon Vickers, engineer and co-owner of Vickers Engineering, a machine shop up the street, and his wife, Jennifer, picked up a taste for foreign and art films while students at Michigan State. Tired of driving to Chicago to indulge their habit, they invested 2 1/2 years in transforming this plain, 350-seat movie theater into a 93-seat art house, with a few extra chairs at tables and in balcony boxes. It's a simple but striking interior, where moviegoers can sip cappucino. Jennifer, formerly a graphic designer, created the futuristic, urban-industrial images in the lobby's tile floor, basing them on Ayn Rand's *Atlas Shrugged.* In booking films and marketing the theater, she aims at the South Bend/Elkhart area as well as area weekend residents and southwest Michigan people who crave the sophisticated, often controversial film fare seldom seen in the region. Some films from the Vickers' debut summer of 1996: *I Shot Andy Warhol,* German filmmaker Doris Dorrie's *Nobody Loves Me,* and *Halfmoon,* based on Paul Bowles short stories. So far, they're off to a good start. Some weekends, their distributor says, they outdraw an art theater in Cleveland. *6 N. Elm. (616) 756-3522. Typical showtimes Fri & Sat 6:30 & 9, Sun 6:30 only.* ♿. *$6 adults, $4 seniors & students.*

Why did all this happen in Three Oaks? For decades Ed Drier gave testimony to how a determined person could shape a small-town business to suit his lifestyle (helped, certainly, by proximity to affluent summer people and tourists). Then Brian Volstorf showed the way to broader community projects. In the early years of his Apple Cider Century ride, he faced a lot of obstacles from local institutions that failed to see the benefits of having thousands of bicyclists in town once a year. But the amiable, unprepossessing former computer technician had a vision. He never gave up. Each year he made the ride and the museum/info center a little bit better. Gradually townspeople came to recognize his accomplishments and support his ideas. As mayor, he has used Downtown Development Authority's tax-increment financing to develop many local projects, most recently a 28-foot gazebo in Dewey Cannon Park for summer events.

Three Oaks' glorious past inspired Volstorf's vision. In the 1890s Three Oaks became a boom town, thanks to a brainstorm of storekeeper E. K. Warren. On a trip to a Chicago feather duster factory, he saw piles of one-sided turkey feathers going to waste. That gave him the idea of splitting the feather shafts and weaving the flexible filaments into improved corset stays that would not suddenly pop the way whalebone ones did.

Soon farm girls were flooding into town to work at the sprawling brick factory buildings of the Warren Featherbone Company. (They're still standing on the northwest edge of downtown, behind Elm Street.) The widely advertised corset stays were endorsed by no less than Sarah Bernhardt. Warren himself was a generous visionary. Seeing the value of wild dunelands then regarded as wastelands, he bought some and donated them to the state. They formed the core of Warren Dunes State Park (p. 27).

Volstorf, a hometown boy who watched a generation of kids move away, wanted to draw attention to the area's quiet beauty and promote small-scale area attractions. After the bike club pays for the depot, the next project to be funded is a community center.

Warren Dunes State Park

Crowded beaches and remote trails,
hang-gliding and dune climbing

THIS REMARKABLE hilly park can handle huge crowds on its beach — often more than 20,000 on hot holiday weekends — and still provide a remote, rugged getaway experience on hiking trails in the dunes. Towards the shore the dunes are bare as a desert. In a textbook example of plant succession as you move inland, they are anchored first with beach grasses, then with quick-growing aspen and willows, and finally with big oaks and hickories. The northern two-thirds of the park is undeveloped except for hiking trails. The southern third contains Michigan's busiest state park facilities, planned to handle crowds of day-trippers from Chicago and South Bend. It makes for a stimulating contrast: people-watching and contemplative nature study.

The **beach** and parking area, though not exactly intimate, are far less overwhelming than most popular beaches within striking distance of urban areas. That's due to the outstanding site planning and design of three bathhouse and concession areas. By the closest parking area is **Tower Hill**, 240 feet above the lake. Kids love to climb this big, bare dune and run down and climb again — exhilarating fun, and a high point of many outings. **Hang-gliders** soar from this hill on weekends, too — more often in the spring and fall, when wind is most likely to come out of the north-northwest. Angelo Mantis gives **hang-gliding lessons** here; $70 gets you a full-day introduction, including four or five short flights. Call (847) 329-8337, and have alternate weekend dates available. Hang-gliders must be certified and have permits from park headquarters. Though hang-gliding isn't nearly as popular as it once was, a good day when the winds are right will still bring out four to six gliders.

Inland the huge dunes here are mostly covered with oak, beech, maple, and hickory woods. It's not hard to get away from the beach's crowds. Walk up the beach from the developed area — the public beach is 2 1/2 miles long — or take

Marram grass anchors the foredunes. Glenda Daniel's *Dune Country* explains how its underground stem/roots spread and send up new shoots. By trapping and holding sand, marram grass can form low dunes up to 10 feet high.

"Great groves of white pines once blanketed the sand hills of Lake Michigan's southern shore," writes Glenda Daniel in *Dune Country*, the ideal introduction to the dunes' fascinating ecology. "Remnants of these huge forests tower. . . from the tallest hills on inland dunes today." Drawing by Carol Lerner.

Although Warren Dunes State Park sometimes attracts more than 20,000 visitors a day on summer weekends, you can get away from crowds just by walking a half mile up the beach away from the developed area.

your car to the deeply shady **picnic area,** along a pretty creek in the relatively secluded back dunes. It has play equipment, grills, restrooms, and a shelter. Come early on holiday weekends — it does fill up.

For the supremely fit and energetic, a foot trail climbs to the top of the **Great Warren Dune**, then descends to an uncrowded beach. Another shorter, 1 1/2-mile section climbs **Mount Randall**. From there on a clear day you can see across Lake Michigan to the Sears Tower and Hancock Building in Chicago. There are **6 miles of hiking** and **cross-country skiing trails** (novice to intermediate difficulty). The trailhead with maps is in the interpretive area with vault toilets, water, and a picnic shelter. Here at dusk on summer weekends, the Adventure Ranger may present a slide show or have a game of nature bingo. Three or four times a week from mid-June until Labor Day, there are dune hikes, beach hikes, or "Sky Watches" where visitors can look at the stars through a telescope. (To find the trailhead, go right on the first drive past the entrance, past the park office.) Trails aren't groomed, but a snowmobile does pack the novice trails. Skiers and tobogganers are welcome to use any areas at their own risk, but only the novice cross-country ski area meets all safety criteria.

The Yellow Birch, a **self-guided nature trail** built in 1996, starts at the parking lot and then loops back to it. The **bird-watching boardwalk** at the north end of the natural area has been laid so that not only can wheelchairs access it but now the trail can be

used when the ground is mucky in the spring and fall. More than a
hundred species of birds can be seen.

The 180 **modern campsites** in the woody area have more privacy than the 122 semi-modern (no electricity or showers) sites near
the beach. Reservations are recommended from mid-May through
September, especially weekends and holidays. For people who don't
have camping gear, three compact, cozy mini-cabins with wood
stove and two double bunks rent for $30 a night.

Dune conditions fascinate scientists because they cover all possible extremes of moisture, from desert conditions to temporary ponds
to constant wetness, in a geographically compact area with the same
general climate. Dunes are home to plants uncommon in Michigan.
Tasty wintergreen berries and cranberries grow in the interdunal wetlands of Warren Dunes and nearby Grand Mere state parks.

Preservation of this extensive area of high dunes is due to the
foresight of E. K. Warren of Three Oaks, the serious-minded son of
a Congregational minister who made a fortune by inventing a flexible corset stay made of turkey feathers. In the late 19th century,
sand dunes were considered worthless, valued only for mining sand
used in foundry molds and building materials. Warren realized the
dunes' ecological value and bought 250 acres of these lakeshore
dunes to preserve them for posterity. He gave them to the state as
the nucleus of this park.

*On the Red Arrow Hwy. 3 miles south of Bridgman. From I-94, take
Exit 16, follow the signs and go south. (616) 426-4013. Beach gates
close at 10 p.m. except in the winter when gates close at dusk.
Campground open at all times. No alcoholic beverages. Restroom
facilities closed Oct. 15-April 15. &: almost everything. For sand
wheelchair, contact beach ranger at the middle concession building.
Call for trail info. $4/car/day ($5 non-residents) or $20/year state
parks sticker residents and non-residents alike (resident senior annual pass $5). **Camping:** $14/night, open all year. Winter camping $8.
Reservations recommended from mid-May thru September: (800) 543-
2YES. ($5 reservation fee.)*

A SPECTACULAR TOUR NEAR BRIDGMAN . . . . on the shore of Lake
Michigan is the **Cook Energy Information Center**. It is one of the largest
nuclear plants in the U.S., providing power to customers in Indiana and
Michigan. Next to its plant, the Indiana Michigan Power Company has built
an impressive tourist center. Visitors can also wander among multi-level
terraces towards the lake, with expensive lighting, wrought-iron tables and
chairs, and abundant, well-maintained shrubs and flowers. Upstairs is a

large assortment of **video games** where visitors can learn about energy and how electricity is made. Every few minutes visitors are taken by a professional guide on a **multi-stage presentation**, through three impressive auditoriums. In the first, a full-sized, computer-driven, android newscaster gives an update on the future of energy. Next, the visitors file into a large circular amphitheater, where a model of the nuclear plant is explained. Finally, in a third and even larger auditorium, visitors see a wide-screen film about the Cook plant. One scene shows the small churning area half a mile out in Lake Michigan where the plant gets its water to cool the steam which turns the giant turbines. A quarter of a mile out, the water is returned 3° F warmer.

Linked to the Cook Center are three miles of forest, dune, and wetland trails along Lake Michigan open to visitors. The Nipissing Dune Trails and the Wetlands Trail, with marked points of interest, are part of the Grand Marais Embayment formed by the last glacial retreat.

Visitors are welcome to **picnic** on a landscaped patio overlooking Lake Michigan, or eat inside on cold or wet days. There's an indoor snack bar and vending machines. *On the Red Arrow Highway 3 miles north of Bridgman and I-94 exit 16. A traffic light is at the entrance. (800) 548-2555. Open mid-January to mid-December: Tues thru Sun 10-5, plus special monthly weekend events. Group tours available. Special* **weekend collectors exhibits** *on quilts, decoys, regional art, and antiques are held once or twice a month. ♿ Free.*

A WILD DUNELAND BIRD-WATCHERS LOVE . . . . . is at **Grand Mere State Park**. Here bogs, a chain of three small lakes, and other wetlands among the dunes prevented cottage development and left the area remarkably wild, though within earshot of I-94. The Michigan Nature Conservancy gave the land to the state for a limited-development natural area. It's wonderful for spring wildflowers and migrating birds (warblers and other songbirds in spring, hawks in spring and fall). Herons, cormorants, gulls, ducks, and even shy loons are regular residents. Now an entrance road leads to a parking lot, **picnic area,** 2,200-foot, wheelchair-accessible **trail**, and 2 miles of **hiking and cross-country ski trails** circling interdunal ponds and cranberry and wintergreen bogs. A trail from the parking lot by South Lake leads to Lake Michigan and back in a mile loop. For **cross-country skiing**, the trail marked "novice" is a two-mile, flat loop, not groomed but packed with a snowmobile. More adventurous skiers and tobogganers are welcome to ski and sled through the dunes on unmarked trails, at their own risk. No camping or swimming. *Take I-94 exit 22 (Stevensville) and follow the signs onto Thornton Rd. (under the freeway to the west). (616) 426-4013. ♿: nature trail. $20 state park sticker or $4/day.*

Fernwood

One woman's enchanted gardens

FERNWOOD has grown into an impressive 105-acre nature center and place to learn about gardening and nature crafts. But its core is a series of very personal gardens begun by Kay Boydston, a schoolteacher from Chicago. This serene, sensuous small universe is an inspiring example of what can be created by years of thinking about plants and working with them. Kay Boydston, a serious, self-taught horticulturist, discovered this ravine and brookside area with her husband, Walter, in the 1930s. From upland fields the land descends 125 feet down to the St. Joseph River, creating an exceptional range of microclimates — perfect for a gardener's and botanist's experiments with diversity. Soils vary from sand to clay, both wet and dry.

Over a 30-year period, Boydston began a **perennial garden**, a **lilac garden**, a **boxwood garden,** a **fern trail** leading to a rustic bridge by a corkscrew falls, and an enchanting **rock garden**. There in April and May bloom primroses, heathers, and many little flowers from the mountains, meadows, and bogs of the world, tucked in pockets of tufa stone. Dwarf conifers add to the effect of a delicate but tough miniature world.

A creek tumbles down a glen in many stages, turning a water wheel in a decorative little mill. A wooded streamside trail follows the creek past marshes down to the wide river and a riverside observation deck, or, turning away from the ferny glen, another trail leads to a sizable pond, where visitors might see turtles basking in the sun. These gardens are a sensory delight, filled with the sounds of splashing

Kay Boydston's Fernwood gardens are relaxed, natural collections of ferns, primroses, Alpine flowers, heathers and other plants, deftly planted in and near the woods going down to the St. Joseph River. It's a serene, sensuous place many visitors long remember.

water and birdsong and the smells of flowers, pines, and leaf mold in the air.

The Fern Trail goes between the Boydston's simple, shingled homes. (One house was oriented to summer views and shade, another to winter sun.) East of the summer house (now used for meeting rooms) is a series of picturesque small spaces like outdoor rooms: a shady perennial garden, a wildflower garden, a boxwood garden, and a lily pond surrounded by lilacs. Throughout the original gardens, arbors, bridges, and benches accent the design and encourage visitors to stay and contemplate a small area. The final "room" is the **North Vista Garden**, planted in 1964 by the late Clarence Gottschalk, longtime director of Chicago's Morton Arboretum. It showcases a fine viburnum collection that blooms in late May, then provides colorful late-summer berries and fall foliage.

Two important trails leave from this building. **The Pine Woods Trail** goes to the arboretum and the tallgrass prairie (see below). The **Wilderness Trail** loops through the woods down to the river and follows it back around to the observation deck not far from the **Fern Trail**. Be sure to study the **trail map**, otherwise you might miss the hidden natural side of Fernwood that puts the cultivated areas into focus. The map's scale helps you estimate distances; the prairie and arboretum are also accessible by car.

The North Vista Garden was the first garden planted after the Boydstons turned their home into a public nature center/garden/ education center in 1964. Fernwood's philosophy, following Kay Boydston's, is to create beautiful gardens while encouraging wildlife and preserving the natural environment. Over half Fernwood's acreage is a diverse nature preserve often coming right up to the cultivated garden. Pesticides are not used to maintain Fernwood's gardens. Pest control here depends on plant selection and knowledgeable horticultural care.

Nature-based education and art programs are the third element in Fernwood's focus, and a key part of the center's growth. The range of **classes** and **expeditions** showcased in the fat, bimonthly *Fernwood News* is truly dazzling — gardening classes on low-maintenance shrubs, prairies, seed-starting for kids, canoe trips on the Dowagiac and St. Joe rivers, Jens Jensen's American landscapes, assemblage sculpture, bird-watching, flower-arranging in low bowls.

Today the extensive **Mary Plym Visitors Center** is the beginning of every Fernwood visit. The center itself houses an extensive garden-oriented **gift shop,** a **fern conservatory** (nice in winter!), a **gallery** for interesting changing exhibits of nature-oriented art, and a **cafe** with outstanding soups, sandwiches, desserts, and muffins for modest prices. Effective new gardens lead to either end of the linked gardens described above. The **South Vista Garden** shines in late spring with snowy white viburnum, deep-hued iris, echoing the blues of the wild hyacinth along the stream. In fall it's also colorful. Smaller theme gardens are around the fern vista garden: butterflies and hummingbirds, pioneer plants, Japanese landscaping, roses.

At the visitor center's north end, visible from the cafe, is a charming **herb and sensory garden** accented by an 18th-century English dovecote, a stone wall, and a wattle fence of woven branches. The herbs, planted with an eye for beauty and bloom, are grouped by use: culinary, medicinal, fragrant, dye, and pest repellents.

In April and May Boydston's rock garden is abloom with the little flowers of mountains and bogs. Primroses, iris, gentians, and wild tulips and daffodils are planted among the dwarf conifers and ferns. The gardens have been planned for year-round interest.

A loop off the main road to the visitor center lets visitors drive and park by the arboretum and prairie. The **tallgrass prairie** is one of the very best prairie reconstructions around. A trail guide explains it. The **overlook platform** a hundred feet from the parking area gets visitors above the lofty grasses for a good view. The prairie is in bloom from May through August.

The 60-acre arboretum, begun in the mid-1960s, has 60 trees recommended for suburban lots, plus comparative collections of pines, maples, oaks, crabapples, firs, spruce, magnolias, hawthorns, dogwood, arborvitae, and various flowering shrubs.

Fernwood is worth frequent visits. The gardens are always different as the growing season progresses, and the three miles of trails are a touchstone with the seasons of the natural world. Bird-watching provides seasonal interest when plants are dormant. Shrubs and trees have been chosen for winter interest.

13988 Range Line Rd. between Berrien Springs and Buchanan.

From Niles or Berrien Springs, take U.S. 31/33 to Walton Rd. turn west and follow the signs. From U.S. 12 and I-94, take Red Bud Trail (in Buchanan) north to River Road, which becomes Walton. Turn left (north) at first intersection onto Range Line. Follow the signs. (616) 695-6491 or 683-8653. Hours: Tues-Sun year-round, 10-6, til 7:30 Saturday during Eastern Daylight Time, 10-5 during Eastern Standard Time. May be open Friday evenings 10-5. $3 adults, $2 seniors (65 and over) and ages 13-19, $1 ages 6-12, 5 and under free. Group rates available. Pick up a free trail map with handy scale to plan your visit.

TWO FINE CANOEING RIVERS . . . . . the small, tranquil **Dowagiac** and the wide, deep **St. Joseph**, can be canoed easily with rental or spotting services from **Niles Canoe Rental** (616-683-5110). It's at their confluence, at 1430 North Bus. U.S. 31. Many trips can be arranged. Some pass through virgin hardwood forests near Dowagiac and Pokagon. **Tubing** can be done in the Dowagiac River.

SURPRISES IN A SMALL NILES MUSEUM . . . . . The interesting **Fort St. Joseph Museum** has many remarkable artifacts. Excavated from the **late 17th-century French Fort St. Joseph** just south of Niles are glass and seed beads, silver crosses, merchants' seals, and pots. The outpost served to protect the Jesuit mission here, to advance French diplomatic interests with neighboring Indians, and to supply them with trade goods in exchange for furs.

Through a historical fluke, the museum also has an outstanding collection of **Plains Indian artwork.** In the late 19th century, Niles military officers and wives, stationed in forts on the Great Plains, became friendly with Sioux leaders. The Sioux gave them many beautiful and fascinating things, including a stunning Victorian-Indian beaded dress, and large autobiographical pictographs done by the illustrious Sitting Bull and by Rain-in-the-Face. (His is in large format on cloth.) Also here: material on famous folks from Niles, including **Ring Lardner**, the **Dodge brothers**, and **Montgomery Ward**; and more about Niles industries and black history. *508 E. Main (U.S. 31/33) at Fifth (M-51), behind the ornate City Hall. (616) 683-4702. Wed-Sat 10-4. ᕈ: first floor only. Donations appreciated.*

Niles' City Hall next door occupies the super-ornate **Chapin Mansion**, a Queen Anne castle of a house, lavish with many patterns of brickwork, in which each room has an elaborate fireplace made of a different imported wood. Henry Chapin was a prosperous Niles grocer in 1865 when he invested in Upper Peninsula mineral land. Years later he raked in profits when a rich iron ore deposit was discovered near Iron Mountain and became the Chapin Mine. Visitors are welcome to look around the during business hours. Ask for the interesting book about it. *Main at Fifth. (616) 683-4702. Open weekdays 8-5. ᕈ: no.*

A PLEASANT WALK THROUGH OLD NILES . . . . . could begin by stopping for candy at the venerable **Veni Sweet Shop** on the southeast corner of Main at Third. (Look up to see the elegant old stained-glass sign on the front and side: black script on lavender and flowers.) The Marazitas have made candy here for 80 years, as the store changed from fruit market to soda fountain (the marble counter remains) to candy store. Favorites are peanut clusters, raisin clusters, and licorice buttons, sugar-free chocolate, plus peanut butter smidgens at Easter, chocolate sponge candy at Christmas. *Open 10-5:30, closed Sunday. (616) 684-1323.* ᕁ.

The St. Joseph River is especially impressive at Niles — almost in a leafy gorge — though it's hard to see it from Main Street, where a shopping strip obscures the view. Walk two blocks south on Third, however, and you'll reach pretty **Island Park**, which follows the river almost a mile. The **boyhood home of Ring Lardner**, humorist and master of American vernacular, is an especially picturesque and well-preserved Gothic Revival house on a bluff overlooking the St. Joseph River. *519 Bond St., off Third four blocks south of Main/U.S. 12.*

Of Niles's four antiques malls, one — and a good one, at that, with 70 dealers – is right downtown in the old Montgomery Ward's at 218 Second just north of Main. **Four Flags Antique Mall** (616-683-6681) is open in summer (and possibly in fall) from 10-6 Monday through Saturdays, 12-6 Sundays. Winter weekdays it closes at 5. ᕁ: *yes.* The three other malls, **Michiana**, **Picker's Paradise**, and **Unique Antiques**, are all on U.S. 33 South on the way to South Bend along with still more antique and consignment shops.

If you walk up the East Main Street hill to the City Hall and Fort St. Joseph Museum, you'll pass the old **Carnegie Library** (now the **Four Flags Chamber of Commerce**, with visitor information; 616-683-3720) and the elegant **Four Flags Hotel** from the 1920s. Now a residence hotel, it's worth a peek inside for its beautiful tiles and carved wood details. The hotel also houses **The Colony** restaurant and **Four Flags Fantastic Flavors** ice cream parlor/espresso cafe. The adjacent **Ready Theater,** remodeled into a quadplex with budget prices, still has the roomy seating and much of the splendid mood of picture palaces from Hollywood's Golden Age. *(616) 683-1112.* ᕁ: *3 of 4 theaters.*

Much of historic downtown Niles has suffered from the success of the homegrown Kawneer Corporation, long America's premiere manufacturers of storefront components. Kawneer pioneered appalling metal panels that gave many old brick commercial buildings a sleek, "modern" look that today makes them look almost sleazy. After covering up much of downtown, Kawneer left town and relocated in the South. Now history-loving new owners are beginning to take the metal panels off.

Also of interest, but farther from downtown, is the magnificent brown sandstone **train station** with its great clock tower and massive Romanesque arches. The last important stop on the old Michigan Central Railroad going into Chicago, it was built as the line's showpiece to impress crowds going to the World's Fair in 1893. More recently, it has appeared in movies, including *Only the Lonely* and *Midnight Run. On Fifth Street six blocks north of Main (Business U.S. 12).*

A BLUFFTOP PARK WITH TRAILS, FINE RIVER VIEWS, PLAYGROUND, AND FRISBEE GOLF. . . . . just south of Niles, **Madeline Bertrand Park** offers **nature programs** from its **visitor center** with **bird-feeding area**. Get a map there to 3 1/2 miles of **trails**, plus more in an adjacent park across the Indiana line. Trails are groomed for **cross-country skiing**, with a warming shelter. Call (616) 683-8280 for program info and ski reports. *From the U.S. 12/U.S. 33 intersection at Niles, go south on U.S. 33 about 2 miles, turn right (west) onto Ontario, follow signs to park entrance. Closed on Mon & Tues from November 1 thru March.* &: *visitor center, all picnic facilities, restrooms, parking, and trails (hard-packed). Non-resident vehicle fee: $5/day.*

TOURS OF SIMPLICITY PATTERNS . . . . . can be arranged for groups of 10 or more (during non-summer months only) by calling (616) 683-4100. Ask for Jo Ann Cabanaw. Simplicity Patterns is headquartered in New York, but all the patterns and promotional material for their world-wide markets are printed here in Niles's 300-employee plant. Visitors see tissue paper being made in Simplicity's paper mill, then printed and folded on big web presses. The color pattern envelopes are printed here, too. &.

A WORKING 1853 GRISTMILL . . . . . complete with wooden waterwheel, can be seen right in downtown Buchanan. **Pears Mill** (pronounced "Peers") has been rescued and restored; the interior, with its massive post-and-beam construction, is handsome. Alas, the old mill stream flows not in a sylvan glade but under an ugly parking lot. Visitors can buy stone-ground flour and cornmeal, and see exhibits about local history. *Open Memorial Day thru September, weekends and holidays 1-5. (NOTE: on Sundays, the mill does not actually run.) Free; donations appreciated. (616) 695-5525. From U.S. 12, take Redbud Trail north into Buchanan; go left (west) onto Front St. (Niles-Buchanan Rd.). In 3 blocks turn south onto Oak and park at mill. From the west, Elm Valley Rd. becomes Front St..*

LIVE ENTERTAINMENT ON SUMMER WEEKENDS. . . . . can be seen and heard at the **Tin Shop Theater** in downtown Buchanan. Plays, music, children's events, and readings are performed from late May through August. Most tickets $5. Call (616) 695-6464 for program, reservations, and directions. Sponsored by the Buchanan Area Fine Arts Council.

MICHIGAN'S ONLY UNDERGROUND CAVE . . . . . can be visited for $3. At **Bear Cave**, north of Buchanan, springs formed unusual formations of tufa (a spongy limestone). Visitors get a competent 20-minute audiotaped tour of the cave's interesting, if unspectacular, chambers, tunnels, and formations. The setting by the St. Joseph River is delightful, but camping is for members only. *At the Bear Cave Campground, off Red Bud Trail 3 miles north of Buchanan. Open at most times, summers only. (616) 695-3050.* &: *no, 40 steps. Adults $3, kids 6-12 $1.50, kids 5 and under free..*

Michigan Wine and Berrien County Wineries

Where you can see it all — from fruit on the vine to wine in the glass, in delightful rural settings

AN EXCELLENT introduction to wine can be had at small wineries where the tasting room is usually staffed by people (often the owner-winemakers) with a hands-on knowledge of wine-growing and winemaking. In Michigan these wineries include **Lemon Creek** and **Heart of the Vineyard** in central Berrien County (see pages 41-44 at the end of this chapter), and around Traverse City **L. Mawby** (page 585) and **Boskydel** (page 585) on the Leelanau Peninsula and **Chateau Chantal** (page 606) and Old Mission Peninsula. These "boutique wineries" offer some noteworthy Michigan wines.

The Michigan wine story is a compelling agricultural drama being played out in our own time. Many factors affect the taste and character of wine. These include quality of rootstock, care of vines, temperature and humidity during the growing season: fall frost; winter weather; sugar content during harvest; manner in which grapes are picked and possibly culled; and winemaking style — whether skin is left in contact with the juice, whether wine is aged in an oak barrel, what kind of yeast is used, and more.

Two crucial factors affecting wine quality are so site-specific as to be impossible to predict without years of experience: the exact composition of the soil on which grape vines are grown and the exact climate of the soil's location. Soil characteristics vary within small areas. And microclimate is affected by elevation, topography, and orientation to the sun, so it can vary considerably within the same neighborhood. To unlock a vineyard's winemaking potential takes years of matching different grape varieties with local soils and microclimates that suit them best.

The great vineyards of Europe have histories of hundreds of years of growing different grape varieties. Michigan and many other U. S. winegrowing regions, in comparison, are just moving beyond the experimental stage.

The officially recognized wine-growing regions of Michigan are the Lake Michigan Shore in southwest Michigan and near Traverse City, the Leelanau Peninsula and the Old Mission Peninsula. Southwest Michigan has sandy soils, rolling terrain, and the same amount of heat units as the wine-producing regions of northern Europe. Michigan winters are colder than those in Europe, but more snow cover here usually protects the graft union on each vine. (That's where the bearing vine is grafted to hardier native root-stock.) Michigan's occasional steamy summer weather encourages fungus, but that can be controlled with species-specific fungicide.

Historically, Michigan has used hardy native grapes like Concord and Catawba to make sweet wines. These bland varieties gave Michigan wines a bad reputation for many years. The first grapes suited to the contemporary taste for drier wines to prove successful here were French hybrid varieties promoted by Michigan State University. Tabor Hill near Berrien Springs showed the way in the 1970s. St. Julian, Michigan's largest and oldest winery and the state's most important buyer of wine grapes, soon convinced its contract growers that French hybrids could be successful on a commercial scale. The hybrids Vignoles and Vidal Blanc (both white grapes) and Chancellor and Chambourcin (reds) are well-suited to Michigan. Since then, young winemakers have emerged, part of the back-to-the-land movement of the 1970s. Noteworthy successes were achieved by blending hybrid varieties to create proprietary blends like St. Julian's popular Simply Red, L. Mawby's excellent blends, and Good Harbor's Fishtown White.

Then Ed O'Keefe at Chateau Grand Traverse north of Traverse City proved that a small winery could succeed growing only vinifera grapes — those prestigious "noble grapes" such as Chardonnay and Merlot from the Old World that are more susceptible to freezes and disease. (It's pronounced "vi [as in 'fib']-NIF-uh-ruh."). Riesling, a white German grape that's more cold-tolerant than most French grapes, and Chardonnay are the vinifera varieties that do best in Michigan. Now more growers are putting more acreage in vinifera varieties, experimenting with the strains resistant to harsh winters and confining them to a small fraction of their overall production.

Sadly, financial difficulties led some daring younger winemakers like Jim Eschner of Madron Lake Hills, a highly regarded premium winery in Berrien County, to get out of wine production altogether.

The recent surprise in Michigan winegrowing has been the success of Michigan red wines. Baco Noir, the first red hybrid variety widely grown here, lacked the body many people expect in a red wine. For a while, that gave rise to the notion that only white wines could really stand out in Michigan. But the hybrids Chambourcin and Chancellor and, just recently, the vinifera Cabernet Sauvignon, have produced full-bodied, award-winning red wines for Michigan wineries. Merlot is a dry red wine grape that has many of the big, round, complex characteristics associated with Cabernet Sauvignon. As Chambourcin becomes better known, Michigan wines will come into their own nationally, says wine-lover Christopher Cook, whose wine column appeared in the *Detroit Free Press* food section for ten years. Lemon Creek's Chambourcin won a National Gold Medal from the American Wine Society.

"It takes a newly planted grape vine five full seasons before it shows what it can produce in local soil like Berrien County's," says Cook. "This is not something you can develop overnight. But we're now seeing a coming of age in Michigan wines. After a long struggle, Michigan wines are genuinely competitive with those of California and elsewhere. What makes them unique is that they have their own personalities.

"Michigan's biggest problem has been a lack of exposure elsewhere. Wine-making states become certified in the public mind once they are contrasted to those that are better known. Thus California became accepted once it was compared to France, Washington to California, Oregon to Washington and so on. No one has compared Michigan to anywhere else yet. But it's going to happen. It's my belief that in five to ten years Michigan will have been accepted across the country as a small, high-quality American wine region. And my bet is that we'll be best known for sparkling wines."

Climate similarities to the Champagne region of France, leave Michigan in some years with underripe Pinot Noir or Chardonnay grapes, Cook says. That's exactly what happens in Champagne. "Typically, Michigan grapes ripen to a point, and then it's a real push at the end of the season to get enough sun to ripen fully. We're

At his highly regarded Heart of the Vineyard winery, winemaker Rick Moersch tells participants in a hands-on winemaking workshop how they can affect their wine's taste by their choice of yeast. At the same time, he draws fresh grape juice into a bottle.

About wine awards

Like so much in the world of PR and media hype, wine competition awards aren't as good indicators of quality as you'd think at first. You never know who has entered which competitions. Some excellent winemakers don't enter competitions at all. Some categories at the Michigan State Fair, the most important competition for the Michigan wine industry, have so few entries that it's insignificant which wine wins. Awards do help new wineries gain recognition, and winning prestigious national competitions does put Michigan wines on a bigger map. But once a small winery has gained a good customer base, entering competitions may not be worth the trouble or money. Wineries have to pay entry fees to be judged. If a winery's output is limited, an award may be counter-productive, if it stimulates too much demand for a particular wine and disappoints regular customers.

seeing several wineries making excellent sparkling wines now."

Exploiting the tourism possibilities of picturesque vineyards is a trend developed in California's wine country that will be popping up more and more in Michigan. Tabor Hill's restaurant has spectacular vineyard views but, in our experience at various times, indifferent food and service. Paw Paw attracts busloads with the St. Julian tour, the idyllic patio area next to Warner Vineyards, and the Little River Cafe with its list focusing on Michigan wines. (See page 46.)

Now a winemaker with lots of experience in Germany has teamed up with a well-heeled partner to build a virtual castle of a bed and breakfast inn in their Old Mission vineyard, Chateau Chantal (page 606). They struggled with rather anemic wines in the first three years, in Cook's opinion, but finally, in 1995, produced a supple, round Merlot that he and many others believe will really put them on the map.

Many wineries' labels allude to the romance of wine and are becoming ever more artistic. Lest consumers get too caught up in the mystique of small boutique wineries, Cook adds, "One of the best consistent wineries in Michigan is St. Julian in Paw Paw." Wine sophisticates may turn up their noses at St. Julian's tasting rooms along interstates and at tourist destinations. Furthermore, it's quite true that St. Julian aims to produce wines for all tastes and pocketbooks. But Cook praises their award-winning Chancellor and Chambourcin, bargains at $8.50 a bottle. "Some will still be excellent wines 20 years from now."

This is an exciting time to taste Michigan wines. "Certain wines shine each year," says Cathy Lemon of Lemon Creek. "We've all got our bread-and-butter wines and our sweet wines, but each year most wineries have one wine that's really good for that year. That's why you don't go to just one winery and drink just one wine. Finding those special wines is the mystique and the fun of wine."

Though wine drinkers can be a supercilious, snobbish lot, tasting rooms are pleasantly democratic places run by people who know that, ultimately, enjoying wine is all a matter of individual taste, varying from person to person. Winery tasting rooms let customers develop their taste inexpensively. If you decide to explore Michigan wine and wineries, it's a good idea to record your likes and dislikes in a permanent notebook.

Michigan wine-lovers seem more aware of small wineries in the Traverse City area. But Berrien County's wineries are a more convenient place to begin exploring Michigan wines, with wines of comparable and even higher quality than those of the Grand Traverse region. The setting is beautiful: hilly, pastoral, and remote in mood, but convenient to Chicago and Detroit. For up-close, personal views of grape-growing and winemaking, visit Lemon Creek, a 150-year-old family fruit farm and the nearby Heart of the Vineyard, Rick Moersch's new winery with 10 acres of producing vines, followed by a visit to St. Julian to see and taste what can be done on a bigger scale using grapes grown on contracts.

Moersch had been the winemaker at the adjacent Tabor Hill, the pioneer in the Michigan's wine industry changeover to drier, more sophisticated wine. Tabor Hill, now a fancy, highly capitalized place that produces mid-priced wines, has become the state's second-biggest winery. It's worth a visit (see p. 44) if you have time, but judging from our recent experience, tours leave a lot to be desired.

LEMON CREEK FRUIT FARMS, VINEYARDS & WINERY

Lemon Creek offers a rare opportunity to taste a good variety of medium-priced Michigan wines (including many award-winners), to buy and pick fresh fruit, and to see most phases of wine production, from grape growing to fermentation and bottling. (Pressing is done at St. Julian's, except for small runs of premium wine.) Just outside the tasting room, you can see vines, neatly labeled by variety, and the tall grape harvester that straddles the rows of vines and harvests the grapes. Visitors can **picnic** at tables outside the tasting room and are welcome to walk in the vineyards and orchards. A duck pond adds to the rural atmosphere. Tours of the winemaking facilities are informal and brief.

Grapes already picked can be purchased for home wine-making, or you can pick them yourself. Varieties produced here include Concord and several French hybrids (Chamborcin, Baco Noir, Vignoles, and Vidal, the Lemons' main stock). Among vinifera varieties are Riesling, Cabernet Sauvignon, Merlot, Chardonnay, and Gewürztraminer. **Fruits** (sold packaged or **U-pick**) include raspberries, four kinds of sweet cherries, tart cherries, nectarines, pears, plums, three kinds of peaches, and eight apple varieties.

The three Lemon brothers grew up on this 225-acre farm. They were among the first in the area to grow grapes for drier wines. With 110 acres in wine grapes, they are quite possibly the largest growers of wine grapes in Michigan. In 1981, after years of falling fruit prices, many other southwest Michigan fruit farmers also replaced their orchards with French hybrid grapes. Prices fell dramatically as a result. The Lemons, like an increasing number of fruit and vegetable producers, realized they'd be more secure financially if they marketed their own produce. They decided to add value to it by producing wine.

Lemon Creek continued supplying Tabor Hill, St. Julian, and Good Harbor with wine grapes but also opened its own winery in 1984. As winemakers, the Lemons have been extraordinarily successful, with well over 100 awards for their wines thus far. Wine prices start at $4.95 a bottle for Ruby Rose (a frequent silver medal-winner). The three Vidal wines (dry, demi-sec, and semi-sweet) have won the most awards; they're $5.95. The Lemons are excited about the 1995 vintage, their best since 1991, they say. Standouts

Tim Lemon (left), his brother Jeff, and Jeff's wife, Cathy, in their vineyard seven miles west of Berrien Springs. For getting a good all-around view of growing fruit and making wine, the informal tour at their Lemon Creek Winery is one of the best.

include the full-bodied, dry red Chancellor at $10 and Lighthouse White at $9, a semi-sweet blend of premium wines. Sparkling juices are $4). *533 Lemon Creek Rd. just east of Baroda, 5 miles east of Bridgman and 7 miles west of Berrien Springs. From 1-94 exit 16 at Bridgman, go north on Red Arrow Hwy. 2 miles to Lemon Creek Rd.. then east 5 miles. (616) 471-1321. Open year-round. May-Dec: 9-6 daily, Sun 12-6. Jan-April: Fri-Sun 12-5 and by appt. A free June festival each* **Father's Day** *weekend includes hayrides, games for kids, arts and crafts booths, and free music.* ♿.

HEART OF THE VINEYARD

Owner/winemaker Rick Moersch, a born teacher, loves talking about the agriculture and chemistry of wine. He was Tabor Hill's winemaker for 13 years. Before that he taught high school science in Berrien Springs. He planted his own eight acres of vines in 1981 on this property, adjacent to Tabor Hill. One Heart of the Vineyard hallmark is esoteric plantings of unusual grape varieties, mostly German, like the fruity, robust Scheurebe, the spicy Gewürztraminer, the delicate Müller-Thurgau, and Pinot Gris. Another distinguishing characteristic is Moersch's drier, French-influenced Alsatian style of making wine with these German grapes. Moersch has been making outstanding champagnes since a French champagne maker showed him how at Tabor Hill, and they continue to be a specialty. Now that he is a boutique winemaker, he enjoys spending less time on the road dealing with distributors and more time educating customers. In America today, wineries are the main locus of wine education, he feels.

There aren't regular tours here, but many special events involve a good deal of wine education. Moersch is regularly quite accessible, either in the tasting room here or at the new Riviera Gardens garden center tasting room on the Red Arrow Highway in Union Pier. (Call to find out where he is.) Wine is served on the terrace behind the farmhouse and winery tasting room, looking out onto the woods. It's a lovely setting, especially when the late afternoon sun illuminates the trees while visitors enjoy a glass of wine on the shady terrace.

It's a treat even for the ignorant to witness Moersch in action, explaining why natural yeasts result in more complex flavors, or giving an insider's view of a revolutionary vine trellising system introduced by Dr. Tom Zabadal of Michigan State University's experiment station at nearby Sodus. "It's a coup for M.S.U. to grab him from Cornell," Moersch says. "He has us growing vines not on a single wire but on multiple wires, so we bring canes up to 42" and

54". We have doubled the canopies [the amount of leaf] so we can produce and ripen more fruit. I'm the only one here who converted 100% of my vineyard, and now I'm harvesting twice as many grapes per vine as my neighbors. Anything to get the fruit into the sunlight! In Michigan we have better ripening and more heat units than comparable areas of Oregon, but we weren't taking advantage of them. Northwest Michigan winemakers feel we're all cultists with Zabadal. To Europeans it's like the Wild West."

A most worthwhile experience is offered in two series of fall hands-on winemaking courses. Enrollees pick grapes and make various choices of yeasts and finishing styles to produce their own wine under Moersch's virtually foolproof guidance — 24 bottles for the $150 fee. Register well in advance. The class making white wines starts the third weekend in September, the reds on the second weekend in October, each with two or three follow-up sessions. Other events include the barrel tasting and **harvest festival** on the last weekend in September ($15 or so covers the lamb, pig, and goat roast, veggies, hayride, etc.), and a free **Nouveau Release** party the first Saturday in December with special discounts on holiday wine gifts. (This "Beaujolais" is actually made with a Chambourcin grape.) In winter, anyone is welcome to **cross-country ski** in the vineyards and along the creek and into the woods. *10981 Hills Rd. just west of Tabor Hill Winery between Berrien Springs and Baroda. From I-94 at Bridgman, take Exit 16, go north on Red Arrow Hwy. to Lake/Shawnee Rd., then east 4 miles to Hills Rd. Turn south (right). Winery is in 1/2 mile. From U.S. 31 bypass at Berrien Springs, take Snow Rd. exit west about 8 miles, follow signs. (800) 716-9463. Open daily year-round 12-6.* &.

TOURING TABOR HILL WINERY . . . . . is pretty and worthwhile if you have time. But don't expect too much from the youthful tour guides hired for busy seasons. If you can catch him at an opportune time, winemaker Michael Merchant is happy to answer questions. He can give group tours by appointment. . . . . Tabor Hill today is a far cry from the creative chaos of Tabor Hill's early, commune-like days under wine visionary and super-salesman Len Olson. Whirlpool heir David Upton rescued the financially shaky operation in the late 1970s. Now it's Michigan's second-biggest winery in volume. Its mainstays have been middle-price wines using French hybrid grapes. Wine experts recommend its Classic Demi-Sec ($6.95), a semi-dry, easy-drinking, summer picnic kind of wine, as an excellent value. Tabor Hill's Late Harvest Riesling was "Best in Show" at the Michigan State Fair in 1994 and their Grand Marque won the Gold at the National Orange show. Merchant especially recommends the vintage Chardonnays of the past four or five years ($15 a bottle), subtler than California

Chardonnays; the Rieslings; and Tabor Hill's successful proprietary Blush blends of Vidal and other hybrid grapes ($6.95/bottle). "They're continually fine-tuned and improved — in our opinion—with each year's grapes," he says. "Of course, what we like may not be everyone's taste. That's the game in market-ing—to anticipate trends in demand and taste." *Between Berrien Springs and Baroda at 185 Mt. Tabor Rd. Same directions as Heart of the Vineyard (p. 43-4), which is just around the corner. Follow Tabor Hill signs instead. (800) 283-3363.* **Wine tastings:** *May thru Sept. or early Oct. Mon & Tues 9-5, Wed-Fri 9-9, Sat 11:30-9, Sun noon-9. Other times by appt.* **Tours:** *May or June thru Sept or early Oct on the half hour, noon to 4:30. It's always best to call ahead.* **Restaurant hours:** *May thru Nov Wed-Sat 11:30-3, 5-9, Sat 5-9, Sun noon-9. Jan-April: Fri 5-9, Sat 11:30-3, 5-9, Sun 12-3.* &.

ALSO RECOMMENDED IN NEARBY BERRIEN SPRINGS . . . . . . From the wave of plain Greek Revival courthouses built shortly after Michigan statehood in 1837, only two survive. The dignified courtroom in the **1839 Courthouse Museum** in sleepy Berrien Springs has been carefully restored. An outstanding museum of Berrien County history is in the lower level. There's a restored **sher-iff's office**, changing exhibits, a large **log house**, and a **book and gift shop** that's very good on regional history, old-fashioned toys, and local crafts.. Recently, two **jail cells** were restored at the site of the 1870 circular jail. Now, visitors can have their picture taken behind bars. . . . . **Summer events** include old-fashioned games, blacksmith demonstrations, and 1860-style baseball games. *On U.S. 31 at Union, 3 blocks north of Shawnee/Ferry. (616) 471-1202. Tues-Fri 9-4, Sat & Sun 1-5. Closed holidays. Adults $2.50, young people (6-17) $1; 5 and under free.* &: *boardwalk connects the four sites together. Courthouse 1st floor with most exhibits is barrier-free.* . . . . . **Wild Birds Unlimited** features a wonderful variety of bird feeding supplies and other bird-related stuff, from books and binoculars to jewelry and sweatshirts. Owner Richard Schinkel, founder of the far-flung bird-feeding franchise, is the former naturalist at Sarett Nature Center. He leads birdwatching trips here and around the world. If he's around, Schinkel is happy to answer questions. He has written several books (*Favorite Wildlife in Eastern U. S.* and *Suburban Nature Guide*) and is a contribu-tor to *Birds of Michigan. 109 N. Main just north of Ferry in downtown Berrien Springs. (616) 471-4031. Mon-Sat 9-5, Sun 9-1.* . . . . . Next door the **Green Wellies Garden Shop** specializes in water gardens, fountains, waterfall equip-ment, and perennials. Seven working ponds, each with a different theme, come with fish, turtles, and waterlilies. Benches let you relax while feeding the fish. *111 N. Main. (616) 471-4037. Hours the same as Wild Birds Unlimited. If you need anything in the winter, just stop by Wild Birds.* & . . . . . For picnics, nature hikes, and cross-country skiing through varied ecosystems, pretty **Love Creek County Park & Nature Center** is way above average. Two staff naturalists lead **weekend programs** on birding, insects, flowers, and the like. Live reptiles and amphibians are on display. The bird-watching window has microphones. Spring's wildflowers and fall's color attract visitors, but summer's deerflies keep them away. Winters, groomed, marked trails are available for both classical and skate-style **cross-country skiing**. (Ski fees: $2 adults, $1 youth. Equipment rental: adults $6, youth $3). *From U.S. 31/33 just east of Berrien Springs, turn east onto Pokagon Rd. and follow signs to park on Huckleberry Rd. (616) 471-2617. Trails open daily dawn to dusk. Center open Wed-Sun 10-5. $3/car from county, $5 outside county, or $20 year. &: not impossible but very difficult. Call.*

SEVENTH-DAY ADVENTISTS IN BERRIEN SPRINGS . . . . . During Battle Creek's fast-buck cereal boom of the early 1900s, the town became far too worldly for the Adventists who had made it the home base of their fundamentalist Christian denomination, started the successful Battle Creek Sanitarium, and launched the health reforms that led to the breakfast cereal industry. The Adventists moved to remote Berrien Springs, then a town without a railroad, and started **Andrews University**. . . . . Many visitors enjoy the Adventists' big, vegetarian **Apple Valley** supermarket by the campus at 9067 U.S. 31, 2 miles northwest of town. There you can buy fake meat, good bakery items and produce, and sample the salad bar. *& (616) 471-3131. Closed Saturday, of course.* . . . . Visitors are also welcome at Andrews' **Horn Archaeological Museum**, focusing on Biblical archaeology. Artifacts from the Biblical period and Palestine are shown in historical context provided by colorful murals of scenes from everyday life, ranging from bronze-age Egypt to the Islamic period. The cuneiform tablet collection is one of the biggest in the U.S. Three exhibits recently added are "History of Writing," "Egyptian Necropolis," and "Tell Jalul". *It's in a small, square building near the circle by the campus entrance. Open during the school year Mon-Thurs 9-12 and 2-5, Fri 9-12, Sat 2-5, closed Sun. Otherwise call (616) 471-3273. The staff is usually there. &: no. Free. Donations accepted.* . . . . Ask for directions to the nearby Andrews **natural history museum** with a fine reconstructed **mammoth**.

WINERY TOURS IN PAW PAW. . . . . are also worthwhile. **St. Julian** is the big player in Michigan wine (see pages 38 and 40), and the family-owned winery does a very good job of wine education and wine tourism. The winery is on a busy commercial strip, not in an idyllic vineyard. The **tour, heavily marketed to tour buses and groups,** begins with an informative audiovisual show on St. Julian and winemaking, then takes visitors to see the bottling line and fermenting room. Wine ferments in containers from a huge, 27,000-gallon tank down to small 50-gallon barrels. At harvest time from late August through September, it's especially busy, as trucks deliver grapes and visitors view the grape crush. Attached to the winery and **tasting room** is the **Apollo cafe** serving wine and Italian fare. *On M-40 a few blocks north of I-94 exit 60 at Paw Paw. (616) 657-5568. Free tours and tastings year-round. Tasting room open Mon-Sat 9-5, Sun noon-5 ('til 5:30 from July thru September). Tours given every half hour from 9:30 to 4. No noon tour. &. When visitors include a wheelchair, the tour is re-routed.* . . . . Next door at **Warner Vineyards**, visitors may take a short self-guided tour of the **champagne cellar** which realistically simulates the chalk storage vaults of the French Champagne region. Brochures are available. They can taste any of

the 27 Warner wines and 6 sparkling juices, now mostly made in nearby
Fennville. Wines range from old favorites like the celebrated Warner Solera
Cream Sherry to an award-winning dry champagne and the popular Warner
Liebestrauben and Holiberry. Visitors can see the complicated riddling or turn-
ing system used in the time-honored *methode champenoise* (fermentation in the
bottle). The **wine deck** next door is a delightful place for having a glass of wine
and a light snack, especially on the shady, sunken brick courtyard between the
rippling Paw Paw River and the renovated 1898 waterworks. *706 S. Kalamazoo/
M-40, just north of St. Julian. (616) 657-3165. Open year-round 10-5 daily, 12-5
Sunday.* ♿.

THE VILLAGE OF PAW PAW. . . . . is worth a look. It's an agricultural and resort
village of 3,200 that's also the Van Buren county seat. Numerous Greek Revival
buildings date from the years after 1835, when the **Territorial Road**, Michigan's
main east-west artery, reached Paw Paw. If it's a weekday, look inside the elaborate **1902 Classic Revival courthouse** just east of M-40 at Territorial. Check out
the grand stairway mural of the goddess of plenty and pulchritude. The **U. S.
Post Office** downtown on North Kalamazoo (M-40) has an especially engaging
WPA mural by Carlos Lopez, full of humorous vignettes of local life. . . . . . **Maple
Isle** is a beautiful island park with swimming beach and changing house. It
would be nicer if there weren't so many geese! It's on Maple Lake off M-40 on
Paw Paw's north side. Look for the small parking area to the east side of the road.

LEARNING MORE ABOUT MICHIGAN WINES . . . . . Pick up the free *Michigan
Wine Country* newspaper. Written in part by noted winemakers, it's interesting
and informative. . . . . . In Ann Arbor, the **Village Corner** on South University at
Forest stocks over a hundred carefully selected Michigan wines and always features some Michigan wines in its promotions. Its super-informative catalog, published six times a year, typically has one Michigan wine feature, too. Ask for a
free subscription at the store, or call (313) 995-1818. . . . . . Many small winemakers only distribute in their own state or a few neighboring states, so **mail
order** is a good way for winelovers across the country to sample a wider variety
of regional wines. The **Village Corner** in Ann Arbor (see above) also ships. . . .
Chain supermarkets may have the best prices on popular Michigan wines.
Meijer, D&W Food Centers in West Michigan, and Osco/Jewel in West Michigan,
Indiana, and Illinois stock Michigan wines. The **Merchant of Vino** gourmet and
wine supermarkets in metro Detroit and Ann Arbor have good prices and big
selections, too. . . . . The **Michigan Wine & Harvest Festival** is held in
Kalamazoo and Paw Paw for five days ending with the weekend after Labor Day.
It has wine tastings from most Michigan wineries — for a fee, to benefit local
charities. The winemakers themselves, however, aren't allowed by law to be on
hand and dispense samples except at the opening-night event on Wednesday.

Michigan's fabulous Fruit Belt

A 270-mile shoreline region of specialty fruits, from wine grapes of increasing note to huge crops of tasty apples, tart cherries, and blueberries.

ONE of Michigan's true glories is the variety and flavor of its fruits and vegetables, available at countless farm stands and many U-pick operations. A finishing touch to every summertime outing in West Michigan should be a visit to a fruit farm to load up on fresh fruit to take home. Farm visits and picking expeditions slow down the all-too-frenetic pace of contemporary life and connect you up to the slower, older world of agriculture.

The Fruit Belt extends inland up to over 30 miles in the south. Up north it's a much narrower zone. Lake Michigan moderates the temperature of the air around it, cooling it in hot weather and making it warmer in cold weather. The lake effect tends to depress spring temperatures 3° to 4° F., delaying early blossoms until danger of frosts are past. The lake also means cooler, longer summers, which let fruit ripen more slowly for more intense flavor. One Georgia native was shocked to discover that Michigan peaches tast-

Growing fruit was and is a family affair. This Michigan family posed with its apple crop in 1891. Many U-pick farm operations in Berrien County have been in the same family for five or more generations, sometimes ever since the land was settled.

ed better than Georgia's
famous peaches. The lake
then elevates tempera-
tures 3° or 4° F. in fall,
extending the growing
season. Wine grape vari-
eties that need a lot of
heat to ripen aren't at
their best in Michigan, but varieties that prefer colder climates, like
the German Riesling and the Pinot Noir and Chardonnay of
Burgundy, make excellent wines.

During most winters Lake Michigan has open water, which
means that westerly winds continue to pick up moisture and
deposit it as snow. Snow protects the fruit trees' roots and graft
unions, while clouds keep winter temperatures some 10° to 20° F.
warmer than those in neighboring Wisconsin. Wisconsin's more
extreme continental climate makes for colder winter and hotter
summer temperatures, and far more sunshine. (The Grand
Rapids/Holland/ Muskegon area is the sixth cloudiest in the U.S.)

The same prevailing west winds crossing Lake Michigan are
what created West Michigan's sandy, well-drained soil that's also
beneficial to fruit. As the most recent glacier was melting some
3,000 years ago, a good deal of the sand and sediment deposited by
rivers and runoff along the shore was blown back onto the land.
That east-blown sand created a wide belt of sandy soil extending as
far inland as Grand Rapids, and the dramatic shoreline dunes, the
longest freshwater dunes in the world.

Southwest Michigan's Fruit Belt first developed in the 1850s,

when early farmers around Benton Harbor and St.
Joseph noticed that their peach trees survived severe
winters that killed off peach trees in other parts of
Michigan. Demand for fruit in booming Chicago across
the lake was so great and shipping from Benton
Harbor so convenient that by the 1860s, productive
peach orchards fetched $1,000 an acre.

Benton Harbor's big fruit market goes back to the 1870s, when
farmers' wagons lined up for a mile to load onto the fruit boats at
the canal then located west of Main Street downtown. Steamers
transported the fruit to wholesale commission houses in Chicago
and Milwaukee. People began buying fruit in quantity direct from
the farmers waiting in line, creating first an informal market and
later a formal one. That market is still operating today. (See p. 52.)

Fruit canneries and factories making baskets and crates sprang up around and beyond Benton Harbor, and fruit-growing spread throughout much of Van Buren and Berrien counties. South Haven was long famous for its **peach** crop. At the turn of the century, 144,000 Michigan acres were planted in peach orchards, more than all other Michigan fruit crops combined.

A devastating freeze in 1919 killed most of the peach trees, and another freeze in the 1920s led many West Michigan farmers to focus more on apples. Then in the 1930s Stanley Johnston developed early, cold-resistant Haven peaches at Michigan State University's South Haven experiment station. Haven peaches revolutionized peach-growing. They have an eye-pleasing reddish color. As a freestone peach, the Haven peach is much easier to eat and slice than earlier varieties, whose flesh clung to the stone. Havens can be picked much earlier, and they produce over an extended period, so eating fresh peaches has become much more popular.

But even the Haven peach failed to halt the decline of peach-growing in Michigan. When Chicago peach processors folded in the 1950s, Michigan peach acreage plummeted to just about 8,000 acres. The exceptionally cold winter of 1994 killed many peach trees. Acreage today is around 6,000, down from 7,500 in 1990.

By comparison, **blueberry** plantations have boomed in recent years. Stanley Johnston also started Michigan's blueberry industry when he domesticated a wild, high-bush variety quite different from low-growing Maine blueberries. Unlike most fruits, blueberries like "junk land": low, relatively chilly, swampish areas with dark, acidic, sandy soil. The area around South Haven and Grand Junction happens to have a lot of this land. It has emerged as the world's leading blueberry producer. (To see a vast array of blueberry products, visit **The Blueberry Store** on Phoenix Street in downtown South Haven. Call 616-637-6322.)

Michigan has produced and sold from 34 million to 87 million pounds of blueberries in recent years. With 15,500 acres yielding from 1.3 to 2.8 tons of blueberries an acre and blueberries wholesaling a typical rate of around 75¢ to a dollar a pint (including packaging), blueberries are Michigan's best-paying legal crop. Those blueberry farmers within 10 or 12 miles of Lake Michigan are especially blessed because they get full benefit of the lake effect. Traditionally, migrant pickers have harvested the blueberry crop, but now $100,000 mechanical berrypickers increasingly do the job.

Michigan has 11,700 acres in grapes, centered around Paw Paw and the big juice plant in Lawton, owned and operated by the nationwide Welch's

cooperative. By far the largest portion of Michigan's grapes are
Concord grapes used for juice.

Especially noteworthy fruit farm destinations in southwest
Michigan's fruit belt include:

◆ **Tree-Mendus Fruit** (page 54). Outstanding orchard tour.

◆ **Wick's Apple House**, just a short distance from Tree-Mendus
Fruit (see page 58)

◆ **Sunrise Farms** near Benton Harbor. From I-94, take exit 30, east
on Napier 2.6 miles. Watch for signs. (616) 944-1457.

◆ **Lemon Creek Winery and Fruit Farm** near Berrien Springs
(page 41).

◆ **Crane's Orchards and Pie Pantry** on M-89 between Fennville
and Saugatuck. Light lunches (616-561-2297), farmy B&B (616-
561-6931) on 5th-generation family fruit farm.

In northwestern Michigan:

◆ **Amon Orchards** near Traverse City (page 610). Excellent orchard
tour.

◆ The beautiful **Bill's Farm Market** in Petoskey (page 642)

◆ **L. Mawby Winery** on the Leelanau Peninsula (page 585)

◆ Wineries and vineyards on the Old Mission Peninsula (page 607)

Apples are widely grown throughout the Lower Peninsula. In a
typical year, Michigan and New York vie for second place in apple

production, behind Washington State, where the eastern desert has been irrigated and planted in orchards.
Michigan's more variable weather lessens their cos-
metic appeal compared with Washington apples, but
the cooler climate produces a sweeter, more flavorful
apple. Big Washington fruit farms mainly stick to Red
and Yellow Delicious and Granny Smith apples, while Michigan
grows 20 main varieties, and another 40 are not uncommon. A single area of West Michigan accounts for 20% of Michigan's apple crop.
Peach Ridge, eight miles wide, extends 20 miles northwest of Grand
Rapids through Sparta. Some 16,000 acres of apples are planted
here. The 200-foot elevation drains the cold spring air which protects
delicate fruit buds.

Northern Spy and Jonathans are used for processing, where
some 60% of Michigan's apples end up. But the small percentage of
the crop sold at farm stands and cider mills is crucial to the survival
of many growers, now that competition is worldwide. Argentina,
Chile, New Zealand, and South Africa export huge quantities of
apples for very low prices.

The Fruit Belt makes for a backroads adventurer's delight. Rows of vineyards and grids of orchards create an orderly, highly cultivated landscape, sprinkled with villages dating from the late 19th-century fruit boom. Much of the Fruit Belt area looks far more like Europe than most of the American Middle West, especially where vineyards and orchards cover high, rolling hills and glacial moraines. The **scenery** can be breathtaking in hilly parts of Berrien County, in Oceana County south of Ludington and along the Hart-Montague Bicycle Trail (page 548), and throughout the Grand Traverse cherry country up north. The Kal-Haven Trail (page 73) also gives a good up-close look at orchards and blueberry plantations.

MEXICAN-AMERICAN MIGRANTS WHO FOLLOW THE HARVEST TO MICHIGAN . . . . . have become residents throughout the Fruit Belt where permanent, year-round jobs are available. Thanks to the big **Heinz pickle cannery** in Holland, the world's largest, over 25% of Holland's residents are Hispanic, still mostly from Texas, but with increasing numbers from Mexico. Little Mexican groceries are fairly frequent sights, and neighborhood Mexican restaurants are becoming more common. **Margarita's** is a block south of Heinz at 495 17th; a cluster of Mexican businesses is on Washington Square between 16th and 17th. One long-established favorite is **Su Casa** on M-89 by the Shell Station in downtown Fennville. Tucked behind a grocery where piñatas and fried pork rind hang from the ceiling, it's a hangout for local cannery workers at breakfast and lunch, and a popular dinner destination for Anglos.

VISITORS ARE WELCOME AT THE WORLD'S LARGEST CASH-TO-GROWER PRODUCE MARKET . . . . . as long as they keep small children at home and stay out of the way of the trucks and hi-los moving around. The **Benton Harbor Fruit Market** is open from May 1 (melons come from south Florida) through October. This big (24 acres), busy wholesale produce market is the largest cash-to-grower market in the world. Especially large numbers of blueberries, strawberries, cantaloupe, sweet and Indian corn, cucumbers, peaches, peppers, tomatoes, and summer squash pass through here. The market isn't set up for outsiders, but you can watch, and you can buy if you get a $5 permit from the **market office**. Prices are low, but you must buy in quantity. (Check out the office for free calendars and pamphlets on buying and using fresh fruits and vegetables.)

　　The most interesting place to watch the action is under the big **market shed** in the center rear. Here growers of produce that hasn't been sold on prearranged contracts negotiate and sell direct from their trucks to day buyers from farm stands, independent grocers, and small chains. Trucks come about 8 a.m. and line up, six abreast, before being admitted to the trading shed at 9 a.m. A U.S. Department of Agriculture reporter takes prices from bidding there. These very prices establish wholesale price guidelines for the entire state.

Behind that shed are direct-sales stalls where bigger growers rent space to sell their produce. Only 7% of market transactions are of the direct, cash-to-grower variety. The rest are deliveries on pre-sold produce. Commission houses representing firms like Meijer and the Spartan co-operative have little trailer-like cubes on long loading docks. Growers deliver produce to these brokers mostly in the afternoon. *The market is about 2 1/2 miles east of downtown Benton Harbor at 1891 Territorial, east of Crystal and just west of Euclid. From I-94 and Kalamazoo, take exit 33, go north on Crystal, east on Territorial. From I-94 and Chicago, take exit 30, go west on Napier to Crystal, north to Territorial, then east. (616) 925-0681. Market opens May 1 with Florida melons, stays open thru October. Daily and Sunday 8-3, except closed Saturdays.* &.

WOOD FRUIT BASKETS AND CRATES . . . . . in a profusion of styles can be purchased singly and in quantity at **Midwest Fruit Package** (616-927-3371), inside the Fruit Market next to the market office. For gift store owners, craftspeople, and home organizer-decorators, this place is a treasure trove, thanks to low prices and the functional, pleasantly country look. Baskets and crates are infinitely useful — for raking leaves, holding mail, storing books and toys — and attractive too. *Open 8-5 daily except Saturday from May through October.* &.

MORE INFO ON FARM STANDS, U-PICKS, AND CIDER MILLS . . . . . For **free guides to orchards and farm stands** in Berrien, Van Buren, and Cass counties, the heart of southwest Michigan's Fruit Belt, call or write **Southwest Michigan Tourist Council**, 2300 Pipestone, Benton Harbor, MI 49022. (616) 925-6301. The "Pick Michigan" booklet lists virtually all farm stands and U-picks, with some coupons. Two big, fold-out **maps** show **scenic routes** past orchards and farms at blossomtime (late April-early May) and in fall, and shows what stands are open. Ask for "Drive among the Blossoms" and "Travel along Jewel-Colored Roads." Inquire here also about **golf** and **events** information. . . . . . The statewide **"Country Carousel"** guide to farm stands and orchards is free at Michigan Welcome Centers.

Tree-Mendus Fruit

No other fruit farm provides visitors with so much to do, from hiking and hayrides to sampling over 200 varieties of antique apples.

IT'S LATE SEPTEMBER, at Tree-Mendus Fruit, the big, energetically promoted U-pick fruit farm in eastern Berrien County between Eau Claire and Dowagiac. The Huffman family has come from suburban Chicago for its annual apple-picking expedition. Orchard owner Herb Teichman, 66, is at the sales counter, as he often is during fall. He's in his element as he slices an apple in disks (the core makes a star in the middle) and gives a condensed version of the Tree-Mendus one-hour farm tour.

"This is from a one-of-a-kind apple tree because we don't know both parents," Teichman explains to a rapt audience of mostly kids. "A bee brought in the pollen, but we don't know from where. We're calling this apple Tree-Mendus #1." He picks up an apple with a rough, blotched skin from the bins of antique apples sold from the porch for a dollar a pound. "You wouldn't buy that, would you? But when you taste it. . . . ," and he passes out more slices, "you say, 'Gee, whiz, that's a good apple.' Someone liked it. Someone in the next generation made a graft of it. I'm just a notch in the chain, but I want to pass it on." Teichman highlights some of the over 200 varieties in his **"old-time apple museum"** that includes the Spitzenberg (Thomas Jefferson's favorite), the Westfield Seek-No Further, the Fameuse (snow apple), Black Gilliflower (sheepnose), and the tasty, tart Calville Blanc d'Hiver, which goes back to 1627. These and many other apples have been overlooked due to modern marketing demands for apples to look uniform and attractive, ship well, and be harvested all at once.

After this inspiring little talk, it looks like old, non-commercial apple varieties may be the focus of this fall's expedition for the Huffmans. Maryellen Huffman plans a lot of activities around their trip here, sometimes even science projects. "We have traditional apple dishes we make each year," she says. "The boys always stir the apple butter. They learn a lot. At first they couldn't believe they could pick the apples off the tree. Now we notice things like how the weather makes better apples some years."

Over the years Teichman followed *his* bliss right here on the family farm. He has developed his dad's progressive orchard into an unusual visitor attraction that's part Mother Nature's classroom, part living museum of antique apples, and part old-fashioned picnic grounds, in addition to being a conventional U-pick orchard and fruit sales room. It now encompasses 250 acres in fruit, plus 150 acres of forest and 50 acres used for recreation and ponds.

Agritourism and farm markets have played an increasingly big role in the health of Michigan fruit farmers for over two decades, as low prices forced farmers to look for additional income sources. Now apples come from New Zealand and South America in the off season. Herb Teichman, actively helped by his energetic wife, Liz, was inspired to use the apple's potent appeal as a rite of autumn as the basis for designing a day in the country for city people several generations removed from the farm. Now their adult children—Lynnell Sage, Cynthia DeValk (and husband Glen), and William (and wife Monica)—work with them in the family business.

The whole Teichman tribe exudes a deep-seated appreciation for the simple joys of rural living, and they all feel the impulse to share it with others. (Herb's brother, John, proprietor of The Candle Factory shop in a beautifully restored Traverse City factory, prepares a wonderful annotated tour map of the Grand Traverse region and distributes it free. His sister Emily Foster, a retired guidance counselor at Niles High School, is an active Fernwood volunteer.)

"We see a lot of Mom in us," Herb says. "She has always enjoyed

Herb Teichman and the rites of autumn: "Lots of good old-time apple varieties like this aren't pretty enough for supermarkets today. But when you taste it, you say, that's a good apple."

natural things like a sunset, watching the clouds, and eating an apple as much as anything else." Leona Teichman, still living in the old home place, was a young secretary in Fort Wayne when she came to the Teichman farm for apples. "She came back for a second bushel, and that's when Dad got her," Herb likes to say on the orchard tour, as he points out the trees in the anniversary orchard, planted to commemorate that meeting.

Herb Teichman, quite unlike the typical German fruit farmer in these parts, is a talker and a natural-born promoter. Justice to the breath and depth of his vision of agriculture isn't done by his folksy, punning style of writing in his widely distributed brochures. (The farm boasts a "scent-sational flower barn" and "seasonal shindigs for the whole gang to enjoy," in addition to the "Tree-Mendus" pun itself.)

The full Tree-Mendus experience involves an orchard tour and a picnic, a slowed-down day of picking, followed by a hike in the woods. The valleys and ravines of this scenic farm are useless for growing fruit because cold air settles in them. So they're given over to recreational uses: the general picnic grounds and a separate, special-event rentable picnic area with frisbee golf and an outdoor chapel, rented for weddings. The 120 acres of mature woods around a steep ravine are laced with trails and full of spring wildflowers, dogwood, and sassafras. Selective cutting of the farm's tulip poplars and other hardwoods yields wood for handsome crates made by a neighbor and sold here in the **Tree House Country Store.**

In addition to the big motorcoach tours, smaller **tours** can be scheduled. A $40 minimum is usual. Sometimes tours in visitors' vehicles can be arranged on short notice. Teichman welcomes all kinds of tourgoers: nursing-home residents, handicapped kids, foreign students. The biggest challenge, he says: "breaking down the barriers to reach people hardened by the city rat race." Visitors are taken on a canopied flatbed trailer with 50 fold-up theater seats to taste some antique apple varieties and learn about the orchard's other fruits, including a plum dating back to the crusades and the native paw paw grown in William's experimental area. He wants to develop more productive strains of this hardy, disease-resistant fruit. Tours also pass the woods, pond, and gathering area on one of the highest points in southwestern Michigan. The **Moonlight Hayride and Cookout** is held on the summer weekends closest to the full moon, complete with stories and skits told to visitors seated on a circle of stones till warm from the day's heat. (This idea was adapted from the Stone Circle poetry gathering near Traverse City.) Prices (roughly between $8 and $20 per person) depend on food served. There's a 15-person minimum; reservations necessary. Visitors are invited to "listen to the sounds of nature as night falls. Watch the stars appear in the clear country sky."

Here's what's available here that visitors might miss.

◆ **Fruit sales**, including the Midwest's biggest selection of antique varieties, for $1 a pound. Mix them for your own home apple-tasting event. Many varieties of farm-grown cherries, peaches, nectarines, plums, apricots, raspberries, apples, and pears are sold. Some ripen in late July and August. Herbs and vegetables are more recent additions. For the **Ripe-N-Ready Report** call (616) 782-7101.

Gift boxes of antique apples can be made up and shipped, or ordered by phone. Most products are available mail order. Here are a special cherry-flavored cider and a delicious cherry dessert made on a local Carbon Malted Waffle. The adjacent **Tree House Country Store** offers the farm's specialty apple and cherry products, small and large fruit crates, and new products like Grandma Zindel's Sweet Pickles and Oak Hill Scorned Woman's Hot Sauce.

◆ The **Flower Barn**, open Friday through Monday 11-5 from June 16 on, has dried flowers, crafts, and perennials. The manager grows all the the dried flowers sold on the farm. The colorful flower garden in front can be seen any time.

◆ **Petting zoo** with goats, chickens, and rabbits. for kids.

◆ **Picnic area**.

◆ **Kite-flying area**.

◆ **U-Pick.** Very well organized. This is not a cozy family affair but a well-regulated, systematized operation. The farm workers giving directions with the foreign accents are exchange students, often from Russia or Ukraine. If you don't have a container, you can purchase one for a few cents. Wear hats and sun protection gear. Take water bottles. Fruits, vegetable, and herbs are all sold on a U-pick basis. Prices may not be much lower than a supermarket, but you can be assured of freshness. To keep the most perishable produce fresh, pick it just before returning home and consider bringing a cooler.

◆ **Rent-A-Tree.** The farm will spray and maintain your semi-dwarf tree, which you can pick. The Notre Dame athletic department does this; so do people from as far as Detroit. Some tree renters pay extra for grafting so their tree produces several varieties. Renters get their own picnic area and trail access. Call (616) 461-4187.

◆ **Special events** take place all season, beginning with the **International Cherry Pit Spitting Championship** around July 4. (Visitors get a big kick out of this Guinness Record event.) Call (616) 782-7101 to hear about special events.

The farm is 2 miles northeast of Eau Claire in extreme eastern Berrien County, 1 1/2 miles east of M-140 on East Eureka Road, **Call first** *for Ripe-N-Ready report: (616) 782-7101. Call 616-782-7101 for reservations for* **tours, hayrides, and special events.**

*Open late June through 3rd week in Oct., then Fri-Sun through the
first three weekends of December. Up to Labor Day: open daily
except Tues 10-6. After Labor Day: Fri-Mon 10-6.* **Group tours** *by
appointment any day, starting in blossomtime (early May).* &: *restrooms, Flower Barn, and Country Store; wheelchairs are lifted up
onto wagon for tours. To pick fruit, some assistance is required. Free
admission to orchard/park. Minimum purchase may be instituted for
some fruits.*

MORE FRUIT AND LUNCH, TOO, NEAR TREE-MENDUS FRUIT . . . . . Scenic
Indian Lake Road leads north off M-62, passing the lake and **Sprague's Old
Orchard** (a beautiful old farmstead and farm market) on the way to **Wicks Apple
House**, another worthwhile destination. It has a good informal restaurant for
breakfast and lunch. It's a glorified farm market, cider mill, gift shop, bustling
and friendly. Glass walls give views of the bakery and, on October weekends, of
the cider-making process. The Wicks family raises its own asparagus, tart cherries, Stanley plums, apples, and Concord grapes. Local produce is featured.
*52281 Indian Lake Rd. (616) 782-7306. Open Memorial Day through October,
Tues-Sun 8-6.*

CANOEING ON THE NEARBY DOWAGIAC RIVER . . . . . has been called by the
book *Canoeing Michigan Rivers* "one of the most interesting trips in southern
Michigan." It's a short (4 hours or less), easy trip though varied, surprisingly
remote terrain. Get an excellent **free pamphlet** on the canoe trip and the river's
geology and history at Olympia Books (p. 58) or the Dowagiac Chamber of
Commerce (616-782-8212) . **Doe-Wah-Jack's Canoe Livery** (616-782-9464) is 3
1/2 miles north of Dowagiac on M-51.

A MAJESTIC REMNANT OF VIRGIN HARDWOOD FOREST . . . . . is along the
Dowagiac River. The Michigan Nature Association's **Dowagiac Woods** is known
for its fabulous displays of spring wildflowers and fall color. It is likely
Michigan's largest moist, virgin-soil woodland. Trees uncommon to Michigan,
including the chinakapin oak, blue beech, and Ohio buckeye, can be seen here.
*From M-62 about 4 miles west of Dowagiac, turn south onto Sink Road. In 1 mile
turn east onto Frost. In about a mile is a parking area on the north side of the
road.* Wear waterproof footgear. The short trail off Frost west of the parking area
is the driest, with a good view of spring wildflowers.

Russ Forest

Primeval oaks and giant tulip trees,
so old they were already huge in pioneer times

AN AWESOME stand of huge oaks, hundreds of years old, surrounds the stately old Newton farmhouse at the edge of Russ Forest. It's in an undeveloped part of undeveloped Cass County. If you come here from the west, from Dowagiac and M-51, it appears by surprise, unannounced by signs. All this contributes to the powerful, out-of-time feeling inspired by these great, primeval trees, a rare remnant of a virgin Eastern hardwood forest.

James Newton, builder of the **Newton House** farmhouse, was an English-born orphan who came to the U.S. as an indentured servant to a Quaker family. Many Quakers came to this part of Michigan. The escaped slaves they helped to settle here, going back to the 1830s, formed **Cass County's old rural black communities** around Calvin Center, Volinia, and Vandalia. The house's older section dates from 1844; Newton's son erected the east wing in 1867. The unrestored house, finished with beautiful local hardwoods, displays historical memorabilia about Cass County and the Grange movement. The Cass County Historical Society runs this museum. To go up the unsettlingly narrow staircase to the house's cupola in the treetops is an adventure in itself. *Open Sundays from 1 to 4:30 from the Sun. after Easter thru October, and by appt. (616) 445-3087. &: no. Donation appreciated.*

Cassopolis businessman Fred Russ purchased the 580-acre Newton Woods Farm during the Depression and donated it to Michigan State University for use as a forestry research station. Such forests of sun-loving oaks and hickories cannot replenish themselves, since only shade-tolerant seedlings can survive here. This majestic stand must have established itself after a fire some 300 or 400 years ago. Gradually the old oaks and hickories are being replaced by young beeches and maples.

Russ Forest's mixed hardwoods also include a stand of immense **black walnuts**, as big as any you'll ever see, and the **biggest recorded tulip poplar** in Michigan, 180 feet high and 15' 6" in circumference. Its sister tree, perhaps 300 years old, was the tallest recorded tree in Michigan until a wind storm toppled it in 1984. The fallen giant and its sister can be seen at the end of a trail that heads due south from near the picnic shelter. The big black walnuts are mixed in with some very old oaks and hickories in the old-growth area that's a little east of the big rock and historical marker along Decatur Road south of Marcellus Highway. This area is the heart of the Newton Woods, 80 acres of hardwood forest that has been set aside as a natural area. The only cutting done here was when some walnut trees were removed for gunstocks in World War I and some white oaks for PT boats in World War II. Tree-rustling of the valuable walnuts presents no threat here; the area is thick with relatives of the pioneer Newton family who long owned this land.

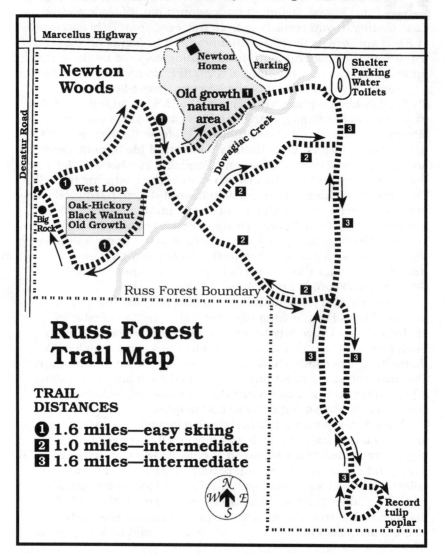

Marcellus Highway

Newton Woods

Newton Home

Parking

Shelter
Parking
Water
Toilets

Old growth ❶ natural area

Decatur Road

Dowagiac Creek

❸

❷

❶

❶ West Loop

Oak-Hickory
Black Walnut
Old Growth

❶

Big
Rock

❸

❶

❷

❷

Russ Forest Boundary

❷

**Russ Forest
Trail Map**

❸ ❸

**TRAIL
DISTANCES**

❶ **1.6 miles—easy skiing**
❷ **1.0 miles—intermediate**
❸ **1.6 miles—intermediate**

N
W E
S

❸

Record
tulip
poplar

They regard the forest as their own and are quick to report any suspicious strangers with chain saws. Many oaks are three feet in diameter, and some up to four feet.

A spectacular **fall color display** in some places is created by the varied trees: oak, hickory, hard maples, flame-orange sassafras, and the clear yellow of tulip trees. **Spring wildflowers** are good, too. Parts of the woods have so many spring beauties in early spring that it looks like it's snowed.

Donor Fred Russ especially valued the property's huge tulip poplars, the giants of the Eastern forest, and wished to encourage research on them. In the 1930s standard forestry practice promoted planting cutover land with pines for timber and conservation. Russ was ahead of his time. He was convinced that tulip poplar plantations were a worthwhile idea. Unlike other softwoods of the poplar family, tulip poplar has a cell structure that keeps it from splintering or splitting when sawn or carved. It works and nails easily, like pine. It's naturally disease-resistant. Today the tulip trees Russ planted have reached usable size. Not all of M.S.U's Russ Research Forest is virgin forest. Most of the tree plantations are on old prairie land that was farmed. Eighty acres were owned and managed by a timber company until their recent purchase by M.S.U. (Hardwood logging is big business in Cass County.)

Cass County's adjacent **Russ Forest Park** provides parking, **picnic tables, play equipment,** a small **shelter, restrooms,** and access to two miles of flat, **scenic trails** through the research forest. Trail loops go over wooden footbridges and through virgin hardwoods and managed stands. **Cross-country skiing** on the flat ungroomed trails is encouraged. The area along Dowagiac Creek (a Class A **trout stream**) is quite open, with some low marshes.

*Park entrance and parking area is on Marcellus Hwy. just east of Newton House, 8 miles west of Marcellus and 5 miles east of Dowagiac. For **information and group tours** about forest ecology and management, contact M.S.U.'S Kellogg Forest. (616) 731-4597. For **park information** or shelter reservations, contact: Cass County Parks Dept., 340 O'Keefe, Cassopolis, MI 49031. (616) 445-8611.*

OFF THE BEATEN TRACK NEAR RUSS FOREST . . . . . The main street of **Marcellus**, 8 miles east of Russ Forest, has lovely old homes, a quaint bank worth a visit, and the **Cozy Cupboard**, a homey restaurant where customers have assembled a collection of souvenir plates from around the world. . . . . . At **Peacewood**, a beautiful produce farm and stand that uses principles of sustainable agriculture, you can find many kinds of peppers and green and yellow beans, plus U-pick for some vegetables and flowers. Recipes provided. Farmers Judy and John Yaeger left the University of Chicago for country living and physical work. *93356 36th St., just inside Van Buren County. (616) 423-8527. From Marcellus Hwy. 4 miles east of Russ Forest and 4 miles west of Marcellus, turn north onto Lawrence Rd. at Thompson Corners Grocery, go 3 1/2 miles north.*

DOWAGIAC'S HISTORIC HOMES AND RESTORED DOWNTOWN . . . . . are remarkable. The small city (population 6,400) prospered with the phenomenal success of **Round Oak** stoves, once America's best-selling wood heater. Then it declined. Now Dowagiac is undergoing a downtown revival. False modern fronts from the Kawneer Company of nearby Niles have been removed, historic storefronts restored, and truck traffic rerouted off Front Street. Gift and decor shops and a discount fashion store make for a modest amount of browsing. Don't miss the 1926 vintage **Caruso's Candy Kitchen** at 130 South Front (open Mon-Sat 9:30-5:30; 616-782-6001) and **Olympia Books and Prints** at 208 South Front, a delightful used book shop. (Open Mon-Fri 10:30-4:30, Sat 10-3 or 4. 616-782-3443). . . . . . Pick up interesting pamphlets about Dowagiac at Olympia or call or stop by the Chamber of Commerce (616-782-8212) in the train station. . Ask for the illustrated **walking tour**, the natural history tour of the **Dowagiac River** (see p. 58 for canoe trip) , downtown businesses, and the Event & Festival Guide, which also describes large nearby natural areas. May's **Dogwood Festival** at Southwestern Michigan College always gives top billing to a **literary luminary** (Alice Walker, John Updike), often ones who hardly ever tour.

The most impressive old houses are west of Front along High, Indiana, and Green. Most unusual of all is **The Maples** at 511 Green, which intersects West Division a block east of West Main (M-51/M-62). Made of boulders, with a great entrance arch, it resembles some of H. H. Richardson's Romanesque masterpieces. This was one of the homes of Round Oak's treasurer, a grandson of founder Philo D. Beckwith. Perhaps their lavish lifestyles left Round Oak's manager/heirs unprepared for the competition brought to their ornate parlor stoves by the advent of central heating, for Round Oak failed to adapt to modern times.

HANDS-ON SCIENCE AND CASS COUNTY HISTORY . . . . . can be enjoyed at the **Southwestern Michigan College Museum** outside Dowagiac. Thirty exhibits like the whisper dish and changing colored shadows convey principles of physics and light. The new **history gallery** spotlights local industries: Round Oak Stoves, **Kitty Litter**, and James Heddon fishing lures, among others. It also covers Cass County's important role on the Underground Railroad and its famous old **rural black community**. (Detroit mayor Dennis Archer grew up in nearby Cassopolis, incidentally.) The museum **shop** is geared to Michigan history and school visits. *From M-51 in Dowagiac, take M-62 east toward Cassopolis. In about a mile, go right (south) onto Cherry Grove Rd. When you come to the college entrance, park in the lot on your left. Museum is at the end of the lot. Go in the cylindrical lobby. (616) 782-5113. Tues-Sat 10-5, Wed to 8. ; Free.*

Downtown St. Joseph

*This quaint old place has a lively downtown,
band concerts, and an old-fashioned park
with a grand view of Lake Michigan.*

OTHER Michigan downtowns have more spectacular architecture or shops, but St. Joseph is overall one of the most attractive. It has healthy small-town and resort retailing, pleasant historic buildings, and a striking setting on a bluff overlooking Lake Michigan. Benches, sculptures, even a hot dog vendor, make State Street a nice place to linger.

"St. Joe," as it's commonly called, enjoys unusual prosperity for a town of 9,000. The Whirlpool world headquarters and some of its facilities are scattered south and north of town. Many old-time resorters live here at least part of the year. And there's been a recent influx of second-home buyers from Chicago who are pricing some locals out of the market.

Lake Bluff Park overlooks Lake Michigan and extends for seven blocks along Lake Boulevard around to the St. Joseph River on the north. Incidentally, the comfortable, elegant Boulevard Hotel (616-983-6600) and the Holiday Inn (616-983-7341) enjoy the park's views. Lake Bluff Park makes a wonderful walk, with flower gardens, a century's worth of sculptures, and overlook benches. The funny, clever **Curious Kids Museum** (p. 65) is a real highlight for children. Get **walking tours** of St. Joseph's public sculpture and downtown historic buildings, along with information about events and attractions, from the helpful **St. Joseph Today.** *(616) 923-6739. 520 Pleasant, around the corner from the Toy Co. on State. Open weekdays 8:30-5, vestibule open longer hours, or ask them to mail you information.*

Takeout food for a **picnic in the park** is conveniently available at **Mama Martorano's** (home-style Italian at 422 State), **Clancy's Deli** at 505 Pleasant, or Caffe Tosi, 516 Pleasant, the snappy in-town *trattoria* of Stevensville's venerable Tosi's Italian restaurant.

Going north, adjoining the park on Ship at Lake Bluff is the elegant **Whitcomb Tower**, once a hotel, now a retirement home. It's on the very site of **La Salle's 1679 fort**, a western outpost in the great French fur-trading empire. Visitors are welcome to peek in and see the mural of Marquette and Joliet's 1669 canoe journey down the St. Joseph River. Still farther north in the park, the **bandshell**, below Port Street between State and Lake, is much used in sum-

❶ Tale of two downtowns. Unsettling & dramatic contrast between trim and prosperous white city and poor black one. **Benton Harbor's** downtown (❶) is finally coming back after nearly becoming a ghost town. Adjacent **St. Joe (❷)** keeps thriving. St. Joe's Krasl Art Center, band concerts in Lake Bluff Park; Benton Harbor has nifty Wolf's Marine and potential to regain fame as art center.

❸ Curious Kids Museum (p. 65). Outstanding small hands-on museum, more kid-centered and playful than most. Zany cartoon decor.

❹ Mama Martorano's. Real Italian home cooking, redolent of garlic and wine, shines at this spot. Excellent food for little money. (616) 982-0387.

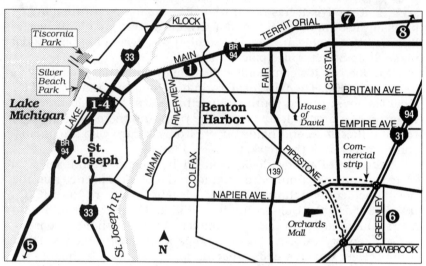

❺ Snowflake Motel. Frank Lloyd Wright conceived this once-luxurious motel which now caters to truckers, & repeat vacationers. Friendly staff, budget rates, pretty courtyard. (616) 429-3261.

❻ The Herb Barn (p. 70). A fragrant natural world one minute from I-94. Good prices on plants; lots of ideas for uses. Pretty display garden. Lunches by reservation.

❼ Benton Harbor Fruit Market (p. 52). Watch the action at world's biggest cash-to-grower fruit & vegetable market. Good retail produce stand. Free posters, recipes

❽ Sarett Nature Center (p. 71). Bird-watcher's paradise, thanks to river wetlands. 5 miles of trails, boardwalks, and elevated viewing seats. Good gift shop, excellent talks & outings.

Highlights of
St. Joseph/
Benton Harbor

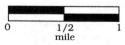

mer. St. Joseph has the only tax-supported municipal band in
Michigan. Audiences can enjoy musical sunsets over the lake. **Free
band concerts** are held here from July through Labor Day, Sundays
and holidays at 3:30 and 7:30 (with free horse-drawn trolley rides
from 1 to 4). More summer concerts are at noon Wednesdays, with
free rides from 11:30 to 2:30, and on August Fridays at 7.

The St. Joseph River curves around St. Joe to the east, making a peninsula of the town. With so much riverfront and the Lake Michigan shore, St.
Joe boasts more boat slips than any other town on Lake Michigan's eastern
shore. At the **Margaret Upton Arboretum**, which descends from the band
shell to the river, **500 boat tie-ups**, free to boaters, have been installed with
rubberized siding and cleats.

A stairway by Ship Street, a block north of Pleasant, descends
to the old Pere Marquette train station, now Zitta's Restaurant,
another stylish casual hangout. From there it's just a few blocks'
walk from **Silver Beach County Park** on Lake Michigan. The
recently renovated park has a wide, sandy **beach**, some picnic
tables, new bathhouses, and a concession stand. There's little natural landscaping and no dunes. Dramatic recent improvements
with bright blue roofs has spiffed up the entire area, from the
blufftop stairway and restrooms to the beach itself. Silver Beach
has access to the 1,000-foot **south pier**. It's a fine place to fish and
get a good view of lake and shore.

Night life has returned to St. Joseph after a long dry spell.
Thursday through Saturday, **Czar's 505** club (616-983-1166) features established regional performers, mostly jazz and blues, with
some reggae, R&B, alternative rock, and comedy. It's in the lower
level of 505 Pleasant, the big building at Lake Bluff. Go in to the
left part of the center entryway.

The heart of downtown retailing is on **State Street** between Ship
and Elm, with its center at State and Pleasant. Typical store hours
are Monday through Saturday from 10 to 5:30, with some stores
open Thursday to 9 and summer Sundays 12-5. Most stores are
wheelchair-accessible. Free parking is along Lake between Ship and
Market, and on Broad *east* of Main. Stores are mostly either small
town standbys (including a department store and a big G. C. Murphy
variety store with a wonderfully creaky wood floor) or women's wear,
gift, and accessory stores catering to fairly conservative, well-to-do
women who expect good service and get it here. Lately more alternative shops have popped up. Here's a selection of noteworthy spots,
mostly downtown, roughly arranged from north to south:

◆ **Curious Kids' Museum.** This small but superior hands-on museum is more tuned into kids and less out to impress their parents

State Street in St. Joseph is both the main street of a pleasant small town and a beach resort.

than many bigger children's museums. Bright, fanciful lobby murals are by Niles cartoonist Nancy Drew, who draws and paints like a kid herself. They set a tone of playful messing-around that's carried on inside by bubble-blowing, face-painting, kaleidoscopes, musical machines, a shadow room, a dinosaur gallery, magnets, a simulated apple orchard, a puppet theater with plays, a 1/6 scale ambulance, and a ship. Costumes and hats add to the fun.

In the handicap area, kids can learn what it's like to go up a ramp or play basketball in a wheelchair, use a Braille typewriter, or wear leg braces. There are also time-tested hands-on favorites: the giant bubble chamber, the toaster-powered hot-air balloon, and tests of heart rate, blood pressure, and so forth. Call about **parties** and **group tours.** There's a busy calendar of enrichment classes and longer workshops. *415 Lake Blvd. between Broad and Elm in downtown St. Joseph. Park next door. (616) 983-2543. Wed-Fri 10-5,*

Sat & Sun noon-5. Also open Tuesdays, June through August. Closed for major holidays and two weeks after Labor Day. &. *$3 for everyone over 2. Kids under 2 free. An adult must accompany kids 13 and under.*

◆ **Once Upon a Time**. Attractive store for quality books for and about children, plus puppets, cassettes, book character dolls, stationery, stickers, and rubber stamps. A separate reading area invites browsing. *515 Pleasant. (616) 983-5055.*

◆ **Elise Marie.** Jewelry, clever T shirts, accessories, floppy hats, gifts, and now more clothing, all with a fresh, contemporary, offbeat look. *521 Pleasant. (616) 982-0550.*

◆ **C&C Clothier.** Understated designer clothing with a look that's young for St. Joe. *220 State. (616) 983-1300.*

◆ **The Toy Company** offers well-chosen "amusements for all ages": colorful basics like Brio trains, dolls and stuffed animals, blocks, puzzles and "Brain Boosters," picture books, plus rubber stamps and nifty crafts supplies. *505 Pleasant at State.*

◆ **Tootie & Dreamers.** Natural cosmetics and skin care, candles and such, essential oils, plus books on personal growth, recovery, Native American and Indian spirituality, and more from the Inner Source Bookstore on Napier Rd. *304 State. (616) 985-5228.*

◆ **The Silver Balloon** is a large, attractive children's clothing and shoe store. *213 State. (616) 983-6044.*

◆ **Majerek's Hall of Cards & Books**. Newsstand/ bookstore/card shop that's well equipped for vacation reading. *219 State.*

◆ **Currie Beads** has infected lots of area working women with jewelry-making mania, thanks to the enthusiasm and good eye of owner Currie Butzbaush. The selection and quality is unusual: designer art glass and ceramic beads, vintage European beads, Japanese and African beads, Czech glass beads sold by the string, and semiprecious stones like garnet and lapis. Kids' summer classes are more flexible. Many books and magazines on bead history and bead art are on hand. *317 State. (616) 982-1948.* &.

◆ **Gallery on the Alley** offers a colorful, upbeat melange of jewelry, contemporary handcrafts, and watercolor landscapes in a tiny space. *611 Broad just half a block east of State. (616) 983-6261.*

◆ The **Krasl Art Center** is an outstanding example of how much a small art center can do with volunteers and well-chosen changing exhibits. The expanded **gallery shop** has hand-crafted jewelry and ceramics plus more art-related gifts, toys, crafts, books, cards, and home and fashion accessories. *707 Lake between Park and Pearl,* *opposite the south end of Lake Bluff Park. (616) 983-0271. Mon-Thurs & Sat 10-4, Fri 10-1, Sun 1-4. &. Free.*

♦ **Everybody's Everything.** Wildly colorful, unexpected juxtapositions of stuff — neckties, ethnic bags and costumes, wigs, some non-wearable curiosities — make this costume shop/clothing resale store worth a trip. Sandra Braddock loves to sew. She creates, assembles, and mends costumes and sells theatrical makeup. Not everything is over the top. Designer resale tends to the classic. *1523 Niles at Wisconsin, in a corner store across from a park. Niles/U.S. 33 is the east leg of the Y made where Main divides south of downtown. (616) 983-3276. Mon-Thurs 11:30-5:30, Fri & Sat to 5.*

A GOOD CHILDREN'S PLAYGROUND . . . . . along Lake Michigan is **Lions' Park,** a few blocks south of Silver Beach in St. Joseph. There's no swimming here, however. *To get there, find the Krasl Art Center at Lake Boulevard and Park up on the bluff. Take Park Street down to the lake and turn left on Lions' Park Lane.*

THE BEST AREA BEACH . . . . . is **Tiscornia Park**, more scenic and secluded than Silver Beach, with low dunes and some natural vegetation. The big old resort hotels are long gone, but there's some historic flavor left, including a Shingle Style **lifesaving station** near the pier. The thousand-foot **North Pier** is popular for perch fishing. The pier is unusual in having **two lighthouses** that comprise one of the last remaining pier range light systems on the Great Lakes. The outer pier light marks the harbor to incoming boats. The inner light is an additional navigational aid.

Tiscornia Park is in two parts: a quarter-mile of Lake Michigan **beachfront** with restrooms, and an area on the St. Joseph River west of Ridgeway by the municipal marina, with **picnic tables** and **new rest rooms**. *In St. Joseph but north of the river. Take M-63 as if you were heading north to South Haven. See map. $2/car. &: some restrooms.*

A TEN-MINUTE WALK FROM DOWNTOWN TO THE NORTH PIER AND TISCORNIA PARK . . . . . . can be taken by walking over the St. Joseph River bridge that carries M-63 to South Haven. This means you don't have to deal withe summer's tight parking in town and at the beach. A bird's-eye view of the busy boat traffic at the river mouth is a bonus. Once across the bridge, cut through the parking area behind the Whirlpool offices, or use Marina Drive, to reach the **West Basin Marina**, which connects to the pier and park. Save some energy for the uphill hike back.

A THOUGHT-PROVOKING SIDE TRIP TO BENTON HARBOR . . . . . Across the

Blossomland Bridge, Benton Harbor is making a comeback from 20 years of fame as one of America's urban basket cases. In fact, many, many other areas have experienced the same levels of poverty, unemployment, and segregation (it's now over 90% black), but they have been part of more populous urban areas, while quirks of history have caused Benton Harbor to be an unnaturally small industrial city, now under 13,000. . . . . .The **Community Renewal through the Arts** program, started by the city and the Cornerstone Alliance of area business and civic leaders, is already bearing fruit. An investment fund has been established to do things like renovate loft space. Chicago-based **Richard Hunt**, one of the most prominent working American sculptors, has started a satellite studio for young artists in Benton Harbor. The old shipping canal is being reopened for pleasure boats, another base for economic development. . . . . Arts renewal linchpins have been Herbert and Audrey Mendel. He turned his family junkyard into an important processor of metal alloys; she's a former ballerina who directs an annual summer seminar with the American Ballet Theatre. (It's striking how many junk dealers are linked with the arts.)

How Benton Harbor went from being a still-prosperous city and resort through the 1950s to become a 20th-century downtown ghost town 20 years later is a story of post-World War II suburbanization at its most extreme. (A nearby township, not St. Joseph, received most of the white flight — and some middle-class black flight, too.) Mutual distrust between the white business establishment and leaders elected by increasingly poor black residents eventually made a shambles of the city and its government. It didn't help that Whirlpool moved all its manufacturing out of the area, mostly to Arkansas. Today, after decades of mistrust and dissension, people are working together in a pragmatic direction of rebuilding the local economy. Traffic signals now work. Vacant office buildings, which had reverted to city ownership for nonpayment of taxes, are being renovated.

A REAL FIND FOR BOATERS AND BARGAIN-HUNTERS . . . . . Savvy boaters detour through Benton Harbor to shop at **Wolf's Marine**, a cavernous marine accessory store that claims to be the Midwest's largest and offers to match or beat any advertised price. Wolf's makes a point to stock several kinds of most accessories, plus hard-to-find-parts and supplies, divers' supplies, and many kinds of smaller boats. Diving lessons are available. Even non-boaters will find lots of useful, fun stuff, like slickers, warm-up suits, seashells and netting, fishing poles, inner tubes, and inflatable boats. *250 W. Main between downtown Benton Harbor and the St. Joseph River. (616) 926-1068. Mon-Fri 9-6; Sat 9-5.*

THE ST. JOSEPH/BENTON HARBOR AREA'S MOST COMPELLING CURIOSITY . . . . . and its most popular attraction from around 1910 through the 1950s won't be found on any current map. The grounds, rockery, and miniature railroad of the **House of David** amusement park and zoo, are now overgrown. The ball diamond where the famous long-haired teams dazzled tourists is long gone. And the fanciful, picturesque band stands and pavilions are rotting and gradually being taken down by the aging members of this once-vital religious commune, whose members were sworn to celibacy.

Followers of this 18th-century Pentecostal cult arrived in Benton Harbor in 1903. Under the leadership of the charismatic and astute Benjamin Purnell, they developed many successful area businesses, including this park. It's a fascinating, complex story, explored in detail in local historian Claire Adkin's *Brother Benjamin*. Still to be seen are the large and ornate communal residences on Britain Avenue. *From downtown Benton Harbor, take Main a mile east to Fair, turn right (south), and in about 3/4 mile, turn left (east) onto Britain.* **No trespassing** *onto private property, but you may use public roads. The houses are on your left.* Take the drive between Shiloh and Jerusalem houses to see whether the **House of David Arts** is open. It's a picture frame shop staffed by a delightful Scottish woman who came to the House of David with her parents in the 1940s. Postcards and other House of David publications are for sale, along with honey still produced by the colony.

MORE HOUSE OF DAVID HISTORY. . . . . can be seen and read at the **House of David Room** at the **Benton Harbor Public Library**. It's one of the most unusual and thorough special-interest archives of its kind, the life work of recently retired librarian Florence Rachuig. Interested visitors are provided with a brief printed history and brought, upon request, documents chosen from the contents list. The photographs are especially compelling. Rachuig's clear-headed, sophisticated, yet sympathetic view of these talented, gullible, misunderstood people and the group psychology that attracted them was a great asset in collecting. *The library is at 213 E. Wall in downtown Benton Harbor, a block south of Main and a block east of Pipestone. (616) 926-6139. Hours: Mon-Wed 9-8, Thurs & Fri 9-6, Sat 9-5. Call first to be sure of seeing the House of David Room.* ♿

Sarett Nature Center

*An extraordinary place to watch birds
that even novices will enjoy*

WHAT MAKES this Michigan Audubon Society sanctuary a paradise for novice birdwatchers are its many benches and elevated towers, strategically located in different habitats. They are comfortable places where it's easy to sit and stay still and quiet enough to observe birds at close range without disturbing ·them. Excellent **trail booklets**, available at all hours at the trailhead by the parking lot, are keyed to views you can often enjoy while sitting. You could even buy a nature book at the top-notch gift shop and read it comfortably sitting by an alder thicket, pond, or tamarack bog, observing the sights and sounds of life around you. A tree house lets you observe from a tree canopy; a bench overlooks a dogwood thicket.

These 350 acres along the Paw Paw River northeast of Benton Harbor include many kinds of prime natural habitats. Here upland meadows and forests overlook lowland marshes and swamp forests going down to the riverbank. In spring and fall the river floods, attracting many migratory waterfowl. A sedge meadow produces a **fine fall wildflower** display. Dead trees, created by rising water levels in swamps, have created plenty of tree holes for wood ducks, owls, woodpeckers, and the uncommon prothonotary warbler. Shorebirds like the Virginia rail remain north in winter if there is open water, provided here by the bayous of the Paw Paw River.

Some five miles of **trails** include quite a bit of boardwalk for good viewing of wetland habitats. The trails are planned as a series of short loops, so you could plan hikes from 1/2 to 2 1/2 hours. **Cross-country skiers** are welcome in winter. Most trails are not wheelchair-accessible because of occasional stairways, but they are otherwise easy. One wheelchair-

Shorebirds like the Virginia rail remain north in winter if there is open water, like the bayous of the Paw Paw River at Sarett.

Towers and treehouses like this let birdwatchers look down on the bird life attracted by the wetlands of the Paw Paw River's floodplain. Hear you may see the unusual Prothonotary Warbler, which nests only in hollow trees close to the water.

accessible trail is directly off the parking lot. Highway noise is occasionally distracting. *Remember, birds are most active in the morning and evening, when the sun is low in the sky. Plan your visit accordingly.*

Sarett's **gift shop** is among the very best for nature publications, note cards, bird feeders, seed, and the like. The adjoining observation room has some well-done displays of mounted birds, seeds, and antlers. A naturalist is usually on hand to answer questions. There's a busy schedule of **talks**, **nature walks**, demonstrations, outings, and adults' and children's summer **classes**. Sarett naturalists lead several adult **eco-trips**; call or write Sarett Nature Center, 2300 Benton Center, Benton Harbor, MI 49022 for details.

*2300 Benton Center Rd. in Benton Township. Northeast of Benton Harbor/St. Joseph on the Paw Paw River, 1 mile north of the Red Arrow Hwy. From I-94, take I-196 north (toward South Haven), but get off in 1 mile at the Red Arrow Hwy. exit, go west to Benton Center Rd., then north. From St. Joseph and downtown Benton Harbor, take Main or Territorial 2 miles east to Crystal, north (left) on Crystal to Red Arrow Hwy. (616) 927-4832. **Interpretive center hours:** Tues-Fri 9-5, Sat 10-5, Sun 1-5. Trails and parking lot open dawn to dusk.*

FOR INFORMATION ON BIRDWATCHING IN MICHIGAN . . . . . call the **Michigan Audubon Society** at (517) 886-9144 weekdays from 9 to 5. Let the friendly, helpful staff know what area you'll be in and they'll supply you with the location of birding sites in that particular part of the state. (MAS has 16 sanctuaries, 2 nature centers, 1 bird observatory , and a couple of Audubon centers.) They can also put you in touch with any of the 46 chapters of the Audubon Society in both the lower and the upper peninsulas who will give you even greater details about bird watching in their respective areas. Michigan Audubon Society, 6011 W. St. Joseph #403, Lansing, MI 48917.

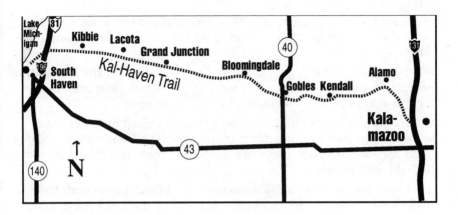

Kal-Haven Trail

The 34-mile bike path from Kalamazoo to South Haven takes you through wonderfully varied terrain.

BIKE PATHS created from abandoned railroad lines are a superb way to travel. Not only are they safer and less stressful than biking on roadways, but many, like the Kal-Haven, diverge well away from highways, opening up more tranquil, less developed settings. Such paths are proliferating across the country, but the Kal-Haven remains one of the very choicest. Its virtues are numerous:

◆ There's an exotic variety of **agricultural scenery**, from onion, celery, and radish farms in the mucklands near Kalamazoo to the big blueberry plantations and peach orchards near South Haven.

◆ There are delightfully cool **woods** to ride through, some with glorious flocks of ferns, some with meandering streams

◆ Near-flat grades make pedaling easy even for occasional bicyclists. The limestone surface is hard enough even for the narrow tires of touring bikes. Though flat, the path ahead is far from boring, as you come upon snakes, chipmunks, groudhogs, birds, and other animals in the quiet, remote areas along the trail.

◆ There's a wonderful assortment of backwater small towns along the way, almost evenly spaced to give welcome respites every half hour or so. Bicyclists can anticipate treats like chocolate sodas at the old-fashioned fountain in Gobles to blueberry pie at the homey Country Fare restaurant in Grand Junction. These little farm communities have a sleepy, almost Southern aura to them, light-years away from the hectic manufacturing centers around Grand Rapids and Detroit.

◆ A tranquil 31-foot deep lake, Lake Eleven, is just off the bike path near Berlamont. Surrounded by woods, the lake is clear and inviting for weary cyclists who want to take a cooling dip.

◆ Climaxing a trip from Kalamazoo to South Haven on a hot, mid-summer day, you can ride down to the lively sand beaches on Lake Michigan and jump in. There are numerous restaurants and bars at this old resort town.

Three towns (Gobles, Bloomingdale, and Grand Junction) have restaurants which make good rest stops along the Kal-Haven. There are eight outhouses along the trail, and hand-pumps provide water every few miles.

Even out-of-shape cyclists can complete the 34-mile trail in a day. It makes sense to start from Kalamazoo and spend the night in South Haven. Bike rentals for $16 a day at Healy True Value Hardware in Gobles (616-628-2584) for a 23-mile trip to South Haven. Bikes may also be rented for $8 a day at Northside Memories just north of the Dyckman Street bridge in South Haven

Lake Michigan at South Haven is a refreshing destination after the 34-mile bike trip from Kalamazoo. Not only beaches but two long piers are a short trip through town from the trail's end. Tight summer parking makes bicycle transportation a real advantage.

(616-637-8319).

Starting from the eastern trailhead just west of Kalamazoo, the trail goes through a hilly, deeply shady oak forest. The terrain flattens out by **Mentha**, named for the peppermint plant. Once a large swamp of tamaracks and black ash, this became the experimental mint plantation of A. M. Todd, Kalamazoo's Peppermint King. Ruins of the company's office and social hall face the trail; other remnants of the company town are south along 23rd Street (formerly Todd Avenue). Mentha operated here from 1900 to 1954, when wilt ruined commercial mint-growing in Michigan.

Bloomingdale (population 500) is the largest town on the route and home of the **Pizza Time** (616-521-6550), open Tuesday through Saturday from 11 to 9 in summer, otherwise Saturday 5-9 and weekdays 11-9. It's across from a central park and the former **train depot**, now held open by volunteers as a bike trail rest stop and little museum on summer weekends. Restrooms are in a nearby caboose.

Grand Junction, surrounded by blueberry fields, is the home of Michigan Blueberry Growers, a large cooperative that markets its 800 members' blueberries within and beyond the U.S. (See page 50 for the Michigan blueberry story.) Here the friendly **Country Fare restaurant** (616-434-6425) is open seven days a week for breakfast, lunch, and dinner. Their tasty biscuits and gravy, available all day is popular with locals. The "small" $1.65 portion is more than most can eat.

On the last few miles of trail through backwater bayous of the Black River, it's well worth planning to linger to take in the wildlife from the railbed's convenient elevated platform of the rail bed.

The variety of natural and agricultural ecosystems make this trail a delight from early spring through fall and into winter. Early May brings **wildflowers** and flowering dogwood (between Kendall and Gobles) to the woods, and **fruit blossoms** to orchards. The trail's well-drained surface is relatively dry when much of Michigan is muddy with spring. **Blueberries** ripen in July and August, and the leaves turn a gorgeous reddish-purple in fall. In winter the red twigs of the blueberry bushes are striking against the snow. **Fall color** along the trail in general is excellent, thanks to the great variety of woods and wetland foliage

The bicycle trail ends at the Blue Star Highway (A-2) just east of South Haven. Oddly, there is no signage to direct cyclists into town. Head south (left) on the Blue Star Highway for about a mile up the Hill to Wells St. and turn right. Stay on Wells to reach the Blue River and bridge to the North Beach area. Turn left onto Bailey to reach the older neighborhood. A right onto Phoenix takes you downtown.

Cross-country skiers and **snowmobilers** are welcome in winter. (Long sight lines mean the snowmobilers won't suddenly come upon skiers.) A 14-mile **horse trail** goes between Kibbie and Bloomingdale.

Kalamazoo trailhead: in Oshtemo township 1/4 mile west of U.S. 131 on 10th St. between West Main and H Avenue. Take West Main from 131, turn north onto 10th. **South Haven trailhead**: *on Blue Star Highway (A2) midway between Phoenix and North Shore Drive at the Black River bridge. From I-196, take the Phoenix exit west, follow signs. Call (616) 637-2788 for an illustrated map/ brochure. &. Trail fee: $2/day individual, $5/family; annual pass $10/$25. Register at trailheads or access points.*

SOUTH HAVEN IS A LIVELY SUMMER BEACH TOWN . . . made more intense because its beaches are the closest to the Kalamazoo metro area. Lots of high school and college kids populate **North Beach** across the drawbridge on Dyckman. **South Beach** is less crowded, more of a family beach. (There's a terrific castle of a play park nearby, on Monroe Blvd. 8 short blocks south of downtown.) . . . . . At the foot of Phoenix and downtown, you can walk out along the Black River channel to the end of the long **South Pier** and its **lighthouse**. . . . . On the river's north side, big yachts and sailboats crowd the colorful **marina**, and a 600-foot **Black River boardwalk** connects the marina with the **Michigan Maritime Museum** on Dyckman, just west of the drawbridge. Highlights include several restored boats, from a dugout canoe to Coast Guard rescue boats, changing exhibits, marine art, well-told exhibits on Michigan's long, diverse boating history, a fine Great Lakes **maritime shop**, and an illuminating series of Great Lakes maps, beginning with one of Louis Joliet from 1673. *Open year-round Wed-Sun 10-5. Call (616) 637-8078. &.* . . . . **Downtown** there's a nifty Art Deco movie theater, the **Michigan** (616-637-1662), the wonderful old-fashioned **Golden Brown Bakery** on Phoenix (which serves the best breakfasts in town), and **The Blueberry Store**, 525 Phoenix (616-637-6322) is owned by a blueberry cooperative. It sells blueberry giftware and oddities like blueberry gum in addition to blueberry preserves and dried blueberries. . . . . Don't miss the huge nutty ice cream bars at **Sherman's Dairy Bar**, on Phoenix just east of I-196.

Michigan Fisheries Interpretive Center

At the Wolf Lake Hatchery see millions of fish,
from tiny fingerlings to huge sturgeons,
and learn a lot about Great Lakes fishing.

EACH YEAR millions of fish are grown at this state hatchery west of Kalamazoo. It and the five other state hatcheries stock Michigan's public lakes and streams. This is one of the nation's most modern computerized and automated hatcheries. Visitors may observe, in season, its many activities, from spawning, incubating, and hatching eggs to rearing and loading millions of fish that will be released. Spawning occurs in October for most trout and salmon, and in late March and April for walleye, northern pike, muskellunge, and rainbow trout. Hatching, beginning in mid-April for walleye, is especially fun to watch.

Some years many millions of walleye are hatched here, quite a few of which are transported to holding ponds around the state. There they grow to a slightly larger size that is much more able to survive in the wild. Over one million chinook salmon are raised for 12 months until they are over three inches long, then released in rivers and streams in early spring along with the three quarters of a million rainbow trout that are spawned in the fall. The salmon swim out into lakes Michigan, Huron, and Superior, where they are joined by salmon from adjoining states' hatcheries. Three and a half years later, those that survive will return to their original stream to spawn.

Huge **tanks** also hold the enormous populations of northern pike,

The bony-plated lake sturgeon at Wolf Lake can grow 200 pounds and more, and live to be well over 100 years old.

muskies, and sturgeon raised here. (The fish-hatching program includes both cold-water and warm-water fish, but varies from year to year.) Trout and salmon in indoor tanks are fed automatically every ten minutes. That's fun to watch, but large groups of people spook the fish, which are unaccustomed to people because the feeding is automatic. Back when an employee fed the fish, they were far less timid, and actually charged after the food.

Other highlights are the 14 **outdoor ponds**, especially the **show pond** with its two enormous sturgeon swimming slowly along the bottom. They are about five feet long and 40 to 50 years old. All the fish here are unusually interesting: big steelheads (also called rainbow trout), from eight to 15 pounds, some very elderly Montana grayling, and other less readily visible sport fish. Visitors can get free pellets to feed the fish. A walkway out into the pond lets visitors look down at the backs of the five-foot sturgeons — even in winter. Flowing well water keeps the pond ice-free in all but the coldest weather. Visibility over the show pond varies. Depending on the weather, the show pond can be either crystal clear or cloudy in the same way visibility in a river or lake varies..

In the central visitors' area are **plaques** of Michigan's record fish, including a 26-pound rainbow trout, a 46-pound chinook salmon, a 193-pound lake sturgeon, and a 47 1/2-pound flathead catfish. Don't miss the excellent 11-minute **multi-image slide show** in the 79-seat auditorium (with room for about 12 wheelchairs) which tells about the mission and workings of the Department of Natural Resources Fisheries Division.

Large **historical photos** and captions tell how, in the late 19th century, Michigan commercial fishermen were taking 30 tons of whitefish a year, which led to an eventual collapse of the fishery. Four play-it-yourself **slide shows** tell the story of commercial fishing in Michigan. The parallels with lumbering are clear; both natural resources were carelessly exploited. They recount the horrid sea lamprey invasion, and describe the recent restoration of the Great Lakes fishery.

In 1921 the Welland Canal bypassing Niagara Falls was finished. It allowed the dreaded sea lamprey to enter the Great Lakes. By 1940 the eel-shaped parasite had spread throughout the lakes. Lampreys decimated valuable food fishes like lake trout and whitefish until a chemical was developed that greatly suppressed lamprey numbers, allowing for the survival of desirable food and sport fishes. The tiny alewives were similarly introduced by accident through the St. Lawrence Seaway. Depletion of large food fish by the lamprey led to the alewife explosion. Huge die-offs, peaking in the memorable year of 1967, threatened to ruin Michigan beaches until coho and chinook salmon were introduced to control the alewife population.

A new slide show demonstrates how to age a fish by the rings in its scales or bones. (Like trees, growth in fish is active in the summer and dormant in the winter, resulting in rings.)

Eight miles west of Kalamazoo on M-43 at Fish Hatchery Road. From I-94, take U.S. 131 north to exit 38B (M-43), go west 6 miles to Fish Hatchery Rd., left (south) to second drive. (616) 668-2876. Open year-round Wed-Sat 10-5. Also open from Mem. Day to Labor Day Sundays noon to 5. &. Admission free.

AN INCREASINGLY ENJOYABLE SCENIC ROUTE FROM KALAMAZOO TO BENTON HARBOR . . . . . is the old **Territorial Road**, also known as the Red Arrow Highway. From the west side of the high moraine west of Kalamazoo, it passes through the **Fruit Belt** with its vineyards, orchards, farm stands, processing plants, and produce farms. Many old buildings in the country and in the villages of Paw Paw, Hartford, and Lawrence are quite interesting. Lately the road has attracted more small businesses like antique dealers and the Paw Paw Food Co-op a few miles west of Paw Paw. Near Benton Harbor the Red Arrow Highway passes by the **Benton Harbor Fruit Market** (page 52) and **Sarett Nature Center** (page 71).

Celery Flats Interpretive Center

A nifty museum remembers the glory and hard work in one of Kalamazoo's most famous products.

KALAMAZOO'S bygone fame as America's Celery City is cele-brated in this inspired little museum built in a creekside park by the city government of Portage. Much of Portage used to be celery farms. Kalamazoo-area growers were the first to popularize celery as an important commercial vegetable. By the 1880s over 300 local growers were shipping huge quantities all over the United States. A quarter of this region's entire populace earned its living from celery.

The Kalamazoo area's huge celery industry got its start in the 1860s, when one Cornelius DeBruyn developed and marketed a sweet but stringy yellow variety of celery. Within a decade other area celery growers were jointly marketing Kalamazoo celery as an appetizer — "fresh as the dew from Kalamazoo." Soon celery was touted as a relaxant in patent medicines, tonics, and sodas. At the train station and on street corners, many boys sold bunches of Kalamazoo's celebrated celery.

At this entertaining museum, the celery story is told not only with gardening tools, tonic bottles, and the like, but by a demon-stration greenhouse, celery beds, family photos, and retired celery farmers as weekend guides.

The museum vividly shows the very hard work of the "celery Dutch." Like almost all of West Michigan's Dutch emigrants, they were poor people from the rural Netherlands. Wetlands, plentiful in southern and western Michigan, had been passed over by the first wave of Yankee pioneers. For little money, poor Dutchmen, accus-tomed to farming wet soils, could buy swamplands and mucklands, then gradually clear them by laboriously grubbing out tamaracks and shrubs, then draining them by hand.

Profitable cultivation of celery depended on having large families (typical among Dutch immigrants) to do the tedious work: first har-rowing the muck fine, then starting and coddling the fussy seedlings, transplanting them, cultivating by hand, and picking off insects, also by hand. (Chemicals injured the plants.) Celery had to be irrigated in dry weather, then blanched by covering with boards in summer and with dirt in fall. Growers had to watch for just the

An old postcard celebrates Kalamazoo, the Celery City, and the many celery fields in and around it. Here in the 1860s celery was first raised as a popular edible vegetable.

right time to harvest. Finally came another round of intense family activity: harvesting before dawn (for fresher celery), cleaning, trimming, and neatly tying and packing each head by elaborately wrapping it in paper: and neatly packaging the heads in crates. Kept in root cellars, celery lasted all winter — one of the few green vegetables reliably available in the 19th century.

World War II, smaller families, and scarce farm labor all hastened the demise of Michigan celery. Celery-growing shifted to California, with its reliable weather and cheaper labor. Today's Pascal celery replaced sweeter yellow varieties. South of town many celery farms were sold for suburban development and became the sprawling suburb of Portage (population 41,000). But elsewhere many greenhouses and small family farmsteads continue as the basis for Kalamazoo's huge bedding plant industry today.

In season you can see a 30' x 100' field **celery field** outside the center. It's planted in May, with a second planting in mid-June during the **family festival**, and harvested in fall.

The celery museum is the centerpiece of the **Celery Flats Historical Area**, which includes several restored buildings and the venues for the City of Portage's extensive **summer entertainment programs** in June, July, and August, including a lively bluegrass festival in July. (Call 616-324-9200 for events info.) Most concerts in the Overlander Band Shell, reached separately off Westnedge just north of Garden Way) are free. The **outdoor amphitheater** presents touring musicals, including the Michigan Opera Theatre cabaret, and the annual Shakespeare Festival in June. Tickets are $8-$10 for adults. The **Hayloft Theater** in a 1940 barn presents family entertainment (some local, some national like Carole King) on weekends for mostly $6/adults, $4 for kids 5-12.

Restored buildings moved onto the site include a brick grain elevator, an 1859 one-room **schoolhouse** with 19th-century furnishings and maps, and the **Stewart Manor**, the 1846 summer home of U.S. Senator Charles Stewart, also furnished in period style. Admission to the interpretive center includes a **one-hour tour** of the manor, school, and interpretive center itself. There's a pretty (if unspectacular) **linear park** along Portage Creek. A two-mile, wheelchair-accessible asphalt **path** follows the stream and connects with the Portage government center on Westnedge. There's an attractive **playground, picnic tables** and **shelter**. For $6 you can take a 45-minute **canoe ride** from a dropoff point back to the center, through woods and marshland that are good for seeing ducks and geese.

7335 Garden Lane in Portage. Easily reached from I-94 exit 76A. (Take S. Westnedge 2 miles south, turn east — left — onto Garden Lane.) From U.S. 131, take exit 31, east on Centre, north on Westnedge, east on Garden Lane. Schedule weekday tours by Parks & Rec. office — 616- 329-4522. Cultural events line — 616-324-9200. May thru September, Fri-Sun & holidays noon-6. Also by appointment during weekdays. $2/adults, $1.50/seniors & children 5-12, under 5 free. &.

FROM CELERY TO FLOWERS . . . . . Gale Arent, the longtime Kalamazoo County extension agent, paved the way for the successful transition from celery-growing to raising bedding plants. He explains that the local celery industry "began to decline in the mid-1950s with the advent of direct seeding in the southern and western United States. . . . Dutch farmers all had small greenhouses used to germinate celery seeds to grow field transplants. As the celery industry declined, the suburbanization of America was creating a demand for flower and vegetable transplants for home garden use. . . . The former celery growers combined their horticultural experience with the knowledge of bedding plant culture provided by Michigan State University scientists and Extension staff to create a profitable and expanding bedding plant industry. Today over five million flats of bedding plants are grown in the Kalamazoo area." . . . . . Bedding plant growers show off their stuff at the **Flowerfest** in mid July. It includes floral displays and horticultural tours in many parts of greater Kalamazoo. Call (616) 381-3597 for details . . . . . For more info on **retail bedding plant greenhouses**, see page 100.

Kalamazoo Air Zoo

The nation's premiere flying museum
of military aircraft creates
quite an experience for both kids and adults.

FOR ANYONE with the slightest interest in flying or in military or aviation history, a visit to the Kalamazoo Aviation History Museum will likely be a real treat. It's among the top ten U.S. air museums, with a big emphasis on education that goes way beyond looking at one plane after another. Adults and kids alike enjoy sitting at the controls of the seven cockpits in the **Simulation Station**. And a trip in the Flight Simulator, so realistic that air sickness bags are provided, is memorable. (See below for details.)

The collection of vintage planes, mostly from the World War II and Korean War eras, is choice, and many of them fly. Some 28 fighters, bombers, troop carriers, reconnaissance planes, espionage gliders, and trainers, restored to tip-top condition, are displayed in the immaculate, brightly lit main building, with more in the Flight Restoration Center. (See below.) On the **"Flight of the Day"** at 2 p.m. daily (May through September only, weather permitting), a vintage plane takes off and flies over the museum's flight deck.

The visitor experience is visually rich. There's some spectacular aviation and military art, plus WWII memorabilia. A **theater** continuously shows a changing selection of videos, half an hour to 45 minutes each. At the **Guadalcanal Memorial Museum**, dioramas with audiotapes tell the story of that long, bloody island campaign, considered the psychological turning point of the land war in the Pacific.

The "Air Zoo" moniker comes from the nicknames of the great vintage aircraft displayed here, including the Flying Tiger, Gooney Bird, and Tin Goose. The P-39 Aircobra here is only one of two in the world known to be airworthy. Four of the museum's famed collection of Grumman Cats — the Wildcat, Hellcat, Tigercat, and Bearcat — have been Grand National champions at Oshkosh, Wisconsin, whose Experimental Aviation National Convention is the American mecca of aviation fans. Air museums like this are focal points for a big brotherhood of aviation fans, and the collections are constantly changing because of loans. The Air Zoo has all the Grumman Cats when Art Wolk's F9F Panther and Dave Kensler's F4F-3 Wildcat are in residence. Exhibition space is limited, so planes on display rotate. *If you hope to see a particular aircraft, call*

(616) 382-6555 to see if it will be on exhibit.

In the **hands-on section,** visitors can climb into any of seven cockpits and manipulate the throttle, buttons, and pedals of an F-106 Delta Dart, a KC-135 Stratotanker, T-28 Trojan, two trainers, or a half-scale Corsair fighter. In another part of the museum, visitors can go inside a DC-3 paratroop carrier, familiar from WWII movies. It's not hard to imagine it full of paratroopers ready to jump. For $3 extra ($1 for ages 3-5), you can be strapped into a seat in the Corsair fighter **flight simulator.** The engine roars, the ventilation system whooshes your hair breezily, and the filmed view out of the cockpit "window" jiggles. The cabin bumps and tilts back on takeoff from the airport here. Later you tilt and rock forward and back as the pilot rolls forward 360 degrees for a spectacular if stomach-churning view of the nearby Lake Michigan shore.

A high level of professionalism and funding sets the Air Zoo apart from most other U.S. aviation museums. A member of the large, wealthy, and energetic Upjohn-Gilmore clan is in the picture, as is so often in case with high-caliber Kalamazoo projects. Suzanne DeLano Parish was a WASP in World War II, flying planes from manufacturers to air bases. Flying a different plane every day made the job demanding and dangerous. She married Pete Parish, a WWII Marine infantryman and pilot in training who later came to Kalamazoo to work for Upjohn. In 1979 Reno air race pilot Gunther Balz offered to donate his rare F8F Bearcat to induce the Parrishes to go ahead with their idea for the museum. They ended up giving seven planes and some money to launch the project. Lots of things, big and small, are done unusually well here. The former director of the illustrious Air Force aviation museum in Dayton, Ohio, has called the Air Zoo the nation's premiere flying museum. When the

museum was expanding, the national organization of Guadalcanal vets approached Pete Parrish, a Guadalcanal vet himself, about installing their museum here.

Though the explanatory signs alongside each plane do a good job, first-time visitors should probably take a one-hour **introductory tour** led by a volunteer docent. Three-fourths of them are WWII vets, male and female, so you often get first-hand perspective on the war. Then take a break at a picnic table on the outdoor terrace or in the theater, and come back to investigate the most interesting things later.

At the Kalamazoo/Battle Creek International Airport south of Kalamazoo by I-94 Portage Rd. exit 78. Go south on Portage past the airport entrance, turn left onto Milham Rd. **Fly-in visitors**: *ask ground control at airport for directions. (616) 382-6555. Open year–round. June-August: Mon-Sat 9-6 except Wed 9-8, Sun 12-6. Sept-May: Mon-Sat 9-5, Sun 12-5. Closed 4 winter holidays.* & *Admission to main building: $5 for adults 16-59, $4 seniors, ages 6-15 $3, ages 3-5 $1. Package (includes museum, simulator, flight restoration center; good on different days): $9 adults, $8 seniors, $7 ages 6-15, $2 ages 3-5. Family membership: $40/year. Free to people unable to afford the fee.*

EXTRA ATTRACTIONS AT THE AIR ZOO . . . . . For $35 a passenger, half-hour **visitor flights** can be reserved on the classic **1929 Ford Tri-Motor**. The "Tin Goose" was Henry Ford's demonstration project to apply mass production techniques to aircraft and prove that commercial aviation was practical. (Flights take off at 2 p.m. Wed-Sun, June-August; and Wed, Sat & Sun in May, Sept. & Oct, *if* there are 4 paying passengers and weather permits.) . . . . . Next door at the **Flight Restoration Center** ($3 separate admission), still more restored aircraft, aviation models, and art are displayed. The museum's four full-time restoration specialists can be seen working on aircraft with volunteers. Busiest days: Mon & Tues. Questions are welcomed. Other planes, including jets still in active use, are on loan from the military as it closes bases and decommissions planes. The Air Zoo's excellent reputation for mechanical restoration gives it an advantage in acquiring vintage aircraft. . . . . . An excellent **museum shop** has good introductory books about flying (in the children's section) and specialized publications. Also on hand: nifty aviation jewelry (the rhinestone planes are great!), famous planes on rubber stamps or mugs, models in plastic or flyable paper, puzzles, videos, and posters. Members can use the 4,000-volume library. The **Michigan Aviation Hall of Fame** is located here. A complete tour and educational materials on "Why Airplanes Fly" is aimed at grades 3-8. Tours alone are aimed at ages 6-15 ($2.40/student) and 16 and up ($4).

Downtown Kalamazoo

*A delightful city park, America's first downtown mall,
a rich array of Victorian architecture, an established
small brewery, and cheap, creative vintage shops*

ALTHOUGH central Kalamazoo features no major visitor destinations, it provides a surprisingly rich urban experience for anyone who enjoys the traditional (and now all too often vanishing) pleasures of city life: walking; browsing interesting stores, people-watching on streets and in a beautiful downtown park, and seeing whole streets full of elaborate, well-preserved Victorian houses and churches. Resale stores here really stand out in originality and value. Beer afficionados think first of Larry Bell's highly regarded Kalamazoo Brewing Company with its brewpub and beer garden. It comes about as close to the inclusive, unpretentious spirit of a German *biergarten* as can be found in the U.S. today.

Kalamazoo is just big enough to support a full range of cultural amenities. The population is 80,000 in the city proper and more than twice that in the metro area, including 41,000 in the sprawling southern suburb of Portage alone.

Western Michigan University, Kalamazoo College, and Kalamazoo Valley Community College form a large educational establishment. People who went to college here often stick around. They form the basis for large art, folk dance, tennis, and blues communities. There's an uncloseted gay community. A substantial black community centered on the north side had its roots in southwest Michigan's old rural black settlements. There are old-line Yankees, more than a few Mexican Americans, Asians, and Latvians, making the town a pretty typical demographic slice of American pie. Liberals and conservatives both have strong constituencies, which means interesting politics and lots of battles over abortion. The large Dutch population includes many religious fundamentalists, yet Kalamazoo was also the home congressional district of liberal gubernatorial candidate Howard Wolpe. Currently Tim Allen, star of TV's "Home Improvement," enjoys most famous alumnus status.

Principal industries are Pharmacia & Upjohn, several paper-making plants, and a big GM plant that's supposed to close. Homegrown Upjohn has long been a key component of the city's surprising cultural life. After its merger with a larger Swedish pharmaceutical firm, Kalamazoo is one of three worldwide products cen-

❶ Bronson Park (p. 93). This wonderful, flower-filled urban park is surrounded by interesting historic buildings and full of fountains and sculptures.

❷ Kalamazoo Mall (p. 89). The country's 1st pedestrian mall is 3 pleasant blocks long, but hasn't thrived over the years, Still, you can see some nifty shops, an ornate old theater,

and a lively mid-day crowd in warm weather. Plenty of restaurants, two big department stores, a good book shops, record shops, and a fine hotel.

❸ Kalamazoo Valley Museum (p. 90). Big new museum offers unusual interactive shows. Learn about stars, space, virtual reality, engaging, local history, wind and waves, and more.

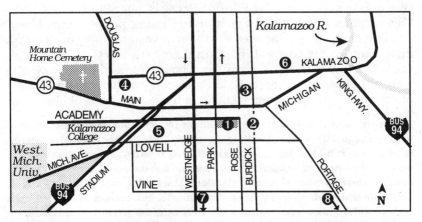

❹❺ Historic districts. On Stuart (❹, p. 99) and South (❺, p. 95), see blocks of showy mansions built by wealthy Victorians. Most are well preserved; 4 are now bed & breakfast inns.

❻ Kalamazoo Brewing Co. (p. 97). Much-praised veteran microbrewery. specializes in delicious, robust ales. Smoke-free cafe & beer garden with games (kids welcome). Saturday tours.

❼ Celery Flat Interpretive Center (p. 80). Kalamazoo pioneered commercial celery. This fascinating museum shows how Dutch families made this once-esoteric vegetable a national staple, also how they grow this fussy plant. There's a nice park for canoeing, biking, and plays

❽ Air Zoo (p. 83). One of the best collections of historically important warplanes. Climb into 7 cockpits & use realistic flight simulator. Daily flights, films. Famous for its dazzling collection of animal-named planes: Flying Tiger, Gooney Bird, Tin Goose. Aircobra, Wildcat, Hellcat, Tigercat, and Bearcat.

Highlights of
Kalamazoo

ters, responsible for marketing in North America, Asia, and Latin America, and for five major therapeutic areas worldwide, including critical care, infectious diseases, and the central nervous system. Kalamazoo's unusually balanced economy and populace is such a cross-section of America that the *Wall Street Journal* featured a focus group of local residents as a regular front-page feature during the 1992 presidential election.

Lately central Kalamazoo is developing a lively alternative scene and a certain panache. To check out the burgeoning local **alternative music scene**, stop by Flipside Records (page 90) or the State Theater office (page 92) and pick up free music publications. Many small, independent businesses with creative ideas have taken hold, more often on the edges of the central area than in the middle. It's not uncommon to meet newcomers who are pleased to have discovered it. To big-city refugees, Kalamazoo can look like heaven: a simple, friendly, heterogenous, visually rich city with great old buildings,

The prestigious biannual Irving S. Gilmore International Keyboard Festival, held next April 25-May 3, 1998, is a secretly juried keyboard artist award funded in part by the estate of a self-effacing Upjohn heir and amateur pianist. Nine days of concerts in and around Kalamazoo, many free or low-cost, celebrate keyboard music: classical, blues, jazz, and more. It's aimed at people who want to learn more about music, and attracts devotees from far and wide. This poster features the first Gilmore artist, David Norris.

Through our non-competitive Gilmore Artist Awards, we quietly search for pianists who deserve a wider international audience.

THE
GILMORE
Irving S. Gilmore International Keyboard Festival
Call us (616) 342 1166 or 1(800) 34 PIANO

compact enough that you can walk everywhere, where social problems are on a manageable scale. And fruit farms and the Big Lake are just a long bike ride away!

Downtown Kalamazoo installed the first U.S. **pedestrian mall** in 1960. Well landscaped and improved over the years, it functions as a popular outdoor living room from 11 to 2 on weekdays in pleasant weather. Despite downtown's two department store and numerous interesting specialty shops, the traffic-choked retail sprawl along South Westnedge has become so prominent in most suburbanites' minds that the downtown mall, even on the nicest summer evenings, can have the feel of a place decorated for a party where too few people came. The city commission has voted to take out the mall, but opponents who fear the effects of still more construction will probably tie up the issue in courts for awhile.

The Arcadia Commons urban renewal and preservation project has refurbished and augmented some stunning historic facades along Rose Street, plopped the massive new Kalamazoo Valley Museum between Rose and the pedestrian mall, and opened up Arcadia Creek, which has all the charm of a tasteful concrete storm sewer. No wonder many confirmed urbanites fear further "improvements" if the mall is removed.

Kalamazoo is one of the few cities in Michigan dense enough to be a good destination for train trips. (See page 101.) Points of interest in central Kalamazoo have been arranged here as a walking tour starting from the train station and proceeding south to Vine at Forest. The route is 1.25 miles one way, plus detours out South Street and East Kalamazoo. Take the Westnedge bus back if you're tired. It's a lot to see and do in one day, depending on how many places you stop at. The best part for pedestrians is along the mall, the park, and South Street. If you're in a car, you might prefer to park on Academy, north of Bronson Park.

KALAMAZOO MALL/BURDICK STREET

This walking tour is written for people arriving by train. In the more likely event that you have driven, use the Eleanor St. parking ramp a block south of Kalamazoo St. and half a block west of Rose near the museum. Rose, Eleanor, and nearby Water are virtually the only two-way streets.

Best way to get downtown: avoid South Westnedge. From west (Chicago), from I-94, go north on U.S. 131, follow Bus. Route I-94 (Michigan Ave.), turn south onto Rose. From east (Detroit), from I-94, take exit 81, which is Bus. Route I-94 (Kalamazoo St.). Out-of-towners in cars should be prepared for one-way confusion — another good reason to leave your car and walk!

◆ **Train station/Metro transit.** Get local bus schedule information here (616-337-8222). Nifty old Richardsonian Romanesque station from 1887. *459 N. Burdick at Kalamazoo.* &.

◆ **Sarkozy Bakery.** The consummate bakery — all sorts of great breads and cookies, often of Eastern European inspiration. Friendly owner Judy S. created a comfortably principle-centered business — a diverse gathering spot that employed and served some mentally impaired people who live at the hotel next door. But too many years of disruption for downtown improvements hurt business and caused (at least temporarily) a radical downsizing. *335 N. Burdick near Kalamazoo. (616) 342-1952. Current hours: Tues-Fri 12-4.* &.

◆ **Flipside Records**. Recommended by new music fans as the best all-around record store in a town becoming known for alternative music. New and used, strong on jazz. Carries more and more new vinyl. *309 N. Burdick. (616) 343-5865. Mon-Sat 10-9, Sun 12-5.* &.

◆ **Kalamazoo Valley Museum.** The long-planned museum, opened in spring, 1996, is an eclectic, not always easily digestible mix of science, technology, history, and culture. It can be a disjointing, frustrating experience if you don't put enough energy into selecting what to see, and then slow down and take it in. The sophisticated wind and water models from The Exploratorium, for instance, require you to follow instructions and contemplate. Be persistent in seeking advice from the volunteer greeter.

Special programs seem to be the big hits. The spectacular,

state-of-the-art **interactive planetarium** ($2) takes visitors on imaginary trips to galaxies and black holes. Shows are Wed & Fri 4 & 4:30, Sat 1:15 through 4:45. **Changing exhibits** in the large third-floor gallery are well worth checking out. The talkative OPUS interactive robot ($2; schedule like planetarium's) bombards visitors in a 90-seat theater with assertively non-linear ideas and info bits about one of eight subject areas chosen by the audience: virtual reality, perhaps, or the information superhighway, or digital computers. If you don't like the group's choice, explore on your own screen. Designer Andrew Dahl aimed the pioneering exhibit at 9 to 15-year-olds who love channel-changing and relish overload. Adults seem to like it, too. Visitors also plan the **Challenger mini-mission**, a 45-minute journey from Earth to deep space. Open sessions are weekend afternoons.

Unfortunately, many of the museum's history exhibits have interactive panels (note that recurring buzzword!) too heavy to lift and read. Still, there are some fine exhibits on Kalamazoo's unusually interesting products, past and present: Gibson Guitars, Checker Cabs, Upjohn's Unicap vitamin, Stryker's hospital bed on a pair of giant hoops that eliminated painful turning of burn patients; and Kalamazoo Vegetable Parchment. (Don't miss the fascinating 1920s film video of the KVP model company suburb of Parchment.) Fans of period interiors should check out the replica of the private museum of A.M. Todd, the world's Peppermint King (see pages 75 and 105). An avid globe-trotter and collector of exotic objects, he donated his collection to form the museum's nucleus. *The museum faces Rose between Eleanor and Water. Park a block west in the Eleanor St. garage. (616) 373-7990. Mon-Fri 9-5, Sat 9-9, Sun 1-5. &. Free except for special programs.*

◆ **Kalamazoo Mall.** *Along South Burdick between Water and Lovell.* Many stores are open Sunday afternoons, and some stay open evenings. Tables and chairs invite takeouts. Recommended: **Caffe Casa coffeehouse/gallery** (128 S. Kalamazoo Mall), **C.W. Michaels** (108 E. Michigan and the mall), or the **Food Dance Cafe** (farther down at 161 E. Michigan). The few blocks of East Michigan east of here, long known as the Haymarket, are downtown's oldest part, a mix of retail and office where much historical rehab has gone on. Turn here if you want to walk to the **warehouse district** (p. 97).

Here are some mall standouts from north to south. The infor-

The State Theater, used mostly for rock, blues, and folk concerts, is a rare surviving example of John Eberson's atmospheric theaters, with an interior that recreates an exotic Mediterranean town, stars that twinkle in a deepening blue sky, and a cloud machine that still works.

mation-filled **Kalamazoo Convention and Visitors Bureau** is across the mall from the Radisson hotel complex. Inside the exceedingly well run **Radisson Plaza at the Kalamazoo Center,** on the Mall at Michigan Avenue, are two art galleries and several good gift and clothing stores. Between Michigan and South, the **Caffe Casa** coffeehouse-gallery is open 'til midnight, except Sun 9-9.Nearby is a large **Repeat the Beat** CD store. **Gilmore's** department store is at 143. New and used mysteries, sci-fi and romance are at **Deadly Passions** (tucked in the rear of number 157). **Petals & Postings** has a huge selection of cards and T shirts, funny and sweet. A few doors west of the mall on South Street, **Something's Brewing** sells coffees and teas and has a small tea room, open in the daytime.

In the next block, an exceptionally large **Mole Hole** is geared to many tastes, from traditional to contemporary to ethnic, with lots of jewelry. **Athena Book Shop** offers good local interest and excellent browsing. Get the 166-page *Walking through Time* ($4.95) if you want a good companion for your historic walking tour. **Jacobson's** upscale department store is in this block; its tea room is open for lunch, including Sundays.

The pedestrian mall ends at Lovell; Pharmacia & Upjohn's big research institute is right downtown, a block east. Our tour turns west on Lovell toward Bronson Park. But first, the 400 block of South Burdick is also worth exploring. The **State Theatre** at Burdick and Lovell is one of only 12 surviving "atmospheric theaters" designed by the famous theater architect John Eberson. Inside is a Spanish courtyard, complete with statues, fountain, and three-dimensional facades of picturesque buildings along the walls. Stars still twinkle in the ceiling-sky when the lights dim, and the cloud machine still works. The theater books live music — rock, jazz, blues, country, and gospel music, plus comedy. Occasionally the vintage Barton theater organ gets a workout at events sponsored by the southwest Michigan theater organ group that maintains the organ. *Call (616) 345-6500 for program information.* &.

Just past the theater and the popular, campus-oriented bar next door, are **La De Da's** appealing vintage clothing shop (open 12-5 Tues-Sat), flanked by **J. P. Collectibles** and **St. Luke's Thrift Shop**. At La De Da's, pick up the flyer on Kalamazoo's excellent resale shops and ask for directions to Souk Sampler.

LOVELL AND PARK TO BRONSON PARK

Walk west on Lovell, then turn north onto Park for a short walk past some interesting places.

♦ **Woodrose Fine Imports** features colorful painted wood masks,

Peruvian jewelry, Guatemalan textiles and ikat-dyed clothing from Indonesia. *115 W. Lovell. (616) 344-8220. Also open Sundays.*

◆ **Pandora's Books for Open Minds**. This rambling store occupies a very old (1846) and unusual Greek Revival home. A wide range of books, cards, etc., some mainstream, is entirely related to feminists and lesbians. *226 W. Lovell. (616) 388-5656.*

◆ **St. Luke's Episcopal Church.** This Gothic Revival church (1884) is exceptionally picturesque. *247 W. Lovell.*

◆ **Ladies' Library Association Building**. One of Michigan's gems of Victorian architecture. An outstandingly bold, richly embellished brick High Victorian Gothic building from 1878-79, it's reminiscent of the strong, gutsy work of Philadelphia architect Frank Furness. It remains a private women's club. In the era before public libraries, when the educational opportunities for women were limited, the Ladies' Library Association sought to stimulate learning and culture. Stained-glass windows depict scenes from Milton, Hawthorne, Shakespeare, and Burns. Don't miss the long-tongued copper gargoyle drain spout on its corner. Free **tours** can be scheduled. Call (616) 344-8429. *333 S. Park.*

◆ **Kalamazoo Institute of Arts.** More about making art, teaching, and thinking creatively than about the passive connoisseurship that dominates most bigger, wealthier museums. There's no permanent collection regularly on display, but the **changing exhibits** are usually stimulating. The **museum shop** emphasizes handcrafts; it's in the rear, off the parking lot entrance. *Park at South. Free parking in rear. (616) 349-7775. Open Tues-Sat 10-5, Sun 1-5. . Free.*

◆ **The Kalamazoo House.** Just behind the Art Institute parking lot is a meticulously restored and furnished 1880s Italianate mansion. It's a bed-and-breakfast inn and Lilie's Provençal restaurant, with lighter fare in the rear carriage house. Passersby are welcome to peek inside to see the rich Victorian interiors. The owners also have a high-caliber historic restoration construction firm. *447 South. (616) 343-5426. .*

BRONSON PARK AND VICINITY

◆ **Bronson Park.** *On the west side of downtown, bounded by Rose, Park, South, and Academy. Extra parking is along Academy.* Even though a deadly 1980 tornado ripped out dozens of its giant oak trees, Bronson Park remains the most interesting of all West Michigan's many old-fashioned, town-square-type parks. Sitting in the park, you see a harmonious collage of architectural styles in the buildings forming the square, from Queen Anne to Art Deco.

Important civic buildings are to the south, historic churches to the west and north. Benches are around the fountain. Tables and chairs make the southeast corner almost like an outdoor public patio.

A century's worth of monuments and fountains immediately convey that this has long been an important focal point for Kalamazoo citizens. The park's centerpiece is Kalamazoo sculptor Kirk Newman's bicentennial **illuminated fountain sculpture,** "When justice and mercy prevail, children may safely play." Nine Kalamazoo children served as models; kids like to play in the fountain today. The **mound** in the southwest corner is the area's last remaining burial site of the mysterious prehistoric Hopewell people. The park's thousands of tulips are usually in bloom by late April through mid May. Later, **bedding plants** and a spectacular **floral sculpture** celebrate Kalamazoo's role as the nation's bedding plant capital.

Once a cow pasture, the rectangular parcel became a park in 1876, part of a great era of American park-building commemorating the nation's centennial. In the northeast corner an imposing eight-foot bronze sculpture of an American foot soldier from 1923 commemorates U.S. military campaigns. **Memorial plaques** sprinkled throughout the park honor people as diverse as Adlai Stevenson and prominent Kalamazoo feminist Lucinda Hinsdale Stone. The 1913 *U.S.S. Maine* Memorial Tablet was cast from parts of that famous Navy ship which exploded in Havana harbor. A dramatic sculpture-fountain, erected in 1939, it commemorates the sad removal of local Indians to the west in 1840.

Special **free festivals and events** fill the park many weekends in spring and summer; call the Convention and Visitors Bureau at (616) 381-4003 for a calendar. Call city parks weekdays for all upcoming Bronson Park events, including Thursday-evening summer **concerts**: (616) 337-8002.

On the park's southern border, the city's distinctive 1931 Art Deco **city hall** has lots of wonderful Egyptian-flavored embellishments outside and in. Along the tops of the four limestone exterior walls are bas-reliefs of events from the city's history. To city hall's west, the **First Presbyterian Church** is a majestic Gothic-inspired structure built in 1930. To city hall's east is the imposing **Park Club**, a Queen Anne castle made of Lake Superior sandstone in 1890. Once the home of a prominent local industrialist, it is now a private club. *Bronson Park is in downtown Kalamazoo, bounded by Rose, Park, South, and Academy streets.* &.

◆ **Michigan News Agency.** A fabulous newsstand with a beat-up wood floors and a been-there-forever atmosphere (since 1947, in fact). It's been brought into the 1990s by the founder's daughter

Because 19th-century Kalamazoo grew steadily, without big booms and busts, homes were built in a succession of historic styles in the same neighborhoods. The Vine, South Street, and Stuart neighborhoods have survived in remarkably good shape, with little demolition. These houses are in the Stuart Neighborhood a mile west of downtown north of West Main.

and her husband. They are utterly devoted to serving *all* their customers, from street people to Kalamazoo's considerable number of literati, such as novelist Jamie Gordon and acclaimed short story writer Stuart Dybek, who both teach at Western. Don't miss the bulletin board! 2,500 magazine titles, with new ones constantly added. Maps, tobacco, comics, lots of out-of-town papers. Noteworthy: job search materials, job banks for many cities, national ad search. *308 W. Michigan, a block north of Bronson Park via Church St. and two blocks east of the Kalamazoo Mall. (616) 343-5958. Open 365 days, 6 a.m. to 9 p.m. &.*

◆ **South Street Historic District.** This remarkably intact historic streetscape, 3/8 of a mile from both downtown and Kalamazoo College to the west, remained a prestigious neighborhood where impressive houses were built between 1847 through World War I. Architectural styles range from Greek and Gothic Revival through Georgian and Tudor. Kalamazoo was a wealthy town with many industries, no booms or busts, and old families who stayed in homes for generations. All this made for stable neighborhoods whose fine homes were unusually well maintained, not chopped into low-income apartments by the 1940s.

The **Red Cross** (616-382-6382) occupies the two **Upjohn houses**. Widowed neighbors Carrie Gilmore and William Upjohn married each other circa 1900, founding a multifaceted business dynasty whose influence remains great. Drop-ins are welcome weekdays; call for tours. *South Street from Westnedge to Stadium.*

VINE NEIGHBORHOOD

This central-city success story is a square mile of southside Kalamazoo, bounded by Lovell, Oakland, Howard/Crosstown Parkway, and Burdick. Some unusual historic homes and some small businesses along South Westnedge are what would interest visitors. In this diverse neighborhood, renters, owner-occupants, students, professionals, and group homes live together in a racially mixed, harmonious, well-organized area. Other college towns could learn a lot about cooperative, self-help community development in low-income and student rental areas from the **Vine Neighborhood Association** (616- 349-8463) and its development arm, **Vine Ventures**, both headquartered at 913 South Westnedge and open weekdays. This dense, turn-of-the century area is on the upswing, with continuing renovation of houses selling for $20,000 to $40,000.

◆ **Cosmo's Cucina.** Delightful, tucked-away second-floor restaurant with great atmosphere and food; a fine spot for a mid-walk break. *804 W. Vine at Locust, a block west of Westnedge. (616) 344-5666. Open 11-10 weekdays, for weekend breakfasts 8:30-3 p.m., also Sat. evenings.*

◆ **Carousel Ice Cream and Sandwich Shop.** Corner store with an original soda fountain. *819 S. Westnedge. (616) 342-8493.*

◆ **Fourth Coast Cafe.** Coffeehouse with international coffees, pastries, etc., plus games to play. *418 S. Westnedge.*

◆ **Bicentennial Bookshop.** Well organized and well stocked with used and rare books and selected old magazines. *820 S. Westnedge. (616) 345-5987. Closed Sundays.*

◆ **Octagon House**. Most unusual for an octagon because it's so well preserved and because it's one story. Hard to see when the leaves are out. *925 S. Westnedge.*

◆ **Pioneer Park.** The site of an old cemetery has been renovated with funds and work crews from the neighborhood. Benches and big trees make for a pleasant place to sit, snack, and view attractive old houses. You may notice small courts of houses built behind main streets here. Dutch immigrants often built extra backyard housing for newly arrived relatives. *Westnedge at Park Place.*

◆ **Attic Trash & Treasures.** Used furniture, jewelry, sheet music, and lots of great middle-class 20th-century nostalgia items. Behind it, **Johnson Piano**, third-generation piano restorers, displays two elaborate small grand pianos and a showcase of miniatures. *1301 S. Westnedge at Forest. (616) 344-2189.*

◆ **Thieves' Market.** A wild mix of used and new stuff, from

sequined dresses to bow ties to accordions, eyeball jewelry, senti-
mental framed pictures, and corny souvenirs, artfully crammed into
quite a small space. For people who miss the Ann Arbor of the
1960s and 1970s, it's a must. The owner stocks tarot cards and
books, does readings by appointment. The bulletin board reflects
her longstanding love of the blues. *1305 S. Westnedge just south of
Forest. (616) 388-6166. Open daily 12-6, Sun 2-5.*

Getting back to downtown: You can walk the 1 1/4 miles back on Park, parallel to Westnedge but a block to the east. Or you could take the bus. It stops on
the half-hour at Park and Forest.

EAST END WAREHOUSE DISTRICT

East of Burdick, extending south from Kalamazoo. A swing east
on Michigan Avenue takes you through the German side of downtown into the industrial area that has spawned some of
Kalamazoo's most interesting businesses. Avoid walking down
Kalamazoo; too much traffic! Many stores stay open to 6, 7, or 9, so
you could stop here before catching an evening train.

♦ **Heritage Company Architectural Salvage & Supply.** Long a
stalwart of Kalamazoo's active historic preservation movement,
Rodger Parzyck has moved his business into a series of 19th-centu-
ry storefronts he and his partners have splendidly restored. In addition to salvage hardware, doors, windows, and light fixtures, there
are some antiques. The connecting **Kalamazoo Antiques Market**
next door features over 30 high-caliber dealers including specialists
in cameras, military memorabilia, costume jewelry, books, trum-
pets, and Arts & Crafts furniture, art pottery, and accessories. *130
N. Edwards, just north of Wendy's between Michigan and Kalamazoo. (616) 385-1004. Heritage hours: Tues-Sat 10-5. Antiques Market
hours: Tues-Fri 11-6, Sat 10-6, Sun 1-6.* &.

♦ **The Emporium.** Three long buildings packed with antique furniture attract antiquers from far and wide. Hand-lettered signs are
everywhere, pronouncing the opinions of the gruff character who
owns the place. *313 E. Kalamazoo. (616) 381-0998. Note odd hours:
2-6 p.m. Sat & Sun; 7-9 p.m. Mon-Fri.* &: no.

♦ **Kalamazoo Brewing Company.** Acclaimed brewer Larry Bell
started brewing unfiltered, unpasteurized, naturally carbonated
beers in 1985. That gives his funky, personal brewery 11 years of
experience on slick new entrants in the current brewpub craze.
Products like Bell's Amber Ale and Bell's Kalamazoo Stout have won
such a following in Chicago (where half his output is sold) and

Two Hearted Ale

Years ago, long before the micro-brew fad, the Kalamazoo Brewery was helped with financing by Lladislav Hanka, Sr. (left), avid fisherman and local resident. Two Hearted Ale recognizes him as "brewery friend and saviour" with a portrait by his son, Llad, the distinguished printmaker who designs Bell's labels.

nationwide that his biggest problem has been keeping up with demand. Current expansion will bring annual output to over 24,000 barrels, up from 6,000 in 1994. **Free tours** ("Beer 101" and a walk through the new plant) are Saturdays at 1, 2, 3, and 4. Within the Brewery is the smoke-free **Eccentric Cafe.** It serves the widest range of beers being produced here. Several seasonal brands are brewed in limited batches; other specialty beers are brewed in two- and six-barrel batches and served only here. Cafe patrons are welcome to play ping-pong, chess, checkers, jenga, and other games. Kids are welcome. Friday and Saturday nights there's live **acoustic music** ranging from jazz to Texas country to polkas. In summer, an enclosed **back-door beer garden** offers bocce and horseshoes. *315 E. Kalamazoo between Michigan and Water. Park in back. (616) 382-2338. Cafe hours are Mon-Thurs 10-a.m.-11:30 p.m., Fri & Sat 10 a.m.-12:30 p.m., Sun noon-7.* &.

◆ **Water Street Coffee Joint.** The interior and mood of this owner-designed coffeehouse is so artistic in every detail, you'd think he was an art student. But no, he studied finance at Western. Working across the street, he had his eye on this spot for years. Pastries, muffins, and light **lunches** are available. Don't miss the inlaid slate and marble sunburst in the concrete floor. *315 East Water at Kalamazoo, across from the brewery. (616) 373-2840. Open every morning. Stays open evenings to 10 at least, except Sun & Mon.* &.

◆ **The Robinson Collection.** Cheerful, friendly shop with an **Afrocentric** focus and widespread appeal: books, tapes (including storytelling, gospel, some African music), collectibles, posters, cards, and dolls, plus some clothing. *505 E. Kalamazoo at Walbridge. (616) 342-8228. Mon-Sat 10-7.*

◆ **Okun Brothers Shoe Store.** This large, colorful shoe store offers discount prices and everything from ballet slippers to firemen's boots, lizard cowboy boots to high-heeled sandals. The 70-year-old store is from a bygone era of retailing — bustling and never fancy. The exterior walls are plastered with painted signs of brand names. The 30 salespeople are willing to bargain even on discounted prices. *South St. at Edwards on the east edge of downtown. (616) 342-1536. Mon-Fri 9-9, Sat to 7.*

🌲🌳🌲

YET ANOTHER MAGNIFICENT LATE 19th-CENTURY NEIGHBORHOOD . . . . is on the west side of central Kalamazoo, just north of the Kalamazoo College campus. The **Stuart Avenue Historic District** is along Stuart and Woodward between West Michigan/Main and North. When a horse-drawn streetcar came out this way in 1884, professional men and business owners built huge suburban homes to display the wealth they gained in the years after the Civil War. . . . Today, the Casteel family's five carefully restored bed and breakfast inns have done much to promote this neighborhood. Many elaborate Eastlake, Queen Anne, and Italianate houses, even student rental properties, boast classy historic paint schemes. Visitors are welcome to walk through the beautiful **gardens** on Stuart at Main, south of the Bartlett-Upjohn House, a bed and breakfast at 229 Stuart, provided they check with the innkeeper first.

ANNUAL EVENTS OF SPECIAL NOTE . . . . . include July's **Flowerfest** in Bronson Park, a celebration of the local bedding plant industry that includes horticultural tours as well as performances and food; the **Black Arts Festival** in August; spinners' and weavers' **Fiberfest** in August; the **Wine and Harvest Festival** in early September; and the new **Allegro Arts Festival**, an interactive, multidisciplinary blend of visual arts, song, and dance (616-342-5059), held on the downtown mall in mid-September . . . . . For a two-month **events calendar** or an annual one, call the **Convention and Visitors Bureau**, (616) 381-2710.

AN ARTS LINE WITH TWO WEEKS' OF UPCOMING EVENTS AND SHOWS . . . . 75 member groups contribute to the **Arts Council of Greater Kalamazoo** arts line. Dial (616) 383-1000, punch in 2787 (that's ARTS), and hold on past the 15-second ad. . . . . . The arts line includes all events at the **Kalamazoo Civic Theater**, in a gem of a theater on the south side of Bronson Park. The multifaceted theater has several programs of musicals and dramas: mainstage, area theater, youth theater, black theater, and summer theater. . . . . **The New Vic Theater** is a professional stock theater, since 1966, presenting a competent, thoughtful mix of off-Broadway hits, cabaret musicals, and folk-related things like an original Harry Chapin revue. *(616) 381-3328. Tickets $14.*

MORE RESOURCES FOR CURIOUS VISITORS . . . . . . You can pick up *Kalamazoo Downtown,* an interesting free tabloid with upcoming events, at area shops. . . . . . History and preservation buffs will want to buy *Walking through Time: A Pictorial Guide to Historic Kalamazoo.* It's $5 at the Athena Book Shop, 300 South Kalamazoo Mall. . . . . The **Kalamazoo Convention and Visitors Bureau** at 128 North Kalamazoo Mall offers visitor information, including a calendar of events and walking tours of historic areas. Stop by the office weekdays, or call (616) 381-4003.

GOOD DEALS FROM THE BEDDING PLANT INDUSTRY . . . . . Family-owned greenhouses are behind nearly every house along certain streets adjacent to the productive mucklands where Kalamazoo's "celery Dutch" grew celery until World War II. (See page 80). In spring you can get **good deals on bedding plants** by buying direct. Some growers sell only wholesale, but others sell wholesale and retail. Their signs will often say whether they sell to the public, what they specialize in, and whether they sell on Sundays. (Many don't.) Look in the Yellow Pages under "Bedding Plants" for a long listing.

To see this interesting variant of family farming, drive out North Westnedge or go to Comstock, just east of Kalamazoo. To get to Comstock, take the I-94 Sprinkle Road exit, go north. After you've passed Bus. I-94/Amvet Parkway, turn right (east) onto Market Street or Comstock Avenue. Two greenhouses have a big retail trade: **Wenke's Greenhouses** on Market at Sprinkle, with annuals, vegetables, and herbs (616-388-2266) and **Bell Flowers** at 5437 Comstock (616-343-6857). Bell's specializes in perennials and sells them in large gallon sizes, in 3" pots, and in small trays, grown like annuals for about $10 a flat, less for additional flats. The selection is enormous — dozens of varieties of clematis, for instance. In winter, house plants and forced bulbs are for sale.

THE CRAFTSMEN BEHIND THE LEGENDARY GIBSON GUITAR . . . . . are still making guitars in Kalamazoo in the old Gibson factory, now known as **Heritage Guitar.** (Gibson left for Nashville and lower labor costs in the South.) A small work force turns out high-quality guitars that sell for $900 to $20,000. Visitors are welcome to stop by the historic factory, northeast of downtown at 225 Parsons. From Kalamazoo or Michigan avenues, turn north on Edwards. When Edwards ends, look down the street (Pitcher) to see "Gibson" on the smokestack.

Amtrak between Detroit and Chicago

A slice of historic Michigan along the Michigan Central: vineyards and factories, quaint towns and depots, and the Kalamazoo River's woods and wetlands.

AMTRAK'S Wolverine run over the historic Michigan Central line is one of the busiest passenger rail lines in the Midwest — and quite possibly the most beautiful. Michigan's historic rail stations are architecturally distinctive and unusually well preserved. They're highlights of this train trip. So is the 1 1/4-hour portion between Jackson and Kalamazoo, when the tracks parallel the Kalamazoo River valley and let you look down at the woods and wildlife by the river. This stretch is especially scenic in **fall color season**, in **early spring** leaf-out time, and in **winter** when snow is on the ground. Late summer's foliage obscures too much; it's the dullest time for this train trip. But good strolling weather makes destinations more fun in summer, especially when they have sidewalk cafes and in-town parks.

On the Amtrak route between Ypsilanti and Kalamazoo, nineteenth-century townscapes and interesting, brief industrial landscapes flash by. They alternate with just the right amount of open farmland and densely wooded river scenes to be diverting.

The trick in planning an outing by rail for a day trip or overnight is finding a destination with enough interesting things to see and do within walking distance of the train station. A trip to the intense metropolis of downtown Chicago is best of all — and the morning train from Michigan cities does allow for six hours in the Windy City without spending the night. That's plenty of time for a walk through the Loop, a visit to the Art Institute, and a stroll down Michigan Avenue's Magnificent Mile.

The Detroit to Chicago corridor is among the busiest in the Amtrak system, a short run that's able to compete effectively with planes. It's often faster to take the train than fly when going from Detroit or Dearborn to downtown Chicago, considering the waiting and ground transportation. But you can't count on getting there on time. The Wolverine's most recent on-time performance figures are 50%, and the definition of "on time" for the complete Chicago-to-Pontiac trip means within half an hour of the estimated arrival time.

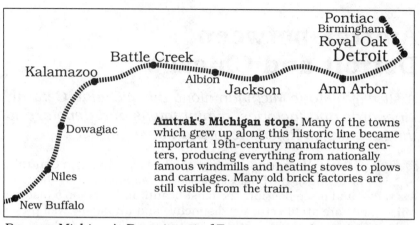

Pontiac
Birmingham
Royal Oak
Battle Creek   Detroit
Kalamazoo
Albion
Jackson   Ann Arbor

Dowagiac

Niles

New Buffalo

Amtrak's Michigan stops. Many of the towns which grew up along this historic line became important 19th-century manufacturing centers, producing everything from nationally famous windmills and heating stoves to plows and carriages. Many old brick factories are still visible from the train.

Because Michigan's Department of Transportation has worked closely with Amtrak, providing studies of signaling improvements, the 71 miles between Kalamazoo and Chicago are currently being upgraded to allow higher speeds — a maximum of 100 mph, contrasted with typical 79 mph top speeds. The goal is to make the Chicago to Detroit trip in three hours, once all track, crossing, and signal improvements have been funded and installed.

In Michigan, here are your choices for interesting destinations:

◆ **Ann Arbor**. The compact, bustling university town has perhaps the state's most interesting central-city shopping and restaurant area, and perhaps the worst parking problem, too. You can be happy here without a car. See pages 149-178. Walk to downtown to connect with the excellent bus system centered on Fourth Ave. near Liberty. It can take you to most outlying destinations and motels. Downtown lodgings include the Campus Inn and Bell Tower Hotel (luxury), the renovated Michigan League, and a bed and breakfast or two. Public transit (available from near train station): (313) 996-0400.

◆ **Kalamazoo** is another excellent rail destination. (See p. 86.) Train schedules from southeast Michigan or Chicago permit a full day's outing or an overnight that's enjoyable in a low-key way. Fine in-town accommodations: the 4-star Radisson Kalamazoo Center and the Kalamazoo House B&B. Busses connect within a half mile of Celery Flats and a mile of the Air Zoo. Public transit center (at train station): 616-337-8201.

◆ **Jackson.** Walk to the bus station for connections every half hour to the Ella Sharp Museum and Park (page 146), an excellent all-day destination for kids because of the museum and village, good restaurant, terrific minigolf, and swimming pool. Busses run less frequently on Saturday. Bus service to the Space Center (p. 144) is limited. Better reserve Dial-A-Ride 48 hours ahead. It's no more than $1 a student each way. Visitors from Ann Arbor and metro Detroit can catch a bus to the Space Center if they take the early train. Public transit

(1/2 mile walk or bus ride from train station): (517) 787-8363.

◆ **Battle Creek.** The downtown train/bus station is convenient to the Kellogg Arena and luxurious Renaissance Hotel, but alas, there's not usually much to see or do downtown, and the bus system doesn't go to the Binder Park Zoo or Gull Lake attractions. (The holiday light display between Thanksgiving and New Year's is spectacular, however.) Walking or local buses could get you to the Kimball House Historical Museum (616-966-2496), a restored house museum with some exhibits on Sojourner Truth, the Willard Library with its excellent local history room, and the worthwhile Kingman Museum of Natural History (616-965-5117). Public transit center (at train station): (616) 966-3474.

◆ **Albion** has one train stop a day in each direction. Rail travelers from southeast Michigan can walk from downtown to some delightful riverside parks, natural areas, and an orchard within their allotted six hours. For overnights, there's nearby Marshall. See pages 117-127. Local cab: (517) 629-5012.

◆ **Niles.** Downtown is a mile from the train station — not a bad walk. A cab can take you to Fernwood Botanical Gardens. See pages 31-6.

◆ **Dearborn.** Amtrak now stops at Greenfield Village itself (see page 355). Greenfield Village and the Henry Ford Museum (see pages 345-55) are 3 miles from the main train station, between Dearborn's two downtowns. For local transportation from the main Dearborn station, call the Dearborn Cab Company, (313-562-6060) or the bus company, SMART (313-962-5515). Lodgings within walking distance to Greenfield Village: Dearborn Inn (pricey), Village Inn (relatively inexpensive). Another big local attraction: terrific Middle Eastern restaurants serving the biggest Arab community in the U.S. (see p. 339-44).

◆ **Detroit.** The new Amtrak station is on Woodward at Baltimore, two blocks south of Grand in the New Center area. The New Center is home of the fabulous Fisher Building (page 000), the Fisher Theater, and several restaurants. It's just 3/4 of a mile down Woodward to the Detroit Institute of Arts, the Detroit Historical Museum, and Wayne State (pages 246-256.) The walk's ugly but not dangerous in daytime, but a cab would be better. Busses are erratic. The People Mover means you can get around downtown at night to the Theater District, Greektown nightlife, and the RenCen observation lounge (neat at night). The Attractions Shuttle connects the DIA, Greenfield Village, and several other major destinations in summer. Call (313) 259-8726 for a pamphlet.

◆ **Royal Oak.** Full of interesting shops, coffeehouses, and restaurants, plus it has the Detroit Zoo. See pages 303-9.

◆ **Birmingham.** Beautiful in-town parks, pleasant downtown for pedestrians, the state's best art galleries, loads of shops and restaurants, and now art movies at the renovated Birmingham Theater. Possibility of group transportation to Cranbrook: call (810) 645-3145. In-town hotels: Townsend (luxury), Village Inn and Holiday Express (merely expensive). See pages 311-316.

TIPS FOR TRAIN TRAVEL

◆ Make a **reservation** ahead of time. Tickets on the Chicago-Detroit-Pontiac train are sold by reservation only. That means that Amtrak can add extra cars at heavy travel times, alleviating the old problem where passengers boarding on busy days in the middle of the line had to stand up. A reservation does not absolutely guarantee you a seat. Fridays and Sundays are busiest. But traveling "custom class" does. It costs $7 extra between Chicago and Detroit and includes a free beverage, newspaper, and curtained-off "custom class" area.

◆ The **ideal vantage point** for looking out train windows is from the table seats in the food service cars that are on most trains. They let you see out left and right without seat backs blocking the view. An extra plus: the train crew hangs out there, and they know a lot about what's on the route.

◆ **Bicyclists** can take their bikes on trains that have baggage cars. On the Chicago to Detroit and Pontiac run, baggage cars are on the morning train westbound from Detroit and the evening train from Chicago around 6 p.m. Some stations don't offer baggage service. Those that do are Niles, Kalamazoo, Battle Creek, Jackson, Ann Arbor, Dearborn, and Detroit. It costs $11/trip to check your bike in Amtrak's bike box. Stations vary as to how long ahead baggage needs to be checked. Call each one for details. Some experienced road cyclists like to ride east from Kalamazoo or Niles to get the prevailing wind from the west behind them. The southern tier of Michigan counties are less populous and offer pretty good backroads cycling if you pick the right route. (See pages 9 and 23 for bicycle planning tips.)

For Amtrak schedule and fares, call 1-800-USA-RAIL. Four trains a day in each direction go between Chicago and Detroit.

RECOMMENDED TOURIST TRAINS . . . . . include the charming **Southern Michigan Railroad** between Clinton and Tecumseh (call 517-456-7677; see page 139); the **Huckleberry Railroad** at **Crossroads Village** near Flint, with its gritty, narrow-gauge old steam engine (517-763-7100; see page 370); and the quarter-size **Junction Valley Railroad** in Bridgeport north of Frankenmuth (517-777-3480), where you can spend the day in delightfully landscaped grounds.

OTHER MICHIGAN AMTRAK ROUTES . . . . . are functional but not as scenic or useful for Michigan day trips. Currently one train a day leaves **Grand Rapids** in the morning, goes to Chicago through Holland, Bangor/ South Haven, St. Joseph, New Buffalo, and Hammond/Whiting. It comes back in the evening. . . . One train a day goes from **Chicago to Toronto**, branching north at Battle Creek and passing through East Lansing, Durand, Flint, Lapeer, and Port Huron. The three other Chicago-Detroit trains connect with East Lansing and Flint via a bus. Call Amtrak for info: 1-800-USA-RAIL.

Gilmore Classic Car Museum

A delightful pastoral setting provides a great stage for a fascinating collection of cars.

EVEN THOSE with only a middling interest in cars should enjoy this collection, one of the choicest anywhere. The location is itself a treat—well off the beaten path northeast of Kalamazoo. Spread over 80 acres of meticulously groomed meadowland are six handsome barns, several of them moved from farms in the region. The late Donald Gilmore, an heir and chairman of the Upjohn pharmaceutical empire, clearly lavished money and attention on his expensive hobby. Far from a grab-bag assemblage of antique cars, it's a connoisseur's carefully chosen stable of historically significant automobiles. Call for each season's **special events.**

What's special here is the opportunity to see how legendary models evolved over the years:

◆ Fourteen pristine **Packards** show the line's dramatic evolution from 1905 through the last model in 1956.

◆ Seven **Rolls Royces** are lined up in a row, from the 1910 Silver Ghost to the 1938 Pack Ward.

◆ Mark I and II **Lincolns** from 1940 and 1956 show how old that

Cars from each of the century's first five decades (left to right): a 1910 Cadillac, 1934 Auburn, 1948 Tucker, 1929 Duesenberg, and 1905 Packard.The big barn is from A. M. Todd's abandoned mint plantation in nearby Mentha, on the Kal-Haven Trail.

sleek line is.

◆ Most historically important is the fascinating evolution of Henry Ford's autos from his initial **1903 Ford Tonneau** to the **1906 Model N** and the record-breaking **Model T** (19 million sold from 1907-1928) to the 1928-31 **Model A.**

◆ You can see the humble 1903 **Cadillac** grow in nine models into the flashy, finny Sixties showboat.

There are two **Stanley Steamers** and a narrow-gauge steam locomotive. (Gilmore loved steam-powered locomotion.) A dazzling display of **hood ornaments** reveal more bared breasts than a *Playboy* magazine. A nifty section called **"Dreams & Failures"** features a grinning 1958 **Edsel,** the infamous 1981 stainless steel **Delorean,** and the last production-line **Tucker** (#78) from 1948.

Another building is devoted to **performance cars**, including the 1967 Indianapolis 500 winner driven by A.J. Foyt and sponsored by Gilmore. Here you'll find a 470 hp **BMW,** a turbocharged **Porsche,** and various **Corvettes**, including the first 8-cylinder model. The centerpiece of a dramatic second-story barn display, complete with historical perspective, is a boxy black Soviet 1978 **Chaika** that was Brezhnev's limousine.

Gilmore's hometown of nearby Kalamazoo is not ignored. The first new car sold in the city, an 1899 **Locomobile,** sits alongside a variety of the high-quality **Roamers,** last made in 1930. And there are three of Kalamazoo's legendary **Checker cabs** from 1922, 1935, and the last Checker that rolled off the line in 1982.

On M-43 at Hickory Rd., due west of Hickory Corners and just north of Gull Lake, 17 miles northeast of Kalamazoo. (616) 671-5089. Open 1st Sat of May to last Sun of Oct., daily 9-5. ♿: yes, except hood ornaments. $5 admission, Seniors 62+ $4, children 7-15 $2.

HERBS AND PERENNIALS IN A PRETTY OLD FARMSTEAD SETTING . . . . are less than three miles from the Gilmore Car Museum at **Braeloch Farms** on the west side of Gull Lake. A big weathered dairy barn is filled with unfussy dried arrangements, floral gift items, books on gardening, and antiques. In spring a variety of perennial herb plants are available. Many gardens and herb plots give visitors ideas for landscaping with herbs and perennials. *From M-43 a mile north of Richland (that's south from the Gilmore Museum), turn east onto County Road C at the Stagecoach Stop Inn. When C ends, turn left. Farm is first drive on right. (616) 629-9884. Open from mid-April to Christmas. Tues-Sat 10-5, Sun 1-5.*

Kellogg Bird Sanctuary

*Where idyllic landscaping has created a paradise
of plentiful food for dramatic big birds*

WALKING into the Kellogg Bird Sanctuary near dusk is like
walking into a dream. It's a lush, romantic landscape.
Peacocks amble freely on the lawn, languorously trailing
tails of brilliant blue and green. Here a normally elusive eastern
wild turkey is so well socialized that it makes an excellent photo
subject if you happen to meet it on its early-morning or late-afternoon foraging strolls. Inside the entrance gift shop, you pay two dollars to enter, plus 50¢ for a generous bucket of corn.

Down a winding path through a wooded glade you come to lovely
Wintergreen Lake. Birdsong fills the air. Squirrels are drawn by
plentiful food from many nut trees, domestic and exotic. Arched
bridges connect lagoons along the shore. Rare trumpeter swans sail
up majestically to you, hoping for corn. When they emerge from the
water, it's a surprise to see them plop along on huge, comical black
feet. It's a thrill to be able to feed these big birds and see them up
close in such a gorgeous setting.

These were barren, overgrazed hills in 1928. At that time cereal
magnate W. K. Kellogg started the sanctuary as a refuge for Canada
geese, threatened by loss of habitat to agriculture and urbanization.
This and other conservation efforts proved so successful that
Canada geese are now pests in many places.

Today the sanctuary is a part of Michigan State University's
Kellogg Biological Station. The excellent **book shop** has toys, posters,
clothing, and gifts, plus an outstanding selection of books geared to
nature-lovers and teachers. Here you can find out how to transform
your back yard into a paradise for birds, following the same landscaping principles and planting materials used in the refuge.

Permanent residents among the free-flying waterfowl by the lagoon include six of the world's nine varieties of swans and 30 pairs
of Canada geese. In spring through fall they are augmented by 20
varieties of migrating ducks, such as bufflehead, ruddy ducks,
hooded mergansers, and northern shovelers. Canadas alone number 5,000 during fall migration.

Interpretive signs along the 1 1/2-mile asphalt loop tell about
the waterfowl in some detail. In a secluded area, away from the lively hubbub of waterfowl at the lake, visitors have an unusual chance
to see over a dozen **birds of prey** up close. There's a threatened

Trumpeter swans, North America's largest native waterfowl, are being rein-troduced to Michigan with birds raised at the sanctuary. Over-hunted by Indians for their quills and skins, trumpeter swans were probably mostly gone from Michigan before English settlers arrived, says KBS's chief wildlife biologist.

red-shouldered hawk, an endangered short-eared owl, and a bald eagle. Modern zoo practice ordinarily prohibits caging such big native birds. These are injured. Some are being rehabilitated; others are so badly hurt they can't survive in the wild.

The sanctuary's residents and their activities change with the seasons, so repeat visits are worthwhile. Spring means the return of winter migrants to nest here or pass through. Swans and geese typically nest in **late March**, ducks start in **early April**. Nesting structures have been built in public areas to be easily observed by visitors. The young are hatched in **May** and **June**. **Summer** residents include many ducks, geese, and swans, along with over two dozen species of backyard songbirds. (To see bobolinks and such, you'd have to go out into the fields of the Biological Station.)

Beginning in **October**, ducks and geese stop here on their way south. **Early November** usually brings the greatest numbers and most varieties. **Winter** isn't dull, either. Over 2,000 resident swans, geese, and ducks stay near the lake, which is kept from freezing by air compressors. (Resident birds have lost their instinct to migrate.) In warm, snowless winters, geese may linger by the thousands, thrown off-kilter by confusing weather signals.

12685 East C Ave. east of Gull Lake between Kalamazoo and Battle Creek. From M-89, turn north on 40th St. In a little over a mile, go west onto East C Ave. (616) 671-2510. Open 365 days. May-Oct: daily 9-8. Nov.-April: 9-5. Early-morning bird-watching by special arrangement. &: *buildings and trails. Wheelchairs available at the office. $2/adult, 50¢/children 4-12.*

SKIERS, HIKERS, AND PICNICKERS . . . . . enjoy the quiet, scenic **W. K. Kellogg Forest**, a Michigan State University forestry experiment station on the hills and valley formed by pretty Augusta Creek. It's about three miles southeast of the Kellogg Bird Sanctuary. Cereal king and philanthropist   W. K. Kellogg started it as a demonstration project in reforesting abandoned farms. Old farms in Michigan's many areas of glacial lakes and hills had the same problems: rocky, hilly land not suited to farming. (When many of these farmers went broke during the Depression, their land reverted to the state for nonpayment of taxes. Many prime state recreation areas consist of such marginal farmland.)

Today the forest's 720 acres are planted in a huge variety of trees, quite possibly the largest genetic archive of temperate plant tree species in the world. From the entrance a dirt road leads back behind the "Maple Manor" sugar shack (used for **mid-March syrup-making demonstrations**) to a series of rustic **picnic areas** beneath big pines along the creek. Artificial ponds and rapids have turned the creek into a designated **trout stream**. A steep 1/4-mile trail leads to a **scenic overlook**. A **2 1/2-mile road loop** continues north from the picnic grounds and circles around, past plantations of Scotch pines for Christmas trees. Seedlings come from stock grown in different cold climates from around the world. **Skiers**, **hikers**, and **bow-hunters** are all welcome to use the forest's 25 miles of ungroomed firebreaks separating experimental stands of trees. *Stop for a **map and brochure** at the forest entrance off 42nd Street, 3/4 of a mile south of M-89 and two miles north of the old canal village of Augusta. Admission is free. Restrooms behind the office are always open. Call (616) 731-4597 for special, **forest-related events**. Open year-round from 8 a.m. until sunset, except Thanksgiving, Christmas, New Year's, and Easter.*

VISIT A MODEL DAIRY . . . . . two miles north of the Kellogg Bird Sanctuary. A free, **self-guided tour** of Michigan State University's **Kellogg Dairy** starts in the milking parlor and ends with a chance to pet the calves in outdoor nursery hutches. Call (616) 671-2507 for current **milking times**. If you miss seeing milking, you can watch an interesting nine-minute video on dairy farming practices. A **free booklet** explains the basics of milk production and nutrition.

This high-tech dairy has an automatic flush system that cleans out the barn in minutes. By hand that's a three-hour job. Dairy farms can be big polluters because of fertilizer runoff and manure. In this integrated waste management system, liquid manure and flushing water are stored in clay-lined ponds, then recycled as fertilizer and irrigation water for fields. Treated manure solids are used for bedding. A high-tech dairy like this could pay off for a herd of 150 or more, the size of a family farm with some hired help. It costs more in equipment but saves on time and fertilizer. *From M-89 east of Gull Lake and Richland, turn north on 40th St. The dairy is 2 1/2 miles north, past B Ave. (616) 671-2507. Open daily, 8 a.m.-sunset. &. Free.*

STROLL THE BEAUTIFUL GROUNDS OF W. K. KELLOGG'S LAKESIDE ESTATE. . . . . at the **Kellogg Biological Station** Manor House (616-671-2356). . It's on 3700 East Gull Lake Drive at B Avenue. (East Gull Lake Drive joins M-89 at the lake's southern tip.) In 1926 Battle Creek's cereal king built a simple, tasteful Tudor home, Eagle Heights, at the highest point on Gull Lake. It became the core of a 3,500-acre, year-round Michigan State University center for biological research (birds, ecology, forestry, agriculture), conferences, and extension programs.

The **Manor House** itself is usually closed to the general public. Call (616) 6781-2356 to find out about occasional tours of the interior, now being restored. Visitors are always welcome to take the health-conscious Kellogg's favorite exercise **walk down to Gull Lake**. A picturesque stone and brick stairway zigzags down the steep, wooded hill to a pagoda and boat dock that juts out into the lake. This walk is especially lovely at sunset. For a dramatic, planned vista, look back up at the house from the pergola. Just before the pergola, there's a perennial garden with a rose arbor and sundial bearing the workaholic Kellogg's favorite saying, "The early bird catches the worm." Kellogg loved to take this walk with his friend and frequent guest, science writer Paul de Kruif, author of the classic *Microbe Hunters*. Kellogg ordinarily insisted on a smoke-free environment, but he let de Kruif smoke his omnipresent pipe on these walks.

SEE HOW RIDING THERAPY HELPS DISABLED KIDS . . . . . Riding therapy is a great confidence-builder for kids and some adults with all kinds of handicaps and learning disabilities, including cerebral palsy, Down's syndrome, and blindness. Powerful yet gentle horses can get through even to children with severe emotional problems. The nation's pioneer in riding therapy is just southeast of the Kellogg Bird Sanctuary. The **Cheff Center for the Handicapped** welcomes visitors to observe its classes, see its stables, and picnic in the playground overlooking the pastures. Besides strengthening muscles and improving coordination, riding and caring for horses teaches patience, responsibility, self-control, and grooming — lessons that apply to kids' own lives. By learning to ride, a disabled child "is doing something that the rest of his friends can't," says a staffer. Results can be thrilling.

Cheff prepares teachers from all over the world to teach therapeutic riding. 35 classes a week are held during the school year. Week-long camps are in summer. Regular volunteers and contributions are most welcome. No tax money supports Cheff. *The Center is on 43rd St., just north of M-89, about 8 miles west of Battle Creek and 2 miles east of Gull Lake's south tip. (616) 731-4471. The barn, at the top of the hill, is open year-round, Mon-Thurs 8-5, Fri 8-noon. Drop-ins welcome, or call to arrange a tour or find out times for year-round classes.*

Binder Park Zoo

A lush environment and big naturalistic settings make this small zoo unusually enjoyable to visit.

THIS SPLENDID, lushly planted small zoo has become a popular regional destination. The animals selected to live here have places where they can feel at home. The gibbons live in a lush, spacious area where they can swing through trees. The handsome zebras have a long enough field to develop a full gallop. The cheetahs' two-acre area resembles their native savannas. The Siberian lynx live in a pine forest; visitors enter a Russian-style log cabin and look at the lynx up close through big windows. Memorable, easy-to-read factoids and signs add to the fun of a zoo visit: llamas recognize each other by smelling their breath. High-flying eagles can look down and see fish three miles away.

Boardwalks add to the feeling that most of this zoo is the *animals'* turf, and visitors are confined to limited areas. The 2/3-mile, interpretive **Michigan Wetlands Encounter Trail,** new for 1997, takes you over bogs, marshes, and swamps. It connects visitors with where they are, balancing zoos' built-in emphasis on the exotic, adding to the feeling that this is not an artificial environment.

Many animals here have been chosen because of their worldwide status as threatened or endangered species. Zoos cooperate to keep and breed threatened species through plans that match animals' requirements with zoo facilities and climates. Chinese red pandas, cheetahs, ruffed lemurs, and gibbons are here as part of a cooperative international species survival plan. Other endangered animals at Binder Park are Mexican wolves, trumpeter swans, ring-tailed lemurs, Formosan sika deer, bald eagles, and gaur, the world's largest cows, native to Indian and Malay bamboo forests. The indoor **Conservation Adventure Station** stresses the ecological implications of everyday consumer choices. Exhibits of live animals dramatize points. A rare cotton-top tamarin lives in a mini rain forest. The indoor beehive and huge snake are hits with kids.

Animals can be petted at the popular **Miller Children's Zoo.** Here are llamas and camels, a draft horse, African cattle, dwarf zebu, Vietnamese pot-bellied pigs, rabbits, and guinea pigs. Kids (even teens) enjoy getting into the goat pen and feeding playful goats. An unremarkable 15-minute **train ride** ($1 per person) takes visitors into the woods and back.

The zoo's landscaped walks and sitting areas make it a pleasant

Spacious, naturalistic settings make the Binder Park Zoo a splendid place to view animals from cheetahs and vultures to the increasingly rare rhinoceros shown here. At the children's zoo, all animals can be petted.

place to linger. There's an attractive restaurant with indoor and outdoor seating. A large **gift shop** by the exit is full of stuffed animals, animal posters and cards, and books and games. A big **picnic area** is out by the parking lot. Inquire about the extensive **special programs** like early-morning nature walks, night life, and kids' zoo snoozes. The big, festive holiday ZooLights extravaganza has many animals out and reindeer to see up-close.

HINTS: use the map to make sure you don't miss exhibits in outlying areas. Keep in mind that animals are most active in the morning or late afternoon, and when the weather is cooler. In summer the zoo stays open until 8 p.m. on Wednesdays. Ask for advice on which animals are most likely to be active. Gibbons are always lively. Patience and a leisurely pace are prime requisites for animal-watching.

In 1976, when zoo president Greg Geise, an animal behaviorist, arrived, the 50 acres of the current zoo exhibits were mostly trees and grass. A tremendous amount of planting since then created the exhibits' natural look. It's easier for newer zoos with big sites to follow today's naturalistic philosophy of zoo design. He began with a tiny budget and is proud to be independent of tax support and the political interference that often goes with it in municipal zoos. Geise believes the zoo will ultimately profit from having to market itself, believes the zoo will ultimately profit from having to market itself, get grants, and support itself like a private business that depends on visitors for revenues. Almost half the visitors come from beyond Calhoun and Kalamazoo counties.

The "Double the Zoo" plan will develop 75 more acres. **The Wilds of Africa** (opening in 1998) will have a spectacular 15-acre savannah with giraffes, zebras, ostriches, antelope, and more.

Zoo is 5 miles south of downtown Battle Creek at 7400 Division Dr. at Beadle Lake Rd. From I-94, take Beadle Lake Rd. Exit 100, go south 3 miles on Beadle Lake Rd. (616) 979-1351. Open mid April to mid October. Weekdays 9-5, Sat 9-6, Sun 11-6. From June thru August open to 8 p.m. Wed. &. Adults $4.75, children 3-12 $2.75, seniors 65 and over $3.75. Family or grandparent memberships $40/year.

THE STORY BEHIND MID-MICHIGAN'S BLACK SQUIRRELS . . . . . is well told at the zoo. **Dr. John Harvey Kellogg**, founder of the famous **Battle Creek Sanatarium** and uncle to Battle Creek's cereal industry, introduced a hundred black squirrels from northern Michigan to Battle Creek in 1915. He used them to help force out the tiny, aggressive red squirrels damaging the San's roof. Black squirrels from Battle Creek were introduced in Lansing in 1958. Black is just a different color phase of the well-behaved gray squirrel. Gray squirrels had all but disappeared from lower Michigan by 1900, after their preferred habitat of maple and oak forests was largely cleared for farming.

THE SPIRITUAL ROOTS OF THE BREAKFAST CEREAL INDUSTRY. . . . . are part of the delightful, fascinating **Adventist History Tour** given free Saturday afternoons at 2:30. Seventh-Day Adventism took hold in Battle Creek beginning in 1855 and became the world center of the dynamic denomination until it moved to Berrien Springs in 1905 (p. 370). Adventism indirectly transformed Battle Creek from a sleepy village into an important industrial center. Hint: skip the cemetery part unless you're an Adventist or a cemetery enthusiast. *Meet at back entrance to Adventist Tabernacle, Washington at Van Buren, a mile west of downtown Battle Creek. Call (616) 968-8101 for groups over 6 or special tours. No tours Dec-Feb.*

Marshall to Monroe

IN THE 1820s AND 1830s, many of Michigan's first settlers moved into this corridor, which stretches almost a hundred miles west from Monroe, on Lake Erie. Energetic, ambitious Yankees from upstate New York sought better opportunities in the emerging West. They traveled to Michigan on the recently opened Erie Canal and on Lake Erie steamships.

These York State Yankees followed long-established Indian trails that became Michigan's first roads. They founded towns along those corridors that often developed into prosperous centers of industry. Ypsilanti, Ann Arbor, Jackson, and Marshall (also Kalamazoo, Battle Creek, and Benton Harbor) developed along the early Territorial Road that turned into the I-94 corridor. Early growth was reinforced by the state's most important railroad, the Michigan Central, which crossed the state by 1849. Its original route is essentially the route used by Amtrak between Detroit and Chicago today. Transplanted New York farmers and businessmen of substance were the core of the young Republican party, which developed from meetings in Jackson and in Ripon, Wisconsin, in 1854.

In the much more rural southern tier of counties, the old Chicago roads were today's M-50 from Monroe through the pretty old town of Tecumseh to the Irish Hills, and today's U.S. 12 from Ypsilanti to Coldwater and on to Chicago, then hardly more than a village.

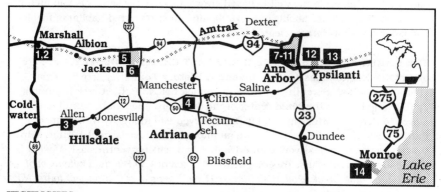

The most visible evidence of the New Yorkers' influence is the clean-lined Greek Revival farmhouses and mansions they built. These can be spotted in many old towns and villages, where there has been less later development pressure to tear them down. Stunning Greek Revival architecture draws many visitors to the town of Marshall, which got off to a fast start but stagnated after its industrial district burned in 1870 — a calamity that preserved its beautiful old homes.

More important are the colleges and universities these well-educated, ambitious Yankees founded: Adrian, Albion, Olivet, the Ypsilanti normal school that became Eastern Michigan University. Most important is the University of Michigan in Ann Arbor. It owes its international research prominence to the influence of its early Yankee leaders, who brought German-style academic research to the innovation-friendly Western frontier. By the 1880s the Ann Arbor frontier institution had become a national leader in higher education.

Information sources: CONVENTION & VISITORS' BUREAUS

Ann Arbor CVB
(313) 995-7281

Lenawee County CVB
Adrian, Blissfield,Tecumseh, Irish Hills
(800) 536-2933 (U.S.),
(800) 682-6580 (U.S. & Canada)

Jackson Con. & Tourist Bureau
(517) 764-4440

Monroe Co. Conv. & Tourism Bureau
(313) 457-1030, (800) 252-3011

Ypsilanti CVB
(313) 4822-4920

Information sources: CHAMBERS OF COMMERCE

Albion (517) 629-5533
Allen (517) 439-4341
Brooklyn/Irish Hills (517) 592-8907
Chelsea (313) 475-1145
Coldwater (517) 278-5985
Hillsdale (517) 439-4341
Jackson (517) 782-8221
Jonesville (517) 439-4341
Manchester (313) 428-7722

Marshall (616) 781-5163;
(800) 877-5168
Monroe (313) 242-3366
Saline (313) 429-4494
Tecumseh (517) 423-3740
Tipton (517) 592-8907
Union City (517) 278-5985
Ypsilanti (313) 482-5920

Marshall

*Michigan's finest historic homes
in a picture-book small town*

PEACEFUL and settled, this town of almost 7,000 retains the pleasant aura of its heyday in the 1850s and 1860s. Its streets are lined with big trees and attractive houses, including Michigan's most outstanding collection of Greek Revival and Gothic Revival homes from the 1840s and 1850s. Its September **homes tour** (page 122) is famous. So is the original **Win Schuler's restaurant**, which capitalized on an Old English theme and a remarkable host to become a favorite destination.

Marshall boomed and grew rich in the mid-19th century, then went to sleep economically until antique-loving mayor Harold Brooks led a pioneering historic preservation crusade, beginning in the 1920s. He succeeded in preserving and publicizing the fabulous stock of historic architecture, and Marshall gained fame as an unusually attractive version of the ideal American small town. The homes tour, started in 1964, is an all-out community effort that continues to promote awareness of restoration, preservation, and interior decorating. Historical plaques pop up everywhere in Marshall, paid for by the enthusiastic historical society that earns plenty of money from the homes tour.

In the 1990s, Marshall has become more of a tourist town in all seasons. Its central location makes the National House Inn and McCarthy's' Bear Creek Inn good rural getaways from Chicago and metro Detroit. Marshall has also grown into an antiques center, with some ten shops and two malls. Downtown has evolved a sweetly romantic Victorian theme so pervasive that browsing in stores is often like seeing a spread of *Victoria* magazine come to life. (In fact, *Victoria* has featured Marshall. So has the *New York Times* travel section, commenting that "Marshall's small-town pride is a genteel descendant of the boosterism that Sinclair Lewis savaged in *Main Street* and *Babbitt*.")

Marshall's quaint image belies both the aggressive real estate speculation launched by the town's founders and its present-day status as a home to large corporations. Marshall is the regional headquarters of State Farm Insurance and the research and development center for Eaton, makers of auto and truck components. It's also a light industrial center. More people work here than live here.

This 1840s Greek Revival mansion, one of Marshall's most imposing, belonged to Mayor Harold Brooks, the man who got Marshall excited about historic preservation in the 1920s. Marshall was settled in the 1830s by industrious Yankees from New York. After an 1872 fire destroyed its industrial district, the town's complex of train repair shops moved to Jackson. The resulting economic slumber preserved Marshall's beautiful houses.

Today Marshall has also become a suburb of choice for commuters to Battle Creek, 15 minutes to the west. And it is the chosen residence of numerous retirees and some 400 traveling salespeople, who can use the two adjacent interstates (I-94 and I-69) to travel to Chicago, Lansing, Detroit, and Indianapolis. All are drawn by Marshall's idyllic small-town image.

Marshall's lovely big homes were built by the town's go-getting early settlers who headed west to Michigan in the 1830s. They were unusually well-educated young people from wealthy New York State families, frustrated by the lack of opportunity in the established and confining East. They went west not to become farmers and till the soil, but to buy up large parcels of land, promote their area, and profit from it.

They liked Marshall's strategic central location, halfway across the state on the Territorial Road, the major artery of Michigan settlement. At Marshall, a creek joined the Kalamazoo River, providing water power for future mills. That site happened to be at the center of Calhoun County, and therefore an ideal spot for the county seat. However, Marshall's splendid old Victorian courthouse was replaced by a boring low box of a building in the 1960s, shortly before tastemakers redeemed the reputation of florid Victorian architecture.

Financial incentives offered by Marshall men succeeded in wooing the Michigan Central Railroad's important machine shops and hotel and restaurant in 1844. These machine shops led to three booming decades that ended after a 1872 fire destroyed the entire factory district. Weakened financially, town leaders couldn't come up with the new subsidy the railroad demanded for improvements. (Subsidies to railroads were a common practice in those days.) In 1874 the railroad shops moved to Jackson, which boomed, while Marshall went to sleep for 50 years.

Thus Marshall was spared the opportunities and stress of an expanding industrial local economy. The town became a kind of haven for a genteel, unhurried lifestyle, a pleasant retreat for old money and for self-employed people like a number of purveyors of patent medicine. Patent medicine enjoyed a boom here from the 1880s to 1906, when the Pure Food and Drug act put a sudden end to it. One lasting legacy of that colorful era is the Brooks Rupture Appliance Company, makers of custom abdominal trusses and the wellspring of the Brooks family fortune. It still occupies its historic quarters on Michigan Avenue next to Carver Park at Marshall Street.

Unthreatened by development pressure, Marshall's blocks of fine old homes remained little affected by competition from new subdivisions (there weren't any until after World War II), or by growing numbers of industrial workers seeking inexpensive housing in rooming houses divided from fine old homes.

Here's a satisfying, do-it-yourself tour of historic Marshall:

◆ **A walking tour map,** authoritative and free, covers a hundred noteworthy homes — dates, styles, and interesting historical tidbits. It, and an interesting cemetery walking tour, are available from the **Chamber of Commerce**, 109 E. Michigan (open weekdays 9-5, Sat 10-4, and Sun 12). Call (800) 877-5163 for the map and a helpful visitor packet. Or get the map at Cronin's or the Marshall House antiques centers.

◆ **The American Museum of Magic.** See page 118.

◆ **The Honolulu House** is a fabulously eccentric 1860 house with a pagoda-shaped observation deck. It's on Fountain Circle on the west edge of downtown. Its builder, State Supreme Court Judge Abner Pratt, fell in love with the Hawaiian Islands when he was U.S. consul there from 1857 to 1859. His wife's poor health forced him to return to Marshall. He built this authentic tropical home with Victorian trim to house their Polynesian treasures and replicate their relaxed lifestyle. His wife soon died, and so did he, reportedly of pneumonia contracted on a cold drive from Lansing during which he wore tropical clothing, as was his wont.

This most peculiar house is lavishly decorated, with beautiful fireplaces. The meticulously restored 1885-1888 murals are a knockout — a late-Victorian reinterpretation of Pratt's original tropical murals. Their lush Renaissance blend of leaf and vine patterns and classical motifs is in rich, subtle greens, reds, purples, and pinks — 120 shades in all.

The interesting furnishings assembled here by the Marshall Historical Society do not reflect the house as it was ever really lived in. The collection's highlight is an elaborate dining-room suite, sent to the 1876 Philadelphia Centennial Exposition to show off each kind of Michigan hardwood and to help publicize the state's burgeoning furniture industry.

The basement rooms are arranged more like a typical house museum, with areas for quilts and needlework, toys, and a kitchen. Don't miss the Marshall Folding Bathtub cleverly disguised as a cabinet. It's a relic of Marshall's patent medicine boom. *Open year-round. Open daily from mid-May to October 31 from noon to 5. Otherwise open weekends only, 1-4. $3 admission. Park behind the house. You may learn more by reading the thorough 25¢ brochure than by asking the amiable volunteer guides.*

◆ **The Prospect Street hill,** two blocks north of Marshall's main street, offered the choicest building sites for Marshall's early elite. An easy hour's walk gives a good look at 29 fine Marshall homes and gardens on the tour map. Take the time to look, and you'll be rewarded. (Look behind the houses, too. This area has some fabulous carriage houses.)

Two blocks north of the Honolulu House on Kalamazoo are two romantic Greek Revival temple-houses facing Prospect. The easterly one belonged to Mayor Harold Brooks for over 50 years, the west one to his brother, Louis, an authority on early chairs in the Middle West. North on Kalamazoo within the next half mile are 15 other noteworthy houses, including some picturesque Gothic Revival ones. Don't miss the square bracketed Italian Villa with the imposing setting at **603 North Kalamazoo.** William Wallace Cook wrote up to a novel a week here between 1903 and 1933.

East on Prospect at Grand, the Gothic Revival houses at **224 Prospect** and **311 North Grand** are straight out of plan books by influential romantic architect Andrew Jackson Downing. Finish your tour by continuing east on Prospect to Division, then going a block toward downtown and turning back on Mansion west toward the Honolulu House. Mansion has the library and other public buildings and a fine Gothic Revival Episcopal church.

◆ **Downtown Marshall** along several blocks of Michigan Avenue has an appealing mix of upscale gift and antique shops, small-town institutions, and elaborate Italianate architecture. (Look up to spot interesting upper-floor details.)

The chamber of commerce has a list of all area **antique dealers**. The biggest stores are open Sunday afternoons, but come on Saturday for the biggest selection. Marshall also has several women's wear stores that offer fairly traditional fashions and good personal service.

Shopping standouts (arranged from east to west) include:

Marshall House Antique Centre. Quality dealers in an historic house. Good mix of furniture (largely 19th century). *100 Exchange at E. Michigan, behind the little park. (616) 781-2112.*

Espresso Yourself. Coffeehouse with good sandwiches, salads, too. *301 E. Michigan at Hamilton, at the light. (616) 789-1136.*

Smithfield Banques. Most charming and personal of all Marshall antique shops, in a pleasantly old-fashioned way. *117 E. Michigan. (616) 781-6969.*

Keystone Architectural & General Antiques. *110 E. Michigan. (616) 789-1355.*

Corner Collections. Big, multifaceted gift store based on tabletop and kitchen things. *103 E. Michigan. (616) 781-3050.*

J. H. Cronin Antique Center. Large antique mall with lots of oak, printed ephemera and prints. Run by Ted and Donna Tear, who put on the monthly Marshall antiques show. He deals in signs and advertising; she has a terrific collection of White Castle mugs, promotional whistles. *101 W. Michigan. (616) 789-0077.*

Kids' Place. A small but interesting children's bookstore that reflects the owner's offbeat sense of humor. Also stocks books on Marshall and related subjects. The late John Bellairs, author of *The House with a Clock in Its Wall* and other popular children's mysteries, grew up in Marshall and effectively appropriated its old spookier spots in his books. Ask for a walking tour map of Bellairs sites. *106 N. Jefferson, half a block north of Michigan. (616) 781-3853.*

Serendipity. Informal but upscale country/Victorian mix of gifts, accessories, coffees and gourmet items, all served up with a decorator's ingenuity approaching Martha Stewart's. *108 W. Michigan. (616) 781-8144.*

Williamson's Gift and Gourmet Shoppe. Opulent Victoriana with the light, airy touch of the 1990s, lavish with laces and flowers, and fine chocolates, too. The place to go for accessories to warm up a grand Italianate mansion. *115 W. Michigan. (616) 781-5641.*

Little Toy Drum. Antiques and gifts, with lots of inexpensive nostalgia cards, books, and paper decorations. *135 W. Michigan. (616) 781-9644.*

Darling V & S Variety. Independently owned dime-store variant, oriented to crafts. Great for trimmings, fabrics, ribbons, buttons, etc. *143 W. Michigan. (616) 781-0122.*

Louie's Bakery. Incredibly inexpensive old-fashioned bakery, especially known for sweet rolls and cookies. A good stop for holiday cookie gifts. Louie's still makes hot cross buns for Lent. *144 W. Michigan. (616) 781-3542.*

The Mole Hole of Marshall. In addition to a general line of gifts, it has antique wood fixtures, a big selection of music boxes, and a seven-rank Barton theater organ. You can ask to have it played and see the pipes operating through a window. *150 W. Michigan. (616) 781-5923.*

National House Inn. One ground-floor room of this historic 1835 inn is an antique shop. The rear herb and perennial garden is worth a look. It's the oldest operating inn in Michigan. *102 S. Parkview at West Michigan on the circle, across Michigan Ave. from the Honolulu House. (616) 781-7374.*

◆ **Postal Museum.** Postmaster Mike Schragg, inspired by his antique dealer grandmother and by Marshall's history mania, has established an impressive museum in several unused basement rooms. His tour begins with a talk about the patronage system used to appoint postmasters as late as the Eisenhower era, then proceeds to survey artifacts like general-store post office cases, books of postwar savings bonds sold to schoolchildren, the first RFD bag ever used in Michigan, and heavy glass mailboxes (so you could see if the mail had come). It's well worthwhile if you have a preexisting interest in the postal service, in bureaucratic systems, or in postage stamps and cancellations.

The post office itself is noteworthy because it's built of Marshall sandstone, in a pure Greek Revival style revived in the 1930s under the influence of Mayor Harold Brooks. The area from here to east of Jackson is the only part of Michigan not on a Great Lakes shoreline where bedrock is at the surface and able to be quarried. Tours can be arranged by appointment or on the spur of the moment if time per-

mits. *Inside the
Marshall Post Office,
202 E. Michigan. (616)
781-2859.*

A judge's stay in Hawaii inspired the Honolulu
House, now a museum, and its tropical murals.

◆ **G.A.R. Hall.** Civil
War memorabilia
and other collections
of Marshall Historical
Society in 1902 hall
of the Grand Army of
the Republic. A
Michigan engineer-
ing regiment created
in Marshall spearheaded Sherman's devastating march through
Georgia. *E. Michigan at Exchange. Open Sun 2-4 in July & Aug.*

◆ **Ketchum Park**, a most pleasant riverside park and playground
on Marshall's humbler south side, is at the millrace of Rice Creek,
just behind the dam — a popular fishing spot. This was the site of
the mill and factory district, whose fiery destruction led to the economic decline of 19th-century Marshall. To get there, take Marshall
Street south from the little park at downtown's east end. **Picnic
tables and grills** are at Ketchum Park, or you could take out a
sandwich from Mancino's on Michigan Avenue.

◆ **Capitol Hill**, the land Marshall set aside for the state capitol, is
on Marshall Street south of the Kalamazoo River. Today it's the
Calhoun County Fairgrounds. The trim little 1839 **"Governor's
Mansion"** at 612 S. Marshall at Washington is now a Daughters of
the American Revolution clubhouse. *Open Sundays in July and
August from 2 to 4.* Also open then is the **Capitol Hill School**, a
well-planned 1860 Gothic Revival schoolhouse, a block east of
Marshall St. on Washington at Maple. Today it contains a nifty period schoolroom and a toy collection with a folk art masterpiece,
Hinkle's Automatic Theater — a traveling marionette show with
mechanical band.

MARSHALL'S BIG EVENT OF THE YEAR . . . . . is the **Marshall Historic
Homes Tour**, held the weekend after Labor Day. A great many of the townspeople pitch in to work on food, musical entertainment, arts and crafts displays,
and tours of half a dozen homes. For particulars on this year's tour, call the
Chamber of Commerce, (800) 877-5163. . . . . . Another smaller, less crowded
homes tour is the **Christmas Walk,** limited to 650 tickets. Call the chamber for
details; sign up by early October. . . . . . Also inquire at the chamber about the

popular July **garden tour**. . . . . . Other big annual events are the **July 4** festivities with free shortcake, a band, and lots of small-town hoopla. The weekend after July 4, the **Fiesta of the Fifties** includes a big regional car cruise, downtown crafts, and more.

EVENING ENTERTAINMENT IN MARSHALL . . . . . Small towns aren't big on nightlife. The Chamber of Commerce (616-781-5163) can fill you in on community events, civic theater productions, etc. . . . . Marshall is unusual in still having an operating movie theater, the **Bogar Theatre**, at 223 E. Michigan. (616) 781-3511. . . . . . **Schuler's Restaurant** offers participatory dinner theater in January, February, and into March, has occasional special dinners, and books performers in the Pub on some weekends. Call (616) 781-0600. Then there's the professional **dinner theater** at **Cornwell's Turkey House** outside of town. Don't expect too much from the dinner beyond the turkey itself. But the theater competently performs light fare, often musical revues. Call (616) 781-4293. . . . . . In Battle Creek, 15 minutes to the west, the intimate, state-of-the-art **Discovery Theatre** downtown next to McCamly Place frequently books a variety of outstanding regional performers in all musical genres. (616) 966-2560. The **Kellogg Arena** books occasional big-name performers; call (616) 965-3308.

AN INDUSTRIAL SMALL-TOWN COUNTERPART TO MARSHALL . . . . is right next door in **Albion** (population 10,000), 11 miles to the east. Its Methodist founders didn't quite have Marshall's money or style, but they did have energy and brains. Their talent went into developing industry and making **Albion College** (birthplace of both "The Old Rugged Cross" and "The Sweetheart of Sigma Chi") into one of Michigan's best private colleges. Albion industries like the Gale Manufacturing Company, makers of a famous steel plow, and the giant Albion Malleable Iron Foundry (now Harvard Industries) attracted workers from Germany, Russia, the Ukraine, Poland, Italy, Hungary, south Texas, Kentucky, and Florida, creating a most ethnically and racially diverse population for a small town.

Albion's prosperity in the late nineteenth century and its location at the **forks of the Kalamazoo River** have resulted in a most **attractive townscape** — well worth a visit. Take Business 94 to Superior, downtown's main street. You can canoe *under* downtown. Also worth a look: the beautifully restored **train station** on West Michigan and the neighborhood along Irwin Avenue. (Irwin intersects with Superior at the south end of town.) But downtown retailing is weak; shopping centers hurt it badly. An interesting **walking tour and map** can be obtained from the Gardner House Museum (see page 124), the Chamber at 418 S. Superior (517-629-5533), or at Local Focus Books & Gifts, 100 S. Superior.

Continue south on Superior and turn left onto River, or turn and you'll reach pretty **Victory Park**, where the river's north and south forks join at a dramatic dam and picturesque series of millraces and waterways. Fishing in the south fork is pretty good. Landscaped by Genevieve Gillette some 50 years ago, Victory Park is quite possibly the prettiest all-around city park in any Michigan town. The best trees are around the bandshell and tennis and basketball court. The most interesting walks are along the complex system of channels and ponds, with some charming bridges and small waterfalls. A Depression-era WPA project created these fishing spots where old water-powered mills once were.

Farther south of Superior, across the river, **Riverside Cemetery** has a most interesting mix of monument styles, from florid Victorian to Russian crosses in the southeast corner. Get an interesting **guide** outside the cemetery office.

A BEAUTIFUL RIVERSIDE REFUGE FOR BIRDS AND WILDLIFE . . . . . is part of Albion College's **Whitehouse Nature Center**. Over half a mile of Kalamazoo River frontage and an unusual variety of ecosystems make the 125-acre center special. In an hour you can visit a tallgrass prairie, marshes, ponds, upland and flood-plain woods, old fields, and an old gravel pit planted to encourage wildlife. The trails, not the interpretive building, make this place special. Best for first-time visitors are the half-mile **Marsh Trail** (a boardwalk path along the river; 20 minutes) and the one-mile **Prairie Trail** (40 minutes) along the river to the prairie. Pick up free trail guides, engagingly written and illustrated, by the building. *Take Erie St. east from downtown Albion. Turn south on Hannah at the train tracks, and immediately look for the signs for Farley Dr. and the nature center. It's through the parking lot and behind the stadium/fieldhouse. (517) 629-2030. Open year-round, dawn to dusk. Interpretive building open weekdays 8 a.m.-5 p.m. Free.*

MICHIGAN'S PREMIERE INSTITUTION SERVING TROUBLED YOUTH . . . . . is outside Albion on the way to Marshall. Visitors are always welcome to tour the beautiful, college-like campus and lake at **Starr Commonwealth**. If it's a weekday, stop in at the impressive main office and conference center nearest the entrance, to learn about Starr and its positive peer culture treatment method. You may be able, even on the spur-of-the-minute, to visit the art collection at the **Brueckner Museum** and see **Gladsome Cottage**, the former home of founder Floyd Starr. The house and its original furnishings give a good look at the earnest, positive, confident world view of **early 20th-century Methodism**. For people who had parents and grandparents from backgrounds like Floyd Starr's, the house is a magical window on a not-too-distant past. Starr believed that beauty instructs. He urged Starr's friends to leave paintings and sculpture to the school. Famous friends memorialized at the Brueckner Museum included Helen Keller and George Washington Carver. *To arrange outstanding student-led tours of Starr, call (517) 629-5591, extension 431. Just south of I-94 exit 119 on 26 Mile/Starr Commonwealth Road, 3 miles west of Albion.*

A TREAT FOR LOVERS OF QUALITY VICTORIANA . . . . . is the **Gardner House Museum** in Albion, with its rich 1880s period rooms of choice furniture, paintings, and objects from local families. Exhibits on Albion's interesting history are featured in upstairs and basement rooms. *509 S. Superior, just south of downtown. (517) 629-5100. Open last weekend April through last weekend October, Sat. & Sun. 1-4 and by appointment.*

American Museum of Magic

*In downtown Marshall,
a passionate fan's tribute
to professional magicians*

THE very best attractions are
often little publicized, the products of dedicated amateurs in
love with their subjects. A premiere
example is the American Museum of
Magic, the creation of the late Robert
Lund, with his wife, Elaine. His life's
mission was to preserve the artifacts
and records of many of the past century's magicians, and to pass along an
appreciation of the wonder they inspired
in others. When Lund was alive, the
museum, housed in an 1868 commercial building with a splendid cast iron
front, kept no regular hours and distributed no brochures. Its fame extends
mainly within the fraternity of magicians. Among them it is world-famous.
Many magicians make annual pilgrimages here when they gather for the
Magic Festival in nearby Colon (see page
128). Magician David Copperfield has
called the museum "one of my favorite
places on earth. No matter how much
time I set aside to enjoy it, it is never
enough." If you want to understand the
soul of magic, he advises, visit this
museum.

Lund, a retired automotive writer,
died in 1995. Elaine Lund has promised
to keep the museum in Marshall, dis-
pelling persistent rumors around town
that David Copperfield will buy it and
move it to Las Vegas. Now Lund's old

friend and fellow magic enthusiast Daniel Waldron gives guided tours on summer weekends. Otherwise, Elaine Lund may be able to accommodate impromptu visitors on the day they call. (She prefers not to be pinned down with advance arrangements.) *Note:* the museum is not intended for children. No tricks are demonstrated. Only patient children or ones with an established interest in magic are likely to enjoy it. Kids under 8 are not welcome.

Even people altogether uninterested in magic may well be won over by the dazzling visuals. Hundreds of posters from the 19th century to recent years cover the walls. There are beautifully decorated magic props, collections of magic sets, toys, packaging that use magic to sell products, and porcelain figures of magicians.

Some highlights of the museum tour, which spans four centuries and six continents, include:

◆ the original prop for the giant milk can stunt that rescued the young Harry Houdini's career. A St. Louis theater owner had threatened to book another act if he didn't draw more customers — soon. Houdini constructed it in a weekend. The audience filled the "milk can" with water, the lid was locked, but Houdini survived — thanks to a specially designed dome top with air holes, so he could tip back his head to breathe.

◆ a century's worth of sets of magic tricks for children.

◆ a bulky 5' x 4' x 4' carrying case, one of scores that famed magician Harry Blackstone traveled with. They filled a 90-foot, double-size baggage car. Each piece, save one, was painted orange for quick identification at train stations. The lone exception was a black tool chest with "Peter Bouton" stenciled on it. It opens to show a neat array of the varied tools of the trade. Bouton was Blackstone's real name. Pete, his brother, was his key offstage man, a gifted carpenter, chemist, painter, even a seamstress. Lund reckoned the Blackstones, senior and junior, as the best all-round magicians he'd seen. He knew Harry, Sr. well. Harry Blackstone, Jr. visits the museum. Many of the Blackstones' papers are in Lund's archives.

Tourgoers are advised to leave some time to stay after the formal tour. Elaine Lund likes to show visitors the basement archive and processing area, where perhaps half a million files and 40,000 photograph negatives are stored. "In my opinion, it's the heart of what my husband's work was about," she says. "He collected faster than

The late Robert Lund and Houdini's milk can, the escape stunt which made Houdini famous. The magic museum Lund created is so filled with significant material about magic that famous magicians make regular pilgrimages to Marshall. His widow, Elaine, is carrying on his archival work.

the building could grow. Magic is mostly moving things. . . [she surveys scores of file cabinets and crates] . . . and I'm still doing it."

In the end, what makes this place special is the spirit behind it.

Teller, the silent half of the Penn and Teller magic team, is a big fan of Robert and Elaine Lund. He has written about them in the *New York Times* magazine and the *Atlantic Monthly*. Today, he wrote, it seems that "everybody is somebody's minion. So few people today have anything they love that's really theirs. Bob and Elaine have this incredible independence, work like crazy, and have this great sense of humor. They have this incredible museum — and their chief fascination is with magicians that you've never heard of."

In downtown Marshall at 107 E. Michigan between Madison and Jefferson, kitty-corner from the post office. Call (616) 781-7674 for current hours or to see if you can tour the museum the day you call. $4/person. $2 for kids from 8 to 12. Not for kids under 8. Children must be accompanied by an adult. &: *call.*

"THE MAGIC CAPITOL OF THE WORLD" . . . . . is **Colon**, Michigan, population 1,700, 40 miles southwest of Marshall. Its claim to fame goes back to when famed magician Harry Blackstone made Colon his summer home. It became a magnet for other magicians. Colon is today the home of **Abbott's Magic Manufacturing Company**, the world's largest producer of magic paraphernalia, the site of Abbott's famous annual **Magic Get-Together**, four days usually around the first weekend in August. For more on Colon and Abbott's summertime **Saturday magic shows** (1 p.m. from Mem. through Labor Day), call (616) 432-3235.

BICYCLING AROUND MARSHALL, ALBION, AND HOMER . . . . . can be fun. Bikes are the ideal way to view Marshall's historic architecture. Back roads into Calhoun County's smaller towns don't generate a lot of traffic, and it's easy to get in and out of Marshall itself. . . . . . **Athens** (population 1,000) is an interesting destination via a series of back roads. . . . . Biking 11 miles to the college town of **Albion** along the **Kalamazoo River valley** is an easy drive, and Albion offers numerous low-key destinations. The best route: Take B Drive North on the south side of Marshall (just north of the river) all the way east to Austin Avenue and into Albion. . . . . The 15 miles from Marshall to **Homer** on Homer Road via the hamlet of **Eckford** are pretty but more demanding for out-of-shape cyclists, and the route jigs and jogs considerably. A good map is recommended. **Bernie's** on Homer's quaint main street has terrific hamburgers and olive burgers. The nearby antique shop, run by a military retiree, is unusually interesting. . . . . . A fine nine-mile route from Homer to Albion takes 25 1/2 Mile Road north out of town. Turn right (east) immediately onto L Drive South, then take the first left onto 25 Mile Road to see an exceptional **octagon house**. At J Drive South jog left (west) back to the pavement on 25 1/2 Mile, which takes you into Albion along Irwin Ave.

Three Gems in Allen

Among all the antiques, a wonderfully funky shop,
a sweet little herb farm, and a whimsical landscape
of orphaned buildings.

FOR ANTIQUERS and people who just like to explore southern Michigan's wealth of pretty small towns and villages, a trip to Allen is increasingly interesting, thanks to three unusual establishments. Allen consists of a four-corners and a strip of 19th-century stores and houses along U.S. 12, the old Chicago Road. Founded in 1827, Allen had 500 people in 1880, but has dwindled to 200 today. Since the 1960s the village, 12 miles east of Coldwater, has been Michigan's self-styled "antique capital," with some 14 independent shops and malls, and over 400 dealers in antiques and country crafts. Now two big malls at either end of Allen's advertised "mile of antiques" add to the wide selection of low- to mid-range antiques.

When you get to Allen, look for the bold black-and-white **brochure and map** to plan your visit. Malls and larger shops are open daily from 10 or 11 to 5 throughout the year. Some shops are open weekends only. **Summer festivals** have open-air antiques, flea market stalls, and barbecues put on by the volunteer firefighters. They are held on Memorial Day, Independence Day, and Labor Day. Winter weekdays are hit-or-miss at many Allen shops. Most of the old buildings are not wheelchair-accessible, though the new malls are.

Here are the three Allen highlights:

OLD ALLEN TOWNSHIP HALL SHOPS

The courtyard and entrance hall signals that the Township Hall is as far from conventional country cute as you can get. There are cases of colorful African trade beads; a baby's denim jacket appliqued with skinhead symbols cornices from old Chicago buildings; and a long, primitively painted commercial sign from the Ivory Coast depicting contemporary geometric haircuts on black male heads.

Farther back on the landing are cowboy kitsch, used saddles, old spurs from Mexico; many kinds of Russian nesting dolls; and a dazzling display of many decades' worth of souvenirs from world travels. One area is given over to religious artifacts, from American plaster statues to Eastern Orthodox icons to Mexican crosses of curled iron and small shrines made of cut-up Ray-O-Vac cases. Some of this is new, some old. All has been chosen and arranged to delight and amuse, with a

Collector extraordinaire: Janine Fentiman has a great eye for creating wonderfully arresting displays. Religious art is a specialty at the Old Allen Township Hall. So is art by and about Indians, as seen in the First People American Indian and Eskimo Museum she and her husband created.

good eye and a sharp wit.

"Furniture. Primitives. Folk art. Artifacts. Rare, collectable and children's books. Religious. Vintage Clothes. Estate Jewelry. Trade Beads.. American Indian. Oriental. African. Ethnic. Cowboy. Knives. Michigan historical. Heisey glass. Military art." That's how the owners advertise what's here. A **Heisey glass show** is held Memorial weekend, an **Indian relic show** in late September.

Janine Fentiman met her husband and business partner, John Alward, at Northwestern, where she majored in design. Sharing with her a love of travel and collecting, he wholesaled paint and insured banks, and she planned store layouts before opening this business. He had grown up up in Camden (south of Hillsdale almost in Ohio), the banker's son. In 1972 they decided to make Allen the home base for a worldwide business built on his interests (knives and trade goods of the muzzleloader-era, plus Native American and cowboy artifacts) and hers in ethnic crafts and religious art. A self-described "visual Catholic," she loves the pre-Vatican II religious art she knew as a child in Chicago and is amazed at how well religious art sells here. They travel three months a year on their collecting adventures.

Visitors can see their **First People American Indian and Eskimo Museum** upstairs by chance or appointment. It's their private collection, arranged with an artistic eye and clever wit: quillwork, papoose

boards, lots of beadwork, garments, weapons, tools, Mexican things —
a dazzling visual treat, punctuated with images of Indians on postcards,
snake oil bottles, tobacco labels, and other printed ephemera that comment (without any exhibit labels at all) about the ways American popular culture has indulged in what Fentiman calls "Indian romanticism."
*Call first: (517) 869-2575. 114 W. Chicago. (517) 869-2575. Open daily,
year-round, 10-5. ໒: call. Museum is only open when the owners are
here. $1.50/adults, 75¢ children. Youth and other group tours welcome
in advance only. ໒: no.*

LITTLE FARM HERB SHOP

A rooted, inner-looking cosmos has been created in the enclosed
rear yard behind a tiny shop that began life as a chicken coop. Here
cottage flowers (hollyhocks, dianthus, campanulas) grow against a
board fence and line paths. **Classes** and **demonstrations** are held in
the charming rear carriage house recently moved to the site. The tiny
front shop is limited to things strictly botanical, often with a simple,
folk art look: topiary herb "trees," handcrafted dried wreaths, metal
sculpture, potpourri (but not the heavily scented, artificial kind), stationery, garden decor, and crafts like leaf-painted whitewashed garden
benches by decorative painter Deborah Nance of nearby Tekonsha. Also
on hand: teas (area's largest selection), jewelry, and aromatherapy items.

Owner Susan Betz had already long been infected by the herb bug
when, ten years ago, she found this garbage-filled, hundred-year-old
chicken coop. Her enthusiasm for sharing information and involving
customers is what makes this place special. A lot of garden problems
and dreams are discussed here, she says. Customers trade ideas and
experiences. Many customers are men; one spouse gets interested and
brings the other. Children are also encouraged, and things like cement
garden statuary can be had for $3 and less. The **newsletter** always has
some interesting tips — like adding a few tangy leaves of bergamot (bee
balm or monarda) to tea and how to make concrete look old and quaint
by growing moss on it. A popular chil-
dren's day each mid-July inspired
kids to garden with crafts and storytelling about the plant kingdom.

Regular customers buy out Betz's
herb plants by the end of May, but the
rear display gardens are a delight up
to fall. Current stars are a growing
variety of thymes (wooly and plain,
creeping and upright,), sages of many
patterns, and many-colored salvias.

146 W. Chicago, half a block west of the main intersection with M-49. (517) 869-2822. Open mid-March to Dec. 24, Mon-Sat 10-5 or by appt. ♿: thru back gate to garden, shop.

Green Top Country Village

This remarkable place thankfully makes no pretense at being a real country village. It's a fanciful collection of some 30 old buildings filled with antiques and used furniture for sale. The buildings include country stores and schools, granaries and barns, a root beer stand and a work-crew trolley car. The effect looks as if pieces of Midwestern towns were sucked up in a tornado, transported to Oz, and rearranged and painted by Munchkins in combinations of soft earthtones and dulled pastels. Maturing lilacs, daylilies, and evergreens serve to root the transplanted village to Earth again. Low stone walls, inspired by the Depression-era roadside attractions along U.S. 12, organize the place into gardens. Woodchip paths wind through a grove of shady young maples to courtyard groupings of the quaint buildings.

This is a much more diverting way to look at a lot of antiques than the usual warehouse-like malls. When looking at stuff gets to be too much, you can stroll through the grounds. They are accented with benches and various ornaments, including an elaborate Italianate outhouse. Pick up a **flyer** on the buildings' origins at the front sales desk in the main building.

The original Green Top Lodge and Cabins (the name comes from their green roofs) are the core of this inspired confection. The one-time roadhouse opened in 1926, the year the Chicago Road was paved. Motor touring was then fast becoming a popular middle-class pastime. Green Top, one of the favorite stops between Detroit and Chicago, hosted salesmen, truckers, and

Tourist cabins and a roadhouse in front of them formed the original Green Top. To them have been added some two dozen orphaned buildings and various rockery like this bird bath, inspired by the rock roadside attractions from the 1930s along this part of U.S. 12. This unusual antiques mall has become a celebrated local attraction.

tourists. The cabins were among the first around to have their own toilets. Jim Klein, a native of nearby Adrian, bought the old place to use as an antique shop in 1982, when the village of Allen was far less lively than it is today. Soon after that, his friend Norma Kaetzel despaired of being able to fix up a dilapidated historic building on her property, a plain little Greek Revival schoolhouse from 1840. Her dilemma inspired Klein to expand Green Top by moving such endangered buildings onto the five-acre site. Since then Green Top has become "a home of last resort for orphaned buildings," says Klein.

Today Green Top as a business is in transition — to what it's not quite clear. It's no longer a mall. All the inventory is the Kleins'. They have a good eye for oddball pieces, primitives, and creations that fall loosely under the "folk art" umbrella, but not everything here is particularly choice. It does tend to be priced to move. Beth has returned to graduate school in her old career of nursing. Jim continues to lavish attention and new plantings on the buildings and grounds, which look more charming each year.

Green Top is on U.S. 12, 12 miles east of I-69 at Coldwater and half a mile west of Allen. (517) 869-2100. Open daily including most holidays, year-round 10:30-5.

🌲🎄🌲

MORE ANTIQUING IN ALLEN. . . . . The very first antique shops, here and elsewhere along the Chicago Road, date from the road's paving in 1925. That spawned tourists courts, gas stations, and curio shops. Many Allen shops from the 1960s, especially the older ones like **Michiana Antiques** and, in the onetime general store and post office, **Andy's Antiques**, have room after room of stuff piled high. For people who like to paw through stuff, they offer the alluring hope of hidden treasures.

At **Hand & Heart Antiques**, woodcarver Brent Barribeau sells decoys he makes along with a general antique line. He started carving because he couldn't afford the old decoys he liked so much. **Simple Treasures Antiques** also has classes and supplies for porcelain dolls. **Chesney's Antiques** in the Olde Chicago Pike Mall sells refinished furniture and cane chairs.

THE AMISH CONNECTION IN ALLEN. . . . . In Michigan's southern tier of counties, many villages are hardly bigger today than they were in their prime in the 1870s. Some, like Allen, almost became ghost towns. Derelict buildings are in good supply in these parts. The land is variously too gravelly, hilly, or wet to pay off for large-scale, mechanized agriculture, but it is well suited to Amish farming methods: small-scale, general, self-sufficient farming. Several Amish communities have moved into the area as the population increases in nearby northern Indiana, one of two Amish heartlands in the Middle West. . . . . . Amish men are excellent **house-movers** and **barn-restorers**. To move the 1,100-square-foot Methodist church to Green Top, teams of Amish workmen carefully pried the walls apart and dug the new foundation by hand. They put the building back together at Green Top after a truck hauled the pieces here. . . . . . Anyone looking to restore an old barn or recycle an old building by moving it should network and get to know their Amish neighbors, Janine Fentiman advises. They're getting to be everywhere in rural Michigan, she says.

A SPRINGTIME DELIGHT . . . . . is the **Slayton Arboretum** at nearby Hillsdale College. Even in winter, this arboretum is exceedingly picturesque. It's the epitome of that informal rock-garden romanticism so popular in the 1920s. In **May** and **June** the arboretum is spectacular with displays of flowering crabs and peonies. In 1929 clumps of white birch and Norway and white spruce were planted in this former gravel pit. Now they loom tall above fieldstone walls and **gazebos**, rustic **footbridges** and goldfish **ponds**. Lagoons and nearby lakes attract many birds. Paths wind up a steep slope from the gazebo and outdoor amphitheater. An overlook terrace permits views of a landscape studded with specimen plantings and quaint little structures like an English cottage-style horticultural laboratory. A new college biology professor has been hired to direct arboretum restoration. For brochure, call the Dow Conference Center (517-437-3311). *On Barber at Union, east of the college. From U.S. 12 at Jonesville, take M-99 almost into downtown Hillsdale, but turn east at Fayette. In about 1/2 mile turn north onto Union. Open dawn to dusk daily. Admission is free.*

A RICH BANKER'S PALATIAL HOME . . . . . has been splendidly restored as the **Grosvenor House Museum** in Jonesville, 5 miles east of Allen on U.S. 12. Elijah Myers, the architect of Michigan's influential state capitol building is said to have designed the house, built in 1874, for Jonesville banker E.O. Grosvenor. It is full of elaborate details and the then-latest tricks in modern engineering and planning. It has that rich layering of exotic objets d'art, patterned motifs, and wood surfaces that gives high Victorian style its eclectic, opulent effect. An upstairs **museum room** presents ordinary Jonesville history well, featuring local products from Jonesville's old cigar factory and dairy to recent plastic dollhouse play sets from Kiddie Brush and Toy — "toys that mold character," says the ad, like Susy's Superette and the Friendly Folks Motel. *From U.S. 12 at the park in downtown Jonesville, take Maumee south 3 blocks to 211 Maumee. (517 849-9596. Open the first full weekend in June through Sept, Sat. & Sun 2-5. A Christmas Open House is the 1st 2 weekends in December.*

Hidden Lake Gardens

*A lovely spot in the Irish Hills pairs
picturesque landscape gardens with woodland trails.*

THIS 755-acre arboretum is a very special place year-round. It was first planted by Harry Fee of Adrian. He used the striking terrain to create memorable scenes with plants. He assembled a property taking advantage of the unusually varied glacial landscape in this band of hills and lakes known as the Irish Hills. In this area huge ice chunks from the last Ice Age left a crazy-quilt landscape of round kettle-hole lakes, steep-sided valleys, and dramatic vistas interspersed with sweeping meadows and marshes.

Fee's plantings, begun in 1926, provide a mature backdrop for the later collections and gardens planted by Michigan State University since 1945. Fee donated his gardens to M.S.U. because of its outstanding landscape and horticulture programs, and left a substantial endowment to provide for their future maintenance. The Herrick family of Tecumseh (Ray Herrick founded Tecumseh Products, a Fortune 500 firm that makes mower engines and refrigerator compressors) donated a handsome and impressive visitor center and separate conservatory. They are used as a **center for landscape education**.

The front part of Hidden Lake Gardens has been landscaped for

One of Hidden Lake Gardens' unusual horticultural attractions is the Harper Collection of Rare and Dwarf Conifers. Fine fall color and in indoor conservatory make for a good year-round destination.

maximum picturesqueness. The back oak uplands, laced with **five miles of hiking trails**, remain in their natural state. (Get a **trail guide** at the visitor center.) Six miles of beautiful **one-way drives** wind through the front part so close to branches of flowering magnolias, crabs, and cherries that even from the car you notice individual flowers. A bike drive through this part lets you stop and smell the flowers. Bikes are prohibited on Sundays, however. You can also park your car on one of many pullovers, and get out and walk.

It all makes for an especially nice blend of the cultivated and wild. You can go for a vigorous hike (a good mix of hardwoods makes **fall colors** gorgeous), then learn about Michigan forest communities in the visitor center, or take in the damp, fragrant atmosphere of the tropical house, or see rare dwarf conifers in a special garden. The gardens are especially beautiful after a fresh snowfall. (Skiing is not allowed.) Everywhere you can glean ideas for your own yard from the many identified plantings. Lists of nursery sources for plants are provided whenever possible.

Here are some highlights not to miss:

◆ The **front road system** artfully invites you into a special world and manipulates the views to give a fresh, intimate perspective on the trees and shrubs you see. Lilacs, flowering crabs, and cherries are wonderful in May. At the far west end is a choice collection of evergreens.

◆ There's **Hidden Lake** itself, beneath overarching willows next to the visitor center. A pair of swans, often with baby cygnets, will come up to the pullover area and eagerly eat bread visitors bring. (No moldy bread, please! It makes them sick.)

◆ **Hosta Hillside** by the lake has been planted and maintained by the Hosta Society of Michigan. Inquire about the society's big May hosta sale, with unusual plants from members' collections.

◆ Naturalized **primroses and daffodils** bloom in the last two weeks of April. The primroses are at the lake's north end; daffodils are all over.

◆ **Exhibits in the visitor center** cover topics like the development of plant aristocrats through hybridization, the life and death of a glacial lake, forest communities in southern Michigan, conifer classifications, and Michigan geology. They're dense yet satisfying to the inquiring lay mind. Take one or two topics on a visit, and you could learn a lot of botany and horticulture basics fast.

◆ The large **conservatory** is unusually enjoyable, especially in winter. Some very large, luxuriant specimens in the **tropical house** make you feel like you're in a rain forest; it's fun to see grapefruit, figs, guava, and tangerines growing on trees. There's also an **arid house** and a **temperate house**, where you can see **orchids, ferns, fuchsia,** and some remarkable **bonsai**, artistically pruned trees up to 25 years old but only a foot high. Well-written signs about plants' culture and uses in food and ornament are good reading. Among the featured indoor plants are bamboo, banana, cactus, camphor, cocoa, coffee, fig, palm, sugarcane, tapioca, and vanilla. After a thoughtful visit to the **temperate house**, you will see familiar house plants in a new way.

◆ **The Harper Collection of Rare and Dwarf Conifers** are behind the conservatory. Some conifers are bluish or gold, some weep or lie flat on the ground. Many come from genetic mutations or witch's brooms: small, thick growths on the limbs of a tree that grow true to form when propagated by cuttings.

A **picnic area** with restrooms has been provided behind the Harper Conifer collection. The excellent visitor center **gift shop** has many books and pamphlets on nature and gardening, plus nature-related notecards, CD's and cassettes of nature sounds such as waterfalls and loons, T-shirts and sweatshirts, rock samples, and bird feeders and houses. Classes and workshops on gardening, birds, and more are held on Tuesday evenings, Saturdays, and in summer on every other Wednesday afternoons. Fees: $4-$29. Family rates available. Call for info. The big **spring plant sale** on a mid-May weekend features lectures on hostas and conifers and choice plants from the collections of American Hosta Society's and American Conifer Society's members.

The Gardens are on M-50 8 miles west of Tecumseh and 7 miles east of Cambridge Junction, the historic crossroads where M-50 joins U.S. 12. From Adrian or Chelsea, take M-52 to M-50, turn west. (517) 431-2060. **Grounds and conservatory** *open 365 days/ year, April thru Oct. 8 a.m.-dusk, Nov. thru March 8 a.m.-4 p.m.* **Visitor center** *open 8-4 weekdays, 10-6 weekends/holidays; in winter 8-4 week-days, 10-4 weekends/holidays. $1/person weekdays, $3/person weekends/holidays, in winter $1 at all times, children under 2 free.* ⅋ *Call ahead to reserve wheelchairs for visitor use.*

🌲🎍🌲

BEEKEEPING SUPPLIES, HONEY, AND CANDLE MOLDS . . . . . along with a **working beehive** (cut away so you can see inside) and all sorts of gifts and books pertaining to bees, are sold a few miles west of Hidden Lake Gardens at

Hubbard Apiaries. $120 buys you everything needed to get started in beekeeping, including a bee suit. Pick up a free catalog. In the spring, there's a greenhouse and in the fall, apples and cider. *On M-50 at Springville Rd., east of U.S. 12. (517) 467-2051. In the summer, open Mon-Sat 9-5, Sun 12-4 Rest the the year open weekdays only, 7-4:30.*

SIGHTSEEING ALONG U.S. 12, THE OLD CHICAGO TURNPIKE . . . . .
through the Irish Hills, can be fun. Along the road is a weird blend of pioneer Michigan history and 20th-century tourism: 1920s gas stations and lookout towers, the Prehistoric Forest, Mystery Hill, water slides, bumper boats, go-cart raceways, and Roger Penske's Michigan International Speedway (517-592-6666), which packs the area four weekends a summer. A few remaining farmhouses and taverns date to the old Indian trail's first round of improvements in the 1830s. Neglect, unsightly sand and gravel pits, and careless development have increasingly taken their toll on this once -interesting route.

Still, it can be interesting if you know where to stop. Here's a short list for a pleasant drive along the 18 miles of U.S. 12 between the interesting village of Clinton on the east and U.S. 127 on the west. List reads from east to west. For other sights on and near U.S. 12, see Allen (pp. 129-134). *Most sights are open daily in summer only. Call (517) 592-8907 weekdays for more Irish Hills info..*

◆ **Irish Hills Fun Center** (Bear's Lair) has go-carts, bumper boats, and a water slide. (517) 431-2217.

◆ **Port to Port Adventure**. Here you can play 18 holes of bank-shot basketball (the only one in Michigan) or mini-golf. Batting cages. *(517) 431-2262.*

◆ **Eisenhower's Presidential railroad car**. Original interiors, memorabilia. Furnished as if Ike were still on the campaign trail. Well worth the modest entrance fee. *(517) 467-2300.*

◆ **Stagecoach Stop**, a make-believe 19th-century village theme park just west of Ike's railroad car, is more of an all-day attraction. It blends soap opera, nostalgia, arcade games, wild game park, and crafts demonstrations. Not for the kitsch-aversive. More for kids today; not nearly as widely appealing to adults since the wonderful antique coin-operated musical devices have been removed. *7203 U.S. 12, near Onsted. (517) 467-2300.*

◆ **Mystery Hill**, where water flows up and trees grow sideways, has a 20-minute tour filled with demonstrations of the "amazing force of gravity." *(517) 467-2517.* &: no. Adults $3.50, kids 4-17 & seniors $2.75.

◆ **Prehistoric Forest**. Water slide & train ride in dinosaur park. *(517) 467-2514.*

◆ **Irish Hills Towers**. Corny, fun lookout is best in fall. Big **adventure golf** course next to it. *(517) 467-2606.*

◆ **St. Joseph's Shrine.** An inspired folk art environment. The Stations of the Cross behind the parking lot leading down the hill to the lake were made of colored tile and cement during the Depression. The way traces Christ's walk to the crucifixion on Cavalry. The historic marker explains, "The footpath begins at a replica of Pontius Pilate's palace, then winds past balconied houses, through the judgment gate and ends at Christ's tomb." The rustic archways and railings were made to resemble logs by two Mexican artisans who did other work in the area. *8743 U.S. 12 in Cambridge Township, Lenawee County, south of Brooklyn.*

♦ **Walker Tavern Historic Complex.** Fine small state historical museum and restored 1832 tavern tell the story of the Chicago Road, a chief route of settlement during Michigan's pioneer boom years of the 1830s. Travelers piled into a few sleeping rooms, shared beds, spent much time in the barroom. Daniel Webster and James Fenimore Cooper stayed here on expeditions to what was then the American west. Pleasant picnic area in large park. *At U.S. 12 and M-50. Enter off M-50 north of U.S. 12. (517) 467-4414. Open summers only due to lack of funds. Call for hours.*

♦ **Michigan International Speedway.** Usually about 4 races a year. *(517) 592-6666. Reserved seats $45-$70. Wheelchair seating $20.*

♦ **Mary's House of Rosaries.** Lots of different kinds of rosaries, and statues of famous and obscure saints. Good religious pictures, too. Well worth a stop for fans of popular religious art. *On U.S. 12 about 3 or 4 miles east of U.S. 127, south side of road. In a house; open daylight hours.*

♦ **Woodlawn Zoo & Wildlife Pets** is a walk-through zoo with black bear, fox, skunk, buffalo, deer, wolf, coyote and other mostly North American animals. In the spring they have baby animals for kids to pet. *(517) 547-7640. Open 10-7 daily in the summer. & Adults $5, kids 10 and under $2.*

♦ **McCourtie Park.** More rustic structures done in cement on the former estate of the cement king of nearby Cement City. Bridges and some remarkable cement birdhouses are along a pretty creek. Poor maintenance is threatening these unusual structures. **Flavor Fruit Farms** (517-688-3455) is an orchard and farm market in a handsome old farm a short ways north on S. Jackson Rd. *McCourtie Park is on U.S. 12 in Somerset Center, in the far northwest corner of Hillsdale County.* **To enter:** *turn north onto South Jackson Road.*

WELL OVER TWO DOZEN ANTIQUE SHOPS . . . . . are in or near the Irish Hills. Among the best are the **Manchester Antique Mall** (313-428-9357) in delightful downtown Manchester, the **Hitching Post Antiques Mall** (517-423-8277) on M-50 near M-52, two miles west of Tecumseh, and the **Brick Walker Tavern** (517-467-4385) on U.S. 12 at M-50 (closed Mon & Tues). Clusters of antiques shops and/or malls are in downtown Clinton, Tecumseh, and Allen, and lately there are more antiques in Jonesville, too. Look up Pluck's in Jonesville, in a big Italianate house a block north of U.S. 12 on M-99. *Ask for a helpful shop guide and map to other area dealers.*

Jackson Cascades

*This huge man-made waterfall in a baroque
pleasure park is a nostalgic sight from the 1930s.*

THERE'S NOTHING subtle about Jackson's best-known sight.
It's an illuminated 500-foot artificial waterfall cascading
down a hill at 3,000 gallons a minute, in three pools and 16
falls. After dark, shifting patterns of colored lights turn the
Cascades into a baroque fantasy in vivid Technicolor.

Every evening from Memorial Day to Labor Day the Cascades offer low-key summer entertainment for $3 a head. The falls, foun-
tains, and music are turned on from 7:30 p.m. to 11 p.m. You can
climb the 129 steps that flank the 30-foot-wide falls and watch the
setting sun produce repeating rainbows in the spray. (Kids love
this!) A hand stamp lets you leave and reenter, so you can picnic,
fish, feed ducks, play, and enjoy the numerous facilities and scenic
hills and waterways of the surrounding **Cascades Park** (see below).

The Cascades are so grand and monumental, you'd expect them
to have been built only in a very large metropolitan area, not in a
small but enterprising city of 55,000. That was Jackson's population at its peak in 1930, two years before the Cascades were finished. (Today the population of Jackson proper has declined to
37,500.) In Jackson's glory years of the 1920s, it prospered and
made many local fortunes in auto parts. "Little Detroit" was
Jackson's nickname. Jacobson's department store, still headquartered here, got its start catering to Jackson's many "poor millionaires" — people with just a million, not a lot more.

One especially forceful and enthusiastic local magnate was
Captain William Sparks. He had immigrated from England with his
family, had grown up in Jackson, and had became rich as a parts
supplier. By 1920, the Sparks Withington Company, originally
formed to make buggy parts, employed over 7,000 people. They
made Sparton radios, electric auto horns (which Sparks pioneered),
and other automotive accessories.

Sparks's lifetime goal was to put Jackson on the map. A three-
term mayor, he was once simultaneously the city manager and
Chamber of Commerce president. His Sparks-Withington Zouaves
(pronounced zoo-AHVS) were a kind of quick-stepping precision drill
team, patterned after a colorful Algerian infantry unit. Many
American towns had their own Zouaves units. "Cap" Sparks (the

At the Cascades, baroque grandeur was brought to Jackson by Cap
Sparks, radio manufacturer and local booster par excellence.

title was honorary; he never served in the military) and his Zouaves
toured the world, bringing fame to their home town. While in
Barcelona, Sparks was so taken by a grand, cascading waterfall
that he later determined to build a version of it on the marshland
behind his magnificent Tudor home. Soon what began as a plan for
a skating pond at the foot of the Cascades blossomed into 465 acres
of lagoons, picnic areas, and an 18-hole golf course and clubhouse.

The **Cascades-Sparks Museum**, just inside the entryway to the
amphitheater, is a quirky, often amusing collection of old Sparton
Electronics radios, colorful Zouaves costumes, and memorabilia,
including photos of the Jackson Zouaves performing in *The Court
Jester* with Danny Kaye, and scenes from the very successful concert Harry Chapin performed here shortly before his death.

The Cascades did succeed in putting Jackson on the national
showbiz map during the 1930s and 1940s, as attested by press
clippings from major U.S. cities about the seven-stage extravagan-
zas staged there. Today Sparks's mansion on West Street has been
replaced by apartments after two feuding women's clubs torpedoed
plans to reuse it. But its impressive Tudor garage and guest house
can still be seen on Kibby Road, across from the matching Tudor
Cascades Manor House (517-784-1500) at the entrance to the
Sparks Foundation Park (or the Cascades County Park, as it is
more commonly known). The main dining room, a contemporary
addition, looks out onto the pond and park. The renovated historic
clubhouse, which Sparks intended for a community gathering
place, is open for weekday **lunch** (Tues-Fri, 11 a.m.-2:30 p.m.) and
Sunday buffet (11:30 a.m.-2:30 p.m.).

Air-conditioned movies and TV took their toll on Cascades
attendance. The concrete crumbled, and Sparks' magnificent gift to

the city threatened to become an obsolete white elephant. But local construction workers restored the Cascades and built the amphitheater and museum building. The new sound system is excellent. A second round of renovations, half a million dollars' worth, was finished in 1993. It includes a new water recirculation system that's both filtered and chlorinated for cleanliness.

Today the Cascades are an entertainment anachronism. Some Jacksonians consider them irredeemably tacky, unsophisticated, and dumb. To others, the Cascades' direct, childlike charm evokes a wonderful, nostalgic period. Gigantic **fireworks shows** with live entertainment are held at the Cascades on the Saturdays of Memorial Day and Labor Day weekends and on the eve of the Fourth of July. For the best seats arrive by 7 p.m. and for a seat, no later than 8 p.m.. The fireworks draw crowds from 25,000 to 30,000. The last weekend of August brings the largest **Civil War Muster** in the Midwest, with major battle re-enactments, camp life, battalion parades, a dress ball, and music festival. It's free; call (517) 788-4320 for a brochure.

S. Brown at Denton Rd. in the Cascades County Park, Jackson. From I-94, take West Ave. exit 138 at Jackson Crossing mall and follow the signs south. (517) 788-4320. At night call (517) 788-4227. Memorial Day through Labor Day, 7:30 p.m.-11 p.m. daily. &. $3 per person, ages 5 and under free.

BY THE CASCADES, A BIG PARK WITH ACTIVITIES AND GREAT GOLF . . . . Inspired by his dream of creating a magnificent landscaped waterfall on his estate, industrialist William Sparks went on to create **Cascades Park**, where meadows and wetlands meet rolling hills. Adjoining the Cascades are a fanciful **playground** with cast concrete animals and a newer plastic playground with slides, etc. similar to those at McDonald's , and an 18-hole miniature golf course with softball and hardball batting cages and a pitching radar gun ($2 a game, open daily in summer 11-11; open fewer days and shorter hours in the spring and fall; 517-782-8006). On special occasions, they have a moonwalker. Across Denton, behind the Tudor-style Cascades clubhouse is a **duck pond**, and two miles of **lagoons** for fishing with a **wheelchair-accessible fishing pier**. Here paddleboats can be rented for $4/half-hour.

Golf is an obsession in Jackson. The high quality of its public and municipal courses makes it available to virtually everybody. Two courses are in Cascades Park. **Hill Brothers Golf Course**, a 9 hole, "executive course" and driving range; $4 for 9 holes, $2 for juniors and seniors, twilight rate $2. (517) 782-2855. No reservations. The **Cascades Golf Course** is an 18-hole course, and quite challenging. Its front 9 are longer and easier, the back 9 shorter and more difficult. Call (517) 788-4323 for reservations and prices.

In winter, the park's glacial hills lends themselves to **cross-country-skiing** (trails begin south of the Clubhouse), **sledding** down the Cascades hill, and **skating** on the duck pond behind the Clubhouse (warming house open weekends 11-7).

FAMOUS FOR ITS GIANT SUNDAES . . . . . the **Parlour** soda fountain at the **Jackson All-Star Dairy** is the most popular spot in town. No super-premium ice cream here, just the basics — chocolate syrup, nuts, whipped cream, good ice cream made at the ice cream plant right next door, and lots of it. (A single scoop here is closer to two normal scoops.) The $4.50 banana split (6 scoops, piled in a foot-high pyramid) is more than three people can comfortably eat. "Dare to Be Great" ($14.95) is a 21-scoop monster. Typical three-scoop sundaes are $2.95. Obliging counter girls will honor requests for extra sides of whipped cream and toppings (you do pay for them) and for special fountain treats — lemon malts, or hot fudge malts, for instance. (Malts are made with soft ice cream unless you specify extra rich.) Expect a wait in summer, longer on weekends or after the malls close and movies are out. The entire fountain menu, plus big $1 cones in 31 flavors, is available at the faster **takeout** line. A few picnic tables are outside. *On Higby at Daniel, just east of Brown and the Westwood Mall. From I-94 exit 138, take West Ave. to Michigan Ave., turn west; in 7 blocks turn north on Higby. (Brown Street runs from the Dairy to the Cascades.) (517) 782-7141. Open daily 10-10, to 11 in summer.* &.

JACKSON'S HIDDEN SECRETS . . . . . hidden to outsiders, that is, include an amazing number of good, moderate-priced **public golf courses** and a wonderful large outdoor sculpture by the late, great **Louise Nevelson**. It's so poorly sited (in front of the closed downtown hotel on East Michigan just east of Mechanic) as to be hard to see from the street. . . . . Call the Jackson Area Golf Association at 800-764-4075 for the **Jackson golf guide**, or stop by the **24-hour tourist info center** by the McDonald's at I-94 Exit 145 east of town. The office is open Mon-Fri 8-5 but the lobby with pamphlets and video machines is always open. Golf is so popular in Jackson it ranks with bowling and softball as one of the three blue-collar sports. . . . . . . Jackson (its rural environs, actually) is the home of Republican rocker Ted Nugent. His musical tributes to hunting and his bowhunting mentor, Fred Bear, are for sale along with archery gear and his published musings on the subject at **Ted Nugent's Bowhunters' World**. In the same building is the **Rock & Roll Bow Hunting Museum** with artifacts from Ted's career along with mounted game from his hunting trips around the world, including two mounted zebra stallions. Quite a few of the photos & memorabilia hail from Ted's heyday in the '70's. Also open to the public: an **indoor archery range** where bows in the shop can be tried out or archery can be practiced off season. Free shooting from 11-1, $3 an hour otherwise. *4133 W. Michigan west of town. Call (517) 750-9060 for directions.Same hours for museum & shop: Mon-Sat 10-6, Sun 11-4, much later in hunting season.* &

Michigan Space & Science Center

A fascinating, up-close view of America's great leap to dominance in space exploration

HOUSED in a big geodesic dome on the Jackson Community College campus south of Jackson, the Michigan Space and Science Center manages to take a complex topic —America's space ventures of the 1960s and 1970s — and illuminate it in a way that entertains and educates rather than overwhelms the visitor. There are background displays on the Solar System and the evolution of rocketry. But most of the displays pertain to that amazing era when the U.S. moved from far behind the Soviets in rocket design to become the first and only country to land humans on the moon.

Liberally scattered throughout the Center is historically important space equipment, such as a NASA prototype of the Mariner IV spacecraft, which flew close to Mars in 1964, and a Lunar Rover Vehicle. Most spectacular is the actual Apollo 9 command module used to link up in space with a test Lunar Excursion Module three months before the first moon landing. You get to look right inside the module to see the cramped quarters. The astronauts aboard the Apollo 13 owe a debt of gratitude to the Apollo 9 for the information that they gathered on the Lunar Excursion Module. Stuck in space , the LEM became the life raft for the crew of Apollo 13 during the attempt at a 3rd lunar landing that gripped the country in 1971 and later became the Tom Hanks movie. An array of spacesuits shows their rapid evolution from the stiff early Mercury suits (1958-1963) to the flexible Apollo suits of the 1970s. Especially fascinating for children is the detailed explanation of how astronauts go to the bathroom. Also interesting are displays of the food eaten in space. Get on a big digital scale and compare your weight on earth with what it would be on any of the other planets. The large but primitive-looking computer console which guided John Glenn's historic first Earth orbit in 1962 shows how much more sophisticated today's space electronics are. A moon rock was brought back by Jackson native Al Worden and other members of the Apollo 15 crew.

Recently, three new computers with interactive software were added. "Return to the Moon." is especially fun because visitors get to do things like launch rockets and decide where on the moon to land.

2111 Emmons Road. Take exit 142 from I-94 to 127. Take 127 to the Monroe and M-50 exit. Turn left onto McDevitt Ave. Turn left onto Hague at the first traffic light on McDevitt. Take Hague to Emmons Road and follow the signs. Plenty of free parking at the Space Center. (517) 787-4425. September 5 thru October: Wed-Sat 10-5, Sun noon-5. November thru

The Apollo 9 command module used for a key test mission three months before the first moon landing. The Space Center's many exhibits illuminate the spectacular American advances in space exploration made from 1960 to 1980.

January: Wed-Sat 10-4. February thru April: Tues-Sat 10-5. May through Labor Day: Mon-Sat 10-5, Sun noon-5. &. Adults $3.85, students and seniors (60 & older) $2.75, children under 5 (with parents) free, two generation families $11.

🌲🌲🌲

A FIRST-RATE NATURE CENTER . . . . . not far from the Michigan Space & Science Center has five miles of **trails** through woods and over streams with excellent interpretive markers. It also has some indoor exhibits and a nature-oriented gift shop. To get to the **John and Mary Dahlem Environmental Education Center** from the Space Center, go south (left) on Browns Lake Road where the entrance drive is. In about a block turn west (right) onto Kummel. In one mile, turn north (right) onto South Jackson Road. Dahlem Center entrance is in two blocks. *Buildings are open Mon-Fri 8-5 during the summer & Tues-Fri 8-5 the rest of the year. Open weekends 12-5 year-round. Trails are open daily from dawn to dusk. Call (517) 782-3453 for info.* ♿

AN OUTSTANDING VICTORIAN HOUSE MUSEUM AND MORE . . . . . is a short, scenic drive from the Space & Science Center. **Ella Sharp Museum** consists of an especially elegant 1857 farmhouse; an authentically furnished settlers' log cabin, circa 1840; a schoolhouse; several 19th-century businesses; and three galleries with regularly **changing exhibits on arts and local history**, plus the hands-on **Discovery Gallery** for children.

Tours of the house, given every half hour, are customized to each small group's interests. They go way beyond Victorian decorating to point out things like how quickly industrialization changed people's everyday lives in the late 19th century and how fascinated the Victorian middle class was with nature and its spiritual power. Ella Sharp's mother was a wealthy Easterner who invested in Michigan land and actually came out to live on it. With her husband she developed Hillside Farm here into a showplace of progressive agriculture. Ella herself was a successful reformer. Her causes were good government, improving town and rural life through women's clubs, and conservation.

The Granary restaurant is a most attractive lunch spot with excellent food (open Tues-Sat 11-2:30). There's a good **gift shop** (open Tues-Fri 10-4, Sat 12-3) in the main exhibit building. *The museum is in Ella Sharp Park on the south edge of Jackson, on Fourth just south of Horton Rd. From the Space Center take Browns Lake Rd. It turns into Stonewall. Eventually Fourth juts off from Stonewall and leads to the museum. Park behind the museum. From I-94, take M-50/Business 127, exit 138 at Jackson Crossing, go south on West, follow the signs. (517) 787-2320.* ♿ *except house 2nd floor, a few historic buildings. Tues-Fri 10-4, Sat & Sun 1-4. $2.50 person, $2 seniors (55+) $1 child 5-15, free under 5, $5 family.*

ADVENTURE GOLF AND SWIMMING AT SHARP PARK . . . . . At the Sharp Park entrance on Fourth Street, just north of the Ella Sharp Museum, a spectacular **18-hole minigolf course** occupies a manmade hill with two cascading waterfalls and rivers emptying into a large pond with a 25-foot fountain. Trees, shrubs, and seasonal flowers turn this into a beautiful three-acre multilevel garden. There's a small snack concession. *The Sharp Park East Miniaturized Golf Course (517-788-4696) is open from April through October. Summer hours are 10 a.m. to 10 p.m.; spring and fall hours start and end with weekends (Fri-Sun) only; call for specifics. Cost: $2.50 per person (all ages), $2 in groups of 5 or more. Half price before noon.* . . . . . Next door, the **Sharp Park Swimming Pool**, an Olympic-size Z-shape pool with diving and instructional wells, is open to all. *Season: school summer vacation, usually from the 2nd week of June to the last part of August. Open swim hours: 1-3, 3:15-5:15, adults only 5:30-7; late-evening hours in hot weather. (517) 788-4040. $1/person.*

THE BIRTHPLACE OF THE REPUBLICAN PARTY . . . . . is Jackson's biggest claim to fame, a claim contested by Ripon, Wisconsin. Local attorney Austin Blair and other dissatisfied local leaders organized a meeting of Free Soilers, abolitionists, anti-slavery Whigs and Democrats, men concerned about the growing power of the railroads, and others was organized. Held in Jackson on July 6, 1854, it proved so large it had to moved outdoors, **"under the oaks"** in a grove just west of town. Though the Ripon meeting had taken place earlier, it was attended only by local people, while the Jackson meeting brought together leaders from throughout the state.

Blair went on to become Michigan's beloved Civil War governor, a staunch backer of Lincoln. Later he was thwarted by Michigan big-money interests who came to dominate the party he helped found. The oak grove was later subdivided and built up, but two city lots now make up a small **park** commemorating the historic site. One of the oaks was hit by lightning during Watergate – the stuff of enduring local mythology. But some big trees remain. *On Franklin at Second just west of downtown. Take West Ave. from I-94 exit 38 to 2 blocks south of Michigan Ave., turn east onto Franklin for 4 blocks.*

1 Downtown. Interesting concentration of restaurants & shops. Lively Main St. weekend scene on into the evening, with plenty of good open-air summer cafés.

2 Kerrytown. Lively restaurant/shop complex. Bustling farmers' market, large kitchenware shop. Nearby Treasure Mart is must visit for bargain hunters.

3 Zingerman's. Extraordinary deli shop. Delicious huge sandwiches, outstanding bread, selections of quality cheeses, meats, olive oils, and other ingredients.

4 State-Liberty shopping area. Anchored by Borders Books. Great record & book shops, coffee houses, and gift shops. Cosmopolitan street scene.

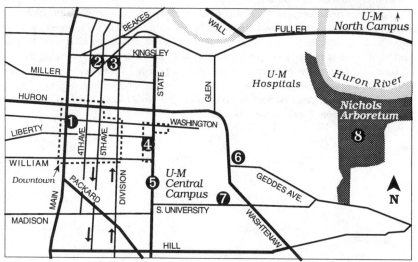

5 Two U-M museums on State St. At the **Kelsey,** priceless art of Egypt, Greece, Rome. **Museum of Art** is tops for Asian art. One of the best overall collections of any university art museum in country.

6 U-M Exhibit Museum. Extraordinary natural science displays with prehistoric dinosaur skeletons, many rare specimens. See vivid scenes of landscapes from thousands of years ago.

7 Middle Earth. Entertaining shop in student-oriented commercial strip. Full of all sorts of amusing items, many outrageous. Nearby **Village Corner** has one of state's best selections of wines.

8 Nichols Arboretum. Delightful hilly 126 acres. Paths down to Huron River. Over 2,000 kinds of plants, outstanding peonies.

Highlights of
Ann Arbor

0   1/2
                                           mile   1

Ann Arbor shopping and nightlife

Michigan's liveliest downtown, cosmopolitan and dynamic, has a dazzling mix of unusually specialized shops, from pop culture of the 1950s to Chinese art.

OVER the past couple of decades Ann Arbor has become one of the most interesting spots to visit in the Midwest. Evenings and weekends, downtown can feel like a tourist spot. Walking down Main Street or State Street, you'll find the sidewalks crowded with a colorful mix of people, from the elegantly attired to street people, from professors to punks. Coffeehouses (18 of them so far, with more on the way) have popped up everywhere. They often have live entertainment, and they're ideal places to observe the local scene. Most shops stay open late, in step with the busy bars and nightspots. Many restaurants spill out onto the sidewalks. The cultural and entertainment options are almost overwhelming. In 1996 the city showed up at the top of ranking charts devised by national media in their endless pursuit of "best" lists and quantifiable (if misleading) rankings. Ann Arbor came out #5 in *Money*'s metropolitan quality of life survey, and #1 in a *Swing* article on the place to be for its twentysomething readers. Newsstands report weekend waves of out-of-towners coming to check out the city and its real estate, some of Michigan's most expensive.

Even on an ordinary winter weekend, central Ann Arbor is alive with activity. Out-of-town visitors are an increasing part of the crowd. Some Ann Arbor store managers say half their customers are from out of town. Lines form outside popular restaurants, and shops on Main Street are full of after-dinner browsers until 10 p.m. Restaurant competition has become fierce, most must be pretty good.

Remnants of Ann Arbor's once-lively counterculture live on at the **Del Rio Bar** at 120 West Washington, the **Old Town** at 120 West Liberty, and upstairs over the **Heidelberg Restaurant**, 215 North Main, where poetry slams are held the first Tuesday of the month. But people who remember the laid-back Ann Arbor of their college days are surprised by its big-city intensity, its traffic (often approaching gridlock, though still light by New York standards) — and the expensive merchandise. It's not hard to find a $1,500 sport coat, a $5,000 painting, or a $20,000 ring in central Ann Arbor.

Ann Arbor has become more than a college town. It has become a regional research and development center. And it's also a suburb of choice for metro Detroit's intelligentsia. Downtown Detroit is barely 45 minutes away. People like Ford Motor president Alex Trotman and many *Detroit Free Press* editors and writers find this the most congenial place in southeast Michigan to live.

What sets Ann Arbor apart from other downtowns that experienced rampant gentrification in the 1980s is that many — maybe even most — stores haven't simply jumped onto the latest hot trend. Stores here are usually owned and run by knowledgeable people with longstanding interests in what they sell, whether it be backpacking gear, running shoes, technomusic clothing, or Chinese art. Upscale specialty chains like Benetton and J. Crew, which threaten to overwhelm downtown Birmingham and Grosse Pointe, have made few inroads in Ann Arbor. Shops with crafts, decorative arts, and home accessories are much stronger in Ann Arbor than clothes. Ann Arbor *really* shines in books (page 170) and CDs (page 176); some say it's the best book and record town in the U.S. Borders, the homegrown bookstore that originated the superstore concept in bookstore chains, took over the Liberty Street space vacated when Jacobson's moved to Briarwood. It has added a sizable music, video, and multi-media department to its huge book inventory. (See page 170.) The Borders/Waldenbook national headquarters has moved next door from Connecticut.

In recent years, the **State Street area** has seen bookstores expand and its retailing mix lose clothing stores and older customers. **South University** has become overwhelmingly oriented to undergraduates. General retailing has nearly vanished from Main Street. The phenomenally successful Zingerman's deli and Sweet Lorraine's restaurant generate daytime traffic that have brought interesting new stores to the **Kerrytown area,** the near north side specialty shopping complex by the Farmers' Market. Central-area parking is so tight that interesting specialty stores geared more to local people are now found in shopping centers along **Plymouth Road**, including Traver Village on Plymouth Road west of Nixon and the Courtyard Shops at North Campus Plaza.

Here are some standouts, arranged by areas. For readers' convenience in planning a route, bookstores and CD stores have been briefly noted here. They're treated more fully in separate chapters on pages 170 and 176.

DOWNTOWN: ON AND OFF MAIN STREET

As recently as 20 years ago, downtown Ann Arbor was dominated by longtime German businesses. But over the past decade it has become a stylish place for eating, drinking coffee, and browsing. The block of South Fourth Avenue between Liberty and Washington attracts interesting start-up stores and is always worth checking out. The 200 block of Washington is becoming a gallery destination. *Parking: street spots are hard to find. There's a big surface lot at Washington at Ashley. The ramp at Ann and Ashley nearly always has space. (Remember that Fourth and Fifth avenues are just east of Main St., Fourth and Fifth streets are just west of Main.)*

◆ **Arcadian II.** Second location of the successful Nickels Arcade antique store has the same sweet flair for displaying things that could look dull and ordinary. Wonderful selection of antique jewelry, including many cameos. Most items are between 1880 and 1930 or so. *322 S. Main. (313) 994-8856. Mon-Thurs 11-6, Fri 11-9, Sat 10-9. Sun noon-5.*

◆ **Generations: The Children's Store.** Great browsing for parents and for kids, who can play at Brio and other playtables. Books, jewelry and nifty toys, puppets, and educational toys that are really fun. Colorful, relatively pricey kids' clothes take up less and less space. A beehive of activity on weekends, Friday night, and summer evenings. Inquire about special events. *337 S. Main. (313) 662-6615.*

◆ **Selo/Shevel Gallery.** Functional and art glass, and perhaps Michigan's best single collection of handmade contemporary American jewelry, from $40 to $1,000 and up. In gold, silver, and brass, with semiprecious and precious stones, including tourmaline and garnets. Back-lit blown glass makes the mood here colorful, clear, and shimmering. Glassmakers include Josh Simpson (his paperweights encasing "little worlds" of freeform colors and shapes) clean freeform, bevel-cut glass sculpture from Blake Street Glass; and Matthew Buechner's Art Nouveau-style trumpet vases in combinations of clear and frosted glass. The gallery's folk art, wood, ceramics, textiles and metal crafts are on Main at Liberty. *335 S. Main. (313) 761-6263. 10-7 Mon-Thurs, 10-10 Fri and Sat.*

◆ **Wilderness Outfitters.** Well-equipped shop features camping, climbing, and backpacking gear. Cross-country ski equipment a specialty. Widest selection of backpacking boots around. Tends toward classic lines of outdoor apparel as compared with flashy new ones. Don't miss the discount clothing rack upstairs. *333 S. Main. (800) 778-3636. Mon-Thurs 10-6, Fri & Sat 10-8, Sun 12-5.*

◆ **Ayla & Co.** *323 S. Main.* Fashion-forward contemporary classic clothing for the rich and the thin. *(313) 665-7788. Mon-Sat.10-6 .*

◆ **Collected Works.** Lots of jewelry, cards, accessories, mostly with a look that's multicultural and hip but soft and on the romantic

Sidewalk seating adds to the browsing and noshing ambiance of both Main Street (above), where the best restaurants, gift shops, and galleries are, and State Street by the U-M campus, the center of book and music stores.

side. Natural-fibers clothing, mostly for women but with some sweaters, shirts, and pants for men. Rayon is considered natural, and there's lots of it, flowery and loose. Relaxed, comfortably sophisticated look plays off ethnic prints and textures against basic solid colors in unstructured clothing, often knit. Prices from inexpensive to moderate. *317 S. Main. Mon-Thurs 10-9, Fri & Sat 10-10, Sun 12-5. (313) 995-4222.*

◆ **ATYS.** Stylish, well-designed, sleekly functional contemporary living accessories, much of it from Europe. Everything from a toothbrush to designer paper clips. *306 S. Main. (313) 996-2976*

◆ **Selo/Shevel Gallery . . . at Liberty.** Stunning corner space at Liberty and Main has an earthy, rich mix of ethnic art and contemporary crafts from leading American craftspeople. Ceramics of porcelain, stoneware, and raku; chimes and Swedish door harps. Ethnic handcrafts include puppets from Bali and Thailand, African masks and sculpture, Turkish and Moroccan kilims, Mexican rugs and pillows, and fantastic carved and painted armadillos, iguanas and such from Oaxaca. Contemporary American wood boxes and furniture are make with exotic woods such as purple heart, padauk, bubinga, and domestic woods. *301 S. Main at Liberty. (313) 761-4620. 10-7 Mon-Thurs, 10-10 Fri and Sat. Summer thru Christmas: noon-5 Sundays.*

◆ **The Conservatory.** This delightfully serene gift shop is run by an architect who emphasizes good design in his merchandise and pleasing historic setting. Jewelry, home accessories, and unusual baskets. The eclectic assemblage emphasizes paper in many forms: cards, unusual playing cards, blank books, stationery, and striking Japanese paper. *111 W. Liberty. (313) 994-4443. Mon-Thurs 10-6, Fri & Sat to 8 or later.*

◆ **Rider's Hobby.** Among Michigan's best hobby shops. Trains, radio-control planes, adventure games, kits. Flagship of the small regional chain with other more spacious locations. *115 W. Liberty. (313) 668-8950. Mon-Fri 10-8, Sat 10-6.*

◆ **Ehnis & Son.** A genuine working man's clothes store, descended from a harnessmaker whose sideline was shoes. Quality overalls, work shirts, and boots. Authentic old-time interior worth a look. *116 W. Liberty. (313) 663-4337. Mon-Sat 8-6.*

◆ **Rage of the Age.** The Thirties through Seventies revisited, with emphasis on vintage designer clothing and fabrics such as printed bark cloth. Funky furnishings and accessories for the home such as brass sputnik chandeliers from the Fifties. Ask about modernist furniture classics. *314 S. Ashley. (313) 662-0777. Thurs-Sat 12-6, otherwise by appointment.*

◆ **Occasionally.** Lots of souvenirs from the U-M (Go Blue T shirts in many languages) and the state of Michigan. *223 S. Main. (313) 769-5151.*

◆ **Falling Water Books and Collectibles.** A store that has its finger on the pulse of the times. Often miscategorized as a New Age store, it's a feel-good gift store that mixes mainstream and New Age self-help, inspirational, personal growth, and women's books with jewelry, cards, fossils, and music. *213 S. Main. (313) 747-9810.*

◆ **16 Hands.** Attractively displayed contemporary crafts and cards at a wide range of prices. Cheerfully sophisticated, often with a colorful primitivism that plays off simple dark silhouettes with glowing colors. Jewelry, furniture and wood accessories, metal work, weaving, blown glass, and other media by talented artists with regional and national followings. *216 S. Main. (313) 761-1110. Mon-Thurs 10-6, Fri & Sat 10-10, Sun 12-5.*

◆ **The Peaceable Kingdom.** Warm, clever, personal shop has become an Ann Arbor institution with its potpourri of imaginatively displayed things, from small inexpensive toys and gadgets to imported and contemporary American folk art. Don't be so distracted by the novelties that you forget to look up on the walls and see Mexican and African masks and compelling one-of-a-kind dolls by Ann Arbor's Charla Khanna. *210 S. Main. (313) 668-7886. Mon-Thurs 10-6, Fri & Sat 10-10.*

◆ **Grace's Select Second Hand.** 4,000-square-foot consignment shop for clean, selected furniture and household goods, from kitchen utensils to bedroom sets and hutches. Unpretentious mix of Middle American furniture, household goods, often from house sales. Offers some good pickings. Akin to the Treasure Mart, but with fewer antiques. Three 80-foot walls allow lots of space for framed paintings and prints, old and new. *122 S. Main, just below Republic Bank. (313) 668-0747. 11-9 Mon-Sat.Noon-5 Sun.*

◆ **Lotus Gallery.** Antique art and furniture of southeast Asia, including Chinese jades, Japanese netsuke and simple 19th-century wood chests of drawers, antique porcelain and stoneware, and unusual things like an opium scale. Also, contemporary Chinese paintings, outstanding Southwest Indian pottery. Owner-collector Les Werbel is available after 5 and on many Saturdays. *207 E. Washington. (313) 665-6322. Wed-Sat 11-5:30.*

◆ **The Artful Exchange.** An eclectic variety of fine art — paintings, sculpture, drawings, ethnic art, and prints — sold on consignment. Prices start as low as $15 and go up into the thousands, for "investment art" by the likes of Chagall, Dali, and Calder. Most are from $300 to $900. Here can be found anything from works by Robert Motherwell and Albrecht Dürer to contemporary Tibetan paintings and Chinese peasant art. A good place to find works by former U-M art school faculty like Emil Weddige, Guy Pallazolla, and Richard Wilt. Frank Cassara, well known in the 1930s and still painting today, is a regular exhibitor. Now about half the gallery is devoted to contemporary gallery artists. *215 E. Washington. (313) 761-2287. Wed-Fri 11-5, Sat 10-5.*

◆ **Barrett's Antiques and Fine Arts.** Victorian antiques, art glass, clocks, quilts, and more, most attractively displayed. There's a good deal of Rookwood pottery, the owner's specialty. Don't miss the toys and collectibles in the basement. Also Pewabic Pottery from Detroit. *212 E. Washington. (313) 662-1140. Fri-Sat 11-5.*

◆ **The Bead Gallery.** A fabulous array of beads is enough to inspire you to make your own creations. Ceramic beads from Thailand, charms, gemstones, Ethiopian silver beads, glass beads, old and new, plus the requisite cords. Books and instructional sheets. *309 E. Liberty between Fifth and Division (lower level). (313) 663-6800. Mon-Sat 10-6, Sun 12-5.*

◆ **Creative Tattoo**. *307 E. Liberty. (313) 662-2520.* Degree-holding artist and former art teacher Suzanne Fauser has won national awards with her beautiful tattoos and relieved a lot of embarrassment by modifying ill-advised body ornament.

KERRYTOWN AREA/NORTH FOURTH AVENUE

This old commercial district just north of downtown has come on very strong recently, with a top Ann Arbor's restaurant (Sweet Lorraine) and many of the interesting shops. The area includes the big Kerrytown complex (actually three connected old buildings), the adjoining Farmers' Market, and nearby shops and restaurants. North Fourth Ave. between Catherine and Ann remains a center of alternative culture. Here you'll find the impressive People's Food Coop, a Birkenstock store, the Wooden Spoon used book shop, and Crazy Wisdom, a center for metaphysics and Eastern Religions. *Parking: often quite tight in this area. Best last resort is the parking structure on Ann Street between Main and Ashley.*

◆ **Near Kerrytown.** The entries below are just south of the Kerrytown complex:

Ann Arbor's Farmers' Market. One of Michigan's most robust, colorful (and crowded) farmers' markets. Not cheap, but quality of the fresh produce and fruits is excellent. Good selection of herbs and other plants. *Open-air sheds run from Detroit and N. Fifth Ave. to N. Fourth. (313) 761-1078. Wed & Sat 7-3.*

DeBoer Gallery. Quirky, whimsical, well-chosen art in all media; many animals. Everything from coffee mugs and T-shirts to jewelry and tiles. Most are one-of-a-kind, handpainted. *303 Detroit. (313) 741-1257. Tues-Thurs 10-6, Fri 10-9, Sat 9-5.*

Gothic Proportions. Reproductions — most of them unpainted — of gargoyles, imps, classical Greek torsos, Egyptian sphinxes, columns and pedestals. An amusing collection, from $8 to $250. *303 Detroit. Tues-Sat 10-6. Sun 11-2.*

◆ **Kerrytown** *(between N. Fourth and Fifth. Most stores are open between 10-8 on Thurs and Fri, Mon-Wed 10-6, Sat 10-5, Sun 12-5.)* Noteworthy shops inside include:

Monahan's Seafood Market. Fresh fish for serious fish-lovers. A quarter of the customers are foreigners accustomed to more fish in their diets. The Japanese like "sanma," a mackerel pike, monkfish livers, and asari. The French like red mullet, flown fresh from Paris. Koreans like skate wings. Germans like smoked eel and a variety of herrings. There's huge shrimp, wonderful flounder. *(313) 662-5118.*

Partners in Wine. Knowledgeable service. Good buys in California, Australian, and French wines. *(313) 761-6384.*

Kitchen Port. An exceptionally fine kitchen store, with considerable selection in everything from utensils to tableware. Largest selection of cookbooks, placemats, napkins, pot racks in southeastern Michigan. Call for times of cooking demonstrations. *(313) 665-9188.*

Moveable Feast. Takeout shop of the bakery of one of Michigan's finest restaurants. Great sourdough French bread, croissants, pastries, and patés.*(313) 663-3331.*

Vintage to Vogue. "Clothing for the body, mind, and soul," the owner likes to say. Considered by some Ann Arbor's top clothing store. New women's fashions, not trendy, not mainstream, much of it by women designers, costing from $40 to $400. Lots of natural and organic fabrics. *(313) 665-9110.*

◆ **Treasure Mart.** Ann Arbor's legendary resale shop has a sprawling array of home furnishings and knick-knacks at all price levels, sometimes at prices far lower than an antique shop would charge. The quality of its used furniture, collectibles, lighting, china, linens, framed pictures, and the like reflects the broad range of Ann Arbor lifestyles, from the ordinary to the affluent. Large and fast-moving stock. *529 Detroit, between Kingsley and Division. (313) 662-1363. Mon-Sat 9-5:30.*

◆ **Zingerman's Delicatessen.** See page 178.

STATE STREET AREA

Although just north of the U-M campus, this area has far transcended a student shopping area. Its shops draw people not just from other parts of Michigan, but other states and countries. It has become the center of Ann Arbor's outstanding concentration of bookstores and CD stores (see pages 170 and page 176). **Nickels Arcade**, an historic 1915 European-style arcade of small shops, runs between State Street and Maynard. *Parking: one of the toughest places to find a space in town. Safest bet is the structure entered from Washington between Main and Division.*

◆ **Renaissance.** Fashion-forward Euro-style and other contemporary clothing and sportswear for men. Sportcoats run from $295-$1295, shirts from $65 to $295. *336 Maynard. (313) 769-8511. Mon-Thurs 10-6, Fri 10-7, Sat 10-6.*

◆ **Matthew C. Hoffmann.** Wealthy folks come from far and wide to buy Matthew Hoffmann's expensive contemporary creations.

Hoffmann calls his jewelry "portable sculpture." *340 Maynard. (313) 665-7692.*

◆ **Chris Triola Gallery.** Very chic pullovers, simple and boldly patterned in themes from African and jazz to Celtic, from $200-$750. Designed by Lansing's Chris Triola. Also skirts, scarves, jackets and sweaters. *5 Nickels Arcade. (313) 996-9955.* Tues-Sat 10-6, Sun 12-5.

◆ **Clay Gallery.** Beautiful pottery, much of it in subdued earthtones, by a cooperative of 12 Ann Arbor potters. Everything from small gift items to large architectural pieces. *8 Nickels Arcade. (313) 662-7927. Mon-Fri 9:30-5:30, Sat 9:30-5.*

◆ **Van Boven Clothing.** Ann Arbor's classic men's clothing store, where professors buy their tweed sportscoats and Oxford shirts. *326 S. State. (313) 665-7228.*

◆ **Bivouac.** Popular outfitters for campers, hikers, climbers, skiers. Big and bustling, with large, knowledgeable staff. *336 S. State. (313) 761-7206.*

◆ **Harry's Army Surplus.** Wild selection of everything from cheap camping gear and East German border guard overcoats to paint splat guns and throwing stars. A neat place to browse. *500 E. Liberty. (313) 994-3572. Mon-Fri 9-8, Sat 9-6, Sun 11-5.*

◆ **Herb David Guitar Studio.** Custom made guitars from Herb's shop range from $200 to $3500. Best repair shop in Midwest. Also for sale here are banjoes, hand drums, acoustic and electric guitars. *302 E. Liberty. (313) 665-8001. 10-6 Mon-Sat, Thurs & Fri to 7. Sun 12-5.*

SOUTH UNIVERSITY COMMERCIAL DISTRICT

Three blocks of stores and restaurants along South University connect the central campus with the fraternity and sorority area along Washtenaw and Hill. Over the past dozen or so years, the area's character has come to be almost exclusively oriented to undergraduates, with a proliferation of fast-food chains. If you are unfortunate enough to arrive by car at the top of the hour when classes are getting out, you'll just have to wait, as there is no doubt in these students' minds that pedestrians have the right of way. *Parking: On South University, the city structure on Forest just south of South University is your best bet.*

◆ **Middle Earth.** One of the most interesting shops in the state. Novelties compete for space with a striking display of beautiful jewelry, some quite expensive, including thousands of earrings. You'll find a wild and outrageous variety of constantly changing "cheap thrills": Elvis troll dolls, inflatable pink Cadillacs. T-shirts are also a big deal here'— with some of the hippest (and funniest) in the country. The first shop in town to sell bawdy greeting cards, Middle Earth still has the most ribald selection, though there are plenty of lovely, artistic cards any mother would love to get. Over 20,000 offbeat postcards. *1209 South University. (313) 769-1488. Mon-Sat 10-7, Thurs & Fri 'til 9, Sun noon-5.*

◆ **Village Corner.** The VC keeps its scruffy, vaguely counter-culture ambiance in the face of Ann Arbor's rampant gentrification. Clerks, often outlandishly clad, wait on you in amusingly surly fashion. You'd never realize a **nationally known wine shop** is in the back. The VC has one of Michigan's most sophisticated and wide-ranging selections of wine, from inexpensive to very fine — 4,000 kinds, along with 600 kinds of spirits. In the wine section, sales people are knowledgeable and willing to take the time to advise customers on their selections, even if it's a $6 bottle to accompany spaghetti and meatballs. Prices are reasonable, and deals on cases of wine are especially good. Masterfully clear and informative shelf descriptions of wines are written in part by Village Corner owner Dick Scheer, a well-known wine authority and judge. Ask for the free annotated **catalog** and **newsletter.** For picnics, the VC has a good selection of convenience and takeout food (fresh fruit, sandwiches, good bread and cheese) and groceries. *Southeast corner of South University and Forest. (313) 995-1818. 7 days 8 a.m.-1 a.m.*

Ann Arbor Nightspots

◆ **The Ark.** Admission is usually $8-$18. Shows begin at 8 p.m. Attracts top acoustic and folk performers from all around the country. New home is in the former Kline's department store, now with its handsome old facade revealed. *316 S. Main. (313) 761-1451.*

◆ **Bird of Paradise.** Pleasant jazz club with live music nightly. *207 S. Ashley. (313)-8310.*

◆ **Blind Pig.** This popular local rock 'n' roll club provided one of the first audiences beyond Seattle to give Nirvana a boost. Live music includes blues, rock 'n' roll, reggae. *208 S. First. (313) 996-8555.*

◆ **The Heidelberg.** This German restaurant uses its top floor for live bands. Thursdays is acid jazz with a DJ playing records plus live music; Fridays and Saturdays (10:30-1:30) often features established Ann Arbor groups and performers: Steve Nardella, George Bedard, Steve Somers, Steve Newhouse, and others. Sundays (7-9:30) there's a big band orchestra. *215 N. Main. Cover up to $5.*

◆ **The Nectarine Ballroom.** A New-York-style dance club with DJs six nights a week. Various themes on different nights: gay, Eurobeat, alternative, disco. *510 E. Liberty. (313) 994-5436.*

◆ **Rick's American Cafe.** Near the U-M campus. Many students flock to this rock 'n' roll club, with strong bookings of out-of-town bands. *611 Church. (313) 996-2747.*

A 1928 PICTURE PALACE . . . . . the **Michigan Theater** was bought by the city in the 1980s for use as a community venue rentable to any group. A Republican mayor took the initiative to rescue it from being converted to a shopping arcade. Now it is a successful community-owned theater, much used for concerts, occasional plays, and films. Splendidly restored to all its gilded grandeur, it has blossomed by filling in gaps in the city's formidable array of entertainment. On weekends, before the main event, the original **Barton Theater Organ** is often played. It's a chance to see movies the way they were once meant to be seen on the big screen. The **drama series** features big-time productions from Broadway and leading regional theater companies. **Not Just For Kids** offers big-name family entertainment. The **Serious Fun** series consists of commercially tested avantgarde performers such as Laurie Anderson, Sankai Juku, and frequently Philip Glass. **Revival films** ($4.50) fill in the off-nights. *Call (313) 668-8397, or stop by the theater entrance on Liberty at Maynard for a schedule.*

INTENSE STREET LIFE . . . . . comes to Ann Arbor each July during the **Art Fair** — actually three big fairs with a thousand artists, stretching from South University to Main Street. There's too much of everything — bargain-priced merchandise, art, food, people, hot weather — but people come back year after year. The Ann Arbor Art Fair and the State St. Art Fair include art of the highest caliber found at street fairs anywhere, while a third is more pedestrian but continually being upgraded. Some terrific area musicians perform on several stages. Wednesday through Saturday, in the last part of July. (313) 994-5260.

THE ANN ARBOR ART SCENE . . . . . is lively, but more oriented to showcasing the area's unusual number of productive artists than to an art-hungry market. There are dozens of places that exhibit visual art, but no single gallery guide. The cultural smorgasbord of **performances, lectures,** etc., is similarly rich. Your best bet for an overview of what's going on is to pick up a copy of the *Ann Arbor Observer* monthly magazine, with a calendar of events and exhibits that's easy to use and comprehensive. The current day's main events are on the *Observer's* **calendar information line,** (313) 665-6155.

GOOD MOVIES DOWNTOWN . . . . . are shown at the small, easy-to-miss **Ann Arbor Theater,** 210 S. Fifth Avenue between Liberty and Washington. (313) 761-9700. Tuesday matinees and weekday shows at 4:40 are a fine alternative to fighting rush-hour traffic.

FUN WITH SCIENCE . . . . is the mission of the popular **Ann Arbor Hands-On Museum** downtown. Over 250 science exhibits for children and adults. Some of the most popular are the giant soap bubble capsule, the "double piddler" (two colliding streams that a strobe light illuminates), the giant zipper, the operating cut-away toilet, and the large PVC pipe organ kids can play. Educational computer games for kids. Good educational **gift shop**. It's in a landmark 1882 fire station. By 1998, it will expand into the adjoining building and triple in size. Call (313) 995-KIDS for info on one-day workshops and free demo topics. *Huron at N. Fifth. Tues-Fri 10-5:30, Sat 10-5, Sun 1-5. Adults $4, seniors, children, and students $2.50.*

University of Michigan museums

On the central campus are three of the state's finest museums — of art, archaeology, and natural history — plus other places to visit.

BECAUSE the University of Michigan has been a leading American research institution for over a century, it has had the collections and research staff to develop three exceptional museums. In recent years they have put real energy into broadening broadening their focus to reach out more to the general public. Ask about their increasing array of special events for families and friends, and sign up well ahead if reservations are required. This happy new thrust is a blend of idealism backed by pragmatic realism about raising funds and increasing resources.

UNIVERSITY OF MICHIGAN EXHIBIT MUSEUM

Not many other natural science museums in the country match the rarity and breadth of items on display here. Areas explored include prehistoric life and dinosaurs, anthropology and Native American cultures, Michigan wildlife, astronomy, biology and ecology. There is much here to interest most visitors. In popular group **tours** kid-friendly docents know how to overcome the exhibit style, mostly still rather stiff until funds permit redesigns.

The second floor holds many museum highlights, including the big draw – the **dinosaur section**. Also here are dozens of meticulously constructed dioramas — miniature three-dimensional scenes which vividly show life on Earth in the distant past. View a lush scene from a Pennsylvania forest 300 million years ago when giant insects abounded, dragonflies had 30-inch wingspans, and huge roaches crawled among gigantic palm trees. Another diorama shows what Nebraska looked

Complete dinosaur skeletons and beautiful dioramas of scenes from their eras are a big draw at the U-M Exhibit Museum. Group tours are excellent.

like 10 million years ago when populated with camels, primitive elephants, short rhinoceroses, and rodents the size of woodchucks. You can see Los Angeles 15 million years ago when sabertooth tigers roamed the region.

A series of seven dioramas reveals the evolution of life, beginning back in the Cambrian age 575 million years ago, when crablike creatures were the most sophisticated beasts around. You also get an intriguing glimpse into the villages of the various people's who inhabited Michigan before Europeans arrived.

The dinosaur section, seven skeletons strong, is highlighted by the looming remains of a big allosaurus that roamed Utah 140 million years ago. The flesh-eating giant had forbiddingly long claws and sharp, menacing teeth. More subtle but also evocative are the various fossil footprints made by dinosaurs millions of years ago.

The fourth floor best shows the museum's new approach. An **interactive weather-wall** display is connected by Ethernet to global weather information and atmospheric phenomena. The transparent anatomical mannequin (a see-through woman whose organs are visible) is the centerpiece of the redone **Human Anatomy Alcove**, opposite the popular planetarium and astronomy exhibits. Weekend **planetarium shows** ($3/adult, $2/kids) change several times a year. They are Saturdays on the half hour from 10:30 to 3:30; Sundays at 1:30, 2:30 and 3:30.

The museum has a nifty **museum shop** on the ground floor, full of inexpensive mineral and fossil specimens, dinosaur items, and all sorts of small items to delight kids, along with nature publications. *1109 Geddes Ave. where it intersects with North University. Parking hints: on weekends the small lot behind the museum, entered off Geddes, sometimes has spaces. It always has **handicap spaces**. Otherwise, public parking is available (about $1/hour) in the Fletcher Street ramp between the dental school and Power Center. (313) 764-0478. Mon-Sat 9-5, Sun 1-5. Free.*

KELSEY MUSEUM OF ARCHAEOLOGY

This small but important museum has two special attractions. The first is the 1891 building itself, made of local fieldstone in the Richardsonian Romanesque style. Originally called Newberry Hall, it was built to house the private Student Christian Association. Great pains were taken in choosing beautiful stones for the structure. The large Tiffany window on the north side, the elaborate woodwork, blue slate roof, and imposing front turret combine to make this a memorable campus landmark.

Inside is stored one of the most important collections of ancient

A Bacchic revel decorates this 2nd-century Roman sarcophagus at the Kelsey Museum. Its exhibits go to great lengths to tell what archaeological objects say about the people and cultures that created them.

Greek, Egyptian, Roman, and Near Eastern artifacts. Only a fraction of the 100,000-piece collection is on permanent display. What you see is very choice indeed, and accompanied by informative explanations of these artifacts' place in ancient life. Colorful Egyptian mummy masks, exquisite Greek black-and-red-figured vase paintings, rare and amazingly intact Roman glass are all presented in a comfortable, intimate setting which encourages close study. Most surprising of all, perhaps, are the early Egyptian sculptures, dating from 2400 to 200 B.C. They reveal remarkable artistic skill.

Good writing in exhibits often shows great understanding and originality in relating ancient world views with current ones on eternal themes like death and fertility. *434 S. State, across from Angell Hall. Mon-Fri 9-4, Sat & Sun 1-4. Call (313) 764-9304 for general information and special exhibits. Summer hours: Tues-Fri 9-4.*

UNIVERSITY OF MICHIGAN MUSEUM OF ART

Among the top ten U.S. university art museums, this has a permanent collection of over 13,000 pieces, rotated regularly. They include works by Dürer, Delacroix, Rodin, Picasso, Rembrandt, Corot, Millet, Monet, Cezanne, Miro, and Klee. At any one time, about 600 can be viewed. Well-known paintings on permanent display include Expressionist Max Beckman's *Begin the Beguine*, the

Italian Baroque painter Guercino's *Esther before Ahasuerus*, Whistler's *Sea and Rain*, and Monet's *The Breakup of the Ice*.

The museum collection is notable for both its range and quality, from Italian Renaissance panel paintings to Han Dynasty tomb figures to African sculpture and contemporary photography. The museum's German Expressionist paintings are outstanding. So are its collections of Asian art and Whistler prints, the bequest of a Detroiter who was Charles Freer's friend and shared the artistic taste of that famous connoisseur who founded the Freer Gallery in Washington. A small version of a Japanese teahouse has been installed in a corner of the Japanese Gallery. The **tea ceremony** is held regularly (no charge) at 3 p.m. on the last Sunday of the month during the academic year.

Making art more accessible and vital to the general public means a lot to Director Bill Hennessey and staff. The museum succeeds splendidly in making even difficult fields of art interesting and relevant. Well-written captions explain what Japanese writing instruments show about that culture. Videos show artists at work. Visitors are invited to make art at some events, and their work is sometimes here, too. "Bringing art and people together — in the service of human understanding." That's the museum's mission statement.

Special exhibitions include both national and international loan shows and small exhibits drawn from the museum's permanent collection. Some examples: "The crisis in Claude Monet's art in 1890" (Jan & Feb 1998); "Sepphoris in Galilee" (Sept-Dec 1997), which recreated an excavation of a Roman town in present-day Israel; and "From Blast to Pop: 20th-c. British Art" (March-April 1998). Interpretive **programs** range from lectures, symposia, and gallery talks by artists and curators to chamber concerts, multimedia performances, and other special events.

The **museum gift shop** has a choice assortment of art publications, posters, handmade and ethnic jewelry, folk art and craft collectibles. An enthusiastic, high-caliber staff of volunteer docents conducts free private tours for school and other groups as well as public **Sunday Tours** of special exhibitions and the permanent collection on Sundays at 2 p.m. During the academic year, the Museum presents **Midweek at the Museum**, a weekly series of gallery talks, art videos, and slide lectures each Wednesday at noon and Thursday evening. For exhibit and program information or to schedule a group tour, phone (313) 764-0395. *525 S. State at South University. (313) 764-0395. September-May: Tues-Fri 10-5, Thurs to 9, Sat-Sun 12-5. From Mem. to Labor Day: Tues-Sat 11-5, Sun 12-5.* ♿ *Free. Donations welcome.*

U-M NORTH CAMPUS

This outlying 800-acre campus, north of the Huron River northeast of the Central Campus, was planned in the 1940s, when residential neighborhoods blocked the university's growth in central Ann Arbor. Architect Eero Saarinen planned the North Campus in the rather futuristic, auto-dominated style of the day. The College of Engineering, School of Music, and the combined School of Art and College of Architecture and Urban Planning are here. The tower Saarinen wanted as the North Campus focal point has now been built, the 165-foot **Lurie Tower** and carillon, the gift of a U-M grad who parlayed a student investment as a campus landlord into a fortune in Chicago real estate. The illustrious Michigan-trained architect Charles Moore came up with the idea for the tower before his death. Its bells were cast by an eminent Dutch bellmaker.

The **North Campus Commons** off Murfin is a good place for lunch or a snack. The art and architecture school snack bar between Murfin and Glacier Way is another possibility,

Thanks to the fundraising energy of recently retired U-M president Jim Duderstadt, the North Campus has achieved a critical mass of density with new buildings and more people. The new Lurie Tower (above) and engineering building is at its center. Near it is the $38 million Integrated Technology Instructional Center, Duderstadt's pet project, intended to be a high-tech playpen and interdisciplinary hangout open to all students 24 hours a day. Will this "Media Union" really get engineers and art students to schmooze and collaborate on nifty computers and virtual reality devices? Check it out! Look for the big glass atrium and the columns shaped like engineering pencils.

and it's always interesting to see current projects of art and architecture students, who work here late into the night. *North Campus is between Fuller Road/Glacier Road to the south and Plymouth Road to the north. Its core is between the two connecting north-south roads: Murfin and Beal. Visitor parking is limited and scattered; North Campus Commons off Murfin has a fair amount of parking.*
    Major public attractions are:

◆ **"The Wave Field."** Created by Maya Lin, who won critical and popular acclaim with her simple, powerful concept for the Vietnam Memorial in Washington. This 70-by-70 foot earth sculpture was designed so that students and visitors can actually lie down in the troughs of the earth waves. *Just east of the François-Xavier Bagnoud Building, 1320 Beal south of Hayward.*

◆ **Phoenix Memorial Laboratory.** The two-megawatt experimental nuclear reactor built here in 1954 was one of the first university reactors in the postwar surge of research interest in peaceful applications of atomic energy. Thirty- to sixty-minute tours are available by appointment (48 hours' advance notice is requested) Monday through Friday. *Bonisteel Blvd. near Beal. (313) 764-6220.*

◆ **Gerald R. Ford Presidential Library.** This is one of only nine presidential libraries in the country. It's here because Ford was a 1935 graduate of the U-M. Interested citizens and scholars from around the world come here to delve into myriad issues affected by the Ford presidency. The library's 15 million pages of documents brought from Washington include all of Ford's White House papers as well as the papers of certain key advisors such as economist Arthur Burns and energy chief Frank Zarb. Some papers remain classified and are kept in locked vaults, but most are available for public scrutiny. *1000 Beal south of Bonisteel Blvd. (313) 741-2218. Mon-Fri 8:45-4:45. ♿ Free.*

◆ **Bentley Historical Library.** Home of the Michigan Historical Collections, one of the three big archives of Michigan history. The others are the State Archives in Lansing, housed in the Historical Museum complex (page 426) and the Burton Collection in the Detroit Public Library (page 255). A gallery shows **exhibits** that change every two months. The general public is welcome to look at original documents, which include the papers of many political figures (governors Frank Murphy and William Milliken, Senator Phillip Hart, and many more), health food progenitor Dr. John Harvey Kellogg, 1960s radical John Sinclair, and the Detroit Urban League. Civil War letters and C. H. Stoner's collection of historical railroad photos are outstanding. Inexpensive photograph copies and enlargements of the over one million graphic images can be made, including postcards of Michigan hometowns of any era and University of Michigan campus scenes. They're nifty gift ideas. *1150 Beal at Bonisteel. Park by building or across the street. (313) 764-3482. Mon-Fri 8:30-5, and from September thru May, Sat 9-12:30.* ᛒ

◆ **Stearns Collection of Musical Instruments.** The core of this unusual collection is 1,400 instruments collected by wealthy Detroit drug manufacturer Frederick Stearns and donated to the university in 1899. They include some extremely rare Asian and African instruments, along with European instruments like a Baroque cello in almost-original condition and a recorder from the time of Bach.

The collection, now over 2,200 items and growing, is encyclopedic, representing instruments of all sorts from throughout the world. New acquisitions, such as the first Moog synthesizer to be sold, reflect an effort to collect 20th-century materials. Interesting **lecture-demonstrations** are held at 2 o'clock on the second Sundays of September, October, January, and February. *In the Dow Towsley south wing of the Moore Building, the main part of the School of Music, at the end of Baits Dr. (Baits is off Broadway at the top of the hill, about 1/4 mile west of Plymouth Rd. Or, from Murfin on North Campus, take Duffield to Baits.) (313) 763-4389. Wed-Sat 10-5, Sun 1-6.* ᛒ *Free.*

TRAVELLING "EDUCATIONAL SUITCASES" ABOUT THE ANCIENT WORLD
. . . . . can be rented for $20 ($25 shipped) from the **Kelsey Museum of Archaeology.** For grades K-4 and 5-12. They include books, games, puzzles, artifacts, and bibliography on subjects like Egypt, writing, Greek mythology, ancient social problems, the Near East, and Greek art. Lesson plans lead up to a play, fair, or festival. Call (313) 747-0441 or 747-4167 information and tours.

THE HEART OF THE U-M CAMPUS . . . . . is the **Diag**, the diagonal walk crossing the original 40-acre campus between the retail districts on State and North University and on South University at East University. Many major classroom buildings are clustered here, backing up to a plaza in front of the **Graduate Library**. (Its eighth-floor map room has one of the best views in town.) Countless rallies and demonstrations have been held here. On pleasant days, this is a good place to see students and their myriad organizations and causes set up here to garner support. The action spills over into the adjacent **Fishbowl**, a large-windowed connecting hall between classroom buildings to the west.

THE FIRST STUDENT UNION . . . . . was the venerable **Michigan Union** on State at the head of South University, built in 1920. On its front steps President

Kennedy first announced the Peace Corps, saying, "Ask not what your country can do for you, but what you can do for your country." For many years women were only allowed entrance to the Union through a side door, and then only for special events. (Women alumnae built the much smaller Michigan League.) The second-floor **billiard room** was the last male bastion to fall, in the late 1960s. It remains one the Union's most interesting areas. With oak paneling and quality tables, the room retains the atmosphere of gentlemen's gaming rooms in decades past. Some of the country's best players still drop in to play here. In the slickly remodeled Union basement is a big **Barnes and Noble student book store** and large **food court**. . . . . . The student-manned first-floor information desk is a helpful place for visitors.

CARILLON CONCERTS BY A PLAYFUL FOUNTAIN . . . . . The Union's feminine counterpart as a student center was the 1929 **Michigan League** on North University at the Ingalls Mall. The mall is a rather grand axis between the graduate library and the monumental Art Deco/neoclassical Rackham Building on Washington Street. Smaller than the Union, the League has long been popular for its well-stocked newsstand at the front desk, its large and excellent **cafeteria**, and its basement grill. The League also houses the 700-seat **Lydia Mendelssohn Theater**, Ann Arbor's most congenial space for theatrical performances. . . . . . In front of the League is the delightful **Cooley Fountain** created by Swedish sculptor **Carl Milles** in 1940, when he was on the Cranbrook faculty. It shows Triton, the Greek god of the sea, frolicking with his children. . . . . . Across from the League is **Burton Tower**, a campus landmark. At its top is the **Baird Carillon**. Its 53 bronze bells weigh from 12 pounds to 12 tons. **Half-hour concerts** begin weekdays at noon when school is in session. During that time you can go up to the top and see the single player pound hand and foot levers in quick succession to ring the bells. The tower offers a fine view of the campus. On the eighth floor is the **Japanese music room**, with tatami mats. Its instruments can be heard when School of Music students practice there Tuesdays between noon and 9 p.m., September through April. Likewise, the **gamelan** or Indonesian orchestra can be heard in practice on the fourth floor Thursday afternoons and evenings.

A BIT OF OXFORD AND CAMBRIDGE IN THE MIDDLE WEST . . . . . Right across State Street from the Union is the **Law Quadrangle**, home of the U-M's highly ranked law school. This picturesque court of Gothic buildings was built between 1923 and 1933 and largely modeled on Cambridge University in England. The Law Quad's quality of workmanship was rare even in the 1920s. The striking reading room of the **old Law Library** at the south side of the quadrangle has richly ornamented blue and gold plaster medallions decorating the ceiling.

A MUST FOR U-M SPORTS FANS. . . . . . is the big, impressive **Margaret Towsley Sports Museum** at Schembechler Hall on South State at McKinley. It's devoted to glorifying Wolverine athletics. The short entrance hallway has a visual timeline of big events in Michigan sports history. (Interesting how the first female athlete appears only in the 1970s!) . . . . . The snazzy visuals go way beyond the usual trophies and action photos. They're accented with objects like an ancient football uniform. The shoes alone weighed several pounds. The teams of Michigan's legendary football coaches get several display cases each, but each minor sport has a case, too. Far more women are seen there, The late Mrs. Towsley, a daughter of Dow Chemical's founder, was an interesting blend of progressivism and conservativism. She had a strong interest in both women's athletics and in the Wolverines. She stipulated that the museum do something on **women in sports**, which is indeed an option on the video monitors. But the show-stopper for most visitors is choosing the **"Great Moments in Wolverine Football"** option and replaying and reanalyzing memorable plays. Among the museum visitors are often former varsity players and their relatives, and high school prospects and their parents. It's a rare chance for the general public to see a little of the subtle, highly regulated, big-stakes recruiting process in action. . . . . A comfortable small theater shows several more **videos**, including a rah-rah Wolverine athletics retrospective extolling the U-M's vaunted tradition of "student athletes, the best and brightest in the land" (!!??), *Hours are Mon-Fri 11-4, Fri evening 5:30-7:30, Sat 10-2,* &.

THE BIGGEST COLLEGIATE STADIUM IN THE U.S. . . . . . . is **Michigan Stadium** on Stadium at Main. It seats over 100,000, but they're packed in mighty tight. The stadium is dug into the side of a valley wall; the football field lies directly over Allen's Creek. If you put your ear down on the 50-yard line when the stands are empty, you will hear the creek running below. Next door is **Crisler Arena**, which seats 1,360. It hosts concerts, NCAA wrestling and gymnastics matches, as well as U-M basketball.

Bookstores in Ann Arbor

The bookstore mecca of the Midwest is centered at Liberty and State, near the U-M campus.

FEW places in the country have as lively and high-quality a concentration of bookstores, both new and used, as does central Ann Arbor. Its anchor is the flagship of the fabulously successful Borders chain, which began here as a humble second-story bookshop. Increasingly the town has become a magnet attracting book-lovers from distant cities.

Connoisseurs of antiquarian books would do well to pick up a listing of area dealers at any used-book store. It will direct them to several distinguished home book shops, such as Jan Longone's internationally known **Wine and Food Library**, which deals exclusively in out-of-print and rare publications on wine, food, and gastronomy. It's by appointment only; call (313) 663-4894.

◆ **Borders Books and Music.** Ann Arbor was a virtual trade book wasteland in 1971 when the two Borders brothers, former grad students, started their store in an obscure second-story retail space on William and kept expanding until it became the first true book superstore in the country. Now one of over 150 Borders nationwide, it remains one of the finest U.S. bookstores, with an impressive 150,000 titles. Secrets of its success: knowledgeable, helpful clerks; a relentlessly attentive manager, Joe Gable; pleasing ambiance; and outstanding back list. Quality remainders include some videos. Big children's and young adult section, with tables. An impressive selection of maps and better posters. The new location features an espresso bar with events bulletin boards, a video and CD section, and a multi-media area. **Weekly events** include a **children's hour** Saturdays at 11 a.m. and **Upstairs at Borders**, with live music, Sundays at 1 p.m. Lots of **free publications** about local happenings in the vestibule. Because Ann Arbor is a huge book market in an influential academic town and also headquarters of the #2 U. S. bookstore chain, the Ann Arbor Borders is a prime stop on authors' book tours, even very short ones. Big draws have included Pulitzer Prizewinner Richard Ford and Walter Mosley, the Easy Rollins mystery writer. But don't expect to see the likes of Jackie Collins here, or Charlton Heston, or Dan Quayle. They read at other Borders in metro Detroit. *612 E. Liberty between State and Maynard. Books: (313) 668-7652. Music: (313) 668-7100. Mon-Thurs 9-10, Fri & Sat 9-11, Sun 10-8.* &

Ann Arbor gets on lots of book tours because it's a huge book market close to the sixth-largest U.S. metropolis *and* it's corporate headquarters of the #2 U.S. book chain. Hillary Rodham Clinton came here to plug her book at the country's first Borders. Founding manager Joe Gable is at the right. Also, many nationally known authors live nearby and speak locally. Pick up monthly events schedules at Borders, Barnes & Noble, Shaman Drum, and Little Professor.

◆ **Shaman Drum Bookshop**. This serene shop specializes in serious books in the humanities, chosen by its highly knowledgeable staff. Departments include literature and literary studies, poetry, Buddhism and Native American culture (owner Karl Pohrt's specialties), anthropology, philosophy, religion, history, psychology, the environment and science, travel, children's, visual and performing arts, classical studies, and Latino/a, Asian America, cultural and gender studies. The store imports books direct, even from India and Sri Lanka, in its specialties. Frequent book signings, poetry readings, and publication parties. Trade manager Keith Taylor, winner of a major poetry award, is most helpful at recommending good books for many tastes. (He's the one with the curly blond hair only none on top.) A fine place to connect up with the area's book people, writers, and scholars. Shaman Drum has been around since 1980. Now it's in a large and much more visible first-floor location, with quadruple the inventory in virtually the same categories. Shaman Drum is trying to lead the way in showing that a highly focused independent bookstore can survive in the shadow of an extremely well-run superstore. *311 S. State. (313) 662-7407. Mon-Sat 10-10, Sun 12-6.* ♿

◆ **Kaleidoscope.** Big space full of oddball old stuff: 40,000 used books, including the best collection in the state of vintage paperbacks from 1940s and 1950s. Strong in science fiction, mysteries, children's books, and modern first editions. Also cameras, toys, magazines, sheet music, posters, and more. A knack for presentation makes it look great. Ample room means you can find things smaller stores couldn't afford to keep around. *217 S. State. (313) 995-9887. Mon-Wed 10-6, Thurs-Sat 10-8, Sun 1-5.*

◆ **David's Books.** Legendary, somewhat scruffy upstairs store, crowded with some 50,000 used books at quite reasonable prices. Strong in general history, political science, literature. An important part of the Ann Arbor book scene. Good collection of new books on chess. *622 E. Liberty at State. (313) 665-8017. Mon-Sat 9:30 to 9 or 9:30, Sun 12-9. &: no.*

◆ **Dawn Treader.** Rambling spaces with general line, specialties in sci-fi, mysteries, natural history, math, science, philosophy, art, Americana, exploration. Some rare and early printing books. *514 E. Liberty near State. (313) 995-1008. May-Oct: Mon-Thurs 11-8, Fri 11-9, Sat 10-9, Sun 12-6.*

◆ **Books in General.** Big, airy, loft-like space. A big, round table makes this a pleasant place to sit and browse through a huge stock of used books in literature, science, humanities. General line, better than usual sections in science and technology, foreign languages. *332 S. State (upstairs). (313) 769-1250. Mon-Sat 10-8, Sun 12-5.*

◆ **U-M Barnes & Noble Bookstore.** Spiffy big college textbook store also has, among its general reading books, a special section with English and American paperback editions of the classics. *In the basement of the Michigan Union, on State at South University. (313) 995-8877. Mon-Thurs 9-6, Fri 9-5, Sat 10-5, Sun 12-5.*

◆ **Ulrich's Book Store.** The oldest textbook store in town, Ulrich's

Shaman Drum owner Karl Pohrt emphasizes readings and publication parties. Allen Ginsberg attracts throngs. Here Janet Kauffman, whose stories and poems appear in *The New Yorker*, talks with fans. She teaches at Eastern Michigan University and lives and farms in Lenawee County.

also has a good art supplies department and a big selection of U-M insignia items and inexpensive posters. *East University at South University. (313) 662-3201. Mon-Fri 9-6, Sat 9:30-5.*

◆ **Adventures in Chess.** 800 chess titles in "Michigan's only full-time chess store studio. Also: mail order, chess sets and supplies, lessons, weekly clubs for adults and kids, tables to play at. 220 S. Main below Elmo's T-shirts. *(313) 665-0612. Tues-Fri noon-8, Wed & Thurs to 10 p.m., Sat 10-10, and by appt.*

◆ **Common Language.** "For women and their friends." Feminist and gay studies, erotica, also mainstream books like detective series where the detective is not a white man. Kids' books stress positives of being different, having a gay parent, etc. *214 South Fourth, downtown between Liberty and Washington. (313) 663-0036. Mon-Sat 10:30-8, Sun 1-5.*

◆ **Aunt Agatha's Book Shop.** Delightful ambiance in this mystery book shop. Knowledgeable owner sells both new and used. Also: true crime books, puzzles, and related items. *213 Fourth. (313) 769-1114. Mon 11-5:30; Tues-Thurs 11-7; Fri-Sat 11-8, Sun noon-5.*

◆ **Falling Water Books and Collectibles.** Books on various forms of spiritual and personal growth, plus crystals, other minerals, gifts. See page 153. *213 S. Main. (313) 747-9810. Mon-Sat 10-10, Sun 12-6.*

◆ **After Words.** Attractively laid out and good for browsing, this good-sized store carries drastically discounted new books. A third are remainders, two-thirds are still in print but at least 40% off. Publishers' overstock of university presses a specialty. So are art and children's' books. Some cheap books on tape, too. Owner Steve Kelly searches out smaller quantities of remaindered books than the big chains, so there are more *219 S. Main. (313) 996-2808. Mon-Sat 10-10, Sun 12-8.*

◆ **Main Street News.** Unslick and personal, this new downtown newsstand has quickly become a gathering spot and destination for all types, including specialists like car designers, political science professors, and fetishists of various kinds. More space, better display, owner involvement make it the top newsstand in a word-oriented town. Standout sections include computer magazines, politics (right and left plus analytical), collectors' specialties, literary journals, auto magazines (from racing to marketing to collecting cars). Demand has created a big foreign section, with lots of German, Spanish-language, Dutch, and Russian magazines and British tabloid weeklies consumed by royal-watchers. Extensive section of out-of-town papers gives clues as to what parts of the U.S. are hot.

220. S. Main. (313) 761-4365. Mon-Thurs 7:30 a.m.-10 p.m., Fri & Sat to midnight, Sun 7:30-6. ♿

♦ **West Side Book Shop.** This delightful shop fits the traditional image of a used bookstore: antique in a comfortable way, cluttered, accented with old prints, and personal — conducive to browsing and chatting. Space constraints make for higher quality. General-line, with nautical topics, exploration, and photography as specialties. Edward Curtis Indian photographs, other old photographs in antique-filled back room. *113 W. Liberty just west of Main. (313) 995-1891. Mon-Fri 11-6, Sat 10-5.*

♦ **Crazy Wisdom.** The owners have expanded and deepened titles in metaphysical and holistic subjects, including holistic health, bodywork, Jungian and transpersonal psychology, Buddhism, and women's spirituality. Also, audiotapes, jewelry, and interesting objects. *206 N. Fourth Ave. (313) 665-2757. Mon & Tues 10-6, Wed-Fri 10-8, Sat 10-6, Sun 12-6.*

♦ **Barnes & Noble.** Another in the fast-growing B&N superstore chain. Especially big children's section. Lots of bargain remaindered books. Espresso bar. Long hours. *Washtenaw at Huron Parkway on Ann Arbor's east side. (313) 677-6475. 9-11 daily.*

♦ **Little Professor.** The flagship store in the Little Professor franchise system. Nowhere nearly as complete as Borders, but better than a mall bookshop. *Westgate Shopping Center (Stadium between Liberty and Huron). (313) 662-4110. Mon-Sat 9-11, Sun 8-10.*

♦ **Geography Limited.** Carries wide selection of maps, including every Michigan topo map. Wide selection of atlases, tour guides, and geography-oriented games. *2390 Winewood (close to Jackson and Stadium). (313) 668-1810. Tues-Wed noon-6, Fri Noon-7, Sat 10-6.*

♦ **Webster's.** Large bookstore in northern Ann Arbor shopping center includes good magazine selection. *2607 Plymouth, in Traver Village. (313) 662-6150. 8-11 daily.*

RARE BOOKS IN A STATELY SETTING . . . . . Next door to the President's House on South University across from Tappan, the **Clements Library** has one of the country's leading collections of rare books, manuscripts, and maps on America through the 19th century. The library is patterned on an Italian Renaissance villa. The style was chosen to reflect the age of great explorers and cartographers who opened up the Americas. Beyond the ornate bronze grilles on the entrance doors is the grand main reading room. Antiques are on display throughout. A grandfather clock comes from George Washington's 1782-83 headquarters at New Windsor, New York, a gift from Carl Van Doren, who used the library to write his *Secret History of the Revolution.* A collection of Amberina glassware, fashionable in the 1880s, was made by the New England firm which eventually moved to Toledo, Ohio, and became Libbey Glass. At the west end of the room is one of the most popular paintings of 18th-century England, Benjamin West's *The Death of General Wolfe.* The painting shows British General Wolfe, fatally wounded, surrounded by his staff. The year was 1759, just after Wolfe had completed a victory over the French at Quebec, sealing British control over North America. *909 S. University at Tappan. (313) 764-2347. Mon-Fri 10:30-12, 1-5.*

A HIDDEN CACHE OF MORE USED BOOKS. . . . . is **The Friends of the Ann Arbor Public Library Book Shop** in the basement of the Ann Arbor Public Library, S. Fifth at Division. In a town that loves its library and ranks at or near the top in U.S. book-buying per capita, a lot of those books end up at the library book shop. *Open weekends, October through April. Sat 10-4, Sun 1:30-4:30.* &

TWO MORE DESTINATIONS FOR BOOK-LOVERS. . . . . are **John King Books** in Detroit, the legendary used and rare book shop (page 242) that fills an old factory with rigorously well-organized stock approaching a million titles, and **Book Beat** (810-968-1190). at 26010 Greenfield in Oak Park just north of Detroit, in a shopping center anchored by K Mart and a fabulous deli. This bookstore/gallery is a highly personal, sophisticated, and creative blend of the owners' interests in art, photography, and children's books. A rare case where "cutting edge" isn't a misnomer.

A HANDY MICHIGAN GUIDE TO ANTIQUARIAN BOOK DEALERS . . . . . in homes as well as shops can be had through the Curious Book Shop, 307 E. Grand River, East Lansing, MI 48823. Stop by, or send a check for 75¢ or a $1 bill plus self-addressed, stamped envelope. The well-organized booklet lists some 150 dealers and specialties (Civil War, cookbooks, radical politics, fishing, Masons, African-American and much more).

Ann Arbor record stores

For CDs, tapes, and even vinyl,
central Ann Arbor is the best between the coasts.

MANY MUSIC-LOVERS from across the U.S. consider Ann Arbor the best place to shop for recordings because of the outstanding comparison-shopping permitted by the concentration of high-quality stores. In its 15 years here, Schoolkids has grown into the musical equivalent of the Ann Arbor Borders in books. Most record stores are open evenings and Sunday afternoons, and most are clustered near State and Liberty just northeast of the U-M Central Campus. Park in the ramp by Borders, entered off Maynard or Thompson, or in the ramp on Washington between State and Division.

◆ **Schoolkids Records & Tapes**. Early on, Schoolkids learned that having a great back list in the right town can build a market dramatically. Its strength is its breadth and depth in everything from rock and jazz to country, folk, blues, and new age, including esoteric labels and foreign pressings. Some CDs it imports direct. Vinyl, which held on longer here, is being phased out. No returns. A good place to pick up information; the staff is knowledgeable and helpful. Now Schoolkids has opened **The Annex** next door for alternative music and used recordings. *523 E. Liberty. (313) 994-8031. Mon-Sat 10-9:30, Sun noon-8.*

◆ **SKR Classical.** Bigger than ever, with 20,000 titles. It's a Schoolkids' subsidiary, managed by Jim Leonard. Passionately opinionated when he was a music critic, Leonard is a most approachable advisor for people who are intimidated by classical music and their ignorance of it. He strives for a user-friendly, anti-snobbish store, started a **newsletter**, and instituted Sunday **music appreciation classes** from 1 to 2 p.m. SKR Classical has the state's biggest collection of classical CDs and a great many tapes. It also has scores and many pirate tapes of live performances. *539 E. Liberty. (313) 995-5051. (800) 272-4506. Mon-Sat 10-9, Sun 12-6.*

◆ **Borders Books and Music.** Following the pattern established by the Borders chain's newer stores, its Ann Arbor flagship is now into CDs in a significant way. Many stations let you hear a good selection of many kinds of music. *612 E. Liberty between State & Maynard. Music: (313) 668-7100. Mon-Sat 9-9, Sun 11-6.* ৬

◆ **Discount Records.** Discount covers all the pop, jazz, and classical bases and keeps local prices competitive. Though part of a chain, its Ann Arbor outlet has an intelligent selection. *State and Liberty. (313) 665-3679. Mon-Thurs 9-9, Fri & Sat 9-10, Sun 12-8.*

◆ **State Discount.** A campus general store, State is known by music buffs not as a source of shampoo and snacks but as the cheapest place in town to buy just-released, mass-volume CDs. *309 S. State. (313) 994-1262. Mon-Fri 8:30-9, Sat 10-7, Sun 12-6.*

◆ **Wazoo Records.** This upstairs store has a well-organized stock of CD records and tapes plus some vinyl (mostly rock, but with big sections of jazz, country, folk, classical). Reasonable prices ($4.50 for most vinyl records, $5-10 for used CDs, tapes $4 to $5). A stock of newly released CDs encourages trade-ins. Everything is guaranteed. The only scratchy records you'll find here are rare ones. Good prices paid for used records. *336 1/2 S. State (upstairs) (313) 761-8686. Mon-Fri 10-8, Sat 10-6, Sun 12-6.*

◆ **Encore Recordings of Ann Arbor.** What used to be the venerable Liberty Music has evolved into a store specializing in used music of all types and in all formats, including sheet music. Not just CDs and vinyl but cylinders, 45s, 78s, and piano rolls, plus books on music and posters. *417 E. Liberty near Maynard. (313) 662-6776. Mon-Wed 10-6, Thurs-Sat 10-8, Sun 1-5.*

◆ **Earth Wisdom Music.** A purveyor of music that used to be considered New Age, for meditation, relaxation, guided imagery, "creative ambiance," and dance. Earth Wisdom pioneered the genre. Also, Native American and world music. *Inside Seva Restaurant, 314 E. Liberty. (313) 769-0969. Mon & Tues 11-7, Wed-Sat 11-8:30, Sun 11-2:30.*

◆ **PJ's Used Records and CDs.** PJ's is a hip, intense used record store run by knowledgeable jazz, R&B, and blues enthusiasts. "Opinions rendered on all subjects," they advertise. Jammed with recordings, it keeps adding more as music fans abandon their vinyl collections in favor of CD. *617B (upstairs above Subway) Packard between Hill and State. (313) 663-3441. Mon-Thurs 10-9, Fri & Sat 10-10, Sun noon-8.*

◆ **Tower Records.** Big outlet of the coast-to-coast outlet. Local manager keeps unusually strong collection of obscure rock imports. *1214 South University just west of Forest (upstairs). Park (if you're lucky) in Forest ramp. (313) 741-9600. 9-midnight daily. ꬱ thru elevator in hall.*

Zingerman's Delicatessen

*This fantastic deli also showcases
choice foods from around the world.*

DEPENDING on who you talk to, this is the best deli in the Midwest or even the world. Sandwiches (over 100 in all) are huge and delicious; the $7.95 corned beef Reuben is the best-seller. The extensive takeout counter offers tempting salads and favorites, from deli classics like coleslaw ($1.99/side), chicken soup, and noodle kugel ($2.50/slice) to inventive potato salads, the popular Thai noodle salad, and salmon-dill pasta salad ($5/side) made with Irish smoked salmon. Bruce Aidells' sausages from San Francisco and unusual hand-made cheeses, domestic and import- ed, help make the deli counter absolutely top-of-the-line. The selec- tion of olive oils, vinegars, and mustards is outstanding. The owners do a great job of searching out exceptional jams, relishes, and good- ies of all kinds. Free **samples** are plentiful, and interesting, educa- tional **promotional events** are frequent. Call (313) 668-2779 ext. 104 or (313) 663-DELI. The fun, information-packed free **handouts** are a short course in food. Call (313) 663-0974 to get their monthly **newsletter** ($10/year). More foods, including fresh produce and an unusual array of dried beans, are sold at **Zingerman's Practical Produce** a block away in Kerrytown o Fifth Avenue. A big part of what makes it practical are recipes about how to incorporate these excellent ingredients in simple everyday fare.

Food writer and *Atlantic* senior editor Corby Kummer enthused in *Eating Well* magazine, "How does a store in such a town offer an unquestionably great selection of the world's cheeses, perhaps the finest teas sold in America, corned beef and pastrami so richly fla- vored as to make even New Yorkers jealous, a brilliantly edited col- lection of olive oils, vinegars, fruit preserves and pastas – in all, between 2,500 and 3,000 of the best foods and flavors anywhere? And why is the service in this remarkable store the sort of utterly professional and knowledgeable service Americans expect to find in Europe – gently blended with the concern and warmth that Europeans think of as American? In short, what has Ann Arbor done to deserve Zingerman's?"

Jim Harrison, novelist and noted cook, seems to come close to a spiritual epiphany in the former neighborhood grocery store on Detroit Street, between Kerrytown and the Treasure Mart. He wrote

An old corner grocery at the edge of the Kerrytown/Farmers' Market area is Zingerman's home Its success is based on a rare mix of knowledge-able employees and enthusiastic service.

in *Esquire*, "In Zingerman's, I get the mighty reassurance that the world can't be totally bad if there's this much good to eat, the same flowing emotions I get at Fauchon in Paris, Harrod's food department in London, Balducci's or Dean and DeLuca in New York, only at Zingerman's there is a warmth and goodwill lacking in the others."

In 1982, when they started Zingerman's, Saginaw (from Detroit) and Weinzweig (from Chicago) wanted to start the kind of deli that would sell the kind of food grandmothers cooked and used, whether they were Jewish or German or Italian. And they wanted to create a workplace that they would enjoy coming to every day.

Those values are in good part responsible for their success — along with a lot of smarts and passion and hard work and study. For years Zingerman's searched out better and better sources for the cheeses and olive oils and meats it sells. Now the business is taking a more active role in supporting emerging producers of hand-crafted foods.

Weinzweig writes much of the catalog and the store's vast amount of promotional and educational material about food. He's the outgoing front man, while the intensely focused, no-nonsense Saginaw deals more with behind-the-scene operations and Food

Gatherers, the leftover food-for-the-poor community service arm Zingerman's founded. Weinzweig has even joined a writers' support group to improve his writing. He is the proud author of a slim and authoritative book on olive oil. Most of Zingerman's treatises on food categories (olive oils, cheeses, olives, salsas, etcetera) are available free as handouts at the deli. The catalog and mail-order business was conceived as a way to build on Zingerman's out-of-town customer base and expand sales without cloning the original store.

But other places can and do carry off the hand-made food thing. What makes Zingerman's stand out from its New York and continental counterparts is its Midwestern-ness. The friendly, knowledgeable staff is astoundingly polite and patient. No matter who you are and what you know or don't know, they are *nice.*

Because Zingerman's refuses to grow by starting branches or franchises, it has legions of imitators intent on ripping off its interior design and display techniques and tracking down its food sources. What these wanna-bes ought to focus on is how Zingerman's hires and trains a staff that serves customers so cheerfully and becomes so knowledgeable about food. In fact, Zingerman's now does consulting for a fee. Savvy local employers in radically different fields (like the University of Michigan art museum) hire Zingerman's "grads" for their outstanding attentiveness to customer service and knowledgeability as basic to marketing.

Zingerman's started its own bakery, **Zingerman's Bakehouse**, in 1992, because Weinzweig and Saginaw weren't happy with the rye bread they could get for sandwiches. "Unfortunately, much of what has passed for rye bread in this country over the years is merely bland wheat bread made with a dash of rye flour and a few caraway seeds for flavor," Weinzweig writes. "They have little in common with the rye bread my grandparents were eating in New York and Chicago 70 or 80 years ago. Jewish-style breads are the core of what we do at Zingerman's. . . . [They] are made with a natural sour starter, a bit of yeast, rye and wheat flours. . . . These rye breads have a shiny, crackling crust when they come out of the oven, a crust that's chewy and satisfying every time you bite into it." Plain Jewish rye is $4.50 for a two-pound loaf. Not all breads are traditional. Some are originals, like the moist, rich chocolate cherry bread ($7 for a 1 1/2-pound loaf), and farm bread with scallions and toasted walnuts ($5 for a 1 1/2-pound loaf). Bakehouse breads are also sold at the bakery near Briarwood; call for directions.

If all this sounds too good to be true, it sometimes is. The down side of Zingerman's can be its customers. Often there are too many of them. Sometimes they are extremely pretentious, self-important, inconsiderate people who are quite comfortable spending what seems like hours tasting and coming to a decision. That's fine when the store is uncrowded, but if you're in a long line behind an overbearing foodie, it's an ordeal waiting to buy your simple loaf of bread to take home to dinner. At the wrong time, Zingerman's can seem far more like hell than heaven — a peculiarly contemporary form of hell, at that.

Straight from Zingerman's deli employees, here are **tips for shopping and eating** at Zingerman's. The store is divided into the deli counter, where groceries are bought, and the sandwich counter, where customers order sandwiches to eat here or to go, and other deli items to eat on the premises. Then they are seated at across the way at **Zingerman's Next Door**, the sit-down area in a spiffily redone old house, or at picnic tables in the court. They are called when their order is ready. The atmosphere at Zingerman's Next Door is quite relaxed, in contrast to the deli's tight spaces. Coffee drinkers are encouraged to linger in the evening over coffee; Community High kids like to come here.

◆ **Order ahead.** Call (313) 663-DELI and leave your name and estimated time of arrival. This works great for sandwiches, but it means you can't taste before you decide on deli items. Piles of take-out menus are at cash registers by every counter, and by the espresso machine at Zingerman's Next Door. Request the mail-order *catalog of good food* from a cashier, but be aware that its selection is more limited than what's in the store.

◆ **Early in the morning and early in the week are less crowded.** Monday and Tuesday mornings are usually the least crowded times, unless it's a holiday. Weekends are unpredictable but usually busy. When the nearby Farmers' Market is underway on Wednesday and Saturday mornings, there's a line by 7 a.m. In winter, weekend mornings are slower.

◆ The **retail deli counter** is busiest from about 9 a.m. to 11 a.m., after work, and probably all day on weekends.

◆ The **sandwich counter** gets busy by 11 a.m. weekdays, with a lull from 2:30 to 3:30 and even 4 p.m. Evenings it slows down after 8

*422 Detroit at Kingsley. From Huron (Bus. I-94) or Catherine, take North Fourth Ave. north to Kingsley, then turn right. Look for a parking place along Kingsley or Detroit. (313) 663-DELI (also call DELI to order ahead). Mail-order: (313) 769-1625; FAX: (313) 769-1235. **Deli** open daily 7 a.m. and 10 p.m. ♿ **Zingerman's Next Door** (313-663-JAVA) open to 11 p.m. ♿: ramp on side.*

Miller Motors

In Ypsilanti's historic Depot Town, a Hudson
auto dealer, little changed from the 1940s.

IN FRONT of this old Hudson dealership is a vintage Hudson sign, and in the show window is a spiffy-looking Hudson coupe. This isn't a mirage — or a museum. It's the business of Jack Miller, whose father started selling Hudsons here in 1933. Though production ceased in 1957, Miller still trades in Hudsons. His place is probably the best in the world to get Hudson parts. A few are still in their original cartons, some half a century old. They have been bought from old warehouses around the country.

In the service area behind the sales room are an array of Hudson cars for sale, as well as Miller's private collection. The inventory of ten to twelve Hudsons constantly changes as buyers for the sedans, convertibles, and trucks are found.

Hudson aficionados often stop by to chat. Miller affably shares his wealth of knowledge about Hudsons with visitors. He explains that they were first manufactured in 1909 and named after financial backer J. L. Hudson, the Detroit department store magnate. The Hudson name was sullied in the mid-1950s when Nash took over the firm and turned out what some consider gaudy imitations of the real thing. But the Hudsons of the 1940s were extraordinary automobiles, Miller points out, they were fast but stable highway cars, engineered and built extremely well.

Looking around the showroom is a treat. The walls are covered with old Hudson promotional posters, as well as with photos and other antique artifacts. Visitors are welcome to browse.

100 E. Cross Street at River just east of the Depot Town historic commercial area. From I-94, take Huron St. exit 183 north about 1¹/₄ miles, then east on Cross. (313) 482-5200. Open Saturdays 9-5 (except for lunchtime). Open during the week by advance arrangement only. Wheelchair accessible.

YPSILANTI'S RICH AUTO-MAKING HISTORY . . . Next door to Miller, the **Ypsilanti Automotive Heritage Collection** celebrates the city's auto history. Apex Motors produced the ACE car here from 1920 to 1922. Preston Tucker made the "Tucker Torpedo," an innovative military vehicle. Kaisers and Frasers

1 Huron St. historic buildings.
Impressive 19th-century mansions line bluff overlooking Huron River. Built before the car industry transformed the city into a blue collar town, they evoke a more scenic, pre-industrial Ypsilanti.

2 Historical Museum.
Humdrum Victorian rooms, but great display of underwear which made Ypsi mills famous. Wonderful arrowhead collection, a giant dollhouse made from Depression-era crates, and other eccentric items.

3 Depot Town.
Old, once-bustling commercial district fueled by two train depots. It's now home to bars and antique shops highlighted by the Side Track with good hamburgers and big ornate bar. Good food co-op around the corner.

4 Miller Motors.
Long after the beloved Hudson auto ceased production, this Hudson dealership keeps trading both parts and cars, retaining its 1940s look. Now there's an auto museum next door featuring the cars and

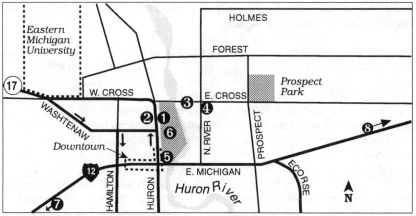

5 Materials Unlimited.
Extraordinarily big selection of vintage architectural items, both antiques and reproductions. Many ornate fixtures, including stained glass, columns, and hardware, makes it a fun place to browse.

6 Riverside & Frog Island Parks.
Scenic Huron River parks host great events—June's Frog Island Blues/jazz Festival, August's big Heritage Festival, and December holiday light display. Call (313) 482-4920 for details.

7 Schmidt's Antiques.
One of the country's best places to get English antique furniture. The monthly auction is a comic treat just to watch. Some tremendous values. You can also buy daily from the showroom. 5138 W. Michigan. (313) 434-2660.

8 Yankee Air Museum/Willow Run Airport.
Terrific collection of old military aircraft at the historic Willow Run airport where Ford built big bombers during WWII See Air Corps veterans refurbishing everything from Saber jets to a hulking B-52.

Highlights of Ypsilanti

0   1/2   1
           mile

were made at the Willow Run B-24 plant from 1946 to 1953. Next door at Willow Run G.M began making trucks in 1955, then Corvairs from 1959 to 1969, and finally Caprices until 1993. Ypsilanti companies made everything from seat belts to convertible tops for the Big Three. Displays remember their role in making Southeast Michigan the auto center of the country. *112 E. Cross St. (313) 482-5200. Sat 10-4, Sun 1-5. Free.*

ANOTHER STOP ON AN AUTOMOTIVE NOSTALGIA TOUR . . . . . is the former home of **Preston Tucker**, father of the innovative **Tucker automobile**, and hero of Francis Ford Coppola's movie *Tucker*. He lived in the big white house at 110 North Park, just north of Michigan Avenue and just a block east of Depot Town. From River Street in Depot Town, go east a block to Park and turn right. As owner of the Ypsilanti Machine Tool Company on Grove Street behind his house, Tucker built a remote gun turret for the Army, in addition to racing Indy cars and customizing automobiles. A rare Tucker car can be seen in the Gilmore Car Museum near Kalamazoo (page 105).

INTERESTING ARCHITECTURE AND ANTIQUE SHOPS . . . . . are in the 19th-century commercial district along East Cross called **Depot Town**. It features some popular bars, several antique and resale shops, a food co-op, and other attractions. Depot Town actually became the city's main downtown for awhile after the railroad arrived in 1838 from Detroit. The passenger and freight depots are still here. The **Michigan Central passenger station** on North River Street, now one story high, is a pale shadow of the ornate three-story building and tower built here in 1863. A fire and train collision have reduced it to its present humble state. . . . . Across the tracks, the **freight depot** is a long Italianate structure from 1875. It is now headquarters for the **Ypsilanti Farmers' Market**, open Wednesdays and Saturdays from 7 a.m. to 3 p.m. Many of the upper stories of the 1850s and 1860s brick storefronts along Cross are now apartments, and the area, with its own sprightly neighborhood publication, has a sense of camaraderie. The 1859 **Follett House** at 17-25 E. Cross was known as one of the finest hotels on the Michigan Central line. The third-floor ballroom hosted Buffalo Bill, Tom Thumb, and other 19th-century celebrities. . . . . The **Side Track** at 56 East Cross is a very popular watering place, with excellent hamburgers and a massive back bar. **Aubree's Saloon** at 39 East Cross is a lively gathering place with billiards, a sidewalk cafe, and a rooftop deck where barbecue ribs, chicken and fish are cooked outside. Call (313) 483-1870 for entertainment. Often it's well worth checking out. Around the corner on North River is the **Ypsilanti Food Co-op**. *East Cross St. between the Huron River and River St. Many stores open Sundays 11-5; some antique shops are closed Mon & Tues.*

SAY IT LIKE A LOCAL . . . . . It's pronounced "IPP-si-lan-tee." Never be tempted to say "YIP-si-lan-tee." Detroit judge Augustus Woodward platted the town in 1825. Ever prone to the magnificently complex (he designed Detroit's circle-and-square street layout), Woodward shrugged off ordinary suggestions like

Waterville. Instead, he christened the town after the Greek general who had just become a hero in the battle for Greek independence against the Turks.

OTHER YPSI STANDOUTS FOR ANTIQUERS . . . . . Materials Unlimited is one of the biggest and best places in the Midwest to find attractive architectural artifacts, new and old: stained glass windows, ornate brass door hinges, carved oak column capitals, 19th-century building ornaments, etc. About half of its 15,000 square feet is devoted to antique American and European furniture, including many Victorian, Art Deco and Arts & Crafts pieces. Also, there are chandeliers, sconces, & other lighting fixtures and eccentric items like wooden masks and cigar-store Indians. *2 W. Michigan Ave. between Huron St. and the river. (313) 483-6980. Mon-Sat 10-5.* . . . . . **Schmidt's Antique Shop** is widely known for its entertainingly funny monthly auctions that often have high-quality furniture. They specialize in 18th & 19th century traditional furniture from England, the continent, and America, and also carry reproductions. *5138 Michigan Ave., 4 miles west of Ypsilanti. (313) 434-2660. Mon-Sat 9-5, Sun 11-5. Auctions are held about every two months. Call for dates & times.*

IN AN IMPRESSIVE MANSION . . . . . perched on a bank of the Huron River, the **Ypsilanti Historical Museum** has an amusing assortment of local artifacts. You can see the long underwear that gave the city a national reputation in the 19th century. A poster touts the woolen garments as "the perfect underwear for progressive people" with the jingle: *"Never rip and never tear/ Ypsilanti underwear."* A back room is full of old dolls. Kids are said to be most intrigued by the large dollhouse made from crates during the Depression. *220 N. Huron St. near Cross. (313) 482-4990. Thurs, Sat, Sun 2-4. Free.*

Yankee Air Museum/ Willow Run Airport

At a legendary aging airport, an imposing collection of famous American fighting planes

PART OF THE FUN of visiting this military air museum is roaming around sprawling Willow Run Airport. It's a remarkable place, built in the early 1940s to test the long-range B-24 bombers built in the huge adjacent Ford factory. Today the airport, now owned and run by Wayne County, has in places a rather seedy, almost disreputable look to it, even though there are still over 150,000 flights a year. Carcasses of old planes are strewn around the fringes of the giant field, some partially devoured for spare parts. The major use of the airport today is air freight. A dozen or so air cargo companies circle the field. Big old four-engine propeller-powered L-188 Electra cargo planes still lumber into the air from the 7,000-foot runways, rushing up to 30,000 pounds of critically needed parts to keep auto plants around the country in production.

Just west of the field is the gigantic **GM Willow Run Transmission Plant**, so big that specially-made divided highways funneled workers in and out of the complex. This was initially the famous **Willow Run Bomber Plant**. Erected by Ford Motor in 1941, it was then the largest building ever built, 3/4 of a mile long and covering 70 acres at the eastern edge of Washtenaw County. Architect Albert Kahn built it in an L-shape to keep it from spilling into Wayne County, which Ford considered unfriendly Democratic territory with higher taxes. The big plant helped boost to American morale after Pearl Harbor.

When the giant facility was planned at the beginning of World War II, it wasn't clear whether or not the Allies would lose their air bases in Great Britain to the Nazis, so Willow Run had to make thousands of bombers big enough to fly missions across the Atlantic to reach Germany. Between 1942 and 1945, some 42,000 women and men worked in the plant. Midgets were hired to fit parts in the nose section and other hard-to-reach areas. By the time the bomber plant closed in June of 1945, it had produced 8,685 B-24 Liberators. Today there are only 12 of these legendary bombers still around, and the Yankee Air Museum has been unable to obtain one.

GM purchased the bomber plant in 1953 to make automatic

transmissions. The big transmission plant has actually been expanded over the years to 4.8 million square feet. It now employs about 6,000 workers. The GM car assembly plant next door, which once made Caprices, has been mothballed.

On the airport's other side, off Beck Road, is the **Yankee Air Museum**, housed in a cavernous 1941 hangar first used as a school to train B-24 bomber mechanics. The museum has the interestingly scruffy atmosphere of a bootstrap creation by dedicated fans of military aircraft. The huge hangar is crowded with aging military aircraft. A recently acquired Lockheed C-60 **Lodestar** was built in 1943 as a paratrooper transport. On weekends elderly volunteer mechanics, veteran Air Force mechanics, are busy making the craft flyable once more.

Three of the 28 planes here already fly. One is a 1945 **C-47**, the cargo version of the classic DC-3. Another is a 1943 **B-25** gunship that saw action in Europe attacking bridges and railroads in Italy. This is the same model used in the Doolittle raid of Japan. A classic **B-17** "Flying Fortress," the Allies' largest heavy bomber during most of World War II, also flies.

On the second floor of the hangar complex are rooms with memorabilia on display: Air Force patches and medals, old newspaper clippings, paintings and photos of planes in action, engines, shells, radios, flights suits, goggles, and so on. Just outside the hangar are even more planes, highlighted by the hulking, rather ominous presence of a camouflaged **B-52** bomber that flew over 600 missions during the Vietnam War. After one bombing mission, a SAM missile was found wedged in one of her wings. Tours inside the B-52 are by appointment only. There's also one of the famous **F-86 Sabre** jets, a **T-33 Shooting Star**, an **F-101 Voodoo**, an **F-84 Thunderstreak**, and an **F-4C Phantom II**.

The museum's **gift shop** is well stocked with books on aviation, model airplanes, postcards, T-shirts, and other souvenirs.

Willow Run Airport, off Beck Rd. Take exit 190 from I-94 and go north on Belleville Rd. to Tyler. Left on Tyler and right on Beck. (313) 483-4030. Tues-Sat 10-4, Sun 12-4. $5/adult, $4 seniors over 62, $3 children over 5, &

TO SEE MORE VINTAGE MILITARY AIRCRAFT. . . . . there's the Kalamazoo Aviation History Museum or **Air Zoo**, page 83. Better funded than the Yankee Air Museum, it has a staff of mechanics who keep many planes in flying condition.

Monroe

It reached its zenith well before the Civil War. Now it's an interesting backwater where you can see a War of 1812 battlefield, well preserved old homes, and Custer memorabilia.

JUST up the beautiful River Raisin from the marshes along Lake Erie, Monroe is a settled old industrial city, originally French. For centuries Indians harvested wild rice in these marshes. Lotuses introduced here by 19th-century settlers blossom here every August, giving a spectacular view to visitors who head east out Dunbar Road just south of town. Hunters and birdwatchers are attracted by the huge flocks of migrating waterfowl stopping at the marshes, home of some of the state's best bird-watching.

The equestrian sculpture of General George Armstrong Custer, on Monroe at Elm just north of the Raisin River, was dedicated by President Roosevelt and the general's spirited journalist widow. The famously impetuous general regarded Monroe as his home town.

Monroe is one of Michigan's most historic cities. Only Detroit was incorporated earlier. But unlike Detroit, Monroe has not grown much over the decades. Today the historic city center seems curiously remote from the busy highways that go past it connecting Toledo to Detroit.

Monroe was founded by French-Canadians who grew disenchanted with life in Detroit under the British after France lost control in 1760. Its first name was Frenchtown. Some natives still speak in the area's distinctive French accent. The Indians taught Monroe's French the custom of eating muskrat (pronounced "mushrat" in these parts), and it is still considered a delicacy here. Trapped before the spring thaw, muskrat is often featured at late winter dinners of Monroe fraternal orders and charitable organizations. Delicious creative dishes of muskrat are regularly on the menu at **Ernie's Gathering Place** 15425 S. Dixie (313-242-2330; &.) Ernie's is one man's unique concept for a restaurant featuring sophisticated regional cooking based on food specialties of his decidedly unhip hometown.

Monroe's most colorful and exciting era was between 1825 and 1837 when thousands of Easterners landed here on their way to settle Michigan, Indiana, and Illinois. The Erie Canal, opened in 1825, brought settlers to Buffalo, where they boarded sailing ships or steamers to make the sometimes dangerous and usually uncomfortable 10-day voyage to Monroe.

Highlights of the Monroe area:

♦ **Monroe County Historical Museum.** Housed in the old post office, this interesting general museum of local history has many memorabilia about **General George Armstrong Custer**, the most famous person associated with Monroe. Custer spent much of his youth in Monroe and visited it often afterwards. Before his famous demise at Little Big Horn in 1876, Custer had been a heroic Civil War officer, promoted to general at the unheard-of age of 23 because of his aggressive, courageous leadership.

Here you can see Custer's swords and beloved rifles, a map he made of a Confederate camp while he was held aloft by balloon, and his big buffalo robe worn during the Washita Campaign of 1868 when he defeated a much bigger band of Sioux. People come from around the world to visit the museum and the Custer collection of

Its pre-Civil War homes are an unheralded treasure of the settled old town of Monroe. A walking tour brochure from Monroe's fine historical museum takes you past blocks of fine mid-19th-century houses south of the courthouse and on the north bank of the Raisin River. Finally there's a bed and breakfast in a fine old house in this district.

the **Monroe County Library** *located one block southeast of the museum in the Dorsch Memorial Library at 18 E. First St. (313- 241-7878; &)*

The museum, outstanding for a town of Monroe's size, has much more than Custer memorabilia of interest. A display about the pride of Monroe, Kaye Lani Rae Rafko, Miss America 1988, features the revealing green sequined Hawaiian costume she made for her hula dance in the pageant's talent competition. The museum also chronicles the history of Monroe county from the early Potawatami settlements thru the Vietnamese War *126 S. Monroe St. (313) 243-7137. May-Sept: Tues-Sun 10-5. Oct-April: Wed-Sun 10-5. & Free in the winter, $2 for adults during the summer. Pick up a* **walking tour brochure** *for a walk through old Monroe.*

◆ **Downtown.** The most interesting part of this faded commercial and civic area is **Loranger Square**, at the intersection of First and Washington, a block east of Monroe Street, the town's main drag. This New England-type square, unique in Michigan, shows how much older Monroe is than other cities in the state. The unusual, impressively ornate 1880 **County Courthouse** is on the square's southeast corner. In front is a cannon that dates from the reign of George II of England. Across First Street is the site of the **First Presbyterian Church,** built in 1846. Next to the church on First is the **Dorsch Memorial Library**, located in the former home of Dr. Eduard Dorsch, a Bavarian physician who fled after the failed 1848 German revolution. On the square's northwest corner, a plaque commemorates the spot where a **whipping post** once stood. Whipping posts were a rarity in the Midwest.

Along Washington Street (one street east of Monroe) are some attractively restored commercial buildings north of the courthouse. **Village Cafe** is a coffeehouse with food, from the same people as the remarkable Ernie's (page 188). The **Monroe Bank & Trust** is a fine example of early 20th-century Beaux Arts architecture. It's worth a peek inside to see the imposing interior. A map on the kiosk outside orients visitors to major Monroe sights.

North of the river across the Monroe Street bridge is the impressive **Custer Monument** at Elm and Monroe. It was unveiled in 1910 by his widow, by then a well-known New York writer, with President Taft at her side. Behind it is **St. Mary's Park,** just north of downtown, a pleasant riverside picnic spot. You can pick up a coney island at downtown's most popular and quaintest eatery, **Coney Island Lunch** *(4 W. Front; 313-241-4904; & one step at entry, restrooms too small)* and saunter across the pedestrian bridge to the park. The impressive complex of Art Deco buildings across Elm

Street from the park is **St. Mary's Center**, a conference and retreat facility, and the Mother House of the **IHM Sisters** (Sisters, Servants of the Immaculate Heart of Mary), the order of nuns which governs Marygrove College in Detroit and taught generations of kids in Detroit's Catholic schools.

Several noteworthy establishments are on Monroe Street. The tidy, well-organized **Thrift Shop** at 119 S. Monroe sells its merchandise (used clothes, furniture, dishes, etc.) at amazingly cheap prices. *(313) 242-1082. Open Mon-Fri 9:30 to 3:30, except for closing at 11:30 on Tuesday; Saturday 10-2.* **Spainhower's Auction House** has a wide variety of antiques for sale as well as newer items. *Open 9-4 Mon-Fri. Call 313-242-5411 about upcoming auctions held every three to four weeks.* The **Book Nook** at 42 S. Monroe sells books and religious articles geared to Monroe's big Catholic community. Lots of material on Custer is available here. Used books and magazines also. *(313) 241-2665. Open Mon-Fri 9:30-6, Sat 9:30-5, Sun 12-4.*

Finally, if you walk west on Front Street past Monroe Street, you'll soon see the home of the *Monroe Evening News* at 201 W. First. Giant glass windows let the passing public see its big web presses in action. Around 2:30 on weekday afternoons, you can see that day's edition roaring off the presses. *Centered at the intersection of Front St. with Monroe and Washington, extending south from the River Raisin.* A **walking tour brochure** available at the museum takes you on an interesting walk through Old Monroe's historic commercial and residential districts.

◆ **River Raisin Battlefields and Massacre Site.** The War of 1812 pitted the British and Indians against the Americans. At stake was the extent of American holdings on the continent. One of the major battles in that often ineptly led war occurred on the River Raisin between today's Dixie Highway and Detroit Street. A sequence of **dioramas** at the **interpretive museum** shows what Frenchtown looked like in 1813 when an American army was badly mauled here in an early-morning surprise attack by British and Canadian soldiers. Nearly 280 Americans were killed, and a brigade of 600 American militiamen surrendered. Wounded Americans, left in the homes of Monroe settlers, were set upon by Indians a day later. Over 60 were murdered. This famous "River Raisin Massacre" later ignited the American troops. A series of metal markers along the river explains its major incidents.

The battlefield interpretive museum houses the Monroe County Historical Museum's most comprehensive exhibits. In addition to a number of dioramas, a fiber optic map program provides a fourteen-minute audio-visual summary of the War of 1812 in the region.

Open daily 10-5, May 15 thru Labor Day; Sat and Sun 10-5 from September thru April, although weekday tours can be arranged in advance. 1403 E. Elm Avenue, just west of Detroit St. (between M-50 and I-75). Call (313) 243-7136 to verify hours. &. Free.

◆ **Navarre-Anderson Trading Post.** The centerpiece of this three-building complex is the plain house built in central Monroe in 1789 by fur trader François Navarre. It's believed to be the oldest surviving house in Michigan, and it has been restored and furnished with simple French-Canadian furniture to look as it might have when the Navarres lived there between 1789 and 1802. The brick schoolhouse built on this site in 1860 has been interpreted as a **country store** from between 1910 and 1920. The third building is a replica of a 1790s **French-Canadian barn.** *N. Custer Rd. at Raisinville Rd., 4 miles west of downtown Monroe. From M-50 (S. Custer Rd.) turn north onto Raisinville Rd. and cross the river. (313) 243-7137. Open Memorial Day-Labor Day, weekends 1-5; other times, by appointment for groups. &.: call. Free.*

◆ **Sterling State Park.** Just north of Monroe, this is western Lake Erie's only park with camping and swimming. From the beach, swimmers and sunbathers get a stark view of the giant cooling towers of the Fermi Nuclear Plant four miles north.

Half of this 1,000-acre park consists of water — lagoons that are excellent habitats for migrating and nesting shore birds. A 2.6-mile loop along the **Marsh View Nature Trail** surrounds the park's largest lagoon. (It's open for **cross-country skiing** in winter.) A new bridge has been built on the trail so the loop is divided into two sections. A mile-long walk leads to its **observation tower.** A causeway leads to the large **beach,** house, parking area and, behind it, the partly shaded **picnic area** and **playground** on a rise offering a panorama of Lake Erie.

Western Lake Erie is often referred to as the "walleye capital of the world." The park has a large **boat launch** area with twelve launch lanes and parking for over 500 cars/trailers. People from all over the U.S. come to camp at Sterling and leave with a freezer full of this delicious fish. The park has 288 modern **campsites** without privacy or shade, overlooking the boat basin. *Camping fee: $12/night. On State Park Rd., off Dixie Hwy. 1 mile northeast of I-75 exit 15. (313) 289-2715. 8 a.m.-10 p.m. $4/day or $20 annual state park sticker. Reservations: (800) 543-2YES. &.: call.*

◆ **Fermi 2 Power Plant & Visitors Center.** Tours of Detroit Edison's only nuclear power plant get high marks from radiation experts for straightforward information about nuclear power and about Fermi 2's much-publicized delays and cost overruns. The visitor center **tours** combine a **film** on how nuclear energy is produced, a tour of the facility, a **bus tour** of the site layout, and lots of chances for questions-and-answers. Not surprisingly, the tour emphasizes safety and environmental issues. There's a scale model of Fermi 2's drywell primary containment system.

Fermi 2 is Detroit Edison's cheapest source of power, so the Christmas Day fire that triggered an emergency shutdown in 1993 really hurt. The plant was shut down for months. *On Enrico Fermi Drive off Dixie Hwy., 7 miles north of downtown Monroe. (313) 586-5228. Advance reservations of 2-3 weeks required for free group tours conducted Mon-Fri between 8 and 4. Individuals may join scheduled group tours. Some evening and Saturday tours may be arranged on request. ふ Free.*

◆ **Horizon Outlet Center.** Discounts of 30% to 70% at 64 stores make this outlet mall Monroe's #1 visitor destination. But the sister mall at Birch Run near Frankenmuth (page 387) has more stores and a neighboring designer outlet mall. Tenant stores here include **Van Heusen**, **Izod**, **Jonathan Logan**, **L'eggs/Hanes/ Bali**, **Bass** shoes, **Famous Footwear**, **Toy Liquidators**, **American Tourister**, **Corning/Revere**, and **Pepperidge Farm**. Places with especially good deals are **Carter's Childrenswear**, **Socks Galore**, **The Paper Factory** (giftwrap and school supplies), and the large **WestPoint Pepperell** store. *14500 La Plaisance at I-75 (exit 11), 2 1/2 miles southeast of downtown Monroe. Mon-Sat 10-9, Sun 11-6. Closed Easter, Thanksgiving, and Christmas. Hours are subject to change. For information call (800) 866-5900 or (313) 241-4813. ふ yes.*

🌲🎄🌲

Metro Detroit

LESS THAN one-thirtieth the area of Michigan, Metro Detroit has some 4.5 million people, half the state's population. It's a mostly flat region of stark contrasts. Oakland County (Birmingham, Bloomfield Hills, Royal Oak, Southfield) is one of the wealthiest counties in the U.S., despite its ailing county seat, the auto manufacturing city of Pontiac. The auto industry continues to dominate the region's economy. Not only do the Big Three have their headquarters here, but hundreds of sizable auto parts suppliers in the metro area and state prosper and languish as U.S. auto sales rise and fall. The city of Detroit, shrunk to about one million people from over two million in the early 1950s, became a national symbol of urban poverty and decline in the 1970s. But the past fifteen years have overall been good ones economically for the region. Detroit too is showing signs of revival in housing, commerce, and the arts, thanks largely to confidence and suburban cooperation inspired by Mayor Dennis Archer, who replaced combative, colorful Coleman Young in 1994.

Detroit was a medium-sized city of 285,000 in 1900, on the eve of the auto boom. As late as 1905 autos were still made in 175 American cities. Then, with surprising speed, Detroit became the nation's dominant auto center. The key was aggressive entrepreneurs and plentiful capital. Henry Ford, the Dodge brothers, the Fisher brothers, and Henry Leland, among others, laid the groundwork for mass-producing reliable cars the middle class could afford. Huge lumber profits from northern Michigan provided capital to invest in the new industry. In addition, Detroit already had a strong base in working with metal and manufacturing engines from its 19th-century shipbuilding, stove, and rail car industries. And the city's central Great Lakes location made it easy to ship iron ore, limestone, and coal to local factories.

By 1910, Detroit had exploded to become the fifth biggest U.S. city. From 1905 to 1924, immigrants flocked to Detroit, giving it a far wider variety of peoples than older Midwestern cities. Today, metro Detroit has more Arabs than any place else in the U.S., unusually large numbers of Albanians, Belgians, Maltese, and Poles, and many Germans, Hungarians, Irish, Italians, Jews, Appalachian southerners, and Mexican-Americans. Detroit, 75% black, has a huge black middle class and is a national center of African-American culture.

Information sources:
CONV. & VISITORS' BUREAU

Metropolitan Detroit CVB
(800) DETROIT; (313) 259-4333

Information sources: CHAMBERS

Auburn Hills (810/248) 853-7862
Belleville (313)697-7151
Dearborn (313) 584-6100

Northville (810/248) 349-7640
Novi (810/248) 349-3743
Oxford (810/248) 628-7591
Plymouth (313) 453-1540
Pontiac (810/248) 335-9600
Rochester (810/248) 651-6700
Utica (810/248) 731-5400
Waterford (810/248) 683-4747

Enormous wealth from the auto industry has left many extraordinary sights in metro Detroit: one of the world's top art museums, the fantastic Belle Isle park, a great zoo, and remarkable historical museums. Elaborately embellished 1920s skyscrapers still loom over the town. Flamboyant mansions of four auto barons are open to visitors.

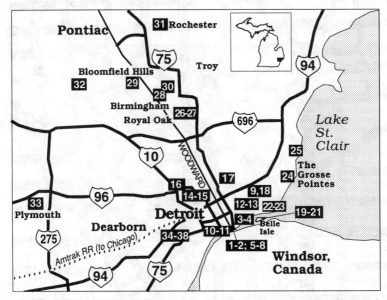

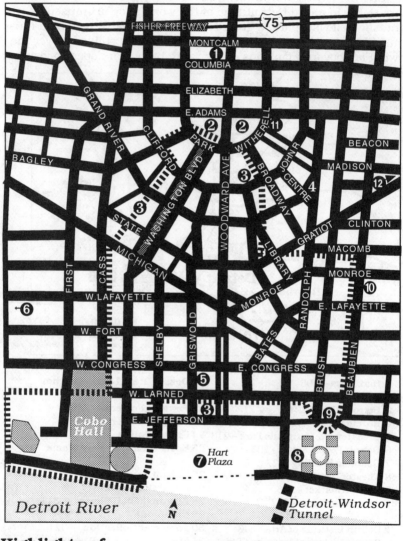

Highlights of
Downtown
Detroit

||||||| Detroit People Mover

0   1/8   1/4
             mile

❶ Fox Theater (p. 197). Restored "Siamese Byzantine" extravaganza, one of the most lavish U.S. picture palaces, has become nation's top-grossing venue for big-name acts. Nearby **Gem** presents clever revues.

❷ Grand Circus Park (p. 216). Once a 19th-century jewel, this old park has many historic statues. This is the heart of Detroit's grand Theater District, now coming to life again.

❸ People Mover (p. 225). A must for visitors, this 2.9 mile elevated train gives a spectacular view of the entire downtown. Terrific public art in the 12 stations. Despite ailing finances, not likely to close.

❹ Harmonie Park (p. 213). Pleasing revival of district of live jazz and blues music with restaurants. Historic buildings have been tastefully renovated in front of a charming old city park.

❺ Guardian Building (p. 227). One of country's great skyscrapers. Flamboyant 1929 Art Deco design has stunning lobby and adjacent banking hall. Ask for nifty brochure.

❻ John King Books (p. 242). Big old glove factory now houses one of country's biggest used book stores. 1 million books plus collectibles like postcards and framed pictures.

❼ Hart Plaza (p. 198). Views of river, city, plus fountain-sculpture. Good free entertainment many weekends from mid-May to Labor Day's great Montreux-Detroit Jazz Festival.

❽ Renaissance Center (p. 201). Huge, disorienting landmark, becoming headquarters of GM, includes large hotel, shops, and restaurants. Great view from the 71st-floor observation lounge.

❾ DuMouchelle Gallery (p. 223). Michigan's premiere auction gallery, featuring expensive possessions of the rich and sometimes famous.

❿ Greektown & Trappers Alley (p. 219). Downtown's liveliest, most colorful spot. Authentic old Greek shops and restaurants next to a beautiful 4-level festival marketplace.

11 Detroit Opera House (p. 233, 225). World-class venue with top acoustics in elegantly restored 1920s vaudeville house. The biggest musical productions can now come to Detroit. Home of Michigan Opera Theater.

12 Eastern Market (p. 236). Hard-to-match mix of shops for cheese, meat, fish, poultry, spices, nuts, produce, wine plus open-air Saturday market. Bargains, selection, earthy atmosphere.

INFORMATION SOURCES

◆ For a **downtown Detroit map and** metro Detroit **visitor packet**, or for information on attractions and events, call the What's Line, (800) 338-7648.

◆ For a **People Mover map** and attractive **Art in the Stations guide**, call (800) 541-RAIL.

◆ For a **Detroit parking guide** to lower-cost city-operated parking, call (313) 224-0300 weekdays, or write Municipal Parking Department, 200 Civic Center, Detroit, MI 48226.

Hart Plaza

At the historic site of Fort Pontchartrain,
it's a lively riverfront scene in the summer.

HIGHLIGHTS of the past and present converge at this attractive riverfront gathering place. Eight acres of multi-level paved park lead down from Jefferson Avenue to the Detroit River and the very spot on which Cadillac built Fort Pontchartrain in 1701. One side of the plaza looks south out onto the river, with views of the **Ambassador Bridge** and **Windsor**, Ontario. This view is especially beautiful towards dusk; the bridge is lit up, the Canadian shore bathed in a warm light, while the American side is pleasantly shady and cool in summer. Neon signs on Windsor's distilleries and busy casinos attest to the symbiotic relationship between the neighboring cities separated by an international border.

To the north Hart Plaza offers a view of Detroit's impressive **skyline**. The bright-painted antique **trolley cars** wait on Jefferson at the side of **Mariners' Church** (page 199) between regular runs to **Grand Circus Park** (page 216) from 10 a.m. to 6 p.m. The giant sculptural fist at Woodward and Jefferson memorializes Joe Louis, Detroit's famous Brown Bomber, who became the world heavyweight boxing champion in 1938.

Hart Plaza is a splendid place to be in nice weather. There are always people fishing for walleye off the river wall. It's easy to be mesmerized by the changing water patterns of the **Dodge Fountain**, by famed sculptor Isamu Noguchi. On weekends, chess games are played on concrete tables nearby. On festival weekends, you may well encounter the perennially dapper Bulldog Joe. A well-known Detroit character, he's the very embodiment of a man-about-town of the 1920s, in a Panama hat, white gloves, ivory-headed cane, and white spats. Lately in the evening he's seen outside the Fox, too.

The 1849 Mariners' Church, just east of Hart Plaza, remains the spiritual focus of a far-flung maritime community of sailors and boat-watchers.

From late May through September, **Diamond Jack cruise boats** leave from Hart Plaza on a 26-mile, two-hour narrated tour. The cruise travels to the St. Aubin Marina, under the Belle Isle bridge, circles Belle Isle, then moves down the Canadian shoreline, passes under the Ambassador Bridge, and loops back along the U.S. side when it reaches Fort Wayne, the star-shaped fort built in the 1840s to insure against a possible invasion from Canada. Detroit maritime buffs from the Dossin Great Lakes museum put together the commentary on the Detroit River history, from Cadillac and his little fort to 19th-century industries to the 1920s, when Gar Wood developed speedboat racing here and Detroit distilleries moved across to Windsor and Michigan's "Prohibition navy" ferried illegal booze to riverfront speakeasies. Line up early for the best seats; the open-air upper deck fills first. Ask where speakers are to hear narration clearly. *Tues-Sun from late May until September at 2, 4, and 6 p.m; in September, Fri-Sun only. Also boards at St. Aubin Park (p. 206) 15 minutes later. (313) 843-7676 (recording); (313) 843-9376 (group reservations). $10/adults, $9/seniors, $7/kids under 16, kids under 5 free.*

Free riverfront festivals are held on selected weekends throughout the summer. Music, dance, food, and national talent fit ethnic festivals themes such as the the mid-May **Downtown Hoedown** (the

At Hart Plaza, the changing spray patterns of the Dodge Fountain by famed sculptor Isamu Noguchi are fun to watch — and run through, perhaps.

world's largest free country music festival), the **World's Largest Free Circus** (mid-June), the **Detroit-Windsor International Freedom Festival** with fireworks (just before the July 4 weekend), the **Latino World Festival** (early July), the **Motor City Praise Festival** (late July), the **Arab** World Festival (early August), and the African World Festival (mid-August). The free **Montreux-Detroit Jazz Festival** on Labor Day weekend elicits raves from critics and fans. It's a wonderful glimpse of Detroit at its best: fabulous music and a mellow crowd.

Hart Plaza is at the foot of Woodward between Jefferson and the Detroit River. People Mover stop: exit at Millender Center and walk across Jefferson or the RenCen skywalk. Best cheap parking: the Ford Auditorium garage, entered from Jefferson's left lanes. (The ramp is in the median of the divided road.) Call (313) 877-8077 weekdays 9-5 for a **Riverfront Festivals schedule.**

UNDER THE RIVER TO CANADA . . . . . It's a bit eerie taking the dark, damp **Detroit-Windsor Tunnel** to Canada under the Detroit River — certainly not as scenic as the Ambassador Bridge downstream. The 5,135-foot-long tunnel was finished in 1930. The center 2,000-foot section was created by sinking nine steel tubes, each 31 feet wide, in a trench 45 feet under the riverbed. At times there are considerable delays waiting to get through customs on either side, made worse by Windsor's much-advertised, state-run casinos. Weekday mornings are least busy. *Foot of Randolph St., just west of the Renaissance Center.*

AN ANCIENT DETROIT CHURCH ON THE RIVER . . . . . Adjacent to the Ren-Cen and at the tunnel to Canada is **Mariners' Church,** founded in 1842 as an autonomous ("free") church by a bequest from Julia Anderson. The building dates from 1849. The church and its charismatic minister remain a focal point for sailors on freighters and for a sizable community of Great Lakes maritime aficionados.

Mariners' Church, "A House of Prayer for All People," uses the traditional Anglican liturgy. At the **Blessing of the Fleet** on the second Sunday of every March, dozens of shipmasters and pleasure-craft owners bring the flags of their ships to be blessed. The closest Sunday to November 10 is a **memorial service** for the crew of the *Edmund Fitzgerald*. Its ill-fated crew was remembered shortly after the ship's mysterious disappearance by the Rector's ringing the Mariners' Church bell 29 times, as described in Gordon Lightfoot's haunting **"Ballad of the *Edmund Fitzgerald.*"** *170 E. Jefferson east of Woodward. (313) 259-2206. Guided tours by appointment. Open for casual visitors Mon thru Fri 10-5. Services Thurs noon, Sun 8:30 & 11.*

Renaissance Center

Henry Ford II's grand effort to jump start Detroit's comeback — and the stunning view it offers

WHEN the Renaissance Center was completed in 1977, it instantly became the most identifiable symbol of Detroit. Located right on the Detroit River, its distinctive four cylindrical office towers grouped around a 73-story cylindrical hotel were intended to signal the rebirth of an uncommonly troubled city. But troubles beset the $337 million project as soon as it opened. The huge concrete berm separating the Center from its entrance on Jefferson Street made the vast complex look all too much like a fortress intended to protect its occupants from Detroit vandals. The unusual multiple-cylinder design, while creating the desired distinctive visual impression from far away, resulted in a maze-like interior that baffled visitors. Moreover, the upscale shops on the first two levels—including Gucci, Cartier, and Mark Cross— were meant to replace downtown Detroit's ravaged retail sector, but failed to attract enough customers and quickly shut their doors.

The project was spurred by the 1967 Detroit riot, which accelerated the exodus of whites from the city's center. Henry Ford II pushed it through, cajoling Ford suppliers and other major area businesses to invest the hundreds of millions to build the riverside complex. Like his grandfather and namesake, Ford had a deep, if erratic, idealistic streak. He felt the RenCen was essential to

An ambiguous symbol of Detroit: the tall, dark towers of the RenCen as seen from Windsor, Ontario across the Detroit River. Financially troubled since its opening in 1977, it was bought by General Motors in 1996 for a mere $75 million. It will become the giant automaker's world headquarters.

Its two top stories, a restaurant and observation deck, provide a remarkable panorama of metro Detroit and the Detroit River.

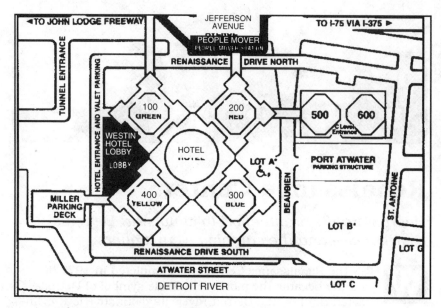

reverse the Motor City's decline.

The architect was John Portman, whose spectacular multi-story interior atriums in Hyatt Hotels in Atlanta and Los Angeles had revolutionized hotel design. But the RenCen quickly became notorious as a good place to get lost. The curving spaces connecting four look-alike round towers around the hotel lacked memorable landmarks to orient visitors. Monied suburbanites were not drawn to the forbidding, confusing place. While luxury retailers pulled out, the huge hotel suffered from a low occupancy rate. To many observers, the RenCen came to symbolize not a renaissance but wrong-headed "magic bullet" urban revitalization schemes cut off from the communities they were devised to serve. By 1983, the original investors had defaulted on their loans.

Today's RenCen is better but still confusing. It still doesn't draw many suburbanites downtown. Nonetheless, the massive complex is credited with helping to launch the succeeding wave of riverfront office and residential projects. The RenCen's over 60 shops and banks and 22 restaurants and eateries have achieved a stable presence, due mainly to the 16,000 people who work for the companies with offices here. Restaurants range from numerous fast-food outlets (some open for breakfast) to the spectacular, 71st-story **Summit Steak House & Lounge** (313-568-8600), with Tex-Mex (promenade), Chinese, Greek, and Italian sit-down restaurants in-between. All restaurants except for the Summit and the two on the promenade are on the street level. The **Renaissance Theaters** (313-259-2370) have four screens and have first-run movies.

The most remarkable RenCen attraction is the **view** from the revolving 71st-floor Summit Steak House or the observation deck just below it. A trip on the glass-sided elevator to the **observation deck** isn't cheap ($3.50/adults). But you can look out from comfortable, pod-like lounges in many directions. The flat Detroit landscape almost looks like a map from this vantage point. You can also see pleasure boats and freighters from miles away. The view is especially impressive toward sunset and at night.

In a final, ironic twist to this controversial complex, G.M. bought the RenCen in 1996 for a deeply discounted $75 million. The center built by the head of Ford will become headquarters for Ford's chief rival.

*Observation deck hours are: Sun-Thurs 11:30 a.m.-10 p.m., Fri & Sat 11:30 a.m.-1 a.m. Cocktails served from 3 p.m. daily. Dinner at the revolving restaurant begins at $29 and lets you take in the view at your leisure. Dinner is served from 5:30 p.m.-10 p.m., Sun-Thurs and 5:30 p.m.-1 a.m., Fri and Sat. Sunday brunch (10:30 a.m.-2:30) p.m. is $26.95/adults, $14.50/children ages 3-10, free/kids under 3. The restaurant is barrier-free as is part of the observation deck. For a quick, **free view** from not quite so high up, take one of the glass-sided elevators attached to each office tower. From the 400 Tower you can see Hart Plaza, downtown, and downriver.*

*E. Jefferson at Brush on the Detroit River. Open 7 a.m.-11 p.m. **Shop hours** vary; most are generally open 10-6. Second-story **bridges across Jefferson** connect with the Millender Center and People Mover Station. **Information kiosk** in Jefferson Ave. lobby. **Park** in Lot A or Lot B off Beaubien, east of Jefferson. Rates encourage short-term and off-hours parking: $1 for 3 hours weekdays 10-6, $1.25 per hour after 3 hours, $2 week nights after 6, 12 hours for $2 weekends. For these lower rates, you need to have your card stamped at any shop in the RenCen. To get a helpful **directory and map,** call (313) 568-5600 weekdays, write Renaissance Center Venture, 100 RenCen #1400, Detroit 48243, or stop at the information kiosk in the Jefferson Ave. lobby. &*

THE REN CEN VISITOR CENTER FOR METRO DETROIT . . . . . is at the Jefferson Street entrance to Tower 100. It has a helpful staff and lots of useful free publications. & *Open Mon-Fri 9-5, Sat 10-5, Sun 12-5. Or call 1-800-DETROIT.*

Detroit River

One of the world's major freighter highways is beautiful on a sunny day.

THIS WIDE, deep river connects the Upper Great Lakes (Huron, Superior, and Michigan) with the lower Great Lakes of Erie and Ontario. Three centuries ago, when French fur-trading interests dominated the region, the river's almost half-mile width made it difficult in wartime for shore batteries to stop ship traffic. So in 1701 the French set up Fort Ponchartrain at the relatively narrow point now marked by downtown Detroit. They perched a cannon on the high northern bank (where Hart Plaza is today) to repel enemy English ships.

For most of Detroit's first two hundred years, shipping from the downtown wharfs was central to its economy, connecting the city with New York to the east and Chicago to the west. The Detroit River is one of the world's busiest waterways in terms of tons carried, but Detroit is no longer a significant port. Today the old riverfront industries that once separated the river from the city are gone. The riverfront between downtown and Belle Isle emerged in the 1970s and 1980s as the magnet for the only new office and residential development in Detroit at that time.

On a warm, not-too-windy day, the banks of this attractive aqua river are a wonderful place to watch the big boats go by. In the 1960s, freighters passed an average of once every 12 minutes. Today it's a busy day when Detroit sees 20 ships between 8 a.m.

The highly recommended Diamond Jack river cruise takes visitors up and down the historic Detroit River, which has been one of North America's busiest waterways for three centuries.

Looking fragile as a toy boat, the *J. W. Westcott* pulls up to a passing freighter to deliver mail. It's the only place in the U.S. where mail is delivered to moving vessels. You can see it in action just below the Ambassador Bridge.

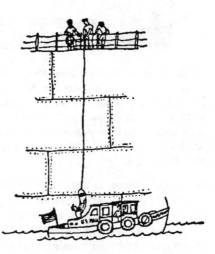

and 8 p.m., including tugs and barges. One reason is the decreased demand for North American grain with the breakup of the Soviet Union. Another is the giant thousand-foot-long Great Lakes freighters, which can do the job of six conventional freighters. It's a thrill to see these massive boats pass by. Some have up to 60,000 tons of cargo. It adds to the mystique that the river traffic also includes ocean-going "salties" that may be coming from any port in the world. They are easily recognized by their rust stains and their groups of three masts angling outwards.

Binoculars add to the fun of watching the passing boats. Good boat-watching sites, arranged southwestward from Windmill Point at the Detroit/Grosse Pointe Park line, are:

◆ **Mariners Park and the Windmill Point Light.** Looks out into Lake St. Clair and across to the east tip of Belle Isle. *Take Jefferson northeast to Alter, about 1/2 mile past Golightly Vo-Tech Center. Turn right (southeast) onto Alter Rd. In a little over a mile, turn right, cross the bridge, look for Mariners Park parking on the left. Walk a block to river.*

◆ **Belle Isle.** See page 278. From the island's east tip and lighthouse you can see out into Lake Clair (page 298). Ships on the horizon are half an hour away. On the island's south side, take Strand out past the Coast Guard Station and park soon after it. A long fishing pier is at the end of Inselruhe just east of the Dossin Museum. The museum itself (page 285) is one of the premiere destinations for Great Lakes maritime fans. *Take the bridge off Jefferson at the foot of E. Grand Blvd., two miles east of downtown Detroit.*

◆ **Chene Park.** Fishing and benches are within view of the big Medusa Cement silos, where every 10 days or so the *Medusa Challenger*, a boat as long as two football fields, unloads cement from Charlevoix on Lake Michigan. The smaller *Medusa Conquest*

Silhouettes from *Know Your Ships*, the newsy, information-packed Great Lakes boatwatcher's guide, enable novices to identify ships of the inland seas. The older 600-foot lakes self-unloader shown above has a boom to unload its own cargo. The Detroit and St. Clair rivers see more tonnage pass than almost anywhere else in the world. *Know Your Ships* ($12.95) is at the Dossin Museum, J. W. Westcott ship store, bookstores, or call (313) 688-4743.

also docks here. It may portend the new age of more flexible Great Lakes shipping with smaller manpower requirements. It's an old tanker cut down into a barge whose stern has been notched so a tugboat fits into it. Call (810) 471-6250 weekdays to find out when deliveries are being made. *At the foot of Chene or Dubois streets east of Jefferson, 1 1 /4 miles past the RenCen.*

◆ **St. Aubin Park**. Two fishing shelters, a picnic area, and two river overlooks abut a 67-boat transient marina. (See page 209.) Creative outdoor **exhibits** relate riverfront history. A scaled-down drydock remembers a seminal Detroit industry, training ground for many automotive pioneers. See page 210.

The *Diamond Jack*, docked here, gives excellent, narrated **two-hour boat tours** of the Detroit and Windsor riverfronts. Leaves daily

Riverside Park, at the foot of West Grand Boulevard in southwest Detroit, is one of the many nooks that reveal less obvious aspects of Detroit life. Here are the J. W. Westcott marine supply company, open around the clock during shipping season, and the Detroit fireboat *Curtis Randolph*.

**The angled booms of an ocean general cargo vessel immediately identify it
as a "salty" — an ocean vessel stained by saltwater**

except Monday at 2:15, 4:15, and 6:15 from Memorial weekend
through August, Friday through Sunday in September. Call (313)
843-7676 (recording) or 843-9376. Costs $9 for adults, $7 for kids.
Take St. Aubin or Orleans from Jefferson south to the river and park.

◆ **Hart Plaza**. The very spot Cadillac chose for Fort Pontchartrain in
1701. See page 198. Fishing, benches and picnic tables along the
river. *At the foot of Woodward. Park free on weekends along adjoining streets west of Jefferson (Shelby, Griswold, Brush, Beaubien) or
use the RenCen lot A off Beaubien east of Jefferson.*

◆ **Riverside Park**. This grassy park, almost beneath the impressive
Ambassador Bridge, is a terrific spot for boat-watching. The little
mail boat of the **J.W. Westcott marine supply company** is docked
next door. It's quite a sight to watch the 45-foot boat sail out and
pull up to passing thousand-foot freighters, looking alarmingly fragile next to the giant it services. The freighter's crew drops down a
line with a bucket for mail and supplies. The Westcott Company
provides ships with everyday supplies, nautical charts, and river
pilots for foreign vessels. Visitors are welcome to browse in its little
Great Lakes bookstore, open 24 hours a day during shipping season (April through December). (313) 496-0555.

Just down from Westcott are the city of Detroit's fireboat, the
Curtis Randolph, and past that, carferries that shuttle railroad cars
between Detroit and Windsor. Also downriver is the Nicholson termi-
nal and dock, below River Rouge, periodically busy shipping and
receiving manufactured parts. Directly across the river are Windsor's
harbor facilities. *At the foot of West Grand a block east of Fort.*

SUMMER KICKS OFF FOR GENERATIONS OF DETROIT FAMILIES . . . . .
with Thunder on the River, the Indy 500 of boat racing, formally known as the
Spirit of Detroit Thunderfest Gold Cup. It's viewed from Belle Isle, downtown
Detroit, and the riverfront parks over four days on Memorial Day weekend. Half
a million people watch these aerodynamic hydroplanes that go over 200 mph.
Some viewing stands are ticketed; call (800) 359-7760.

East Jefferson Avenue and the riverfront

History, good music, Detroit's oldest historic architecture, and striking scenery in a series of riverfront parks

IN 1980 the three-mile stretch of riverfront between the RenCen and Belle Isle bridge was industrial. The river was blocked off from public use by old warehouses and factories, and by remnants of docks and shipyards. Today the departure of most industry has paved the way for the **Rivertown entertainment district** on the most expensive land in Detroit. Scattered nightspots and restaurants range from famed chef Jimmy Schmidt's' flagship Rattlesnake Club in the handsomely renovated old Parke-Davis complex to the Woodbridge Tavern (an old speakeasy with a nifty terrace) and the earthily casual and eclectic Soup Kitchen Saloon blues and jazz club. Ample parking and safe streets are plusses. For more on the Detroit River and shipping, see pages 204-207.

The city's **riverfront parks** at the feet of St. Aubin and Chene streets have proven aesthetic and popular successes. Chene Park outdoor jazz and pop music concerts at sunset are a don't-miss attraction worth a visit to Detroit.

Harbortown and River Place, two large mixed-use luxury housing developments, have proven popular with upper-income empty-nesters and young professionals. More new apartments are being built — a welcome trend in a city passed over by the 1980s building boom. Enough old buildings and businesses like the Medusa Cement silos remain to give the place a kind of gritty, real-world visual atmosphere.

Here are Rivertown highlights, arranged from west (the RenCen end) to east, toward Belle Isle. Easiest access is from Jefferson; all the mentioned streets that end at the river (Chene, St. Aubin, etc.) intersect with Jefferson.

◆ **Jefferson Avenue historic buildings.** Pre-Civil War Detroit, with its gentle Federal-style townhouses and Gothic revival churches, has largely been erased by the industrialization spurred by the War between the States. But scattered pieces of antebellum Detroit can still be seen on Jefferson, especially on the two blocks east of the Chrysler Freeway (I-75/I-375). The parade of old houses is occasionally interrupted by turn-of-the-century apartment buildings and clubhouses built by the wealthy before they left the city for the suburbs in the 1920s.

Two fine old buildings are regularly open to the public:

◆ **Christ Episcopal Church** is a beautiful 1863 Gothic Revival church designed by Gordon Lloyd. A star of 19th-century Michigan architecture, Lloyd was known for his picturesque Episcopal churches all over the state. Weekdays ask at the office to look inside and see the beautiful stained glass windows. A Tiffany window depicts the legend of St. Elizabeth of Hungary. A portrait window honors the family of the church's first rector, William Lyster. As a missionary in pioneer Michigan, he coined the name "Irish Hills" for the

Christ Episcopal Church on Jefferson welcomes casual visitors interested in its beautiful stained glass. It's one of 15 members of the Detroit Historic Churches Association featured in an interesting free brochure found at the Metro Detroit Visitors Center in the RenCen or by calling 1-800-DETROIT.

glacial hills of Jackson and Lenawee counties. *960 E. Jefferson just east of I-75. (313) 259-6688. Sunday morning services 8:15 and 10:30.* &

◆ The 1840s **Moross House**, Detroit's oldest existing brick dwelling, is the headquarters of the **Detroit Garden Center**. Portions of it have been furnished with mid-19th-century antiques from old Detroit families. Its walled rear garden is a lush, vine-clad oasis planted with favorites from the mid-19th century: peonies, lilacs, spring bulbs, and wisteria. There is an excellent **horticultural library**. The center sponsors classes and workshops, trips, lectures on things like flower-arranging and butterfly gardens, and hosts special events like a Christmas open house, a Valentine's orchid show, and a March tea. A brochure permits self-guided **tours** of the house. *1460 Jefferson west of Riopelle. (313) 259-6363. Open Tues-Thurs 9:30-3:30.* &

◆ **St. Aubin Park.** This attractive, well-maintained park features two **river overlooks**, two fishing shelters, and a grassy **picnic area**, plus a 67-slip transient pleasure boat marina (the only one in

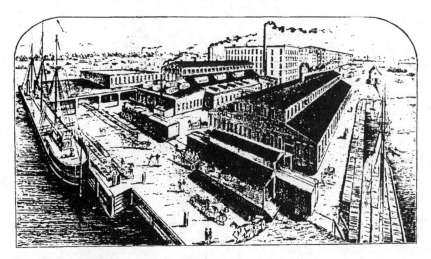

The riverfront was lined with heavy industry in the late 19th century, like the Detroit Stove Works just west of the Belle Isle bridge (the old Uniroyal site). The Rivertown area has some of the flavor of the old brick buildings, shown in an 1884 city history, and St. Aubin Park has outdoor exhibits about the river's industrial past. Experience in metalworking and engines lay behind Detroit's sudden rise to dominate automobile manufacturing. Detroit had led the nation in making stoves.

Detroit) handy to downtown. The **Diamond Jack River Cruises** originate at Hart Plaza and board from St. Aubin Park at 2:15, 4:15, and 6:15 in season (page 199).

History plus riverfront scenery make the park a fine place for a leisurely stroll. A series of **outdoor history exhibits** interpret the Detroit riverfront. Many exhibits are on the river's edge buffer between the river and the marina. A path to it starts at St. Aubin and Atwater. Along the riverwalk, on the north end of the river's edge buffer, are inscriptions with a dozen key **moments** in the riverfront's history. On a curved wall on the north end of the park, three markers give a historical overview of **African-Americans in Detroit**.

Some of the largest marine steam engines ever made were built across the street at the Detroit Drydock Company. In fact, the city's auto boom of the early 20th century built directly on skills and technologies of shipbuilding. A seven-foot **model of a drydock** shows an 1892 freighter being worked on.

By the marina office and restrooms is a play area with "**Land of Boats**," the first play sculpture designed by the internationally known sculptor **Vito Acconci**. *On Atwater between Orleans and St. Aubin about a mile north of the RenCen. Open for fishing during day-*

light hours. For marina reservations and docking fees, call (313) 259-4677 or 1-800-338-6424.

◆ **Chene Park.** Chene Park combines low-key fishing and riverfront access with an expanded, 6,500-seat riverfront amphitheater that is a beautiful **concert venue** for top performers in blues, jazz, classical, and adult contemporary music, plus an annual June Gospelfest. For concert info, call (313) 393-0066 24 hours. Concertgoers can get up during concerts and walk along the river and small pond. At sunset and after dark, the effect of lights reflected in the water is fabulous. And during a concert, the combination of spectacular scenery, good music, and mellow crowds along the river is hard to equal.

Every 10 days or so, the ***Medusa Challenger***, a freighter as long as two football fields, unloads cement from Charlevoix to the Medusa silos next to the park. Its smaller sister ship, the *Medusa Conquest* (p. 205), also unloads here. Call (313) 496-0555 to find out when these interesting events occur. *On Atwater at the foot of Chene and Dubois, between St. Aubin Park and Stroh River Place.*

◆ **River Place.** The giant Parke-Davis pharmaceutical company began here in 1873. Architect Albert Kahn's handsome brick buildings from the early 1920s were stylishly renovated and developed by the Stroh Brewery. River Place has offices (including Stroh corporate headquarters), apartments and townhouses, the elegant River Place Hotel, and Jimmy Schmidt's celebrated **Rattlesnake Club**, with innovative American regional food. *At the foot of Joseph Campau, corner of Atwater. Valet parking, or park on a nearby street and walk.*

Changing exhibits are held in the gallery space of the **Detroit Artists Market**, next to the Rattlesnake Club. Shows feature new and established artists in the area. Some examples: "Detroit Underground Pulp Visions & Icons," the big March all-media show, and landscapes dealing with artificial light. The Detroit Artists Market was established by collectors and art-lovers to provide a place where new art could be seen and sold. Board members typically include leaders of the Detroit Institute of Arts and other notables, not artists. The **gallery shop** carries two-dimensional art, sculpture, and jewelry, hand-crafted by Michigan artists. A special spring show is aimed at families: artist-designed dollhouses, dog houses, and, twice, mini-golf, with each artist designing a hole. *Enter 300 River Place building from Joseph Campau, go upstairs, through doors, past info desk. (313) 393-1770. Tues-Sat 11-5. Closed August. ♿: call.*

◆ **Atwater Block Brewery.** Not yet finished at press time, this microbrewery with tap room and restaurant sounds like more than just another follower of the current fad. Owner-developer Scott Henderson is an avid home-brewer and former Coopers & Lybrand specialist in mergers and acquisitions. His brewmaster and brewing equipment are from Germany. They aim to work from the German brewing tradition of Pilsner-type beers, "jazzed up for American tastes." They plan to produce wheat, smoked, and bock beers and to market widely their Kräusen beers, fermented Pilsners to which fresh, cloudy beer is added for a fresh taste. Henderson liked the way the long tables at the old Mr. Flood's Party in Ann Arbor brought strangers together, and plans the same for his renovated factory here. The food menu is planned to complement beer. *237 Joseph Campau between Jefferson and the river, next to Dunleavyz. (313) 393-BEER.* &

◆ **Mt. Elliott Park.** The Lighthouse Depot built here during the 1870s became a Coast Guard center of operations for the entire region from Lake Erie to Lake Superior. Today a Coast Guard station for maintaining lighthouses and river channel markers is head-quartered at the foot of Mt. Elliott. It's not open to the public, but its ships are readily observable from the park, which is finally being completed after years of delays. A building formerly owned by the Coast Guard will be open to the public. *On Atwater at the feet of Mt. Elliott, Iron, and Meldrum.*

🌲🌳🌲

IN THE VICINITY AND WORTH A LOOK. . . . . The well-known **Capuchin monastery and soup kitchen** is a few blocks southeast on Mt. Elliott. . . . . For almost two centuries Detroit notables have been buried at picturesque **Elmwood Cemetery**, entered off Elmwood just north of Lafayette. At the cemetery office, pick up information on graves of noteworthy burials. Notice, too, the gentle rise and fall of the land. Much of Detroit looked like this in the 1840s, before it was leveled for high-density real estate developments. . . . . If you take Mt. Elliott all the way southeast to the river, you'll be at **Mt. Elliott Park**, one of the new riverfront parks. It's a good place to fish and watch river traffic and activities at the **Coast Guards station** for ice-breaking, rescue, buoy-tending, and policing operations.

Harmonie Park, Greektown, and beyond

A growing number of nightspots and galleries make parts of Detroit an increasingly pleasant place to visit.

DOWNTOWN DETROIT — parts of it, anyway — is beginning to feel like a real urban place. On a fine summer night you can walk down Monroe from Greektown and along Randolph, crossing Gratiot into the Harmonie Park area. The sidewalks are lively with cafes and pedestrians, and live music spills out into the street. It no longer seems silly to imagine a downtown not limited to big, isolated "silver bullet" renewal projects or daytime-only office towers or small, clearly defined urban pieces like Greektown. Perhaps parts of downtown will fill in to the point that some active, pedestrian-friendly streets will connect up the dispersed activity nodes: Harmonie Park, the theaters around Grand Circus Park, the men's retailers on Broadway, Greektown, the art gallery corridor behind the old Hudson's, the splendid 1920s office towers of the "Financial District," and even Washington Boulevard, in all its faded Beaux Arts grandeur.

There are many grounds for optimism. The continuing growth of the Theater District (page 230) has already led to the second-biggest concentration of theaters in the U.S., after only New York. Finally, Harmonie Park redevelopment is more than plans. The little neighborhood's potential as an attractive urban place is being realized.

Detroit has experienced a new mood of confidence and enthusiasm, and new investment, since Dennis Archer became mayor in 1994. Downtown's specialty retailers are busier on weekends, not just with their regular customers but with new ones, too. G.M.'s move to the RenCen will draw many employees who now work in the suburbs and beyond. Many offices displaced by G.M. (like Ford) must find space elsewhere. Some will relocate downtown — a boon for older office buildings that have suffered from growing vacancy rates when recent large new office buildings have opened.

Finally, more artists have studio-lofts right downtown and near it. Artists' energy and artists' visions of urban life have been the initial chapters of more than a few urban success stories.

In truth, it's too early to dub Detroit "comeback city," in the mass media's dumb overgeneralizing way of simplifying things as complicated as cities. Some parts of downtown seem to be losing energy at this moment. Greektown and the Financial District come to mind. Windsor's casinos suck entertainment dollars out of the city, yet the effects of legalized gambling in Detroit are a mixed bag at best. Furthermore, it should be said that in the boom years of the 1920s Detroit wasn't exactly a hub of urban culture. It had a lot of people (over 1 1/2 million in the city alone in 1930) and money, and many grand buildings and movie theaters, but Detroit in the 1930s couldn't support a legitimate theater. Culturally, the metro area is much more interesting and arts-friendly today, now that the children and grandchildren of the huge groups of migrated autoworkers have had time to mix up their genes and cultures, have additional life choices beyond factory work, and shape the mainstream of American life.

Here's a quick overview of some of downtown's interesting spots by day and by night. (Space unfortunately doesn't permit detailing downtown's riches of early 20th-century architecture.) There's also nearby Rivertown, across Jefferson. The free quarterly *Metro Detroit Visitors Guide* does a fine job of surveying the scene, in terms of shopping, nightspots, hotels, entertainment, events, and more. Get it from the Visitor Information Centers in the RenCen or Detroit Historical Museum, or call 1-800-DETROIT.

HARMONIE PARK AND GRAND RIVER

Judge Woodward's 1805 circle and spokes plan for Detroit created some odd triangles designated for parks. This one is just north of Gratiot where Grand River starts at Randolph. (That's the same Grand River Avenue that goes through Howell and passes the Michigan State University campus and crosses the river at Lansing's Old Town.) The turn-of-the-century buildings around Harmonie Park form a delightful backdrop for a lush urban oasis. The little park is home to a pleasant, cascading waterfall-wall fountain. The handsome four-story Beaux Arts-style **Harmonie Club** at Grand River and Centre was built by a German social club formed in 1849 as the Gesang-Verein Harmonie. Metro Detroit's huge German population first located on downtown's east side and moved east along Gratiot. Singing societies were key components of German-American social life, along with beer gardens and rural shooting parks. The 1895 Harmonie Club set a high standard for quality building in the area. Pewabic Pottery had its showroom across the way on Randolph in what's now the Harmonie Studios. (Look for the decorative tiles on the exterior.)

By the 1970s and 1980s Harmonie Park had become a low-rent center of artists and theater people, residential hotels and street people. Landscape architects/developers SVM (Schervish/Vogel/

Merz) spearheaded acquisition of most Harmonie Park property and planned to redevelop it as loft offices, apartments, and studios, with ground-level restaurants aimed at theatergoers. Now most of the original artists — and all the street people — are gone. Streetscaping and landscaping makes the area look wonderful, day and night. **Intermezzo Italian Ristorante** (Randolph at Centre; 313-961-0707) has proven a hit. It's a partnership between chef Nick Apone and restaurateur Nick Cutraro, a leader in area restaurantainment with his trendsetting Metropolitan Music Cafe in Royal Oak and Industry nightclub in Pontiac. Cutraro plans a similar music-themed restaurant for the Harmonie Club, but perhaps with a more sophisticated or urban theme than the Music Cafe with its pop-rock artifacts. A brew pub is planned for the club's historic rathskeller.

Also facing the park is the alcohol-free **Cafe Mahagony** (1645 Centre, 313-235-2233). It offers cappuccino, deli sandwiches and salads, and a mix of comedy, poetry, and on weekends live jazz. It's open from 11 a.m. until midnight, 3;30 a.m. on weekends. A Middle Eastern breakfast, lunch, and snack spot, **Harmonie Gardens** (313-961-7255) is a block north on John R at Centre. After years of delays, Harmonie Park is finally happening, with more restaurants probable.

The area's old-timer and keeper of collective memory is antiques dealer Dell Pryor. Her beautiful **Dell Pryor Galleries** (313-963-5977) occupies the large, two-level space at 1452 Randolph, across from Intermezzo. It's open Tuesday through Saturday, 11-5. As a widow with six children, Pryor built up Cluttered Corners antiques in

Dell Pryor's gallery mixes dramatic antiques, estate and contemporary jewelry, handcrafted furnishings, and fine art.

Greektown using her interior design background and her love of the old Greektown's artistic ambiance. Then her charming old alleyway was developed into the rehabbed Trappers Alley. The Attic Theater and later Pryor herself had to move. (The Attic is now back in Trappers' Alley.) Her gallery mixes unusual accent antiques with contemporary crafts, all displayed in striking room settings. The mezzanine and front exhibit space permit changing **shows** of regional artists. Also on hand: interesting estate and modern jewelry, including African-face cameos.

A stately downtown park: Grand Circus Park on Woodward and Adams. Its semi-circular shape was created by Judge Augustus Woodward's neo-Parisian, circle-and-spoke plan for rebuilding Detroit after the 1805 fire. This view is from 1886.

Two additional nightspots are just beyond Harmonie Park. For many years **Bo-Mac's Lounge** (313-961-5152) has attracted jazz-lovers with its clean, well-run club, reasonably priced, down-home food, unusually friendly atmosphere, and good music. Music starts early. It's at 281 Gratiot between Broadway and Randolph. Now there's a new club a few doors down at 1314 Broadway. **The Network** (313-963-2180) has

Once a jewel, the park remains a fine blend of old and new sculpture, a fountain, and pleasant trees, set against a backdrop of handsome buildings from downtown Detroit's apogee between 1915 and 1925. The staffed underground parking garage is reasonably safe, inexpensive, and never full.

a sidewalk cafe in summer and live weekend entertainment with Saturday dance parties.

Half a block south from Harmonie Park on Grand River, **Spectacles** is the quintessence of cool, urban hip. It features "underground gear" or "street wear" — pricey Ts, sweats, jackets, and caps. Sportswear, jewelry, accessories, leather goods, and shades are also on hand. *230 E. Grand River. (313) 963-6886. Mon-Sat 11-6* *except Fri to 7.*

◆ **Along Washington Boulevard**, designed about 1915 to be the Paris of Detroit and now a poignant shadow of its former glory, two upscale apparel stores stand out. They are "fashion-oriented but not trendy." Meta Fluker-Yett says, "We buy New York-inspired clothes for fashion staying power." Her **Rio Boutique** offers contemporary women's clothes and accessories for play, career, and after 5. Image consulting and free makeup consultation are extra services offered to customers. *222 West Grand River at Washington Blvd. Times Square People Mover Station. (313) 961-6056. Mon-Sat 10-6.* ⬥ **Rio Kids** offers cleanly styled, contemporary clothes for infants through size 14, boys and girls. Kids love the play area with videos. *1258 Washington Blvd., kitty corner from the Rio Boutique. (313) 963-0180. Mon-Sat 10:30-5:30.* ⬥

GRAND CIRCUS PARK/THEATER DISTRICT

Beautiful buildings and historic sculptures in the park make for a pleasant walk, even though stores are scattered. Perhaps this area will turn into a neighborhood within a few years. Note the seated likeness of Hazen "Potato Patch" Pingree, mayor and governor, surveying Woodward Avenue from the park. Initially the candidate of the Republican machine, the paunchy shoe manufacturer turned out to be a steadfast supporter of the common man — against the streetcar syndicate, and ready to help jobless residents grow food during the depression of 1893, hence his nickname.

◆ Facing **Grand Circus Park**, the **David Whitney Building** has unfortunately lost many interesting tenants in its beautiful arcaded spaces. But on the other side of the park, east on Adams from the Central Methodist Church, the church-sponsored **Swords into Plowshares** peace art gallery and thrift shop a few doors down are worth checking out. The gallery space permits some passionate multimedia explorations of the themes of war and peace that can be very moving. Gift Shop. *45 E. Adams. Tues, Thurs, & Sat 11-3. Also open 2nd Sun 12-3. For info, call (313) 963-7575.* ⬥

◆ **Little Foxes.** This tiny, luxuriously layered gift shop/flower shop behind Tres Vite restaurant in the Fox Theatre Building is worth checking out not just for the sterling jewelry, crystal, cards, and gifts, but for the miniature fountain and beautiful, ivy festooned ceiling paintings. *2211 Woodward at Montcalm. (313) 983-6202. Tues-Fri 10-6. Also open about 2 hours prior to shows on weekends.*

◆ **21 Ten Elizabeth's** is a tucked-away treasure, charmingly cluttered with interesting jewelry, baskets, pottery, stationery, and

cards — multi-cultural in origin, arranged
with a gentle sort of Victorian flair.
There's so much to see, you might easily
miss the nifty rubber stamps, and beads
for necklaces and earrings. Also, lots of
bath items, candles, and incense.*Moved to
downtown Royal Oak, 200 W. Fifth Ave.
near Washington. (248) 548-4600, Mon-Sat
11-6, summer evenings and some Sundays
by chance.* ♿

DETROIT GALLERY CORRIDOR

On Grand River at Library, two blocks
toward Woodward from Harmonie Park, a
gallery center has developed behind the
old Hudson's. The **Sherry Washington
Gallery** represents three internationally
acclaimed African-American painters,
Benny Andrews, Richard Mayhew, and
William T. Williams, as well as Shirley
Woodson, Charles Burwell, David
Driskell, Robert Freeman, Cheryl Hanna,
and David Fludd, all with national reputations and all of African descent. Big windows and a splendidly restored Beaux Arts
building make this a fine place to look at
art. *1274 Library St. (313) 961-4500. Open
Tues-Fri 10-5, Sat 12-6, Sun & Mon by
appointment.* ♿

**Pam Duvall in front of her
charming gift shop, 21Ten
Elizabeth's. Displaced by
the new stadium, it's now
in Royal Oak.**

Kitty-corner from it, **Gallery Biegas**
presents an eclectic mix of established artists from around the
world and emerging artists. The setting is a striking, modernistic
former bank building. Occasional one-person shows highlight
artists from other countries. *35. E. Grand River at Library. (313)
961-0634. Tues-Fri 12-6, Sat 12-5.*

Building owners Christine and Miguel Biagas have reached out
to enable several other galleries to open in the adjoining storefronts.
The storefronts are looking frayed around the edges as we go to
press. Next door is the respected **Detroit Focus Gallery**. The artist-
run, nonprofit gallery shows the work of established and new
artists, including some big environmental installations, in about
five shows a year and three nights of performance art. Current
director, Cranbrook graduate Robert Chrise, sees the gallery's focus

as cutting edge or ground-breaking. For info on the Detroit art scene, stop by and talk to him. Get the **Detroit Gallery Guide** here or from the Visitors Center (1-800-DETROIT) to track down some 35 in the city. *On 33 E. Grand River, one block east of Woodward just north of the old Hudson bldg. (313) 965-3245. Thurs-Sat 12-6. Closed in August.* Every 3 months, Detroit hosts **Art Night** during which the galleries in Detroit stay open from 5 p.m. to 9.pm. Call for dates. &

At the **International Artists Gallery**, another Biagas' tenant, partners Julian Chiu (a Romanian painter) and Richard Griesbeck show work by American and international artists, thus far from East Africa, Hungary, Romania, and Russia. *27 E. Grand River. (313) 961-1188. Thurs-Sat 12-5.* The final gallery in the Biagases' building is **AC, T** (that stands for Artists' Cooperative, The). AC,T is run by about 50 artists who fund the gallery by membership dues rather than grants or donations. In addition to exhibiting the works of its members, AC,T has invitational and juried shows. *29 E. Grand River. (313) 961-4336. Thurs-Sat 12-5. &: call.* If you're doing downtown galleries, don't forget the interesting **Urban Park** in Trappers Alley (page 221) and Swords into Plowshares peace art gallery (page 217).

BROADWAY AT GRATIOT

This busy intersection has long been a center of men's clothing, and a half a dozen good shoe stores and menswear stores remain. The range of styles is enormous, from the carefully elegant to the urban hip. **The Broadway** at 1247 Broadway is loaded with designer names, leather coats, and beautifully accessorized displays — the GQ look, and quite probably Detroit's top menswear store in terms of fashion. A branch is on Northwestern Highway in Southfield. It's favored by style-conscious men, including famous rock and sports stars and occasional drug dealers like the one assassinated in the store itself. Despite that incident, it's a friendly place, with terrific sales. *(313) 963-2171. Mon-Thurs 9:30-6 p.m., to 7 on Fri & Sat. &*

Across Gratiot, **Henry the Hatter** was started over a hundred years ago, in 1893. "Everything that's made, we carry," claims its owner, including $8 wool berets, British silk hats, Western hats, and the flat-top black hat with a snap brim ($65) favored by jazz great Dexter Gordon, a favorite with women and men. *1307 Broadway at Gratiot. (313) 962-0970. Mon-Sat 9-6. &*

GREEKTOWN

With its many Greek restaurants and the Trappers Alley shopping and restaurant complex, this bright block of Monroe Street has long been one of Detroit's most popular tourist attractions. It's one of the few areas in Detroit where the 19th-century city holds its own. It's brightly lit and busy. Taking a cue from the neon People Mover art by the Greektown Station, the street's neon signs look better every year, creating real visual excitement. Proximity to the city's police headquarters and courts make Monroe Street a round-the-clock place that attracts downtown workers, suburbanites, and guests at nearby hotels. Trappers Alley shops have come and gone — and the International Center's promising incubator for apparel designers failed to take hold. But area developers Ted Gatzaros and Jim Pappas have scored some enduring successes with their beautiful, conveniently located **Atheneum Suite Hotel** (313-962-2323; 1-800-772-2323) a block away at Brush and Lafayette, and their popular New Orleans-style **Fishbone's Rhythm Kitchen** on Monroe at Brush, in the International Center Building. (The elegant, multistory waterfall behind the restaurant is quite amazing.)

Gatzaros and Pappas have been lobbying long and hard to establish gambling in Greektown. Detroit's powerful black churches successfully fought gambling for years, but with Windsor casinos sucking money out of the city, the climate has changed. Mayor Dennis Archer is no longer against gambling (though he hasn't supported it, either), and the issue is on the ballot.

This area is the core of a Greek neighborhood going back to 1915, with its bakeries, grocery stores, and coffee houses where a few old-timers still come to drink coffee and play cards. The Greek coffeehouses are now tucked away behind more profitable ventures. A block south, at 349 Monroe is **The Old Shillelagh,** an Irish pub with darts and weekend folk music (313-964-0007).

The neighborhood, like much of Detroit's east side, was originally German. The beautiful red-brick **St. Mary's Catholic Church** complex at 646 Monroe houses the city's third-oldest Catholic parish, dating to 1835. Almost as old is the congregation of the **Second Baptist Church** at 441 Monroe, founded by 13 former slaves in 1836. Its first pastor was an antislavery activist, its basement the last stop on Michigan's underground railroad.

Overpopulation caused hard times that drove over a fourth of the Greek labor force off their native rocky farmlands between 1890 and 1920. Greek men found their way to then-booming industrial towns throughout Michigan, from Detroit and Flint to Dowagiac and Calumet. They parlayed earnings from factory and construction work into small businesses opening up in a rapidly urbanizing America: shoe repair, groceries, rooming houses and downtown commercial property, and above all, confectioneries and restaurants. Greeks did it so quickly and successfully that it's hard to believe that they were mostly farmers from primitive Greek villages thrust into a totally unfamiliar environment.

Greektown families have long since moved onward and upward. They are scattered throughout the metro area. But many Greek-Americans still patronize Greektown establishments. Restaurant menus feature gyros, shish kebab, spinach pie, Greek salads, egg-lemon soup, rice pudding, baklava, and the like. Always a good value, the food has been upgraded in recent years.

Here are Greektown points of interest in addition to restaurants:

◆ **Trappers Alley** is a pleasant, well-maintained place to wander around even though it has fewer shops. The rich brick facades of old buildings are juxtaposed with crisp, colorful tiles and lush foliage. These buildings once were part of the huge tannery operations of Traugott Schmidt and Sons, one of the country's largest tanneries in the late 19th century. A leading attraction here is the **Blue Nile** Ethiopian restaurant. Tucked away on the second level is **Urban Park** (313-963-5445), a nonprofit art gallery. It mounts changing shows of local, regional, and national artists who are often on hand to talk about their work. Don't miss the lively bulletin board and handouts on the local arts, music, and coffeehouse scene. **D'jenne Beads & Art** (313-965-6620) deals in African imports from trade beads, mud cloth and other fabrics, Yoruba bead work, and batik. Across the way, **Comix Oasis** (313-964-4450) puts together arresting windows of pop art and collectibles. Shops have changed a lot lately; current ones feature things from South America and China. Women's fashions and lingerie are staples. On the ground level, the **Athens**

Lots of neon has long been a Greektown signature, which artist Stephen Antonakos picked up on in his swirling People Mover station art.
New restaurant signs add an arty, sophisticated note to the neon streetscape.

Bookstore (313-963-4490) is *the* place to find Greek-language publications, cassettes of Greek music, ornate coffee urns, and gaudy religious icons, along with lots of tacky Detroit souvenirs.

The Attic Theatre, after years of financial difficulties and the departure of its longtime director, has returned to Greektown from the New Center and staged some very well received plays and musicals. It's well worth checking out **year-round performances** at this respected local theater. At 180 seats, its attractive new Trappers Alley home gives an intimate theater experiences. Some productions in 1997: *God's Country* (about white supremacists), *Always Patsy Cline*, a long-awaited production of Sondheim's dark musical *Sweeney Todd*, and humorous *Compleat Works of Wm Shakspr. Trappers Alley, 3rd floor. (313) 963-9339. Thurs-Sun, usually with weekend matinees.* &. *$20 & $25.*

Trappers Alley is on Monroe at Beaubien, five blocks north of the Renaissance Center and 2 blocks west of I-75. Follow I-75 South to 375 South and take the Lafayette exit. If you turn right on Lafayette and go up 1 1/2 blocks, you'll come to an entrance for the parking lot located behind Trappers Alley. The Greektown People Mover station is on the third level of Trappers Alley. (313) 963-5445. Mon-Thurs 10-9, Fri & Sat 10-11, Sun noon-7. &.

◆ **International Center of Apparel Design.** When you go out Trappers Alley's south door, you're right across from the International Center. Here four classy shops remain on the first floor from this ambitious experiment to showcase local designers of clothing, jewelry, and accessories designers. **By Sharrone** (313-961-9334) shows "wearable art" in bold, African-inspired prints. Custom designs welcomed. It's a knockout. *Main entrance at 1045 Beaubien at Monroe. (313) 963-3357.* &.

◆ **Astoria Pastry Shop.** This old Greek pastry shop has been expanded and spiffed up to appeal to strolling Greektown crowds, with ice cream, cappuccino, and quite a few tables. The spinach pie is a nice snack if you don't feel like buying an entire meal at nearby restaurants. Crusty yet soft Greek breads are made for sopping up salad oils and pan juices. All the traditional Greek and Middle Eastern filo-honey-nut pastries are here, some with a new twist, like chocolate baklava. Astoria offers a wide range of baked goods, including American favorites and Italian standards like toasted biscotti (some dipped in chocolate and walnut), tiramisu, and cannoli. Napoleons, Baba Rum, tortes, and other French pastries also available. *541 Monroe. (313) 963-9603. Sun-Thurs 8 a.m.-11:00 p.m., Fri-Sat 8 a.m.-1:30 a.m.* &.

◆ **Athens Grocery and Bakery.** Both Greektown groceries enjoy good reputations among Greek-Americans, and they smell wonderfully of fresh bread (in the morning) and spices. The crusty loaves, soft in the middle, sell for under a dollar apiece. The Athens' old-fashioned front window, filled with neatly arranged groceries, nicely balances Greektown's neon glitz. *527 Monroe. (313) 961-1149. Mon-Thurs 9-9, Fri & Sat 9-11, Sun 9-7.*

◆ **Monroe Grocery and Bakery.** Open the beat-up wood screen door, and you feel you're in a time warp. Ornate, shiny tins of olive oil and imports have a turn-of-the-century look, *573 Monroe. (313) 964-9642. Sun-Thurs 9:30-8:30, Fri & Sat until 10 or 11.* &: no.

*Greektown is on Monroe St. between St. Antoine & Beaubien. Follow 75 South to 375 South and take the Lafayette exit. Most restaurants open 11 a.m.- 2 a.m. or later, 7 days a week. **Park** at the large, 24-hour city structure just east of Greektown, entered off Monroe or Macomb. **People Mover Stations:** Greektown (Monroe and Beaubien), Bricktown (Beaubien and Fort).*

BRICKTOWN

"Bricktown" is the designation for the mixed area of 19th- century buildings and parking structures along Beaubien near Jefferson. It has its own People Mover stop.

◆ **Muccioli Studio Gallery.** An elegantly renovated Italianate town-house serves as the studios of jeweler Nate Muccioli and his mother, Anna Muccioli, both graduates of the Center for Creative Studies. She's a painter and sculptor; he does custom creative jewelry and uses the gold and stones in customers' old jewelry in new designs. *511 Beaubien near Greektown. (313) 962-4700. Tues-Fri 11-6, Sat 11-4.* &: call.

◆ **DuMouchelle Art Galleries.** The region's premier auction spot is where the furniture, art, jewelry, and bibelots of the very rich are put on the block. Once Detroit's first Cadillac dealership, the building has big display windows today full of things like chandeliers, porcelain, paintings, cut crystal, silver, rugs, and furniture. These are priced items for sale right from the floor.

Auctions take place once a month, usually the second or third week. The event attracts collectors from all over the world. Items may be inspected the week before the auction from 9:30 to 5:30. The three-day auction begins Friday at 6:30 p.m., Saturday at 11 a.m., and Sunday at noon. Items go for anywhere from $10 to $400,000. A Tiffany lamp recently sold for $49,000. A silk Oriental rug from the Shah of Iran's palace was picked up for $60,000. And the high bid for an Andy Warhol "slipper collage" was $10,000. *409 E. Jefferson at Brush across from the RenCen. (313) 963-6255. Mon-Fri 9-5:30, Sat 9:30-5:30. Free valet parking on auction dates. Pick up a **free illustrated brochure** for the upcoming auction here, at the RenCen visitor information booth or at the Detroit Historical Society.* &

◆ **The Beaubien House,** a beautifully renovated Italianate townhouse from the 1870s, is a good first stop for people interested in making their own tour of **Detroit historic architecture**. The historic home is now headquarters of the **American Institute of Architects of Michigan**. In the elegant front parlor are worthwhile **changing exhibits** related to architecture or people involved in architecture in Michigan. *553 E. Jefferson just east of Beaubien. (313) 965-4100. Mon-Fri 8-5.* &*: back entrance.*

GROCERIES IN GREEKTOWN . . . . . Hours at Greektown's two old-world grocery stores are so long ('til 9 p.m. at the earliest) that you can both dine and shop for groceries. Greek bread, cheese, and wine can be the center of simple, delicious meals. **Greek feta cheese**, made from sheep's milk, is richer and quite unlike the domestic variety. Creamy white **kasseri cheese** is like a mild cheddar. It can be cut into cubes, dredged in seasoned flour, and pan-fried 'til it's soft. Greeks serve it with lemon, crusty Greek bread, and a **red wine** like the dry red from the highly recommended Nemea (pronounced "nuh-MAY-uh") region. An excellent, very light white wine is made by Boutari. Both are about $7 a bottle. **Retsina wine**, flavored with resin, is admittedly an acquired taste even when served correctly (very, very cold). Greeks like to drink it with fish, or with olives, bread, and fresh tomatoes.

THE CRIMINAL JUSTICE SYSTEM AT WORK . . . . . Criminal mystique has been one of Detroit's hottest cultural exports, thanks to area detective writers Elmore Leonard and Loren Estleman, who have set many of their stories here. **Detroit Recorder's Court** is where Leonard and Estleman get much of their material, and where Harrison Ford hung out to pick up atmosphere for the movie *Presumed Innocent*. A model of efficiency under difficult conditions, the court won a prestigious national award for its operation. "Watching criminal investigations in Recorder's Court is better than going to the movies, and it's free," says a Leonard character. Now Wayne County voters will elect the judges, but visitors will see the same interesting cast of characters: incredibly stupid criminals, mostly; theatrical lawyers; and judges and staff who have seen it all. See if you can find the Wayne County sheriff wearing a wig to hide his flowing, Ted Nugent-style locks. *Frank Murphy Hall of Justice, 1441 St. Antoine south of Gratiot, a block northwest of Greektown.*

Detroit People Mover

Get a spectacular bird's-eye view
of downtown on one of the country's
most lavish public transportation systems.

THIS elevated rail system runs in a 2.9-mile loop around downtown. It offers extraordinary views of the central city, the Detroit River, and Windsor. Even in winter, it's a memorable ride. As a bonus, big, colorful works of art make it an adventure to enter the platforms in each of the 13 stations. Call the People Mover for a splendid brochure on **"Art in the Stations."** Especially memorable are Stephen Antonakos's neon at Greektown, Charles McGee's African-inspired *Noah's Ark* at the Broadway station, and rich, new dynamic designs in Pewabic tile at Millender Center and Times Square, as well as 1955 Pewabic tile originally made for Stroh Brewery at the Cadillac Center.

The People Mover is the most expensive public transportation project in history. The 2.9 miles cost federal and state taxpayers a whopping $200 million, vastly more than initial projections. Unfortunately, there were fewer riders than projected, requiring the financially strapped city to subsidize it heavily.

Vibrant art, mostly in tile and richly colorful, makes the People Mover experience even more exciting. Views of art alternate with slice-of-life reality as you look into the buildings and streets along the route. Art is in each station. Pewabic tile is often featured in this important and successful public art project. Here are (left) Al Loving Jr.'s subtly colorful work in Millender Center and Kirk Newman's hurrying commuters in the Michigan Avenue station.

Still, the People Mover is a visitor's delight: beautifully designed, clean, safe, and frequently patrolled. It's a smooth- working system which gives the rider an unparalleled view of the glories and desolations of downtown Detroit. The entire loop takes only 15 minutes. Cars come at least every two to three minutes. Maps with all the stations and what's near them are available in each car.

You may want to make several trips to take it all in: the beauty of the aqua Detroit River on a sunny day, the ornate 1920s skyscrapers, the VIPs' cars double-parked for lunch at the elite Detroit Club, historic Grand Circus Park, the once proud and now sadly abandoned hotels and office buildings on the north part of the loop, the towering Renaissance Center, lively Bricktown and Greektown. Special highlights: the swing out over the Detroit River by the Joe Louis Arena and the up-close glimpse of City-County Building employees at their desks.

Downtown Detroit (see map for route). 1-800-541-7245; from Detroit, 962-RAIL. Current operating hours: Mon-Thurs 7 a.m.-11 p.m., Fri 7 a.m.-midnight, Sat 9 a.m.-midnight, Sun noon-8 p.m. Hours are often extended for special events. Call for information. Fare: 50¢, seniors & physically challenged 25¢, children 5 and under free. &

FOR A HANDY PEOPLE MOVER MAP . . . . . with clear indications of nearby destinations, call (800) 541-7245 or, from Detroit, 962-RAIL. Ask for the "Art in the Stations" brochure while you're at it.

Guardian Building

*A most remarkable
Art Deco skyscraper
is a visual feast.*

THIS COLORFUL, richly decorated Art Deco skyscraper, finished in 1929, is a flamboyant banking tribute to Detroit's go-go years of the 1920s. It also is linked to the financial excesses of that time, for its occupant and owner, Guardian National Bank, was the very first in a domino-like chain of banks across the United States to close in 1933, greatly intensifying the national Depression.

The notched Aztec façade is unusual in itself. The 32-story building is faced with specially-made reddish-orange bricks, enlivened by bands of green and white Pewabic tiles. Using bricks, less costly than the granite or limestone exteriors of most skyscrapers of the era, allowed architect Wirt Rowland to spend the savings on a variety of spectacular visual effects, designed to make the building seem inviting while standing out — both on the street and within the skyline.

Most stunning are the **main lobby** and the adjacent **banking room** half a story up which visitors may look into. When you walk into the lobby, the building takes you by surprise, even when you've been there before. It's so rich, so saturated. The greens and blues, golds and reds of the lobby ceiling tiles are echoed in the back-lit stained glass seen in the elevator alcove. Every detail reinforces this vibrant, strong impression: the Pewabic tile in the half-dome outside over the entrance; the blood-red Numidian marble at the interior walls' base (an African quarry was reopened for this job alone); the stylized white pine mosaic bearing the bank motto. Reinforcing the image of Guardian Trust as the people's bank, the

Blue, green, and red tiles in geometric Indian motifs decorate not only the Guardian Building's outside entrance but its roof line and lobby. Inside a Michigan map mural, one of many contributions by noted artists, dominates the grand banking hall.

effect was designed to be strong but warm.

In the same vein today, visitors are approached by security guards and given a beautiful four-color brochure about the building and the era that produced it. The Guardian's present owner-occupant, the MichCon natural gas utility, has restored the building and removed paneling that hid its glorious ornaments. Though the onetime banking hall is off-limits office space, visitors are welcome to look in at this cathedral of finance and take in the geometric ceiling murals and Michigan map. In the basement, the snazzy **Aztec Cafe** lunch room, open to the public, carries out the Art Deco look with a stainless steel ceiling and incorporates the old bank vaults. Lunch specials are under $4.

Ernest Kanzler, brother-in-law and close friend of Henry Ford's son, Edsel, built the Guardian Building. His Guardian Group became the major banking power in Detroit. Edsel Ford put millions of his and Ford Motor Company's money into Kanzler's banking syndicate. So successful was this group that there was even talk that Detroit would overtake Chicago as the financial center of the Midwest. Then the 1929 stock market crash put increasing strain on the overextended bank. Despite a personal plea from President Hoover, Henry Ford refused to bail the bank out at a critical juncture, even though his son lost up to $20 million with its failure.

500 Griswold at Congress. (313) 965-2430. Lobby open 24 hours a day, 7 days a week. &

OTHER FINE DOWNTOWN OFFICE TOWERS AND BANKS FROM THE EARLY 20TH CENTURY . . . . . The 1925 **Buhl Building** across Griswold from the Guardian Building feels like a church, a true temple of commerce, with the dark, enclosed, rich effect of heavy medieval masonry and Romanesque decorative embellishments. Italian bronzes accent the marble lobby. The Buhl Cafe and Bar has the quiet, cozy feel of a private club. *Southwest corner, Griswold at Congress. Open Mon-Fri . . . . .* In the 47-story **Penobscot Building**, finished in 1928, architect Wirt Rowland designed one of Detroit's most endearingly appealing buildings. Setbacks above the 30th floor form an interesting cubistic pattern topped by an observation deck (now closed) and a big, illuminated ball, once a hallmark of the city. Inside, the warm-colored marble floors feature geometric designs, with Indian eagles on the elevator doors and mailboxes. The interior shops include **L&L Books** (open weekdays 9-6) and **John T. Woodhouse Sons** tobacconist, whose wood-inlaid interior is a period delight. In the basement, entered off Fort St., the **Epicurean Cafe** is a big place with breakfasts and lunches that are a terrific deal. *Corner of Griswold and Fort. (313) 961-8800. Mon-Fri 8 a.m.-6 p.m.* &

CRIME IN DETROIT . . . . . is what outsiders worry most about. But downtown Detroit, Rivertown, and the New Center are frequently patrolled. The People Mover is constantly monitored. Recent national statistics confirm the notion held by most people who live and work in Detroit that crime downtown is no worse than in other big American cities. . . . . Normal discretion about being aware, avoiding deserted places, likely targets of holdups at night, bad neighborhoods, etc., is advisable, of course. (In Detroit, however, it's not so easy to tell a bad neighborhood. The lower Cass Corridor look awful but isn't. Crime is much lower in some desolate parts of the depopulated east side than in better-looking, younger west side neighborhoods. . . . At night, know where you're going and take advantage of lighted, guarded parking whenever possible. . . . . The biggest danger in Detroit at night, insiders say, is **car theft**, not muggings. GM products and snazzy trucks are most in demand. . . . .

The Theater District

A restored Siamese-Byzantine-Hindu picture palace and a world-class opera house anchor the revival of one of America's great entertainment centers from the 1920s.

DETROIT'S EXTRAORDINARY auto boom decade of the 1920s resulted in an unusual concentration of theaters — second to New York in total seating capacity. The downtown theater district is again attracting crowds to the central city. And 1996 saw a huge step taken in realizing the dreams of a reborn theater district with the spectacular transformation of the Grand Circus Theater from a water-damaged wreck into the world-class Detroit Opera House.

In Detroit the auto boom's explosive population growth coincided with the era of palatial movie theaters put up across America by Hollywood studio owners. Detroit's Grand Circus Park area attracted many opulent theaters, each designed to outdo the last. None was more utterly and unabashedly gaudy than the 5,000-seat **Fox Theatre** on Woodward, opened in 1928 and restored in 1988. Part of the nationwide 250-theater Fox chain, this picture palace, built for $6 million, was the flagship of the empire and the pinnacle of Detroit architect C. Howard Crane's successful career as one of the nation's preeminent designers of movie theaters.

The eclectic Asian interior was designed by owner William Fox's wife, Eve Leo. She humorously called it "Siamese Byzantine." The six-story lobby was intended to look like an ancient temple in India. In the main auditorium you can see a two-ton stained-glass chandelier. Walls feature peacocks, serpents, Buddhas, Chinese tomb guardians, Greek masks, Egyptian lions, and other motifs from Hindu, Persian, Indian, Chinese, and southeast Asian art. This era of unbridled opulence was not to last long. William Fox lost control of his theaters during the Depression, which left him $91 million in debt.

The Fox was designed for both movies and live performances. A careful $15 million restoration was completed in 1988 thanks to hometown boosters Mike and Marian Ilitch, owners of Little Caesar's Pizza, the Detroit Tigers baseball team, and the Red Wings hockey team. From the start the Fox packed in crowds with over 250 acts a year. It was a heartening boon for a troubled downtown abandoned by major retailers. Next Ilitch business and family interests established North America's third **Second City comedy troupe** in the building next door and launched three new restaurants in and around the Fox: **Tres Vite**, superchef Jimmy Schmidt's Mediterranean restaurant in the Fox office building; **America's Pizza Cafe**, where specialty pizzas are made in a wood-fired oven, also in the Fox building; and **Risata**, a contemporary Italian restaurant in the Second City building.

For several years in a row, the Fox has been the top-grossing venue in the U.S. Wide-ranging attractions have included Barbara Streisand, David Copperfield, the New York City Ballet, Bonnie Raitt, and President Bill Clinton speaking to the G-7 economic conference. The Ilitches renovated the 10-story office building attached to the Fox as the world headquarters of Little Caesar's, their pizza

In terms of lavish splendor, it seemed nothing anywhere could outdo the Fox, the largest and most exotic of the 1920s picture palaces, dreamed up by movie magnate William Fox and his wife Eve, with help from architect C. Howard Crane. This is its lobby.

But in booming Detroit, even it was upstaged by the Fisher Theater, for opulence if not size. And then came the Great Depression.

Theater District savior Chuck Forbes, in his State Theater: he assembled the key properties and restored two (so far) himself.

chain of over 4,000 stores. It was the first suburban firm to move into Detroit in recent years, and one of the largest.

Now the Ilitches, as owners of the Detroit Tigers, are building a new Tiger Stadium behind the theater as "Foxtown," a broadly conceived entertainment district. The plan has been controversial because some state tax money would be required to make it work. However, in early 1995 the proposal survived both a ballot referendum and a legal challenge. It now appears to be on the way toward opening perhaps in 1999.

Much of the credit for this district revival goes to Detroit real estate executive/investor Chuck Forbes, a former Ford Motor real estate executive. He has nurtured his long-held dream to save the grand theater district he had loved growing up in Detroit. First he bought several threatened theaters, including the Fox. Brought together by the city of Detroit with bigger investors, including the Ilitches, he made deals to assure the theaters' preservation and reuse. His own flagship is the intimate, stunningly restored 1927 **Gem Theater** (designed by George Mason) across Woodward from the Fox, home to musical revues that bring in visitors by the busload. On a bigger scale, Forbes's 1925 **State Theater** (another Crane design), half a block down Woodward from the Fox, has cabaret seating, a 64-screen video wall, and a dance floor. Designed by Crane in an opulent Renaissance style, the theater is now used for rock concerts, dancing, and private parties and meetings.

The $36 million **Detroit Opera House** developed by the **Michigan Opera Theater** has created a world-class opera house that played host to Luciano Pavarotti, Dame Joan Sutherland, and other luminaries on opening night in spring, 1996. Its acoustics are naturally excellent, thanks in large part to the way sound bounces within its shoebox shape, longer than it is wide. The theater was designed for

David Di Chiera outside the stagehouse of the newly restored Detroit Opera House: 25 years of developing an audience and support for opera have paid off in a world-class opera house for the world's preeminent factory town.

the human voice — for vaudeville, but the effect's the same for opera. The renovation restored the historic interior with its delicate neoclassical plaster decorations and built a new stage house, dressing areas, classrooms, etc. The 7,000-square-foot stage, 65 feet deep, and the backstage facilities compare with other world-class opera houses. The orchestra pit can hold the entire Detroit Symphony Orchestra — over 90 musicians. These facilities mean that now there's nothing being staged that couldn't be performed in Detroit — even the most spectacular megamusicals. With 2,700 seats, the Opera House is one of the Midwest's largest venues for legitimate theater and musicals, though locally the Masonic Temple has far more seats (4,444). An extra bonus: many Opera House seats are quite affordable. The cheapest season-ticket seats are $17.

This grand accomplishment is due to the vision, tenacity, and untemperamental charm of David Di Chiera. Then an Oakland University faculty member, he founded the Michigan Opera Theater in 1971 to bring opera to schoolchildren. Initially, the MOT reopened the Music Hall as a regular tenant — actually the first step in the Theater District's revival — and then used larger venues. Di Chiera developed the MOT into a nationally respected opera com-

pany that presented its own productions, sometimes staged together with operas he simultaneously headed in Dayton and Orange
County. Di Chiera was determined that MOT should have its own
home, one built for the human voice. His conservative fund-raising
plan got early, critical financial support from Ford, Kmart, Detroit
Renaissance, and General Motors. Di Chiera (pronounced DEE key
AIR uh) credits much of the MOT's success to the sustaining support of his ex-wife, Karen VanderKloot, who still heads the MOT's
community outreach department.

As landlord, the MOT supports its own season on revenue and
profits from leasing the house to traveling shows and local events.

Yet more theaters may be in store for the district. Forbes plans
to renovate the **Century**, a turn-of-the-century women's club with
playhouse next to the Gem, into a 200-seat dinner theater, planned
to open in 1997. Forbes also owns the nearby YWCA, which houses
both a 200-seat theater and a 500-seat auditorium. He hopes to
someday operate both as commercial venues and turn upper floors
into condo apartments. Meanwhile, the Detroit-based building firm
run by the McLemore family has bought the **Madison Theater** on
Grand Circus Park and plans to turn it into a Motown Cafe-style
entertainment club, with its own corporate offices on top. The
Ilitches own the defunct Adams Theater on Grand Circus Park and
may someday renovate it.

A most welcome bonus of Theater District redevelopment is
demand and plans for new housing. For the first time in decades,
there is demand for housing *away* from the river. Additional housing is happening in **Harmonie Park** — the charming, intimate corner of downtown between the Theater District and Greektown
whose restaurants and coffeehouses are an important part of the
Theater District's revival. See page 230. There's even revived interest in the grand old buildings on Washington Boulevard, including
the sumptuous Book Cadillac Hotel, site of John F. Kennedy's last
speech before Dallas, closed for nearly 20 years.

Here's information about attending events at current theater
district venues. For freeway directions to the Theater District, see
end of theater entries.

◆ **Fox Theatre.** *Woodward at Montcalm at the northwest edge of
downtown. (313) 396-7600. Parking (maximum daily or evening rate
$5) is off Woodward across the street or in the eight-story parking
deck behind the theater off Montcalm.*

◆ **Second City Theatre.** Young actor/comedians on an empty
stage create topical sketches and improvise. Second City developed
talent and set the style for *Saturday Night Live.* Incidentally, the

father of Gilda Radner, one of its most talented alums, managed a Grand Circus Park hotel a few blocks from here. *Woodward at Montcalm, next to the Fox. (313) 965-2222.*

◆ **Gem Theatre.** Splendidly detailed restoration of the intimate, 450-seat Spanish Revival theater built for the 20th Century Club. The Gem now books long-running revues like *Forbidden Broadway, Beehive,* and *Shear Madness.* Historical note: in the early 1960s, actor George C. Scott founded and directed a theater company at the Gem, then known as the Vanguard. *58 East Columbia across Woodward from the Fox. (313) 963-9800.*

◆ **State Theater.** Call (313) 961-5450 for concert and nightclub information. *On Woodward a block east of the Fox.*

◆ **Michigan Opera Theater.** Tickets for the Michigan Opera Theater 1996-7 season *(Carmen, West Side Story, Rigoletto, The Marriage of Figaro, The Flying Dutchman)* range from $86 (Sunday matinees) to $357 for weekend-night orchestra seats. For the cheap seats, sight lines and acoustics are great, but bring binoculars! The house hosts some 200 evenings of entertainment, thanks in large part to a history-making arrangement in which the Nederlander and Ilitch organizations are both booking traveling shows *(Chorus Line, Carousel, Damn Yankees)* at a single venue, the Opera House. *1526 Broadway at Witherell & Madison near Grand Circus Park. (313) 874-7464.*

◆ **Music Hall Center for the Performing Arts.** This elegant theater, built as a legitimate theater in 1928 by Dodge widow and heiress Matilda Dodge Wilson, now books a wide variety of music, dance, and dramatic performances. (313) 963-7680. Weekends it's home to the very popular **Detroit Youtheatre**, with Saturday children's programs and the Wiggle Club on Sundays (both October through May). *350 Madison at Witherell on Grand Circus Park. (313) 963-7663.*

*Freeway directions to Woodward and the Theater District: **From I-94 east or westbound**, take the Woodward exit, go south on Woodward (toward downtown), theater is on the right after 2 miles. **From I-75 southbound**, take Mack Ave. exit, go right onto Mack, go about 3/4 mile to Woodward, turn south onto Woodward (toward downtown); the Fox is on the right in 1/2 mile. **From I-75 northbound**, take Woodward exit, follow signs to Fox Center, taking two immediate right hand turns and you'll see the theater. **From I-96**, go toward Detroit to I-75 north and follow directions above. **From Lodge Freeway**, take I-75 north and follow directions above.*

Eastern Market

A colorful, earthy vestige of old Detroit, with wonderful food appealing to the city's diverse population

SINCE the 1890s, this colorful, bustling market has been where Detroiters come to buy vegetables and produce from area farmers and to purchase groceries from the stores surrounding the market sheds. Up to 800 farmers can sell their produce at the large, municipally-owned open-air stall area called "the sheds." The sheds and the market square (used for parking) are surrounded by wholesale-retail specialty shops, up to a hundred years old, selling meats, fish, coffee, nuts, produce, fruit, spices, wine, and cheese.

Today Eastern Market shoppers take advantage of all kinds of bargains. They can buy in quantity in 50-pound bags. They can buy seconds, or buy discounted produce late in the day on Saturday when vendors need to sell out. They can bargain with vendors. The wholesale-retail stores have prices well below standard retail prices. These stores are also the nucleus of a thriving gift basket cottage industry that buys candies, condiments, and more from R. Hirt, Rafal Spice, and Rocky Peanut Company.

The Market is a genuine vestige of old Detroit: a great medley of smells and sounds and colorful sights, and a vast variety of food appealing to the city's diverse cultures. In front of **Ciaramitaro's**, the third-generation Italian produce business on Market and Winder, you'll see dozens of crates of onions being unloaded, followed by piles of burlap bags of potatoes. Customers buy fruits and vegetables from the stand that's in front of the store, winter and summer.

Across the recessed Fisher Freeway, the aroma of nuts pervades the air at **Germack's**, the oldest pistachio importer in the U.S. Pungent spices greet you in several shops. An Islamic slaughterhouse is a few blocks away. Nearby at **Capital Poultry**, live ducks (a favorite with Detroit's many Poles) and chickens cackle away. Feathers are mixed in the dirt in the gutter outside.

Wholesalers at the market today are likely to be descended from Belgian, German, and Polish farmers who sold at the market generations ago, or from Italian produce peddlers who first catered to Detroit's booming population of industrial workers beginning about 1910. In a city that's known great ups and downs, people love the Eastern Market because it's still pretty much the same. More and more of the vendors are from that nearby part of Canada that's

The market sheds are surrounded by wholesale houses, often 100 years old. Ciarmitaro's Produce (center) is in an 1840s building used by the Underground Railroad. That's a mural of a chicken face on the market shed.

actually *south* of Detroit. The area around Leamington on Lake Erie is known as "the sunpiler." Its produce is two to three weeks ahead of southern Michigan's, and its tomatoes are often ripe by July 4.

In the past two decades artists have been moving into the market area. The five-story building on Gratiot with Fuchs Religious Goods on the ground floor is almost entirely occupied by artists, as is a good deal of second-story space near Rocky Peanut Company. More studios are in the Russell Industrial Center. Detroit's Center for Creative Studies near the Detroit Institute of Arts attracts art students and faculty, but space in that busy area isn't cheap.

The market changes with the time and day of the week. Something's happening almost around the clock.

◆ **Saturday mornings.** The market is a madhouse, especially from 7 to 10, when the crowds are largest. Food-lovers from far and wide converge here for weekend shopping.

◆ **Weekend and weekday nights.** The market area's energetic night life is epitomized by the literally 'til-all-hours activity at **Bert's Marketplace.** This jazz club serves soul food. Ribs and baked chicken are popular items. Musicians perform throughout the week. *2727 Russell. (313) 567-2030. Mon-Thurs 11 a.m. until about 2 or 3 a.m. Fri-Sat 10 a.m. until 5 or 6 a.m.* &

◆ **Early weekday mornings.** The wholesalers' weekday work is mostly over before sun-up. Around 1 a.m. trucks from the South and Southwest arrive to be unloaded. Throughout the early-morning hours, trucks of all sizes are coming and going, unloading and loading. Some produce is already destined for distributors like I.G.A., Spartan, and Abner Wolf, and some is sold at the market. By the time restaurants open around 6 or 7 a.m., the main part of the work day is over, and it's time for a break.

Farmers in market stalls compete with these out-of-state producers for retail buyers, and a lot of bargaining takes place. They are prepared to sell wholesale to distributors, retailers, and restaurants, and retail to the general public. But consumers can try their hand at bargaining down to wholesale prices, especially if they buy in quantity.

◆ **Weekdays in the mid-morning and afternoon.** Now the atmosphere is leisurely — a good time to get the undivided attention of clerks at market shops. The farmers are gone by late morning, but wholesale/retail produce places remain well stocked.

The thickest concentration of retail stores is on Russell just north of the market. There, low new buildings house a variety of retail stores, including the venerable and highly recommended **Al's Fish and Seafood** (2929 Russell, 313-393-1722) and **B & S Produce** (3111 Russell, 313-833-6133). There you can get big bags of onions and potatoes, five pounds of raw peanuts for under $5, fresh-roasted peanuts for little over a dollar a pound, or choose from five kinds of watermelon in season.

North of the market between Gratiot and Mack are several more blocks of wholesalers and meat packers, who cut up and package carcasses for retailers. Every odd turn reveals something else: **Berry & Sons Islamic Slaughterhouse**, **Fuchs Religious Goods** across Gratiot from the Gratiot Central Market (where you'll find jinx-removing incense and herbal remedies), the popular **Farmers' Restaurant** on Market and Division, and the **Meat Cutters Inn** at 2638 Orleans ("Fine Food, open 7 a.m.-7 p.m., Hires Root Beer").

Here are some of the Eastern Market's most noteworthy shops, arranged from east to west:

◆ **Cost Plus Wine Warehouse.** It's a real pleasure to deal with Irishman Tim McCarthy. Knowledgeable without being condescending, he is a terrific guide to wines. Imported and American wines; imported beers. *2448 Market. (313) 259-3845. Mon-Fri 8:30-6, Sat 7-4:30.* ₺.

◆ **R. Hirt Jr. Company.** This century-old Detroit grocery has a great range of merchandise: cheese, sausage and ham products, crackers, bottled waters, beans and rice, coffees and teas, mustards and condiments, chocolates and cookies, and all sorts of imported pastas, jams, sparkling waters, olives, and fancy foods. As at many Eastern Market wholesale/retailers, prices are somewhere between

wholesale and normal retail prices.

Hirt's is resolutely old-fashioned, even when old-fashioned means somewhat inefficient. Here's the system for shopping at Hirt's: take a basket, load up on shelved merchandise, then go to the counterperson. He or she gets your cheese from the ancient, walk-in wood refrigerator, cuts it straight from the wheel (you can ask for samples), wraps your purchases, and writes up a bill. This you pay at the separate cashier's, then return to pick up your purchases. Saturdays are crazy, what with the big, convivial crowds who seem to enjoy the opportunity to socialize in line and pick up food ideas. On weekdays, it's quiet, and the service is faster.

Hirt's non-food treasure trove is the third-floor **wicker and basket department**, where you can find decorator items (including decorative tins, hampers, Adirondack chairs, soaps, lotions, and more), and a huge variety of shapes and sizes of all kinds of baskets. *2468 Market at Windsor. (313) 567-1173. Mon-Fri 8-5, Sat 7-4. Closed on Mon. from Jan. thru Aug. &: ask to use freight elevator for upper floors.*

◆ **Ciaramitaro Brothers Produce.** Ciaramitaro's (pronounced "SHERM-uh-ta-ro's) and many other market old-timers started as commission houses that took farm produce and resold it at a percentage. Today Ciarmitaro's is mainly a wholesale food purveyor to independent groceries, restaurants, and more. The colorful, year-round produce stand on the sidewalk is more of a sideline run by retirees. The ancient-looking frame building was used as a tavern and inn going back to the 1840s. Slaves fleeing to Canada were housed in its basement. *2506 Market at Winder. (313) 567-9064. Mon-Sat 7:30 a.m.-2 p.m. &*

◆ **Eastern Market Trade Center.** Indoor bazaar of small merchants who sell everything from West African sculpture and musical instruments to antiques to baseball cards to gold jewelry to African-theme sportswear. *2530 Market, next to Farmers' Restaurant and Adelaide St. (313) 259-0042. Mon-Thurs 8-5, Fri-Sat 8-6. &: first floor.*

◆ **Rafal Spice Company.** Be sure to stop in here just to smell the cumulative effect of over 400 herbs and spices on hand. It's a visual treat, too, to see row upon row crammed with everything from asafetida powder to burdock root. Rafal also carries 85 kinds of coffee beans (at attractive prices), 60 kinds of bulk teas, and a large assortment of hot sauces and other condiments, plus potpourri, oils, and books with recipes for concocting your own scents. Pick up a **mail-order catalog**, and you can conveniently inventory and restock your spice rack from home. You can also get a catalog by calling (800) 228-4276. *2521 Russell. (313) 259-6373. Mon-Sat 7-4.* &.

♦ **Rocky Peanut Company.** In addition to a very wide variety of bulk nuts, snack mixes, and dried fruit, this updated grocery stocks many oils, vinegars, condiments, packaged cookies, and tinned and packaged gourmet items, coffees, teas, spices, etc. What's especially dazzling are the bins of bulk candies – over 400 kinds, perfect for assembling your own gift baskets. A **coffeehouse** with espresso, cappuccino, and more is open during regular hours. *2489 Russell facing the marketplace. (313) 567-6871. Mon-Fri 7-4; Sat 7-5.* &

♦ **Gratiot Central Market.** A 1995 fire destroyed this colorful landmark in the white terra cotta-faced building with the cow heads over the entrances. It's hoped that most parts of that colorful amalgam of butchers and other shops will reassemble in the new Gratiot Central Market being built upon the site. Meanwhile, **Joe Wigley's Meats** has permanently moved. (See below.) **Ronnie's Meats** (313-874-5796() is temporarily at 1445 E. Kirby at Russell, a mile north, next to Thornapple Valley. Ronnie's specialties are shish-kebab meat and baby-back ribs once deemed the best in town by *Detroit Monthly*. It also butchers goat to Islamic halal standards and offers organ meats that most Americans don't consider edible — tripe and sheep testicles, for instance.

♦ **Capital Poultry.** Here you can actually pick out a live chicken to be dressed and picked up later. Free-range chickens grown by northern Indiana Amish are sold for very reasonable prices. Other poultry is also available, including guineas, pigeons, and wild game in season. *1466 E. Fisher Freeway next to the Gratiot Central Market. (313) 567-8200. Tues-Sat 8-5.* &.

♦ **Germack Pistachio Company.** America's oldest pistachio processor (since 1924) offers natural and red pistachios and many kinds of nuts, seeds, and dried fruits. Roasting is done on the premises. *1416 E. Fisher Freeway, near the Gratiot Market. (313) 393-0219. Mon-Fri 8:30-5, Sat 8-12 (til 3 during the holidays).* &.

♦ **Joe's Wine and Liquor.** Known for its extensive collection of beers. *2933 Russell. (313) 393-3125. Mon-Sat 7-6, Fri until 7.* &

♦ **Joe Wigley Meats** has a reputation and a half for its kosher-style corned beef and lamb. For years, it was in the Gratiot Central Market until the 1995 fire. Its retail outlet is now located inside

Diamond Produce and seems destined to stay there. For years, it was in the Gratiot Central Market until it burned down. After the fire, Joe Wigley built a new processing plant a few blocks away and now has begun selling its famous corned beef nationally. *In Diamond Produce, 3405 Russell at Erskine. (313) 833-3030. Open Mon-Sat 8-6 and Sun 8-3. Closed Xmas & New Years.* &

The Eastern Market is just north of Gratiot 1 mile east of downtown. From Gratiot, take Russell north over the Chrysler Freeway. From the freeways, get onto the eastbound Fisher Freeway/I-75. It ends by depositing traffic onto Gratiot just east of the market. Turn around and go back on Gratiot. Signs clearly direct visitors from Gratiot to the market. **Parking** *is tight on Saturday in the market square but plentiful in the structure just behind the sheds, entered from Riopelle at Russell. Eastern Market Central Administration: (313) 393-2000.* **Market hours:** *Mon-Fri 5 a.m.-noon (but most farmers arrive at 3 or 4 and are gone by 7 or 8), On Sat., open air market is open 5 a.m.-5 p.m.* **Retail store hours:** *typically 8 a.m. (earlier on Saturday) until 4 p.m. or 2 p.m. Sat.* &

EASTERN MARKET RESTAURANTS . . . . . There are a variety of popular eating places in the market to pick up a breakfast or lunch. The **Russell Street Deli** (2465 Russell, &, 313-567-2900; current hours Mon-Fri 11-2:30, Sat 8-2:30) stands out above the rest with its excellent homemade soups, changing daily, and fresh-roasted turkey and classic deli sandwiches. The same owner-chef has started **Flat Planet Pizza** (313-567-7879), two doors down at 2457 Russell, with carryout gourmet pizza, pasta & salads. **The Farmers' Restaurant** (313-259-8230) at 2542 Market opens early and has good breakfasts, superior pancakes. . . . . Also in the vicinity: the venerable **Roma Cafe, Joe Muer's** outstanding fish restaurant on Gratiot at Vernor, and, on the inexpensive, takeout end, the highly regarded **Louisiana Creole Gumbo** (313-446-9639) just north of Joe Muer's on the opposite side of Gratiot.

EASTERN MARKET FLOWER DAY. . . . . is a big Detroit tradition. Crowds flock here for wide selection and good prices. It's on the spring weekend at the peak of planting season when growers and vendors from Michigan and beyond sell bedding plants and vegetables. It's Saturday and Sunday from 6 a.m. to 4 or 5 p.m., but the date varies with the weather. Call (313) 833-1560.

John King Books

In an old glove factory near downtown, one of the best and biggest used book stores in the country.

HOUSED in a former work glove factory just west of downtown, John King Books has put Detroit on the map for many faraway booklovers who otherwise would give the city short shrift. *New York Times* wordmeister William Safire has called it "the great used book store in Detroit." Workaholic bookseller John King flies around the country tracking down estates, closed book stores, and other sources of used and remaindered books to fill his store's over 30,000 square feet. A separate warehouse has another 20,000 square feet. King also owns the Big Book Store on Cass near Wayne State University (it sells comic books, magazines, and paperbacks) and a Ferndale store with a scaled-down version of his Detroit stock for those too timid to venture to the city. At perhaps a million volumes, his may be the biggest book store in the country. He says he no longer has time to read for pleasure — he's too busy buying and researching stock. The stock is rigorously well organized and the staff knowledgeable and helpful. Browsing on four floors is comfortable despite a sign that warns, "You have to be tough to shop here

Bookseller John King, with Sparky. King flies around the country buying large lots of books for his huge but well organized bookstore.

— we don't serve coffee." On the second floor, tables of irregular Penguins sell for $1 each.

King also sells a fascinating variety of framed pictures, **printed ephemera**, **postcards**, and **collectibles**, artfully displayed in several first-floor rooms of this pleasant catacomb. There's lots of Detroit and Michigan material here, not surprisingly. Ask to see the **catalog** of rare books and letters. The store will **search** for hard-to-find titles for a dollar. A box of free books is always out front.

King's philosophy for acquiring books is to stay general, partly because he finds it "too boring" to specialize, partly because he's not limited by lack of space. He and his staff do a good job weeding out the drivel. Prices can vary widely. One serious book collector says you can occasionally get some terrific bargains here, like the first English edition of Chekov letters he found for $12.50.

901 W. Lafayette at Fifth St. Take the southbound Lodge Expressway (U.S. 10) to the Howard Street exit ramp. Store is at the top of ramp service drive. (313) 961-0622. Mon-Sat 9:30-5:30. ♿: *call first, elevator in back to all four floors.*

Tiger Stadium

One of very last of the legendary old ball parks,
it's got atmosphere the new ones can't beat.

IT LOOKS like the old ball park at Michigan and Trumbull has only a few more years before it's replaced by a new stadium downtown. (See page 232.) The exploits of Tigers past — Ty Cobb, Charlie Gehringer, Mickey Cochran, Al Kaline, not to mention Lou Gehrig's last game and Reggie Jackson's 1971 All-Star home run onto the upper-deck roof — all these resonate in the minds of knowledgeable visitors to the venerable park. Tiger Stadium has no plush suites for corporate entertaining, and more cheap seats than any other major league ball park. That jeopardizes it in the new economics of baseball.

However, just *when* a new ball park may open remains in doubt. Both the city of Detroit and the state of Michigan have agreed to contribute part of the construction costs. And the plan for a new stadium has withstood a ballot referendum and a lawsuit in Lansing, both engineered by fans who wish to preserve the historic ball park. Odds are that a new ball park would open during the 1999 season.

So see the old ball park while you can. The Tigers were already playing at this site (then called Bennett Park, capacity 8,500) when a 23,000-seat stadium was built in 1912. It is the core of today's Tiger Stadium. In 1924 double decks were constructed from first to third base. They extend all the way out over the lower deck, providing some of baseball's best upper-level seats, right on top of the action. In 1936 more double decks were added in the right field pavilion and bleachers, and in 1938 still more seats, bringing the capacity to 53,000. Today Tiger Stadium is the only major league ballpark with upper deck and lower deck outfield seats. That, experts say, makes it "the best fan ballpark in the country."

On the other hand, the old ballpark has its problems. Up to 7,000 seats are obstructed. And restrooms and concession stands in the concourse levels are dank, dark, and uninviting. And then there's the **Corktown** neighborhood — a typical Detroit landscape consisting of a few old buildings and too much vacant space. That puts off the suburbanites who are baseball's biggest fans. In truth, those old bars on Michigan Avenue are lively remnants of an Irish community that still comes back to the neighborhood to get together in places like the **Irish-American Club** (313-964-8700) at 2068

Michigan Avenue, known for traditional music, dance, and drink. As the Irish have moved out, they have been replaced by Maltese — a little-known ethnic group initially drawn by the auto plants. (Metro Detroit has more Maltese than anywhere else aside from the Mediterranean island nation itself.) Corktown is a remarkably stable, mixed neighborhood, home of many professionals. But the bleak view on and off Michigan Avenue is so off-putting, it's hard to convince suburban visitors that the area is pretty safe.

Tigers owner Mike Illitch oversees a flourishing entertainment empire that also includes the Detroit Red Wings hockey team, various minor league clubs, and the Little Caesar pizza chain. Known as a marketing genius, Ilitch has done much to attract fans. (Too bad his Tigers have become the worst team in baseball, without the panache of the original Mets!) He brought back live organ music to Tiger Stadium, rectifying one of many PR blunders by former Tiger owner and rival pizza baron Tom Monaghan. He has introduced a host of promotions. Monday night, kids can run the bases after the game. Friday nights bring **fireworks** from Memorial Day to Labor Day. **Seniors** 62 and over pay $7, not $11, for weekday day games. There's an **alcohol-free family seating section**.

Michigan Ave. at Trumbull, one mile west of downtown. From I-75 and the south or from the westbound I-75, take Rosa Parks exit 49A. Other freeways take Trumbull exit from right lane. For schedule, tickets, group discounts, call (313) 962-4000.

TASTES OF MEXICO AND IRELAND NEAR TIGER STADIUM . . . . . Just half a mile southwest of the stadium on Bagley is **Mexican Town**. Businesses here and on Vernor serve southwest Detroit's Hispanic population of over 30,000. Standouts among restaurants: **Los Galanes** (23rd & Bagley, 313-554-4444, patio, lunch buffet, live Latin music & dance Thurs-Sun); **Las Brisas** (8445 Vernor near Lawndale, 313-842-8252, mariachi bands Fri & Sat); **El Comal** (1414 Junction near Vernor, 313-841-7753, Guatemalan & Central American cooking & art). Among stores: **La Plaza Market** (1139 Clark near Clark Park, 313-843-1211, Latin groceries & beers); the new **Mexicantown Bakers** (4300 W. Vernor, 313-554-0001). . . . . The **Mexicantown Mercado** open-air market brings imported crafts, clothing, etc. to Bagley at 21st Sundays from late June to early Sept. (313-842-0450). . . . . In the heart of Corktown, near the Irish mother church Holy Trinity, is the charming **O'Leary's Tea Room**, (1411 Brooklyn at Porter, 313-964-0936; not just lunch but dinner too).

Detroit Institute of Arts

One of the nation's most extraordinary collections of great art, with special strengths in American art, German Expressionism, and Italian Renaissance art

DETROIT'S art museum is blessed with one of the world's great art collections. It is encyclopedic—virtually every period of Western art is creditably represented, from the Mesopotamian through modern eras. In nonwestern art, the Asian and African collections are especially strong. Works by every major American artist are here.

The museum's greatest strengths are in American, Italian Renaissance, Dutch-Flemish, and German Expressionist art. While there are dozens of masterpieces throughout, the following (arranged in chronological order) are considered the museum's most important:

Gudea of Lagash (Mesopotamian), ca. 2141-2122 B.C. Superb stone sculpture of the ruler of a city-state.

Early Autumn (Qian Xuan), 13th or 14th century from China. Delicate handscroll in ink and color of insects in autumn.

Nail Figure (from the Western Kongo), ca. 1875-1900. 46-inch wooden icon served an African community's mystical needs.

Saint Jerome in His Study (Jan van Eyck), ca. 1390-1441. Small, richly symbolic oil painting by the great Flemish painter.

The Wedding Dance (Pieter Bruegel the Elder), ca. 1566. Colorful, realistic view of a peasant wedding.

The Visitation (Rembrandt), 1640. Dramatic presentation of the Biblical scene in which Mary and Elizabeth encounter God.

Cotopaxi (Frederic Church), 1862. Grand, mystical oil painting of an active volcano in the Andes.

Self Portrait (Vincent van Gogh), 1887. One of the great artist's sunnier self-portraits.

Seated Bather (Pierre-Auguste Renoir), 1903-6. Sensuous, languid nude painted when the artist was in his sixties.

Detroit Industry (Diego Rivera), 1932-33. Rivera's masterpiece. An enormous series of frescoes focusing on Detroit's auto industry.

Reclining Figure (Henry Moore), 1939. Large female sculpture in elmwood.

Many other important works are worth mentioning — major

pieces by Whistler, Picasso, Modigliani, Miro, Kokoschka, Gauguin, Seurat, Degas, Cezanne, and Matisse, among others. A popular favorite is Romare Bearden's **Quilting Time** (1986), a large, colorful work showing African-Americans and their quilts outside a tiny house in a cotton field.

To find specific works, ask a staff person to note their locations on a map as you enter. The museum's huge size and disorienting labyrinth of halls and corridors present the visitor with the problem of excess. You need to be careful not to become numbed by the thousands of pieces on display. One helpful antidote is a free one-hour **guided tour** *(given Wed-Sat 1 p.m., Sun at 1 & 2:30, groups over 15 by reservation, call 313-833-7981)*. It gives a quick view of the highlights.

Detroit was merely a medium-sized city until the auto boom took off around 1910. The late 19th-century wealth that launched most great American museums wasn't widespread enough here. When Detroit did finally open its museum, in 1927, it had the talent and resources to build a great museum quickly. Its first director, William Valentiner, a friend of many German Expressionists, bought their work before the art market escalated its cost. In Detroit, Valentiner proved a gifted teacher of wealthy, well-connected Detroiters like Robert Hudson Tannahill and Eleanor Clay Ford, cousins belonging to the J. L. Hudson department store family. They contributed enormously to the museum, not only through their donations, but through their advice, taste, and connections.

Edsel Ford, Henry's son and Eleanor's husband, had the enthusiasm to take up Valentiner's suggestion and commission Diego Rivera, the great Mexican socialist muralist, to create his masterpiece, *Detroit Industry*, in the DIA's main courtyard. And Edsel Ford had the courage to stand up to virulent criti-

To make family museum visits into adventures, go to the Rivera Court info desk (10 a.m.-3 p.m.) and pick up free, cartoon-style gallery guides and games like this popular Indiana Jones-style archaeological adventure kit with five mysterious three-dimensional fragments.from ancient Egypt, Babylon, Greece, and Rome.

Diego Rivera's masterpiece, *Detroit Industry,* was made possible through the patronage of Henry Ford's son, Edsel, with the encouragement of his friend and art mentor, museum director William Valentiner. Radical in its critique of capitalism, the mural accurately depicted manufacturing processes and conveyed Rivera's admiration for the possibilities of the machine age. Ford defended *Detroit Industry* against the predictable outcry of criticism, while the Rockefellers capitulated and destroyed the Rivera mural they commissioned for Rockefeller Center.

cism of this powerful but controversial celebration and critique of Detroit's economic base. Its social criticism and modernist look went way beyond the bounds of the genteel good taste wealthy Detroiters expected from art.

The down side of Detroit's late entry into the art museum game is the DIA's still-skimpy endowment. The DIA remained far more dependent on government subsidies than most museums. A recent funding crisis cut back hours, eliminated blockbuster shows, and had museum galleries open in shifts for awhile. Now, thanks to volunteers, all galleries are open, and a scaled-back program of **special exhibits**, often drawn from the museum's own collections, is in place. For the many **lectures** and **events** on weekdays, evenings, and weekends, call (313) 833-7978 .

The museum is making the right moves to broaden and deepen its audience and supporters. (Often it has felt like a stage set for a fashionable crowd of suburbanites who dash into the underground garage and never connect with the city.) It is also reaching out — belatedly, but with sincere enthusiasm — to the black community right around it. For the time being, thanks to the Michigan Council for Arts & Cultural Affairs, the DIA offers a full, broadly appealing, affordable schedule of **year-round art classes** and longer **workshops** for families, for children in three age groups from 9 to 18, for adults, and for teachers. Call (313) 833-4249. **Drop-in workshops** for all ages, related to current exhibits and popular areas of art, are free with museum admission.

The DIA staff knows it has had a problem being user-friendly. The huge museum with its multiple additions is made even more confusing and hard to grasp because the ground-level side entrance on Farnsworth has become the major entrance. Visitors have to thread their way through hallways, stairways, and elevators to the main first-floor galleries. A map is essential here.

The museum has created a **visitor center** off the Farnsworth lobby. It's easy to miss. Here in a short video, museum director Sam Sachs, hand in blazer pocket, invites visitors to "have fun. You're going to have a great experi-
ence." He urges them to think and explore art, points out that reproductions are no substitute for seeing the orig-inal, and dispenses sensible advice. The museum can't be seen in a day. Choose a part to look at more closely. When concentration wanes or arch-es collapse, take a break. The museum has two restau-rants. The striking **Kresge Court Cafe** (Wed-Fri 11:30-

Portraits of art patron Edsel Ford (left) and his friend William Valentiner, founding director of the Detroit Institute of Arts, are depicted in a corner of *Detroit Industry.*

3:30, Sat-Sun 11:30-4:30) is a vast, open dining area inspired in part by the courtyard of the Bargello Palace in Florence. Here you can eat cafeteria-style, sip coffee, or drink beer and wine. The upscale **American Grille** restaurant offers table service and a Sunday brunch (Wed-Fri 11:30-2, Sun brunch 11-3); for reservations, call (313) 833-1857.

The **Museum Shop** by the Farnsworth entrance carries a sophisticated selection of art books, cards, reproductions, jewelry, souvenirs, and gift items. Shops are becoming a major revenue source for strapped museums; the DIA shop has outlets at Novi's Twelve Oaks mall and the Somerset Collection (page 321). *(313) 833-7944. Open Wed-Fri 11-4:30, Sat & Sun 11-5:30.*

*5200 Woodward between Kirby and Farnsworth, 1/4 mile southeast of I-94. From I-94 east or west, take the Woodward/John R exit, go south on John R approximately 4 blocks. From I-75 south, take the Warren Ave. exit, proceed on Warren 5 blocks to Woodward, and go north 1 block on Woodward. From U.S. 10 north or south, take the Forest Ave. exit, go east on Forest, then north on Woodward 1/2 mile. (313) 833-7900. Wed-Fri 11-4; Sat-Sun 11-5. & Pay what you wish, but you must pay something. Suggested admission: adults $4, students and children $1. Occasional charge (typically $3) for special exhibitions. **Parking** in a secure, lighted parking garage on Farnsworth. Unpaved lot east of museum on Frederick Douglass between John R and Brush.*

OTHER NEARBY MUSEUMS . . . . . The handsome **Museum of African-American History** documents the history and culture of African-Americans from pre-slavery life in African villages through the Underground Railroad to the Civil Rights Movement. The museum's most dramatic display is a full-scale mock-up of part of a slave ship below deck, complete with sound effects. *301 Frederick Douglass between John R and Brush. From Woodward, take Kirby to John R, turn right, then left. (313) 833-9800. Wed-Sat 9:30-5; Sun 1-5. Suggested donation: $2/adults, $1/children. . . . . .* Some time in 1997 the museum will move into its vast **new home** a block away on East Warren at Brush. (See page 264.) It will be closed for three months during the move. . . . . . **The Detroit Science Center** has many hands-on exhibits: computer games, a giant soap bubble device, anatomical displays, geological formations, fossils. The big draw is the **Omni-Max Theater**, a huge tilted screen which conveys a sense of motion in specially filmed movies. Science-related films are included in the admission fee. Call for topics and times. *5020 John R. From Woodward, take Kirby to John R. (313) 577-8400. Mon-Fri 10-4, Sat & Sun 11:30-5. & Adults $6.50; ages 4-12 $4.50; under 4 free.* **FOR CURRENT GALLERY SHOWS . . . . .** see listings in the Friday *Detroit Free*

Press and *Detroit News.*

THE DIA'S DETROIT FILM THEATER. . . . . Variety has called "this superbly equipped theatre. . . . . the best buy for cinéastes in America." It's comfortable, elegant, cheap ($5.50), and stimulating. And the **Crystal Gallery Cafe** on the balcony serves coffees, snacks, sandwiches, and pastries from an hour before each day's first performance (that means 6 p.m. on Fri & Mon, 3 p.m. on weekends) until the last show begins. . . . . In its own words: "Important premieres by both new and established directors will share the screen with restored, rarely-seen classics. All showings are in the DIA's exquisite, 1,150-seat theatre, which is equipped to show all films in their correct aspect ratios, exactly as their directors intended." . . . . . The **Monday series** shows "independent features, documentaries, challenging new visions, and freshly restored classics." . . . . . *Typical* **show times**: *Fri 7 & 9:30-10, Sat 4, 7 & 9:30, Sun 4 & 7, Mon 7.* **Tickets** *at the door and in advance. Books of 5 are $20. Call (313) 833-2323 for tickets and* **schedule info.**

Detroit Historical Museum

*From fort to Motor City, Detroit's past
is illuminated with bold, insightful exhibits.*

THERE is no better overview of the birth of the American auto industry and how cars changed Detroit than the sweeping, spectacular **Motor City Exhibition** — "How cars built Detroit. How Detroit builds cars." This permanent exhibit, center-piece of the museum, was installed to commemorate the centennial of the American automobile in 1996. It has all the requisite special effects of a major museum exhibit. There's a computer-aided design station that lets visitors "create" a car and a nifty interactive "Where Would You Work?" display that shows various real jobs in action and describes their pros and cons. A chunk of assembly line from the old Clark Street Cadillac plant includes a moving two-story body drop and appropriate sound effects. In a contemporary twist, the visitor/autoworker is empowered to stop the line if quality problems arise.

Best of all, there's real depth and breadth here, and lots of ideas, pithily expressed. A satisfying hometown touch is coupled with meaty concepts — a hard thing for many museums to get right. Overlooked but key auto pioneers like Henry Leland are given their due. Experienced in building gasoline marine engines, he persuaded unhappy early Ford investors to put their money into his Cadillac company. He was the leading auto engineer of his day, credited with implementing interchangeable parts. The industry's booms and busts eliminated smaller auto makers like Packard and Hudson; their achievements are detailed. The success of Ford's low-cost strat-egy is made clear. In 1904 2,735 Ford workers made 9,125 vehicles. Ten years later, 67,538 Ford workers made 442,982 vehicles, 78% of the total U.S. production.

TV ads and promotional materials, and snapshots of cars with their owners, reflect the enormous role of cars in American popular culture. Autoworkers don't get left out, either. Efficiency expert Frederick Taylor visited Detroit shortly after 1900 and complained that "the shops were really run by the workmen and not the boss-es." He wanted — and Detroit soon got — a workplace where work-ers wouldn't think. Justice is done to Detroit's epic drama as a magnet for immigrants from large parts of the world — not just Poland and Italy, but Malta and Syria, not to mention disparate parts of America like Mississippi cotton fields, Kentucky coal fields,

Though the spectacular, interactive, and illuminating Motor City
Exhibition is the museum's new centerpiece, there's also a lot about the
interesting early part of Detroit's 300-year history. This engraving shows
Detroit in 1796, when it came into U.S. possession. The village, though
nearly a hundred years old, consisted of fewer than 200 houses inside the
log stockade around St. Anne's Church.

and Upper Peninsula mines. On a big map of ethnic Detroit, vector
arrows show the movement of ethnic communities out from the core
city and into the suburbs. The immigration experience is personalized with displays. Don't overlook the exhibit's **upstairs gallery**.
There's a fascinating display on parts suppliers and their unsung
role in providing half of a car's content, and on communities built
by proximity to major automotive facilities (Detroit's Chalmers
neighborhood, Highland Park, Hamtramck, Dearborn, Ypsilanti,
and Warren).

Grants from many firms and foundations paid for this impressive exhibit. It's not the place to look for much about the automobile's dark side — the effect of cars and freeways on human interactions and neighborhood life, for instance, or on people unable to
drive for reasons of age, poverty, or disability.

There's more to the Detroit Historical Museum — and to Detroit
— than cars, of course. Founded in 1701, Detroit is one of the
Midwest's oldest cities, with an especially rich, eventful history. Five
times its sovereignty has changed. Detroit's strategic location at a
narrow point on the Detroit River made the fort town a keenly
fought-over prize, ruled by France and then England before joining
the U.S. in 1796. This museum captures much of that history quite
well. The **Furs to Factories** exhibit traces Detroit's development over
200 years from a fur-trading outpost to an industrial city about to
become the center of American industry. Wall murals and life-size
scenes recreate the French wilderness settlement of the 1700s —
quite a contrast to the big firms at the Detroit International Fair of

1889-92, such as Ferry Seed, big stove and rail car manufacturers, and Detroit Dry Dock.

On the second floor, **Doorway to Freedom** traces the Underground Railroad routes leading to Detroit, just across the river from escaped slaves' ultimate destination in Canada. It highlights area churches, homes and other buildings where they found refuge. The **Tavi Stone Fashion Library** (limited hours) is a rare resource for fashion historians, with magazines, videos, books, and slides about all areas of fashion. Beyond it, the **Booth-Wilkinson Costume Gallery** has interesting **changing exhibits** and a wonderful evocation of the late, lamented **Boblo amusement park.** A parade of Detroiters dressed for summer marches through the years, next to Dodg'em cars, swan boats, carousel pieces, and Capt'n Boblo. Videos give glimpses of the island park. At Home in Detroit has four large, furnished doll houses and interesting photos and artifacts from rooms of many eras.

The basement is geared to kids. A longtime highlight is **The Streets of Detroit**, a three-quarters-scale, realistic nighttime recreation of commercial storefronts in the 1840s, 1870s, and 1900. It's dusk as you walk along cobblestone and then brick streets.The settings seem lifelike and compelling in the dim light. It's a rich step into the past, no doubt magical for many children. Particularly wonderful is the old Kresge & Wilson Big 5 and 10¢ Store, first in the chain that became Kmart. The **National Toy Gallery** shows changing exhibits from one of the world's largest collections of toys, including Barbie. Too bad there aren't more insightful captions. The notable **Glancy Trains** are an impressive Lionel layout in constant motion. Also a kids' favorite: a 15-foot-high carved mahogany **clock**, circa 1900, near the main floor front door. At its noon concert, a procession of figures marches in native costumes around a globe.

The attractive first-floor **gift shop** features a well-chosen assortment of antique reproductions, posters of Detroit scenes, books, toys, and souvenirs. The side entrance on Kirby has a most helpful **visitor information center** with brochures on many metro Detroit destinations.

5401 Woodward at Kirby (across from Detroit Institute of Arts). Park free behind museum off Kirby. If you park on the street and your meter runs out, expect a ticket. (313) 833-1805. Wed-Fri 9:30-5, Sat & Sun 10-5. &: mostly. Call. Freewill donation: adults $3,seniors $2, kids $1.

DETROIT HISTORICAL TOURS, LECTURES, DINNERS, AND EVENTS . . . . .
are previewed in the plump annual program guide, available at no cost through
the **Detroit Historical Society.** Call (313) 833-1805 or write the Society at 5401
Woodward Avenue, Detroit, MI 48202. Behind-the-scene tours (mostly by bus)
include black historic sites, the auto industry and its unions, lavish mansions,
Latino Detroit and other ethnic neighborhoods, Eastern Market, the Theater
District, and neighborhood strolls from Corktown to Northville and Wyandotte.
Meals and performances sometimes included. Typical costs: $20-$40. . . . .
School group tours ($2/person) highlight everyday life, the Motor City Exhibit,
and storytelling on the Underground Railroad, auto migration, and more. Call
(313) 833-1419.

DETROIT HISTORICAL SOCIETY MEMBERSHIP . . . . . brings free admission
to the Detroit Historical Museum and Dossin Great Lakes Museum, a free subscription to *Michigan History* magazine and the society's quarterly, a 15% discount at the Old Detroit Museum Shop, the annual program guide, and invita-
tions to special events. Call (313) 833-0481.

**FOR A SURPRISINGLY PLEASANT WALK THROUGH THE WAYNE STATE UNI-
VERSITY CAMPUS . . . . .** walk down Kirby (it's the side street between the his-
torical museum and the library) to Cass. The Wayne campus doesn't look like
much from the street, but the interior is a successful urban space. Across Cass,
Kirby has been turned into part of a beautifully landscaped **campus pedestrian
mall,** studded with sculptures. Its main corridor is along what used to be Second
Avenue, parallel to Cass. Points of visitor interest: changing exhibits at **Walter
Reuther Library of Urban Affairs** and in the gallery at the **Art Building** (both at
Kirby); **Student Center** with food court and campus events info (on the mall at
what was Kirby). For events info during the school year, call (313) 577-8934.
   Campus hangouts on Cass include **Alvin's Finer Delicatessen,** 5756 Cass
near Palmer (known for blues, rock; 313-832-2355); arty new **Twingo's** cafe/cof-
feehouse and unpretentious, multiethnic **Cass Cafe** in the 4600 block of Cass
south of Warren (313-313-831-1400). A block over from Cass, there's the perennially surprising restaurant/bar/dairy/bakery **Traffic Jam & Snug,** Canfield at
Second (313-831-9470). . . . . For takeout sandwiches, Middle Eastern salads,
and more, there's the friendly, cheerful **Cass Corridor Food Co-op,** 4201 Cass
at Willis (313-831-74562), open long hours. . . . . This part of Cass merges into
Detroit's longtime skid row, anchored farther down by many residence hotels.
The Wayne/Cass Corridor area was a hotbed of social activism and avant-garde
art in the late 1960s.

VISITOR HIGHLIGHTS AT AN OUTSTANDING PUBLIC LIBRARY . . . . . The
Detroit Public Library, across Woodward from the art museum and across
Kirby from the historical museum, is in a Beaux Arts building (1921), designed
by Cass Gilbert to resemble the Boston Public Library. Italian Renaissance-style
murals decorate the grand staircase. **Romantic historical scenes** of early

Detroit are in the second-floor Adam Strohm Hall, home of interesting **changing exhibits**. *Library hours: Tues-Sat 9:30-5:30, except Wed 1-9. (313) 833-1000.* . . .
. . The library's **Burton Historical Collection** (Detroit history; limited hours) and **National Automotive History Collection** (limited hours) are tops of their kind.

PRESERVATION WAYNE'S DETROIT HERITAGE TOURS . . . . . give the general public an insider's view of some of Detroit's grand architecture and exciting renovation projects, in tours given by the city's main historic preservation organization. . . . . For information on upcoming tours and events, or to volunteer for tour guide training, call the Preservation Wayne 24-hour **tour and events line** at (313) 222-0321. Handouts mailed upon request. Saturday walking tours are generally at 10 a.m. Reservations recommended. Most tours are $10, $8 to members. Some popular tours are **"Magnificence on Woodward"** (with a look inside the sumptuous French chateau of a house designed for railroad car magnate Frank Hecker), a **Theater District tour** of restored theaters, an **Eastern Market** tour, **1920s skyscrapers**, and **"Mansions of Ferry Avenue,"** in which visitors can go inside famed art collector **Charles Freer's 1893 Shingle Style house,** one of the finest works of noted Philadelphia architect Wilson Eyre. One room was built to house Whistler's Peacock Room before Freer started Washington's Freer Gallery and moved it there. Preservation Wayne has convinced Wayne State University to invest $2 million in restoring and renovating that important building. By 1998 several neighboring mansions will be restored for use as a bed-and-breakfast inn and conference center.
     Occasional Preservation Wayne bus tours cover **Detroit stained glass**, Cranbrook's origins in **Detroit's Arts and Crafts movement**, and the emergence of the auto industry and unions in Detroit.

HISTORIC FORT WAYNE . . . . . remains closed due to budget cutbacks. The old, star-shaped U.S. Army fort, built in the 1840s and 1850s, is owned and used by the city of Detroit as a group of historical museums on Great Lakes Native Americans, the WWII Tuskegee Airmen, and Detroit's military history. The fort is on Jefferson at the foot of Livernois, overlooking the Detroit River. Its design, based on 17th-century principles of warfare, is closer to a medieval fortress than a 20th-century military base. . . . . Fort Wayne may be open for **special events** and more. Call the Detroit Historical Museum, (313) 833-1805.

Fisher Building

An office building with 1920s-style Persian grandeur,
thanks to the brothers who started Fisher Body

THE FISHER BUILDING ranks with the Guardian Building downtown as the most fantastic of Detroit's remarkable collection of 1920s office buildings. The seven Fisher brothers had become enormously rich by developing the enclosed auto body and then selling Fisher Body to GM. They planned the New Center complex across from the General Motors headquarters as the city's second major commercial center. It was supposed to rival the increasingly congested downtown area.

Here the brothers set out to create the world's most beautiful office building. The architect was Albert Kahn, famed for his factories. Plans called for erecting another identical 26-story building, with a 60-story tower between them. But before these other buildings were begun, the Depression stopped them cold.

When the Fisher Building opened in 1928, it sported one of the

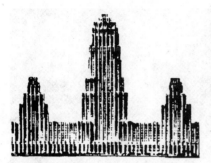

The depression curtailed the Fisher brothers' grand plan to build a copy of the existing Fisher Building and connect them with a much taller 60-floor tower.

most fabulous interiors of any office building in the world. It's full of what Detroit architectural historian Hawkins Ferry called "pagan splendors" — mosaics and inlaid marbles patterned in geometric and stylized naturalistic motifs. "Upon the walls gleam 40 different varieties of marble that would dazzle even the most jaded Roman emperor," remarked Ferry. In the magnificent three-story arcade of shops, the ceiling and walls are covered with cherubs and muses, orange trees and hemlocks, eagles, vines, and folk art motifs. These are best observed from the second and third stories of the arcade. Rich greens and oranges, lavishly gilded with gold leaf, make for a warm and welcoming effect that makes an ordinary office worker or shopper feel like royalty.

The original interior decorations of the adjoining **Fisher Theater**, which uses the arcade as its lobby, were based on Central American art. In visual splendor they rivaled those of the fabulous Fox. They were removed in 1961, at the end of the theater's moving picture days, when it was transformed into Detroit's preeminent legitimate theater. Its acoustics, stage, and orchestra pit make it superb for even the biggest and most elaborate musicals. Hits including *Hello, Dolly* and *Fiddler on the Roof;* originated here before moving to Broadway. Now the Fisher is again launching some new Broadway productions. Call (313) 872-1000 for box office info.

As in most fancy office towers of the 1920s, elevator doors and mailboxes are treated as works of art. Unusual amenities here included free babysitting in a richly decorated nursery, white-dressed parking attendants, and, in the theater lobby, banana trees, a pond of goldfish and turtles, and wandering macaws fed by moviegoers.

In an era and a city where a good many historic jewels have faded or disappeared, it's a pleasure to visit the Fisher Building, impeccably maintained by the Canadian real estate firm, Trizec Properties.

A bank's sumptuous Aztec plaster decoration and ornate vault are now part of the beautiful, affordably priced **Pegasus at the Fisher** Greek restaurant facing Grand Boulevard. Shops catering to office workers and theatergoers line the main arcade and elevator

wing. Most are open Mondays through Saturdays 10-6 and on theater nights. The **Detroit Gallery of Contemporary Crafts** (313-
873-7888) offers a select and beguiling array of American contemporary crafts by top craftspeople, priced from $25 to $500 and up.
Displays mix media to good effect: jewelry, ceramics, rugs, toys, a
little furniture, clothing, quilts, and dolls. Don't miss the sunburst
of tiles from Detroit's famous Pewabic Pottery (page 288) on the
floor in the rear. **The Poster Gallery** (313-875-5211) includes a
well-chosen selection of quality posters mostly focused on area
artists; on Detroit history and events, including William Moss's
super-detailed time trips to the Boblo dock, Hudson's parade, and
city of 1948; and on African-American culture and jazz. Next door,
Cultural Accents (313-872-5540) carries African-American collectibles, dolls, jewelry, and gifts. **Facets Jewelry Design Studio**
features unusual designs and stones from award-winning jeweler
Todd Terwilliger. By the Lothrop (rear) entrance, **Detroit Floral
Designs** (313-874-1700) has created a glowing interior that takes
its cues from the 1928 architecture, Spanish-tiled stairway and fireplace, and wrought iron of what was once an elegant law office. It's
the perfect setting for the simple elegance of the shop's orchids and
exotic tropical flowers.

Don't forget to go upstairs to get the full effect of the murals and
mosaics. A worthwhile stop is #216, the office and gallery of the
National Conference of Artists (313-875-0923), open Mon-Sat 11-
5. Promoting African-American culture through the visual arts is
the mission of this group of artists, teachers, and enthusiasts. They
organize school programs and videos and artist residencies.

*W. Grand Blvd. at Second Ave. Rear entrance on Lothrop. Open Mon-
Fri 8 a.m.-9 p.m., Sat 9-6. Freeway directions: take the Lodge (U.S.
10) to Pallister exit, turn left onto Lothrop. 3 hours free parking in New
Center One lot, Lothrop between Second and Woodward with valida-
tion from any New Center store.* **Fisher Theater:** (313) 872-1000. &

THE REST OF THE NEW CENTER IS ALSO WORTH A LOOK. . . . . The grand,
Renaissance-style lobby of the **General Motors world headquarters** (1922;
Albert Kahn, architect) across the street is open to the public. The massive,
sprawling office building is in transition as the automaker moves its headquarters to the RenCen and other firms move into the impressive, impeccably maintained building. **Current-model GM cars** and **historical exhibits** have been displayed on the lobby's east hall (toward Woodward). . . . . **New Center One** is an
attractive small shopping center anchored by Crowley's Department Store, with

Winkelman's, Gantos, Waldenbooks, and several fast-food restaurants. (It's across from the Fisher Building on Grand Boulevard at Second.) . . . . . North of the Fisher Building, **New Center Commons**, a mix of new and renovated housing, is a successful GM project to rehabilitate the neighborhood around it.

NEW CENTER RESTAURANTS AND A JAZZ CLUB. . . . . Il Centro (313-872-5110) is pretty, arty, fresh, and Northern Italian-influenced. In a renovated house across Lothrop from the Fisher Building. . . . . A former Detroit Piston started **Macon's Music Cafe**, a restaurant and club in the Fisher Building lower level where Club Penta used to be. It serves up food at lunch and dinner, and entertainment most nights, with comedy, reggae, jazz, and more. Call (313) 972-3760 for upcoming events. . . . . That's in addition to Greek and American food at the beautiful, Art Deco **Pegasus at the Fisher** (page 258) and the fast food in New Center One, the GM Building, and **Gertie's Garden** lunch counter at the Fisher Building's Third Ave. corridor.

Motown Museum

In a house on Grand Boulevard, hits were churned out with assembly-line regularity. Hitsville USA takes you back to when one nation came together under a groove.

POP MUSIC legends by the dozens were created during the Sixties in these two adjacent homes. The genius behind Motown's amazing hit factory was Berry Gordy Jr. a former boxer and autoworker. His father, a Georgia farm worker who came to Detroit in 1922, was a part of the Great Migration from the agricultural South to the industrial North.

Under Berry Gordy, Motown Records launched stars whose music is part of American life today: Michael Jackson, Stevie Wonder, Diana Ross and the Supremes, Marvin Gaye, Martha Reeves and the Vandellas, Smokey Robinson and the Miracles, the Four Tops, the Temptations, Lionel Richie, Gladys Knight and the Pips, the Isley Brothers, Junior Walker, and many more. Motown's Black Forum label made the only authorized recording of Martin Luther King's "I Have a Dream" speech. "Lift Every Voice and Sing," considered the black national anthem, with lyrics by poet James Weldon Johnson, was first recorded by Motown's Kim Weston, who is today a tireless organizer and supporter of local talent in Detroit.

Records produced in the small rear studio were among the first 45s by black artists to break out of the R&B charts into mainstream popularity. Within a few years of its founding in 1959, Motown be

Though fans will find lots of early photos and memorabilia of Motown stars like the Supremes (here), the museum "goes well beyond the usual easy allusions to stars and hits," wrote *Michigan Monthly.* "It brilliantly joins artifacts and historical details about black Detroit in the 1950s . . . with close-up interviews . . . to create a memorable idea of the energetic, cooperative Motown spirit."

came America's biggest black-owned company. In 1972 Gordy left Detroit for Los Angeles to pursue movie and television projects. Music industry analysts date the decline of Motown Records to its departure from Detroit and its inability to develop new talent in Los Angeles to replace its increasingly independent stars and songwriters from the Motor City. In 1988 Motown sold its recording arm to MCA-linked investors for $61 million.

Esther Gordy Edwards, Berry Gordy's sister and herself an early Motown executive, kept Hitsville USA as Motown's Detroit office. And she never threw anything away. Motown fans sometimes showed up on the doorstep from Europe, having come to Detroit just to see Motown. That's how the idea for the museum was born, she says.

For years the museum was an admittedly homespun operation. But the museum effectively made the point that Motown's genius was in organizing and marketing talent that was already right here in Detroit, for the most part, and that its success was the work of many, many people, not just the stars.

Now a pioneering partnership with the Henry Ford Museum has restored and enlarged Hitsville USA. Go into Berry Gordy's tidy upstairs apartment and it's 1959, with a orange Naugahyde sofa, playpen in the living room, and the very formica table from which he and his first wife shipped records. The office is vintage 1964, when the house never closed and musicians and songwriters worked round the clock. So is Studio 4, where Motown's biggest hits were recorded, and the modest four-track board from which most of them were engineered. Original sheet music is on the music stands.

After seeing the snapshots, costumes, and video footage of the huge Motown revues that went on the road to build audiences, it's easy to imagine the simple house in that time, filled with creative energy. So many local kids flocked to the Motown studio here that traffic on West Grand was jammed for blocks. Some wanted to glimpse the stars who recorded here. Others hoped to audition informally on the front porch, an approach that had succeeded for more than one Motown star.

An excellent introductory **video** outlines the inspiring story, beginning with the Great Migration from the American South and the way Detroit's black neighborhoods in the 1940s and 1950s were alive with music. The dream of Pops Gordy (Berry Gordy, Senior) was to pass on to his eight children the ambition, hard work, financial acumen for business success. He trained them in his own Booker T. Washington Grocery.

Berry Gordy grew up in the neighborhood behind the Detroit Institute of Arts. Each member of the hard-working Gordy family contributed $10 a month to build an enterprise fund from which any family member could draw. After Berry Gordy's jazz-oriented record shop went bankrupt, he began focusing on writing and producing rhythm and blues songs for local groups. Singers Jackie Wilson, whom he met boxing, and Smokey Robinson got him involved in the record business. At a critical juncture, Gordy borrowed $800 from the family fund to start his own record production company. "Shop Around," written by Robinson, was the first big hit he produced.

A talented manager and an autocratic disciplinarian, Gordy perfected the assembly-line style of hit production. His inspiration, he has said, was his experience working on the assembly line at Ford. Gordy's Motown was three companies: music publishing, record producing, and artist management. (Tamla, his music publishing company, was named after "Tammy," Debbie Reynolds' hit song, which he greatly admired.) He hired teams of writers who, as one critic describes it, put out "a wholly mechanical style and sound that roared and purred like a well-tuned Porsche." The Supremes recorded 12 #1 pop hits in five years, all written by the great songwriting team of Lamont Dozier and Eddie and Brian Holland. Maxine Powell, already well-known in Detroit for her modeling school and sense of classic style, polished the manners and posture of singers so they could comport themselves comfortably with anyone, even kings and queens.

The museum is a rich experience, designed either to be browsed quickly or delved into for hours. Kids enjoy seeing one of Michael Jackson's gloves and the natural echo chamber made for recordings by opening into the attic. Visitors who want to learn more have an outstanding resource in the soft-spoken, deeply informed Chris Alexander, the usual tour guide in the second-floor gallery.

The main parts of the big 11,000-square-foot **Henry Ford Museum Motown exhibit** will come back to the Motown Museum, perhaps in May, 1997. **Interactive exhibits** let visitors learn choreography to songs from Cholly Atkins, just like Motown stars did; introduce records like Detroit deejay legend Martha Jean the Queen; and mix soundtracks like the exacting Berry Gordy himself. Visuals and history are detailed enough to satisfy the most ardent fans. One memorable highlight: a film showing **black Detroit in the 1950s**: neighborhoods, streets, and the fabled Hastings Street business and entertainment area before it succumbed to I-75.

The museum **shop** sells many CD sets by Motown stars, selected books and videos, and an intriguing $35 educational package with timeline posters, tapes and lesson plans for conducting oral history and analyzing songs and their lyrics.

2648 W. Grand Blvd., a few blocks west of the New Center, and Henry Ford Hospitals. From the Lodge/U.S. 10, take W. Grand Blvd. exit, head west. From I-96, take West Grand exit, go east. From I-94, take the Lodge/U.S. 10 north, get off at the next exit (Grand) and go west. (313) 875-2264. Sun & Mon 12-5, Tues-Sat 10-5. & Fan club membership ($30 individual, $45 family of 4) includes free annual admission, Grapevine newsletter, notices of museum events. Admission: adults $6, 12 and under $3.

A TERRIFIC FREE GUIDE TO AFRICAN-AMERICAN DETROIT. . . . . . is available from the Metro Detroit CVB at visitor centers at the RenCen (page 203) and Detroit Historical Museum (254), or call 1 (800) DETROIT. Ask for **"Detroit: The Northern Star,"** a guide to African-American Detroit. It includes not only the well-known destinations but info on smaller galleries showing art of Africa and the African diaspora in the Western Hemisphere, bookstores, nightclubs, leading soul food and African-related restaurants, the Black Cinema Gallery, clubs, and annual events like the Detroit Institute of Art's Bal Africain in May, the world's largest fundraising dinner (April's NAACP Freedom Fund Dinner, serving 10,000), and music festivals (often free) at Hart Plaza and elsewhere. Three museums across the river in **Windsor, Ontario,** are related to its role as a major terminus of the **Underground Railroad** and place of settlement for escaped slaves. Rev. Josiah Henson, better known as the prototype for Harriet Beecher Stowe's Uncle Tom, established a settlement in Windsor before the Civil War whose remains can be visited today. . . . . Additional information sources are detailed, from archives to the weekly *Michigan Chronicle* to the **Detroit Black Yellow Pages**, available at the Shrine of the Black Madonna or by calling (313) 342-1717. . . . . The booklet also describes options for special **group tours** focusing on areas of special interest to African-Americans and notes famous Detoiters past and present, from Ralph Bunch, Joe Louis, and Dr. Ben Carson, the first neurosurgeon to perform brain surgery on conjoined twins, to current Detroit residents Rosa Parks, Anita Baker, Aretha Franklin. . . . . People planning a trip to Detroit can get a 10-minute **video version of this guide** to black Detroit, "Detroit: The Northern Star," from the Metro Detroit CVB, (313) 259-4333.

THE LARGEST AFRICAN-AMERICAN MUSEUM IN THE U.S. . . . . . is the **Museum of African-American History**, a block behind the Detroit Institute of Arts. The vast new museum opened in spring, 1997. It incorporates exhibits popular at the previous museum, including **"Field to Factory,"** the story of the Great Migration to Detroit and other northern cities, and a life-size slave ship (complete with unsettling audio effects). No admission fee required; donations appreciated. Afro-centric **museum shop** and research library. The museum has developed a big reputation as a venue for **special events,** lectures, and presentations. It's open daily at **Kwanzaa** (between Christmas and New Year's) and during **Black History Month** in February. Call for details. *(313) 833-9800. New museum on Warren at Brush. Wed-Sat 9:30-5, Sun 1-5* &

A BASTION OF THE U.S. BLACK MIDDLE CLASS. . . . . High-paid auto jobs and government jobs largely account for Detroit's role as one of the centers and spawning grounds of talented, successful black Americans. Five U.S. zip codes are characterized by marketers as large-scale, real-life versions of Bill Cosby's TV neighborhood. One is in northwest Detroit, the University District/Palmer Park area west and north of Palmer Park and north of the Jesuit-run University of Detroit. (It's also the home of Mumford High, whose athletics logos pop up in movies and TV thanks to a phalanx of nostalgic Jewish alums from the 1960s, now in the entertainment business.) . . . . . Livernois between Seven and Eight Mile roads, once dubbed "The Avenue of Fashion," has regained a number of interesting small businesses recently.

A RETAIL ARCHIVE OF POP MUSIC AND POP CULTURE. . . . . on Detroit's east side is **Melodies and Memories** .in St. Clair Shores. Look for the yellow-green awning. Here's where to find half a million 45s, new & used CDs and vinyl (not just pop but jazz & country), jukeboxes, TV show memorabilia, and things you had as a kid that your mom threw away. Museum-like displays feature lit-up figures of Detroit musicians (Motown, Madonna, Bob Seger and more) and treasures like Supreme bread wrappers (made in Detroit), Motown autographs, and metal lunchboxes. *23013 Gratiot 3 blocks north of Nine Mile Rd. (810) 774-8480. Mon-Sat 10 a.m.-9 p.m., Sun 12-6.* &

Shrine of the Black Madonna Bookstore

A terrific selection of books on Africa and African-Americans, plus African fabrics and artifacts

THE ATTRACTIVE cultural centers/bookstores of the Shrine of the Black Madonna present the largest selection of books on Africans and African-Americans anywhere in the U.S. The Detroit store, though not as big as the Shrine's Houston facility, is most impressive: spiffy, well-organized, and serene in mood. The staff is knowledgeable and friendly to customers of all races. Long before multicultural chic and African fashions showed up in malls and department stores, people who cared about African cultures came here.

The Shrine is a black church founded in Detroit over 40 years ago by the Reverend Albert Cleage to promote African-American self-sufficiency and to stress black Americans' connectedness with African culture. It describes itself as a Pan-African orthodox Christian church; today it's part of the United Church of Christ with

Long before African design became chic, the Shrine of the Black Madonna bookstore and gallery carried traditional African artifacts like the sculpture store manager Ayele Bennett shows here.

churches in Detroit, Atlanta, and Houston.

The large bookstore and import shop is also a **gallery** (on the second floor) with space for occasional lectures and readings by visiting authors and others. Here you can find an unparalleled range of books on Africans and African-Americans, from mainstream bestsellers like Taylor Branch's biography of Martin Luther King, to obscure publications by small political and literary presses here and abroad. This is the place to find the complete works in print of Langston Hughes, Zora Neale Hurston, and James Baldwin, as well as a passel of biographies of Motown stars and numerous scholarly and popular histories by black and white historians. Egyptology is another specialty. The children's book section is large and especially inviting.

Scott Nearing's 1930s classic on subsistence farming reminds visitors that self-sufficient agriculture is what the Shrine's Beulahland project is all about. Beulahland is an 5,000-acre farm planned for the South, where young African-American boys can grow up off the streets and help feed the poor in American cities.

Other sections of the store feature jewelry, imported fabrics, and handcrafted objects from Africa. Prices are lower than what you'd expect to pay at gift shops. Fabrics, mostly $7 to $12 a yard, include woven kente cloth strips, once worn only by Ghanaian royalty; vivid aso-oke from Nigeria, accented with metallic threads; heavy cotton mudcloth in bold patterns and muted, neutral colors; long pieces of khorogo cloth, with designs of animals, birds, and village life; and batiks from Nigeria and Ghana. For inspiration on how to use these beautiful fabrics, there's a book on 101 ways to wrap kanga cloth.

The shop offers quite a range of African artifacts: little thumb pianos, wonderful wood elephants for $8, copies of Ashanti kings' stools, and carved stone chess sets for $96 to $145. Considering the craftsmanship, prices are low. Kissi stone plates, incised with etched designs of plants and fish, are $35. Handpainted papyri in beautiful golds and bronzes are copies of ancient pictures of Egyptian deities.

13535 Livernois just west of Davison in Detroit. From I-96, get off at the Davison ramp and go east. Turn left at Livernois and immediately look for the sign and guarded parking lot. This is a rough part of town but OK in daytime. (313) 491-0777. Tues-Thurs 11-6, Fri & Sat 11-7. Closed Sun & Mon. &: *first floor only.*

Hamtramck

This Polish autoworkers' enclave, now also home to diverse artists and Eastern European immigrants, has a bustling commercial district with good food.

JUST two square miles, totally surrounded by Detroit, Hamtramck has been a Polish stronghold since the First World War. Drive along its bustling main street of Joseph Campau and you'll see Polish bakeries, Polish meat shops, Polish bookstores, Polish clubs. At the corner of Belmont and Joseph Campau is a tribute to the Polish Pope, a large statue of Pope John Paul. For a **free guide to Hamtramck** – its Polish and its artistic aspects – stop at the Polish Art Center, 9539 Joseph Campau (page 270).

For years now, Detroiters have been discovering the gritty charm of a trip to Hamtramck: eating heartily in its good, cheap restaurants; browsing in the small, budget-oriented shops, bakeries, and meat markets; stopping at coffeehouses with acoustic music; and dancing to some of the area's most innovative rock music at Lili's 21.

For years numerous artists have had studios in second-story storefront space, invisible to public view. Now two cool coffeehouses on side streets, the Shadow Box Cafe and Planet Ant, cater to working artists in the daytime and to alternative music-lovers at night.

Joseph Campau's long retail blocks still have some of the aura of a thriving blue-collar commercial district from the 1930s or 1940s, before chains came to depersonalize retailing and before malls had sucked the vitality out of most American downtowns. Many of its vintage features have been replaced by recent remodeling. Hamtramck's downtown today presents an amazing contrast with the boarded-up bleakness of similar 1920s shopping strips in nearby Detroit. Many value-conscious Detroit-area shoppers, black and white, do a large part of their shopping for clothes and household goods in Hamtramck's shops.

Though Hamtramck is still identifiably Polish, with new Polish immigrants moving in as the first generation of Polish widows dies off, the Polish population is nonetheless declining, from a high of 60% to under 40% today. Taking up the slack are Albanians from Yugoslavia. They are now over 20% of the population.

The dense workers' neighborhoods here were built for autoworkers' families in one amazing gush between 1914 and 1920, when the village's population skyrocketed from 3,589 to 45,615, the largest increase in that decade anywhere in the U.S. The sudden growth occurred because in 1910 the Dodge Brothers built Dodge Main, a huge auto factory on the south edge of what was then an old German farming village.

Today, even with the declining Polish presence in Hamtramck, its commercial district has a distinctly Polish feel to it. But city services are suffering as the city's population, which peaked in 1930 at 56,000, has dropped to just 18,400 today. A major blow to the community was the closing of Dodge Main in 1979. The GM Poletown plant, built on some of the same land, sits two-thirds over the Detroit border. Its approximately 5,200 jobs haven't come close to replacing the 11,000 Dodge workers.

Hamtramck highlights, arranged from south (near Holbrook) to north, include:

◆ **Cadillac Detroit-Hamtramck Assembly Center.** The highly roboticized new Poletown plant makes Cadillac Sevilles, Buick Rivieras, and Oldsmobile Toronados. An extended, wrenching controversy and much pain were created when the city of Detroit condemned and tore down a whole neighborhood and the Immaculate Conception church so GM could build its big new Poletown plant, incorporating the site of the old Dodge Main plant. A vital retail district along Chene Street south of I-94 was turned into a ghost town in the process. Plant tours have unfortunately been suspended. *Just north of I-94 between Mt. Elliot and I-75.*

◆ **Holbrook Cafe/Polish-American Citizens' Center.** The history of Poland is colorfully portrayed in a big, two-part mural by Dennis Orlowski. His murals pop up everywhere in his hometown. *3201 Holbrook a block east of Joseph Campau. (313) 875-1115.*

◆ **Henry the Hatter.** Like its downtown parent store (page 219), this shop offers a wide range of hats, from wool berets to Western-style. *9307 Joseph Campau. (313) 875-5587. Mon-Sat 9-5:30.* &

◆ **Kowalski Sausage Co.** The Hamtramck sausage maker has 11 outlets around metro Detroit, including this local one. Kowalski's smoked kielbasa rated tops of eight in the *Detroit Free Press* taste test judged by five mostly Polish food people. Kowalski stores also offer takeout golabki (cabbage rolls), pierogi, blintzes, and soups. *9405 Joseph Campau. (313) 871-9060.*

A cherished Detroit landmark on Kowalkski's Hamtramck factory on Holbrook.

Images from Polish history and Polish folk life are seen on murals all around Hamtramck, not just at the Polish Art Center, which uses this drawing as its logo.

◆**Polish Art Center.** This delightful shop has such an attractive array of arts and crafts from Poland and neighboring countries that people visit it from all over the U.S. Owner Joan Bittner sometimes imports direct and adds new items frequently. The displays get better and better. Whole areas are devoted to traditional religious icons; to peacock-patterned blue-and-white stoneware from Boleslawiec, now in Silesia; to beautiful mouth-blown Polish Christmas ornaments revived by Christopher Radko. Here you can find Polish carved wooden boxes and plates, Polish leaded crystal, folk dolls, and many kinds of brightly painted Russian nesting dolls. Sparkling and intricate tinfoil nativities, called *szopka*, are $75.

Colorful Polish and Ukrainian Easter eggs, including goose and ostrich eggs, are on hand, as are egg-decorating supplies (dyes, wax, tools, unfinished eggs). There are inexpensive paper cuttings (and books on creating this cheery Polish folk art), amber jewelry, replicas of antique Polish swords, and Polish greeting cards.

Recently the store has added many Polish videos ($25-$79) and thousands of Polish-language books – everything from Polish translations of American popular fiction to Polish-language courses. Books on crafts, folklore, customs, cooking, history, and art are in English, too. It probably has the largest selection of Polish, European, and polka cassettes (from $6.50) and CDs (from $16) around. Poland's famous posters of movies are back, too, for $12 and up. Ask for the newsletter. FAX inquiries are welcome (313-874-1302). *9539 Joseph Campau at Norwalk. (313) 874-2242. Mon-Wed 9:30-5, Thurs to 7, Fri-Sat 9:30-6, winter Sun 11-3.*

◆ **St. Florian Church.** This magnificent Gothic church, completed
in 1926, is on the scale of a great European cathedral. Serving one
of the region's largest parishes, it holds 1,800. The church was designed by Ralph Adams Cram, America's high priest of the 20th-
century Gothic Revival. The interior is awesome, with an enormously high ceiling. All the windows are true stained glass windows – not
the painted colored glass of most American churches, but windows
where the designs and figures are made of individual small pieces of
glass of different colors. Seen in daytime with only natural light fil-
tering through the windows, the effect is the same as in medieval
churches. *2626 Poland. Faces Florian St. one block west of Joseph
Campau. (313) 871-2778. Church is open to visitors 8:30 a.m.-6 p.m.;
enter from back door on Poland St. (next to the rectory).* ♿: *no.*

◆ **Roadrunner's Raft.** Musician Brian Holvey has transformed a
corner bar into "Hamtramck's folk and acoustic music club." Its
motto: "music of the people, by the people and for the people." Here
beer is $3 a pitcher from 4 to 8 p.m. Call for current schedule, likely
to include a weekly open-mike night and a blues jam, plus special
events like benefits for the Hamtramck art festival and green movement. *2363 Yemans at Brombach, a block west of Joseph Campau.
(313) 873-RAFT.*

◆ **New Palace Bakery.** Hamtramck is known for its Polish bakeries,
and the New Palace is a favorite among the locals. One Polish specialty is *chrusciki* ("angel wings"), a very light dough fried with a
powdering of sugar. Another favorite are *paczki*, those jelly-filled
doughnuts now getting mainstream promotion. On the day before
Lent, lines form by 7 a.m. to buy them. Lemon tortes, cinnamon-
raisin breakfast rolls, and pumpernickel and Polish rye breads are
other standbys, and cookies come in many, many shapes. A popular cookie is the soft *kilaczki* filled with fruit. *9833 Joseph Campau
between Yemans and Evaline. (313) 875-1334. Mon-Sat 5 a.m.-7
p.m., Fri 'til 8.* ♿

◆ **Monument to Pope John Paul II.** It's not surprising that this
distinctively Polish city would want to do something special to
commemorate the installation of the first Polish pope. Much of the
funding has come from the proceeds of an annual festival held for
four days around Labor Day, when over 700,000 visitors flock to the
city. The austere little park is enlivened by the colorful and well-
executed mural of costumed folk dancers in a historic Polish street
scene. The fence is formed by the original entrance gates to the late,
lamented Dodge Main plant, Hamtramck's reason for being. *Corner
Belmont and Joseph Campau.*

◆ **Shadow Box Cafe.** College students, artists, teachers, and more mingle at this intimate, 40-seat cafe, where jazz and folk artists and alternative bands play on weekends starting at 9. Sunday night is poetry night. Charmingly improvised decor, mismatched furniture, games and magazines, in what was formerly a Moderne-styled bar. *2917 Trowbridge south of Caniff and just east of Joseph Campau. (313) 891-0703. Open Mon 4 p.m.-midnight; Tues-Thurs & Sun 11 a.m.-midnight; Fri-Sat 11 a.m.-4 a.m.*

◆ **Planet Ant.** This busy spot seats 50 or 60 inside and, in summer, opens a back patio with a garden and tables sculpted by Detroit artist Brian Lehto. Call about open mike nights and scheduled bands. *2357 Caniff between Joseph Campau and I-75. (313) 365-4948. Sun-Thurs 11 a.m.-1 a.m., Fri-Sat until 3 a.m.*

◆ **Fredro Market.** In a *Detroit Free Press* kielbasa taste test judged by mostly Polish food people, fresh kielbasa from this well-known neighborhood meat market topped every other entry. Their smoked kielbasa ranked high, too. So far north in Hamtramck, it's actually in Detroit. *4540 Fredro at Fenelon, near Conant and Carpenter. Call for directions. (313) 366-6276.*

GETTING TO HAMTRAMCK . . . . . isn't all that easy. It's isolated by freeways, a rail line, and the big G.M. Plant. From Woodward in Detroit, turn east onto Holbrook, a mile north of I-94. From northern Detroit, take McNichols (6 Mile) 1 1/2 miles east of Woodward to Joseph Campau. From the east side, take Mt. Elliott north and veer to the left onto Conant, on Hamtramck's eastern perimeter. **From freeways**, take I-75 (the Chrysler Freeway) to Caniff, about 1 1/2 miles north of I-94. If you're northbound, from Detroit's downtown/New Center, turn right onto Caniff, then right onto Joseph Campau in three blocks to reach the main drag. If you're southbound from the suburbs, turn left onto Caniff. If it's late at night, pay attention to these directions, or you'll end up lost in a creepy part of Detroit.

LATE-NIGHT HAMTRAMCK ROCKS . . . . . The streets are empty, all the Polish widows are asleep, and the serious drinkers in the after-work crowd are lingering in the front rooms of their favorite taverns when they're joined by the late wave of hip young people from every social class, from Birmingham and Royal Oak and Detroit. They've come to hear new music – not oldies and covers of current hits. The opening band plays around 10 p.m., followed by the headliner at midnight, so sometimes people first stop by **Planet Ant** or the **Shadow Box Cafe** or **Roadrunner's Raft** (see above), where an acoustic act might be playing. The club that books the best-known acts is **Lili's 21** at 2930 Jacob, 3 blocks south

of Holbrook (313-875-6555). This nightclub/neighborhood bar hosts groups like
Sponge and Those Darn Accordions out of San Francisco. A small bar built in
the 20s, it retains its old look. *Mon-Fri 3 p.m-2 a.m., Sat & Sun 8 p.m.-2 a.m.* ♿:
no. Paycheck's Lounge (see below).also books well-known bands. . . . . Genuine
Euro-techno-disco with its pulsating beat, strobes, lasers, and smoke (from a
smoke machine and cigarettes) happens around midnight in the upstairs hall of
the **White Star Cafe**, 9819 Conant. (313)-872-8888. Here's where Poles, Roman-
ians, Russians, Bosnians, Georgians, Hungarians, and more come together.

NEIGHBORHOOD TAVERNS . . . . . off the main drag are enduringly popular
Hamtramck institutions best observed right after work. Many have inexpensive
food and/or entertainment. They include:
♦ **Artie's Locker Room,** *3141 Caniff at Charest. (313) 893-8088. No food. Open
4 p.m.-2 a.m.* ♿
♦ **The former G's Place,** *2764 Florian. (313) 871-9641. Call for details about* big
changes underway.
♦ **Paycheck's Lounge.** Entertainment Friday and Saturday nights. *2932 Caniff.
(313) 874-0909.*
♦ **The Attic Bar.** Popular hangout for blues musicians who drop by to play and
listen. Live blues featured seven nights a week. Call after 5 p.m. for listings. No
food. *11667 Joseph Campau. (313) 365-4194. Open daily 5 p.m.-2 a.m.* ♿

The Heidelberg Project

Color and castoffs turned a decaying neighborhood
into a curiously moving fantasy environment.
Now the art here is limited to private property, but
the artist is spreading his vision out into the world.

TYREE GUYTON'S art environment on Heidelberg Street, just east of Mt. Elliott, has been a regular tour bus stop for years. Suburbanites drive by and even get out of their cars. In this neighborhood are street after street of modest worker homes from the 1880s. Most are old and run-down. A few look well-maintained. Pheasants thrive in the many weedy vacant lot. The near east side is the oldest and most decrepit part of Detroit. Its aging population makes for a crime rate well below that of the city's younger, newer west side.

Guyton grew up on Heidelberg Street. In an area where curbside piles of mattresses and junk were common, he started creating remarkable inner-city environmental art. In his first work, "Fun House," he splashed color over an abandoned house next to his grandfather's neat home and covered it with old toys, dollhouses, pictures, signs, plastic bottles and the like. The project became a way to work out Guyton's own personal demons. As a child he had lived in poverty. Family responsibilities overwhelmed his mother. Lonely and overlooked, Guyton was teased for his interest in art and secretly abused by a family acquaintance. Only his grandfather encouraged the boy's art.

As an adult, Guyton studied briefly at Detroit's Center for Creative Studies and has pursued art as a career. "Fun House" got him started using color, imagination, and cast-off toys to transform a depressing environment into a wild and appealing fantasy of the childhood he never enjoyed. Sometimes his work becomes a social critique. Always, the effect is loose and not conventionally cute. It evokes strong reactions — pro and con — especially from neighbors. "I'm glad it's not in my neighborhood," says one black Detroit art teacher who admires Guyton's work.

The city has now made Guyton remove his assemblages from sidewalks, street trees, and all property not owned by himself or consenting landlords.

Guyton's late grandfather, Sam Mackey, lived for 40 years in the neat gray house that has now been transformed into The Dotty

The Dotty Wotty House, inspired by Martin Luther King Jr. saying, "We are all the same color on the inside." Artist Tyree Guyton says the celebratory statement of color represents the common unifying spirit among us.

Wotty House, covered with multicolored polka dots. He saw the neighborhood become spotted with abandoned homes that invite arson, drugs, and other crimes. Sam Mackey, and later Guyton's then-wife Karen, encouraged his environmental art as a way to stabilize the neighborhood by boarding up and decorating abandoned houses and by bringing more eyes to the street, always the best crime-stoppers.

A philosopher and preacher, Mackey was often out on the park bench he installed for the steady stream of visitors to the Heidelberg Project. Happy to share his stories and thoughts, he added a wonderful dimension to the art experience. His grandson's art inspired him to take up a brush and create shapes and figures in a child-like fashion; a gallery in Paris exhibited these works.

Tyree Guyton's Heidelberg Project has grown beyond individual buildings. It pops up on a few houses and yards on nearby streets. The pavement of Heidelberg Street, meticulously swept each day, sports a tangle of colored lines. Bright shoes march up tree trunks. Vacant land where several houses once stood has trees that are incorporated into the changing art environments. Currently, smiling faces are painted kid-style on propped-up car hood "canvasses." Other images strike a disturbing chord. Clothes dangling from trees remind many visitors of lynchings. Some dolls and stuffed animals are ashen gray. New discards arrive regularly, dropped off by Guyton's many fans. The project is always evolving with new ideas and new material.

Photos can't convey the magical, powerful feeling of this place. Coming here can be a very special experience. Heidelberg Street has to be seen in real life, and not just from a car, to best work its often powerful effect. Some people never do feel it, but skeptics may very well be won over. One such skeptic, ever alert to pretensions and no fan of most current art, has come to enjoy the experience. Guyton, he feels, does seem to be a real artist, driven to create.

Former Detroit mayor Coleman Young hated this project and the publicity it brought. It was so far from the shiny, new image he wanted Detroit to project. In the spring of 1992, the city, responding to unidentified neighbors' complaints, gave Tyree Guyton 15 minutes to salvage bits of his assemblages before demolishing Fun House and several other city-owned buildings he had decorated. Deflated and despirited, Sam Mackey died in June. Guyton turned his attention to the trees, pavement, and other landscape elements, considering them less vulnerable than the houses.

Not long after that, a wrong turn led to the support infrastructure so helpful to environmental artists. Jenenne Whitfield discovered the project and got to know Guyton, his dreams, his frustrations, his difficulties in furthering his career. She knew she could help. ("A yearning for greatness colors everything Guyton says and does," wrote Michael Hodges in a long, appreciative, insightful *Detroit News* article from July 5, 1995. "The conviction that he hasn't received the recognition he deserves gnaws at him.") Soon she quit her good bank job to organize a nonprofit group to support Guyton. Now the Heidelberg Project has a very well-written, visually fresh web site: http://www.ddc.can/heidelberg/ Group tours can be scheduled; participants may do some painting themselves. Guyton is "brilliant with kids," says reporter Hodges.

The web site and printed tour guide deal with the inevitable questions about what it all means. Some examples:

◆ **On Guyton's work in general:** "a synthesis of an unusual array or artistic styles — from modernist traditions like Dadaism to Pop Art, to Folk Art and African-American Yard Art (a Southern tradition in which houses, yards, vehicles, and trees are decorated with found objects)."

◆ **On two tree works,** "Changing Time" and "Non-Stop": "These demonstrate the uplifting messages prevalent in most of Guyton's art. Bicycles, cars, even clocks climb upward — out of the streets.

One's ability to be transported . . . from a dangerous and unwel-coming world is experienced as our eyes are drawn up to the tops of these tree works."

◆ **On "The OJ House"** — for "Obstruction of Justice": "Symbols of the chase, faces of the jury, and mocking, chaotic references to how the media has showcased this trial address the absurdity of such a focus when atrocities and injustices abound all around us every day."

◆ **On "A Lot of Shoes":** "Guyton lines the sidewalk with the souls of those standing in unemployment lines, leading to the soles of the wandering homeless."

Shoes standing for people play a big role in Guyton's current work. In August, 1996, Guyton oversaw the creation of a Shoe House in St. Paul, Minnesota's multiethnic Frogtown neighborhood. The work is called "Soul People . . . *How beautiful are the feet of them who carry glad tidings.*" Here's the Heidelberg Project statement: "Each shoe a history of a forgotten life, a missing presence, the house becomes literally a house of lost 'soles.' Yet the sheer scale and playfulness . . . evokes a childlike sense of wonder and joy."

On Heidelberg between Mt. Elliott and Ellery. From downtown, take Gratiot to Mt. Elliot, turn right. Three blocks past Mack, turn right onto Heidelberg Street. Or, go east on Jefferson, turn left onto Mt. Elliot, and turn left onto Heidelberg in about a mile. To schedule tours, make donations, or contact the artist, call (313) 537-8037 or write The Heidelberg Project, Box 1937, Detroit, MI 48219.

ANOTHER MEMORABLE HOME-BASED ART ENVIRONMENT . . . . . is in Redford Township, between Detroit and Livonia. Here in a courtyard between Silvio Barile's **Redford Italian Bakery and Pizzeria** and his house, he has used Kwikcrete to create an elaborate sculptural homage to things he cares about: America, freedom, family, mama's love, Roman and Italian heroes, and selected American presidents (Washington, Lincoln, Roosevelt, and Kennedy). Another part of the magic on this modest city lot: productive fruit trees and vines, includ-ing things like figs that ordinarily don't grow in Michigan. The bakery is also an Italian grocery. You can sit at tables and eat Etruscan pizza, his specialty, with pop. *26417 Plymouth Road. From I-96, take the Beech-Daly Exit 178, go south on Beech-Daly to Plymouth, then right (west). Bakery is across from Long John Silver. (313) 937-2288.*

Belle Isle

A top Michigan attraction, this 3-mile-long island features great views, a splendid small zoo and aquarium, a nature center, conservatory, and much more.

FROM this splendid park in the middle of the Detroit River, you can get a dramatic **view of downtown Detroit,** a panoramic **view of the Detroit River** with its international freighter traffic, and an equally sweeping **view of Canada**. Right across the river is the big Hiram Walker distillery, moved from Detroit to Windsor during Prohibition.

On the 981-acre island itself are waterfront **picnic areas** throughout, two long **fishing piers,** and an elaborate **playground** for kids along with a **giant slide**. Frederick Law Olmstead, planner of New York's Central Park and the father of American landscape architecture, had a hand in laying out the curving drives and waterways. There's a delightful **zoo**, an extraordinarily beautiful freshwater **aquarium**, a fascinating **Great Lakes shipping museum**, a sizable plant **conservatory** and formal gardens, and a **nature center** with nature trails through forests filled with deer. A quaint **floral clock** still graces the entrance in summer. Even if you don't get out of your car, it's pleasant to drive around the park with its antique cast-iron street lights, fanciful old picnic pavilions, and frequent monuments. A herd of some 90 fallow deer, tame and very small, roam the island, especially around the nature center.

The crush of visitors (at least 3 million cars a year) and limited budget creates problems on this attractive island. At times maintenance personnel cannot keep up with the accumulation of trash. Some areas are scarred and need upgrading. On warm evenings teenagers cruising with loud portable stereos can create so much congestion that this is one of the last places you would want to be. Evenings and weekend afternoons from the first warm days of spring into midsummer are best avoided. There is a quaint **police station** on the island, at Inselruhe and Central Avenue, with enough patrols to make it safe for visitors day or night. (The island is never closed.) By big-city standards, Belle Isle is quite safe.

The city bought Belle Isle in 1879 for $200,000. A century earlier, it had been a common grazing ground for the French farmers whose narrow ribbon farms fronted on the river. Today the major thoroughfares are around the island's perimeter and lengthwise down its center. Originally swampy throughout, most of the park

At Scott Fountain on Belle Isle's western end there is a splendid view of downtown Detroit.

has been elevated with fill. Only the eastern wooded area looks the way it did a century ago. Canals allow **canoeists** to traverse the length of the island, but the canoe livery is currently closed.

The one-way **perimeter road** goes counter-clockwise. Sights are arranged in the order in which you come to them. Of special interest on Belle Isle are:

◆ **Scott Fountain.** To make room for this huge and ornate fountain, Belle Isle's western end was extended a thousand yards. From that western tip you can see not only the fountain but its reflection in the specially constructed lagoon. Italian white marble — some 20,000 square feet of it — was used to create the monument, which the city was at first reluctant to build. The half million dollars were supplied in the bequest of James Scott when he died in 1910. But Scott was viewed as such a scoundrel that the city at first refused his request to spend the donation on an imposing monument in his honor. Eventually the city held an international competition, won by the eminent Beaux-Arts architect Cass Gilbert. (The following year he also was hired to design Detroit's Public Library.) For the fountain, Gilbert came up with a complex series of bowls, basins, and fountains, complete with spewing turtles, dolphins, lionesses, Neptunes, and animal horns. Sculptor Herbert Adams created the required bronze statue of Scott. It's on the fountain's west side. Some say the spot was chosen so that prevailing winds keep him wet much of the time. Now, for the first time in decades, all four pumps work, and the central spray reaches a height of over 75 feet.

◆ **Dossin Great Lakes Museum.** Not to be missed. One of the country's leading maritime museums. Outstanding river views, in all weather, from the pilot house of the *William Clay Ford.* See separate entry, page 285. *Open Wed-Sun 10-5.*

◆ **Aquarium.** Another must-see, both for dramatic tanks of fish and its striking architecture. See separate entry, page283. *Open daily including holidays 10-5.*

◆ **Whitcomb Conservatory.** Capped by an imposing 85-foot glass dome, this building was made of parts from an exhibit at the St. Louis World's Fair of 1904. The **giant palms** in the central space are spectacular. Adjoining rooms feature cacti, ferns, tropical plants, a large collection of orchids, and seasonal floral displays. The bulletin board is a good place to catch up on **horticulture events** in the area.

In front are **formal gardens** and a delightful fountain capped by a **bronze gazelle**, created by Marshall Fredericks in 1936. At the base are four animals native to the island: a hawk, rabbit, otter, and grouse. *Inland from Dossin Museum. (313) 267-7134. Open 9-5, every day of the year. $2 for 13 and over; $1 ages 2-12. Keep receipt for free access to the Aquarium next door.*

◆ **Belle Isle Zoo.** Set amid splendid, shady trees, this small, 13-acre zoo is an exceptionally pleasant place to spend a summer day. The key to its charm is the 3/4-mile-long **elevated walkway** from which most of the animals are viewed. Looking down onto the animals and their living spaces gives a more three-dimensional, interesting view. The naturalistic settings are ample enough to allow most of the over 30 species to roam freely. For brief visits or for people with small children, a visit to the Belle Isle Zoo may well be more satisfying than seeing the much larger Detroit Zoo. Lions and tigers are a

'The Belle Isle Conservatory (above) and Aquarium are wonderful places to visit any time of year. $2 gets you into both.

recent attraction. The rare Sumatran tigers are extremely endangered; one lion came from a local crack house.

Among the other rare animals on display are endangered spectacled bears, the only bear native to South America, and maned wolves, also from South America. These wolves are known as "foxes on stilts" because their long legs enable them to see over tall vegetation. The popular **"World of Spiders"** showcases many kinds of spiders, including some that are much, much bigger than tarantulas. *On Vista, just south of Central Avenue in center of island. (313) 398-0900. Open May thru Oct, 10-5 daily. Probably open to 6 on weekends in July & August.* & *Admission: 13 and older $3, seniors $2, ages 2-12 $1.*

The Mobassa starburst spider is part of the popular, expanded "World of Spiders" exhibit at the delightful Belle Isle Zoo.

◆ **Nature Center.** Belle Isle's nature center is on the island's eastern side, where the forest and marsh remain in their natural state. Two self-guided **nature trails**, one 3/4 of a mile long, the other 1/4 mile, give good views of the native wildlife in the 200-acre natural area. In April the trails are likely to be underwater. For **wheelchair users** there's a short paved trail as well. Here you can also see the now tame and abundant European fallow deer, brought to the island in the1930s.

Though the indoor part of the nature center isn't large, it's well worth a visit any time of year. Intelligent, clear displays explain the area's interesting natural history and dramatically spotlight selected aspects of animal anatomy and behavior. Lively bulletin boards make this a good place to learn about area natural history programs. Most of the snakes, birds, turtles, and mammals inside are temporarily held injured animals or illegal confiscated pets such as ferrets and foxes. *North end of island on Oakway. (313) 267-7157. Wed-Sun 10-4. Donations welcome.*

◆ **The Livingstone Memorial Lighthouse**, made of Georgian marble, is topped by a bronze lantern cap. It's almost 70 feet tall; its light can be seen 15 miles away in the middle of Lake St. Clair. *The light is on the east tip of Belle Isle. As you follow the island perimeter road to the right around the island, past the Coast Guard station and park where the road veers left. Walk the asphalt path to the island's tip.*

To get to Belle Isle *from the intersection of I-375 and Jefferson in downtown Detroit, go 2 1/2 miles east to East Grand Blvd. Turn right onto the MacArthur Bridge to Belle Isle. From I-94, take the Mt. Elliot exit 217, go south, turn left immediately onto East Grand, take it to the bridge. (313) 267-7116.*

A BROCHURE WITH MAP . . . . . "Detroit's Beautiful Belle Isle Park," describes the full range of activities and sights. It is available weekdays 8-3:30 at the park office, which is in the White House on Inselruhe, or by writing Detroit Recreation Dept., 735 Randolph #2006, Detroit, MI 48226.

KEEPING BELLE ISLE NATURAL . . . . . and keeping it a clean, attractive, public pleasure park is the aim of **Friends of Belle Isle**. They organize a spring clean-up and other volunteer activities, raise money for island renovation projects, publicize the many activities and events held on the island, and act as a watchdog advisory group to Detroit Common Council about the many development projects proposed for the island. Their **newsletter** is newsy and excellent. To get involved, call (313) 331-7760 Mondays or Fridays, or become a member ($15 individual, $25 family). Write Friends of Belle Isle, 8909 E. Jefferson, Detroit, MI 48214.

INDY CARS ON BELLE ISLE . . . . . That's the **Detroit Grand Prix,** held in the city since 1981 on the first weekend in June. Free admission to the time trials on the first day (Friday). Call (313) 259-7749 for ticket info.

Belle Isle Aquarium

*A fantastic freshwater world of strange fish
and a noisy electric eel in a most beautiful setting*

NOT ONLY is this the oldest public aquarium in the U.S. but
it's one of the most visually striking. Built in 1904, it's an
early work by Albert Kahn, the architect who shaped much of
Detroit. Carved dolphins, now mostly covered by vines, grace the
entrance. The interior, with muted, indirect lighting, has a delightful
aura created by the serene green-tiled ceiling contrasted with the
black-tiled wainscoting. The effect, enhanced by the many strange
fish in crystal-clear aquaria, is that of entering a fantastic new world.

Colorful tropical fish now swim in a new, 20,000-gallon coral
reef tank, thanks to recent improvements that solve the corrosion
problem from salt water. Fiji damselfish, pennant coralfish, and
anemones now join 100 species of freshwater fish. The rarest is the
tiny and endangered desert pupfish from the southwestern U.S.,
where rampant development is dangerously lowering the water
table. Most popular is the huge, ugly **electric eel**, which delivers a
hefty 650 volts to stun prey. Through a speaker visitors can hear
the big eel's electric output when it is fed at 10:30, 12:30, and 2:30
daily (and at 4:30 Sunday). Often big crowds gather to experience
the noisy performance.

Informative signs in this striking aquarium are well written, and
interior "waterscaping" in the big tanks realistically emulates the
fishes' natural environments. The signs, neither frustratingly brief
nor overly long, provide interesting nuggets of information like:
"Outside of the movies, piranhas have never been known to kill a

The longnose gar fish (below) is one of many large Great Lakes fish you can
see in their huge 2,800-gallon tank. New in 1996: colorful tropical fish. The
Belle Isle Aquarium's biggest attraction of all remains the noisy electric eel
at feeding time.

person. In fact, people swim and bathe in rivers where piranhas live. Piranhas use their razor-sharp teeth and strong jaws to feed on fish. An injured animal that falls into piranha-infested waters may be reduced to bones in minutes."

Most major groups of freshwater fish are here, including a big 4,000-gallon tank of Great Lakes fish: largemouth bass, lake sturgeon, spotted gar, and long-nose gar. Ten thousand gallons of refrigerated water is used to keep pike, walleye, perch, bass, panfish, and trout.

Inland from Dossin Museum. (313) 267-7159. 10-5 daily, including holidays. & $2 admission for 13 and over; $1 for ages 2-12. Keep receipt for free admission to the Whitcomb Conservatory next door.

FISHING ON BELLE ISLE . . . . . The island has four special fishing spots. The two long piers at either end of Inselruhe are especially interesting. Fishing bulkheads are at the island's east end, one on the south side (just west of the Coast Guard Station) and one on the north, across a channel from the Detroit Yacht Club. Sizable catches are common. Among the fish caught are silver bass, bluegill, perch, sheephead, catfish, salmon, pickerel and pike. A bait shop is four blocks west of the MacArthur Bridge: **Jefferson & Meldrum Service** (6220 E. Jefferson, 313-259-1176). It can fix you up with a pole, hook, line, and sinker for under $10. Don't forget a fishing license. Minnows are $2 a dozen, worms $1.50 a dozen. Worms are used in summer, while minnows are used in the winter for pike and pickerel.

Dossin Great Lakes Museum

It spotlights Detroit's important role in Lakes shipping with an elegant 1912 passenger lounge, meticulous models, changing exhibits, and a pilot house with a grand river view of the Detroit River.

THIS SUPERB museum is an ideal place to launch a season of boat-watching. It ranks among the top Great Lakes maritime museums. All sorts of questions can be fielded by its knowledgeable staff and, on weekends, by its enthusiastic volunteers. Broad-based support by maritime fans has kept Dossin fresh and vital in the face of budget cutbacks at the city of Detroit's Museums Department. A **bookstore/souvenir shop** is housed in an elegant tobacco stand from an old passenger ship. Groups of 10 or more can call ahead for a tour. (Donations appreciated.)

Outside are two big cannons from Commodore Perry's key naval victory in the Battle of Lake Erie, the turning point of the War of 1812. In the room leading toward the river, a giant three-dimensional relief map of the Great Lakes shows the relative depths of the five lakes, from shallow Lake Erie (only 210 feet at its deepest) to Lake Superior (1,333 feet).

Among models of Great Lakes ships and large photos of boat christenings and spectacular wrecks, a display promotes Great Lakes shipping, which today takes a back seat to railroads and trucks. It points out that a boat delivering 15 million tons to Chicago from the East Coast takes just 24 million gallons of fuel, compared with 35 million gallons by rail and 123 million gallons by truck.

Three to five **changing exhibits** a year are mounted. A fascinat-

Not only does the Dossin Museum have lots of information about Great Lakes shipping, it's an exceptional place to watch ships, thanks to a working freighter periscope and radio.

In the pilot house of the *William Clay Ford* bulk freighter, built out over the river at the Dossin Museum, you can steer and hear nearby ships on the ship's radio. Imagine what it was like to be here, like Capt. Donald Erikson, anchored in Whitefish Bay, waiting out the terrible storm that sank the *Edmund Fitzgerald* and listening to the Fitzgerald's last matter-of-fact radio message, then watching in vain for her safe arrival on the radar screen.

ing semi-permanent exhibit, **"Michigan's Prohibition Navy,"** traces rum-running from Detroit to the Soo.

Museum highlights include:

◆ the splendid smoking lounge, all fitted out in oak and stained glass from the 1912 steamer, the *City of Detroit.* This was the **Gothic Room**, where male passengers came to smoke and talk. The ornate room brings back to life that vanished era when passengers cruised the Great Lakes in luxurious comfort.

◆ the **modern-day working pilot house** of the *William Clay Ford* (1953), flagship of the Ford fleet that hauled taconite pellets, coal, dolomite, and limestone to the automaker's Rouge Steel in Dearborn. Visitors can steer the surprisingly small wheel, check the chadburns at the front for direction and speed, and look up and down the river. Over the functioning **ship's radio**, you can actually hear nearby ships radioing their expected time of arrival to the *J.W. Westcott* mail boat station four miles downriver. (See page 207.)

On the river's near bank are signs showing the distance and direction to frequent freighter destinations:

< Marquette 481 miles
< Green Bay 507 miles
< Alpena 219 miles
< Duluth 728 miles
Montreal 618 miles>
Toronto 299 miles>

◆ a **working submarine periscope** at the base of the stairs to *William Clay Ford*'s pilot house is the museum's most popular exhibit. Looking past crosshairs designed to guide torpedos at enemy ships, you can get a great view of what's on the river.

◆ Big **picture windows look out and down the river** in **De Roy Hall**, to the right of the pilot house. Here too are detailed **displays** of things like torpedo boats at Detroit's Fisher Boat Works (once the most complete boat works on the Lakes), and superbly detailed **ship models** of ships associated with Michigan, from LaSalle's ill-fated *Griffon* through the Boblo *S.S. Columbia*, the famous luxury passenger *S.S. South American*, and the *Edmund Fitzgerald*.

◆ *Miss Pepsi* (1963), the first hydroplane to break 100 mph, is in the pavilion opposite the entrance. (The Dossin family, who paid for half the original museum, owned *Miss Pepsi* and the local bottling company that was bought out by Pepsi-Cola.)

For information on the Detroit-based **Great Lakes Maritime Institute** of maritime fans, and for many of their publications, stop at the Dossin Museum's excellent **shop**. Call to find out about year-round **weekend programs** featuring ship model makers, retired captains, lighthouse restoration groups, and more.

Open Wed-Sun 10-5. (313) 852-4051. Closed holidays. ⎣ *Adults $2, seniors and ages 12-17 $1, ages 11 & under free. Wednesdays free.*

🌲🎄🌲

OTHER TOP GREAT LAKES MARITIME MUSEUMS . . . . . are the Great Lakes Historical Society's museum in Vermilion, Ohio; the *William G. Mather* museum ship in Cleveland; and the Manitowoc [Wisconsin] Maritime Museum, easy to visit if you take the Lake Michigan car ferry from Ludington to Manitowoc.

THE GREAT LAKES BOATWATCHERS' BIBLE. . . . . . is the handy, super-informative *Know Your Ships* (126 pp., about $13). Not only does it have vessel listings for every ship on the lakes and the smokestack markings to help identify them, but it's packed with tidbits like meanings of boat whistles, the locks system and how locks operate, maritime museums, and an annual update of changes in ships and shipping. New color photos each year. . . . . Available here and at other maritime museum shops, or phone (313) 668-4743.

Pewabic Pottery

Since 1903, some of the world's finest pottery and tile has been made at this quaint studio.

THE ART and architectural tile made here since the early 20th century is famous for its beautiful, subtle glazes. Pewabic's founder, Mary Chase Perry Stratton, perfected her six iridescent glazes, which were used extensively on both vessels and tile. She had been encouraged by Charles Freer, a Detroit industrialist who became one of the world's foremost connoisseurs of Oriental art. He showed Stratton a piece of Babylonian pottery which had a mysteriously beautiful patina. After years of experimentation, she was able to emulate it.

Stratton was an important figure in the Arts and Crafts movement that flourished in Detroit at the turn of the century. It promoted a return to simple, pre-industrial handcraftsmanship. True to its ideals, Stratton never attempted to exploit her glaze formulations by mass-producing her art. Her work maintained its artistic integrity, involving constant experimentation and change. Some of Stratton's most striking work was in architectural tiles, which can be found in public places, from the Nebraska State Capitol to the Shrine of the Immaculate Conception in Washington, D.C. Pewabic tiles are all over Detroit, on many grand public buildings like the entrance of the Guardian Building in downtown Detroit and Christ Church in Bloomfield Hills, and in countless homes.

Stratton named the fledgling pottery "Pewabic" after a Keweenaw Peninsula copper mine near Hancock, Michigan, her hometown. Her work was so well received that she was able to build this pleasant gallery and workshop. Its style is that of an old English country inn. She later married its architect, William Stratton. The pottery made here declined after her death in 1961.

But since 1981 there has been a revival under the auspices of the nonprofit Pewabic Society. Production is again underway, in the spirit of Stratton's work. To see what contemporary artists do with tiles commissioned for their work at Pewabic, take a look at the UAW Monument in downtown Flint (page 364) or two People Mover stations, Detroit's Times Square and Millender Center (see page 226). Vintage Pewabic murals are at the Cadillac Center station in downtown Detroit.

Continuing to reflect Mary Stratton's vision, Pewabic today is a multifaceted place involved in education, exhibits, museum collections and archives, and in increasing production of handcrafted architectural tile for buildings. Designers and craftspeople make tiles for homeowners and design professionals who want distinctive custom tiles for fireplaces, countertops and backsplashes, bathrooms and spas, and for walls. Pewabic also offers **classes**, workshops, lectures, internships and residency programs for studio potters and other artists, as well as outreach to students from preschool through high school. **Historical exhibits** here tell the story of Pewabic's role in the history of Detroit, the growth of the American Arts and Crafts movement, and the development of ceramic art.

Visitors can wander freely throughout the two-story building, which looks much as it did decades ago. A brochure is available for a **self-guided tour**. In its **production studios**, artists mix clay, create molds, press and glaze tile, shape vessels, and fire a variety of kilns. The **exhibit gallery** usually features one or two local, national, or Canadian clay artists. The exhibit changes about every six

Pewabic founder Mary Chase Perry Stratton in her studio. Her glaze for pottery and tiles became a celebrated part of Detroit's Arts and Crafts movement early in this century.

weeks. The artists usually give a workshop on opening day. In July, the faculty and staff exhibit their work. Pewabic's **consignment galleries** showcase ceramic works in varying styles and techniques by established and emerging artists nationwide. The **gift shop** features reasonably priced Pewabic gift tiles and vessels in both reproductions and adaptations of its historic designs. Motifs include animals, themes from fairy tales and fables, and geometric shapes. There are displays of tile tables, garden ware, jewelry and commemorative tiles.

10125 E. Jefferson between Cadillac and Hurlbut, across from Waterworks Park and about 1 1/2 miles east of the Belle Isle bridge. Park in courtyard in front of the building. (313) 822-0954. Mon-Sat 10-6. &: no. Free admission; donations welcome. Call for group tours: $3.50 adults, $2 seniors and students.

AN ENDURINGLY ELEGANT NEIGHBORHOOD . . . . . is **Indian Village**, between the Belle Isle bridge and Pewabic Pottery. The large mansions on three long streets were built between 1895 and the mid-1920s on land that used to be 18th-century French ribbon farms. Many pioneers of the auto industry built magnificent homes here. The annual **homes tour** (313-922-0911) showcases noteworthy architecture, renovations, decorating, and gardens. . . . . Indian Village is on Burns, Seminole, and Iroquois between Jefferson and Mack. The older homes are closer to Jefferson. . . . . Nearby **Van Dyke Place** (313-821-2620) offers elegant cuisine in a sumptuously decorated mansion. . . . . . **The Harlequin Cafe** (313-331-0922) in an old West Village apartment building at 8047 Agnes has a more informal interior, rich and dark, and eclectic good food.

Fisher Mansion

Amusingly lavish, this auto baron's mansion recalls the excesses of the Roaring Twenties.

THIS fancifully lavish mansion is one of the extraordinary sights of Detroit. It was built in the 1920s by the talented playboy head of Cadillac Motors. Its style has been described as "glitz bordering on garish." Neglected after owner Lawrence Fisher's death, the mansion has been purchased, restored, and maintained as the Bhaktivedanta Cultural Center by Alfred Brush Ford, great-grandson of Henry Ford, and Elisabeth Reuther Dickmeyer, daughter of legendary UAW chief Walter Reuther. Ford and Dickmeyer donated the mansion to the International Society for Krishna Consciousness (ISKCON), to which they belong. It is one of 300 ISKCON centers world-wide.

A small community of ISKCON members use the ballroom for their temple room. They are pleasant, gentle people who do not proselytize visitors in any way and don't wear orange robes, either. They do offer, upon request, an audio-visual presentation on the spiritually-based Bhaktivedanta way of life. On the second floor is the excellent **Govinda's vegetarian restaurant**. It's open Friday and Saturday noon to 3 p.m. and 6 p.m. to 9 p.m., Sunday noon to 7. The grounds and gardens with their fountains and wandering peacocks are peaceful retreats in the Spanish style of the house.

The Fisher Mansion is a cozy, comfortable version of San Simeon, the California palace of Lawrence Fisher's friend, publishing magnate William Randolph Hearst.

From this silver head of Neptune, champagne flowed continuously at the parties of Cadillac Motor chief Lawrence Fisher. The variety of dramatic tile designs in this foyer only hints at the exuberant, eclectic decor throughout this amazing mansion.

Lawrence Fisher was one of the seven Fisher Brothers who helped revolutionize the auto industry in the early 20th century by building enclosed bodies for cars. Lawrence was a big, beefy bachelor who squired the likes of Jean Harlow and threw opulent parties. No elitist, he invited local tradespeople as well as celebrities to these events. Champagne flowed continuously during parties from the mouth of a solid silver head of Neptune in the entryway.

The home of publishing magnate William Randolph Hearst, Fisher's good friend, inspired this mansion on the Detroit River. Hearst's San Simeon then set the standard for California opulence, mixing an eclectic array of florid architectural styles. Fisher's mansion follows suit. The effect of all the pattern, texture, and color is dazzling and surprising, not overwhelming or pompous. The scale is intimate; the house only has three bedrooms. The entranceway has black Majorcan tiles on the floor with gold insets. Tiles in Art Deco patterns surround the silver head of Neptune. Long Roman tiles alternate with Pewabic tile. The marble columns are Corinthian Greek. The bathrooms are especially memorable. In all, 75 ounces of gold leaf and 140 ounces of silver were used on the mansion's ceilings and moldings.

Always impeccably dressed, Fisher remained a bachelor until, at 62, he married his childhood sweetheart, then 67. One of his great loves was his dogs. He frequently dined alone with his cocker spaniel, who ate out of a silver bowl. When the dog suddenly disappeared one day, the disconsolate auto baron personally went door to door in the neighborhood, offering a $10,000 reward for its return, to no avail. Later, when another dog drowned in the adjacent swimming pool, he had the pool filled in. He buried two of his beloved pooches in signed, silver Tiffany caskets on the mansion's grounds. One of the first things a subsequent owner did was to dig up the caskets, dump the bones in the trash, and sell the silver.

Sailing was another of Lawrence Fisher's passions. Hence, the mansion is strategically situated with canal access to the Detroit River. Fisher had the Grayhaven Canal built up to the house, with large enclosed boat houses on each side. The larger held his 106-foot yacht. The smaller housed the vessel which later became President Kennedy's presidential yacht.

The ballroom emulates a Spanish courtyard, complete with Venetian parapet and delicate white clouds painted on the blue ceiling. During Fisher's festive parties, a machine projected stars on this ceiling, and lighting was adjusted to simulate dusk or dawn, whichever time it might be. Some of the world's top wood-carvers were brought to work on detailing. In some cases a carver would spend over a year on a single door. Not much of a reader, Fisher ordered the hand-tooled leather books in the library by color rather than title.

Amazingly, this splendid mansion was sold by a bank in the early 1960s for just $80,000. ISKCON has respected the historical integrity of the place. Its own colorful religious paintings hang on some walls, but they don't obscure the feel of the place when Fisher lived there. In fact, they are well suited to the vivid, exotic atmosphere.

383 Lenox, off E. Jefferson in Detroit, about 3 miles east of the Belle Isle Bridge and 5 miles east of downtown. From Jefferson, turn onto Dickerson. Look for the sign to Victoria Park, Detroit's new showplace subdivision. Dickerson becomes Lenox. From I-94, take the Conner exit; go south on Conner, which ends at E. Jefferson, and turn left onto E. Jefferson. At the second traffic light, turn right onto Dickerson, where you will see a billboard for Victoria Park. (313) 331-6740. Tours Friday thru Sunday at 12:30, 2, 3:30, and 6; also at other times by prior arrangement. &: no. $6 adults, $5 seniors, $4 children.

Grosse Pointe

A haven for Detroit's old money, the Pointes offer lovely views of Lake St. Clair, and lavish estates from the early 20th century.

THIS FAMOUS string of five affluent suburbs is a splendid place to tour by car or bicycle, thanks to beautiful Lake St. Clair and the many handsomely landscaped homes. "Grosse Pointe" is actually five separate municipalities stretching along and off the lake just east of Detroit. Driving out Jefferson from Detroit into Grosse Pointe Park, there is a dramatic change. As you cross Alter Road, you go from close-packed depressed Detroit blocks and enter a green, kempt domain of big trees and beautiful homes.

The prominent old families of Grosse Pointe, Grosse Pointe Shores, and Grosse Pointe Farms are about as close as Metro Detroit comes to having an aristocracy. Many scions of the founding auto barons still live here. This is definitely George and Barbara Bush territory, with the tone set by low-key people with inherited money. Actually, there's more diversity of income and ethnicity here than the WASP stereotype suggests. Away from the lake, especially toward Detroit in the planned buffer suburb of Grosse Pointe Park, there's a good deal of modest, middle-class 1920s housing. The Grosse Pointes offer better housing deals on comparable houses than Ann Arbor. Grosse Pointers reflect the ethnic mix of Detroit's old east side: Italians, Belgians, Poles, and Lebanese, plus a few old French families — and lots of executive transfers.

Property on the lake is always expensive — often over a million dollars per home. Some of the choicest streets are Vendome, Provençal (overlooking the Country Club of Detroit), and Lake Shore Road. There still aren't many Jews or Democrats or blacks in the Pointes, though their numbers are gradually increasing. For years through the 1950s, prospective Grosse Pointe home buyers were screened by the Grosse Pointe Realtors' infamous point system – a source of much embarrassment today. Private detectives hired to fill out reports didn't even bother to rate blacks or Asians. They were automatically banned. Other prospective home buyers were secretly rated on such issues as:

1. Is their way of living typically American?
2. Appearances—swarthy, slightly swarthy, or not at all?
3. Accents—pronounced, medium, slight, not at all?
4. Dress—neat, sloppy, flashy, or conservative?

The screening maintained a dependably population of white Protestants.

The shoreline of these affluent communities was first settled by French who left Detroit after England took it over in 1760. The French established distinctive ribbon farms along Lake St. Clair. Only 300 to 600 feet wide, they extended a mile or more inland, permitting each farmer crucial access to Lake St. Clair for transportation.

Wealthy Detroiters began building summer homes in the Grosse Pointe area as early as the 1840s, but few who worked in Detroit dared live year-round so far out. Wealthy businessmen often commuted by yacht to Detroit from their summer Grosse Pointe residences. A few of these fine old Victorian mansions still stand, such as the 1895 Queen Anne house at 365 Lake Shore.

Beginning around 1910, wealthy Detroiters withdrew from the city, from its booming factories they themselves built, and from the masses of immigrants whom they brought to work there. Grosse Pointe became famous for its magnificent lakeshore estates that imitated elegant country houses in England, France, and Italy. More typical were regular blocks of large, ten-room Tudor or Georgian Revival houses. Some of the most spectacular lakefront mansions have been razed to make way for more modest half-million-dollar homes. But many remain.

A trip out Jefferson and Lake Shore Road from Detroit to Grosse Pointe Shores is a fine drive, especially when the sun is shining on the stunning turquoise blue of Lake St. Clair. The wonderful Art Deco storefronts on Jefferson remind you just how urban

Grosse Pointe is famous for its lake-front mansions, though many of the grandest have been demolished for subdivisions. One choice mansion you can visit is the Grosse Pointe War Memorial at 32 Lake Shore, built for a Packard Motor founder.

these close-in suburbs of the 1920s really are. They were laid out along streetcar lines, in fact. To see Windmill Point or the house built by Pewabic Pottery founder **Mary Chase Perry Stratton** and her architect husband, turn right from Jefferson onto Three Mile Drive, about a mile west of the entrance to Grosse Pointe Park. The Strattons' informal multi-level house at 938 Three Mile is oriented to the garden. It combines Arts and Crafts principles with balconies, bays, and beamed ceilings of Mexican architecture.

To see one of the prettiest parts of the Pointes, continue on Three Mile to Esser. Go right onto Esser, left onto Bedford or Harcourt, and right onto Windmill Pointe Drive. It terminates at a small park. The **Windmill Point Lighthouse**, where Lake St. Clair joins the Detroit River, sits at the south edge of Mariners' Park in Detroit. From Windmill Point Drive, turn left at Alter Road to get to the lighthouse.

Where Jefferson becomes Lake Shore Road, no houses obscure motorists' views of the lake. You could park on a side street and walk along here. But don't venture into the public parks. They're for card-carrying residents only — and always have been. (Suburbs of this era throughout the U.S. were developed with the explicit intention of providing a wholesome, healthy life for "our kind of people" and keeping the growing central cities and their exotic immigrant populations at bay.)

Stop in at the **Grosse Pointe War Memorial** (313-881-7511) at 32 Lake Shore Road in Grosse Pointe Farms for a peek at one of the best of the old estates. It's a fine example of the neoclassical villas that were the architectural specialty of the prominent New York architect Charles A. Platt. The house and gardens take advantage of a beautiful view of Lake St. Clair. Originally the home of Russell Alger, Jr., a Packard Motor Company founder and son of the Governor/Senator/Secretary of War, the estate is now a community center. Its lectures, concerts, and classes are open to anyone whether or not they live in the Pointes. (Black Detroiters often learn to play golf through War Memorial classes.) Summer **outdoor concerts** in this lovely setting would be the perfect ending for a day in the Pointes. Visitors are welcome to peek inside the meeting rooms and see the stunning lake views, framed by elegant, formal interiors in 15th-century Florentine, 16th-century Venetian, and Italian Baroque styles.

A particularly striking sight is the private **Grosse Pointe Yacht Club** off Lake Shore at the foot of Vernier Road. What began as a ice boating club in 1914 had, by 1929, become an Art Deco version of Venetian splendor. The picturesque tower, almost 200 feet high, has ship bells which strike the hours during sailing season. This remarkable yacht club, finished just before the Depression, turned out to be Grosse Pointe's last gasp of gilded grandeur. The Thirties ushered in a sober Georgian neoclassicism, which set the tasteful, albeit dull, tone for nearly all Grosse Pointe construction ever since. A visit to the Cotswold-inspired **estate of Edsel and Eleanor Ford** (page 300) is a worthwhile culmination of the drive out Lake Shore. Shortly before you get there, look for the new lakefront French chateau with the sweeping curved entrance stairs, and steep, slate mansard roof. Built by Art Van Elslander of Art Van furniture, it's far larger than anything else around. It has to be, to fit in all the extras like indoor and outdoor pools, toy room, game room, massage room, etc.

To get from Jefferson to **Kercheval, Grosse Pointe's main shopping street**, is tricky. You have to go west on a street going in from Lake St. Clair that is south of the Country Club of Detroit. In Grosse Pointe Farms to the north, Moran is a good cross street. So is Maryland, in Grosse Pointe Park to the south. The rest of the Pointes' retailing, restaurants, and services are on Mack Avenue, the major artery which goes from downtown Detroit to St. Clair Shores and beyond. Mack is on or near the Pointes' northeastern border.

Shopping in the Pointes is pleasant, friendly, and famously dull, compared to glitzy, trendy Oakland County's nouveau riche affluence. Request a helpful **brochure/map** by calling (313) 886-7474. The Pointes' pervasively preppy look — traditional good taste, little makeup — barely changes from one generation to another. **The Hill,** on Kercheval in Grosse Pointe Farms between Fisher and Muir, has non-chain shops and upscale services. **The Village**, Kercheval's chief shopping area, is between Cadieux and Neff in Grosse Pointe. It's now almost completely dominated by chains: Talbot's, Laura Ashley, Jacobson's, Waldenbooks, Winkelman's, etc. Just south of the main retail area, at 11 Kercheval, is a **Brooks Brothers** discount outlet (313-886-2300), where suits retailing for $400 to $500 sell for $300 and $40 ties are $10. Next door at 15 Kercheval, the showroom of **Kennedy and Company** (313-885-2701), decorators, displays its trademark look, traditional but not timid, with rich fabrics and saturated, deep colors. Of the accessories sold here, candles and votives are a specialty. On Kercheval at Fisher, the mostly glass **Grosse Pointe Public Library** stands in striking architectural contrast to the conservative revival styles favored in the Pointes. No wonder – it was designed by Bauhaus-trained Marcel Breuer, a master of the International Style. Dexter Ferry, Jr., an heir to the Detroit seed company fortune, donated it to the school system. Breuer wanted to make the main reading room homelike by furnishing it with art, including a tapestry based on a Kandinsky painting and a Calder mobile.

Grosse Pointe's most interesting browsing is on **Kercheval in the Park**, between Wayburn and Beaconsfield in Grosse Pointe Park, just across from the Detroit line. The popular Sparky Herbert's restaurant inspired its revival. Now higher rents have forced some really distinctive tenants, like James Monnig Booksellers (313-884-7323), to relocate to nearby Detroit. Still, there are some distinctive old and new spots here.

◆ **Grosse Pointe Reliques.** Crowded consignment shop full of quality antiques and used furniture at reasonable prices. It contains **Shaw's Books**, specializing in automotive books and ephemera, open by appointment (313) 0824-0816. *(313) 822-0111. 14932 Kercheval. Mon-Sat 11-5.*

◆ **Reading in the Park.** A delightful children's bookstore often frequented by favorite children's authors and characters like Dr. Seuss's Cat in the Hat. *15129 Kercheval. (313) 822-1559. Mon-Sat 10-6.*

◆ **Cup A Cino**. A coffeehouse that brings a touch of bohemian life to the staid Pointes. *15104 Kercheval. (313) 822-3888. 8 a.m.-midnight.*

◆ **Gallerie 454**. An eclectic gallery that shows works by new and emerging artists as well as traditional favorites. *15105 Kercheval. (313) 822-4454. Thurs-Fri 12-6, Sat 10-5 and by appointment.*

◆ **Rustic Cabins Bar.** In the early 1930s, when this onetime blind pig went legit, the façade was adorned by two northwoods cabins outlined in round log slabs. Inside, this favorite hangout has barely changed. It has original booths and beat-up old tables, a moose head and mounted fish on the knotty-pine walls, and an Art Deco bar. There's pool, foosball, pinball, but no food. Old-timers stop by in the afternoon, a young crowd comes in the evening. 15209 *Kercheval. Mon-Sat 11 a.m.-2 a.m.*

◆ **Mulier's Omer Market.** Fourth-generation grocer-butcher has evolved from a neighborhood store geared to nearby Belgians into a gourmet grocery, without losing any of its earthy character. They make liver paté, meat loaf, sausage, and Rose Mulier's famous potato salad. *15215 Kercheval. Mon-Sat 8-6.*

LAKE ST. CLAIR . . . . . named by La Salle in 1679, is a heart-shaped body of water 400 square miles, sandwiched between Lake Erie and Lake Huron. It separates the Detroit River from the St. Clair River above. The lake is shallow, averaging just 10 feet in depth. A 700-foot-wide shipping channel has been dredged for 18 1/2 miles, giving freighters the needed 27 feet of water to pass through. Water quality problems have caused a stir by occasionally closing popular beaches in recent summers.

TWO WONDERFUL BAKERIES ON MACK AVENUE . . . . . Top-of-the-line baked goods, from danish and rye breads to cookies and beautiful whipped cream pastries, can be enjoyed at tables at **Josef's French Pastry Shop**. Fresh fruit, semi-sweet chocolate, good cream and custard fillings, and not too much sugar make the pastries stand out. Prices are reasonable. Quiche, pizza, and pasta salads are available for quick lunches. *21150 Mack at Brys, a few blocks past the Farmer Jack at the northeast edge of Grosse Pointe Woods. Look for the purple awning. (313) 881-5710. Tues-Sat 8-6, Sun 8-1:30.* & . . . . . An Italian bakery with all the trimmings (lemon ice, candy almonds, pizza by the slice, Italian bread, a substantial section of imported pastas, canned goods, and wines), **Bommarito Bakery Dolceria Palermo** is advertised as "the original Italian bakery, family owned and operated since 1925." There's nothing fancy or pretentious about this place. Eastside Italians agree their cannoli are outstanding. Chewy sub rolls make their subs terrific, too. A boon for busy families: Mrs. Turri's frozen ravioli, around $3 a pound. *21830 Greater Mack at Avalon, east side of street, just inside St. Clair Shores, across from Meldrum Bros. Nursery. (810) 772-6731. Open Tues-Thurs 9-8, Fri-Sun 8-8.* . . . . . **Freeway directions** for both bakeries: take I-94 to Vernier exit, east on Vernier to Mack, then west onto Mack.

Edsel & Eleanor Ford Home

*A beautiful Cotswold manor house and grounds,
just as they looked when the Fords lived there*

BUILT on 87 acres at Gaukler Point, overlooking Lake St.
Clair, this splendid mansion takes the prize for knowledgeable good taste among the homes of Detroit auto barons. A
large, rambling house designed by the eminent Detroit architect
Albert Kahn, it mimics on a much larger scale Cotswold cottages
and country homes a hundred miles west of London. Much of the
interior paneling and furniture come from distinguished old English
manors. The roof is of imported English stones expertly laid by
Cotswold roofers. Interior hallways are of limestone, which gives
you the feeling of entering a centuries-old manor, though the house
was actually completed in 1929.

What makes this house especially interesting is that it remains
as it was when the Fords lived here. Edsel, Henry Ford's son and the
president of Ford Motor, died in 1943. His wife, Eleanor Clay Ford,
left the estate virtually untouched. "Henry the Deuce," their oldest
son and the legendary savior of the company, whose bywords were
"Never complain, never explain," grew up here with his three sib-
lings. A diligent and well-educated student of art history, Eleanor
was a niece of department-store magnate J. L. Hudson. Tutored by
William Valentiner (see page 247), first director of the Detroit
Institute of Arts, she and her husband became true art connoisseurs. Their influence on the visual arts in Detroit, through his
public and financial support, was tremendous. Some of their priceless paintings — by Renoir, Degas, Titian, Van Gogh — have been
donated to the Detroit Institute of Arts and replaced by copies. Originals by Cezanne, Matisse, Diego Rivera, and others remain here.
And the original furniture and carpeting are intact.

Tourgoers first see a 15-minute **video** about the Fords and their
house, then go on an informative, entertaining two-hour guided tour.
New in 1996 is a **permanent Ford family exhibit area** in the south
cottage and gatehouse, with memorabilia and photographs.

Most rooms have a stately, formal feel. Striking exceptions are
two stylishly sophisticated yet comfortable rooms executed in a
serene, harmonious Art Deco style in 1938 by famed industrial
designer Walter Dorwin Teague. What the Fords called the "Modern
Room" was their favorite casual gathering place. The other Teague
room was shared by Henry and his brother.

The grounds of Edsel and Eleanor Ford's estate were designed by Jens Jensen, one of America's most influential landscape architects, a proponent of naturalistic design and native plant materials like these American elms. The grounds make a pleasant place to linger and enjoy the splendid view of Lake St. Clair.

Eleanor left Edsel's personal study unchanged after his early death from stomach cancer. It was here that the capable executive was reportedly seen bent over his desk, weeping in frustration from the abuses heaped on him by his father. Edsel, an intelligent, modest, gentle man, was Henry and Clara Ford's only child. President of Ford Motor since he was 25 years old, Edsel was widely respected at Ford. His work in developing the 1940 Lincoln Continental resulted in a classic automobile honored by the Museum of Modern Art.

As the years went by, Edsel was at times sadistically treated by his father, who became more curmudgeonly and autocratic as he aged. More than once Henry publicly demolished badly needed auto innovations that his son had spearheaded. Edsel and his co-workers had to watch helplessly as Henry refused to upgrade his Model T while Chevrolet surged into the lead as the nation's best-selling automobile. Ford Motor didn't begin to rebuild until Edsel's son, Henry II, with Eleanor's backing, wrested control from company thugs after Henry died.

The estate's lakefront setting is as remarkable as the manor house. The **grounds** ($3 fee without house tour) were planted in native Michigan trees and shrubs by **Jens Jensen**. Based in Chicago,

Jensen was extremely influential in the landscape architecture of parks and large homes. He advocated loose, natural landscaping using only native species. Now his plantings are mature, and the effect is hauntingly serene. Here Jensen created a large meadow, a lagoon, a peninsula that formed a cove, and plants to enhance the property at all times of year. Printed and audiotaped **guides to the grounds** are now available for visitors. Plan to take a tour before 4 p.m. or even 3 so there will be plenty of time to enjoy the grounds and see the pool house and gardens.

Another treat is daughter Josephine's **playhouse**, a gift on her sixth birthday. It is carefully crafted in a the same Cotswold style as the main house, but executed in 3/4 scale so that the ceiling is only six feet high. The furniture is similarly proportioned. Boys weren't permitted in the playhouse, the tour guide says, but Josephine sometimes spent the night there, alone except for her two bodyguards.

Eleanor Ford left her beloved home to the public when she died in 1976. Call for customized **group tours** and **children's activities**. The inexpensive **family summer concerts** are said to be wonderful. Michigan history tours to groups of fourth-graders are free. A separate **exhibit gallery** mounts occasional shows of wide-ranging interest, for example, "In the Spirit of Resistance: African-American Modernists and the Mexican Muralist School" (March 26-May 25, 1997). Jens Jensen promoted the practice of having a Council Ring in the grounds he planned, a outdoor gathering circle for getting in touch with nature. None was actually installed here, but the name is used for a wide variety of year-round **events** held outdoors and in: garden walks and lectures, astronomy, bird walks, art, historic preservation lectures, and more. For info on upcoming exhibits and events, call (313) 884-4222. An **activity center** with meeting rooms encourages additional public use.

The **Tea Room** serves a lunch of reasonably priced soups, sandwiches, salads, and desserts Wednesday through Saturday from 11:30 to 2:30 at least. The expanded **Gallery Shop** offers an interesting illustrated booklet on the house ($4) and many gifts and books on topics related to the Fords, including cars, dolls, historic preservation, art, gardening, and souvenirs.

1100 Lake Shore Rd. at the north end of Grosse Pointe Shores. (313) 884-4222. Tours Wed-Sun 1, 2, 3, 4 p.m. A noon tour is given from April thru December. Adults $4, seniors $4, children under 12 $3. Grounds only: $3 adults. &: first floor of house.

Detroit Zoo

Known for its pioneering chimp colony, the zoo now has an indoor area with a butterfly garden, coral reef aquarium, theater, and interactive stations.

THE DETROIT ZOO, one of the nation's 20 largest, was the first American zoo to emphasize more naturalistic barless exhibits when it opened in 1928. It offers some wonderful opportunities to observe a very wide variety of animals in natural settings that have been made possible in part by the zoo's unusual size (125 acres). One of the zoo's first displays, enormous Bear Hill, remains dramatic today.

The four-acre outdoor exhibit **Great Apes of Harambee** includes **chimpanzees** and now **gorillas**. Renowned chimpanzee researcher Jane Goodall dedicated it in 1989. It remains one of the finest and largest of its kind anywhere. From a variety of observation points the chimps can be seen in three environments resembling their natural habitats: forest clearing, meadow, and rock outcrop. The big, complex environment and opportunities for privacy allow the chimps to establish a natural social order. Visitors can see them acting as they would in the wild — playing, courting, and raising their young. "Termite hills" have been provided. If you are patient, you can witness a tool-using chimp slide a blade of grass into the hill for a tasty snack. The chimps are outside almost every day, often even in winter, but when weather is too severe, they can be viewed in two large indoor day rooms behind one-way glass.

Gorillas are new residents of the realistic Harambee ape environment that lets them establish a natural social order.

Splashy, playful young mandrills inhabit an airy, newish multi-level exhibit with a glass front. These members of the baboon family are fun to watch because of their wildly hued faces and rumps in shades of blue, red, and purple. Other recent arrivals are aardvarks, anteaters, rare sloth bear cubs, and Komodo dragons.

The zoo's newest area is the **Wildlife Interpretive Gallery**. It's indoors in the beautiful old glass-domed bird house. The renovated building itself has lots of nifty old architectural touches, like the floor's nautilus mosaic (best viewed from the rotunda), fossil-etched limestone walls, and Pewabic tile peacocks over the entrances. Here also is an **exhibit area** for changing shows, a **gallery** of animal art, a **theater** with changing presentations (call the info line for current events), a 2,000-gallon **coral reef aquarium**, and a **butterfly-hummingbird garden**. Visitors are surrounded by hundreds of big, colorful butterflies native to Florida and South America plus colorful finches and two pairs of hummingbirds and colorful finches flying freely about. Multimedia **interactive exhibits** let visitors direct camera monitors to interior spaces in the aquarium and zoom up onto fish, hummingbirds, and butterflies. Once a month a **multimedia arts program** takes place here.

Passing through the garden, you enter the **Wilson Aviary Wing**, where 30 species of colorful, exotic tropical birds fly free in a lush tropical environment landscaped with a waterfall, stream, and pond. Here the visitors are the caged ones, separated by an enclosed walkway from the birds.

Immediately next door you can view birds swimming in the **penguinarium**. The exhibit's outer triangular "ring" is water, through which penguins can swim continuously. Visitors see up close the swimming, sleekly streamlined birds, so different from their awkward waddling on land. Four species of penguins (Blue, Kay, Macaroni, and Rockhopper) live here together.

Nearby is another popular indoor exhibit, the **Holden Museum of Living Reptiles**. It houses a wide variety of snakes, crocodiles, frogs, and lizards,

Flamingos have become such a common ornamental motif, it comes as a surprise to see how they move and behave in real life.

PLANNING A ZOO VISIT

The zoo's complexity and size (125 acres, with 12 miles of paths) demand some planning. *If you only have a day,* follow the white **elephant tracks** painted on the pavement. They take you to zoo highlights mentioned above and also to bears, lions, tigers, giraffes, elephants, seals and sea lions, and giraffes, ending up at the African Station for a free train trip back. Other tips for zoo visits:

◆ **Spring** and **fall** are good times to visit because crowds are thinner, and the cooler weather means outdoor animals are more active.

◆ In **summer**, animals are more active earlier and later in the day. Indoor visits offer relief from the sun and heat. Air-conditioned buildings include the reptile house, penguinarium, and Wildlife Interpretive Center.

◆ In **winter** active outdoor animals include polar bears, arctic foxes, hyenas, and snow monkey. The hippo and giraffe houses are open to visitors. The Wildlife Interpretive Gallery and nearby indoor areas make the zoo even more of an any-time, any-weather attraction.

◆ Use the free **zoo train** (it runs from May through September) to reduce walking. It goes 1 1/2 miles from the entrance to the African station and back without stops.

◆ **Strollers** and **wagons** can be rented here or brought and used in outdoor areas, but not inside.

◆ About **food:** though the food stands scattered throughout the zoo offer more than hot dogs, zoo food is expensive, and service is slow on busy days. **Picnic tables** are provided near the Penguinarium. You can spread a picnic cloth on any grassy area. Bring **water bottles** to slake thirst without soft drinks, which make you thirsty.

◆ If you try to take in too many exhibits too fast, your head will swim. Starting with the gardens, there are a lot of low-key things to enjoy at the zoo so you don't overload yourself with too much information. Volunteers help to plant and maintain many gardens with ideas about encouraging wildlife in urban and suburban habitats.

In Royal Oak at 10 Mile and Woodward, just north of I-696 (take Woodward exit). Enter from Woodward off I-696 service drive. Open daily, year-round, 10-5. Information line: (810/248) 398-0900. Membership, volunteer & travel opportunities: (810/248) 541-5717, weekdays. Administration: (810/248) 398-0903. ♿ *Single admission: $7.50 ages 13-60, $5.50 seniors, $5 students 13-18, $4.50 ages 2-12. Parking: $3. Reservations required for group discount. Membership: $55 family or grandparent, $40-50 individual.*

Royal Oak shops and galleries

The hippest retailing in Metro Detroit

THROUGH the 1970s, Royal Oak's twin commercial boulevards, Main Street and Washington Avenue, had fallen into decline, like most aging American downtowns upstaged by shopping malls. That trend began to reverse itself in 1980 when energetic Patti Smith started her vintage clothing shop on Washington. Hip and affordable, Patti Smith Collectibles attracted customers from far and wide with both its interesting vintage clothing and its inexpensive original designs. Smith set a successful example, and her Sixties-style, community-minded spirit has been infectious. Antiques and collectibles, part of the attractive original mix, have attracted more galleries and home accessories shops.

More and more interesting shops have popped up in Royal Oak, which is one of Detroit's larger suburbs at 65,000. Prices for even its modest bungalows have soared. Design-conscious professionals gut them and open up their interior spaces. Shops paved the way for the area's emergence as Metro Detroit's restaurant center. Now coffeehouses are everywhere, beloved by teens who are under drinking age. Weekends Royal Oak is quite a scene. All these developments lead to the questions of whether the higher rents restaurants and coffeehouses can pay will hurt the offbeat shops that launched ther area. Here are some of the shops that make Royal Oak's downtown one of the Midwest's most interesting. Keep in mind that Washington and Main, both of which parallel Woodward several blocks to the east, are twin main streets a block apart. All the stores are open Monday through Saturday, some until 9 p.m.

ON AND OFF WASHINGTON

◆ **Patti Smith.** Known by many for her creative designs, Patti Smith (not the rock poet, who also lives in metro Detroit) now focuses on 1920s-1970s vintage clothing for men and children as well as women. What's hot currently are nylon print shirts, bell bottoms, and, of all things, polyester leisure suits. There's a "$4 Room" in back full of irregular and slightly damaged vintage clothes that attracts lots of teenagers. She also features a small collection of promising young designers from New York, Chicago, L.A., and Great Britain. Prices are inexpensive to moderate. *405 S. Washington. (810/248) 399-0756.*

◆ **Dave's Comics and Collectibles.** A colorful clutter of Fifties and

Sixties juvenile collectibles form the heart of this shop. At the back is the metal lunchbox collection. Another mainstay are the action figures, including Starwars and Superheroes. A more recent nostalgic collectible: kids' metal wastebaskets decorated with colored TV or movie heroes. There are also rings from cereal-box promotions, vintage toy trucks, sports cards, and comic books from 1938 on. *407 S. Washington. (810/248) 548-1230.*

◆ **Gayle's Chocolates.** Gayle's was the first to offer espresso and cappucino in Royal Oak, something now found on just about every downtown block of this trend-conscious place. Gayle's decor, at first a stunning Art Deco, has evolved into what one employee calls a "soda fountain/plantation" motif. The expansion has made room for a juice bar (most popular: carrot-apple-ginger, $3.75 a glass). You can also get tasty sandwiches, led by the tomato-mozzarella-basil ($4). Loose tea is now on hand, along with all sorts of coffees. There's homemade ice cream, hot chocolate, and steamed milk with honey. But the heart of the operation remains the chocolate. Some fifteen workers toil on the second floor overhead making chocolate that is shipped all over the country. Outstanding chocolate truffles

Deborah Roberts in front of her shop on 11 Mile just east of Main. She's a more recent example of the creative energy that has made Royal Oak into an exceptionally exciting place to browse and eat.

($1.25 each) are the main attraction. Some say Gayle's are the best available. *417 S. Washington. (810/248) 398-0001.*

◆ **Lotus Import Co.** Ethnic jewelry, clothing, and decorative accessories from all continents, with quite a few Asian selections, especially Indonesian — all appealingly displayed in this visually rich shop. Big selection of aromatherapy and bath products. *419 S. Washington. (810/248) 546-8820.*

◆ **21 Ten Elizabeth's.** A bright spot of downtown Detroit displaced by the stadium, this charming gift shop is now in Royal Oak. *200 W. Fifth Ave. near Washington. Mon-Sat 11-6, later by chance.*

◆ **Vertu.** Vertu is known for its collection of furniture from the mid-1930s to the late 1950s, especially pieces by Eames, Nelson, and other Herman Miller designers. Vertu deals in objects of modern design (largely furniture and ceramics) from 1900 to 1960. Roger Ellingsworth and Robert Rozycki are quite knowledgeable about mid-20th-century design. *511 S. Washington. (810/248) 545-6050.*

◆ **Dos Manos.** Well-chosen, affordable handcrafts from Latin America. Tin mirrors from Mexico, Mexican pottery, jewelry from Mexico and Peru, wool and cotton purses from Guatemala and Bolivia. Terra cotta planters in the shapes of frogs and turtles are $18 to $65. *210 W. Sixth. (810/248) 542-5856.*

◆ **Deco Doug.** Radios, clocks, lamps, vintage watches, and some furniture, exclusively Art Deco from the 1920s into the 1950s. *106 W. Fourth. (810) 547-3330.*

◆ **Stamping Grounds.** Rubber stamps here are taken as serious fun, a means for inspired creative expression, and not just a passing fad or cute gift item. Plenty of nifty examples and idea books to get you started, and special inks for stamping on fabrics. *228 W. Fourth. (810/248) 543-2190.*

◆ **Chosen Books of Michigan.** Metro Detroit's only gay bookstore. Well-stocked with books, magazines, cards, novelties, gifts, videos, and various paraphernalia. *120 W. Fourth. (810/248) 543-5758.*

◆ **Deborah Roberts.** This small, crowded gift shop is a visual delight. New York native Roberts has an uncommon eye for finding and arranging interesting things from toothbrushes to toys. *206 W. 11 Mile Rd, just east of Main. (810/248) 543-7372.*

ON MAIN

◆ **Bright Ideas.** The Midwest doesn't have many contemporary home furnishings stores featuring original new Italian, Swedish, and German furniture designs. Bright Ideas has them, plus accessories like halogen lighting. *220 S. Main at Third. (810/248) 541-9940.*

◆ **Carol/James Gallery.** An exceptionally pleasing contemporary arts and crafts gallery, Carol/James carries glass, decorative and functional ceramics, wood, jewelry, and fiber by 75 craftspeople. The blown glass paperweights and perfume bottles ($55-$365) stand out. *301 S. Main. (810/248) 541-6216.*

◆ **Incognito.** Clothing related to popular music (rock 'n' roll, hip-hop) takes up most of the space in this shop, but there is also an extraordinary selection of sunglasses in over 300 styles. *323 S. Main (at Fourth). (810/248) 548-2980.*

◆ **Noir Leather.** Downtown Royal Oak can boast of some genuinely eccentric shops. Noir Leather is the most notorious. "It is certainly one of the few places in the Midwest where you can buy how-to videos on body piercing and tattooing, underwear that glows in the dark, and a range of political buttons fit for everyone from peacenik to storm trooper," wrote *Detroit Free Press* reporter Lewis Beale. "Where else could you see in-store signs that read, 'Absolutely no return on Bondage items for sanitation reasons'? " Most Noir customers are interested in fairly conventional things like its big selection of leather motorcycle caps and leather sheath skirts, but there's an ample supply of handcuffs, ominous-looking leather masks, and crops for customers with kinky sexual tastes. Owner Keith Howarth is no punk himself but an art historian and former art conservator with exceedingly polite manners. Also check out Vintage Noir around the corner at 124 N. Fourth, which sells everything from Catholic schoolgirl uniforms to shrunken heads. *415 S. Main. (810/248) 541-3979.*

◆ **Aquarium Shop.** Owners Dave and Mike have a reputation for good service and a quality selection of well-cared-for pets. Tropical fish and birds are the main attractions, but they also now sell ferrets ($160), small pets that remain as playful as kittens even as adults. One of the most popular birds is the quaker, a smart, small parrot ($249). Lily pads ($20-$30) and Japanese koi (colorful fish which grow up to two feet) are sold to stock backyard ponds, an increasingly popular home hobby. *504 N. Main. (810/248) 544-FISH.*

◆ **Lulu's.** This beloved antique shop, several blocks north of the heart of downtown Royal Oak, specializes in antique buttons. The thousands on hand range from 50¢ to $250 for hand-painted enamels. Lulu is not the least bit pretentious. "If it's beautiful and interesting, I'll get it," she says. The result is a pleasing store to visit.

There are lots of ceramics, including pieces made in the 1930s and 1940s by McCoy of Zanesville, Ohio. *405 N. Main.*

GETTING TO THE ZOO AND ROYAL OAK . . . . . Now that I-696 links Metro Detroit's east and west sides, it's a snap. Take I-696 and get off at the Woodward/Main St. exit, go north on Main, less than a mile. The retail area is just south of 11 Mile Road. To get to Washington, go left on Fourth. Peripheral parking is clearly marked. From I-75, take the 11 Mile exit 62, go west on 11 Mile about 1 1/4 miles, then south on Main or Washington.

GOOD FRESH FOODS AND GOOD STUFF . . . . . Many discriminating cooks shop for in-season produce and fruit at the year-round, 110-stall **Royal Oak Farmers' Market**. Most stalls are indoors, and there's a big parking lot. Sundays year-round from 10-5 the market changes into a highly regarded **flea market** that's better than the name implies. A number of the 75 dealers have permanent booths set up, from which they sell everything from dried flowers and crafts to precious metals and coins. Lots of clothes (both old and new) and antiques and collectibles are always on hand. *Open May through October on Tues, Fri, Sat 7 a.m.-1 p.m. Open year-round on Saturday. 316 East 11 Mile Rd., 1 1/2 blocks east of Main St. (810/248) 548-8822.*

A DEMAGOGUE'S LEGACY . . . . . The impressive **Shrine of the Little Flower** Catholic Church at Woodward and Roseland just north of 12 Mile Rd. was built by the famous **radio priest Charles Coughlin**, whose listenership in the 1930s was not unlike Rush Limbaugh's today. The theatrical priest sympathized with the Depression-era plight of his autoworker parishioners and became an influential New Deal backer. But by 1935 Coughlin had become a blatant anti-Semite and almost a fascist. He denounced Roosevelt as a tool of Jewish bankers. When World War II began, his popularity plummeted, and by 1942 he was off the air. His admirers contributed to the church, completed in 1933. Stones from each state are inscribed with that state's flower. Antiwar activist Tom Hayden was an altar boy here.

ENTERTAINMENT IN ROYAL OAK . . . . . is anchored by the metro area's leading comedy club, **Mark Ridley's Comedy Castle** (810-542-9900); the **Royal Oak Music Theater** (810-546-7610), a major venue for various rock/pop genres; and the **Main Art Theatre** (810-542-0180), limited distribution art and foreign films.

NEW AREA CODE. . . . . . Oakland County's area code changes from 810 to **248** in 1997.

Birmingham galleries

One of the most important concentrations of art galleries in the Midwest

DURING the Eighties, Birmingham became a major Midwestern center of important art galleries. They focus on everything from museum-quality ancient artifacts to contemporary art by internationally known artists. Catalyst for this convenient concentration was the prestigious Donald Morris Gallery on Townsend, which moved from Detroit in 1975. So many galleries came to occupy a charming strip of small shops on Woodward north of downtown that it's now known as "gallery row." A number of galleries also located near Donald Morris, which eventually closed its public gallery in 1994, a victim of rising rents. High overhead (rents, staffing) makes public galleries vulnerable institutions. There's been a trend in high-rent places like New York for public galleries to give way to parties, salons, and temporary events as ways of showing and marketing new art.

Birmingham is Michigan's version of SoHo — a cluster of mini-museums with enthusiastic, knowledgeable staffs and a wealth of fine artists. Call galleries for shows and dates of openings and artists' receptions.

ON AND NEAR TOWNSEND STREET

◆ **Susanne Hilberry Gallery.** One of Birmingham's oldest galleries shows contemporary American artists with national reputations. Some are Michigan-based: Ellen Phelan, Judy Pfaff, Michael Luchs, Judy Linn, Mike Kelley. In the back is an exquisite small ceramics exhibit. *555 S. Woodward. (810/248) 642-8250. Tues-Sat 11-6.*

◆ **Robert Kidd Gallery.** The talent at this large gallery is so deep, it's like a quick trip to the Museum of Modern Art in New York. Works by major figures like Harry Bertoia, Helen Frankenthaler, Sam Gilliam, James Havard, and Ida Kohlmeyer, and emerging artists as well. *107 Townsend. (810/248) 642-3909. Tues-Sat 10:30-5:30.*

◆ **David Klein Gallery.** In a new, much larger location, Klein focuses on contemporary realism, American modernism of the 1930s and 1940s, and 20th-century European and American modern masters. New shows every month. *163 Townsend. (810/248) 433-3700. Tues-Sat 11-5:30.*

◆ **G. R. N'Namdi Gallery.** Paintings, sculpture, and a good number of collages by contemporary artists with national and international reputations. Many African-American and Latin-American artists are featured, such as Jacob Lawrence, Perez Celis, Al Loving, Jean Miotte, and Howardina Pindel. This gallery also fills an important role in highlighting some unusual artists who wouldn't be seen elsewhere. *181 Townsend. (810/248) 642-2700. Tues-Sat 10:30-5:30.*

◆ **Hill Gallery.** Hill has become a leading Michigan gallery. It shows major working artists like Frank Stella, Mark di Suvero, John Walker, and Donald Sultan, plus important Michigan-based artists. Its new space has dramatic, high, skylit ceilings that enhance the art and many sculptures. That's in addition to the Hills' longtime base of museum-quality American folk art. *407 W. Brown at Chester, 4 blocks west of Woodward, closer to Southfield. (810/248) 540-9288. Tues-Sat 12-6 or by appointment.* ♿

◆ **Donald Morris Gallery.** Now by appointment only, Morris primarily sells the established 20th-century American and European masters: Milton Avery, Alexander Calder, Joseph Cornell, Jean Dubuffet, and Piet Mondrian, among others. Also: classical African art and turn-of-the-century decorative arts. *(810/248) 584-3445.*

GALLERY ROW ON NORTH WOODWARD

On North Woodward between Harmon & Oak, a few blocks north of downtown.

◆ **Lemberg Gallery.** Contemporary paintings, drawings, and graphics by artists who are locally and nationally prominent. A $30,000 Jasper Johns print may hang on one wall, and on another a $4,000 Jane Hammond drawing or a $1,000 oil painting by Stephen Magsig. *538 N. Woodward. (810/248) 642-6623. Tues-Fri 11-5:30, Sat 11-5.*

◆ **Halsted Gallery.** This gallery has a national reputation for its 19th- and 20th-century photography. It also carries out-of-print and rare books on photography and books from current exhibitions. It's a rare collection, with a view of important works rarely exhibited in most museums because photography has been ignored and undervalued during its development. *560 N. Woodward. (810/248) 644-8284. Tues-Sat 10-5:30.*

◆ **Donna Jacobs Gallery Ltd.** This fascinating upstairs gallery specializes in ancient art: Greek, Roman, Egyptian, Etruscan, Near Eastern, and Pre-Columbian objects. These include glass, bronzes, stone. If you have ever wanted to visit a museum back room where the collection is stored, don't miss this. *574 N. Woodward. (810/248) 540-1600. Thurs-Fri 11-5:30, Sat 1-5.*

◆ **Elizabeth Stone Gallery.** Original art by illustrators of children's books— mostly contemporary, and some old masters of the genre. Numbered, signed lithographs, prints, posters, and fine children's books are here, along with watercolors, pastels, engravings, etchings, collage, and oils. Elizabeth Stone was the children's librarian at Cranbrook's elementary school for many years. The staff extends a warm welcome to interested visitors. Prices range from $100 for spot illustrations to $7,500. *536 N. Woodward. (810/248) 647-7040. Tues-Sat 10-6.*

◆ **Mettal Studio.** Highly original sculptural art jewelry by nationally recognized Patrick Irla and Cary Stefani, both Center for Creative Studies alums. Their studio/gallery provides a look at the process of making art. Customers can also collaborate with the artists and come up with custom designs. *534 N. Woodward. (810/248) 258-8818. Tues-Fri 10-6, Sat 10-4.*

◆ **Arkitektura/In-Situ.** Reproductions of classic 20th-century modern design, mostly furniture and lighting. It was started in 1984 by the grandson of Eliel Saarinen and two other alums of nearby Cranbrook, where the great Swedish designer lived and worked for many years. In addition to Saarinen designs, Arkitektura/In-Situ sells authorized reproductions of furniture by great architect/designers of the past like Le Corbusier, Mies van der Rohe, and Charles Rennie Macintosh, and current names like Phillippe Starek, Antonio Citerio, and many Italian designers. Prices range from $100 to over $15,000. Don't miss the collection of playful, low-voltage lighting. *474 N. Woodward. (810/248) 646-0097. Mon-Fri 9:30-5, Sat 1-5. Closed Sat in summer (Mem.-Labor Day).*

🌲🌳🌲

OTHER SPECIALIZED GALLERIES NEARBY . . . . . Other art centers are on or near Woodward in **Pontiac** and **Ferndale** (see below), **Royal Oak** (pages 306-310), and **Detroit** (page 218).

THE REVIVAL OF DOWNTOWN PONTIAC . . . . . is coming about because of restaurants, art galleries, and the Industry dance club in an old movie theater. The ailing automaking city (population 71,000) is the county seat of wealthy Oakland County. Historic buildings from the car companies' golden age of the 1920s have been the nucleus of redevelopment. . . . . Many new galleries are housed in the **Oakland Arts Building** at 7 North Saginaw, Pontiac's main street. Their anchor is **The Habatat Gallery**, which enjoys a national reputation in the relatively new field of contemporary art glass. The field got its start at workshops held in a garage behind the Toledo art museum in 1962. A Libbey Glass chemist gave University of Wisconsin art professor Harvey Littleton technical information enabling artists to work in glass using only small kilns, without big factory facilities. Glass can be cast, blown, sandblasted, or slumped. Some is clear, some is brilliantly colored, some is like a painting. Prices can run from $3,000 to $80,000 for works by leading glass artists like Dale Chihuly, Joel Philip Myers, Howard Ben Tre, and Klaus Moje. *7 N. Saginaw. (810/248) 333-2060. Tues-Sat 11-6, Fri to 8. May close Tues in July & Aug.* &. . . . . . In the same building, the **Shaw Guido Gallery** shows sculptural ceramics by young artists and recognized names like Michael Lucero (New York), John Mason (California), and Karen Karnes (Vermont). Ceramics has become well established as an art medium in museums, but it is rarely shown except in crafts galleries, which tend to emphasize decorative versions of functional items like plates, teapots, etc. *7 N. Saginaw. (810/248) 333-1070. Tues-Sat 11-6, Fri to 8. May close Tues in July & Aug.* &. . . . . Another neighbor is the **Riki Schaeffer Gallery**. Its unusual specialty: one-of-a-kind contemporary doll art from all over the world, all handmade. Also, unusual gift items by artists: pins, books, tiles, and more. *7 N. Saginaw. (810/248) 745-9494. Tues-Sat 11-6, Fri to 8. Call for summer hours.* &

IN FERNDALE . . . . . The Woodward streetscape has been claimed by **Revolution: A Gallery Project** and its large billboard, designed by a different artist each month. The billboard responds to the current show. Revolution's proclaimed mission is to "provide a vehicle for dissemination of ideas. . . , to be an educational tool which allows everyone to experience and challenge the aesthetic and cultural judgments of our time." Changing shows may include artists' installations, or functional ceramics, paintings and sculptures by new and recognized artists. *23257 Woodward half-way between 9 and 10 Mile roads. (810/248) 541-3444. Tues-Sat 10-6, Thurs to 8.*

MICHIGAN'S MOST FASHION-CONSCIOUS, GLITZIEST DOWNTOWN . . . . is in **Birmingham**, centered at Woodward and Maple. Blessed with virtually the only functioning downtown in this booming suburban region of central Oakland County, the prestigious residential suburb of 20,000 assumed a new role in the late 1970s and 1980s as the shopping mecca for one of the 10 wealthiest counties in the U.S.,

As of 1996, downtown Birmingham faces a challenge. Adjacent Troy's Somerset Collection (page 321) has expanded into a fashion power center so vast and choice that Birmingham's retail offerings look pale by comparison. Consultants suggest that Birmingham's new role may be in various forms of entertainment and shopping-as-entertainment, rather than straight retailing.

In any case, Birmingham offers a beautiful urban environment, with natural beauty close at hand in the park along Quarton Lake and the upper Rouge River. Proximity to Cranbrook (page 315) is a big plus. An offspring of pizza/sports magnates Mike and Marian Ilitch have turned the **Birmingham Theater** (810-644-3456) on Woodward into an eightplex that always includes family choices in its lineup. . . . . Easiest parking is in city ramps; look for signs. Request a helpful **Birmingham parking map** and **annual events schedule** from the Metro Detroit Convention & Visitor Bureau, 1(800) DETROIT.

Cranbrook

*Here the famous architect Eliel Saarinen
created a total environment of extraordinary beauty
for artists and students.*

THIS EDUCATIONAL complex on 315 rolling acres has several claims to fame. Internationally, Cranbrook is known for its Academy of Art, which is a graduate school of art, design, and architecture. Locally it is known for its prestigious private elementary, middle, and upper schools, as well as for its art and science museums.

Finally, Cranbrook is known throughout the world for the total aesthetics of its built environment — a careful integration of buildings, gardens, sculpture, and interiors. The noted architectural photographer Balthazar Korab, who lives nearby, expressed this nicely. "Cranbrook is my place of recreation. Walking there, you find yourself in a different atmosphere. It's like a large private estate that has been opened to us pedestrians, where you can inhale a time past, an era of great patrons and great ideas. . . . The gardens, the grounds, and the buildings have a definite, luxurious cohesiveness."

Two remarkable men, a patron and an artist, joined their energies to create this special place. The patron was Detroit newspaper magnate George Booth. The artist was Eliel Saarinen. In 1904 Booth bought a run-down Bloomfield Hills farm and commissioned Albert Kahn, on his way to becoming Detroit's leading architect, to build a large, Tudor-style mansion there. Booth, the grandson of an English coppersmith from Kent, was a leading proponent of the Arts and Crafts movement, which stressed a greater unification of life and art through handcrafted artistic production by individual craftspeople. It was a total approach to design that blurred the distinction between fine arts and crafts. Before Booth married into a newspaper family, he had owned a successful ornamental ironwork factory in Windsor. Curiously, the Arts & Crafts sensibility took hold in Detroit at the same time as the city's great industrial growth.

A trip Booth took to Rome in 1922 was the catalyst for the Cranbrook schools, which would gain worldwide attention. There he saw the American Academy and decided to create a school of architecture and design. He persuaded the well-known Finnish architect, Eliel Saarinen, along with Saarinen's wife and children, to move to Bloomfield Hills in 1925 and lay the groundwork for the Cranbrook community.

Saarinen's Brookside elementary school, built up close to Cranbrook Road, shows the rustic charm of the cottage style. It has a wonderful iron gate, Scandinavian-style brickwork, and numerous sculptural accents. Saarinen's first designs were for an Academy of Art and Cranbrook School for boys in 1925. His blend of the familiar English Collegiate Gothic style with Finnish Romanticism is distinctive. In 1928 Saarinen designed his own house (now completely restored, along with the furnishings designed by him and his wife,

Loja, and open to the public) and a second house along Academy Way off Lone Pine Road. Saarinen and Booth had begun to bring distinguished artists to teach at the Academy, which opened in 1931, and to assist in creating and furnishing many buildings within the complex. (Most are not viewable by the public. But one of the best interiors, at the Kingswood School, can be viewed on a regular Sunday tour. See page 318.)

The Cranbrook Academy quickly gained a reputation as one of the world's top artistic communities. It continues today to be an important advanced art institute, with internationally known artists in residence in nine departments: architecture, ceramics, design, fiber, metalsmithing, painting, photography, printmaking, and sculpture. A high point of Cranbrook was just before World War II, when two faculty, Charles Eames and Saarinen's son, Eero, who soon became a famous architect himself, created a new, leaner interior design look in frankly machine-made furniture. By the 1950s, Cranbrook alumni Charles Eames, his wife, Ray, Florence Knoll, and Harry Bertoia, had popularized the look so much that it has become the very essence of "modern" design. Examples of their work can be seen at the Academy of Art Museum (see below).

Cranbrook is a wonderful place to take walks at every time of year. Covered with fresh snow, it's magical. In spring and summer the formal gardens at Cranbrook House are a special delight. The distinctive buildings, many with engaging decorative details, combine with the hilly setting, mature landscaping, and decorative iron gates to create a memorable environment. Throughout the grounds are 60 sculptures by the prominent Swedish sculptor Carl Milles, who headed the sculpture department for 20 years, and Marshall Frederick. Fredericks was Milles' protegé. His "Spirit of Detroit" and other sculptures are familiar Detroit-area landmarks. A map of the grounds clearly shows what areas are open to the public. (The schools and faculty residences are not.) Get the map from the Cranbrook House or museums. A highly recommended **architecture and sculpture tour** takes visitors through the art museum gardens and the boys' school campus, and then visits the **Kingswood School** library and dining room (1931), a real treat for interior design fans. The entire Saarinen family, Eliel and Loja and

Now restored and open to the public: Saarinen House, designed by and for Eliel and Loja Saarinen. He was Cranbrook's Finnish-American architect in residence (1925-1950) and the head of its art academy (1932-1946). She was an influential weaver. The dining room here, done in coral, red, dark and light woods, and a gold ceiling oval, shows their rich yet simple style. He designed the furniture; her tapestry is on the wall.

their adult children Pipsan and
Eero, brilliantly designed and
furnished the school's major
rooms and their rugs, draperies,
interior paneling, and furniture .
Kingswood combines aspects of
the Prairie School, Art Deco, and
Nordic folk art in a warm,
appealing way. *$6 adults, $4
seniors & students (includes art
museum fee). May-Oct: Sundays
2 p.m. at the art museum. Call
(810) 645-3323 for private tours
for 8 or more.*

Four Cranbrook areas are
regularly open to the public:

◆ **Cranbrook House &
Gardens.** The 1908 mansion
designed by Albert Kahn is now
the Cranbrook community's
administrative office. It features
leaded-glass windows and tapestries, Pewabic tile, and art
objects collected by Cranbrook
founders George and Ellen
Booth. The stunning **gardens**
around the house, impeccably
maintained by volunteers, are
marked by dramatic vistas,
fountains and cascades, sculp-

Before Saarinen came to Cranbrook,
newspaper owner George Booth
already set a high standard for landscaping and environmental design
with carefully planned fieldstone
walls, ornamental ironwork, and statuary at his home, Cranbrook House,
and its garden.

tures and architectural fragments. In early June the gardens are
said to be at their peak with lilacs and peonies in bloom, but a
vibrant combination of perennials and petunias makes them really
wonderful in August, a difficult time for many gardens. Don't miss
the tiny rock garden by the sunken garden. Daffodils and thousands of tulips make spring spectacular, too. *380 Lone Pine Road.
(313) 645-3149. Gardens open: May thru August, Mon-Sat 10-5, Sun
11-5. September, daily 11-3. October, weekends only 11-3. Combined
house and garden tour: $6. Call (313) 645-3149 by Tues. for Thurs.
lunch in the Oak Room. Park at Christ Church Cranbrook.*

◆ **Saarinen House.** The 1930 home, studio, and garden of Eliel
Saarinen, Cranbrook's resident architect from 1925 to 1950. Now
completely restored down to the important decorative accessories,

the extraordinary interiors feature Eliel's furniture and architectural detailing and tapestries, rugs, curtains, and other textiles designed by his wife, Loja. *Open May through October. One-hour tours held Thurs, Sat & Sun at 1, 1:30, 2:30, 3 and Thurs also at 11. Private tours by reservation for 8 or more: Wed & Fri 10-5, Thurs 5-9, Sat 10:30-12. (810/248) 645-3323. Adults $6, students & seniors $5. Includes art museum admission.* ♿: no.

◆ **Academy of Art Museum.** On permanent view are works by the Cranbrook Academy's many prominent faculty and students, including Carl Milles, Florence Knoll, Charles and Ray Eames, Maija Grotell, Eero Saarinen, and Marshall Fredericks. Many examples of Eliel Saarinen's decorative work and architectural drawings are here. **Changing exhibits** focus on contemporary trends in the visual arts, with one-person and group shows of nationally and internationally known artists and emerging artists and designers. The impressive **bookstore** offers books and some gifts about art, architecture, and design for adults and children. *(810/248) 645-3312. Turn right and park behind the museum. Open Wed thru Sun 1-5.* ♿ *Adults $4; $2 students & seniors. Call for information on frequent **lectures** and exhibits.*

◆ **Institute of Science.** By the year 2000 "The New Institute" will have emerged from a major construction and renovation program that will add 50% more space and four more halls to this family science and anthropology museum. The Institute began as a teaching museum adjunct to The Cranbrook School. Many of its current permanent exhibits date from an earlier, less interactive museum approach that gives a complete three-dimensional overview of a subject area such as geology.

In recent years Cranbrook has become the premiere destination for area school trips, with 250,000 visitors a year. **Changing exhibits** prepared by outside exhibit development companies attract publicity and many family visitors. The main show always has a family focus appealing to children *and* to adults. It's common on weekdays to find adults who live in the area and belong to the Institute dropping by to mess around, by themselves, with special-event demonstrations, like the popular one on how music is made. *Note:* the entire museum, not just the planetarium, stays open Friday and Saturday nights.

As for the current permanent exhibits, the **Physics Hall** is the most popular. Elegantly simple hands-on demonstration devices show how things work: pulleys in various applications, electricity, waves, light. The museum shop stocks books and games that reinforce learning here and elsewhere in the Institute, including the changing exhibits. The **mineral collection**, one of the most exten-sive and well arranged in the country, will dazzle rockhounds and overwhelm most others. The more accessible **hall on Native American culture** has a full-scale tipi and many interesting arti-facts and dioramas showing what life was like in villages of various native peoples. Other displays illuminate key aspects of earth sci-ence, botany, and biology.

The **observatory** is open to the public Saturday evenings after dark, weather permitting. An astronomer is there Saturday to field questions. Call (810/248) 645-3200 for weekend planetarium shows ($1 extra) and evening laser light shows to rock music ($2 extra). One show is always aimed at ages 3 and up. The other deals with current astronomical events: a comet approach, a recent stop of the space probe Galileo, etc. *Mon-Thurs 10-5; Fri-Sat 10-10, Sun 1-5. & Adults $6, seniors & kids 3-17 $4. Memberships $20-$50. (810/248) 645-3200. Recorded events line: (810/248) 645-3236.*

Cranbrook is at 1221 North Woodward Avenue between Lone Pine Rd. and Long Lake Rd. in Bloomfield Hills. The new **public main entrance** *on Woodward is marked by a sign. If coming from the south and Birmingham,* stay left. *There's a separate lane for turning through the median. Signs direct visitors to the various public attractions. A* **map** *of the grounds and brochure about the Cranbrook Educational Community is at each attraction, or call (810/248) 645-3142.*

NEAR CRANBROOK . . . . . Christ Church Cranbrook, an imposing English Gothic-style Episcopal church, was the gift of Cranbrook founder George Gough Booth and his wife. The extraordinary craftsmanship throughout the building speak to their interest in the English side of the Arts and Crafts movement. Booth sought out the finest artists and craftspeople to work on the church. Although most of the woodcarving, stained glass, and mosaics are from the 1920s, the Booths brought back many older objects from Europe. . . . . The 118-foot tower holds the Wallace Carillon, whose 50 bronze bells weigh between 16 and 6,720 pounds. **Sunday summer carillon recitals** are offered free of charge at 4 p.m., usually from July 4 weekend through Labor Day weekend. **Tours of the tower**, which offers a spectacular view of Bloomfield Hills and Cranbrook, are available by appointment. *Main sanctuary open to visitors 8-6 Sun-Thurs, 8-4 Fri, 8-5 Sat. Sunday services at 8, 9:15, and 11:15 a.m.; 8 and 10 a.m. during the summer. Weekday services at 10:30 a.m. Tues & 7 a.m. Wed. 470 Church Road, at Lone Pine and Cranbrook Roads (across from the Cranbrook House entrance). (810/248) 644-5210.*

NEW AREA CODE. . . . . Oakland County's area code changes from 810 to **248** in 1997.

Somerset Collection

Newly enlarged, Michigan's premiere shopping complex is now a dazzling concentration of the best stuff.

EVEN IF SHOPPING is not your thing, these twin tasteful retail palaces are likely to be a treat to visit. Its beautiful architecture and artwork make most malls look ordinary. Somerset North, new in 1996, adds a family dimension and choice retailers found nowhere else in the state: F.A.O. Schwartz, Restoration Hardware, Pottery Barn, and April Cornell, an upscale version of Pier 1. This concentration of elite stores is rare in the Midwest, and access is much easier than in Chicago. Anchors are Nordstrom, Neiman Marcus, Saks, and a Hudson's honed to contend with the competition, Here too are Henri Bendel, Barneys New York, Bebe, Jaeger, Mundi Collection, Caché, MAC Cosmetics, Tiffany, William Randall Cashmere, Bruno Ricci, Bally of Switzerland, to name a few. Fitness and outdoors, shoes, and home furnishings are other strong categories. Neiman Marcus has even dedicated a third-story room to display nothing but beautiful Steuben glassware ($2,000 and up). There's plenty to interest a man, including The Sharper Image, Brookstone, Hear Music, Rand McNally Map & Travel, Bang & Olufsen audio and video; Doubleday, Eddie Bauer. NM's little lunchroom provides $10 lunches (open 11-5) comparable to many of the area's best restaurants. The Peacock Cafe food court in Somerset North will no doubt set the standard for these often pedestrian eateries. Jimmy Schmidt's Stelline is a standout in Somerset South.

2801 W. Big Beaver Road at Coolidge in Troy. 2 miles west of I-75, exit 69. (810) 643-7440. Mon-Fri 10-9; Sat 10-6; Sun 12-5. ₺ Valet parking (3 stations) to arrive at Somerset South, leave at the North or vice-versa. For nearby hotels, call (810/248) 641-8151.

The Skywalk's moving walk connects Somersets South and North.

Oakland University's Meadow Brook Hall

Imagine the lifestyle of the very, very rich in a carefully concocted Tudor estate with its original furnishings.

A TOUR of Meadow Brook Hall, the 103-room Neo-Tudor country estate built by the widow of Detroit auto pioneer John Dodge in 1926-29, gives visitors an excellent look at the scope and detail of the fantasy architectural projects of wealthy American industrialists. Mechanics John Dodge and his brother Horace were among the half dozen car makers responsible for Detroit's remarkably sudden automotive dominance by 1910. John Dodge had begun construction on a manor of similar scale on Lake St. Clair in Grosse Pointe when he suddenly died in 1920. Five years later his widow, Matilda, married Alfred Wilson, a wealthy lumberman who belonged to her church. They spent their honeymoon researching English manor houses with architect William Kapp of the Detroit firm of Smith Hinchman & Grylls. A whole industry of art dealers, designers, and craftsmen had developed to help newly wealthy Americans build their 20th-century princely homes with taste and style to match the European aristocrats who were regarded as their natural counterparts.

Seventy years later, Meadow Brook is unusual in remaining intact and completely furnished, because Mrs. Wilson left the entire estate to Oakland University, which she also helped endow. As a conference center, Meadow Brook today actively uses its dining rooms and guestrooms.

Unfortunately, the volunteer-led guided tour focuses too much on details: a secret stairway, hidden panels and heating systems, checkerboard handles on the door of the game room, and many paintings by artists great and not-so-great. Everything gets equal weight on this tour: the player Aeolian organ, the Goebelin tapestry, the younger Wilson daughter's collection of Storybook and Madame Alexander dolls (which added a refreshing contemporary note), the paneling in Alfred Wilson's study depicting scenes and mementoes from his boyhood on an Indiana farm and his years at Beloit College, and lots of carved gargoyles on the grand stair hall.

Like many tours of grand homes, this one gave no perspective, no ideas, and little notion of the lives or personalities of most of the people connected with Meadow Brook. (We learn more about

Frances, the Dodge daughter who became an outstanding horse-woman and developed a well-known Kentucky horse farm, than anyone else.) Expect a change when Meadow Brook's new director, who has an art history background, hires a curator and settles in.

As for now, there's barely a mention of John Dodge and his fortune, the source of the wealth for this great house. The company he started with his brother Horace (John did the business deals and presentations, Horace was an outstanding machinist) was a key supplier to Henry Ford before the Dodges started assembling their own cars and trucks and making machine gun mechanisms for the French in World War I. John Dodge had been widowed for years when Matilda Rausch became his secretary and then, at the age of 20, his wife. She was the tiny, resourceful daughter of a German saloonkeeper on the Detroit riverfront. Matilda had grown up on a Canadian farm and gone to business school in Detroit. In 1920, when John and Horace both died of influenza, Dodge Brothers was making 500 cars a day. *The John F. Dodge Story* by Jean Maddern Pitrone and Joan Potter Elwart, is an interesting little booklet sold for $3 at Meadow Brook. It gives a good overview of Dodge's life, career, and generous if temperamental personality. The tour will be more enjoyable if you spend 15 minutes reading it, sitting in the beautiful rear garden or the comfortable entry hall.

People who love all kinds of nooks and crannies or who enjoy "Lifestyles of the Rich and Famous" will love the Meadow Brook tour as it is, starting with the basement "entertainment area": the Fountain Room (a rec room), the two-story ballroom with its leaded oriel windows, and the game rooms copied from two old English pubs. Conspicuously absent from the tour were the rooms for the

Meadow Brook Hall was built in the late 1920s for $4 million (an astonishing sum in those days). Interiors were planned from measured drawings of English country estates.

Meadow Brook's gardens are worth checking out. Landscape firms contribute small theme gardens for a summer garden show. The Pegasus Fountain by favorite Detroit-area sculptor Marshall Fredericks is in the peaceful rear garden.

staff. (Some 20 maids and 2 butlers lived in quarters over the kitchen.) We'd been on quite a hike by the time we had seen the dining hall, the Wilsons' studies, the vast 40' by 60' living room, the conservatory, the library with case after case of matched bound leather sets and a hidden room for shelving newspapers, the grand stair hall, the children's suites, guest rooms, and the Wilsons' connecting bedrooms. Wheelchairs, a real convenience on this tour, can go on elevators from floor to floor.

A definite highlight are the gorgeous bathrooms. Mostly they are in richly contrasting colors of Pewabic tiles (see page 288), with a simpler, more Arts & Crafts look than any other part of the house. The nursery bathroom with its colorful animal tiles is wonderful, but the piece de résistance is Matilda Wilson's Art Deco retreat in lilac and green, with a romantic landscape of Rookwood tiles behind the bath — a complete contrast to her dim, ornate bedroom, writhing with curvey French lines and draped fabrics, glinting with the only gilding in the house.

As a boy John Dodge had loved roaming the woods and fields near his home in Niles. He was deeply attracted to having an extensive country farm and started buying the farms that comprised Meadow Brook in 1907.

After Meadow Brook's construction was underway, Matilda and Alfred Wilson devoted a second trip to inspecting Tudor, Elizabethan, and Jacobean interiors in English manor houses. She used American woods in nearly all its paneling, and said with conviction, "To me, Meadow Brook Hall is really American."

Though Mrs. Wilson lived until 1967, she didn't spend the rest of her life in her dream house. The Wilsons lived in the original Meadow Brook farmhouse during the depression. World War II fuel restrictions and staff shortages also made Meadow Brook impractical and much of it was closed off. In 1957 the Wilsons moved into Sunset House, the much more modest contemporary house they built closer to Adams Road.

Matilda Dodge Wilson donated the Meadow Brook estate and $2 million to help start **Oakland University** on these grounds. Keeping up this stately home has been a challenge. Running it costs $3,000 a day. Groups (including small tour groups) can arrange to have breakfast, lunch, or dinner in the dining areas. Volunteers staff the **gift shop** in the charming courtyard by the long garages.

Visitors first see Meadow Brook at the end of a drive cut through a woods, as if it were a great nobleman's country estate set apart from the workaday village. To take in this grand effect, resist the urge to take the most direct path from the parking area to the cobbled entrance court. Instead, take the path through the woods to the entrance drive. There a six-room, 3/4 scale playhouse, **Knole Cottage**, was built for John and Matilda's daughter, Frances — and her bodyguard. (Especially after the Lindbergh baby's murder, kidnapping was a constant concern for the very rich.) The kitchen appliances really worked, so Frances could learn to cook. Knole Cottage is open during Meadow Brook Hall tour hours, June through December, weather permitting and for groups who make advance arrangements.

Over a dozen small **garden areas** installed by landscapers for June's garden show (see below) are by the entrance court and the terrace behind the house, overlooking the golf course. These and the woods are open to the public at no charge. Not to be missed: the boxwood **Pegasus garden** outside the breakfast room, adorned with a statue by favorite Detroit sculptor Marshall Fredericks, and the adjoining **rose garden**. Ask for directions. A big grant from Mrs. Wilson's estate means parts of the grounds are being redone in keeping with the 1928 landscape plan. (One is a garden for dancing.)

*On the east edge of the Oakland University campus 3 mile northeast of downtown Pontiac via University Dr., or 13 miles due north of downtown Birmingham via Adams Rd. (being reconstructed in summer 1996). From I-75, take Exit 79 (Pontiac Rd./University Dr.) east to Oakland U. entrance. Turn left onto Squirrel Rd., right onto Walton, right again onto Adams at the campus's edge. In 1/3 mile look for entrance to Meadow Brook Hall. (810/248) 370-3140. **Tour info:** Year-round (except Xmas) Sun 1-5 (last tour leaves at 3:45) and* *weekdays at 1:30. No reservation necessary. July & August, Mon-Sat at 10:30, 12, 1:30 and 3. Sun 1:10, 1:30, 2, 2:30, 3:05, 3:45. **Tea room** open July & August, Mon-Fri 11:30-3. &. Adults $6, children under 12 $3. Group tours can be planned to include lunch, dessert, theater matinee (see below), and/or dinner.*

SPECIAL EVENTS AT MEADOW BROOK . . . . . Unless otherwise stated, call (810/248) 370-3140 for details. . . . . At the **Meadow Brook Landscape & Garden** show on a June weekend ($7), participating landscapers and other experts answer questions and give gardening talks. . . . . Meadow Brook's grounds are the perfect setting for festive events. In June, July, and August the **Meadow Brook Music Festival** presents pop, country, Big Band, and classical performers, including the Detroit Symphony Orchestra, in a natural outdoor amphitheater just beyond the woods at Meadow Brook Hall. Food is served and picnic baskets are welcome. Music starts at 8 p.m. $12-$40. (810/248) 370-0100. . . . . Held on the first Sunday in August, the **Meadow Brook Concours d'Elegance** is considered one of the world's top three classic auto shows, with cars valued at between $50 and $100 million. . . . . For 10 days around early December, Meadow Brook is **Holiday Theme Walk** and Knole Cottage becomes Santa's house.

ON THE OAKLAND UNIVERSITY CAMPUS. . . . . The well-known **Meadow Brook Theatre** on campus offers professional theater (mostly contemporary dramas and comedies) between October and May. Call (810/248) 377-3300 for information. . . . . For information about **Oakland U. student performances** in music, theater, and dance, call (810/248) 370-3013.

FOR MORE STATELY HOMES OF DETROIT'S PRINCES OF INDUSTRY, ... see the flamboyant but relatively cozy **Fisher Mansion** on Detroit's riverfront (p. 291), the well-mannered Cotswold estate of art connoisseurs **Edsel and Eleanor Ford** on Lake St. Clair (p. 300), and Henry Ford's eccentric **Fair Lane**, more interesting for its gardens and power plant than its furnishings (p. 356). Only the Grosse Pointe Farms mansion of Packard Motor vice-president Russell Alger, Jr. (now the **Grosse Pointe War Memorial** community center, p. 296) approaches Meadow Brook in making a Big Impression.

NEW AREA CODE. . . . . . Oakland County's area code changes from 810 to **248** in 1997.

Holocaust Memorial Center

*Grim and disturbing, this outstanding museum
illuminates what led to the mass murder of Jews.*

THE MURDER of 6 million Jews by Hitler's Nazis during
World War II is documented in a chilling, almost low-key
manner in this multifaceted, superbly designed museum.
The $7 million center opened in 1984 after decades of planning. It
was the first freestanding Holocaust museum in the U.S.

Visitors begin the **self-guided tour** hearing the sweet, haunting
voice of a mother singing a Jewish lullaby. You enter a darkened,
ominous-looking tunnel and pass a video of Hitler bombastically
shouting to a throng of Germans his racist message and world view.
Displays put into historical context Germany's suffering after World
War I and the punishing peace imposed by the French. It becomes
clear how humiliation and economic distress led many Germans to
turn upon their Jewish fellow Germans as scapegoats.

Displays use a sophisticated combination of historical artifacts,
photos, dioramas, and film footage, so that no visitor can escape the
Holocaust's horror. **Films** on video monitors give glimpses into the
Warsaw Ghetto, site of the first Jewish resistance. Warsaw was the
first of several walled-off ghettos in major cities where Jews were
brought and imprisoned under conditions of terrible overcrowding

**The knock at the
door: what Jew-
ish families in
Nazi-occupied
Europe dreaded.
Nazi attempts to
eradicate the
impact of Jewish
culture were
futile, so deeply
interwoven was
it with the histo-
ry of Western
science, art, and
thought. The
Holocaust Center
takes a long,
broadly humanis-
tic look at the
Holocaust, from
multiple per-
spectives.**

and hunger. More films show the very scenes that Allied troops found when they liberated concentration campus. A video theater presents **testimonials of Holocaust survivors**, continually being collected by the center's archives.

What comes across is the almost incredible act of the systematic extermination of millions of men, women, and children by an industrialized, Western society quite similar to our own. The Nazis' blatant sadism is also evident. These victims not only died but experienced extraordinary suffering before death. Some "righteous gentiles" are introduced near the eternal flame; more are remembered in the outdoor garden (below).

Free group tours are given for groups of 10 or more. They book early. Volunteer docents with an interest in the subject become very well informed and can answer with wisdom and understanding the inevitable questions about what the Holocaust tells about human behavior. Why didn't Jews leave or fight back earlier? Why didn't more Germans protest? Why was the U.S. government so late in confronting this issue? A Holocaust survivor speaks to the group at the end of each tour — a special opportunity that will vanish with time. Independent visitors are welcome to tag along on tours if it's OK with the group leaders. A general public tour is held each Sunday at 1 p.m.

This obviously isn't a pleasant place to visit. Children under 12 aren't advised to come unless they already have some background about the Holocaust. But the museum exposes us to sad truths about what the human race is capable of.

6602 W. Maple in West Bloomfield Township, 2 miles west of Orchard Lake Rd. In the Jewish Community Center Campus across from Henry Ford Hospital. From I-696, take Orchard Lake Rd. exit 3 miles north to Maple, turn left. (810/248) 661-0840. Sun thru Thurs 10-3:30. Fri 9-1 from Sept-May only. 1 1/2 -hour **public tour** *held Sundays at 1 p.m.* ♿ *No admission charge.*

ALSO AT THE HOLOCAUST MEMORIAL CENTER . . . . . is the Benard L. Maas **Garden of the Righteous**, where marble plaques commemorate the heroism and unselfishness of only a handful of the many who helped save lives. Among those honored are governments, diplomats, communities, and individuals. . . . . The **Morris and Emma Schaver Library-Archive** is one of the most comprehensive collections of Holocaust materials in the U.S. Everyone is welcome to read, browse, or do research here. Many researchers come from abroad, especially Germany. Copy service is available. The **documentary video collection** can be viewed here by anyone. Teachers and others may borrow videos for group use.

The **communities retrieval service** can provide a printout highlighting the history and inhabitants of 1,200 European Jewish community of 500 families or larger. Cost: $10 per retrieval. The center book shop, events, and Holocaust research information is on the web. The address is http.//holocaust center.com.

NEXT DOOR AT THE JEWISH COMMUNITY CENTER . . . . . The JCC presents a huge range of classes and lectures, often on subjects related to Judaism, and also sports, chess, bridge, etc., sometimes old movies in Yiddish. All are open to nonmembers. The facilities resemble those of a large community college. There's an **exhibit gallery** with changing shows, a **sports hall of fame** for Michigan Jews, and a cappucino and **snack bar**. Call (810/248) 661-1000. . . . . The professional, highly regarded **Jewish Ensemble Theatre** does four productions a year from September through June, plus an annual Festival of New Plays with staged readings. Plays range from comedies and musicals to dramas. They are of interest to Jews but not necessarily only about Jews. Performances Wed, Thurs, Sat & Sun evenings, Sun matinees. Tickets $15-$23. (810/248) 788-2900.

100 KINDS OF YARMULKES . . . . . plus sterling menorahs, Israeli recorded music, books and games on Jewish subjects are a few miles away at **Esther's Judaica Giftworld**, in Crosswinds Mall on Orchard Lake at Lone Pine Road (810-932-3377).

THE EPICENTER OF JEWISH BAKERIES . . . . . is at Greenfield and Ten Mile in **Oak Park**, one of the first postwar suburbs of choice for Jews, long before the move to West Bloomfield Township. Three well-known, old bakeries are near here: **Star Bakery** (in New Orleans strip mall on the northwest corner; 810-559-4808), **Modern Bakery** (nearby at 13735 W. Nine Mile, 1 1/2 blocks west of Coolidge; 810-546-4477), and **Zeman's Kosher Bakery** (in the strip mall on the northeast corner). . . . . Today Oak Park has large communities of Orthodox Jews and recent Russian Jewish immigrants, along with many Chaldeans and African-Americans. **Minsk International** (810-559-0545), a grocery in the same mall as the Star Bakery, attracts Russians (Jewish and not) from the entire region with its unusual caviars and other specialties.

Plymouth

*A sedate suburb's downtown has blossomed into
a center of interesting and unusual shops.*

THIS bedroom community of 10,000 with its bustling downtown and tidy, prosperous-looking neighborhoods reminds
one of the classic white middle class suburbs in 1950s sit-
coms like "Leave It to Beaver." For years, Plymouth was home of the
Daisy Air Rifle Company and known far and wide as the air rifle
capital of the world. Daisy was initially the Plymouth Windmill
Company, but when sales declined, the firm decided to make and
give away an all-metal air rifle to any farmer who would buy its
windmill. The air rifle sold briskly while windmill sales languished.
So the company stopped making windmills and began focusing production on air rifles in 1895. You can still see its big brick buildings
off North Main close to the railroad tracks. But they no longer make
air rifles here; the factory moved to Arkansas in 1958.

Today Plymouth's neighborhoods of well-maintained, unpretentious homes are considered so safe some residents don't even
lock their doors. Summer evenings find entire families walking
downtown to visit the park, the bookstores, and coffeehouses. A
community band still gives concerts weekly on Thursday evenings
in Kellogg Park at 8 p.m. Now more and more visitors are coming to
town, attracted by a variety of surprisingly exciting shops and good
restaurants.

Highlights of Plymouth are:

◆ **Kellogg Park** is a shady triangular downtown park that creates a
pleasant center to the city. It was donated by John Kellogg, who
arrived in 1832 with a chest full of gold coins, having just sold a
hotel and warehouse on the Erie Canal in Palmyra, New York.
Opposite the park on Penniman is the **Farmers' Market**, where
fresh produce is sold Saturdays from 8 a.m. to 1 p.m., May through
October. At the **Penn Theatre**, facing the park, not-quite-first-run
movies are shown, usually at 7 and 9, for $2. *(313) 453-0870.*

◆ **Penniman Showcase,** located on a pleasant street just west of
Kellogg Park, is a handcrafts shop with exceptionally striking and
colorful handcrafts. The work of some 150 American craftsmen in
porcelain, stoneware, fibers, and jewelry is attractively displayed.
The richly colorful display of blown glass is a special treat. Prices
range from $10 to $500. *827 Penniman. (313) 455-5531.*

Right across from Main Street is delightful Kellogg Park. Plymouth residents walk here for free summer concerts Wednesdays at noon and for Thursday-evenings band concerts. Call (313) 453-1540 for details.

◆ **Muriel's Doll House.** The downstairs is crammed with a big selection of dolls ranging from $10 to $9,000. Upstairs you'll find elaborate dollhouse kits (some costing as much as $3,600) and an enormous selection of accessories. This place has customers from all over the world. *824 Penniman. (313) 455-8110.*

◆ **Plymouth Coffee Bean Co.** Sip cappuccino in inviting overstuffed chairs and sofas. Newspapers, books, and board games are also on hand. *884 Penniman. (313) 454-0178.*

◆ **Gabriala's** is a country decor shop with something of an upscale edge to it. Beginning with the inviting scents when you enter, this is a pleasant place to visit. A big seller here are the Cat's Meow Village silkscreened building façades that feature major Plymouth landmarks. *322 S. Main. (313) 454-3612.*

◆ **Memory Lane.** Of Plymouth's many antique shops, this one stands out for jewelry and china. *336 S. Main. (313) 451-1873.*

◆ **Chameleon Galleries.** This contemporary art shop features wood, porcelain, pottery, among other things. Most striking are the blown glass and strikingly beautiful handcrafted kaleidoscopes ($125-$500). In back is a **coffeehouse**, which also connects to the adjoining **Little Professor bookstore**, a major Plymouth hangout and source of newspapers from far and wide. *370 S. Main. (313) 455-0445.*

◆ **Maggie & Me.** Maggie LaForrest designs wonderfully exuberant,

Daisy's 1947 American Boy's Bill of Rights responded to post-World War II anti-gun sentiment by proclaiming a boy's right to learn to shoot safely.

oversized women's shirts, pants, and dresses. They're so distinctive you can spot a design a mile away. Not trendy, this is what some call "fun clothing," sometimes embellished with lace, baubles, beads, and buttons. Women from 30 and up flock to the shop, where prices range from $38 for a tank top to $350 for a coat. *880 W. Ann Arbor Trail, one block south of Penniman.*

◆ **Native West.** Well selected Native American art, mostly Southwestern, includes hot pepper wreaths, drums, Navajo sand paintings, and alabaster sculptures. The shop also carries lodge pole furniture made of sturdy pine. *863 W. Ann Arbor Trail. (313) 455-8838.*

◆ **Harvest Moon.** A combination juice bar, coffee and sandwich shop, this place has an inviting counterculture flair unusual for Plymouth, with homespun aphorisms tacked to the walls. Try the $2.25 "Red Roar" — "NOT too much beet but the right amount of this iron-rich, blood-cleansing, nutrient-rich powerhouse." The yummy Yamalicious salad combines apples, yams, cabbage, walnuts in a tangy sauce. *545 Forest Ave. (313) 454-7593.*

◆ **Georgia's Gift Gallery.** This vast emporium of collectibles— 15,000 square feet in all—grew out of a modest shop opened in 1983 to become one of the biggest volume dealers in the country. The big three lines are Disney, Dept 56, and Bradford Exchange, but there are dozens of other makers of limited editions here, including John Hine Studios, Hummel, and Lladro. Even if you're not into collecting limited editions, this is a remarkable place to visit. *575 Forest Ave. (313) 453-7733.*

◆ **Plymouth Historical Museum.** A highlight here is the BB-gun room displaying the locally manufactured Daisy and Markham BB guns and the fascinating advertising for them. One 1910 Daisy Air Rifle ad insists, "Boy, you ought to have a gun this summer. Make up your mind to get one, and learn to shoot straight." In the basement is a wonderful model of the countryside along the Middle Rouge River showing the village industries Henry Ford built. Two bargains in the **gift shop** are a $2 paperback on the history of Daisy Air Rifle and an especially well written hardbound history of Plymouth by Sam Hudson for $8. *155 S. Main St. (313) 455-8940. Wed, Thurs, Sat 1-4, Sun 2-5. Adults $1.50, children 5-17 50¢, families $4.*

ALSO IN PLYMOUTH . . . . . are two notable restaurants which attract people from many miles around: the **Sweet Afton Tearoom**, 450 Forest, and the **Cafe Bon Homme** on Penniman across from the Penniman Showcase.

ANOTHER CHARMING TOWN NEARBY . . . . . just four miles north of Plymouth, **Northville** has a smaller, older downtown with a number of upscale gift and antique shops in various traditional styles. . . . . For entertainment there's the **Marquis Theatre**, with professional productions (313-349-0868). For amusing mystery whodunits, check out the casual, funny **Genitti's Hole-in-the-Wall** restaurant. *108 E. Main. (810) 349-0522,*

Ford Rouge Complex

*An awesome historic symbol of American industry
at its most vibrant and oppressive*

THIS HISTORIC COLOSSUS of American industry is, sadly, no longer open for tours, but you can drive around the complex to take in its awesome magnitude and powerful visual forms. The Rouge was where Henry Ford put it all together. It was the world's first vertically integrated factory, an idea much copied but later discredited as too centralized and massive. At one end iron ore came in by ship; at the other cars rolled out the auto assembly plant.

The shallow River Rouge was dredged for three and a half miles up from its mouth at the Detroit River to enable freighters to deliver limestone, coal, iron ore, and other raw materials to the 1,100-acre site. The huge factories Ford built here turned the raw materials into auto parts made of steel, plastic, rubber and glass. They were then assembled into Ford automobiles.

By the 1920s this had become the world's biggest manufacturing complex. 10,000 cars a day were made here. The Rouge became a potent symbol of the machine age.

Henry Ford's historic Highland Park Plant, where just a few years earlier he introduced the assembly line, was only five years old when he started planning for the much bigger Rouge plant in 1914. The Rouge was located not far from the Dearborn farm where Ford grew up. The 1,100 acres were marshy farmland when Ford sent his agents to buy up the component parcels all in a single day. The Rouge's first products were submarine-chasing Eagle boats made at the tail end of World War I.

By the late 1920s, 75,000 workers were making Model As at the Rouge, turning raw materials into completed vehicles in just 33 hours. Immigrants from much of Europe and the Middle East flocked here to work. Just east of the factory gates, on Salina Street, were bars for nearly every nationality. Fifty languages were said to be spoken at the elementary school serving Dearborn's South End. As older immigrants left, they were replaced in the 1960s and 1970s by countrymen of the Syrians, Lebanese, and Palestinians who had long worked at Ford, and by fellow Arabs from Yemen and Iraq. They form the largest Arab community in North America. Since Arabs eschew alcohol, the bars have vanished.

It was an extraordinarily bold move for Henry Ford to invest the hundreds of millions of dollars needed to make this giant car-

The Rouge River, still a natural-looking waterway as it passed Henry Ford's home a few miles upstream, was deepened and straightened at the Rouge complex to admit giant freighters. They brought the coal, iron ore, and other basic materials that built the 10,000 cars a day produced in the huge plant. This view is from the 1940s.

manufacturing complex. It included a state-of-the-art steelmaking plant. Another Rouge plant turned 210,000 bushels of soybeans a year into paints, plastics, and binders. An electrical power plant added in 1920 was one of the world's largest. One plant made the tires for Ford cars, while another made the glass windshields. Yet another made the famous Ford V-8 engine, Henry Ford's last engineering triumph.

But the Rouge was also the scene of terrible labor strife. The aging Henry Ford lost interest in industrial production. And he couldn't relate to the new immigrants and their foreign cultures. "The Rouge isn't fun any more," he explained, and he turned his interests to Greenfield Village, *McGuffey's Readers*, and an idealized American past — ironically, the pre-industrial, rural past of Ford's hometown of Dearborn before his own factories transformed it. Ford had developed his Fordson tractor to liberate farmers from the bondage of caring for farm animals. Yet Greenfield Village celebrated the rural communities, knit tight by their isolation, his cars helped weaken with the allure of the road and the options automobiles offered.

As Henry Ford aged, the dark, suspicious side in him grew. It allowed little sympathy for his workers. They were pushed to exhaustion and spied upon. At Ford Motor Company, Henry's capable son, Edsel, was cruelly frustrated by his father, while Henry empowered the notorious Harry Bennett and his security department — virtual thugs and spies who infiltrated many potential organizing meetings. Symptoms of oppressive working conditions were many. Innocent protesters were slaughtered during the 1932 Hunger March. In the 1937 **Battle of the Overpass,** Walter Reuther and other union organizers passing out leaflets were flagrantly beaten up by Bennett's goons, even though photographers were present. The resulting photographs helped turn public opinion in the union's favor. Finally, a strike in 1941 prompted the company to recognize unionized workers.

Labor difficulties, along with the threat of German bombing attacks at the huge complex, led Ford management to decentralize operations after World War II. The Rouge's equipment grew outdated. The plant's very existence was threatened during the auto depression of the early 1980s. Workers at the complex dwindled to about 15,000.

But a 1983 labor-management agreement prompted the company to invest $500 million to modernize its Rouge Steel operations, including Double Eagle Steel Coating. They now make galvanized (rust-resistant) steel. Rouge Steel is the new blue-colored plant you see at the east side of Miller Road near Rotunda Drive. Finally, Rouge Steel became profitable. Ford sold it in 1989.

The soybean and tire plants were scrapped long ago, but the Rouge Power House still generates enough power to serve a city the size of Boston. Mustangs roll off the assembly line at the rate of nearly one a minute. Each year freighters carry 5 million tons of coal, iron-rich taconite pellets, and limestone to the complex. The blast furnaces can produce over 2 million tons of iron, and the steelmaking facilities make 3 million tons of molten steel a year. Ford's Dearborn Engine Plant makes some 500,000 of the 1.9 liter, four-cylinder engines for Ford Escorts each year.

A DRIVE AROUND THE ROUGE . . . . . Start at the north. Take Miller from Michigan Avenue, or take the Rotunda Drive exit from I-94 (Exit 209). As Miller Road passes high over the rail lines, a vast panorama of this awesome industrial complex opens up. Unfortunately, it's almost impossible to park near here and take in the view. A little farther on, by Gate 4, the main gate, you can pull over to look at the Dearborn Historical Society's marker — which neglects to mention the historic Battle of the Overpass that took place on a bridge near here. The attack on labor organizers played a key role in the history of the United Auto Workers. That bridge is gone, but it looked like the current overpass you see leading to the employee parking lot.

Turn west onto Dix Avenue just as it passes over the River Rouge. The drawbridge here rises to let big freighters come in from the Great Lakes. The once-meandering river is now dredged straight and so polluted with chemicals that it never freezes in the winter. In the distance you can often see freighters unloading at the huge steel foundry to the north.

Along Dix west of here is an ugly but powerful and fascinating landscape created by piles of raw materials and byproducts of industry. Firms like a refinery and Detroit Tarpaulin are mixed in with factory-gate bars and junkyards advertising for wrecked cars. At this point you may want to turn around and head back on Dix into Dearborn's Arab South End (page 339), the working-class neighborhood at the factory gates. Or you can continue onto Schaefer Drive and back to I-94 or Michigan Avenue.

A SNACK OR MEAL IN THE NEARBY MIDDLE EAST . . . . . Directly in front of the Rouge is a bit of the Middle East, not five miles from Greenfield Village. There you can buy delicious, healthy breads, meat pies, meals, and ingredients for Middle Eastern cooking. The **Red Sea** Yemeni restaurant at 10307 Dix at Salina serves huge portions of good food in pleasant surroundings.

❶ Greenfield Village (p. 351). Henry Ford's extraordinary assemblage of American buildings. See 18th c. farm, Wright brothers bicycle shop, much more.

❷ Henry Ford Museum (p. 345). Provocative displays use superb collections, videos to illuminate American life relating to autos and manufacturing.

❸ Fair Lane (p. 356). Quirky home of idiosyncratic industrialist. Highlights: rustic Field Room, 1915 power plant, vast grounds. Letdown: Clara's boring formal decor.

❹ Arab Shops on W. Warren. Main retail area for largest Arab community in US. has waterpipes and coffee sets, fresh figs, elaborate pastries, great food.

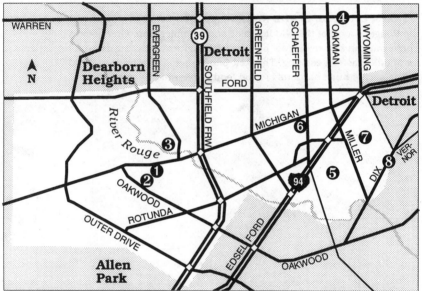

❺ Ford Rouge Plant (p. 334). Awesome complex an icon of industrial history. Iron ore came in ships, cars rolled out. 100,000 from around the world worked here.

❻ Alcamo's Market (p. 344). Outstanding Italian grocery with wide range of cheeses, sausage, imported pastas.

❼ ACCESS (p. 340). Arab support group has museum of Arab culture. Interesting displays of textiles, calligraphy, other arts. Weekends only.

❽ South End (p. 340). Port of entry neighborhood for newer immigrants, often from Yemen. Groceries, restaurants with low prices. Mosque on Vernor at Dix.

Highlights of
Dearborn

0   1   2
miles

Two Arab neighborhoods in Dearborn

The largest Arab community in the U.S. offers exceptional bakeries, a variety of good restaurants, and Arab hospitality in a familiar but exotic setting.

TODAY Dearborn's South End seems as exotic as anyplace in the U.S. The working-class neighborhood near the Ford Rouge factory gates is the point of entry for Dearborn's large (20,000) and growing Islamic Arab community. Signs are in Arabic as well as English, head scarves are common among women, and Yemeni men wear traditional skullcaps. The call to prayer can be heard from a the mosque on Vernor at Dix five times a day. Storekeepers uncover small prayer rugs on their counters and pray.

And yet, in other ways, the area seems quite familiar to anyone who grew up in a city neighborhood where kids played pick-up games of ball and went to the corner store for their mothers, where several families on every block had fabulous rose gardens in their small yards, and where, on summer nights, grown-ups sat on their porches after dinner and talked.

People from around much of the world came to work in Detroit during its original auto boom, from around 1910 until immigration was virtually cut off in 1924. The first mosque in the U.S., in fact, was near Ford's Highland Park plant. For a long time most Arabic-speaking immigrants to the Detroit area were Christians, usually from Lebanon or the Chaldean part of Iraq. Then in the 1960s, 1970s, and 1980s wars in the Middle East caused a surge in refugees, mostly Muslim, largely from Lebanon, Palestine, and Iraq. At the same time, as the nearly medieval country of Yemen opened up, many Yemeni men came to work at Ford, taking the least desirable jobs, especially in the now-roboticized paint shops. These widely varying immigrant streams made for an exceptionally diverse Arab population. Beirut business classes have been among the most cosmopolitan people anywhere. The Yemeni were largely peasants, thrust into an urban environment. It's easy to forget how many Arabs are Christian, and in fact, most of metro Detroit's early 20th-century Arab immigration was Christian, as are metro Detroit's many Chaldeans from Iran, who run so many urban food and liquor stores. The Dearborn community is Muslim. The Arabic language, not religion or ethnicity, is what distinguished Arabs from non-Arabs. Some Detroit Arab groups make great efforts to cooperate within the metro area across religious divisions.

One legacy of metro Detroit's big and diverse Arab population is an increasing number of very good Middle Eastern restaurants and a few really outstanding ones, including La Shish in West Dearborn, Al-Berdouni in Dearborn, Phoenicia in Birmingham (and now in Fairlane mall), and Steve's Back Room in Harper Woods. For a nifty **guide** and **map** to area restaurants and shops, call *(517) 629-4494.*

THE SOUTH END

Dearborn's South End residential neighborhood grew up quickly in the early 1920s around the factory gates of the famous **Ford Rouge plant**, which once employed some **100,000 workers.** The Rouge's smoke stacks loom over the neighborhood's modest houses. The South End was a true American melting pot of dozens of nationalities working at Ford, until well after World War II. Today newly arrived Arab immigrants have replaced the older-generation autoworkers who have died or moved to better housing elsewhere.

Now that the South End has become a port of entry for Muslim Arabs, especially Yemeni, the dozens of bars on Salinas Street have disappeared. The children of Muslim autoworkers who started building the mosque in 1939 have mostly moved on "into business" — the second stage of many Arabs' preferred career pattern that ends up, one or two generations after immigration, in "the professions," especially law. Now the South End is the reception area for a continuing stream of immigrants. When they can afford it, they'll likely move to the middle-class part of east Dearborn around Warren and Schaefer, where roomy brick houses were originally built for Ford foremen and craftsmen. The Lebanese and West Bank Palestinians, escaping wars at home, have come to America as families. Yemeni men usually come alone. They frequent the South End's coffeehouses, patronized by Arab men only. Yemenis in America long dreamed of saving enough money to return and live comfortably with their families in their beloved but impoverished homeland. Now, finally, they're resigned to a life across the ocean in America.

To learn more about Arab culture over the centuries, plan a weekday visit to the excellent **Arab-American Community Center for Economic and Social Services** (better known as **ACCESS**). Mainly it helps immigrants with visa problems, health services, and adjusting to life here. Outstanding **displays** of interesting artifacts, photos, and text feature Islamic contributions to science, coffee-drinking, beautiful embroidered garments, and calligraphy. One interesting exhibit tells how Arab culture is rooted in a common

language, not ethnicity or religion, and explains how the Virgin
Mary is revered in Islam as the mother of one of its great prophets.
More exhibits are in the library on music and local Arab history
(Arab peddlers' wagons were a neighborhood staple in much of
Detroit, and the beginnings of many successful businesses). Self-
guided tours (by tape or brochure) are available. Staff is happy to
answer questions. An exhibit on Detroit's Arabs and their hundred-
year history, prepared for the Smithsonian in 1995, is here. So is an
exhibit about **Hajji Aliya Hassan**, a teacher of Malcolm X and a private investigator in New York. She's considered the mother of
ACCESS and the Detroit Muslim Arab community. ACCESS's comprehensive **library** of books, videos, and artifacts, including costumes of the Arab world, is open to the general public and available
for teachers to borrow. *Take Dix east of Miller 7 blocks, turn north
(left) onto Saulino Court. It's in the former Catholic school across from
the church. Open weekdays 9-5. Call (313) 842-7010 for weekday
group tours. Pick up the* **guide** *to area shops and restaurants.* ⓑ

   South End stores are on Dix and Vernor just east of Miller. Take
Miller south from I-94 or Michigan Avenue. *Many stores are open from
9 a.m. to 9 p.m., 7 days a week.* Two shops that stand out are:

◆ **Arabian Village Bakery.** This small, family-run, homestyle bakery occupies part of a neighborhood grocery. Meat pies are about a
dollar each. (For takeout eating on the run, the clerk will microwave
them and squirt on a hummus sauce.) *Zahtar* are delicious flat
breads flavored with oregano, sumac, and sesame. *10045 W. Vernor
at Dix. (313) 843-0800. Open Mon-Fri 9-7, Sat to 5:30, Sun 9-2.* ⓑ

◆ **Arabian Gulf Market.** At Middle Eastern groceries like this, you'll
find many kinds of rice — in bulk (mostly 50¢ a pound) or in huge
bags, imported olives at $1.29 a pound, unusual baked goods and
candies, chunks of pressed tobacco, exotic tins of olive oils and fruits,
and other staples, along with brass coffee boilers for making Turkish
coffee. *1001 W. Vernor near Dix. (313) 841-7888. 9 a.m.-11 p.m.* ⓑ

WEST WARREN BETWEEN SCHAEFER AND MILLER

   Arab culture, with its long tradition of trading, dovetails with
the American dream of success through entrepreneurial energy and
hard work. Storefronts along West Warren were largely empty 15
years ago. Today they are bursting with immigrant energy. Signs
are in Arabic and English, giving the ordinary 1920s shopping strip
an oddly exotic air.

   Arabs set great store by fresh fruit, good breads, and pastries.
Prices are often astonishingly low. "Shopping is a social event," says

an Arab woman, "and the price is always questioned." Bargaining is never considered rude.

Competition is fierce, and most Arab restaurants here are good, with similar menus. Many are quite popular with non-Arab customers, who enjoy the healthy food and hospitable service. Generous hospitality and entertaining at home are hallmarks of Arab culture. In Arab homes it's important to have a tray of pastries on hand to serve with Arabic coffee, that thick, cardamom-flavored brew served in tiny cups. Honey-nut-filo pastries akin to the more familiar Greek baklava are traditional. Beautiful, light French pastries with whipped cream and icing flowers are a legacy from the era when the French dominated Lebanon in the 19th and early 20th centuries. (In fact, the French colonial government shoulders the blame for stirring up rivalries between previously peaceful peoples by elevating the Maronite Christians above the Muslims.)

The restaurant scene here is in constant flux. New ones are opening all the time, and ownership changes frequently. (The restaurant business lacks status among most Arabs.) Some restaurants still have good reputations among outsiders after they have gone way down hill.

From the car, everything blurs together on this busy street. The area is best enjoyed on foot — window-shopping, buying food, stopping for pastry or coffee. Gift shops featuring fashions, household accessories, coffee sets, games, and gold jewelry are becoming more common. Many stores stay open late, so you can shop after dinner.

West Warren businesses are patronized mostly by Arab speakers from the metro area and beyond. A surprising variety of non-Arabs also come here to shop and eat out, attracted by the tasty, healthy food and extremely reasonable prices. The meat stores offer lamb and goat, slaughtered to halal standards akin to kosher rules.

Here is a selection of noteworthy shops, arranged from north to south and east to west:

◆ **Eastborn Fruit Market.** Arabs eat prodigious quantities of fresh fruit, and Dearborn produce markets offer low prices and unusual things like fresh figs and crunchy, tart-sweet fresh dates in season. This popular store is the area's first Arab produce store that's fairly large and well lighted. It also carries imported oils, rice, and other grains. *7431 Wyoming north of Warren. 8 a.m.-9 p.m.* &

◆ **Afrah Pastry**. Small shop well thought of by locals. Afrah offers beautiful honey-filo-nut pastries, and some French pastries, at lower prices. The bird's nest with pistachios (60¢) is excellent. Tables make this a nice place to stop in an interesting area. *12741 W. Warren. (313) 582-7878.* &

◆ **Express Jewelry.** Middle Eastern jewelry and gold. In the fluid, war-torn Arab world, gold jewelry is as esteemed as a portable form of wealth as it is for display and status. *12817 Warren at Appoline.* &

◆ **Coffee and Nut Gallery.** The smells of coffee beans and spices in this tiny grocery are wonderful. *13029 W. Warren next to the Cedarland Restaurant.* &

◆ **New Yasmeen Bakery.** New Yasmeen's pita bread has become a familiar staple at many metro Detroit groceries. Arabs not lucky enough to live in metro Detroit order UPS from here. New Yasmeen's *fatiya* (spinach pies) are considered the best around. Lebanese spinach pies are much simpler and healthier than the familiar Greek spinach pies in filo dough that's flaky with butter. The dough is plumper and more substantial, and the spinach filling is deliciously lemony. One and a half or two *fatiya* make a handy, satisfying lunch. Meat pies, filled with a ground lamb mix, come in the same plump triangular pocket and also cost 75¢. The same dough is used for round, 10-inch open pies topped with cheese, meat, or thyme mixed with sesame and oil ($1.25 each), and 5-inch tomato-onion-parsley pies (75¢).

New Yasmeen has a deli and large streetfront **seating area.** (The door is on the side.) It's easy to stop for a quick meal and go home with an array of breads, spreads like hummus, and salads like tabooli and fatoush, so you wouldn't have to cook for days. Big refrigerator cases have deli items like stuffed grape leaves, and several kinds of olives and cheese.

The helpful, friendly staff is happy to provide samples and advise non-Arabs about what to eat with what and when. *Labne,* for instance, is a thickened form of yogurt that makes a terrific, healthy breakfast when spread, with or without jam, on date-filled bread rings, raisin bread, and other breakfast breads. But ask first what you're getting. A fair number of those beautiful-looking breads are flavored with cardamom, a taste many Americans can't deal with for breakfast. *13900 West Warren at Horger, 3 blocks west of Schaefer. (313) 582-6035. Daily 5:30 a.m.-p.m., Sun to 7.* &

◆ **Sultan's Bakery.** Meat and spinach pies, fried kibbee, and such, not fancy pastries, are the focus of this attractive bakery/deli. The owners of the Arabian Village Bakery, a longtime fixture in Dearborn's South End, started this venture to reach a broader, more affluent market. Also on hand, to take out or eat in at tables: olives, cheeses, and such, plus garlicky hummus chickpea spread, babaganoush (eggplant spread), falafel sandwiches, fried kibbee, rotisserie chicken, and deli salads like parsley-rich fatoush and tabooli. "They have become a favorite in East Dearborn," says a resident. "Their prices made them popular." *6851 Schaefer. Watch for the red awning. (313) 581-6688. Open daily 7 a.m. to at least 7 p.m.* &

◆ **Shatila Bakery.** Long the big name among Dearborn's Arab bakeries, Shatila was founded by a noted pastry chef from Beirut. Shatila is particularly known for French pastries. The bakery also serves coffee and has a few tables which are great places for people-watching, since so many people in the line at the counter know each other. *6914 Schaefer two blocks south of Warren, opposite L'Opera Banquet Hall. (313) 582-1952. Daily 8 a.m.-11 p.m.* &

◆ **El-Masri Bakery.** Founded in Palestine shortly after the turn of the century, and recently moved to Dearborn. Known for *kanify*, a Palestinian delicacy something like a pizza made with sweet, soft cheese — sold by the slice or by the pie. Also on hand: an extensive variety of traditional honey-nut-filo pastries and beautifully decorated French pastries (actually lighter and less buttery) with whipped cream, at incredibly low prices like 60¢. Tables let you sit, eat, drink coffee, and watch people. El-Masri has fast become a very popular local gathering spot. *5125 Schaefer 1 block north of Michigan. (313) 584-3500. Daily 8 a.m.-11 p.m.* &

OTHER GOOD ETHNIC FOOD SHOPS IN AND NEAR EAST DEARBORN . . . . .
When you walk in the door of **Alcamo's Market,** East Dearborn's celebrated Italian specialty store, you're overwhelmed by the beguiling fragrances of spicy salamis, garlic, cheeses, coffee beans, and breads. There are two aisles of imported pastas in this spiffily updated old-time grocery, along with Italian specialties like fava beans, imported Italian cookies, crackers, appetizers, and sauces. Produce is gorgeous. There's some Greek food, too. *4423 Schaefer, 2 blocks south of Michigan in downtown East Dearborn, (313) 584-3010. Mon- Sat 9-6, Fri to 7. Easy to miss. Look for the red awning. Park in lot on Schaefer and Osborn.* . . . . In the stable Polish neighborhood in a part of Detroit's west side wedged between East Dearborn and Dearborn Heights, two longtime retail neighbors have combined. **Kowalski Sausage** sells takeout Polish favorites like stuffed cabbage, in addition to its well-known kielbasa and such. At the **West Warren Bakery** good pumpernickel and rye breads are just over a **dollar a loaf.** There are Polish specialties like angel wings and jelly donuts, and a very good sourdough French bread, great for toast, also baked as **submarine rolls.** They're chewy, with a crunchy crust that holds in the juice from tomatoes, and only a quarter apiece. Order ahead to be sure of availability. *15708 W. Warren at Montrose, 2 blocks west of Greenfield and about a mile east of the Southfield Freeway in Detroit. (313) 584-2610.* **Mon-Sat 5 a.m.-7 p.m.** &

Henry Ford Museum

A world-famous collection of American products, along with remarkable exhibits that entertain and explore the American cultures of cars and manufacturing

HENRY FORD'S squadrons of pickers spread over the Midwest and New England to come up with an astounding array of artifacts for this vast (12 acres) indoor museum next to Greenfield Village. The museum's dignified exterior is an exact copy of Philadelphia's Independence Hall. Inside is one colossal collection after another. There's the world's greatest collection of 19th-century farm and kitchen implements. The exhibit on the history of lighting, from candles through electric bulbs, is immense enough to comprise a substantial museum in itself. The same could be said for the large collection of airplanes and cars. Nowhere will you find a more complete collection of American tractors.

Over the years the museum staff has worked to give shape to this huge, at times bewildering, hoard of items. Harold Skramstad, who headed the Henry Ford Museum/Greenfield Village from 1980 to 1996, came here with the mission of reinvigorating the institution and reviving it financially. Its new direction is to use the splendid collection to illuminate people's work lives and social lives. This approach has only become apparent since 1987, with the opening of the immensely popular **"The Automobile in American Life."** This lavish series of full-scale displays nostalgically shows the car's effect on the American roadside landscape. It was updated in 1996 as part of the celebration of the American auto industry's centennial. There's a vintage McDonald's sign, complete with oversized golden arches, a Holiday Inn guest room, and a diner plucked from Marlboro, Massachusetts, lovingly refurbished to its pristine state in 1946, when an egg salad sandwich cost 15¢. At a gleaming green and white 1940 Texaco service station, you can even peer into the full-scale garage and see the tools used at the time.

The **evolution of the auto industry** is vividly explained by using a sequence of TV monitors showing short historical film clips alongside splendidly restored automobiles from each period. To see the restored cars/auto history in chronological order, find the ramp in front of the Oscar Meyer Wienermobile and follow it up. Videotaped **interviews about design concepts** with illustrious automobile designers like Gordon Buerig, Raymond Loewy, and Harley Earl are fascinating even for people with little previous interest in car design.

How the automobile changed the American landscape is one of several themes of the Henry Ford's sprawling, riveting exhibit on "The Automobile and American Life." This giant, neon-trimmed McDonald's arch from the 1950s is a crowd favorite.

But the exhibit's tone remains celebratory and barely touches on the negative aspects of America's love affair with the automobile: urban sprawl, impersonality, dependence on foreign oil, pollution, and increased isolation of the poor and old.

The **"Made in America"** permanent exhibit, opened in 1992, goes beyond mere celebration. It deals with American manufacturing – its technological development and social impact. It presents the subject in such an entertaining and illuminating way that there's something in it for everybody: a film clip from the "I Love Lucy" show of Lucy messing up the candy-making production line; a huge operating painting robot used in auto factories; a life-size clean room where microchips are made; and 1930s miniature furniture (used by salesmen) of the trend-setting Herman Miller trend-setting modular system.

Video stories are told in the voices of people who came to America from all over the world. The factories they worked in that epitomized the American System of manufacturing first developed here in Southeast Michigan. The **American System** came to feature long production runs, low prices, a mass market, and eventually plenty of styling and advertising to promote planned obsolescence. Here, finally, is the Big Picture about the American age of industry from the 18th-century crafts era to today and into an uncertain future— honestly represented, replete with tradeoffs about industrial growth and its impact on the environment and the quality of work life. Visitors can look through the 19th-century *Scrapbook of Censure* and see that criticism of materialism and consumption is far from new. A video show on efficiency expert Frederick Winslow Taylor and the assembly-line speed-up he inspired shows its terrible effects on worker morale. Henry Ford emerges with some warts in the museum he founded.

"Made in America" is meant to be grazed. There's no designated sequence. But it's easy to miss a lot, including the exhibit's centerpiece video, "America in the Making."

Here is some useful advice for a visit.

◆ **Buy an annual ticket and come back several times.** Single-day admissions to either the museum or Greenfield Village are expensive ($12.50/adult, $6.75/child 5-12), and the new exhibits are so extensive and interesting, return visits are well worthwhile. The Henry Ford Museum/Greenfield Village combined annual ticket ($28/adult, $14 child) and $90 family membership are bargains if you go four or five times a year and attend a few of the many special weekends with no additional charge.

◆ **Look for the "Made in America" layout map** as you enter the main entrance. Getting an overview of what you most want to see will keep you from missing out on personal highlights. (A printed map for visitors is in the works.)

◆ **See the first section (up to the raised platform) carefully and thoroughly.** It incorporates large and sophisticated machines, several of which operate. The display cases spell out the problems and trade-offs involved, without oversimplifying. For instance, robots can substitute for human workers in dangerous, unhealthy jobs like spray painting, but they also take away good jobs workers enjoy. Small items like book covers, pamphlets, ads, and objects are effectively used to illustrate and amplify ideas. If you skim over the display cases, you'll miss some of the exhibit's most interesting parts.

◆ **Talk to presenters.** The staff who greet visitors in the entry area are trained to demonstrate and explain many parts of the exhibit. They can show how things work that you might well not understand by yourself. They are also free to offer candid personal perspective on the big questions raised here. It's quite a surprise to hear a retired GM engineer say, "It took three million years to develop the fuel resources we use, and we're using them up so fast, I think we need to slow down and smell the roses. We're such a pell-mell society, rushing headlong into what could be a real calamity."

◆ **Watch the frequent short videos.** They can be the exhibit's highlight, because they add a thoughtful dimension of historic depth, with lots of old film footage. The 1950s smarmy, smug advertising pap about the wonders of American consumerism is shown for what it is. Over an hour's worth of videos are shown on a dozen small video monitors and two large theaters.

◆ **Choose "The Craft Era" and "The Making of Mass Production"** over the exhibit on Power. These complete the historical overview of where we are and how we got there. Manufactured goods illustrate points like "Americans have always preferred or relied on foreign products" (18th and 19th century Chinese export porcelain) and "Silversmiths catered to customers who used silver to illustrate their wealth and taste" (Paul Revere pitcher). The giant interior photo of the revolutionary Ford Highland Park plant is impressive; the **"Workers' Lives"** video is not to be missed.

The **power exhibit**, replete with several huge steam engines, is visually impressive. But unfortunately it assumes some familiarity with the basics that aren't explained – like knowing that boilers made the steam and used coal to do it. Having an interpreter explain what you don't understand might make this come alive.

A new, permanent exhibit as of November, 1996, is **"Henry's Story: The Making of an Innovator."** It's on the main concourse. Artifacts highlight Ford's life as an innovator and industrialist. The exhibit is intended as a primer for innovation. It tells stories about his experiences and shows his style of learning by doing. Inspired self-educated tinkerers like Ford were a key component of American industrial dominance in the 20th century.

In counterpoint to these mammoth display areas and the long-time collections of items by category (glass and dishes are in front, for instance), the museum also holds an assortment of fascinating isolated items. There's the rocking chair in which Lincoln was murdered. You can see the huge, 600-ton 1941 "Allegheny" steam locomotive, one of the last and largest of a proud era, displayed to great effect next to the cute life-size replica of the third-oldest train in the U.S. A Lunar Roving Vehicle, one made by NASA to transport astronauts on the moon, is in the concourse.

Hands-on exhibits are generally entertaining but don't add much to big-picture ideas. The elaborate **Innovation Station** participatory production line, aimed at kids, requires getting a free ticket and takes about half an hour. At the supervised **Activities Center** children can operate an assembly line, pedal a high-wheel bike, and do other hands-on things.

At the end of the walk from the entrance, the **American Cafe** and soda fountain is open 9-4:30, year around. No museum ticket is required. Here the hot dogs cost almost $2, but the beef stew lunch at under $6 is hearty and filling. Thrifty visitors are well advised to bring bag lunches to eat at the Corner Cupboard **picnic area** within the museum. The **Plaza Store** within the museum sells handcrafts (many made in Greenfield Village) and a wide range of toys for children and adults.

Temporary exhibits are quite elaborate, semi-permanent in nature. A major exhibit on the **Motown Sound** is here into spring 1997 before moving to the Motown Museum in Detroit. (See page 261.)

See Greenfield Village (page 351) for directions, phone, and prices. To learn about upcoming events, order an info packet, or talk to a live operator, call (800) 835-5237. &

A NOTEWORTHY MUSEUM STORE . . . . . You don't have to have a museum ticket to shop at Henry Ford Museum's **Museum Store** (open 9-5 daily). Its outstanding book section is especially strong on automobiles and roadside architecture, Henry Ford and Ford Motor, antiques, crafts, Detroit history, and inexpensive Dover paper toys and coloring books. Many of the dolls, crystal, china, and other gift items reproduce objects in the Museum's collections.

TO UNDERSTAND THE EPIC DRAMA OF HENRY FORD . . . . . and a good deal of Detroit, along with the fascinating ironies of the museums he created, you have to *read* about it. A good place to start is with Robert Lacey's *Ford: The Men and the Machine* or with *The Fords* by Peter Collier and David Horowitz.

In many ways, Henry Ford himself is the most fascinating story of all, rich in paradoxes. Ford, the genius of mass production, wanted to develop a popular priced automobile and tractor to help free farmers from the burdens of animal power and rural isolation. A few miles downstream from his boyhood home and later baronial mansion on the River Rouge, he built the world's biggest factory, the Ford Rouge, the consummate example of vertical integration. Iron ore came in by ship, finished cars rolled out. A hundred thousand workers from all over the world came to work there, creating a polyglot proletariat Henry Ford neither understood nor respected. Then Ford then declared, "The Rouge isn't fun anymore," and set about developing Greenfield Village and the Henry Ford Museum to recreate the rural world of middling people, farmers and craftsmen, a world he had done much to destroy.

The museum, village, and related elementary school were at once Ford's personal retreat and a very forward-looking vision, museum staffers say. By drawing on the past and on the history of change and innovation, Ford wanted to train people to continue to be resourceful in the modern industrial era he had helped create.

Ford insisted on keeping control of Ford Motor Company while he was absorbed by his museums, and by experimental interests like exploiting the manufacturing possibilities of soybeans and developing seasonal "village industries" to enable people to stay on the farm. He actively thwarted plans of his astute son, Edsel. The results for the company were disastrous. (See pages 300 and 335.)

OTHER THINGS TO DO IN DEARBORN . . . . . if you're staying over on a trip to Greenfield Village/Henry Ford Museum: **Visit Fair Lane,** the Henry Ford Estate, and have lunch (weekdays only) in the dramatic swimming pool room. See page 356. . . . . **Explore Arab Dearborn** for dinner and food shopping; pastry shops and groceries are open until 9 at least. West Warren between Schaefer and Wyoming is the main drag. See pages 339-344. Call (517) 629-4494 for a shopping and **restaurant guide** to Arab Dearborn.

HELP IN CONSERVING YOUR HISTORIC ARTIFACTS . . . . . Conservators at the Henry Ford Museum are happy to share their expertise. **Preservation fact sheets** ($2 each, prepaid) include care and cleaning tips, plus a resource list and bibliography. They cover archival material, autos, brass, clocks, textiles and clothing, furniture and wood, glass and ceramics, structures, iron, paintings, phonographs, photos, plastic, silver, and art on paper. . . . . . Consultations about artifacts brought to the museum ($50/hour in donation to museum and village) require filling out an order/info form in advance. . . . . Call (313) 271-1620 for conservation particulars.

AN INEXPENSIVE SHUTTLE TO MAJOR AREA DESTINATIONS, ... including Henry Ford's estate, Fair Lane, the Detroit Institute of Arts, RenCen, Greektown, New Center, and Greenfield Village, runs from Memorial Day through Labor Day. Last bus returns at 5 p.m. $5 per person, under 5 free. For info on the **Attractions Shuttle**, call the Metro Detroit CVB 24-hour info line (1-800-DETROIT and hook up with the appropriate line.

Greenfield Village

*A product of Henry Ford's great interest
in American history, it's a major American attraction.*

THIS FAMOUS outdoor museum is a direct outgrowth of
Henry Ford's desire to show how technology has changed
the lives of ordinary Americans. Its indoor counterpart is
the Henry Ford Museum next door. As Ford entered his sixties, he
developed a passionate interest in the tangible manifestations of
American history. Ford had a different collecting agenda from most
of his wealthy contemporaries, who sought out the pinnacles of
achievement in the arts and crafts. In the Henry Ford Museum and
Greenfield Village, Ford wanted mainly to document ordinary life
from the past, that of farmers and shopkeepers and artisans, the
more common people. He focused on America's industrial transformation in the late 19th and early 20th centuries.

Not only did Ford spend millions to obtain the many buildings
and artifacts assembled here, but he also personally spent years
actively seeking them out. He supervised their placement here, and
would spend hours in these historic buildings — often alone —
savoring their connection with the past.

Over the years, however, a certain implicit nostalgia settled over
the place. Today the staff is working to bring more parts of Greenfield
Village to life, to go beyond the costumes and look of the past. They
want to bring to life for visitors the experiences of eccentric giants
like Ford, Edison, and the Wright brothers, and also the everyday
lives of real people whose names never appear in history books. It
takes time and money, but changes are ongoing. Ask about what's
been finished lately. *Be aware that during summer and at certain
other times of year more areas have demonstrations and people
working on the site.* Call if this matters to you.

Village highlights include:

◆ **Firestone Farm.** A real Ohio working farm from 1882, concentrated on seven acres. The house is the boyhood home of tiremaker
and Ford friend Harvey Firestone. Merino sheep were the farm's
main cash product. Visitors can see big Percheron draft horses at
work. Short-horned Durham cows and Poland China pigs, slaughtered in the fall, provide household food. From 9 to 5, museum
employees actually "live" there, doing normal farm work: milking,
working with the animals, laundry, gardening. If you come at noon,
they're eating the noon meal the women have prepared. Inquire

Percheron draft horses do much of the work at the Firestone Farm, restored and operated as it was in the 1880s. It was the boyhood home of tiremaker Harvey Firestone, a close friend of Henry Ford.

about the dates for **Spring Farm Days** that kick off the season and **Fall Harvest Days** each October.

◆ **Wright Cycle Shop.** Here, in the famed birthplace of aviation, Orville and Wilbur Wright built kites, gliders, and ultimately the world's first successful flying machine. By 1903, the American bicycle craze of the 1890s was on the wane. The Wrights eked out a living selling bicycles and bicycling paraphernalia from the store and repairing bikes in the room behind it. In the very back, they built their flying machines. Moved here from Dayton, Ohio, in 1936, the building has been restored to look much as it did in 1903, the year of their first motorized flight.

◆ **Susquehanna Plantation.** This Maryland plantation house is shown as it was in 1860. It illuminates the economic and social basis of slavery — who the slaves and masters were, their various roles, and the relationships among them.

◆ **Glass, pottery, printing, tinsmithing, and textile demonstrations**. Using 19th-century techniques, craftspeople show how these important products were made.

◆ **Ford's birthplace.** This simple Greek Revival farmhouse was built on Ford Road in Dearborn by Henry's father William in 1861. Widespread fascination with Henry Ford makes this exhibit popular.

◆ **Ford Mack Avenue Factory.** In 1903 the first production-model Fords were manufactured in the original of this building. This factory turned out up to 18 cars a day and quickly made Ford wealthy. The 4- horsepower vehicles started at $800.

◆ **Mrs. Cohen's millinery shop.** A Detroit widow ran this shop at the turn of the century to support her family. Visitors enjoy seeing hats made and trying them on.

◆ **Armington & Sims Machine Shop.** Many visitors are unexpectedly fascinated by the awesome turn-of-the-century steam engines demonstrated here.

◆ **Edison's Menlo Park Compound.** In this complex of six plain New Jersey buildings, one can relive one of the most extraordinary phenomena in American history. Thomas Edison's 1880 laboratories were the world's first commercial research and development center. Edison gathered chemists, machinists, craftsmen, glass blowers, and other specialists and gave them a wide assortment of tools and materials. The results were spectacular. In just 10 years, more than 400 of Edison's 1,093 patents came from here, including the electric light bulb, phonograph, and electric sewing machine.

◆ **Noah Webster House.** Here Noah Webster completed his famous dictionary. An upstairs room displays the extraordinary number of his accomplishments, from founding Amherst College to serving in his state legislature.

◆ **Eagle Tavern.** Transported from Clinton, Michigan, this 19th century tavern is complete with ladies' parlor, sitting room, and bar. Here you can buy weak versions of authentic drinks from the 1850s such as a "Jersey Lightning" ($3.75). In back, a **restaurant** serves huge, reasonably-priced meals from recipes of the era such as stewed rabbit and pork loin. Recommended: lemon trout. Entrees around $9.

◆ **J.R. Jones General Store.** Waterford, Michigan's general store has been meticulously restored to the year 1886, when the proprietor retired. Most museum stores have a range of contents that date over several decades at least. Here the shelves are stocked with 3,000 authentic artifacts and 2,500 reproductions of merchandise available in 1886, when consumerism and brand names (Heinz, Arm & Hammer, Borden's Eagle Brand condensed milk, Louisville Slugger baseball bats) were beginning to take hold. Authentic local notices are posted on the wall. Visitors can banter with the clerks and feel the fabrics stocked here.

◆ **Cotswold Forge.** A gifted blacksmith/interpreter fascinates visitors of all ages as he explains his work (two hundred years ago, most everyday tools and fasteners were made by hand by the village blacksmith) and bends heated iron to fashion useful objects. Things made here are used in the village and sold at the gift shops. The nearby 17th-century stone cottage and barn were brought from southwestern England, 175 tons in all. Some of Henry Ford's ancestors came from the Cotswolds.

◆ **Daggett Farmhouse.** Kids and adults love seeing the everyday activities of this spare New England farmhouse from the 1760's: spinning (visitors help card wool), cooking on the open hearth, gardening in the beautiful big garden, where many plants are unfamiliar. Medicinal herbs grown and used include hyssop (for coughs) and angelica (used in liquors and perfumes, also believed to ward off evil spirits). The household talks about topics of the day.

◆ **Suwanee Lagoon.** Idyllic, shady park-like area with a snack bar and terrace seating overlooking the lagoon where the paddlewheel steamboat, Suwanee, docks. Boat rides are $1; rides on the **antique carousel** are 75¢.

Greenfield Village's mammoth size is a strength and a weakness. The quality of interpretation is uneven. You may only want to see part of the big complex at one visit. Plan on making a day of it. Pace yourself. Take a break and sit in the park-like areas scattered throughout the village. Slow down. Don't see so many buildings that they blur together. The **annual ticket** and **membership** allow for repeat visits and bring the cost per visit way down. Study the map and daily activities upon arrival and decide what you want to focus on. Visitors can break up their walking tour with a narrated **train ride** on the village's splendid steam locomotive that circles the entire complex. It stops only at the entrance and the Suwanee lagoon. $2 gives you unlimited rides for the day. Or you can take a horse-driven **carriage ride** ($4 per person) or **bus ride** ($3 per person); both are narrated and last 30 to 35 minutes.

Another good way to take a break is to have a meal or a snack. Picnics are encouraged. The snack bar food, scattered throughout the village, is uneven and not cheap. Food is served at the historic Eagle Tavern and the **Taste of History** cafeteria (open 10-5) right next door. Here you can sample some of the dishes also prepared at the Firestone Farm and 18th-century Daggett Farmhouse and try Dandy Weed Salad (George Washington Carver's favorite), Abraham Lincoln's chicken fricassee, or Elvis Presley's favorite pound cake. Entrees are around $5; soups and pastries between $2 and $2.50; tastings 50¢-75¢. Bag lunches (around $5) reflect themes from the

Firestone Farm, Carver's peanuts, or a railroader's meal. The big, airy room, by the inventive metro Detroit restaurant design firm Peterhansrea, is something to see. It combines some carnival glass and Haviland china from the museum with corn-art murals and a pie clock.

The **Greenfield Village Store** gift shop has many toys and games for children in addition to reproductions of antiques and jewelry in the collection here, handcrafts made in the village, and an outstanding book store like that in the Henry Ford Museum.

Greenfield Village is in West Dearborn, about 8 miles west of down-town Detroit. From I-94, take the Southfield Freeway north and follow signs for the Village. From Michigan Avenue, turn south onto the Southfield Freeway and follow the signs. (313) 271-1620. A real person will talk to you. TDD for the Deaf: (313) 271-2455, 10-5 daily. **Open** *daily 10-5. Buildings are closed Jan-mid-March, but the exteriors can be viewed for free with a ticket to Henry Ford Museum.* &: *some but not all historic buildings; call.* **Admission** *to either Henry Ford Museum or Greenfield Village: adults $12.50, seniors 62 and over $11.50, youths 5-12 $6.75, under 5 free. 2-day unlimited-admission ticket to Museum and Village $11 youths, $22 adults. The Museum/Village annual pass ($28 adults, $14 youths) makes frequent visits affordable. Call for membership options. Members get free admission, discounts in shops, classes, members-only events. Sample family rate for 2 adults (can be parents or grandparents) and children: $90/year.*

A S A

TAKE AMTRAK TO GREENFIELD VILLAGE AND THE HENRY FORD MUSEUM . . . . . One Amtrak train a day stops within the Greenfield Village complex itself at the Smith Creek Depot — *if* passengers have ticketed it in advance. The morning eastbound train from Chicago and Kalamazoo (#350) stops around 1 p.m. Westbound run #355 leaves in the late afternoon. Call Amtrak for details: (800) USA-RAIL.

Fair Lane, Henry Ford's Estate

Here's the huge, quirky home the industrial legend created once money was no object.

BY THE TIME his estate was completed in 1914, Henry Ford's interests were already expanding beyond manufacturing cars. His wife Clara and son Edsel moved into Fair Lane without him in December while he was taking his peace ship to Europe in a quixotic attempt to stop World War I. Fair Lane is a gigantic, park-like spread, 1,600 acres in all. For some the splendid natural landscaping is the high point of a visit. For others it's technical quirks like the self-sufficient power plant.

The home itself shows that aesthetics were not the legendary auto magnate's strong suit. It's a strange amalgam of Frank Lloyd Wright's naturalistic Prairie Style and the medieval-influenced Scottish baronial style. Ford changed architects in midstream, and it shows. Much of the grand home reflects Clara Ford's preferences for a fitting setting for formal entertaining. It is a bad fit for Henry Ford's down-to-earth tastes, but he deferred to her taste, desiring peace at any cost. His favorite room, and the most interesting to see, was the rustic Field Room with its Navajo rugs, Windsor chairs, trestle table, and carved likenesses of the "Four Vagabonds" (Ford and his friends Harvey Firestone, Thomas Edison, and John Burroughs).

Although his father and uncles auctioned off most of the original furniture after Henry and Clara died, Edsel Ford II is leading the Ford family and the community in a restoration effort that has recovered many of the furnishings and placed them back in their original spots. Fees from tours, weddings, and such further the restoration. A posthumous painting of Henry's mother, Mary Litogot Ford, once again hangs in the music room. The English Room, where Thomas Edison stayed, has been restored, as has the dining room. The restored **garage** will soon house a Fordson tractor, kiddie cars driven by Ford's grandchildren, and the station wagon the Vagabonds took on their famous camping trips, complete with early refrigerator. Future plans include taking visitors for a short **ride in a Model T**.

The tour involves a lot of walking. The house can get very hot and muggy. A good introductory **video** sets the scene well, but the tour itself, led by knowledgeable volunteers, tends to become immersed in details without painting the broad strokes of Ford's character — full of fascinating contradictions, a complex mix of good and bad, and his relationship with his wife, a key figure in his motivation. Knowing more about Ford makes the tour far more interesting.

Ford applied his restless, creative energy to the estate's huge hydroelectric power plant and laboratory. It occupies a separate structure, connected by a long underground tunnel with the mansion. Ford teamed up with friend Thomas Edison to create an extraordinary 110-kilowatt electric system — quite a feat, given the small size of the River Rouge which powers it. The 1915 plant once again generates all the estate's electricity. The independence provided by having his own power plant must have fulfilled a deep-seated need in Ford. He later built another 20 hydroelectric plants on small rivers in southeastern Michigan.

Nature was one of Ford's many passions. He installed hundreds of birdhouses — eight even heated in winter! Almost 600 deer roamed the woods and fields. Clara Ford's taste was for more formal English gardens. She appropriated one of Jensen's meadows to create a fantastic rose garden that gained national attention in its day. Today you can see its ruins, for it would cost $400,000 a year to maintain.

Fair Lane overlooks a beautiful, wooded portion of the River Rouge at the point of a delightful man-made **waterfall**. The **Ford Discovery Trail,** a 45-minute outdoor walk, acquaints visitors with Ford, his friends, and highlights of the grounds, including a reconstructed **tree house**. Ford and naturalist John Burroughs dedicated the **Burroughs Grotto** 1918. After seeing garbage floating past his mansion, Henry Ford persuaded the upstream towns of Plymouth and Northville to stop dumping raw sewage in the river. The famous landscape architect Jens Jensen transformed the surrounding 1,600 acres were transformed into a series of naturalistic meadows and forests. At the gift shop or reception desk get the well-designed $1 **map of the grounds** to tour remnants of this vast area, largely occupied by a community college and the University of Michigan at Dearborn. It's worth having lunch at **The Pool**, a pleasant, popular restaurant in the bright, airy space which housed the mansion's swimming pool. It's open weekdays from 11 to 2. Entrees, salads, and sandwiches are $7 or so.

In west Dearborn, west off Evergreen between Michigan Ave. and Ford Rd. From I-94 or I-96, take the Southfield Freeway (M-39) to Ford Road in Dearborn, go west on Ford to Evergreen, south to Fair Lane. Park at the Henry Ford Estate lot, marked by a brown sign. (313) 593-5590. Open year-round. From April thru Dec: daily tours. Mon-Fri at 10, 11, `1, 2, 3. Sat on the hour from 10-3. Sun 1-4:30. Jan-April: Sunday tours on the half-hour, 1-4:30, Mon-Fri at 1:30 only (call to confirm), no tour Sat. &: except for 2nd floor. $7/adults, $6/seniors & kids, 5 & under free.

Flint, Saginaw Valley & the Thumb

THIS WAS one of the country's most important lumbering regions in the late 19th century. Millions of logs were floated down the Saginaw river to mills in Saginaw and Bay City. Logging generated huge fortunes, which later helped fund the start of the auto industry.

Among the many area factories using lumber was Flint's successful Durant-Dort Carriage Company, started by Billy Durant. That visionary entrepreneur later brought together Buick, Oldsmobile, Cadillac, and Oakland Motors (renamed Pontiac) to create General Motors.

Saginaw and Bay City are classic lumber towns, where lumber barons built elaborate houses, libraries, and churches. They are good examples of how lumbering and foundries developed in tandem. Lumber towns with extensive sawmills needed nearby foundries that could make replacement parts immediately available. Saginaw's foundries expanded into huge facilities incorporated into General Motors.

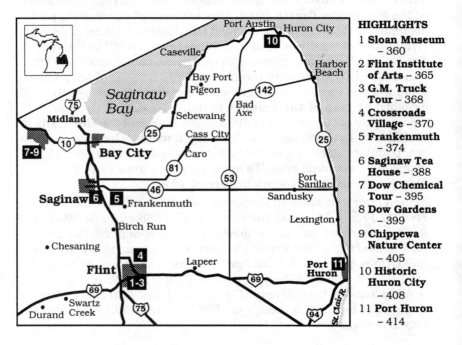

HIGHLIGHTS

1 **Sloan Museum** – 360

2 **Flint Institute of Arts** – 365

3 **G.M. Truck Tour** – 368

4 **Crossroads Village** – 370

5 **Frankenmuth** – 374

6 **Saginaw Tea House** – 388

7 **Dow Chemical Tour** – 395

8 **Dow Gardens** – 399

9 **Chippewa Nature Center** – 405

10 **Historic Huron City** – 408

11 **Port Huron** – 414

Bay City today is a poor but remarkably preserved city with an interesting industrial past. (See page 398.) Bay City made giant cranes and hoists, and kit homes from Aladdin and other makers. The many Poles who worked in those factories give the town an enviable, well-kept solidity.

Nearby Midland enjoyed little of the money reaped from logging. When Herbert Dow came to develop its bromine deposits into a chemical industry, the devastated landscape of tree stumps challenged him and his family to use landscaping and nature to make Midland a better place to live. The Dow legacy lives on in the unusual Dow Gardens and the architecture of Dow's inventive son Alden.

After the Thumb was logged off, professors at East Lansing's Michigan Agricultural College (now Michigan State University) drew on their climate and soils research to encourage the Polish, German, and Canadian farmers moving into the area to grow sugar beets and dry beans. Today the Thumb's flat skyline is dramatically punctuated by huge bean silos, by the spires of Catholic churches and the stubby towers of Lutheran ones, and, in fall, by colossal piles of sugar beets.

Information sources: CONVENTION & VISITOR BUREAUS

Bay Area CVB
Bay County
(517) 893-1222, (800) 424-5114

Flint Area CVB
Genesee County
(313) 232-8900, (800) 288-8040

Huron County Visitors Bureau
(517) 269-6431, (800) 35-THUMB

Frankenmuth CVB
(517) 652-6106, (800) FUN-TOWN

Midland County CVB
(517) 839-9901, (800) 678-1961

Blue Water Area Tourist Bureau
St. Clair County
(313) 987-86897
(800) 852-4242 (MI only)

Saginaw County CVB
(517) 752-7164, (800) 444-9979

Information sources: CHAMBERS OF COMMERCE

Algonac (810) 794-5511
Caro (517) 673-5211
Caseville (517) 856-3818
Cass City (517) 872-3434
Chesaning (517) 845-3055
Durand (517) 288-371
Fenton (810) 629-5447
Lexington (810) 359-2262

Marine City (810) 765-4501
Marysville (810) 364-6180
Pigeon (517) 453-2551
Port Huron (810) 985-7101
Sandusky (810) 648-4445
Sebewaing (517) 883-2150
Swartz Creek (810) 635-9643

Sloan Museum

Flint's local history, of unusual interest and importance to American labor and manufacturing, is told with uncommon candor, sympathy, and perspective.

THE VIBRANT new 10,000-square-foot permanent exhibit on **"Flint and the American Dream"** adds new dimensions of Baby Boom nostalgia and contemporary social relevance to an already outstanding museum of local history and culture. An extra bonus for car-lovers is a **choice collection of cars,** including the oldest production-model Chevrolet in existence, a sporty red 1910 Buick "Bug" raced by Louis Chevrolet, the famous Chevy "490" (the world's top-selling line in 1918), and a futuristic 1959 Cadillac Cyclone, a non-production concept car that still looks avant-garde.

As long as Flint's G.M. plants were booming, the local official popular culture consisted of a bland, self-congratulating (and usually dumbed-out) faith in the status quo, in GM, and in a basically sunny future. But by the late 1980s, that confidence had been fundamentally rocked – by severe unemployment, made worse by decades of easy living; by prospects of continued corporate downsizing; and by global competitors and GM's internal problems, long masked by lack of competition.

Flint has been accurately billed as the town that built General Motors, not the town that GM built. Its story, as told in the Sloan Museum, begins like that of many Michigan towns: first, with Native American hunting and agriculture, in tune with the seasons; followed by Europeans exploiting natural resources through commercial fur-trapping, then through lumbering, which spawned heavy industry needed to make equipment for sawmills and logging equipment. Each of these eras is illustrated by a fully furnished, **life-size interior** of unusual interest. The **tipi** can be entered, a great hit with children. A vast and realistic miniature model of a logging company, from camp to mill, is compelling for anyone interested in the subject.

In the 20th century, hometown carriage manufacturer Billy Durant created General Motors with his stock market winnings. Flint history becomes so dramatic and fascinating that it's nationally significant. First, more than any other event, the 1937 Flint Sitdown Strike was the birth of the modern labor movement. It led to the UAW becoming the only recognized negotiating representative of

Flint's dramatic, important labor history is well told at the Sloan Museum and at the Labor Museum and Learning Center. This photo shows the famous 1937 Sit-Down Strike, an event that led to unionization of all American autoworkers.

labor in the auto industry, ushering in a long era of high wages and good benefits for Michigan's many autoworkers. Flint had the highest concentration of autoworkers of any metropolitan area in the United States – and probably still does.

What makes this new exhibit so compelling is its honest, complex look at Flint's evolution into a company town and a consumption-oriented boom town without equal – and at the painful shock that came when jobs dwindled and the GM market share plummeted in the 1980s. This local museum stands out by not flinching at many less attractive aspects of local history. Americanization campaigns of the 1920s bordered on harassment of foreign immigrants. Easy credit sold more cars but made the Depression worse by repossessing workers' homes and cars. The postwar suburban dream of the 1950s was available to white people only. The local government and press were all too willing to support GM corporate goals without criticism. The AutoWorld indoor theme park and downtown festival marketplace, supposed to launch tourism to bolster the local economy, proved embarrassing failures.

Highlights of "Flint and the American Dream" include:

◆ pennants for Good Roads Day (1912): "No more mud!"

◆ factory life shown in huge photos and a movie

◆ compelling quotes from many kinds of observers on labor issues. "I ain't got no kick on wages," said a GM worker in 1935, "but I just don't like to be drove."

◆ a 1930s home movie tour of downtown Flint

◆ a newsreel of the 1937 Sit-Down Strike and two front pages (one from the UAW, one from the GM house organ) to take home

◆ consumer ads, signs, and products from Flint's 1950s boom, photos and memorabilia of drive-ins. Teen car culture was an especially lucrative market in Flint.

◆ a lobby display for **"Roger and Me,"** Michael Moore's documentary movie hit satirizing Flint and General Motors.

It's too bad the exhibit didn't draw on Moore's comments or those of other gifted culture critics from the Flint area. They include 1960s activist and White Panther Party founder John Sinclair; Ben Hamper, "the Rivethead," celebrated autoworker/ columnist; the late raconteur and novelist Ed Love, author of *Subways Are for Sleeping* and several funny, poignant reminiscences; comedienne Sandra Bernhard; and gadfly/philanthropist Stewart Mott.

Even for people who don't care much about cars, the **car collection** is worthwhile for its business and social history. The cars convey the principles of **"Sloanism,"** as developed by Durant's successor in the 1920s, the young M.I.T. grad who had developed a reputation for turning around troubled companies. The principles: clearly segment the market by price and prestige, and introduce the annual model change.

The Sloan Museum also includes an exhibit on human health and anatomy that lays out the basics of reproductive health. Short, clear displays show birth-control methods and explain how effective each is; tell in vivid detail about sexually transmitted diseases; and show the stages of gestation in three-dimensional models, from a tiny embryo to a nine-month fetus. It could be a boon for parents who find it hard to discuss sex with their kids. The sensible blue sheets on "There's No Place Like Home . . . For Sex Education" are available to take home.

Finally, in 1996, the Sloan unveiled its "Hands On Science Discovery Center," a large room filled with "science boxes," each devoted to illuminating a different subject such as magnets, electricity, light, and properties of physics. Less entertainment oriented than most hands-on museums, these subject centers can give kids a better grounding in fundamentals of science.

1221 East Kearsley in Flint's Cultural Center. From I-75, take I-475 north to Exit 8A (Longway Blvd.), turn right at the first light, turn right at the next street (Forest). To park in free lot down the hill from the museum, turn right onto Matthew and left into the lot. (810) 760-1169. Mon-Fri 10-5, Sat-Sun 12-5. ♿ $4 adults, $3 children 5-12.

THE STORY OF WORK AND WORKING PEOPLE IN MICHIGAN . . . . . is told in huge photo panels of exceptional interest, with well-chosen, accessible text, at the **Labor Museum and Learning Center of Michigan.** You may opt for a **guided tour** by a UAW retiree that's simpler but also interesting. Written material is objectively presented and no more pro-labor than a state historical museum might be. Thoughtful displays begin with the egalitarian crafts era of small shops, where owners and workers labored together. By the late 19th and early 20th centuries, the crafts era was replaced by impersonal mass production; productivity and profits increased and wages decreased as a result. Early labor leaders disagreed on how to organize – trade by trade (the American Federation of Labor's approach) or the Wobblies' "One Big Union."

Displays look at work and conditions in lumber mills (lumber barons greatly influenced Republican state politics), in Upper Peninsula mines, and in the huge manufacturing plants of the stove, railroad car, and automobile industries. Strong-arm tactics, blacklists, and Flint's well-meaning welfare capitalism were all used to keep out unions. Grievances behind the historic 1937 Flint Sit-Down Strike that paved the way for the United Auto Workers Union are explored: wages, unpaid down time, speed-ups, seniority (foremen often fired older workers and favored younger ones), and piece work.

This museum is still in progress. It now ends just after World War II, which brought more women and minorities into the workforce. It has a small labor book shop and gift shop. *711 N. Saginaw in the Walter Reuther Bldg. on the Mott Community College Campus 2 blocks north of downtown. From Saginaw and downtown, turn left onto Fifth, then immediately into parking lot. From I-475, take the Longway Blvd. exit. Go west 6 blocks on Longway, look for Reuther Bldg. between Saginaw and Martin Luther King Blvd. (810) 762-0251. Tues-Fri 10-5. ♿ $2/adults, $1/children and seniors.*

A SCENIC PICNIC SPOT IN DOWNTOWN FLINT . . . . . Riverbank Park along the Flint River is an unusually elaborate urban park, the outgrowth of needed flood-control measures. Four and one half blocks long, it has flower gardens, picnic sites, a **playground**, a large amphitheater, and a fish ladder for the big salmon migrating upriver in the fall. There is even a water-powered **Archimedes screw** which lifts water to create multiple waterfalls. In the fall it's exciting to see the **fish ladder** and watch for giant salmon swimming upriver from Lake Huron to spawn. The greatest migration is usually from late September through October. . . . . The 50th anniversary of the **UAW Flint Sitdown Strike** is commemorated in a nifty pictorial **monument**. It's across the river from the University of Michigan Flint, at the park's east end. The handsome display features big, rather primitive mural paintings on Pewabic tiles. One shows the great Flint Sitdown strike of 1936-37 at Fisher Body Plants 1 & 2. The other shows workers in an automobile plant. An amusing touch is the benches in front of the displays: tan concrete car seats.

HISTORIC MIDWEST PIPE SHOP . . . . . **Paul's Pipe Shop** (810-235-0581) at 647 S. Saginaw in downtown Flint stocks over a million pipes ranging from a $1.49 corncob to a $5,000 Dunhill. Pipes cram the shop. Upstairs is a pipe museum with over a thousand pipes, including the pipes of former customer and legendary philanthropist C.S. Mott and pipes from world champion pipe smokers. Owner Paul Spaniola's best selling tobacco is his "58th Anniversary" blend — $3.25 for 2 ounces. Cigars fill another climate-controlled room. Paul boils his own Cayuga pipes in a special South American nut oil and claims flatly that it is "the best pipe you ever smoked." Paul himself is a six-time winner of the world pipe-smoking title. (The person who can smoke his pipe the longest wins.) Neither pipe-smoking nor downtown Flint is what it used to be. Paul's has more the air of a party store than a gentleman's pipe shop. *Mon-Sat 9-7.*

A GOOD WEEKEND FAMILY DESTINATION . . . . . There's so much to see and do in **Flint's Cultural Center** alone, what with the museums, planetarium, events at the Whiting Auditorium, Flint makes a worthwhile destination any time of year. Call the **visitors' bureau** at (810) 232-8900 for upcoming events. Call **Whiting Auditorium** (810-760-1138) to receive info on the coming seasons of its Classical, Broadway, Showcase, and Family series. Flint offers an impressive array of reasonably priced offerings, and visitors won't have a hard time finding their way around. In summer, with **Crossroads Village** and related areas in gear, you could just about spend an enjoyable week in Flint, and camp at the county's attractive campground. The failed AutoWorld theme park was derided when it sought to build on that tourism infrastructure.

Flint Institute of Arts

Splendid 19th-century French paintings help make this a leading Midwestern art museum.

GENEROUS donations from wealthy Flint citizens have built this into the state's second most prominent art museum, behind only the Detroit Institute of Arts. It's an unusually appealing museum, worth a look even for people who don't think they like art. It's small. Admission is free. The changing exhibits are interesting and diverse. The permanent collection is strong in accessible but radically different areas.

The **contemporary paintings and sculptures**, nearly all representative in some way and often quite realistic, are bold and stimulating. Often they incorporate pop images or optical tricks. Look at them and you see things in a new way, without having to be inducted into an arcane art theory.

Broadly appealing in a much softer, more romantic vein, is the exceptional collection of **19th-century French paintings**, mostly landscapes. It includes works by Corot, Courbet, Renoir, Toulouse-Lautrec, Bonnard, Pissarro, and Vuillard.

The **Bray Renaissance Gallery** is a Renaissance-style hall, with an ornate coffered ceiling and marble floor. It houses an impressive collection of 15th- to 17th-century European works of art, including furniture, paintings, a monumental set of ten 17th-century French tapestries, and an angel by Rubens. A

American art at the Flint Institute of Arts is appealing, even for people who don't think they like art. John George Brown's *How D'Ye* (circa 1875-1880) is an uncommon depiction of an African-American boy.

Philip Pearlstein's
*Entrance to Lincoln
Tunnel, Daytime*
(1992) is an important
neorealist work. The
artist rented an
apartment to paint
this scene from life.

series of six Sunday-afternoon **classical music concerts** is held in
this stately marble hall.

Other highlights include African art, an American Gallery with
works dating back to Benjamin West and John Singer Sargeant,
and a European Gallery that includes a Goya and a collection of
19th-century paperweights. The museum's Asian Gallery with its
collection of Chinese and Japanese pottery and sculpture is also
noteworthy. Some exhibition highlights: "Painters of the Great
Lakes Scene" (March 31 through May 11, 1997), and "Art from the
Driver's Seat: Americans and Their Cars" (May 25 through July 13,
1997). Call for upcoming **events**, which include frequent workshops, a Wednesday noon film series, and evening lectures.

The **museum shop** includes decorator items, handmade
contemporary jewelry, scarves, art books, toys, and cards.

*1120 E. Kearsley, in Flint's Cultural Center. From I-475 from the
south, get off at the Court St. exit, turn right, go to 2nd light, turn left
onto Crapo. At the next light, turn right onto Kearsley. Park in lot
south of museum. (810) 234-1695. Tues-Sat 10-5, Sun 1-5. Gift shop
open all museum hours plus Mon 9-5. &. Free admission; donations
appreciated.*

OTHER ART STOPS IN FLINT . . . . . Right down a hall from the Flint Institute
of Arts in the sprawling DeWaters Art Center is the **Mott Community College
Fine Arts Gallery**. From October through December and February through April,

it mounts one-person shows by prominent Michigan and occasionally national artists. For info, call the Fine Arts Department at (810) 762-0443. ᕦ . . . . . It's not exactly art, but the **Flint Public Library**, just west of the art museum, hosts crafts and collectibles exhibits and a huge range of free talks, readings, workshops, and performances for all ages. The library holds many musical events like the annual summer Blues Festival and the winter Jazz concerts. Also held yearly is the **Julia A. Moore Worst Poetry Contest.** Call (810) 232-7111. The library on school nights is a lively place that sheds a more hopeful light on urban education than you get in the media. ᕦ . . . . . The **Buckham Gallery** in downtown Flint is one of Michigan's premiere alternative galleries and performance spaces. It is run by artists to show "contemporary, cutting-edge art . . . with no censorship or interference." Though some art is for sale, it has not been chosen for its marketability. Its big space encourages large environmental installations and dance performances. (Poetry is also featured.) Artists and poets may have international reputations or local ones. *The gallery is at 134 1/2 W. Second a block off Saginaw in downtown Flint. Phone (810) 239-6334 for upcoming shows and events. Hours: Wed & Thurs 11:30-5, Fri 1:30-7, Saturday by appointment.* ᕦ: *no.*

MICHIGAN'S LARGEST PLANETARIUM . . . . . is the **Longway Planetarium**, with a 60-foot domed screen for an especially realistic depiction of the skies. It's the same size as the big planetaria in Chicago and New York. Entertaining multimedia shows change every three to five months and explore the skies, ancient mythology and the constellations, science fiction, and space travel. An excellent **gift counter** has astronomy- and space-related T-shirts, stickers, books, posters, and hard-to-find educational items. Gift and **exhibit areas** are open 9-5 weekdays and on weekends when there is a show. Individuals are welcome to tag along with any school group coming to see shows during the week. *1310 E. Kearsley in the Cultural Center. From I-475 from the south, take Longway Blvd. exit, go 2 blocks east to Walnut and turn right. (810) 760-1181. **Regular astronomy shows** ($3.50/general admission. $2.50/kids 12 and under) are scheduled Saturday and Sunday afternoons at 1 and 2:30. Spectacular **laser light shows** with rock music can be seen on Fri. and Sat. evenings. The first show begins around 8 and the last at midnight.* ᕦ: *theater but not restrooms. $6 adults, $5 kids 12 and under. Call for current program info.*

GM Truck & Bus Flint Assembly Plant Tour

An old auto plant shows a new, participatory management philosophy at work.

FOR ANYONE interested in seeing a real, unscripted look at a typical auto assembly plant, this tour comes highly recommended. The guide, veteran autoworker Ed Campbell, encourages visitors to stop and ask questions at any point on the 1 1/2 mile, 1 1/2 hour walking tour. (The tour is also fully wheelchair accessible; call for details.) Workers enjoy talking about what they do. The tour is so unstructured that if you don't ask questions, you won't get much out of it.

This historic plant was built to make Chevrolets in 1947. The first Corvairs were made here; so were military vehicles used in World War II and in Desert Storm. After the tour, visitors are welcome to linger in the **display area** where interesting photos and text illuminate the plant's history. Books and plant souvenirs are for sale at the nearby **gift shop**. GM Truck & Bus has been through a lot of changes since the days when Ben Hamper, "the Rivethead," worked on its rivet line. From 1977 through 1987, the celebrated gonzo autoworker/author riveted frames of GM Suburbans and Blazers, which are now made in Janesville, Wisconsin. The rivet line is gone, replaced by the plant's only robots.

Products are always being shuffled among auto plants because it takes a year to install new manufacturing lines for redesigned products. Most new product lines are installed in available empty space, so that production of popular models can keep going without interruption on the old manufacturing line.

From mid-1993 to mid-1996, this plant made GMC and Chevrolet "G" vans, moved in from plants that were closed in Lordstown, Ohio, and Scarborough, Ontario. In 1996, the plant made a summertime conversion to make Chevy CK-type full-sized pickups, including crew cabs.

Fifty-six acres (3.3 million square feet) are under one roof here. The plant used to employ up to 8,500 workers making several products, compared to today's work force of 3,500. Seven rail lines ended here; now only one is in use. The current just-in-time manufacturing system means far fewer large deliveries by rail, but hourly deliveries at four or five truck docks.

An auto assembly plant like this assembles several thousand parts and subassemblies. On each 10-hour shift, 340 workers build 34 vehicles per hour. Each worker has 1 minute and 47 seconds to complete his or her operations, which range from bolting on separate parts (gas tanks, body parts, etc.) to applying seals and filling each brake cylinder with brake fluid. There's a surprising amount of variety within that 1 minute and 47 seconds. Several tasks may be performed. And not all vehicles are the same. They have been ordered to different specifications. Workers check the manifest for each vehicle and the directions on their computer screens.

The tour starts with the most dramatic assembly step, gate-keeping, where the side (gate) is married to the floor panel. (The old body-drop construction, where a completed auto body is dropped onto the chassis, has been abandoned.) Then the tour goes back to the ladder line, where the frame is riveted together, and across to the finishing line, where vehicles are road-tested on rollers.

Everyone here is consistently busy, unlike workers at Flint's heavily roboticized Buick City, who have time to read on the job. Maintenance workers with walkie-talkies circulate on bicycles. Occasional supply baskets of fresh parts roll down wide aisles to workstations. The whole scene is like a calm, steady, complex ballet choreographed by engineers for a cast of hundreds. That's the industrial aesthetic that mesmerized artist Diego Rivera when he was researching and creating his vast *Detroit Industry* mural at the Detroit Institute of Arts.

Tour visitors are impressed with how clean the plant is, and how mature and serious the workforce is. No wonder – the minimum seniority is 15 years. Most of the $38,000-a-year workers are well over 40. Many look like casually dressed college teachers.

The plant is on Van Slyke at Bristol Rd., on the southwest side of Flint near Bishop Airport. From I-75/U.S. 23, take the Bristol Rd. exit 116A, go east, in 1 mile turn north onto Van Slyke. Enter Gate 6, park in visitor parking. From I-69, turn south onto I-75, then take first exit at Bristol Rd., follow above directions. (810) 236-4978. &: call. Free one-hour tours are available at 9 a.m., but only by advance request.

Crossroads Village and Huckleberry Railroad

A charming 19th-century working village and the grit, noise, and smoke that went with it.

THIS museum village is an attractive destination for families and history-lovers, and a good value, too. It's the only place in Michigan where you can see a big variety of 19th-century industries in action every day. There's a pre-Civil War **gristmill**, a **sawmill**, and a **cider mill**, along with more commonly seen things like a **print shop** and **blacksmith shop**. Outside the **Toy Barn** kids have great fun walking on stilts, rolling hoops, and playing with other old-fashioned toys. Some longtime demonstrators are experts in their fields. Competent costumed workers make simple tools, cornmeal, beautiful and functional small brooms, and cider, which visitors can purchase. A vintage ferris wheel, carousel, and Venetian Swing effectively recreate the core of an old-fashioned amusement park on Mott Lake. The *Genesee Belle* paddle wheel riverboat leaves from there on 45-minute cruises of the man-made lake. Next door, farm animals can be seen up close at Mott Farm ($1/adults, 50¢ kids).

A special attraction is a 35-minute ride on the **Huckleberry Railroad,** a train drawn by a narrow-gauge steam engine similar to those built for logging camps and mines. The train ride's grit and jolts do much to de-romanticize 19th-century train travel. Watching the old steam-powered machines in action sheds a perspective on how hard people had to work under noisy, dangerous conditions to make basic products. The smell of coal smoke and sawdust can be irritating.

Bees swarm around the apple pulp at the cider mill. Belts whir

Historic Genesee County buildings threatened by demolition were moved to Crossroads Village and restored. The three-story brick buildings (right) were moved when Fenton replaced much of its downtown with a shopping center. The depot in Davison (left) dates from lumbering days. The 1854 Buzzell House (center) is one of several authentically furnished houses.

overhead in the grist mill. Most historic recreations are never confront all your senses the way these do.

Other things at Crossroads Village, however, can be annoying. Suburban-style landscaping near the train station is bright and cheery but completely inauthentic. The staged train robbery melodrama is corny, even for some children. The general store has country merchandise from the Far East and hardly anything about Genesee County. If things like this bother you, plan to concentrate on the buildings and activities on the periphery first, and save the downtown for later, or skip the train trip.

Spend a few minutes upon arrival to plan your visit by studying the demonstration and performance schedule. A large cafeteria between "downtown" and the mill serves reasonably priced food.

Crossroads Village highlights include:

◆ **Atlas Mill.** An 1836 grist mill sits on a splendidly lazy "mill pond" that's actually part of Mott Lake. The whole building shakes when the watergate is opened up to move the grindstones and make cornmeal. The complicated system of pulleys and line shaft is visible. So is the sifter. There's enough dust in the air to show why gristmills often exploded.

◆ **Vintage amusement park rides.** Music from an antique organ imitates a whole band and accompanies the chariots and 36 horses of this 1912 **carousel**. It was manufactured by Charles Parker, "America's Amusement King." Next to it are a 1910 Parker **ferris wheel** and a **Venetian swing**. Rides on all are 75¢. In Village Park, tucked away beyond the chapel and sawmill, they're easy to miss.

◆ **Genesee Belle.** A 45-minute ride on this new, 500-passenger paddlewheel riverboat leaves from Village Park, crosses to Bluebell Beach and Stepping Stone Falls, and offers a fine view of the gristmill. Nice in fall color time. *Leaves at noon, 1:30, 3, and on weekends at 4:30. $3.75/adult, $2/kids 1-12.*

◆ **Huckleberry Railroad.** Line up early for a seat in the caboose. The ride goes through not-very-interesting woods and fields and through the village of Genesee. Train ride included in admission fee. *Leaves from 11 a.m. weekdays, noon weekends & holidays.*

◆ **Sawmill** with demonstration.

◆ **Cider mill** with demonstration. A pulley system operated the press. Good candy apples, cider, and popcorn is for sale.

◆ **Restored, 19th-century buildings,** authentically furnished with antiques, include a lawyer's office and home, a church, a school, and a doctor's office that gives a startling look at medical practice of a hundred years ago. (These are quite well done, unlike other historic buildings which conceal souvenir and snack shops.) Costumed interpreters encourage questions.

◆ **Fenton Opera House.** When you climb up to this second-story auditorium, it feels like going back in time. The competent Pritchard Productions of Marshall, which also puts on Cornwell's Dinner Theater at Turkeyville, stage mostly musical revues that change with the seasons. A spring magic show is a hit with kids. *Free.*

◆ **Durant barn** with toymaking demonstrations.

◆ **Print shop** in the Manwaring Building downtown. The Crossroads Chronicle is a good read in the lively, folksy style of small-town journalism.

Weekends have more activities than weekdays. In addition, most weekends from June through September feature a **special show** of some sort at no extra charge. Call for a brochure on these **annual events.** Highlights include bluegrass bands and a mule race (Father's Day weekend), a Civil War Weekend, Antique Machine Show, Colonial Life Weekend, and Railfans' Weekend with tours of the Huckleberry Railroad's maintenance shops. February **ice harvesting** is something unusual.

*Bray Rd. north of Coldwater Rd. east of I-475. From I-475, take Saginaw St. (exit 13) and follow signs. (810) 763-7100. (800) 648-7275. **Summer season:** mid-May through Labor Day. Mon-Fri 10-5:30, weekends & holidays 11-6:30. **Sept:** open weekends. &*
Regular season rates: adults $7.50, children 4-12 $5.50, seniors over 60 $6.50.

MORE FAMILY SUMMER ATTRACTIONS NEARBY . . . . . make Crossroads Village an ideal low-cost summer destination. (All these destinations, including the village itself, are operated by Genesee County Parks and Rec.) There's nearby scenic camping on the Flint River at the **Timber Wolf Campground.** . . . . .
Penny Whistle Place is a spiffy, creative play environment with 10 activities aimed at toddlers to pre-teens — easy, fun ones like the Ball Crawl, Cloud

Bounce, and Music Machine (a sort of giant calliope with keys you step on), or challenging, scary ones like climbing high on a net, or swinging from platform to platform on a gliding cable. A real hit with kids. **Bluebell Beach**, using the same parking area, provides a convenient place to swim, but without much shade. *Penny Whistle Place and Bluebell Beach are on Bray Road just south of Crossroads Village. Open Memorial Day to Labor Day, daily 10-7, $3/person.* . . .
. . **Stepping Stone Falls** has wooded picnic spots. It's especially nice near dusk, when the man-made falls at the outlet of Mott Lake are illuminated with **changing colored lights.** The water flows over rectilinear platforms with stepping stones across the shallow parts. *From Crossroads Village and Penny Whistle Place, take Bray south to Carpenter, then east, north on Branch. From I-475, take Carpenter exit 11, go east 1 1/2 miles to Branch, north briefly on Branch to falls. Open daily from Memorial Day to Labor Day, noon-11. Free.* . . . .
For info on all these destinations, *call 1-800-648-PARK.*

HALLOWEEN AND CHRISTMAS AT CROSSROADS VILLAGE . . . . . Two popular holiday family programs draws some 60,000 visitors; tickets should be purchased ahead for the festive train ride option. **Crossroads Ghosts & Goodies** runs for 10 days before Halloween and two earlier 3-day October weekends. **Christmas at Crossroads** combines decorated historic homes, holiday lights, Santa, music and entertainment, crafts. Runs every weekend after Thanksgiving, almost daily from mid-Dec. *Call 800-648-PARK for events info. Admission to village only $3.50-$4/adults, $3.25 for kids. Village & RR: $6.50-7/adults, $4.75-6.50/kids.*

Frankenmuth

A guide to the real Frankenmuth —
and the best things to do there

THIS FORMER German farm town of 4,400 has become Michigan's top tourist draw, thanks to a lot of hard work and heavy promotion. An estimated three million visitors a year flock to its Bavarian-themed street of gift shops, now two miles long. There's Bronner's, the world's largest Christmas shop, advertised on billboards from Canada to Florida. It's the size of four football fields; the year-round Christmas light display costs over $500 a day in electricity bills. (Statistics are thrown around with gusto in Frankenmuth.) Two mammoth restaurants anchor the bustling pedestrian strip. Zehnder's and the Bavarian Inn rank among the 10 biggest-volume restaurants in the U.S., serving up to 10,000 guests on a weekend. With its new Heritage Dining Room and Garden Room addition, Zehnder's now seats 1,500, making it the largest family-owned restaurant in the U.S.

The entire commercial area is dolled up in a relentless Alpine manner: chalet-type buildings with cutout wood balconies and wavy trim on the eaves. Gift shops abound. Geraniums are everywhere in warm weather. The streets and sidewalks are Disneyland-clean.

It's easy to dismiss Frankenmuth as an overcommercialized tourist trap.But it would be a shame to miss some delightful experiences here: an outstanding small American brewery; an excellent local museum; shops to delight woodcarvers, quilters, and dollhouse fans; and some good German food, especially sausages. The slice-of-life, Italian-style nativity scene at Zeesenagel Alpine Village is straight from the heart and worth a trip in itself. The best shops here are small and personal.

The secret to enjoying Frankenmuth lies in being selective. The town works on two levels at once. The applied surface is completely phony, a marketing ploy pure and simple. That Alpine motif is completely inauthentic, and even the Bavarian connection is pretty thin. Actually, the Germans who settled Frankenmuth in 1845 were devout Lutherans, serious and extremely hard-working, just like their descendants today.They were from the German region of Franconia (*Franken* in German), which wasn't part of Bavaria at all until Napoleon reorganized his German conquests in 1803. Then Franconia became the northern part of the kingdom (and now state)

The scene outside Bronner's, Frankenmuth's most famous attraction. Started by signpainter Wally Bronner in his garage, it has grown to become the world's largest Christmas store, as big as four football fields.

of Bavaria. Those fun-loving, exuberant, sometimes outrageous Bavarians are Catholics who have quite a different regional culture from Franconians. Franconia certainly doesn't have chalets designed to stand up under the heavy snows of the Bavarian Alps over a hundred miles to the south.

But on a deeper level, Frankenmuth is quite genuine, and friendly, too. It's very German. You can meet locals under 60 who speak English with a slight German accent even though their ancestors have been in Michigan well over a hundred years. They often didn't learn English until school.

Frankenmuth is very much a community, though so many G.M. managers and other new families are coming to town that locals are feeling like a somewhat beleaguered minority. "Plastic people" is what one successful 40-ish hometown boy calls these suburbanized outsiders. Among the native-born, everybody knows everybody else, and quite a bit about their family history, too. Cleanliness and local pride are pervasive. Even the bank president picks up stray trash on his way to work; it's bad form in Frankenmuth to ignore litter. After the June, 1996 tornado that did $6.6 million worth of property damage, hundreds of volunteers showed up, unrequested, and were dispatched by city hall to help homeowners clean up debris. The unassuming Zehnder brothers Ed and Tiny, who own Zehnder's and the Bavarian Inn and much of their respective sides of main street, live right in town in the main visitor area. They are hands-on managers and models of fraternal cooperation. Growing up in the restaurant business, everybody learned to pitch in.

Little in the commercial district still resembles Frankenmuth before it became a tourist mecca. It was a plain, sober Lutheran farm town, like many others in the Saginaw Valley and the Thumb today. It was founded in 1845 by a band of young Lutherans from the villages of Rosstal and Neudettelsau near Nuremberg. They followed their pastor's call to become missionaries in America. Their plan was to minister to the many Germans already in the Saginaw Valley and to the area's Chippewa Indians. Not surprisingly, the settlers failed in their efforts to Germanize local Indians.

Once the forest was logged off, Frankenmuth's German settlers, like their countrymen throughout the Saginaw Valley, settled into farming, which they continue to pursue with characteristic industry and devotion. New subdivisions of expensive homes have been built on low, wet land and woodlots, and very seldom on farmland. Frankenmuth remains closely linked with the surrounding farm producers. Star of the West milling company is one of Michigan's largest flour mills. The brewery, the Zeilinger Wool Company, and the cheese- and sausagemakers all use products from local farms.

Frankenmuth's fame began with chicken dinners at several hotels that took advantage of their convenient location between Detroit, Flint, and Saginaw. Their all-you-can-eat dinners attracted lots of traveling salesmen at first. Then, in the 1920s and 1930s, when auto touring was a novelty, families started coming out for a drive and dinner on weekends. During the 1950s, the Christmas decorating shop begun as a sideline of Wally Bronner's sign shop quickly grew into a famous institution advertised on billboards as far away as Pennsylvania and Florida.

The interstate highway program of the 1950s was what caused Alpine Bavarian architecture to be taken up with such enthusiasm in Frankenmuth. The new I-75 missed Frankenmuth by seven miles. Worried that their big chicken-dinner restaurants might be bypassed, the Zehnder family decided upon a dramatic theme to help business. They remodeled their Fischer Hotel in the picturesque Bavarian style. As the new Bavarian Inn, it offered German specialties like sauerbraten and schnitzel, served by waitresses dressed in dirndls. (Zehnder's, the family's first restaurant styled after Mount Vernon, retains its Early American decor and emphasis on fried chicken.)

By the 1970s Frankenmuth's downtown had been transformed and expanded by dozens of gift shops that built on the reputation long established by Frankenmuth breweries and sausagemakers. Today, with Michigan's largest discount shopping mall at Birch Run, seven miles away on I-75, the Frankenmuth phenomenon has gained momentum, benefitting motels in Flint and Saginaw. Canadian shoppers come and stay for a week. With a new 18-hole golf course, The Fortress, the big, resort-style Bavarian Inn Lodge, and an ever-increasing number of visitor attractions, the area has grown way beyond a day-trip destination.

TIPS FOR ENJOYING FRANKENMUTH

Certainly Frankenmuth today is in the great American tradition of too much of everything. The best way to enjoy it is to stick to a short list of sights and not allow yourself to drift into too many, too-similar shops.

Park in the big lots behind the Bavarian Inn or Zehnder's. (Overflow parking is across the wooden bridge, reached by driving between the river and tall brick tower of the closed Heileman brewery.) At the Bavarian-style **Visitor's Information Center** north of the Bavarian Inn, pick up a helpful map and well-organized advertising guide. *635 S. Main. (517) 652-6106. June, July, and August, open from 8-6 Mon-Wed, 8-8 Thurs & Fri, 10-8 Sat, and 12-6 Sun. Closes at 6 rest of year.* &: *pick up complete list of all accessible sites in Frankenmuth.*

Take a **snack and rest break** in the park at Main and Tuscola, at the Main Street Tavern, or at the Tiffany Biergarten with its original turn-of-the-century decor. (See locations below.) Or take the relaxing Riverboat Cruise. Finish with a trip to Bronner's to see the lights.

To get to know the town, stay in a local bed and breakfast. Here B&Bs are typically the homestay kind, where guests usually have a spare bedroom in a plain, comfortable brick ranch house.

MUST-SEE SIGHTS

◆ **Zeesenagel Alpine Village.** It's worth coming to Frankenmuth just to see this wonderful miniature re-creation of everyday Italian life, and to hear the simple Christmas legend told with it. Interior designers David Zeese and Don Nagel were so inspired by the 18th-century *presepio* or nativity scene they saw in a Roman church over 25 years ago that they decided to create figures for a permanent diorama of their own. It was first displayed at Comerica bank in downtown Detroit. Later they decided to move to Frankenmuth and install the tableau in a dramatic permanent setting. It is a miniature town nestled into the mossy slopes of a steep hillside. They enlarge it every year.

Traditional Italian *presepio* were commissioned by wealthy nobles. They often included representations of entire villages or estates. Realistic individual portraits honored the nobles' loyal retainers or especially productive farmers.

Zeesenagel's 1/6 scale scenes have come to fill over ten scenes with 550 realistic figures. Their Alpine village expands each year. It includes all segments of society, including dignitaries with their noses in the air and beggars (a reminder to others to share). The fool, ignored by all, in the end delivers the message about the true spirit of Christmas. On the guided **tour**, each staff person tells the story in his or her own way. Special lighting effects and music add to the drama and magic. You could enjoy seeing and hearing this several times.

Colorful scenes of Italian street life and festival days are everywhere — a customer sniffing a fishmonger's wares, a fruit vendor arguing with a customer, a puppet theater, a lacemaker. Recent additions include a troupe of commedia dell'arte clowns who have arrived — on stilts — to celebrate the Epiphany. Zeese and Nagel

This vignette in a glassblower's workshop is one of hundreds of richly evocative details from the entrancing northern Italian nativity scene at Zeesenagel Alpine Village.

create the highly individualized figures with much feeling. Facial expressions and gestures are so vivid, you can almost hear the figures talk.

A delight in itself is the eclectic Zeesenagel **gift shop** of international crafts and Christmas figures. The staff here knows so much about the merchandise, you could get a short course on cloisonné — or see a furry Folkmanis raccoon come to life. A house specialty are Italian-style angels ($11, $20, and $30) whose stiffened fabric wings and bodies are sculpted and painted here. The effect is dramatic when the angel is suspended to float free, lighted from below. *780 Mill, at the bottom of the hill between Zehnder's and the river. (517) 652-2591. May 1-Jan. 6: open daily 10-6. Otherwise: weekdays 12-5, weekends 10-6. Tours ($2 adults, $1 12 and under) on the half-hour between 10:30 and 5:30 (last tour). <u>Winter tours</u> only on weekends.* &

♦ **Bronner's CHRISTmas Wonderland.** For years it's been the world's largest Christmas store. In 1991 it became twice as big — 200,000 square feet in all. Bronner's is a phenomenon. The year-round illuminated **outdoor display** is extensive. Indoors there are more than 260 decorated Christmas trees and 800 animated figures. In many categories — Advent calendars, nutcrackers, 6,000 kinds of glass ornaments, 500 styles of Nativity scenes from 75 countries — Bronner's selection is stupendous. Much is from Germany, Italy, and the former Czechoslovakia. But Bronner's goes to great lengths to emphasize the international aspect of Christmas. Bibles come in 33 languages, and ornaments and banners in 70. Children's books and Christmas stories in world languages are on hand. Chanukah and Kwanzaa are also included. Inclusiveness, in fact, is a Bronner's hallmark and a key secret of its success. Nativity scenes of all sizes come in versions with brown skin, and so do some Santas.

Bronner's is not a discount store. But it imports in such quantity that some prices — for instance, on glass ornaments ordered direct from German factories — are very attractive.

Not everything relates to Christmas. Decorations for other seasons and holidays are on hand, along with gifts and souvenirs from around the world. Collectibles like Hummel and Precious Moments attract post-Christmas shoppers.

The place is so big *it's easy to become disoriented.* Take note of which entrance you used (there are two, south and west) so you can find your car. Refer to the store directory to find what you're especially interested in. And break up your visit by going to the **refreshment area** (it's near the west exit by the nativities, books, and nutcrackers) or by seeing **"The World of Bronner's,"** an 18-minute, multi-projector slide show tells the Bronner's story with folksy family photos. It's shown every hour or so, from 10 or 11 until 4 or 7 (more frequent showings over a longer time period from June through December). The store's own 500-figure **Hummel collection,** complete **Precious Moments collection**, and other interesting displays are in the auditorium room.

A 1993 addition at the south end of the parking lot is the **Silent Night Memorial Chapel**. It's an exact replica of the chapel that replaced the church in Oberndorf, Austria, where the world's favorite Christmas hymn was written. Plaques with "Silent Night" in a hundred languages line a walkway to the chapel, which is open daily for visiting and meditating. *Bronner's is on S. Main at Weiss on the south end of Frankenmuth. Events line: 1-800-ALL-YEAR. Open 361 days. June thru Dec: Mon-Sat 9-9, Sun 12-7. Jan thru May: Mon-Sat 9-5:30, Fri until 9, Sun 12-5:30. Christmas Tree Lane lit up from dusk to midnight every night.* ♿

CRAFTS AND MANUFACTURING DEMOS & TOURS

Fudgemaking, cheesemaking, woodcarving, wool-carding, milling, beermaking, taffypulling — a visit to Frankenmuth has become a great place to see a variety of free crafts demonstrations. Now the city has started a Agriculture Tourism Park on Weiss Street behind Bronner's. Only agricultural production facilities can locate there, and only if they offer public tours of the entire manufacturing process.

The following demonstrations and tours stand out:

◆ **Frankenmuth Brewery.** This small brewery, which bills itself as Michigan's first microbrewery, traces its roots to 1862. Today it's the largest operating brewery in Michigan. (Stroh's tore down its original brewery in a cost-cutting move. Heileman's shut its big Frankenmuth brewery down the hill and across the river.) The Frankenmuth Brewery is the same size as local German breweries, with a capacity of 50,000 barrels a year. Its German brewmaster makes distinctive, flavorful German-style beers using state-of-the-art German equipment. Frankenmuth Pilsener, Frankenmuth Dark, and Frankenmuth Bock (a dark, rich, beer traditionally brewed only in springtime) have won awards; Old Detroit Amber Ale won the Chicago Beer Society's best of show two years in a row. They sell for under $9 a six-pack at stores like Meijer. Frankenmuth's motto: "Brewed in Michigan, where quality doesn't have to be imported." Freshness improves the taste of beer, so it's a real advantage to buy quality beers locally. Half-hour **tours**, given on the hour, include a video on brewing and a short tour of the tanks and bottling line, followed by two beers of your choice in the hospitality room.

In June 1996, a tornado badly damaged the brewery. The repairs were so extensive that tours resume only in spring 1997. Call to verify. Left intact by the tornado, the next-door **gift shop** remains open. It sells many logo items, glassware, and beer-related gifts. *425 S. Main, just south of Tuscola. (517) 652-6183. Jan-Mar:*

One of many worthwhile demonstrations in Frankenmuth is at master woodcarver Georg Keilhofer's shop on Main Street.

Thurs-Mon noon-5. Mid-May thru Dec: Mon-Fri 11-5, Sat 11-6, Sun 12-5. &: *gift shop but not tour. $2.50 21 & up, $1.25 12-20, under 12 free. For tour info, call (810) 652-2088.*

◆ **St. Julian Winery.** This facility has two parts. One is the free tasting room for the many noteworthy wines and sparkling fruit juices from the mid-range St. Julian Winery, Michigan's largest. (See wine chapter on page 38.) It is also an actual small winery where solera cream sherry is aged from wine made in the main winery in Paw Paw. Visitors can see a 10-minute **video** on solera and the history of St. Julian. *127 S. Main, 1 block north of School Haus Square. (517) 652-3281. Tasting room open Mon-Sat 10-6, Sunday 12-6, closes at 5 daily Jan thru April. Tours of the winery are available to large groups.* &

◆ **Frankenmuth Woodcarving Studio.** This workshop/store is one of Frankenmuth's special places. It's small, personal, and authentically German. Here, you can watch noted German sculptor Georg Keilhofer execute commissions for churches and individuals. **Woodcarving instruction** is offered in once-a-week nine-week courses and intensive one- and two-week summer seminars. Most of Keilhofer's work is for commissions. He doesn't have many popularly priced examples sitting around for sale. But his shop, managed by his wife, sells many wood carvings from Europe, both religious and secular. It also carries a large selection of top-quality woodcarving tools and supplies.

In the little park next door, a delightful **gazebo** commemorates the Brothers Grimm with fairy tale scenes carved on oak panels. *976 S. Main, south of the river but north of Jefferson. (517) 652-2975. Mon-Sat 9-5.* &

◆ **Zeilinger Wool Company.** For over 80 years Zeilinger's has processed raw wool, straight off the sheep, and used it as batting in custom comforters. A **self-guided tour** shows visitors all steps of the process, from washing and air-drying wool to carding it and making hand-stitched quilts and comforters. On weekends, however, manufacturing employees are off. Quilting supplies and fabrics are here, too. *1130 Weiss (north of Bronner's). (517) 652-2920. Mon-Sat 9-5:30, Sun 12-5.* &*: store but not tour. Free.*

◆ **Frankenmuth Pretzel Company.** Watch pretzels being twisted from the gift and snack shop. Both hard and soft styles are baked here. Groups can sign up for pretzel-twisting lessons.

◆ **Bavarian Inn Doll & Toy Factory.** Nobody does toys better than Germans; they've been exporting toys in a big way for centuries. Here are all the top-of-the-line classics: teddy bears, puppets, wooden trains, mechanical toys, and dolls. *713 S. Main. (517) 652-9941.* &.

◆ **Frankenmuth's Historic Woolen Mill.** Today this old mill is more of an upscale sweater store, though you can see wool-filled comforters being made in a large workroom, and see how wool is processed — right on Frankenmuth's main pedestrian drag. *570 S. Main between Cass and Tuscola. (517) 652-8121. Open daily. June thru Labor Day: 9-9. Otherwise: 9-5.* &.

FRANKENMUTH HISTORY

◆ **Frankenmuth Historical Museum** is a strikingly intelligent exception in the world of small local museums. It focuses on the most important aspects of Frankenmuth's history: the motivations for immigration and the immigrants' Christian values. And it uses objects to help tell these and other significant stories. Revamped exhibits use dramatic life-size tableaus and dramatized readings from authentic immigrant letters. They bring the immigration experience to life. Who came? Why? How often were their hopes fulfilled?

Elsewhere, a well-done video surveys the town's history. Other exhibits deal with logging, Prohibition (highly unpopular here!), chicken dinners, and local brewing. An entire case is devoted to

Frankie the dachshund, trademark of the original Frankenmuth Brewery. The good-size **museum shop** is strong on old-fashioned, simple toys and on publications relevant to Frankenmuth. Herman Zehnder's *Teach My People the Truth* ($10) is well worth reading. One gallery is for **special exhibits** that change yearly. The museum is refreshingly peaceful and plain in contrast to the street fair atmosphere outside. *613 S. Main. (517) 652-9701. Labor Day thru Mem. Day: Mon-Sat 10:30-7, Sun 12:30-7. Rest of the year: Mon-Sat 10:30-5, Sun 12-5. & Adults $1, kids 50¢.*

◆ **St. Lorenz Church and Log Cabin Church.** This much-enlarged 1880 brick Gothic-style church houses the largest congregation east of the Mississippi — 4,300 strong — in the conservative Missouri Synod of the Lutheran Church. You can stop in any weekday for a **self-guided tour** of the sanctuary, where splendid contemporary stained-glass windows show scenes of Lutheran history, from St. Paul to Luther to Frankenmuth's missionary ministers on horse-back. If you call in advance, volunteer Sharon Bickell will give you a most interesting look back at the settlement's early days. You'll visit a **reconstruction of the original log church** and parsonage, com-plete with packing-case pulpit. Nearby is the cemetery where the first settlers were buried and the first brick church, used until 1865 and now a museum. St. Lorenz still holds a **German-language ser-vice** with hymns each Sunday at 9:15 and on Wednesdays in Lent and Advent at 9:30. *On Tuscola at Mayer, about a mile west of down-town. Park in rear and go in back door. Call (517) 652-6141 for tour. &: current church only.*

PLACES TO TAKE A REST

◆ **Willkommen Park.** A pleasant, shady spot on downtown Frank-enmuth's main intersection at Main and Tuscola. Benches, drinking fountain, but no restrooms. (Use restrooms at Visitor's Center or at nearby restaurants.) Carryout food from Willi's, Main Street Tavern, or Satow's.

◆ The historic **Tiffany Biergarten** saloon at 656 S. Main, the unpretentious **Main Street Tavern** at 310 S. Main up the hill, or the **Riverview Cafe,** 445 S. Main are nice places to sit and rest and have refreshments. The cafe has shady decks going down to the Cass River.

◆ **Frankenmuth Riverboat Tour.** Festive Dixieland music and informative commentary by tour guides make this 45-minute cruise up the pretty Cass River especially enjoyable. The boat is a diesel-powered, two-deck paddlewheeler. A fine way to rest your feet while learning more about Frankenmuth. *Leaves from the Riverview Cafe, 445 S. Main. (517) 652-8844. Runs May thru Oct. Leaves at 12:30, 2:30, 4:30, 7 (6 in May, Sept & Oct). ⅋ $6/adult, $3 12 & under. Tip: buy tickets early. $12 cocktail cruise, 8 p.m. Saturday nights in July & August, includes minstrel, hors d'oeuvres.*

◆ **Fischer Platz.** This pretty, popular Bavarian-style "town square" with many benches was created as part of the Bavarian theme campaign circa 1960. Seven times a day (at 11, noon, 3, 5, 6, 9, and 10) the Glockenspiel does its thing: first it plays, then the Pied Piper tale is told (in German and English), then more music, then the moving figures rotate and play out the legend. Though the whole thing was imported from Germany, this doesn't compare to the wonderful antique German moving clocks it was modeled on. Here too are **restrooms** and visitor information kiosks. *Behind the Bavarian Inn, next to the Visitors' Center. ⅋*

◆ **Picnic facilities in public parks.** Picnic tables and barbeque grills are in tip-top shape at both convenient city parks. **Heritage Park** at the north end of Weiss has long, scenic frontage along the Cass River, and more playground equipment. Restrooms. **Memorial Park** on East Tuscola, 1/4 mile east of downtown, is a hilly area with a creek running through it. (Tobogganing here is the best around.) Amenities include a **swimming pool** open to all, **rose gardens**, and an **exercise trail**. Restrooms. Get good bratwurst and franks, rolls, potato salad at Willi's Sausage Haus (page 385).

OLD FRANKENMUTH

Beneath tourism's thick icing, there's still a very German small town in downtown Frankenmuth. Here's where to find it.

◆ **Satow's Drug Store.** The lunch counter is a popular local hangout where you can get an earful of German, and of the distinctive Frankenmuth dialect of English, in which "just" may be "chust" and nearly every sentence sounds like a question. The soups are homemade, and the prices can't be beat; lunch specials are $3 or so. *308 S. Main, just north of Tuscola. Mon-Fri 7-10, Sat 7-8, Sun 8-4. ⅋*

◆ **Main Street Tavern.** An utterly plain German-American gasthaus where the food's as important as the beer. Owner Keith Boesnecker, who was Zehnder's baker for years, spotlights local products whenever possible. He makes all the bread and buns on the premises. That all makes for quality bar food. The $2.50 quarter-pound cheeseburger is made from local beef and cheese. Willi's next door supplies the excellent bratwurst ($2.75) and the beef stix and Italian sausage used on the Willi Pizza. (Square pizzas are a house specialty.) Frankenmuth pilsner ($1.50) and dark ($1.25) are on draft, while Carling's (still a local favorite even if no longer locally made) is 75¢, or 50¢ on darts night (Wednesday). *310 S. Main, just north of Tuscola. (517) 652-2222. Mon-Sat 9 a.m.-2 a.m., Sun noon-2 a.m.* &

◆ **Willi's Sausage Haus.** As soon as you walk in the door, the smell and the plain, super-clean appearance tell you how German Willi's is. The main decoration consists of photos of Willi playing his accordion. A master sausagemaker, he turns out sausages, hams, and bacon — over 100 items in all — here in his shop and smokehouse, and in his wholesale plant in Vassar. Locals shop here for their traditional favorites from bratwurst and weisswurst to head cheese and a famous beef jerky made from carefully trimmed top round. Non-traditional innovations include many turkey products, made without fatty skin, such as turkey pepper loaf and smoked turkey bratwurst. Prices compare favorably with suburban delis.

A sausage of your choice can be grilled to eat at the Schnell-imbiss stand-up counter or in the park across the street. A line of imported German specialties is on hand: chocolates, mustards, cookies (good holiday gifts), and Rudolph's excellent rye bread from Toronto. Small-group tours may be arranged. *316 S. Main, just north of Tuscola. (517) 652-9041. Mon-Sat 8-6, Sun 11-5.* &

◆ **Star of the West Milling Company.** Michigan's wheat fields once made it a breadbasket of America, but Michigan wheat has been relegated to niche markets since Minneapolis became America's milling center at the turn of the century. That niche is strong, because Michigan soft winter wheat has the lowest protein of any east of the Rockies. Low protein means low viscosity, and a flour that's good for cookies and pie crust. The Star of the West is one of only six commercial mills left in Michigan, all enormous. Its big silos are right downtown. Customers include commercial bakers and Battle Creek's cereal makers, who buy bran. At its interesting store across the street are 25-pound sacks of Nightingale brand pastry-type flour — white, graham, wheat germ, and bran. This is also a garden shop with bird feeders, seed, and the like and a farm-supply store where you can get (among other things) numbers to put on cows' ears. *121 E. Tuscola. (517) 652-9971. Mon-Fri 7-5. Also open Sat. 7-noon in April, May, and June,* &

GIFT AND SPECIALTY SHOPS

Competition has made for a very broad market. Many shops focus on high-ticket collectible lines, character dolls, wood carvings, German beer steins and cuckoo clocks. There's some good stuff here, if you focus on finding what really interests you. Here are some highlights:

◆ **Rau's Country Store.** A rambling, appealing mix of many gift categories and price levels. Hard candies, a vast array of vintage advertising reproductions on tin boxes, posters, and metal signs (one room for Coca Cola alone), plus reproduction Victorian lamps and glassware. There's lots more farther back and downstairs, including cassettes of polkas and German folk songs, a nice selection of Chinese baskets, die-cast toys, oak shelves, miniature cottages, and, in the basement, loads of inexpensive scrapbook cutouts. **Doll house miniatures**, displayed in well over a hundred room settings, are fabulous here and across the street at Pinocchio's. *656 S. Main. (517) 652-8388. Summer hours: Mon-Sat 9:30-10, Sun 11-9. Shorter hours rest of the year.* ⎣: *ground floor only.*

◆ **Kite Kraft.** In its big new location, this interesting store has two parts. The kite shop is in back, with hundreds of kites, windsocks, and wind toys, staffed by kite-flying enthusiasts. Up front is an activity-oriented toy store. Here are Brio trains, funny wind-ups, fantasy construction toys, and cheap, entertaining novelties like the $1.25 balloonocopter (helicopter blades powered by balloons). **Toy demonstrations** happen all the time. The owner, a longtime elementary teacher, follows up customers' suggestions. *576 S. Main, just at the bottom of the hill. (517) 652-2961. Mem. Day-Christmas: Mon-Sat 10-9, Sun 10-6. Otherwise: 10-6 daily.* ⎣

COLLECTORS' MUSEUMS

Frankenmuth's huge flow of customer traffic makes possible some wonderful displays of serious collectors' stuff. Highlights include:

◆ **Memory Lane Arcade.** Kiss-O-Meter, The Egyptian Mummy Answers Your Question — here are favorite coin-operated games and music from amusement parks and saloons going back 90 years. They're playable, though you don't always get enough time for your quarter. Still, it's magical to go back in time and play all these evocative devices: Play Golf, the Mystic Swami, a 1933 Personality Indicator, player pianos, pinball games. The place swarms with kids playing video games and using the photo booth (4 photos for $2). *626 S. Main. (517) 652-8881. Open daily 12-9 in summer, until dark in fall, after Xmas weekends only, weather permitting.* ⎣ *Free admission.*

◆ **Michigan's Own Military Museum.** Highly regarded exhibits show off uniforms and memorabilia of state veterans distinguished in war (370 thus far, from six wars, with accompanying biographies), plus uniforms of all 11 Michigan astronauts. Also here: the world's largest collection of "Polar Bear" artifacts. The "Polar Bears," the "forgotten" 339th regiment of the 85th division of the U.S. Army, were the only American soldiers to ever fight in Russia. Fighting in Archangel from 1918 to 1919, 94 soldiers died. Curator Stan Bozich, author of *Detroit's Own "Polar Bears,"* began collecting in 1945. Exhibits in the World Wars Room are changed quarterly. *1250 Weiss (the road that parallels Main Street on the other side of Bronner's). (517) 652-8005. 10-5 Mon-Sat 11-5 Sun.* ♿ *$2.50 adults, $2 seniors, $1 Children 6-18. Under 6 free.*

DISCOUNT SHOPPING AT BIRCH RUN . . . . . Before 1986 it was an obscure village at the I-75 Frankenmuth exit. Now Birch Run is Michigan's premiere discount shopping capital, the Michigan flagship of the very successful Muskegon-based Horizon Group, which now has 35 discount malls nation-wide. With about 200 stores, Horizon's **Outlets at Birch Run** (517-624-4868; 800-866-5900) is bigger than its sister malls at Holland, Monroe, Traverse City, and Lansing. Horizon's Birch Run mall has merged with the neighboring designer outlet mall. Its **impressive array of stores** includes new stores Sony, Tommy Hilfiger, Nautica, Ann Taylor, and Ultra Golden Jewelry (all 14k), clothing outlets Liz Claiborne, Anne Klein, Evan-Picone, Capezio, J. Crew, Adolfo II, Bugle Boy, Van Heusen, Polo, Eddie Bauer, Esprit, Oshkosh, Guess?, Woolrich, and, in hard goods, Corning, American Tourister, Lenox, Villeroy & Boch, Mikasa, and some kitchen stores. For food, there's a new Pizzeria Uno, quality popularizers of the Chicago deep-dish pizza. . . . . Now more amenities are planned (golf, indoor hockey & ice skating, movies) to make this a family outing destinations, building on shopping's longstanding role in American culture as a "bonding thing," in the words of Horizon's PR person. Moms and daughters, husbands and wives, sisters, friends. More and more large motels are locating at Birch Run.

Birch Run has a food court, a food vendor outside in good weather and umbrellaed tables on a terrace. Its revamped indoor "relaxation room," geared for guys, offers a comfy, living room setting with sofas, oriental rugs, tables to work at, TVs for sports events, and a vending area.

Malls like Horizons' deal mostly in manufacturers' overruns not bought by non-discount retailers. Fashions typically show up six to eight weeks later than in department stores, though some are last year's models. Prices range from 20% to 70% off, which often can be beat by special sales at department stores, but the selection of discounted goods in one place is so far unparalleled in Michigan. *At I-75 exit 136; go west on Birch Run Rd. Village Shops are just west of Horizon Outlets. Both malls have similar hours. Mon-Sat 10-9, Sun 11-6.*

Awa Saginaw An

*An authentic tea house is a serene introduction
to the essence of Japanese art and culture.*

ONE of Michigan's unheralded gems is the meticulously
detailed Japanese tea house and garden in Saginaw. It has
been designed and built strictly according to the principles
of the Urasenke School of Tea developed in 16th-century Japan.
Here, as in very few other places in the U.S., visitors can see a formal Japanese tea ceremony performed in a setting that's completely
authentic. The public tea ceremony is performed one Saturday a
month, or by reservation for groups of 15 or more. At other times,
five days a week from March through November, visitors can tour
the tea house and Japanese garden and examine the myriad of
carefully conceived details of architecture and design that contribute to *Chado*, or the way of tea.

"A bowl of tea, when prepared according to the principles of
Chado, is a ritual developed to meet man's need for inner tranquility." So says the excellent little pamphlet from the Urasenke Foundation, with which the Saginaw tea house is affiliated. A worldwide
nonprofit institution devoted to promulgating the Urasenke tradition of tea, the Urasenke Foundation is one of the three large, traditional tea schools in Japan. The current national Grand Tea Master
follows the Urasenke tradition.)

In Japan, the tea ceremony is a social occasion and an aesthetic
exercise linked to meditation. Its settings and rituals were developed by Zen masters on the spiritual foundation of Zen Buddhism.
The Urasenke branch of this aesthetic was developed in Kyoto by
Sen Rikyu (1522-1591), a tea master and leader in politics and art.

The ceremony separates participants from the pressures and
cares of the everyday world. Its rituals create a harmonious, peace-

**The old lumber
and foundry
city of Saginaw
is the unlikely
home of one of
the very few
authentic Japa-
nese teahouses
in the U.S.**

ful state of mind through the aesthetic of tea. The traditional tea house emulates a Zen monastery in design. ("An" means "primitive hut"; "Awa" is the ancient name of Tokushima, Saginaw's Japanese sister city, which joined with Saginaw in building the tea house.) Guests enter the tea house through the *roji* or inner garden, designed to purify the spirit, even if it is built in a busy city. Randomly placed stepping stones make guests pay attention and concentrate the mind. At the washing basin, ritual etiquette has them squat, reach for the ladle, then wash hands and mouth.

Japanese gardens, like this one outside the Saginaw tea house, evolved in the 16th century as places to contemplate natural beauty and escape the pressures of the everyday world outside.

Guests enter the tea house quietly, through a small door, some three feet high — "to instill humility." Our hostess says, "samurai warriors were required to leave their swords outside. Everyone was treated equally" — quite a feat in the extremely class-conscious Japanese society. The tea ceremony developed among the aristocracy. It penetrated to the level of ordinary people and took on an egalitarian tone under the influence of the great tea masters of the 15th and 16th centuries.

The way of tea is based on these principles:

◆ *wa* — "harmony between people, and of people with nature"

◆ *kei* — "respect paid to all things, coming from sincere feelings of gratitude for their being"

◆ *sei* — "purity of mind and heart, implying both worldly and spiritual cleanliness." Or, as our tea house hostess sad, "We would like your mind to be as uncluttered as this room."

◆ *jaku* — tranquility or peace of mind, which comes from practicing the first three principles

Behind Saginaw's tea house is the Friendship Garden. It's an approximation of a traditional Japanese garden, with an arched footbridge over a stream. Japanese gardens like this depend on the landscape's forms and textures, not flowers — except when the cherry trees blossom in early May. The garden seems to have earned a spot in the hearts of local people. On my visit, a festive crowd of high schoolers in party clothes posed for a photo on the footbridge to help commemorate the *quinceañera*-like Sweet 16 party for a Hispanic girl.

The old industrial city of Saginaw, home to vast G.M. parts plants and the huge G.M. grey iron foundry, doesn't seem a likely place to find a corner of a public park given over to an aesthetic practice of rigorous refinement. There's no Japanese community of any size here. The tea house grew out of Saginaw's sister city relationship with Tokushima, an agricultural trading center of some 250,000 on the island of Shikoku, near Kobe. Yoko Mossner, wife of a Saginaw attorney active in the Democratic party, was able to nurture the sister-city relationship for many years. (Often these relationships wane when key people move on and leave town.) The Saginaw People to People chapter developed the Friendship Garden, which led to the tea house idea. Funds were raised in Tokushima and Saginaw, a Japanese architect came to Saginaw to work on the design, and the teahouse was built in 1986. For a time its operation languished under shifting volunteer groups, until Mossner became its permanent volunteer director. Since then the tea house has been open regularly.

Mossner has been happy to have been able to help support and spread the tea ceremony tradition here. "It's the essence of Japanese culture," she says, yet "Japanese who live in the U.S. are getting away from it. Some don't even own a kimono."

Tea houses are made of simple, natural materials to promote a sense of harmony with nature. They need not be large. Some may be only as large as two tatami mats. (A mat is about three by six feet.) The idea is to be a quiet retreat. In a tea house, the *tokonoma* or niche is the place of honor. It serves as a focal point for a scroll, a sculpture, and a flower or branch. Saginaw's tea house is designed in the *sukiya* style with a two-layered roof. It uses traditional methods and materials. It has a ceiling made of woven cedar strips; paper and bamboo lighting; and interior joinery made the Japanese way, without nails. Mud for the exterior walls was imported from Japan. The effect is subtle, restful, and contemporary, though a building like this could have been constructed a hundred years ago. It has one traditional tea room with tatami mats and no benches, and another with benches to sit on (the Western style that became prevalent after Commander Perry opened Japan to the outside world.) The tea utensils themselves have developed according to the same aesthetic of simplicity and harmony.

Not all Japanese society was as pure and high-minded as the tea ceremony, however. At the same time it developed, Japanese palaces were decorated in as elaborate and worldly a way as Renaissance palaces. The tea aesthetic was a reaction to this luxury. And the tea ceremony's ideals, Mossner said, "unfortunately were used for political gain, as a clever way of gaining support for a powerful lord."

The tea ceremony lies at the basis of the minimalist style of Japanese art which has so greatly influenced the Western art and architecture of the past hundred years. James McNeill Whistler and Frank Lloyd Wright were among the prominent figures who studied Japanese art and transmitted some of its ideas into our popular culture, either in their own time or later. Charles Freer, the Detroit stove manufacturer and friend of Whistler whose collection of Asian is the basis of the Smithsonian's Freer Gallery, had a special simple gallery built in his Detroit home (see page 256) where he drank tea and contemplated his paintings, one at a time.

Normally, visitors to Saginaw's tea house are given a **guided tour**, followed by a cup of tea and a traditional Japanese sweet. The powdered green tea, quite different from the leaf tea we associate with China, is actually quite bitter. "It's an acquired taste," our hostess smiles. "It's an experience even if you don't like the taste." The **formal tea ceremony** can be seen monthly on the second Saturday at 2 p.m. or arranged for groups of 15 or more. It lasts about an hour.

In either case, a little advance preparation helps visitors tune into the subtleties of this most understated aesthetic. A good, inexpensive introduction to the way of tea (including its connections to religion, art, and flower-arranging) is *The Book of Tea* (Dover, 76 pp., $3.95) by Kakuzo Okakura, a curator of Asian art in Boston at the turn of the century.

Two miles south of downtown Saginaw at the east on Washington/M-13 at Rust Dr./M-46 in Ezra Rust Park. (517) 759-1648. Tea house open March thru Nov., Tues-Sat 12-4, for tours of at least 25 minutes. Dec-Feb: group tours by reservation only. Formal tea ceremony ($6) by arrangement for groups of 15 (at least a month notice preferred) or 2nd Sun. each month at 2 p.m.; reservations advised. Group tours can be customized for small children, but they will be bored by the adult tour. ᕔ $3 includes tour, traditional tea, and sweet. $1.50 for students and children under 12. Garden *hours: April-Nov, Tues-Sat. April & May 9-4; June-Sept 9-8; Oct & Nov 9-4. ♿ Free.*

🌲🎋🌲

RELATED TO THE WAY OF TEA. . . . . Principles of Japanese landscape gardens have been expanded onto a much larger scale in much of the **Dow Gardens** in Midland, just 25 miles from Saginaw. The Dow chemical founder and his son learned much from Japanese garden planners. See page 399. . . . . The Asian Gallery at the **University of Michigan Museum of Art** features a 2/3 scale Japanese tea house, tea utensils hundreds of years old, a monthly tea ceremony, and an outstanding collection of Japanese scrolls. See page 162.

OTHER THINGS TO DO IN SAGINAW. . . . . A **rose garden** grows on top of the reservoir in Rust Park, across Court St. from the tea house. Across Washington from the tea house, the **children's zoo** is getting a boost from a newly formed civic group. . . . . The **Montague Inn** (517-7523-3939) is an elegant inn and restaurant in the Georgian mansion of a sugar beet magnate just north of the tea house. . . . . The **Saginaw Antiques Warehouse** (517-755-4343) has 70 dealers and 9 specialty shops including a children's book store and a tea room. It's on the west side near the river, at 1910 N. Michigan just south of I-675 (take exit 3). Open daily 10-5, Sun 12-5. The **art museum** is just a few blocks south on Washington. . . . . In the 19th century, two cities on either side of the Saginaw River competed for dominance; Old Town on the west side was surpassed by the other downtown on the east side. **Old Town** consists of several blocks south around Michigan and Hamilton at Court. Here are more antiques and thrift shops, a used book store, the excellent **El Farolito** Mexican restaurant (115 N. Hamilton), a bar that goes back to lumbering days (now known as **Zinggers**, 301 N. Hamilton), and the **Red Eye Coffeehouse**, 205 N. Hamilton. 517-793-1411. (Hamilton intersects with Court/M-46 just west of the river.) On Washington, **Bear Necessities** has loads of teddy bears, including some intriguingly scrawny collector bears selling for $180. . . . . Saginaw's splendid 1929 **Temple Theatre** (517-754-2575) is a gilded neoclassical extravaganza with its original crystal chandelier, drapes, fixtures, and wall treatments intact. It shows $3 **classic movies** and occasional art films every other weekend. Films start at 8 p.m., Barton Theatre Organ overture at 7:30. *203 N. Washington, north end of downtown, east side of river. (517) 754-2575.* ♿: *call (517) 754-2575 or 793-8941.*

FIVE RIVERS MEET . . . . . at Saginaw to form the Saginaw River: the Tittabawassee, the Shiawassee, the Bad, the Cass, and the Flint. Their confluences create, south of town, some unusually rich, marshy environments full of birds and fish. . . . . Nine miles of footpaths, some on dikes, go into the **Shiawassee National Wildlife Refuge** (517-777-5930) southwest of Saginaw, but it takes about a 2 1/2-mile hike to reach the observation tower from the west end of Curtis Road off M-13 southwest of town. . . . . **Imerman Memorial Park** on the Tittabawassee towards Freeland, offers easy river access, **picnic spots** (one pavilion juts out over the river), and **canoe rentals**. It's about 11 miles west of downtown on M-47/Midland Rd., reached via M-58/Davenport/ State or M-46/Gratiot. . . . . *Natural Michigan* by Tom Powers (Friede Publications, $14.95) directs visitors to other nearby tucked-away natural areas. In St. Charles the **Hartley Outdoor Education Center** (517-865-6295) trails go by a coal mine and expanses of wetlands where over 200 species of birds have been seen. Just 1/4 mile north of downtown St. Charles off M-52, the large, enclosed **St. Charles Waterfowl Observatory** lets birdwatchers get up close to 30 pairs of waterfowl.

SUGAR BEETS, TEJANO MUSIC AND MEXICAN FOOD. . . . . In the Saginaw Valley logged-off timberlands were followed by sugar beets, thanks to late 19th-century research at Michigan Agricultural College (now MSU) which indicated soil and climate favorable for the hefty root. Many later Saginaw fortunes were based on sugar beets and their byproducts. . . . . Employment at sugar refineries beckoned Hispanics, who first came as railroad construction workers. Michigan today is the fifth biggest sugar beet producer in the U.S. Michigan Sugar (Pioneer brand) is headquartered in Saginaw, Monitor (Big Chief) in Bay City. The Tri-City area (Saginaw, Bay City, and Midland) is home to an estimated 23,000 Hispanics. . . . . For a closer look at the **Hispanic community** and its night spots, restaurants, dances, record shops, groceries, etc., pick up a free copy of the English-language *Mi Gente* ("my people") monthly newspaper around town. It's at the excellent **El Farolito** restaurant on 115 N. Hamilton in Saginaw's Old Town, or at **Rodriguez Party Store**, 3558 Hess, off M-13/Washington/East on the southeast side (517-752-7458). Rodriguez has take-out tamales, barbacoa, and Mexican sandwiches. . . . . Every Saturday afternoon, Delta College public radio, **WUCX-FM 90.1,** has four hours of lively Tejano music and Latino programming. Volunteers and college students make for a high-caliber small station with heart. . . . . The Saturday nearest May 5 is Michigan's largest **Cinco de Mayo** parade celebrating Mexican independence, followed by a free **festival** from 12:30 to 6:30 on Ojibway Island behind the tea house in Rust Park. The **parade** leaves around 10:45 from Genesee at Michigan, goes down Michigan through Old Town, then crosses the Court St. bridge to the island. *Charros* (Mexican cowboys in tight, braid-trimmed suits) and their trained palominos are an annual hit.

MICHIGAN'S ONLY PULITZER PRIZE-WINNING POET. . . . . Saginaw was the hometown of **Theodore Roethke**, one of the 20th century's great poets, and its rivers, natural areas, and his family's greenhouse were subjects of some of his most memorable poems. *Roethke's Saginaw*, a richly evocative short, self-guided biographical tour booklet, is a good introduction to the influential teacher-

poet and his work. Buy a copy for a dollar or two at the Red Eye Coffeehouse in
Old Town. (See above.) . . . . . The Sunday closest to the May 25, 1908 birthday
of Theodore Roethke, Michigan's only Pulitzer Prize-winning poet (see p. 393), is
the **Rouse for Roethke** at Imerman Park Pavilion 2 (see p. 393). For several
hours beginning at 1 or 2 p.m., local and regional poets and performing artists
read all of Roethke's poems. Call the coffeehouse for details. . . . . Saginaw's relative isolation makes for an arts community that tends to create its own events.
Poet and Roethke-booster Al Hellus helped organize the monthly **Poetry Slam**
(Michigan's second). It's at the Red Eye Coffeehouse (above) on the third Tuesday
(usually) from September through May.

THE MARSHALL M. FREDERICKS SCULPTURE GALLERY. . . . . at Saginaw
Valley State University displays many, many sketches and plaster models for
works by Detroit's most widely recognized sculptor. If you know Detroit's logo
"The Spirit of Detroit" or the bronze gazelle by the Belle Isle conservatory (or the
world's largest crucifix at Indian River), you know Marshall Fredericks.
Unfortunately the collected mass of so many white sculptures here in one big
room, not in the architectural or landscape settings for which they were intended, can be rather overwhelming. But it's a good chance to see how the works
evolved, and see photos of bronze sculptures installed around the world.
(Scandinavian-American, Fredericks studied under the famous Swedish sculptor
Carl Milles and often had studios in Scandinavia.) A growing collection of bronze
casts is in the **sculpture garden** by the gallery. *On the Saginaw Valley State U.
campus, 7 miles north of Saginaw and 2 1/2 miles north of Fashion Square Mall
on Bay St/M-84. (Go over a mile west out Court St. from the river to reach Bay St.)
After passing Pierce Rd., turn right at the light onto the campus. Gallery is first
building on right. Open year-round, Tues-Sun except holidays and some university
vacations. No charge except for some tours. (517) 790-5667. &: call.*

Dow Chemical Tour and Visitor Center; H.H. Dow Historical Museum

Top-notch industrial history at a primitive brine well and a sprawling modern chemical complex

GOOD MUSEUMS of industrial history are a new and unusual phenomenon. Industrial tours of any kind have become increasingly rare because of widespread liability and industrial espionage concerns. Visitors to Midland can be treated to not one but *two* exceptionally interesting looks at Dow Chemical, the world's sixth-biggest chemical firm. Dow was founded here in 1897, and out-of-the-way Midland (population 38,000) remains its headquarters today.

The **H. H. Dow Museum** tells the dramatic story of Dow's origins at a replica of the simple old grist mill and brine well where founder Herbert Dow started out in 1890. **Dow's plant tour** shows visitors parts of its Michigan Division, one of the world's largest and most diversified chemical complexes. At the 1,900-acre complex along the Tittabawassee River just east of downtown Midland, about 3,500 people work, including Dow's world-wide research and development staff. Finally, there's the **Dow Visitor Center,** open week-

As a student in Cleveland, Herbert Dow figured out how to use electricity to extract the newly valuable chemical bromine from salt deposits, common in parts of Michigan. He arrived in Midland in 1890 and scraped together investors to develop a brine well, the beginning of Dow Chemical. A reconstruction of that well houses the unusual H. H. Dow Historical Museum.

days, which shows interested visitors an overview of Dow consumer products and an interesting illustrated summary of its history.

These are probably the most intelligent exhibits of corporate industrial history in Michigan. They're made even more interesting by exploring the character and motivation of its founder, a remarkably persistent, independent, and creative man. Herbert Dow was more than a good scientist and collaborator with others. As a hard-headed businessman, he was able to break the lock German cartels had on the American market for chemicals, thus paving the way for a strong American chemical industry.

Still, you won't get the *whole* Dow story at the museum or visitor center. There's little official mention of "Crazy Dow." That's what skeptical Midlanders called 24-year-old Herbert Dow shortly after he arrived in town with a suitcase, a few hundred dollars, and an idea for extracting the valuable chemical bromine from the bromine-rich brine deposits under Midland. His studies at the Case School of Applied Science in Cleveland had convinced him that he could use electricity to extract commercial quantities of bromine from such salt deposits. Its use in photo processing and pharmaceuticals had made bromine valuable.

You *do* hear a lot on the tour about good walleye fishing these days now that chemical contaminants in the Tittabawassee River have been dramatically reduced and about Dow's advanced methods of waste treatment and ingenious uses for turning waste into new products.

DOW CHEMICAL TOURS

Dow's Midland operation, like many chemical facilities, is an amazing-looking labyrinth of buildings, industrial equipment, and pipes. Just driving by is impressive. Forty independent plants, each with its own production facility, quality control analysis lab, and warehouse, are joined by a network of insulated overhead pipes that carry steam, water, and raw materials to each plant. This open-air plant design differs from conventional plants enclosed in huge buildings. It allows for good ventilation, easy maintenance access, and great flexibility. Buildings and equipment are constantly being changed.

Visitors who make tour reservations are driven through this interesting complex in a van or bus for an up-close (if selective) view of operations. Tour stops include the Saran wrap plant and a state-of-the-art analytical lab. If everything is presented with an ideal, picture-perfect glow, down to happy-looking workers viewed on break in a snack room with a giant, deer-in-forest photo mural —

well, that's more or less the way working at Dow really is, to hear most locals talk about it. Dow workers are well paid. Its big research staff gives Midland the educational and income demographics and international population of a university town. Midland residents enjoy fabulous sports and cultural facilities. *Reservations required for free public tours, held Mon 9:30-11:30. (517) 636-8658. Call early; availability limited, especially for spring and summer tours.*

Dow Visitors' Center

Many of the 500 products made in Midland are displayed here — including Saran Wrap (introduced in 1953) and Dursban insecticide. Less famous products include plastics, agricultural products, and specialties like ceramics materials, latex, and Methocel. To move away from producing mainly bulk chemicals with lower profit margins and big price swings, Dow is increasingly stressing consumer products, both through new research and through acquiring makers of personal care products and pharmaceuticals.

There's a touch-screen program on plastics recycling. The interesting panels of photographs and text on company history are of considerable general interest. *500 E. Lyon Rd. at Bayliss, in the Dow complex just east of downtown Midland. From I-75, take U.S. 10 into town. After you've passed Washington Street and much of the Dow complex, look for Bayliss and turn left. Center is on the next block. (517) 636-8658. Open Mon-Fri 8-4:30.*

H. H. Dow Historical Museum

The life and accomplishments of Herbert Dow are engagingly presented in replicas of the rough wood buildings where he launched Dow Chemical. These include a primitive grist mill, brine well and derrick with handmade wooden pumping machinery, and pegged wood brine storage tank. The museum, owned and operated by the Midland Historical Society, uses some slick presentation techniques — voiceovers of actors who play family members and associates, a worthwhile 12-minute film on Midland shown in a nifty little 1890s theater, and a spectral image of Dow himself, fancifully revisiting Midland 60 years after his death and talking about an exhibit of products he developed. (Family members said it sounds like Dow, informal and down-to-earth.)

This isn't the pompous puffery you might expect, and it's not only for chemists and engineers, though they will be especially interested in the big display on the great Corliss steam engine exhibited at the 1876 Centennial Exhibition in Philadelphia (it fascinated the young Dow and a generation of nascent American inventors and technobuffs) and the reconstructed 1890 lab/manufacturing plant showing the bromine-extracting process on which Dow Chemical was built. There is a recreation of the workshop where, in his youth, Dow happily spent hours working on the inventions and projects of his mentor father, who was a master mechanic for a Cleveland shovel works. In a ghostly life-size tableau, early Dow scientists, recruited by Herbert Dow from his old alma mater, Case, sit around in shirtsleeves late at night brainstorming to solve a problem. *From downtown Midland, take Main Street west about 1 1/4 miles to Cook Road, turn left, and you're there. (517) 832-5319. Wed-Sat 10-4, Sun 1-5. Adults $2, $1 children, $5 family.*

CANOEING ON MIDLAND'S THREE RIVERS . . . . . is made easy with the **City of Midland canoe livery** (517-832-8438). It's at the foot of Ashman, which crosses Main in the very center of downtown Midland. You can paddle up the Chippewa to the Chippewa Nature Center, and from there up the Pine and back. They flow into the Tittabawassee, which is lined by city parks and golf courses northwest of downtown and by Dow Chemical to the southeast. But don't think you can get a duck's-eye view of the giant chemical complex. Canoeists will be met by Dow security who will transport them and their canoe around the plant and deposit them by the Mapleton boat launch to the east.

TUBING DOWN THE RIVER . . . . . is a popular recreation in these parts. Mount Pleasant, 30 miles west of Midland, has so little industry and such a modern sewage treatment plant that Central Michigan students like to float on inner tubes all the way through town. Tube and canoe rentals and transportation are available through **Chippewa Valley Canoe Livery and Campground** 13 miles west of Midland. (800) 686-2447.

MIDLAND'S OPPOSITE . . . . . attractive in a very different way, is the old lumber and industrial center of **Bay City** (see p. 358-9), near where the Saginaw River empties into the bay. An old retail area on Midland St. just west of the Saginaw River has become a lively entertainment district, popular with boaters. Center Street has the finest lumber barons' mansions. Downtown attractions include a large antiques mall, the venerable St. Laurent peanut shop, the remarkable Mill End (a sort of an updated army surplus store), and Karras' Red Lion diner, which metamorphoses into a French-Asian-influenced fine dining restaurant at night. It's worth finding the way to **Krzysiak's House** restaurant (517-894-5531) in an old Polish neighborhood. Polish specialties stand out.

Dow Gardens

A place of year-round beauty and harmony,
it fosters exploring and playful creativity
and shows what's possible in your own yard.

AS SOON as you enter the Dow Gardens, you're aware of how unusual they are. Signs and brochures invite you to explore the gardens by walking anywhere, including on the grass. (But don't climb rocks and waterfalls!) One of the first things you see is not flower beds or a striking vista but a stand of tall pines with remarkable chunky bark. That's a clear hint that texture, form, and contrasts are as important here as more obvious displays of colorful blooms. Some staffers even like the gardens best of all after a fresh snow without any flowers whatsoever.

The design of the place beckons and draws you in, to explore an unfolding array of environments. Past the pine grove, the trail squeezes between massive boulders crossed by a splashing waterfall. Then it opens out to the beds of annual flowers and the rose garden on your left. To your right is a maze formed by viburnums. Beyond that, an Oriental-looking red bridge draws your eye up a meandering creek.

In the rarefied ranks of great American gardens, the Dow Gardens are *most* unusual — fresh and creative. They owe little to the European gardens imitated by the usual American industrialists of great wealth. Typically industrialists were coached in imitative connoisseurship by art dealers, architects, and their own aspiring wives. They built Italian palazzi or Norman French castles or English country houses and installed formal gardens to go with them. The Dow family were never followers or imitators. Dow Chemical founder Herbert Dow and his architect son, the late Alden Dow, were broadly creative people. They shaped these gardens for over 70 years.

Visitors often call the Dow Gardens Japanese or oriental because of the striking red bridge, the emphasis on textures and rocks, and the design principle of inviting you to explore without showing an overview of the entire place. Director Doug Chapman bristles at the idea that these gardens are Japanese. He wastes no time in explaining that these are *American* gardens and nothing else. Japanese gardens are small and very, very controlled miniature environments of highly selected plant materials, he explains. They are fussily main-

The beautiful studio-home of the late architect Alden Dow, son of the Dow Chemical founder, overlooks the gardens which he and his father painstakingly developed over 70 years.

tained, pruned, and raked, down to the last detail.

The Dow Gardens are big — 100 acres, quite enormous when compared with gardens that seem large but are really just half a dozen acres. Yet the staff of gardeners here is quite small. Maintenance is relaxed. Occasional weeds are allowed to invade the lawn. Sprays and pruning are minimized. This is no minimal, sparse, symbolic landscape like a Japanese garden. The famous red bridge here is red because red is the natural complement of green, not because it's supposed to look Oriental.

A broad range of plants, not just choice specimens, are allowed to grow here, but only if they do well in Midland's cold winters and sandy soils, and only if they help create a sense of balanced harmony. "There is no such thing as a bad plant, just a bad place" is an operating principle, illustrated by the presence of a big silver maple, often considered a weed for its messy habits.

The gardens began as Herbert Dow's extended back yard. Creative and questioning by nature, he had always been interested in shaping his surroundings. When he arrived in Midland (see page 396), a landscape of stumps surrounded the declining lumbering town. Beginning in 1899, he landscaped his house here to show what fellow townspeople could do with their own yards. He kept the grounds open to the public. Dow's forest green house, facing West Main, can be seen from the far side of the gardens.

An enthusiastic traveler, Herbert Dow became friends with a noted designer of Tokyo parks, who visited Midland frequently and shared landscaping ideas with Dow and other Midlanders. Lack of money early in his life prevented Dow from studying architecture. It was no surprise when his youngest son, Alden, forsook engineering and a Dow Chemical career for architecture.

Alden Dow became one of Frank Lloyd Wright's original Taliesin fellows. In his own long (1934-1973) architectural career, based in Midland, he remained absorbed in harmoniously joining architecture and nature — a clear debt to Wright, and to the Japanese. "Gardens never end, and buildings never begin," he liked to say. He found many ways to bring the outdoors inside and extend architecture out, via retaining walls, paving, bridges, and other garden structures.

No better example exists than these gardens and **Alden Dow's own studio-home**, one of the most celebrated 20th-century houses. You glimpse it from the gardens beyond the red bridge. It's a long, low house with extending copper-green eaves. It seems to float on the pond that surrounds most of the house.

Renewing and extending the Dow Gardens, which had fallen into disrepair, became Alden Dow's retirement project in the 1970s. Working with director Doug Chapman, a former Michigan State University extension horticulturist, he refined favorite design ideas. Over a thousand different trees and shrubs were added to the garden. New greenhouses, a maintenance building, and a visitors' center with library were built. The reorganized gardens extended Herbert Dow's original philosophy of helping and inspiring the backyard gardener.

In the gardens Alden Dow developed smaller fantasy environments that bring out the playful child in visitors. (The Dow family — Herbert, Alden, and his sister Margaret Towsley, founder of an Ann Arbor children's play school — considered creative play an important part of adult life.) A **"jungle walk"** through a hilly thicket leads to a hidden pool and wildflower garden. There's an irregular **maze** through viburnums, and a **land sculpture** of rounded miniature mountains.

Visit the gardens in the gentle, playful spirit of Alden Dow. Follow your instincts and explore. Don't stay on the main path. Don't let the map guide you. And don't pay much attention to the plant labels. Instead, follow the sound of splashing water or the scent of

Even before spring leaf-out, the Dow Gardens offer striking vistas with pine groves, waterfalls, and boulders. The gardens' Asian influence is apparent, but the scale and relaxed informality is American.

wet pine needles. If a distant vista beckons, go there.

If you only have a little time, visit the interesting **sensory trail** (designed with sightless and other handicapped visitors in mind) by the main entrance and the nearby **boulders and waterfall**. If you have more time, you can check out the special areas like the **herb garden**, or the **All-America display garden** of annual flowers, or the **rose garden** or **perennial garden**. The sizable, attractive **gift shop** emphasizes books on horticulture, garden planning, and nature, with some plant-related gift items and cards.

An annual, free Christmas Walk (with luminaries and music) is held nightly the first Thursday, Friday, and Saturday of December. In early summer, a free night of entertainment with a picnic is held in the gardens. Call (517) 631-5930.

The Gardens are next to the Midland Center for the Arts on Eastman Rd. (Bus. Rte. 10) at West St. Andrew's, just northwest of downtown Midland. (517) 631-2677. Outside Midland, (800) 362-4874. Open 7 days a week at 10 a.m., closes at sunset. Closed Thanksgiving, Christmas Eve and Day, New Year's Eve and Day. ♿ $3 daily admission fee 18 and older. Ages 6-17 $1. Children 5 and under free. Annual card $5.

MORE OF ALDEN DOW'S BEST WORKS . . . . . including Dow's studio, are part of an interesting, worthwhile **Midland Architectural Tour** (the Legacy Tour) on cassette tape, meant for your car's tape deck. If you haven't got a tape deck, they will lend you one. It may be rented for $5 at the Midland Center for the

Arts, right next to the Dow Gardens. (The center is open from 10 a.m. until 6 p.m.) The homes Dow designed in the 1930s and 1940s are a must for anyone interested in his teacher, Frank Lloyd Wright. The narrated tour takes you through Midland's elite neighborhoods and surveys noteworthy historic architecture from the 19th century to a 1957 space-age dome, insulated with Dow Chemical's Styrofoam. The tour takes at least an hour and a half — with options, two hours or more. It's like having a well-informed local resident show you around. . . . . The **annual tour of Dow's architectural designs** in October always includes a visit inside his studio-house — a fascinating place, full of playful surprises including a toy train collection and the so-called "Submarine Conference Room." (The pond outside comes up to its windows.) *Call the Alden B. Dow Creativity Center (517-837-4478) for info or to make required reservations. The two-hour tour also involves a bus and visiting two private homes. $15/ adults, $12.50/students. ♿: no.* . . . . The Alden B. Dow Archives hold a **tour** of the **Dow home and studio** every 1st Friday and 3rd Saturday. It also includes family history, and a little on his organic style and philosophy. *(517) 839-2744. 10 a.m. By reservation only. Tours fill quickly in the summer. Sometimes a second tour is added. $7.50 Adults /$5 students . ♿: no.*

A LAVISH COMMUNITY CENTER FOR THE ARTS . . . . . is one of Alden Dow's ugliest buildings, the **Midland Center for the Arts,** next to the Dow Gardens. The interior space is much nicer, something like Wright's Guggenheim Museum. It includes a splendid performance space, changing **art and history exhibits** (on the 4th floor), and an attractive **gift shop** with items relating to science, art and history that also includes handmade and ethnic gifts and jewelry. The unusual **Hall of Ideas** (levels 1-3) has recently been renovated and made somewhat more accessible to younger and less focussed visitors. Exhibits start with geological eras in Michigan and a Foucault pendulum and end with *you* and your possibilities for contributing to the future. It's a typically dynamic, Dow approach that joins art and history, business and science in an idiosyncratic synthesis. Highlights include a replica of a full-size **mastodon** on the 1st floor, a Great Lakes sailing vessels exhibit with a birchbark canoe and 14' sailing skiff in the on the second floor, and a **history of communications** covering oral communication, radio, film, television, and computers on on the third floor. The **hands-on exhibit**s are unusual. There are 14 **interactive computers** throughout the hall and a small movie theater. The exhibits are geared toward all ages, including pre-schoolers. *On Eastman Rd. (Bus. Rte. 10) at St. Andrew's, just northwest of downtown Midland. Call (517) 631-5930 for **performance and exhibit information.** Hall of Ideas open 10-6 daily except major holidays. ♿. $3 adults, $1 students to 25, $8 families of 4 or larger.*

PICNICKING . . . . . is encouraged in the **park by the Tridge**, architect Alden Dow's unique three-legged arched footbridge at the confluence of the Chippewa and Tittawabasse rivers in downtown Midland. There are picnic tables and grills, and you can walk across the Tittabawasse to a playground in Chippewassee

Park. Take Ashman from Business Route 10 west into the heart of downtown all the way down to the river. The Tridge is right there, along with a lively **farmers' market**, open Wednesdays and Saturdays from spring through fall, 7 a.m.-noon.

PERE MARQUETTE RAIL-TRAIL . . . . . for bicyclists, wheelchairs, strollers, rollerbladers, and joggers. The 22-mile asphalt/glassphalt trail, 14 feet wide, starts at the Tridge in Midland and follows Saginaw Road all the way to Coleman, passing through Averill and Sanford. The first three miles pass Emerson City Park, the Brady historical home (517-832-5319), and Dow Historical Museum. . . . . **Sanford**, about eight miles from Midland, has a **Centennial Museum** with restored historic buildings (depot, small church, log cabin, country store, school, railroad cars). **Sanford Lake Park,** about 1/8 mile from the museum, has a sandy public beach, bathhouse, concession stands, boat launch, playground, and picnic area. Turn at Smith; when you reach Irish, follow the signs. Just past Sanford, a marked path leads to the 300-foot-long **Arbutus Bog Boardwalk** and out to an observation deck in the 19-acre bog. . . . . Also on the trail is a **coastal plain/wet sand prairie.** . . . . Bikers cross the **Tittabawassee** and **Big Salt** rivers on four former railroad bridges, including one high truss. The first part of the trail is woodsy with birds and wildflowers that change throughout the year. The second half of the trail goes through farm country which is especially spectacular during fall color season. . . . . . Only a few miles from the trail between Sanford and Coleman are two county parks, **Pine Haven Recreation Area** with 8 miles of trails and **Veterans Memorial Park** with 175-year-old white and red pines. . . . . Eventually the trail will reach Clare and cross the state. Near its current end in **Coleman** is a **bike shop**. The trail has picnic tables, but so far only porta-potty, between Sanford and Coleman. More toilets are in the works. . . . . For trail details, call. (517) 832-6871. & *Free, no pass required.*

A BLEND OF MUSIC, ART AND SCIENCE THAT'S QUINTESSENTIALLY MIDLAND . . . . . is the 17-day **Matrix: Midland Festival** held each June in the Midland Center for the Arts. For info on the unusual mix of science, dance, jazz, film, classical music, and more, call (517) 631-8250 weekdays and Saturdays.

Chippewa Nature Center

Michigan's best all-around nature center
has a good natural history museum, interpreted trails,
and an authentic 1870s log homestead.

MIDLAND'S Chippewa Nature Center clearly stands out from the rest of Michigan's many fine nature centers. First, it has a fabulous classroom and museum building. A comfortable lounge, shaped like a riverboat pilot house, seems suspended over the Pine River. Long views look upstream and down to the nearby confluence of the Pine and Chippewa. Using the bird-watchers' telescope provided, you can look out and see birds patrolling the river, hoping to catch a fish. The Center's architect, Midland's creative Alden Dow (see pages401), learned from his teacher, Frank Lloyd Wright, how to design buildings that seem to melt into the living world around them when you're inside them..

Displays, trails, and programs are all intelligently planned and user-friendly, with good signage to help you understand what you're looking at. Furthermore, Chippewa offers an unusually rich mix of things to do and see, including an authentic log homestead and displays of items as old as 7,000 years, discovered from on-site archaeological digs. Other nature centers have more interesting sites than this flat riverside bottomland of second-growth woods. But Chippewa probably provides the best all-around introduction to the natural history of its area, outdoors and in, and man's use of the environment. (The Gillette Sand Dunes Interpretive Center at Hoffmaster State Park near Muskegon is more dramatically situated, comparable in many ways, but more tightly focused.)

Highlights include:

◆ **Outstanding indoor wildlife observation areas** that look out onto feeders, shrubs, and flowers that attract many birds and chipmunks. Bright annuals attract hummingbirds to the river window. The museum's wildlife window is busy year-round. Even the most infirm visitors could sit here and enjoy nature for hours.

◆ **A museum** of colorful, well-done **dioramas** shows **Michigan geology** and scenes from **Saginaw Valley Indian cultures** of different eras. The geology exhibits nicely illustrate the notion that, seen in geological cross-section, Michigan is like a set of nesting bowls formed during different eras, mostly overlaid by a heavy layer of glacial till. Shown with each diorama are rocks or artifacts that go

Partly perched over the Pine River, the nature center's fine museum illuminates Michigan geology and the everyday lives of Indian peoples who settled the Saginaw Valley.

with that geological age. Unusually vivid displays on Indian cultures show scenes from everyday life in the Saginaw Valley at different periods, together with objects excavated from the nature center's **archaeological sites** and the archaeological methods used to uncover and identify them. The Saginaw River system, abundant with game and fish, was one of Michigan's most important centers of indigenous peoples before European settlement.

The museum displays are intelligent and clear but dense and best absorbed a little at a time. Easier to enjoy is a scene with a giant beaver. Just after the last ice age, Michigan was home to beavers 3 1/2 feet tall.

♦ **"The Naturalist's Challenge,"** a nifty exercise in slowing down and making observations of natural objects. It starts with an indoor hands-on display, followed up with outdoor observations made with the help of a borrowed bird whistle, magnifying glass, and bug box. Parents are well advised to try this out first to get the hang of it.

♦ The expanded **River's Edge Gift Shop** is strong on the natural and cultural history of the Great Lakes area, and on nature study accessories. Also on hand: gifts and souvenirs.

♦ A **14-mile trail system** on flat terrain often parallels the Chippewa River. Highlights are the .4 mile **Arbury Trail**, wheelchair-accessible, and a wooded, fern-filled **oxbow**. In winter the trails are used for **cross-country skiing; and hiking**. They're ungroomed and sometimes rough.

♦ A **man-made wetlands** was begun in 1990 as a replacement for wetlands destroyed to build a shopping mall north of Midland. The marsh vegetation is lush and wetland wildlife plentiful. Trails circle two basins; a boardwalk/dock lets you walk out over the water. *It's on Badour Road South of the Visitor Center, with its own parking*

area. Open roughly dawn to dusk as are all trails.

◆ **An 1870s log homestead** from Midland County. The house is well crafted, not a temporary cabin, and authentically furnished. (The nature center staff includes an historian.) Other log buildings moved here are a **barn**, a **log schoolhouse**, and a **sugarhouse** used every weekend in March for very popular maple syrup-making demonstrations. *The homestead buildings are open for special events and on Sunday afternoons, 1:30-4:30, mid-May through mid-October. Walkers are otherwise welcome to look in the windows.*

◆ **Weekend programs**, generally free and geared to families, are usually on Saturday and Sunday afternoons. Typical programs are similar to the presentation on insect metamorphosis which includes a puppet show and an outdoor walk complete with nets for the kids. October's **Fall Harvest Festival** (first full weekend/$4 adults, $2 kids) and March's **Maple Syrup Festival** (third Saturday/$3 adults, $1 kids) are big annual events.

The Nature Center is southwest of downtown Midland on Badour Rd. at the Chippewa River. From downtown, take Poseyville Rd. across the bridge, turn right immediately onto St. Charles, turn left onto Whitman. In 3 miles, turn right at sign for nature center. (517) 631-0830. Mon-Fri 8-5, Sat 9-5, Sun and holidays (except Thanksgiving, Christmas, and Christmas Eve) 1-5. &: *visitors center, sugarhouse, barn, Arbury Trail. Free.*

Historic Huron City

*A look at the civilized, relaxed summer life of Yale's
Billy Phelps, "America's favorite college professor"*

TIME moves slowly in Michigan's Thumb. The landscape is utterly flat, and the Lake Huron scenery is pleasant but unspectacular, no match for the Grand Traverse region or West Michigan's sand dunes. So even vacation development is blessedly low-key. In the absence of pressure to sell and develop property, old households have often survived intact, with all their everyday furnishings. They are natural museums maintained by heirs over the decades, until, sometimes, they emerge as organized museums with public hours. Examples, described at the end of this chapter, are the Sanilac Historical Museum in Port Sanilac (with the local doctor's home, furnishings, records, and library) and the Harbor Beach law office of Frank Murphy, Michigan's most illustrious leader of the Depression era.

But the **House of the Seven Gables** in the historic **Huron City** museum village is the most wonderful survivor of all. The big, comfortable Italianate house, built by lumberman Langdon Hubbard, sits behind a picket fence atop a long hill overlooking Lake Huron. When you enter this informal house and walk into the cozy, memento-filled library, the tea cart by the fire is set for afternoon tea. Books are piled on the center table waiting to be read and reviewed by Hubbard's son-in-law, William Lyon Phelps. A 1930s *Life* magazine feature called Phelps "America's favorite college professor." Classic Adirondack chairs look out across to the lake. It's easy to imagine that it's 1932 and Billy Phelps is about to come back from his afternoon game of golf.

Visitors immediately feel that this interior is no historical reconstruction. It's simply an old house that had, until 1987, been lived in by the same family ever since it was built in 1881. It was a very interesting family at that, sure of themselves and unconcerned with fashion. Langdon Hubbard had come to Michigan from Connecticut as a young, high-minded, and ambitious young man hoping to make his fortune in the West. He bought 29,000 acres of timberland and an old sawmill, which he developed into a lake port with a half mile-long dock.

By 1880 Hubbard's two sawmills produced 20,000 feet of lumber a day. But the great Thumb fire of 1881 burned up the area's remaining timber. Such fires were common in logging regions.

Loggers left treetops and other waste wood behind in the ravaged stumplands. Dried over the years, they caught fire easily.

The 1881 fire hastened the growth of inland towns like Bad Axe and Sandusky. The area's burned-over forests proved excellent for growing navy beans, potatoes, and, later, sugar beets. Old lumber ports like Huron City, however, were destined to languish except as modest resorts. In this area, brine wells and salt-making had been a byproduct of lumbering, and the process ended up contaminating well water with salt. The only sources of fresh water for port communities were Lake Huron and shallow, easily polluted wells. That limited lakeshore development.

After the fire, Hubbard rebuilt his big Italianate house and sold off his timberland to German and Polish farmers. He didn't rebuild his sawmills, which could have salvaged the dead trees and provided some local employment. A general store, inn, church, and school were built for the farm village Hubbard hoped would prosper on the site. Today they survive, fully furnished, as components of Historic Huron City. Hubbard provided unusual amenities for villagers: a social parlor in the inn, a roller rink near the store, and books from

Layers of history and generations of interesting possessions make the House of the Seven Gables a memorable time trip. It's easy to imagine that it's 1932 and you're visiting the family summer home of Anabel and William Lyons "Billy" Phelps, the phenomenally popular Yale English professor.

his personal library to borrow. But by 1883 Huron City had less than two dozen residents, down from 1,500 before the fire.

Huron City did prove an ideal summer retreat for the Hubbard descendants, who lived in Grosse Pointe, and their friends. The daughter, Annabel, married William Lyon Phelps, who became a phenomenally popular English professor at Yale. To generations of Yale students he was Billy Phelps. They flocked to his interesting, easy-to-take lectures. Phelps was also an American Baptist preacher and a prolific writer of book reviews and literary appreciations for the general reading public. He and Annabel summered in the House of the Seven Gables. His non-denominational, Sunday-afternoon sermons attracted so many vacationers that the little church was expanded to hold 600. Seven Gables remained in use through the death of the Phelps's heir in 1987.

Physical evidence of the Hubbards' and Phelpses' affluent, civilized, and relaxed lifestyle is everywhere. There's an ornate 1886 pool table in the double parlors, and above it a print of a Raphael Madonna. Parlor amusements range from a music box with huge discs, circa 1885, to Mah-Jong tiles from that craze. There are portraits of favorite dogs and cats, and racks of croquet mallets and tennis rackets in the study. The ladies' fancy work, seed pictures, twig shelves, and Annabel Phelps's almost Expressionistic landscape paintings are all interesting. The books and magazines in Phelps's large, airy upstairs study give a good idea of the literary fare of well-read people in the 1920s and 1930s.

A house like this required an upstairs maid and a parlor maid. Also, a cook and a kitchen maid worked in a cheerful, practical kitchen. State-of-the-art in 1915, it hardly changed thereafter. Enthusiasts of authentic period decor won't be disappointed by things like the 1915 dishwasher or the series of bedrooms from different decades.

The genial Billy Phelps stuck to a productive daily routine in summer, beginning with calisthenics at six a.m. (All guests were awakened to join in.) He then retired to his study to write until noon. After lunch, he played golf. Grazing sheep clipped the golf course between the house and Lake Huron, but were rounded up at game time and herded under the old roller rink. Edgar Guest, the *Detroit Free Press* columnist famed for his light verse, was a frequent golfing buddy, and eventually built a summer cottage in nearby Pointe aux Barques.

After Billy and Annabel Phelps's deaths, the property came into the hands of Annabel's niece, Carolyn Hubbard Parcells Lucas. The dynamic personality of Billy Phelps and the public's great interest in

Phelps was also a dynamic Baptist preacher. His summer sermons attracted such enormous crowds that the old Huron City church had to be expanded twice.

him inspired her to furnish and preserve Huron City's church, inn, and general store. A trim brick **museum building** was erected to house exhibits on local history and on Phelps's career. All the buildings are simple and attractive, painted white with green trim, giving them a neat New England look.

Huron City's buildings are more fully and authentically furnished than most museums'. That's a result of local people's long memories and many contributions. Much of the merchandise in the **general store** was left over from Langdon Hubbard's stock. The original **post office** and **lumbering office** remain in back of the store, while a large room is given over to displays of tools for lumbering and cutting ice.

The **lifesaving station** built next to the lighthouse at nearby Pointe aux Barques has been moved here to Huron City. Here a breeches buoy and other lifesaving equipment can be seen, along with displays on local maritime history. Teenage tour guides are pleasant and competent.

The buildings of Huron City make up one tour; the Seven

Gables summer house is a separate tour. Seen alone, Huron City is impressive. But it is overwhelmed by the compelling intimacy of the House of the Seven Gables, which seems too real to be a museum. Each 1-hour tour would probably be more enjoyable if taken on a separate day, or if separated by a trip to the beach.

If you do take both tours on the same day, bring a snack or lunch to eat at a picnic table. No refreshments except soft drinks are nearby, and each tour lasts 1 hour.

Huron City is on M-25 8 miles south of Port Austin and 8 miles north of Port Hope. (517) 428-4123. Open July 1 through Labor Day, every day but Tuesday and Wednesday, 10-5. Group tours available in June through Sept. ♿: church, lifesaving station, log cabin, general store, 1st floor of house (video for 2nd). Admission to each tour (Huron City or Seven Gables): $6 adult, $5 seniors, $3 10-15, under 10 free. Both tours: $10 adult, $8 seniors, $5 10-15.

ANOTHER TRIP BACK IN TIME, TO THE 1920s AND 1930s, ... is the **Frank Murphy Birthplace** in Harbor Beach. Murphy was the Michigan governor who refused to use the National Guard to quash the 1937 Flint Sit-Down Strike. By initiating collective bargaining, he paved the way for the United Auto Workers union. This is a very simple frame house, to which the storefront law office of Murphy's father is attached. Walk in and you feel like you're in 1910, what with the potbelly stove, kerosene lamps, and plain wood chairs.

Murphy's father made enough money to move into the impressive Gothic Revival house next door, where his children grew up. His famous son, a true labor hero, started his career in Detroit, became mayor (no Depression-era mayor did more to alleviate hunger among the jobless), governor (1936-38), U.S. Attorney General, and U.S. Supreme Court judge (1940 to his death in 1949). Murphy seems to have used the little house as a home base and repository for books and gifts, souvenirs and snapshots.

The houses are treasure troves of interesting historical objects. Everything in the houses has been kept the same as it was the day Murphy died. You can learn a lot about Murphy's character from the things he left here, and from talking to the UAW retirees who, as true keepers of the flame, run the museum. Inspirational books, pairs of riding boots, crucifixes and religious statues, countless autographed photos of Murphy with celebrities and labor leaders — all add up to a picture of his political ambition and concern for achievement and high principles, his Catholic faith, and his love of challenge and hard work. While governor of the Philippines from 1933 to 1935, he received some most unusual gifts displayed here.

In 1996, the city of Harbor Beach acquired the Frank Murphy Birthplace and is now making the site barrier-free, creating new tours, and re-organizing the museum. The city also recently bought the Murphys' Gothic Revival house next door, once used as a summer cottage. All its contents remain, including a huge crystal chandelier from the Royal Palace in the Philippines and other artifacts from Murphy's travels. *142 S. Huron in central Harbor Beach, across from Norm's Place. For info, call Matt Armentrout at the Parks Dept.: (517) 479-9554. Open Memorial Day thru Labor Day, Wed-Sun 10-6. ᕳ : not yet. $2 adults, $1 children 6-17, under 6 free.* . . . . . While in Harbor Beach, you might want to seek out the interesting **Community Building** on M-25 just north of downtown. Its murals depict the disastrous Thumb fire of 1881, scenes from Murphy's career, and other events of local significance.

A **PRETTY PARK AND LIGHTHOUSE** . . . . . just 2 1/2 miles east of Huron City on Lighthouse Road is the **Pointe aux Barques lighthouse** (1848) and the **Lighthouse County Park** with campground, boat yard, picnic area, and lawn down to the **beach.** (517) 428-4749. *From June 1st thru Labor Day, the lighthouse museum is open Sat, Sun, and holidays 11-6. At other times, knock on the door to the keeper's house and if it's not too busy, you'll get a tour of the lighthouse. ᕳ: lighthouse museum. In 1996, a one-mile wheelchair accessible walk is being built along the beach and will include several lookout piers over the lake that provides barrier-free access. Free. Donations appreciated.*

A **NICE PLACE TO LINGER AND WATCH BOATS** . . . . . is shady **Harbor Park** overlooking the busy transient marina at **Port Sanilac** (population 650), some 33 miles north of Port Huron on M-25. Get the feeling of being out on Lake Huron by walking out to the long **breakwater** past the pretty Victorian **lighthouse** and the **Old Bark Shanty** (a favorite local landmark from pioneer days, not open to the public). Mornings and evenings the breakwater is usually well populated by fishermen, and for the October salmon run it's packed.

THE FINE ITALIANATE HOME OF A PIONEER DOCTOR . . . . . and most all his things, from a massive curio case full of bird's nests, Indian pipes, and coral specimens to medical books and his original medicines, make the **Sanilac Historical Museum** special. The doctor's grandson and only heir became a ship's captain, and never threw anything out or modernized much, since he only stayed here occasionally. Some rooms are given over to museum display. There's a first-rate **quilt collection**, a Victorian display of stuffed birds with a painted backdrop, a good **marine history room** about the area's famous shipwrecks, and odd donations like a Mexican bullfrog mariachi band of stuffed bullfrogs wearing sombreros. There's a lot of high-quality stuff to see here: carriages, an old log cabin, a display on the fishing industry, a general store, a blacksmith shop, a country schoolhouse, a little dairy museum. Sanilac is Michigan's #1 milk-producing county. Two-hour tours are guided by girls dressed in period costume. Pleasant **picnic area** and grounds with Victorian garden, too. *On the west side of M-25 at the south edge of Sanilac. (810) 622-9946. Open from Memorial to Labor Day, Tues-Fri 11-4:30, Sat & Sun 12-430, closed Mon. ᕳ: no. $6 adults, $5 seniors & AAA, $2 kids, 6 and under free. $15 family.*

Port Huron

*Striking views of freighters and water
in one of America's earliest inland outposts*

STRATEGICALLY sited where Lake Huron pours into the St. Clair River, this city of 34,000 is a grand place to watch passing freighters and a good jumping-off place for exploring the bucolic charms of the Thumb and the Lake Huron Shore. This site became one of the earlier outposts in the American interior when the French built Fort St. Joseph here in 1686 to seal off the upper Great Lakes from the English. In 1814 the Americans built Fort Gratiot on the same site, also to keep the British out of Lake Huron and Lake Superior. American friction with British-controlled Canada had changed to cooperation by 1891 when the St. Clair Railroad Tunnel was built beneath the St. Clair River to join Sarnia with Port Huron. Located a mile south of downtown between Johnstone and Beard, the tunnel has recently been replaced by a larger tunnel next to it. This is big enough to accommodate the many double-decker auto carriers that cross the border. The line's owner, the Canadian-owned Grand Trunk Railroad, had its big railroad car repair shops (now abandoned) a mile west of the tunnel on 25th Street

Despite its strategic position, Port Huron has been something of a backwater in this century. No nationally prominent manufacturers sprang up here as they did in Midland, Battle Creek, and Kalamazoo. For environmental reasons, the city rejected the bids of chemical companies to build plants here; they settled on the laxer Canadian side of the river instead.

Port Huron's main claim to fame is that it's the hometown of Thomas Edison. (Novelist Terry McMillan, author of the megahit *Waiting to Exhale*, was born and raised here and got her first exposure to black authors shelving books in the public library.) The one big event which attracts thousands is the **Mackinac Race Day** in late July, when a flotilla of sail boats races to Mackinac Island.

Here are Port Huron highlights, arranged roughly from north to south. *Note that the main north-south street and business route of I-94, has four names:* Gratiot and Electric/Military south of the Black River and downtown; Huron (downtown north of the river); and Pine Grove where it angles northwest north of downtown.

◆ **Blue Water Bridge.** One of the most stunning sights in all of

The Fort Gratiot lighthouse still guides ships from Lake Huron into the St. Clair River, a tricky maneuver because of its narrow width and rapid current. Until 1971 sailors were also aided by the Huron Lightship, moored on the shoals six miles from the river entrance.

Michigan is the panoramic view at the crest of this imposing bridge. You're 152 feet over the water, looking down to the north at Lake Huron where it meets the St. Clair River. To the south are the cities of Sarnia (Ontario) and Port Huron, as well as a lengthy stretch of the river. The bridge's vantage point allows you to see freighter traffic for miles both ways. Just to the north on the American side you see the Dunn Paper facilities. Even better than a car ride across the bridge is a walk along the bridge's sidewalk (temporarily curtailed during construction). There's no need to report to customs until you get to the other side, and there's no charge for walking.

Traffic has grown so much across the bridge that a new $79 million bridge will be completed in mid-summer of 1997. Also over a mile long, this companion bridge will handle the U.S.-to-Canada traffic. *U.S. entrance is the northern terminus of I-94. From town, take Pine Grove 2 miles north. Toll: $1.25 per car.*

◆ **Thomas Edison Park.** Port Huron's strategic location where Lake Huron flows into the St. Clair River provides an exceptional visual setting in this new park by an historic train station. To the east, facing Canada, looms the enormous **Blue Water Bridge**, and beyond that, the great expanse of **Lake Huron**. Directly ahead, the river is quite narrow, less than a quarter mile wide. It therefore flows quite swiftly, up to five miles an hour. The river's narrow width brings the big freighters up close.

In the shadow of the bridge is the restored 1858 **Grand Trunk**

Depot. From here in 1859 Thomas Edison, a Port Huron boy of 12, boarded the train daily to sell fruits, nuts, magazines, and newspapers on the way to Detroit and back. He used much of his earnings to buy chemicals for the small laboratory he set up in the train's baggage car. The depot now houses the local visitors' bureau. In the lobby are historical photos and displays, including artifacts excavated from the yard of Thomas Edison's boyhood home that once stood nearby. Just south of the old depot is the new **Thomas Edison Inn,** a pricey 150-suite dining/hotel complex built by the owners of the popular St. Clair Inn downriver. Just south of the inn's parking lot is where **Fort Gratiot** (1814-1879) stood. *Just south of the Blue Water Bridge. From Pine Grove Ave. take Thomas Edison Parkway just north of the tracks. Parking spaces and boardwalk by the river.*

◆ **Sarnia, Canada.** Port Huron's neighbor across the St. Clair River is a pleasant, if rather unexciting, place to visit. No longer are there great buys on Commonwealth products to lure Americans across the border. The flow is now reversed, and Canadians flock to Port Huron's malls for good deals. The community at the bridge is actually Port Edward; downtown Sarnia is actually a mile to the south. The economy of Sarnia (population 80,000) is based on the petrochemical industry, whose fascinating-looking plants sprawl for some 20 miles below the city along the St. Clair River. At night, the spaghetti-like complex of lights and tubing is quite a sight from the American side. An elaborate government-run information center is just to the south of the Canadian side of the bridge. *Take I-94 to the Blue Water Bridge; once in Canada, go south on Hwy. 402 and then 40 B. No passport necessary for American citizens.*

◆ **Lighthouse Park**. This park, a quarter-mile north of the bridge, is next to a picturesque 1861 brick lighthouse and keeper's dwelling that are on the site of Michigan's first lighthouse. The tower is open to visitors a few times a year; call (810) 982-0891. The park is another good vantage point from which to enjoy the splendid view of Lake Huron as it enters the St. Clair River. Lights illuminate a short asphalt path leading to the sandy swimming **beach.** (The water is clean but swift; **Lakeside Park**, a mile north off Gratiot, is the big beach for swimming.) Along the way, you pass a small Coast Guard complex, complete with an 1874 lightkeeper's dwelling of red brick and a white clapboard Coast Guard station. Also in the complex is the 86-foot-tall **Fort Gratiot Light**. (Call the Lightship, below, to find out about occasional Sunday open house.) The light still flashes a warning to freighters coming south from Lake Huron into the river, a tricky maneuver because of the river's narrow width and swift current. On foggy days, it's eerie to see giant northbound freighters quietly churning past and becoming quickly engulfed in the mist on the lake. *Off Omar St. between Robinson and Riverview Five blocks north of the Blue Water Bridge. From Pine Grove north of I-94, take Garfield east to the park.*

◆ **Pine Grove Park.** This older park in town fronts the St. Clair River and provides a wonderful view of the big bridge, the Canadian shoreline, and boat traffic. On the concrete walk right at the river-bank, fishermen with big landing nets fish for walleye and steel-head. At the park's northeastern edge is the **Huron Lightship,** a retired floating lighthouse. For many years it was stationed at the treacherous freighter pas-sage beginning six miles north of Port Huron. The light from the 97-foot-long vessel could be seen for 14 miles. The last lightship on the Great Lakes, retired in 1970, it has been lovingly restored by retired sailors and Coast Guarders. The self-guided **tour** takes you through the engine room, crew's quarters, mess, and galley. The lightship's high main deck is also a great outpost for watching freighters, although there

Today the Huron Lightship, carefully restored, is permanently docked next to Pinegrove Park. The deck and cabins can be toured from May through September.

is no predicting when or how often ships will come by. *On the river by parking lot. Open weekends at least, May thru Sept. May, June & Sept: Sat & Sun 1-4:30. July & August: Wed-Sun 1-4:30. (810) 982-0891. &: no. Adults $1.50, students 50¢, 6 & under free.*

North of the lightship you can see a red **pilot house,** quarters for the American freighter pilots who take the wheels of foreign ves-sels heading into U.S. waters. The vacant lot behind the pilot house was where Thomas Edison's family home stood.

Looking south across the river, you can see the beginning of Canada's 20-mile-long **"chemical valley,"** Canada's greatest con-centration of chemical factories. It's a spectacular nighttime sight reflected in the water. Chemical valley creates most of the pollution in the lower St. Clair River. *On the east side of Pine Grove between Prospect and Lincoln, north of downtown. From I-94, take the very*

*last exit, the one past the exit to the Blue Water Bridge. Go south
(away from the lake).*

◆ **Diana Sweet Shop.** Fine woodwork abounds in this beautifully
preserved 1926 sweet shop. The ornate tapestry, the lighting, the
pressed metal ceiling, the pictures — all combine to create an extraordinary atmosphere. It is still owned and operated by the sons of
the founder. Sweet shops flourished in the 1920s as the tempo of
American urban life sped up and people stopped going home for
lunch. Elegant interiors were a
mark of success. Port Huron looked
like an emerging boom town in
1926, so Gus Deligianis and George
Dallas, Greek immigrants who first
found work as railroad water boys,
moved here from Flint, where they
had worked in sweet shops.

"The original decor would have succumbed
to the competitive pressures of cushions and
chrome in the '50s if the sons had not been
sidetracked by their participation in the Korean
War," states the menu. Diana's preserves not only
the decor but the menu: sandwiches, ice cream, pastries, phosphates and sodas, and fudge. Don't miss the original 1926 "Violino
Virtuoso" up front as you enter. For 25¢ it will play one of five
tunes, plucking at a violin and hammering on strings. *Downtown at
307 Huron between Grand River and McMorran. (810) 985-6933.
Mon-Sat 7:30 a.m.-5:45 p.m. exc except Fri to 7:30 p.m. Sat 7:30-6.
MC, Visa, Am Ex. No alcohol.* &: *at front tables.*

◆ **Port Huron Museum**. This sizable museum in the impressive
1904 Carnegie library building has a little bit of everything, from
7,000 B.C. Indian artifacts to recent paintings for sale by local
artists. A noteworthy array of Indian stone points and tools is from
the area. Archeological digs have recovered objects from Edison's
boyhood home (which burned down), including evidence of his boyhood laboratory. In the McMorran Room are ornate turn-of-the-century furnishings that illuminate Port Huron life in that era. The
biggest attraction in the Cooper's Marine Gallery on the second floor
is the **freighter pilot house**, restored piece by piece over a two-year
period by the same volunteers who have rebuilt the Huron
Lightship. Most haunting are the objects brought up by divers from
nearby **Lake Huron wrecks**, some from the previous century.
Among the items available in the **gift shop** are books written by

Thomas Edison and a history of Port Huron, *The Reflection* ($18.50). *1115 Sixth St. between Wall and Court, south of the Black River and downtown. Sixth is one block west of M-25, the main artery. (810) 982-0891. Wed-Sun 1-4:30. $1.50/adults, $1/seniors, 50¢/students, children under 6 free.*

CRUISES ON THE ST. CLAIR RIVER. . . . . The *Huron Lady*, a 65-foot excursion boat, takes you under the Blue Water Bridge out onto Lake Huron to view the lighthouse (see above), then goes along the river to St. Clair to see giant freighters loading and unloading along both sides. Order $4.75 box lunches in advance. Also can be boarded from St. Clair. *Departs Tues-Sat 1 p.m. & Wed-Sat 7 p.m. from the Port Huron dock on the Black River's south bank, next to the Military St. entrance to Michigan National Bank on the corner of Water. Adults $11, kids 5-12 $6, seniors $9. Picnic lunch $4.75. Reservations recommended. &: call. (810) 984-1500.*

TO IDENTIFY PASSING FREIGHTERS . . . . . several books are available. *Know Your Ships* ($12.95) is a compact boat-watcher's bible. Each year's edition includes an overview of the St. Lawrence Seaway locks and waterways and a chronicle of each year's major events in Great Lakes shipping, plus flag markings, whistle codes, and much more. The color photos change each year. You'll find many books on Great Lakes shipping at the front counter at **Dean's Book Center**, 234 Huron Ave., downtown. (810) 982-8686.

Mid-Michigan

THE TERRAIN of mid-Michigan is among the least interesting in the state. The flat to gently rolling landscape is home to large farms, occasional wooded river valleys and farm towns. There's a splendid county courthouse in Mason. St. Johns and Ithaca are also attractive, settled old county seats. The Grand River, lengthiest in the state, winds past some interesting old towns with pretty wooded riverside parks. Eaton Rapids has quaint old woolen mills. Grand Ledge is famous for its exposed sandstone ledges. Portland, Ionia, and Lowell all have pleasant riverside locations. Owosso, hometown of 1940s presidential candidate Thomas Dewey, has a similarly picturesque location on the Shiawassee River. There James Oliver Curwood, an Owosso boy who became rich and famous writing outdoors novels, built a miniature castle, now open to the public.

But there is only one sizable city in mid-Michigan: Lansing. In 1847 the wilderness hamlet of Lansing was chosen as state capital purely for its central location. None of the bigger, older Michigan cities could get a majority vote from the state legislature for the

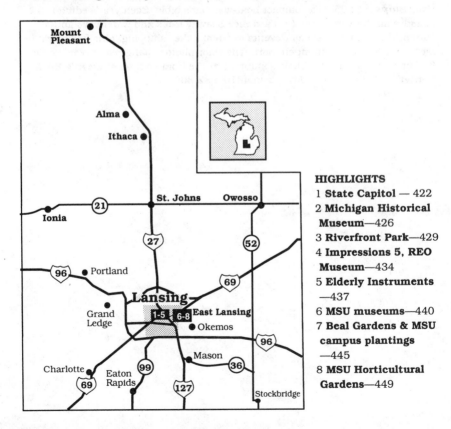

HIGHLIGHTS
1 **State Capitol** — 422
2 **Michigan Historical Museum**—426
3 **Riverfront Park**—429
4 **Impressions 5, REO Museum**—434
5 **Elderly Instruments** —437
6 **MSU museums**—440
7 **Beal Gardens & MSU campus plantings** —445
8 **MSU Horticultural Gardens**—449

honor. Though Detroit was clearly Michigan's metropolis, it was on a potentially unsafe international border where a war with Great Britain had been fought just 35 years before. Nationwide, many Americans shared Jefferson's mistrust of cities.

Today Lansing is defined by its status as the seat of state government. It is also defined by another perk won by default. In the 1850s Michigan farmers successfully lobbied to start an independent college of scientific agriculture, one of America's very first. (See page 445.) The tiny college that became Michigan State University was carved out of the woods east of Lansing.

Lansing is also a center of auto manufacturing, the headquarters of GM's Oldsmobile division. It shares the characteristics of auto boom towns: rapid growth and low-density sprawl from 1905 to 1930, considerable ethnic variety, and economic decline since 1970.

Downtown was hurt by the massive disruption of urban renewal in the 1960s and by freeway construction on the near south side. Relatively little historic preservation or gentrification has occurred in central Lansing. Although Lansing has often put its worst foot forward, it actually has a lot to offer visitors. It's affordable. Lansing museums, events at M.S.U., the respected Boars Head Theater, all make for an interesting weekend. Pretty spots are tucked away, many of them along the Grand and Red Cedar rivers that wind through town. On the Michigan State campus, landscape architects have fashioned some of Michigan's loveliest and most accessible gardens.

Hopes are now high that Lansing's image is poised for a change. A handsome new multipurpose stadium, home of the Lansing Lugnuts minor-league baseball team, stands on land on East Michigan Avenue where the embarrassingly visible skid row was bulldozed. There's talk of more restaurants, another downtown hotel for conferences, and a revitalized downtown entertainment district.

Information sources: CONVENTION & VISITOR BUREAUS

Greater Lansing CVB
(517) 487-6800, (800) 648-6630

Mount Pleasant Area CVB
(517) 772-4433, (800) 77-CHIEF (MI only)

Information sources: CHAMBERS OF COMMERCE

Charlotte   (517) 543-0400
Grand Ledge   (517) 627-2383
Ithaca   (517) 875-3640

St. Johns   (517) 224-7248
Williamston   (517) 655-1549

Michigan State Capitol

A tour de force of rich Victorian decorating
that's intense with political energy

MICHIGAN'S state capitol is an exciting place to visit for the spectacle it presents of seeing lawmakers in action in a richly decorated Victorian setting. The high-domed exterior looks like a state capitol ought to look: formal and impressive. Finished in 1879, it was one of the first state capitols modeled after the nation's Capitol, which had itself been remodeled during the Civil War. Lincoln insisted that capitol construction continue despite the war because the Capitol stood for the union. The tall central dome was made possible by using cast iron, then a new and relatively inexpensive building material.

Before Michigan's capitol was built, state capitols had come in many styles, including Greek temples and Gothic castles. Michigan's use of the national Capitol as a model helped establish that building form as the very symbol of the democratic form of government. The central dome stands for the executive branch and the balanced wings for the senate and house of representatives. This form set the standard for virtually all state capitols to come.

Even on the exterior, details like the oval windows in the dome hint that this building is no stern exercise in Roman dignity, but a product of the Gilded Age. The interior is rich in vivid colors, with contrasting decorative textures and patterns like plaster swirled like tight waves, and lots of gold leaf. Ornamental details include chandeliers embellished with stags. It was a tour de force for its cost-conscious architect, Elijah Myers, who called for very little marble, stone, or cabinet-grade wood. Most of the opulent effect was achieved with paint in elaborate designs on plaster. Pine was grained to resemble walnut. Myers' success with Michigan's capitol enabled him to win later commissions for capitols in Texas, Idaho, and Colorado. The capitol was designated a National Historic Landmark in 1992, in part for its remarkable decorative paint, over nine *acres* in all. It is the nation's preeminent example of Victorian decorative paint.

A monumental restoration, begun in 1987, is now complete. It received the 1992 Honor award by the National Trust for Historic Preservation, the nation's highest preservation award, for its challenge, complexity, and accuracy. The beautiful painted wall decorations and the elaborate ceilings in the **Senate and House chambers** have returned. The Senate walls, no longer a cautious, conservative

In 1847, weary legislators placed the state capital in Lansing, a centrally-located wilderness hamlet, after many fights in favor of major cities. The capitol remains Lansing's defining landmark. After a spectacular restoration, it is the preeminent U.S. example of Victorian painted decoration.

forest green, have returned to their original colors, predominantly a rich Prussian blue, several shades of warm yellows, gold, and rose used for the elaborate plasterwork. (An electronic display board is concealed in the wall until the board is illuminated. It shows proposed legislation and records the legislators' votes on it.) Ceiling panels of white and ruby glass etched with seals of all the states can again be seen — a favorite with visitors. The House has received a similar treatment in its original color scheme: vibrant corals, teals, and metallic silver, bronze, copper, and pewter.

Now that the scaffolding is gone from the restored interior **rotunda,** you can again get the spectacular full effect of looking straight up at the richly patterned dome with its starry inner eye. The governors' full-length portraits are back, and so are the flags carried in battle by Michigan Civil War regiments. (Replicas now stand in for the badly deteriorated originals.)

The capitol building is a magnificent stage set for the drama of everyday government. Controversies are played out and laws are made right here. When important legislation is being voted on, the entrance lobbies to the house and senate chambers are filled with lobbyists — so-called because they must wait in the adjacent lobbies. Barred from the legislative floor, they send messages to legislators via pages and confer with them in the lobby.

The capitol and all its public meeting rooms are open to all Michigan citizens. As the memorable late tour guide, Tony Dodos, loved to point out, "Everyone here — the governor, your representative, me — works for *you*. You pay us every time you pay a state tax." Some retirees attend legislative sessions regularly and keep scorecards of the proceedings as if they were at a ball game.

Here's what you need to know to be able to observe the legislature in action and figure out what's going on:

◆ Call the **Capitol Tour Guide and Information Service** at (517) 373-2353 to find if the legislature is in session and to find out who your representatives are if you don't know. Normally the legislature is in session Tuesdays through Thursdays, occasionally well on into the evening and early morning. Breaks are at Christmas (3-4 weeks), Easter (2 weeks), and summer (from June or July into September).

◆ Your representative will be happy to phone or mail you info on what's happening on a given day, or when action is scheduled on particular bills, or the dates of hearings on subjects that concern you.

◆ Bring your binoculars. Otherwise, sitting in the balcony, you probably won't be able to read the nameplates on each legislator's desk.

◆ If at all possible, go on a free **capitol tour** when the legislature is in session. Tours leave every half hour from the tour desk on the ground floor, east (front) wing. Call (517) 373-2353 for groups of 10 or more. From March through May, you'll probably be with an elementary school group, but you'll still learn a lot you didn't know. When the tour group is on the gallery, your guide can show you how to figure out what's going on. Tours generally last about 45 minutes. You'll get an overview of Michigan history as it relates to the Capitol, information on the decorative painting techniques, and a participative story of the legislative process.

◆ Stop by your senator or representative's office for a look around and to pick up interesting free material, including a capitol walking tour, a coloring book for kids, and an introduction to state government. Especially helpful for your visit and for having input on legislation is *A Citizen's Guide to State Government*, with lobbying tips and legislators' photos and addresses.

◆ At the ground-floor **tour guide desk** in the east (front) wing, get a **map**. The printed journal of yesterday's legislative proceedings and **today's agenda** can be had for no charge at the Documents Room in the ground floor north wing, off Ottawa Street. (You can also ask for copies of any state laws.)

◆ Visitors are free to sit in the balconies in the rear of the senate or house, and in the senate and house fourth-floor conference rooms during any **public proceedings**. In the house, speakers' voices come over a p.a. system, so it's hard to tell who's talking. Look for the microphones on the side aisles, where representatives come to speak. A light goes on by the speaker's microphone. What's being considered on the floor is displayed on the electronic display board; refer to your agenda to learn more about it.

On Capitol Avenue at the head of Michigan Avenue in downtown Lansing. **From I-496,** *take Grand or Walnut exits and go north.* **Hours:** *weekdays 9-4, Sat from 10 to 3, closed Sun & holidays.* **Tours** *are every half hour. Last one leaves at 3:30 or 2:30 on Sat. Tour guide desk is on ground floor, east (front) wing. For* **group tours** *and* **questions** *on state government, contact the Capitol Tour Guide and Information Service, Box 30014, Lansing, MI 48909. (517) 373-2353.* **Parking** *structures are at S. Capitol and Allegan (just south of the Capitol), at Capitol and Kalamazoo, and at Grand north of Ottawa.* &. *Free.*

BEFORE YOUR GROUP VISIT TO THE CAPITOL . . . . . you can see a **video** about its construction, history, and the renovation process. The Michigan Capitol Committee will mail it to you free of charge. Sign up early, especially in spring. Call (517) 373-5527, or write the committee in care of Capitol Tour Guide Service, Box 30036, Lansing, MI 48909.

LUNCH WHERE THE MOVERS AND SHAKERS HANG OUT . . . . . at the **Parthenon** restaurant at 227 S. Washington in downtown Lansing. The food — Greek and American, meat and vegetarian — is pretty good. Breakfast meetings are big (the mayor's here a lot). At lunch the place is packed with legislators and state employees. The sound isolation isn't very good; keep your ears open and you can pick up some interesting tidbits! Political meetings and receptions are often held here, too. The **Radisson restaurant** is another schmoozing spot.

THE LIBRARY OF MICHIGAN . . . . . in the west wing of the historical center (page 426) is Michigan's version of the Library of Congress. It was founded as a research institution for legislators and state employees. Collections of this beautiful and very user-friendly library focus on all areas of state government, from social services to highways and sewers, and on local history and Michigan authors. **Michigan residents** can easily get **library cards.** Materials may be checked out for a month and mailed back. Pick up a pamphlet about the unusually powerful **art works** in the building, and take a look around. *(517) 373-5400. Mon-Fri 9-6, Sat 9-5, Sun 1-5, closed state holidays.* &. At the adjoining **Archives of Michigan,** anyone can look through thousands of historic photographic images on many Michigan subjects and order prints made.

Michigan Historical Museum

Michigan history told with pizzazz and drama.

AFTER A CENTURY of being relegated to makeshift quarters, the state historical museum enjoys a stunning new space and has become a major Michigan tourist destination. The combined museum/state library/archives complex, opened in 1989, is a real architectural and artistic show-stopper. Detroit architect William Kessler brilliantly played off contrasts between polished and rough surfaces and natural elements associated with Michigan. These include limestone, copper, granite, and a 70-foot white pine, Michigan's state tree, dramatically planted in the central court.

Many of the expensive, expertly made displays are visually memorable: an Indian canoe pulled into a stretch of marsh and cat-tails in front of a realistic diorama of a lake; a lumberman's big wheel, 12 feet in diameter, used to move logs out of stump-filled forests; a two-story replica of the front part of Muskegon lumber baron Charles Hackley's elaborate Queen Anne home (see page 528). This dramatic exhibit style of thrusting the viewer in life-size environments is the hallmark of the influential Canadian museum designer Jean André, who worked on this project. **"Growing Up in Michigan: 1880-1895,"** in the mezzanine, uses diaries and reminiscences of five children who grew up in various kinds of Michigan homes. (One was Della Thompson Lutes, author of the delightful *Country Kitchen* cookbook memoir, recently republished.)

The historical narrative itself is honest and intelligent. No punches are pulled. It explains how within a few generations of contact with Europeans, Native American culture was nearly destroyed and their self-sufficient way of life changed to dependence on manufactured goods. "Give the least to get the most" was the business motto of John Jacob Astor, whose fur empire dominated the Michigan wilderness's economy in the first part of the 19th century.

For those who take the time to read and look, many basics — especially in geology, Indian cultures, and mining — are clearly explained and engagingly illustrated. The copper mining exhibit is particularly detailed and satisfying (better than anything found in Copper Country today), down to specifics and samples of rock types and diagrams of the mining and smelting process. Visitors walk through a life-size passage of a **copper mine**, supported by leaning timbers, to see miners and carts and hear the boom of a distant blast. Interesting **video shows on lumbering and mining** by the

**Striking sculpture and murals relating to Michigan's natural features are an
extra bonus on visits to the impressive state history complex. It contains
the state history museum plus the state archives and library — both treasure troves of local and regional history. Michigan residents are welcome to
use all three free of charge. The Stonhenge-like pylons and boulders is**
Polaris Rising **by David Barr.**

state Bureau of Michigan History illuminate life in camps. Small sit-
down **theaters** give your feet a rest.

The recently opened third floor covers the **20th century.** It's
more superficial, covering subjects mostly national in scope—the
dawn of the automobile age in Michigan, World Wars I and II, the
Depression, the Fifties. Though often interesting, it gives visitors little in the way of insight. Nor does the museum bring the shapers of
Michigan to life as fascinating, often contradictory individuals.

On the lower level there's an **exhibit gallery** for changing
shows, a large **snack area** with sandwiches (weekdays only) and
vending machines, and an attractive small **museum store** (closed
Mondays) with books and gifts which relate directly to the exhibits.
The museum store has one of Michigan's best selections of books
on the history of blacks in Michigan. Occasional **special activity
days** and **programs** usually relate to the **changing exhibits** in the
lower-level gallery by the entrance.

*The museum is between Washtenaw and Allegan southwest of the
capitol and east of Logan. See p. 428 for directional map. Park (free
on weekends) just south of the building off Allegan. (517) 373-3559.
To schedule free* **tours** *of the Library and Historical Center for 10 or
more, call (517) 335-1483. Mon-Fri 9-4:30, Sat 10-4, Sun 1-5. &. Free.*

❶ State Capitol (p. 422). Dazzling masterpiece of Victorian decorating, splendidly restored. See politicians in actions Tues.-Thurs. Tours Mon.-Sat.

❷ Michigan Historical Museum (p. 426). Fine visuals present state history with flair. Lumbering, mining, & pre-history stand out. Best copper-mining exhibit in state.

❸ Washington Street. Lansing's downtown alive only in daytime, but the architecture here makes it worth a look. Check out scene at Dancing Goat coffeehouse, 301 S. Washington.

❹ Riverfront Park and River Trail (p. 429). 5 1/2 mile pedestrian/bike path connects lively riverfront destinations, from the Zoo and museums to the fish ladder and North Lansing.

❺ North Lansing (p. 439). Striking turn-of-the-century commercial area finally has been reborn. Coffeehouse, galleries. Fish ladder at scenic dam south of Grand River is an old favorite during fall salmon run.

❻ Elderly Instruments (p. 433). America's headquarters for folk recordings & acoustic instruments. Amazing selection and savvy staff.

❼ Museum Drive (p. 434).Three museums: Impressions 5—Michigan's biggest hands-on museum. A car museum featuring Lansing's Ransom Olds, & the only U.S. surveying museum.

❽ Oldsmobile Stadium. Home of K.C. Royals farm team, the Lansing Lugnuts. Nuts & Bolts shop at SE corner sells popular Lugnut logo items.

❾ Potter Park & Zoo (p. 433). Pleasant riverside location with enlarged zoo (just $1 for kids), canoe rentals, great picnic grove.

Highlights of
Lansing

0   1/4   1/2
     mile

Riverfront Park and Trail

*A six-mile riverside path and bike trail
through Lansing connects museums and market,
fishing spots and zoo.*

LANSING'S real beauty spots are a number of distinctive
parks along the Red Cedar and Grand rivers, which join in
downtown Lansing. These places are so hidden away, you
must already know about them to see them. Riverfront Park, an
award-winning linear park along the Grand and Red Cedar rivers, is a
marvelous rarity in the Midwest: an urban park and pathway that
dramatizes a natural feature and connects interesting destinations.
Accents enliven the route for walkers, joggers, and bicyclists.
Fishermen and canoeists enjoy it, too.

Here, as in most American cities, rivers attracted early industries
and railroads. Although sources of water and means of transportation, they also became sewers and
dumps. Warehouses and factories
blocked the rivers from public view
as long as industrial activity
remained centered downtown. The
notion of an urban greenway in
Lansing, discussed since the 1920s,
was finally realized as a 1976
Bicentennial project.

For a dramatic walk, start by
the north end at the dam and head
toward the market and city center,
with Lansing's surprisingly impressive skyline ahead of you. Park in
the lot off Grand River just east of

**Walkers, rollerbladers, and bicyclists
enjoy Lansing's path along the Grand
and Red Cedar rivers. It passes interesting industrial landmarks like the
municipal power plant (in background)
as well as serene natural areas, the
North Lansing fish ladder, three museums, the city market, and the recently expanded Potter Park Zoo.**

the river. A vivid landscape really comes together here. There's the wide river and, behind it, the skyline, dominated by the capitol dome, some new glass office buildings, and the warm orange and yellow bricks of two fine Art Deco buildings, the Michigan National Bank tower and the **Board of Water and Light,** Lansing's city-owned utility, with its landmark stack. Though many old warehouses were demolished for the park, enough industrial relics remain to give the walk some character. There are **coal silos** by the dam and the frame and girders of the old **salt sheds** by Lansing Community College.

North of Shiawassee Street the Grand's riverbanks haven't been artificially straightened and channeled. Here they have grown up wild with small, moisture-loving poplars, willows, and maples. This accidental landscaping softens the urban views and creates some lovely seasonal effects that look wonderful against the river's sparkling surface on sunny days: the spring-green of buds, bright yellows in fall, snow-traced branches in winter.

Highlights along the six-mile riverwalk (arranged from north to south) include:

◆ **Turner-Dodge House**, near the northern end of the trail, is one of Lansing's most historic homes. Its core was built in 1858 by a Lansing pioneer and later enlarged by prominent architect Darius Moon into a three-story Classic Revival mansion with wooden Ionic columns and leaded French windows. Owned by the city since 1974, it is now used for community events. *106 E North St.*

◆ **The North Lansing dam, canoe and fishing platform, and fish ladder**. Some fishermen can nearly always be found at this beautiful spot, where a water-level platform provides easy access for canoeists and fishermen. The Grand's natural species here include catfish, suckers, carp, bass, bluegill, and perch. Walleye, coho, and steelhead have been planted. Fine organic sediments in runoff make for water that's typically murky, but the Department of Natural Resources says without reservation that fish caught here are edible. **Grand River Bait and Tackle** (517-482-4461) is a block away at 1201 Turner, at the corner of Turner and East Grand River. Most popular live bait: nightcrawlers for $1.35 a dozen, used to catch the rivers' population of walleye, smallmouth bass, catfish, and carp.

Off to one side, by the stone generator built to power Lansing's street lights, is an elaborate sculptural **fish ladder**. It is is on the very site of the cabin and dam built by Lansing's first settler in 1843. During the fall salmon run from late September to mid or late October, it's usually crowded with people scrutinizing the roiling waters of the fish ladder steps to get a glimpse of big fish heroically struggling upstream to deposit eggs. The coho and chinook salmon can be as large as 25 pounds. In the spring the steelhead trout, up to fifteen pounds in size, use the ladder. **Benches and picnic tables** make the fish ladder a nice place to linger. Park off of Race, which goes south off Grand River Avenue just east of the river itself. ♿

♦ **Innovations** is a nifty conversion of a stately old North Lansing bank on Grand River Avenue into a studio/showcase for artist Thomas J's eye-catching copper-clad sculptures ($30-$4,000). Gentrification is beginning to occur in this interesting old commercial district, which could well become one of the niftiest parts of Lansing in the coming years. *Instead of taking the boardwalk under the Grand River bridge, head up onto Grand River. 226 E. Grand River. (517) 484-0456.*

♦ The famous **Elderly Instruments** (page 437) is a good destination if you're walking north along the park from the market and museum area. It's just west of the river on Washington south of Grand River Avenue. For a return trip downtown through what was Lansing's most elegant neighborhood circa 1900, go south on Washington.

♦ **A pedestrian bridge** across the Grand is just south of the Saginaw Street bridge, near the tennis courts. Here you can cross the river to the busy **Lansing Community College campus** and the outdoor performing space by the salt sheds. For upcoming LCC **performances, lectures, and exhibits,** call (517) 483-1880 weekdays.

♦ For delicious, spicy, quick **Thai food**, eat in or take out from **Bangkok House**, on the south side of Saginaw in Riverfront Mall just east of the park. Benches (but no tables) overlook the river.

♦ The **Lansing City Market** occupies two enclosed market halls built in 1938. A smaller, enclosed version of Detroit's fabled Eastern Market, it also continues the tradition of big-city markets as places where a broad spectrum of social classes and ethnic groups come together to shop. The market operates year-round, so even in winter there's fresh produce brought in from the south, along with locally produced maple syrup, eggs, apples, root vegetables, baked goods, and such. A cheese shop, meat market, and florist are more like stores than stalls. A good bakery features cookies, breads, and a number of meat, vegetable, and cheese pies. There's a snack bar and lunch deli. Sit down and eat at indoor picnic tables or the **picnic/restroom/playground area** by the river across the parking lot.

From spring through fall, the colors and smells of the plants and farm produce are wonderful. The number of agricultural growers and producers is increasing. Only juried handcrafted crafts are now allowed. Women from Lansing's Hmong community of Laotian refugees sometimes sell their intricate geometric and storytelling embroideries and appliques here, usually around Christmas and in summer. *On Cedar (one-way southbound) at Shiawassee. From Michigan Avenue, go north on Larch, and west on Shiawassee, then south on Cedar. (517) 483-4300. Free parking on market days. Tues-Thurs-Sat 8-5 p.m.*

◆ **A picnic area and small playground** are between the market and the river. For takeout food, try the market itself or **Roma Bakery and Imported Foods**, a longtime Italian grocery at 428 North Cedar across from the market.

◆ **The Lansing Center** convention facility has been built between the market and Michigan Avenue. The Riverfront Trail squeezes alongside it by the river to get to the museums. Walkers can cross the river to the Radisson Hotel and Grand parking garage on a handy **skywalk**, reached by stairs or elevator in the Lansing Center parking garage.

◆ **Impression 5, the REO Museum, and the Michigan Museum of Surveying** — see page 434 for all three — are just off the riverwalk south of the Michigan Avenue bridge. This cluster ends the intensely developed section of the riverwalk with many.

◆ **Potter Park** (see page 432), $1^1/_2$ miles southeast of downtown along the riverfront path, has a big playground, a **picnic area** and nifty **zoo** in a grove of large oaks, and **canoeing** on the river.

◆ Getting to **East Lansing** via the Riverfront Trail is easy until you get to East Lansing's city limits. East of Potter Park is a wild natural area. But the nicely paved bike trail ends at the city limits. For a half mile or so going east on Kalamazoo you have to share the road with cars. Then you get to the M.S.U. campus, with an excellent bike path system. (See pages 440-451.)

◆ **Rental canoes** and **information on canoeing** can be obtained from the **Potter Park canoe livery** (517-374-1022). As they flow through Lansing, the Red Cedar and Grand are good beginner's rivers, shallow enough that most adults could stand up in them. You lose sight of the city along much of the waterway. Fall color along the riverbanks is good.

*Riverfront Park's current northern terminus is is about one-half-mile past the Turner Dodge House. Park in the lot off Race or Factory just south of Grand River Ave. and east of the river. In the **market area**, park at the market, the Lansing Center lot ($2/all day) or in the Grand garage just west of the river and north of the Radisson. The riverwalk enters **Potter Park** at Pennsylvania Avenue south of the Olds Freeway and the Grand Trunk tracks and goes all the way to the East Lansing city limits at Clippert, for 5 1/2 miles of paved river-*

front bike path separate from streets.

🌲🌳🌲

A NIFTY PARK AND ZOO . . . . . is at Lansing's **Potter Park.** The park's pleasant setting (in a mature oak grove on the Red Cedar River) and the zoo's low fee (just $1 for kids) make it good for short visits and letting off steam. There's plenty of playground equipment and space for games, along with picnic tables and grills, and food concessions. Canoes can be rented here, too. (517-374-1022.)

The **Potter Park Zoo** has been expanded and modernized in recent years. It still enjoys an unusually shady and attractive setting that somehow makes the animals seem happier, as chipmunks and squirrels scamper about. . . . Popular **recent additions** are gray wolves, which can be observed up close from the windows of a log cabin, and funny meerkats, made popular in *The Lion King.* Active and curious, they stand like prairie dogs and seem to enjoy watching people as much as people like watching them. Other new residents: binturong (Asian "bear-cats," with long tails), rhinos, and sunni antelopes. . . . . The zoo has a **tropical bird and reptile house**, many monkeys and larger **primates**, big **cats** that look comfortable in natural-looking outdoor displays, and a **farmyard**. Kids can feel friendly goats and take camel and pony rides. Especially fun to watch are the penguins in their pool; many playful, cat-like lemurs with long ringed tails; raccoon-like red pandas; and spider monkeys. . . . . Pick up a self-guided **tour** and **map** at the Zoovenir Shop. There's a new, expanded **concession stand** with picnic tables and a **center for backyard gardeners**, located by the eagles. *Park entrance is at 1301 S. Pennsylvania just north of the Red Cedar River and four blocks south of the Olds Freeway (I-496). Zoo open 365 days/year from 10-5 at least. Expanded hours during daylight time: 9-5 in April, May, Sept. & Oct.; 9-6 from Mem. Day weekend to July 4; 9-7 in July & Aug. (517) 483-4222.* **Tours:** *(517) 371-4155.* ♿ *Family membership: $40/year, reciprocates with zoos & aquaria. $2.50 adult. $1 ages 3-15 & seniors.*

COFFEEHOUSES & GALLERIES . . . . . instead of adult videos and lingerie. North Lansing's long-awaited transformation into a lively urban arts center has finally happened, as of 1996. The turn-of-the-century commercial subcenter is on Grand River at Turner and the Grand River. One everyday anchor is the soft-serve dairy stand on Grand River near Turner. **The Brick House** cafe (372-FOOD), at 311 E. Grand River four doors east of Turner near the tracks, serves hearty, healthy, inexpensive breakfast burritos, soups, wraps, quiches, cornbread, cheesecake, and more. It's open Tues-Fri 7 a.m.-2 p.m., Sun 9-2. ♿ . . . . . **Lamai Thai Eggroll Kitchen** (517) 374-6390 at 401 E. Grand River a block east of Turner, doubles as a Thai cultural center for occasional events. Good food in an unpretentious atmosphere in this former lunch counter. . . . . For food with drinks, the nearby choice is **Ramon's** (517-482-6690) at 718 E. Grand River, where the guacamole is thick and real and the homemade red and green salsas are *hot.* . . . . For more on Old Town, see pages 439 and 431.

Museum Drive

The state's best hands-on museum is next to two other interesting museums, all on the Grand River.

ON A BANK of the Grand River just east of the state capitol and downtown Lansing are three noteworthy museums all in a row. This was an old warehouse district, and before that the mill district, powered at first by the river itself. The museums have made use of the roomy old brick mill buildings for their displays. Visitors can also embark on the interesting **Riverfront Trail** from here (see page 429).

IMPRESSIONS 5

Hands-on museums are difficult to do well. Especially when the emphasis is science, as is the case here, the tendency is to allow corporate benefactors to influence the displays and activities, too often destroying the interest value for kids. Impression 5 has successfully blended meaningful instruction with absorbing activities. It's targeted to grades four through six, but it's so large and diverse, anyone can find something to enjoy. **Kids' Space** is a new area for toddlers. Seek out a uniformed staff person to help orient your group.

There's a lot of space here — 40,000 square feet. It's full of interesting, informative things to do. There are classics found in many hands-on museums such as the giant soap bubble maker and the spinning momentum chair along with uniquely ambitious projects. Some of the exhibits, like pulleys lifting 30-lb. weights, demonstrate important principles with elegant simplicity. Big satellite dishes allow one person to communicate by whispers with another person 50 feet away. The new 2,000-square-foot **Heartworks** exhibit features a huge, walk-through heart and many interactive stations. At an impressive **chemistry lab**, kids make slime and other concoctions. The popular multi-media Macintosh **computer lab** puts technology at your fingertips.

The interesting second-floor museum **shop** can be visited without paying admission. So can the ground-floor **Sara's deli**, open weekdays 11-4, Sundays 12-4.

200 Museum Drive (see p. 436). (517) 485-8116. Mon-Sat 10-5, Sun 12-5. & $50 annual family membership admits you to over 180 U.S. science & children's museums. Adults $4.50, seniors and children 4-18 $3, children 3 and under free.

Ransom E. Olds' pioneering Oldsmobile (shown here in 1904) was the first mass-produced car that could reliably climb hills — a feature that made it the country's best-selling auto from 1901 to 1907. Olds' second automotive venture, REO, is now defunct. Even its famous trucks are no longer made. But Lansing remains Oldsmobile headquarters today. Olds and his auto ventures star in the R. E. Olds Museum.

R.E. OLDS TRANSPORTATION MUSEUM

Not many people realize that Lansing native Ransom E. Olds was one of the towering pioneers of the auto industry. The Oldsmobile curved-dash runabout was the world's first mass-produced car. From 1901 to 1907, it sold more than all other models combined. Although Olds is responsible for Oldsmobile's headquarters remaining in Lansing to this day, he left after disagreements in 1904 and formed the REO Motor Car Company (named after his initials), also in Lansing. The REO automobile proved fabulously successful, too, but succumbed during the Depression.

The museum displays over 50 Oldsmobiles, REOs, and less well known automobiles built in Lansing. Here you'll see the **1897**

Oldsmobile (the very first production Oldsmobile); a famous 1904 Curved Dash model, a concourse-class **1931 REO Royale** convertible; and a rare concourse-class **1911 Olds Limited.** It's fascinating to see the clunky early models evolve into powerful, sleek, flashy models like the 1959 Super 88 and the 1970 Cutlass Supreme. A separate room filled with Olds engines chronicles their growing power, climaxed by the last Rocket V8 engine made in 1990.

Another room features the trucks made by Olds's REO company. A jaunty **yellow REO Speedwagon truck** was once viewed here by the popular rock group REO Speedwagon, which had not been aware of the source of its name. The lively **gift shop** features an usually wide offering of Olds-related gadgets, toys, and other collectibles. *240 Museum Dr. (see below). (517) 372-0422. Mon-Sat 10-5, Sun noon-5. Adults $2.50, students/seniors $1.50.*

Michigan Museum of Surveying

This, the only surveying museum in the U.S., shows what a feat it was to survey Michigan by foot in the 19th century and what hardships surveyors endured. From 1815 to 1857, surveyors plotted out the state's 1,900 townships, each 36 square miles. At the museum is the rock which marked the spot southeast of Lansing from which all other measurements for the state are taken. Surveyors back then were paid $3 a day, with which they had to buy equipment and supplies and pay a field cook, hunter, rod man, chain man, and brush cutter. Historical photos show some of these intrepid men, who had to push straight through dense swamps to follow lines.

Michigan's famous surveyor, William Burt, was first alerted to the presence of huge iron lodes in the Upper Peninsula by deflections in his compass. His solar compass, invented in 1835, is on display here. A revolutionary improvement in the accuracy of field surveying, it allowed much more accurate meridian measurements just by sighting the sun. *220 Museum Drive (see below). (517) 484-6605. Mon-Fri 8-5. Donations welcome.*

Directions to MUSEUM DRIVE: *Museum Drive is just east of the Grand River and downtown Lansing, south off Michigan Avenue. Quickest, easiest freeway directions: from U.S. 127, I-96, or I-69, take I-496 to downtown Lansing. Take Washington Ave. exit north to Michigan Ave., then east (right), then right again after you cross the river. Museum Dr. is south off Michigan Ave. just east of the Grand River and downtown. Free parking, now better controlled to save space for museum. If full, turn left onto Museum Dr., go under Michigan Ave. into Lansing Center structure.*

Elderly Instruments

*America's mail-order center for traditional music
is also the retail hub of a lively local folk scene.*

THE SQUARE brick Oddfellows' Hall in North Lansing has
been reborn as a folkies' heaven — 35,000 square feet full
of string instruments, recordings, sheet music, and much
more. Expanding into a connecting building next door has given
more room for more stock. Here you can find obscure recordings of
bluegrass, blues, country, folk, jazz, and music with traditional
roots from many countries and cultures, plus sheet music and
instructional videos. There's Tex-Mex and Celtic, African and Arab,
and many more. Even more remarkable is the fact that musicians
can try out almost any kind of acoustic instrument that exists, from
the complete line of legendary Martin guitars to pennywhistles and
concertinas, zydeco washboards and musical saws, simple rhythm
instruments and kazoos. There are over 1,600 guitars alone, 60% of
them new. You can find everything from an $87,000 Gibson Flying
V prototype to a simple starter guitar. Gift items include related
postcards, rubber stamps, trading cards, musical toys, dozens of T-
shirts featuring blues masters, and bumper stickers with sayings
like "String band music is a social disease" and "Hammer dul-
cimists never fret." The five-person repair shop is nationally known.

Though acoustic and traditional music have always been the
major focus at Elderly, the musician/staffers are no strangers to
rock 'n roll or gospel or jazz. They sell more electric guitars than
any other music store in Michigan. The front hall **information area
puts** customers in touch with regional folk-related festivals and
workshops. Early evenings the place is busy with lessons. Some
customers drive a long way just to visit Elderly.

It may seem improbable to find the world's largest dealer in
stringed instruments in a medium-sized Midwestern city. In fact,
much of Elderly's business comes from catalog sales. Its **four catalogs** (recordings, acoustic instruments and accessories, books and
videos, and amplified instruments) are themselves full of interesting
reading on such topics as recommended recordings or ukuleles
(billed as *the* instrument of the 90s). A more frequent publication
lists Elderly's current supply of used instruments, their prices, and
descriptions. Ask for the latest catalogs by calling (517) 372-7890.

The idea for this extraordinary institution occurred in Ann

Some Elderly staff out front with a collection of vintage Gibson guitars made in Kalamazoo. Elderly slowly built a national reputation for traditional acoustic instruments and music.

Arbor, at the open-mike nights at The Ark, the now-legendary folk-music coffeehouse. There Sharon McInturff met graduate student and banjo player Stan Werbin. A chance purchase of a guitar at a yard sale prompted them to think about starting a business selling used acoustic instruments (hence the "Elderly" name). But a store already occupied that niche in Ann Arbor, so they moved to East Lansing and, in 1972, set up shop in a tiny space across from the Michigan State University campus. They couldn't afford to stock much, but they would order anything — and at a discount. Werbin hailed from the aggressive business environment of New York City, so discounts were natural to him.

Although the popularity of folk music had waned just about everywhere since the boom years of the late '50s and early '60s, a solid core of folk fans and performers still existed, thanks to a number of popular festivals and a small but active coffeehouse circuit. Many local performers like Sally Rogers and Joel Mabus, M.S.U. undergraduates who went on to become well-known folk singers and musicians, inspired enthusiasm by teaching at Elderly and performing on or near campus.

Without a big local market, members of Lansing's growing folk community had to organize for themselves volunteer-run coffeehouses in churches and on campus. Thus developed an active folk community, less vulnerable to shifting mass-market taste than audiences attracted by big trends in entertainment.

Interest in folk music increased in the Lansing area as the boom ceased nationally. Elderly grew in its own grassroots way. By 1975, the big folk-oriented music stores were fading, and Elderly was well positioned to introduce a mail-order catalog and become a dominant force in the shrunken field of folk.

1100 N. Washington a block south of Grand River and a mile north of downtown Lansing. (517) 372-7880. Mail order phone (Mon-Fri 9-5): (517) 372-7890. Store hours: Mon-Wed 11-7, Thurs 11-9, Fri & Sat 10-6. &

THE NEARBY COMMERCIAL DISTRICT OF NORTH LANSING, ... , now called **Old Town,** is picturesquely clustered at the intersection of Grand River and Turner two blocks from Elderly, has become a weekend arts spot with two eateries open daily (page 439). . . . . **Bach Dor coffeehouse**/gallery (517-267-0606) books live folk, blues, and jazz almost nightly. . . . . Galleries to check out: **Otherwise Gallery**, a showcase for local artists with monthly Sunday openings that are big events (see page 443); the **Creole Gallery** featuring largely art of the African diaspora; the **Bare Bones Studio** (often women's art); and the **Real World Emporium** (517-485-2665). Its gallery and performance space is for "the lesbian and gay community and our friends," while the book and gift store focuses mostly on lesbian books. Coming, perhaps: a coffeehouse. Real World and the old gay bar up Turner give a gay flavor to the entire area on weekend evenings, though tolerant straights certainly won't feel out of place. . . . . Browsing and shopping highlights include the **Innovations Gallery** (page 431), **Pleats** custom interiors, and **Foibles Antiques and Uniques**, all on Grand River east of the river. Everyone's waiting to see who can put a deal together to buy the old Estes Furniture building on Grand River west of the river. With six storefronts, it will have a big impact on the area.

GOOD ANTIQUING IN THE LANSING AREA . . . . . in terms of quantity and quality. **The Wooden Skate** (517-349-1515) is a big shop occupying several buildings of an old farm at 1259 W. Grand River, a mile or so east of the Meridian Mall in Okemos. Five or so miles farther east, the attractive small town of **Williamston** has more shops and small malls. Call (517) 655-5621 for info. **Mason**, the Ingham county seat south of Lansing off U.S. 27, has a district of four large, quality malls in old warehouses along the train tracks northwest of downtown. Call (517) 676-9753.

Michigan State University museums and more

Natural history, art, Michigan history, folklife, astronomy – all are presented to the general public with intelligence and enthusiasm.

COMPARED with universities that have had over a century's worth of archaeological and natural history expeditions, Michigan State hasn't received the rare artifacts, unusual specimens, donations of art, or bequests that build up the most prestigious museum collections over generations. Up through World War II, Michigan State's alumni body was made up mainly of farmers, teachers, and such — not lines of work likely to result in gifts of magnificent buildings or choice libraries of rare books to the old alma mater.

But what M.S.U.'s museums lack in accumulations of rare and costly possessions, they usually make up in spirit — a real excitement about teaching and an enthusiasm for reaching out and connecting up with the everyday experience of the general public. M.S.U. museums are unusually well suited for family outings with children.

MICHIGAN STATE UNIVERSITY MUSEUM is M.S.U.'s many-sided museum of natural science, history, folk life, paleontology, and anthropology.

On the first floor, **Heritage Hall** has small dioramas of Michigan logging camps and locks, a fishing wharf, forts and copper mines, along with appealing, authentically detailed life-sized re-creations of a country kitchen, a general store, and a fur-trading post. A shed houses a 1904 Oldsmobile curved-dash runabout, the world's first popular-priced car, which turned Lansing into a center of the auto industry. The interesting **Special Exhibits Gallery** generally highlights folk culture: the likes of African-American quilts, or Finnish saunas, or duck blinds and decoys. There's a good, small **gift shop**.

Upstairs, seven North American habitats, from forests to grasslands, tropics to tundra, are represented in huge dioramas in **Habitat Hall**. Sweeping scenes with large animal specimens, and tiny insects and plants make it fun to examine these in detail. The hall's central area has two complete skeleton models of the North American dinosaurs, allosaurus and stegosaurus. Changing major exhibits in the **East and West Galleries** include natural and cultural history topics related to Michigan.

On the lower level, the **Orientation Room** offers well-chosen films, often on nature or Michigan history. **The Hall of Evolution** does a good job of illustrating every geological time period with scenic dioramas and with samples of animal and plant fossils formed in that time. **The Hall of World Cultures** has colorful, interesting displays of artifacts: shadow puppets from Java, swords from many cultures, the ritual uses of African masks, South American clothing, and more. The **Great Lakes Indians Gallery** features changing exhibits on woodlands Indian culture. *On West Circle Drive on the old part of the campus. Call (517) 355-2370 for directions, information on* **classes**, **activities**, **exhibits**. *Open Mon-Fri 9-5, Thurs until 9, Sat 10-5, Sun 1-5. & Free; donations welcome. Metered visitor parking in front, sometimes scarce. See page 442.*

THE KRESGE ART MUSEUM, select and intimate, makes up in clever presentation what its collection lacks in depth. Highlights are wide-ranging: Zurbaran's dramatic "Vision of St. Anthony" and a gigantic 1967 color-field canvas by Morris Louis. The introductory gallery of Greek through medieval art has a wonderful way of getting you to really look at individual small objects. A strength of this art museum is its collection of 1960s and 1970s art. On display is Andy Warhol's famous lithograph "Marilyn" and Keinholz's "Aperitif Suze." *Just east of Collingwood and Farm Lane on the old part of the M.S.U. campus. Call (517) 355-7631 for directions, changing exhibits, special events. School-year hours: weekdays except Thurs 9:30-4:30, Thurs 12-8, weekends 1-4. Summer hours: weekdays 11-4, weekends 1-4. Closed Thanksgiving vacation, mid-Dec.-early Jan., Easter, Mem. Day and July 4 weekend, and for a month during the summer (call to check dates). & Free admission, donations appreciated. Limited visitor parking in front of museum. See also page 442 for parking.*

ABRAMS PLANETARIUM. Enthusiastic presenters and top-notch projectors in the 150-seat auditorium make planetarium shows a popular form of entertainment for area families. Astronomy exhibits in the black light gallery are open weekdays (8:30-4:30) and before regular weekend shows. *Call (517) 355-4672 for this week's* **program**, *directions. At the corner of Shaw Lane and Science, south of the Red Cedar River. Look for the dome just east of Farm Lane. Closed a month in summer. Show times: Fri & Sat 8 p.m., Sun 4 p.m. Special shows for children at 2:30 Sun. Adults $3, students $2.50, kids 12 and under $2.* **Starline** *(star-gazing info on this week's skies): (517) 332-STAR.*

THE DAIRY STORE. Students in the M.S.U. dairy program manufacture and sell their own ice cream, yogurt, and cheeses right here. If you come by at the right time, you can look through the plate-glass window and watch. Students love the generous cones of rich ice cream; black cherry is a special favorite. Weirdest item: chocolate cheese (it's something like a dairy-based fudge), developed for kids who won't drink their milk. *On the west side of Farm Lane just south of Shaw Lane and the Abrams Planetarium. (517) 353-1663 (info line), (517) 355-8466 (dairy store). Mon-Fri 10-6, Sat noon-5. Free group tours need 2 weeks' notice, minimum of 10.*

CANOE THE RED CEDAR THROUGH CAMPUS . . . . . and up to the dam at Okemos or (if you portage around a dam) down to Potter Park. The **M.S.U. canoe livery,** also known as the Red Cedar Yacht Club, is behind Bessey Hall at Farm Lane. Call for hours. (517) 355-3397.

VISITOR PARKING ON CAMPUS. . . . . . is easy if you're willing to walk from two convenient **visitor lots** just south of the Red Cedar River. The **Spartan Stadium lot** at the very east end of Kalamazoo Street at Red Cedar Drive has a manned booth. It's a short, pretty walk to the Beal Garden and circle campus across a foot bridge or the Kalamazoo Street bridge. Another lot is on Farm Lane at Shaw, in front of the **Planetarium.** On weekends, spaces along the circle drives can often be found.

ANIMAL BARNS ARE OPEN TO THE PUBLIC. . . . . . Involving the public is a tradition that goes back to M.S.U.'s roots as Michigan Agricultural College and one of the oldest land-grant colleges. South of Mount Hope Road, much of the vast campus is devoted to animal husbandry. Visitors are welcome to stop by the barns any day, look at the animals, and ask questions of the staff.

FINE CRAFTS AND ART, AND GREAT PINBALL . . . . . are in downtown East Lansing across from Michigan State University, along Grand River and Albert, one block behind it. M.A.C. Avenue (it stands for "Michigan Agricultural College") is a connecting spine. Though still overwhelmingly oriented to undergraduates, with the predictable CD stores, fast food and ice cream shops, and bars, downtown is much more interesting than it was ten years ago. In comparison with hubs of sophistication like Birmingham and Ann Arbor, there can be a "we try harder" friendliness about East Lansing that's refreshing. But high rents have hurt the area's interest value. Competition from book superstores in Okemos has left East Lansing without a good general bookstore. .
   Retail standouts along M.A.C. include **Brother Gambit** (leather and wood

crafts and jewelry, 517-351-0825), **Campbell's Smoke Shop** (an old-fashioned tobacco shop with candy, knives, and gadgets, too, 517-332-4269), **Prints Ancient and Modern** (517-336-6366, a gallery of antique and contemporary prints), and the original **Pinball Pete's** (517-337-2544, Michigan's biggest and best games arcade, also with lovingly maintained pinball machines and bargain pop) with entrance around the corner on Albert. **Mackerel Sky Gallery of Contemporary Craft** (517-351-2211) is in the diagonal row of stores at the little plaza at Ann and M.A.C. A big survey of American craftspeople has named it one of the 100 best crafts galleries in the U.S. It also has cards and inexpensive gifts. Don't miss the back gallery space focusing on the work of one gallery artist.

A block east of the Marriott hotel at 433 Albert, the **Saper Galleries** (517-351-0815) has won a national following among collectors of international art for their friendly art search service and unusual frame design. Roy Saper, a former MSU music therapy student, and his staff buy paintings, sculpture, and original prints by artists from around the world — famous and not so famous, old and new, traditional and avant-garde, Western and non-Western. The gallery features changing shows, planned with little advance notice. Often very well-known artists like Peter Max appear in person. In the back are drawers and boxes of unframed prints, watercolors, etc. for customers to see. *Mon-Sat 10-6, Thurs to 9.* &

Just east of M.A.C. in the 300 block of East Grand River, the **Curious Used Book Shop** (517-332-0112) appealingly blends serious reading, comics, science fiction, sports memorabilia, and all sorts of old magazines and printed ephemera; It fills three floors and has an annex, too. **Jacobson's** department store at 333 E. Grand River (517-351-2550) has a second-floor restaurant overlooking the campus. . . . . **In Flight** at 507 E. Grand River (517-351-8100) combines Hackey Sacks and Frisbees with alternative clothing and Grateful Dead stuff. . . . . **Toomuchfun** (517-351-2030), the inventive rubber stamp store at 515 E. Grand River, is the progenitor of the similarly named Ann Arbor store. . . . . Still farther south, near Taco Bell, the second-story space of 541 East Grand River houses a changing but interesting collection of offbeat businesses like **Thomas & Sons Gallery** (517-333-4267). It reflects longtime arts activist David Thomas's interests in Mexican folk art, Michigan history, and antiques. The mainstay here is **FBC** (formerly Flat, Black & Circular), an excellent used CD store (517-351-0838). *There's a great deal of attended parking in ramps and lots along Albert, so you needn't worry about getting a ticket. Many downtown stores stay open Sunday afternoons and Thurs & Fri evenings.*

FOR FREE COMMUNITY CONCERTS AND OTHER EVENTS IN EAST LANSING. . . . . call the community events coordinator at City Hall, (517) 337-1731.

FIRST SUNDAY GALLERY WALK IN EAST LANSING AND OLD TOWN . . . . . bring an **arts open house** at some 18 galleries, museums, and restaurants. It's featured in a handy monthly **cultural calendar** available at Brother Gambit, Mackerel Sky, and elsewhere, or call (517) 351-2211. Openings are coordinated to happen at this time; Mackerel Sky and Old Town's Otherwise Gallery are said to have the best parties. In good weather, there's generally a live music concert at Fountain Square in front of the Radisson, M.A.C. and Albert.

GOOD FOOD AND DRINK. . . . . Here's a short, varied selection. . . . . In downtown East Lansing, **The Peanut Barrel**, 521 E. Grand River (517-351-0608), is the perfect good-time bar, in the opinion of one astute M.S.U. restaurant management grad: good burgers, good service, cold beer. **El Azteco** (517-351-9111), long a favorite subterranean hangout, remains a hot spot in its larger, brighter quarters at 225 Ann near M.A.C. Big Mexican menu goes beyond the usual; big servings, beer, margaritas keep customers forever. **Beggar's Banquet** (517-351-4573), at 218 Abbott between Grand River and Albert, has long been an idiosyncratic mix of haute cuisine and offbeat bar, frequented by governors Blanchard and Engler alike. Recently it has put more energy into their menu's lower end. . . . . Four miles east, at the old four-corners of Okemos Road and Hamilton that was downtown Okemos before the area on Grand River became mall city, The **Travelers' Club International Restaurant & Tuba Museum** (517-349-1775) has got to be Michigan's most naturally unusual restaurant. It features a different world cuisine each month — in addition to the small-town diner menu (burgers, hot dogs, malts) and healthy vegetarian-inclined fare. Now there's beer and wine (six beers on tap, 50 in bottles), and live music some weekends. One owner grew up in the Middle East; hence the international home cooking. The other's father played tuba, which led to the museum of tubas and euphoniums on the walls. Open daily, breakfasts, too.

ANOTHER CENTER OF LANSING'S ALTERNATIVE CULTURE . . . . . can be found at some of the shops on the friendly block of **East Michigan Avenue between Clemens and Fairview**, about 1 1/2 miles east of the capitol. In the early 20th century, these small storefronts were geared around a streetcar stop on the busy car line between Lansing and East Lansing. Today their attractive off-campus rents and convenient location have attracted an interesting variety of businesses, including **Wolfmoon Food Co-op** (517-482-0038), the delightfully old-fashioned **Gnome Sweet Shoppe** (517-372-8455), and **Capital City Comics and Books** (517-485-0416; good prices on good books). Many are open daily, including Sundays, and evenings. Stores with shorter hours include several worthwhile resale shops and Raupp Campfitters. **Gary's Kitchen** (517-484-5135) is a promising new takeout spot, 80% vegetarian, with a few tables. Limited menu (4 sandwiches, 4 salads, 4 entrees, plus desserts). No salt, no fat, from scratch. *Mon-Fri 11-7, Sat 11-6.*

A DESTINATION FABRIC STORE. . . . . probably the best in Michigan, is **The Fabric Gallery** (517-655-4573) at 146 W. Grand River in Williamston, 10 miles east of East Lansing. It's the place to find unusual cottons, silks, and wools, plus hard-to-find buttons and findings and patterns like Folkwear, Neue Mode, Burda and Sewing Workshop that aren't widely distributed. *Open Mon-Sat 10-5, Thurs to 8.*

W.J. Beal Botanical Garden and M.S.U. Campus Plantings

At America's first college of scientific agriculture, a gorgeous campus combines beauty and learning in a demonstration landscape.

THE OLDER PART of Michigan State University's campus fits the popular image of what a college *should* look like. It has curving drives and Collegiate Gothic buildings in a park-like setting full of stately trees and flowering shrubs. Huge beeches and some gnarled white oaks over 200 years old are between the Student Union and Beaumont Tower, just south of Grand River Avenue along West Circle Drive. Students walk to class through what has become a true arboretum over the years, with some 5,000 varieties of woody plants. Among M.S.U.'s huge, largely undergraduate student population, appreciation of the gardens, the majestic trees, and the beautiful displays of lilacs, azaleas, and viburnum is surprisingly widespread — partly because the tucked-away nooks of the Beal Botanical Garden and the winding paths along the Red Cedar River are popular trysting spots.

Campus plantings have here been a central part of the institution's mission for well over a hundred years. Michigan State started in 1857 as the first U.S. agricultural college to teach scientific agriculture (a distinction shared with Penn State). The campus has long been regarded as a great outdoor laboratory for teaching, research, and observation. Horticulture, botany, and landscape architecture classes take advantage of the campus always increasing display of the widest possible variety of trees, shrubs, and woody vines suited to this climate. Very few planted environments in the Middle West have enjoyed such sustained commitment for virtually 150 years.

Highlights of campus plantings include:

◆ **The Beal Botanical Garden**, an outdoor museum of living plants arranged by family and by economic use. See plants used for dyes, flavorings, and perfumes, along with flowering plants good for honeybees, and select landscaping and vegetable species.

Exotic flowering landscape specimens have been planted on slopes descending from the gazebo entrance on West Circle Drive. The steep banks were created when clay was dug here in the 1850s for the fledgling college's first brick buildings. Below is a flat, sunken garden. Here specimen plants and signs march like columns of soldiers in rows of regular rectangles of soil. The signs, well written and informative, are a big part of what makes visiting this garden so enjoyable.

One section focuses on common weeds — plants that invade field crops. In the injurious plant section, there's poison ivy, neatly staked and marked with a red sign of warning. There are plants used in modern pharmaceuticals; cotton, flax, hemp, and other fiber plants; and plants used as food by Indians — all described as to origin, use, and culture. Don't miss the display of endangered Michigan plants below the entrance stairs by the IM Building.

By a charming **goldfish pond** around behind the library, there are benches and a plaque commemorating botany professor William James Beal, his 40 years of service to Michigan Agricultural College (as M.S.U was known into the 1920s), and his pioneering experiments in hybridizing corn. In 1873 Beal established this garden. According to the staff, the Beal Garden is "the oldest continuously operating botanical garden" in the U.S. *Look for the entrance **gazebo** by the IM Sports Building on West Circle Drive, not too far from the*

The Beal Botanical Garden is an outdoor museum of plants, neatly arranged and labeled according to use (pharmaceuticals, herbs, dyes, etc.), family, or, in the case of weeds, according to where and how they grow. The beautifully landscaped valley setting by the Red Cedar River attracts many non-botanists, too.

Beal Entrance off Michigan Avenue. A box along the walk usually contains a free brochure about the gardens, with map and general introduction. (517) 355-9582. No charge. Guided group tours ($1/adults; 50¢/child with $15 minimum) can be arranged in advance. &: enter from Kalamazoo St. on the west side or from the south side of the Library on the east side.

◆ **The azalea and rhododendron garden** has soil adapted to acid-loving plants. Its displays are spectacular from late April through May and even into June. *By the music school just north of the Beal Garden across West Circle Drive. &: no sidewalk, but can be entered via lawn area.*

◆ **Landscaping groupings and collections of dogwoods, viburnums, and clematis.** These beautiful paths with their secret nooks show the lush, sensuous effects that can be achieved with screens and ground covers in narrow, shady spaces. The display of spring bulbs and early-blooming woody plants begins in March and gets into high gear from mid-April through May and early June. *Behind and alongside the I-M Sports Building just west of the Beal Garden. &: yes, from Kalamazoo St. the west entrance to Beal.*

◆ **The Old Horticulture Gardens** are gorgeous in spring because of all the lilacs and flowering crabs around the pool. "Old Hort," was redesigned and planted to reflect a park like setting. *On East Circle Drive at the northern end of Farm Lane. &*

◆ **The Botany Teaching Greenhouses** contain plants used to teach M.S.U. botany classes. Interpretive labels tell you a lot about what you're looking at. Inside are a **tropical rainforest room**, complete with mountain waterfall and stream; a Florida-like **subtropical room**; a **desert house**; and a **butterfly house** aflutter with activity. Zebra and monarch butterflies are here year-round, joined by swallowtails and other kinds in spring. Wear bright colors, stand still, and a butterfly might alight on you! Behind the Natural Sciences Building on the north side of East Circle Dr. just east of Farm Lane. Tours may be scheduled year-round for $1.50/adult, $1/child. Open Mon-Fri 8-5, Sat & Sun 10-2. (517) 355-0229. &

◆ **The Horticulture Demonstration Gardens** are so extensive and so spectacular, even in fall and winter, that they deserve their own chapter. See page 449.

The campus has been planted to be attractive at all seasons, and it is. Early bulbs and flowering witch hazel are out in March, followed by a panoply of flowering shrubs and vines, plus annuals, that extend the season up to frost. The dramatic grasses in the new

Horticulture Demonstration Gardens look good well into winter. Fall color and winter bark textures and branch forms are important considerations in plant selection.

Plant-lovers could get a good horticultural education just by studying campus plantings on a series of fine days throughout the year. Many campus plants are labeled; some have excellent explanatory signs for gardeners about which varieties to choose and what plant materials go well together. **"Campus Plantings,"** a map and complete guide to 15 shrub and tree collections and 200 individual specimens, is available from Campus Park and Planning. The brochure is ten years old; it will be updated early in 1997. Meanwhile for a current list of the campus woody plant collection, call or write Dr. Frank Telewski at Campus Park and Planning, 412 Olds Hall, M.S.U., East Lansing, MI 48824. (517) 355-9582. For info about the collection on the worldwide web, visit http://www.cpp.msu.edu/beal.htm.

A BEAUTIFUL, LEAFY PATH . . . . . for walking, biking, and jogging runs along the south side of the Red Cedar River almost the entire length of the campus, from the Kellogg Center on Harrison Road past the statue of "Sparty," the M.S.U. Spartan, to Hagadorn Road.

WHY MICHIGAN'S AGRICULTURAL COLLEGE WASN'T STARTED IN ANN ARBOR OR YPSILANTI. . . . . . Michigan State has such a splendid campus because it has long been one of the nation's premiere colleges of agriculture. Credit goes to the enlightened Michigan farmers who in 1849 began lobbying for a state college to promote modern agriculture. The University of Michigan in Ann Arbor and Michigan Normal in Ypsilanti both wanted the new agriculture school, but its farmer backers insisted on an autonomous college. They chose as its site 677 acres of forest five miles east of the new state capital in Lansing, conveniently located just south of the old plank road to Detroit (now Grand River Avenue).

Michigan's agriculture leaders became important backers of the 1862 Morrill Act. It established land-grant colleges to be funded by sales of federal lands and geared toward broad-based, practical education and public service for all levels of society. Michigan State and Pennsylvania State share honors as the first land-grant colleges.

For many decades, manual labor, three hours a day, was expected of all students — part of the hands-on laboratory approach which also enabled poor students to afford a college education.

M.S.U. Horticultural Demonstration Gardens

*Plants and designers work their magic
to create a delightful floral environment
and a fun introduction for kids to the world of plants.*

THE HORTICULTURAL GARDENS at Michigan State University testify to the transforming power of plants. Here on a generally bleak-looking, post-1960 part of the campus, the expanded horticultural gardens have wrought their magic on the utilitarian, boxy Plant and Soil Science building. In their former home on the picturesque old campus, where graceful lampposts accent handsome Collegiate Gothic buildings, the gardens were a beloved campus landmark, a secret nook created by mature shrubs. Cramped quarters necessitated the move to the present, 7.5-acre gardens. Energetic fundraising from the private sector enabled the impressive new gardens to be built. Funds for the endowment are still being sought.

The new gardens, opened in 1993, work the same civilizing magic on this huge campus, considered a party school even by its most loyal and intellectual alums. The gardens' variety of visitors is remarkable. New as they are, the gardens create a striking environment, thanks largely to the great, tall sprays of ornamental grasses, with their dramatic background texture. Up to 10 and 12 feet tall and four feet across, they are planted in islands as large-scale background foils for detailed, small foreground plantings.

Towards dusk is an especially nice time to visit the gardens. The scents are stronger in the cool air, and those flowers that are brightly colored seem to shimmer with their own light as your eyes' receptors change from using cones to rods. (See page 502 for the explanation.)

There's so much to see here that repeat visits are in order at different times in the growing season. In fall, after a killing frost, the grasses turn golden and reddish, forming a colorful background for cold-resistant flowers and leaves. Michigan gardeners will find lots of ideas for new plants and plant combinations here. Customized tours lasting 45 minutes to 1 1/2 hours are offered June through September. They cost $1/adult, 50¢ for children, with a $15 minimum and two-week notice required.

A lot of garden architecture – pergolas, gazebos, arbors, topiary frames, even an artificial hill – was used to enliven a part of the campus that's as flat and bare as the most unpromising subdivision.

To help plan your visits so you won't miss tucked-away areas, here's a checklist and brief description of the garden complex.

◆ **Parking** and **entrance pavilion** off Bogue south of Wilson Road. Parking surrounds the **floral peacock**, 14 feet high. The body, built on a frame stuffed with packaging peanuts and eight to 12 inches of dirt, is planted in begonias and ageratum. Colorful annuals make up the 35-foot tail along the ground.

First, get your useful gardens map (and your weekday parking token) at the **Visitor Information Center** just inside the side wing of the Plant and Soil Sciences Building to the right of the round entrance pavilion. A select garden bookshop is inside, with free information on special **gardening programs** and classes for the general public. **Sparty's Flowers & Garden Barn** (517-353-3770), run by horticulture students and open Mondays through Fridays from 11 to 5:30, is in this building; ask for directions.

◆ The **4-H Children's Garden**, alongside the parking area, is such a novelty it seems sure to become a popular regional attraction. Gardens relate to plant themes – 62 in all – designed with kids' interests and questions in mind. The **Pizza Garden** shows the herbs used in America's favorite school lunch. The **Sense-a-tional Garden** appeals to all the senses, with plants like aromatic ginger and luffa sponges. There's a **pharmacy garden**, a **perfume garden**, and a "small world" globe around which radiate gardens growing important foods for various parts of the world. An **African-American garden** grows plants used in Africa and plants introduced from Africa to America (including hibiscus, okra, black-eyed peas, watermelon, and cucumbers).

Everything is sized for children, and there are no "NO" signs. This type of children's garden is a first on any college campus. Children can wind through a maze, dance on chimes, and swing a gate that makes frogs in a pond spit water. Topiary teddy bears grow on frames designed by the topiary maker for the movie *Edward Scissorhands*. Group **tours** and **workshops** here are most welcome. Call (517) 355-0348. *Open April through October. Free.*

◆ The **Idea Gardens** are another small area of specialty gardens, just west of the 4-H Children's Garden on the south edge of the main perennial garden. Volunteer master gardeners tend themed plots: vegetables, companion planting, cacti, herbs, plants for special needs children, and butterfly-attracting herbs.

◆ The **DeLapa Perennial Garden** of over 1,800 labeled varieties, already described, is behind the large, round entrance pavilion. Don't miss the water lilies by the pond. In back, to the west, **Frank's Nursery and Crafts Rose Garden** includes the latest All-America Rose selections and hundreds of other roses. (Outside financial support from individuals and institutions has permitted the Horticultural Gardens' grand expansion.)

◆ It's easy to miss the large and impressive **Carter Annual Trial Garden**. From the rose gardens, take the axial path north between the Teaching Greenhouses and the Pesticide Research Center. Past the houses, you'll come to a fountain and sunken garden. From here to the distant pool, over a thousand varieties of bedding plants are at their best in July and August. Among them are the **All-American Selection Trial Garden**, part of a nationwide program to test seed companies' new flowers in different climates, and **Fleuro Select**, European selections on trial.

Visitors are welcome to look inside the **teaching greenhouses,** full of student horticulture projects. They're open weekdays, 8 a.m.-4:30 p.m. Gardeners are well advised to bring cameras and notebooks; these gardens are full of examples of plant varieties and planting combinations that will work well in many Michigan yards.

*On the southeast side of the Michigan State campus, south of Wilson Rd. off Bogue St., one street east of Farm Lane. Enter off Bogue just north of the railroad tracks to find inexpensive visitor parking. Open from April through October, dawn to dusk. Though the gardens open April 1, it takes a good deal of warm spring weather before even the perennials and grasses amount to much. Planting annual beds is delayed until after Memorial Day. Guided **tours** $1/adult, 50¢/student. Call (517) 355-0348 to arrange. ♿ Free admission.*

A SURPRISING ALL-SEASONS WORLD OF TEXTURES AND SHAPES . . . . . can be explored just south and across the railroad tracks from the Horticultural Demonstration Gardens. On the site of the old campus nursery, the **Clarence E. Lewis Landscape Arboretum** creates some wonderful effects. "In springtime the redolent trail through the flowering magnolias, viburnums, and witch hazels accentuates a spectacle of pastels," writes Victoria McAree. "Dogwoods, crabapples, and spireas offer their characteristic white, pink, or purple blooms. During summer, compare and contrast foliar textures and numerous shades of green. Yellow, red and russet tones abound in the fall. . . . . In the wintertime, the prominent forms of deciduous trees and shrubs stand out against a backdrop of snow-laden evergreens." *Park off Bogue just north of the tracks.*

West Michigan

WHILE West Michigan is best known for its sand dunes and sugar-sand beaches, its history and development have been greatly influenced by a strong Dutch subculture. Holland and Grand Rapids form the center of the conservative Dutch-American subculture, which has a strong work ethic and a deep streak of cleanliness and environmentalism. Unlike the auto plants' history of bitter labor relations on the eastern side of the state,

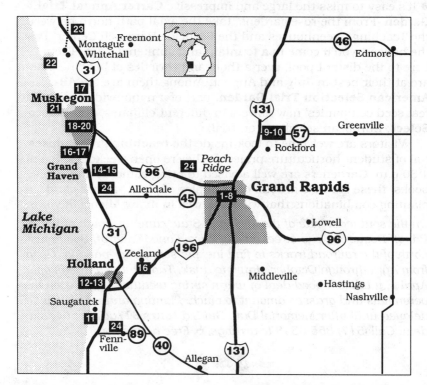

labor relations in West Michigan are generally quite good. Before participatory work practices were in vogue, they were already being practiced here.

In Grand Rapids, once known as America's furniture city, and Holland, locally-owned companies have prospered and grown into internationally-known firms. Office furniture manufacturers Steelcase and Herman Miller have two of the most respected management cultures in the U.S. A Holland High School shop teacher founded Haworth in his basement and developed it into another big office furniture maker. The Meijer family has successfully pioneered the dual grocery/discount store business. Donnelly and Prince have become major auto parts suppliers. Amway took direct sales to a new worldwide level. All have contributed much in the way of civic improvements to their home towns.

Ethical principles are discussed more here than most other places because many people have had a rigorous religious education. Many business leaders come from Holland's Hope College (affiliated with the Reformed Church of America) or Grand Rapids' Calvin College (run by the Christian Reformed Church). Grand Rapids is also the U.S. center of religious publishing. Its four reli-

Information sources: CONVENTION & VISITOR BUREAUS

Allegan Co. Tourist & Rec. Council
(Saugatuck, Allegan, Fennville, Glenn)
(616) 673-2479

Mecosta County CVB
(Big Rapids, Remus)
(616) 769-7640, (800) 833-6697

Grand Haven-Spring Lake CVB
(616) 842-4499, (800) 303-4094

Grand Rapids Area CVB
(616) 459-8287, (800) 937-8837

Muskegon County CVB
(Muskegon, Whitehall, Montague)
(616) 722-3751, (800) 235-FUNN

Saugatuck-Douglas CVB
(616) 857-1701

Information sources: LOCAL CHAMBERS OF COMMERCE

Allegan (616) 673-2479
Big Rapids (616) 796-7649
Cedar Springs (616) 696-3260
Evart (616) 734-5555
Fennville (616) 561-5013
Fremont (616) 924-0770
Grand Haven- (616) 842-4910
Grandville (616) 531-8890
Greenville (616) 754-5697
Hastings (616) 945-2454
Holland (616) 392-2389

Hudsonville (616) 896-9020
Ionia (616) 527-2560
Pentwater (616) 869-4150
Plainwell (616) 685-8877
Spring Lake (616) 842-4910
Wayland (616) 792-6644
White Cloud (616) 689-6607
Whitehall (616) 893-4585
Wyoming (616) 531-5990
Zeeland (616) 772-2494

❶ **Gerald Ford Museum** (p. 455). Superb profile of Ford & his presidency. Revamped with more on the 1970s, fall of Saigon, loss to Carter. Much for fans of Betty Ford.

❷ **Amway Grand Plaza.** Posh union of ornate old Pantlind Hotel & new tower. Several excellent restaurants, two floors of fine shops. (616) 774-2000.

❸ **John Ball Zoo** (p. 464). Dramatic hillside setting with. Pacific Northwest aquarium, African forest edge, Patagonian penguinarium. Other hits: nocturnal animals, playful otters, chimps.

❹ **Ed's Breads** (p. 463). Marvelous Eastern European breads in Polish/ Lithuanian neighborhood setting.

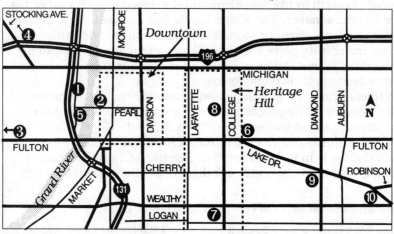

❺ **Public Museum** (p. 458). Spectacular new place perched over river. Fine displays on Michigan Indians, planetarium; carousel; neat macro/micro dioramas of dune, river, forest, field. Fascinating **Furniture City is** multifaceted look at industry, styles, workers.

❻ **Heritage Hill** (p. 470). Grand Rapids' elite residential area from 1840s to 1920s. Many architectural styles and detailing for the city's style- and craftsmanship conscious business leaders. Also one of Frank Lloyd Wright's best preserved homes.

❼ **Meyer May House** (p. 467). Meticulous restoration of 1908 Frank Lloyd Wright house with original furnishings is worth a trip to Grand Rapids.

❽ **Voigt House** (p. 474). Victorian chateau with all the original trappings.

❾ **Heartwood** (p. 476). Choice Arts & Crafts and moderne pieces, proprietor who knows a lot about local. Mission manufacturers.

❿ **Eastown** (p. 476). Urban subcenter with offbeat shops.

Heritage Hill B&Bs (p. 476). Personal lodgings in a variety of superb historic homes furnished in period style.

Highlights of
Grand Rapids

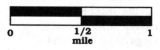

0   1/2   1
           mile

Gerald R. Ford Museum

Refocused to give new perspective to the 1970s,
this superb museum illuminates the short, eventful
presidency of Grand Rapids' native son.

ALREADY one of Michigan's most interesting museums, the Ford Museum has undergone dramatic renovations. By late April, 1997, it should become more prominent nationally. Meanwhile, it remains open. The building itself enjoys a striking setting on the west bank of the wide Grand River across from downtown Grand Rapids.

Gerald Ford was only president for two and a half years, but he enjoyed a rich political career and confronted a number of important challenges as president. He earned a reputation as an honest politician, which was why Nixon chose him for vice president after Spiro Agnew resigned in disgrace and soon was convicted for taking bribes. The museum reveals both high and low moments in his life and shows the role of Ford's exemplary namesake and stepfather, who had a Grand Rapids paint and varnish business, in forming his character. The display explores Ford's fateful 1974 decision to pardon Nixon in order to get the affair behind the nation and avoid months of court proceedings. It includes some of the many letters of outrage Ford subsequently received.

At Ford's suggestion, plans are in the works for a display to include recently declassified cables between Washington and Saigon that dramatically bring back that horrific time when Saigon was falling to the North Vietnamese. The display on Ford's fateful 1974 decision to pardon Nixon includes some of the many letters of outrage Ford subsequently received.

Ford's 1976 loss to Jimmy Carter, when he came from 20 percentage points behind and almost beat the Georgia governor, is colorfully documented. New displays will show one reason for the loss: the strong challenge by Ronald Reagan in that year's Republican convention weakened Ford's chances considerably. Visitors will be able to enter a room that recreated the convention's noise and visual bedlam.

Betty Ford's courage and candor as First Lady is also nicely captured on a wall of photos, text, and memorabilia. Pro-choice and pro-ERA, she was the first First Lady to publicly profess opinions different from her husband's. She became as controversial in her

President Gerald Ford in the Oval Office. A full-size replica of the room during Ford's presidency lets visitors feel what it's like to be in that intimidating space.

time as Hillary Clinton. Her outspokenness is captured here in a dramatic video of a *60 Minutes* interview with Morley Safer before the 1976 election.

The museum's most popular display is the full-size **replica of the Oval Office** in the White House, just as it looked while Ford was president. It effectively gives the visitor a sense of what it's like to be in that room, known to intimidate even seasoned politicians. It is being augmented with Ford's voice, just as if it were a normal work day during his presidency.

Most prominent of all: a huge **interactive world map** that allows visitors with a push of the button to see what was happening globally during the 1970s. A vibrant introductory exhibit recreates the 1970s, showing everything from an episode from "The Mary Tyler Moore Show" to CBS news clips.

Every hour, a **28-minute film** on Gerald Ford's life and presidency is presented in the comfortable auditorium. A small **gift shop** is tightly focused on presidential items, including real campaign buttons ($3 each, both parties), postcards of past presidents and their wives, lots of inexpensive souvenirs for kids, and many books (some autographed) by and about Ford.

A gallery offers **changing exhibits** on subjects that may have nothing to do with Ford or the presidency, such as the Civil War (spring, 1997).

North side of Pearl Street on the west bank of the Grand River; another entrance is off Bridge. From U.S. 131, take Pearl St exit 31B. By foot from downtown: less than 1/2 mile via a pedestrian bridge behind Welsh Auditorium and the Amway Grand Plaza. By car from downtown, take the Pearl Street bridge west and turn right, or take the Michigan Ave./ Bridge St. bridge and turn left. (616) 451-9263; Mon-Sat 9-4:45; Sun 12-4:45. &. Adults $2 ($3 after April 1977), seniors $1.50/$2, children under 16 free.

NEAR THE FORD MUSEUM . . . . . Ah-Nab-Awen Bicentennial Park in front of the Gerald Ford Museum is pleasantly open to the sky and cityscape. It's studded with interesting landscape features and sculptures, including a fountain and a giant button children can climb through. The interconnected, curved walkways are favored by strollers, dog-walkers, and joggers. . . . . A **pedestrian bridge** (a former interurban trestle, actually) lets you cross the Grand in leisure, look down at the water, and walk over to downtown and the Riverwalk behind the Grand Center complex.

MINOR LEAGUE BASEBALL HAS COME TO WEST MICHIGAN . . . . . A Class A affiliate of the Oakland Athletics, the **West Michigan Whitecaps** play at Old Kent Park in Comstock Park just north of Grand Rapids. Tickets ($3-$6) are available through Ticketmaster or at the park, off U.S. 131 on West River Drive. Call (800) 227-7946 (within area code 616 only) or (616) 451-6166.

GRAND RAPIDS EVENTS & VISITOR INFORMATION . . . . . is conveniently available from the super-helpful **Visitor Information Center**. It's at 134 Monroe Mall downtown, just south of Monroe at Pearl, kitty-corner from the Amway Grand Plaza hotel. Open 10-5:30 weekdays, or call (800) 678-9859 for a visitor packet and events calendar. . . . . *On the Town* magazine, free at many hotels and visitor destinations, is an excellent source of events and entertainment at large and small venues. . . . . . **Calvin College** offers a meaty cultural calendar of music, theater, and lectures, many free. For events info and tickets, call (616) 957-6282 weekdays from 8 to 5, or later for recording. Calvin's January Series of free noonday lectures by many nationally prominent authors and commentators in the Fine Arts Center is widely appreciated. Former Surgeon General C. Everett Koop has been an annual speaker. Moral aspects of current affairs is a common theme.

Van Andel Museum Center/ Public Museum of Grand Rapids

An exceptional city museum offers the fullest look at Michigan Indians, a brilliant, rich view of the city's furniture industry, and more.

THERE'S SO much to do at this monumental and accessible "entertainment/educational center," as the new museum describes itself, it can be the focus of an entire weekend — especially for someone with a great interest in furniture ("Furniture City" is the museum's centerpiece) or for a family. The rich, dense exhibits can be browsed quickly or studied in depth and visited repeatedly. The spectacular building offers interesting cityscape panoramas across the Grand River to downtown — a welcome dose of natural light in winter — and the moderately-priced **cafe** has unusually good soups, sandwiches, and salads, plus espresso and desserts. A change of pace is offered by 50¢ rides on a big 1928 carousel perched over the river.

The museum building alone cost $35 million. A large gift from Amway co-founder Jay Van Andel resulted in its new name, a matter of some local controversy. Museum staff made a big point of including emotional community touchstones in the new museum: a popular whale skeleton from the old museum, for instance, and the

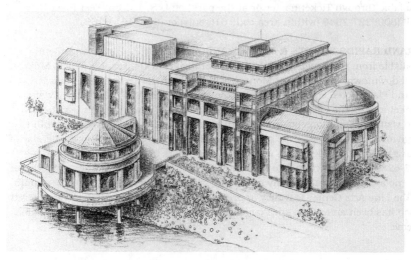

Grand Rapids has Michigan's largest Indian population. The big permanent exhibit "Anishabek: The People of This Place" shows how West Michigan's many Odawa, Ojibwa, and Potawatomi continue a living culture despite huge obstacles. Here are five generations of one family: Rosie Holmberg, baby Sadie Olsen, Christa Olsen, Stella Gibson, and Rose Shalifoe.

Romanesque clock tower and pieces of patterned tile flooring from the late, lamented Victorian city hall, destroyed for urban renewal in the Calder Plaza area. The Public Museum has been collecting broadly since 1854. The extent and quality of its collections is outstanding.

Highlights are:

◆ **"Anishabek: The People of the Place"** is the most extensive, fullest, and most satisfying illumination anywhere of Michigan's indigenous Odawa, Ojibwa, and Pottawatomi peoples. In excellent introductory video interviews, they present themselves as our neighbors, links in a chain of culture that has survived very difficult challenges like boarding schools designed to replace family tradition with mainstream American culture. Grand Rapids, as the industrial metropolis drawing workers from the hinterlands of western and northern Michigan, has the largest Indian population in the state. The exhibit also explores in detail and concept traditional crafts like beadwork, basketmaking, and quillwork, and tackles ideas like how Buffalo Bill's Wild West shows popularized the stereotyped image of Plains Indians, which became mistakenly applied to native peoples of Michigan's Eastern Woodlands as well.

Belts and drive shafts attached to the Corliss-type steam engine (rear) powered woodworking machinery from the Phoenix Furniture Factory circa 1910. It's part of the Furniture City permanent exhibit.

◆ **Habitat Exhibits** about the natural environment are the biggest hit with kids. (Adults will enjoy them, too.) Huge dioramas of a dune forest/lakeshore, a Grand River bayou near Grand Haven, a woods, and cropland let viewers lose themselves in a scene that's full of push-button sounds (bullfrogs, rushes rustling in the wind) and details kids love to pick out. Some things are seen through underground peepholes: muskrats in their lodge, a mole hole, a dead mouse teeming with maggots (a particular favorite). Dramatic magnified models show what sand, a drop of clear marsh water, and a slice of farm soil are like.

◆ **"Streets of Grand Rapids,"** as seen at night, dramatically and authentically recreates 11 Grand Rapids shops of the 1890s with antique merchandise chosen from the collections and interestingly displayed. It includes city sounds of the era.

◆ **"Furniture City,"** the largest exhibit of all, is a real tour-de-force. An entire section of the 1910 Phoenix Furniture Factory shows machines at work stations attached by belts to a line shaft moved by a dramatic, big Corliss steam engine in the lobby. (Silent electricity powers it now.) The exhibit tells how, starting in the 1870s and

1880s, Grand Rapids provided a rapidly growing America with affordable, stylish furniture — thanks to its location at the edge of the North Woods but nor far from the big mail-order houses in Chicago. 1920s film clips bring to life scenes in the city and surrounding lakeside lodges as toured by buyers to the big annual Grand Rapids furniture market (now held in High Point, North Carolina). By the early 1920s the exodus of middle-market home furniture manufacturers to the South had already begun. "Furniture City" shows how the boost World War II gave to the remaining office and institutional furniture sectors more than made up for jobs lost earlier. Big Grand Rapids-area furniture firms include not only famous names like Steelcase and Herman Miller but giants in the more obscure fields of auditorium, school, and automotive seating. Fascinating futuristic prototypes of office systems offer intriguing perspectives on changing office work life as it becomes more decentralized and flexible and less hierarchical.

Cheap but ornate furniture is what made Grand Rapids first prosper. A fancy-looking, machine-carved desk is shown to have a back like a packing crate. Excellent videos use local amateur actors to portray people who worked in the furniture industry, from lumber rippers to salesmen to owners. Each tells about his work and how he felt about the divisive 1911 strike, turning it into an event of high drama. Additional displays don't shrink from showing the industry's least attractive aspects: child labor, unfair treatment of blacks and Indians, and workplace dangers.

More videos at the Phoenix Furniture work stations show the actual work in progress, explained by retirees. Plans call for live furniture-making demonstrations with retiree docents.

People who love the furniture itself won't be disappointed. There's loads of great furniture here, interpreted in displays like "The Hollywood Fantasy" (movies influenced what people wanted in their homes; furniture from the *Gone with the Wind* set makes the point) and "The Designers Anointed" (about Charles Eames, Florence Knoll, and other luminaries involved in office furniture design). Folk art from Italy, Germany, and Eastern Europe inspired a vogue for painted furniture in the 1920s and 1930s. Museum reproductions helped keep the upper end of domestic furniture alive in West Michigan, where Baker and Widdicomb remain.

◆ The **Chaffee Planetarium** shows astronomy programs ($1.50 extra) that change every three months. Viewings of the main show are typically at 11, 2, and 4 daily plus Friday and Saturday evenings at 8. Special shows for children run weekends at noon and 3. Laser light shows with rock music are weekend nights when the museum is closed; $5 admission. A narrated introduction to the season's brightest constellations and planets is shown daily at 1. No children under three, please. Call (616) 456-DOME for program information.

The museum is on Pearl St. just west of the Grand River downtown. From U.S. 131, take the Pearl Street exit 85B. From I-196 and the east, use Ottawa Ave. downtown exit 77C, take Ottawa south to Pearl, then west across the river. From I-196 and the west, take Lake Michigan Dr. exit 75. Lake Michigan becomes Pearl. (616) 456-3966 (programs). (616) 456-3977 (office). Open 9-5 daily, including holidays. ♿ $5/adult, $4/senior, $2 ages 3-17. $50 household pass admits to museum, Voigt House, planetarium, nature center.

GRAND RAPIDS' ETHNIC WESTSIDE . . . . . Hardly anyone thinks of Grand Rapids as a rich multi-ethnic city, so strong is its image as the epicenter of America's conservative Dutch Reformed subculture. But it is, and people who know where to look will be rewarded with good, authentic ethnic food at popular prices. Mexican-Americans live in many parts of the city. There are substantial Asian communities. African-Americans dominate the near southeast side. West of the Grand is the home turf of Lithuanians, Ukrainians, Germans, Latvians, more than a few American Indians, and enough Poles to build **St. Adalbert's**, a splendid domed, multi-towered basilica church as big as many European cathedrals. Seen from the freeway coming over the Grand's east bluff, it's memorable.

The commercial district around Bridge and Stocking is the most obvious ethnic area. (Bridge is the same street as Michigan Ave. on the east side. It's the street just north of the Gerald Ford Museum.) It's home to Polish and Mexican bakeries, two Mexican groceries, and Mexican and Polish restaurants. A nerve center of the West Side's huge Polish community is **American Bread**, a popular lunch counter and bakery (good enough, but no equal to Ed's). This was the home turf of Rocky, Max Apple's baker grandfather and hero of his autobiographical bestseller *Roommate*. (In the movie this westside neighborhood was transplanted to Pittsburgh.) *712 Bridge, a block west of Stocking. (616) 458-3201. Open daily 6:30-6:30, Sunday 7:30-6:30.* ♿

◆ **El Matador Mercado** is a small retail outlet of El Matador Tortilla Company, now moved out of the neighborhood into a $3 million factory. Its corn chips are sold here in quantity, along with basics like salsa, many sizes of canned refried beans, chorizo, and a half-gallon of picante sauce for around $6.50. Hispanics are the fastest-growing segment of Grand Rapids' population, and Hispanic businesses have flourished. El Matador's founding family, Mike and Isabel Navarro, are among a dozen Mexican-American millionaires in the area. They came to western Michigan to pick celery after World War II. *653 Stocking. (616) 454-2163.*

Open daily 9:30-5, closed Sunday.

◆ **Moctezuma Cash and Carry** and **Maggie's Kitchen.** 636 Bridge. See p. 466.

◆ **Ed's Breads.** Ed's outstanding traditional East European breads are dense and flavorful, especially the sourer doughs, like the fabulous Latvian rye. At $1.75 to $2.50 for a big loaf, the breads here are a terrific value, and very good. So are the cookies, sweet-rolls, and rolls. Basics here, baked daily, are the huge, 2 1/4-pound loaf of Polish rye and a 2-pound whole wheat loaf. These are heavy, nutritious breads, truly the staff of life.

Customers from all walks of life, from as far as Muskegon and Holland, come here regularly. Founder Ed Parauka first baked and improved his Lithuanian and Polish grandmothers' recipes in his basement. When he got them right, he opened this shop. Eventually the baker's long hours got to Ed. Current owner/bakers are Barb and Oran Rankin, who were trained by Kathryn Kelly, who was trained by Ed. Their hand-rolled loaves are made without preservatives, rolling machines, or yeast stabilizers. Traditional baking is "more by instinct and experience — more alchemy," Kelly said. It's more time-consuming and more challenging.

Here is Ed's weekly schedule of specialty breads. *Come early in the day for best selection.* Load up on bread for your freezer on your way home. You won't be sorry. **Tuesday:** health bread, sourdough French bread. **Wednesday:** cream cheese-raisin, pumpernickel, oatmeal-honey bread **Thursday:** Latvian rye, sourdough French, health and potato bread. **Friday:** Lithuanian rye, oatmeal-honey. **Saturday:** bundukies. *1204 Leonard on Grand Rapids' northwest side, just west of Garfield across from Burger King. Leonard is a major east-west artery on the north side. From U.S. 131, take the Leonard St. exit and go west one mile. From downtown, take Division to Leonard, then west. (616) 451-9100. Tues-Fri 8 a.m.-6 p.m., Sat 8-noon.* ♿: one step. . . . . See also **Lewandoski's Market,** page 466.

NEXT TO ED'S ON LEONARD STREET . . . . . a large, well-stocked used book shop, **The Book Gallery,** carries a general line that includes everything from 50¢ books to expensive hard-to-find books. *(616) 459-4944. Open Tues-Fri 10-8, Sat 10-8. Call to confirm hours.* ♿: one step. . . . . Clean and well-organized, the **Tried and True Consignment Shop** on the corner carries quality furniture for resale. *(616) 774-9052. Mon-Fri 10-6, Sat 10-5.* ♿: one step.

FOR DUTCH IMPORTS . . . . . the places to go are **The Dutch Store** (616-452-9403), a cozy place in an old Dutch neighborhood, now Hispanic, at 1505 Grandville on the near south side, and **Peters Import Marketplace** (616-243-0649) in new quarters at 370 36th St., almost 5 miles south of downtown. Because of much Dutch immigration in the mid 20th-century, there's a big market for old country products: candy (double-salt licorice and Wilhelmina peppermints are classics); cheeses; butter cookies in fancy tins; an astounding array of scrub brushes and cleaning supplies; laces; and jewelry and other gifts.

John Ball Zoo

A gem of a zoo with a lush setting and wonderful views of playful otters, monkeys, and penguins.

WHAT gives this medium-size zoo its powerful and memorable sense of place is the way it winds up the steep glacial hill that rises abruptly from the adjoining level park on the flat valley floor of Grand Rapids' west side. Most zoos are flat. This one is vertical. Animal exhibits are tucked into grotto-like areas built of rocky shelves, some natural, some artificial. The rest of the hillside is in a semi-wild, natural state, covered by shrubby growth and shaded by trees. A 60-foot waterfall emerges from the hillside. On a summer day, the place seems like a lush oasis rising above nearby streets of closely-spaced bungalows.

The zoo has been here for a hundred years. Its effect on visitors is dramatic, as if they are entering an enchanted realm as they wind their way up the hill. Now years of construction projects are coming to a close. New and revamped exhibits are nearly all open, and the zoo's appeal to out-of-towners is far more potent. Another plus: walkways have been reconfigured with more frequent rest areas and wheelchair turnouts.

The zoo has over 600 animals. There are black bears and zebras, lions and tigers, and exotic birds. Here are some highlights.

◆ A **Michigan northwoods stream**, visible indoors and out, empties into the new **bald eagle aviary**. (Only hurt birds are confined to zoos.) Fish in the stream can be seen from all angles. In one place, zoo-goers are *below* the fish, looking up.

◆ The new **habitat immersion aquarium** will simulate the environment of the coastal Pacific Northwest. Colorful saltwater fish, including leopard sharks, swim through an underwater kelp forest. Other parts have octopus, and a crashing wave creates a tidal pool where anemone and starfish can be seen.

◆ The **penguinarium** shares a building with the aquarium. It recreates a rocky environment in far southern Patagonia, where playful penguins swim and strut. The cutaway underwater view shows how their streamlined bodies are adapted to water.

◆ **African Forest Edge.** This new exhibit shows a mixed environment where a savannah would meet the forest around a water hole. Here forest animals like the shy bongo (a large antelope adapted to move easily in the forest) meet zebras, vultures, crown cranes, and sitatunga (smaller antelopes whose long hoofs are well suited to muddy areas).

◆ **Great Ape Exhibit.** The new chimpanzee area next to the African Forest should be finished sometime in 1998.

◆ There's a wonderful **display of otters** whose playful antics can be seen from above and below water, thanks to a glass-walled tank.

◆ At **Monkey Island,** an elevated boardwalk gives a spectacular view down onto a rocky hill over which a big band of monkeys cavorts.

◆ The darkened **herpetarium** lets you see nocturnal animals like foxes, jungle cats, and bush babies, under conditions in which they are naturally active.

Some visitors accustomed to newer zoos with more space, or to bigger zoos lucky to have a lot of acreage, may feel spaces here for big animals like lions and tigers look small and depressing. Zoo professionals point out that lions in the wild don't budge an inch unless they're hunting. They sleep 22 hours a day. Much of what zoo exhibits involve is done for visitors. Animals don't necessarily require a natural setting to be content. The John Ball Zoo has been especially successful with its big cats in terms of breeding, health, and temperament.

John Ball, pioneer, legislator, and lawyer, was one of the many people who came west to Michigan in the last century to speculate in land. A delightful bronze **statue** at the zoo entrance shows him as an old man with his children at his knees. It commemorates his gift of 40 acres to the city for a park. Today the **park** part of the 100-acre complex is a large, shady, flat expanse with **picnic facilities**, ball diamonds, playground, tennis courts, and some playful contemporary sculptures.

Fulton St. and Valley Ave., 1¹/₄ miles west of the Grand River. From U.S. 131, take the Fulton Street exit and go west. (616) 336-4300 (recording); (616) 336-4301 (office). Open daily 10 a.m.-4 p.m. ('til 6 in summer), year-round, including holidays. ♿ *Strollers and wheelchairs available. Current fees: adults $3, children 5-13 and seniors $1.50, under 5 free.*

SUMMER THEATER IN JOHN BALL PARK. . . . . is next door to the zoo at the **Circle Theater**. Three **children's shows** (tickets $4) run from June through August, Tuesday through Saturday at 10 a.m. and 12:30. . . . . Five **mainstage shows** (four musicals and one play) run from May through September, Tuesday through Saturday at 8 p.m., Sundays at 7. . . . . Call (616) 456-6656 for program and ticket information.

WESTSIDE ETHNIC FOOD FOR PARK PICNICS AND MORE. . . . . **Moctezuma Cash and Carry** and **Maggie's Kitchen** share a very large, bright space on Bridge near Stocking. The store has all the basic Mexican groceries, exotic canned juices, and Mexican soda pop. Frozen tamales come from Chicago. A full line of spices for Mexican cooking in institutional sizes is imported and distributed. The basement is full of Spanish-language **videos and recordings** and lots of bright piñatas. Maggie makes pastries and a range of **tortas**, authentic Mexican sandwiches, for $3.05. Many are meal-size. The sweet rolls look great on a plate and go well with coffee for breakfast. Table seating now lets customers eat in. *636 Bridge. (616) 458-8583. Open Tuesday-Saturday 9-6, Sunday 9-4, closed Monday.* ♿: *use front entrance.* . . . .At the **Lewandoski's Market,** in a plain, inconspicuous neighborhood grocery, butcher-owner Vic Hill makes widely admired sausages: German-style wieners; ring bologna; smoked kielbasa; delicious, super-spicy pepperoni; and kiska (a Polish sausage made of buckwheat, pork, and blood). *1107 Walker at Powers. From Ed's, go south on Garfield to Walker (the diagonal street), then left for two blocks. (616) 454-2281. Tues-Fri 8-6, Sat to 5.* ♿: *call.*

Meyer May House

*Serene and sublime, it's a remarkably complete
example of Frank Lloyd Wright's famous Prairie Style.*

SEEING PHOTOS of Wright interiors — or seeing objects he designed taken out of context — leaves people unprepared for the emotional impact of the places he designed. Wright was famed for designing total environments, including leaded glass and furniture. He worked with favorite craftspeople and dictated to his clients just what kind of pictures and ceramics his rooms should have.

The May House was designed for the owner of a Grand Rapids menswear store in 1908, the same year as Wright's famous Robie House in Chicago. The eminent architectural historian Vincent Scully has called this the most beautifully and completely restored of any of Wright's Prairie houses: serene and suffused by a gentle unity. "To come suddenly into that interior environment is an overwhelming experience. It is to be wholly caught up and carried along by something rarely experienced: absolute peace, integral order, deep quiet grandeur and calm — all of it achieved in a house of no more than moderate size, . . . set in the typical grid pattern of the American town." It's a vivid testament to Wright's originality to see this house in the context of its more conventional Heritage Hill neighbors in their late Queen Anne, Craftsman, and Classical Revival styles.

The quiet generosity of Steelcase, the nationally famous Grand

The Meyer May House shows the total environment designed by America's greatest architect. The meticulous restoration by Steelcase features the original Wright-designed furniture, leaded-glass windows and lighting, plus the textiles, murals, and other accessories he chose.

Rapids office furniture manufacturer, made this amazing restoration possible. Except for the kitchen, it virtually duplicates the house's 1916 appearance. The ambitious project employed scholars and top local and national conservators and restoration craftsmen in everything from furniture and art glass to pottery and linen. With typical modesty, Steelcase officials never mention the cost. They say the restoration is honoring a debt to Wright. In his celebrated Johnson Wax Administration Building (1939), Wright insisted on designing a total work environment. That was the beginning of the modern workstation, the bread and butter of today's office furniture manufacturers centered in and near Grand Rapids. Wright contracted with Steelcase to manufacture desks and chairs for Johnson Wax.

Visitors on the $1^1/_2$-hour tour first come to the visitor center in the house next door and watch an interesting **video** showing the Meyer May house before, during, and after restoration. It focuses on techniques and puts the house in historical context.

The top-notch **tour** effectively illuminates the rationale for Wright's design idiosyncrasies. He designed each house as a private family refuge. This house has a hidden entrance to the side. The deep balcony overhangs let occupants sit on porches in shady privacy. The bedroom ceilings, like little tents, work to promote a settled feeling of enclosed security. In contrast, downstairs ceiling and molding details emphasize the flow from room to room and a sense of richly expansive vistas.

The **perennial flower garden** — a striking geometric design in bloom spring through fall — is behind the house off Logan. People are welcome to look at it any time.

450 Madison S.E. at Logan southeast of downtown Grand Rapids in the Heritage Hill historic district. Take Fulton, Cherry or Wealthy to Madison, turn south. From U.S. 131, take Wealthy St. (616) 246-4821. Tues & Thurs 10-2 (last tour begins at 1), Sun 1-5 (last tour begins at 4). Closed some Sundays; call ahead. Reservations required for groups of 10 or more. &: visitor center and 1st floor Meyer May House. Free.

PUT TOGETHER A FRANK LLOYD WRIGHT TOUR . . . . . over four or five days, and you'll see a lot of interesting places along with the Master's own architecture. Grand Rapids is well situated for making a pleasant loop, via the relaxing Lake Michigan Carferry (see page 556).

◆ **Taliesin** (608-588-7900). Wright's famous summer office/residence in his family's home turf at bucolic Spring Green on the Wisconsin River, an hour west of Madison in Wisconsin's beautiful Driftless Region. There, no glaciers filled up the deep valleys with glacial till, as they did in most of the Upper Midwest, including Michigan.

◆ The **Johnson Wax Administration Building** (414-260-2154) in Racine, Wisconsin, an architecturally rich and underappreciated old industrial city on Lake Michigan. Call the local convention and visitor bureau at (414) 634-3293 for more on historic Racine. Its 19th-century density didn't suit Wright, who designed his masterpiece office building to ignore the handsome nearby factories of Milwaukee cream brick. The nearby former home of the Johnson CEO, Wingspread conference center, is undergoing major structural repairs and is not open to the public in 1996.

◆ **Oak Park, Illinois** offers many tours of Wright's buildings (including the Unity Temple and the studio/residence he used until 1909), Ernest Hemingway's boyhood home and museum, and other noteworthy buildings in this turn-of-the-century suburb just west of Chicago. Call (708) 848-1500 for a helpful brochure.

Heritage Hill

Grand Rapids' historic neighborhood
of superbly detailed homes is probably
the richest and most varied in the U.S.

HERITAGE HILL is one of America's most extraordinary historic districts. It numbers hundreds of uniquely detailed houses in an amazing variety of styles — over 60, from Greek Revival and Gothic Revival of the 1840s to Arts and Crafts and Spanish Revival of the 1920s. As a manufacturing city with many locally owned businesses, Grand Rapids generated considerable wealth and wasn't shy about displaying it. Prominent families, including design-conscious owners of the city's famous furniture factories, built these hillside homes up and away from their factories' smoke.

The historic district is six blocks wide and nearly one and a half miles long. It rises up and along the crest of the hill east of downtown Grand Rapids. Nearly every street has uncommon and rare architecture to dazzle old-house fans. Here are unusually heavy and ornately detailed Italianate doors and window caps; unaltered Stick Style cottages; rambling Shingle Style lodges; Chauteauesque castles; and a most peculiar Queen Anne house constructed of logs for a rustic effect. The Hill has two **Frank Lloyd Wright houses** and one adapted from one of his *Ladies' Home Journal* plans for small, moderate-priced houses. Wright's Meyer May House (page 467) is one of the most authentically furnished Wright designs in existence.

From the 1840s into the 1920s, "the Hill" remained Grand Rapids' residential area of choice — a long period for any prosperous American city. In many cities, the elite neighborhood of choice changed every generation — even more often in fast-growing boom towns like Detroit.

By the time people could afford to build on Grand Rapids' prestigious hill, they were already middle-aged and wealthy. Families competed in devising unusual details to distinguish their big residences. Grand Tours in Europe acquainted them with many prototypes, which were seldom literally copied. Especially on the Hill's south end, developed after 1885 or so, you can see strange blends of architectural styles.

In the 1920s the Hill was supplanted as Grand Rapids' best address by East Grand Rapids — part of the nation-wide retreat of the upper classes to less public life in the suburbs. By the 1950s the Hill had become an aging neighborhood. Here and in other similar neighborhoods in older cities elsewhere, historic streetscapes were being chewed away by urban renewal and neighboring hospitals, churches, and schools eager for parking and new building sites. Much of the prime block of College Avenue was wiped out. The threat to this nationally significant neighborhood prompted the Grand Rapids city council in 1970 to create one of the country's earliest and largest historic districts and a neighborhood support agency. For awhile, an innovative revolving fund enabled many houses to be renovated and sold without use of any public grant money.

Houses of special historic or architectural interest are listed from northwest to southeast. * means you can look inside during business hours.

◆ **Rowe House.** *226 Prospect north of Lyon.* Prairie Style. Built from a 1907 Frank Lloyd Wright *Ladies' Home Journal* design as "A Fireproof House for $5,000."

◆ **230 Fountain** *just west of Lafayette.* 1872, Italianate, with 1894 Classic Revival modifications. The onion-domed garage (visible from Lafayette) shows the kind of detail lavished even on fences and accessory buildings on Heritage Hill. From 1907 to 1964 Edmund Booth of Booth Newspapers fame lived here.

◆ **Holt House.** *50 Lafayette.* 1886. Unusual house in fieldstone and shingles, with many inventive touches. Reminiscent of rambling Shingle Style summer cottages in New England.

◆ * **T. Stewart White House.** *427 E. Fulton.* 1907, Tudor Revival. A lumber baron built this house and installed a gold leaf dining room ceiling by Tiffany. Three sons became famous: Roderick White as a concert violinist, Gilbert White as a sculptor in Paris, and Stewart Edward White as a popular, nationally known writer of adventure stories. Drawing on his father's experiences, Stewart White chronicled Michigan lumberjacks and the early West. Gilbert painted murals in the house's library with scenes from King Arthur's court, using faces of family members. As Warren Hall, the building now houses **Davenport College of Business** offices. Call ahead (616-451-3511) to look at the murals.

◆ **264 College.** 1889 Queen Anne with eccentric log construction. Built by an architect as his own home.

◆ **Gay House.** *422-426 E. Fulton.* 1883. Built for the co-founder of Berkey & Gay, Grand Rapids' leading furniture manufacturer in the early decades of its furniture boom, for $50,000 — then an

Heritage Hill might have been eaten away by demolition from land-hungry institutions if it weren't for the efforts of self-described white-gloved Republican ladies like Barbara Roelofs (right) and Linda DeJong. They lobbied successfully for a historic district. A revolving fund restored this stately house, which had had an addition wrapped around it while it was a synagogue.

astounding sum.

◆ **Sweet House/Women's City Club.** *254 Fulton.* The cast-iron fence and drooping camperdown elm in front of this 1860 Italian villa-style house were popular Victorian lawn accents. Its builder, lumberman Martin Sweet, was long the richest man in town, until the financial panic of 1893 ruined him. He died here in near poverty. Later the house became a music school attended by young Arnold Gingrich, who became *Esquire* magazine's brilliant founding editor. He set his 1935 novel, *Cast Down the Laurel*, in this house. Today it's a private women's club.

◆ * **Voigt House.** Overstuffed Victorian chateau with original furnishings, now a house museum. A rare look at all the accoutrements of a grand, public lifestyle. Its suffocating decor helps you understand what modernism was all about. See page 474.

◆ **Byrne/Hanchett House.** *125 College.* Circa 1891. Attractive landscaping complements the rose stone and ornate detailing of this beautiful English manor house, built for a single woman. Private chapel has sumptuous stained glass windows.

◆ **The Castle.** *455 Cherry at College.* 1884. This rugged granite Norman chateau is a neighborhood landmark. It was built by bachelor brothers who got rich selling lumber for railroad ties.

◆ * **Sanford House.** *540 Cherry,* 1847. Greek Revival. This imposing house was once a country estate on the outskirts of town. Now it's a counseling office, and visitors can see the stair hall's splendid handpainted mural of a tropical scene.

◆ **McKay House.** *411 Morris.* 1924. Plain but impressive tile-roofed house built by banker and Republican boss Frank McKay. His control of the state Republican party was finally broken in 1948, when a progressive reform candidate, the young Gerald Ford, defeated his candidate for Congress.

◆ **Amberg House.** *505 College at Logan.* 1910, Prairie Style. Frank Lloyd Wright started design work on it, but Marion Mahoney, his first apprentice, finished after Wright abruptly left his wife and six children to spend a year in Europe with a client's wife.

◆ **Meyer May House.** *1908.* Most completely furnished and restored Frank Lloyd Wright house in existence. See page 467.

*See Grand Rapids map. Get a **free walking tour brochure with map** from the Heritage Hill Association office, 126 College S.E., Grand Rapids 54903. From downtown, take Fulton up the hill to college on the crest, turn south on one-way street to 126 College. Turn into the driveway of WOTV and look for the little house in the rear (the servant's quarters) with the purple mailbox. Brochures available from purple mailbox 24 hours a day. Office open Mon-Fri 9-5. (616) 459-8950.* **Homes tour:** *first full weekend in Oct. $12, $10 in advance.*

GETTING TO HERITAGE HILL . . . . . From U.S. 131, take the Wealthy Street exit and go east. From I-196, take College Avenue exit and go south. . . . . For boundaries of the **National Register Historic District**, see the dotted line on the map to central Grand Rapids, page 454. . . . . Call or write the Heritage Hill Association (above) for a **detailed neighborhood map** with notes to 76 houses.

Voigt House

On Grand Rapids' Heritage Hill, a complete Victorian mansion — from the velvet scarf on the library table to the pills and tonics in the medicine chest.

HERE, remarkably preserved, is a Victorian household in a big, turreted 1895 chateau, complete down to the last fringed piano scarf. It brims with the excess that epitomized Victorian decor. A table with carved lion legs is diagonally draped with a fringed velvet cloth. Antimacassars decorate the tops of every upholstered chair. Oriental carpets rest on parquet floors with elaborate inlaid borders. Doorways and windows are draped or festooned with heavy multi-layered window treatments and portieres. Patterns on patterns are everywhere. Rich reds and greens predominate.

Some visitors love the Voigt House's richness. Others experience it as claustrophobic and stifling, and feel like running out into the sunshine and fresh air.

This fascinating place is a monument to family prosperity. It's a gem of a historic house because of the authenticity of its furnishings. The two generations of Voigts who lived here until 1971 saved just about everything: letters, receipts, dresses, the entire contents of medicine chests. Everything is here the way it was. Most of the elaborately styled furniture is from Grand Rapids. It's the conventional best that America's Furniture City had to offer. There's a heavy, masculine library and hallway accented with exotica like an Arabian figure holding calling cards; a delicate French parlor; a rather Germanic dining room with loads of Bavarian china; and a comfortable, casual music room. In the basement is the original laundry, fully furnished with soap, along with interesting Voigt flour mill memorabilia.

The German-American Voigts made their fortune milling flour. They were supremely fussy, according to accounts from a former housekeeper. Cotton wads at the corners of pictures protected the walls. Except for cleaning, servants never used the main staircase to avoid unnecessary wear on the carpet.

The possessions of Ralph Voigt, the son and heir to the family flour mills, extend the house into the 20th century. They include a banjo and a simple bedroom suite with mementos of his years at Yale. The yard is planted and landscaped with plants of the Victorian era, a rose bower, and an iron geranium stand. During

A Victorian chateau with all the original furnishings: the Voigt House real-istically conveys the atmosphere of a wealthy bourgeois American house-hold. Rich and solid, or suffocating? Judge for yourself!

the warm months (May-September), the Carriage House, complete with garden tools, bird cages, and a carriage untouched by time, is open to visitors. Different tours take place throughout the year. The Christmas and Mother's Day tours are the most popular.

115 College just southeast of downtown between Fulton and Cherry. (616) 456-4600. Tues 11-3, 2nd and 4th Sundays 1-3. &: with 2 weeks notice. 1st and 2nd floor. Admission includes guided tour: $3/adults, $2/seniors and children.

FOR A MEMORABLE CONTRAST . . . . . plan to visit Frank Lloyd Wright's serene Meyer May house after seeing the Voigt House. The Voigt House is just the kind of architecture Wright detested: a mock European chateau encrusted with ornament borrowed from the past. His own architecture reacted to that revivalist esthetic in every way. Both homes are fully furnished — a rare treat. It's hard to believe that they were built and furnished just 11 years apart. They're both open at the same time on Tuesdays and alternate Sundays.

OTHER RECOMMENDED ATTRACTIONS NEAR HERITAGE HILL . . . . . Take

Fulton or Cherry east to diagonal Lake Street, turn southeast (right), and you'll soon reach two interesting commercial subdistricts. Turn south (right) onto Diamond and you'll be at the **Gaia Coffeehouse** (209 Diamond; 616-454-6233), a pleasantly laid-back counterculture hangout. It's a vegetarian restaurant (breakfast, lunch, and dinner) with a gallery. ♿ Take a harder right onto Cherry to find the exceptional **Heartwood** antiques (616) 454-1478), known for its Arts and Crafts, Art Deco, and moderne furniture and accessories. ♿: *no*. Farther out Lake Street, at Robinson Road and Wealthy, is **Eastown**, an offbeat collection of snack shops, offbeat shops, and bookstores. Especially worth checking out: the quality hot dogs and amusing soda shoppe atmosphere at **Yesterdog** *(1505 Wealthy)*; **Argos** used books *(1405 Robinson just east of Wealthy, 616-454-0111, ♿)*; **Eastown Food Co-op** *(1450 Wealthy, 616-454-8822, ♿)*; and **McKendree** hand-crafted jewelry *(1443 Wealthy, 616-458-0267, ♿)*, in a fascinating woodsman's baroque building where Grand Rapids' fabled wood craftsmanship took off on a wildly organic, 1960s bent. Be sure to see the bone-like interior staircase.

PROMOTING URBAN LIVING . . . . . is a tough job in Grand Rapids, where an insular suburban mindset is especially prevalent. Fortunately the city has enough people of all ages who appreciate Heritage Hill's exceptional environment to keep the area in demand and improving. Prices for very large multi-unit homes are often in the $90,000 to $200,000 range. . . . . The **Heritage Hill Association** has community organizers who promote their neighborhood, which is racially and economically quite mixed. The group works with residents to lobby for the neighborhood and resolve concerns and problems with crime, land use, housing maintenance, and preservation. Reach them at (616) 459-8950, or stop by weekdays at 126 College (in rear), Grand Rapids, MI 49503.

SEE INSIDE HERITAGE HILL HOMES . . . . . Stay at one of the beautiful **bed and breakfasts** on the hill. Call (616) 458-6621 for info on the Italianate **Fountain Hill B&B**, (616) 454-8000 for **Peaches**, a Georgian manor at 29 Gay, and (616) 451-4849 for the **Shingle Style house** at 455 College, the **Georgian Revival** at 516 College, and the **Arts & Crafts house** (with period furnishings) at 243 Morris. . . . . Attend the annual **fall homes tour** on the first weekend in October. Tickets are $10 in advance from the Heritage Hill Association (see above), or $12 on tour day. Meet at Davenport College, 415 E. Fulton between Prospect and College. . . . . **Group tours** by bus of the area and downtown Grand Rapids can be arranged by calling Joyce Makinen at (616) 456-7121.

Meijer Gardens & Sculpture Park

In a region of avid gardeners, a spectacular new setting for plants and sculptural animals

PLANTS AND SCULPTURES come together in this spectacular facility: a 15,000-square-foot conservatory (the largest in Michigan) and an outdoor area of colorful flower gardens. Ponds, woods, and wetlands in the back will be enhanced over the next few years with plantings. The gardens opened in 1995.

This ambitious complex is the fruit of the inspiring visions of Meijer stores' owner Fred Meijer and of Betsy Borre. West Michigan has had no large public garden, indoors or out, within recent memory. In a place where the dominant Dutch have such a passion and gift for nurturing plants, that's been a noteworthy void. Borre wanted to see a botanical garden happen. The small West Michigan Horticultural Society had grown to 400 under her leadership by the time she approached Meijer for financial help and influence in launching a fundraising campaign.

Borre's dreams clicked with Meijer's. He had collected dozens of sculptures, mostly by Marshall Fredericks, whose bronze animals and allegorical figures have graced Cranbrook and many other Michigan sites since the 1930s. Then Meijer saw a Swedish sculpture garden of works by Carl Milles, Fredericks' mentor. It started him thinking about a similar project in West Michigan. He gave some land his firm had purchased for a store. And he gave an impressive amount of money to get the ball rolling. After that, the gardens happened quickly, and without any public money.

The gardens hum with activity that draws in many kinds of people. Clubs meet here for lunch and visit. The gardens draw upon the many retirees who live in the immediate area for docents, and they are most helpful and enthusiastic. (That was one reason Meijer liked the site.) Mothers take their toddlers to the outdoor sculptures, which attract kids like magnets. (Many are intended to be cuddled or climbed.) Indoors, sculptures are tucked and perched throughout the conservatory. Occasional quotations from Michigan poets (Theodore Roethke, Jim Harrison) deal with the connections between people and plants.

Grouped around the main conservatory are a series of smaller garden spaces: the **Arid Gardens**, the **Gardener's Corner** where spe-

cialty plants are sold; and the **Victorian Gardens Parlor**, an expanded recreation of the collections of exotica favored in homes of wealthy
Victorians. Another space is for **changing plant displays**. The palms
in the big tropical conservatory are new and relatively small, but the
conservatory dome with waterfall and winding paths will be a welcome oasis, moist and fragrant, during the dry winter months.

Don't miss the introductory **multi-image show** "Natural
Affections." You might miss the theater off to a side. Simple and
serene, this show effectively invites visitors to relax and open themselves to the quiet power of plants. It blends close-up views of
plants with two appealingly plain-language narrators: the garden
director and a 92-year-old plant enthusiast.

The extremely pleasant **Garden View Cafe** offers tasty sandwiches, soups, coffee, salads, and desserts. Plant-related gifts,
books, and tools are in the good **gift shop**. A hallway gallery is
given over to **changing exhibits** that can be wonderful. Call for
information about exhibits and **special events** that include a summer music series, garden tours, classes, and more.

Outdoors a wheelchair-accessible half-mile **path** opens up to
views of attractive ponds, woods, and wetlands. Future plantings
will make this area more of a garden.

The Gardens are northeast of downtown Grand Rapids off I-96 at
East Beltline. From I-96, take exit 38 to Bradford (the first street on
your right). Go down Bradford. The Gardens are shortly on your left.
(616) 957-3535 (information), (616) 957-1580 (office). Open 9-5 daily,
Wed to 9, Sun 12-5, except Christmas and New Year's. ௶ $4 ages 14
and up, $1.50 ages 5-13. No fee to visit outdoor areas.

🌲🌸🌲

CUTTING-EDGE ATTRACTIONS THAT KEEP THE HOMETOWN TOUCH. . . . .
That's a difficult trick to pull off, and it's what visitors can expect in Grand
Rapids. Grand Rapids owes much to the special characteristics of the civic and
philanthropic leaders of this deeply Middle American city, who have given gener-
ously to the city's visitor attractions. In this age of corporate mergers, Grand
Rapids is most fortunate to have retained a big complement of resident business
princes who own their own companies: **Amway**, **Steelcase**, and **Meijer**, which,
unnoticed by Wall Street, pioneered the hypermarket in the 1950s and 1960s
when its grocery stores became vast discount stores. . . . . Now their owners are
reaching the age when they want to leave their philanthropic marks on future
generations at home. They are becoming the Middle American version of
Renaissance Florence's great patrons of art. "These entrepreneurs are driven,
passionate people," says a local fundraiser. "When you get one of them behind a
project, you're really lucky."

Jerry's Diner Village

*Vintage diners, moved and restored by a diner fan
and ceramics artist, now sell art and diner food.*

JERRY BERTA still marvels at how he, a ceramics artist, has
become the savior and owner of three vintage diners — and a
successful restaurateur to boot. Rosie's Diner, known to millions from a popular series of Bounty towel TV commercials, reopened
in Michigan in 1991, and served its millionth customer in 1996 —
quite an accomplishment for a 92-seat diner. Bathed in neon, Jerry's
Diner Village sits on a busy stretch of M-57 just north of Rockford, 15
minutes north of Grand Rapids and half a mile east of the U.S. 131
superhighway that heads north to Big Rapids and Cadillac.

   If you've only seen pictures and video images of diners, it's a
thrill to experience the stainless steel sunburst surfaces, cozy booths
and counter, and classic accoutrements (thick china mugs, ketchup

**Diner museum: of Berta's three vintage diners, The Diner Store, made by
the O'Mahoney company, is an Olds; the Delux, from Silk City, is a
Chevy;. and Rosie's, from Paramount, is a Cadillac, full of jazzy details.
Summer Wednesdays are cruise nights with hot rods and 50s cars.**

bottles, menu boards, etc.) of the real thing. Jerry Berta studied diners intensively to glean accurate details for the playful, cartoon-like ceramic diners that have been his artistic signature. For years he and his wife, Madeleine Kaczmarczk, have been familiar artists in regional and national art fairs. In addition to diners, Berta does other images of roadside Americana: tail-finned cars, movie theaters, gas stations, and tiny blue plate specials, worn as pins.

Diner research precipitated Berta's unexpected debut in the restaurant and tourism world. He came upon Uncle Bob's Diner in Flint, derelict and awaiting destruction. It seemed an ideal studio/gallery because of its unusually large size (74 seats), so Berta bought it for $2,000. Construction work is second nature to Berta. He grew up helping his dad, a Detroit-area autoworker, build a house a year on weekends and model-changeover time. He found a highway lot a half a mile from his studio/home in the woods. For another $14,000 he moved the diner to Rockford and went about remodeling it into a studio and gallery. "NO FOOD — JUST ART," proclaimed the neon window sign. The original Formica counter and booths and the pie shelf soon displayed Berta's porcelain diner night lights ($150 and up), gas stations, salt-and-pepper sets ($45-$75), fantasy diners shaped like hotdogs and hamburgers ($200-$2,000), and diners with neon "EAT" signs. In a similarly playful vein are patterned teapots and slab vases by Berta's wife, Madeleine Kaczmarczk, neon clocks and signs by his friend, Ian McCartney. Today they're joined by souvenir mugs, pins, T shirts, and a vast and increasing array of diner books, diner calendars, and more.

Berta wasn't looking for another diner when he revisited the celebrated **Rosie's Diner** on Route 46 in Little Ferry, New Jersey, long familiar from commercials starring Nancy Walker as Rosie the waitress. But owner Ralph Carrado asked him if he wanted to buy it. Carrado had already sold the lot to a neighbor and had unsuccessfully offered the diner to the Smithsonian. He was thrilled that the landmark diner would survive in good hands.

Rosie's, manufactured in 1946, gained its present name after TV stardom. It's an unusually large diner — the long camera angles made it a favorite with ad directors for many products — and in excellent condition. The Paramount Dining Car Company included in this diner most of the design hallmarks of the best of the golden age of diners, that period shortly after World War II when America took to the road and returning GIs found diners attractive investments. Rosie's has curved glass-brick corners, a rounded Pullman-style roof, and an interior full of reflecting stainless steel sunbursts and a jazzy combination of ceramic tile, vintage Formica, and leatherette in red, pink, light blue, and black.

Berta was thrilled and captivated with the idea of adding real food to the diner concept. Never lacking in self-confidence, he plunged into the totally new restaurant business, despite his wife's apprehension. The results are surprising. The classic diner food is far better than that found in most popular-priced restaurants, from the roll to the fresh green beans and fresh strawberries for pie in season. Waitresses, clad in pink uniforms, are energetic and competent. Just like the original Rosie's, Rosie's opens at 6 a.m. and serves burgers, meat loaf, pies and puddings, and blue plate specials. The clientele is a real cross-section of society, just like diners were. And the price is right – $5.95 for a meat loaf dinner with potato, vegetable, salad, and roll. (This is West Michigan, after all, home of famously thrifty folks.)

Buoyed by Rosie's success, Berta bought yet another diner for his complex: a 50-seat diner in Fulton, New York, named the Garden of Eatin'. A late diner, it dates from the 1950s and combines porcelain with stainless steel exterior, and maroon and cream-tiled interior, for a softer, less reflective look. As the **Delux Diner**, he envisioned it becoming a "upscale, fine dining special-occasion restaurant in a classic diner setting," patterned along the lines of San Francisco's Fog City Diner. But custom Art Deco wood booths, reminiscent of the earlier style of Worcester oak diners before streamlining took hold in the 1930s, and private-label wines set a dressier tone that Rosie's customers didn't like. Now the Delux features "fun dining, not fine dining," with barbeque, stir-fries, and pastas in the same price range as Rosie's ($5 to 7 for a complete lunch, $7 to $10 for dinner). Thursday nights are Parrot Head nights with margaritas and Jimmy Buffet music. Summer Wednesdays "Cruise to Rosie's" night attracts Fifties cars. A **miniature golf course** is diner-themed with holes using such motifs as fried eggs and hamburgers.

The diners are at 450014 Mile Rd. (M-57) 5 miles north of Rockford. 1/2 mile east of U.S. 131, 1/2 mile west of Beltline. **Rosie's** *is open Sun-Thurs 6 a.m.-9 p.m., Fri & Sat to 10, winter Sundays open at 7 a.m. Delux Diner hours: weekday lunch 11:30-2:30, dinners Wed-Fri 5-10 p.m. Sat 11:30-10, Sun 11:30-8. (616) 866-FOOD.* ♿*: side doors. Visa, MasterCard. The* **Diner Store** *is generally open 10-6 daily, later in summer. (616) 866-ARTS.* ♿ **Minigolf** *is open in good weather 10:30 a.m.-10 p.m.*

SPECIALTY SHOPPING IN A MOST SCENIC SPOT . . . . . is the big attraction of the **Squires Street shops** in downtown Rockford. An old mill, now **Arnie's Old Mill Restaurant** (part of the Arnie's Bakery Restaurants chain), is at the center of an informal group of mostly gift shops. *Shops are one block east of Main on Squires between Bridge and Courtland. If parking's tight, try the lot off Monroe, one block east of the principal business block on Main. Hours are mostly 10-5 daily, to 8 Fridays, and 12-5 Sundays. Summer weekdays to 8.*

Behind the shops by the Rogue River and dam is an attractive little **park**. Just east of Squires Street is Rockford's main business block, with a great old hardware store and **The Corner Bar** with its well-known Hot Dog Hall of Fame. Connecting them is Courtland Street. The **post office** there has a WPA mural, "Along the Furrows," with an unusual, cubist-tinged version of Midwestern farm life.

The Melting Pot, 63 Courtland, resembles a fudge, cookware, and gourmet shop like many others, but its owners are committed to doing things right — and not for maximum profit, either. They're extremely knowledgeable about coffee. You may see snapshots from their recent trip to a supplier plantation in Costa Rica, for instance. As a wholesaler, they roast a day's supply of many kinds of beans fresh each day. (Freshness is paramount for great coffee.) Mail-order (616-866-2900) is available. Good fudge and chocolates are also made fresh daily, as are bagels — a boon to transplanted urbanites in the area. Open at 8 a.m. except Sundays, 12-5.

Baskets in the Belfry at 46 East Bridge (616-866-2890) has evolved from a basket shop into the ultimate, all-round feminine gift shop that makes the most of the familiar Victorian-country genre and expands it without ever seeming slavishly imitative or hackneyed. The romantic tone is set by grapevines and flowers, potpourri and soaps, lace and cutwork (an outstanding selection, from runners to dollies). But you'll also find African and South American stone and wood carvings, nature books, afghans, an extensive selection of picnic baskets, and more.

THE ATTRACTIVE ROGUE RIVER DAM . . . . . is where many things come together. It's a very popular **fishing spot**. There are spring steelhead runs and fall salmon runs below the dam. Above the dam are pike, bass, and panfish. A big **platform for handicapped fishermen** is on the west bank. The Rogue is clean enough for swimming and tubing. Trips can be arranged through AAA Rogue River Canoe Rentals at 8 West Bridge, (616) 866-9264. (Warning: there's not much current. You have to do a lot of paddling even downstream.)

You can enjoy the scenery and activity from a park bench behind the Squires Street shops, or take a cloth for a regular picnic. Takeout recommendations: coffee and bagels from The Melting Pot, or hot dogs or burgers from the famous Corner Bar downtown on Main at Court. The **Rockford Historical Museum** (open May through October, Tues-Sun 1:30-3:30) fills the former powerhouse on East Bridge with a more-interesting-than-usual mix of old stuff.

A SEPARATE BIKE PATH FROM ROCKFORD TO CEDAR SPRINGS . . . . . is part of an eventual **rails-to-trails bike path** from Grand Rapids to Cadillac. The Rockford segment, which starts between the dam and the depot near Squires Street, is hard-packed dirt, good cycling for all but the narrowest tires.

Hush-Puppy Tour

An informative factory tour in Rockford
shows how Hush-Puppies are made.

THE FACTORY TOUR at Hush-Puppy shoes offers a slice-of-life glimpse of an interesting manufacturing process from start to finish. (Many tours just show the packaging process.) And it's delivered by a veteran employee familiar with all aspects of plant operation. Here you see already-cut shoe uppers being shaped on a last (a form that's sized for different lengths and widths of feet). Shoes are made with a lot of heat, steam, and pressure. Heat softens the leather. Steam shapes it on the last. And pressure applies the cement and tacks that hold the shoe together. Then you see the shoes polished, inspected for quality, and packaged.

Wolverine World Wide began as the Krause tannery here in Rockford and remains headquartered here today. It's one of the leading U.S. shoe companies, with factories in the U. S., Puerto Rico, and the Dominican Republic. The uppers of the shoes you see assembled here may come from the Caribbean. The firm's big breakthrough came when it invented a new process for getting skin off pigs sent to slaughterhouses. The old method had immersed them in boiling water, thereby ruining the pigskin for any other use.

Pigskin, with its bristle pores, *breathes* more than cowhide — a real asset at work and in summer. Pigskin's extra comfort prompted the Hush-Puppies name and the well-known logo. "People who know

Saddle

We're classic.
Your Hush Puppies® shoes. Colorful, in waterproof, stain-resistant "Worry-free" suede - with Scotchgard® Leather Protector. They're one of the ways - we invented casual.®

HUSH PUPPIES®
We invented casual.®

wear pigskin work shoes in summer," McIntyre says. As soon as you walk into this busy, noisy factory and see the degree of hand work in the labor-intensive 14-step shoemaking process, it's clear why so much U.S. shoe manufacturing has been relocated to countries with cheaper labor. Workers in this factory are highly competitive piece-rate workers. Each worker can perform at least two jobs and knows the basic procedure on 40 different shoe patterns at a time.

Wolverine World Wide employs 500 people in its Rockford factory, including 300 in the tannery, one of the world's largest. Many employees commute from towns like Greenville and Belding, which have been badly hurt by plant closings.

Recently Wolverine World Wide has scored a huge success in freshening its image among younger buyers. A talented designer reintroduced the original thick-soled, waterproof pigskin suede classics from 1958 in colors like hot red-orange, violet, lemon, and scarlet, in addition to black, gray, and brown. They retail for $70, $90 in golf shoes. Styles include high-vamped loafers, saddle shoes, desert boots. Designer Anna Sui — called "a good barometer of hipness" by the New York Times —used Hush Puppy desert books in her spring 1996 show. Relaunching the original Hush Puppies struck a retro chord that surprised the manufacturers, especially after they won a prestigious fashion award. For years, Hush Puppies strove to keep up with Rockport and downplay its stodgy image. But fashion cognoscenti figured they were due for a comeback. Some trendy retailers work with Wolverine World Wide to create special styles and colors. Now a long list of celebrities wear Hush Puppies (Demi Moore, Ziggy Marley, Jodie Foster, Jim Carey) and some have at least a dozen (Ellen Degeneres, Sharon Stone).

To schedule a free tour, usually Tuesday and Thursday at 9:30 and 1 p.m., ask for the person in charge of tours, Norma Moore, at least a few weeks ahead of time, weekdays at (616) 866-5514. Young children must be very well supervised (2 adults for every child). ♿: *call.*

Saugatuck

One of the state's most picturesque resort towns, with interesting shops and galleries, a lively street scene, and beaches and forested dunes close at hand

SAUGATUCK is one of the state's jewels, a little resort town blessed with a combination of natural and man-made beauty. For a delightful blend of shady backdune beech woods, beautiful sand beaches, village charm, good browsing in art galleries and shops, and a lively boating scene, Saugatuck is hard to match — provided this arty, fun-loving town isn't too crowded. On summer weekends it certainly is. Saugatuck shines in spring, when in-town gardens and wildflower woods are in bloom.

The town is nestled along the Kalamazoo River on a half-mile-long plain between hills and Lake Michigan dunes to both east and west. South of the Kalamazoo River lies Saugatuck's less intense sister community of Douglas. It too has about 1,000 year-round residents.

Because both villages were bypassed by railroads and late-19th-century commerce, they have the quaint look of pre-industrial Michigan, like parts of New England. Small-scale clapboard buildings are often embellished with Victorian gingerbread trim. In downtown Saugatuck, paths lead to tucked-away shops, patios, and balconies set back from the sidewalk activity. The public gardens and parks are delightful.

An island of hedonism near the center of America's Dutch Calvinist heartland, Saugatuck's reputation goes back to when it was an art colony. **Ox-Bow**, a summer school of art connected with the Chicago Institute of Art, operates at the picturesque remote tip of the peninsula across the river from downtown. It opened in 1910 and continues to attract serious students of art. Visitors are welcome to look around. The 1940 WPA guide to Michigan also mentions a "group of tumble-down shacks and cabins" on the river opposite downtown Saugatuck, "in which artists live with Bohemian informality. [It] is said to have been a 'hobo jungle' before they took it over."

The area's most visible artistic presence today is its unusually interesting art galleries. Retailing has been invigorated by gays and other talented urban refugees, often from Chicago. Ever since the turn of the century, when lake steamers brought summer visitors

❶ Saugatuck Dunes State Park (p. 497). Wild, pristine dune country, 2 mi. of uncrowded beach, 14 mi. of hiking trails. Dune tops offer nice lake views.

❷ Downtown Saugatuck (p. 487). Lively mix of quality galleries, gift & clothing shops, restaurants along with delightful town common and gardens.

❸ Star of Saugatuck (p. 497). Informative cruise on fake steamboat highlights marine geography of Kalamazoo Lake and Lake Michigan shoreline.

❹ Wicks Park & boardwalk. Civilized little park looks across busy river to Mt. Baldhead.

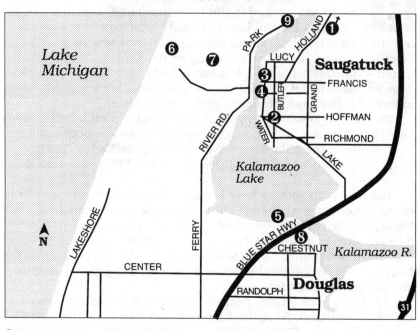

❺ S.S. Keewatin (p. 493). Bygone glories of elegant Great Lakes cruise ships live on in this 336-foot steamship, now a museum.

❻ Oval Beach. Costs $5 a car on weekends to join the crowd at this popular beach. Well-stocked concession stand, pleasantly natural setting.

❼ Mt. Baldhead (p. 495). Reward of short but strenuous climb is splendid views of city and lakes. Big beech trees. Pleasant picnic site below on river.

❽ Joyce Petter Gallery (p. 492).
❾ Ox-Bow (p. 485).

Bed and breakfast inns. Outstanding quality & variety. Call Chamber at (616) 857-1701.

Highlights of
Saugatuck

0   1/4   1/2
mile

from Chicago, Saugatuck has been a favorite and convenient get-away destination for Chicagoans. It also functions as a magnet for homegrown free spirits who find nearby Holland, Grand Rapids, and Ottawa County too confining. In recent years, the local tourism momentum has tilted in a fairly upscale direction. Inspired by the success of the romantic, year-round country French restaurant Toulouse, more restaurants are making an effort to serve good food year-round. *Most shops and many restaurants stay open year-round, at least weekends.*

DOWNTOWN SAUGATUCK

Saugatuck is unusual in having a **town common**, deeded by town founder William Gay Butler, a Connecticut Yankee. Today these three corner parks on Butler at Main continue to have a small-scale New England charm. The temple-like facade of the Christian Science church is an attractive backdrop for the delightful little garden in the southwest park. A bronze statue of a girl with a puppet commemorates the late Burr Tillstrom, creator of 1950s TV puppets "Kukla, Fran and Ollie." He was a beloved Saugatuck summer resident. Across Main Street is a pleasant children's playground. **Tennis courts**, a **basketball court**, and a gaily painted **restroom** building are on the other side of Butler.

Peaceful **Wicks Park,** on Water Street at Main, offers some lovely views over the river and across to the old cottage colony clustered around Mount Baldhead. **Riverside benches,** away from the summer crowds in downtown Saugatuck, make this a nice spot for a takeout picnic.

Saugatuck's downtown along Butler and Water streets has a strong mix of gift shops, resortwear, and traditional casual clothing. A stroll up one side and down the other reveals shops geared to many tastes, also to ice cream, fudge, and not a little schlock. Here are some highlights, arranged along Butler from its south end at Culver to its north end. It's always worthwhile exploring the nooks and crannies and side streets off Butler, since new shops are always opening and the odd corners are among the village's most charming spots. There are interesting old churches and houses on the bluff up the steep hill above downtown. They make for a pleasant walk.

◆ **Swell Times.** Artful arrangements of 1950s and modernistic collectibles, genuine and reproduced. *322 Culver. (616) 857-8320. Open daily in summer, 11-6 at least. Closed Tues & Wed otherwise.* ⌖

◆ **Tuck's of Saugatuck.** Delightful shop devoted to fine Christmas ornaments and accessories, including Christopher Radko and Dept. 56. Many are designed especially for the shop. Each year Tuck dramatically changes the decor, which alone is worth a look. *249 Culver. (616) 857-4594. Open all year. May-Dec: open Mon-Thurs 10-7, Fri & Sat to 9, Sun 10-6. Jan-April: Thurs-Sun 10-7.* &

◆ **The Butler Pantry.** A kitchen accessory shop of unusual quality, the Pantry was created by ex-Chicagoans Ron Aure and the late Fritz Helman. Gourmet foods, wines, and gift baskets are on hand, too. Upstairs the owners have fashioned a beguiling little mini-mall looking out onto a delightful alleyway courtyard. *121 Butler. (616 857-4875. Open year around. Mem.-Labor Day: Sun-Thurs 10--7, Fri-Sat 10-9. Fall thru Dec. 31: Sun-Thurs 10-6, Fri & Sat 10-7: Jan-March: 10-5 daily. April & May: 10-7 daily.* &

Small-scale charm: a streetscape of interesting small shops, courtyards and alleyways on and just off Butler Street makes Saugatuck fun to explore.

◆ **2nd Home.** Simple things with a highly refined sense of style — that's the idea behind this distinctive interior accessories store. It's the kind of place that can take a few candles or hand-blown glass vases and some shells or rocks, and arrange them so elegantly on a rough cocoa mat that you lust after them. Not surprisingly, the owner is a Chicago-based design consultant for store window displays in North America and Europe. Fabulous cut flowers have always been part of 2nd Home's simple, refined look. The charming rear courtyard connects with Ralph's Garden (below). Ask to see their quarterly **newsletter**. *146 Butler. (616) 857-2353. Open year-round. Summer hours: Sun-Thurs 10-7, Fri & Sat 10-9. Call for winter hours.* &*: store, not courtyard.*

◆ **Ralph's Garden.** The owner, a horticulturist and floral designer, shares the spare and elegant design approach of his friends at 2nd Home. He grows and buys topiary, herbs, blooming plants (tropical and winter-hardy), presented in unusual containers. Also on hand:

gardening supplies and pots for patios and indoor plants. Ralph Graham consults and designs, too. The rear courtyard shows what can be done with a tiny space. *231 Mason. (616) 857-3806. Open year-round. Mem-Labor Day: Sun-Thurs 10-6, Fri & Sat 10-9. &: crowded.*

◆ **Hoopdee Scootee.** This outrageous, amusing shop does a booming business in unisex clothing, Art Deco reproductions, T- shirts, sculpture, and adult cards. Custom-designed neon sells for $150 to $400. The checkout counter is made out of the front of a 1 1/2 ton truck. A car door shields the dressing room. *133 Mason, a few doors west of Butler. (616) 857-4141. Open April 15-Dec 31: Mon-Fri 10-9. Sat 10-10, Sun 11-7. &: no.*

◆ **Good Goods.** "Global art and artifacts" from American artists, accented with some traditional ethnic handcrafts from around the world. Everything from $5 Chinese papercuttings to fine contemporary gold and silver jewelry to handblown glass perfume bottles. Increasingly known for handpainted clothing and other wearable art, often handwoven. A back room has some African stringed instruments and drums, pottery flutes and ocarinas. Another part of the mix is classic Eames seating, hand-crafted George Nelson designs, Noguchi tables, and other furniture from the newish Herman Miller for the Home line. (A good number of Saugatuck designers work at nearby Herman Miller.) The upstairs fine arts **gallery** features **changing exhibits** by well-known area artists. Regular exhibitors include Bob Fagan of public TV's "Painting on Location" and Irving Stettner, whose work as a street artist in Paris was once collected by Henry Miller. The new year-round **cafe** offers cappuccino, espresso, pastries, and cookies on an indoor porch and a pretty outdoor **courtyard**. *106 Mason at Water, a short block west of Butler. (616) 857-1557. Memorial Day thru Labor Day: 10-10 daily. Off-season: 10-6 daily. &: first floor.*

◆ **Coral Gables,** on the Kalamazoo River in downtown Saugatuck, is the **Coral Gables**, a vast, rambling dance hall/restaurant, reminiscent of the big old nightspots built up and down the coast to attract Chicago summer visitors. The **Crow Bar** rock 'n' roll dance hall featuring a DJ weekends from 8 p.m. to 2 a.m. It packs in a young crowd of hundreds. In the **Rathskeller** below, a blues band entertains a more sedate, smaller crowd of dancers. The **El Forno** dining room (lunch and dinner) has the best water view in town. **The Bootlegger** bar features shrimp and oysters when available. *220 Water near Mason. (616) 857-2162. Open April thru Oct. &: not restrooms.*

◆ **Saugatuck Drugs** is the town hub — a vast old drugstore with soda fountain and video arcade, the expected beach gear, art supplies in back, big selections of kites and costumes, and all kinds of diverting things. *Northeast corner, Butler at Mason. (616) 857-8241. Year-round pharmacy hours: Mon-Sat 9-6, Sun 10-5. In summer, store stays open to 10 Mon-Sat, to 7 Sun.* ♿

◆ **Old Post Office.** A card shop extraordinaire (plus some puzzles, bags and boxes, giftwrap, rubber stamps, stationery, etc.) in the former post office, complete with antique mail slots. *238 Butler. (616) 857-4553. Open Mon-Sat 10-5, Sun 11-5, later summer & holidays.*

◆ **Uncommon Grounds.** Charming coffeehouse with displays of original art is a year-round gathering place. It has a deck, games, a good bulletin board, and free reading. Next door: Cafe Dona, a terrific lunch spot. Down the street at the corner of Water: an amply funded doll shop. *Sun-Thurs 9 a.m.-10:30 p.m., to 11:30 Fri & Sat. Jan-March: closes at 10 (Fri & Sat) or 9 p.m.* ♿

◆ **Singapore Bank Bookstore.** Saugatuck's biggest bookstore, a cozy, personal place run by an avid sailor, is in the old Singapore Bank building. Moving the structure here from the buried town of Singapore saved it from entombment by dune sands. General reading plus lots of local lore. *317 Butler (2nd floor). (616) 857-3785. May thru Dec: Sun-Thurs 10-6. Fri & Sat 10-8. Winter: may close Tues-Thurs. Call first.*

◆ **Cain Gallery.** The summer home of a gallery in suburban Oak Park, Illinois, Cain shows paintings and prints, jewelry, sculpture, and art glass by living artists with national reputations. *322 Butler. Open Mother's Day thru second weekend Oct. June 1 thru Labor Day: 12-5 daily. Weekends only in May and fall. (616) 857-4353.*

◆ **Animalia Gallery.** Everything in this striking American handcrafts gallery has an animal motif of some sort, without being cloying or dumb. Prints, paintings, sculpture, and also earrings, teapots, platters, cards, and the like. **Shows** change every two weeks. *403 Water at Main. (616) 857-3227.* ♿

◆ **Water Street Galleries.** Big upstairs gallery with a stimulating mix of contemporary art from mainly American artists. Paintings by William Aiken of San Francisco, prints by Tony Saladino of Texas and Wimsi Van Wyck of South Africa, bronze sculpture by Jean Jacques Porret of Chicago, still lifes by Catherine Maize and landscapes by Chuck Parsons. *403 Water. (616) 857-8485. Mon-Sat 10-5, Sun noon-5. Closed Thanksgiving, Christmas, and New Year's Day.* ♿

◆ **DeGraaf Fine Arts.** Sophisticated one- and two-person shows highlight works by artists including Bill Barrett (sculpture), G. Elyane Bick (tapestries), Charlie Brouwer (wood sculptures), and Stefan Davidek (paintings), and Steven MacGowan (painted wood relief). For the many people who enjoyed Dan DeGraaf's Ann Arbor gallery in the 1970s and early 1980s, it's like coming upon an old friend. After years in the gallery business in Chicago, he has returned to his native West Michigan. *403 Water Street on Main (enter around the corner on Main). (616) 857-1882. Open May thru December, Mon-Sat 11-5, Sun 1-5. Closed January thru April.* ♿

♦ **Open Door Music.** "Music to soothe the soul" and a little bit of many relaxing things, reflecting owner Ron Elmore's outlook on life. Cassettes and CDs of all forms of unusual piano music, from classical to jazz, Scottish and Irish, and what's loosely called New Age. These have become a mail-order specialty. The store offers some 500 demos. "They call me the music physician — I prescribe," Elmore jokes. Jewelry, wearable art, and supplies for massage and aroma therapy are also on hand, and Elmore provides spiritual consultations. Visitors are welcome to sit and examine "story stones" — mixes of calcite and hematite found in beachside banks. They suggest stories and characters, viewed in some ways. A former geologist, Elmore says these are far more fascinating than Petoskey stones. *403 Water St. (616) 857-4565. Summer hours are generally 10:30-5:30 daily, open evenings Wed-Sat. Call to check seasonal hours.* ♿

♦ **Polka Gallery.** Genial, European-trained oil painter John Polka has been a Saugatuck fixture since 1964. In his studio/ gallery you can see him at work on his own dreamily romantic, impressionist paintings of flowers, landscapes, animals, and figures ($100 to $5,000). Many scenes are local. Polka also does commission portraits and teaches classes in his studio. *731 Water. (616) 857-2430. Year-round, daily 9-8.* ♿: *2 steps, assistance available.*

DOUGLAS

Downtown Douglas has in recent years been spiffed up, with some attractive antiques and design shops, a coffeehouse, and two modestly priced restaurants popular with summer people. Unlike Saugatuck, you can still find a parking place here in summer. Douglas has some attractive historic buildings in and around the town center near the river, and up the hill from downtown. West off Center, on the other side of the busy Blue Star Highway with its commercial strip, a peaceful, shady shore drive is lined with turn-of-the-century summer houses. Spring wildflowers through the

Art in a former lumberyard: The Joyce Petter Gallery has openings every other week. The buildings are interesting in themselves.

woods here are delightful. *To reach downtown Douglas, turn east onto Center from the Blue Star Highway at the light on the hill south of town, or exit from the rear of the parking lot of the Joyce Petter Gallery at the bridge.*

◆ **Joyce Petter Gallery.** Often humorous or richly decorative, this art is meant to be "a delight to live with," as manager Mary Hart says. Eclectic, accessible, and interesting, the Petter Gallery showcases some five dozen American painters, printmakers, sculptors, glassmakers, and ceramicists. Landscapes often show ordinary subjects, urban and rural, in fresh new ways. The gallery's home is now a beautifully remodeled lumberyard by the Kalamazoo River bridge in Douglas. There's more room to show off the art, plus space for a fireplace, sofa and chairs, coffee, and antiques to show how the art would suit a traditional home. Windows frame beautiful real-life views: a garden, a pretty street of old houses. Don't miss the striking, light-filled **glass gallery** at one end, or the separate remodeled barn that has lots of sculpture. Weather permitting, **croquet** can be played on the gallery green.

From May through September, the gallery hosts **bi-weekly openings** on Sunday afternoons from 12-5:30 p.m., with the artists present from 2-4. Recent additions are the huge floral watercolors of Cathleen Daly (they measure 7 feet by 4 1/2 feet) and joyful figurative oils on shaped canvas by Joyce Paul. Prices range from $300-$8,000. The staff enjoys explaining processes of printmaking, ceramics, and such. *161 Blue Star Highway at the bridge in Douglas/Saugatuck. (616) 857-7861. May thru December Mon-Sat 10-5:30, Sun noon-5:30. January thru March: weekends and by appointment.* &

♦ **S.S.** *Keewatin* **ship museum.** The 350-foot *Keewatin,* permanently moored here, is a rare vestige of the wonderful era of Great Lakes steamship travel. The passenger and freight steamship was one of the last of the big boats, in service until 1965. The *Keewatin* (it's pronounced "key-WAY-tin") sailed from Port McNicoll on Georgian Bay to Fort William on western Lake Superior. The six-day round trip cost $30 in 1908, including meals. Tour guides gives visitors a thorough look at the Scottish-built vessel: the mahogany interiors, the compact staterooms, the forward lounge for female passengers only, the Edwardian dining room; the captain's suite; the wheelhouse. The spartan galley had Chinese chefs. (The original French cooks drank too much.) On top is the great 50-foot funnel. Fired by coal, the boat's 3,300 horsepower engine took 150 tons of coal a week.

The S.S. *Keewatin* **took 288 passengers from Georgian Bay to Fort William on western Lake Superior. The Canadian Pacific Railway was its owner.**

The lower deck has many cases of interesting memorabilia about the ship's history. Alongside the *Keewatin* is the *Reiss*, the last of the coal-fired Great Lakes steam tugs. *On Blue Star Highway at the Kalamazoo River. See map. (616) 857-2107. Guided tours 10:30-4:30 daily, Mem. Day thru Labor Day. Adults $4.50, children 6-12 $2. &: no.*

◆ **Australian Galleries, Ltd.** Donald Stoltz and Jane Vandervelde have assembled an interesting range of merchandise on Australian culture — everything from jars of Vegimite, a strange concentrated yeast extract Australians love to spread on crackers, to Crocodile Dundee-type hats and $250 long Drizabone waxed dusters to boomerangs from $5 up. Books, videos, T shirts, fabrics and aprons by aboriginal artists in adaptations of traditional patterns of swirling dots, koala bear stuffed toys, opals — you could spend hours here, and sample that Vegimite, too. Ask for a demonstration of musical instruments like the didgeridoo and clap sticks, and buy some tapes to learn to play them. The **gallery** mounts changing shows of Australian art and culture. *95 Blue Star Hwy. (north side), in a new, steep-roofed building on the hill. (616) 857-6022. Open daily 1-6 year-round. &*

◆ **Button Galleries.** The site alone is so attractive, it's worth the drive to Douglas's leafy area of summer homes along Lake Michigan. Visitors can walk through the garden filled with rhododendrons and azaleas. Features contemporary oils and watercolors by national and regional artists. *955 Center in Douglas, one block east of Lake Michigan. Turn west from Blue Star Hwy. onto Center at the light, proceed toward lake. (616) 857-2175. Usually open daily 11-5 between mid-May and mid-Oct. In winter, Sat hours are noon-5. Call first. &: east door.*

◆ **The Ark.** Not in Douglas at all, but on the Blue Star Highway just northeast of Saugatuck and east of I-196/U.S. 31. Marcia Perry's own creations in wood range from big, earthy treetrunk figures to switchplates to massive carved-out seats such as a surprisingly comfortable rocker. She works instinctively. "The trees talk to me. I translate so other people can see what they say," she says, without a hint of pretentious mysticism. "Trees give us so much, and ask for nothing." Lately she's been producing handmade books of poems and tree images as another way to getting the tree message across. Exhibits in the upstairs **gallery** feature theme shows like "The World Tree" and the Goddess Invitational. It favors neglected art forms (like books) and artists who are just getting going.

Ask for directions to **Thirdstone**, the studio of her friend Bruce

Cutean, an assemblage sculptor. He assembles recycled stuff into bizarre and fanciful constructions. His gallery represents some 25 or 30 working artists that commercial galleries wouldn't touch. Cutean and Perry sponsor **workshops** (led by themselves and others) on glass bead-making, bookmaking, paper-making, clay, jewelry and metalsmithing techniques, stained glass, woodcarving, and assemblage art. *Blue Star Hwy. just east of I-96. (616) 857-4210. Open 12-5 daily except Tues. Jan-April: call for hours.* ♿: *workshop but not gallery.*

Marcia Perry sits in one of her massive (and suprisingly comfortable) treetrunk chairs that encircle the body. Her mission: to interpret to humans what trees have to teach us.

◆ **Thirdstone Gallery**. Bruce Cutean assembles recycled stuff into bizarre and fanciful constructions. His gallery also represents some 25 or 30 working artists that commercial galleries wouldn't touch. See above for workshops. *3995 64th St. near Saugatuck. Call for directions. (616) 335-8027. Open year-round. Mon-Sat 11-5, Sun 12-5 and by appointment. Closed Tues & Wed Nov-March.* ♿: *call.*

MOUNT BALDHEAD AND OVAL BEACH

A fine panorama, a pretty picnic spot, dune trails, and a well-equipped beach are just across the river from Saugatuck. You can easily get there from downtown Saugatuck by taking the **chain ferry,** which runs from Mary and Water in downtown Saugatuck to Ferry Street, across the Kalamazoo River. *Mem.- Labor Day 9-9. Adults $1; children 50¢ one way. Call (616) 857-4243 to confirm hours.*

For a **delightful car-free picnic**, pick up tasty sandwiches at Loaf & Mug, 236 Culver, or at Pumpernickel's, 202 Butler in downtown Saugatuck. Take the chain ferry across the river and head north along Park Street to the foot of Mt. Baldhead. You can picnic

on the pleasant deck overlooking the river and downtown Saugatuck. The **Saugatuck-Douglas Historical Museum**, open seasonal-
ly, is in the small brick building nearby.

A short, steep wood stairway and path leads to the top of
Mount Baldhead, named for its sandy crown before trees were
planted on top. This 262-foot dune is the tallest in the region. It
provides a superb **view** of Saugatuck, Lake Kalamazoo, and
Douglas. On top of Mt. Baldhead is a **radar dome**, installed in 1957
as part of the DEW line that once stretched across northern
America to warn of Soviet attack from the north. The dome now
holds a ship-to-shore antenna. From the top, two interesting **trails,**
one to the north and one to the south, lead to **scenic views** of the
lake and forested surroundings. The South Ridge Trail leads across
the dune and down to the road to the popular city-owned **Oval
Beach**, just west of Mt. Baldhead. A beautiful natural setting with
low dunes and marram grass adds visual interest. There's a pretty
overlook by the restrooms, changing rooms, and **snack stand** (616-
857-1991) with beach paraphernalia. You can rent chairs and
umbrellas. The beach gets increasingly crowded around the third
week in June, when Chicago schools let out and urban vacationers
arrive in large numbers, especially on weekends.

*To climb Mt. Baldhead, take the chain ferry from downtown
Saugatuck on Water at Mary. See directions above. OR drive by car.
Take the Blue Star Hwy. through Douglas, turn west on Center, right
on Park. Park at the Mt. Baldhead parking lot on Park St., 2 blocks
north of Perryman Beach Rd.*

*To reach Oval Beach by foot. take the chain ferry across the river,
head south on Park St., turn left onto Perryman for a leisurely hike
through scenic dunes. By car take the Blue Star Hwy. through Douglas,
turn west on Center, right onto Park. At the dune's base, turn left onto
Perryman Beach Rd., follow signs to Oval Beach. Beach season runs
Mem.-Labor Day. Lifeguard & concession hours usually 11-6. $5/car.
Season pass $25. Walk-ins free. &: restroom, dune overlook.*

EVENTS IN SAUGATUCK . . . . . In Wicks Park there are chamber music concerts, a summer music festival (usually jazz), and art exhibits. . . . . For an
events calendar, call (616) 857-5801 or stop by the Saugatuck-Douglas
Convention & Visitor Bureau at 303 Culver. On weekends stop at the kiosk on
Butler at Culver, across from Town Hall. . . . . $5 a day introductory **drop-in art
lessons** are offered at Ox-Bow for a week in July and August by well-known
Michigan painters and potters. Call Ox-Bow at (616) 857-5811 for details, or

check out the posters around town. &. . . . . Twenty galleries have open houses for **Gallery Stroll** the second weekend in October.

ONE OF THE VERY BEST LAKE MICHIGAN BOAT CRUISES. . . . . Interestingly varied scenery makes the **Star of Saugatuck** an enjoyable $1^1/_2$-hour voyage. The 67-foot, 82-passenger boat goes out on Lake Michigan when the waves aren't too high. The informative guide comments colorfully on passing sights. He explains how the little flags on charter fishing boats tell how many fish were caught on the last outing, how the Lake Michigan shoreline has eroded 300 feet over the past 88 years, how the soft-sounding foghorn at the end of the channel going into Lake Michigan sounds much louder in a fog. It's best to take this pleasant voyage when it isn't too windy; then the boat can go farther out into Lake Michigan. In general, the earlier in the day, the calmer the water. There are restrooms, ships, candy, drinks, beer, and wine on board. *716 Water near Spear next to Gleason's Party Store, in downtown Saugatuck on the Kalamazoo River. (616) 857-4261. Daily early May thru Sept; weekends thru mid-Oct., weather permitting. $8 adults, $4.50 children.* &: *except no electric or extra-wide.*

AN EXCEPTIONALLY NATURAL AND PEACEFUL BEACH . . . . . the **Saugatuck Dunes State Park** is protected from hoards of beachgoers by its remote location. It's one of western Michigan's most beautiful yet uncrowded nature spots. The 866 acres include over two miles of Lake Michigan **beach** and 18 miles of groomed **cross-country skiing trails** (from beginning to expert levels) through the wild, pristine dune country to wonderful dune-top views of the lake. There are a few picnic tables, but no restrooms or changing areas. The parking lot is a mile from the beach, and the sandy, hilly path makes it seem even longer. *3 1/2 miles north of Saugatuck. Take Blue Star Highway to 64th St., go north 1 1/2 miles to 138th Ave., west 1 mile to park. (616) 399-9390. 8 a.m.-10 p.m. daily. $4/car/day, $20 annual state park sticker.* **No camping.**

THE SAUGATUCK DUNE RIDES . . . . plunge you through shifting sands in a converted 3/4 ton Dodge pickup. The 35-minute ride emphasizes amusement, not nature appreciation. Roaring up and down steep slopes, the driver is likely to suddenly shout things like, "No brakes! We've lost the brakes!" *Blue Star Highway, 1/2 mile west of I-196 on exit 41, 1 mile northeast of Saugatuck. (616) 857-2253. Open May 1 thru mid-October. Through September Mon-Sat 10-5:30, Sun 12-5:30. In July & Aug. open until 7:30. In October weekends only. $10 adults; $5.50 children 3 to 10. Cash only.* &: *call.*

MORE STUDIO GALLERIES . . . . . are along the **Blue Star Highway** between Saugatuck and South Haven. It's a delightful drive past blueberry fields and through old villages with a fair number of antiques shops. Flags and signs indicate which studios are open. Summers it's most of the time, on weekends in fall.

Holland

Not just tulips and wooden shoes,
Holland has a lively, picture-perfect new downtown
and a pretty, old-fashioned park.

IT'S THE CITY'S Dutch heritage that brings visitors to Holland – that and the beaches at the very popular state park just north of town. The big draw is Tulip Time in May, when Holland is jammed with half a million tourists who have come to see millions of tulips. Other Dutch attractions are in high gear all summer. **Windmill Island**, a sort of mini-theme park, has the only authentic old Dutch windmill allowed to leave the Netherlands. **Dutch Village** (a recreated village out on U.S. 31 by the Horizon Outlet Center) and the **Holland Museum** offer some interesting glimpses of Dutch culture. Even the two **wooden shoe factories** – tourist traps in the nostalgic style of several decades ago – have a certain charm and sincerity.

Holland's downtown, one of the state's most pleasant, has reoriented itself to feature appealing specialty shops in the face of mall competition. Architectural details from the Northern Renaissance are in evidence as you walk around the downtown business district. You can take nice downtown walks to **Centennial Park**, the **Holland Museum**, the attractive **Hope College campus**, and the lovely **historic neighborhood** along Twelfth Street west of River. It's especially nice in spring, when block after block is lined with tulips.

Few American industrial towns remained as ethnically pure for so long as Holland. Founded by Dutch religious dissenters in 1847, it remained 90% Dutch for over a century. Holland's founding

Hope College logo: the college's mission was to be an anchor of the Reformed Faith in the New World.

Separatists were rural artisans and farmers. They had resisted the 19th-century Dutch movement to modernize the state-controlled church. Some were actually jailed by the Dutch government for their belief in a more literal interpretation of the Bible. The opportunity in the 1840s to form their own self-run community in America had the same appeal it had for the Puritans two centuries earlier. Times were hard in the Netherlands then, and the success of the industrial revolution in England had weakened the Dutch economy.

❶ **Kirk Park**
(p. 509). Area's best beach combines natural scenery, pretty picnic spots, good playground, splendid beach backed by high dunes and dark beech woods. Bike path from Holland.

❷ **Veldheer Tulip Gardens** (p. 502). Costs $3 to enter the formal garden, but the 30-acre tulip field out back is also magical. Visit at dusk, when tulips glow. Next door is only Delftware factory outside the Netherlands.

❸ **Bike path to Grand Haven**
(p. 519). 29 miles. Passes shady back dunes, cottages & homes, estuary with wildlife at Port Sheldon. Connects beaches at Holland State Park, Tunnel and Kirk parks. Nice ride in 2 days even for the fairly unfit.

❹ **Dutch Village**
(p. 510). Beguiling mix of history, nostalgia, and storybook kitsch. Small theme park; 18th-19th c. village setting with adroit details. Wonderful antique carnival rides, street organs. klompen dancers.

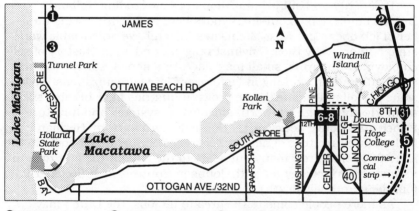

❺ **Wooden Shoe Factory** (p. 503). Fun, old-timey tourist trap has Holland's best demonstrations of wooden shoe making. See antique French sabots and Dutch klompen; sample Dutch sweets and cheese.

❻ **Centennial Park** (p. 507). Old-fashioned park with lighted fountain, rock grotto, windmill-shaped flower beds, potted palms from city greenhouse, all beneath canopy of century-old trees.

❼ **Holland Museum** (p. 500). Dutch bourgeoisie was the Western World's first to create cozy, private homes. See their cheerful 18th-c. sitting rooms, outstanding collections of Delftware, pewter. Displays on multicultural Holland & its vaunted work ethic.

❽ **Eighth Street** (p. 504). Renovated downtown with beautiful buildings, good shopping, bakeries, restaurants. Don't miss **Till Midnight** restaurant-bakery (p. 504) on College for soup or an elegant meal.

Highlights of
Holland

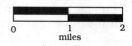

0   1   2
                        miles

Hard times and religious oppression in the Netherlands led increasing numbers of pious rural folk, an estimated 250,000 in all, to emigrate to the U.S., mainly in an arc around southern Lake Michigan. Often whole congregations or neighborhood units arrived together and established their own communities. By 1849, new arrivals had founded the nearby villages of Zeeland, Vriesland, Groningen, Overisel, and Drenthe, named after the newcomers' place of origin.

Loyalty to home and neighborhood are characteristic of the Dutch. In Holland, Michigan, this was reinforced by the immigrants' strong religious convictions and by intentional isolation in their own small, self-contained city. As a result, Holland remained unusually homogeneous four and five generations after the first immigrants arrived. Natural blondes were the rule.

Prosperity and suburbanization are now eroding Holland's Dutch complexion as outsiders move here to fill the growing number of job openings. West Michigan's Dutch have an enviable work ethic reinforced by their Calvinist religion, and a long history of self-employment in farms, small manufacturing shops, stores, and services rather than working in factories or large organizations. Now some of Holland's many home-grown industries have become spectacularly successful: Haworth office panel systems and furniture, Prince automotive accessories, Donnelly auto mirrors, Herman Miller office furniture of nearby Zeeland. They created a boom in the late 1980s that drew many outsiders to the city for the first time in its history. Prince merged with Johnson Controls in 1996, after its founder's untimely death.

As more people come to the area to fill jobs, the Dutch may actually become a minority of Holland's residents. The hundreds of high school kids who practice for months to perform as klompen dancers at Tulip Time now come in a very broad range of hair colors and skin tones. Most noticeable are the Mexican-Americans, who now make up a quarter of all public school students.

DUTCH ATTRACTIONS

♦ **Dutch Village.** Evocative, appealing interpretation of a 19th-century village. A real highlight. See page 510.

♦ **Holland Museum.** What used to be the Netherlands Museum has moved into Holland's grand old post office. It now goes beyond Dutch culture to tell the story of the entire city of Holland, including its numerous Mexican-American and Asian residents. Exhibits focus on Holland's remarkable economic development and the cultural values that created the climate for growth.

Rare sight: a operating Dutch windmill, the only one allowed to leave the Netherlands. It's a majestic sight at dusk, seen from the Black River causeway and park on North River Street north of downtown. Five stories high, it grinds flour sold at Windmill Island.

Windmills and wooden shoes symbolize Dutch ingenuity and hard work that made a difficult, wet environment productive.

Many of the charming artifacts from the old museum are on display: a quaint tiled Dutch living room first recreated in the Cincinnati apartment of a Dutch immigrant; a large doll house, furnished down to inkwells and cookie cutters; and many things shown in the Dutch exhibit of the 1939 World's Fair, including an 11-foot clock surmounted by the Queen and her ministers. Press a button and it plays the Dutch national anthem. *Downtown at Tenth at River in the old post office facing Centennial Park. (616) 392-9084. Mon-Sat 10-5, Thurs to 8, Sun 2-5. Closed major holidays.* ♿ *$3, $2 seniors & students, family rate $7.*

♦ **Windmill Island Municipal Park.** This city park, built for tourists, features De Zwaan ("The Swan"), five stories high, the only **working Dutch windmill** outside the Netherlands. It grinds whole wheat flour sold at the park, but operates only when supplies are low and the wind is between 15 and 20 knots. Call before coming to find out whether it's in operation. The park's other unique highlight is **"Little Netherlands,"** a delightful folk art model of a canal-laced

Dutch town in 1847, the year Holland's settlers left for America. Local artisans built and carved it as a Tulip Time project in the 1930s and put in lots of jokey scenes and corny comments. Windmill Island has loads of tulip beds, **klompen dancers**, a 1910 **carousel**, a pleasant **terrace** by the cafe. But a lot of tacky merchandise and dated displays spoil the effect. Plans for overhauling the city-owned attraction are in the works. As for now, the privately owned Dutch Village, where more attention has been paid to details, is a better overall family entertainment value. *Just northeast of downtown Holland at Seventh and Lincoln. (616) 396-5433. Open May into late October. May, July & August: Mon-Sat 9-6, Sun 11:30-6. June & Sept: Mon-Fri 10-5, Sat 9-6, Sun 11:30-6. Oct: Mon-Fri 10-4, Sat 9-5, Sun 11:30-4. Adults $5, children 5-12 $2.50. &: yes, except restrooms & windmill's upper stories.*

◆ **Veldheer Tulip Gardens.** Veldheer's spectacular mass of tulips attracts throngs of tourists in May. The longtime Holland tulip-grower has a very pleasant **formal garden**, complete with draw-bridges and the inevitable ornamental windmills, which are also sold in the adjoining garden shop. The large **windmill** is an authentic copy of a traditional Dutch drainage windmill. In summer the gardens are filled with many varieties of lilies, peonies, and Dutch iris that Veldheer's propagates and sells here.

But the truly spectacular sight is the 30-acre **tulip field** behind the warehouses. Evenings, when the tour buses are gone, the locals come out after work to enjoy the tulips. At dusk, the sweeping masses of flowers, almost as far as you can see, seem to glow and shimmer with their own light, especially on overcast days. This striking phenomenon, known as the Purkinje Shift, comes just at sunset, when the receptors in your eye's retina shift from using cones (for color vision) to the more accurate, black and white rods at the retina's periphery. For a brief time, you still perceive color, but differently, more toward the red end of the spectrum.

Beds in the formal gardens are numbered to correspond with Veldheer's mail-order catalog, so you can place orders for fall bulbs after seeing the real thing in bloom (the first three weeks in May). Veldheer claims to grow the world's largest selection of tulips, over 100 varieties in all, plus various daffodils, hyacinths, crocus, and the new peonies and lilies. Prices average $5 for 10 tulip bulbs. *On Quincy just east of U.S. 31, 4 miles north of Holland. Clearly visible from the highway. (616) 399-1900. Open year-round. During Tulip Time (1st 3 weeks of May): daily 8-dusk. April thru December (except Tulip Time): Mon-Fri 8-6, Sat-Sun 9-5. January thru March: Mon-Fri 9-5. &: grass paths in gardens, fields are too soft. Admission to formal* *gardens: $3 adults, $1 children 6-16.*

♦ **DeKlomp Wooden Shoe and Delftware Factory**. Next to Veldheer's, under the same ownership and management. It's the only place outside the Netherlands where earthenware is hand-painted in the Dutch style using genuine Delft glaze. In the 17th-century, during the short time of Dutch dominance at sea, blue-and-white Delft imitating expensive Chinese porcelains was manufactured for middle-class Hollanders. Painters here are happy to answer questions and explain the difference between real, handpainted Delft and much cheaper look alikes with printed decal transfers. Popular items include personalized wedding and retirement plates (up to $80 when completely handpainted), tiny shoes and figurines ($8), house portraits, and wedding or baby tiles.

De Klomp also has a **wooden shoe demonstration workshop** with picture windows. The large stock of plain and decorated wooden shoes ("klompen" in Dutch, "sabots" in French) is made in the Netherlands; prices here ($16.45 for a women's size 7) are somewhat cheaper than at other outlets. Devised as sturdy, dry footwear in the wet, low fields of northern Europe, these serve perfectly well as gardening shoes today. The usual Dutch sweets and souvenirs are also for sale. *See Veldheer Tulip Gardens on previous page for location and hours.*

♦ **Wooden Shoe Factory**. A giant, old-timey tourist trap features Holland's best wooden shoemaking demonstrations. The only American member of the Dutch guild of klompenmakers works in a

The epitome of cozy: few if any peoples in history have lavished more attention on the cozy amenities of home than the Dutch. This rural living room can be seen at the Holland Museum.

sawdusty, sneezy wood shop. The specialized wood-turning equipment used here in making wooden shoes was manufactured in the Netherlands and France at the turn of the century. An interesting **display** shows many kind of wooden shoes worn in damp, low-lying areas of France, Holland, and Belgium. *(616) 396-6513. On U.S. 31 just south of 16th St. 8 a.m.-6 p.m. daily. Demonstrations run from 8 a.m. to 4:30 daily except Sunday.* ♿

DOWNTOWN POINTS OF INTEREST

Holland's main street, Eighth, is today a picture-perfect scene of unusually handsome and distinctive turn-of-the-century buildings. For years downtown Holland was the only major shopping area within 25 miles. In a foresighted response to two shopping malls that opened in 1988, the city launched a massive streetscape improvement project involving pleasant benches, beautiful flower beds, attractive street lamps and paving, and Snowmelt, a costly underground heating system to keep sidewalks clear of snow.

For awhile it looked as if downtown was being kept alive by good intentions and money from the late Ed Prince, a successful automotive accessory maker who insisted on anonymity for his downtown project. Today downtown is remarkably lively, with many interesting and creative new businesses. It's designed for browsing, with book and CD stores, galleries, lots of places to eat and snack, two excellent bakeries, and four little parks. Better women's wear and men's wear and shoes are especially well represented. There's also a downtown bowling alley, the **Holland Bowling Center** (616-392-1425) and art movie theater, the Dutch-style **Knickerbocker Theater** at 86 E. Eighth (616-395-4950; ♿). Pick up a store location map at area stores to get the full picture. And remember, most stores are *closed on Sunday. On Eighth Street some are open in summer only. A growing core of stores are staying open until 9 p.m. at least on Mon, Thurs, and Fri.*

Five **parking lots along Ninth** make it a handy place to park. The good shopping starts on River at Ninth, a block south of Eighth.

Selected shopping highlights, arranged from west (River St.) to east, include:

◆ **Three Chairs Co.** The owner, a former product design manager at Herman Miller, opened a retail store showing contemporary classics at good price points. Its strong suit: upholstered pieces with washable slipcovers that are suited to family life. That casual, elegant simplicity can deal with popcorn, dog hair, and kids. Also shown: Shaker-inspired pieces, handcrafted black iron metal beds, accent lamps, and more. The only really luxurious merchandise are the bed linens. The name comes from Thoreau. The building itself is interesting: brick walls, and a mix of old and new patterned floor tiles. *215 S. River at Ninth. (616) 393-9433. Mon-Sat 10-5:30, to 9 p.m. Mon, Thurs & Fri.* &

◆ **The Shaker Messenger of Shaker and Folk Art.** Country crafts of very high quality from makers individually known to the proprietors. The effect is simple and spare, like the store's Shaker namesakes. Noah's ark is a favorite motif. For do-it-yourselfers, there are books and plenty of inspiration and encouragement. Pick up a **newsletter** featuring special talks, demonstrations, workshops, and artists' receptions. *210 S. River. (616) 396-4588. Open Mon, Thurs & Fri 10-9; Tues, Wed, & Sat 10-5:30; Sun 12-4.* &

◆ **Reader's World.** An exceptionally well managed and attractive newsstand with a good selection of books, including local and regional titles. *194 River at Eighth. Mon-Fri 9-9, Sat 9-6, Sun 8-5. (616) 396-8548.* &

◆ **Tower Clock Accents.** Beautiful, wide-ranging gift and tabletop store in downtown Holland's most striking building, erected in 1891 of blue-gray local Waverly stone. *190 S. River. (616) 393-0305. Mon & Fri 10-9; Tues, Wed & Sat 10-6. Open Thurs to 9 in summer.* &

◆ **Holland Arts Council.** The **gallery** typically shows work by several Michigan artists in one medium at a time. The **shop** is crammed with unusual jewelry, cards, and art-related toys and gifts. Pick up the **newsletter** with upcoming workshops, performances, and dances visitors can join in. **Free First Friday** workshops from 5-6:30 invite families to try out art projects on the second floor. *25 West Eighth. (616) 396-3278. Summer hours: Mon & Fri 10-9, Tues-Thurs 10-5, Sat 10-4. Winter hours: Mon-Thurs 10-9, Fri 10-5, Sat 10-4.* &

◆ **The Bridge.** Self-help crafts store supplied by artisans from 40 developing countries. Textiles, wall hangings, rugs, and jackets especially stand out. Merchandise is reasonably priced and attractively displayed. The store is run by a volunteer ministry of Western Theological Seminary, the Reformed Church in America school connected with Hope College. *18 West Eighth. (616) 392-3977. Mon-Sat 9:30-5:30, Mon & Fri to 9.* &

◆ **Booksellers on Main Street.** Good browsing and an attractive mix of books, cards, and gifts. Pleasant, sit-down section for kids. *49 East Eighth. (616) 396-0043. Mon-Sat 9:30-9.* &

◆ **Sand Castle.** A toy store where nearly every toy can be played with, and virtually none appear on TV. Nifty decor highlights kites, sand toys, dolls, marionettes, puppets, games, and creative playsets like Toobers & Zots, a colorful wired foam construction set. Brio and Brio Mec tables encourage kids to sit down and play. *2 E. Eighth at Central. (616) 396-5955. Mon-Sat 10-6, to 9 Thurs & Fri. Summer: Mon-Sat 10-9.* &

◆ **Alpen Rose.** A genuine Austrian *konditorei* in front of a large restaurant. The co-owner is an Austrian who came to the U.S. to work as pastry chef on Mackinac Island's Grand Hotel and met his American wife and partner there. Pies, cookies, plus terrific European-style whipped cream pastries and butter tortes. *4 East Eighth at Central. (616) 393-2111. Summer: Mon-Thurs 9-9:30, Fri & Sat 9-10, Sun 10:30-2. Winter hours vary.* &

◆ **Tikal.** Alternative and ethnic women's clothing from many countries, including Mexico, Guatemala, Indonesia, Thailand, and Nepal. Also sterling silver jewelry. *6 E. Eighth. (616) 396-6828. Open 10-5:30 Tues-Sat, to 9 Mon, Thurs & Fri.* &

◆ **Castle Park Gallery.** After spending many summers in Holland, owner Tom Stevens moved his gallery of fine arts and crafts up from the Carolinas in 1993, and began adding western Michigan artists. Over 150 artists are now represented. The gallery is becoming especially known for its art glass from Michigan, Santa Fe, Seattle, and elsewhere. Oils, watercolors, sculpture, pottery, and jewelry are in all price ranges up to around $4,000. Hand-made cards start at $2. A new hit: table-size waterfalls of slate and stone. *8 E. Eighth. (616) 395-0077. Mon & Fri 10-9; Tues thru Thurs & Sat 10-5:30.* &

◆ **The Tin Ceiling.** Cooperating owners pool their resources to create 5 shops under one roof. Folk art and traditional, Victorian and Scandinavian crafts, with a little touch of country. *10 E. Eighth. (616) 395-2623. Mon & Fri 10-9; Tues thru Thurs & Sat 10-5:30.* &

◆ **Lokers Shoes.** Wonderful motto ("Shoes that fit.") and huge stock includes hard-to-find sizes, quality brands. The bargain basement has some great values in shoes and handbags, too. *31 E. Eighth. (616) 392-1749. Mon-Sat 9:30-9.* &

◆ **Butch's Drydock.** Big, bustling deli/bar with lots of seating, good breads, many imported cheeses and other foods, deli salads, frozen takeout entrees that could be a boon to vacationers. Entertainment some nights. A favorite with Hope College students. *44 E. Eighth. (616) 396-8227. Mon-Wed 10-11, Thurs-Sat to midnight.* &

◆ **Moynihan Gallery and Framing**. Artist-in-residence Kathleen Moynihan and her husband, Larry Weller, who specializes in custom framing, offer original art, posters, hand-crafted cards, books

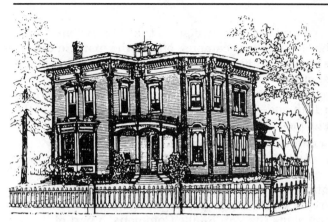

Furnishings and family memorabilia at the 1874 Cappon House tell about a prosperous Dutch family c. 1885. It's open first Saturdays 1-4, and Fri & Sat 1-4 in summer. Call (616) 392-6740 for teas & events.

and artistic gifts. *48 E. Eighth. (616) 394-0093. Mon- Fri 10-8, Sat 10-6, Sun 12-4.* ♿

◆ **Till Midnight.** Bakery arm of Holland's creative and very popular cafe/restaurant. Especially known for French, sourdough, and herb breads. The sidewalk cafe is a nice place for dessert and coffee. *208 College just south of Eighth. (616) 392-6883.* ♿

◆ **Jacob's Ladder.** Comes close to being a New Age/Late Punk/ Christian CD store, an unusual combination, to say the least. In West Michigan, where so many people are steeped in the Christian Reformed subculture, you come to expect occasional offbeat twists on conventional Christianity. *214 College. (616) 392-3303. Summer: Mon-Fri 11-7, Sat 10-6. Winter: Mon-Sat 10-8.* ♿

◆ **The Holland Museum.** See page 500. *31 W. 19th at River, over-looking Centennial Park.*

◆ **Centennial Park.** The leafy canopy of trees over this old-fashioned, leisurely downtown square comes from the commemorative tree-planting done for the nation's centennial in 1876. The park occupies Holland's original market square. Over the years numerous picturesque adornments have been installed: a rock grotto, central fountain (illuminated at night), old-fashioned carpet beds of flowers in the shapes of a windmill and wooden shoe, and palm trees brought out each summer from the city's Victorian greenhouse. A sesquicentennial addition: a statue of Domanie Albertus Van Raalte, Holland's founder. *Between South River and Central between Tenth and Twelfth streets.* ♿

◆ **Walks of historic Holland.** Holland's stock of 19th-century homes, businesses, and institutional buildings is often beautifully detailed and very well maintained. Three worthwhile **walking tour**

brochures on the central area are available at the library: one on downtown and the Hope College campus, one on the **historic district** of Holland's most beautiful historic homes and churches along West Twelfth west of River, and one on things seen between the Holland Museum and historic Cappon House. *Herrick Public Library on River between 12th and 13th. Open Mon-Thurs 9-9, Fri 9-6, Sat 9-6 in winter, 9-1 in summer, Sun 2-5 in winter, closed in summer.*

♦ **Hope College campus** and **De Pree Art Center and Gallery.** Small (2,500 students) liberal-arts college founded by and affiliated with the Reformed Church of America. (Today, actually, the single largest denomination of students is Roman Catholic.) The campus is an attractive architectural hodge-podge dating from 1857. See the campus by walking along the Van Raalte Commons, a part of Twelfth Street converted to a mall connecting College and Columbia streets. The **DeWitt Center** off Columbia has a cafeteria, student bookstore, and game arcade. The De Pree Gallery, named in honor of former Herman Miller furniture chairman and Hope alum Hugh De Pree, mounts changing shows, sometimes student and faculty shows, sometimes nationally known artists and leading Dutch artists. *The art center is behind the visitor parking lot off Columbia between Eleventh and Twelfth. Summer hours: Mon-Fri 9:30--5:30. Weekend hours: Mon-Thurs 10-10, Fri & Sat 10-7. Call (616) 394-7500 for gallery exhibits.* &

THE GRANDMOTHER OF LOCAL FESTIVALS . . . . . was started in the 1930s by a Holland schoolteacher who wasn't Dutch. **Tulip Time**, begins most years on the second Thursday in May. Depending on the weather, it draws from a half-million to a million visitors, largely seniors in tour busses. On Thursday the Town Crier declares the street too dirty and in need of a public scrubbing. The next day, there is a Salute to the Volunteers with a huge fireworks display at dusk, free entertainment, and at 8:30 p.m., the largest Dutch dance exhibition in the world (1400 synchronized dancers). The following Wednesday, the 1st **parade of street scrubbers** and bands goes into action followed by a Children Story Parade on Thursday, and the Parade of Bands (award winning) on Saturday. All parades start at two. There are loads of **shows** (from Lawrence Welk and Christian music to barbershop, vaudeville, and 50s songs), displays, **folk dancing in wooden shoes**, historic **tours**, etc. The biggest crowds are Saturday. It's impeccably organized, a real volunteer-powered community event locals go all-out for. For many visitors, the most enjoyable part is staying in local homes — a tradition of hospitality that goes back for decades. *Call 1-800-822-2770 or (616) 396-4221 for information. Brochure available in October.* &

TULIPS WITHOUT TOURISTS . . . . . Consider visiting Holland the week *before* crowds jam the town for Tulip Time. Flowers are likely already in bloom all over town. (Bulb varieties are planned to bloom during Tulip Time no matter how the weather may vary.) **Tulip Lane**, 8 miles of clearly designated tulip-lined streets, starts at 12th and River, by the Herrick Public Library, and winds through historic and suburban neighborhoods. You can see **klompen dancers** being told how to smile at the 6 p.m. dress rehearsals at Centennial Park (Thurs, Fri, Mon & Tues before Wed's kick-off parade). Dancers are recruited from Holland High, a much more cosmopolitan place than it once was, so today's klompen dancers include Irish and especially Hispanic faces intermixed among a lot of blonds.

HOLLAND'S 150th BIRTHDAY . . . . . brings year-long events in 1997, starting with a February walk from Allegan commemorating the trek of Van Raalte's band through waist-deep snow and ending with the annual **Dutch winterfest** with Sinterklaas. Many lectures and events stress the Dutch connection, like a summer games festival with Dutch games.

WHICH LAKE MICHIGAN BEACH? . . . . . On the north side of Lake Macatawa at Lake Michigan, **Holland State Park** is probably the most crowded, and there's nothing but asphalt behind the sandy beach, but the big red lighthouse and channel with boat traffic is a highlight. You can fish off the pier by the light. . . . . **Tunnel Park**, so-called because a tunnel under a dune goes to the beach, is favored by local families. It's a mile north of the state park on Lake Shore Drive. . . . . Some 10 miles north of the state park and channel, on Lake Shore between Holland and Grand Haven, **Kirk Park** has the most beautiful natural setting. The beach is backed by high dunes; a dune stairway affords a good view of the lake. A shady picnic area is behind the dunes.

FREE BIKE MAPS . . . . . of several recommended bike paths and routes can be had at **The Highwheeler**, 380 Chicago Dr. (Bus I-196). (616) 396-6084. . . . . An **off-road bike path goes from Holland to Grand Haven**, passing the three popular beaches (Holland State Park, Tunnel Park, and Kirk Park). There are no Lake Michigan views along the path itself, but the shady back dunes and huge beech trees are beautiful. A marshy estuary at Port Sheldon is a good place to see waterfowl. See page 519.

FOR A YEAR-ROUND VISITOR PACKET . . . . . contact **Holland Convention & Visitors Bureau**, downtown near the Knickerbocker Theater at 100 E. Eighth, Suite 120 (rear). Open Mon thru Fri 9-5. Call (800) 506-1299.

HIGH-CALIBER SUMMER THEATER . . . . . **Hope Summer Repertory Theatre** is a favorite vacation highlight, with its popular and interesting plays and musicals. Single tickets cost $12-$17; a 4-show coupon is $48 (seniors $44). Early reservations are advised. Call (616) 394-7890.

Dutch Village

*The charm and music of an old Dutch street carnival
in a recreated 19th-century village*

IF YOU go to only one tourist sight in Holland, Dutch Village
should be it. This recreation of a 19th-century Dutch village
is a beguiling combination of fantasy, nostalgia, education,
and gentle kitsch. It's a private, family-run attraction that grew out
of a tulip farm. Dutch Village does a good job of entertaining visitors
while illuminating the 18th- and 19th-century village life Holland's
immigrants left behind — a better job, in fact, than Holland's
municipally owned Windmill Island currently does.

The brick buildings that line Dutch Village's four canals look
authentic, with their careful detailing and imported tile roofs. They
are sandwiched between truck-filled U.S. 31 (noise buffers would be
a nice improvement) and the sprawling Horizon Outlet Center mall.
Despite the busy location, an illusion of leaving the 20th century
behind is effectively created by the big willows and cheery brick
houses. Perennial gardens with over 250 varieties make the grounds
even more attractive throughout the growing season.

The best part of Dutch Village is the operating, antique street
carnival, free for the cost of admission to the grounds. There's a
carousel, two splendid, ornately carved Dutch **street organs**, and
the **Zweefmolen**, a swing something like an antique carousel. It's
just scary enough for older kids to want to ride it again and again —
conveniently allowing adults to look longer at interesting exhibits
and shops. For little children, there's a wavy **slide** descending from
a wooden-shoe house. **Ducks** can be fed on the pond, and **goats**
and **sheep** in the half- scale barn.

High-kicking, adept **klompen dancers** perform at 10:30, 12, 2,
4, and 6 to waltzes and gallops played on the **Gauen Engel organ**,
an oversized 1880 Amsterdam street organ restored by the famous
Carl Frey in 1960. For organ-lovers, this alone is worth the cost of
admission. Visitors can go behind the organ to see the bellows,
wood pipes, and punched music paper (much like a player piano's)
in action. Recordings of street-organ classics are for sale in one of
the gift shops. Attached to the barn is a typical 18th-century **farmhouse**, realistically furnished, with an alcove bed in the stairwell,
and a root cellar down below. The nearby garden area has a
European-style grape arbor, roses, loads of tulips in season, and a

Dutch street carnival circa 1900: this ornate antique street organ plays popular songs of the day. See the punched music rolls from the back. Rides on an antique carousel and giant swing are included in the admission price. So are klompen dancers performing in wooden shoes.

giant stork holding a diaper. Visitors can sit and pose for photos — one of many such planned photo opportunities.

Tucked away and easy to miss are old-fashioned displays of **Dutch regional costumes** and a well-done **windmill diorama** in a building across the way, along with a **cheese-making exhibit.** Next to it, in a grisly allusion to medieval superstitions that survived in 17th-century Holland, is a scale where suspected witches were weighed. If they were unusually light, they were suspected of being able to fly. Near the entrance, the **Bioscoop** (movie theater) shows a 20-minute free movie on the Netherlands.

The gift shops at Dutch Village cover an enormous range. The **Souvenir Shop** covers the low end. The **Arts and Crafts Building** goes upscale with lead crystal, Dutch lace valences, a lot of pricey English and French collectibles (interesting carved figures, quaint porcelain villages), beer steins, Delft-trimmed Dutch copper and brass cookware, and cases of stunning Royal Delft, including a $900 plate after a Rembrandt painting. In the same building is a small **wooden shoe factory** (for demonstration only) and shop.

Imported cheeses, Belgian chocolates, Dutch cookies, and jams are for sale in the **Gourmet Food Shop** and **terrace** overlooking the Horizon Outlet Center pond.

Holland's only restaurant serving Dutch food is the attached **Queen's Inn.** Don't miss the section of real **thatched roof.** It comes down to near eye-level so you can see just how thick and tight-bundled it is.

Every year, starting the day after Thanksgiving and ending Christmas Day, Dutch Village has a free display of 50,000 Christmas lights daily from dusk until around 9. Running concurrently with the Christmas lighting display is a special **Dutch**

Dinner Theater Christmas program Thursday through Saturday, available with or without dinner. Times vary.

James at U.S. 31, 2 miles northeast of downtown Holland. (616) 396-1475. **Shops** *open year-round 9-5:30, in summer until 8. (No entrance fee for shops.)* **Grounds** *are open from the last weekend of April through mid-October. Gates open at 9 a.m. and close at 6.* ♿ *Admission: $5 adults, $3 children 3-11.*

50 OUTLET STORES . . . . . are next door to Dutch Village at **Horizon Outlet Center**, open Mon-Sat 10-9, Sun 11-6, closed Thanksgiving, Christmas, and Easter. In addition to name-brand outlets like Bass Shoes, Van Heusen, Eddie Bauer, Carter Childrenswear, American Tourister, Casual Corner, Champion Hanes, Faberware, Hush Puppies, Jockey, Jonathan Logan, and Pfaltzgraff, some stores offer deeper discounts on miscellaneous closeouts. Outlets offer wide selection on discounts you might have to wait for sales to find locally. But everything's a trade-off. How do your purchases at outlets affect local businesses you care about? *(616) 396-1808 or (800) 866-5900.* ♿

Grand Haven's Boardwalk

At the mouth of the Grand River, Michigan's liveliest pedestrian promenade connects a fine historical museum, the famous musical fountain, and the dramatic Lake Michigan light and pier.

FROM EARLY morning until late evening, both visitors and townspeople stroll along this interesting waterfront walkway. It extends along the Grand River's mouth over a mile, terminating at the Lake Michigan pier and light by Grand Haven State Park. Active boat traffic on this part of the Grand ranges from large freighters to million-dollar yachts. The boardwalk (actually it's mostly asphalt) makes a terrific walk because it's punctuated with pleasant places to sit and many interesting sights, from an extraordinary variety of expensive pleasure boats to ice cream stands to a good museum and the drama of going out on the pier. Lake Michigan piers are grand places to get in touch with the incoming weather, the big lake, and the wide variety of people who come to fish for perch. Piers can be fatally dangerous in storms, however.

Large crowds descend on the town of Grand Haven (population 18,000) because it has the closest Lake Michigan beach to Grand Rapids, Michigan's second largest city. On summer weekend evenings, especially on a holiday, the scene on the boardwalk can be intense, not just with pedestrians but with the low throbbing of powerboats in the adjoining channel and cruising cars along Harbor Drive. Towards sunset, crowds gather to see and hear the illuminated Musical Fountain. For some, it's great

Climax of a boardwalk stroll: the Grand Haven pier and lighthouse. Locals rallied to save the obsolete catwalk, built to reach the lighthouse during stormy high water.

❶ North Beach Park. Much less crowded beach than the state park just south. Terrific dune to climb, with splendid view of lake.

❷ Arboreal Inn. Out of the way, but worth the drive. Excellent food, great atmosphere in quaint, rustic setting. (616) 842-3800.

❸ Boardwalk (p. 513). Lively and scenic, with lots of boats, views, strollers, snacks, good museum. Snug Harbor Restaurant.

❹ South Pier (p. 517). Dramatic walk out to 2 lighthouses. As popular with strollers as fishermen. But dangerous when stormy!

❺ Grand Haven State Park and city beach. Trees are scarce, but these beachside parks are packed with swimmers, kites, and RVs.

❻ Highland Park (p. 520). Haunting Victorian summer colony in wooded dunes. Great old cottages, with scenic boardwalk winding through them.

❼ Lake Forest Cemetery & Duncan Park (p. 521). Beautiful 19th-c. setting with hills, dales, majestic beeches & interesting monuments.

❽ Idyllic drive along the Grand to mid-19th c. river villages of Eastmanville & Lamont. See bayous on south bank, by taking Robbins to Mercury.

Grand Haven

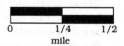

0   1/4   1/2
mile

fun to be where the action so clearly is. For others, it can seem like the All-American nightmare. They're advised to visit the boardwalk in midweek, in the off-season, or in the morning.

Many highlights accent this pleasant walk. They are arranged from east to west toward Lake Michigan, starting at the boardwalk's east end on Jackson at Second Street and ending at the pier. You can **park** at the lot by the Farmers' Market off Jackson. (See page 517 for more parking hints.)

◆ A striking **historic railroad display** on North Harbor Drive just north of Chinook Pier includes a huge coaling tower and a 1941 steam locomotive, with tender and two old cabooses.

◆ The **farmers' market** is off North Harbor just east of the city marina at Chinook Pier. Expect terrific produce in this lakeshore garden spot, where generations of Dutch farmers have had green thumbs. *Open Wednesdays and Saturdays June through October from 8 a.m. until everything's sold.*

◆ **Chinook Pier**, two blocks north of Washington at 101 North Harbor, is home of the large **Chinook Pier sports fishing fleet** (616-842-2229), Grand Haven's municipal **transient marina** (616-847-3478), and **Chinook Pier Miniature Golf** (616-846-2445). Chinook Pier is also the departure point for two summer sightseeing tours, one by bus and the other by boat. (See notes on page 518.) Alongside popular Mac's Cafe convenience store and sit-down deli are shops selling cookies and ice cream and some of the coolest T-shirts and beachwear to be found at any Michigan resort.

◆ The famous **Musical Fountain** across the Grand River is seen from a viewing stand by the boardwalk, behind the old depot and historical museum at the foot of Washington downtown. The sprays emanate from a plain fountain part-way up Dewey Hill on the other side of the river. Every evening at approximately 9:30 p.m. from mid-May through Labor Day, the half-hour display of changing colored lights and spray, and the recorded music concert (40,000 watts worth) attract crowds of pedestrians and flotillas of pleasure boats for a coordinated half-hour concert of recorded music. The program of pop favorites changes each night; Sunday night is hymn night. Pleasure boats crowd together in the river to view the event. The fountain even speaks! "Good evening, ladies and gentlemen. I am the Grand Haven Musical Fountain." Built by volunteers, financed by donated funds, the fountain represents much that is near and dear to this community. To criticize the distant visual display as "insipid" and the sound quality as "fuzzy" is to experience the enduring wrath of local boosters.

The crush of boats and jet skis in the water and the tanned bodies on shore make Grand Haven State Park and City Beach magnets for the exhibitionistic and the gregarious. This scene was during the big Coast Guard Festival.

◆ The **Tri-Cities Historical Museum** is on the river at the head of Washington Street in the old Grand Trunk Depot. It has a wonderfully rich assortment of local artifacts illuminating the area's colorful past, from trapping, lumbering, and shipping to manufacturing, railroading, and the Coast Guard past. Don't miss the tourism display in the basement, or Spring Lake folk artist Lewis Cross's huge, striking, and poignant painting of hunters and one of the vast flocks of now-extinct passenger pigeons that used to fly up the Lake Michigan shore. There's also some great reading, like this newspaper article about the arrival of Grand Haven's first railroad: "The railroad has put an end to our solitude. For twenty long, tedious, dreary winters we have been shut up in solitary confinement for no fault of ours . . . like bears in their hibernation. But now we believe we are on the high road to advancement. We see no reason why we should not become the Milwaukee of Michigan." The museum **shop** has a good selection of books and walking tours to the area. *(616)* *842-0700. Open daily except Mon, Mem. Day thru Labor Day, 10-9:30, Sun noon-9:30. Sept-May: open Tues-Fri 10-5 and noon-4 on weekend afternoons. Adults $1 donation, ages 17 and under free. &: main level.*

◆ The **Brass River Display** is between historical museum and the Chamber of Commerce on South Harbor Drive at Washington. It's a wonderful brass sidewalk map, 50 feet wide, of all the tributaries which feed into the Grand River. This splendid brass map vividly shows how the immense catchment area of the mighty Grand River extends all the way to the Irish Hills south of Jackson. It was made with volunteer help by employees of the local Grand Haven Brass Foundry.

◆ **Downtown Grand Haven** extends along Washington Street from Harbor Drive and has some of West Michigan's best specialty shopping. (See note, page 518.) The first two blocks are largely geared to visitors. The long building of cream-colored brick is **Harbourfront Place,** a shopping/restaurant/office complex in the converted 1906 Story & Clark piano factory.

◆ **The Coast Guard Search and Rescue Station** at 601 S. Harbor (616-847-4500) lacks the excitement it used to have, before the cutter *Acacia* was transferred to Charlevoix to replace its cutter, which ran aground and sank near Marquette. The small boats you're likely to see here are the Coast Guard's primary search-and-rescue boats, a 44-foot motor lifeboat and a 41-foot utility boat.

◆ The striking **South Pier** with its **catwalk** and **lighthouse** is at the end of the boardwalk, a mile from downtown and the historical museum. The long pier's catwalk, once used to get out to the lights during storms, has great nostalgic value to locals, who pitched in to pay for restoring it. The pier is a great place to stroll — except during storms, when it can be very dangerous. It's also popular with fishermen for perch in summer and for steelhead, salmon, and brown trout in fall and spring.

◆ **Grand Haven State Park.** Stunt kites from the Mackinaw Kite Company on Washington Street are demonstrated almost daily on the popular **beach** next to the pier here. A concession stand, playground, and restrooms are nearby. The 174-site modern **camping** area, pure asphalt and sand with hardly a tree in sight, is one of the most popular in Michigan. Come early to park here on weekends. It's open from April through October. The social meat market where tanned bodies are on display is farther south in front of the concession building of **City Beach.** *On South Harbor Drive a mile west of downtown. Also accessible from the south via Lake Ave. which goes west off Lake Shore/Sheldon/Fifth. (616) 798-3711.* &: *restrooms, picnic tables, some campsites.*

PARKING TIPS. . . . . Come early in the morning or just after noon to find a place in the two big lots along Franklin. The Grand Haven trolley (see below)

transports people from downtown parking to the beach. Overflow beach parking extends out Lake Ave. to the cemetery.

GRAND HAVEN'S HIDDEN INDUSTRIAL WATERFRONT AND BEAUTIFUL ESTATES COME ALIVE . . . . . if you take the relaxing and surprisingly interesting 1 1/2-hour narrated harbor cruise on the **Harbor Steamer.** (Actually it's a diesel-powered paddle-wheeler.) The scenery isn't much until the boat gets to Spring Lake, though the effects of the changing light and setting sun at the evening cruise are beautiful everywhere. At the trim suburb of Spring Lake you see pretty waterfront homes and parks and the beautiful red-roofed Tudor Robbins estate. But good historical narration makes the industrial harbor seem interesting, too. Grand Haven's lumber boom days are vividly recalled. Maritime fans will enjoy the knowledgeable commentary on hard-working ships and barges seen on the trip. There's good stuff for rail fans, too. Bring a jacket; it can get windy on the water. A shorter, 45-minute cruise leaves twice each afternoon. A third option is on Fri & Sat 7 p.m.-11 p.m: full bar, passengers can get on or off at any time. *Leaves Chinook Pier at 301 North Harbor Drive. Call (616) 842-8950 for schedule and price information.* **&:** *to 28 1/2" wide.*

INEXPENSIVE BUS TOURS . . . . . on the **Grand Haven Harbor Trolley** line are far less interesting (the narration is slight and jokey) but enjoyable if you have the time and don't expect too much. You'll see some interesting parts of the Tri-Cities you'd probably miss. . . . . From Memorial Day through Labor Day, Harbor Transit (616-842-3200) runs trolleys from Chinook Pier to Grand Haven, leaving on the hour and on the half-hour approximately from 11 a.m. to 10 p.m. daily. From the pier, the trolley travels out Harbor Drive to the state park, turns around there and comes down Washington Street to center town, turns around in the Bookman municipal parking lot across from Eighth Street, and returns along Washington Street to Chinook Pier. The trolley can be flagged down. . . . . . A second tour goes to **Spring Lake** and its beach. . . . . The regular fare is $1; seniors over 59, handicapped, and children 12 and under ride for 50¢. **&:** call.

DOWNTOWN GRAND HAVEN . . . . . has some of West Michigan's best specialty shopping. Closest to the boardwalk is **Harbourfront Place,** a shopping/restaurant/office complex in a big 1906 piano factory. Many other visitor-oriented gift and t-shirt shops are near the boardwalk, while galleries and clothing stores are east a block or so. . . . . The town's top gourmet shop for good wines, cheeses, fancy foods, and freshly roasted peanuts is **Fortino's,** an old grocery store at 114 Washington with a been-there-forever atmosphere. Next door, the **Mackinaw Kite Company** (616-846-7501) has an awesome selection of kites and other wind toys, from indoor versions to traditional Chinese kites to stunt kites and power kites that lift the flier off the ground. You can get instructions for making your own kites, too. The third weekend of May it sponsors a national kite-flying contest, in which kites fly in formation to music. . . . . **G. Louise** (616-847-0045; **&**) is a fashion-forward women's boutique at 121 Washington.

Don't miss the clever, eco-friendly, multicultural new fashion and accessory stores across the street from it, near Buffalo Bob's. . . . . The **Michigan Rag Company** at 121 Washington (616-846-1451) prints and sells colorful, sturdy beach and boating wear, screen-printed on cotton fabrics in bright, punchy repeat designs like fish, log cabins, Michigan lighthouses, umbrellas, and more. Designed here by Richard Sweet, they're sold in summer resorts throughout the U.S. Seconds are substantially marked down. Big windows let passers by see screenprinters at work. . . . . **Buffalo Bob's** at Washington at Second (616-847-0019; &) has taken over the former downtown drugstore and come up with a really idiosyncratic retail mix: beach store, rollerblade store, novelty shop, upscale Western wear and outdoors store, and soda fountain with soups, sandwiches, ice cream sodas, and old-fashioned phosphates. **Bicycle and rollerblade rentals** are available. . . . . **Ad Lib**, 218 Washington (616- 842-7300) carries quite a gift mix, currently crystal and silver, paisley table linens, Italian ceramics, Russian painted boxes, Mexican earthenware. . . . . In the same interconnected complex at 214-222 Washington, **Whims and Wishes** (616-842-9533) carries an original medley of contemporary and antique gifts, furniture, and jewelry, and **Bach's Lunch** (616-846-2224) is a charming coffee and lunch spot looking onto a pretty landscaped courtyard. It now has a gourmet grocery with jams, pastas, salsa, etc., and take-out suppers. Mon-Fri 11-5, Sat 12-5. &: call.

FOR ART WORTH CHECKING OUT. . . . . A cooperative of area artists is in a large, attractive series of rooms upstairs at 715 Washington. (Enter off the parking lot in back.) **The Gallery Upstairs** (616-846-5460; open Mon-Fri 10:30-5:30, Sat 10:30-4) features over 30 participating artists, largely painters, potters, sculptors, and jewelers. Flowers and landscapes are particularly strong here and elsewhere in West Michigan, where the area's passion for horticulture, linked with the Dutch, comes together with the resort art market. &: *no.*

BICYCLING AROUND GRAND HAVEN. . . . . Two beautiful off-road bike paths now make the Grand Haven area a good bicycling destination for family bicyclists. . . . . A **bicycle path to Holland** (22 or 29 miles, depending on the route) along Sheldon Road/Lake Shore. Sheldon begins downtown as Fifth Street, and eventually turns into Lake Shore Road. The path starts about half a mile south of the hospital on the east side of Sheldon. You pass big beech trees and attractive houses near the lake, then reach **Kirk Park** with its beautiful, wooded dunes and beach (see page 509) at 9 miles, **Pigeon Lake** (11 miles), Tunnel Park, and **Holland State Park** (21 miles). The Butternut turnoff leads from Pigeon Lake more directly to the city of Holland for a 22-mile trip (one-way). . . . . A **bike path around Spring Lake** is some 16 miles long. Highlights include many water views, several bridges over bayous, and a stop at the pretty Fruitport city park. You can park at Central Park, half a block north of Savidge. . . . . **Free bike maps** with these paths and suggestions for several loops over lightly traveled roads may be had at **Rock 'N' Road Cycle**, *300 North Seventh at Elliott. (616) 846-2800. Open year-round. Mem.-Labor Day: Mon-Fri 11-8, Sat 10-5, Sun noon-4. Otherwise Mon-Fri 11-7, Sat 10-2.* &

Highland Park

Grand Haven's enchanting 19th-century cottage colony has magical boardwalks through steep, forested hills and shady valleys.

THIS HAUNTING summer colony of a hundred cottages sits among dunes overlooking Lake Michigan. Since 1886 Highland Park has been a summer retreat for well-to-do families. Many longtime cottagers come from as far away as St. Louis and Louisville, as well as Chicago and Grand Rapids. Today these cottages command fancy prices — from $100,000 to $250,000. Many family cottages, especially those in from the lake, retain a rather austere simplicity that hasn't changed for decades. What's special here are the quaint narrow roads, the striking dune environment with steep hills and shady valleys, and the old beech and maple forests.

The best look at Highland Park is from the rambling **boardwalks** that go back and dip through the steep, heavily wooded back dunes. It's dark and cool here, a nice respite from too much sun on the beach. The dunes drop off so dramatically, the boardwalks seem suspended in the treetops as they pass by the cottages' ample porches. From them you can look down on wildflowers and scampering chipmunks. The quaintest cottages are back away from the lake. Some are only approachable via the boardwalk and numerous steps.

Finding Highland Park's boardwalks can be a trick. If you are on the beach, look for the stairs climbing the bluff just south of the

The leisurely atmosphere of plain, rustic summer retreats lives on at Highland Park's Khardomah Lodge. The rooms are small and simple, the public spaces rambling and inviting — the opposite of most contemporary lodgings.

busy Lake Avenue intersection. They lead to an **overlook** with benches, a popular place for viewing sunsets, in front of the pink Highland Park Hotel. (Actually this was the annex for the stately main hotel, which burned in 1967.) Walk briefly back along Lake Avenue; behind the hotel, you'll see Lover's Lane. Go down it a ways, and a little to your left you'll see the white painted railing to stairs that look like a private cottage entrance. This is actually part of the boardwalk, maintained by the Highland Park Association. The boardwalk winds around among the cottages, sometimes ending on a road. (The roads themselves are oriented to parking, not views, and much less interesting.)

To more fully experience the beauty of Highland Park, you may want to stay either in the **Khardomah Lodge**, which dates from 1873, or the **Highland Park Hotel**, a bed and breakfast.

Along and off of Highland Rd., south of Lake Ave., overlooking Lake Michigan. Just east of the Bil Mar Restaurant, which is at 1223 S. Harbor.

BEHIND HIGHLAND PARK . . . . . Duncan Park is a dark and mysterious-looking beech-maple climax forest on the back dunes about half a mile from Lake Michigan. It's for walking, cross-country skiing in winter, and picnicking. Entrances are on Lake Drive and Sheldon Avenue (the southern extension of Fifth). . . . . Just west of the park's Lake Drive entrance, entered off Lake, is **Lake Forest Cemetery**, established in 1872 among the hills and dales of the forested back dunes. Few cemeteries can approach this one for the combination of beautiful setting, interesting plants and monuments, and varied strands of local history and American immigrants' experience represented in the dates and birthplaces of people buried here: Yankee, Scotch, and Irish pioneers, soon followed by numerous Dutch. The deep shade of majestic beeches contrasts with the play of light on their elephant-smooth trunks. The great trees anchor the winding paths and are effective natural foils to the elaborate post-Civil War monuments. To get a splendid **map and history** of Lake Forest Cemetery, complete with 35 identified sites, ask at the Tri-Cities Historical Museum (page 521).

Hoffmaster State Park and Gillette Visitors' Center

An inspired nature center expands enjoyment and understanding of Lake Michigan's splendid dunes.

PART of the dunes' magic is their contrast of sun and sand with deep, dark shade. The beach and foredunes are sunny and windswept, with only dune grass and occasional shrubs and scrawny trees. The back dunes are dark and cool, mysterious beneath the canopy of huge maples and ancient-looking, elephant-barked beeches. Hoffmaster State Park, more than most Lake Michigan parks, gets you interested in the complete dune environment, not just the beach and foredunes.

What makes Hoffmaster so very special is the top-notch nature center at the **Gillette Visitors' Center**. It provides one of the best views of Lake Michigan's dunes, which are the longest stretch of freshwater dunes in the world. And it tells their story in an unusually compelling way that makes you respect their fragile ecology and grandeur.

The best part of the story is told outdoors, on the dunes themselves, through excellent diagrams and explanations of the very view you are seeing. A **boardwalk** and 200-step **dune stairway** lead visitors up through a beech maple forest so towering, dark, and shady that it seems to have been there forever. There are frequent seats for resting and looking down on the trees. At the summit is a spectacular 180-foot-high overlook with a bird's-eye view of a vast landscape. To the west and north you see Lake Michigan and the two lines of dunes paralleling it. East you see sandy, low-lying blueberry farms and pretty Little Black Lake.

On the walk up the stairway and back down and out to the beach, you see how the back dunes vary from desert-like conditions on their west-facing slopes to virtual rain forests of perpetual dampness in the troughs and east slopes, where moist winds off the lake drop their moisture as they hit land. These diverse biologic zones fascinate naturalists. The basic principles of plant succession were, in fact, based on observations of Lake Michigan sand dunes by University of Chicago biologists.

The nature center here is one of the best in Michigan. If you're short on time, pass over the elaborate but jargon-filled displays of the Exhibit Hall, prepared by an outside firm of museum professionals. (One exception is the impressive interactive Spinning Cube that tells how sand dunes are formed and shows samples of different kinds of sand.) Opt instead for the outstanding multi-image slide show, **"Michigan Sand Dunes and Hoffmaster State Park,"** shown every hour on the half hour in the comfortable, 82-seat theater. Written and produced by the talented naturalists who developed this place, Earl Wolf and the late Sandy McBeath, it tells Lake Michigan's sand dune story through the 19th-century logging and resort eras, up into the present time. The dunes were formed by prevailing westerlies some 3,000 years ago, piling up sand deposited by glacial meltwaters. Every hour on the hour, a second beautifully photographed slide show features seasonal wildflowers or other natural subjects in the park.

Downstairs, the well-thought-out **hands-on classroom** is a great rainy-day destination. Kids seem fascinated cuddling a stuffed owl to see how soft and plumped-up its layers of feathers are. Here from late spring through Labor Day are numerous live cold-blooded animals and fish to watch. Visitors can request to see **videos** on shoreline erosion and on moose, loons, and bluebirds — all species at risk due to increased development of their natural habitats.

The excellent **bookstore**, run by an enthusiastic volunteer organization, focuses on nature publications for all ages. It has a fine

The long dune stairway behind Gillette Visitor Center offers a spectacular panoramic view of dunes and Lake Michigan on the horizon. Interpretive signs give a good, on-the-scene idea of sand dune formation and ecology.

array of posters, notecards, and nature-related gifts, too.

Spring wildflower displays in backdune forests like these are spectacular. On Mother's Day each year the **Trillium Festival** offers many special events. Call (616) 798-3573 for a schedule of **special programs** and guided walks at Gillette; group tours are by appointment. In summer there's a guided walk or program every day.

Adjoining the visitors' center are 10 miles of wonderful **hiking trails** through beech-maple forests, up dunes and down onto fairly remote beaches. At some time during 1997, a dune trail for wheelchairs will open. In winter, three miles of intermediate cross-country **ski trails** through the forests begin by the picnic shelter at the end of the drive past the Visitors' Center.

Hoffmaster has 2 1/2 miles of **beach** with beautiful dunes as a backdrop. The beach is most crowded by the concession stand and bathhouse, close to large parking lots and an unshaded **picnic area**. But if you walk south down the beach, in 10 minutes you can be away from the crowds and close to the beautiful boardwalk that leads back to the spectacular dune overlook connected to the Gillette Visitors' Center. Much nicer **picnic areas**, deeply shaded and relatively private, are along the main road past the beach turnoff.

The 333-space modern **campground** ($14/night) is one of the nicest in Michigan, despite its large size. It's in a separate part of the park to the north, off Lake Harbor Road, beneath a shady canopy of pines and hardwoods. Its beautiful setting and proximity to a campers-only beach make it quite popular. Reservations are advised on all summer weekends and on weekdays especially during special events. The campground is open all year, but water and showers are turned off from mid-October through mid-April. In 1997, the number of campground spaces will decrease when the park builds a bigger playground, full-service sites, and pull-through sites.

See map for location of Hoffmaster State Park. It's 6 miles south of Muskegon and 7 miles north of Grand Haven. From U.S. 31, take the Pontaluna Rd. exit and go west. (616) 798-3711 for information. (800) 543-2YES for reservations. &: pit toilet, picnic shelter. State park sticker required: $4/day, $20/year. **Gillette Visitor Center:** *(616) 798-3573. Open all year: mid-June to thru Labor Day 10-5 daily, closed Mon; Labor Day thru mid-June Tues-Fri 1-5, Sat & Sun 10-5, closed Mon. &: 2nd floor accessed by service entrance ramp; in 1997 dune trail. No extra fee.*

Pleasure Island and Michigan's Adventure

Two good water parks near Muskegon —
one with roller coasters, too

BECAUSE of Michigan's northern location on a peninsula off to the side of most other Midwestern population centers, there is no major amusement park on the scale of Ohio's Cedar Point. There are, however, a couple of decent minor-league amusement parks. Pleasure Island and Michigan's Adventure are both near Muskegon. Both have water parks, and both give unlimited rides for one entrance fee.

PLEASURE ISLAND, Michigan's largest water park, is quite different from an urban water park, where concrete and chlorine seem to dominate. It's built on Little Black Lake around three lagoons, not far from Lake Michigan and Hoffmaster State Park. It's a nicely landscaped park setting, with lots of flowers — a place where families come to spend the day. There's something for everyone — thrills for older kids and teens, and gentle river rides for grandparents and small children who don't meet the 42" height requirement for many rides. In the newer, River Country part of the park, the **Lazy River ride** is slow and relaxing, like a miniature float trip in inner tubes, while **Thunder Falls** is like going over a cliff in an inner tube. At the **Runaway River** family inner tube slide, tubes with one or two riders (little kids can sit on laps) go down a long, winding slide.

Over 13 waterslides are the park's big attraction. They range from two long, gentle **Corkscrews** (410 feet long, they start from Michigan's tallest slide tower) to the terrifying **Black Hole**. It consists of a green translucent tube that goes through the side of a hill, where it's all black, makes several harrowing loops, and emerges, depositing its victims in water at high speed. Almost as scary is the **Rampage**, which hurls you in a small sled steeply down a slide and sends you skidding across a pond. In the **Twister**, two slides spiral around each other, enclosed at the top, then opening up. It's fun, not scary. There are also two speed slides and three kiddie water slides. A **sandy beach** is for picnicking and swimming. Other attractions include 18 holes of **miniature golf**, a kiddie **water play area**, and **pedal boats**. **Water cannons** are personal giant squirt guns, used in a confined area.

Advice: this place is especially enjoyable and uncrowded if you visit in the morning or after 4 on a weekday, when rates go down. Summer weekends between July 4 and the middle of August are busiest, and Saturday is busiest of all.

Pleasure Island is on Pontaluna road on the way to Hoffmaster State Park, between Grand Haven and Muskegon. From U.S. 31, take the Pontaluna Rd. exit, go 1 1/2 miles west. (616) 798-7857. Open daily from Mem. Day to the week before Labor Day. In the first half of June: open weekdays10:30-3:30, weekends 10:30-6. After that, closes at 8:00 p.m., 9 p.m. on Saturdays. &: free admission for all in wheelchairs, toilets, paddleboats. $15.95 admission and all rides for anyone over 42" tall. $9.95 for kids under 42" or kids 2 to 4. Discounts after 4 p.m.: $10.95, or $7.95 for kids 2 to 4. Senior saver: $8.95 admission for age 60 and up.

MICHIGAN ADVENTURE has smaller crowds and shorter lines than Pleasure Island. It has 20 rides, including two scary roller coasters, in addition to water park attractions. On the other hand, the setting isn't as attractive, making it less of an all-day family destination. But area teens and preteens prefer it. Sixth-grader Colin Wolf likes the water slides at Pleasure Island but says Michigan's Adventure is "110 times better" because "it's a water park *and* an amusement park. Everybody I know who goes to Michigan's Adventure always goes back."

The **water park** has a wave pool with six-foot waves; a kiddie water play area; the Lazy River and the Action River (inner-tube rides on streams of different speeds); and 11 water slides: speed slides, inner-tube slides, and body slides.

The **amusement park's** scariest ride is the **Wolverine**, a big, wooden coaster, which takes you on a long ride, lulls you into a false sense of security, then drops you by surprise. The **Corkscrew**, Colin's favorite, turns you upside-down twice and has other sudden turns.

To him, the **Log Ride** stands out among the other rides. "You get in a log and drop really fast down a waterfall by surprise." In addition, there's a giant gondola wheel similar to a Ferris wheel; a Tilt-a-Whirl; a Scrambler; the Flying Trapeze swing ride; a Falling Star; a carousel; and Muttley's Putt-Putt car rides.

Michigan's Adventure is 8 miles north of Muskegon. From U.S. 31, take the Russell Rd. exit, follow signs. (616) 766-3377. Open weekends in May, daily beginning in June thru Labor Day. Hours are 11 a.m.-7 p.m., to 8 p.m. from late June thru Labor Day. &: some rides have ramps, toilets. $16/person; children 2 and under free.

❶ **Muskegon S.P./ Scenic Dr.** (p. 541). Beautiful park, un- crowded 3 miles of beach, dunes, inland beach & camp- grounds.

❷ **Winter Sports Complex** (p. 539). Learn to use 40 mph **luge.** Scenic lighted x-c ski trails, warm- ing lodge. In beauti- ful state park.

❸ **Museum of Art** (p. 533). Outstand- ing small museum geared to a broad public. Don't miss Curry's "Tornado over Kansas."

❹ **Hackley House** (p. 528). Exuberant, spare-no-expense Queen Anne fantasy mansion built by Muskegon's great benefactor.

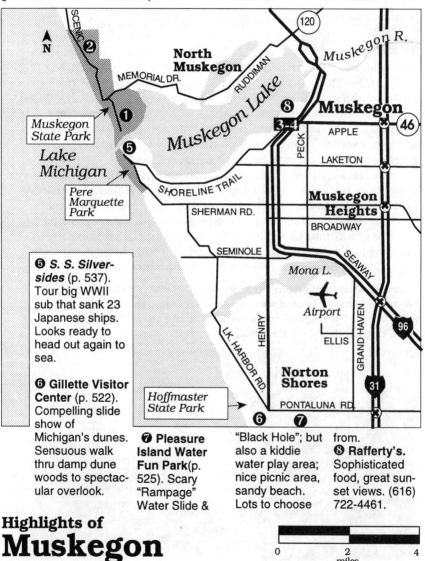

❺ *S. S. Silver- sides* (p. 537). Tour big WWII sub that sank 23 Japanese ships. Looks ready to head out again to sea.

❻ **Gillette Visitor Center** (p. 522). Compelling slide show of Michigan's dunes. Sensuous walk thru damp dune woods to spectac- ular overlook.

❼ **Pleasure Island Water Fun Park**(p. 525). Scary "Rampage" Water Slide &

"Black Hole"; but also a kiddie water play area; nice picnic area, sandy beach. Lots to choose

from.
❽ **Rafferty's.** Sophisticated food, great sun- set views. (616) 722-4461.

Highlights of
Muskegon

0   2   4
miles

Hackley & Hume Houses

Gems of Victorian architecture — the exuberant legacy of Muskegon's rich and generous lumber baron

VICTORIAN love of ornament may have reached a new height in the 1888 home of Muskegon's great benefactor and richest lumber baron, Charles Hackley. When the restoration now underway is finished, it will be the finest restored Queen Anne house in North America. That's the belief of Muskegon County Museum director John McGarry, who oversees the project. "When it's done, it will be Charles Hackley's house in 1890, restored down to the cigar in the ashtray," he says. The complex Victorian paint scheme involves 28 shades of paint, mostly in the green-yellow green-gold-brown spectrum, with some red accents.

The Hackley House shares an elaborate carriage house with the impressive but less opulent home next door of Hackley's business partner, Thomas Hume. The three buildings form a remarkable urban ensemble. Their many towers give it the many-turreted silhouette of a romantic walled town, rich in colors and textures. Inside it is almost completely restored and fully furnished, often with the Hackleys' own furniture. Noted architectural historian

Quintessential lumbermen's mansions: the Hackley (left) and Hume houses are being restored with unusual accuracy, thanks to an enormous amount of original documentation about them. This photo shows them shortly after they were finished in 1888.

Wayne Andrews called the Hackley and Hume houses "peerless specimens of the flamboyant style" and devoted nine pages and the cover photo to them in his fascinating *Architecture in Michigan*.

Houses of this size and splendor were usually made of brick or stone, but Hackley and Hume built in wood, the material that made their fortunes. In the Hackley house, surfaces are alive with carved and tiled ornament. Stained glass filters outside light for a dreamy interior look in the elaborately carved entry hall. Correspondence between the architect and Hackley reveals the hall's theme of welcome and the architect's little architectural jokes and comments. Carved figures of the Victorians' five races of man greet the visitor. Less obvious are caryatid portraits of Hackley and the architect. Over them all squats Darwin's monkey, looking down from the stairway.

The dining room is another highlight. Plain peach walls enlivened with simple stenciling play up the elaborate decorative detail of the tile fireplace and buffet, carved with widely used Victorian dining room motifs of hunting, fishing, and fruit. Deer, hunting dogs, fishing creels, and apples can all be spotted.

Hackley (1837-1905) refused to take his money and run from the stump-scarred north country when its timber ran out. In Muskegon's greatest boom year of 1886, Hackley and Hume were among the few who already realized that Michigan's timber would soon be gone. To perpetuate their fortune, they bought vast acreages of timberland in the West and South. Hackley apparently regarded his great wealth as a trust fund to be administered for society's benefit — though some small-town cynics attributed his generosity to vanity and a wish to rename Muskegon "Hackleyville." At any rate, Hackley decided to invest in Muskegon and try to develop it as a modern, enlightened industrial city.

A retiring and enigmatic personality, Hackley often deferred to the advice of a trusted circle of friends. He started by giving the city a superb library, park, hospital, and new industrial arts school, then promoted the city as a superior place to live and do business. He and his friends used those model institutions to attract industrial companies that could, and did, turn Muskegon into an important industrial city, the biggest on Lake Michigan's eastern shore. Modern-day Muskegon's leading employers – Sealed Power (now SPX), Brunswick bowling, S. D. Warren paper, and Shaw-Walker office furniture — all originally located in Muskegon because of the Muskegon Improvement Company started by Hackley and his friends.

In all, Hackley's gifts to Muskegon between 1888 and 1912

Muskegon's great benefactor, Charles Hackley, withdrew from the public eye. But he made a ceremony of personally issuing to Muskegon residents library cards to the monumental stone library he built downtown. To get their card, citizens were ushered to his second-story office (shown above) to see Hackley.

totaled nearly $6 million — a stunning testimony to the wealth of successful capitalists before income tax. In appreciation, Muskegon has celebrated Hackley Day (May 25) as a school and city holiday since 1888. (Generations of Muskegon natives can still sing the Hackley Day Song!) Hackley's monumental legacies dominate central Muskegon.

Now, when restoration of the two houses is in progress, is an especially interesting time to view the houses. Research on the 1915 interior of the Hume House has started as has the actual interior restoration. Exposed layers of wall treatments reveal the house's decorating history. The Hume House is being restored to 1915 to take advantage of a wonderful resource found in the Michigan State University archives: an insurance inventory taken in that year which lists every piece in every room. The structural work on the Hackley House was completed in June of 1996 and for the next couple of years lighting fixtures and furnishings will be restored to their original condition.

Volunteer guides give uneven tours focusing on various details of the houses, of the restoration process and everyday life for the Hackleys and Humes. Charles Hackley usually preferred to take a behind-the-scenes role in local affairs. A limp from an old logging accident made it hard to get around. But he did assume one idiosyncratic public role. He asked everyone who applied for a free library card to his splendid public library (see page 535) to come to the second-floor study of his house and get it from him in person.

During the Christmas season, the houses are decked in period decoration and there are special holiday tours from Thanksgiving on. Free carriage rides around the block are offered on the first weekend of the Christmas tour. Call for special holiday hours.

484 W. Webster at Sixth, in downtown Muskegon, 2 blocks west of Hackley Park. From U. S. 31, take the Muskegon exit for Bus. U.S. 31 (Seaway) to Sixth. Follow signs. (616) 722-7578. Open late May through September, Wed, Sat & Sun 1-4. Group tours by appointment at other times. Free tours for school groups and scout troops. $2/adults. 12 and under free. &: no.

FOR MUSKEGON'S FASCINATING LUMBERING HISTORY . . . . . go to the **Muskegon County Museum** (page 536). In the Lumber Queen gallery, first request to see the outstanding half-hour **tape/slide show.** It clearly conveys the lumber barons' business strategy, along with the colorful, dangerous life in lumber camps. Then look at the dioramas of lumbering scenes in Muskegon.

BIG CHANGES NEAR THE HACKLEY HOUSE. . . . . After decades of suffering under a negative self-image as a declining foundry town, Muskegon has waked up to its positives: West Michigan's most extensive lakeshore parks, less expensive boat slips, historic gems and tremendous cultural resources, a downtown that is reorienting itself to Muskegon Lake now that key foundries are gone, and a multiethnic lumbertown populace that likes to party and drink beer. That can be refreshing when so much of West Michigan is dominated by the Dutch, who mainly only drink at home. (It's still hard to get a good meal with wine on Sunday in Holland and Grand Haven.) The SPX headquarters and gorgeous **Rafferty's restaurant** *(616) 722-4461; &)* offer a grand sunset view looking west down Muskegon Lake. . . . . **Heritage Village,** the neighborhood around the

Hackley House, is coming back after years of devolving into low-rent apartments. Two pleasant bed and breakfasts are on the same block as the Hackley House. Houses are being moved onto vacant lots. The historic **Fire Barn Museum** *(616-722-4461) at 510 W. Clay* is open the same hours as the Hackley House. Retired firefighters can show kids how to use replica equipment. **&** *Free.* Business Route 31 has been rerouted near the lake, so high-speed traffic won't tear through the historic neighborhood. . . . . . The historic buildings remaining along **Western Avenue,** down the hill from the Hackley House toward the lake, are showing signs of life. **Seeback's Deli** and coffeehouse (616-722-4362) at 477 W. Western Avenue is delightful. *In winter, it's open Mon through Sat 8:30 a.m.-2:30 p.m. In summer, it's open Mon through Sat 8:30 a.m.-4 p.m. and Wed through Sat 5p.m.-8 p.m.* The handsome Romanesque Revival **Union Depot** (1895) is now the home of the Chamber of Commerce/Visitors' Bureau.

FOR VISITOR INFO. . . . . Call the **Convention and Visitors Bureau** at 1-800-235-FUNN or (616) 722-3751 for events info. It's in the Union Depot at 586 W. Western at Sixth, down the hill from the Hackley House. . . . . For **films, plays, exhibits, lectures,** etc., call the Hackley Library (616-722-7276).

CHEAP SIGHTSEEING TOURS OF THE MUSKEGON AREA . . . . . are available via the **Muskegon Trolley Company.** All major destinations are connected by trolley buses. For $1 a person, you can get an hour and a half tour. Catch them daily from 11 a.m. to 6 p.m. You can flag down the trolley. The north route goes around Muskegon Lake from the state park on the north to downtown, the Hackley-Hume houses, and Pere Marquette State Park. Another goes south to Hoffmaster State Park and Pere Marquette. Call (616) 724-6420, or stop by the bus kiosk in Muskegon Mall downtown. An informative brochure/map tells you want you're looking at. **&:** *lift.*

EVENTS IN AND AROUND MUSKEGON . . . . . include the **Cherry County Playhouse** in its new home in the superb Frauenthal Theater, Friday-evening summer parties in Hackley Park, concerts by the **West Shore Symphony** and the summertime Blue Lake Fine Arts Camp special guests, a top-notch civic theater, the Muskegon Fury professional hockey team, a big air show, and more.

Muskegon Museum of Art

Western Michigan's top art museum —
small, stimulating, geared to a broad audience

THANKS to the beneficence of museum founder Charles Hackley (page 529) and two astute early directors, Muskegon has long had the finest art museum in western Michigan. It's a very pleasant place, accessible and stimulating. The Hackley Gallery (the original 1912 museum building) contains the permanent collection, strong on realistic paintings that are interesting and complex. The much newer Walker Gallery is a big, open space well suited to changing shows, sometimes very large in scale and quite powerful.

Some choice paintings are here, mostly purchased many decades ago. The best-known is the dramatic "Tornado over Kansas" by John Steuart Curry, a prominent proponent of the regionalism that dominated American art in the 1930s. Whistler's famous "A Study in Rose and Brown," a simplified, unpretty portrait of a young woman, created such a controversy in Muskegon that the museum's talented first director, Raymond Wyer, quit in a huff. He then went to Worcester, Massachusetts, and proceeded to build its museum into one of national prominence. The extraordinary "Tea Time," by Whistler's contemporary William Merritt Chase, was also avant-garde in its day. Winslow Homer, Edward Hopper, and Andrew Wyeth are among the other prominent American painters represented here.

The European holdings, not as extensive, also include some choice works. The most important is "St. Jerome in Penitence," painted circa 1516 by Joos Van Cleve. The saint, in a fascinating, vivid landscape, is surrounded by symbolic and anthropomorphic forms. Don't miss another important Dutch painting, Jan van der Heyden's haunting "The Moat of a Castle with Drawbridge." Portraits of Martin Luther and his wife, Katharina von Bora, were painted by their friend, Cranach the Elder.

Unusual treasures for a small museum on the geographical periphery of the art world include a set of Rembrandt etchings and the largest collection of works of Françoise Gilot, both generous gifts. Gilot was part of a circle including Matisse (who influenced her style), Braque, and Picasso, with whom she lived for years. (Paloma Picasso is their daughter.)

Some fourteen **changing exhibits** a year cover topics from Old Masters to children's book illustration to porcelain and Native American art. They make it worthwhile to stop in when you're in the vicinity. (Access and parking are easy.) Accompanying the exhibits are a wide range of programs from parent-child workshops to scholarly lectures. Call the museum for a brochure on future activities.

"We've always been a cutting-edge, open museum, geared to a broader public but ahead of the crowd," said former director Al Kochka with pride. Recently the Hackley Gallery has been restored to its original 1912 appearance. Dark, rich green and cranberry fabrics cover main gallery walls and set off the paintings like vivid jew-

Today the Hackley Gallery has been restored to look much as it did in 1912: paintings hang over one another, brilliantly set off against walls of dark green and cranberry. Astute purchases by its first director formed the nucleus of this outstanding small museum.

els. The deep, saturated colors are a radical departure from the white walls that became de rigueur for museums in the 1960s and 1970s. Over the past 15 years, museums have gradually introduced colors on gallery walls especially where pre-20th century works are exhibited. Muskegon Museum staff thought long and hard before returning to the dark colors, but everyone is pleased with the stunning results and the way they make the marble wainscoting stand out. By comparison, the one light gray gallery seems dull. The renovation also included installing state-of-the-art climate control systems and removing drop ceilings to reveal the English box-style ceiling system for skylights.

The lower-level **gift shop** has a nice selection of notecards, books, posters, jewelry, and inexpensive gifts for children.

On West Webster just east of Third and Hackley Park in downtown Muskegon. Park alongside the towered building on Third. (616) 722-2600. Tues-Fri 10-5, Sat & Sun 12-5. ♿ Free; donations appreciated.

FABULOUS VICTORIANA NEAR THE ART MUSEUM . . . . . Right next door on Webster at Third is the first and most splendid of all Charles Hackley's gifts to Muskegon, the **Hackley Public Library**, a Romanesque Revival castle from 1890. Don't miss the impressive main reading room sparkling with leaded glass, the huge oil painting of the library's dedication (a hundred deft portraits of Muskegon society at the twilight of the lumbering era), four stone fireplaces with Art Nouveau touches, and the upstairs children's room mural of a parade of colorful literary characters from around the world. For those who prefer self-guided tours, a booklet is available ($2) which will take you through the library and its stone towers. Regular tours can be arranged by calling the Reference Desk at (616) 722-7276, ext. 228. *Winter hours: Tues & Wed 8:30 a.m.-8 p.m., Thurs & Fri 8:30 a.m.-6 p.m., Sat 9 a.m.-5p.m., closed Sun & Mon. Summer hours: Mon 10 a.m.-6 p.m., Tues & Wed 10 a.m.-8 p.m., Thurs & Fri 10 a.m.-6 p.m., closed Sat. & Sun. Hours may vary so call to doublecheck.* ♿ . . . . . Across Webster is the **Torrent House**, a massive stone chateau built in 1892 for the then-astonishing sum of $250,000 and now used by the Library to house its collection of 17th and 18th century books. Lumberman and mayor John Torrent located his magnificent pile here to show up his rival, Hackley. Although the Torrent House is closed to the public, you can call the Reference Desk at the Hackley Public Library (see previous page) to arrange a tour. . . . . . At Webster and Third is shady **Hackley Park**, Hackley's entry in the competition among aspiring cities of the late 19th century to erect monumental public sculptures honoring the veterans who served their country. At the corners, bronze figures of Lincoln, Grant, Sherman, and Admiral David Farragut were radical for their day because of their realistic poses. Popular

Parties in the Park with live music, food, and beer are held here Fridays from 5 to 9, from early June through early September.

A CURIOUS DOWNTOWN MALL. . . . . A block down Third at Clay is one of the nation's most unusual malls. In the 1970s **Muskegon Mall** put a roof over four principal downtown retail blocks. It incorporated several large office buildings and the stately old Century Club and tore down 96 surrounding buildings to provide free parking in the heart of downtown. The only trouble is, there's not much of downtown left except for parking lots and large institutional buildings. It was a dramatic — or desperate — solution for a depressed industrial city. Unlike many such cities, downtown Muskegon is not deserted at night. Nearby frontage along Muskegon Lake has finally been developed for recreation and entertainment, and the mall is being expanded to stay competitive.

AN AMBITIOUS AND CREATIVE LOCAL HISTORY MUSEUM. . . . . New directions make downtown's **Muskegon County Museum** an outstanding rainy-day destination. An ambitious new **multimedia gallery** deals with local history in terms of the **changing environment** and ecological issues. It starts with geology, rocks and minerals, and mastodon bones found by salt deposits in northern Muskegon County, and ends with zebra mussels, otters at play on an old foundry site, and the nature in a typical backyard. "The Powers of Ten" film puts **geological time in perspective.** Upcoming permanent galleries deal with human history and recreate a factory setting. The museum can do a lot because it produces its own exhibits in-house, then recycles many to out-county sites. Every two months there's a new **changing exhibit,** often devoted to collectors with delightfully folksy captions: Your Favorite Christmas Gift, Tiny Objects You Saved, yo-yos, etc. . . . . Other highlights include the lumber exhibits (see above) and the poignant display on the extinct **passenger pigeons** that once darkened the skies here along the Lake Michigan shore, and the successful **Body Works hands-on gallery** of the human body. Its food and calories game is a hit. A dramatic, oversized painting by folk artist Lewis Cross of nearby Spring Lake shows a swirl of the docile birds being shot at by farmers. Also, on the lower level, Victor Casenelli's 19 dreamily impressionistic **murals of Muskegon's history,** done for Lumberman's Bank in 1929. The **gift shop** in the museum, the Muskegon Mercantile, carries Victorian jewelry, toys, and books. *430 W. Clay at Fourth, downtown, 1 block west of Hackley Park. (616) 722-0278. Mon-Fri 9:30-4:30, Sat & Sun 12:30-4:30. Closed major holidays. &: call. Free.*

U.S.S. Silversides
Maritime Museum

*In Muskegon, tour one of World War II's fightingest
subs, which looks much as it did on its many missions.*

FOR ANYONE interested in World War II or naval warfare,
this is a major attraction in western Michigan. Military
equipment that survives a war has usually seen little
action, but this big sub was a Pacific workhorse. Completed just
after the attack on Pearl Harbor in 1942, the *Silversides* went on to
sink 23 ships. It went on 14 patrols in all, losing only one man while
sinking over 90,000 tons. During one reconnaissance mission, crew
members even watched a Japanese horse race by periscope.

The ship's excellent condition and the fact that its furnishings
are nearly complete make the tour especially worthwhile. As you go
below and walk from bow to stern, it looks very much as it did during World War II, with the same bunks, sonar equipment, brass
torpedo doors, radios, and charting table. The tour gives a good feel
of what it was like in those very cramped spaces to go out on a 45-
day tour deep into enemy territory.

Next to the sub is a small museum exhibiting WWII memorabilia and artifacts from the *S.S.N679 Silversides*, a decommissioned
nuclear sub named in honor of the WWII *Silversides*. The centerpiece is the actual helm from the nuclear sub. When it was decommissioned, parts of it including the helm were sent here to sit along
side its namesake. Kids can sit at the helm complete with panel
and gages and see what it feels like to "steer" a submarine. In the

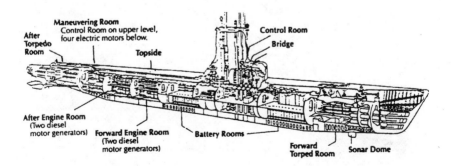

Maneuvering Room
Control Room on upper level,
four electric motors below.

After
Torpedo
Room

Topside

Control Room

Bridge

After Engine Room
(Two diesel
motor generators)

Forward Engine Room
(Two diesel
motor generators)

Battery Rooms

Forward
Torped Room

Sonar Dome

museum is a souvenir shop with a nautical theme that has a number of books and periodicals relating to ships and submarines.

In the near future, as part of the *U.S.S. Silversides* tour, visitors will be able to enter the **conning tower** and look through the periscope at the surrounding countryside. The museum has also acquired a 1927 Coast Guard cutter, the last of its kind left in the world, which it hopes to have ready for touring soon. Meanwhile, visitors can view it at the dock.

1346 Bluff, in Pere Marquette Park on the channel wall's south side. Take U.S. 31 to the Sherman Rd. exit; turn west onto Sherman, which becomes Beach St; follow Beach St. to Pere Marquette Park. (616) 755-1230. Jun-Aug daily 10-5:30. April and Oct, Sat & Sun 10-5:30; May & Sept, weekdays 1-5:30. &: no. Adults $4, students 12-18 $3; seniors 62 and older $2.50, children 5-11 $2; under 5 free.
***Overnight camping program** 6 p.m.-9:30 a.m. Mon-Thurs $12.50 per person, Fri-Sun $17.50 per person.*

Muskegon State Park & Winter Sports Park

A quarter-mile of Olympic sledding thrills, delightful cross-country skiing even at night, and wonderfully uncrowded beaches in summer

LARGE SNOWFALLS and beautiful, forested scenery make Muskegon State Park ideal for winter sports. Due to the lake effect of Lake Michigan at its western edge, the park commonly has at least some snow when most of southern Michigan is completely snowless. In a dark, snowy evergreen forest, the golden glow of dots from the lighted ski trails and the big golden beacon of the warming house's huge windows are enchanting. The low lampposts make intimate pools of light – much more beautiful than the floodlit effect of high parking lot-style lights typical of ski areas. A family-oriented ice rink is also maintained, weather permitting.

Centerpieces of the beautiful Muskegon Winter Sports Complex in Muskegon State Park are a

Muskegon State Park enjoys a long cross-country ski season thanks to the lake effect snow that gets dumped along the lakeshore. That makes it a good place for the luge run, too.

luge run (the only other one in the U.S. is at Lake Placid) and some of the longest lighted **cross-country ski trails** in Michigan. In the luge, an Olympic sport, a small, one-person sled of wood, metal, and canvas is steered down an iced chute that has wooden walls. The side walls are contoured with snowy slush, and the luge run is iced nightly after each day's use with a mix of snow and water, then misted for a slick, even surface.

The helmeted driver lies down facing up on the sled and steers it by bending one flexible front wood runner support and raising the opposite shoulder. Everything goes by in a blur. On the Muskegon course, sleds can go up to 40 m.p.h. And that seems even faster when you're four inches from the ground. Anybody can experience the thrill of luging.

A volunteer group of outdoors enthusiasts started and developed this remarkably attractive facility in order to develop interest in the sport in the Midwest. Among them was Mark Grimette from North Muskegon. His team's fourth-place finish in the 1994 Winter Olympics was the best an American team has ever done in the luge.

Anyone can buy a day's pass, which includes a sled, helmet, and coach. You don't need reservations. Just show up in light-weight shoes or boots, gloves, warm clothes, and proof of health insurance. First-timers are fully supervised; they start at the base of the starting ramp of the shorter, slower lower track, so they can become accustomed to the sensation and gradually build-up speed without being terrified. Careful volunteer coaches observe and instruct all lugers and decide when they can advance to a higher level. Waits are not long. By the end of the day beginners will be completing the entire lower run in 10 seconds, a speed of about 25 m.p.h. The faster (40 m.p.h.), twisting upper track has far more turns and banks.

"It was an incredible experience – the speed!" said one happy novice who traveled from Jackson to learn to luge. "As long as you felt comfortable, they moved you right along! We did the [lighted] 5K ski trail as it was getting dark. The trail was really nice; it goes into pockets of trees."

The **ski trails** were laid out specifically for skiing. Many state park ski trails are really hiking trails, with turns too sudden for all but the best skiers. The trails here are ideal for novices, because they combine easy turns and interesting scenery. The 2 1/2 kilometer trail is flat to rolling; the 5K trail has three hills that provide a challenge for better skiers. (A bypass lets less skillful skiers avoid the short, steep hill.) Trails are tracked for both ski-skaters and conventional skiers. Sheltering pines protect skiers from the wind and preserve the snow from the sun. Design details have been better thought out on this volunteer project than on many professional jobs. **Ski rentals** are available for adults and children. For skaters, there is a lighted family **skating rink**. If you would like to skate and don't have a pair of skates, there is self-serve box of assorted skates available to anyone.

For directions to Muskegon State Park, see below. The Winter Sports Park is at the north end of Muskegon State Park, off Scenic Dr. across from the Lakeshore Campground, around the curve north of the landmark blockhouse. (616) 744-9629. Season from mid-Dec. to mid-March, depending on weather. Park hours: daily 10-10. **Luge open hours**: *Fri 5-9, Sat 12-9 & Sun 10-6. Competitions and meets held on Sat. a.m.; public welcome. State park sticker required: $4/day, $20/year. Ski trail fee: Mon-Fri $3 adults, $1.50 children; Sat-Sun $4 adults, $2 children. Luge fee (including equipment rental): lower track, $15 adults, $12 age 17 and under; upper track, $25 adults, $20 age 17 and under. Skating: $2 adults, $1 age 17 and under.*

BEAUTIFUL BEACHES THAT ARE NEVER CROWDED . . . . . are what **Muskegon State Park** is known for. There's also plenty of space to spread out — three miles of Lake Michigan beach along Scenic Drive, 1165 acres of mostly woods, and 11 1/2 miles of hiking trails. When Holland and Grand Haven are packed, this is the place to reliably find waves, sand, and solitude. **Snug Harbor** (off Memorial Drive) is a pleasant, quiet bay of Muskegon Lake with warmer water and a perfect place for small children to swim, swing, and fish. Boaters and fishermen favor the 139-site, modern **Muskegon Lake Campground** (south site) by the boat launch on the channel's Muskegon Lake side. (Although you can launch a small boat from the boat launch, the majority are launched from Snug Harbor.) The 110-site **Lake Michigan Campground** (north site, also modern) is among the most scenic state park campgrounds, nestled in a grove of towering maples and beeches, an easy walk across the dunes from a campers-only beach. The **East Campground** has 52 semi-modern sites (bathroom & shower but no electricity). Campgrounds fill on summer weekdays as well as weekends. Reservations recommended. *On the north side of the Muskegon Lake channel. From U.S. 31, take M-120 southwest and follow the signs through North Muskegon onto Memorial Drive (the park's south entrance). Or take Scenic Dr. from Whitehall. (616) 744-3480. Camp reservations: (800) 543-2YES.* &: *toilets; bathhouse possible in 1996. State park sticker required: $4/day, $20/year.*

THE PERFECT PLACE FOR A SNACK AFTER SKIING . . . . . is the cozy **Bear Lake Tavern** in North Muskegon. 360 Ruddiman at the *Bear Lake channel. (616) 744-1161. It's about three miles east of Lake Michigan on the shore road along Muskegon Lake.* &

White River Lighthouse Museum

An unspoiled and picturesque setting — amid the relaxed, old-fashioned resort life of the White Lake area

TUCKED AWAY behind huge beech trees at the channel from Lake Michigan to White Lake, this old limestone and brick lighthouse looks so simple and homey, it seems the keeper could still be there. Today this delightful little museum owned by Fruitland Township is still a home — of the curator. Maybe the lived-in feel, and having a child around, is part of what gives this place its special aura. Part of the magic is getting there: taking the winding lane out through the old summer houses, and walking through the deep shade of the beeches into the lighthouse's sunny yard, where you see the big lake for the first time.

Tightly spiraled in the narrow tower is a beautiful wrought-iron stairway. After a somewhat spooky, claustrophobic ascent, it leads you to a fine view of Lake Michigan.

Low-key displays include photographs, maps, ships' models, and nautical artifacts, mainly about White Lake's maritime history. The curator is happy to explain how the museum's navigational devices are used. The first boats in the area were Indian fishing canoes, followed by fur-traders' canoes, lumber schooners, and the resort-era steamers beginning in the 1880s. Big steamers brought summer people from Chicago, Indiana, and St. Louis to White Lake's summer hotels and cottages. A **changing exhibit,** based on the curator's ongoing research and new historical resources, is mounted each season.

A museum highlight is the station's original Fresnel lens, which reflected and magnified the oil lamp in the tower. These beautiful big crystal lenses, handmade in France, were the lighthouse keepers' crown jewels, kept clean and polished, along with the brass mountings. A Fourth Order Fresnel lens like this magnified the oil lamp so it could be seen 14 miles away. Today an electric light has been installed inside the lens. When it's turned on at dusk, as it is on fall afternoons when the museum is open, the lens projects beautiful rainbows around the room.

A **shop** goes well beyond mass-produced souvenirs. It offers watercolors and prints of the lighthouse by various artists, and pop-

The White River lighthouse and a lumber schooner are shown at the
channel between White Lake and Lake Michigan in this late 19th-centu-
ry painting by Frederick Norman. Many of his fascinating paintings
about the White River logging era can be seen at the Whitehall branch
of First of America Bank at 119 S. Mears.

ular ties handpainted with the lighthouse and other nautical
designs. **Lee Murdock**, singer of old and new Great Lakes sailing
songs, comes yearly for a day of afternoon storytelling and evening
concerts. Call for time.

Year-round, people come to the lighthouse to walk along the
channel wall and get to Lake Michigan. (The beach up to the water
line is privately owned.) This "Government Channel" was created in
1871, during the lumber boom. Lumber schooners leaving Lake
Michigan's lumber ports had become so numerous that the federal
government financed many navigational improvements, including
this lighthouse, erected in 1875.

Civilized simplicity still sets the tone for White Lake resort life,
which feels far away from today's harried pace. Cottages here are
likely painted brown, or classic white with green trim, seldom
mauve or pink. Trees and green are everywhere. These charms are
showcased on the drive out South Shore Drive from Whitehall to the
lighthouse.

The direct channel here bypassed the White River's circuitous
old channel north of here. Today the **Old Channel Trail** starts in
Montague and goes west along White Lake. Then it turns north near
Lake Michigan, making for an exceptionally scenic drive. Consider a
stop at the Old Channel Inn. A road alongside it leads down to a
good swimming beach. To get to little **Medbury Park** and the beach
across the channel from the lighthouse, take Old Channel Trail, but
turn west at Lau Road when the main road turns north.

The lighthouse is at the south side of the White Lake channel, at the end of Murray Rd. Murray Rd. goes west from the junction of Scenic Dr. (along Lake Michigan from Muskegon) and South Shore Rd. (along White Lake from Whitehall). Or come from U.S. 31 via Duck Lake State Park (see below). (616) 894-8265. (**Museum** *open June through Labor Day Tues-Fri 11-5, Sat & Sun noon-6. Memorial Day-June 1 and in Sept.: weekends only.* &: *no. $2 admission ages 19 and over. Ages 10-18: $1. 10 and under free. Tours of museum and dune ecology are available by arrangement.*) **Grounds and channel walk** *are a* **public park** *open year-round.*

A SCENIC DRIVE AND NICE BEACHES . . . . . Public beach access isn't a strong point of the White Lake area. To get to two pleasant public beaches, go south along the aptly named Scenic Drive to **Duck Lake State Park**, an old scout camp. It has beach frontage on both Lake Michigan and on pretty Duck Lake, which is unspoiled by development and good for fishing. Take Michillinda Road to the main park entrance on Duck Lake. The picnic area is beneath big oaks. The park has no camping at this time. . . . . . All the major east-west roads lead to **Scenic Drive**, which parallels Lake Michigan from Muskegon State Park in North Muskegon to White Lake. For a pretty, winding way to Muskegon, continue south on Scenic from Duck Lake State Park through the wooded dunes of Muskegon State Park into the beautiful lakefront suburb of North Muskegon. *To get to Duck Lake State Park from U.S. 31,, take the Lakewood Club exit 10 miles north of Muskegon and follow signs. (616) 744-3480. State park sticker required: $4/day, $20/year. .*

THE LOW-KEY CHARMS OF WHITEHALL AND MONTAGUE. . . . . . Friendly and unfussy, the twin towns at the head of White Lake offer two rival weathervane manufacturers (both on Water Street in downtown Montague), two drugstores with soda fountains (**Lipka's** and the bustling **Todd Pharmacy**), both on Ferry in Montague, and two eat-in bakeries, both in Whitehall. **Riverview Cafe and Bakery** (616-893-5163) at 115 North Mears overlooks the White River marsh (&), and **Robinson's Bakery** (616-894-5979) at 1019 S. Mears makes outstanding, authentic Swedish breads and cookies. &

The weird, wonderful **Montague Historical Museum**, a community attic in a church on Meade and Church up the hill in Montague is open summer weekends 1-5. &: *no.* Also worth checking out is **American Sampler** gift shop at 124 S. Mears and inside the First of America Muskegon Bank at 119 S. Mears, the remarkable, accurate **paintings chronicling White Lake's lumbering industry**, done from life by an area signpainter in the 1870s. . . . . . The local claim to fame, the **world's largest weather vane**, is less appealing than its setting on **Ellenwood Landing.** That new marina is on the causeway between Whitehall and Montague that separates White Lake from the sweeping marsh of the White

River. It offers fine sunset views. Sailboats set the tone of boating here. Fast motor boats don't like to contend with these pokey vessels, so they gravitate elsewhere. . . . . Take in the views and the marsh's many swans from the asphalt boardwalk or the **Dog and Suds** parking lot, across the causeway from Ellenwood Landing.

FOR MORE INFORMATION ABOUT THE WHITE LAKE AREA . . . . . stop by the **Chamber of Commerce**, in the old depot on the causeway, for more information about this attractive, unspoiled resort area. Or call (616) 893-4585. . . . . Summer events include **concerts** at **Blue Lake Fine Arts Camp** (800-221-3796 or 616-894-1966) on Twin Lake, outside Whitehall, and summer theater at the **Howmet Playhouse** (616-894-2540) in Whitehall, affiliated with Blue Lake. . . . . For info on the pretty **Hart-Montague Trail** for bicycles, rollerblades, and wheelchairs, see page 549.

AN ACCESSIBLE TREASURE FOR CANOEISTS. . . . . . Famous as a logging river, the **White River** today is less canoed, less fished, and more remote in feel than some better-known, longer rivers up north. A quiet river trip here puts you in touch with wildlife that usually flees at the sound of hikers. Especially in the early morning and late afternoon, you can see blue heron, sandhill cranes, many kinds of ducks, and occasionally beaver.

The narrow White winds across a floodplain that's a half-mile to a mile wide. Sometimes it's up against a steep, forested bank. Sometimes it's surrounded by marshy flats. Other times it flows through hardwood and conifer forest that has not been logged in this century. Within **the Manistee National Forest**, it's a designated **wild-scenic river**, which means that timber on the floodplain can't be cut. Fishing is good for bass, northern pike, and salmon and steelhead runs.

There aren't many public access points to the river. By far the easiest way to canoe it is to use the **Happy Mohawk Canoe Livery**, which rents canoes, tubes, rafts, and kayaks. Sample prices, including all equipment and transportation: $13/person for a canoe trip of four hours paddling time; $6.75-$8.25/per tube (the more tubes you rent, the cheaper the price) for a 2 or 3-hour tubing expedition. Prices and particulars vary, so call or write for a brochure.

The Happy Mohawk owners also own and operate the exceptionally picturesque **White River Campground**. It's in the heavily wooded valley of pretty little Sand Creek where it joins the White River. *735 E. Fruitvale Rd., 5 miles east of U.S. 31 northeast of Montague. From U.S. 31, take Fruitvale Rd. exit, go 5 miles east. (616) 894-4209. Campground open May through October.*

Northern Michigan

TOURISTS AND RESORTERS have flocked to northern Michigan to escape the summer heat ever since the forests were cut over and logging gave out, beginning in the 1880s. At that time, the same railroads and Great Lakes shipping lines that had hauled lumber out began advertising the region as a vacation paradise and teaming up with business leaders to develop cottage colonies. Railroads and lakes steamers started transporting vacationers north. Wealthy families from Chicago, Detroit, St. Louis, Indianapolis, and other hot, steamy Midwestern cities built big summer cottages up here, some quite large. Most of these old cottages are still in use, many enjoyed by descendants of their original owners.

Driving north, you can often feel the temperature drop as you enter the upper half of the Lower Peninsula, the beginning of the North Woods. The landscape changes. Farms become farther apart and forests more extensive. Above **Clare** at least half the land is in state or national forests.The lakes and rivers are cleaner here, and population density lower (though sprawl is an increasing problem.) The fresh, cool air and the abundance of shoreline have made this region continue to grow in tourism, second homes, and more recently in year-round homes for urban refugee professionals, especially in the areas around **Traverse City** and **Petoskey**, a North Woods Gold Coast. In no other part of Michigan does tourism so dominate the local economy. With interstates, the North has become accessible for

Information sources: CONVENTION & VISITORS' BUREAUS

CVB of Thunder Bay Region
(517) 354-4181, (800) 4-ALPENA

Mescota County CVB (Big Rapids)
(616)796-7640, (800) 833-6697

Cadillac Area Visitors Bureau
(616) 775-9776, (800) 22-LAKES

Charlevoix Area CVB
(800) 367-8557 (MI only)

Cheboygan Area Tourist Bureau
(616) 627-7138, (800) 968-3302

Gaylord Area Tourism Bureau
(517) 732-6333, (800) 345-8621

Grayling Area Visitors Council
(517) 348-2921, (800) 937-8837

Houghton Lake Area Tourist Bureau
(517) 422-3931

Indian River Tourist Bureau
(616) 238-9325

Ludington Area CVB
(616) 845-0324, (800) 542-4600

Mackinaw Area Tourist Bureau
(616) 436-5664, (800) 666-0160

Greenbush-Oscoda-Au Sable Lodging Association
(800) 235-GOAL

Boyne Country CVB (Petoskey area)
(616) 348-2755, (800) 845-2828

Rogers City Visitors Bureau
(517) 7334-2535,
(800) 622-4148 (MI only)

Tawas Bay Tourist Bureau
(517) 362-8643, (800) 55-TAWAS

Traverse City CVB
(616) 947-1120, (800) 872-8377

West Branch-Ogemaw Visitors Bureau
(800) 755-9091 (MI); (517) 755-9091

getaway weekends and year-round second homes. (Locals regard hurried weekend "trunk-slammers" with far more disdain than established summer people with cottages.) Hunting and snowmobiling drives tourism in some inland counties.

Other economies up here have failed to thrive. Significant agri-

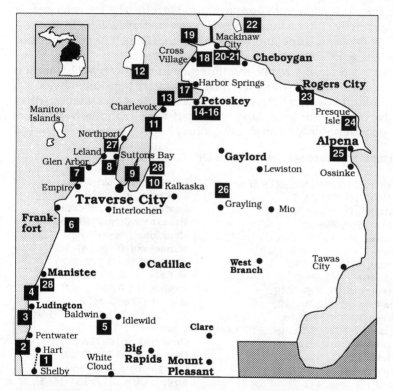

culture is limited. The **Lake Michigan fruit belt** and potatoes near **Rogers City** stand out. Little industry developed. But tourism continues to grow, with more and more resort developments and golf courses. The fate of many people up here is to work like crazy and endure crowds for short, intense tourism seasons (**July** and **August**, and for some the ski season from **January** into **March**). The fall color season bustles briefly. Top destination **golf courses** draw golfers from May through October. **June** and **September** are the real sleeper months for people who want nice weather and no crowds.

There's a lot of poverty and illiteracy in northern Michigan. It's hidden from visitors who stick near the water, but quite obvious along inland roads, where weather-worn trailers and shacks with huge woodpiles are seen. Love of the outdoors is the universal common denominator for everybody up here.

Information sources: CHAMBERS OF COMMERCE

Alpena (517) 354-4181; (800) 582-1906
Arcadia (616) 723-2575
Atlanta (517) 785-3400
Baldwin (616) 745-4331
Bear Lake (616) 723-2575
Bellaire (616) 533-6023
Benzonia (616) 882-5802
Beulah (616) 882-5802
Big Rapids (616) 796-7649
Boyne City (616) 582-6222
Brethren (616) 723-2575
Cadillac (616) 775-9776, (800) 22-LAKES
Central Lake (616) 544-3322
Charlevoix (616) 547-2101
Cheboygan (616) 627-7138
Clare (517) 386-2442
East Jordan (616) 536-7351
Elk Rapids (616) 264-8202
Frankfort (616) 352-7251
Gladwin (517) 426-5451
Harrison (517) 539-6011
Harrisville (517) 724-5107
Hillman (517) 742-4341
Honor (616) 882-5802
Houghton Lake (517) 366-5644
Idlewild (616) 745-4331
Indian River (616) 238-9325

Kaleva (616) 723-2575
Kalkaska (616) 258-9103
Lewiston (517) 786-2293
Mackinaw City (616) 436-5574
Mackinac Island (800) 4-LILACS
Mancelona (616) 587-5500
Manistee (616) 723-2575
McBain (616) 825-2755
Mesick (616) 885-1280
Mio (517) 685-7129
Northport (616) 386-5806
Onaway (517) 733-2874
Onekama (616) 723-2575
Oscoda (517) 739-7322
Otsego (616) 694-6880
Rogers City (517) 734-2535
St. Helen (517) 389-3447
Scottville (616) 757-4729
Standish (517) 846-7867
Tawas City (517) 362-8643,
  (800) 55-TAWAS
Thompsonville (616) 882-5802
Traverse City (616) 947-5075
Trufant (616) 984-2597
Wellston (616) 723-2575
West Branch (616) 345-2821

Hart-Montague Trail State Park

A beautiful, easy bike path
through woods and orchards, hills and villages

THIS 22 1/2-mile asphalt path leads bicyclists (rollerbladers and wheelchair users, too) past a pleasant variety of rural scenery and small-town sights. The trail leads north from Montague, on White Lake, to the village of Hart, the county seat of Oceana County. The high sandy hills and orchards of Oceana County, between Muskegon and Ludington, make for beautiful scenery that's not widely known. (Horses are also permitted on the trail, but not on the 10-foot-wide asphalt strip.) In the northern reaches of Michigan's fabulously diversified fruit belt (see page 48), Oceana County is a top U.S. producer of apples, tart cherries, asparagus, and Christmas trees.

Along the trail, farming is much in evidence. There's the sight and smell of cherry and apple blossoms in mid-May. Wind-sown wild asparagus is along much of the trail, hidden and succulent in spring, feathery and gold in fall. The cherries ripen in July, the apples from September through October. A common sight are fruit crates stacked along side the long brick canneries.

Contrasted to orderly fields of asparagus and orchards are stretches where trees and shrubs have grown up along the trail. They harbor wildlife, which is fun to see while bicycling. And they

Fields of asparagus: the trail passes through Michigan's center of asparagus production. The asphalt surface makes the trail ideal for rollerblades, wheelchairs (racers practice here) and strollers.

buffer road noise along the trail's southern third, where it parallels Oceana Drive (Old U.S. 31). In the north, between Mears and Shelby, the trail goes through a high oak forest and looks down on a lake.

The very railroad line that has been converted into the Hart-Montague Trail launched the area's agricultural market economy in the 1870s. Today the string of five small market centers along the trail were spawned by the railroad. Today, they remain no more than villages. Hart, the biggest, has a population of just under 2,000. Their small, simple scale makes these towns ideal for bicyclists to explore. The entire landscape has the nostalgic simplicity of rural America in the1940s and 1950s, a time before sprawl and rural decay, when the countryside looked like the pictures of Dick and Jane visiting their friendly, apple-cheeked grandparents down on the farm. On summer weekends and holidays, the trail can be a busy place indeed. You might plan an early start to avoid crowds.

Scattered along the trail are four picnic shelters and unsheltered tables every two miles for trail users. About every four miles, there is a toilet visible from the trail (portapotties or restrooms built in shelters), the one exception being the shelter at Rothbury which is about 250 feet off the trail.There are no phones along the trail, but every town has a restaurant. Bikes can be rented at several places along the trail. (See note below.)

Which direction to start in? None of the bike rental places currently offers shuttles, so unless you have two cars, you'll have to make a round trip. The views from the north to the south are definitely the best. The distant hills are so dramatic and striking, it hardly seems like Michigan. You might want to enjoy that while you're fresh. On the other hand, the grade on the trail's northern third is slightly downhill from north to south—so you might prefer to save that for a boost when you're tired. South from Rothbury, it's flatter and less interesting. As for overnight accommodations, restaurants, and events, the twin towns of Whitehall and Montague have more to offer. Whitehall's Howmet Theater has summer stock productions. (From May through September, call 616-894-2540; the rest of the year, call Blue Lake Fine Arts Camp at 616-894-1966.)

If you've been on rails-to-trails bikeways before, you're aware of how easy, almost effortless, the bicycling is, thanks to the gentle railroad grade. The only exception is when there's a strong wind in the wrong direction. Even a 10-year-old in not very good shape could accomplish a round trip with an overnight. Hart, at the northern trailhead, is a pleasant town with a beautiful, wooded park and campground overlooking a small lake and swimming beach. At the south trailhead, the twin towns of Montague and Whitehall sit at the east end of White Lake, a drowned river mouth that empties into Lake Michigan, just seven miles away. (The best bike route to a Lake Michigan beach is following Garfield Road due west out of New Era to the Stony Lake area.) Whitehall/Montague is well supplied with motels and bed and breakfast inns.

Two helpful **map-guides** may be requested by calling (616) 873-3083 weekdays. A little booklet with ads has lots of tips, ads for most area bed and breakfasts, and a trail map. An area map for bicyclists shows the **best bike routes** to area attractions like **Silver Lake** and **Stony Lake**. These routes are quite busy in summer and are for experienced cyclists accustomed to auto traffic.

Here are points of interest in each town along the trail, arranged from north to south. Every town has at least one cafe. Many establishments are closed on Sundays.

HART. John Gurney Park offers roomy camping with all the amenities (electricity, water and sewer, showers; $16-18/night, less for rustic sites), in a beautiful wooded setting overlooking a lake with fishing. The wading beach is a bit weedy. There's tennis and a playground. *Northeast of downtown Hart at 407 State. (616) 873-4959 or (616) 873-2488 (in winter). Camping reservations taken; fills on holiday weekends. ᕀ: call ahead.*

Hart has a pleasant downtown with some fine old houses and the excellent La Fiesta Mexicana restaurant. (Come early at mealtimes or be prepared to wait.)

MEARS. Smallest of the trailside towns. Home of the **Oceana Co. Historical Museum** with changing displays of local history, two blocks west of the blinker light on Fox Road. *It's open between Memorial Day and Labor Day weekends, on weekends from 2 to 5 and on July and August Wednesdays, also 2-5. (616) 873-2600/(616) 861-2965. ᕀ: call. Donations appreciated.*

SHELBY. Right by the trail, **Shelby Gemstone Factory** makes "the ultimate simulated diamond" and shows visitors how it's done (except for certain secret chemicals) in a **continuous slide show** in a 50-seat auditorium. Simulated emeralds and synthetic rubies and sapphires are also made here. Like the diamonds, they can be set in 600 styles of 14K gold jewelry, displayed in the showroom. *On Industrial Dr. northeast of downtown Shelby. (616) 861-2165. Open year-round, Mon-Fri 9-5:30, Sat noon-4. Call ahead for tours of 10 or more. Sat: no tours but slide-show available. ᕀ: auditorium,, shop, and toilets. Free.*

Downtown Shelby, along a north-south street just east of the trail, is a lively little place. More businesses are along Oceana Dr.

(Old U.S. 31), another north-south road farther east. There on the northeast side of town, across from the high school, the **Shelby Pavilion** (616-861-2300) is a nifty, old-fashioned roller rink and ice cream parlor. It includes the **Fireplug Restaurant**.

MONTAGUE. See pages 543-544.

Hart trailhead is just east of the U.S. 31 Polk Rd. exit at the parking lot to Hansen's supermarket. ***Montague trailhead*** *is on Eilers Rd. just east of Bus. Route 31 at the northeast edge of Montague. Administered by Silver Lake State Park; call (616) 873-3083 for information.* &. *Motorized wheelchairs and training for wheelchair racing OK.* **Trail pass:** *$2/day, $10/year, or $5/day, $25/year family pass, available at vendors in each town: in Hart, the Amoco Station downtown or the Shell/Subway halfway between the express way and the trail; in Mears, at The Woodshed; in Shelby at the Shelby Hardware; in New Era at the Country Variety gas station; in Rothbury at Dominic's Grocery; in Montague at the Bicycle Depot. The easiest way to get a pass is on the trail from the ranger as he passes by.*

BIKE RENTALS ALONG THE TRAIL are, as we go to press, ...

◆ in **Hart** at the Wells 602 House Bed & Breakfast, 602 State. (616) 873-3834.

◆ in **Rothbury**, Rothbury Hardware & Farm Supply has a couple of bikes. (616) 861-2418 or (616) 894-8590. Closed Sunday.

◆ in **Montague** at the Bicycle Depot on Bus. U.S. 31 on the northeast side of town. No phone but they never seem to run out of bikes.

◆ in **Mears** at the Woodshed.

WINTER ON THE TRAIL . . . . . **cross-country skiers** and snowmobilers are both permitted on the trail. Because of the railroad right-of-way's long sight lines, the snowmobilers can't come upon the skiers by surprise. The trail parallels nearby Lake Michigan, so snow is plentiful, thanks to the lake effect.

A DOUBLE DECKER BUS FROM HART . . . . . to **Silver Lake** and **Pentwater**, with their **beaches** runs about every two hours from Memorial Day through Labor Day. Call (800) 845-1232 or (616) 845-1231 to get a schedule. ; *Adults $4; 60 and over, handicapped, and 11 and under $2. Ticket allows you to ride all day on three bus tours: Ludington State Park (1 hour, 10 to 5), Ludington-Pentwater (2 hours, 11 to 8), and Pentwater-Silver Lake -Hart (2 hours, 10 to 8). On each tour a tape describes the sights.*

Mac Woods' Dune Rides and Silver Lake State Park

Thrills and insight on the ghostly dunes,
with sunset's pinks and purple shadows

THIS 35-MINUTE ride up and down the sand dunes at Silver Lake offers thrills, hauntingly eerie scenery, and surprisingly intelligent commentary. It's actually worth the money, unlike most of the overpriced go-kart rides, water slides, and family attractions that could make a Silver Lake vacation a thrifty parent's nightmare.

The eight-mile tour conveys the drama of these unusual dunes west and north of Silver Lake. They are *live* dunes, constantly moved by the wind. On a windy day you can feel the dunes in action as you're peppered with wind-borne sand. When the shoreline timber was logged off in the 19th century, hardy dune grass restabilized most denuded sand dunes enough that new vegetation eventually stopped most wind erosion and created "dead" dunes. But in a few places the dunes were so high and windblown that dune grasses couldn't get established.

Crescent-shaped Silver Lake itself is filling in with windblown sand about four feet a year. It's really becoming "Sliver Lake," the tour guide jokes. Eventually the high dunes that separate Silver Lake from Lake Michigan will be cut down by the wind to a more typical height. A few sandblasted pine stumps remain from the logging era. Treetops buried by shifting dunes look like bushes. The buried jack pines die, but poplars survive by sending out additional root systems from their trunks.

Mostly, though, what you see here is a treeless desert, more like the Sahara than normal Michigan dunes with their diverse plant life.

Courteous, well-informed drivers take visitors in safe, fat-tired trucks that have been modified as long, open-air vehicles. The ride includes some moderately thrilling dips and climbs, stops for picture taking, and a pause at the beach to wade in Lake Michigan. *Towards sunset is by far the best time to go on the ride.* The flaming sky and blue lake are dramatic behind the rosy dunes. The slanting light delineates the dunes' shapes and patterns. Oddly, crowds are smaller at this spectacular time.

Old-fashioned tourism prevails here. The dune rides' gift shop is a classic, genial tourist trap. The Burma-Shave-type signs as you enter the dunes have corny mother-in-law jokes. In the 1930s, resort operator Mac Woods bought a thousand acres of this duneland cheap. When the state of Michigan bought the land as part of an expanded Silver Lake State Park, the dune rides company retained concession rights to continue operations. Since the dunes are already actively moving, the rides don't contribute to extra erosion.

On 16th Ave. at Scenic Drive just south of Silver Lake, Mears, MI. From U.S. 31, take Shelby or Hart exits, turn west, and follow the signs. (616) 873-2817. Open daily from mid-May thru mid-October. hours from mid-June thru Labor Day: 9:30-sundown. Shorter hours otherwise. &. Adults $10, children 3-11 $6, under 3 free.

THE MIDWEST'S ONLY DESIGNATED OFF-ROAD-VEHICLE AREA IN SAND DUNES . . . . . is at the north end of the dunes at **Silver Lake State Park**. Here the 300-space parking lot is frequently filled as four-wheelers, dune buggies, trucks, and motorcycles from all over the Midwest create a constant whine and roar that's heard for miles. This goes on from April 1 through October 31. Sandy Korners (616-873-5048) offers **Jeep rentals** and guided drives. The first three weeks in October, there's a 3-hour color run that starts through the sand dunes, goes into Manistique National Forest, and comes back by way of the Pentwater Plain. The $50 per person fee includes lunch in Pentwater. &, call for info. . . . . For info on Michigan's other **designated ORV areas** and hundreds of miles of marked trails, call (517) 373-4175.

WALKING THROUGH THE DUNES . . . . . is permitted in a third section of Silver Lake State Park. The distant roar of off-road vehicles is omnipresent on weekends. During the week the dunes can be peaceful. Wilderness-seekers will prefer the undeveloped **Nordhouse Dunes** north of **Ludington State Park** (page 563).

THE SILVER LAKE SCENE . . . . . involves commercial tourism and active recreation of an intensity seldom found in Michigan. Minigolf, go-kart rides, Jellystone Park, waterslides, trout farms, frozen yogurt stands, and such are everywhere, and hardly anything is cheap. But when the sun is low and the sky illuminated, it is lovely to look across the genuinely silver lake to the ghostly bare, dunes. Blue shadows are cast on the pink dunes. . . . . **Pontoons, sailboards, jet skis, and more can be rented** from the Wave Club (616-873-3700) . . . . The **Silver Lake State Park beach** along Silver Lake takes advantage of the beautiful dune view and provides an island of some serenity. It's a kempt, suburban little park with lawns. Some good-sized pines provide up-north vacation atmosphere and shade. *From U.S. 31, take Hart/Mears exit at Polk Rd., go west on Polk through Mears, follow signs to Silver Lake State Park beach. (616) 873-*

3083. ♿: except for beach. State park sticker required: $4/day $20/year.

A LOVELY, SECLUDED LAKE MICHIGAN BEACH . . . . . away from the hubbub of Silver Lake, but nearby, is **the Little Sable Point Beach** section of the
state park. (Sable is pronounced "SAH-bel" and means sand.) It's a long beach
with an open landscape of poplars, beachgrass, and low dunes, dominated by
the tall red brick shaft of the handsome **Little Sable Point Lighthouse**. Get
there by taking Scenic Drive along the south shore of Silver Lake. Past the Mac
Woods Dune Rides building and many cottages, it becomes Channel Drive. The
paved road stops by Silver Creek. Look for the signs and the narrow dirt road at
the left. It goes alongside the creek, through a heavily wooded area of surprisingly dramatic cottages, to **Golden Township Park** and then on to Little Sable
Point. In the peak summer season, plan on arriving by 10 a.m. to find a spot in
the smallish lot of this attractive beach. *State park sticker required. $4/day,
$20/year.*

PRETTY PENTWATER . . . . . a resort village of charming clapboard storefronts
and pleasant houses, looks a lot like Saugatuck without so many shops. It's
about 15 miles north of Silver Lake, just off U.S. 31. There's a nice **park** for picnics by the marina on Pentwater Lake. The sugar-sand Lake Michigan beach at
Charles Mears State Park is an easy walk to downtown shops and a nifty ice
cream bar with minigolf. A **double-decker bus** (♿) goes to Ludington. For particulars on Pentwater, call (616) 869-4150.

The S.S. *Badger*
Lake Michigan carferry

*The only scheduled cross-lake passenger ship offers
a relaxing mini-cruise between Ludington, Michigan,
and Manitowoc, Wisconsin.*

FOR ANYONE who wants to get a taste of what the Great
Lakes passenger cruises of the first half of our century were
like, a four-hour, 60-mile trip on the refurbished S.S.
Badger, the carferry between the ports of Ludington and Manitowoc
is in order. There's nothing else like it on the lakes today.

Crossing Lake Michigan, even at one of its narrower points,
makes you realize just how *big* the Great Lakes are. Sailing at an
average speed of 18 knots an hour (just under 21 mph), it takes anywhere from 45 minutes to an hour to lose sight of land. Then for
another 45 to 60 minutes there's no land to be seen in any direction.

Granted, the *Badger* has no white-tablecloth dining room or luxury lounge, like the Great Lakes passenger steamers from 1910. But
the *Badger* has enough well-done amenities aboard ship that it completely lives up to its billing as "a unique and affordable travel experience with many of the features and amenities of an ocean cruise."
These include a **cafeteria** and upper-deck **snack bar**, an intelligent
mini-museum on carferry history, and the shipboard **theater** with
free G-rated family films. In keeping with the "family fun" theme,
there are also board games on loan, a video arcade,and a **maritime
puppet theater** and **storytime**. **Badger Bingo** is played on each
daytime and early evening trip, also at no extra charge, with prizes.
There's a **bar** with beer, wine, and cocktails. **Singalongs** are led by
crew members.

Still, the main attractions are the views from the deck. Large
groups gather on the bow of the promenade deck, where there's an
old-fashioned holiday air that comes from the pleasure of having
nothing to do. Along the sides, there's lots of space for anyone who
wants a railside seat. Crew members enjoy showing passengers
around the ship. Forty-two staterooms, arranged like Pullman cars
with two berths each, can be rented for $25 extra each way. (That's
per stateroom, not per person.) They're especially in demand for the
nighttime Manitowoc-to-Ludington run. But the four-hour trip
doesn't provide a good night's sleep. Many people stretch out on
sleeping pads on the deck during the night run. Blankets are

The renovated carferry S. S. Badger comes closer to being a Great Lakes cruise ship than anything else on the lakes today. Staterooms, bingo, movies, meals, and other amenities are offered on the four-hour trip.

advised! A helpful on-board **travel service** advises passengers of what there is to see and do on the Michigan and Wisconsin sides of the lake. It stocks lots of maps and brochures.

The atmosphere is completely different from the latter years of the *Badger's* operation by the Chesapeake & Ohio Railroad. The interior is bright and fresh, and the crew is uniformly cheerful and enthusiastic. The railroad company had the *Badger* and its sister ship, the *Spartan*, built at Sturgeon Bay, Wisconsin, in 1952. The streamlined, machine-age styling continued the look of an earlier generation of carferry from 1939. At that time they were the largest carferries ever built, and their passenger accommodations were equal to the first-rate train service of the day. But by the 1970s, the car ferries' main emphasis had become hauling freight cars across. Bad service and dingy surroundings were part of a plan to discourage passengers and justify discontinuing passenger service altogether. The C&O abandoned service between Muskegon and Milwaukee in 1980 and between Ludington and Manitowoc at the end of 1981. From 1983 through 1990 Ludington investors operated the Ludington run but went bankrupt and stopped operations. 1991 was a sad year for Ludington. After a hundred years of local pride centered on its carferry, the town lost its daily morning and evening bustle, as the crowds gathered by the dock and the beautiful boat steamed out of the harbor. (In many ways watching the *Badger* sail off, a proud plume of coal smoke streaming behind it, is around Ludington when it sails, by all means plan to see it.) The *Badger* is the last coal-fired steamer built on the Lakes. Diesel engines were already well-established when the Chesapeake & Ohio built the *Badger* in 1952. But it preferred a coal because it hauled so much coal. The boiler furnaces burn 70 tons of coal a day, continuously during the ship's sailing season.

It took a man with a dream and a lot of money to make the Badger into the pleasant experience it is today. Not surprisingly, he was a Ludington native. A good number of kids who grow up around the big Great Lakes boats are emotionally imprinted for life and go to great lengths just to be around them. The late Charles Conrad made his money by founding and developing Thermotron Industries in Holland, Michigan. It made ultra-cold test chambers for environmental simulation, largely in aviation and space programs. In retirement Conrad bought and upgraded several Ludington-area resorts. When the ferry stopped, he was aghast, like most of Ludington. His father had been a chief engineer on the carferry trains, and he had gone along on many cross-lake trips.

The *Badger*'s first season in 1992 was a smashing success. It buoyed widely held hopes for a revival of Lake Michigan passenger service. Now that the effects of the initial publicity barrage and novelty have worn off, it's clear that demand for cross lake has to grow to support new ferries and routes. (The *Badger*'s sister ship, the *Spartan*, is moored next to the *Badger*'s Ludington dock, awaiting possible renovation but currently used a a parts source.) Today the Lake Michigan Carferry is owned by Conrad's son-in-law and two Ludington businessmen.

At peak times in July and August, the ferry can be full. *Reservations are advised* to avoid disappointment. A new 40-car deck has been added to increase auto capacity to 180.

Ludington dock: *at the east end of downtown Ludington, a few blocks south of U.S. 10 at the foot of William Street.* **Manitowoc dock:** *in downtown Manitowoc, south of the river. From I-43, take U.S. 151 east from Exit 149, turn right on 10th St., then left onto Madison. Follow signs to dock. Call for 1997 schedule.* **Passenger fares:** *adults $35 one-way, $55 round trip; seniors 65 & up $32/$50; children 5-15 $15/$25. Under 5 free. Groups of 20 or more with one vehicle: 20% to 40% discount. Staterooms $25.* **Badger mini-cruise** *(round-trip without vehicle in 2-day period): adult $40, child $20.* **One-way vehicle fares:** *autos, vans, pickups $45. RVs, trailers: $3/foot (under 7' wide), $5/foot (7'-8'6" wide). Motorcycle $25, with sidecar or trailer $30. Bicycle $5.* **Reservations & info:** *(800) 843-4157 or (616) 845-5555.*

♠ ☗ ♠

HOW MUCH TIME AND STRESS IS SAVED BY TAKING THE CARFERRY? . . .
. . It all depends on where you're coming from and where you're going. One thing
is certain: it's a most relaxing trip. You'll feel 1000% better getting off the ferry
than driving through Chicago, with its constant traffic and construction. The
boat trip lasts four hours, and it's at least an extra half hour on either end to
load and pick up your car. Bicycles are simpler and cost $5 each way. To help
calculate, it's 7 1/2 hours driving time from Ludington to Manitowoc around
Chicago under optimum conditions. Drive times to Ludington (at the speed limit)
are 4 1/2 hours from Detroit, 1 hour 40 minutes from Grand Rapids, 3 1/2
hours from South Bend. Drive times from Manitowoc are 2 hours to Madison
and Milwaukee, 4 1/2 hours to Minneapolis, 3 1/2 hours to Chicago. For drivers
from metro Detroit and southern Michigan, the carferry *really* pays off if you're
going to Door County, Minneapolis, the western Upper Peninsula, or the Apostle
Islands. For North Shore Chicagoans and Wisconsinites going to northern
Michigan, Ludington is 1 hour to Cadillac, 1 1/2 hours to Leland or Traverse
City, and 2 1/2 hours to Charlevoix.

FOR MORE ON LUDINGTON & VICINITY . . . . . call (800) 542-4600 or (616)
845-0324. Ludington has one of Michigan's nicest in-town beaches and, just five
miles north of the ferry, Michigan's biggest, most diverse sand dune state park
and natural area. (See page 561.)

BICYCLING FROM THE carferry . . . . . works well in both Michigan and
Wisconsin. Save money by leaving the car and taking the 48-hour mini-cruise
($15 off per person) or organizing a group of 20 and keeping the same schedule
($22 off). . . . . Ludington is a small town free of the noose of high-traffic arteries
and freeways that make larger places so hard for bicyclists. Call the **Trailhead
Bike Shop** (616-845-0545) for advice on good bike routes. The northern trailhead of a rails-to-trails bike path is in Hart, just 15 miles away. (See page 000.)
. . . . . Wisconsin is justifiably famous as a bicycling paradise, with far more
rails-to-trails paths than any other state, sometimes linked for great distances.
Also, the dairying industry means virtually all back roads in dairy areas are
paved for year-round reliable daily access by milk trucks. Good, low-traffic roads
for bicycling are clearly marked on a super-detailed bike map published by the
state. Call (800) 432-TRIP to ask for it and any other information on Wisconsin.
2-3 week delivery time. . . . . A **short Wisconsin bike trip** could take in the 5-
diamond **American Club resort** (414-457-8000) and other destinations founded
by the **Kohler family** of plumbing fixture fame: the Kohler Design Center (a fascinating museum of plumbing fixtures), and more. Kohler and Sheboygan are
just 30 miles from Manitowoc. Call (414) 457-9495.

TWO RECOMMENDED DESTINATIONS IN MANITOWOC . . . . . are within easy
biking range of the ferry. Manitowoc's long shipbuilding history culminated in

TWO RECOMMENDED DESTINATIONS IN MANITOWOC . . . . . are within easy biking range of the ferry. Manitowoc's long shipbuilding history culminated in WWII submarine construction. Life on a sub and home life during WWII are two themes stressed at the **Manitowoc Maritime Museum** (414-684-0218), which includes a 45-minute tour of a **WWII submarine** . . . . . The CEO of Manitowoc Shipbuilding (makers of legendary cranes today) designed and built a contemporary house in 1934 which his wife planted in a most original manner. Today their **West of the Lake Gardens** (414-684-8533) are open to the public free of charge in season, from Memorial Day or earlier into early October, daily from 10-5, to 7:30 Thursday, with a 6 p.m. tour. Ruth West seems to have adapted Gertrude Jekyll's style of English gardens and Tom Jensen's California look based on dry streambeds and natural features (in this case, Lake Michigan). Sweeping vistas and massive perennial beds are united by flowing annual borders. The inventive color scheme shifts from red and white through pastels to hot colors of orange, purple, and gold. . . . . . Call (414) 683-4388 for Manitowoc area visitor info.

A CARLESS VACATION IN LUDINGTON . . . . . is made easy by the system of summer doubledecker English busses that run from Ludington to the state park; from Ludington to Pentwater; and from Pentwater to Silver Lake and Hart. The $4 round-trip rides ($2 for kids, handicapped, and seniors) are narrated (tapes) . . . . For schedules, call (800) 845-1232 or (616) 845-1231 or pick them up at area lodgings and restaurants. ⅋

Ludington State Park and Nordhouse Dunes

The best all-round state park in Michigan has a long Lake Michigan beach, a large inland lake, a river, extensive trails, a nature center, and more.

LUDINGTON STATE PARK offers the most satisfying mix of natural scenery and popular activities — swimming, boating, hiking, fishing — of any single state park. The 5,300-acre park has six miles of sandy, dune-backed Lake Michigan beach with a handsome lighthouse; an outstanding fishing lake; an inland beach; a fine nature center; and 18 miles of hiking trails. For people who really want to get away from it all, it joins the 3,400-acre **Nordhouse Dunes**, where cars are not permitted.

You don't have to camp here to enjoy the park. The town of Ludington has a big variety of motels. (They often fill on summer weekends.) Nearby campgrounds don't usually fill up. Backpackers can camp along any of the Nordhouse Dunes' trails.

Of special interest here:

♦ The park's six-mile **Lake Michigan beach,** backed by low to high dunes, is longer than any other in Michigan's state park system. The designated swimming area stands out because of a handsome shingle **bathhouse** and **concession** building built by the Civilian Conservation Corps during the Depression. Beachgoers can pull over, park anywhere along the 3 1/2-mile main entry road and walk over to the beach, or walk another mile and a half up the beach from the bathhouse to the beautiful **Big Point Sable Lighthouse.**

♦ An **inland beach** is good for swimming on days when Lake Michigan is too cool. It's by the dam at the west end of **Hamlin Lake.**

♦ The mile-long **Big Sable River** joins Hamlin Lake and Lake Michigan just south of the main swimming beach. It's shallow and clear, ideal for **tubing.** A newly expanded **bike and jogging path** parallels it and the road to Hamlin Lake. A pretty **picnic area** is midway.

♦ **Hamlin Lake** is a 4,500-acre lake, 10 miles long, with excellent **fishing** (panfish, some walleye and pike). Several coves and inlets make for interesting boating, too.

♦ **Canoes and boats** can be rented at Hamlin Beach. The park

Room to spread out: Ludington State Park has miles of sandy beach that's easy to reach by car.

offers the only canoe trail in the state park system. The marked path takes canoeists through ponds, lakes and secluded wetlands.

◆ The **trail system** is one of the very best in the state parks system. It's long — 18 miles altogether. It's varied, passing through dunes, by Hamlin Lake, along the river, and through the woods.. Interconnected trails go to all the park's major activity centers, for hikes of 1 to 8 hours. Trails are dotted with occasional **scenic lookouts**, shelters, and toilets. Designated **cross-country ski trails** include a 6-mile beginner/intermediate trail and an 11-mile advanced trail.

◆ The attractive **Great Lakes Visitor Center** is tucked between deeply shady back dunes and the south bank of the Big Sable River, behind the windswept entry area of scrubby jack pines. Its highlight is outstanding multi-screen **slide/tape shows**, the topic changing frequently, often weekly.

Exhibits include displays on area natural history and natural resources and detailed three-dimensional maps of the bottoms of all the Great Lakes that are of special interest to sailors. The one-mile **Skyline Loop** starts with a dune stair by the parking area and climbs the dune ridge for views clear to the Ludington lighthouse and down into the treetops below. A small **gift shop** is well-stocked with nature books. Call for times of scheduled **nature walks** and **interpretive programs**. *Easy to miss; look for the sign three miles into the park, shortly before you come to the river. Typically open May-Oct. Open daily 10-5 from Memorial Day through Labor Day. Call to confirm spring & fall hours.* &

◆ **344 modern campsites** and **3 rustic mini-cabins** in three mostly shady campgrounds, offer little privacy but are always full between Memorial Day and Labor Day. Campgrounds are equipped with electricity, fire pit, along with water and bathhouses. Electricity is available in the winter but the bathhouse is closed. Those without reservations generally have to wait 2 to 3 days to get in.

Ludington State Park is 7 miles north of Ludington on M-116. (616) 843-8671. ⚥: modern campground, mini-cabins, fishing on wooden walk by Lake Hamlin, 1-mile paved hiking trail. State park sticker required: $4/day, $20/year. Camping fees: $14/night in season, $8 otherwise. For reservations, call (800) 543-2YES.

A DUNELAND WILDERNESS . . . . . where all wheeled vehicles (including mountain bikes) are forbidden is the 3,400-acre **Nordhouse Dunes**, just north of Ludington State Park. Some 15 miles of **trails** here go through areas rich in wildlife and wildflowers. A long, sandy **beach** (5 miles) is fine for swimming. In his helpful little *Natural Wonders of Michigan* (Country Roads Press, $9.95), Tom Carney recommends walking in from the south entrance by the Nurnberg Road parking area to avoid campers who use the north end. First you'll cross a hardwood forest, then pass a marsh before reaching the piney back dunes and, finally in nearly an hour, the beach. You *may* be the only one there. Trails aren't marked except at the trailhead, so pay attention. Take water and wear a hat, of course. **Back country camping** is permitted along the trails. The adjoining, drive-in **Lake Michigan Recreation Area** operated by the U.S. Forest Service has 100 of the nicest rustic campsites in the U.S.: very large, shady, and close to the beach. New playground equipment was recently installed. *$10/night, May 15-Oct 1; $7/night, off season. No reservations except for groups. Lake Mich. Rec. Area and the trailhead for Nordhouse Dunes trails are about 10 miles south of Manistee, then west off U.S. 31. Lake Mich. Rec. Area Rd. leads to campground in about 12 miles. Call (616) 723-6716 or (616) 723-2211 or write P.O. Box 502, Manistee 49660 for information on the dunes and recreation area. ⚥: flush and vault toilets, observation deck on Lake Michigan, fire rings, and picnic tables.*

FOR RAINY DAYS . . . . . there are movies at the **Lyric** at 208 S. James St. in Ludington (616-843-8811; ⚥). . . . . **White Pine Village** is a collection of 20 historic museum buildings. Twelve predate 1900; some are 150 years old. All are furnished with period artifacts from the Mason County Historical Society. There's a blacksmith shop, courthouse, schoolhouse, chapel, research library, and an old-fashioned ice-cream parlour that also serves light food. *On S. Lakeshore Dr. south of Pere Marquette Lake, a few miles south of Ludington. Follow signs from U.S. 31 or main roads. By reservation mid-April thru May. June thru mid Oct. open Tues-Sun 11 to 4:30. Closed Mon. (616) 843-4808. ⚥ Adults $5, children 6-12 $4, under 6 free.*

Shrine of the Pines

Overlooking the Pere Marquette River, an idiosyncratic memorial to the forest's ravaged grandeur and to the beauty of wood itself.

T HE NORTH WOODS of Michigan and Wisconsin are dotted with heartfelt rustic architectural tributes to the inspiring power of nature and the beauty of wood. One of the most striking is the Shrine of the Pines, just south of Baldwin. Here Raymond "Bud" Overholzer decided to build his own personal shrine. He was a small-town farm boy who fell in love with the North and became a hunting and fishing guide. He had seen the aftermath of the logging era's terrible destruction. Logging companies left the cutover forests littered with vast amounts of unusable wood. Stumps, treetops, and bard slabs, left for decades, became vast, dry tinderboxes for forest fires.

Overholzer's passion was making amazingly organic furniture from the leftover roots and stumps. He pursued it from the 1930s into the 1950s, working in the same vein as Stanley Smolak, the creator of Legs Inn north of Harbor Springs. (See page 654.) He drew on the same Central European tradition of withdrawing from society into the peace of the woods. And he too adopted a Central European woodworking style which sometimes blended the rustic and picturesque with touches of the grotesque.

Overholzer, with the help of builder Louis Merrill, had a natural feel for designing a total environment. The site, buildings, and interior furnishings complement each other. The area around the hunting-lodge "shrine" is a delightful place to walk and linger. The lodge takes in the view of a beautiful bend in the Pere Marquette River from its site on a high bank. The first American stocking of the German brown trout *(Bachforelle)*, in 1884, helped turn the Pere Marquette into a noted fishing stream. Today it has been designated a National Scenic River. The stand of pines around the lodge, planted by Overholzer, are not yet majestic, but they do contribute a pleasantly piney smell. **Trails** lead along the top of the bank, off to a small **gift shop**, and down to the river.

Set in the symmetrical log lodge are freeform windows and dormers. They give the place the look of organic 1960s back-to-nature architecture, though actually the lodge is much older.

The enjoyable guided tour that takes visitors into the lodge to see the sensuously handcrafted furniture is a form of folk art itself.

Tree-trunk gun rack: and cabinet: from the 1930s into the 1950s, Bud Overholzer made freeform, organic furniture from tree trunks and roots, in tribute to the great pines fallen during the logging era.

It encourages visitors to admire Overholzer's enduring vision, painstaking craftsmanship, and ingenuity in using only materials of the forest. He avoided nails and glue. Pieces of root form door handles. Hand-rubbed like all the furniture, they are smooth and sensuous to the touch. Other roots, carefully selected, form a balustrade on the stairway that spells out "REST."

There's a huge, 12-seat dinner table formed from a single root. And there's the poker table with little shelves for each player to set cards and a drink. None of the furniture apparently was ever used except for his wife's rocking chair and one other piece of furniture. Woven into the tour is the story of a persistent individualist with a dream, and an unusual and enduring romance whose surprising secret is revealed at the tour's end.

By the parking area are a pop machines, a modern barrier-free restroom, and picnic tables for visitors.

On M-37, 2 miles south of Baldwin, 35 miles east of Ludington on Lake Michigan and 20 miles west of Reed City on U.S. 31. ((616) 745-

7892. Open May 15 thru October 15: Mon-Sat 10 a.m.-6 p.m., Sun 1:30-6 p.m. & $3.50/adult, $2.75 for ages 55 and over, $1 ages 6-12, groups of 30 or more $2.75.

FOR MORE NORTHWOODS MYSTIQUE . . . . . stop at the interesting **Newaygo County Historical Museum** in Newaygo, 41 miles south of Baldwin on M-37 on the way to Grand Rapids. *The museum is in the powerhouse to the dam on the south side of town, and it's open daily from June until school starts (September). In May and September-October, regular hours are on weekends; weekday tours available on request. Hours: 8:30-5, Mon-Sat and 1-5 Sun. (616) 652-9281. & first floor.* There's lots of material on the late **Earnest Jack Sharpe**, popular versifier and creator of *Newaygo Newt*. A sample of Sharpe's appreciative verse is this tribute to the Shrine of the Pines:

> *Near the forest's edge the temple stands*
> *Upon a grassy bank, where it commands*
> *A gorgeous view of swiftly flowing stream,*
> *Where tired souls may sit awhile and dream.*
> *Dreams of the past in keeping with this shrine*
> *Created in honor of the pine.*

Newaygo is an old logging center on the Muskegon River. Just east of town on the river's south side, the **High Rollway Scenic Panorama** offers wonderful views in fall color season. Rollways were where loggers rolled logs down to the river, to float down to the many lumber mills at the river's mouth.

CANOEING THE PERE MARQUETTE . . . . . Baldwin has two canoe liveries. **Ivan's Canoe Rental** (616-745-3361) is at the Pere Marquette bridge three miles south of town. **Baldwin Canoe Rental** (616-745-4669) offers canoeing and rafting on the Pere Marquette and Pine rivers and weekday Christian retreats at its campgrounds. They also have a new motel, Canoe Country Motel. . . . . . . The entire river is very beautiful. It has been designated a *National Scenic River* by both the National Forest Service and the State Forest Service. It is one of the cleanest rivers in the state. You can see the gravel bottom. It has a good current — it's not boring, nor is it dangerous. The Pine is faster and more exciting but requires a more experienced canoeist.

A FAMOUS BLACK RESORT AND ENTERTAINMENT MECCA . . . . . was developed four miles east of Baldwin at **Idlewild** for middle-class black Americans who were barred from owning vacation property at most resorts. One of many land developments started to make money from cutover timberland, Idlewild was marketed with testimonials from respected black professionals who already owned property there. Simple vacation cottages and a few stores developed around four lakes. The resort's wide fame was based on the big-name black entertainers who performed at Idlewild, especially after World War II. Segregation caused the resort to flourish. The civil rights movement of the 1960s offered black people more options and helped send Idlewild into decline. Today longtime residents, however, have helped stabilize it as a low-key vacation and retirement community.

A HAVEN FOR WILDFLOWERS OFF M-37 . . . . . An unusual variety of habitats around Loda Lake north of White Cloud led the Federated Garden Clubs and the U. S. Forest Service to develop the **Loda Lake Wildflower Sanctuary** in 1938. Native Michigan wildflowers have been encouraged here and also transplanted to this thousand-acre preserve. A brochure interprets plants at numbered posts along the one-mile trail. The wildflower display begins with the usual woodland wildflowers in early May and continues until early June. Orchids and carnivorous plants may be viewed on special marked stops along the trail at this time. Many kinds of ferns can be seen throughout the growing season. **Picnic tables** overlooking the lake are by the parking area at the trailhead. Bring your binoculars to see a variety of songbirds and waterfowl, too. *From M-37 six miles north of White Cloud, turn west onto Five Mile Road. In one mile, turn north onto Felch Ave. (dirt). Entrance is in a mile, on right side of road. Brown signs for sanctuary are on M-37. Request the* **brochure** *that goes with the numbered trail from the Manistee National Forest/Baldwin-White Cloud Ranger District, 650 N. Michigan Ave., Baldwin, (after Jan. 1997 or so). (616) 745-4631.* ♿: *no.*

CAMPING PUBLIC LANDS AROUND BALDWIN . . . . . Many National Forest campgrounds once managed by the National Forest Ranger Districts are now managed by concessionaires. **Ivan's Canoe Rental** (616-745-3361) manages, takes reservations, and provides information on 20-site **Bowman Bridge Campground** on the **North Country Trail** and the 4-site **Gleason's Landing** (both on the Pere Marquette National Scenic River). Reservations are recommended in the summer. . . . . . . Concessionaire for the 24-site **Benton Lake Campground** and the 28-site **Nichols Lake Campground**, both 4 1/2 miles off M-37, is Bill Heyser. He also manages the High Bank, Pine Point, and Old Grade sites. No reservations — first come, first served. (616) 745-3337. ♿ . . . . . The **Baldwin-White Cloud Ranger District** at 650 N. Michigan Ave., Baldwin 49304, still oversees one site, **Timber Creek**. (616) 745-4631. Also, no reservations — first come, first served. . . . . .Three campgrounds northeast of Baldwin are part of the **Pere Marquette State Forest**, Route 1, Cadillac, MI 49601. (616) 775-9727.

The Gwen Frostic Studio

In a workshop/store that seems to grow out of river-bank and woods, a crusty artist-philosopher-entrepreneur has created a domain based on nature.

GWEN FROSTIC'S remarkable business is an extremely successful studio/shop that mass-produces original linoleum block prints of simple natural subjects. It's run, hands-on, every day, by Gwen Frostic, the pithy artist-entrepreneur-philosopher-printer. Born in 1906, she was a feminist long before the current movement emerged. Her domain is her studio-salesroom-factory-home, built into the side of a riverbank hill in a completely organic style that reminds many people of Frank Lloyd Wright's work.

In summer up to 1,200 people a day come here to buy Gwen Frostic's line of note cards, giftwrap, napkins, blank books, prints, and books written and illustrated by Frostic – at prices so low they seem like wholesale.

The studio overlooks the valley of the Betsie River, just south of Crystal Lake and west of Benzonia. It has a sod roof and walls made of local stones and boulders, contrasted with rustic wood. Plashing water from fountains sets a peaceful mood. Free-form rock pillars add to the inventive, natural atmosphere. Deer tracks and leaf impressions are in the concrete floor.

The cards are arranged by color (the papers are soft pinks, yellows, beiges, and blues) to become a completely integrated part of the overall design, like a pattern of wallpaper or carpet.

A set of large windows by the sales counter lets visitors look

Printmaker Gwen Frostic has used her many design talents to create an autonomous fiefdom — her home, studio, shop, and manufacturing facility built into the valley wall of the Betsie River near Frankfort.

down on 13 old Heidelberg presses that print all Frostic's cards and papers. The air is filled with the smell of ink when the sheet-fed presses are in action between 9 and 4:30, Monday through Friday. The Round House was added in a wing by the entrance to handle crowds at peak seasons. Its big windows look down on ponds and nature trails. Downstairs from the entrance is Frostic's **library**, where visitors are welcome to sit and read. Or they can go out from here onto the **trails** by the pond and the Betsie River. This is the ultimate in an integrated, values-based system of life, art, and livelihood. It fits right into Frostic's grand theme, a holistic view of life that ultimately revolves around nature and its many kinds of power. "All things are part of the whole," she summarizes her philosophy. "Nothing can exist alone. I have never felt any separation between my business and me."

Nature never goes out of style. "Keep it simple" is another business principle. There are no UPS or no credit cards in her mail-order business, and no wholesale prices, either. (Frostic cards sold elsewhere are simply marked up from prices at her store.)

"She's a genius in her art and business," says a longtime admirer. "Nature has always been her theme. She's faithful to her principles. She's studied people and knows what they like. All her prints are technically originals; she gets 40,000 reprints from her linoleum blocks. Everybody else in her line of work depends on outside offset printers to print their images. In her poetry, she really gets down to the essence of life. She's her own publisher and printer. I don't know any other artist who's doing all that." Such rare independence and persistence could well stem from Frostic's determination to overcome early childhood handicaps.

After spending childhood summers on Crystal Lake, Frostic moved north in 1955. She developed her successful business in a Frankfort storefront before building the studio in the early 1960s. Today, with a staff of 30, Frostic is able to spend a good deal of her energy in writing books about her philosophy of life – books, she says

with a smile, that hardly anybody reads. But they're for sale at the studio, along with the cocktail napkins and gift enclosures. Every two years she produces a new book of prints and thoughts. In 1995's *Synthesis* she wrote, "Activity — the essence of the universe/the continuous activity of growth/ keeps life alive . . ./All seems to be in a constant state of /motion — even the elements . . ."

On River Rd/CR 608, 2 miles west of U.S. 31 and Benzonia. In Benzonia, River Rd./608 is where the old Congregational Church faces the green. In Frankfort, River Road intersects with M-22 between Frankfort and Elberta. Go east to studio. Drive down to studio is just west of Higgins Rd. intersection. Open year-round. Open daily from 1st Sun of May to 1st Sun of Nov, 9-5:30. Otherwise open Mon-Sat 9-4:30. (616) 882-5505. ♿

A CITY UPON THE HILL . . . . . in the Biblical sense of a holy place elevated above crass trading and sensuality. That's what the idealistic Congregational founders of **Benzonia** hoped to build. Their plans to develop Northern Michigan's version of Oberlin College failed, however. Famed Civil War historian Bruce Catton told the story in ***Waiting for the Morning Train***, his compelling personal history of his hometown and region at the end of the lumber boom. Today Benzonia is a backwater compared with Leelanau County resorts not far to the north. The charming cluster of **art galleries** and **Northern Delights** bakery/restaurant, just west of U.S. 31 by the main four corners, is worth a visit. Ferries, gliders, and more appear in the **Benzie Area Historical Museum**. It's in the large old Congregational Church on River Road/Homestead Road. Don't miss Lou McConnell's wonderful folk-art sawmill model in the basement. In 1997 or 1998, the museum will expand its exhibit space. (A Gwen Frostic exhibit is being planned which will include a partial reproduction of her Presscraft building, original blocks, and an oral history.) *Open May thru Dec : Tues-Sat 10 a.m.-4 p.m. (616) 882-5539.* ♿: *elevator to come in 1997 or 1998. $2/adult, 50¢/children, $5/ family.*

DOWNTOWN FRANKFORT IS BOUNCING BACK . . . . from hard times that began with the loss of the Ann Arbor Railroad carferries in 1982. A grassroots economic development group purchased the closed Pet cherry pie plant and has its Gateway products in many supermarkets. New Main Street **shops** along Betsie Bay are worth checking out. **The Bookstore** is a pleasant spot for browsing. . . . . It's fun to walk out on the **pier** leading to the breakwater light. Just north of it are a nice **beach** and playground. Inside the **post office**, a WPA mural depicts a carferry caught in a fierce storm. Across the bay in Elberta is moored one of the last remaining railroad carferries, ***The City of Milwaukee***. As we go to press, there are plans to sell it and renovate it as a museum.

Sleeping Bear Dunes National Lakeshore

Beaches and trails with splendid views;
maritime and lumbering history;
and two uninhabited islands to explore

CENTERPIECE of this sprawling national lakeshore is the most famous of Great Lakes dunes, Sleeping Bear. The National Lakeshore, visited by some 1.25 million people a year, is a varied 35-mile stretch of scenic shoreline extending some two miles inland. It includes:

◆ a scenic drive
◆ a variety of simple, beautiful beaches with high Lake Michigan overlooks
◆ a dozen hiking trails to many outstanding overlooks
◆ smaller lakes
◆ rivers
◆ an attractively woodsy rustic campground
◆ a state-of-the-art modern campground
◆ two large carless islands, North and South Manitou

Sleeping Bear once was larger, looming 600 feet above Lake Michigan. Topped by trees, the dune did look like a bear. It sat back from the shore, protected by a bluff of sand. But dunes and shore-lines are marked by alternating periods of stability and change. Since the early part of this century, wave action has devoured the bluff's edge, eroding the glacial plateau beneath Sleeping Bear itself. Winds, having destroyed the plant cover on top, send sands sailing over to the Dune Climb, an area so volatile that human footsteps can do no additional harm. By 1980 Sleeping Bear was down to 400 feet.

The area offers a hard-to-match blend of outstanding natural areas and civilized amenities. No matter how crowded the towns are, there's plenty of room to spread out in the national lakeshore. Here's how to acquaint yourself with the area:

◆ Begin your visit with a stop at the **Sleeping Bear Dunes Visitor Center** just outside the village of Empire. Rangers are happy to advise visitors about recreational opportunities. Visitor information currently can be mailed upon request. New **displays** and **videos** give good overviews of the lakeshore's wildlife, plants, geology, and human history. Its **book shop** is excellent. Budget cutbacks have reduced the number of free publications on the Lakeshore, but some are sold for nominal prices. "Hiking Trails" summarizes all 13 trails and directs you to the trailheads. Visitor maps from the Empire and Glen Lake chambers of commerce include a lot of helpful information. **Free daily programs** and **guided walks** about the area's natural and human history are held in July and August. A volunteer friends group has stablilized programming in the wake of federal budget cutbacks. *Off M-72 at M-22 just east of Empire. (616) 326-5134. Open daily except for off-season federal holidays, at least from 9:30 to 4. Inquire for possibly longer summer hours. &: visitor center, wheelchair available for use in park, park accessibility brochure. Call accessibility coordinator for info. Free.*

◆ Next, take a short, marvelous hike along the **Empire Bluff Trail.** This highly recommended 1.7 mile round trip goes up into a deeply shady beech-maple climax forest, out into the high, perched dunes, and to an observation platform some 400 feet above the lake. The **trail guide** from the visitors' center makes it even more enjoyable. Your reward is a view that includes two-thirds of the entire National Lakeshore, from Platte Bay on the south to Sleeping Bear itself on the north, out to South Manitou Island. *From M-22 about 1 1/2 miles south of Empire, turn northwest onto Wilco Road and look for the sign.*

◆ A third good introduction is the 7.4-mile-long **Pierce Stocking Scenic Drive**, named after the area lumberman who developed it as a private visitor attraction in the 1960s. An excellent **interpretive brochure** is available at the entrance. The valley overlook and picnic spot looks down on Glen Lake and a three-mile stretch of duneland leading up to Sleeping Bear itself. The first Lake Michigan overlook (wheelchair accessible) offers closer views of the vanishing big dune, a mile away; the second Lake Michigan overlook also has a fine view of the shoreline to the south, down to the Empire Bluffs and Platte Bay. *From M-22 2 miles north of Empire, turn north onto M-109. Drive entrance is in 1 mile. Drive open May to mid-October. In winter it's a groomed ski trail. Open 9 a.m. to 1 hour after sunset. For early-morning walks, park by the entrance. &: parking and restrooms at Picnic Mountain, and North Bar Lake Overlook; Dunes Overlook has accessible path; Lake Michigan Overlook is steep. Free.*

◆ Another aspect of the National Lakeshore it its historic rural landscapes. Now that the lakeshore is 25 years old, the farms are mostly inactive, and building are boarded up, which gives them a poignant, slightly spooky aura. Neal Bullington, manager of Lakeshore interpreters, points to the rural community of **Port Oneida**, northeast of Glen Arbor, as a historic landscape of World War II vintage, before fence rows were removed so massive machinery could make turns.

Michigan's most famous dune, Sleeping Bear, towers 400 feet above Lake Michigan. The splendid Sleeping Bear National Lakeshore incorporates many hiking trails, beaches, and scenic vistas.

Port Oneida's back roads make for pleasant bicycling. Take loops off M-22 on Thorson Road, about two miles north of Glen Arbors, or on Port Oneida Road and Basch Road a mile or so farther away. The **Bay View Trail** for hiking and cross-country skiing (7 miles long, in several loops) goes past farmsteads through old fields and wooded hills. **Lookout Poin**t offers a good Lake Michigan view. *The trailhead is on Thorson Rd. just north of M-22.*

Here are highlights of the Sleeping Bear Dunes area. All noteworthy attractions are arranged by activity category.

BEACHES (arranged from south to north). Most have no lifeguards.

◆ **Platte River Point Beach.** Kids enjoy this beach because the Platte River winds around behind Lake Michigan to make a shallow, warm-water area for wading and making sand architecture. There's a **picnic area**, flush toilets, and drinking water available. *About 10 miles south of Empire and 14 or 15 miles north of Frankfort, From M-22 just east of the Platte River bridge, take Lake Michigan Rd. about 2 miles to Lake Michigan. &: picnic area has restrooms, picnic shelters, river walk, fish cleaning station. Free.*

◆ **Esch Road Beach.** A simple, barely-developed beach in a pretty, natural setting. Vault toilet. Otter Creek makes a shallow, warm backwater good for wading. *From M-22 4 miles south of Empire, take Esch Rd. a little over a mile to Lake Michigan. Free.*

◆ **Empire Beach.** This pleasant village beach with grassy lawns offers a fine view of Sleeping Bear, South Manitou Island, and passing freighters. Sandy beach frontage is on both South Bar Lake, for a nice cool-weather swimming alternative, and on Lake Michigan. There's a **picnic area** with grills, gazebo, restrooms, volleyball net, basketball court, and **playgrounds** on both beachfront areas, plus a **boat launch** and shore fishing. A historical marker fills you in on Empire's boom years as a lumbering center, 1873-1917. The trim little **Manning Memorial Light** was erected in 1991 in memory of an avid fisherman and lifelong Empire resident who always wanted a light to guide his fishing boat home. *From the west end of Front Street in downtown Empire (the westward extension of M-72), turn north onto Lake to reach the beach. No charge. Beach parking can fill up on nice summer days; come by noon.*

◆ **Glen Lake Beach.** This sandy inland beach has a fine view of Little Glen Lake, with hills in the background and the Dune Climb across the road. **Picnic tables**, grills, changing house, vault toilets. Geese can be a problem. *Take M-109 from M-22 at either central Glen Arbor or 3 miles north of Empire. Beach is about 4 miles from either end. Free.*

◆ **Glen Haven Beach.** By the now-deserted pilings of the Glen Lake Canning Company pier, this extremely simple little beach at Sleeping Bear Point has good swimming and nice views of the Manitou Islands. It's a favorite **sunset walk**, year-in and year-out, for many area residents. The distant islands are striking, set against the rosy sunset sky. **Picnic table**s, vault toilets. Most of the village of Glen Haven is boarded up, awaiting possible future restoration by the National Park Service. *From central Glen Arbor, take M-109 west to Glen Haven, turn in by the parking area by the old cannery. Free.*

◆ **Good Harbor Bay Beach.** Lots of surrounding natural vegetation and striking views of the bluffs of Pyramid Point and North Manitou Island make this very simple, uncrowded beach attractive. Before you come to the **picnic area**, look for the trailhead to the **Good Harbor Bay Hiking Trail**, a 2.8 mile loop. It goes past low dunes and across low ridges into a forest along a creek. *Take M-22 about 8 miles northeast of Glen Arbor or 9 miles southwest of the intersection with M-204. Turn north at County Road 669 (you'll see the sign to Cedar; go in the opposite direction). When you get to the lake, turn right. Free.*

◆ **Good Harbor Beach.** Like Good Harbor Bay Beach, but on the east end of the bay. Vault toilets. *At the end of County Road 651, a mile west of M-22, 7 miles due north of Cedar and 4 miles southwest* *of the intersection of M-204 and M-22 near Leland. Free.*

ADVENTURES

◆ **Dune Climb.** Sleeping Bear today is a live dune. As the wind cuts
down its top, sand spills over the back. This 150-foot wall of sand is
a strenuous climb, more so for adults than lightweight kids, but
climbers are rewarded with a view of Glen Lake and the surrounding countryside. To see Lake Michigan from the top of
Sleeping Bear, however, it's a two-mile walk across hot sand, and
two miles back, three to four hours altogether. Water, hats, and sun
protection are advised. **Picnic tables** and a **refreshment and souvenir stand** are near the parking lot at the dune climb's base. A
measuring beam placed at the dune's base measures its rate of
eastward advance.The Warnes family, souvenir stand proprietors,
have been in the area for generations. They're a fine source of local
history. *Take M-109 from M-22 at either central Glen Arbor or 3 miles
north of Empire. Dune Climb is about 4 miles from either end.* &: *restrooms; Duneside Trail has 6-foot-wide hardened surface. Free.*

◆ **South Manitou Island.** In the early days of Great Lakes shipping,
this small island (about 3 1/2 by 3 1/2 miles) and others like it
bustled with activity, while the mainland away from shipping routes
remained a wilderness. Woodcutters on the island supplied fuel for
steamers. (On each trip through the Great Lakes a ship consumed
from 100 to 300 cords of wood). South Manitou farms supplied provisions for ship crews. The island had a village with stores, a busy
harbor, and a lighthouse to mark the entrance to the Manitou
Passage, a much-used but potentially dangerous shortcut. By 1960
the last farms were gone and the Coast Guard station had been
closed. Some old-timers remained and catered to the summer people and boaters who came to the island. In 1970 the National Parks
Service began buying the island as part of the Sleeping Bear
National Lakeshore. The island's natural life slowly came to an end
as property owners sold out and life lessees died. Today abandoned
farm buildings, a school, and a cemetery remain as evocative testimony to changing times.

As part of the National Lakeshore, the island has been open
since 1970 to primitive, low-impact campers, to hikers, to boaters
(who must anchor offshore and come in by dinghy), and to day-trippers who take the 1 1/2-hour voyage over, spend three hours on
the island, and return to Leland. Manitou Island Transit, the ferry
service, is owned and operated by the Grosvenors, whose family
lived for generations on the island. They know it well and offer a 1
1/2 hour **island tour** in an open-air vehicle. It can be customized
for special interests. The tour focuses on everyday details of bygone

island life, then ends with a cemetery visit about the real people who lived it. Sign up for the tour on the boat; it's $7 for adults, $4 for children.

Near the docks, rangers give **talks** about the **lighthouse** and shipping (currently at 1 p.m.) that include a trip up the 100-foot lighthouse tower. The **Visitor Center** in the old village post office tells the island's natural and human history.

Day-trippers can also choose to explore the island on their own. If you don't plan your time carefully, you'll find yourself running to catch the ferry, or faced with the prospect of spending the night in the open. Three hours enables you to see the grove of **virgin white cedars** (ask rangers how to find the world record-holder, 17 1/2 feet around), get to the huge **perched dunes** overlooking the rocky coast on the island's west side, and see **the wreck of the *Francisco Morazan***, run aground in 1960 off the island's south tip. On a sunny day, seen from a bluff, its rusty hulk is dramatic against the blue waters of the Manitou Passage, a tempting but treacherous shortcut for ships. If you're inclined to hike along the beach, wear wading shoes. All-day **natural history tours** of South Manitou ($35 including ferry) are led every other Thursday (and sometimes on Saturday) mid-May through September by the Leelanau Conservancy. Call (616) 256-9665 for info. and fall schedule.

No food is available on the island; bring your own. Ten miles of marked **hiking trails** go through dense, mature forests and old fields. Some forests, far from the harbor, have never been cut. Wildflower colonies there have grown undisturbed, so you can see jack-in-the-pulpit and trillium of enormous size. Sandy **beaches** are plentiful; the protected east bay is especially popular. The island's small size makes it hard to get lost for long; South Manitou is a good place for families' first big backpacking adventure. Careful planning and disposal of waste is imperative, to avoid trashing the island. Camping is permitted at three main **campgrounds** (from one to four miles from the dock; campers hike there), at scattered **back-country campsites** for up to 6 people, and at a few larger group campsites. No reservations are taken; get a permit at the visitor center. Try to go on a sunny day when the scenery shows to best advantage. **To help plan a trip** to either Manitou island, call the National Lakeshore at (616) 326-5134 for free handouts or to order one of two helpful visitor guides: Steve Harrington's ***Visitor's Guide to South Manitou Island*** (24 pp., $1.50) or Robert Ruchhoft's ***Exploring North Manitou, South Manitou, High and Garden Islands of the Lake Michigan Archipelago*** (362 pp., $14.95). Ask about various historical books on the Manitous. *Manitou Island*

Transit leaves from Fishtown in downtown Leland. Daily service June thru August; no Tues. or Thurs. trips in May, Sept., Oct. Check in at 9:30 a.m., depart at 10 a.m. Reservations recommended. (616) 256-9061. &: assistance needed for ferry, motorized tour, and village area. Call both park and ferry for info. Day trip: $19 adults, $13 children 12 and under. No bicycles.

◆ **North Manitou Island.** Logging, farming, cherry-raising, and the Coast Guard have all vanished from North Manitou, where two towns once were. All that remains are abandoned and ruined buildings, a few private camps, and a small visitor staging area in the east village with a ranger station for emergency assistance. Most of the island was a private hunting preserve; seven deer introduced in 1927 have proliferated into a herd once as high as two thousand. Their overbrowsing destroyed young trees and shrubs and made the island look like a park — pretty, but ultimately ruinous. Liberal hunting seasons in recent years have reduced the deer herd, and vegetation has recovered. Topography varies from low, open dunes to rugged bluffs.

Since the National Parks Service bought the hunting preserve in 1984, it is managing the island as "a primitive experience emphasizing solitude, a feeling of self-reliance, and a sense of exploration." That means: no cars or wheeled vehicles; water at only one place; two outhouses; one campground; fires only at two fire rings. Low-impact camping (burying human waste, packing out trash) is required. Thirty miles of **marked trails** make three interconnecting loops around the island. To go elsewhere, a compass is essential. Campers are free to choose backcountry sites under certain limitations. *Manitou Island Transit leaves Leland at 10 on Sunday, Wednesday, and Friday, June thru August and returns immediately, without a layover. In July and August, departures on Monday and Saturday also. Call (616) 256-9061 for other times and for **hunting information**. &: no. Round-trip fares: $19 adults, $13 children 12 and under. No bicycles.*

◆ **Canoeing or kayaking on the Crystal River.** Short, 2 1/2 hour trip on the beautiful Crystal River as it goes from Fisher Lake through cedar and balsam forests on state land with lots of wildlife. A good family trip. Lots of places to get out and swim or wade. Some portaging across roads. *Crystal River Canoe Livery, at the Glen Arbor Shell Station on M-22 just northeast of Glen Arbor. (616) 334-3090 or (616) 334-3831. 9-5 daily in season.*

◆ **Canoeing on the Platte River.** A delightful, easy 1 1/2-hour trip through hardwood forests, wetlands, sand dunes, and Loon Lake. Much animal and bird life can be seen if you go before noon or after

6 p.m. The gentle current of this shallow river makes it ideal for canoeing novices; the wildlife makes it attractive to veteran naturalists. Start by the M-22 bridge at the Platte River between Empire and Frankfort. **Canoe rentals** from the Riverside Canoe Livery (same location), (616) 325-5622. Parking is scarce; come early.

◆ **Hiking.** The 13 hiking trails lead through distinctive environments to scenic overlooks. The Parks Service's "Hiking Trails" brochure summarizes the special features of each trail; separate hiking and cross-country skiing maps are available for each. Three trails are especially recommended. The 1 1/2-mile **Empire Bluffs Trail** (page 572) gives the best overview of the entire shoreline. The 4-mile Otter Creek loop of the 15-mile **Platte Plains Trail** goes alongside a stream full of wildlife, including beavers, and through a fragrant cedar swamp. The **Dunes Trail**, a strenuous 2.8 mile loop, starts near the Glen Haven Maritime Museum. It explores the spooky, desolate dunescape atop Sleeping Bear, including a ghost forest of trees that flourished before being buried in sand. Wind-sculpted patterns in the sand are striking. (Water, a hat, sunscreen, and shoes are recommended for hot dune hikes.)

Two easy, 1 1/2-mile, one-hour hikes come with interpretive brochures to put you in touch with sand dune ecology (**Cottonwood Trail**) and the rich variety of species found where forests meet fields (**Windy Moraine Trail**). The new Duneside Accessible Trail (1.8 miles round trip from the Dune Climb's north end, page 575) is designed for wheel chairs. An audiocassette and player can be borrowed at the visitor center for nature interpretation without reading.

INDOOR ACTIVITIES

◆ **Empire Area Historical Museum.** See page 601. A local museum showing the results of lots of energy and some great stuff. A good rainy-day destination.

◆ **Sleeping Bear Point Coast Guard Station Maritime Museum.** Worth a visit for the beautiful setting alone. "The [Coast Guard] surfmen became folk heroes, greatly respected for their courage and skill," interpreters said. "Neighbors often came by to watch their drills." You can see a **video** of the breeches buoy drill and relive the crew's rigorous weekly schedule. The **Manitou Passage** off Sleeping

Bear was a favorite shipping shortcut, deep but narrow and therefore the scene of many wrecks. The big historic photos and spartan quarters of the lifesaving crew and keeper are dramatic. There's no hint of the personal lives of these self-sacrificing men except the intriguing audio reminiscence of a Coast Guard admiral whose father was a lighthouse keeper. Don't miss the **boathouse**, restored to about 1905, with a beach cart, surf boats, and other rescue items. A short distance away on the same road, the old **Glen Haven Cannery** has historic boats from rowboats to a 36-foot Coast Guard lifeboat. *Open same hours as Maritime Museum. West of Glen Haven. Take M-109 to Glen Haven, 2 1/2 miles west of Glen Arbor, and follow signs to the Museum on Sleeping Bear Point. (616) 326-5134. Open weekends10:30-5, Memorial thru Labor Day. (May be open weekdays in July and August; call first.)* &: *boathouse and restrooms. Free.*

◆ **Shopping in Glen Arbor.** See page 599.

BEST STOPS FOR PICNIC FIXINGS . . . . . In **Empire**, Deering's Market on Front at La Rue has a big meat counter and produce section and its own smokehouse. . . . . In **Glen Arbor**, Steffen's IGA at M-22 and M-109 has the best selection and prices on groceries and meats. . . . . . Both are open year-round. In **Leland**, **Stone House Breads** at the south entrance to town on M-22 has the region's best breads, crusty and full-flavored. The **Mercantile** downtown has an amazingly diverse grocery selection for a small store, and the **Village Cheese Shanty** in Fishtown offers samples of a wide range of cheeses. See p. 595.) The **Manitou Market** on M-22 just south of M-204 is a handy stop with good local produce in season. . . . . At the south end of Suttons Bay off M-22, **Hansen Foods** (616-271-4280) has an outstanding deli with housemade salads and terrific subs, plus housemade hot dogs and smoked meats, Stone House Breads, a good wine department, and more. Open 8-8, to 9 in summer.

VISIT THE PEACEFUL, RURAL STUDIO . . . . . of watercolorist and woodcarver **Rod Conklin** not far from Empire and the Esch Road beach.near the south end of the Sleeping Bear National Lakeshore. Here in a trim, tidy outbuilding of a hillside farm, he carves charming smooth sumac birds, using both colors of the wood to good advantage. His framed prints ($25-$75) and paintings are clean, simplified distillations of nearby shoreline scenes and farm vignettes. *7339 Valley Rd./C.R. 677. First house south of C.R. 610. From M-22 by Fowler Rd., go 4 miles east on Fowler. From M-72/Fowler Rd., go south 4 miles on CR 677. (616) 325-6482. Open regularly June thru color season, 11-5 daily. Stop in or call ahead any time.* . . . . . . On summer weekend afternoons, the Benzie County Historical Society holds open the pretty brick **schoolhouse** at the corner of C.R. 610 and C.R. 677 just north of Rod Conklin's studio.

CROSS-COUNTRY SKIING . . . . . is very popular at the National Lakeshore. Though trails are not groomed, heavy use means there's usually a track. Get trail maps at the Visitor Center (p. 571). Call (616) 326-5134 for **snow report.**

Leelanau Peninsula

One of the state's major attractions, this picturesque
spit of land draws large number of visitors annually.
Here's how to enjoy its many delights.

THE LITTLE FINGER of lower Michigan's mitten, the
Leelanau Peninsula extends 30 miles into Lake Michigan,
forming the west shore of Grand Traverse Bay's West Arm.
Here history and geology have combined to create a delightful landscape. The most recent glacier, as it retreated north, formed streamlined long hills called drumlins. "From every hillcrest, a panorama
of carefully tilled farmlands and wooded slopes unfolds before the
visitor's eye, with the ever present lake waters as a background,"
described the Michigan W.P.A. guide of 1940. "Off the western shore
of the peninsula, the Manitou Islands rise, hazy green, above the
horizon." Cherry orchards, joined more recently by vineyards, create
a beautiful, orderly, highly cultivated landscape, dotted with nine
pleasant villages.

The interior's striking hilliness is reminiscent of upper New
England. It's lovely at every time of year. Winter reveals the shapes
of trees and buildings with great clarity. Fruit trees blossom in the
early green of spring. In fall, long views of distant barns and lakes
are framed in hills glowing with color, with enough evergreens to set
off the flaming reds and yellows. Summer, when the area is most
crowded with visitors, may well be the least interesting season,
when the landscape is reduced to vacation basics: lots of greens,
blue water, and sand. The blue itself can be stunning. On sunny
days it's a vivid turquoise, created by light reflecting from the white,
sandy bottom of Grand Traverse Bay.

The area's diverse economic activities from the 1850s into the
early 20th century created distinctive small towns and attracted
many kinds of peoples. Today that diversity makes the peninsula
more interesting and varied than many other areas dominated by
resorts. Leelanau's first settlements were three separate Indian missions founded south of Northport, around **Omena**, between 1849
and 1852. The name Leelanau was not an authentic Indian place
name but a poetic invention of Henry Schoolcraft, Indian agent,
scholar, and advisor to Governor Lewis Cass. Protestant missionaries brought Indian congregations here. They hoped, in vain, that the
isolated area would remain free of white settlers, away from the cor-
rupting influence of alcohol. Intermarried offspring of these Ojibwa

and Odawa bands remain here today, largely in the reservation at **Peshawbestown**, between Suttons Bay and Omena.

Leland (the county seat) and **Northport** developed as ports for commercial fishermen and provisioners of Great Lakes vessels. Supplying cordwood and food to ships was the original livelihood for many remote ports. The Homestead Act of 1862 was what finally opened up the remote peninsula to widespread settlement. Immigrants, often seeking to avoid conscription in the post-Napoleonic reorganizations of their homelands, homesteaded the area and soon changed from subsistence farming to raising fruit. **Suttons Bay** first prospered with sawmills, then became a cherry-processing center. Many nationalities, including Bohemians, Norwegians, Belgians, and Poles, were recruited to work in lumber camps and mills, of which the Empire Lumber Company in **Empire** was by far the largest. Today the Polish town of **Cedar** is locally famous for its sausage and its Polish Festival each August. French-Canadians, Bohemians, and German-Catholics made up the village of **Lake Leelanau**. Lumber companies, thinking the county's hill, landlocked interior was worthless, sold land cheap.

The peninsula's visual charm and its small-scale, small-town ambiance is due to the area's economic paralysis since 1910 in every sector but tourism and agriculture. The only non-agricultural industries were sawmills and, in Leland, 19th-century charcoal iron smelting. The transition to tourism occurred when Chicagoans came north to escape the pressures of city life and find cool weather and solace. Resort development was in full swing by 1890, well before the lumber ran out.

For most of the 20th century, Leelanau enjoyed a

successful balance between local people and nature-loving, privacy-seeking cottagers and resorters from big cities, who provided incomes for old Leelanau families. The 1970s saw a new influx of outsiders — urbanites seeking a simple life in tune with nature. These included writers, artists, and craftspeople, whose studio/shops add greatly to the pleasure of drives in the country.

At the same time, the seeds of change were planted that now disrupt the old balance. Second homes, long an important part of the local mix, began to change in character from leisurely summer cottages to condos for people driving up for the weekend, mostly from metro Detroit. These so-called "trunk-slammers" don't have the old-time cottage-owners' concern and commitment to the area, engendered by years of personal ties. The resort economy, which had been on a ma-and-pa level, started attracting big-time developers with large projects like The Homestead and Sugar Loaf resorts and condo complexes. Establishing the Sleeping Bear Dunes National Lakeshore in 1970 helped promote the change to more intense development. So did the booms in downhill skiing and boating.

Today Leelanau's population has doubled to 18,000 from its longtime low of 8,900 in 1968. Suttons Bay, with easy access to Traverse City via M-22, has become a virtual suburb. Peshawbestown and its heavily advertised casino are booming. Leland, long an attractive mix of pleasant but modest houses and old summer homes, has become so slicked up and gentrified, with so many gift shops, that many year-round Leelanau residents consider it ruined and avoid it altogether, especially in summer. Zoning policies as far away as Northport are now set by exurbanites intent on fending off threats of development, with the ironic result that cherry farmers attempting to survive by selling fruit and crafts at farm or small locally owned businesses on side streets are thwarted by strict township regulation of signs.

To the casual visitor, the results of all this development are mixed. There are a lot more shops everywhere, and some are quite interesting. Most cater to visitors and second homeowners. (Everybody else depends on weekly trips to Traverse City discount stores.) Suttons Bay and Glen Arbor are outstanding places to see the latest ingenious trends in interior design for second homes. Artists' studio-shops are now plentiful; at any one, pick up a free copy of **Arts and Crafts Trails in Northern Michigan**, a listing and map of various studios. There are two fabulous restaurants — Hattie's in Suttons Bay and La Becasse in tiny Burdickville, on Glen Lake — and many others that cater to well-heeled outsiders, while year-round neighborhood hangouts are few and far between.

The negatives are the traffic in towns and on much of M-22 in summer, and the anger and depressed resignation you encounter among people who love this place. Pick up a copy of the interesting weekly newspaper, the *Leelanau Enterprise*, and you'll realize how intense the local political battles are. It's full of letters by concerned local residents about the perils brought by development and tourism to a precious, vulnerable rural way of life.

Still, Leelanau remains a place with no fast food restaurants, no tanning booths, no traffic lights (except for a new one on the outskirts of Traverse City), and three bookstores – a point of local pride.

You can enjoy the Leelanau's beauty without the crowds by seeking out less convenient beaches (see below and page 573), by hiking, by biking on scenic roads in the morning, and — perhaps best of all — by planning a visit in May or June or September or January. Winter is beautiful here, and the **skiing** is excellent – downhill at **Sugar Loaf Resort** (616-228-5461), with a 500-foot vertical drop, and cross-country in the Sleeping Bear National Lakeshore and Leelanau State Park. A lot of interesting people live up here and get into retailing to make a living. The people, in many ways, are a big part of what make Leelanau special. When you visit in the off-season, they have plenty of time to talk.

Travel brochures sometimes suggest a 93-mile driving tour of Leelanau to be done in a day (or a half day!). These miss the charms of the area entirely. Leelanau is a special blend of nature and simple man-made diversions, best enjoyed slowly — by lingering and walking, swimming and bicycling.

Here are some of the peninsula's highlights, arranged along M-22 from Traverse City north through Suttons Bay to Northport and south from Northport to Leland and Glen Arbor. By the way, that amazing horse farm on the west side of M-22 south of Suttons Bay belongs to area restaurateur Barry Boone and his wife.

BETWEEN TRAVERSE CITY AND SUTTONS BAY

◆ **The Leelanau Trail**, 15 1/2 miles between Suttons Bay and Greilickville outside Traverse City, is now open but not paved. The Leelanau Trails Association of bicyclists has purchased the railroad branch line, once used by cherry canneries, with private funds. Opposition from abutting homeowners torpedoed DNR help in purchasing the costlier northern segment from Suttons Bay to Northport, despite strong community support.

The trail, seldom visible from M-22, goes past wetlands, woods, orchards, and fields, offering occasional scenic vistas. Improvements take place as funds permit: eventually the trail will

The hilly, high interior of the Leelanau Peninsula offers an unfolding succession of delightful views: simple old farms and barns; cherry trees marching over curving hills. Printmaker Rod Conklin gets to the essence of farmstead scenes. His charming studio home is between Glen Lake and Honor.

be paved. The entire trail is currently groomed for **cross-country skiing**. The graded trail is sandy, suited to mountain bikes, runners, and hikers. Want to support the effort? Call Dave Monstrey, *(616) 946-0018*. The southern trailhead, which in the future will begin in Traverse City, now begins at Cherry Bend Road and includes a parking lot. The northern trailhead is at the stone depot on M-22 at the south entrance to downtown Suttons Bay. In 1997, a parking lot is planned for Forest St. at Suttons Bay.

♦ **Monstrey's General Store and Sport Shop.** Ideal first stop for lots of free printed information and local travel advice from owner Dave Monstrey, avid bicyclist and leader of the local bike trail group. Bicyclists will find a $5 **bicycling guide** to six counties of northwestern Michigan invaluable. Just finding this shop is an adventure that gets you off the beaten path of M-22 and into the hilly, scenic interior overlooking Lake Leelanau. There are **rentals** of bicycles, tandem bikes, bike carts for small children, sailboards, tubes, and small boats. Amish furniture and classic toys, books on the region and on bicycling and adventure travel. *8332 Bingham Rd./C.R. 618 in the hamlet of Bingham. From M-22, about 10 miles north of Traverse City, turn west on 618. Store is between 633 and 641. (616) 946-0018. From May thru color season at least. Hours at least Tues-Sat 10-6. From Mem. to Labor Day Mon-Sat 10-6, Sun noon-5. Other times call first. &: call.*

♦ **Bellwether Herbs.** Gail Ingraham was a commercial banker in Traverse City until 1984 when she decided what she really wanted to do was grow things. Now she has quite an extensive set-up – three acres of herbs and perennials. You can buy over 350 varieties of potted herbs and perennials, plus everlasting annuals and dried everlastings ready to arrange. "We consider our gardens a living picturebook of ideas for our customer," says Ingraham, who is happy to advise customers about garden design. *On northwest corner of Shady Lane and Elm Valley Rd. toward Suttons Bay. Take M-22 north 8 miles from Traverse City. Turn left (west) on Shady Lane and head 1/3 mile west. Northwest of Traverse City south of Suttons Bay. Open from May to Christmas. May 1 to Labor Day: Tues thru Sat 10-5, Sun 10-3 except closed Sun in august. Call for fall hours. (616) 271-3004. &: gardens only.*

◆ **Nature's Gifts.** Wide-ranging rock shop, from inexpensive mineral specimens and rough rocks to polished agate slabs and large mineral specimens, handcrafted jewelry, bookends, and belt buckles. With gemstones and semi-precious beads, you can design or make your own jewelry. An extra bonus: the spectacular view of Grand Traverse Bay from the patio. *On Hilltop Rd. 1/2 mile west of M-22, 10 miles north of Traverse City and 5 miles south of Suttons Bay. (616) 271-6826. Open June thru Dec., Mon-Sat 10 a.m.-5 p.m. or by appointment. &: call first for directions.*

◆ **L. Mawby Vineyards.** At this well regarded small winery, the owner-winemaker-publicist-poet will give you a tour if arranged ahead. L. Mawby is known for rich, full-bodied dry Vignoles, fermented and aged in oak, and for sparkling wines made like champagne. Michigan's wine-making reputation will eventually be based on them. Mawby, considered by many to be the unofficial spiritual leader of the wine community, once told Detroit Free Press wine writer Christopher Cook that in his wines he was seeking "a oneness without sameness" with other Michigan wines. Cook calls Mawby the Zen Winemaster of Michigan. Striking wine labels, prints and poems, designed by his wife, Peggy Core, are also for sale at the tasting room, along with her drawings, cards, baskets, and jewelry. *4519 Elm Valley Rd. 5 miles south of Suttons Bay. From M-22 2 miles north of 618, turn west on Hill Top Rd., then north on Elm Valley. (616) 271-3522. Tastings from May through October, Thurs-Sat 1-6 an other wise by appointment. &*

◆ **Boskydel Vineyard.** The wine is good, the view is terrific, and the atmosphere – Old World in flavor but not in the least imitative – is unequalled at the winery of retired Northern Michigan College librarian and pioneer winemaker Bernie Rink. He was the first to grow wine grapes anywhere in the Grand Traverse region. "Such Boskydel varietals as Vignoles, Seyval Blanc, and De Chaunac will have a magic all their own," he states. "Boskydel Red, White, and Rose blends will approximate and many times exceed good ordinaires from France." *7501 E. Otto Rd. at corner of Lake Leelanau Drive (C.R. 641) about 3 1/2 miles south of the town of Lake Leelanau, on the east shore of the lake. From Traverse City and M-22, take C.R. 633 west at Greilickville,* *turn north in 3-4 miles onto Lake Leelanau Drive (C.R. 641). (616) 256-7272. Open daily year-round 1-6 p.m.* &

SUTTONS BAY

This village of around 600 was not so long ago considered the slummier part of the Leelanau Peninsula. Here is where migrant cherry-pickers would hang out on summer evenings. Then mechanical pickers displaced the migrants, and Suttons Bay became gentrified to the point where it is fashionable. The row of nouveau Victorian main street storefronts sports a color-coordinated pastel paint scheme by local architect Larry Graves and now looks like "a set from a Hollywood movie," as one shopkeeper puts it. Professionals living here appreciate the convenient commute to Traverse City while living on or near the water.

Now that Suttons Bay has a "horsey set" and a "BMW crowd," the creative free spirits who liked its friendly ambiance are drawn towards humbler communities like Lake Leelanau. Says one, "Being a fashionable address has attracted all these dull, affluent people who hang around Cappucino's Cafe and don't have to work for a living. These people are followers of trends. If it's something they're supposed to have, they want it. It's no fun being here any more." Another craftsman-merchant sees a similar cultural change toward an adversarial community (seen in local zoning disputes focused on the letter of the law, not its spirit), and toward consumerism in local customers. His customers used to show more curiosity and disinterested appreciation of what they saw. Vacationing gamblers driving from lodgings in Traverse City to the Peshabestown casino have also contributed to changing the customer mix.

The pleasant **municipal beach** and park is north of downtown. Two exceptionally enjoyable events take place here: the **Jazzfest** (fourth Saturday of July, featuring musicians who played with bands of the Big Band Era) and the **Suttons Bay Art Fair** (first weekend of August) with very good food booths and superior arts and crafts. In town, don't miss the big old trees and substantial Victorian houses in the picturesque neighborhood up the hill just west of downtown on St. Mary's and Lincoln avenues.

For access to the bay in a less busy setting, go out to Stony Point, reached by taking M-22 south of town but staying near the bay and going east onto Stony Point Road when M-22 goes south. Soon you'll come to **Sutton Park**, a nice, shady small suburban park with a sandy **beach** and good views of boats in the harbor. Three more miles and you're at the point, where **Vic Steimel Township Park** looks across to the tip of the Old Mission Peninsula. The shore is stony, and poison ivy grows in the rocks, but the natural setting beneath cedars and birches makes this a fine destination for a **picnic** at the tables here. Light traffic and interesting houses along the road make this a good, easy **bicycle ride**.

Suttons Bay is a year-round town, more of a suburb than a resort, and many of its stores are open all year. Here are some highlights (arranged from south to north on St. Joseph/M-22). Most stores are open daily from mid-June through Labor Day. Stores open year-round, six days a week, unless otherwise noted.

◆ **Hansen's Foods.** The "good cook's store" and perfect picnic stop. See page 579.

◆ **Suttons Bay Bookstore,** now in addition to new books, has used books, CDs and cassettes, and lots of Native American books and posters, along with the usual good personal service, strong regional section, unusual cards, and rainy-day activities for kids like puzzles and Mad-Libs. They also have art by local artists featuring local subjects. *100 Cedar. Go to the blinker light at the South end of town and turn left. Directly opposite Boone's. (616) 271-3923 or (800) 850-2945. Open Mon-Sat 10-5 at least. From mid-June to Labor Day open Sun noon-4.* ♿

◆ **Sew Central** fabric store focuses on hard-to-find fabrics for garments — everything from Polartec and ripstop nylon to fine wool suiting and beautiful silks. Lessons and examples for home sewers are featured. *117 Broadway west of St. Joseph at the south end of town. (616) 271-6331. ♿: no.*

◆ **Bahle's Department Store.** Founded in the 1870s as a dry goods store with farmers' work clothes, now a bastion of Woolrich, Nautica, and other fashionable casual wear for men and women. The Bahles renovated and reconstructed this block and turned the movie theater into an arts center. *210 St. Joseph. (616) 271-3841.* ♿

◆ **Enerdyne Nature and Science Playthings**, owned and run by a former teacher, is based on the premise that nature and science are fun — and that educational toys aren't just for children. Also has garden furnishings and bird feeders. *212 St. Joseph St. (616) 271-6033.*

◆ **Bay Theater.** First-run and foreign/art films and occasional live performances. *216 St. Joseph. (616) 271-3772.* ♿

◆ **The Painted Bird.** Unusual clothing and contemporary crafts — housewares, furniture, and sculptural pieces — mostly by local and Great Lakes craftspeople. Kate Fiebig's colorful jackets and vests are appliqued with bugs that have gossamer wings. Bill Perkins' bent willow rockers are remarkably comfortable. When the staff isn't busy with customers or stock, they're likely weaving at the big loom (handed down in owner Karen Bahle's husband's family), finishing custom orders for their heavily textured rag rugs and hangings of contemporary design. *216 St. Joseph next to the theater. (616) 271-3050. Open daily, year-round.* &

◆ **Suttons Bay Galleries.** Original antique prints (birds, architectural, botanicals, maps, European and American city views, *Harper's Weekly* Civil War engravings, Japanese woodblock prints, and more), along with Russell Chatham's lithograph landscapes, similar to his paintings seen on the covers of Jim Harrison's books. The jazz-loving English owners enjoy explaining about engravings, etchings, and other printmaking techniques. Saxophonist Harry Goldson frequently performs classic jazz in the area. *102 Jefferson, one door down from St. Joseph on the way to the harbor. (616) 271-4444. Open year-round. May-mid Jan: daily 10:30-5:30 at least. Otherwise open Thurs-Sat.* &

◆ **Will Case-Daniel Jewelry.** Tucked off a courtyard behind the main street shops, silversmith Will Case-Daniel has created an idiosyncratic world that spills out of his diverting shop into a charming courtyard. There David Grath's Leelanau landscape commemorates the late Western Michigan University art professor Robert Sweeney. Look up to see Case-Daniel's weathervanes. His shop sells cards and accessories plus jewelry made by himself and others. *305 St. Joseph St. (rear). Open yea-round, Mon-Sat 10-5:30. (616) 271-3876.* &

◆ **Inter-Arts Studio** was the first gift shop in Suttons Bay. Now owner Ken Krantz, an artist and architect, has remodeled and moved into the back of his building. He sells only things he likes: colorful Polish rugs and other area rugs, glassware, lots of bedspreads and fabrics (including India print bedspreads, those cheap, multipurpose standbys of the 1960s), and other classics of contemporary and folk design. *On Adams behind BG's Saddlery at 326 St. Joseph. (616) 271-3891. Summer hours: 10-5, closed Mon. Call for other times.* &: *entry, restrooms, and part of the shop.*

Between Suttons Bay and Northport

◆ **Busha's Brae Herb Farm** and **St. Wenceslas Church.** For a **scenic interior drive** to Northport with wonderful vistas and less traffic than M-22 with its casino-goers, turn west from M-22 onto Dumas Road a mile north of Suttons Bay and M-204. It merges with Setterbo Road, which continues northwest to join CR 637. You see fieldstone houses and cherry orchards, especially delightful in blossomtime in mid-May and in late June and early July when the fruit is ripening. Stop and look back for a grand bay view.

Busha's Brae occupies an old farm. Display gardens include a children's garden, big perennial gardens, and well-researched gardens of herbs in Shakespeare and the Bible. New owner Danielle Vachow became interested in herbs because of the need for tasty low-salt, low-fat foods for her husband, a meat-and-potatoes kind of guy. Now she's hooked. She sells several kinds of herb jellies. Her no-salt Brae seasoning blend has found many uses. A retired elementary teacher, she gives classes in preserving herbs and making wreaths. Occasional **teas** with herb talks ($15), held in the farmhouse, fill up soon. *232 Setterbo Rd. Open May-Christmas, Tues-Sun 10-6. (616) 271-6284. &: call.*

When you come to the striking **Saint Wenceslas Catholic Church** at the T intersection of CR 637 with CR 626, get out to look at the beautiful scrolled iron monuments in the Bohemian cemetery. 637 rejoins M-22 at the popular **Happy Hour Tavern** (&). Turn right and you'll soon be in Northport.

♦ **Leelanau Sands Casino and Super Bingo Palace.** A 1991 expansion briefly made this the largest of Michigan's casinos on Indian reservations, with space for 500. The Grand Traverse band runs it to create jobs, fund tribal government, and promote economic development. It advertises "Las Vegas-style gambling." But don't expect bright lights and glamorous shows. This is pretty sedate stuff, geared to conservative Midwestern tourists. The right to gamble on Indian reservations is based on tribal rights to self-government. The tribe recently open Easgle's Ridge restaurant next door serving breakfast, lunch, and dinner buffet style ($4, $6, and $12). *On M-22 in Peshawbestown, about 4 mi. north of Suttons Bay. (616) 271-4104. Open year-round. Mon-Thurs 8 a.m. -2 a.m., Fri & Sat 8 a.m.-3 a.m., Sun 9 a.m.-2 p.m. Tables open at 11 Mon-Sat, 12 Sun. & Must be 21 (liquor on premises).*

OMENA

This picturesque small hamlet at the head of Omena Bay was first settled in 1852. The name means "Is it so?" in Indian, a phrase often used by a suspicious early white settler when talking with the local Indians. Steamers made use of the bay to take on cordwood, potatoes, beans and apples from the region. The first dock was built in 1868. Later, hotels and resorts, long since gone, were built to accommodate vacationers. Old photos are displayed in a case in front of the combined **post office/general store.**

♦ The **Tamarack Craftsmen Gallery** occupies the old Omena general store, perched on a hill surveying the beach and bay. The building was what inspired owners David and Sally Viskochil to start their extraordinary gallery of American crafts over 20 years ago when they got out of the Peace Corps. They are committed to displaying work by artists they believe in. Much of it is interestingly strange. The place has a vivid, imaginative look, with lots of hand-blown glass. They were the first to show the twig furniture of Clifton Monteith. Dewey Blocksma, who is gaining a national reputation for his outsider art, is another longtime artist. So is Catherine Baldwin, the last quill basket-maker in the area. Though prices go into the thousands of dollars, there are plenty of little things like earrings and mugs for $20 and under. *On M-22 in Omena. (616) 386-5529. Mem.-Labor Day: Mon-Sat 10-6, Sun 12-5. Otherwise: Tues-Sat 11-5, Sun 12-5. &: call.*

◆ **Leelanau Cheese Co.** For Detroiter John Hoyt, travels in Europe led to working in vineyards, where hard-working harvesters partied with wine and raclette, that traditional Swiss dish of melted cheese over boiled new potatoes. Since 1995 he and his French wife, Anne, have made their own raclette (a semi-hard cheese akin to Gruyere) and a soft fromage blanc (like a boursin but made with milk, not cream, and fluffier), which is flavored with garlic, pepper, herbs, or (for a dessert cheese) cherries. Milk comes from a single area farmer. When they're making cheese, visitors are welcome to watch. The retail shop sells only their cheese and various accompaniments for the dish raclette: gherkins, onions, and other pickled items. Raclette is made in 10" wheels; it sells for $8 a pound and can be shipped. *In the former gas station where M-22 curves around Omena Bay. Open year-round. May-Oct: 10-5 at least, to 6 weekends. Otherwise call first. (616) 386-7731. &*

NORTHPORT

Summer people have long been attracted to this pretty village and port. Being so far from Traverse City (25 miles) thins the traffic in summer and keeps Northport less of a suburb and more of a resort. It offers visitors a number of galleries and antique shops, mostly seasonal, and two unusually attractive picnic spots.

◆ Anchoring a lively collection of downtown gift and antique shops is **North Country Gardens** in the village's former grocery store. It now concentrates on gifts and cards with a lush, luxurious look often based on vegetables, fruits, and flowers. *On Waukazoo at Nagonaba, where M-22 turns. (616) 386-5031. &*

Most Northport shops are right along M-22 and easy to check out. Two interesting artists' studio/shops might be missed, however. **Photo Arts**, on the south side of Nagonaba just west of

Waukazoo is a group of 20 photographers from Michigan working in a wide variety of contemporary fine art techniques who were invited by proprietor Sue Copka to join her in displaying their work. The walls are exclusively photography while the floor space is devoted to 3-D objects functional and non-functional made by local artists and artisans *(616) 386-9240. Open June thru Oct and around the holidays: Mon-Fri 10-5:30, Sat 10-8. All other times, call 616-271-3229 for appointment.* &

ZO:ON Gallery shows Char Bickel's soft sculptures of fish and shadowbox col-

A big tree like the one at the Beech Tree Gallery creates its own cosmos. Coffee and dessert are served beneath it.

lages of angels, bears, and other animals in themes of mythological inspiration, alive with shimmery color and pattern hand-painted on silk. They have a fresh but mysterious appeal. *122 W. Naganoba next to City Hall. (616) 386-5937. Open July & Aug. Call for times. Also by appointment (616-386-7510).* &: *one small step.*

◆ In a Victorian cottage a block south on Waukazoo, **The Beech Tree Gallery and Cafe** is a wonderful spot to enjoy coffee and dessert beneath a huge copper beech. Popular two-week summer **cafe** features Leelanau foods. Call for time. Inside are fiber and ceramics, furniture, clothing, and jewelry, often with a contemporary, updated, sophisticated country theme. Quilts are featured. *202 Waukazoo. (616) 386-5200. Memorial Day to mid-Oct. Open 11-5 Wed-Sat and Mon, 11-4 Sun, closed Tues.* &: *use kitchen entrance.*

◆ At the marina, **Bay Front Park**, a couple of blocks east of the commercial district, is right on Grand Traverse Bay, with a good view of tiny Bellow Island in the distance. It has a pleasant **beach** and **playground**. Free summer **concerts** are held here every Friday at 7 from July 4 weekend through August.

Some really impressive sail boats can be seen at the marina, along with all the charter boats and smaller craft. Northport is where Great Lakes sport trolling was pioneered in the early 1920s by George Ruff. Methods he and his wife developed for catching trout and other gamefish set the pattern for other charter services. The tall ship **Manitou,** a 114-foot two-masted topsail schooner, similar in design to 19th century ship that once transported passengers and cargo, is berthed here when it's not out on three- and six-day windjammer **cruises**. Call (616) 941-2000 for info on sailing/hiking cruises to nearby islands.

At the Leelanau Peninsula's tip, the Grand Traverse or Cat's Head lighthouse in Leelanau State Park is now a museum. From its tower you can see east across to the top of the Old Mission Peninsula, north to the Medusa cement silos in Charlevoix, and west to the Fox Islands.

Two wonderful old-timey souvenir shops have been at the marina for decades. Nautical decor, from tiny treasures to dramatic objects to do-it-yourself craft kits, is the thing at **The Shipwreck** (616-386-5878). ♿ **Nature Gems** (616-386-7826) sells rocks and seashells, minerals and Petoskey stone jewelry at all price levels. They also carry Native American jewelry and souvenirs. *Open daily 10-10 June through Sept., 10-5 weekends only in Oct. In the winter, call (616) 383-5189 & the owner will open the shop.* ♿

◆ A few blocks north up from downtown at Third Street and Fourth is a serene, picturesque **mill pond and park**, shaded by a big old apple tree. A picnic table and short footpath are here.

◆ **Joppich's Bay Street Gallery**, tucked in a neighborhood north of the town center, has focused on Michigan artists long before regional art became a popular cause. Owner Edee Joppich, a painter herself, travels throughout the state during the off season searching out 50 artists to participate in the coming year's exhibit. Most have never been shown here before. Typically a third of the participants are on college or university faculties. Paintings, sculpture, original prints, and fine art crafts are displayed in airy galleries inside a remodeled house. Prices range from $20 to $10,000. Every year in August, the gallery has an open house with chamber music, free food, and many of the exhibiting artists in attendance. (In 1996, it will be on August 10th.) *109 N. Rose (also called Bay), one street over from M-201, Northport's main street, and a block north of the marina. (616) 386-7428. Open from 11-6, weekends in*

June and Sept thru mid-Oct, daily July and Aug. &: *call.*

Beyond Northport

♦ **Woolsey Airport.** Aviation with a charming Fred Flintstone look. This small, picturesque fieldstone airport from the 1930s is fun to explore. There's a picnic table outside. *About 4 miles north of Northport on C.R. 629.*

♦ **Leelanau State Park (south section).** Here the beautiful sandy **beach** on Cathead Bay and the spectacular views of the Fox and Manitou islands are blissfully peaceful and uncrowded, because a mile's hike through a dark beech-maple forest is required to get there. It's an easy, pretty walk, well worth while. You can climb the **Lake Michigan Overlook** first for an even better view – especially memorable at sunset.

Most of the park's 1,500 acres are in this unspoiled section of diverse habitats. Eight miles of **trail loops** through low dunes and hardwood forests are well marked with colored posts, and with maps at major intersections. But other confusing trails have been informally made. *Only turn where you see a post!* The hilly, 2-mile **Mud Lake Loop** reaches a platform for viewing migratory waterfowl in spring and fall. **Cross-country skiing** here is very popular. Beachgoers here will be rewarded with an astonishing number of Petoskey stones from the ancient coral seas. *Just past Woolsey Airport on C.R. 629, turn north on Densmore Road. Trailhead is in about 1 1/2 miles. (616) 386-5422. State park sticker required; $4/day, $20/year.* &: *toilets; trails are dirt/woodchips.*

♦ **Leelanau State Park (north section).** At the Leelanau Peninsula's very tip is an interesting rocky beach and memorable **Grand Traverse lighthouse museum** with a pleasant **picnic area**. A former lightkeeper's son who grew up here is now a retiree and the museum curator. His father made some of the remarkable **pebble lawn ornaments**, including an elaborate flower bed in the shape of a crown and a miniature lighthouse that's a purple martin house. From the lighttower you can see across to the tip of the Old Mission Peninsula and out to the Manitou and Fox islands. *Open from May thru October, 12-5 weekends at least. In July & August, open 11-7 daily. (616) 386-7553.* &: *no, but you can see a free video of the tour in accessible Fog Signal Building/gift shop. Adults $1.*

The adjoining campground offers some of the state parks' most picturesque **campsites**, overlooking Grand Traverse Bay and a rocky beach. Here it's unpleasant for swimming or wading unless you bring wading shoes). Though rustic, these campsites are in great demand, with early summer reservations advised.

The stony beach by the Grand Traverse Lighthouse offers good pickings
for rockhounds and fine views at both sunrise (on the east-facing campground side) and sunsets looking west.

   Lighthouse and *campground* *are at the end of C.R. 629, 8 miles
north of Northport. From town, take 201 north to 629. (616) 386-5422.
&. toilets. State park sticker required: $4/day, $20/season.*

◆ **Kilcherman's Christmas Cove Farm.** Third-generation fruit
farmer John Kilcherman has become intensely interested in the history of old apple varieties. He grows over 200 varieties of antique
apples and sells many of them at this attractive farm stand. For
special occasions he makes up sampler boxes of antique apples,
complete with a brochure he has written. His wife, Phyllis, helps
with the 85 acres of apples and cherries. It's a pretty place to stop
and sample good apples, and to hear about the travails of fruit
farming. *On Kilcherman Rd (formerly De Long Rd.) off 201 n. of
Northport. (616) 386-5637. Open Sept. 15 thru Nov. or until cold
weather sets in. After Nov., call.* &.

◆ **Peterson Park.** A remote, pretty park — a big, grassy area on a
bluff, from which the Manitou and Fox islands can be seen. An
amazingly large maple is the park's focal point. There are picnic
tables, a small play area, and restrooms tucked away in a woods.
Stairs lead down a long ways to a stony **beach** with lots of Petoskey
stones. *From 201 in Northport, take either the North or South
Peterson Park Rd. No fee.*

LELAND

Fishtown is a picturesque group of weathered old fishermen's
shanties along the Carp River, where Lake Leelanau empties into
Lake Michigan. The harbor here is a lively place, busy with charter
boats and Manitou Transit's ferries to the Manitou Islands (p. 574-7).
Fishtown's transformation into tourist shops around 1970 changed
this pretty resort village into Leelanau's first and most intensely
developed tourist shopping hub. Novelist Jim Harrison, who lives on
a nearby farm, was wont to say that Leland was ruined by "trinket-
sellers" of the worst kind, in frequent letters to the local weekly.

With enough old boats, fishnets, and fishy smells to seem
authentic, Fishtown is still an interesting place when it's not
packed with people, which is to say in the early morning or the off-
season. People come not just to shop or sightsee but to fish by a
dramatic little waterfall and dam. Two commercial fishing boats
continue to operate out of Leland. (The commercial fishing peak was
during the first three decades of the 20th century.) **Carlson's
Fishery** (616-256-9801) sells smoked whitefish and fresh whitefish
fillets. Interesting photos on the wall show Bill Carlson's forbears at
work on their fishing tugs. Next door, another Carlson runs the
Village Cheese Shanty (616-256-9141), a friendly cheese and wine
shop with a bakery. The thoughtful selection of American and
imported cheeses are at all price levels; the wines are local. The
municipal **beach** is just north of the harbor. *From M-22 just north of
the bridge in Leland, turn west onto River or Pearl. Come early; parking is limited.* &

Since the early part of this century, Leland has been the summer retreat for many old-money Midwestern families – and some
Easterners, too, but especially people from northern Indiana. A sudden family illness on vacation forced one of the Ball brothers of the
Muncie canning jar company to stay here awhile. His family was so
taken with Leland, they spread the word to friends and family.
Compared with Harbor Springs, the tone here is not at all grand,
but quite low-key and unpretentious in a traditional sort of way.
Now, after several generations, summers are like a big reunion of
far-flung kith and kin. This clubby crowd can be seen around town
picking up mail at the post office, shopping at the Merc (the **Leland
Mercantile** grocery on Main at River), meeting with townspeople for
morning coffee at the volunteer fire department, and having dinner
and drinks at the Leland Lodge, adjoining their golf course.

Perhaps that old-money heritage and image are what led Leland
shops to adopt their generally traditional, rather preppy tone compared with the more art- or nature-related images of other Leelanau

towns. Most shops in the small shopping area are seasonal, open daily in summer. In addition to the fudge and gift shops, there are over half a dozen women's wear specialty stores.

Shopping standouts (arranged from north to south) include:

◆ **Leelanau Books.** A year-round general bookstore with good personal service. It recently doubled in size to incorporate a cappucino cafe and to emphasize more Northern Michigan authors and regional history. New York Times and Chicago Tribune available Sunday mornings along with coffee. *109 N. Main. (616) 256-7111. Hours from late June to Labor Day: 10-9 Mon-Sat, 8:30-6 on Sun. Winter hours: daily 10-5.* ♿

◆ **Nell Revell Smith Studio.** The local favored painter of cherished summer scenes, a sort of latter-day Marcel Prendergast with brighter colors. Her images appear on prints, posters, T shirts, and more. *107 N. Main. (616) 256-7689. Call for off-season hours.*

◆ **Inland Passage.** A thoughtful, imaginative selection of Up North gifts, crafts, maps, graphics, shirts, and books. Typically simple and useful, with clean, colorful designs and often a sense of humor. A current favorite is a $125 blanket with one of many Woodland Indian legend designs. Mail-order catalog available. *(800) 626-5432 or (616) 256-9900. 104 N. Main (in rear courtyard). June thru Oct. open 10-9 daily; to Christmas Tues-Sun; otherwise Saturday at least.* ♿

◆ **Tampico.** The Mexican and southwest Indian jewelry and crafts shop, earthy, carefully edited, and beyond trendy, has taken a great leap forward by purchasing a building and greatly expanding its space. Now there's room not just for the Navajo and Mexican silver jewelry, Oaxacan painted wood animals, masks, glassware, and ornamental tinware, but for bigger things. More folk art, more ceramics (colorful Talavera tiles, sinks, candlesticks are big), furniture from Mexico, and textiles — Navajo blankets, Mexican rugs, blankets, pillows, and beach blankets. Kathy Telgard and her husband, Cris (who has introduced the popular ethnic evenings to his family's Bluebird restaurant) spend two winter months buying in Mexico and the southwest — a nice contrast to Northern Michigan. *112 N. Main (formerly Statice Seekers). Open daily:10-5 May and June, 10-10 July thru Labor Day, 10-5 after Labor Day. Closed Jan-April. (616) 256-7747.* ♿

◆ **Becky Thatcher Designs.** Leland branch of the Glen Arbor jeweler. See page 600. *In Harbor Square, the shopping complex across from the marina. Memorial Day through Labor Day open daily10-6. at least, opens at 11 Sun. (616) 256-2229.* ♿

◆ **Stone House Bread.** Former Detroit newsman Bob Pisor is devoting himself to producing crusty sourdough and authentic French baguettes, thereby ending Northern Michigan's dearth of fresh, chewy Old World-style breads. They're wholesaled to Folgarelli's Market on West Front in Traverse City, Hansen's Foods in Suttons Bay, and elsewhere. Here in a special Matador steam-injected oven, which makes wonderful crusts, are produced his signature North Country bread (a blend of unbleached white, whole wheat, and rye flours in a

A historic lumber schooner by Pyramid Point in a storm: logo of the Leelanau Conservancy, the multifaceted Leland-based land trust. Preserving natural and manmade landscapes is the conservancy's focus. Its staff and nature specialists conduct several walks and programs a week, year-round.

secret recipe), plus herb bread, raisin walnut, cracked wheat, and a white sourdough round. He buys stone-ground organic flour from a Mennonite farmer in Kansas, and still manages to sell bread for $3.25 a 1 1/4 pound loaf in spite of the droughts that have recently hit wheat growers. Helped by two excellent bakers, he aspires to become the equal of Acme breads in Berkeley, California. There's a coffee area, and weekend sweet rolls. Come early in the day for widest availability. *405 S. Main (the southernmost retail building in town). June-Aug: open daily 6-6. May & Sept: closed Tues. Winter hours: Thurs-Mon 6-3. (616) 256-2577.* &

Except for the Mercantile, Leland's local life is sequestered away on the side streets away from the shops. **The Leelanau Conservancy**'s office is worth a stop, to pick up a schedule of their many interesting nature walks and talks, and to check out the attractive posters, T shirts, mugs, notecards, and wildflower sculpture. Proceeds support this active, successful land trust. Its current project is raising funds to pay for a 50% interest in Whaleback, the whale-shaped, tree-covered hill south of Leland. (It's one of the coastline's three landmarks, along with Sleeping Bear Point and Pyramid Point.) Thanks to purchases and gifts of land and conservation easements, the conservancy owns 500 acres of natural areas outright and has easements to limit development on another 1,000. It has protected the south side of the Carp River across from Fishtown, or Leland would be even more congested than it already is. *In the small gray building at 102 N. First, a block over from Main, around the corner from the post office. Open weekdays about 8 to 5. (616) 256-9665.* ♿:

The little **Leelanau Historical Museum** is not to be missed. It's on the south side of Carp River, next to the town library (whose riverfront picture windows make a most delightful place to sit and read). Well-done permanent exhibits tell the story of Leelanau's settlement and development from the first lighthouse on South Manitou Island. There's a hands-on display of old-fashioned toys, and interpretive material on the **Manitou Passage State Underwater Preserve**. (Divers can get additional shipwreck information here.) A significant **changing exhibit** is mounted each year. The excellent small **shop** offers local history books, old-fashioned toys, and locally produced needlework kits and crafts, many not to be found elsewhere. *From M-22, 203 East Cedar, next to the library. Turn east just before the bridge. (616) 256-7475. Open year-round. June thru Labor Day: Tues-Sat 10-4, Sun 1-4. Otherwise: Fri & Sat 1-4 or by appointment. $1/adult, 50¢/student.* ♿

LAKE LEELANAU AND VICINITY

The quiet, unpretentious village of Lake Leenanau, centered around St. Mary's Church and school, is made up largely of French-Canadian, Bohemian, and German farm families. It's looking more and more attractive to many area artists and writers because it's affordable and because of the caring values manifest in the church community. The big annual event is the **homecoming** and **chicken dinner** with a high-quality quilt raffle the second Sunday of August. **Dick's Pour House** is the longtime local gathering spot. The **Provement General Store** has some interesting antiques in the corner store down from the church. **Basket Expressions** on the highway is a good place to stop for local information and regional food, including owner Ken Denoyer's Old Geezer soup mixes.

◆ **Good Harbor Vineyards.** From the tasting room of this small winery you can go on an instructive self-guided tour. Not only does owner-winemaker Bruce Simpson make good wines, he has become renowned in the small world of Michigan wines as something of a marketing genius. His Trillium, a semi-dry mix of Seyval, Vignoles, and Vidal grapes, is Michigan's most successful blended, proprietary wine. Another white he developed in recent years, the crackly, fruity dry Fishtown White, has become immensely popular in restaurants and homes as a great match with spicy foods like Mexican, Thai, and Chinese. *On M-22, 1/2 mi. s. of the intersection with 204. On a hill behind Manitou Market. (616) 256-7165. Open*

mid-May thru Oct., Mon-Sat 11-6, Sun 12-6; Sat 12-5 in Nov. &. Dec.;
also by appt. ㋐

◆ **Sleeping Bear Dunes National Lakeshore.** See chapter beginning page 547. The National Lakeshore extends as far north as
Good Harbor Bay, with a sandy public beach at the end of CR 651,
just six miles south of Leland.

GLEN ARBOR

Never a town in the typical sense, Glen Arbor evolved more as a
crossroads expanded into a collection of services for nearby Glen
Lake summer people and tourist shops for visitors to nearby
Sleeping Bear. An old Christian Science summer community founded the private, secondary Leelanau School. The school's original
location has developed into **The Homestead**, a condo resort that
fits unusually well into its striking setting. Its developer, Bob Kuras,
has stirred up an enduring political hornet's nest with his plans to
build a golf course involving wetlands along the Crystal River

Today, fueled by growth in second homes, the exurbanization of
Traverse City, and increasing National Lakeshore tourism, Glen
Arbor seems to be dividing into quite separate areas. The old-time
tourist shops along M-22 near the lake have metamorphosed into
plush, nouveau rustic affairs that close in winter. The old soda
shoppe is the Western Avenue Grill. A modest restaurant has
become the massive Boone Docks restaurant, part of the area chain
known for huge portions of beef. Even its gazeboed deck overpowers
its modest neighbors. It's been painful for local nature-lovers to witness Glen Arbor's woodland ambiance give way to ever more asphalt.
Art's Tavern, once the epitome of a personal Northern Michigan bar,
is part of a local hospitality mini-empire that never misses a chance
to cross-market its goods and services to its customers.

The Totem Shop, a souvenir shop/general store of the old
school, anchors the visitor-oriented main street. It has something
for everyone; art and crafts materials are a hidden strength. *Open
daily in season. (616) 334-3533.* ㋐ Three superior women's shops
are scattered among the T shirt emporia: **Sandi's**, the **Black Swan**,
and **Cottonseed**.

Year-round artists and entrepreneurs have gathered on Lake
Street, a less costly side street which forms the corner at Art's
Tavern. **Leelanau Coffee Roasters'** coffeehouse has become a popular local gathering place, with baked goods, magazines to read all
day if you like, and an array of coffee drinks made from beans
roasted on the premises. Brothers John and Steve Arens have chosen to use only the highest grade of arabica coffee from each coun-

try, so prices start at $8.50 a pound. They use a hot air bed roaster, not a rotating drum, which makes for more even roasting and less foreign matter in the coffee. They remain busy year-round, roasting for the region's restaurants and for their mail-order customers. *6026 S. Lake. (616) 334-3365. Open daily year-round, at least 8:30 to 4, Sun to 2. Open 7:30 a.m. to 11:30 p.m. mid June to mid Sept.* &

Next door at **Cherry Republic**, the ebullient Bobby Sutherland took a cue from the popular motto of his "Life, Liberty, Beaches and Pie" T shirt to switch his focus from the fast-changing T shirt business to making and marketing cherry-based candy, jams, and trail mixes to summer visitors, in person or by mail. Try some samples; the sour cherry candy is terrific. His wife, Amy, is starting a side garden of medicinal herbs and flowers next to the store; when it's more mature, she plans to sell teas. **Bibb's Farm Market** sets up behind the garden in summer. workshop/gallery next door. *6026 S. Lake. Open daily 10-5 in summer, open winter weekend. Call for fall hours. (800) 206-6949.* &: no.

In the classic white general store building next door, **Arbor Lights** Gift Shop (616-334-3165, &) shares space with the **Cottage Book Shop**, a general book store with a good regional section, out-of-print books, and ordinary used books. Owner Barbara Siepker has installed a cafe area, too, and schedules frequent summer readings. The store's e-mail book discussion group links participants in Glen Arbor and Yekatrinburg, Russia, where Yarn Shop owner Mary Turek's son is vice-consul. Original work by area artists is shown at the **Glen Lake Artists Gallery** *(616-334-4230, &: no)* cooperative, behind the book shop. *5970 S. Lake. (616) 334-4223. Open daily 10-9, Sun 12-4 in summer; til Christmas and in May Thurs-Mon; Jan-April Sat 12-4.* &

Across the street, the **Lake Street Studios/Center Gallery** is an artists' working/teaching studio coordinated by resident painter Suzanne Wilson. **Classes** for children and adults are offered in various media, with workshops up to a week long. Weekly one-person **painting shows** are mounted throughout the summer; visitors are welcome at Friday-evening openings. Other artists with studio/galleries here include silversmith Ben Bricker, fiber artist Majel Obata, and Ananda Bricker, whose three-dimensional sculptures of porcelain flowers and oxidized copper leaves on a wood base, as seen in the Smithsonian catalog. *6023 Lake on M-22 at Lake. (616) 334-6112. 10-5 daily in summer. Otherwise by chance or appointment.* &

On Lake Street toward the beach, across M-22, **Becky Thatcher Designs** is the friendly workshop/gallery of jewelry designer Becky Thatcher. After spending childhood summers in Glen Arbor, she developed this successful business, largely based on translating

Sleeping Bear legends and memories of sunsets, islands, and lakes, into jewelry. She likes to use beach stones, often carved into bears, beavers, birds, and fish. Unusual colored gemstones like tourmalines and opals are another specialty. Ask about her summer teas. Her newsletter makes her annual gem-buying expeditions to Hong Kong, Australia, Sri Lanka, and elsewhere seem like wonderful adventures. *5975 Lake. Turn onto Lake toward the lake. (616) 334-3826. Open year-round, daily in summer. &: not without assistance.*

Furnituremaker Paul May and his wife, who illustrates the beautiful American Spoon Foods catalogs, show their work at a gallery behind their home on M-22 as it turns away from Lake Michigan to Glen Lake. Look for the sign **Kristin Hurlin Illustration/Paul May Furniture Company**. A quiet, contemplative appreciation of nature and wood pervades both their work. Kristin's pen-and-ink drawings and watercolors of Leelanau landscapes and botanicals are for sale as originals and as cards, and limited edition prints. Paul's custom furniture, cabinetry, lamps, and clocks are mainly Shaker- and Mission-inspired designs. *South Ray St. (M-22) on the south end of downtown Glen Arbor. (616) 334-3128. Open May thru Oct. daily 11-4 or by appointment. &: no.*

The Village Sampler shopping complex across the street seems new and unremarkable, but it does house Glen Arbor's oldest continuing business, **The Yarn Shop.** Mary Turak teaches knitting and designs distinctive sweaters for customers to knit or to buy knitted by her. There's no charge for knitting lessons. *On M-22., Open Mon-Sat 10-5 and Sun 1-5 in the summer; open Mon-Sat 12-5 in the winter. (616) 334-3805.*

The south end of Glen Arbor, on M-109 on the way to Glen Haven and Sleeping Bear Point, is growing into the "decorator district." An increasing number of galleries and studios here, including a new branch of a Grand Rapids gallery, seem geared to condo owners who want the look of Northern Michigan for their place.

EMPIRE

This lakeshore village is admired for its community spirit. Natives are largely descended from the Belgians, French-Canadians, and Norwegians recruited by the local lumber company, the peninsula's largest.

◆ **Empire Area Historical Museum.** A vast collection of interesting things has been built up by an energetic group of summer folk and Empire natives (a mix of Belgians, Frenchmen, and Norwegians recruited by logging companies). The museum displays antique vehicles, a nifty model of the big Empire Lumber Company where the public beach now is, and a turkey feather Christmas tree. Centerpiece of the museum is the splendid back and front bar from Andrew Roen's saloon that flourished during Empire's logging heyday, along with a coin-operated music box and horse race game. Headlines from newspapers across the nation tell the story of the discovery, after the old man died, of $125,000 in cash, plus this disassembled bar and "a lot of great stuff that belonged in Empire," according to the museum's founder, service station owner Dave Taghon. Many unusually interesting old photos of everyday life in these parts help make this a fine place to spend a rainy day. An inexpensive **gift shop** features local history and reproductions of antique books and cardboard ornaments. Museum publications include several photo albums and a book of 1860 letters between a soldier and his wife in Glen Arbor, discovered as a house was being demolished. They illuminate early life in northern Michigan. *On M-22 at the intersection of La Core and Salisbury, on the north edge of Empire. (616) 326-5316 or (616) 326-5181. Mem. Day thru June: open Sat & Sun 1-4. July & August: daily except Wednesday 10-4 (Sun 1-4). Sept. thru color season: Sat & Sun 1-4. Also open by appt. Free admission; donations welcome.* &

◆ **The Secret Garden** is worth checking out in downtown Empire. It's a clean, contemporary gallery of nature-inspired arts, including watercolors and prints of birds by Empire native and wildlife artist Tom Ford, and watercolors of flowers, fish, and local scenes by Paul St. Denis. A fellow of the American Watercolor Society, he teaches winters at the Cleveland Art Institute. *10206 Front St. Open mid-May thru color season: daily to Labor Day, weekends in fall. Summer hours: Mon-Sat 10-8, Sun 10-5. (616) 326-5428.* &

◆ **Taghon's Corners.** Not to be missed is the gas station museum tucked in back of this busy convenience store and gas station. The 1928 Standard station of owner Dave Taghon's parents has been duplicated, down to the pumps outside and the road maps and products glimpsed through the windows. Also on hand: lots more roadside nostalgia and die-cast cars and trucks. *M-22 and M-72. (616) 326-5181.* &

BEACHES AND BOOKS . . . . . They go together, especially in Leelanau County where beaches are generally quiet and natural, and three good bookstores (pages 587, 596, and 600) do a good business in local history and lore. Especially recommended: Kathleen Stocking's **Letters from the Leelanau** ($15.95 paper) and **Lake Country** ($14.95 paper), essays of blended personal reflection and portraits. They capture in great depth the worlds (rooted and rural, exurban seekers and artists) and issues that make this area so fascinating. An in-depth Leelanau guide that combines places and shops with vignettes of people is *Seasons of the Leelanau* by Sandra G. Bradshaw ($9.95 paper). Also recommended is *Ghost Towns of Michigan* ($16.95 paper) by another local author, Larry Wakefield.

A SUMMER OF CHAMBER MUSIC, FOLK, AND RAGTIME . . . . . takes place in over a dozen concerts at various Leelanau locations. Cost per concert: $8-$10. The **Manitou Music Festival** was founded by an Interlochen faculty member and a summer resident. Call the Glen Arbor Art Association at the Lakestreet Studios (616) 334-6112 to get a brochure. Folksinger Claudia Schmidt seems to be a regular favorite. *Tickets also sell 4 for $20, children under 12 free when accompanied by parent.* ♿: *varies, call.*

NATURE HIKES AND WORKSHOPS. . . . . are offered year-round through the **Leelanau Conservancy**. (See p. 597.) Prominent area birders, ecologists, and academics lead these programs, which are either free or reasonably priced. Topics range from bird-watching and nature interpretation to forest ecology, weather, bog ecology, and medicinal plants. Free **Wednesday hikes**, usually at 8 a.m. or 6 p.m, often interpret **Kehl Lake**, the conservancy-owned, undeveloped lake and wetland by Leelanau State Park, once a favorite site of Indian ceremonies. Other events include full moon hikes, $10 **Cedar River float trips** to an extensive wetland, and $35 **South Manitou Island natural history trips**. (Education director Molly Grosvenor is familiar to many vacationers through her family involvement in Manitou Transit to the islands.) . . . . . Pick up a **schedule** at many area businesses or at the conservancy **office** in the small gray building at 102 N. First, a block over from Main, around the corner from the post office. Support conservancy projects by purchasing its fund-raising souvenir t shirts, mugs, prints, maps, and caps. Hours are about 8 to 5. (616) 2567-9665.

BIKE RENTALS AND MORE. . . . . In Leland, **Geo Bikes** rents bikes in summer, cross-country skis in winter. Recumbent bikes, where the cyclist sits with legs in front, are a specialty. *Up the hill on River at Grand. (River is the street by the Bluebird and Fishtown.) Open daylight hours. (616) 256-9696.* . . . . . **Monstrey's General Store** near Suttons Bay rents bikes, bike carts, canoes, small boats and sailboards, and much more. See p. 584.

Old Mission Peninsula

Perfectly suited for growing cherries, Old Mission is one of the most scenic areas in Michigan.

THIS NARROW, high ridge of a peninsula, 18 miles long, bisects Grand Traverse Bay. It's more intimate than its neighbor to the west, the Leelanau Peninsula. The scenery on a drive to the tip is spectacular, as each rise in the road offers new, panoramic views of hilly vineyards and orchards dropping down to the blue bay. The hilly land is some of the finest in the country for growing cherries and grapes. The bay moderates temperatures and prevents early spring warming that endangers fruit buds. So suitable is the soil and climate for cherries that once there was no denser concentration of cherry trees in the country. Now wine grapes are proving more profitable and sometimes replacing cherry trees.

The orchards and vineyards are a pleasant foreground for the hilltop vistas of the bay to the east and west. A white sandy bottom makes the water so turquoise that it seems artificially enhanced when seen in photographs. The roads hugging the east shore — East Shore Road, Bluff Road, and Smokey Hollow Road — are less developed and more scenic than those on the west shore. Highway M-37 follows the central spine to the northern tip and provides plenty of spectacular panoramas.

The peninsula is named for the first settlement in the Grand Traverse region, a Presbyterian mission started in a log cabin in 1839. A replica of the cabin is now a small museum (see below).

The peninsula has experienced a fierce, drawn-out struggle between cherry farmers who want to sell off land to developers and residents concerned about preserving the rural landscape. Cherries have been the major crop for well over a century, but overproduction has made the orchards' economic viability tenuous. Every year over 50 new homes are built on the peninsula, and the population has jumped to nearly 5,000 from just over 2,500 in 1970. Recently Old Mission voters made history in agreeing to tax themselves to obtain development rights on agricultural land so it can remain agricultural without unduly penalizing landowners. Underwood Orchards, long a popular tourist spot at the peninsula's base, is now a housing development. Thanks to vigilant township planners, the views from the hillcrest remain unobstructed.

Elegance in agritourism: Chateau Chantal, sited on the hill crest of a
former cherry orchard. It functions as the a wine tasting room (the view of
both arms of the Grand Traverse Bay is exceptional), a winery, the co-owners' home, and a bed and breakfast.

◆ **Chateau Grand Traverse.** This 80-acre winery is known for its
domestic Rieslings. Owner Ed O'Keefe was for many years the only
Michigan vintner to grow exclusively vinifera grapes — prestigious
Old World varieties that are more susceptible to frost and disease
than hybrid or native grapes. Current wines include five Rieslings
(from $8 to $50/bottle), three Chardonnays, four red wines (Gamay,
Merlot, Syrah, and Pinot Noir), and Mission Blush ($4.99). Chateau
Grand Traverse is now sold in 23 states. The vineyard's much-
praised cherry wines ($4.99) are a tasty novelty and good Michigan
gift item. Spicy cherry makes a good hot winter drink; the new cherry Riesling is a terrific picnic wine. 25-minute **winery tours** are
held on the hour from Memorial Day through Labor Day; weekends
only in spring and fall; in winter by appointment only. Free tastings
are year-round. Call to schedule large groups. Mail order available.
*M-37 at Island View Rd. 8 miles out of Traverse City. (616) 223-7355;
(800) 283-0247. Open regularly April thru Dec. April & May: 10-5.
June-Dec: 10-6. No Sunday sales before noon.*

◆ **Bowers Harbor.** Midway up the western shore of the peninsula,
Neah-Ta-Wanta Point creates this well-protected harbor. One of the
better restaurants in the Traverse City area, the Bowers Harbor Inn,
is in an old summer home here. There's also a **public beach**, a
marina, and a picnic area. The old summer hotel at the point has
become a bed and breakfast and the Neahtawanta Center for Peace
Research and Education. *Reached by Peninsula Dr. on the west
shore, or turn west off M-37 at Bowers Harbor Road, then right onto
Peninsula.*

◆ **Bowers Harbor Vineyards.** This small, family-run operation
grows a few grapes but mainly markets Chardonnay, Riesling and

sparkling wines made for them at nearby Chateau Grand Traverse. Linda Stegenga says their wines aren't the same as Chateau Grand Traverse's, and urges visitors to taste and compare. The Stegengas have made a good start at disproving the adage that if you want to make a small fortune in wine, start with a big fortune. Doubters wrote off the Stegengas' project as a plaything for a couple who just wanted to dabble in wine. But Bowers Harbor has consistently produced quality wines since it started, winning medals in competitions year after year. The drive from M-37 to the tasting room offers some grand views. *2896 Bowers Harbor Road a ways east of the bay. From M-37/Center Rd., go 8 1/2 miles north of Traverse City to Seven Hills Rd. Turn left, go 1/2 mile, turn left on Bowers Harbor. Winery is on left. (616) 223-7615. Open daily 11-6. Jan-March, open weekends only or by appointment.*

◆ **Chateau Chantal**. This is Michigan's first taste of California-style wine tourism on a grand scale. This big brick French Provincial-style winery, conspicuously perched like a castle on the hillcrest of a former cherry farm, combines production facilities, wine cellars, a luxurious tasting room, the co-owners' large apartment, and three bed and breakfast rooms. Call it "Napa Valley-ization if you will, but this magnificent structure and its winery is Michigan's premiere agri-tourism stop, copy-catting northern California wine country." says wine writer Chris Cook.

Principal partners are winemaker Mark Johnson, the former winemaker at nearby Chateau Grand Traverse, and financial backer Bob Begin, a former Catholic priest. Both have loved living in European wine regions. (Johnson is a graduate of the prestigious wine institute in Geisenheim, Germany.) Chateau Chantal grows only vinifera grapes. Riesling, Chardonnay, Gewurztraminer, and Pinot Noir are currently in production. They also make an ice wine, a sparkling wine, and a cherry wine. From the first few years of rather anemic Gewurztraminers and Rieslings, the now mature vines are " beginning to produce more and more robust, complex, and intense juice," says Cook, who also judges wine.

The tasting room is furnished like a sunny, elegant living room, with sofas and a piano. Visitors are welcome to sit and enjoy the spectacular views of *both* arms of Grand Traverse Bay. Visitors are given escorted **tours** of the entire facility. From July into October, the winery offers **"Sunset on the Terrace"** evenings ($8.50/person), for enjoying wine, cheese, bread, and fruit while listening to jazz from the excellent Jeff Haas Quartet (all days but Tuesdays). It's Tuesdays and Thursdays in July and August, Fridays in September and October. Call for info on off-season **wine seminars**.

On Center Rd./M-37, 2 miles north of Mapleton, (616) 223-4110.
Open daily year-round, noon to 5. In summer open 11-5.

◆ The **Old Mission Church.** This little historical museum is a replica of a log church built in 1839 by the Presbyterian missionary to the Chippewa Indians. Its original bell is in this belfry. The informative historical displays inside were done by the Old Mission Women's Club — another example of how enthusiastic amateurs can outdo professional museum curators.

Visitors learn that until 1900, many residents of the peninsula's eastern shore would get two or three months' provisions at a time by boating across the bay to Elk Rapids. A brief history of local cherry farming points out that because the soil here is so perfect for cherries, that's what everyone grew. So when an early frost occasionally wiped out the cherry crop, the peninsula was thrown into a profound depression. Another disadvantage of a single-crop economy was having to pick all the cherries at the same time, straining the available labor supply. At first local Indians were used as pickers, then Jamaicans, then Japanese, then Mexicans. By 1965 cherry-picking machines were becoming widespread and migrants were no longer needed. *On Old Mission Rd. in the hamlet of Old Mission. 18 miles out on M-37, turn right onto Old Mission Rd. Open daily from 8 or 9 a.m. to 6 p.m. or so, from Mem. Day through color season.*

◆ **Old Mission Cellars.** Dave and Joan Kroupa have over 150 acres in cherries on their Old Mission farm, so the low cherry prices of recent years have really hurt. Observing the success of local wineries, they planted wine grapes, intending to sell to wineries. Then they decided to get into winemaking themselves. Their cherries and apples can produce much more income in the form of wine. Old Mission's four wines (Chardonnay, Riesling, apple, and cherry) are currently only available in their tasting room, which shares space with their Old Mission grocery store and post office. Winemaker Lee Lutes seems to have a knack; his first vintage of Chardonnay (1994; sold out) was judged the top Chardonnay at the 1995 Michigan State Fair. The Old Mission's longer growing season means its Chardonnay grapes (and those of the Leelanau Peninsula) have a better chance of ripening than other Michigan Chardonnays.

Production is still limited. Old Mission's leading blend is made of red wine grapes from a Leelanau grower. Lutes likes wines to be "food-friendly." Even his apple and cherry wines are made less sweet to go with food. He's working on a "white cherry wine" made from Old Mission yellow cherries. *18250 Mission Rd. in the hamlet of Old Mission. (616) 223-4310. Open Mem. Day thru color season, daily 10-6, Sun 12-6, with shorter Oct. hours. ♦: no.*

♦ **Haserot Beach.** A local calls this 250-foot public beach the best swimming in northern Michigan. A lifeguard is provided by the township. The beach is protected from chilly winds by the cove. *North of Old Mission. From M-37, take Swaney Rd. east to shore.*

♦ **Old Mission Point and Light.** This quaint old lighthouse, not open to the public, dates from 1870. The original frame lightkeeper's dwelling remains. The 45th parallel of latitude intersects here, halfway from the North Pole to the Equator. At the peninsula's rocky point is a swimming **beach** (really more of a wading beach), a simple, pretty spot. There's a fine view west across to Omena on the Leelanau Peninsula, and east to Eastport at the outlet of Torch Lake. The state has acquired the surrounding 513 acres, but it remains a day-use facility with no camping.

A REAL DOWNTOWN IN A RESORT AREA . . . . . downtown Traverse City is well worth exploring. As Northern Michigan's biggest city, and the hub of the increasingly affluent Grand Traverse region, Traverse City has a range of specialties, services, and arts organizations found nowhere else in the region. It looks a lot like Ann Arbor on a bay. **Horizon Books** (616-946-7290) took over the vacant Penney's at 243 E. Front between Park and Cass. It's open daily from 7 a.m. to 10 p.m., to 11 p.m. Friday and Saturday. . . . . . Entertainment is another downtown strength. Look in local tabloids for info.. . . . . . In addition to the four principal shopping blocks of Front Street between Pine and Boardman, explore West Front on the way to U.S. 31/Division and take Union Street from downtown across the Boardman River into "Old Town."

LOCALS ARE EXCITED ABOUT . . . . . Northwestern Michigan College's exhibit and auditorium space, the **Dennos Museum Center**. The displays are unusually interesting, and the building is open, airy, and beautiful. The three permanent displays are the **sculpture gallery**, the **Inuit Gallery**, showing a selection from former NMC librarian (and winemaker) Bernie Rink's collection of contemporary Eskimo art, one of the nation's largest; and the very popular hands-on **Discovery Gallery**. (See the colors of your on-screen image change; make sounds by touching different colors on a wall.) Call also for lecture and performance schedule. . . . . . In summer, the Dennos Center is home to the **Michigan Ensemble Theater**, nonprofit professional summer stock. Its comedies and revues run from mid June through early October. Individual tickets: $19. Call (616) 922-1552. *On the campus of Northwestern Michigan University, off U.S. 31 roughly two miles east of downtown Traverse City, and follow signs. (616) 922-1055. Open Mon-Sat 10-5 (to 8 in summer), Sun 1-5. $2/adults, $1 under 18.*

The Music House

From music boxes to nickelodeons and giant organs,
take in the nostalgic sounds and visual glamor
of mechanical music-makers at a top-notch museum.

THE STORY of the automation of music, from the elaborate music boxes of the 1870s to the Victrola and talking movies of 1929, is told — and better yet, played — in this impressive, intelligent museum created by two collectors. The one-and-one-half hour guided tour includes satisfying demonstrations of music on 12 instruments. The giant Regina music box has interchangeable punched metal discs and a delicate, tinkling sound. There's a reproducing player piano, briefly popular in the 1920s. Its piano roll was punched to exactly recreate, for example, George Gershwin performing *Rhapsody in Blue*. Musicologists come here to hear just how Grieg and Rachmaninoff really played the music they wrote.

It's a thrill to see and hear these instruments in action. Many are lavish with carved ornament and gilt. The music conjures up scenes in shoebox theaters, saloons, and dance halls. Some music is meant to blow you away with a throbbing bass and penetrating, clear melody. It's fascinating to watch the inner workings of these clever mechanical devices, with their bellows and hammers.

The magnificent and rare Amaryllis organ — a great, gilded confection of pipes, carved foliage, and moving louvers — imitates a dance orchestra and vibrates the floor with its bass notes. Built for a big Belgian dance hall, it looks like it belongs in an 18th-century Rococo church. A similar instrument in a less elaborate case was once strategically positioned on a rooftop at an amusement park in New Jersey to provide background music throughout the park.

One co-founder of this museum is an architect who has recreated antique room settings for some instruments. The electric player piano (known by many names, including nickelodeon) is in an elaborate saloon from the 1890s, all mahogany and mirrors. The tiny, make-believe Little Lyric Theater showcases a Reproduco piano-organ combination, used as a popular and inexpensive accompaniment for silent movies.

Restoration of additional instruments is ongoing. Work is under way on a large Wurlitzer theater organ, soon to be enjoyed from the museum lobby. Six of the twenty vintage jukeboxes which will eventually appear in the "Big Band Era Gallery" are currently displayed.

Before or after the tour, visitors can examine extensive **displays**

Big on visuals and music: the outer cases of the Music House's mechanical music machines are show-stoppers, too. The Amaryllis organ built for a Belgian dance hall resembles 18th-century Baroque organs

on the evolution of the Victrola, the radio, and early TVs. (No audio demonstrations go with them.) The **gift shop** carries many tapes of music played on music boxes, chapel bells, player pianos, and street organs.

The Music House occupies the hay barn and granary of the cherry and dairy farm where one founder grew up. That's been the story of Grand Traverse, he points out — cherries and agriculture replaced by tourism, condos, and golf.

The Music House is in a complex of barns on the west side of U.S. 31 about 8 miles northeast of Traverse City and 1 1/2 miles north of M-72. (616) 938-9300. Open May through October, Mon-Sat 10 a.m.-4 p.m., Sun 12-4. Open weekends Thanksgiving thru New Year's Day. Call or write for details on holiday program. ♿ $6.50/ adults, $2/children 6-16, children under 6 free. Allow 2 hours per tour.

A FINE CHERRY ORCHARD TOUR . . . . . is just north of the Music House at **Amon's Orchards and U-Pick.** Here in the center of U.S. tart cherry production, overproduction perennially depresses wholesale cherry prices. To stay profitable, orchards have had to turn to marketing their cherries and cherry products direct to visitors. Family-run Amon's has reoriented itself to tourism while retaining a pleasantly farmy flavor. Half-hour **wagon tours** by knowledgeable employees cover area cherry history and how cherries are grown and marketed. There's also a **petting zoo** of common farm animals kids can feed. In the sales room and bakery, you can buy sweet and tart cherries, apples, and plums, raspberries, and nectarines in season. Plenty of knowledgeable people are around to field questions about cherry cookery and cherry agriculture. Amon's offers **free samples** of some fairly exotic cherry products like cherry pepper jelly, cherry steak sauce, and Mexican cherry salsa, the current best-seller. Cherry mustard is awfully good, too. Splendid views of the East Arm of Grand Traverse Bay make this an outstanding place for an afternoon of cherry-picking. Fall brings u-pick pumpkins and press-your-own cider. **Fall festival time** is Sept. thru Oct. *On the east side of U.S. 31, 2 1/2 miles north of M-72. (800) 937-1644 or (616) 938-9160. Open for tours from July 4 thru October. Free admission to u-pick orchards and sales room. Call for tour times, availability,reservations, and rates. **Tours** on request during May. ⅰ $1 donation suggested for tour. Cherry dessert at end of tour extra.*

Fisherman's Island State Park

*An uncrowded up-north Eden
just south of bustling Charlevoix*

THIS LITTLE-DEVELOPED state park is a stunning bit of pure, unmessed-with natural beauty that occupies a prime spot along six miles of Lake Michigan shore south of Charlevoix. Although this region has become uncomfortably developed, Fisherman's island is uncrowded, thanks to a lack of amenities like flush toilets, a bathhouse at the beach, and the showers at the campgrounds.

As at many beaches in the Charlevoix-Petoskey area, stretches of rocky piles of limestone gravel alternate with pockets and little bays of sand. Rocky limestone outcrops make for a more rugged shoreline than vacationers expect. Occasional boulders are dramatic accents. This area south of Charlevoix is actually better for finding **Petoskey stones** than the Petoskey area itself. (Hint: the distinctive markings show up much better when the stones are held under water.)

What you gain in scenery and privacy, you give up in convenience. There isn't much of an official trail system, either. But in from the shore 20 miles of paths wind through the dense woods. Here they are mainly birch and aspen, along with spruce, balsam fir, and occasional hardwoods. The many low, swampy areas are full of tamaracks and fragrant cedars.

Most everywhere around here are the simple, beautiful basics conveyed in the romantic image of northern Michigan: the big blue lake and long beaches, accented with birches, aspens, and pines. You have it all to yourself, the way it would have been in Hemingway's time — actually better, since the North Country had been recently logged over in Hemingway's day. The trees are much taller today.

The main day-use beach and **designated swimming area** is at the end of a two-mile drive past the two campgrounds. Its parking area is very seldom full. People are welcome to pull over anywhere along the road and get out and swim. The park's northern section off Bell's Bay Road contains the two sections of **campsites** and a simple **scenic overlook** near the entrance. Of the 90 rustic campsites, 14 directly overlook the beach. The others are across a road but a very short walk to the beach.

The **southern part of the park** is a secret treasure, undeveloped and unmarked by signs. But it's a trick to reach. *13 miles southwest of downtown Charlevoix on U.S. 31, go west on Norwood Road until you get to the Norwood Township Park in the village of Norwood. The two-track road behind the park goes north along the shore.* Conditions are rough; check ahead at the park office. With "potholes the size of a truck", there's a good chance of getting stuck. (Towing charges run about $100.) You may be able to drive 2.3 miles north along the beach to Whiskey Creek. Or you may want to pull over and walk the rest of the way.

In his *Michigan State and National Parks* guide, outdoorsman Tom Powers says this lovely, isolated stretch of creek and beach is among his very favorite places in all of northern Michigan. He suggests planning on spending at least the better part of a day here. If you're very lucky, you may come upon what was perhaps the Woodland Indians' most important source of chert stone, used in weapons and tools. The quarry, consisting of holes the size of bushel baskets, is almost impossible to find in the heavy forest with its fern-covered floor.

The **main entrance** *to Fisherman's Island State Park is off Bell's Bay Road, which joins U.S. 31 two miles south of Charlevoix, almost across from the Brumm Showroom (616) 547-6641. Reservations: (800) 543-2YES. State parks sticker required: $4/day or $20/year. Park open May thru November. 90 rustic campsites (no electricity or running water except for a hand pump) fill up on weekends and weekdays in season (mid-June through late August), when reservations are advised. $6/night. &: outhouses in 2nd loop.*

ARTS AND CRAFTS FROM NATURAL MATERIALS . . . . . are the focus of the **Norman Brumm Showroom** on U. S. 31 southwest of Charlevoix. Brumm is well known for copper enamel bird and wildflower sculptures, and suncatchers made of sliced agate in black metal frames, often shaped like birds. The vast, rambling store also carries a very wide range of jewelry, notecards, prints, baskets, pottery, and other decorative gift items, nature-themed. Even people who aren't drawn to the gift items may well enjoy looking through drawers upon drawers of mineral and shell specimens plus books and drawings on natural subjects. *Old U.S. 31 South, 2 miles south of Charlevoix. Open daily, May through Christmas 9:30-5:30. Open same hours Mon-Sat in April. (616) 547-4084. &*

Beaver Island

A two-hour ferry ride from the mainland,
this simple place is heaven for island-lovers.

OF ALL MICHIGAN'S permanently inhabited islands, Beaver Island (14 miles long, almost seven miles wide, year-round population 450, summer population over 2,000) is the only one that's over five miles from the mainland. Eighteen miles from the nearest Lower Peninsula shore, it's the biggest island in the Beaver Archipelago; five other islands are within five miles. Beaver Island has much more of an island feeling than islands connected by a bridge or a short ferry ride. It's completely different from summertime Mackinac Island with its huge and stylish Victorian summer "cottages" and hotels.

How you feel about Beaver Island depends a lot on how you feel about the pace and huge variety of choices of contemporary life — how much you like things slowed down and simplified. Beaver Island has cars, but not very many. It costs $94 to take them over and back on the ferry. You have to plan ahead to get here. The ferry from Charlevoix takes two hours and costs $29 round-trip. The plane is $52 round-trip and may not fly five or six days a year. The ferry vibrates and sometimes tosses unpleasantly. In late fall and early spring it only runs three times a week. From late December through March it doesn't run at all. If you just want to look around Beaver Island, you can make a $29 day trip and have 7 1/2 hours on the island. But it doesn't really add up, spending four hours on the ferry to see a few low-key sights on the run. You're better off to stay a few days, or at least overnight, and unwind. Most of the lodgings are simple but pleasant enough. The rustic campgrounds and beautiful, and there are many vacation houses to rent.

Beaver Island is occasionally promoted as something of a natural wonder. It's true that some rare wildflowers are profuse on the island, and that loons nest in Font Lake. But the essential Beaver Island is a plain, pleasant, sandy piece of Michigan's north country —largely flat to rolling, with some bluffs and dunes on the west, covered with second-growth pines and hardwoods. The island's isolation has protected those Up North qualities of woods, water, shore, and rural landscape that Northern Michigan's summer people hold dear. Only in the past 30 years have the beaches gained the inevitable rim of cottages.

What you see when you arrive at St. James, Beaver Island's port

This old boathouse is now a museum about Beaver Island's once-active role as a fishing, boat-building, and lumbering center.

and only town, is a collection of mostly plain, small buildings — either clapboard houses and storefronts built over the years by the descendants of Irish fishermen who first settled in 1856, or aluminum-sided motels and ranch houses of the 1960s. That's when the man who had been buying property at tax sales over the years divided some of it into vacation lots. Gentrification, though occurring, has been far, far less ostentatious than elsewhere in northwestern Michigan.

All that's left of the island's brief, bizarre period as the only kingdom in the United States — the self-proclaimed kingdom of breakaway Mormon leader King James Jesse Strang — are a few old frame buildings (the Mormons' print shop is the local museum) and some place names: Paradise Bay (the harbor's official name), Font Lake where baptisms occurred, Lake Genesrath, and St. James, named after Strang himself. Most of the names you see — Erin Motel, O'Donough Grocery, Donegal Bay — reflect the island's strongly Irish past and present.

Beaver Island is about slowing down and relaxing, getting in tune with nature, family, and neighbors. It's a place so small that acquaintances cut across social class distinctions. Summer people have built many handsome contemporary cottages tucked off the perimeter roads south of St. James. A large number of academics and writers summer on the island, which accounts for the high caliber of writing in the local historical society's publications and in the *Beaver Beacon*, the island monthly. There's little entertainment, except for the local bands that play Saturday nights in summer at the **Shamrock Pub** and folk music at the **Circle M restaurant**, now that it's been purchased by folk singers Claudia Schmidt and Kevin White and their spouses.

The charm here is that "much of what Beaver Island offers is free for the finding," as the Chamber of Commerce's fine little **brochure/map**, "Beaver Island Pure & Simple," points out, That includes "beachcombing, camping, bird-watching, hunting, fishing, hiking, boating, or cross-country skiing. . . . Many miles of walking trails can lead to close-up views of beaver dams or other wildlife. There are shipwrecks for divers to explore, abandoned log cabins to photograph, miles of beach to walk."

This subtle place needs a personal guide, an insider who knows the little, everyday things that make island living different, not just the island's geography and exotic history. First-time visitors are lucky to have such a guide in Jim Willis, a crusty but amiable retiree and island resident who has been familiar with the island since 1939, when he came to spend the summer as a boy. Willis is the only full-time employee of **Beaver Island Tours.** (Tours are arranged through the Beaver Island Boat Co., 616-547-2311.) He'll meet visitors at the dock and take them to all the major sights. Later you can make longer, more leisurely expeditions to those places that interest you the most. You'll see the Old Mormon Print Shop and Marine Museum, the lighthouse, Barney's Lake, the fateful dock former Tiger baseball star Norm Cash fell off of after a night of drinking and drowned. Willis will fill you in on Beaver Island's peculiar history, about how the charismatic James Jesse Strang (by all accounts a gifted and intelligent if autocratic leader) moved his band of some 2,000 followers from Wisconsin to Beaver Island in 1850. The Mormons soon took over the fledgling county government by virtue of their numbers, moved the county seat to St. James, and drove off the fishermen from their "kingdom" before Strang was killed by a rebel of his own group. The Mormons were then driven out by non-Mormon mainlanders. Homeless and dispossessed, they eventually scattered across the country. Their descendants sometimes show up on Willis's tours.

In a laconic, philosophical sing-song, Willis talks about island life today. How the bank is open from 9 to 1 Tuesday mornings, except during the summer season. How "there's no crime here. Most of the sheriff's problems come when someone has too much to drink at the Shamrock Bar." How the resale shop operated by the Beaver Island Volunteer Fire Department Auxiliary is a very popular social spot.

Beaver Island was long the center of northern Lake Michigan's profitable fishery, Willis explains, but overfishing and alewives killed off the industry. The island's population dropped dramatically. Now that long decline, a concern for every small community, has been reversed. Opening-day school enrollment rose from 84 to 104 between 1994 and 1995 as younger urban refugees experimented with island life. The new medical center has a permanent nurse-practitioner and a visiting doctor. Thanks to one of the first federal grants of gas-tax funds to smaller islands, a larger ferry should be running in 1997. "Sophistication — a word that never would have been linked to the old island — is not out of place," commented *Washington Post* political columnist David Broder in 1995, in his annual column from his island summer home. "First-class crafts-men, quilters, potters, painters, jewelry makers, have set up [year-round] studios." Celebrated quilter and Dover author **Gwen Marston** offers occasional **quilting workshops** (616-448-2565). Singer-songwriter Claudia Schmidt, a longtime folk favorite, and her husband, a former public radio staffer, have restored a very old farmhouse, turned it into the **Bluebird bed and breakfast** (616-448-2600), and purchased the old rectory, formerly called the Circle M restaurant, now renamed The Old Rectory restaurant. Musical per-formances are part of their agenda.

Building vacation homes has kept the island economy going for the last two decades. Development battles are now intensifying between "islanders" (natives who grew up here and who need jobs to stay) and "off-islanders" (people from somewhere else, who usually favor limiting development to preserve the island's natural environ-ment). "The island is changing, and some of these people aren't ready for it," says one longtime observer, a blue-collar retiree. "The old ones think the island's here to use. They see logs and we see trees," comments a year-round artist resident. The islanders have the majority vote in St. James and the northern fourth of the island, but in the southern three-fourths, Peaine Township, off-islanders now outnumber islanders.

IN AND AROUND ST. JAMES

Visitors could happily spend a vacation in and around **St. James**, with perhaps a day's island exploration in a rented car. The village extends over a mile around the crescent harbor. Here's a **quick tour** from the **ferry dock**. A number of Main Street gift shops and some businesses in the woods have not been mentioned; more exploring could be done. Be prepared to hike 2 1/2 miles, or rent a bike.

Almost across from the ferry is the **Shamrock Bar**, a family-type place with good food, a dance floor, **live music on Saturday nights,** and front tables with a terrific bay view. Left (south) from the ferry, stop in at the **Chamber of Commerce** for information and a detailed island map if you plan to explore interior paths and two-tracks.

The **Old Mormon Print Shop** museum of the Beaver Island Historical Society tells the story of island people: Indians, Irish immigrants, Mormons, and "interesting characters who have sought seclusion," like the beloved Estonian refugee actor/ writer, Dr. Protar. He practiced alternative medicine here. Island activities, including lumbering as well as boating, are covered in the Maritime Museum (see page 619). The museum's visual jewels are sketches of early island residents by the late Helen Hoffman Collar, longtime island historian and David Broder's mother-in-law. A free **treasure hunt** is offered for children. Rainy days would be well spent here, reading interesting documents and browsing in the book shop with maps and books pertaining to the island. *The Print Shop Museum is on a corner opposite the bay south of the ferry. Both museums are open daily, mid-June to Labor Day, 11-4, Sundays 12-3. (616) 448-2254. ♿ Combined admission: $3/adult, $1/children.*

A little ways south of the museum is the public town beach. Up the cross street a short ways is the **Holy Cross Catholic Church** and **hall**, a hub of island social life, with the school and library nearby. The first side road leads past the tennis courts to **Beaver Island Lodge**, a small, woodsy resort whose public dining room offers nice sunset views. In two miles the dirt Donegal Bay Road ends at the sandy bay. Right takes you in a mile to **Indian Poin**t, a favorite sunset overlook. Left soon leads to a **public beach** (it also faces west for sunsets), a wild dune landscape, and some striking contemporary summer homes. Other close-in west side biking or hiking destinations are Barney's Lake and, farther west almost to Bonner's Bluff, the Protar home and tomb. Get directions from the map. The pleasant **Barney's Lake Nature Preserve** and picnic area in a picturesque old orchard overlook the lake.

Back in town at the corner between library and school, you could go north along the **Back Highway** for a fuller look at town, an interesting old cemetery and church, assorted studios, and small homes of the island's longtime Indian residents. Their activities spread out into their yards, in much the way that Greek villagers live their lives half outdoors. **Boyle's Family Fun Center**, on Back Highway past the fire hall,is a magnet for kids, with pizza, ice cream, roller skating, video games, and bike rentals.

North still farther, at the corner, nonfiction writer Mary Blocksma (*Naming Nature, Yoo Hoo Moon*) has turned her back room into **Beaver Island Books**, a personal shop strong on thoughtful current fiction and nonfiction, nature, and children's books and activities. Her *The Fourth Coast: Exploring the Great Lakes Coastline* (Penguin, $12.95) has several pages about Beaver Island. *Open summers 10-5 mostly, otherwise call first. (616) 448-2876.*

At Beaver Island Books, head down to the harbor. The **Gillespie Dock** is where barges arrive with cargo that can't come on the ferry: house trailers, logs, lumber, and other building materials. In another block is the extensive **McDonough's Market**, half a mile east of the ferry dock, another community hub. It offers rentals of VCRs and movies, custom meats, books, souvenirs, and now a deli and bakery. Next door at the **Beaver Island Boat Shop**, visitors can stop in and watch Bill Freese making birch and cherry canoes, paddles, and cherry buckets, a useful item on boats too small to have a head or restroom. His neighbor at **Maritime Collectables**, Carl Felix, makes ship models to order from customers' photos.

As late as the 1950s, the harbor was a picturesque jumble before it was cleaned up and beautified. A bit of the old atmosphere remains around the old boathouse that's now the **Maritime Museum**, on the way to the harbor entrance and light. A restored fish tug, the *Bob S.*, is outside. Inside are exhibits about ferryboats, boat-building, lumbering, and fishing, with a full-scale fish shanty. *Same hours, fees as Old Print Shop Museum, p. 618.* ♿ A working Indian gill-net fishing tug is sometimes docked nearby.

Don't leave the island without visiting the **Beaver Island Toy Museum and Store**, overlooking the harbor a little past the Marine Museum. Inside this simple bungalow, the golden age of dime stores lives on. You'll find charms like tiny coppery baseball mitts, cheap plastic necklaces, magic tricks, whistles, glow bugs, cowboy stuff — it's like returning to the 1950s, with bits of the 1960s and 1930s thrown in. Watercolor sets, simple games, coloring books, and more make this a great vacation stop for kids. Most things are for sale, but some are for display only. The deadly categorizing of the typical serious collector is altogether absent. Owner Mary Rose has avoided any sense of real-world monetary value and make her cache of warehouse finds into a fantasy realm — "the last five-cent store in America," she likes to say. Along the back path to her house and henhouse of exotic birds are little creations of cement, broken china, plastic toys, and beach stones. Examine them and you may be tempted to create some backyard fantasies of your own. *Open in season, 11-4 daily, noon-3 on Sunday.* ♿ *: no. In the off-season, inquire in the residence out back.*

Just past the Toy Museum, Sue Thomson's charming **Livingstone Studio** showcases her own beautiful creations: jewelry, occasional masks, collages with images of empowering women, stones and driftwood painted in a Celtic-looking stream--of-consciousness style. Works by other artists fit right in. *Open daily 11-4, Mem. to Labor Day, or by appt. (616) 448-2975.*

The 1856 brick **lighthouse** still stands at the harbor entrance; the keeper's house has been taken down. The Irish laborers who built the lighthouse started the island's Irish community. They wrote back to hungry relatives about plenty of fish and plenty of land for potatoes.

PLANNING A STAY AT BEAVER ISLAND . . . . . The **Chamber of Commerce** is an excellent clearinghouse for any inquiries, including cottage rentals. (616) 448-2505. Box 5, St. James, Beaver Island, MI 49782. Get a **free map** when you get off the boat; the complete **$4 map** is worthwhile if you intend to bike or hike. . . . . For the ferry schedule and reservations, call the **Beaver Island Boat Company**, (616) 547-2311. The ferry runs from April thru December and costs $27 round trip ($13.50 for kids 5 to 12). From late June through August boats leave Charlevoix at 8:30 a.m. and 2:30 p.m. at least. Inquire about the very attractive spring and fall package ($140 per couple for a night's lodging, ferry, breakfast, dinner, tour, and museum fee). The $38 day-trip summer package includes ferry, lunch, tour, and two museums. . . . . . . **Island Airways** makes frequent flights ($52 round-trip) on demand from Charlevoix. Call (616) 448-2326). Flying off the island it quite a delightful experience. One of the airport's buildings is a log barn. The amiable pilot opens the door of the 10-passenger plane for you. The seat ahead of you might be taken by a dog. The island's shores appeal as beautiful rings of green, tan, and blue. Flying over Medusa Cement in Charlevoix is fascinating. . . . . . . **Beaver Island Tours'** excellent 1-hour tour is available daily at the dock as the ferry disembarks or by appointment. $7/adult, $4/children 5-12. Package tours and custom tours are also available. (616) 547-2311.

GETTING AROUND THE ISLAND . . . . . Outlying restaurants provide **free taxi service** to and from motels. . . . . A **bike** is perfect for getting around St. James, the nearby campground and public beach, and Font Lake. West Side Road to the island's south tip is bicycle-able, but the East Side Road to the Peaine Township campground, Central Michigan camp, and beyond is very poor. You can bring a **bike** on the ferry for $10 round-trip. **Bike rentals** are from **Boyle's Family Fun Center** (616-448-2266) or **Lakesports Gear & Rental** (616-448-2616), which also rents canoes, wave runners,snorkeling gear, windsurfers, and canoes.. . . . . A car or **rental car** is the preferred transportation on the east side. They are available for about $40 to $55 and up from Armstrong Car (616-448-2513), Gordon's Auto Service (616-448-2438), and Beaver Island Jeep (616-448-2200).

CAMPING ON THE ISLAND. . . . . Both **campgrounds** are rustic and beautiful. Fees are $5 a night, first-come, first served. Both have pay phones and firewood. Both are wheelchair-accessible. The **Township Campground** on the island's north side, a mile north of St. James near Beaver Lodge, is smaller (12 sites), perched on a bluff, with sunset views, breezes, and adjacent beach below. The 22-site **Bill Wagner Memorial Campground**, seven miles south of St. James, has a gorgeous beach but a potentially bad black fly problem on cloudy days through early July.

IRISH TRADITIONS LIVE ON . . . . . at Beaver Island, where many islanders are descended from fishermen who came from the islands of Aran in County Donegal in 1856. The island's **St. Patrick's celebration** lasts for days. . . . . Irish country dancing is done at the church. . . . . . Irish music is much in evidence at the annual **homecoming** on the second weekend of August. Call the Chamber of Commerce for details: (616) 448-2505.

GATHERINGS ON BEAVER ISLAND . . . . . A traditional small-town **homecoming** is held the second week of every August. . . . . . **Museum Week**, the third in July, involves nature walks, Music on the Porch put on by any interested island musicians, and lectures, slide shows, and demonstrations pertaining to all aspects of island life. Admission is charged to these events. It culminates with a Saturday-night pub concert. . . . . . The **Shamrock Pub** and the **Catholic church** are the main social centers. Look for posters around town advertising events.

TOURING THE REST OF THE ISLAND. . . . . Much of the island's northern third is a pretty rural landscape of log farms and abandoned barns. The two largest inland lakes, Font Lake near St. James and Lake Genesrath at the southeast tip, have ample bass, pike, and some big muskies. The island's interior is public land administered by the Mackinaw State Forest. It's crisscrossed by hiking trails and some faint two-tracks. (Mountain bikes are ideal for these interior roads.) There's good berry-picking.

From King's Highway, the north-south road extending south from St. James down half the island, a **perimeter road** (East Side or West Side drives) goes around the lower three-fourths of the island. It offers water views intermittently along the island's east side and most spectacularly for 3 1/2 miles at the south end. Here are highlights of the perimeter, going clockwise from St. James. A day's or half-day's outing including some time at a beach is in order. **Picnic supplies** are at McDonough's Grocery or Clarkston's Deli (a new touch of gourmet sensibility on the island) next to the Shamrock. King's Highway leaves south from town, passing the **Old Rectory restaurant**). Turn right at the four corners onto East Side Road. You pass the charming **Welke Airport** and the nine-hole public **golf course**. Across from the first tee a footpath leads to the beautiful **Little Sand Bay Nature Preserve**. (Better walk and avoid the terrible road.) Cottage drives, but few cottages, are visible from the road. Much later, seven miles south of St. James, is the **Bill Wagner Memorial Campground** (above) with its beautiful sandy **beach** and low dunes. The Central Michigan University research station and conference center is in a few more miles. To find the beautiful, mile-long sandy **public beach**, look for the "public access" sign near Cable Creek, some 12 or 13 miles south of St. James. Then go through the forest to the parking lot. A pretty half-mile walk passes the creek and through the fragrant balsam forest and dunes. Mossy boulders and exposed roots give the creek ravine a magical, medievally woodsy look. Enjoy this sylvan solitude view while you can. "This will get all housed up," an artist told me. "It's all for sale for *big* prices."

A trip to the **Beaver Head Light** on the island's south tip is the highlight of a round-the-island trip. Youth groups are restoring the large brick keepers' residences.(A Charlevoix/Emmet County alternative school is here during the school year.) The handsome tower, open to visitors daily from 10 a.m. to 9 p.m. in summer, offers a fine view of the island interior and shore. Just west of the lighthouse, the road borders beautiful Iron Ore Bay and its sandy, easy-to-reach swimming **beach** with picnic tables and volleyball net. A creek provides a warm backwater for wading.

In a mile, the perimeter road turns north and stays a mile inland. Several roads and two-tracks lead west toward the lake, bordered on the west shore by a bluff. Take any of these roads or the trails that lead west from the road ends, and you'll be almost sure to have the beach all to yourself. **West Side Highway** itself is a beauty spot here, as it goes through breeze-cooled, fairy-tale woods of white birches contrasted with the dark hemlock green. The road surface here is good for bicycles — less gravelly, and not dusty in summer. This is a spectacular place in early spring, and in fall when the birch and maples fire up yellow and red. The summer look of green leaves illuminated by dappled light is also pretty

EXPLORING THE BEAVER ARCHIPELAGO. . . . . "Some of the wildest places around Lake Michigan exist on the islands surrounding Beaver Island," say John and Ann Mahan, photographer-naturalists in their beautiful, interesting *Wild Lake Michigan*. **Hog, Garden,** and **High islands** are open to the public, and primitive camping is permitted. (Register at the Beaver Island deputy sheriff office out toward the harbor light.) Reefs typically circle the islands, the Mahans point out, so it takes rowing or wading to get ashore. . . . . High Island, once farmed by the House of David religious sect, has trails through varied terrain: woods, farms, dunes to the west and a sandy spit to the northeast. . . . . **Scenic Island Tours** (616-448-2527) arranges half-day, all-day, and overnight trips to these islands.

Earl Young Houses

*Charlevoix's beguiling "Mushroom Houses" look
like they were designed by gnomes or Smurfs.*

IT HAS BEEN called "Charlevoix the Beautiful" ever since
the dawn of Charlevoix's resort era in 1879, when the humble lumber port of Pine River was renamed to honor a
Jesuit priest. Rampant overdevelopment has spoiled the nice little
resort town on three beautiful lakes. Today it's condo city along
many stretches of central waterfront. The small downtown is so
crowded in summer that locals and longtime summer people try to
avoid it altogether. The drawbridge on the busy channel to Round
Lake raises every half hour, adding to the traffic. But people love to
watch it in operation.

Fortunately, the look of Charlevoix's leisurely, lovely past survives in places. The private **Belvedere Club** occupies a prominent
hill at the southwest edge of Lake Charlevoix. Its old-fashioned
Victorian houses are ample and gracious. The winding paths along
immaculately trimmed lawns and trees make it special. Inspired by
the success of Bay View (page 608) as a Methodist camp meeting
and resort, local developers successfully approached a Kalamazoo
Baptist group to launch the resort
in 1878. Summer colonies like this
seem untouched by the hectic,
hurried lifestyle ushered in after
World War II; so does the **Grey
Gables** restaurant in a big
Victorian house at 308
Belvedere on the north
edge of the Belvedere
Club. The club is
closed to the pub-
lic in July and
August, but you
can see some of it
east of U.S.
31/Bridge Street
just at the south
end of downtown.
Turn east onto
Belvedere and fol-

**Houses designed and built by
Charlevoix's Earl Young seem
to grow organically of their
own accord, built of local
stones and boulders.**

❶ Fisherman's Island State Park (p. 612). Outstanding scenery along 5-mile rocky beach, good for finding Petoskey stones. Sandy swimming area. 90 idyllic rustic campsites in pines, some right on lake.

❷ Downtown Charlevoix. Now more interesting & year-round. Standouts include Koucky Gallery of fun, playful crafts; Bridge St. Book Shop; Northern Possessions. New restaurants with flair: Acorn Cafe, On the Edge, refreshed Gray Gables.

❸❹ Earl Young gnome homes (p. 623). Inspired, eccentric rustic architecture. Smurf-like roofs, huge stones, fascinating details. Self-taught architect/ realtor Young built clusters in Boulder Park (❸) & on Park. (❹).

❺ Channel walkway. Very pleasant path leads from busy Bridge St. to Michigan. Ave. Beach. Wooded park and Earl Young homes above it. Good for viewing boats, drawbridge, sunsets.

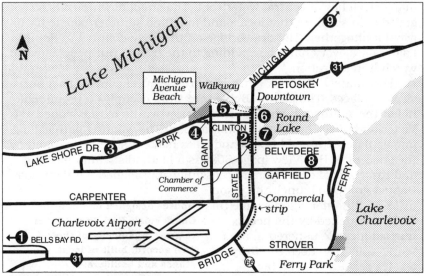

❻ East Park/ City Dock (p. 627). Colorfully diverse harbor. See Beaver Island ferries, Coast Guard cutter *Acacia*, commercial fishing boats, many sailboats, power boats, big yachts.

❼ John Cross Fisheries (p. 626). Picturesque landmark famed for good fresh and smoked whitefish, trout, perch, salmon, all locally caught. Fishing boats dock here.

❽ Belvedere Club. Stately row of Victorian cottages on Ferry St. overlook Lake Charlevoix and Yacht Club. Impeccable old resort. Interior closed to public in summer.

❾ Mount McSauba. Highest dune in area. Scenic downhill and cross-country skiing with lights. 547-3253. Hiking trails, viewing platforms, wonderful beach with wild, natural, open feel.

Highlights of
Charlevoix

0   1/2 mile

low it around the corner onto Ferry. A similar summer resort development established by Congregationalists from Chicago is the **Chicago Club**, on the north side of Round Lake west of the little Pere Marquette Depot on Lake Charlevoix. It too is off-limits to the general public, but some houses can be seen at the end of East Dixon Avenue, the first through street to the east on the north side of the drawbridge.

What makes Charlevoix worth a trip today are some beautiful waterfront parks, the most interesting harbor in northern Lower Michigan, and the wonderfully strange stone homes designed by Earl Young, a real estate broker and self-taught architect. He built them from the 1920s through the 1950s. These are the most surprising and original of all the wonderful northwoods architecture inspired by northern Michigan's natural beauty and encouraged by the 1920s' quest for the picturesque.

Young used natural materials — mostly different kinds of local limestone and glacial fieldstone, with cedar shake roofs. Rather than relying on variations of typical rustic style — log hunting lodges, for instance, or Shingle Style blends — he took popular vernacular styles of the day and fitted them so ingeniously and organically to the materials and sites that they look like they grew of their own accord, following rules devised by gnomes and elves.

Irregularly curving roofs mark all Young's homes. He must have had accomplished craftsmen — maybe boatbuilders accustomed to curving hulls — to make these amazing roofs. The smallish, medievally picturesque 1920s houses in Boulder Park are off Park Street along Lake Michigan on the west side of town, just past the hospital. They are made of oversized rose and gray fieldstone boulders, sometimes fully three and four feet long. The stones' great size gives the houses a fairytale, dollhouse look. Don't miss the tiny bungalows along Park at Clinton, across from the beautiful woods of shady Lake Michigan Park. Park Street can be reached by taking Bridge or the parallel residential streets of State or Grant north almost to the channel, then turning west onto Park.

By the entrance to Boulder Park are two much later Young ranch houses, faced with long, thin pieces of local white limestone. Young's flowing roofs and sinuous retaining walls give them a sensuous, romantic appeal that's rare in ranch houses.

To appreciate the details — the roofs, the playful chimneys, the quaint doorways, the inventive retaining walls — plan on parking your car and walking by each group of houses. For a **free map and brochure** on Earl Young's homes, stop at the **Charlevoix Chamber of Commerce** at 408 Bridge, corner of Belvedere; or call (616) 547-

2101. His daughter, Irene, also designed homes that look like his.

Young's only public buildings are the **Appletree** gift shop at 224 Bridge (next to the movie theater), with an unusual stone interior, and two hotels overlooking the Pine River Channel — the **Weathervane Terrace** and **The Lodge**. The lobby interiors are worth a look for their almost incredibly massive fireplaces, but they lack the intimate charm of the house interiors.

FOR VISITOR INFO ON THE CHARLEVOIX AREA, ... on the prestigious July Waterfront Art Fair and the popular fall Apple Festival, call the extremely helpful **Chamber of Commerce** at (616) 547-2101, or write them at 408 Bridge, Charlevoix, MI 49720. *Hours: Mon-Sat 9-5, to 6:30 in summer except for Saturday.*& . . . . Ask about the area's pleasant waterfront parks and natural areas tucked away from the main roads.

A LOOK AT OLD CHARLEVOIX . . . . . and the present-day beauty spots remaining from the old resort days is presented in the chatty, beautifully illus- trated little booklet, *Historic Charlevoix: A Guide to Walking and Driving Tours of the Charlevoix Area's Most Historic Sights*. It's available at the Chamber of Commerce (see above).

A CONVENIENT LAKE MICHIGAN BEACH AND SCENIC WALKWAY . . . . . is the **Lake Michigan Beach** on Grant north of Park. The beach has changing rooms, a concession stand, playground, picnic area. No fee. Plenty of parking. The hillside park behind it provides a lovely backdrop of pine woods, nice for a picnic or a stroll to see the Earl Young homes on Park Street (page 592). A water- side **walkway** curves around along the channel for a good view of the busy boat traffic. The **pier** gives a good view of the activity at the big **Medusa Cement** port a mile west,. This is a fine spot to watch the sun set over Lake Michigan.

ONE OF LAKE MICHIGAN'S LAST FISHERIES. . . . . . is the **John Cross Fishery**. This simple, highly regarded Charlevoix landmark gives an idea of what fishing was like in the days before World War II, when Northern Michigan's econ- omy was more balanced with non-tourist enterprises like commercial fishing. Overfishing and then alewives brought an end to most commercial fishing, except for Indian fishing boats permitted by treaty. Indians own and operate the tugs docked here. They catch the fish that John Cross supplies to leading area restaurants. *John Cross Fishery is down off a drive at 209 Belvedere just east of Bridge. (616) 547-2532. Summer hours: daily 9-5. Winter hours vary; call.*

SHOPPING IN CHARLEVOIX. . . . . Charlevoix is a seasonal town, and most shops on its three busy downtown blocks south of the drawbridge are branches of resort-area chains seen elsewhere: **Mettler's** upscale, updated traditional clothing; **Splash Alternatives; Bananarama; Bahnhof Sports; Northern Possessions'** handcrafted contemporary furniture, clothing, and gifts; **American Spoon Foods'** intensely flavored fruit preserves and condiments; the worthwhile **Rocking Horse Toy Company**; fudge shops; and a host of other stores. The **Koucky Gallery** is one-of-a-kind. Its decorative art — mostly playful, fun, and accessible — comes from some 300 artists and craftspeople: ceramics, sculpture, weaving, furniture, jewelry, painting, and prints. Many artists live nearby. Charlevoix has long been a favorite base for artists who do the circuit of better art fairs. Some pieces here are huge, like local favorite Todd Warner's earthy four-foot llamas and caricatures of Western icons. Many pieces use odd materials and techniques, like jewelry made of rubber and glass beads. These are things you don't see everywhere. Jewelry and mugs begin in the $20 range. *The Koucky Gallery is at 319 Bridge in downtown Charlevoix.&. (616) 547-2228. Open Mon-Sat 9:30-5:30, Sun 10-4. In summer open until 9.* Downtown browsing has become more interesting lately, thanks in part to the large, new year-round **Bridge Street Book Shop** (616-547-7323) on Bridge between Mason and Antrim, and the coffeehouse next door. A number of interesting **antiques** and interiors shops now occupy houses up the hill south of downtown.

CHARLEVOIX'S BUSY HARBOR . . . . . is one of the most diverse and interesting in Michigan. It's home port to the Beaver Island ferry, a commercial fishing boat, the Coast Guard buoy tender *Acacia*, and a dazzling array of sailboats and some yachts. To get to the **City Dock**, just south of the U.S. 31 drawbridge, turn east and go behind downtown stores. . . . . Benches and tables make **East Park** a nice place to sit and observe the action. For frequent **summer band concerts** at the park, look for posters or ask at the Chamber of Commerce. A **walkway** along the south side of the Pine River channel connects the harbor with **Lake Michigan Beach**. Once a month a huge freighter, the *Myron C. Taylor*, goes through the channel and up to the head of Lake Charlevoix taking coal to a power plant. It's quite a spectacle; the Coast Guard can tell you when it's scheduled. Call (616) 547-2541. . . . . . The **Coast Guard cutter** *Acacia* welcomes visitors whenever it's in port, which is often from July into October. A seaman is always on watch. Call (616) 547-4447 to make sure it's not out on a buoy-tending run (in fall or spring) or being repaired, or gone to a summer festival.

LEARN TO SAIL INEXPENSIVELY. . . . . with **4-H sailing lessons** offered for children ages 8 to 18 in Boyne City the last two weeks of June and Charlevoix in July and early August. Week-long courses take place for three hours in either the morning or afternoon. Cost: $25-$45/week. Call (616) 582-6232 for more information. . . . . **Adult sessions** ($40) are held over a two-week period.

CHARLEVOIX HISTORY. . . . . comes alive at the **Harsha House**, home of the historical society, *103 State near Park, a block west of downtown. (616) 547-0373. Open mid June-Labor Day Tues-Sat 1-4. Sat only thru Dec. $1.* See resort-era photos, nifty local memorabilia at **shop**. Ask about new depot museum.

BOAT RENTALS . . . . . allow anyone to spend a few hours or more on beautiful Lake Charlevoix. Rates at **Ward Brothers' Boats** (616-547-2371) are from $40 for two hours on a 13-foot 4-person Boston whaler to $275 a day for the 19' Larson Bowrider that holds 10 for a day of waterskiing and sport. A 12-person pontoon boat rents for $165 a day. The dock and boat shop are at the harbor on the foot of Antrim, off Belvedere.

SAILING CRUISES ON THE TOPSAIL SCHOONER *APPLEDORE*. . . . . leave the City Dock in Charlevoix at noon, 3 p.m. and 7:30 p.m. in July and most of August. The 85' sailboat goes as far down Lake Charlevoix's north arm as time permits — no farther than Hemingway Point. Rates are $25/adult, $14/child. $5 extra for wine & cheese on sunset cruise. Call (616) 547-0024 for reservations.

WHAT MEDUSA DOES AT CHARLEVOIX. . . . . . Limestone and shale are quarried here, then crushed, blended with much smaller amounts of sand and iron ore, ground fine, and baked in a 2800° F kiln. The resulting clinker is stored and eventually ground so fine that it passes through a sieve that's able to hold water. Pneumatic pipelines take this cement powder to storage silos where it awaits shipment on the *Medusa Challenger* or the *Medusa Conquest.* (See page 205.) these freighters take cement to Chicago, Cleveland (Medusa's headquarters), Milwaukee, Manitowoc, and Detroit, 32 hours away. The Medusa silos and ships are familiar sights in Detroit's Rivertown entertainment district, next to St. Aubin Park. To find out when the *Challenger* or *Conquest* is in Charlevoix, call (616) 547-9971. Cement shipment by lake boats is an important factor in concrete's low cost. (Cement is concrete's basic ingredient.)

POTTERY IN A LIGHT-FILLED OLD SCHOOLHOUSE. . . . . . six miles south of Charlevoix on U.S. 31. The **Bier Art Gallery** shows David Bier's animal sculptures, nativity scenes, and more. Other artists, including Bonnie Staffel, again in Michigan, continue the mood of natural images and often whimsical animals. *(616) 547-2288. Open daily 10-6, late April thru October; weekends thru Dec.*

FLOWER-PETAL CANDLES. . . . . with a luminous glow are a hallmark of nationally distributed **Bullfrog Light Co.** (616-547-4407). At their small factory outlet on M-66 a mile east of Charlevoix, they sell seconds and the odd experiment not in mass production, along with their first-quality handcrafted candles.

EXTENSIVE DISPLAY GARDENS . . . . . and many **classes** on using herbs in skin care, crafts, and more are found at **Wintergreen Herbs & Potpourri** between Charlevoix and Petoskey. There's a butterfly garden, English cottage garden, fabric dye garden, medicinal garden, biblical garden, edible flower garden, Shakespeare garden, shade garden, and fragrance garden, with many component plants for sale. Nice gift shop, too, with flowery hand-painted things. *From U.S. 31 a mile west of Bayshore, take Murray Rd. to Old U.S. 31, then up Burnett. (616) 347-7399. Open May-Oct. Mon-Sat 9-5.*

Petoskey and its Gaslight District

A landmark museum, a splendid chain of waterfront parks, and good shopping give Petoskey one of Michigan's most enjoyable downtowns.

THE OLD RESORT TOWN of Petoskey is one of the jewels of northern Michigan. Like Saugatuck or Marquette, it's has retained its distinctive character in spite of being a major tourist spot. Because it's a year-round town, a regional medical center, and the county seat of Emmet County, Petoskey has a more authentic small-town character than many resorts. It enjoys a lively if small homegrown arts scene. In the late 1990s, residents worry about the impact of continuing development on their attractive community. Granting site plan approval for the new Wal-Mart was most controversial. Alternatives for a bypass for traffic-clogged U.S. 131 have been a matter of great concern, since they would affect many rural areas. Bay Harbor is building a "world-class golf resort" and luxury hotel echoing Newport and Mackinac Island's grandest 1890s "cottages" on what was a horribly polluted cement plant site. Its 800 homes, averaging $500,000, makes Bay Harbor a third as large as the entire town of Petoskey. Local people welcome Bay Harbor's environmental upgrade, two lakefront public parks, and low density. (A previous proposal was much larger.) But the new houses add to the

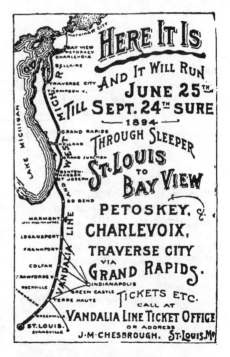

1894 advertisement. Railroads companies, seeking to replace lost lumber business, played an active part in developing major Michigan resorts like Petoskey and Mackinac Island.

❶ Gaslight District. Over 75 mostly upper-end resort shops in attractive old storefronts. Watch famous American Spoon kitchen in action.

❷ Bayfront Park (p. 632). Lively waterfront park with marina, refreshments. West of the museum is a historic mineral spring, scenic Bear River valley & iron bridge.

❸ Little Traverse Museum (p. 631). Handsome depot now home of stimulating historical museum. Splendid displays on passenger pigeons, Odawa quill boxes, Hemingway.

❹ Bill's Farm Market (p. 642). 3 miles east of downtown out Mitchell. Tiny veggies, 25 kinds of squash, flowers, more, grown here & arranged with an artist's eye.

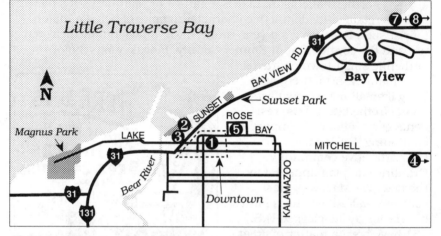

❺ Perry Hotel. 81-room, 1899 brick hotel/restaurant, jazzed up Victorian-style by famed innkeeper Stafford Smith. Long, old-fashioned porch, great Gaslight District location. (616) 347-2516.

❻ Bay View (p. 636). Peaceful, well-preserved 1875 Methodist summer retreat for relaxation and moral uplift. Wonderful old cottages. Eat and stay at Bay View Inn or Terrace Inn.

❼ Petoskey State Park (p. 641). Delightful view of bay from 1.25-mile beach with occasional Petoskey stones at south end. Scenic campsites and picnic sites among pines, boardwalk atop wooded dunes.

❽ Indian Hills Trading Co. Choice array of Indian crafts. Southwest, Eskimo, plus local Odawa specialties like sweet grass boxes and hot pads, quality quill boxes & ash baskets. 1681 Harbor Springs Rd.

Highlights of
Petoskey

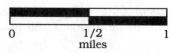

0   1/2   1
miles

worry that Petoskey may approach the Traverse City area in the scope of its sprawl and traffic.

Here are area highlights:

LITTLE TRAVERSE HISTORICAL MUSEUM

Petoskey's impressive Shingle Style 1892 depot houses this large, interesting local museum. It's an eye-catching reminder of the importance of railroads in developing Petoskey and other fashionable northern Michigan resorts for Midwesterners who grew rich in the post-Civil War era. The waterfront museum, just north of U.S. 31 and below that busy road, is a good introduction to the area.

In the mid-1870s, the timber on which the local economy depended was running out. Railroads teamed up with lumbermen and local business leaders to promote the Little Traverse Bay area as a resort. The museum commemorates Petoskey's railroad era with a reconstructed railroad station manager's office, complete with clicking telegraph key.

Virtually all the giant white pines in the region were logged. A museum display suggests their grandeur with a cross-section of a 225-year-old tree that's almost four feet across.

A vivid old mural depicts passenger pigeon hunting, so popular and lucrative here before the turn of the century that farmers neglected their crops to pursue it. The meat was a delicacy in fancy big-city restaurants, and the feathers were used to make pillows and mattresses. An estimated three billion to five billion of these plump birds were here before settlers arrived. One flock was 240 miles long and a mile wide. The birds were so docile that hunters simply clubbed them to death. By 1878 whole boatloads were being shipped from Petoskey. The last flock was seen in 1900. The last passenger pigeon died in 1914 in a Cincinnati zoo.

Probably the most important collection here is the **quill boxes** made by area Odawa over a hundred years ago. These small boxes of birchbark are completely covered with beautiful patterns and images of animals and flowers, made of dyed porcupine quills punched into the bark. Boxes of this quality predate the era of commercial Indian crafts made for tourists. It took an immense amount of time to make them. One small box uses ten porcupines' worth of quills. They were bestowed as important gifts for people the makers especially wished to honor.

The museum's recently expanded Bruce Catton exhibit includes all of his books, a Pulitzer Prize, and original galleys along with biographical information on Catton, who was born in Petoskey.

But what draws the most visitors here is an extensive collection of material on **Ernest Hemingway**, who spent each of his first 18 summers at his family's cottage on Walloon Lake south of town. Later, after Hemingway was wounded as an ambulance driver in World War I, he spent the winter in Petoskey, writing *The Torrents of Spring* and collecting materials for the famous Nick Adams stories that appeared in *In Our Time*. Hemingway met his first wife, St. Louisan Hadley Richardson, in this area; they were married in the little church in Horton Bay.

The museum also has changing exhibits which in the summer of 1996 will include a history of early 19th century hotels in the area and a history of golf in Emmet County. Periodically through the summer, special events had held. During the third week of June, there is the Historic Festival with Folk art, music, and hands-on demonstrations of old-time artifacts, the third week of July, there is the Garden Tour, and in August, the Historic Church Tour takes a look at the artwork, architecture, and the history of the early settlers in the area. An interesting **gift shop** with many good regional books adds to visitors' enjoyment of the area. *From down-town business district, make a left on to West Lake Street and follow it to the marina. Located on the waterfront of downtown Petoskey, west of the marina. (616) 347-2620. Ample parking by museum. Open May 1-November 1, Tues-Sat 10-3. Between Memorial Day and Labor Day open to 4 except on Thursday when open to 8; also open on Mondays. ♿ $1 donation. Research material available in winter by appointment.*

BAYFRONT PARK AREA

For an enjoyable stroll on the waterfront and up the leafy banks of the rushing **Bear River**, park in the public lot at the mouth of the river on West Lake Street. **Bayfront Park** is the dazzlingly trans-formed waterfront that once was an industrial eyesore. The park extends a half mile east from downtown out to the limestone cliff by Sunset Park. It connects the marina, the Little Traverse Museum, and to walkways along the Bear River valley. Start at the **Bayfront Park Resource Center**, where a short **video** tells about the park's past and present. The illuminated, four-headed, 60-foot Bell Tower next to the Center can be seen from Little Traverse Bay and from the bypass. In front of you are the 90-slip marina and sailboats on the bay. An unusual **playground** is tucked in a sunken sand pit near the marina.

Go east to reach the shady **picnic area** with the 35-foot **water-fall**. The stairs by the waterfall lead up to a scenic overlook that connects to **Sunset Park**, off U.S. 31, with a gazebo and telescopes.

Go west along the shore and you'll come to the **Little Traverse Museum** (page 631), City Hall, and the **Bear River mouth**, often lined with fishermen. The river is stocked with brook trout and steelhead. In **City Hall**, you can see a300-pound Petoskey stone, one of the largest known. Beautifully patterned when polished, it is fossilized coral, a remnant of the Devonian seas that covered Michigan some 250 million years ago. Across the drive is picturesque **Mineral Well Park**, a shady, old-fashioned gazebo and **picnic area** built so that health-conscious Victorian resorters could take in the foul-smelling sulfur waters. The Bear River rushes dramatically, dropping 75 feet within a mile, through a natural area that's wild with otter, beaver, minks, and waterfowl. It's hard to imagine that it once was an industrial mill district. **Trails** on either side of the river extend back a mile and a half; hikers can make a loop by using the Bridge Street bridge at the inland end. The east bank can be used by cross-country skis and mountain bikes. The city has built a tunnel from Bayfront Park to the Gaslight Shopping District. Enter east of the museum in the park and exit by Grampa Shorter's Gift Shop. Well lit, the tunnel is wheelchair accessible with a ramp. &: *yes, except stairs to Sunset Park.*

GASLIGHT DISTRICT

For people who choose to spend their vacation time doing resort-area shopping, the Gaslight District in downtown Petoskey stands out for its size (almost 80 stores in a six-block area geared to visitors), for setting (well preserved two-story Victorian brick storefronts and a pleasant park), and for tradition. A recent round of streetscape improvements have spiffed up the entire downtown.

This shopping district has catered to the Midwest's wealthiest resorters since the turn of the century, when steamers took Harbor Springs summer people across the bay to Petoskey stores to be fitted for fall suits and dresses. You don't see as many independent boutiques with "Petoskey and Naples" on their signs as 25 years ago, and there's more ordinary gifty stuff, but a good deal of the old flavor of serving the carriage trade remains. Fudge shops haven't taken over.

The area is geared to browsing. Prices are high because rents are high and the season is short, but there are some terrific markdowns at the end of the season in October. Shops now stay open year-round. This is a good place to find fashionable skiwear and after-ski wear, as well as other sports gear and clothing. One favorite shopping destination of well-heeled resorters: the large **Penney's** on Mitchell, old-fashioned but well maintained, with excellent service.

Antique shops are mostly clustered around Bay at Howard, at the district's north (bayside) end. Don't miss **Longton Hall Antiques** (616-347-9672), across from the Perry Hotel at 410 Rose. It specializes in antique wicker, rustic hickory, Indian things, and primitives. Interior furnishings are more likely to be loose and contemporary, sometimes in a folkish vein, in keeping with a relaxed, summer-cottage feel. Updated traditional clothes for men and women an area strength, in shops like **Mettler's** (400 Bay) and **Pappagallo** (402 E. Lake). Gifts and collectibles are becoming a bigger deal here, especially if they have ducks and fish on them, or if they have an Up North flavor (Petoskey stones, moccasins, birch boxes). For toys and novelties, **Games Imported** (206 Howard), **The Rocking Horse Toy Company** (325 E. Lake), and **Grandpa Shorter's** (301 E. Lake) all carry things you're not likely to find at your local mall.

A handy **Gaslight shopping guide** is available at the helpful **Chamber of Commerce** in the little office with columns on the corner of Mitchell and Howard. Or call (616) 347-4150 for a visitor packet. The Chamber is open 8:30-5, Monday through Friday; from June 3-Labor Day it closes at 6. **Store hours** are typically 9:30-5, Monday through Saturday, with evening hours and Sunday hours in summer. Only about 20 stores are open Sunday year-round; hours vary. &

Stores worth special mention include:

◆ **Grandpa Shorter's**. The consummate, old-fashioned Northern Michigan souvenir shop: big selection of moccasins, Petoskey stones, rubber tomahawks for kids — all the classics, plus well-chosen new novelties and some quality gifts. Lots of inexpensive toys and games for kids. Incorporates junk without being junky. All the fun of a good old-time dime store. *301 E. Lake at Petoskey. (616) 347-2603.* &

◆ **McLean & Eakin Booksellers**. General bookstore focused on customer service, amenities like free coffee, chairs for browsing. Call for special **events**, held monthly at least. First Fridays are poetry, second Fridays singles. B7est children's section in the area. On the lower level, there is a travel, map, and globe section with a nice fireplace where special gatherings are held. *307 E. Lake. (616) 347-1180. Extended hours: to 8 weekdays, Sundays noon to 4.* &

◆ **Ward & Eis Gallery**. Works by top leather craftspeople from across the U.S. include practical, beautiful handbags from 30 individual craftspeople, many kinds of calendars and organizers, and amazing decorative masks. Handbags run from $40 to $200, with

many in the $50-$80 range. All come with lifetime guara
There's a growing array of leather jewelry, including real
size leather feathers of birds of prey. They also carry leather and
pottery from various Indian craftspeople who have become friends
of the owners. There are Lakota (Sioux) beaded leather rattles and
axes, things from Huichol artists living in the Sierra Madre, and
pottery from Steve and Leigh Smith of the Mohawk Six Nations. New
additions: Navaho and Zuni jewelry; carved antler and stone
(turquoise, amethyst, and marble) fetishes believed by the Zuni to
bring luck. Co-owner Don Ward loves to talk about crafts of Native
American peoples and the workplaces and methods he has seen.
The one store in Petoskey not to miss. Beautiful bay view from rear
window. *315 E. Lake. (616) 347-2750. &: one step.*

◆ **Arktos Fine Arts Studio & Gallery.** Dana Costand loves animals
and creates colorful, rich watercolors of animals in natural settings.
Prints ($22 to $150) of many images are also available. H er rich

textural style is akin to stained
glass and batik. The borders
give the pictures a folklorish
look, in which the animals are
both playful and somewhat
magical. Her favorite animals
are bears. She works here, too.
*316 E. Lake. (616) 347-5199.
Open daily, year-round.*

Justin Rashid has built American Spoon Foods into a highly regarded maker of gourmet sauces, condiments, and fruit toppings, based largely on Michigan-grown fruit, herbs, and mushrooms.

◆ **Symons General Store**. A
friendly gourmet grocery in a
charmingly cluttered old storefront with high tin ceilings.
There's a good wine and cheese
selection, plus breads, muffins,
deli items, and imports and
Michigan products for gift baskets. . Three breads are baked
everyday are blue cheese sourdough, cheddar cheese vegetable, and goat cheese/dried
tomato/pesto wholewheat. *401
E. Lake at Howard. (616) 347-
2438. Open daily; in summer,
open evenings. &: call.*

◆ **Whistling Moose Studios.**

The natural northwoods theme is done with sincerity and simplicity here in the studio/gallery of John and Hanni Yothers. He makes boats — canoes hanging from the ceiling, boat models, and more. She makes handbuilt stoneware and porcelain plates, mugs, and functional things in a pleasant pinetree pattern. The boat that launched this business — a 38-foot sailboat John built, which so impressed a partner that he helped them buy this building — is stored in a barn. The energy required by the business means the boat has hardly been in the water. Other interesting nature-inspired handcrafts and jewelry round out the gallery: beaded and other jewelry, wooden boxes, wildlife carvings and prints, cards, baskets, gourds, and functional pottery. By the way, this shop pre-dates The Quiet Moose, that heavily advertised decorator studio on the way to Charlevoix. *209 Howard. (616) 347-5281. Open daily, year-round.*

◆ **Gattles**. Custom linens for the carriage trade — for instance, here you could have pillowcases embroidered to match your wallpaper. Also, ladies nightwear. In 1996, Gattles expanded by moving to its new location with more floor space. In past years when they put out a catalog, they had a big mail-order clientele for unusual merchandise and services. *210 Howard. (616) 347-3982.* ♿

◆ **Great Lakes Design**. Geared to informal summer residences. A good deal of hand-decorated furniture. Each year features a changing array of unusual accents, hand-painted in Mexico in folk art styles: colorful flower and fruit designs on large plates, blue and white bathroom ceramics in a loose, informal pattern, from $20 toothbrush and towel holders to a lavatory basin. *406 Bay (also in Harbor Springs). (616) 347-9831.* ♿

◆ **American Spoon Foods.** Justin Rashid's highly regarded company is Michigan's biggest culinary success story. Its nationally famed fruit preserves and all-fruit, no-sugar spreads concentrate the natural-fruit taste by using top ingredients and minimizing sugar. They're on the pricey side (roughly $5.25 for a 9-ounce jar), but they are souvenir gifts with cachet. Until a few years ago, the shop here doubled as the kitchen, where everything was produced. A greatly expanded product line now includes condiments, pasta sauces, salad dressings, and more, devised by chef/co-owner Larry Forgione, in addition to Michigan-grown fruit toppings. Small bottles of concentrated Salad Dazzlers will go a long way to enliven the blandest, dullest food. The company has added fruit butters (blueberry, pineapple-passion fruit, mango) and a line of vinaigrettes. On the counter: a vast array of opened jars for sampling. If there's anything you'd like to try and it's not open, just ask. Most popular: sugar-free sour cherry spoon fruit. Other big sellers: dried cherries, strawberry preserves, and smoky Southwest Salsa, rated in the *New York Times* top four salsas. Also for sale: pretty birchbark gift baskets, evocative prints of Northern Michigan scenes by artist Kristin Hurlin, and more. *411 E. Lake, almost at Park Avenue. (616) 347-1739.* &

♦ **Horizon Books**. Large branch of the Traverse City bookstore also has a good selection of better magazines. *319 E. Mitchell. (616) 347-2590. Open daily 9 a.m.-9 p.m.* &

To get to the Gaslight District, follow signs from U.S. 31 to downtown. Large parking lots are at the foot of Bay Street and between Bay and Lake just east of the tracks. But <u>come by 10 in summer for easy parking</u>. Get a free parking map from the Chamber of Commerce (p. 634).

FOR A PLEASANT LUNCH BREAK . . . . . treat yourself to a meal in the elegant bayview dining room of the **Perry Hotel** on Bay at Lewis. The big old brick building, directly across from the old train station and the tracks, has been beautifully restored by area restaurateur Stafford Smith. Its new exterior paint scheme brings out its architectural detail. . . . . . Or you could make up a picnic lunch from the imported cheeses, deli items, and fresh-baked muffins and sourdough bread at **Symons General Store**, Lake at Howard. (See page 635) . . . . . Picnic spots: the **waterfront park** (get there safely by finding the tunnel under U.S. 31 down from the intersection of Bay and Petoskey streets) or **Pennsylvania Park**.

A SHADY DOWNTOWN PARK . . . . . is alongside the railroad tracks that define the Gaslight District's eastern edge. **Pennsylvania Park** runs between Mitchell and Lake. It has benches, picnic tables, and a gazebo where **summer band concerts** are held Tuesdays and Fridays at 12:15 and Tuesdays at 7 p.m. between June thru late August. Restrooms and pay phones are across the tracks at the Chamber of Commerce, Mitchell at Howard.

MOVIES IN PETOSKEY . . . . The **Gaslight Cinema** at 302 Petoskey, down the hill at the Gaslight District's west and, has five screens for has five screens for first-run movies. Call (616) 347-3480 for program information. **Children's Saturday matinees** are a regular feature. . . . . . The **Petoskey Film Theatre** screens art films on Friday and Saturday night and Sunday afternoon at the McCune Arts Center, 461 E. Mitchell. Each series (spring, fall, and winter) of films last about two months. (616) 347-4337. &

Bay View

*A charming, peaceful 19th-century religious resort
that keeps its special atmosphere.*

THIS REMARKABLE colony of 438 cottages and 28 public buildings overlooks Traverse Bay just east of Petoskey. Most of the cottages were built before 1900, and the resort, with its big trees and winding lanes, retains the aura of an earlier era. Michigan Methodists organized Bay View in 1875 as a place for summer camp meetings. Initially a tent camp, it grew within 20 years to included elaborate cottages, a hotel, chapel, and eventually a fine library. Famous speakers at Bay View have included William Jennings Bryan and Booker T. Washington.

Camp meetings came out of the Second Great Awakening of early 19th century America. It ignited the fires of religious fervor and swept across much of the new nation, typically on frontiers. Methodists and other groups encouraged camp meetings, often in the woods, as ways "to come together for religious refreshment and revival." They were especially concerned about establishing an atmosphere conductive for their children to have conversion experiences.

Earlier Methodist summer camps had been established in the East. Bay View was the very first formally organized summer colony in the logged-off North Woods of Michigan. Unlike earlier East Coast summer camps, Bay View adopted a romantic, curving street plan instead of a geometric grid or circle. In her remarkable *Buildings of Michigan*, architectural historian Kathryn Eckert writes, the plan "exagger[ates] the site's rugged topography to get a sense of other-worldliness — all to aid relaxation and religious feeling."

Bay View's influence was enormous. When later associations of Midwestern businessmen planned Wequetonsing and Harbor Point in nearby Harbor Springs, for instance, they carefully studied the Bay View model — its common spaces and community buildings and its paths and roads.

Bay View cottages were built on a series of natural terraces, those ancient beach lines created by higher lake levels in eras when glacial meltwaters were gradually receding. The Methodist founders were not wealthy people. The first houses were tents and simple 12' by 16' cabins. By the 1890s, prosperity had enabled property owners to enlarge their cabins in style, with big front additions. The Queen Anne style is dominant, with lots of gingerbread trim on wide porches across the front, and on small second-story porches above.

Evelyn Hall, one of Bay View's meeting areas, was built in 1890 by the Women's Christian Temperance Union. Bay View today continues the extensive summer programming that started in the Chautauqua tradition of spiritual uplift and educational enlightenment.

All cottages originally had views of the bay, now blocked by trees. Many of them face away from the drives, so to really experience Bay View, you should get out and walk across the central campus. (Parking spaces are plentiful along most drives.) Don't miss the impressive, wonderfully complex **Evelyn Hall** from 1891.

"The spiritual atmosphere of Bay View has always been highly moralistic, with a stern interdiction of Demon Rum, cardplaying, dancing, and other fleshly pursuits," wrote the late John Rauch, a longtime observer and chronicler of the area's resort history. "Sundays were dedicated to worship and everyone attended three services. . . . As late as 1910, no deliveries in Bay View or other traffic was permitted to disturb the pious Sabbath. There was much hymn singing and prayer meetings on weekday nights."

Today's Bay View is considerably more relaxed, and its social tone has become far more luxurious than the old days Rauch remembered. Just about half of the current residents are Methodists, some of them the sixth generation descendants of original Bay View summer residents. Members of the Bay View Association have taken great care to preserve the community's

Victorian look. Cottage owners are required to get association approval for even minor exterior changes. Residents own their own cottages (costing from $40,000 to $200,000) but lease their land from the association. Bay View is occupied only from May through October, although two inns are open year-round.

Days are filled with courses, sports, lectures, plays, and concerts, just as they were in the colony's early years. A small but select summer school of music attracts gifted musicians from around the country. The 2,000-seat auditorium is where **concerts** are held at 8 p.m Wednesday and Sunday. To receive a free program of services, vespers, concerts, and events open to the public, call (616) 347-6225. Daily events schedules are published in each day's *Petoskey News-Review*. A **museum** on the main campus in the two oldest buildings is open beginning in July and August from noon to 1 on Sundays, and 2:30-4:30 Wednesdays.

A popular place for visitors to stay and eat is **Stafford's Bay View Inn** close to Little Traverse Bay. Less fancy, quieter, and more in the original spirit of Bay View is the **Terrace Inn**, facing the central campus. Two bed-and-breakfasts are in vintage rooming houses.

The main part of Bay View is just south of U.S. 31 on the eastern edge of Petoskey. Encampment Drive takes you to the central campus. To reach the Bay View main campus from Petoskey, take U.S. 31 past the S curve by the train tracks and turn south (right) on Fairview Avenue. Take it to the T intersection. The campus is just ahead of you. Park anywhere. For information on summer concerts, plays, or events, call the Bay View business office at (616) 347-6225.

RENT MOUNTAIN BIKES, CROSS COUNTRY SKIS, SNOWSHOES, AND MORE
. . . . at **Adventure Sports**, 1100 Bay View Road east of Bay View. Prices are reasonable ($20/day for a mountain bike and helmet), and the staff can advise you on the many good trails and routes in the area. Open daily in summer and ski season. (616) 347-3041.

A PAVED BICYCLE PATH WITH A BEAUTIFUL VIEW, ... especially spectacular at sunset, runs along side Little Traverse Bay east 1 1/2 miles from Bayfront Park. It passes through **Bay View** and eventually meets with U.S. 31 as a parallel off-road trail. . . . . If you take back roads through quiet neighborhoods near the water for about half a mile, you can connect up with another link of the bike trail that will, in the future, go all the way **to Harbor Springs**. The second link is a mile, off-road trail parallel to M-119 that goes to **Petoskey State Park**.

Petoskey State Park

Convenient to upscale resort towns, it has a woodsy setting, scenic beach, dunes, and a wonderful bay view.

PETOSKEY STATE PARK manages to combine convenience of location and facilities with a wonderful natural atmosphere in only 305 acres. It enjoys a choice site among and behind the wooded dunes at the funnel-like end of Little Traverse Bay. The mile-long **beach** not only has soft sand but a fabulous view of nearby Harbor Springs and Petoskey in the distance. The shoreline frames the setting sun for spectacular sunsets, followed by the twinkling town lights reflected in the water.

Be forewarned, however, that sometimes west winds across the funnel-shaped bay concentrate all sorts of floating refuse from boats right here. Parks employees clean up regularly, but it can occasionally be a problem.

There's a **concession stand**, **bathhouse**, and **playground**. The parking lot is big enough to handle demand on all but the hottest days of the year. There's plenty of room to walk down the beach and get away from crowds. If you're lucky, you may be able to find a Petoskey stone along the south end of the beach, among the stones and gravel.

It's gorgeous in fall here. A mix of hardwoods makes for especially rich colors contrasting with the conifers' dark green and the white paper bark of birch trees.

A stand of big pines gives the **picnic area** in a hollow behind the dunes its own special aura. It's deeply shady, unlike the open beach, and filled with piney scents and scampering chipmunks.

The two **campgrounds** nestled in wooded dunes behind the beach manage to offer 178 sites and 2 mini-cabins with modern amenities (electrical hookups and showers) while retaining a good deal of privacy and a wonderful, woodsy feel.

Two trail loops start by the campground registration office. At the .7-mile **Old Baldy Trail**, a stairway climbs steeply up into heavily wooded dunes for a spectacular view of the bay through the trees. When you climb the dunewalk stairs into the rustling, dark, cool forest of pines and maples, you feel remote from the traffic along 119's commercial strip half a mile away. The much easier 2.7-mile **Portage Trail** goes through lower dunes to Lake Michigan and a little inland lake. It's recommended for **cross-country skiing** in winter.

For more of a real wilderness experience, Wilderness State Park (page 657) and the Bliss Township beach (page 658) are not too terribly far away — about 35 miles north on county road 81. But for combining natural beauty and convenience to two of northern Michigan's most attractive old resort communities, Petoskey State Park is tops.

The park is at 2475 Harbor-Petoskey Rd. (U.S. 119) about 1 1/2 miles north of U.S. 31, 4 miles east of Petoskey and about 8 miles east of Harbor Springs. (616) 347-2311. Reservations: (800) 543-2YES. Although the park is open year-round, the campground is only open from April 1 to December 1 with running water and flush toilets shut off in April, May, and November. ♿: *picnic tables, picnic shelters, toilets, and showers. State park sticker required: $4/day or $20/year. Camping $14/night.*

A BEAUTIFUL FARM STAND WITH A GORGEOUS VIEW . . . . . Take Petoskey's main drag, Mitchell Street, up the hill and east about three miles to **Bill's Farm Market**. (This is a great low-traffic way to I-75; just stay on C-58 until the Wolverine exit.) Here, arranged with an artist's eye, are all the basics and a lot more – miniature vegetables grown for restaurants like the Stafford's group and Tapawingo; 25 kinds of squash, including the delicious Sweet Dumpling; and finger-size ears of sweet corn that are edible. *445 Mitchell Road. (616) 347-6735. Open mid-June through mid-December, Mon-Fri 9-6, Sat 9-5, closed Sun.* ♿

A SCENIC DRIVE TO HORTON BAY . . . . . takes in Hemingway lore. Take U.S. 31 west out of Petoskey toward Charlevoix along Little Traverse Bay. In four or five miles, look for Horton Bay Road (C-71), which goes due south to the old lumbering village of **Horton Bay** (population 39) on Lake Charlevoix. . . . . . Just after the lumbering era's end, young Ernest Hemingway used to walk from his family's cottage on Walloon Lake to fish and hunt near the Point at Horton Bay. The classic **Horton Bay General Store** (616-582-7827), where he sometimes stopped, is well supplied with Hemingway memorabilia along with groceries and a lunch counter. ♿: ramp to not-very -wide side door. . . . . . Several of **Hemingway's Nick Adams stories** are set in and around Horton Bay. Its little church was where Hemingway married Hadley Richardson of St. Louis, another resorter. Three popular restaurants kept Horton Bay alive when lumbering was gone. Today it owes its fame to its weird and wonderful **Fourth of July** parade, a totally home-made affair that attracts some 14,000 spectators.

Harbor Springs

*The Midwest's most exclusive old resort area
has an interesting downtown, lovely resort colonies,
and wonderful views of bay, town, and woods.*

THIS FAMOUS old resort town — "the Newport of the Middle
West" — still manages to hold onto its great physical beauty
and small-town charm. This remains true despite the vastly
increased development, in the 1970s and 1980s, of nearby second
homes, golf and ski resorts and the resulting new intensity of retail
activity. Harbor Springs lacks the disturbing sense of development
gone rampant. It has avoided the four-story condo complexes in
Charlevoix and the busy fast-food strips abutting Bay View and
Petoskey.

East Bluff Drive still has a stunningly picturesque view.
Overlooking the turn-of-the-century downtown, you see a crescent
harbor full of sailboats and, on the point, a leafy, lovely summer cottage colony and lighthouse. To the east, in the century-old resort
association of Wequetonsing, a stately parade of large, picture-perfect summer homes have gracious verandas looking out across
flower-bordered lawns and paths to the sailboats on Little Traverse
Bay. There are extensive areas of golf course, woods, and wetlands
along the main entrance to Harbor Springs from Petoskey, buffering
the east edge of town from development. Many of the wooded areas
are now public preserves that have been donated to the **Little
Traverse Conservancy** (see page 652) by individual landowners, or
bought with Conservancy funds.

At the height of the season in July and August, downtown traffic and crowds can spoil the tranquil aura of the place. Some people
prefer the quieter times — midweek in summer, or in the morning,
or any time in the lovely spring and fall. Winter bustles again with
skiers who come to the two ski slopes built on the dramatic, steep
hills north of town the **Boyne Highlands** ski resort (616-526-2171)
on Highlands Drive or **Nub's Nob Ski Area** (616-526-2131) on
Pleasantview Road.

Downtown Harbor Springs still has enough old-timey places
with character to maintain the leisurely, civilized sociability of an
old resort town. To see it in action, stop for coffee and doughnuts
between 9 and 10 a.m. at Mary Ellen's lunch counter and magazine
stand on Main Street. The plywood magazine racks and general
ambiance are straight out of the 1940s. Here you'll witness a conge-

❶ Bluff Gardens. (p. 652) Fancy farm market with choice tiny vegetables, jams and jellies & a huge stock of peasanty, gay Quimper earthenware.

❷ East Bluff Drive (p. 651). Best view of the charming downtown and harbor is from this stairway between the high school on bluff and Spring St. down below.

❸ Downtown shops (p. 646). Attractive retail area with pricey resortwear and traditional clothing. Creative surprises in handcrafts and home accessories.

❹ Hoover Flower Shop (p. 651). Cut flowers, plants, and dried arrangements for stately summer homes come from these colorful fields and greenhouses.

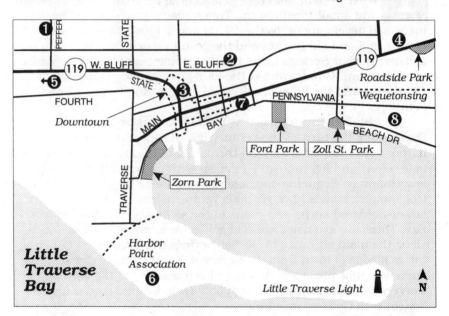

❺ Tunnel of Trees (p. 656). Twisting highway along Lake Michigan is one of the state's most scenic drives.

❻ Harbor Point. No outsiders allowed at this elite summer colony favored by old Detroit and Lansing money. Only horses provide summer transportation.

❼ Blackbird Museum (p. 649). The Indian postmaster built this post office in 1876. Curator Veronica Medicine tells about the traditional life of local Odawa.

❽ Wequetonsing (p. 650). Glimpse traditional resort life of the affluent. There's sailing, golf, flowers, drinks on the veranda — at this grand old cottage colony.

Highlights of
Harbor Springs

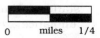

0   miles   1/4

Holy Childhood Church at the head of Main Street was erected by the Indian mission that was the basis of the first permanent settlement at Harbor Springs. The present church was intentionally sited as the street's focal point, getting around the wishes of resorters to straighten the street and reduce the Catholics' visual impact on the town.

nial coffee klatsch that includes all spheres of permanent residents, from natives to "trust-fund babies."

Harbor Springs' identity as the Midwest's premiere resort community began just five years after the railroad first arrived at Petoskey in 1873. Lumber, the main freight of Northern Michigan railroads, was running out, and the railroads aggressively promoted the area's recreational virtues to hayfever sufferers and wealthy Midwestern families escaping hot summers at home.

The success of nearby Bay View (page 638) inspired the formation of two resort associations in Harbor Springs, Harbor Point and Wequetonsing. (Its local nickname is pronounced WEE-kwee.) Both were tonier and more fun-loving than earnest, education-minded Bay View. But both were patterned after the Methodist colony in that the associations own the land and approve the cottage owners. That control gives resort colonies like these a century-old visual and social continuity that's almost unheard of in fast-changing American society, where suburbs can boom and decline within a generation.

A much earlier group of residents are the Ottawa (Odawa) Indians, who moved into the area between Harbor Springs and Cross Village in the 1700s and remain here, in diminished numbers, today. The Odawa were able to hold on to these villages while Indians in the more desirable farmlands of southern Michigan were forcibly moved west by the U.S. government in the 1840s. Wealthy Harbor Springs resorters and tourists actually helped maintain the local Odawa community during the early 20th century by buying the famous quillwork and crafts.

The old resort families hailed from big Midwestern cities where technical know-how of German immigrants had combined with Yankee enterprise to create great manufacturing fortunes in the decades during and after the Civil War. Townspeople protect the privacy of the famous old families who come here — they include some automotive Fords, some glass-making Fords of Toledo, and some Gambles of Proctor & Gamble — while they readily divulge the presence of newcomers like Detroit Piston Bill Laimbeer and rock star Bob Seger, all of whom have second homes in the newer areas just outside Harbor Springs.

Highlights of the Harbor Spring area include:

◆ **Downtown shopping.** *Downtown is centered along two blocks of Main St. between State and Gardner, with an increasing number of shops on Bay and on the adjoining three blocks of State.* **Parking lots** *along Third and Bay.* **Seasonal hours.** *Summer hours: daily from 9 or 10 a.m. to 5 or 5:30 p.m. and often into the evening. Many stores stay open Sundays through fall color season.*

The delightful, small-scale historic storefronts and cottages, combined with the choice merchandise and some fresh ideas, make for pleasant browsing in Harbor Springs. Many of the familiar, upper-end resort retailers in Northern Michigan have shops here, but what makes Harbor Springs stand out are an unusual number of individualistic galleries and specialty shops. Antiques, home accessories, and clothing especially are worth seeking out. Stores change from summer to summer; high rents and a short season make for high turnover.

Main Street's year-round businesses are centered in the main business block east of the major intersection with State. Here they are listed from west to east. At **Hilda of Harbor** (just west of State at 107 W. Main; 616-526-9613) clothing is art, but practical, too, often with a fashionably folkish look: Giesswein Austrian loden coats made to stand up to cold weather for decades; Linda Lundstrom's four-season theme coats from Canada; sheared beaver hats; unusual Coogi sweaters from Australia in fabulous random textures; and Gay Ellis's Polartec Lapland-look Samii line. Hilda's is for women and kids; adjoining **Eager Beaver** has similar look of clothing for men. Both have shoes and boots. **Huzza** *(136 E. Main; 616-526-6914)* creates a smart, eclectic style that plays off good contemporary design with antiques and freely painted earthenware in its mix of interior decor, tabletop accessories, expensive and simple women's clothing, and gifts. In the sale room, the same top-quality clothes are more affordable.

Between the Covers *(152 E. Main; 616-526-6658)* book store offers good browsing, a cozy, literate atmosphere, an excellent regional section, and even a backyard terrace with seats. Service is informed and personal, and the selection is much more discriminating than the usual resort bookshop. *Open daily 9:30-9:30, Sun 10-4 in July & August; otherwise open Mon-Sat 10-5, Sun in color season.* **The Coyote Woman** gallery *(160 E. Main; 616-526-5889)* makes nearly every list of noteworthy shops with its mix of Southwest and contemporary art, jewelry (in sterling silver and 14-karat gold, often with semi-precious stones), and accessories like pottery, Navajo rugs, and sculptural works in stone, bronze, and raku pottery. Along with the strong Southwest element are local artists like Chuck Parsons, well-known for his scenes and abstract images. Stop in for a **brochure** of Harbor Springs' seven other year-round galleries.

By the Bay (172 E. Main, 616-526-3964) has a broad, deep, and discriminating selection of nautical and lighthouse things: art (not just up-north, but Detroit and East Coast scenes), books, maps, sculptures, antiques, the requisite brass instruments and artifacts, and jewelry.

Some alleyways and back entrances lead to a pretty courtyard between Main and Bay. More shops face Bay — a pleasant walk, with the marina and city park on the street's other side, and sailboats in the bay. **Mercado Imports** (131 E. Bay) has a fresh look with its wide-ranging Latin American folk art and sterling silver jewelry. **Birds on the Bay** (137 E. Bay; 616-526-5039) has a vast variety of birdhouses and feeders.

In the 200 block of East Main, most shops are summer-only, from June through August — too bad, because fall is such a pleasant time to visit the area, and many of these shops in converted houses and small storefronts are delightful.

A core of old-line Harbor Springs institutions have managed to escape escalating rents by owning their buildings. **Cassidy Hardware** *(135 E. Main; 616-526-24441)* is a classic, with wood fixtures, squeaky floors, and all sorts of paraphernalia for wild birds. **Hovey's Pharmacy** *(205 E. Main; 616-526-5971)* displays interesting historic photos by its entrance. **Gurney's Harbor Bottle Shop** *(215 E. Main; 616- 526-5472)* is known for its wonderful sandwiches, thick stacks of roast beef or ham with a distinctive sauce on a fresh homemade bun. Order a half-sandwich (with half the meat) so you can get your mouth around it. **Mary Ellen's Place** *(145 E. Main;*

The block of summer shops in downtown Harbor Springs has some delightful, quirky nooks like the courtyard leading to Tom's Mom's Cookies.

616-526-5591) is a newsstand and soda fountain that's the premiere local institution for keeping up with everyone in town. It's a fine spot for an inexpensive snack in this pricey town. Summer residents have their personal cubbyholes for their hometown papers. The **Harbor Springs Library** *(616-526-2531)* is upstairs on Main at Spring; enter around the corner at 206 Spring. It's open daily in summer, otherwise most afternoons and Saturday mornings. This light-filled, comfortable, old-fashioned space has a fine view of the harbor. There you can browse through back copies of the *Harbor Light* weekly newspaper, a literate, leisurely chronicle of town and resort life. It's an all-too-rare continuation of the tradition of serious small-town journalism.

Several unusual shops you might miss are on North State near the bend at the bluff. At the nonsensically named **Pooter Olooms** , owner Jenny Feldman and manager Anne-Gaelle Maizeray buy bare pine and colorfully painted country antique furniture in France, Austria, and Scandinavia. (More furniture is at a second location down the street.) These pieces form the basis of an inspired assemblage of collector quilts, garden sculpture, and folk art, antique and contemporary. The folk art, both naive and sophisticated, often has a spiritual aspect and occasionally verges on the darkly mysterious. It includes a lot of tramp art purchased in Europe, idiosyncratic one-of-a-kind pieces, and work from a dozen gallery regulars. This includes Kim Nicolas's vases and candlesticks and lamps made of Michigan stones, embellished with woven willow or hickory; Kelli Sniveley's muted paintings incorporating postage stamps like religious icons; Liz Galbraith's elegant lampshades of Japanese-style paper she makes; and North Creek Creations — fish, birdhouses, and other primitives made by a family that home schools in Northern Michigan. *339 N. State; (616) 526-6101) Open daily year-round.*

Behind Pooter Olooms, **Primitive Images** (616-526-9026) show-cases the owner-made birch and twig furniture and interesting lamps with woven shades. Toward town, **Boyer Glassworks** *(207 N. State; 616-526-6359)* features Harry Boyer's handblown glass vases, paper-weights, and ornaments, plus his wife's paintings and some less expensive crafts and jewelry. Boyer's glass earrings are striking. Harry Boyer was close to the 1970s beginnings of the contemporary art glass movement in Toledo. Visitors can watch him at work.

♦ **Holy Childhood Catholic Church and School.** This striking complex — a simple, Gothic clapboard church and adjacent three-story brick school — is the direct descendant of the Catholic Indian mission that was the basis of the first permanent settlement at Harbor Springs. French Catholic missionaries had converted area Indians in the 1700s. In 1823, residents in the nearby Ottawa vil-lage of L'Arbre Croche asked the U.S. government to send them a Catholic missionary. By 1833 the mission had become the largest Indian mission in the northern U.S. Franciscans took over in 1886 and built a large school and dormitory for Indian students. Indians today resent such institutions because they did so much to weaken Indian families. *150 W. Main. 616- 526-2017. Masses at 8 a.m. weekdays, 5:30 & 7 p.m. Sat., 9:30 and 11 a.m. Sun, year-round.*

♦ **Andrew Blackbird Museum.** Odawa chief Andrew Blackbird start-ed Harbor Springs' first post office in his kitchen here in 1862. Indians held the paid government jobs in Harbor Springs' early years. But as whites moved in, they took over the Indians' positions. When they claimed Blackbird's house couldn't handle the volume of mail, he built the adjoining storefront. But he lost his job anyway. Blackbird continued his career as a writer and lecturer. His works and some possessions are on display, along with various stone points, baskets, and Indian clothing from here and elsewhere. Now the Little Traverse Bay Band has taken over the museum. Changing exhibits explore other aspects of their culture. The collection of beau-tiful Odawa birchbark boxes covered with dyed porcupine quills is a point of pride. *368 E. Main, next to the Shay hexagon house. 616-526-7731. Mem.-Labor Day: Mon-Sat 10-5, Sun 12-5. Weekends in color season. Otherwise by appt; call the band at 616-348-3410. &: call. $1.*

♦ **Shay House.** This odd hexagonal house with projecting hexago-nal wings (1892) illustrates the inventive mind of its owner and designer, Ephraim Shay. In 1881 he had invented a revolutionary new locomotive. Small and versatile, it enabled narrow-gauge track to be laid easily to remote mines and stands of timber. The Shay locomotive made logging much more efficient — so efficient, in fact, that Northern Michigan's forests, considered so vast they would last a thousand years, were nearly gone by 1910.

In his adopted home town of Harbor Springs, Shay devised an early household water system and experimented with steel-hulled boats. The pleasant, light-filled house, sheathed inside and out with embossed metal in many patterns, is now used as offices. Visitors are welcome in the lobby. *373 E. Main.*

◆ **Harbor area.** Many sailboats and a grand view of the Harbor Point lighthouse and Little Traverse Bay behind it make this harbor exceptionally picturesque. The waterfront park has many benches, a small **local museum** with limited hours, restrooms, and a small **swimming beach** west of the piers and State Street. A boat ramp is just east of the **Irish Boat Shop**, which even has a staff sailmaker. A board sail ramp is at the foot of Zoll Street, east almost at Wequetonsing.

◆ **Wequetonsing.** Unlike many other exclusive summer colonies, Wequetonsing (pronounced WEE-kwee-TON-sing) isn't a gated enclave that's off-limits to the public in summer. It gives you a rare glimpse of the living continuation of a very leisurely, very private, very privileged summer world. Routines for some are generations old. One older banker habitually enjoys a newspaper with breakfast, then spends an hour on the phone with his private secretary back home. Backgammon is at 10, then lunch at the club, followed by golf and bridge, shopping, or a fashion show for his wife. Cocktails on the veranda are followed by dinner, often at the club, and then to bed.

For townspeople and retirees, it can be an education to work for these old guard families, usually so charming and considerate in their private lives. Teams of summer workers start opening the vacation homes in May and June, painting and repairing, grooming the perfect lawns, installing bedding plants. Then eight hectic weeks in the service of the resorters: cleaning, cooking, shopping, and serving. After Labor Day, a deep collective sigh — of relief and regret that the whole magical show is over for another season.

Wequetonsing was laid out on the Bay View plan, with a common activity building (the casino), playgrounds, and tennis courts clustered along Second Avenue between Pennsylvania and Central. The golf course is across the Petoskey Road. The bayside houses grew grand and showy, but simpler places, closely spaced, line the pedestrian walkways that lead back from the water. Just to the

The pretty summer resort of Wequetonsing, just east of Harbor Springs, was established by Presbyterians from Allegan, Michigan, and Elkhart, Indiana, so that "worn-out and sweltering humanity could repair to recover health and enjoy rational recreations." The most impressive houses (left) face Little Traverse Bay, while smaller cottages line pedestrian walks (right).

west is town. To the east and north of Wequetonsing, along Beach Road, are a series of wooded **nature preserves**, open to the public, interlaced with paths and boardwalks. The spring wildflowers are beautiful, but the trails are often wet. Parking is by the A.C. Fischer Preserve sign. *To reach the nature preserves and Wequetonsing from town, take Main or Bay east to Zoll, go south to the shore and turn left onto Beach Drive. To take a scenic, slow alternate route from 119 and Petoskey, look for Powell Road to your right about 2 miles north of U.S. 31. As soon as you pass it, look for the inconspicuous Beach Drive to your left. Turn onto it and take it into town.*

◆ **Hoover Flower Shop.** Fresh-cut and dried flowers, bedding plants, and shrubs for the carriage trade are supplied from these five greenhouses and five acres of fields. Fields are filled with color in July and August. You can buy dried flowers and grasses by the piece. The color range of dried sweetheart roses (75¢/stem, reduced in spring) may be unequaled. *M-119 (Petoskey Rd.) just east of Harbor Springs. (616) 526-2992. Open May through mid-October and Thanksgiving to Christmas.*

◆ **East Bluff Drive.** This part of Bluff Drive boasts a splendid view of town and bay, along with Harbor Springs' most elaborate non-resort Victorian houses. A stairway descends from the high school up on the bluff down to Spring Street. *State east to Arbor.*

◆ **Bluff Gardens.** A produce stand catering to the entertaining
needs of Harbor Point and Wequetonsing resorters has evolved into
a purveyor of homemade fancy foods, sold at this glorified farm
market and by catalog. There are jams, dressings, and relishes
(about $4 an 8-ounce jar). Even the tiny carrots and beets are dis-
played like jewels in the carpeted sales area. Bluff Gardens' pride is
its stock of Quimper, the French earthenware famous for its peasanty motifs in blue, yellow, and red-orange. *721 W. Lake. From
downtown Harbor Springs, take State up the hill to West Bluff (M-
119). In about a mile turn right onto Peffer, then left onto Lake. (616)
526-5571.*

◆ **"Tunnel of Trees"** (M-119) to Bliss Township Park and
Wilderness State Park. *See page 656.*

◆ **Thorne Swift Nature Preserve and Beach.** These 30 acres of
beautiful beach, dunes, and fragrant cedar swamp have been
donated for use as a park and nature center. A **dune stair and
overlook** offer close-up looks at pioneer dune plants, and a
panoramic view of the bay. The small swimming **beach**, seldom
crowded, is reached by a 1/4-mile trail. **Boardwalks** pass shallow-
rooted cedars leaning crazily in the swamp for a surreal effect. The
wonderful cedar aroma makes this a special destination. So do the
outstanding interpretive signs and pamphlets for three short nature
trails. Naturalist-rangers give **scheduled guided tours** and are
often around to field casual questions. Call to arrange a nature
walk anytime in summer. *Lower Shore Dr. 3 1/2 miles west of
Harbor Springs. Take M-119 to Lower Shore Dr. (616) 526-6401.
Open daily Mem.-Labor Day 10 a.m.-sunset; weekends Sept. & Oct.
Call for permission to enter other times. $2/car for non-residents.*

THE BEST BEACHES. . . . . if you like the away-from-it-all mood and natural,
windswept dune environment, are at **Bliss Township Park** and **Wilderness
State Park** on Sturgeon Bay, north of Cross Village. See pages 657-8. The beach
at **Thorne-Swift Nature Preserve** (above) is natural, close to Harbor Springs,
but small.

FOR A MINI-GUIDE TO NATURE PRESERVES . . . . . some dozen in all, stop by
or call the **Little Traverse Conservancy** outside Harbor Springs. (616) 347-
0991. The office is open weekdays 8-5. It's just off the Harbor Springs-Petoskey
Road (M-119) at 3264 Powell Road on the north shore of Round Lake, at the
headwaters of the Inland Water Route to Lake Huron. There's a self-guided

brochure to a short trail near the lake, a good area for spring wildflowers, birds — and mosquitoes. Other good-size preserves are near Harbor Springs, on Burt Lake, on the lower Pigeon River (where a cabin can be rented by groups), and near Lake Charlevoix. . . . . A **complete directory** to all Conservancy preserves — all open to the public — is $10 at the office, $12 by mail.

FOR A DOWN-TO-EARTH CONTRAST TO HARBOR SPRINGS. . . . . take U.S. 31 to Alanson on the Inland Waterway, visit **Bob's Place** restaurant (it draws folks from all around), the excellent **Dutch Oven** bakery and yarn shop, or **Spanky's** snack bar, with a nice deck overlooking the waterway at the swing bridge. To see the waterway, turn east onto River in the center of Alanson. A little park with a dock is across from Spanky's. You can come upon some interesting, offbeat shops in and around Alanson. . . . . West of Alanson, the **Oden State Fish Hatchery** in Oden is right off U.S. 31 across from Crooked Lake. Interpretive signs tell about what fish are being reared there. . . . . Going to Mackinaw City, U.S. 31 shows you a slice of life in the real northern Michigan that is as much trailers and roadside bars and welfare as it is condos and marinas and art galleries.

THE INLAND WATERWAY. . . . . Indians used the Inland Water Route through interconnected Crooked Lake, Burt Lake, and Mullet Lake to get from Little Traverse Bay to Lake Huron. Later, little steamers took resorters to their summer cottages on the lakes. Today navigation ends at Crooked Lake, just a few miles from Lake Michigan. It's a popular route for power boaters — often *too* popular, if you enjoy quiet — and most of the route is lined with cottages. . . . . A good deal of the way between Crooked Lake and Burt Lake is pretty and natural, full of wildlife, especially in the morning, before the boaters are out in force. Rentals of fishing boats, pontoons, and ski boats are available from the nice people at **Ryde Marine** (616-347-8273), a mile south of Alanson off U.S. 31. Look for the sign. They can point out visitor highlights on Burt Lake or sell you a little guide.

Legs Inn

North of Harbor Springs, the pinnacle of Michigan rustic folk architecture is also a warm Polish restaurant

THE NORTH WOODS is full of inspired folk-art creations. None is more improbable than Legs Inn in Cross Village, along the Lake Michigan shore 20 miles north of Harbor Springs. It's a Polish restaurant and bar created by Stanley Smolak, who came from Poland as a young man to work in a Detroit auto factory. He got to know the Odawa Indians in Cross Village, which in the 1920s was still a living center of the Odawa culture. What fascinated Smolak was the Odawas' close connection with nature, and the intimate linking of the material and spiritual worlds.

In the late 1920s Smolak started work on the inn. It grew in stages to encompass many moods and environments. What's seen from the road verges on ugly. There's no landscaping to soften the busy exterior façade of small, irregular fieldstones, accented by totem poles and a fanciful row of curved upside-down stove legs on the roof (hence the "Legs" of the name). Hand-painted lettering on piled-up boulders advertises "BEER, LIQUORS, SOUVENIRS, DRiftWOOD."

The interior is far more compelling. The barroom is dark and grotto-like, easy to pass over on your way to the restaurant in the rear. After your eyes are acclimated to the dark, you'll make all sorts of discoveries. Phone booths are made of hollowed-out trees. A lacey, tangled lattice of shellacked roots above the balcony disappears into the dark. Faces and figures seem like spirits emerging from branches and roots. This blend of the rustic and picturesque with touches of the grotesque hearkens back to a pre-Christian style still found in the mountains of Switzerland and Central Europe. The restaurant's picture windows overlook a beautiful rear terrace with outside dining, pines, and a cheerful flower-filled rock garden, the passion of George Smolak, Stanley's nephew. He gave up his engineering career to revive this unique place ten years ago with his wife Kathy. In the distance is Lake Michigan; on the north horizon stretch the low islands off Waugoshance Point, eighty miles north. Legs Inn is a popular spot on summer evenings at sunset. Children can run around the extensive grounds and play while their parents linger over dinner and dessert. Sunday from 4 to 8, there's music in the garden — maybe contemporary guitar, maybe singalongs.

The restaurant's atmosphere is cheerful and warm. There's a

big stone fireplace and interlacing rafters of sticks. Dining areas are separated by screens of intertwined driftwood, glistening with shellac. Here and there primitive, pixyish faces painted on the driftwood peek out.

The food has been Polish home cooking, the equal of Hamtramck or Chicago's favorite Polish restaurants. The cabbage rolls are outstanding. Whitefish is also available. Expect some new dishes from the new Polish chef. Dinners (with soup or salad, bread and potato) are around $10 to $15 or so, sandwiches and lunch entrees $5 to $10. A world-wide selection of over 100 beers, imported and regional, is on hand.

If you time your dinner visit right, you can enjoy the sunset over the lake, and then linger in that amazing grotto of a barroom. Legs Inn is also known for **live music**.

Barroom at Legs Inn. Creator Stanley Smolak borrowed from popular Indian motifs like the totem pole of the Pacific Northwest that had nothing to do with his friends among the local Odawa.

Sunday evenings through Labor Day the Jelly Roll Blues Band, one of northern Michigan's best bands, plays at 9. Other bands (aimed at people over 30) play Friday and Saturday, plus Wednesday and Thursday in July and August. No music after Labor Day except for the season-closing Halloween party over the third weekend in October.

Smolak's Depression-era art is based on found materials, inspiration, and persistence. "He claims that any man can do what he did if he only keeps his eyes open and his hands busy," stated one appreciative article. "For the world is filled with fine and great wonders, things which people take no notice of because they have eyes yet do not see and hands that lie idle."

After Smolak's death, Legs Inn devolved into something of a dive. Today it has been rejuvenated into a family restaurant and local meeting place that's a refreshing change from the carefully traditional interiors so evident in nearby Harbor Springs and Petoskey. The **gift shop** offers souvenirs and items imported from Poland.

Legs Inn is on 119 just north of Levering Road, 22 miles from Mackinaw City and 20 miles along the lakeshore route from Harbor Springs. (616) 526-2281. Open the weekend before Mem. Day through 3rd weekend in Oct. Summer dining-room hours 11-10, Sun. noon-10. Fall hours noon-9. Bar open until 2 a.m. Full bar. Visa, MC. &

A LOVELY DRIVE TO LEGS INN . . . . . is along the lake, through the celebrated **Tunnel of Trees**, narrow M-119 (Northlake Shore Drive) that twists above the shoreline. The overarching trees, the glimpses of Lake Michigan from the bluff, the aroma of cedars and pines, some huge beech trees and lots of paper birch — all combine to make this very special. Bicyclists favor the drive in morning when traffic is rarely heavy or fast. Colonies of trillium cover the woods around Memorial Day for a spectacular show. After dark, you're better off avoiding the twists and turns and taking the inland route back to Petoskey. Take 66 (Levering Road) east from Cross Village; in 9 miles turn south at 81. It eventually ends at Harbor Springs-Petoskey Road. . . . . . To explore what was once a center of Great Lakes Odawa culture, take a scenic detour at **Good Hart**. Its quaint **post office/general store**, which has deli sandwiches and takeout for picnics, caters to local cottagers' paradoxical preferences for primitivism and luxury. People come to the bakery from far away to buy apple-cinnamon bread, swiss rye bread (makes a great Rubin), and the home-made chicken pot pies. If you ask to use the restroom, be prepared for an outhouse. *(616) 526-2281. Open daily 9-7 summer and 10-5:30 winter.* & . . . . Go down the shady dirt shore road behind the post office. After 1 1/2 miles you pass a few tiny log houses and come to a clearing with a simple wood church surrounded by a cemetery of homemade wood crosses and markers. This may have been the site of the **17th-century mission** the Jesuits called L'Arbre Croche or Crooked Tree. Later, in 1839, Father Baraga built a church here. There's a beautiful Lake Michigan beach behind the church. . . . . To piece together the complex, unhappy story of the dispersal and destruction of Indian culture here, visit the Blackbird Museum in Harbor Springs (p. 649). Read *The Land of the Crooked Tree*, a first-person account from the 1870s by noted horticulturist U.P. Hedrick (his take on Indians will shock modern sensibilities) and *Night-Flying Woman*, a first-person Ojibway account of the missions' effect by Minnesota Ojibwa teacher Ignatia Broker.

Wilderness State Park

30 miles of unspoiled coast, picturesque cabins,
sandy beaches with no crowds,
and rugged backcountry trails for skiing and hiking

WILDERNESS STATE PARK is a state treasure — a world apart from Mackinaw City's densely commercialized motel-land, yet barely 15 minutes away. It combines a location near major destinations around Petoskey and the Straits with an exceptional expanse of varied natural beauty. Rocky limestone shores face the straits, backed by cedars and birches that can sustain themselves on these thin, rocky soils. A series of inlets stretches out into Lake Michigan. A long crescent of a sandy beach faces west on Sturgeon Bay. The wild, low dunes here give these simple, undeveloped beaches a special aura that draws local people from Petoskey and Harbor Springs. The remote, forested back country is laced with trails. At a little over 8,000 acres, Wilderness ranks as one of the Lower Peninsula's largest, most complex, and least developed parks.

Wilderness Park Drive leads from Mackinaw City past the campgrounds and main beach to Waugoshance Point. Along the shore and point are **five lighthouses**, some abandoned, some still functioning, all erected to warn vessels away from the shallow shoals as they turn into the straits The point and the two long offshore islands near it extend almost five miles out into Lake Michigan, just 15 miles from the Upper Peninsula. A newly improved gravel road enables you to drive out to the point. The point is a favorite spot for birders because over 100 species either nest here or migrate through. Certain areas along the shoreline are closed during the rare Piping Plover's nesting season.

A beach that's sandy, although more crowded on good days in the summer, and more natural, backed by dunes, is reached at the park's southwest corner, where M-119 joins Lakeview Road. Look for the sign to **Sturgeon Bay Picnic Area.** It has grills, tables, and pit toilets. The sandy **beach** along Sturgeon Bay stretches five miles north within the park. In the rugged interior backcountry, many paths and old logging roads cross a glacial landscape of wetlands and high hills, including Mount Nebo. Check with park staff for tips on combining trail segments to suit your requirements, and to be sure that the popular trail to Waugoshance Point (2 miles each way) is open. The park has over six miles of groomed **cross-country ski trails** and 12 miles of separate **snowmobile trails**.

Lakeshore Campground (150 modern sites) is an open, suburban-style campground with lake views. Across the road, the 100 large modern sites in the **Pines Campground** are shaded and not far from the trails. Both fill up in summer and cost $14/night. Five rustic 4- to 8-person **log cabins** in scenic beach spots along Point Road and one cabin 2 miles inland are for rent, along with three 24-person cabins near the campgrounds. Although not always necessary, camping reservations are recommended from the last week in June through Labor Day. (800-543-2YES). Reservations are needed well ahead for all cabins.

Main entrance and booth with park maps are on Wilderness Park Dr. (C-81), 12 miles west of Mackinaw City. Write: Wilderness State Park, P. O. Box 380, Carp Lake, MI 49718. (616) 436-5381. State park sticker required: $4/day, $20/year. &: no.

A SURPRISING, QUIET, NATURAL SIDE TO MACKINAW CITY . . . . . can be seen by taking the **shore route** from town to Wilderness State Park and avoiding Trail's End Road. To see the quaint, rustic cottages of the Wawatam Association, follow the south perimeter of Colonial Michilimackinac west to Straits Avenue and Lakeside Drive. This old Indian trail is today a charming but bumpy drive by back doors of cottages. . . . . . To continue out to Wilderness State Park, turn left at Cedar to avoid a long detour, and go right (west) out Central. At the T, the right (north) road end out to McGulpin Point offers a terrific view of the Mackinac Bridge. Then go back (south) and turn right (west) briefly onto Trail's End. A beautiful, simple **public beach** lies ahead where the road turns; another similarly sandy **public beach** is in a couple of miles. Both have toilets. Follow the signs from here to Wilderness.

A DELIGHTFULLY REMOTE BEACH . . . . . with a backdrop of wild-looking dunes, is at **Bliss Township Park** on M-119 about 10 miles north of Legs Inn on Sturgeon Bay. It's not fancy; amenities consist of two outhouses. From Mackinaw City, take County Road 81 southwest, but keep going west on Lakeview when 81 turns south. See also **Sturgeon Bay Picnic Area** at **Wilderness State Park**.

Colonial Michilimackinac

Living glimpses of frontier life of the French, Indians and British at this reconstructed 18th-century fort, built to control the lucrative fur trade.

BY 1779-1781, the British had abandoned and burned this old stockaded fur-trading post and fort overlooking the Straits of Mackinac. But so many bits and pieces of everyday life and military armament were left buried in the sand and so many accounts of life at the old fort had been written, that it has been possible to reconstruct the fort's buildings with great accuracy and to recreate the colorful frontier life here. Many superficially similar reconstructed forts are far less authentic. Colonial Michilimackinac gives a more relevant and more interesting view of the fur trade and straits history than the more dramatic fort on Mackinac Island, which interprets military life in the far less significant Victorian era.

Fur-trading in the upper Great Lakes caused competitive friction between France and Great Britain through much of the 18th century. A small fort at the northern tip of Michigan's Lower Peninsula was built here in 1715, part of France's ongoing efforts to keep the

Bird's-eye view of Fort Michilimackinac as it looked in the 1770s. Many but not all of these buildings have been reconstructed. New buildings are added as archaeological excavations are completed and funds released.

British out of this lucrative trade zone. There was never a big military force here, usually about 20 soldiers. Still, as the present reconstruction of the old site shows, it was a typical fort of the day, surrounded by an 18-foot-high stockade. As many traders as soldiers lived in the community, which was cut off from the outside world six months a year.

The French finally surrendered their northern territories to Great Britain in 1760. The British occupied Fort Michilimackinac for another 20 years until they built a more defensible fort on Mackinac Island. The most notable event during their stay was the 1763 massacre of most of the fort's British soldiers by the local Indians, part of Chief Pontiac's ultimately unsuccessful plan to repulse the British.

Former interpreter Annette Naganashe at the Indian encampment outside the fort. Interpreters here work at various everyday tasks: weaving mats, cooking, and (here) making a rope.

The fort has been restored to the 1770s. At that time, British soldiers were garrisoned here but the traders continued to be a polyglot mix of British, French, several Indian peoples, mixed-blood descendants of them all, and even some Jews, the first to live in Michigan. Millions of artifacts have been excavated here since 1959, along with the foundations of the burned buildings, in the oldest ongoing archaeological site in the U.S.

New interpretive exhibits and recreated events are continually being added, thanks to the fort's favorable status as one of the three Mackinac State Historic Parks. These parks are well funded by the ample gate receipts at these popular tourist attractions. Even if you have been here before, return visits can be worthwhile. The past seven years have seen the reconstruction of the 18th-century **rowhouse** home of 18th-century fur-trader Ezekiel Solomon, the addition of a recreated French **colonial wedding** to the fort's scheduled daily events, and a new underground **archeological exhibit**, "Treasures from the Sand."

Most interesting is the **Indian encampmen**t outside the palisades. Here visitors can go inside a wauginogan (a tipi with a rounded top) and a nasaogan (a tipi with a pointed top), simply furnished with a few bowls and utensils, furs, and a cradle board, all of which visitors are welcome to examine. Costumed interpreters who are Michigan Indians are busy at assigned tasks.

Costumed re-enactors play actual people such as fur trader Peter Pond, who summered at the fort after spending winters in Minnesota, and a representative British wife who gives a most interesting talk about the 18th-century vegetables she grows in her garden. All the re-enactors have jobs like preparing food, cooking, and making and fixing things. It's fascinating to watch them and ask questions. Though they may have scripted demonstrations, these interpreters are broadly informed, often longtime students of their subject matter, and they can field many kinds of questions.

Plan on starting your visit with a 30-minute **guided walking tour** to familiarize yourself with the village inside the palisades of the fort. Then explore it at your leisure, taking in the re-enactments and talks that interest you the most. The **cannon-firing and muzzle-loading demonstration** is a great favorite with kids. The fort is fully staffed and presents its full schedule of re-enactments from mid-June through Labor Day.

Like many historical reconstructions, Colonial Michimilimackinac focuses on the details of daily living, military history and technology, and trade networks, rather than on ideas and the social consequences of historical events. Little mention is made of the fur trade's vast impact on the Indians it touched, who quickly became dependent on useful trade goods, and on the alcohol which too many traders used as a trade good.

An excellent array of books on the area and on the fur trade are in the **museum shop**, along with crafts and souvenirs that reflect the fort's history and the culture of Straits Indian peoples. The shop, in the Visitor Center under the Mackinac Bridge approach, is also open to people without museum tickets.

Take northbound I-75 to exit 339 just before the bridge, follow signs to fort. (616) 436-5563. Information pack mailed upon request. Open daily from mid-May to mid-Oct. Hours: Spring and fall, 10-4. Summer 9-6. Adults $6.75, children 6-12 $4, family $20. **Mackinac State Park combination ticket** *(for here, fort on island, mill): adults $12.50, children $7.50, family $38 (unlimited admission throughout the year).* &: *call for a detailed guide to both forts and mill Questions? accessibilty coordinator, at (616) 436-7301.*

ACCESSIBILITY AT MACKINAC STATE HISTORIC PARKS. . . . . is taken very seriously. It's pretty good, despite the challenges of historic buildings and the island fort's blufftop location. Call the **access coordinator** at (616) 436-7301 for a **guide to access** for visitors with disabilities, for additional details, and to make special arrangements like getting a **sign language interpreter.**

TWO PLEASANT PARKS FOR WATCHING BOATS AND THE BIG BRIDGE . . . . A shady park stretches east along the shore from Colonial Michilimackinac to the **Old Mackinac Point Lighthouse** and along the shore past a few motels. Plenty of benches and **picnic tables** make this a fine place to sit and enjoy the bridge and Straits view, or walk along the beach (the white limestone rocks are full of fossils), or read a book about the area's rich history. **Regional books** are at the Island Bookstore at 215 East Central or at the Colonial Michilimackinac museum shop at the visitor center under the bridge approach. You can see the sunrise and sunset from this park because of its unusual location at the tip of a peninsula. The reflection of bridge lights in the water is memorable. . . . If you walk east down Huron Avenue from the lighthouse towards the docks, you will pass the less touristy, older neighborhoods of Mackinaw City. Little public areas at the ends of streets offer changing perspectives on the big bridge. **Wawatam Park** at the foot of Jamet and Etherington east of Huron has play equipment and interesting outdoor exhibits about fishing history and the Mackinaw boat.

SHOPPING IN MACKINAW CITY . . . . . is a lot more interesting than it used to be. There are still lots of general gift shops that could be just anywhere, but several places have their own distinctive personalities. Standouts include:
♦ **Island Bookstore**, *215 East Central. (616) 436-BOOK.* Part nature store, part rock shop, part toy and gift seller. Book department is strong on nature and regional sections. The new owners of the one-time Copper Lantern. who also run a bookstore on Mackinac Island, have kept the science and nature theme of former owner Peg Smith and have added some best-sellers and general books. &: *no.*
♦ **Tundra Outfitters**, *221 E. Central. (616) 436-5243.* Gifts and limited edition prints related to Alaska and wolves, a large book section, plus Alaskan-style clothing designed for serious cold weather. Owners sponsor a sled in the Iditarod race. It's also the headquarters for the Mackinaw Mush which takes place the first week in February. &
♦ **Sandpiper Alley**, *113 N. Huron (another entrance is on Langlade). (616) 436-5309.* Michigan gifts and crafts. &
♦ **Mackinaw Kite**, *105 N. Huron. (616) 436-8051.* Inspired and inspiring array of kites, from fun toys to stunt kites that can do amazing loops and lift a person off the ground. Also: wind-powered toys, windsocks, and books on kite-flying and kite-making through the ages.&
♦ **Mackinaw Bakery**, *110 Langlade (near McDonald's). (616) 436-5525.* Old-fashioned, full-line bakery with tables to sit down at for coffee. &
♦ **Traverse Bay Woolens**, *312 S. Huron. (616) 436-5402.* This up-north tourist center chain has switched to natural fibers and greatly upgraded the quality of its blankets, sweaters, and sportswear. New: a garden room. &: *front door.*

Mill Creek State Historic Park

A beautiful trail overlooks a reconstructed
1790 sawmill powered by a working waterwheel.

A RECONSTRUCTED 18th-century sawmill in an unusually scenic location makes this park an extraordinary place to visit. The extensive trails, interestingly interpreted with nuggets about nature and area history, are a welcome attraction in themselves. This point of entry to the natural world of northern Michigan is a relief from the bustle and crowds nearby.

The original mill was built by a Scottish trader in 1790 to supply lumber for the British fort on Mackinac Island just to the north. It was powered by Mill Creek, which flows into the nearby Straits of Mackinac linking Lake Huron and Lake Michigan. The mill has been rebuilt to duplicate the original, complete with a big wooden waterwheel. **Demonstrations** show what noisy, shaking contraptions water-powered mills were. A **visitor center/museum** by the

entrance and parking lot puts the site in historical context and displays items uncovered on the site by archaeologists. The excellent **museum shop** features books, activities, and gifts related to nature and to logging.

A highlight is a 15-minute walk on **Mill Pond Trail**. It forms a loop from the visitor center to the sawmill and around the

Perched over picturesque Mill Creek, this replica of a 1790 lumber mill gives visitors a dramatic and noisy view of how sawmills worked before steam power. A bonus is the beautiful location in a hilly area close to Lake Huron.

mill pond. On the way are two delightful **overlooks** from which you can look down on the sylvan scene and even see the Straits and Mackinac Island. Another 25-minute **trail**, also a loop, takes you through a forest along the top of the bluff paralleling the mill stream. An hour-long **trail** follows the stream farther back to some beaver dams.

On U.S. 23 1/2 mile southeast of Mackinaw City. (616) 436-7301. Open mid-May to mid-Oct. Summer hours (June 15-Labor Day) 9-6. Otherwise 10-4. &: call. Ramp leads to trails. Wheelchairs available at site. Adults $4.50, children 6-12 $3, 5 & under free, family (two adults and children under 14) $14. See page 661 for information on combination tickets.

TWO OUTSTANDING PRIVATE MUSEUMS IN MACKINAW CITY. . . . .
Teysen's **Woodland Indian Museum** features gorgeous beaded leather clothing, baskets, and other artifacts in a very interesting, to-the-point display done by Michigan State University museum specialists. It tells you a lot more about Michigan Indian cultures than many bigger, more tedious museums. Teysen's Restaurant, the museum's old home, now has different owners. Teysen's Gift Shop, now at 300 Central Ave. downtown, expects to reopen the museum in 1997. *(616) 436-7011. Fees not announced. . . . . .* The **Mackinac Bridge Museum** was started by an ironworker who helped build the bridge. It's over his pizzeria. The displays aren't professional or slick, but the project has both intelligence and the heart of grassroots history. There are hundreds of workers' personalized hardhats, photos (taken before the bridge was built) of the ferries and huge lines of waiting cars during hunting season at the Straits, and an excellent half-hour film about designing and building the bridge. Not to be missed. *Over Mama Mia's Pizzeria, 231 E. Central at Henry. (616) 436-5534. Free.*

HOW TO SAY IT. . . . . "Mackinac" and "Mackinaw" are pronounced the same way. The letter "c" is silent, so the last syllable is "naw." "Mackinac" is the way the French spelled the Indian word, "Mackinaw" the way the English spelled it. It's *never* right to say "MACK-i-NACK" when you're talking about **Mackinac Island.**

Mackinac Island

*This celebrated resort features an 18th-century fort,
the famous Grand Hotel, striking rock formations,
wonderful bike and carriage rides, and no cars.*

AN 18-MINUTE BOAT RIDE from either the Upper or Lower
Peninsula, this three-mile-long island is a major Midwestern travel destination for many reasons. Its interestingly rugged terrain provides many pleasant panoramas and views of
striking limestone formations.

The island's military and economic history is equally colorful.
Various Indian peoples met there to trade. The British built a big
fort here in 1781, and American and British forces fought a battle
in 1812. For 50 years the island was the center of the North
American fur-trading network. The legendary fur-trading tycoon
John Jacob Astor had his main trading office here in the fur trade's
waning years, from 1817 to 1834. One of the world's most famous
Victorian hotels, **Grand Hotel**, is perched on the side of a bluff, visible from the mainland.

The absence of autos and the use of horses and bicycles for
transportation give the island the aura of another age. Actually, the
decision to ban autos was made for practical, not aesthetic, reasons
in the 1920s. By then the automobile's potential for destruction of
the sensitive island environment was becoming apparent.

Even inexperienced cyclists enjoy the scenic but undemanding
trip on the paved road that hugs the lakeshore all the way around.
There's the additional adventure of having to take one of the many
ferries from St. Ignace or Mackinaw City to the island's harbor and
resort town at its southern end, giving passengers a striking view of
the large Victorian summer houses, the big fort, and the majestic
Grand Hotel, all situated on steep limestone slopes.

Most of the island is a park, laced with roads, bike trails, and
foot trails that are clearly signed. The free **visitor map** identifies
them all. Because the island is mostly limestone, with only a thin
layer of topsoil, it has been little farmed. The rocky terrain, eroded
by wave action from earlier, higher lake levels, includes many interesting formations such as Arch Rock, Devil's Kitchen, Sugar Loaf
Rock, and Chimney Rock.

The island was a popular meeting and trading place for
Ojibway, Odawa, and Huron people. They called it the great turtle
(Michilimackinac), because of its humped, oval shape. French mis-

sionaries began setting up missions in the Straits area to convert the Indians in the 17th century. At the same time, exporting Great Lakes furs to Europe became a highly profitable enterprise, pursued by both the British and French. In 1781 the British moved their mainland fort here, and the island became the center of Great Lakes fur trading until the 1830s. By then the beaver population was decimated.

Mackinac Island's unusual limestone formations led late 19th-century tourists to explore the island's interior. Here two boys have climbed Sugar Loaf Rock. Fresh, cool air and outdoor activity contributed to the island's reputation for invigorating refreshment.

Tourists escaping the summer heat began visiting the picturesque island in 1838. By the 1870s Mackinac Island was just a three-day steamer trip from Detroit and a two-day train trip from Chicago. Congress made the island the country's second national park in 1875. Tourism boomed along with the Midwest's industrial economy, which developed greatly during the Civil War. Fort Mackinac was closed in 1894, and a year later over 80% of the island was designated Michigan's first state park. That protected it from further development.

Under 400 of the island's 2,300 acres remain privately owned. The handsome huge, Victorian summer "cottages" just to the east and west of the harbor now sell for up to $700,000. Even some of the modest workers' homes in Harrisonville, toward the center of the island, sell for over $100,000, forcing some of the 500 year-round residents to leave the island for cheaper housing elsewhere. The biggest issue now facing the island is overdevelopment as new shops and housing have created low water pressure, power outages, and landfill problems.

Some 900,000 "fudgies," the locals' sardonic term for visitors, come to the island each year. Getting off a ferry in the harbor, they are confronted with a bustling street full of carriages and tourists, fudge and souvenir shops. It's easy to get drawn into the tourist shuffle, going from sight to sight and shop to shop. But that's not what makes the island special.

Follow this advice for a really enjoyable trip:

1. Read up on the island ahead so you have a rough itinerary worked out when you arrive. Call or write ahead for a map and information packet from the Mackinac Island Chamber of Commerce (906-847-6418 or 906-847-3783) and from the Mackinac State Historic Park (616-436-5563). *Mackinac Connection: An Insider's Guide*, by longtime summer person Amy McVeigh, is a chatty, informative 160-page book with many helpful tips and candid info on all lodgings, restaurants, shops, outings, events, walks, bike rides, and much more. Highly recommended pre-trip reading. It's available at many bookstores, or see our mail-order book section in the front of this book.

2. Consider spending a night on the island so you can have two days of activities and time to relax and explore the island's natural interior. Many people have the mistaken idea that Grand Hotel, where a special deal is $145 per person, is the only hotel on the island. That's far from the case.

Most hotel rooms are $80 to $100 and up, but there are simple tourist homes with rates of $50 or $60 for two. Get a lodgings list from the Chamber or an annotated list from *Mackinac Connection*.

3. Take a carriage tour first to see what you most want to visit.

4. Get a free Mackinac Island map at the **Chamber of Commerce** in the center of town. Walk right on Main Street a block from the docks and stop at the foot of Fort, beneath the fort. The **Visitor Center of the Mackinac State Historic Park** shows a good introductory video and offers more info. *(Open 9 a.m. to 6 p.m. in summer, reduced hours in spring and fall. &)*

5. Walks are a real delight. Figure out how to alternate walks and rest periods where you can sit and take in the many splendid views. Walks through the village along Market Street and the east end of Main are exceptionally enjoyable; so are walks along East Bluff and West Bluff. *Mackinac Connection* outlines several walks. Wear good walking shoes!

6. Take a break. These are some good spots for rest and relaxation: *benches* scattered along many paths; *Marquette Park*, on Main Street below the fort; the fort's *terrace restaurant*; the porch and gardens of *Grand Hotel* (anyone can use them for $5); the *garden* next to *St. Anne's Church* on East Main; *church sanctuaries*, held open for visitors; the *Chippewa Hotel*'s Harbor View dining room, inside and out, at Main and Fort; at the other end of Main at French Lane, the *Iroquois Hotel*'s Carriage House, with a grand Straits view.

7. Get a good book to read about island history, nature, or architecture from the Island Bookstore in the Lilac Hotel on Main Street, or at the gift shop at the fort. Reading breaks get you planted in a place and slow you down from the numbing tourist pace. Two fascinating novels set in part on the island during the fur trade are *Enemies* (English trader Alexander Henry's story) and *Loon Feather* (with a shifting Indian perspective).

8. Take the bike ride around the island (see pages 675 and 678). If you're in shape for the hills, explore the interior. The nature center and snack stand at *British Landing* makes a good break half-way round the island.

9. Early mornings and evenings are especially beautiful, and less crowded in peak seasons — another good reason for spending the night.

10. Consider a visit in fall or spring. (Before mid-June the wildflowers are wonderful.) The pace then is slower and things are less crowded. Most shops stay open all season. The only thing you'll miss is the Market Street historic buildings, open only from mid-June thru Labor Day. From the last week or so of August through Labor Day the crowds drop off considerably.

11. Have a picnic. Prices for island food are on the high side, restaurants can be crowded, and sometimes the food isn't very good. If sticker shock gets you upset, pick up a sandwich at Doud's Mercantile, the island's only grocery, at Main and Fort, or bring food from the mainland. Mackinaw City's Mackinaw Bakery, next to McDonald's on Langlade just north of Central, has good pasties and bread.

Highlights for visitors to the island are:

♦ **Carriage tour.** Thirty local families pooled forces over 40 years ago to start a cooperative carriage company. Today they operate about 75 carriages, using some 300 horses, to transport visitors around the island. The narrated tour, approved by the city and the state park, lasts 1 hour 45 minutes. It's a pleasant, informative, slow-paced drive which takes you by most sights. Stops at Fort Mackinac and Arch Rock let you get out and enjoy the wonderful view. You can be dropped off at Grand Hotel at the tour's end. (It's a pleasant half-mile walk back to town.) *Begins downtown at the Mackinac Island Carriage ticket office on Main Street opposite the Arnold docks, next to Chamber of Commerce. Open from mid May through mid Oct. Summer hours (from mid June thru-Labor Day) 8:30-5:30 or so. Otherwise 9-3. Call (906) 847-3307 for further info or to make special arrangements. &. Adults $12, children 4-11 $6.*

♦ **Fort Mackinac.** Perched on a bluff overlooking the harbor, this historic fort is well worth visiting. Its views of town and harbor below are delightful. The well-preserved fort has been restored to look as it did in the 1880s, when the army garrison's main duties were to take care of the national park and entertain wealthy summer people. Seen from that perspective, the fort's military significance seems trivial. But that wasn't the case in 1780-1781, when the British built the fort to protect their fur trade interests west of their breakaway colonies, or in the War of 1812, when the British captured the fort from the Americans.

A short **slide/tape show** is a good introduction to the fort. The views from the blockhouses and parapets are wonderful. Of the scheduled **historical demonstrations and recreations**, the cannon firing by an enthusiastic and expert costumed guide is always a hit. Audience questions are encouraged. The military music concert/talk is a lot more interesting than the court martial. Musicians played important roles in signaling. Skilled buglers were often recruited from immigrants at Ellis Island. On the **children's tour**, kids roll hoops and play other games from the 1880s. In the **Children's Discovery Room** in the Officers' Stone Quarters, children can try on military hats and coats and period costumes and pose for photos in them. Other hands-on displays introduce what things associated with the fort's history sounded like and felt like (beaver pelts, for instance).

Down below, in the same Officers' Stone Quarters from the 1780s, is a delightful **tearoom.** The tapered masonry walls are from two to four feet thick, so the windows are like little niches. Food is

The parapets of Fort Mackinac offer splendid views of the town below and the Straits of Mackinac and freighter traffic in the distance. Some interpreters wear the uniforms of the soldiers stationed here in the 1880s, when Prussian spiked helmets were adopted by the U.S. Army.

also served on the terrace, which has a fabulous view. The excellent food, prepared by Grand Hotel cooks, includes soup, salads (fruit, Caesar, and spinach are under $7), personal pizzas (around $5), hot dogs ($3.95), and the sandwich of the day ($5.75). The $4.50 pecan fudge ice cream ball is enough for two. Gratuity included in prices. &: *outdoor patio with waitresses.*

You can go inside 14 original buildings, furnished as they were in 1880. These include a barracks, blockhouses, a canteen, and a post commissary. The **officers' quarters** are quite a contrast to the enlisted men's spartan rooms. They're much more interesting, appointed with a good deal of Victorian bric-a-brac to make families feel at home at this remote outpost. The social niceties among military wives are explained in fascinating detail. *Same hours, prices as Fort Michilmackinac (page 661). The joint pass to all three historic parks is a good deal. The helpful **visitor center** to the fort is below the fort on Main at Fort, opposite the park. It's open 9 a.m. to 7 p.m. in summer, reduced hours at other times.* &: *yes, see note on Fort Michilimackinac (page 662).*

◆ **Market Street** parallels Main a block inland. While Main Street's dense storefronts and hotels were built for the busy Victorian tourist trade, Market Street's detached houses reflect the much simpler Mackinac Island of fishermen and fur-traders before the Civil War paved the way for the industrial boom of northeast America. Many buildings on Market Street are furnished as museums today, though there are tourist homes, a few shops, and public buildings. It's a refreshing summer contrast to the throngs on Main Street.

The ticket for the fort also admits you to several historic or reconstructed Market Street buildings, open from June 15 through Labor Day from 11-5. The **McGulpin House** is a French-Canadian log house from the 1780s. At the **Beaumont Memorial** (not authentic), dioramas show the startling investigations of Dr. William Beaumont. He became the first doctor to observe how the stomach functions, thanks to a gunshot wound to Alexis St. Martin which left a hole that never healed. Spinning and baking are demonstrated at the 1780 **Edward Biddle House**. Behind it, a blacksmith is at work at the **Benjamin Blacksmith Shop**. Many **demonstrators** at the Mackinac State Historic Parks have made lifetime avocations of these summer jobs and are extremely knowledgeable about their subjects. Don't miss the **Robert Stuart House**, the local museum of the city of Mackinac Island. It's full of photos and memorabilia, with a knowledgeable staff of local people who love to talk about island life. The Stuart house along with the warehouse (now community center) next door is where Stuart once stored John Jacob Astor's furs. &: *the Biddle House and the first floor of the Beaumont Memorial. At McGulpin House, one step leads to the 31-inch door. A steep ramp leads into the Blacksmith Shop — exit the yard through the Biddle House. In 1997, Stuart House will have a ramp.*

◆ **Huron Street and East Bluff.** One of Mackinac's most delightful walks goes past Marquette Park, at the fort's foot, where Main turns into Huron Street and goes to Mission Point. Prim, simple pre-Victorian houses are mixed with later summer places, often used to house the island's legions of summer workers. The yards and gardens are beautiful. **St. Anne's Catholic Church**, the island's biggest and most active church, has a delightful public garden and little basement **museum** with lots of island photos and some St. Anne's artifacts going back to when the parish was at Michilimackinac. A marker commemorates **Magdelaine De La Framboise**, a prominent and generous French-Indian fur trader whose legacy helped build the church.

Cut through St. Anne's garden path to get back to McGulpin Street and visit **The Mackinac Island Butterfly House**, in a greenhouse that once supplied many of the island's bedding plants and geraniums. Visitors pass through antechambers with two curtains to enter the large greenhouse. It's a magical place where butterflies fly freely around. Big, colorful, exotic-looking butterflies from rain forests of Costa Rica and Malaysia now join their more familiar, smaller North American relations. Butterflies eat nectar from the greenhouse's flowers.

In the new indoor-outdoor caterpillar garden, milkweed, fennel, and collard greens provide food for caterpillar varieties native to Michigan, to increase the island's butterfly population. If you sit still awhile, they'll land on you! Proprietor Doug Beardsley views the butterfly house as a livelihood and a mission that capitalize on the butterfly's natural charm to get an ecological message across. "The butterfly is a spokesman for the insect world," he maintains. "People may wonder why there aren't as many as there used to be. Today you can buy enough chemicals at the hardware store to kill the whole town's insects. If you interrupt the food chain by eliminating the insect biomass, you've got trouble. We have to get away from the mindset that everything ought to be perfect, without insects on it." There's also a terrific **butterfly gift shop.** *Open daily from Mem. Day weekend thru Sept. at least, about 9 a.m. to 8 p.m.; butterflies are more active when it's warmer, from 9:30 or 10 to 7 or so. (906) 847-3972.* ♿ *Admission is $3 for adults, $2 for children.*

Come back out onto Huron Street and continue east at least to stop inside at **Mission Church**, a New England colonial church with a pretty octagonal belfry. It was built by the United Foreign Missionary Society in 1829-30. The mission was established in 1822 to "civilize and educate" Indians who came to the island to trade, and to uplift the soldiers at the fort and the local people. *Wheelchair accessible: no, stairs make it difficult.* A few blocks farther (skip this if you're tiring) is the **Mission Point Resort** (906-847-3312), a sprawling family-oriented resort that enjoys a fine view

If you take a seat at The Mackinac Island Butterfly House, like proprietor Doug Beardsley here, chances are a butterfly will light on you, too.

of the shipping lanes. Its contemporary buildings of natural materials were erected in the 1950s and 1960s by Moral Rearmament, a murkily patriotic crusade. They have been improved by the resort. The library and public areas are fine for relaxing, and two of the three restaurants have a good view of freighter traffic. ᕃ

Return by taking the back streets (Mission or Truscott) to Mission Hill at the top of Truscott. There you can get a closer look at the massive late 19th-century "cottages" on East Bluff and enjoy the view looking down at the Huron Street buildings you've just passed. Go west and take the second stairway down to go past the tourist homes on Bogan Lane, which leads you to Huron Street again. Or continue walking along the bluff to the fort and governor's summer house (see page 674) and return on Fort Street.

◆ **Grand Hotel**. This is a living American vestige of the late-19th-century European tradition of elegant summer resorts. When a consortium of railroads and steamship companies finished the hotel in 1887, it became the world's largest summer hotel and the world's largest pine building, with the world's largest porch — 660 feet. At least, those are the firsts claimed by the hotel's avid publicists, who still claim the records today.

The formalities of a bygone era live on here. The hotel still requires dresses or skirts for women and jackets and ties for men at and after dinner. The $5 fee charged non-guests to visit the hotel and grounds is a reasonable cost if you spend the better part of a day here, exploring the lovely Victorian gardens, enjoying the lobby and porch with their splendid views of the Straits, and having lunch in the varied restaurants and bars (all top-notch). A swim in the pretty but small pool is $10 extra. But the overpriced ground-floor shops, gussied up with Anglophile status symbols and self-important Grand Hotel souvenirs, with little pertaining to the rest of the island, can leave a bad taste in your mouth. Enter upstairs at the central entrance for a better first impression of the hotel and its busy, courteous desk staff.

Smaller rooms start at around $145 per person, double occupancy, modified American plan, including breakfast and dinner; an extra 18% gratuity is added. (The Grand is a non-tipping hotel; this includes restaurants.) To get the most out of a Grand Hotel stay, guests should take advantage of all the **special facilities** and **daily events** that were part of resort life in the grand tradition. There's the big breakfast and five-course dinner, the **parlor and porch** (popular for late-afternoon and evening cocktails and just sitting), golf at the expanded **18-hole public course** (the first nine has wonderful views and some challenging holes; the second nine, reached by a carriage ride, is in the woods), **tennis**, swimming in a beautifully landscaped **pool**, a 4 o'clock **tea concert** with champagne, sandwiches, and pastries, **dancing** at dinner, and a library of early edition nature books to read with wine, cordial, or cappucino in the den-like **Audubon Wine Bar**, the vintage Art Deco **Terrace Room** (dancing with a seven-piece swing orchestra), and the **Cupola Bar** (dancing to a jazz trio in a rooftop room with a dazzling view).

Grand Hotel has long had a mystique as a summer locus of fashion, power, and political activity. Hotel history, chiefly photos of famous guests and important conferences, is displayed in a two-room **museum** on the lower level. (Having the **Governor's summer mansion** on Mackinac Island adds to the power mystique.)

The old hotel wasn't always so snazzy. Most of its original furnishings were replaced by inexpensive Art Deco furniture. By the 1970s, it was looking worn. Famed decorator Carleton Varney began revamping the hotel in 1977 and has been creating new rooms for the Grand ever since then including 26 name rooms. Each suite reflects its name (Governors Milliken and Williams, Lincoln, Teddy Roosevelt, Napoleon and Josephine, Versailles, China, etc.). He created a punchy, decorator version of Victorian summer resorts — a look that's been widely imitated in northern Michigan. Every September during Antique and Decorators Weekend, Varney gives tours of his work.

Varney drew on his own memories of seaside summers in Massachusetts to emphasize the mood of a Victorian summer resort. He uses motifs like the hotel's signature red geranium, repeated boldly on black carpets and trellis wallpapers.

The governor's summer home: one of the many large and interesting "cottages" built on the east and west bluffs overlooking the island village was this post-1900 variant on the Shingle Style. The state of Michigan bought it for $15,000 in 1945 to use as the governor's summer residence. Summer visitors can tour it Wednesday mornings from 9:30 to 11:30.

Vibrant summer colors enliven the tiny guest rooms: daffodil yellow, sky blue, deep green, and geranium pink. The effect of all this clever decorating is cheerful. The interiors feel warm and lively even on rainy days.

Web users can catch up on the history of the Grand Hotel and Mackinac Island in general through: http://www.mackinac.com/. Call for a brochure on special theme weekends. *(800) 334-7263. Open mid-May through October.* ♿

◆ **Bicycle tour around the island.** Rent either single or tandem bikes for this delightful, easy eight-mile trip. Roughly half way around the island on the western shore is **British Landing**, the place where Indians and British soldiers landed in 1812 in their successful surprise attack on Fort Mackinac. You can get a bite to eat at the well-equipped **snack shop** here. There are also **rest-rooms**, a **picnic area**, and **nature center** staffed in summer by a naturalist who's happy to answer questions. A half-mile **nature trail** with many interesting explanatory markers and nature displays goes through forests and up a bluff. The bluff here has a good view of the Mackinac Bridge. The trail then goes on to the beautiful **Croghan Water wetland** area.

British Landing is where, during the winter, an ice bridge forms to St. Ignace, allowing year-round residents to snowmobile off the island. *For bike rental information, see page 678.*

◆ **Bicycle tour into the island's interior.** Island-lovers agree that to really get to know the island, you need to explore its natural areas and appreciate their beauty. The interior has some steep bluffs, and bicycling may be a challenge. Don't be embarrassed to push your rental bike up some hills.

Here's a short but challenging tour to the island's highest point, not too far from town. Start behind the fort where several trails come together. Take the South Bicycle Trail, not the road, to the dramatic limestone **Arch Rock.** (That way you'll avoid the carriage tours). From there, take Rifle Range Road inland, turn right onto Garrison Road, and you'll come to **Skull Cave**. The island's caves were formed when water from higher lake levels thousands of years ago eroded parts of the limestone. Continue on Garrison Road past the **cemeteries** (always interesting for amateur historians). Turn right onto Fort Holmes Road and you'll soon reach **Fort Holmes**. On this spot during the War of 1812, the British, who had landed unnoticed on the island's north end, surprised the American fort. When the British got their cannon on this high point aimed at the big American fort below, the Americans didn't even consider defending the fort. They surrendered without a shot. The British built a small stockade and blockhouse here. The spectacular **Straits view** from the reconstructed stockade is worth the arduous trip.

Now go back to Garrison Road. When you reach it, you can go right and end up at British Landing (close to two miles north), or turn left and go back to town. Consult your free map for other options. Wherever you go, it's downhill from here!

◆ **Shopping.** *Mostly along Main, with some shops on Market.* Mackinac shopping has improved greatly in recent years. Many visitors' impressions of the island are unfortunately dominated by the fudge and ice cream shops and generally ordinary souvenir stores that line Main Street. Sidewalks are crowded in season; service mostly depends on untrained summer help. For generations, shopkeepers did well enough appealing to the captive market of passive day-trippers who visited the fort and Grand Hotel, then browsed in the shops by the ferry docks. Time-honored souvenirs like rubber tomahawks and moccasins, humorous wood plaques and souvenir teacups are fun and nostalgic but get tiring fast.

The 1980s' continuing boom in upscale island inns and mainland motels has brought some new and tony shops. Most are big on updated traditional clothing and accessories that run heavily in the direction of traditional duck prints and decoys, dolls for collectors, Victorian-styled luxuries, and fancy soaps. But better stores of this kind can be found elsewhere, especially in Petoskey and Leland. The short season and high rents necessarily tend to increase already high prices. Consider limiting shopping time in favor of the taking advantage of the island's unique scenery and its hiking and bicycling opportunities. Or save shopping for a rainy day.

Four shopping highlights are:

Maeve's Arts & Antiques. Contemporary American handcrafts in a whimsical, folkish vein mix well with colorful handcrafted artifacts and clothing from many cultures. On hand: ethnic musical instruments and bells as well as masks from Bali, Africa, and Jamaica. The outstanding jewelry selection is strong on handmade silver from Mexico, Bali, and India. Shop owner Maeve Croghan, whose paintings of the island are don the walls, has spent many summers on the island where her Irish ancestors lived and worked. *Main Street near Astor, between the Arnold and Shepler docks. (906) 847-3755.* ✆: *one step.*

Island Scrimshander. The proprietor is one of three brothers to make a living at the ancient whalers' craft of engraving ivory. In the mid-1700's, New England whalers stuck on a windless ocean without chores to do or whales to catch, began the craft of engraving the teeth of sperm whales to pass the time. Concern in the past few years for the survival of different whales species makes it difficult to obtain legal whale teeth. Instead, ivory from mammoths and mastodons, extinct some 10,000 years, is being used now. Most of the Island Scrimshander's ivory comes from Russia. When the Siberian-Western European natural gas pipeline was being laid a few years back, 250,000 tons of mammoth and mastodon remains were uncovered. Other sources of ivory are the Alaska pipeline project and goldmining in the Yukon. Sometimes you can see the owner at work engraving miniature local scenes and inlaying jewelry. *Opposite Opposite the Drug Store in the lobby of the Chippewa Hotel beside the Pink Pony. (906) 847-3792.* ᕃ

Island Books. A personal, complete bookstore, with everything from vacation reading and regional titles about Mackinac and much of northern Michigan to books on computers, investments, and gardening. *Main between Astor and Hoban, closer to Astor, in the Lilac Tree Shops. (906) 847-6202. Open from May thru Oct. from 10 to 5 at least. Summer hours 10-10.* ᕃ

Fort Mackinac Museum Shop. One of three very good museum shops of the Mackinac State Historic Parks. All go way beyond the usual gift shop in their efforts to illuminate chosen themes and historic periods with a choice selection of books and authentic historic-reproduction artifacts. Specialties here are pre-industrial cooking and crafts, along with military, Civil War, and Indian history and popular culture of the Victorian era, when the fort was still in operation. Excellent regional selections. Out-of-the-ordinary items include replicas of Indian trade silver pendants ($10-12), tin fifes and harmonicas with instructions, hooked rugs in colorful scenes ($170-$350), and tiny birch boxes with quill turtles ($10-$20). Many toys and gifts are $2 and under. *In the barracks of Fort mackinac. (906) 847-6610. Open from May thru Oct. from 10-4 at least. Summer hours 9-6.* ᕃ

GETTING THERE. . . . . The many highway billboards show how competitive the **ferry** lines to Mackinac Island are. The three ferry companies have similar prices (adult round-trip $12, children 5 to 12 $7, bikes $4). All offer valet parking for $3 or less. But their schedules vary. If you anticipate a tight schedule or want to get on or off the island early or late, compare schedules before buying your ticket. (The schedules are at virtually every motel, restaurant, or visitor information center in the area.) Other variables are atmosphere and speed. A 14- to 18-minute trip from Mackinaw City is the rule. Local commuters often use all three ferries, depending on the circumstances. In all cases, *be sure your luggage gets on the boat.*

♦ **Arnold Transit** (906-847-3351) is the biggest line, and its *catamarans* are newest and fastest. They make the trip from Mackinaw City (they depart from the southern of Arnold's two Mackinaw docks) in 14 minutes, from St. Ignace in 9. One veteran island commuter prefers the stable catamarans when winds and waves are high but avoids Arnold in peak summer season because of the crush of daytrippers. A lot of people who really enjoy leisurely boat rides prefer Arnold's slow boat that takes 35 minutes from St. Ignace. Overnight parking is $1 a day outdoors, $3 fenced, $10 indoor, valet parking $3. ♿

♦ **Shepler's** (616-436-5023) is the second ferry in size, with a 16-minute ride from Mackinaw. Service is a passion for owner Bill Shepler, who also organizes service seminars for Mackinaw City businesses. Shepler's parking and loading systems are streamlined, and there's free overnight parking up to 5 days or secured parking for $3.50 a day outdoors, $5 indoors, valet parking $2..50 round trip. Shepler's Car Care will fill up and wash your car while you're on the island and even change the oil and do minor repairs. ♿

♦ **Star Line** (616-436-5044) is the newest and smallest ferry line, with a more laid-back atmosphere and less of a crush. That can be refreshing in midsummer. Its boats are the ones with rooster-tails of water behind them. Valet parking is cheaper, but overnight parking is from $2 (guarded, at the dock) to $3 (outdoor valet)/$4 (indoor valet). ♿

RENTING BIKES . . . . . If you plan on doing a fair amount of bicycling, it's better to *take your own bike* and lock to the island for $4 (Star line, $3.5) a round trip. (Take off flags; they scare the horses.) *Take your own helmet*, in any case. They can't be rented for sanitary reasons. . . . . **Bike rental businesses** are at several points along Main Street and at the Iroquois and Mission Point hotels. Standard rates are pretty much the same ($4/hour for single-speed or three-speeds, $5-$6 for mountain bikes, $5-6 for tandems), but the equipment can vary considerably. Calling around can help you find what you want. **Ryba's** (906-847-6261) is the biggest, with three locations. It offers single speed, three speed and mountain bikes (18 and 21 speed), along with pull-behind Burley kids carts. All day rates range from $35 to $50, depending on the bike. **Orr-Kids** (906-847-3211), on Main across from the Haunted Theater, is the only bike rental which takes Visa and Mastercard. They have Burley carts for 1 or 2 kids (up to 90 lbs.), mountain bikes, 6-speed bikes, child carriers, child strollers, and adult strollers. All day rates start at $20. **Island Bicycle Livery** (906-847-6288) is near the Shepler Dock on the lake side. It offers all-day rates, which begin at $16, as well as hourly, weekly, and 24-hour rates. Tandems, children's bikes, and baby seats are available.

Rogers City

A spectacular quarry, freshly caught whitefish, fabulous smoked pork loin, and miles of uncrowded beaches at this unpretentious Lake Huron port

THIS TOWN of 4,000 is home to the largest limestone quarry in the world. Despite the abundance of beautiful Lake Huron beaches both in and around the city. Few tourists come here compared to the northwestern coast of the Lower Peninsula. That gives Rogers City a refreshingly authentic, down-to-earth personality. The conservative Polish, German, and Italian populace attends the huge Catholic and Lutheran churches in town, each having congregations over a thousand. Some 300,000 acres of commercially harvested timberlands here in Presque Isle County create the biggest employment sector. German and Polish farmers raise huge quantities of beans. Eight per cent of the U.S. crop of kidney beans comes from this county alone. The cool, moist climate is also excellent for potatoes.

Over the years, so many Rogers City men have become sailors in Michigan Limestone's big fleet of carriers, based here, that Rogers City has styled itself as "The Nautical City" and called its downtown mall "Mariners Mall."

Highlights of Rogers City and vicinity include:

◆ **Michigan Limestone & Operations quarry.** It can be viewed from two strategic locations (see map). The **viewing stand** off Business 23 south of town reveals the vast expanse of the 6,000-acre quarry. Over the decades the company has dug down over 250 feet to mine the almost-pure limestone. View huge shovels scooping up blasted chunks of limestone and loading large dump trucks. From the **harbor view**, open daylight hours, you can better see the screen house, where the chunks are sorted by size, and the harbor, where up to two freighters at a time can be loaded. Some 400 freighter trips haul away the 10 million tons excavated annually. Call (517) 734-2117 to find out when freighters will be in port.

◆ **Lakeside Park/Rogers City Harbor.** A pleasant, long lakefront park has a nice, sandy **beach** and many amenities: **playground**, concession stand, picnic tables, basketball, a **bandstand** where summer concerts are held. It overlooks the busy marina and **fishing pier**.

◆ **Gauthier & Spaulding Fisheries.** On the front of G&S's Bradley

❶ Seagull Point Nature Area (p. 682). Picturesque setting on Lake Huron with sandy 2-mile interpretive trail and beach.

❷ Gauthier & Spaulding Fisheries (p. 679). Buy inexpensive whitefish fresh from Lake Huron at one of the few remaining Great Lakes fisheries.

❸ Plath's Meats (p. 681). Famous for smoked pork loin, made in the smokehouse back of the 78-year-old German shop.

❹ Historical Museum (p. 681). Striking old bungalow where Mich. Limestone presidents lived for over 5 decades. 1920s flappers' hats a highlight.

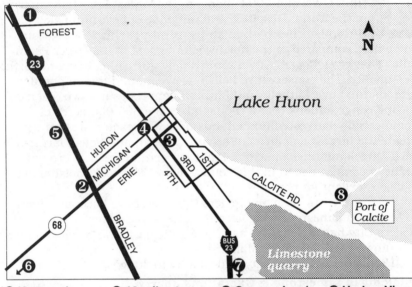

❺ Kortman's Restaurant. Pleasing family eatery with good, modestly-priced homemade dishes and plain, down-home atmosphere. (616) 734-3512.

❻ 12 miles to Ocqueoc Falls (p. 683). Erosion has leveled these waters to a frisky rapids, but it's a pretty picnic site with a 7-mile hiking trail.

❼ Quarry view (p. 679). 1 mile south. Dramatic bird's-eye view of 5,000-acre, 200-feet-deep limestone quarry, the world's largest. Bring binoculars.

❽ Harbor View (p. 679). See big freighters load up with limestone at this 5,000-acre quarry. Big brick structure sorts stones by size. See also p. 683.

Highlights of
Rogers City

0   1/2 miles

Highway/U.S. 23 retail outlet is a colorful painting of the boat used to catch the whitefish sold here. From April to the end of October, the 46-foot *Viking* pulls up a 1,500-foot trapnet from 90 feet of Lake Huron water. A good haul is a ton of fish. Either smoked or filleted, the fish are around $3.50 a pound. Cleaned and dressed fish is $1.75 a pound.

Third-generation fisherman John Gauthier says northern Lake Huron has the cleanest water in the Great Lakes. Recently, the firm has moved its docking site from the city harbor to the Michigan Limestone docks. Around noon daily the *Viking* returns with its haul. Buy fish right off the boat for about $1 pound at the factory (521 Park Drive off US 23 south of Erie). Looking like small submarines, the wooden fishing boats are totally enclosed with no deck, so the crew never has to be exposed to the often hazardous, frigid waters of the upper Great Lakes. *103 S. Bradley Hwy/U.S. 23 (retail outlet). (517) 734-3474. Open Mon-Sat, 10 a.m.-5 p.m.* &

◆ **Presque Isle County Historical Museum.** (Familiarly known as the Bradley House.) This handsome bungalow, built in 1914, was occupied until 1957 by Carl Bradley, first president of Michigan Limestone & Chemical, and his successors. Some rooms are now furnished with period furniture and accessories. Others have selected local artifacts. Don't miss the flamboyantly colorful 1920s flapper hats discovered decades later in the back of a local clothing shop. In the basement is a beautiful, authentic Indian birchbark canoe. The new maritime exhibit focuses on the *Carl D. Bradley* which sank mysteriously off Beaver Island in 1958, leaving only two survivors out of a crew of 35. Recently, controversy was stirred when the group that explored the *Edmund Fitzgerald*, Deep Quest, announced that it would try to enter the Carl D. Bradley.To many, the ship is the grave of their lost family and friends and they would like it left undisturbed. The exhibit includes the sinkings of the *Cedarville* (whose homeport was also Roger's City) and the *Edmund Fitzgerald* along with a model of the still afloat *John G. Munson*, who's namesake was one of the presidents of Michigan Limestone & Chemical who lived in the Bradley House.There are also changing exhibits and a gift shop with books on shipwrecks, Great Lakes storms, and maps of lighthouses and shipwrecks. *176 W. Michigan Ave. at Fourth St. Open June through Oct., 12-4 weekdays. Also open Sat from 12-4 in July and August. (517) 734-4121.* &*: no. No admission charge; donations appreciated.*

◆ **Plath's Meats.** A modest-looking meat market on Rogers City's main street, Plath's is famous for the smoked pork loin prepared in the smokehouse behind the retail shop; it's also served at the Buoy

Restaurant and Lounge and almost every other restaurant in town. Third and fourth generation Plaths use the same recipe for preparing the smoked pork that Emil Plath brought over from Germany in 1913. *Open Mon thru Sat 9-5. 116 South Third. (517) 734-2232.* &

◆ **Three beautiful beaches north of Rogers City along U.S. 23**. Gently sloping, sandy beaches and some low dunes mark much of the Lake Huron shore north of Rogers City. That contrasts with the broken, fossil-rich limestone rubble that predominates to the south. Going north along U.S. 23 from Rogers City, at the edge of town you come to **Seagull Point Park**, an uncrowded beach backed by low dunes with an interesting variety of tough little shrubs. A two-mile **interpretive trail** close to the lake explains the area's natural history. Soft sand here can make walking slow going. Across the road, the **Herman Volger Nature Preserve** is a quiet, vehicle-free foot travel area along the impounded Trout River. There's **cross-country skiing** here in winter.

About three miles northwest of here, **P.H. Hoeft State Park** offers not only 144 shady, modern **campsites**, a picnic area, playground, and CCC-era shelter, but a mile-long **beach**, again backed by low dunes. One **trail loop** (1.2 miles) passes behind the dunes and then goes along a creek in a .75 mile loop, revealing quite a variety of wildflowers. Another trail loop (1.5 miles) crosses U.S. 23 and goes into a forest. Both are available for **cross-country skiing** in winter. *On U.S. 23, 5 miles northwest of Rogers City. (517) 734-2543. Campsites are $8/night; reservations advised (800-543-2YES). Mini cabin in campground sleeping four available, $30. State park sticker required. $4/day, $20/year.* &: *call.*

Two miles north of Hoeft State Park, the **Presque Isle County Lighthouse Park** is a delightful picnic spot, with tables and grills in the birches and pines overlooking the **sandy beach**. The Forty Mile Point Lighthouse and tower, though not open to the public, are a nice focal point for the park. *Look for the brown park sign between Hoeft State Park and Manitou Beach Road.*

THE POSEN POTATO FESTIVAL . . . . . Posen (population 260), a Polish farming village 15 miles southeast of Rogers City, enjoys a reputation for growing exceptionally tasty potatoes on its rocky limestone soil. On the first weekend after Labor Day each year, it hosts a delightful festival. Polka and country bands play continuously from noon to 1 a.m. Saturday and to 9 p.m. Sunday. As many as 25,000 watch a mile-long parade at 1:30 Sunday. But the big draw is the potato pancake smorgasbord beginning Sunday morning at 10:30. Signs lead visitors to local farmers who sell 100-pound bags of their potatoes.

"THE LARGEST WATERFALL IN THE LOWER PENINSULA" . . . . . is the title bestowed on **Ocqueoc Falls** — testament to how little competition for the honor there is. It looks more like a rapids than a waterfall, but despite its puny drop, it's a fine place for a picnic because of the picturesque site. A seven-mile **hiking and cross-country skiing trail** starts next to the falls. *On M-68 at Ocqueoc Falls Highway, 12 miles west of Rogers City.*

LIMESTONE IN NORTHEASTERN MICHIGAN . . . . . Cartographer David Brown told the story in his *Atlas of Northern Michigan Cities*, now unfortunately out of print: "For millions of years, ancient seas covered most of Michigan. In parts of these seas were many coral-forming organisms. By long accumulation and compression they formed large limestone deposits. One of these formations, called the Dundee, comes to the surface at Rogers City [and also Alpena and its namesake, Dundee, in extreme southeastern Michigan]. It took 300 million years for this 250-foot stratum to form."

Rogers City limestone that had been too crumbly to be a construction material was discovered, in tests in 1907, to be unusually pure – a great asset as a key agent in making steel and many chemicals. The **Michigan Limestone and Chemical Company** began operating in Rogers City in 1910. Later it was bought by **Carl D. Bradley** and **U.S. Steel**, and eventually owned entirely by U.S. Steel. The Bradley Transportation Line it founded is a major Great Lakes carrier.

Presque Isle lighthouses

Two of the Great Lakes' most unusual lighthouses are tucked away on a scenic stretch of Lake Huron shore.

PRESQUE ISLE — "almost an island" — is a beautiful, old, and almost completely undiscovered resort area *way* off the beaten track between Alpena and Rogers City. You could pass near it on U.S. 23 and never know it was there. It's wedged between Grand Lake (seven miles long) and the Lake Huron shore, which here consists of picturesque points and beaches of broken, fossil-rich limestone. A large limestone quarry at Stoneport inconspicuously occupies a third of the area.

Two delightful and distinctive lighthouse museums are Presque Isle's chief public attractions, along with the new, 84-slip transient **marina** at Presque Isle Harbor, open May 15 through September 15 (517-595-3069). Both lighthouses are at the edge of cedar forests on the two-mile spit of land that forms the Presque Isle Harbor, one of Lake Huron's best natural harbors. The lights here were important parts of the federal government's early system of navigational aids in the Upper Great Lakes.

Two unusual **natural areas** add to the area's appeal for more adventurous explorers. The Besser-Bell Natural Area has trails around a ghost town and a sandy beach. Thompson's Harbor State Park is an undeveloped state park with seven and a half miles of Lake Huron shore and an unusually large concentration of the threatened dwarf lake iris.

THE OLD PRESQUE ISLE LIGHTHOUSE PARK goes all the way back to 1840. Its thick, squat stone tower served for 30 years.Then it was replaced by the "new" and much taller Presque Isle Light farther out on the spit, which developed into a Lifesaving Station and later a Coast Guard Station. The Stebbins family of Lansing purchased the property in the early 1900s. They fixed up the light tower and reconstructed the simple stone and stucco house as a vacation home and repository for their many antiques. For many years they opened it to the public. In 1995 Presque Isle Township purchased the property with help from the DNR. It will continue operating the museum.

There's a storybook mood about this place, beginning with the old **front range light** that has been moved to the road to mark the

The Old Presque Isle Lighthouse and Museum overlooks the entrance to Presque Isle Harbor, shown here with winter's eerie lake ice formations.

entrance. After going along a dirt road through a dark cedar forest, visitors park and emerge from the trees to the sunny, grassy keeper's cottage surrounded by a trim stone wall. A flagstone porch overlooks a rocky coast and the Presque Isle Harbor. Picturesque additions and improvements inside have made the place a reflection of its owners' tastes and collecting interests more than anything authentic. It's completely charming in its own way. Slate floors, leaded glass, a big stone fireplace, and exposed timbers salvaged from Lansing's old post office give the place an almost medieval English look. Wood doors come from a shipwreck.

The Stebbinses collected a lot of interesting old stuff, but it was museum manager Lorraine Parris's inspiration to make the little museum hands-on. "You tell kids they can't do something and they do it anyway," she says. She got tired of watching out for all the antiques. "When I made it a **hands-on museum**, the artifacts more or less stayed." She shows visitors how to use the old brass sextant. She lets them play the pump organ, and ring the cowbell. She encourages questions and likes to tell local shipwreck stories. And she delights in describing the mystery of how the light in the tower can be seen from the walkway of the harbor lately, even when there's no bulb and no power to the light.

Scattered throughout the yard are various other antiques: fake stocks, anchors, and the ton-and-a-half bronze bell from the old Lansing City Hall, which visitors are welcome to ring. But the real highlight is a trip up the winding stone steps of the two-story tower. Visitors can walk out on the parapet surrounding the lantern room for a beautiful and thrilling view. Recently, the township installed

At the New Presque Isle Lighthouse, enterprising museum manager Dan McGee plays the part of lightkeeper for special occasions. He will demonstrate his collection of ship steam whistles for interested visitors.

benches and picnic tables or visitors are welcome to spread a blanket on the grounds for their picnics. *Off U.S. 23, 23 miles north of Alpena and 20 miles south of Rogers City. There should be signs to the lighthouses. From Rogers City, turn left onto Hwy. 638 before you reach Grand Lake and turn left again at the harbor. From Alpena, take the right Y at the Hideaway Inn onto Hwy. 405 and continue north past the harbor to lighthouse. (517) 595-2787. Open in early May thru Oct. 15. 7 days, 9 a.m.-6 p.m. Open to 7 p.m. between Mem. and Labor Day. &: one step at the entry (ramp in near future). $1.50/adult, 50¢ ages 6-12.*

THE NEW PRESQUE ISLE LIGHTHOUSE AND MUSEUM sits amid a hundred-acre township **park** with **picnic tables, restrooms** and **nature trails** through the woods of pines and cedars. On the limey soil here and at the nearby state park, the endangered blue pitcher thistle and dwarf lake iris flourish.

This is another delightful spot, which another enterprising museum manager has developed into something original. Dan McGee, the son and grandson of Great Lakes sailors, was hired as a caretaker by the group who took over the abandoned light and Coast Guard station here. Now he convincingly plays the part of a turn of the century lightkeeper for group tours and special occasions. He has collected **steam whistles** from many different Great Lakes boats and assembled them under a gazebo. He'll demonstrate them for interested visitors.

The 100-foot lighthouse **tower** is the tallest on the Great Lakes. Despite Coast Guard concern about liability, it's still open to the public from noon until 5 during two special events: the Fourth of July picnic and barbecue and the Labor Day pig roast. Both events are held on Saturday of the holiday weekend. Restoring and stabilizing the lighthouse here has been a successful community project. The **museum shop** is unusually good. *The New Presque Isle Light is a mile beyond the Old Light (see above). (517) 595-2059. Open May 1 thru Oct 15, daily 9-6. &: gift shop, restrooms; museum has 4 steps. Free; donations appreciated.*

GRAND LAKE . . . . . has four public fishing sites, three picnic areas, and abundant perch, bass, pike, walleye, and muskies. For an area **brochure**, write Presque Isle Area Commerce Committee, Box 74, Presque Isle, MI 49777, or request it at either lighthouse museum.

VIRGIN WHITE PINE, A SANDY BEACH, AND THE GHOST TOWN OF BELL . . . . . are part of the **Besser-Bell Natural Area.** Trails go through a dark cedar forest, soon to emerge on Lake Huron's shore. It makes for a pleasant hour's walk and a nice afternoon at a remote beach. A house is used as a clubhouse for local functions. It's best reached from U.S. 23 south of Grand Lake. Turn east at the Hideaway Inn onto Grand Lake Rd. At the Township Hall, turn right (you're still on Hwy. 405) and look for the signs in about a mile. Park at the main parking area.

WET MEADOWS, INLAND DUNES, AND ROCKY BEACHES. . . . . make undeveloped **Thompson's Harbor State Park** a naturalist's delight. Its four miles of hiking trails are marked, although a compass might be well-advised, and the hiking is not strenuous. The trailhead is one mile inside the park entrance, which is twelve miles southeast of Rogers City or five miles from the junction of U.S. 23 and M-65. The park, which awaits future development, is the last legacy of Genevieve Gillette, ardent parks promoter and landscape architect. The state bought it with money she left to the people of Michigan. Thompson's Harbor is administered by managers at P. H. Hoeft State Park in Rogers City. (517) 734-2543.

The Alpena area and the Jesse Besser Museum

*An old lumber and cement town
with unusual architecture, a fine museum,
excellent diving, and a Lake Huron shoreline
of great natural beauty.*

FOR ENJOYING the natural beauty of the Great Lakes with nary a trace of trendy gentrification, there's no place else in the Lower Peninsula that comes close to the Alpena area, overlooking Lake Huron's Thunder Bay. Two undeveloped state parks nearby (Negwegon to the south and Thompson's Harbor to the north) have 14 miles of completely undeveloped Lake Huron shoreline between them.

Alpena is not easy to get to. It's 74 miles from the nearest interstate, and 104 miles up the two-lane U.S. 23 from Standish on Saginaw Bay. The atmosphere, like that of most old lumber towns, is definitely unpretentious, working-class, and friendly, with lots of corner bars in the Polish north end along U.S. 23. There is a surprisingly lively cultural scene, thanks to spirited local arts advocates.

After the turn of the century, lumbering was in decline in this region when a group of lumbermen realized that Alpena had all the necessary ingredients for making portland cement: pure limestone, marl, shale, and clay. They formed the first portland cement plant. A local competitor eventually became the largest cement plant in the world. Herman Besser and his son, Jesse, invented and manufactured an enormously successful machine for making concrete blocks. The Besser Company remains the world's leading producer of such machinery.

Jesse Besser became an active area philanthropist; his gifts of buildings and land always stipulated that buildings on the site be erected of concrete. As a result, many 20th-century public buildings and houses are made of concrete, often with unusual finishes. The 1930s concrete courthouse at First and Water, for instance, was sand-blasted and treated with "Resto-crete" for an enriched color. Herman Besser's bungalow home at 403 South Second was the first to use Bes-Stone Split Block that resembled long, narrow blocks of rough-faced limestone.

Buoyed by the big cement industry, paper mills, and also by Wurtsmith Air Force Base 35 miles south in Oscoda, the local economy perked along into the 1970s without having to develop the tourism that most of northern Michigan was forced to rely on much earlier. But Wurtsmith closed in 1992, and the big cement plant, under its new owners, La Farge, today employs a fifth of the workforce it once did. Visitors can get a terrific value in the Alpena area and feel like they're making a valuable contribution to local economic development.

Major attractions of the Alpena area include:

◆ **Bay View Park and the Thunder Bay Shores Marine,** downtown just south of the Thunder Bay River. Both have been handsomely redone. The marina (800-332-9204) has 77 transient slips, a boat launch, charter boat service, a fish-cleaning station, and restrooms and showers. Just south of it is Bay View Park with tennis courts, basketball, volley ball, a bandshell (**summer concerts** are Tuesdays at 6:30 and Thursdays at 7:30 in July and August, ♿), a **playground**, and a swimming **beach**.

◆ **Historic homes on State Avenue/U.S. 23,** the main entry into town from the south. Built along the shore are impressive and often unusually elaborate homes of lumbermen, bankers, lawyers, and other business leaders who promoted Alpena and profited from its prosperous decades around the turn of the century. Fans of historic architecture will enjoy walking down State from Bay View Park to Richardson Street, then heading inland a block and returning along First. Cement block king Jesse Besser's own Moderne house, a 1939 testament to the durability and versatility of concrete block, is at 232 South First. Today it's the **Besser House bed and breakfast** (517-356-0592). ♿: no. Three more lakefront parks are to the south, in the older part of town.

◆ **Old Town,** north of the river across the Second Avenue bridge, has many handsome old commercial buildings. Entrepreneurs John and Connie Van Schoik have invested in renovating some and developing the noteworthy **John A. Lau Saloon** and restaurant (517-354-6898) at 414 North Second (♿) and the **Display Case** (517-356-2758), a gift/gourmet/import store at 428 North Second (♿: no). You can watch candles being made at **Sonlight Candles**, at 309 North Second. Another popular visitor stop is **Jeannie's Sweet Shop**, an ice cream parlor with homemade chocolates. It's downtown – south across the Second Street bridge and up half a block at 109 West Chisholm. (517) 356-6541. ♿: no.

The **Thunder Bay Theatre** *at* 400 N. Second (517-354-2267) is northern Michigan's only year-round professional theater company. It also hosts many shows and performances. ♿ The three-screen **Royal Knight Cinema** is at Second and Chisholm (517-356-3333).

Newly renovated is the **State Theater**, with five screens, 204 North Second Avenue at Park Place (517-354-3500). &: *with 2 hours notice, films showing in the 2 upper theaters can be brought downstairs.*

◆ **Jesse Besser Museum and Planetarium.** One of Michigan's most impressive museums, Besser combines historical, scientific, and art exhibits on two levels. A striking three-story-high Foucault pendulum greets entering visitors, vividly showing the effect of the Earth's rotation.

The museum's highlight is its spectacular collection of artifacts from **Great Lakes Indians**, particularly in the historic era. It's one of the finest in the country. A local state highway employee and his son, now a museum curator, gathered the 20,000-item Haltiner Collection. Their most remarkable discoveries were found right across the street: copper artifacts dating back 7,000 years, made by a still-mysterious people known only as the Copper Culture.

Local history highlights include a recreated avenue of Alpena shops from the 1890s, a popular diorama with mounted indigenous birds and animals, and a room devoted to Jesse Besser and his roles in concrete technology and Alpena-area philanthropy.

Changing exhibits, 23 a year, showcase widely varied subjects. Call for information on related **lectures**. Many exhibits showcase emerging Michigan artists.

The **Sky Theater Planetarium** (75¢ additional admission) has shows at 1 and 3 p.m. Sundays and in July and August Thursdays at 7:30. Shows change throughout the year. An example: *Tle'eho- onaa'ei: The One Who Governs the Night,* Native American stories combined with the astronomy of the fall sky (Oct 6/Nov 24, 1996). *On the north edge of Alpena, 1 block east of U.S. 23 North, at 491 Johnson. East of Holiday Inn, next to the Alpena Community College campus. (517) 356-2202. Open Mon-Fri 10-5, Thurs to 9, Sat & Sun noon-5. &: partial. $2/adult, $1 students & seniors (60 & older), hand- icapped & under 5 free, maximum $5/family.*

◆ **Sportsmen's Island** is in a bay of the Thunder Bay River, right in town by the Holiday Inn across from the Besser Museum and the Chamber of Commerce. It's a handy place to fish from platforms, bird-watch, and see wildlife from a canoe or along a one-mile perimeter **nature trail.** *Parking is on roadside park at U.S. 23 and Long Rapids/Johnson.* The **Washington Street Park** off M-32 just west of downtown offers another good view of the river, with lots of geese who greet people, hoping to be fed.

◆ **Presque Isle Lighthouses.** See page 684.

◆ **Squaw Bay.** U.S. 23 goes right through a big marsh south of town. You can pull over and get out to watch some beautiful water birds.

◆ **Dinosaur Gardens.** This roadside attraction is no kitschy tourist trap but a moody, eerie place, a sensitively executed folk art installation that was the life work of the late self-taught artist and sculptor Paul Domke. Through a dark, primordial, ferny cedar swamp wind built-up trails. A plashing creek bisects the forty acres. Every so often a huge, life-size dinosaur is seen around a bend. The creatures are realistically fashioned of concrete, Alpena's favorite building material, here mixed with gravel and deer hair and applied on substructures of metal and lathe.

Domke had a fine feel for creating a complete environment. He took good advantage of the cedar swamp. That natural setting evokes the imagined mood of dinosaur time, a part of creation deeply bound up with his own religious beliefs. Occasionally he combined images of dinosaurs and Christ — "as a testimonial to his belief that Christ was the master planner of an Earth that included dinosaurs," according to an explanatory sign. The Gardens' effect is greatest toward dusk. *Dinosaur Gardens are north of the center of Ossineke on U.S. 23, 10 miles south of Alpena. (517) 471-5477. Open May 15 thru Oct 15, 10-4 daily (10-6 during peak season). $3/adult, $2/children 6-12, $1/children under 6. Funds go to maintaining the concrete sculptures.* ⴑ

◆ **Negwegon State Park.** This undeveloped gem of a state park is, so far, the delightful secret of local people and a limited number of outdoors lovers who eschew the crowds and conveniences of developed parks. "Many believe the most beautiful and possibly the most isolated beaches on Lake Huron lie [here]," writes Jim Du Fresne in his comprehensive and useful guide, *Michigan State Parks.* "Words like 'paradise' are often used . . . to describe the park's shoreline, a string of bays and coves stretching 6.5 miles." Rocky points separate the coves; the interior is pine, cedar, and white birch. Ten miles of signed **trails** in three loops go along the shoreline and through the interior. (Because the park is so heavily wooded, park rangers recommend that you bring along a compass.) They start at the parking lot. There is a pit toilet. No camping. *Park is off U.S. 23 (but not signed), 12 miles north of Harrisville and 18 miles or so south of Alpena. From U.S. 23, turn east onto Black River Road. In 1.5 miles you'll see a cemetery on the left. Just past it, turn north (left) onto Sand Hill Trail.* **Warning:** *this sandy, unimproved road can be difficult in very dry or very wet weather. In about 2 1/2 miles, watch at your right for a good gravel road with park entrance signs. Go east 1 1/4 miles to parking lot. If you do get stuck, the nearest phone is about 5 miles away on U.S. 23. For information, call (517) 739-9730.* ⴑ: *no. No fee.*

GOOD INFORMATION SOURCES FOR THE ALPENA AREA . . . . . The **Alpena Chamber of Commerce** (1-800-582-1906) is on U.S. 23 North at Johnson St., just south of the Holiday Inn, in the Alpena Civic Center Building. Ask here for info on **cross-country skiing** in nearby state forests. **24-hour visitor information centers** are at principal entries to town: on U.S. 23 South at *Dawn Donuts*; on U.S. 23 North at *Kurvan's Restaurant* and Mini-Mart; and on M-32 West at the *Bagley Marathon Station.* Call for a helpful visitor's packet. The Northern Radio Network puts out the handy **Sunrise Side Vacation Guide** of some 50 pages, widely available at chambers of commerce and participating businesses in Lake Huron communities.

A POPULAR PLACE FOR DIVERS . . . . . because of its clear waters and interesting underwater limestone formations, the **Thunder Bay Underwater Preserve** contains 80 shipwrecks in a protected area of 288 square miles just off Alpena. Fourteen of these are moored shipwrecks that can be explored with the help of a charter wreck-diving service. The unusually dense concentration of shipwrecks is due to the number of hazardous shoals and rocky islands here. Also, at this point in Lake Huron, upbound ships must turn to the northwest. "If captains overestimated their ship's capabilities during northwestern gales, they sometimes found themselves in trouble," writes Steve Harrington in his useful *Divers' Guide to Michigan.* In 1981 the state made the area a preserve, prohibiting divers from taking artifacts from wrecks.

Right on the Thunder Bay River is **Thunder Bay Divers**, offering charter wreck-diving service at a cost of $55 per day for a walk-in, per diver. Discounted rates for groups. (517) 356-9336. Located at 405 East Chisholm (the Alpena city marina), they have rental equipment, dive store facilities, and an air station. Group boat tours are available if arranged in advance. New owner Lee Barnhill will have night tours of Thunder Bay this year. The 2 1/2 hour tour aboard the 54-foot utility boat lasts begins at 7 p.m. Cost is $15 per adult, $10 for 10 and under with a minimum of 10 people. Alcohol permitted. July and August are the best months for diving. A favorite dive is the American steamer *The Grecian,* under 90 feet of water. It sank in 1904 while returning back to Detour from Detroit for repairs.

Hartwick Pines State Park & Michigan Forest Visitor Center

*See a rare, majestic stand of 200-year-old pines,
a remnant of the awesome forests
that once covered a third of the state.*

BEFORE THE RUSH of settlers to Michigan in the 1830s, over 13 million of the state's 38 million acres were covered with white pine. Thriving in poor, sandy soil, these majestic trees grow up to 200 feet tall and could live 500 years. They were prized because the tall, straight trunks make excellent building lumber and are light enough to float down rivers to lumber mills. It took the white man half a century to transform these forests into the lumber that built towns from Michigan to the treeless Great Plains and rebuilt Chicago after the fire of 1871. By the 1920s the once-huge forests were cutover wastelands.

One of the very few virgin white pine forests remaining is the 49-acre stand at this state park. Actually it's a mix of white pine, red pine, and eastern hemlock. Taking advantage of the park's handy location on the main highway for vacationers heading up north, Hartwick Pines has long been a place where visitors could learn about lumbering days. Now the popular state park has been revamped and reconfigured, with a single entrance, new campground, and big new visitor center building.

Here's an overview of the park's chief visitor attractions.

◆ The beautiful big **visitor center**

The majestic white pine, Michigan's state tree, provided much of the capital invested in the automotive industry and other important early-20th-century businesses.

seems to float in the forest. In its 100-seat **auditorium** a 14-minute, nine-projector audiovisual show "**The Forest: Michigan's Renewable Resource**" is presented every half-hour throughout the day. (Be aware that forestry products companies have helped pay for this and certain other interpretive exhibits. This is not the place to find a consideration of all the environmental and social consequences of logging — like the great forest fires of the 1870s, searching for new uses for cutover land, and the unsuccessful attempts to farm much of northern Michigan.) For a look back at logging, visitors can request to view in a small classroom some fascinating **historical videos** showing logging drives and camp life in Michigan, Minnesota, and Maine.

The **exhibit hall** deals with Michigan forests and forest management. A cutaway view of an artifical tree shows how its vascular system works. Hands-on **computer games** present the choices of various forest management scenarios in game form. The **museum shop** features books and educational materials on logging, Michigan flora and fauna, and state parks. Many **presentations** and demonstrations of crafts take place on weekends, especially in summer. The park now has a full-time historian and another natural-history interpreter who give tours and talks.

If at all possible, visitors should plan to take advantage of the free **guided tours** that leave from here. Call (517) 348-2537 after Mondays at 11 a.m. for that week's schedule. Call about off-season, "special request" group tours. &

◆ The **Big Pines** down a hill are now connected with the visitor center by blacktop trails, so wheelchairs and strollers can use them. **Guided walks** through the Big Pines take one to 1 1/2 hours and leave from the visitor center.

These virgin pines were saved by the national panic of 1893. It so depressed demand for lumber that the logging outfit cutting it suspended operations. When the economy improved, it wasn't worth the trouble to set up a new camp for so little acreage. In 1927 Karen Hartwick purchased 8,236 acres from the Salling Hanson Lumber Company and donated it to the state for a state park.

The imposing parcel is a big enough area to give the visitor a sense what awesome forests covered the state. The white pines are so tall that their wide, dark trunks dominate a walker's view. You have to crane your neck to look high up and see where the trees' branches begin eight or nine stories in the air. *Follow signs from park entrance. Open 9-4 daily year-round, to 7 from Mem. to Labor Day. (517) 348-2537.* &

◆ The **Logging Museum**, with its life-size, compellingly realistic recreations of a mess hall, kitchen, bunkhouse, and office, has been revamped. The Civilian Conservation Corps erected the original log buildings in 1934-35. In an authentic logging camp the kitchen/mess hall and bunk room would have been in separate buildings, but generations of visitors mistook this for the real thing. Now display cases with photographs let them know it's a museum. A **big wheel**, used to haul logs over rough ground, can be seen in the woods nearby. The museum tour shows the high level of organization it took for a 75-man crew to clear an acre a day, and conveys the colorful lingo. Kids love the synonyms for lice: "seam squirrels" and "crotch crickets," for instance. Longtime logging interpreter Wendell Hoover, incidentally, is now at the interesting **Civilian Conservation Corps Museum** at nearby North Higgens Lake State Park: (517) 821-6125.

The logging museum area and the outdoor **steam sawmill** come to life on special weekends. Centered around various handcrafts demonstrations and old-time string music, these events have developed into friendly social gatherings of kindred spirits who camp and share stories in the evening and look forward eagerly to next year's event. Crafts demonstrators are apt to be experienced professionals; their works are for sale at wholesale prices. The two-day events, held from 10 a.m. to 4 p.m., currently include ; **Wood Shaving Days** (3rd weekend in July, features woodcarving) and **Black Iron Days** (4th weekend of August; blacksmithing), when a team of horses and a driver with a log-driver's excellent sense of balance put the big wheel to use. Call (517) 348-2537 to confirm dates.

Renovations on the second museum building with the blacksmith shop, an essential part of every logging camp, may be finished for 1997. *The museum is now reached from the visitor center (above). Open April thru Oct, daily 9-4. From Mem. to Labor Day, open 9-7.* ⅛

THE REST OF THE PARK

The Big Pines and interesting interpretive displays are such a heavily used draw that they overshadow the rest of the park, which itself is exceptional. At 9,672 acres, Hartwick Pines State Park is the largest state park in the Lower Peninsula. It's accessible (200 miles from Detroit, about 150 from Lansing or Grand Rapids). And it combines an extensive and typical stretch of prime north woods habitats— forest, three stocked fishing *lakes*, and streams —is with the conveniences of a modern state park campground — a matter of great importance to some families.

For motorists, a good way to see the rest of the park is along the eight-mile **Scenic Drive**, entered from M-93 some two miles north

Prime habitat for the rare little blue-gray Kirtland's warbler is in young jack pine forests in and near Hartwick Pines State Park in Crawford and Oscoda counties. Breeding grounds are off-limits except for free guided tours led by Forest Service naturalists from mid-May through July 4.

of the main park entrance. Here interpretive signs and turnouts encourage visitors to get out of their cars and take in the natural world. The drive crosses the Au Sable River and passes an area with some individual white pines that are now over 200 years old but were considered too small by early loggers. A stand of virgin jack pine – an unusual group of elderly members of that short-lived species – is along the Scenic Drive. **Cross-country skiers** are finding Hartwick Pines State Park a superior destination. On the north side of M-93, some 17 miles of intermediate loops are groomed. (These are open to **mountain bikes** in summer.) Narrow bridges make it impossible to groom the Au Sable Trail and Mertz Grade Trail, but skiers use them, too. **Ski maps** are available at the main entrance contact station, open year-round.

Two especially nice times to visit Hartwick Pines are mid-May into mid-June when the variety of **wild flowers** in bloom is greatest, and at the end of September, when **fall color** is usually at its peak. There's a good mix of colorful hardwoods through most of the state park: maple, beech, oak, aspen, and birch, which makes for a full range of reds and yellows, especially near the river. In the winter there is almost always snow on the ground, and a visit then shows what it was like during the logging season.

A trail system leads visitors to the park's less obvious charms.

◆ The **Au Sable River Trail** is an easy three-mile loop that begins on the south side of M-93, opposite the main vehicle entrance. It crosses the East Branch of that legendary river twice. Famous for **trout fishing**, the Au Sable was originally full of grayling until they were fished to extinction in the late 19th century. Stocked trout thrived so well that fishing parties earlier this century would often catch over 500 fish an outing. Today the North Branch and main stream of that famous river are so heavily canoed that only the shallow and uncanoeable **East Branch** and the upper reaches of the North Branch retain the mystique of yesteryear. About three miles of the East Branch passes through the park. "Here the river is a crystal-clear stream that gurgles over gravel banks and undercuts the banks around deadheads and trees," says veteran outdoorsman Jim Du Fresne in his highly recommended *Michigan State Parks: A Complete Recreation Guide for Campers, Boaters, Anglers, Hikers & Skiers.* It's an excellent but overlooked stream for rainbow and brook trout, he says, fished with flies and short, six- to seven-foot rods, or with worms or spinners.

The trail also passes a rare forest of **virgin hemlocks** 80 to 90 feet tall, saved from the saw by a sudden drop in the price of its bark, which was used for tanning leather. An optional, steep **scenic overlook** at the northwest extreme of the walk gives a panoramic view of the area.

◆ The easy two-mile **Mertz Grade Nature Trail** loops through a variety of forests, on part of an old logging railroad grade. It links up with the Big Pines trails behind the visitor center.

Hartwick Pines State Park is off I-75 at Exit 259, a little north of Grayling. Go north on M-93 three miles to park entrance. Or take M-93 7 1/2 miles north of Grayling. The park and campground are open year-round. (517) 348-7068. State park sticker required: $4/day or $20 year.

FREE GUIDED TOURS TO SEE THE RARE KIRTLAND'S WARBLER . . . . .
attract birders from all over the world to Grayling and tiny Mio, 30 miles east on M-72. The particular preferences of the little blue-gray bird with the yellow breast and male's beautiful song have made it an endangered species. The Kirtland's warbler will nest only in Jack Pines, between five and 15 feet tall, or roughly between eight and 20 years old. Each breeding pair requires at least 30

acres. Jack pines cones release their seeds only when burned. Modern fire control has allowed the Jack Pine to mature where it was once periodically burned and renewed through forest fires. No new habitats for Kirtland's warblers are naturally created.

A section of northeast Michigan centered at Mio is the only place in the world where Kirtland's warblers breed today. Since 1975, 23 areas of public land have been managed to encourage Kirtland's warblers. A 1993 census identified 486 singing males (assumed to be half of a mating pair) – a big gain from the low of 167 in 1987, but hardly enough to put the little bird off the endangered list.

Kirtland's warbler breeding grounds are off-limits except for these free guided tours, led by U.S. Forest Service naturalists between May 15 and July 4. **From Grayling** at the Holiday Inn on I-75 Business Loop South, they leave daily at 7 a.m. and 11 a.m. (517) 337-6650. **From Mio**, they leave Wednesday through Sunday at 7 a.m., with an extra 11 a.m. tour on weekends. Meet at the Forest Service office, 401 South Court at the corner of M-33, across from the Mio Motel. (517) 826-3252. Reservations only necessary for groups.

CANOE THE MANISTEE . . . . . to avoid the crowds on the popular Au Sable and have an equivalent canoeing experience. Both rivers pass through Grayling and are well served by area liveries. Call the **Grayling Area Visitors' Council** at (800) 937-8837 for a Grayling area information packet.

FOR OTHER, LESS DEVELOPED CAMPGROUNDS NEAR GRAYLING . . . . . ask for maps and information from these state and national forest offices:
◆ **Au Sable State Forest**, Route 1, Box 146, Mio, MI 48647. (517) 826-3211. 10 campgrounds with 260 campsites in Crawford County.
◆ **Huron National Forest, Mio Ranger District**, 401 S. Court St., Mio, MI 48647. (517) 826-3252. Two campgrounds with 36 campsites between Grayling and Mio. Request the large and elaborate map/guide of all facilities and trails (hiking, snowmobiling, horseback riding, cross-country skiing, and more) in the Huron National Forest and adjacent state forests between Grayling and Oscoda. It's a goldmine for outdoorsmen. Campgrounds are on the Manistee and Au Sable Rivers and on many nearby lakes.

IN NEARBY GAYLORD . . . . a convenient stop is the quarter-century-old **Call of the Wild Museum.** Here you can see dozens of scenes of stuffed wild animals native to the area. Interesting descriptions by each exhibit tell such things as how Michigan's wild turkeys disappeared in 1888 and weren't restocked until the 1950s, or how the American elk was hunted almost to extinction. A large gift shop sells everything from saddles to clothing. *850 S. Wisconsin. Take exit 282 from I-75, east 1/4 mile. (517) 732-4336. June 15-Sept 2: daily 8:30 a.m.-9 p.m. 9:30-6 rest of year. Adults $4, children 5-13 $2.50.*

FOR MORE ON LOGGING HISTORY. . . . . Other must-see destinations for any-one interested in lumber history are the **Muskegon County Museum**, page 536, and the fabulous **Hackley House** lumber baron's mansion in Muskegon, page 528 . . . . . . Other noteworthy destinations are the **Michigan Historical Museum** in Lansing (page 426), the **Sloan Museum** in Flint (page 360), the won-derful homemade model of a logging camp in the **Benzie County Historical Museum** (page 570), the **Empire Area Historical Museum** near Sleeping Bear Dunes (page 601), and the **Tahquamenon River Logging Museum** in Newberry (page 749). . . . . . Logging employment brought people from many parts of the world to Michigan (Scandinavians stand out, but there were also many Germans, Belgians, Irish, and French-Indians from Canada.) And lumber capital got the auto industry off to a fast start in Detroit and Flint.

STAY IN A GRAYLING LUMBERMAN'S MANSION . . . . . The mansion built by Karen Michaelson Hartwick's business partner is now a beautifully restored bed and breakfast known as **Belknap's Hanson House** (517-348-6630). It's three blocks north of downtown Grayling on the corner of Lake and Peninsular. The owners and staff are up on local history and interesting things in the area.

The Upper Peninsula

IN MANY WAYS Upper Michigan is a world apart from the rest of the state. It's a big place — 300 miles across— and often quite wild. It has over 11,000 miles of Great Lakes shoreline on lakes Superior, Michigan, and Huron. Detroit is closer to Philadelphia than it is to Ironwood, which is not only north but so far west it's west of Madison, Wisconsin. All the Upper Peninsula counties along the 200-mile Wisconsin border are on Central Time. The U.P. has its own state fair, in Escanaba in August. There's been a surprising amount of farming here. Farming was a first step out of mines and logging camps.

It is in an entirely different bioregion, the northern mixed forest, adapted to a short growing season and long winter. Huge banks of snow aren't melted until summer has almost begun, along with the black fly season. The annoying flies are mostly gone by early July. July through color season up to the first part of October are the prime visitor seasons here, though skiing and snowmobiling are also potent draws. Logging

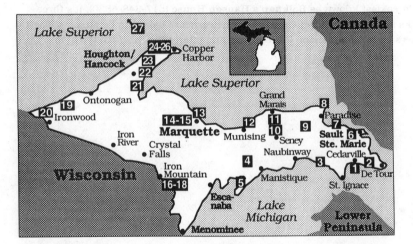

continues to be big business here, largely to supply pulp for paper mills centered in **Iron Mountain** (Champion International), **Escanaba** (Mead), and **Munising** (Kimberly Clark).

Many people appreciate the area's small population and vast open spaces. Only 300,000 people live up here year-round. The biggest city, **Marquette**, is under 22,000. (But individual populations can mislead; there's a lot of sprawl, and old mining towns cluster together.) Most of the land is government-owned, as part of the **Hiawatha** and **Ottawa national forests** or the **Copper Country**, **Escanaba River**, and **Lake Superior state forests**. You can drive through miles of forest without seeing a single building. Most land owned by paper and mining companies is also open to public hunting, gathering, and recreation, in return for lower taxes.

Logging has never remotely approached the riches generated by the region's huge copper and iron mining industries in the latter 19th and early 20th centuries. The western Upper Peninsula is ancient volcanic rock, known as the Canadian Shield. Michigan's **Porcupine** and **Huron mountains** are the worn-down remains of the Laurentian Mountains, once higher than the Rockies, the core of the first North American continent. The volcanic and conglomerate rock contain rich deposits of copper in the **Keweenaw Range** (first mined over 5,000 years ago) and iron in the **Gogebic**, **Menominee**, and **Marquette ranges**, plus enough

Information sources: VISITORS' BUREAUS

Delta Co. Tourism Bureau
(800) 437-7496

Les Cheneaux Islands Tourist Assn.
(Escanaba) (906) 484-3935

Tourism Assn. of Dickinson Co.
(Iron Mountain)
(906) 774-2002, (800) 236-2447

Iron Co. Tourism Council (Iron River)
(906) 265-3822, (800) 255-3620

Ironwood Tourism Council
(906) 932-1000

Keweenaw Tourism Council
Calumet: (800) 338-7982
Houghton (800) 338-7982

Western Upper Peninsula CVB
(906) 932-4850, (800) 272-7000

Baraga Co. Tourist Assn.
(L'Anse) (906) 524-7444

Manistique Area Tourist Council
(906) 341-5838, (800) 342-4282

Marquette Country CVB
(906) 228-7749, (800) 544-4321

Munising Visitors Bureau
(906) 387-2138

Newberry Area Tourist Association
(906) 293-5562, (800) 831-7292

Ontonogan Tourism Council
(906) 8844-4735

Paradise Area Tourism Council
(906) 492-3927

St. Ignace Area Tourist Association
(906) 643-8717, (800) 338-6660

Sault Ste. Marie Tourist Bureau
(906) 632-3301, (800) MI-SAULT

gemstones and agates to make the area a major U.S. destination for rock-hounds. Eastern capitalists drawn by mining were the original settlers in the western U.P. Marquette, in fact, was originally called New Worcester after the Massachusetts home of its founders. Mining companies like Calumet and Hecla (managed by the son of famed Harvard scientist Louis Agassiz) and Cleveland-Cliffs developed not only mines but most communities. They recruited immigrants from Scandinavia, Croatia, Cornwall (the font of mining know-how), and many other countries.

This ethnic mix flavors the area in many ways. There are distinctive **ethnic foods** like the Cornish pasty (the famous meat-and-potato-filled folded pastry carried by miners); Finnish cinnamon toast; and spicy Italian cudighi sausage. The **regional accent**, sometimes so strong it sounds foreign, blends Finnish and Canadian rhythms. The Finnish sauna is a common sight behind many homes in the western U.P., where Finns are by far the dominant ethnic group. The significant Indian population means there are a dozen places with gambling and that public radio stations in Houghton and Marquette pick up news from an interesting North American tribal network.

The mining ranges are only in the rugged western Upper Peninsula, with its dramatic worn-down mountains. The eastern Upper Peninsula is largely flat and more monotonous. Here the indigenous population has roots in fishing and logging. Many share French and Indian ancestry. The Au Train Basin forms a clear divide between the western and eastern parts of the peninsula. It is a series of streams and lakes between Lake Superior's Au Train Bay near Munising and the head of Little Bay de Noc on Lake Michigan near Escanaba. Lake Superior once emptied into Lake Michigan through here, it's thought.

Today virtually all the underground mines have closed. Ore is too far down to be mined economically. Only the vast open-pit Tilden iron mine

Information sources: CHAMBERS OF COMMERCE

Bergland (906) 575-3265	**Iron River** (906) 265-3822
Bessemer (906) 663-4542	**Ironwood** (906) 932-1122
Caspian (906) 265-3822	**Ishpeming-Negaunee** (906) 486-4841
Cedarville (906) 484-3935	**Manistique** (906) 341-5010
Crystal Falls (906) 265-3822	**Marquette** (906) 226-6591
DeTour Village (906) 297-5987	**Menominee** (906) 863-2679
Drummond Island (906) 493-5245	**Munising** (906) 387-2138
Escanaba (906) 786-2192	**Ontonagon** (906) 884-4735
Garden (906) 786-2192	**Rapid River** (906) 786-2192
Gladstone (906) 786-2192	**St. Ignace** (906) 643-3301
Grand Marais (906) 494-2766	**Sault Ste. Marie** (906) 632-3301
Houghton (906) 482-5240	**Wakefield** (906) 224-2222
Iron Mountain (906) 774-2002	

remains, and a Keweenaw mine that supplies copper for Wolmanized lumber. The U.P.'s largest single employer today is the Soo-based Kewadin casino, now that K. I. Sawyer Air Force Base near Marquette has closed. State prisons are Michigan's big growth industry thanks to mandatory sentencing. The Upper Peninsula has a lot of them. Tourism is very important everywhere, even is summer is short. Towns promote snowmobiling to bring new business during the six-month winter.

People here really know how to stretch a dollar — one positive byproduct of the mining heritage of boom and hard times, both beyond local control. That's probably behind the relaxed "one day at a time" attitude so different from the striving and fretting of people down below. There's a whole different attitude toward the outdoors up here. Hunting or fishing are likely to be serious, lifelong pursuits. There's a shared sense of this being a place, not unlike Alaska, where a person can live a freer, more independent, simpler life away from the pressure of careers, fashion, materialism, high-power entertainment, and status. Nothing infuriates local people as much as a fence, unless it's a bureaucrat from Lansing. Still, reasonably affable visitors often encounter a down-to-earth friendliness here that's quite amazing — is it a holdover from another era, or some ethnic-influenced thing? — even if the visitors come across looking like college-educated environmentalists themselves.

Every so often, local sentiment builds up to form a 51st state, to be called **Superior**. When you look at a map, it seems quite logical. How did the Upper Peninsula, once part of Wisconsin Territory, end up in Michigan, anyway? Because of the bloodless **Toledo War** of 1835. Fuzzy language and inadequate surveys were behind the 1805 establishment of Michigan Territory's southern boundary. Ohio wanted to control the mouth of the Maumee River, a strategic site for economic development. In 1835 the state of Ohio had far more political clout than Michigan, still a territory. Ohio won the Toledo Strip. Michigan received the Upper Peninsula as a consolation prize, first thought worthless. But discovery of iron and copper deposits in the 1840s launched mining booms that generated many times the wealth of California's gold.

Information sources: MISCELLANEOUS

Upper Peninsula Travel & Rec. Assn.
(906) 774-5480, (800) 562-7134
Ask for helpful U.P. travel guide

Hiawatha National Forest
Rapid River/Escanaba (906) 474-6442
Manistique (906) 341-5666
Munising (906) 387-2512
St. Ignace (906) 643-7900
National forest offices have recreation info sheets on many areas & activities.

Ottawa National Forest
Ironwood (906) 932-1330
Sylvania Wilderness Area/Watersmeet
(906) 358-4551

Copper Country State Forest
Baraga (906) 353-6651

Escanaba River State Forest
Gladstone (906) 786-2351

Lake Superior State Forest
Newberry (906) 293-5131

Les Cheneaux Islands

Off Hessel and Cedarville, a maze of channels between rocky isles and peninsulas is an unhurried paradise for sailors, boaters, and fishermen.

AN UNTRUMPETED treasure of the eastern Upper Peninsula is the Les Cheneaux Islands area, with its rocky islands and peninsulas, wildflower meadows, and cedar forests. Within just 45 minutes of the Mackinac Bridge and Sault Ste. Marie, this old resort area makes a fine base for a week of relaxation augmented with some sightseeing as far away as Tahquamanon Falls and Whitefish Point.

The second Saturday of August the Antique Wooden Boat Show at Hessel puts the area in the news. Otherwise, Les Cheneaux is *way* off the beaten tourist track. There's not a big golf resort or shopping district to be found — and that's the way the people who have had summered here for decades want things to stay. About the only signs of recent development are a nice new supermarket and a two-story Comfort Inn in Cedarville — this despite the fact that increasing numbers of retirees and urban refugees are making their permanent homes here.

Les Cheneaux means "the channels" in French. It's pronounced "Lay SHEN o" and known as "the snows." Here rocky fingers of limestone, sand, and gravel stretch out southeast into Lake Huron's most northwestern waters and break up into a series of 36 islands along 12 miles of shore. Some islands are quite large. Others are big enough for just a few cottages. Tiny Dollar Island in the Snows Channel is a perch for a single fantastic Arabian-inspired house that extends its verandas and docks out into the water and seems to float without terrestrial support.

The sheltered bays and channels make for ideal sailing and boating — protected from the Great Lakes' winds and waves. (Waves are much higher out on Lake Huron than within the Snows.) Constantly changing vistas created by the complex shorelines of many islands and inlets make for interesting boating even at very slow speeds — in a rented fishing boat with an outboard motor, or even a canoe. (A paddler in good shape can canoe from Hessel to Cedarville in two hours.)

The area's idiosyncratic shoreline architecture adds interest to cruising. Along Les Cheneaux Club and Snows Channel are wonderful old boathouses, weathered gray or painted brown or dark

Famous for wooden boats: Les Cheneaux Islands Antique Wooden Boat Show celebrates the area's tradition of building, maintaining, and restoring wooden boats. It's at Hessel on the second Saturday of August.

Island cottagers depended on boats for transportation and fishing. That kept local boat shops busy long after commercial fishing declined. This 1906 photograph shows photographer Andrew Tanner, his wife, and son in their Mackinaw boat.

green, elaborately rustic like the big summer houses they are connected with.

The Snows has been a favorite summer retreat since the late 19th century. Then, at the end of the logging era, older Middle Western cities were establishing themselves as industrial and commercial powerhouses and centers of great wealth. Hay fever relief and escaped from city heat led many wealthy people, from Chicago, St. Louis, Pittsburgh, and especially Ohio, to build rambling summer houses, modestly referred to as "cottages." Favorite locations were 6 1/2 mile by 3 1/2 mile Marquette Island, off the onetime fishing port of Hessel, and on 4-mile La Salle Island off. Cedarville. Tucked away on these wooded islands, these summer homes aren't as ostentatious as their counterparts on Mackinac Island or Harbor Springs. Les Cheneaux has always enjoyed a very low-key charm. The area's good fishing, natural beauty, and tranquility also attracted academics with free summers, artists, and fishermen from many walks of life.

Boats have always been, of necessity, the primary form of transportation here. Through the 1930s, summer people arrived by D&C steamer from Detroit or Cleveland. Into the early 1960s the old route of M-134 from St. Ignace was just a gravel road. Today, there are no cars on the islands, even the big islands. Summer islanders use runabouts to get to the mainland, where marinas park their cars.

The area has the largest number of restored wood-hulled boats in the United States. Cottagers' boats are in storage nine or ten months a year, so they're spared a lot of wear and tear. Thanks to family tradition, nostalgia, and natural thrift, it's de rigueur in these parts to keep that old mahogany Chris-Craft for 40 years and to maintain it in excellent condition. (Mertaugh's Boat Works in Hessel is the oldest Chris-Craft dealer in the U.S., since 1925. New owners have given it a contemporary look, however.) Another source of vintage wood boats is the local boat-building trade, which developed to serve fishermen and was kept alive by purchases from summer visitors.

It all makes for a pleasant little paradise for environmentally-conscious sailors and fishermen who hate the noise and posturing of macho powerboats and the boaters who go with them. At the municipal marinas at Cedarville and Hessel during July and August, wooden boats can be seen in all directions, with more and more sailboats all the time. The attractively designed marinas have plenty of benches that make them nice places to linger.

Viewed from water or from land, the shoreline of Les Cheneaux makes for a tranquil landscape. (See page 709 for the drive along beautiful M-134 from Cedarville to Detour.) White boulders and mostly gravelly beaches are played off against a blue summer sky, the bright greens of poplars and birches, and the contrasting dark cedars and spruces. In late summer, splashes of goldenrod and purple asters make for a simple beauty that's an ideal antidote to overstimulated lives. Fall colors, more yellow than red, stand out against the evergreen and water.

This sense of sweet simplicity and harmony with the natural world is captured in *Hollyhocks and Radishes*, the delightful and hugely successful cookbook inspired by author Bonnie Mickelson's many summers in the Snows and by the generous, life-loving spirit of Julia Chard. For years Mrs. Chard dispensed fresh vegetables, coffee, cooking tips, and country wisdom from her front-yard produce stand near Hessel. Her observations on life and the world around her give the book a wonderful depth.

Beautiful old boathouses like this, photographed in 1906, adds to the fun of boating in Les Cheneaux. Picnic tables and campsites on picturesque Government Island may be used at no charge.

Summer people and longtime residents have intelligently and observantly showcased their favorite place in the two museums of Les Cheneaux Historical Association. They are well worth a close look by anyone interested in their subject areas.

◆ **Les Cheneaux Historical Museum** offers a remarkable range and quality of projects on the area's social and natural history. 1996 exhibits emphasize native wildflowers. The **videos** really stand out; many are also for sale for $28. Ask to see videos on the area's natural history and **unusual glacial geology**, on wildflowers, and on its long history of **building wooden boats**.

Local boatbuilders have been interviewed. Local limestone fossils of unusual interest have been collected. It's all here: lumber camps, commercial fishing, native peoples (and dugout and bark canoes), old summer hotels, beautiful boat models. The simple joys of resort life circa 1906 — fishing and boating, picnics, and fish fries — are recorded in detail in the Tanner Collection of historic photographs. Historian Philip Pittman, tired of academia, has devoted himself to capturing the sweep of history of this small place in the massive and surprisingly engaging *Les Cheneaux Chronicles: Anatomy of a Community* and *Ripple from the Breezes,* an anthology of past stories about the place. Real students of natural and human history could spend a rainy day here without the least regret. (Kids are likely to last about 10 minutes, however.) The **museum shop** is strong on books and notecards of local interest. Inquire about occasional Monday-evening programs. *On Meridian Rd. in Cedarville, one block south of light at M-134 and M-129. (906) 484-2821. Open from*

*Memorial Day thru September. In June & September, Tues-Sat 11-4.
In July & August, daily 10-4, Sun 1-4. &. Donations appreciated.*

◆ **Les Cheneaux Maritime Museum.** A relocated and remodeled
boathouse contains boats and boat-related items from the 1920s to
the present. A new addition dwarfs the original building and permits
more boats to be displayed. There are sailboats, rowboats, Old Town
canoes. In the works for 1997 or 1998: a boat-building shop with
viewing windows. Now museum volunteers can work on boats like the
Navis, a 43' passenger boat from the 1920s. *In Cedarville, on M-134
two blocks east of the light and just east of the high school. (906)
484-3354. Open June thru Sept. In July & Aug., Mon-Sat 10-4:30, Sun
1-4:30. Otherwise weekends only. &. Donations appreciated.*

RENTING BOATS . . . . . Most resorts and cottages rent boats to guests.
Otherwise, go to Paul's Waterfront Cottages in the heart of Cedarville. Paul
Sjoberg has fished here since 1957. He rents boats and tackle and sells bait.
(906) 484-2868. . . . . We haven't found any boat shops that rent sailboats. Some
years Frank Ingram on Marquette Island rents his small sailboat in summer.
Call (906) 484-3493 or (517) 337-2532.

BOATING IN LES CHENEAUX . . . . . can be fun, but tricky navigating. Is that
an island ahead, or a point? A channel or a bay? You have to keep track of
where you are! Every motel and resort has a map. . . . . **Picnicking** and **camping**
are encouraged on beautiful **Government Island,** just off La Salle Island and an
easy 4 1/2 miles straight out of Cedarville. The shore is surprisingly rocky and
steep, though there are some flat picnic sites and campsites with fire rings and
beat-up picnic tables. Birch and conifers dominate the two mile island; its
southeastern tip overlooks Lake Huron and the yacht entrance to Cedarville Bay.
No charge.

PUBLIC GOLFING . . . . . at the golf course of **Les Cheneaux Club,** founded by
original resorters. The course is on the mainland. On Four-Mile Block Road
south off M-134 between Hessel and Cedarville. (906) 484-3606.

FOR A GOOD SWIMMING BEACH . . . . . go east on M-134 past M-48. See
page710. Or stay at a resort that has developed its own swimming beach.

FOR GOOD EATING . . . . . there are two similar reliable restaurants with water
views, The Landing in Cedarville and Hessel Bay Inn in Hessel, plus the seasonal
Hessel Home Bakery on M-134 in Hessel (906-484-3680) and the delightful **Nye
Vegetable Farm** half a mile north of Hessel. Take 3 Mile Road half a mile north
from M-134, turn left on Nye Road. The farm is on corner.

M-134 from Cedarville to De Tour

An idyllic stretch of beaches, dunes, rocky points, and woods makes for a pleasant drive or bike ride.

JUST EAST of Les Cheneaux, the 24 miles of M-134 from Cedarville to De Tour pass a series of rocky points and little bays, some with sandy beaches and low dunes, others with marshes full of wildlife. The village of De Tour (population 400) overlooks the De Tour Passage, where the St. Marys River that leads from Lake Superior and Sault Ste. Marie empties into Lake Huron. ("De Tour" means the turning place. The word is pronounced correctly in the French way, with the accent on the second syllable — "de-TOUR," though just as many say "DE-tour.") Two parks along the passage are ideal for watching up-close the big freighters that come by every hour or so. (See page 205 and 285-7 for background about Great Lakes shipping, and why there are fewer but bigger freighters on the lakes today.)

So much state land abuts M-134 (it's part of the Lake Superior State Forest) that the highway seems part of a beautiful, magically under-used park. Frequent pulloffs make it easy to stop and watch birds, or to swim, or to beachcomb for the area's plentiful limestone fossils, or to walk into the low natural areas of birch, cedar, and hemlock.

Although there's no separate bicycle path, M-134 has extra-wide, two-foot paved shoulders that make for good bicycling. There's still not very much traffic here, and summer residents are often seen walking along the shoulders enjoying the pristine scenery. Another plus for out-of-shape cyclists: it's quite flat. Mountain bikes would allow additional adventures: taking the often rough, unimproved roads south off M-134 out to the points.

For a delightful, lazy day, wear your swimsuit or shorts and good wading shoes, and bring binoculars for watching birds and boats.

Dwarf lake iris grow only here and in similar Great Lakes wetlands. Artist Oliver Birge's wood engravings (above) of it and other wildflowers are sold at the Les Cheneaux Historical Museum. Ask to see the beautiful video of the area's natural history.

Take a picnic lunch, and stop often along the way. Recommended provisioning points on M-134: the Hessel Home Bakery (the pasties are excellent) or the big Cedarville Foods supermarket.

Here are points of interest along M-134 and approximate mileage from the blinker light at M-134 and M-129 in Cedarville:

♦ **Les Cheneaux Historical Museum.** (One block south on M-129.) See page 707.

♦ **Les Cheneaux Maritime Museum.** (1/4 mile, just east of the high school.) See page 708.

♦ **Michigan Limestone**, Cedarville Plant. (4 miles.) If you're lucky, you may see a freighter being loaded and pulling out of Port Dolomite at McKay Bay, on the eastern edge of Les Cheneaux.

♦ **Prentiss Bay marsh.** Here Prentiss Creek forms a wide marsh. The scores of nesting boxes are for tree swallows. They are among some 300 in the area made from scrap by longtime resident Harry Harris, a former gunsmith, a birder, and dedicated ecologist. Each spring he deploys the boxes from his boat; each fall he takes them in. (Every year, the Les Cheneaux Historical Society presents his bird slide program to a "standing room only" audience. Many of these exceptional photographs are on display at the Les Cheneaux Historical Museum. Ask for date of his next slide show.)

♦ **Highway department roadside park.** (18 miles; 1 mile east of M-148.) Much more than a typical roadside park. There's a beautiful, sandy **beach**; a shady, grassy **picnic area** with lots of pleasant picnic tables and grills; plus vault toilets and a water pump. The beach is past some birches and cedars and over some low dunes. The view is accented by occasional offshore rocks and the square Martin Reef Light seven miles to the southwest. It warns boaters away from shallow water.

♦ **De Tour State Forest Beach, picnic area, and campground**, formerly De Tour State Park. (17 1/2 miles; 3 1/2 miles east of M-48.) A real find for picnickers, swimmers, and campers who don't require a lot of conveniences. Out of sight of the highway towards St. Vital Point are a nice, sandy **beach**, a few picnic tables, a hand pump, pit toilets, and 21 large, private campsites in a mature coniferous forest. *$6 camping fee. Self-registration.* &: no.

♦ **Boat launch.** (At the outskirts of De Tour village.) Parking area, vault toilets, and launch are in a woods well away from M-134.

♦ **Picnic area and dock.** (At the outskirts of De Tour.) A pleasant, shady natural area with a grand view of the De Tour Passage. Vault toilets.

♦ **Dr. Shula F. Giddens Memorial Gardens.** (10 miles east of M-148 on west edge of De Tour village.) A sunny park and gazebo over-look the De Tour Passage and resemble an ambitiously landscaped front yard that's colorful with flowers. Benches let you sit and enjoy the view, which occasionally includes freighters.

♦ **Ferry landing** and **museum** in De Tour village. The big back windows of the Fogcutter restaurant look out directly at the passing parade of small boats and the occasional Lake Superior freighter entering and leaving the North Channel. The Gull's Landing restaurant, east by the new public marina, has a similar view and better food. The **De Tour Passage Historical Museum** across the road has exhibits, a very helpful volunteer staff, and lots of free publications about the area. *(906) 297-3404. It's open most days and Friday nights in season.* Best source for local information: the **Dockside Cafe** (906-297-5165) on Elizabeth (the street by the ferry) at Ontario (the main street up the hill). It's the only year-round restaurant, and it had good food and big portions. &: *cafe yes, toilets no.*

FOR MORE OFF-THE-BEATEN PATH SHORELINE EXPLORATIONS . . . . . look for visitor information on the **Sweetwater Trail**. This National Endowment for the Humanities project interprets a very broad and interesting range of sights, natural and man-made, along northern Michigan's Great Lakes shore-lines. This part of the eastern Upper Peninsula is the pilot project. An easy way to find when it's out: call or stop at the super-helpful Michigan Welcome Center in St. Ignace at the north approach to the Mackinac Bridge: (906) 643-6979.

A BOATER'S TRAIL GUIDE . . . . . to the St. Marys River near **DeTour** and **Drummond Island** is available at the DeTour info center by the Drummond Ferry, or call DNR Forest Management, (517) 373-1275, which can also send detailed trail info on the area. . . . . At the tip of **St. Joseph Island**, the big Canadian island on the St. Mary's River, **Fort St. Joseph National Historic Site** has an excellent museum on the fur trade and British history. Call (705) 949-1231 for season and hours.

ABOUT DRUMMOND ISLAND . . . . . At De Tour, the ferry crosses the one-mile channel to Drummond Island. It's yet another piece of low-key northwoods vaca-tionland. It's a boater's and outdoors-lover's paradise, thanks to protected bays, inland lakes, and extensive state lands laced with trails. Drummond Island is the largest U.S. island in the Great Lakes. Ferries run about every hour. The round-trip is about $8 for car and driver. Call or write the Chamber of Commerce, Box 200, Drummond Island, Mi 49726; (906) 493-5245. It's a misconception that the island was wrecked by pizza magnate Tom Monaghan's Domino's Lodge (a 3,000-acre golf resort now sold and renamed **Woodmor**). For more info on Woodmor, call (906) 493-1000. ⚭ A charming tearoom, antique shop, and bed and breakfast on an otherworldly cove is the **Wayfarer's Mart**, on Scammon Cove near the end of Johnswood Road. Call (906) 493-5935 to reserve accommodations and lunch. Follow signs to sandy, remote Big Shoal Beach a couple of miles beyond it. . . . . Drummond Island campgrounds include **Drummond Township Park**, close to the ferry, with toilets, showers, and picnic area (it's pretty busy) and the **Maxton Bay State Forest Campground** (no drinking water). . . . . A little **museum** is in Drummond village on Maxton Bay.

SPRING FISHING . . . . . is famous around Les Cheneaux and Drummond Island. The perch and smelt run roughly the last week in April and the first part of May. The burgeoning cormorant population has hurt fishing in recent years. . . . . . Summer and fall fishing off Drummond Island is for northern pike, walleye, perch, and small-mouth bass. . . . . Summer fishing at Les Cheneaux includes salmon, pike, and herring.

FOSSILS ARE PLENTIFUL . . . . . in the dolomite limestone forming the bedrock and much of the beach gravel from here to St. Ignace and beyond. Fossil coral and shellfish are common.

FOR OTHER SMALL LOCAL MUSEUMS . . . . . in the eastern Upper Peninsula, get the new **pamphlet/guide** of the Eastern Upper Peninsula History Consortium at the Les Cheneaux museums. Member museums extend east from Manistique and Newberry. Nearby Kinross has a good one with a restored log house. Since so much of the fun of the Upper Peninsula is meeting people and getting out to explore and read the landscape, small volunteer-staffed museums are good places to begin making connections with people and history.

U.S. 2 from St. Ignace to Naubinway

*See 17th-century sites in St. Ignace,
followed by long stretches of beach and dunes
and beautiful, convenient campgrounds.*

FOR MOST of the 42 miles between the Mackinac Bridge and Naubinway, U.S. 2 parallels Lake Michigan. Naubinway is the plain little fishing village at Lake Michigan's northernmost tip. The highway passes right alongside long, sandy beaches and low dunes alternating with forests and marshes and stony points. It's punctuated with high overlooks and dramatic vistas. Outstanding campgrounds invite visitors to linger and make this centrally located area their base camp.

An Upper Peninsula trip will be off to a mellow start if you plan to slow down here and take time out from driving. If you don't learn to stop, get out to swim or walk or just enjoy the beautiful scenery, much of your trip is likely to blur together from too much driving. This delightful stretch of U.S. 2 is ideal for switching gears. Bring binoculars to see offshore islands and lighthouses.

A short stop in St. Ignace can help tune you in to the 350-year recorded history of this still-sparsely populated part of Michigan. Here a substantial portion of the native-born locals are descended from a mix of native peoples, French trappers and voyageurs, and fishermen and loggers from various backgrounds.

Recorded history of the Straits area goes back to 1634, when Jean Nicolet passed through the Straits trying to find a route to the Orient. Soon French fur traders had superimposed a far-flung fur-trading

Father Jacques Marquette founded a Jesuit mission at St. Ignace in 1671. Two St. Ignace museums deal with the impact of the French on Straits history, from the French and Ojibwa points of view.

system on the preexisting trade network of native peoples. The fur trade's center had long been on the Straits, first at Michilimackinac (Mackinaw City), then on Mackinac Island. Jesuit priests were troubled about the harm done to native peoples by the fur trade and by trade goods, especially alcohol, which Indians couldn't tolerate. Led by Father Jacques Marquette, the Jesuits established a mission at St. Ignace in 1671 and named it after their order's founder, St. Ignatius Loyola.

"It is difficult for us to comprehend the . . . flaming zeal of the French missionaries to save the souls of the 'savages,'" commented the late historian Willis Dunbar in his *Michigan: A History of the Wolverine State* (1965). "They regarded life as a torture, and death as a great release. They not only endured hardship, they courted it. . . . It did not matter to the Jesuit how hopeless it might seem to convert the Indians to Christianity. . . . His job was to carry out the will of God, to forgo all bodily pleasures, and to labor unceasingly to convert the Indians, all as much for his own soul as for that of the Indian. When a man has not the slightest desire to live any longer than God ordains, he is not only unafraid to brave danger but he welcomes it."

For years St. Ignace has been oriented to Mackinac Island tourism, with all three ferry lines and numerous gift shops, including the remarkable Indian Village. (See p. 715.) Today the branch casino of the Sault Ste. Marie Tribe of Chippewas, the Upper Peninsula's masters of gambling savvy, has stimulated construction of lodging rooms and increased traffic. Though visitors driving down State Street may not realize it, St. Ignace (population 2,500) is also a year-round town, not just a tourist town, and the county seat of Mackinac County. Here's a recommended itinerary that can be compressed to a couple of hours or expanded to last a day or more. It begins in downtown St. Ignace on State Street/Business I-75

◆ **Museum of Ojibwa Culture/Marquette Mission Park.** This intelligently done small museum is in a former Catholic church. It focuses on the simple subsistence culture of the Ojibwa (Chippewa) people, the original residents of the upper Great Lakes. Exhibits depict their ingenuity in surviving in a cold, harsh climate and deriving the necessities of life from the water and land around them. In the back room, the exhibit "Currents of Change in the Straits" deals with the arrival of the Hurons, the Odawa (Ottawa), and in the 1760s and 1770s the French, who sought beaver fur for fashionable hats. The museum takes the viewpoint of native people and shows how they allied with the French against their common British enemy.

The museum and church occupy the very site of Marquette's Jesuit mission (1671-1701). Here, too, in this vicinity were villages of Huron and Odawa people, driven from their homes in southern Ontario in the 1640s by the hostile, expansionistic Iroquois.

A memorial to Father Marquette occupies the park by the museum. Significant archaeological digs have occurred here. An **authentic Huron longhouse** and other outdoor exhibits describe how Huron and Odawa refugees adapted their culture to this new land. At that same time French traders and voyageurs were introducing changes that would forever destroy the native peoples' way of life, which was difficult but ecologically balanced.

An expanded **museum shop** in the building next door features area Woodland Indian handcrafts and a good selection of books on Native American and French history of the Straits area. For the summer of 1996, at least, live crafts demonstrations will be held by the museum, culminating in a **Native American Cultural Festival** August 24 and 25. On Labor Day weekend, a well-regarded traditional **pow-pow** is held here by some members of the Sault Ste. Marie Chippewa tribe. Without competitions, it's more like a big family reunion attended mostly by Native Americans. *500 N. State/Bus I-75 at the north end of downtown St. Ignace. (906) 643-9161. Open from Memorial Day thru 1st weekend in Oct. From mid June thru Labor Day open daily 10-8. Otherwise open daily 1-5. &. $2/adults, $1/student, $5/family.*

♦ **St. Ignace Chamber of Commerce.** Helpful people and a new, convenient location sharing the Ojibwa museum shop. *560 N. State. (906) 643-8717. Winter hours: Mon-Fri 9-3 at least. July & August: Mon-Fri 9-7, Sat 9-5. &.*

♦ **Indian Village.** A classic of picturesque tourism, Indian Village appears to be the creation of Indians who have faced the outside with cedars. Inside, rubber tomahawks and other longtime staples of the tourist trade are appear in a remarkable context. The ceilings and walls are sided with birch bark and decorated with twigs and pictographs. The 1970s building resembles the earlier building from 1927. *499 N. State, across from the Ojibwa Museum. &.*

♦ **St. Ignace Boardwalk.** This new mile-long path is a nice way to disconnect from the traffic of the main street and to connect up with Lake Huron. The Kiwanis Beach is at the north end, and the city marina at the south end, by the new American Legion Memorial Park. It has a gazebo, picnic tables, and a dive platform. *North end across from Ojibwa museum. Park at Museum. Look for flags by the American Legion Park at the south end. &.*

Visitors are welcome to visit the Coast Guard icebreaker *Biscayne Bay* in summer at the station on the southwest end of St. Ignace. It belongs to an improved class of more efficient icebreaking tugs. The curved hull, wider on top, breaks ice by applying pressure from above.

◆ **Father Marquette National Memorial and Museum.** This simple, spare museum focuses on the achievements and spiritual motivation of Jacques Marquette (1637-1675), who founded Sault Ste. Marie and discovered and mapped the Mississippi River in his nine short years in North America. It shows the French perspective on Straits history. In the 17th century the Straits were vitally important to international politics and economics. **French Heritage Days** are celebrated here on the second weekend of August. A new **outdoor interpretive trail** focuses on the 17th and 18th century environment of the Straits area and how it was used by native peoples and by the newly arrived Europeans. At the **bridge overlook**, panels bring to mind the 1673 canoe exploration of Father Marquette and fur trader Louis Joliet, a skilled navigator and mapmaker, as they passed below en route to the Mississippi. *The memorial/museum is south off U.S. 2 just west of I-75 and St. Ignace. (906) 643-8620. Open from Mem. Day thru Labor Day at least. Hours: daily 9:30-5; from mid-June thru mid-Aug. to 8 daily. Call for fall hours.* ♿: *building & pathway. State park sticker required: $4/day, $20/year.*

   For many visitors, St. Ignace can go by in a blur of pasty shops and older motels that sprawl west for miles on U.S. 2. If you have time to start poking along, it can be fun to stop at some of these places (here arranged from east to west).

◆ **Boulevard Drive/Point Labarbe Road.** To avoid the distractions of U.S. 2 just west of St. Ignace, take the shore road out of town. You'll see sweeping views of Lake Michigan, with an occasional freighter. The most dramatic **views of the Mackinac Bridge** are from the parking area at the foot of Boulevard Drive. (Telescopes are available there.) In a few miles the shore road joins U.S. 2. About a mile west of where Point Labarbe Road joins U.S. 2, you can turn south onto **Gros Cap Road** and follow the shore for another four miles or so. *To reach the shore road from U.S. 2 just west of I-75, turn south onto Boulevard Drive at the Howard Johnson's/Marquette Memorial Drive. Boulevard Drive is gravel for a mile or so. To continue onto Point Labarbe Road, turn right before you get to the parking lot and stay along the shore.*

◆ In the **McDonald's restaurant** a quarter-mile west of the bridge is a richly nostalgic series of displays by artist Morten Fadum III of Harvard, Illinois. They evoke collective memories of vacations up north with artful assemblages of old illustrations from the likes of Field & Stream, road maps, hand-carved ducks and fish, assorted fishing, canoeing, and hunting paraphernalia, and custom-made "antique" signs and props from Indians and tourists. This nifty blend of nature, nostalgia, and U. P. history won a McDonald's design award and netted Fadum a commission for an even more elaborate display at the Munising Hardee's. Fadum's work can also be seen at the landmark log Hack-Ma-Tack restaurant near Cheboygan, Lakeside Charlie's in Cadillac, and at summer art fairs in Suttons Bay, Charlevoix, and St. Joseph.

◆ **Suzy's Pasties.** *(906) 643-7007.)* This super-spiffy, trim spot on the north side of U.S. 2 is well positioned for takeouts for picnic stops along U.S. 2. Here are all the classics: pasties, smoked fish, slaw to go with it, and fudge for dessert. A man from Iron Mountain, known for its pasties, rates these high.

◆ **Curio Fair**. (906-643-8626). Another old-timey tourist trap, built just after the Mackinac Bridge opened in 1957. The style hearkens back to a much earlier era. The building is encrusted with seashells and rocks on the exterior, with birch bark and twig Indian pictograms on the inside. The tower (8 stories up) has a grand view of the bridge and straits to the south and woods to the north— beautiful in color season. It's 50¢ to climb the tower. Worth a stop any time.

◆ **Riverside Park and Helena Island overlook.** This blufftop park

and picnic spot takes in a grand view of St. Helena Island two miles
offshore. French fishermen from Gros Cap (the shoreline village that
once stood below the bluff here) established a prosperous town on St.
Helena in the 19th century. This beautiful island's north shore enjoys
a natural harbor that made it an ideal fueling stop for wood-fired
steamship. Later it became a pleasant destination for outings by boat
or sleigh. On the south shore are a classic, tapered light tower and a
brick keeper's house, built in 1873 and abandoned for 60 years. A
noteworthy Boy Scout service project has renovated it. The island
makes a fine destination for small boats, provided the water is calm.
With rocky and sandy shorelines, forests and wetlands, meadows and
sandbars, it offers much variety in a small (1 mile by 1/2 mile) space.
Drawbacks for adventurers: snakes and poison ivy.

♦ **Point aux Chenes River Marsh.** Just east of Point aux Chenes,
this river's many twists between Round Lake and Lake Michigan form
an usually large and undisturbed marsh. It's inaccessible, except by
canoe during high water. Loons, osprey, eagles, and terns live there.
An osprey nest is visible from the road near the river bridge.

♦ **CCC Camp Round Lake Interpretive Site & Sand Dunes Cross-
Country Ski Trail.** Half a mile north of U.S. 2 on H-57/ Brevort
Lake Road is this trail-laced forest within the Hiawatha National
Forest. It offers 15 miles of **trails** and an excellent outdoor **exhibit**
about the **Civilian Conservation Corps** and the camp that was
here in the 1930s. It was one of 2,650 camps across the U.S. that
employed 600,000 men in 1935. Flat gravel walks connect large,
engraved metal signboards marking the sites of various camp buildings. Well-written interpretive signs convey what camp life was like
for jobless young men here. They worked on CCC reforestation projects, made trails, and built many of the Michigan State Parks' most
beautiful rustic buildings — all for $30/month plus food and cloth-
ing. "City boys surrounded by trees," says one sign. It describes typical CCC crews as "boys that didn't know an ax from a baseball
bat." At Round Lake some 200 young men built roads, planted
trees, made the dam and campgrounds at Brevort Lake, and cleared
logging debris to prevent fires. The site is now a meadow, filled with
wildflowers in late summer. The philosophy and politics behind the
CCC are clearly conveyed through excellent writing and graphics.
This is an inspiring place, in a very quiet way. &: *site yes, toilets no.*

Six **trail loops** (each a couple of miles) go through open areas
and wooded old oak forests on the backs of dunes. In summer,
loops A, B, and C offer more stable footing; D, E, and F go through
more bare sand. The **ski season** here usually lasts from early
December through March. Trails are **groomed** on Mondays and

Fridays, and there's firewood for building a fire at the **warming cabin** by the entrance. Call (906) 643-7900 for trail conditions. ♿: *no.*

♦ **Lake Michigan beach between Point aux Chenes and Brevort.** U.S. 2 passes right along eight miles of beautiful, sandy, wide beach Between H-57/Brevort Lake Road and Ozark Road in Brevort. Low dunes lead back from the north side of the highway and invite exploration by nature-lovers. Wide shoulders make it easy to pull over and stop anywhere. There are no picnic or restroom facilities here. Maybe that's why this fabulous beach is so reliably uncrowded.

♦ **Lake Michigan Campground beach and picnic area** (Hiawatha National Forest). Low dunes separate the sandy beach from a shady, mature forest *On U.S. 2 about 6 miles west of Brevoort Lake Road and about 3 miles east of Ozark Road. (906) 643-7900.*

♦ **Brevoort Lake Campgrounds** (Hiawatha National Forest). **Spencer's Landing**, an extraordinarily helpful camp store before the main campground, rents **canoes** and **fishing boats** ($10/day, but bring your own motor) and **kayaks** ($3/hour). (906) 292-5471. Open from second weekend of May through last week of September. Hours: 8 a.m.-9 p.m. Nearby is the beach and lakeside **picnic area** with tables and grills.

Big **Brevoort Lake** (4,233 acres) has a man-made spawning reef that has helped create a good walleye fishery. *20 miles northwest of St. Ignace off U.S. 2. Turn north onto Brevoort Camp Road for 1 mile to park. (906) 643-7900.*

♦ **Cut River Bridge and picnic area.** Motorists on U.S. 2 notice the striking, deep limestone gorge formed by the Cut River as it empties into Lake Michigan. But the attractive, shady picnic area at the bridge's east end isn't quite so obvious, nor is the paved path and stairway that descend 147 feet to the river. A striking stretch of asphalt path, wheelchair-accessible, goes under the dramatic stone bridge supports to the splendid stairway. The stairs are in flights, with large landings and overlooks to make the trip back up less arduous and more interesting. As you descend, the sound of waves replaces highway noise. It's beautiful to look down through the tree-tops and glimpse the beach and water below. From the bottom, it's an easy walk along the river to the sandy beach. Kids enjoy diverting water to make their own channels and lagoons. You can also walk across the bridge on a pedestrian walkway. The view down is terrific. Be advised that the sway and vibration from big trucks may be thrilling or alarming. *On U.S. 2 about 4 miles west of Brevoort. Vault toilets are by the picnic area.*

♦ **Hog Island Point, Lake Superior State Forest.** A sandy Lake

Michigan **beach** is served by vault toilets, picnic tables, and a shady, spacious rustic campground. *Half-way between Epoufette and Naubinway on U.S. 2. (906) 293-5131. &: some gravel sites. Camping $6 night. No reservations.*

◆ **Prinski Roadside Park.** This pleasant picnic spot beneath the pines looks out onto a sandy beach and a point of rocks that march out into Lake Michigan like a series of stepping stones. *2-3 miles east of Naubinway off U.S. 2.*

FOR PEOPLE WHO LIKE BEACHES THAT ARE REALLY OFF THE BEATEN PATH . . . . . try these two west of Naubinway, off U.S. 2 about 14 miles southwest of town. . . . . Look for the sign to the **Big Knob Campground** of Lake Superior State Forest. The 23-site rustic campground is at the end of a road that winds at least six miles through forest and wetlands, to emerge on a **beach** overlooking Lake Michigan. . . . . **Scott's Point** is the closest mainland point on either peninsula to the Beaver Archipelago, which is clearly visible on the horizon. Squaw Island and its light are barely 10 miles offshore, and Beaver Island is another six. The wide, sandy **beach** descends so gradually into the water that adults can wade out for a hundred feet without getting their knees wet. Shore birds are abundant in this idyllic and remote place. A state forest picnic area is in a cedar grove. *From U.S. 2 at Gould City, go south 9 miles on Gould City Rd. Park is at road's end.*

ANTIQUARIAN BOOKS NEAR BREVORT . . . . . Mary and Eugene run an interesting used bookstore, **First Edition**, and the Black Letter Press from their country home on 461 Worth Road. From U.S. 2 in Brevort, go north just past Gustafson's restaurant on Ozark Road for half a mile until you reach Worth Road. First Edition's main specialty is Michigan and Great Lakes history, but there's lots of good general reading on hand. Open daily from Memorial to Labor Day. The rest of the year is by chance or by appointment. Hours are casual; when the first customer knocks on the door in the morning, the bookshop opens. Often it stays open until 10 or so in the evening. (906) 292-5513.

LAS VEGAS-STYLE GAMBLING IN ST. IGNACE . . . . . takes place in a converted motel north of town, now the **Kewadin Shores Casino**, run by the Soo Tribe of the Chippewa Indians. It offers the usual craps, black jack, keno, roulette, and big-six in a facility that's smaller than the band's original spread outside Sault Ste. Marie. Besides the usual slot machines, they have $5 and $25, progressive (5¢, 25¢, and $1), and megabucks slots connected to Las Vegas. Call (906) 643-7071 for information. Must be 21 (liquor served). &

DIVING IN THE STRAITS AREA . . . . . Fourteen wrecks are buoyed for divers and another 11 can be found with sonar. Still more are described in Chuck and Jeri Feltner's authoritative, interesting *Shipwrecks of the Straits of Mackinac*

. . . . . For a **dive brochure**, call (906) 643-8717. For more info and for reservations on the 42-foot *Rec Diver*, call Straits Scuba Center, (810) 558-9922. The Center has some diving accessories and air but no diving equipment. Ask about off-shore dive sites.

FOR PROOF THAT INFORMED AND INFORMATIVE SMALL-TOWN WEEK-LIES ARE STILL POSSIBLE . . . . . pick up a copy of *The St. Ignace News*, infused by the principles of its longtime publisher, the late Wesley Maurer Sr., who headed the University of Michigan journalism department for many years. First he bought the *Mackinac Island Town Crier* in 1957 and turned it into a training laboratory for journalism students. In 1975, years after his retirement, he fulfilled his lifelong dream of publishing a year-round newspaper when he bought the *News* and ran it with his son and daughter-in-law, who continue to do it today. On its masthead are its stated principles, adapted from the words over the entrance of the *Detroit News* building: "Upbuilder of the Home — Nourisher of the Community Spirit — Arts, Letters and Science of the Common People." They still reflect the paper's values. Expect to see small-town banquets and *Christian Science Monitor* editorials sharing the front page.

VISITORS ARE WELCOME . . . . . to tour the **U.S. Coast Guard's Cutter *Biscayne Bay***, when it's docked at its home port in St. Ignace. The Coast Guard Station is at 1075 South Huron. This relatively new class of icebreaking tug uses a wider beam and greater horsepower to break more ice, and a "blubber" hull lubrication system to do it more efficiently. Air is slowly forced through ports in the hull, which makes water flow upward, reducing friction between the hull and ice. Call (906) 643-6435 to arrange a tour. &: call.

Kitch-iti-kipi (Big Spring)

*A deep, crystal-clear forest pool
where 10,000 gallons of water bubbles up each minute*

FEW NATURAL SIGHTS in Michigan compare with the beauty and mystique of this enormous, bowl-like spring. Through a picturebook forest of cedars and pines, you come upon an amazing, emerald-green spring, oval and jewel-like, some 200 feet wide. Visitors pull a cable on a simple 18' x 20' raft to reach the middle, then gaze down through 45 feet of crystal-clear water. Bubbling up from the bottom is a constant flow of about 10,000 gallons of water a minute or more. Huge brown lake trout swim lazily around. Lime-encrusted logs, mossy and fallen to the sandy bottom, look like piles of sticks so close you could almost touch them.

The water here stays 45° F. year around, so the spring can be viewed in any season. If it's the off-season and the gate is closed, it's necessary to hike 300 yards to the spring. Summer is a delightful time to visit. This cool glade is a delightful contrast to warm days. In the morning, mist hangs over the water and turns the surrounding woods into abstract, mysterious shapes. Come either before mid-morning or near dusk to experience the serenity of the place. In mid-day it's a popular spot, much loved by children. The water is *so* green and clear, the fish *so* big. And a kid of six or seven can make the raft move! One enraptured toddler called out, "Hello, fish! Hello!. . . . I see a *humongous* fish! A see *five* of them!!" There's a pleasant **picnic and playground area** and a well-run **concession stand** (open May 15 up into October) with snacks and gifts.

Kitch-iti-kipi (pronounced "KITCH-i-tee-KI-pee") is Michigan's biggest spring. Its name means "big cold water." It is not known where this enormous volume of water comes from. Hydraulic pressure forces the groundwater to the surface. The spring's bowl is similar to other sink holes except it is connected with aquifers (underground streams). Sinkholes are created by underground water dissolving limestone bedrock to create caves. When the top layer of limestone finally dissolves, the cave collapses. The state acquired this beautiful place in 1926, thanks to John Bellaire, owner of a Manistique dime store. He fell in love with the place, which loggers had used as a dump. Seeing its potential as a public beauty spot, he persuaded the Palms Book Land Company to sell the spring and 90 acres to the state for $10. *Palms Book State Park* *and Kitch-iti-kipi are northwest of Manistique. From U.S. 2, take M-149 8 miles north. (906) 341-2355. Open for day use only, 8 a.m.-10 p.m. &: only sidewalk to restrooms and raft. One step onto raft. State Park sticker required: $4/day, $20/year.*

SWIMMING NEAR KITCH-ITI-KIPI AND MANISTIQUE . . . . . On the Upper Peninsula's fourth-biggest lake, **Indian Lake State Park** has two modern campgrounds and beaches, and good fishing for walleye and perch. **Indian Lake** is quite shallow and therefore warms up sooner than most Upper Peninsula lakes. **South Shore Campground** has 157 sites with little privacy but right on the lake; reserve in advance. The adjacent **Chippewa Trail** comes with a brochure about wild foods used by native peoples. **West Shore Campground** has 144 secluded sites farther from the lake; it's rarely full. *A few miles west of Manistique. At Thompson, turn north off U. S. 2 onto M-149; park is in 3 miles. Follow signs to west unit. (906) 341-2355. State Park sticker required: $4/day, $20/year.* . . . . Public Lake Michigan beaches are **Roger's Beach** (on U.S. 2 about 3 miles west of town), **Manistique Township Park** (4 miles east of town; the park road is off Dock Inn Rd. which branches off U.S. 2 where U.S. 2 swings north), and a beach south of Gulliver Lake off CR 434.

MANISTIQUE'S BEAUTIFUL BOARDWALK . . . . . goes two miles east from the lighthouse pier near downtown. It lets you walk from motels to town and back, enjoying the view out across the water all the way. Parking is by the three-story apartments near Hardee's on the west end.

GOOD BIRDWATCHING FROM BOARDWALKS AND AN ELEVATED PLAT-FORM . . . . . is across Indian Lake from Kitch-iti-kipi. Especially during spring and fall warbler migration, songbirds are plentiful at the Rainey Wildlife Area, where Smith Creek creates a slough before entering the lake. The *Michigan Wildlife Viewing Guide* (see p. 855) suggests calling warblers into view by standing still and softly going "pssh pssh pssh." There's a good chance of seeing bald eagles and ospreys from the observation platform, spring through fall. Take M-94 north from Manistique and U.S. 2. In about 5 miles, turn left (west) onto Dawson Rd. In 1 1/2 miles you'll get the access road that goes north to the parking lot.

AN UNUSUALLY BEAUTIFUL LIGHTHOUSE WITH A TOWER TO CLIMB . . . . . is the **Seul Choix Point Light** almost 20 miles east of Manistique. It's 8 miles off U.S. 2 on a dead-end road but well worth the trip. Seul Choix Point is at Lake Michigan's northernmost tip, surrounded by water. It's a grand view from the 78-foot tower (97 steps up!). The light still functions. The dedicated **Gulliver Historical Society** has worked hard to raise donations and grants to restore the lighthouse complex. The Romanesque-style keeper's dwelling has been furnished in 1920's decor. The new 1/10 scale model of the light, made with 30,000 tiny bricks and a miniature Fresnel lends, is said to be remarkable. The gift shop is well stocked with clothing, book, and memorabilia of special interest to lighthouse lovers. . . . . The fog signal building is a museum with Coast Guard and local history items, big on logging and fishing. . . . . Seul Choix (pronounced "SISH-wah") means "only choice" and refers to the harbor of refuge northeast of the rocky shoals that the light warns sailors to avoid. . . . . The surrounding 10 acres is the **Mueller Township Park**, with **picnic** tables, a swimming **beach**, a **boat launch**, and trails through the rocky woods of fragrant cedars. *From U.S. 2 and CR 432 at the blinker in Gulliver, go south on CR 432 about 4 miles to CR 431 (gravel). Turn right (south) on CR-431 and go 4 miles to lighthouse. (906) 283-3169. Open daily mid June-mid Sept. 12-4, assuming volunteer staff is available. &: fog signal building & museum, park restrooms. Donation appreciated.*

A FINE PLACE FOR FOOD, RUSTIC ATMOSPHERE, AND LOCAL INFO . . . . . is just off U.S. 2 12 miles east of Manistique on Gulliver Lake. **Fischer's Old Deerfield Inn** was built in 1930 as the focal point for a big northwoods cottage development. Co-owner Marilyn Fischer spearheaded the Seul Choix Lighthouse restoration, runs the bar, restaurant, and resort with her husband, and is the area's designated loon ranger. Food ranges from pasties and a salad bar to whitefish and steaks. *On U.S. 2 12 miles east of Manistique and around 28-30 miles west of Naubinway. At blinker light, turn south onto U.S. 2. In 400 feet, go right onto Gulliver Lake Road to inn. (906) 283-3169. &: no.*

MANISTIQUE ITSELF . . . . . is an unprepossessing lumber and paper milltown whose longtime claim to fame is its **siphon bridge** supported by water. The roadway is actually *below* water level. It's next to the landmark Roman Revival water tower, on M-94 in town. . . . . The **museum** in the adjacent park, open occasionally, was a hit with Mary Blocksma, author of *The Fourth Coast* (p. 855) and a fan of oddball artifacts. . . . . Manistique is also the commercial center for a sizable area of lakes and resorts with a wide variety of motels, many with beach frontage on U.S. . . . . Manistique has a nice transient marina with showers (906-341-6841) and two movies, **Cinema I** (downtown at 114 S. Cedar, 906-341-5541) and **Cinema II drive-in** on East U.S. 2. (906-341-5920). . . . . Stop by at the helpful **Chamber of Commerce Information Center** on U.S. 2 just west of the river. . . . . For information on the beautiful **Pine Marten Run** mountain bike trail, contact **The Bicycle Shop**, 315 Deer St, (906-341-2234).

Fayette Historic Townsite

*Once a filthy worksite for iron furnace laborers,
this 19th-century ghost town on the Garden Peninsula
is scenic today.*

THIS PICTURESQUE industrial ghost town curves around
pretty Snail Shell Harbor, on a bit of land jutting out into
northern Lake Michigan. Its heart is the great limestone
stacks and beehive charcoal furnaces of a charcoal pig-iron operation started in the 1860s. The silvery, weathered frame buildings
and restored stone furnaces have been preserved as ghosts, not
repainted and spiffed up as if they were new. From the main road
and visitor center, visitors take an asphalt path down a steep limestone bluff. Here limestone was quarried for building and for flux to
remove impurities in the iron smelting process.

Fayette is a peaceful
place today, all green with
leaves and grass. It's a far
cry from its productive
years in the 1870s and
1880s, when soot and
smoke, noise, mud, horrible
smells, and stockpiles of
materials made a visitor
compare Fayette unfavor-
ably to Cleveland's worst
slums. Imagine those
quaint cabins surrounded
by soot-covered children
breathing air so dirty wives
couldn't hang wash out to
dry. (Managers' homes were
thoughtfully located away
from the soot and smoke.)

Fayette boomed after
demand for high-quality
iron escalated during the
Civil War. Fayette Brown,
general manager of the
Jackson Iron Company (the
Jackson-based pioneer of

Upper Peninsula iron mining), studied ways to reduce the tremendous cost of shipping bulk iron ore all the way to foundries on the lower lakes. He chose this place for a new blast furnace because the site had limestone to purify the molten iron and abundant hardwood forests to fuel the furnaces. Iron ore was shipped by rail from the Marquette Range to Escanaba. From there steamers took it 25 miles to Fayette's iron furnaces.

Fayette set production records during its heyday. But by the mid-1880s, nearby forests were depleted. Improved methods of making coke iron and steel were making charcoal iron too expensive to produce. The smelting operation here closed down in 1891. The hotel lived on as a resort for many decades, and Fayette survived as a fishing village through the 1920s.

You have to plan a visit for Fayette to be a real highlight. The scenery won't automatically carry the day, though the view across the harbor to the exposed limestone bluffs is beautiful, especially at dusk. There can be lot of walking here, so plan what to see if your energy is limited.

1. Come early or late in the day when the slanted light is dramatic and there aren't many people. Sometimes a morning mist rising off the harbor gives a soft, romantic, ghostly look to the place. Evening sunsets are spectacular.

2. Stop at the visitor center. Interesting, quick exhibits place the Fayette operation in the context of Michigan's iron industry. A big model orients you to the village down the hill. The 5-minute audio orientation is being upgraded.

3. Get a free townsite map and buy *Fayette: A Visitor's Guide* at the visitors' center front desk for $3. Sophisticated, honest interpretive displays in the village are based on careful historical and archaeological research.

4. Wander around the buildings and look inside. The hotel, the town hall with its interesting opera house and shops, and one supervisor's home are presented with satisfying period accuracy and detail, down to the suitcases of traveling salesmen. You really can have that window-in-time feeling if conditions are right and you have learned enough from the exhibits to flesh out your imagination. Some other buildings, like the office, are full of interesting and detailed exhibit panels. Read them, and you'll learn about subjects as diverse as the butcher business, medicine before the acceptance of antiseptics, ladies' entertainments, traveling shows, passenger steamers and excursion boats, and labor history. (When orders for iron were slow, workers didn't get paid — sometimes for weeks on end!)

5. After 11 a.m. the village will likely be filling up with tourists. You can take a worthwhile 25-minute free **guided tour** of Fayette's main street. The competent, college-age guides may well be descended from Fayette's laborers and commercial fishermen. That personal dimension makes history more vivid. These tours depend on parks staffing and funding. They're offered in July and August, through Labor Day if possible. The **carriage tours**, contracted to a concessionaire, can be much less satisfying. The carriage top obstructs views, and the ride is horribly bumpy.

If you have time, take your booklet, sit down on a bench or at the picnic tables at the parking lot's edge, and read through it for a good overview of the charcoal iron-smelting process, the town, and the interesting ongoing **archaeological investigations** of the area. They reveal much about workers' lives and daily activities that hasn't been recorded in surviving letters and diaries.

6. Scenic walks are another attractive aspect of Fayette. The cedar forest by the superintendent's house feels like the forest primeval, a dark canopy offering occasional peeks at the lake. The effect is eerie in fog, with the sounds of the unseen bell buoy made louder by the fog. Big old apple trees behind some houses are bearing edible fruit by mid-August. You can walk inside the massive stone furnace walls by the harbor. Don't miss the **hiking trail along the limestone bluffs** east of the harbor. It's 1/4 mile each way. Four spots offer beautiful views of the village and look clear across Big Bay de Noc to the Stonington Peninsula to the west. The state park has **seven miles of hiking trails** in all.

Snail Shell Harbor offers a **transient marina** (there's no pump-out station but it is a scenic setting for overnights), a **boat ramp**, and **fishing** for perch and smallmouth bass.

Two special events are held at Fayette. At the **Blessing of the Fleet**, the Bishop of Marquette blesses fishing boats and pleasure boats. **Heritage Days** (2nd Sat. in August) features costumed reenactments like 1880s baseball, bands, and a traveling medicine show.

The townsite is only part of a 750-acre park. A 7-mile **trail system** of several loops connects the beach, campground, and townsite, and winds through a beech-maple hardwood forest. Terrain is basically flat. It's groomed for cross-country skiing.

Fayette State Park is 16 miles south on M-183 from Garden Corners and U.S. 2, between Escanaba and Manistique. (906) 644-2603. State park and grounds of townsite are open year-round. Buildings & visitor center open 9 a.m.-5 p.m. from the 3rd weekend in May thru the 2nd weekend in Oct. Fayette Townsite is open from 8 a.m. to 5 p.m., until 9 in July & August. &: *planned — 2 buildings, smoother paths in townsite,. State park sticker required; $4/day, $20/year.*

A 2,000-FOOT WHITE SAND BEACH . . . . . backed by low dunes is about a mile south of Fayette Townsite, in a different part of **Fayette State Park,** reached by another road off M-183. There's a large **picnic area** and a **changing house**. State park sticker required; $4/day, $20/year.

ANOTHER BEACH AND PICNIC AREA . . . . . even less crowded, is the **Sac Bay County Park** off M-183 about five miles south of Fayette. The facilities are no match for those at the state park beach's. But it's an interesting view off to the islands dotted between the Garden and Door peninsulas at the mouth of Green Bay. Continue south to the end of M-183 and you'll be at **Fairport**, almost at the very tip of the Garden Peninsula. It's **a commercial fishing village**, one of the few left in Michigan. There's no store or restaurant, but you can stop by the fish shed and buy **fresh whitefish to cook out.**

A LITTLE FARMING AND FISHING VILLAGE . . . . . that's looking more and more like a ghost town itself is **Garden** (population 268), the peninsula's hub. As small farms and orchards decline, so does its year-round population. Quaint frame storefronts are increasingly empty. Cottagers and retirees bring some life to the place in summer. There's the **Village Artisan**, an attractive little crafts gallery and consignment shop; the small, summer-only **Garden Peninsula Historical Museum** (where genealogy, especially French-Canadian, is a specialty); and two popular restaurants: the **Garden House Saloon** (starring a great old bar from Hamtramck) and **Rosie's Place.**

EXPLORING THE GARDEN PENINSULA. . . . . Fayette is near the tip of the 21-mile-long Garden Peninsula, so called because the moderating waters of Lake Michigan made it well suited for farming and orchards. Marijuana is Garden's best-known crop today — an indication of how economically pressed and alienated some farm families have felt. Don't be surprised in early August if the normally quiet area swarms with state troopers and helicopters confiscating pot.

Lake Michigan is surprisingly seldom seen from the Garden Peninsula's improved roads. But for people who really like to poke around, the peninsula is a relaxing, congenial place. Stop in at **Garden Orchards** and its market store for its apples, apricots in season, and samples of homemade preserves. (It's in the former school, a contemporary building on M-183 between U.S. 2 and Garden Village. . . . . The **beach** at **Lake Superior State Forest's Portage Bay Campground** can hardly be beat for its low sand dunes, adjacent forests of mature pines, and peace and quiet. From M-183 17 miles out the peninsula, look for Portage Bay Rd., go 6 miles east to beach. The campground's nifty **Ninga Aki Pathway** (that means "Mother Earth" in Ojibwa) shows visitors 15 important plants used constantly in traditional Ojibwa life. Loops are 3/4 mile and 1 1/2 miles. The wildflowers are so wonderful here in June that nature-lovers Lon and Lynn Emerick make an annual camping trip here a rite of spring. Lon describes it in an appreciative essay in *The Superior Peninsula*. (See p. 855.) . . . . . Two-track roads indicated on the **DeLorme** *Michigan Atlas and Gazetteer* can lead you to other shoreline discoveries.

A DOOR COUNTY BIKE TRIP FROM FAYETTE . . . . . Thursdays in summer a passenger ferry makes a day trip from Washington Island, at the tip of Wisconsin's

Door Peninsula, to Fayette. That means bicyclists *could* take it from Fayette to Washington Island if they wanted to spend a week. Call (414) 854-2972.

SEE TROUT AND SALMON BEING "REARED" . . . . . They're fed and grown until they're big enough to be stocked in lakes and streams — 6 to 9 inches for trout and 3 1/2-4 inches for salmon —at the **Thompson State Hatchery** about 8 miles west of Manistique. *It's just off U.S. 2 a little ways north on M-149, just east of where U.S. 2 turns away from Lake Michigan. (906) 341-5587. Open daily 8-4:30, weekends and holidays 8-4.* . . . . . See the indoor incubation room and tanks, and the 12 outdoor raceways. Each holds about 85,000 trout or salmon. The necessary cold water comes from a 47° spring and two 59° deep wells. In spring and fall you might see fish being transferred to a truck (via a special fish pump; it reduces the stress of handling) that takes them to streams to be stocked. Each year this modern hatchery, built in 1977, produces about 800,000 yearling trout (browns, steelhead, and rainbow), 600 chinook for stocking, plus 10-15 million walleye fry released in lakes or taken elsewhere to be raised in rearing ponds.

A BEAUTIFUL NATURAL AREA AND NIFTY HOTEL . . . . . are just west of the historic Garden Peninsula at **Nahma**. (Pronounced "NAY-muh," it means Sturgeon in Ojibwa.) In the early 20th century, the Bay de Noc Lumber Company built a mill and small company town here. Today the Groleau brothers, Warren, Ron, and Pat (Nahma High classes of '54, '59, and '64) and their wives have purchased the hotel, store, and half of the nine-hole golf course. Their **Nahma Hotel** (906-644-2466) is refurbished and very pleasantly decorated, with a bar and year-round restaurant, and some **Lake Michigan beach** frontage next to the new DNR boat launch. The lower part of the Sturgeon River, through thick pine and hardwood forest, is recognized in Tom Powers' *Natural Michigan* (see p. 855). It now has a **wildlife observation platform** off CR 497, the scenic, super-bumpy riverside road from Nahma Junction on U.S. 2. Plans call for resurfacing it as an official "scenic road," with a covered bridge over the river. A canoe livery may open. As it is, the low-traffic peninsula is perfect for bicycling. Country roads 495 (from U.S. 2 at Isabella) and 499 (from St. Jacques) have good surfaces and go along the shore past cottages.

Soo Locks

*A key link between the Great Lakes
gives a close-up view of giant freighters.*

FOR WATCHING BIG BOATS up close, there's hardly a more dramatic place anywhere than the Soo Locks at Sault Ste. Marie. The St. Marys River connects Lake Superior to Lake Huron, then to the lower Great Lakes, and ultimately to the Atlantic. The locks, four in all, enable vessels to bypass the falls, an undramatic, gradually descending drop of 21 feet. Visitors may be a scant 20 feet or so from 800-foot-long freighters moving slowly into the MacArthur Lock, the closest lock to shore. Going over the impressive **International Bridge** to Sault Ste. Marie, Canada, gives a wonderful aerial view of the falls and locks just east of the bridge. (Pedestrians are permitted only for the June 29 bridge walk celebrating Canadian independence.) The bridge, nearly three miles including approaches, is a worthwhile sight in its own right. It offers splendid views west to Lake Superior and down on the sprawling Algoma Steel plant.

The locks are on the American side of the river. The U.S. Army Corp of Engineers operates them. Their elaborate and interesting **Soo Locks Information Center** is open long hours from mid-May through mid-November. (See below.) In 1995 it doubled in size and added new displays combining the locks' story with interesting visuals going back to construction of the very first lock in 1853-5. The Upper Peninsula mining boom created a pressing need for efficient shipping, even though the remote frontier location made it hard to get a federal land grant to be able to fund lock construction. Senator Henry Clay scoffed that a canal here would be "a work quite beyond the remotest settlement of the United States if not in the moon."

Visitors can see a short **video** on the locks' history and operations. Also on view is a large working model of the locks. A display about the environment of Lake Superior added in 1996. A sign on the wall tells which freighters are due the next two to three hours. The elevated **outside viewing platform** allows you to get a close-up, bird's eye view of the big vessels as they wait the few minutes it takes for a chamber to go 21 feet up to the Superior level or 21 feet down to the Huron level.

Twelve thousand vessels pass through these locks each year. About one fourth are huge cargo vessels, some carrying as much as 70,000 tons. The principal cargo of the oceangoing vessels coming

The Soo Locks give boatwatchers a good, close-up look at boats, and the
visitor center provides lots of background about Great Lakes shipping.
There are far fewer big bulk carriers on the lakes today, due to new vessels' huge capacities and currently decreased shipping tonnage.

from Lake Superior is grain grown in the North American heartland.
Downbound lakers take taconite pellets from the iron ranges to
industrial users on the lower Lakes. while upbound Great Lakes
freighters are most likely to be carrying manufactured steel, cement,
stone, fuel oil, and road salt.

Alongside the locks, the **Soo Locks Park**, also maintained by
the Army Engineers, is a beautiful place to linger, especially in the
evening when lights reflect on the water and illuminate the trees.
Benches and a fountain with colored lights and music in the
evening make this a peaceful, pleasant place, in contrast to the
cluttered tourist shops on the other side of Portage Avenue. They
continue to be among Michigan's most uninspired tourist traps.
(Portage Avenue is so named because voyageurs in the fur trade
portaged along this route in the 17th and 18th centuries.)

Nowadays you should expect to wait a while to see a big boat
pass through the locks. Only 120 U.S. and Canadian cargo vessels
are registered on the Lakes — down from 300 just 10 years ago.
That's largely because efficient, high-volume thousand-foot bulk
carriers are gradually replacing 600-footers with the same number

More to the Soo than gambling and locks. It's a good place for birding and fishing. Rarely seen this far south, Arctic-bred gyrfalcons hang out by the Edison Sault power plant in winter, feeding on unlucky ducks. The Whitefish Point Bird Observatory gift shop (page 744) sells an inexpensive area bird guide and this print by Gary Wright. Sugar Island, connected with Sault, Michigan, by a ferry, has several small fishing resorts.

of crew but less than half the capacity. Also, the collapse of the Soviet Union means much less Great Plains wheat is being shipped overseas. One big cargo ship comes through the locks every hour and a half on the average, though ships sometimes bunch due to bad weather. *To reach the locks, take the I-75 Ashmun Street exit and go to downtown Sault Ste. Marie. At the T intersection, turn left onto Portage. Locks are in one block. Dates of opening and closing the locks each year vary with the weather. Usually they open in mid-March and close in mid-December. Park along Portage or adjacent streets. If space is tight, look west on Portage beyond shops.* **Corps of Engineers information center** *is from mid-May through mid-November, 8 a.m. to 10 p.m. Extended hours, 7 a.m.-11p.m. from mid-June through Labor Day. (906) 632-3311. &. Free.*

For a ship's perspective of the locks, take the interesting **Soo Locks Boat Tour.** Come early to get seats at the front of the boat if possible. The two-hour excursion takes you through the locks up to the level of Lake Superior, passing under the 2.8-mile-long

International Bridge to Canada. You are treated to a rather surreal-istic view of Canada's huge riverfront Algoma Steel Mill, with its 10,000 employees and five blast furnaces. On the wharf are enor-mous piles of purplish taconite iron pellets from Lake Superior's iron-mining regions. Across the river, you see downtown Sault Ste. Marie, Canada, and its seaplane station for fighting forest fires. The planes swoop down onto lakes and in just seven seconds fill their two water tanks on the move. You also pass the quarter-mile-long Edison Sault Electric Company. (See page734.) ***Boat tour docks** are along Portage east of Ashmun Bus. I-75 and the locks. One is next to the Museum Ship Valley Camp on Portage, half a mile east of Ashmun; another is 1.7 miles east of Ashmun, beyond the Edison Sault powerhouse. For the complex, changing **schedule,** call (800) 432-6301 or pick up a brochure — they're everywhere. Boats leave hourly or more often between 9 a.m. and 5:40 or 6:40 p.m. in July & August. & Buy tickets ahead of time. Adults $12.50, senior 62 and over $12, kids 8-13 $10, kids 5-12 $6, 4 and under free.*

The American and Canadian settlements at the Soo have always been strategic outposts. The recorded history of the area goes back to 1618. Father Jacques Marquette started a mission at the Soo in 1668. The Straits of Mackinac soon became the center of a vast fur-trading network. In 1855, the first canal around the rapids actually caused an economic tailspin by taking away local residents' liveli-hood portaging freight around the rapids.

In the late 19th century, there were plans for Michigan's Sault Ste. Marie to become a major northern metropolis by using the St. Marys River as a power source. Francis Clergue from Maine pur-sued this dream but went bankrupt in developing the striking, quarter-mile-long **power plant** where the waterpower canal meets the river, on East Portage two-thirds of a mile east of Ashmun. The anticipated new industries never came. Despite Clergue's ultimate financial failure, deals and alliances he made with Canadian investors transformed Sault Ste. Marie, Canada into a major indus-trial center. He helped create the Algoma Central Railroad (the famous Snow Train that is disappointedly dull to some), St. Mary's Paper, Algoma Steel, and Algoma Central Marine. Clergue's story is poignantly told at the Tower of History.

In recent years Sault, Michigan has experienced a boom from the **Kewadin Casino** of the Sault Ste. Marie Tribe of Chippewa Indians. The multifaceted vision of tribal chairman Bernard Bouschor has developed the casino into a spectacular entertainment/lodging/cul-tural complex with an art gallery. It sets a high standard for Indian casinos, and is worth a look as a cultural phenomenon. The casino has funded the tribe's non-gambling spinoffs such as a new school, a $12,000,000 medical clinic, and 800 new houses for tribal members and has stimulated much lodging development.

For a good overview of the area, take the Twin Sault Tour (see below), and then visit the weird but worthwhile **Tower of History**. This 21-story concrete tower, in an architectural style of the 1960s known as Brutalism, was built as the bell tower for the planned new building of the church next door. In 1967, after the $660,000 tower was finished, the governing Catholic bishop said enough already to the grandiose parish project. A local nonprofit historical society turned it into a museum — still a very uneven museum but new direction may rectify that. The best part is the amazing **view** from its top of the locks, waterways, and hills. The museum is currently showing a film about the early history of the area. On exhibit are the local history and Native American culture. *326 E. Portage, 3 blocks east (right) from Ashmun/Bus. I-75. (906) 632-3658. Open mid-May thru mid-Oct, 10-6 daily. &: no. $2.95 adults; $1.75 ages 6-16.*

Don't leave without driving a few blocks east on Portage to see the monumental, quarter-mile-long **Edison Sault Power Plant**, Clergue's glory and downfall. It was built of reddish-brown sandstone excavated from the Power Canal that makes an island of downtown Sault Ste. Marie and powers the plant. But the project failed to attract enough industries to the area, Clergue went bust, and Sault Ste. Marie, Michigan, is today not another Minneapolis but a town of 15,000.

ENTERTAINING AND INFORMATIVE . . . . . but bumpy, the **Soo Locks Tour Trains** take you through both the U.S. and Canadian Sault Ste. Marie. In the U.S. the conveyances are open trailers pulled by a mock-train truck; in Canada they are double-decker buses. You learn a lot about both cities. The American city (population 15,000) was larger until the turn of the century, but now is dwarfed by its Canadian neighbor (population 83,000). The Canadian guide explains how that country's high taxes on cigarettes, alcohol, and gasoline help pay for the country's universal health insurance and how even a modest home there costs well over $100,000. At 40%, Italians are the largest of Sault Canada's many ethnic groups. The two-hour **Twin Sault Tour** is the one to take. It can give you time to shop and eat in Canada, if you choose. *Tour depot is at 315 W. Portage, across from Soo Locks Park and next to the Haunted Depot. (800) 387-6200. Opens Mem. Day, closes around Oct. 10. Tours leave between 10 and 4 hourly in June, every half hour in July & August. Call for fall times. &: no. One-hour tours: adults $5.50, students $3..50. Two-hour tours: $9.75 and $6.*

A FREIGHTER AND A MUSEUM . . . . . The **Museum Ship Valley Camp** is an old Great Lakes freighter whose large cargo holds have been converted into a Great Lakes theme museum. In one cavernous space an **Edmund Fitzgerald display** effectively captures the eeriness with which that huge freighter disappeared suddenly from the view of a trailing freighter. A torn lifeboat, one of the few remnants of the wreck to surface, is displayed. Especially interesting is the Valley Camp's **pilothouse,** which contains one of the lakes' first radar systems. Also on view are the captain's quarters, the quarters of the other officers and crew, the mess hall and galley. Exhibits are uneven, and some are dated. The place is so big, it's really a "find-it-yourself" museum that depends on the visitor's intuition, luck, or pre-existing interest and knowledge of the subject. It's a great place to visit on a rainy day. With more rigorously user-friendly interpretations, it could become an outstanding museum. Look for changes under its new direction. *(906) 632-3658.* &: *no. Adults $5.95, kids 6 thru 16 $3.50, 5 and under free. Group rates available upon request.*

SIMILARLY UNEVEN . . . . . is the ambitious **River of History Museum** in the old Beaux Arts post office building. Spoken stories at a few compelling life-size dioramas focus on key periods of area history. The enterable replica of a French fur trader's cabin has clothes to try on and other hands-on items. Other displays include a fishing diorama. Going through all eight of the museum's galleries takes about 30 to 45 minutes . It's a good rainy-day destination, with a fine museum shop of educational materials and local crafts. *209 E. Portage, a block east (right) from Ashmun/Bus. I-75 downtown. (906) 632-1999. Open mid-May thru mid October. By appt. in winter. Basic hours: Mon-Sat 10-5, Sun 12-5.* & *$2.50/adult, $1.25 ages 8-16. 7 and under free, $8 family.*

On the shores of Whitefish Bay

*A drive with many points of interest
and gorgeous views of Lake Superior and ships*

BETWEEN PARADISE and Brimley near Sault Ste. Marie and Paradise, Lake Shore Drive is a shoreline road along Whitefish Bay that's beautiful and most interesting. It offers terrific Lake Superior views looking out onto shipping lanes, plus a lighthouse museum with a stunning view from its tower, a remarkable scenic overlook, a fish hatchery, a beautiful short section of the North Country Trail with a swinging bridge, and several picnic areas, campgrounds, and beaches. There's little development. Most of the area is part of the Hiawatha National Forest.

It all makes for a lovely day's drive, especially magnificent in color season, when maples, birches, and dark green conifers make rich color contrasts. The resort and retirement village of Paradise is a fine vacation base from which to explore the eastern Upper Peninsula and visit nearby Tahquamenon Falls.

If you're going between Tahquamenon Falls and Sault Ste. Marie, it's well worth the extra time to take this east-west scenic route instead of the direct but dull M-28. Here are directions and highlights, arranged from east (Sault Ste. Marie) to west (the mouth of the Tahquamenon River and Paradise):

◆ Take Bus. I-75/Ashmun/Mackinaw Trail out of Sault Ste. Marie. Stop to pick up brochures and information sheets at the helpful **Hiawatha National Forest office** on Bus. I-75 (906-635-5311). Do not turn onto I-75. Instead, continue south on Mackinaw Trail and turn right (west) onto Six Mile Road at the blinker and cemetery. In seven miles you might enjoy stopping at well-known Great Lakes marine artist Mary Demroske's **Mushroom Cap Studio and Gallery**, (906-248-6632). There baskets, pottery, and her own prints and cards of freighters and lighthouses are for sale. Look for the blue garage on the north side of the road. After eight miles on Six Mile Road you will reach Lake Shore Road and Brimley.

◆ **Brimley** is in two parts: a resort hamlet where the Waisko River empties into Lake Superior, and a village a mile south on M-221, which joins Lake Shore just west of the river. Look for the "Cedar Shop" sign just before you reach the big lake, turn down a forested lane, and you'll come to the **Cedar Shop** home business (906-248-3392). At this charming little spread, lumber dealer Steve LePine sells classic and **updated versions of rustic Adirondack furniture made of local white cedar.** Fridays and Saturdays in the summer, if Steve isn't at his home shop, he's at his warehouse on Bay Mills Point Road which he opens for shoppers. &: most of the furniture is on his lawn at home; the warehouse is accessible.

◆ **Brimley State Park** is a tidy, 157-acre park with a mile of Lake Superior shoreline. The developed part feels suburban, not at all wild. The **picnic area** has an **outstanding view of freighters** heading to and from the Soo Locks. Modern camping. The **beach** here is one of the warmest places to swim in Lake Superior. *Entrance off Six Mile Rd. just east of Brimley. (906) 248-3422. &: one building at the camp ground. State Park sticker required: $4/day, $20/year.*

◆ **Willoughby's** restaurant has a nice deck at the Waiska River mouth in Brimley. It's a pleasant spot for a snack or meal. The owners also own Munising's popular Dogpatch. (906) 248-3800. &

◆ **Kings Club Casino** is on the shore road just west of Brimley run by the Bay Mills Indian Community. About a mile away is the brand-new **Bay Mills Resort & Casino** with an 18-hole golf course. (906) 248-3227. &

◆ **Wheels of History Museum.** Trains of the Duluth, South 12 Shore & Atlantic RR once brought logs to the milltown of Bay Mills and took finished lumber to distant markets. The Bay Mills - Brimley Historical Research Society, instrumental in restoring the Point Iroquois lighthouse, has now turned its attention to the local history of railroads, fishing, logging, milling, and early telephones. Its new museum occupies a turn-of-the-century wooden coach from the Algoma Central RR. The **gift shop** and **info center** is in a caboose. *In Brimley village at Superior Township Park, M-221 at Depot St. From Lake Shore, turn south onto M-22 just west of the river mouth. (906) 248-3665. Open mid-May thru mid-Oct. Open Wed-Sun 10-4 from mid-June thru Labor Day. Otherwise open Sat & Sun only. &. Donations appreciated.*

◆ **Mission Hill/Spectacle Lake Overlook** offers one of the most memorable scenic panoramas of the entire Upper Peninsula, almost on a par with Brockway Mountain Drive. Here a steep sand dune dramatically towers over the Lake Superior shore. To the left, the white tower of the Iroquois Point lighthouse stands out among the dark pines and hardwoods. If you're lucky, you can see some freighters heading in and out of the Soo Locks, visible to the far right. Behind the locks are the Algoma Steel stacks and, blue in the distance, the rugged Laurentian hills of the Algoma Region of Ontario. Just below is Spectacle Lake. A plaque remembers Herman and Frances Cameron, an inspirational, community-minded Ojibwa couple from Bay Mills who liked to come here "for contemplation and renewal." Follow their example. Don't hurry from this serene spot. The inconspicuous turnoff from Lake Shore Drive to Mission Hill is a little west of the Bay Mills Indian Cemetery. If you continue due west up on the hill, you will arrive at the Dollar Settlement on Whitefish Bay in five bumpy miles.

◆ **Monocle Lake Campground** of the Hiawatha National Forest centers around 172-acre Monocle Lake, stocked with walleye, bass, pike, and perch. Lots of recent improvements, including a floating **fishing dock** and hard gravel paths, make the area about as wheelchair-accessible as a rustic camping area can be. There's a **beach**, boat launch, and **picnic area** with charcoal grilles. From it starts a two-mile **hiking trail loop** through natural hardwoods that include some very old white pines and hemlocks. It goes on a boardwalk across a beaver dam and wetland. When the trail comes to a bench in a quarter mile, a spur leads left up the bluff to another grand **view** overlooking the shipping channel. The **campground** offers 39 rustic sites (picnic tables, fire ring, pit toilets, hand pump, cold-water shower). It fills only on summer weekends. Lake Superior and the Point Iroquois light are just a mile away. *From M-28, take M-221 to Brimley, go west on lakeshore 7 miles. (906) 635-5311. &: campground (call). $6/night.*

◆ **The Point Iroquois Light Station and Museum** brings together all the elements that create the lighthouse mystique for so many people. The site is memorable. It's in a woods just back from a beautiful beach with ample deposits of driftwood and colored rocks. The 65-foot **tower** offers a fine view of the shipping lanes at the St. Marys River entrance.

One apartment of the 1870 lighthouse has been furnished to give an idea of the life the lightkeepers led, while other museum rooms show lighthouse technology, the history of navigational aids, and photos from the lighthouse from the 1890s until its closing in 1962. This important light station housed three families. Betty Byrnes Bacon, who grew up here, recalled her life at this self-sufficient homestead in the 1920s in a delightful book, *Lighthouse Memories*. It's available here at the attractive small **museum shop**. The Bay Mills-Brimley Historical Research Society has worked with the Forest Service to develop this museum. New resident managers, true lighthouse devotees, are also terrific info sources on area destinations. *On Lake Shore Dr. 5 miles west of Brimley and east of Paradise. (906) 437-5272. Open from May 15 thru October 15 daily from 9 a.m. to 5 p.m. Often the tower but not the museum is open*

Fabulous views: the tower of the Point Iroquois Light Station overlooks the shipping traffic entering the St. Marys River and the Soo Locks.

until 7 or 8 p.m. &: no. Donations appreciated.

◆ **Big Pine Picnic Area.** Yet another beautiful **beach** is beyond the pines of the picnic grounds. Picnic tables, grills, and benches make this a fine place to linger and see **sunsets.**

◆ **Bay View Beach and Campgrounds** of Hiawatha National Forest. Except for campers, the sandy Lake Superior beach is virtually empty and the forest behind it has some really big red pines. Here 24 rustic, private campsites (**picnic tables**, fire ring, vault toilets, hand pump) are steps away from the **beach.** *From M-28 at Raco, take Forest Road 3154 to Dollar Settlement, turn west (left) 2 miles. (906) 635-5311. &: no. $8/night. Fills on many summer weekends and sometimes during the week in hot weather.*

◆ **Pendills Creek National Fish Hatchery.** Some 800,000 lake trout stocked in the Great Lakes each year come from this hatchery and one nearby. Long tanks are covered with round plastic roofs. Six million eggs go into egg-seeding programs in lakes Superior, Michigan, and Huron. Here fry are reared for a year, until they are five to eight inches long. Then they are released. Visitors can enter the tank buildings and walk across metal catwalks to look down at the masses of little fish. More interesting is the pond of big, dark brood fish, from five to 12 or so years old. They weigh from four to 10 pounds. Eggs are taken from them in fall, fertilized, incubated for 40 days, and then shipped to the Jordan River Fish Hatchery near Gaylord to be raised to 2 1/2 inches before coming back here for further fish rearing.

Displays and pamphlets show eggs developing into fish and tell the story of how parasitic sea lamprey from Lake Ontario nearly destroyed the Upper Great Lakes fishery in the 1930s before being partially controlled by a combination of lampricide chemicals and natural predators like the coho salmon. *On Lake Shore Rd. 4 miles west of Dollar Settlement and Forest Rd. #3154. (906) 437-5231. Open Mon-Fri 8 a.m.-4:30 p.m. Weekend outdoor visitation allowed but visitor center is closed. &. Free.*

◆ **Indian Fishing Historical Marker** and **Whitefish Bay roadside park.** This spot offers a sweeping view and the interesting story of how a 1981 Supreme Court case brought by Big Abe LeBlanc of Bay Mills confirmed his contention that Michigan Indians gave up their *land* in an 1836 treaty but not their rights to *fish* and *gather*. As a result, Indian commercial fishermen can continue to fish while state policy otherwise severely limits commercial fishing in favor of sport fishing. *A little west of the Pendills Creek Hatchery and Rexford Rd. on Lake Shore.*

◆ **North Country Trail Segment.** A short and especially scenic part of the long-distance hiking trail is clearly marked at a **parking area** by Lake Shore Road west of Menekaunce Point. From there it's a one-mile hike to the **swinging bridge**, and another half mile to Tahquamenon Bay, before heading back to your car.

◆ **Rivermouth Unit of Tahquamenon Falls State Park.** Good fishing, rustic and modern campgrounds, and a Lake Superior beach. See page 747.

◆ **Paradise** is a pleasant little resort community with several simple motels, resorts, and restaurants strung along M-23, where it veers west to Tahquamenon Falls. Due north is the Great Lakes Shipwreck Museum at Whitefish Point (see page 741). Many resorts overlook Whitefish Bay.

Great Lakes Shipwreck Historical Museum and Whitefish Point

A moody, dramatic museum and outstanding spring and fall bird-watching attract throngs to a sandy, scenic point overlooking treacherous Whitefish Bay.

ON A POINT of land that forms the entrance to Lake Superior's Whitefish Bay, this museum is close to an expanse of water to the north called "the graveyard of the Great Lakes." A local diving enthusiast has marshalled volunteers and grants to develop the museum into a nationally prominent organization that continues to look for new shipwreck sites and to organize diving projects like the retrieval of the *Edmund Fitzgerald* bell. That's in addition to its role as an outstanding visitor attraction. Over a thousand visitors a day come here in July and August. Whitefish Point Bay's geography concentrates both ships and migrating birds at Whitefish Point. Birds flying along Lake superior's shoreline often cross north into Canada here where the straits are narrow. Whitefish Bay is a funnel for ships entering and leaving Lake Superior via the St. Marys River at the Soo to reach the lower lakes.

Shipwrecks were common here because the shipping lanes were congested with ships entering and leaving Lake Superior during the mining booms. High seas from 200 miles of open water to the west compounded the poor visibility from fog, forest fires, and snow. Most wrecks are from the 19th century, when over 3,000 much smaller commercial vessels plied the lakes, compared with just 120 today. Skippers were less experienced. Wood-burning steamers stayed close to the fueling stations on the shore, so they often ran up on rocks and shallows.

In an 80-mile stretch from Whitefish Point to Pictured Rocks, there have been over 300 shipwrecks, killing 320 sailors. The first to go under was the *Invincible*, a British schooner which went down in an 1816 gale; the last was the *Edmund Fitzgerald* in 1975.

The view at the sandy point is beautiful. You can see the Canadian mainland, across water 600 feet deep. Along the beach are countless colored stones worn smooth by water. This was a stopping place for Indians, 17th-century French voyageurs, and Jesuit missionaries.

The dramatic Shipwreck Museum grew out of Tom Farnquist's Lake Superior diving experiences. It has gathered outstanding photographs of the many wrecks off Whitefish Point, including the *Edmund Fitzgerald*.

The original lighttower at Whitefish Point was the first on Lake Superior, dating from the early copper boom of 1849. That first light was replaced in 1861 by the unusual iron tower within a framework of triangulated metal supports.

GREAT LAKES SHIPWRECK HISTORICAL MUSEUM

A sizable Coast Guard Station developed around the lighthouse. In 1985 it became the home of the Great Lakes Shipwreck Historical Society, founded by Tom Farnquist. Then a Sault Ste. Marie junior high biology teacher, he is a longtime diving enthusiast. He and other Great Lakes divers, concerned about the loss of shipwreck artifacts, wanted to share the excitement and history of shipwrecks with a wider public. He had also become expert at underwater photography. Mysterious, evocative photographs of dives, enlarged as backgrounds for exhibits, make this impressive small museum unusually compelling. An exhibit designer for the prestigious Milwaukee Public Museum was so taken by the ship wreck museum that he now volunteers his services.

The museum interior uses eerie, somber music and dramatic lighting in an otherwise dim room to convey the haunting world of underwater shipwrecks. Models of boats which have sunk in

Superior are juxtaposed with items brought up from the depths, such as a ship's bell from the schooner *Niagara*, sunk in 1897, or a carved bird from the steamer *Vienna*, sunk in 1892. Noting causes of shipwrecks (excessive speed, anchoring inadvertently in a shipping lane, violent storms) add to the drama. The center piece Fresnel lighthouse lens is a second-order giant dwarfing ones typically seen. Its light casts patterns on the dim floor and ceiling. The *Edmund Fitzgerald* exhibit caps the museum. Families of lost crew members turned to the museum for help when they decided to raise the ship's bell to draw attention to their pleas to divers to leave in peace the wreck and its bodies, preserved by Superior's cold water. A ship's bell symbolizes the connection of crew and ship. The *Fitzgerald's* bell is now on display here.

An adjoining **theater** shows an excellent film, *Edmund Fitzgerald "1995 Bell Recovery"* on Great Lakes shipwrecks. Highly emotional, the film includes the ceremonies and the families' responses to the recovery. The duplex **lightkeeper quarters** has been carefully restored, one unit to the 1890s, another to the 1920s, thanks to the detailed memory of a keeper's granddaughter. The **museum shop** sells a well-chosen array of Great Lakes maritime books and gifts and Upper Peninsula souvenirs. *Take M-123 north to the end of Whitefish Rd. past Paradise. (906) 635-1742. Open May 15-Oct. 15, daily 10-6. &. Adults $6, children $4.*

WHITEFISH POINT BIRD OBSERVATORY

Michigan's best birdwatching for birds of prey is when the hawk migration peaks at **Whitefish Point** during late April and May. Birds use the point poking out into Lake Superior to minimize flying over open water. 15,000 to 25,000 hawks have been counted in a season. Some 7,000 loons come a little later, with ducks and grebes, followed by songbirds through May and early mid June. The Michigan Audubon Society's **Whitefish Point Bird Observatory** is open year-round next to the old Coast Guard Station, conducting research and banding of raptors and songbirds. Over 300 species of birds in all have been counted here, including bald and golden eagles, merlin and peregrine falcons, and unusual Arctic birds. All summer long the point, almost surrounded by water, also attracts unusual numbers of water birds, such as common loons, grebes, cormorants, and sandhill cranes.

Low, windswept dunes, miles of undeveloped beach, and the fun of watching ships make Whitefish Point a fine place to spend the day. For an excellent map of the point's trails, and for helpful tips for bird-watching at the point, stop at the excellent **gift shop**, a treasure trove for bird lovers. and buy the observatory's checklist. (Map is in back.) A small indoor **nature center** interprets the area. Don't miss the trail to the **hawk dune** (behind the shipwreck museum) and the **trail** to the **point** (north of the observatory center. Here the dry forest of jack pine and sweet fern meets the wind-shaped dunes and beaches. It's a glorious place to linger and spend the day watching birds and gathering Lake Superior's colorful beach stones. Birders advise bringing warm clothing year-round for this windy, cool environment. *Observatory is in a small building on the east side of the shipwreck museum parking lot. (906) 492-3596. Open daily 9-4:30 from mid-April thru the end of May; open daily 10-6 from the end of May to mid-Oct. Gift shop hours are the same as the nature centers. Mail-order available: HC 48 Box 115, Paradise, MI 49768.* &

MAGNIFICENT VIEWS OF WHITEFISH BAY . . . . . can be had from the **Point Iroquois lighttower** (page 738), some 25 miles by car southeast of Whitefish Point on the scenic shore road to Sault Ste. Marie. The nearby **Spectacle Lake Overlook** (page 737) offers a similar view, with a foliage foreground that's beautiful in autumn.

Tahquamenon Falls State Park

Spectacular views of Michigan's most majestic falls are a tourist magnet in a huge wilderness park.

MOST MICHIGAN WATERFALLS are attractive but puny affairs compared with the mighty falls of the world. Michigan's one really substantial waterfall is the **Upper Falls** here at Tahquamenon. The falls are nearly 200 feet across. As much as 50,000 gallons of water a second plunge 48 feet into a canyon below. The state park has constructed an exciting platform that allows you to stand right at the brink of the falls, so you can take in the dramatic contrast between the serene meanderings of the upper Tahquamenon River and the roaring foam below the falls. The river is darkened by tannic acid from the many hemlocks, cedars, and spruces along its banks, which gives the initial spill of water an interesting brownish hue.

Park visitors are concentrated so intensely at the Upper Falls and the Lower Falls four miles downstream that it's easy to forget that this 40,000-acre park is Michigan's second-biggest state park. It stretches 13 miles west from Whitefish Bay at the Tahquamenon

At the Upper Tahquamenon Falls, the Tahquamenon River drops dramatically down from the sandstone cliff that underlies the glacial soils of the area. This is the same sandstone cliff or escarpment that forms the Pictured Rocks, only here it is inland.

River's mouth. Most of it is a designated **wilderness area** where you won't see a power line or hear a car. Maps are available at the fee stations at the Upper and Lower Falls or at park headquarters on M-123 between them.

The stairway to the memorable vantage point at the Upper Falls is reached by turning right as you go from the parking lot to the falls. It's a .4 mile wheelchair-accessible walk to the falls. From this same viewing platform you see, far downstream, the once-again peaceful river as it flows between reddish bluffs another 20 miles towards Lake Superior's Whitefish Bay south of Paradise. The left trail from the parking area leads to a less spectacular view of the falls from the lower river.

A .8 mile **interpretive nature trail** leads from the platform at the Upper Falls. The entire area around the falls is a 300-year-old beech-maple climax forest, but visitors miss out on this unless they think to look up.

In midday in July and August, the crowds and cars by the Upper Falls can be overwhelming. In color season it's also a well-trod tourist path. If you don't like being part of a herd, consider coming in the real off-seasons. Early May, with its active birds and wildlife, is nice. (Black flies can be a problem from late-May through the third week in June; mosquitoes can always be bad if it's been damp.) Another nice, quiet time is the end of October, when some leaves are left. Spectacular **fall color** peaks here well into October, later than in much of the U.P. A mix of maple, birch, and conifer makes for rich yellows and reds contrasted with dark green. An easy, flat trail into the forest is the four-mile **Giant Pine Loop** that begins at the brink of the Upper Falls and passes by some very old white pines. It is groomed for **cross-country skiing** in winter, and skiers are welcome to make their own trails. **Snowshoers** often take the trail between the falls. In his book of meditative U.P. nature explorations, *A Superior Peninsula* (p. 855), Lon Emerick highly rec-ommends an all-day inspection of the falls in midwinter, when most of the falls have frozen into huge daggers and the colors at close range are breath taking. Winter camping and visits are becoming increasingly popular.

If you *are* here in July or the first half of August, try coming before 10 a.m. (the earlier the better) or after 6 p.m. Remember, it stays light until 10 p.m. up here. Another reason to go earlier or later: the light effects and birds and wildlife are best in the early morning and evening.

Energetic and fit hikers might well prefer approaching the Upper Falls by foot, for maximum dramatic impact. An up-and-down **riverside trail**, recently improved, follows the Tahquamenon River for four miles upstream from the trailhead at the Lower Falls to the Upper Falls, crossing smaller streams on boardwalks along the way. Once at the Upper Falls, of course, you would need to walk four miles back.

At the Upper Falls parking area, visitors are greeted by an unusually striking log building, called **Camp 33** to recall the logging company that originally owned a large parcel within the state park. The high-ceilinged timberframe structure was built with oak posts and beams (no nails), which are exposed on the interior. The concessionaires who erected the building and run the store are descendants of the lumberman who gave the land for the park. The buildings and seating of the **picnic area** and restaurant terrace outside Camp 33 look out into the surrounding forest of big trees, well separated from the massive parking area. The **takeout restaurant** serves pasties, cooked-to-order hamburgers, and similar fare. There is also a recently-constructed **sit-down restaurant** and brewpub.

The **Lower Falls**, four miles downstream, is smaller but, in its own serene way, equally delightful. Here the Tahquamenon River drops 22 feet in a series of cascades that surround a sizable island and a series of boulders. You can view the series of falls from a high bluff, but for about $1.50 a person you can rent a rowboat from the concession which takes you much closer. A **footpath** goes right up to the falls. There's a **picnic area** along the river and a restaurant by the parking lot.

Trails up to 13 miles long enable hikers to get away from the crowds. They pass by many habitats, including conifer forests, sandy ridges, and boggy lakes typical of the eastern Upper Peninsula. Four miles of the twelve-mile **North Country Trail** (see page 759) pass through the park. Thanks to a round of funding for trail work, trails are all now very well marked and cleared. The four miles connecting the Upper and Lower Falls now has boardwalks, bridges, and steps on slippery hills. Wet areas outside the park may not be bridged, so waterproof footgear is recommended. A series of three **wilderness lakes** with northern pike and perch can be reached by an access road to Clark Lake and a half-mile portage to Betsy Lake. Park staff is happy to recommend hikes to suit your interests.

Below the Lower Falls, the Tahquamenon River offers the park's best **fishing**: northern pike, muskies, and walleye run in early spring and late October. A third developed area of this vast park is the Rivermouth Unit south of Paradise, where the Tahquamenon empties into Whitefish Bay. **Swimming** can be done from the park's beach on Whitefish Bay — if you can tolerate cold water. The shal-

low bay can warm up nicely when the weather is warm and sunny.
Campgrounds are at the **Rivermouth Unit**. They are wooded
and modern (electricity, hot showers, the works). Sites are not large.

*Headquarters is on M-123 a mile or so west of the **Lower Falls**
entrance, which is 12 miles west of Paradise. **Upper Falls** entrance on
M-123 is 2 miles west of Lower Falls and 21 miles east of Newberry.
The Rivermouth Unit is on M-123 4 miles south of Paradise. (906) 492-
3415. Open year-round. &: concession buildings, vault toilet at Upper
Falls, path from parking to Upper Falls, boardwalk at Lower Falls.
State park sticker required; $4/day, or $20/year.*

TWO BOAT CRUISES TO THE UPPER FALLS . . . . . Both come with recommendations. Neither offers such easy access to the falls, nor such a good view as
the state park on the river's north side. yet they may be worthwhile excursions
or good rainy-day options if your schedule permits. Both tours highlight local
Ojibwa lore, Tahquamenon logging history, and above all, nature. Bear and deer
are sometimes seen on the trip. Bring your binoculars! Expect a knowledgeable
narrator/pilot who's a longtime local resident and good at wildlife identification.
The 250-passenger double-deck river boats are similar. They are quiet — no bad
vibrations. Both have food and bar service (and excellent grilled hamburgers),
restrooms, covered decks, and open and enclosed seating. Line up early to get
the best seats, up front in the bow. The atmosphere on these leisurely cruises is
congenial; you may learn a lot of Michigan history from the mostly older crowd.
     The all-day **Toonerville Trolley and Riverboat** trip (begun in 1927) uses a
narrow-gauge train over old logging track. A 5-ton diesel originally used in mines
pulls the train through an interesting mix of northwoods habitats: spruce
(scrubby and majestic), tamarack, and birch and young maples. It's a bumpy
ride, 35 minutes each way. The four-hour cruise on the wide river passes mature
second-growth forests and a few cottages. The boat docks quite a ways upstream
from the falls. A 5/8 mile path goes through a beautiful old conifer forest and
looks down on the river. This walk is not for the infirm. It has hills, some roots
and some steps, before a long series of stairways down a dramatic sheer cliff to
the falls overlook platform. *Train leaves Soo Junction (about 2 miles north of M-28
and 12 miles east of Newberry) at 10:30 a.m., returns at 5. Come by 10 or so.
Operates daily , June 15-October 6. (906) 876-2311; (906) 293-3806 (winter).
Reservations recommended for holiday weekends. &: no, but help is available to
climb in and out of train cars. Boat trip need not involve steps. $16/adult,
$15/seniors 62 and up, $8 children 6-15. Under 6 free. AAA discount.*
     The **Tom Sawyer Riverboat & Paul Bunyan Tour Train** (founded in 1947)
is similar but two hours shorter. The trip starts on the river, then uses a tractor-
pulled rubber-tired train to go through a mature forest to the falls. *Starts from
Slater's Landing 12 miles north of M-28 at Hulbert Corners, which is 6 miles west
of M-123. From Mem. weekend through Oct. 10. Leaves at 10:30 through June 30.*

*Weekends only through June 14. In July & August, leaves at 9:30 a.m. & 2 p.m.
Mon-Fri, 10:30 a.m. Sat & Sun. In Sept. & Oct. leaves at noon. (906) 876-2331 and
(906) 632-3727. Reservations advised for holiday weekends.* &: *see Toonerville,
above. Adults $14. Kids 5-15 $7. Under 5 free.*

CANOEING THE TAHQUAMENON . . . . . The **only canoe livery on the
Tahquamenon** is just north of Newberry, at M-123 and CR 462. **Mark's Rod &
Reel Repair and Canoe Livery** offers very beautiful, 2-hour paddles from the
Dollarville Dam east to the Tahquamenon River Logging Museum in Newberry.
Longer trips go farther down the river into the gorgeous, wild country below the
dam. It's a four-day or so trip to the falls, with camping anywhere you can find a
clear spot. This is easy, flat water, with no portaging, well suited to beginners
with good camping skills. There's good fishing for pike, muskie, walleye, and
panfish. Bows and bow repair also available. Cost: $25 (slightly higher for dis-
tant points) for spotting (that is, taking you and your canoe to the put-in point)
plus $20/day rental fee. (906) 293-5608.

A SURPRISING FIND . . . . . is the unassuming roadside **Tahquamenon River
Logging Museum** and **Nature Study Area** just north of Newberry on M-123.
Parts of it are typically tiresome displays of tools and equipment without vitaliz-
ing ideas or stories. But the **local history displays** in the old house are excellent, and the **interpretive nature trail** leading back through a woods and
swamp to a scenic river overlook gives a remarkably clear explanation of northwoods tree species. If you can see the top-notch logging **video** done by Wendell
Hoover, Hartwick Pines' logging historian, you'll gain a new appreciation of the
social history of logging and the lives of shanty boys. (They never called themselves "lumberjacks.") Lively old-time **music jamborees** are held on the fourth
weekends of July and August (the Lumberjack Festival). The music starts about
noon and lasts until everyone gets tired. *On M-123 at Tahquamenon River, 1 1/2
miles north of Newberry. (906) 293-3700. Open 9-5 daily from Memorial thru Labor
Day.* &: *museum and the trail up to the river. $3/adults, $1.50/kids 6-12, 5 and
under free. Includes tour of nature trail and buildings and video show.*

FOR LOCALLY MADE INDIAN CRAFTS . . . . . and for supplies, too, stop in at
the **Luce County Inter-Tribal Center for the Arts** in Newberry. You'll find
black ash baskets, porcupine quill boxes, and leather and beaded items. Classes
are held here too. *Take M-123 to downtown Newberry. The Center is next to the
Ford Garage on the east side of Main St. (906) 293-3491. Open year round Mon-Fri
8-5, Sat 10-4, by appointment at other times.* &

GOOD CANOEING NOT FAR FROM THE FALLS . . . . . **Two Hearted Canoe
Trips** can arrange a wonderful, easy four- to six-hour family canoe trip
($25/canoe) to its rustic Rainbow Lodge and Campground at the Two-Hearted
River's mouth on Lake Superior, or two- and three-day trips for experienced
canoeists. The 1 1/2 hour canoe trip for two people is $18. If you bring your own
canoe, shuttle service is $15. (906) 658-3357.

Seney National Wildlife Refuge

*For seeing a splendid range of northwoods wildlife,
little can match this vast domain
of managed wetlands, bog, and wilderness.*

EVEN FOR PEOPLE with a casual interest in wildlife, the enormous 95,000-acre refuge southwest of Seney is a magical place, where it's easy to get an intimate look at many different northwoods wildlife habitats. Motorists driving along special lanes built on dikes can see bald eagles, trumpeter swans, and loons feeding. For mountain bikers, Seney is a paradise. Bicyclists use the nearly eighty miles of mostly flat trails along dikes and back roads. Signs of elusive wolves and moose who use the Refuge may be seen in the backcountry. Birders intent on expanding their lists of birds sometimes drive thousands of miles to spot the yellow rail or black-backed three-toed woodpecker found here. Seney may be the very best place to see woodcock in the entire United States.

Hints for finding wildlife to watch are conveyed through excellent interpretive displays in the Visitor Center and through signs along the trails and wildlife drives. Knowledgeable staff and volunteers can direct visitors to unusual habitats such as recently burned areas and different kinds of bogs. Common birds include mergansers, ring-necked ducks, American bitterns, black terns, and pine warblers, which can often be heard along the tour route.

The story of the north woods is essentially many variations on one epic theme: exploiting natural resources, by trapping from about 1650 into the 1830s and by logging in the 19th and early 20th centuries. There was the Big Cut and the boom that went with it, and then there was the inevitable bust: the cutover land and devastated local economies, and all the different ways various people responded, from local and state political leaders to railroads to agricultural

Fish in the Refuge's wetlands are managed to provide plenty of food for bald eagles and other fish-eating birds and mammals. Visitors have a very good chance of seeing bald eagles.

researchers to early conservationists to loggers-turned-farmers to real estate promoters.

The story of the Seney National Wildlife Refuge is told in a well-written display at the Refuge's Visitor Center. The Refuge is a huge (95,455 acres or 150 square miles) and peaceful wetland that drains into the Manistique River between Seney and Munising. From 1881 to 1900 the area was logged off. Fires swept many cutover lands, including the Great Manistique Swamp here. A decade later, land speculators started to drain this marsh to develop it for farming. They failed, but waterfowl diminished because their habitat was lost. Most of this land — like much poor land across the U.S. — reverted to the government for nonpayment of taxes during the Depression. Such land, through farsighted parks and recreation plans of the 1930s, became the cores of many public parks.

Conservationists organized to try to protect the threatened waterfowl. The State of Michigan asked the Roosevelt administration to include the Seney land among the submarginal farmlands to be developed as waterfowl refuges. In 1935, using funds from duck stamps and labor from the Civilian Conservation Corps (CCC) and Works Projects Administration (WPA), an intricate system of dikes and dams created thousands of acres of permanent marshes for waterfowl at Seney. CCC crews planted aquatic plants favored by ducks and geese: pondweed, bulrushes, duck weed, wild rice, wild celery, and more.

Today the Refuge is managed to encourage waterfowl production. Controlling water levels creates wet and dry cycles that mimic nature. (Because the pools are man-made, wet-dry cycles can't occur naturally.) Controlled fire imitates the beneficial effects of lightning-caused fires. For instance, fires clear underbrush which creates tender young growth for deer. Fires also heat jack pine cones until they open and release seeds.

Though wildlife management is the Refuge's main purpose, much has been done for visitors. The Visitor Center and seven-mile marshland Wildlife Drive have become popular Upper Peninsula attractions. The Refuge's back roads and dikes have been opened to bicyclists and hikers. Nearly **eighty miles of bike and hiking trails** are ideally suited for viewing wildlife. **Canoeing** is encouraged along the Manistique River. For information on canoe and mountain bike rentals, see page 747.

Plan your visit so you'll be able to view wildlife in the early morning or evening, when birds and mammals are most active. The outstanding Visitor Center is open from 9 a.m. to 5 p.m. seven days a week from May 15 to October 15. The wildlife drive and trails are

Nearly eighty miles of back roads and dikes make it easy for mountain bikers to get away from road noise and traffic and increase their chances of seeing wildlife.

open from sunup to sundown. Over 200 species of birds and 50 species of mammals, including the eastern timber wolf, have been recorded here. A bird list is available at the Visitor Center, along with a detailed **map and guide** to the entire refuge. Off-hours it's in the rack in front. In the off-season, it's at the main office next door. As part of the Refuge's **"Watchable Wildlife Program,"** the map includes hints for seeing wildlife and marks places and habitats where certain kinds of wildlife are often seen.

Main visitor attractions include:

◆ **Visitor Center.** Excellent displays, a knowledgeable staff, and the Seney Natural History Association's small **bookstore** make this a good first stop for orientation. A new multi-projector **slide/tape introduction to the Refuge**, 14 minutes long, tells visitors what they can expect to do and see at Seney. The **loon exhibit** invites visitors to hear the loon's four main calls while seeing a beautiful diorama of a loon swimming with its chick on its back. A short video shows loons in action. Loons are plentiful in the refuge because it meets their three main requirements: 1) clean water; 2) quiet, undisturbed nesting islands; and 3) a good supply of fish to eat.

Free **brochures** describe the Refuge's policy and opportunities for hunting and fishing. Northern pike, bullheads, and perch offer anglers a challenge. Get information on the nature trail, driving loop, and back roads (closed to vehicles). Visitors can **borrow binoculars**, a bird guide, and a flower guide at no cost. *Open May 15-October 15, 9 a.m. to 5 p.m. (906) 586-9851. &: marginally. Free.*

◆ **Marshland Wildlife Drive.** This seven-mile **self-guided auto tour** on a one-way gravel road connects three **observation decks** in favorite habitats where trumpeter swans, loons and osprey, and bald eagles can sometimes be seen. Scopes are provided at each observation deck. (Both the decks and the scopes are barrier free.) The speed limit is 15 mph. **Interpretive signs** are most informative. Deer, beaver, turtles, waterfowl, and wading birds are also plentiful. Motorists are encouraged to get out of their cars and walk along the dikes and back roads to improve their chances of seeing more wildlife. Binoculars can be borrowed at the visitor center. The **fishing loop** adds three more miles and one barrier-free **fishing platform** (with a barrier-free scope) to the drive. Narrow clearances and car traffic here make it more enjoyable for bicyclists to use back roads instead. They'll see more wildlife on back roads, too. *The wildlife drive starts near the visitor center and ends on M-77, just south of the main Refuge entrance. It's open from May 15 through October 15, daylight hours only. The drive is closed to motorized vehicles (but not to walkers or bicyclists) during nesting season and fall migration to leave birds undisturbed.*

◆ **Pine Ridge Nature Trail.** A 1.4 mile loop (&: no) with interpretive signs takes visitors along high, dry pine ridges that weave through the pool system. A **boardwalk** traverses a marshy area, excellent for viewing waterfowl. Spring and summer wildflowers are abundant. It's a peaceful experience except for nearby road noise.

◆ **Backcountry paths** along dikes and service roads offer hikers and bicyclists nearly eighty miles of prime wildlife viewing. Intersections are clearly marked so users can easily plot their routes and see where they are on the detailed Refuge map. Surfaces are varied. Hard-packed gravel and sand work fine for bikes with narrow tires in most conditions, but mountain bikes would be better, especially after rain.

◆ **Northern Hardwoods Cross-Country Ski Area.** Ten miles of groomed trails are usually skiable from mid or late December through March. Trails start at the parking lot west of M-77, 1/3 mile south of the blinking light in Germfask. For snow conditions, call (906) 586-9851.

◆ **Canoeing** can be done on the Refuge's rivers. The Manistique River is the only conveniently reachable stream section that can be canoed during the allotted daylight hours. Canoeing is not allowed on the Refuge pools or marshes. There are three popular places to put in: Northland Outfitters on the north edge of Germfask off M-77 (906-586-9801); Big Cedar Campground on the south edge of Germfask off M-77 (906-586-6684); and the pretty picnic area on M-77 about a mile south of Germfask. Canoeists end up at the 10-campsite **Mead Creek Campground** of Lake Superior State Forest on County Road 436 south of the wildlife refuge.

Although there are no picnic tables, grills, or trash cans on the

Refuge, picnicking is allowed. Bring a blanket, take your trash home with you, and don't light any kind of fire.

The main entrance to the refuge is on M-77, 2 miles north of Germfask and 5 miles south of Seney. (906) 586-9851. Between May 15 and October 15: Marshland Wildlife Drive open between sunrise and sunset. Visitor Center open 9- 5. <u>Visitor use of the Refuge is limited to daylight hours.</u> In the off-season, the entrance to ski trails is off the parking lot on M-77, half a mile south of Germfask. &: visitor center, viewing platforms along wildlife drive, indoor & outdoor toilets. Free.

CANOE, KAYAK AND MOUNTAIN BIKE RENTALS . . . . . are at **Northland Outfitters** on the north edge of Germfask just east off M-77, 1 1/2 miles south of the Refuge entrance. (906) 586-9801. Northland's large, shady campgrounds for RVs and tents are near the river in a pretty, grassy spot. The proprietors (transplanted suburbanites who also sell local real estate) can arrange for short two- and four-hour trips on the Manistique River and for long, multi-day canoe trips on the Manistique and Fox rivers and the Big Island Lake Complex. &: campground. . . . . Canoes may also be rented at the **Big Cedar Campground**, a private campground on M-77 just south of Germfask. On the site of an old CCC camp, it's open from May 1 thru March 15. (906) 586-6684. The most popular canoe trip, a 4-hour paddle through Seney Wildlife refuge, is $20 for 2. &: no.

THE TOWN THAT WAS SOLD ALL AT ONCE . . . . . Twelve miles south of the Seney National Wildlife Refuge on M-77, the town of **Blaney Park** began as the company town of the Wisconsin Land and Lumber Company. In 1909 the townsite and some 33,000 acres were acquired by the Washington Earle family, designers of the machinery that first produced tongue and groove flooring, sold under the IXL trademark. ("I excel.") Company headquarters, between Escanaba and Iron Mountain, are a time capsule you can visit; see page 783. The Earles stopped logging in 1926, and decided to develop Blaney into an outdoorsman's fishing and hunting resort. With a restaurant, tennis, golf, and riding to broaden its appeal, the Blaney Park Resort thrived into the 1950s but then declined. The Earles auctioned off the land (in 1984) and town buildings (in 1985). Now the new owners of Blaney Park, a diverse crew largely of urban refugees, have breathed new life into the store, the excellent Blaney Inn Restaurant, the charming **Blaney Camp 9 Cabins,** and Celibeth House Bed & Breakfast (a delightful respite for nature-lovers). **Paul Bunyan's Country Store**, right on   M-77, has aspects of a funny, funky museum.

WRONG RIVER . . . . . Hemingway appropriated the Two-Hearted River's memorable name and gave it to the river his fictional alter-ego Nick Adams fished, in his famous story **"Big Two-Hearted River."** Actually Hemingway fished the Fox. It flows through Seney into the Manistique River and Lake Michigan.

Grand Marais and vicinity

A tranquil, picturesque refuge on Lake Superior

THE SIMPLE little village of Grand Marais (population 400) is the gateway to the eastern end of the Pictured Rocks National Lakeshore, with the Grand Sable Dunes. The village (M-77 from Seney). sits in splendid isolation on an unusually well protected Lake Superior harbor. West Bay offered such good protection to 17th-century French explorers that they gave it the name "marais," which means "harbor of refuge." Today the harbor is shoaling in because storms have destroyed its century-old breakwall. A local committee is pressing to fund federal harbor improvements.

The older houses in Grand Marais date from its boom years between 1860 and 1910, when it was an active fishing and lumber port full of saloons and lumber mills. It then lay nearly dormant for over half a century until revived by resorters and tourists attracted to the quiet scenic beauty. Their aluminum-sided ranch homes now seem to outnumber the simple older homes.

Today Grand Marais makes for a tranquil, out-of-the-way base from which to explore the unspoiled forests, dunes, and beaches that surround it. At the end of a single blacktop road, this village is really at the end of the line. Roads do go east and west, roughly along the lakeshore for a ways, but they are unpaved and sometimes very bumpy. H58 going west is the worst. And a surprising number of nature-loving artists, writers, and urban refugees are well aware of its special quality. Novelist and poet Jim Harrison escapes to his cabin near here when his Lake Leelanau home gets too busy with summer visitors.

You would expect Grand Marais to be at its most tranquil in winter. Ironically, snowmobiles make it a jarring time to visit. The noisy machines converge weekends, and lodgings and restaurants report doing as much business as during the height of summer. Weekdays are likely to be a good deal quieter.

The short peninsula that forms West Bay leads to a windswept beach over low dunes from a parking area. Here too is a lighthouse and Coast Guard station, home of the Grand Marais **Maritime Museum** *(open weekends 10-6, July through Labor Day)*. Displays in the small museum are done in the minimalist style typical of the National Parks Service that spotlights a few objects: the third-order Fresnel Lens from the nearby Au Sable light tower, a breeches buoy used by lifesavers, some photos of local fishermen and the lifesaving station. The toilet in the ladies room is in almost the very place where the Coast Guard radioman last made contact with the *Edmund Fitzgerald*. With recent budget cutbacks and the dependence on volunteers now, museum hours vary from year to year. Currently, the museum is open from July 4 to August 15, Thursday thru Monday from 10 to 6 . Call (906) 494-2660 or (906) 387-3700 to confirm hours. &

Nearby, a stone **pier** protecting the harbor entrance holds the front range light. A nearby lighthouse keeper's bungalow houses the folksy museum of the **Grand Marais Historical Society.** Furnished

with the artifacts from a working class family of 1899, it reflects the boom time of 1900. Tours by volunteers include stories of the house and the area. *Open daily from 1-4 from July 4 thru Labor Day, weekends only in late June and September, and by appointment. (906-494-2355). &. Free. Donations accepted.*

Go west along the shore to come to another beach extending miles to the west, the well-known **agate beach**, where even novices may find the variegated, translucent stones of quartz while strolling along the shoreline looking through the clear water. Banded agates are formed by liquid quartz in cavities of preexisting rock. They may have a pitted potato-skin texture. Most common are shattered pieces with distinctive agate banding. (The colors are formed by different impurities.) Some people find more where the bank meets the beach. A one-mile walk down the beach and you're at the mouth of **Sable Creek**. A short path along the creek leads up to the delightful **Sable Falls**. (Camping hint: stay at Grand Marais' modern Woodland Park Campground for ready access down to agate beach.)

Several highlights of the Pictured Rocks National Lakeshore are most accessible from Grand Marais. Get information at nearby Grand Sable Visitor Center (page 758). Going west from town, these include:

♦ **Sable Falls** is off H-58 about a mile west of Grand Marais. A delightful half-mile walk and stairway take you through a forest and reveal the falls and Lake Superior in tantalizing glimpses before letting you look down on the entire cascade from the rocky shelf that forms it. Continue down and along Sable Creek, then go right (east) to get to the **agate beach** (see above).

♦ **The Grand Sable Bank and Dunes** are best seen by taking the footpath back from Sable Falls a ways and picking up another half-mile walk across the creek to the dunes. "Grand Sable" means "big sand." The banks are a huge formation along Lake Superior, up to 275 feet high, created when sand and gravel filled in a deep rift in the ice of the last glacier. Dunes are perched atop the banks, rising another 80 feet. They were formed when wind and waves piled up sand at the edge of lake Nipissing, forerunner of Superior. First you pass through a jack pine forest, then enter a bleak dunescape where only a few hardy plant pioneers like marram grass can take hold. Excellent **interpretive displays** explain the principles of plant succession in the beach's harsh, dry, hot/cold, nutrient-deficient environment. You can also see a small **ghost forest** of trees over-

The Log Slide, 300 feet above Lake Superior, offers distant views of the Au Sable Point Lighttower and the Grand Sable Banks. Decades ago, loggers rolled logs down from it to waiting lumber schooners.

whelmed by sand.

The banks and dunes, seen from this vantage point midway up
their height, seem dramatic and overwhelming. They are entirely
bare and blindingly blank on a sunny day, slanting into Lake
Superior at the steep, 35 ° angle of repose common to all piles of
dry sand. The banks stretch west for five miles, down to the Log
Slide. Don't be tempted to walk down to the lake here; walking back
up the sand would be very difficult. &: *no.*

◆ At its **Grand Sable Visitor Center**, on H-58 about five miles west
of Grand Marais, you can find free information on the National
Lakeshore, including campgrounds, day hikes, and backcountry
camping along the 43-mile **Lakeshore Trail** along the entire shoreline. (See page 763.) Displays and a small **bookstore** focus on the
area's natural and human history. *On H-58 about 5 miles west of
Grand Marais. (906) 494-2660. Currently open from mid-May thru
mid-October, from at least 10-6 daily.* &

◆ **Log Slide.** This high point of the ridge along Lake Superior is
almost 300 feet above the water. In the late 19th century loggers
rolled and slid logs down a 500-foot slide on the sharp incline, to be
loaded on Great Lakes lumber schooners. It is well located for fine
views of the Grand Sable Banks and Dunes to the east and the Au
Sable Point lighthouse to the west. *Off H-58 about 8 miles west of
Grand Marais and 24 miles east of Munising.* &: *no..*

◆ **Au Sable Point Light and Lighthouse**. The red brick lightkeeper's house and attached white cylinder of a tower sit atop picture-
perfect red sandstone rocks. The lighthouse and tower with lens,
recently restored to its 1910 condition, is now open to the public.
From July 1 through Labor Day free **tours** are held ever half hour
Thursday through Sunday. Call (906) 494-2660 or (906) 494-2669
to check tour times, which are subject to change. The easy 1 1/2-
mile walk from the Hurricane River Campgrounds (3 miles round-
trip) is worthwhile. Climb down the rocks from the lighthouse and
go west a ways, and you'll come upon some shipwreck skeletons
sticking out of the sand. &: *no.*

◆ **Twelvemile Beach.** This long sand and pebble beach is
approached from the road through a beautiful white birch forest.
Swimming here is awfully cold, but the beach is fine for picnics and
walks along the Lakeshore Trail. At the Twelvemile Beach campground, 38 shady, private rustic campsites with tent pads and hand
pumps ($8 a night per car) sit on a bluff overlooking the lake. A
two-mile interpretive **nature trail** takes you through the beautiful
and unusual **White Birch Forest** of large birches. Sun-loving pio-

neers after forest fires and cutting, birches are normally soon shaded by more adaptable maples. Here they have thrived longer, thanks to moist soils and plenty of sunlight. (The birches can also be seen from H-58.) *Take H-58 (unpaved) about 15 miles west of Grand Marais or about 37 miles east of Munising.*

THE TEENIE WEENIE PICKLE BARREL COTTAGE. . . . . is a connected pair of rather large barrels that today serve as **Grand Marais's tourist information center.** It's in town next to the Sportsman Restaurant. It was built as the summer home on Grand Sable Lake of William and Mary Donahey, creators of the band of elfin Teenie Weenies who starred in a 1920s comic strip of that name. . . . . For laminated Tweenie Weenie cartoon placemats and a real trip back in time, to somewhere in the 1940s, stop in across the street at the **Superior Hotel** (906-494-2539). There you can get ice cream, penny candy, and a long perspective on the local scene from Bess Capogrossa — and a clean room with a firm mattress for about $20 a night.

HIKE FROM MARQUETTE TO ST. IGNACE . . . . . over 200 miles along the completed sections of the **North Country Trail**. It goes from Marquette through the Pictured Rocks and Muskallonge State Park on Lake Superior and the through the Hiawatha National Forest, passing by the Upper and Lower Tahquamenon Falls along the way. For a brochure, contact the National Parks/National Forest Service visitor center, (906) 387-3700; Box 400, Route 2, Munising, MI 49862. Eventually the trail will extend from the Appalachian Trail in New York State to North Dakota.

Pictured Rocks National Lakeshore and Grand Island

Colorful cliffs meet clear, green Lake Superior in a series of memorable views, with many waterfalls and miles of wilderness hiking and canoe trails nearby

THIS EXTRAORDINARY 43 miles of Lake Superior shoreline, extending from Munising to Grand Marais, contains some of Michigan's most remarkable scenery. Most famous are the **Pictured Rocks**, only visible from the water. Red and yellow sandstone bluffs up to 200 feet high have been shaped by wind, waves, and ice into dramatic columns and watery caves, then variously stained into colored "pictures" by mineral-rich water seeping between sandstone layers. The colors of the sandstone cliffs are subtle. Blues and greens are created by copper, the reddish hues by iron. In mid-day on a glary day they can be washed out. Five waterfalls are formed when short streams (characteristic of the Upper Peninsula) tumble down the escarpment near the lakeshore. Because the scenery is so striking, Pictured Rocks was designated the first National Lakeshore in the U.S. in 1966.

Most see the Pictured Rocks by taking a three-hour boat cruise from Munising. Late-afternoon light is best for seeing the colors. The 5 p.m. cruise in July and August would be best. Arrive early to get a seat on the top deck, the best place to view the scenery. The cruise begins by passing 14,600-acre **Grand Island**, once the private retreat of Cleveland-Cliffs Iron Company, now part of the Lakeshore. (See page 764.) *Pictured Rock Boat Cruises leave from downtown Munising from Friday before Memorial Day thru October 10. Call for times and reservations. (906) 387-2379. Adults $21, children 6-12 $7, 5 and under free. The 37-mile trip takes 2 hours and 40 minutes. ᕙ: one chair.*

Just as dramatic but less famous are the Grand Sable Dunes, perched atop the Grand Sable Banks that stretch seven miles at the National Lakeshore's east end, toward the remote village of Grand Marais. The National Lakeshore's third distinct area is a sand and pebble beach, far less dramatic but also beautiful. It stretches east to Au Sable Point and its picturesque lighthouse, close to the Grand Sable Banks.

No road goes through the National Lakeshore. County Road H-58 twists through the back country from Munising to Grand

Marais, providing access to *park highlights* and campgrounds via side roads. H-58 is paved for 18 1/2 miles east of Munising. but then it turns to gravel. South of the lakeshore's midsection, H-58 can be very rough and washboarded. Lack of a good road divides the lakeshore into two sections for all practical purposes. It looks as if H-58 may be paved (who knows when?) as a compromise solution to a bitter controversy over building a shoreline road through the national lakeshore. For the time being, you need to carefully plan visits to the national lakeshore to minimize driving.

Scope out what interests you and plan to stay or camp at the end that suits you best. (See page 759 for camping tips.) The isolated Grand Marais area is detailed in a separate chapter, pages 710 to 714. A good many naturalist-writer-artist-academic types prefer Grand Marais' less developed, less conventionally touristy personality. (It's a place where one local bar is a funky brew pub, and the other serves veggie burgers along with hamburgers.) Munising (population 2,800) has a lot of food places (and a terrific, big 24-hour Glen's Market) pressing in on a plain little town that has one of the most beautiful sites in all of Michigan. It offers easy access to the Big Island Lake Wilderness Area, the pretty Au Train area, and Marquette, just an hour west on scenic M-28.

PLANNING YOUR VISIT

Stop in or phone year-round to the **Hiawatha National Forest/ Pictured Rocks National Lakeshore Visitor Information Center** in Munising (906-387-3700). The helpful staff is happy to mail information sheets on activities and natural features upon request.

Shoreline erosion at different lake levels created these caves near Bridal Veil Falls. The Pictured Rocks boat cruise enters one of the caves if waters are calm enough.

The center has a wide range of information not only on the national lakeshore but on the less heavily used Munising District of the Hiawatha National Forest. Its campgrounds consist of popular, easily accessible ones on Lake Superior at Bay Furnace and on Au Train Lake, as well as four more remote ones on lakes, accessible from Highway 13.

The Visitor Center has maps and handouts for the Hiawatha National Forest's **Big Island Lake Wilderness Area** in an area of cottages and fishing resorts south of Munising. There's no road access to these 23 small lakes, from 5 to 149 acres, which are linked by waterways or by marked portage trails. Motors are banned. Canoeists can camp in designated spaces or choose their own sites. Abundant wildlife includes eagles and many loons.

Maps to some 16 miles of groomed **cross-country ski trails** are available. Skiers, be aware that winter's silence may often be broken by the whine of snowmobiles. Munising is a snowmobile

Long before tourists came to the area, the 1872 book *Picturesque America* depicted the Pictured Rocks area as a romantic landscape of inspirational beauty.

hot spot. A stimulating array of free **guided nature walks and programs** are held daily (often two times a day and at a campground at night) from late June through Labor Day. The over 70,000 acre national lakeshore is a four-season destination. Its highlights attract considerable crowds in summer and **fall color** season, while its diverse charms are subtle enough to bring back nature-lovers, waterfall enthusiasts, and backpackers again and again. Lon Emerick, who devotes a chapter of *The Superior Land* (page 851) to Pictured Rocks, hikes the Lakeshore Trail each spring for its wildflowers.

The Visitor Center has some displays and an excellent small **bookstore** of relevant nature books and area history, plus USGS maps and trail maps for hiking and canoeing in the national forest and national lakeshore. *The Visitor Center is at M-28 and H-58. Forest Service district office just east of downtown Munising. Look for brown signs. (906) 387-3700. Open year-round. Daily from June thru mid Sept., 8-6; Mon-Sat from 9-4:30 the rest of the year.* &

Two routes connect Pictured Rocks' major sights and camp-grounds. The 43-mile **Lakeshore Trail** is the only route that follows the shoreline. It connects major sights with spurs to to camp-grounds. Several designated backcountry campsites are along the way. (Permits, available from either visitor center, are necessary for this.) Trailheads are at Sand Point or Munising Falls at the Munising end, and at the Grand Marais Visitor Center. Typical hik-ing time: three nights and four days. Alger County's **Altran shuttle** runs Monday, Thursday, and Saturday with a 10 a.m. pickup at Munising Falls and 11:30 a.m. pickup at Grand Marais. It will drop off hikers at any point along H-58. No bicycles are allowed on trails. Hikers might well consider hiking part of the trail — say, from the Munising trailhead to Sand Point and Miners Castle (about 6 miles) and an additional mile through the woods to Miners Falls, for a 12- to-14 mile round trip. Or time your hike so the Altran trolley can take you back. (Call 906-387-4845.) $10 per person. You might even ask them if they could drop you off somewhere else. Shuttle service from Munising to Little Beaver requires a 24-hour notice.

Here's a summary of sights of greatest interest along the shore, arranged from Munising to Grand Marais. In summer these may also be the busiest, so you may want to include other spots accessi-ble only by foot.

◆ **Munising Falls.** This slender, exceptionally attractive falls has a dramatic 50-foot drop into a small, rocky canyon. In winter the sight is equally spectacular when the column of water is frozen. A pleas-ant, 800-foot path leads to the falls. The excellent **interpretive cen-ter** at the parking lot gives historical perspective on the region's geol-ogy and logging history. It's next to the site of an **1868 blast furnace** which made 16 tons of pig iron a day. *On H-58 about 2 miles east of downtown Munising and the intersection of M-28 and H-58. Unstaffed center is open May 1 through Oct. 31, daily 8:30-4:30.* &

◆ **Sand Point and beach.** From this point of land jutting out toward Grand Island, you get a good view of the island and the city of Munising. In the evening there is a distant **view of the Pictured Rocks**. (They're shaded in the morning.) The beach just south of the point is one of the warmer **swimming spots** in Lake Superior. Local swimmers point out that once you get acclimated to the chilly water, you don't feel the cold. The half-mile, barrier-free Sand Point

Marsh Trail crosses a scenic wetland that's alive with waterfowl, herons, and water-loving songbirds. Beaver lodges can be seen. Come near dawn or dusk to glimpse the nocturnal creatures themselves. *East of Munising a little over a mile on H-58, then left on Washington St. 1/2 mile to Sand Point Rd. North 2 miles. &: trail.*

◆ **Miners Castle and Falls.** A spectacular view looks down at an emerald-green Lake Superior cove from high upon a majestic, castle-like cliff, a single great stone some nine stories tall. The clearness of the water lets you see the rocky bottom even at considerable depths. The Pictured Rocks cliffs can be seen from land here, but the orientation means the light is never right for a good view. Another trail leads to a nice, long **beach** just northeast of Miners Castle. Farther inland, off Miners Castle Road and accessible via a steep half-mile trail and stair way, is **Miners Falls**. Water drops some 40 feet and forms interesting shapes in the stone at its base. Towards the end of the trail to it is a panoramic view of Lake Superior in the distance. *Take H-58 east from Munising. In about 7 miles, turn north on Miners Castle Rd. for 6 miles to Miners Castle. &: overlook platform and trail to castle.*

◆ **Grand Island.** Protecting the entrance to beautiful Munising Bay is unspoiled Grand Island with its remarkable scenery. In *Natural Michigan* (p. 855), Tom Powers waxes rhapsodic about its spectacular shoreline, waterfalls, 200-foot sandstone cliffs, caves, and huge white pine and beech trees. "Most visitors come away from a trip to this 8-mile long, 3-mile wide island agreeing that nature has created one of the most beautiful spots in the world," he writes.

Grand Island has a 3,000-year history as a Native American fishing and hunting ground, fur-trading location, steamship fueling station, resort, and game ranch. Recently, it became a national recreation area administered by the national lakeshore. After much debate and local input, the National Park Service has opted for very limited development focused mainly on the shoreline. (Its 27-mile shore is bigger than Mackinac Island's.) A ferry runs from Grand Island Landing just outside of Munising to the island's Williams Landing at least three times a day from early May into October. Get a map at the Visitor Center for up-to-date details. There are six interim campsites for four to six campers each (first-come, first-serve; no permits necessary). Roads and trails are not yet marked. By 1998 there will be more campsites, plus marked hiking and mountain bike trails. The island and protected bay, with its many interesting shipwrecks close to the surface, is ideal for **sea kayaking**. Some campsites are being developed with sea kayakers in mind.

The colorful sandstone cliffs on the south shore and the picturesque East Channel Light, its wood weathered to a dark gray, can be seen on both the Pictured Rocks Cruise (page 760) and the shipwreck cruise (page 766). Altran's **Grand Island van tour** focuses on the island's natural and human history. Seven stops include Williams Landing opposite Bay Furnace, the beach and overlooks at Trout Bay, an inland lake, and Mather beach. It's offered daily, currently from early July into September. ♿ The $16 cost includes the ferry ride. Kids under 12 are $8. Call (906) 387-4845 weekdays for reservations; otherwise call (906) 387-3503.

Grand Island Ferry operates from early May into October. Between late May and early Sept. departs from Grand Island Landing one mile west of Munising on M-28 at 9,12,3:30, 6:30 for Williams Landing. Departs from the island at 9:15, 12:15, 3:45, 6:45. Spring & fall: departs from Grand Island Landing at 9, 12, 3:30, leaves island at 9:15, 12:15, 3:45. (906) 387-3503. Reservations advised. ♿: ferry, restrooms on island. $10 round-trip for adults, $5 ages 6-12, $3 bike.

◆ **Au Sable Point Lighthouse, Hurricane River Campground, Log Slide, Grand Sable Dunes, Sable Falls, and Maritime Museum** are all most easily accessible from Grand Marais. See pages 710-714.

*Pictured Rocks National Lakeshore's helpful **main visitor center** is at the junction of M-28 and H-58 in Munising. See page 761 for hours. Open year-round. Call (906) 387-3700 to get a general or backpackers' visitor packet. The **Grand Sable visitor center** is on H-58 about 5 miles west of Grand Marais. open from late May thru mid September. See page 758 for hours. No fees for National Lakeshore except for developed campgrounds.*

10 MILES SOUTHEAST OF MUNISING . . . . . take a quick **tour of Iverson Snowshoes** in Shingleton. It's one of only two wood-frame snowshoe factories remaining in the U.S. You will see how workers take long strips of white ash, steam them to increase their flexibility, bend them around a form and dry them in a kiln overnight. The labor-intensive job includes hand-lacing with traditional rawhide or more durable neoprene. Snowshoes are easy to use and practical. Iverson's makes nine models for different purposes. Primitive furniture and fishnets are also made on site. *Turn north on Maple St., two blocks west of Shingleton's only blinker. (906) 452-6370. Open Mon-Fri 8-3:30. Large groups should call first. ♿: call first, narrow passages.*

SHIPWRECK SIGHTSEEING AND DIVING . . . . . in the **Alger Underwater Preserve** off Munising is easily arranged through Capt. Pete Lindquist's **Grand Island Charters** (906-387-4477). Interesting **shipwreck cruises** at 10 a.m., 1 p.m., and 3:30 p.m. leave from the Munising dock and take visitors out to look down at three wrecks close to the surface, in clear water, and also offer views of sandstone bluffs on Grand Island and the Pictured Rocks. The viewing portal in the boat's bottom has been enlarged for 1996. The pilot may well invite kids to "help" him at the helm. Visitors are encouraged to reserve places on the 2 1/2-hour cruise the night before. $18 adults, $7.50 5-12, 5 and under free. Lindquist also takes divers out to wrecks (there are eight); a diving instructor is on his staff. &: no. . . . . Clear waters and eroded underwater "caves" are other area attractions. Call the Alger Chamber of Commerce, (906) 387-2138, for a **dive brochure**.

Marquette and vicinity

Blessed with beautiful views, imposing old buildings, a craggy peninsula park, and a lively downtown

IN CONTRAST to the sleepy, still somewhat depressed look of many Upper Peninsula towns, this city of 23,000 is an uncommonly attractive place to visit. Marquette has been an important port since the 1850s, when the Soo Locks opened up shipping throughout the Great Lakes. The city rises sharply from Lake Superior, giving beautiful views of Presque Isle harbor and Marquette Bay. These are punctuated by dramatic landmarks: the ore docks, the old red lighthouse, and Presque Isle, a beautiful park whose red rocks and pines jut out into Lake Superior.

Marquette has more for visitors to see and do than any other single place north of the bridge. **Northern Michigan University**, with its 8,000 students, gives economic stability to the city, as does a large regional hospital complex and a maximum-security prison. Thanks to the area's logrolling former state representative, the late Dominic Jacobetti of Negaunee, the U.P.'s patron saint, NMU's campus now has the "Yooper Dome" (officially known as the Superior Dome). Seen from many vantage points it seems to hover like a weird space station on the horizon. The 8,500-seat enclosed stadium is big enough for football games.

Certainly the 1995 closing of K. I. Sawyer Air Force Base south of town has been a blow. It was the equivalent of Upper Michigan's fourth largest city. Some businesses have moved into the complex while state and local officials argue and vie to control the redevelopment process and make the Air Force deal with cleaning up the environmental messes they say it has left.

Marquette is one of those frontier boom towns found scattered throughout the Middle and Far West that developed because of the money and influence of Eastern investors — in this case, three men from Worcester, Massachusetts, who, in 1849 organized the second iron mining company in the Marquette Range.

In erecting public buildings, churches, industrial structures, and their own homes, Marquette's business powers chose many of the leading architects of Detroit, Chicago, Milwaukee, and Cleveland. Marquette attracts architecture buffs with its impressive stock of elaborate 19th-century buildings concentrated in a very small city. Many buildings are made of richly detailed Lake Superior sandstone, deep red in color — what's known as brownstone in New

Awesome sight and sound: at one of Marquette's long ore docks, railroad cars from Ishpeming's Tilden Mine empty iron-rich taconite pellets into the dock's 200 pockets. When a giant freighter pulls up to the dock, chutes are lowered from the dock into the boat's cargo hold. Loading is a noisy, interesting process to watch. Call (906) 226-6122 to find out when a freighter will be at the ore dock by Presque Isle Park.

York City. (See page 771 for historic walking tours.)

The billions of tons of iron ore shipped from Marquette since the 1850s helped pay for many of these fancy buildings. In the second half of the 19th century, 40% of the world's iron ore came from here, fueling America's transition from an agricultural to an industrial society. From April through mid-December, two to three freighters a day still pick up enormous loads of ore, processed and condensed into taconite pellets, at the north ore dock just below Presque Isle Park. You can watch the noisy process from Lakeshore Boulevard or Presque Isle.

For over a hundred years, Marquette has reigned as "Queen City of the North" – of Upper Michigan, at any rate. To a visitor it feels more cosmopolitan than anyplace else in the U.P., and far less Yooperish than other towns based on mining. The nearby mining towns of Ishpeming (population 7,200) or Negaunee (4,700), on the other hand, stand out for regional color in among the citizenry. (See page 779.)

Marquette highlights include:

♦ Two **spectacular views** of the city. From the south, see the city, bay, and lake from **Mount Marquette**. You can drive to the summit. *Take Highway 41 south until you come to the Tiroler Hof hotel and make a right. The road will very quickly become a "Y". Veer to your left onto the dirt road (Carp River Drive) and follow the river for a half mile or so until you see a sign on your right that says "Mount Marquette". Turn and drive to the top where you will find space to park and paths to walk. Come down on the road on the other side of the mountain which will bring you to CR 553. On your left will be Marquette Mountain. Turn right to get back to Marquette .* From the north, **Sugarloaf Mountain** offers an equally grand view looking south and east to the lake, the city of Marquette with its steeples, and the green forests beyond. It's a 15- to 20-minute walk to the peak — a view best enjoyed when the morning sky is still dawn-rosy. The trail is well marked. Steps built by Boy Scouts as well as benches and a deck at the peak make this climb less strenuous than it might otherwise be. Many other trails for combinations of hiking, cross-country skiing, and mountain biking, link up in this general vicinity. (See page 775.) The second parking area is by the **Mead-Wetmore Pond Nature Trail** trailhead (3 loops of 12 miles) leading to a floating bog. *Sugarloaf Mountain is north of Marquette on CR 550. In town, BR 41 becomes Front Street. Take Front to Washington, turn west and go to Fourth Avenue. Turn north onto Fourth, which becomes Presque Isle Ave. At Wright turn west. In 8 or so blocks, look for Sugar Loaf Rd./CR 550. Park at the first parking area, closest to Sugar Loaf Mt.*

♦ **Downtown**. Centered on Washington between Front and Third, downtown Marquette is well worth exploring for its interesting shops, striking architecture, and fine views down to the harbor. The recent growth in new, locally-owned specialty shops, including a kitchen shop, clothing imports, and beads, has made Washington Street much more lively. It now has a critical mass for strolling, snacking, and browsing. Monday through Saturday, most stores open at 10 and stay open until at least 7 in the summer and 5:30 in the winter. On Sunday some shops stay open while others are closed. With many of the shops in older buildings, barrier-free accessibility varies also. The elaborate 1883 **Vierling Saloon** on Front at Main (now also a brew pub) has a great view of the bay from its back windows. In the historic Harlow Block at 102 W. Washington at Front, the **Italian Place and New York Deli** (906-226-3032) is a much-talked-about restaurant. ♿ **Sandpiper Books** (112 W. Washington) is a general bookstore with in-depth sections on U.P., Upper Great Lakes, and Native American topics. *(906)*

225-0400. Open Mon thru Wed 10-6, Thurs thru Sat 10-8. Next door,
Michigan Fair (114 W. Washington; 906-226-3894) features a nice
selection of Michigan products and Upper Peninsula handcrafts.
Wattsson & Wattsson (118 W. Washington) draws visitors with a
replica of the old Ropes Gold Mine in nearby Ishpeming, displays
about the mine, and jewelry made of gold from that mine. (906)
228-5775. &. **Snowbound Books**, around the corner and up the
hill at 118 N. Third, is a large, well organized, and friendly used
book shop with an excellent regional and maritime section. *(906)
228-4448. &: no.* **Red Earth Gallery** (127 W. Washington) has an
interesting collection of authentic Scandinavian trolls, gnomes,
teddy bears, and Santas in sizes from 6" to over 3'. Dressed in recycled old fur coats and carrying little leather pouches with driftwood
and such, the raggedy trolls and the scenic photographs of
Marquette and the U.P make for interesting browsing. *(906)
228-7420.* &. **Donckers Candy & Gifts**, 137 W. Washington (906-
226-6110) sells candies (many homemade, including candy canes)
by the pound in a charming old store with vintage cases and mirrors. Locally made carmel corn dipped in dark chocolate makes a
great gift basket item.

In the next block, **Babycakes** at 223 W. Washington is a cappuccino bar with a rotating selection of 80 kinds of muffins and many
delicious specialty breads, all made on the premises. *Open Mon thru
Fri 6 a.m.-6 p.m., Sat 7 a.m.-5:30 p.m. (906) 226-7744.* The oldest of
Marquette's three movie theaters, the **Delft,** is at 139 W. Washington
(906-226-3741). Across the street at 136 W. Washington, a big new
general-line bookshop, the **Washington Street Bookstore**, (906-
228-9490) occupies what used to be the Nordic Theater. *Open 9-9
Mon-Fri, 9-5 Sat & Sun.* &

Art and architecture fans might enjoy these stops: the 1936
post office at 202 W. Washington, which has a WPA mural of
Father Marquette exploring Lake Superior's shores; the splendid,
twin-towered 1890 **St. Peter's Catholic Cathedral** two blocks
south on S. Fourth at Baraga (see below); and the dignified, beautifully restored 1902 Beaux Arts **Marquette County Courthouse** on
Third at Baraga. (Scenes from the 1959 classic *Anatomy of a Murder*
were filmed here. Peek inside the elaborate second-floor courtroom
if you can!) At Baraga and First, **Angeli's Bakery-Deli** (906-
226-7335) still bakes cross-shaped, crusty *cornetti,* designed for
dunking and sopping up pan juices.

The south side of town was — and is — where the immigrants
and Catholics lived. With **St. Peter's Cathedral** the Catholic
Church wanted to make a strong architectural statement to coun-

terbalance the unusually large and elegant St. Paul's Episcopal Church on the northside hill at Ridge and High where wealthy Easterners lived. The twin-towered Romanesque cathedral took 10 years to complete in 1890. It was rebuilt in part in 1935, after a fire. The beautiful interior, lavish with stained glass and woodwork, may be visited weekdays. &

♦ **Third Street**, leading north up the hill from downtown toward the edge of Northern Michigan University, has another noteworthy retailing district that visitors might miss. It's too spread-out to be walkable. Here's where to find sport shops, campus hangouts, and popular restaurants like Sweetwater Cafe, Vango's, and Casa Calabria. **Bittersweet Gifts** at 424 N. Fourth fills a big yellow house with dried wreaths and decorative accessories that are as elegant as it gets in the Upper Peninsula.

♦ The **Marquette County Historical Museum** focuses on the cultural development of Marquette County, including the social impact of fishing, shipping, logging, and mining. Its excellent collections are used to mount exhibits that change twice a year. A life-size diorama, made with help from area Chippewas, lets kids crawl inside an authentically furnished wigwam. Another realistic life-size diorama shows the Burt survey party, outfitted with a very early solar compass. Don't miss the huge 1881 bird's-eye view of Marquette and its busy harbor. There are good regional history books at the **gift shop**, including *Dandelion Cottage*, Carroll Watson Rankin's delightful popular girl's book from 1904. Pick up easy-to-use **walking tour guides** of downtown and the Ridge-Arch Historic District for $1 each. *213 N. Front at Ridge, 2 blocks north of Washington. (906) 226-3571. Mon thru Fri 10-4:30, open 3rd Thurs to 9 p.m.* &: *no. Adults $3, ages 12-18 $1.*

♦ **Fresh fish** from a downtown dock. **Thill's Fish House** (906-226-9851) is located just north of the downtown ore dock, at the foot of Main. It's the last commercial fishing operation in what was once a thriving Marquette-area fishery. Buy fresh whitefish fillets for **$3.65-$4/lb.; smoked whitefish sausage is $4.50/lb.** &

♦ **Maritime Museum**. Located in the big old Water Works Building not far from the lighthouse. Outboard engines were first developed in Marquette, and the museum has some very old ones. A typical Finnish fishing shanty has been reconstructed. Photos and exhibits explain how taconite pellets, a condensed form of iron ore, have made it more economical to ship iron. There is a 3 1/2 foot model of an ore carrier. There's a well-stocked **gift shop**. Large, colorful ship flags hang from the high ceilings. *E. Ridge at Lakeshore Blvd. just* *north of downtown. Open daily June 1 thru September 30, 10-5. (906) 226-2006. $3, kids 12 and under (accompanied by adult) free.* &

◆ **Marquette Harbor Light**. One of Michigan's most picturesque lighthouses perches atop a red stone bluff at the Coast Guard station at the foot of Ridge. *Not open to the public, but worth viewing from nearby parks.*

◆ **Lakeside bike path**. You can rent 5-speed bikes and take a pleasant 12-mile bike ride along a shoreline **bike path**. It extends 7 miles south of downtown and 5 miles north to Presque Isle. *Rent bikes at Lakeshore Bike & Kite, 505 Lakeshore Blvd. just west of the lighthouse. It's on the bike path, near the Lower Harbor just north of downtown. (906) 228-7547.*

◆ **Ridge and Arch Historic District**. East of High and Pine Streets, Marquette's mining and shipping magnates built their homes on a high bluff overlooking the harbor and Presque Isle. The dramatic site and the concentration of grand homes make this a fine place for a leisurely walk. Pick up a **$1 printed walking tour** at the historical museum (page 771), or call (906) 226-3571 to find out about **guided walking tours** held Tuesdays and Thursdays from early July through August at 10:30 a.m. (Tour leaders are often district residents who invite the group home for interior tours.) Although are not necessary, reservations are appreciated. Adults $3, students 6-12 $1, 5 and under free.

Architectural highlights include: an elaborate 1880 Italian villa at **410 E. Ridge**; the elaborate Gothic Revival house at **450 E. Ridge** built for early Cleveland mining investor Henry Mather; the 1875 stone Gothic Revival house at **430 E. Arch**; and the 1887 Shingle Style house at **425 Ohio**, one of the few surviving houses designed by the important Chicago architect John Wellborn Root. One of the grandest houses in the entire Upper Peninsula, John Longyear's house at Arch and Cedar, was dismantled and shipped on 190 railroad cars to Brookline, Massachusetts, after other business leaders rebuffed his plan to donate all his bluffside property down to the shore as a memorial for his dead son. Today the rebuilt mansion houses a Christian Science museum.

◆ The **Lake Superior & Ishpeming RR Ore Dock** on Lakeshore Boulevard, shortly before the entrance to Presque Isle Park, is a monumental sight to see and hear. The steel-framed dock juts out almost a quarter of a mile into Lake Superior, 75 feet above the water. The railroad approach is a mile-long earth embankment. Railroad cars come from Cleveland Cliffs' taconite processing facility near their vast Tilden (page 781) and Empire open-pit mines south of Ishpeming. The rail cars continually move out along the top of the ore dock and empty taconite pellets (a concentrated form of iron-bearing rock) down into the ore dock's 200 pockets. Usually once or twice a day, a bulk ore carrier comes to the dock to load. Chutes from each pocket are lowered into the cargo hold, and taconite thunders down into it. Then the ship shifts 20 or 30 feet (winches being tightened or loosened let it move), and new pockets empty into the hold. It's a noisy, impressive spectacle — a worthwhile opportunity to view giant 600- to 1,000-foot ships in action, at close range. This particular ore dock, built by a Cleveland-Cliffs subsidiary in 1912, revolutionized the shipping of iron ore. *To find out when an ore carrier will dock, call (906) 226-6122.* Nearby is the giant, coal-fired generating station of Wisconsin Electric Power. It's the main electrical plant in the Upper Peninsula.

◆ **Presque Isle Park.** This rocky, wooded, and extraordinarily picturesque peninsula just north of town is a splendid setting for an outing any time of year. A **gazebo** and **picnic area** on a promontory overlook near the entrance look out into the lake and back at the ore docks and harbor. The green of pines contrasts with the red rock and great blue lake. A one-way, two-mile-long **interior road** has turnouts and footpaths at especially scenic points. Northwest of the peninsula are several craggy, dark islets and the Huron Mountains, blue in the distance. It's a grand view, especially at sunset. The high cliffs plunging into Lake Superior prove tempting, and sometimes fatal, for overadventurous rock climbers and divers. Five miles of **trails** go up and down through woods of hardy conifers kept small by wind and rock. From December into March, four miles of **groomed cross-country ski trails** wind through the woods with occasional views past the ridges and peaks of lake ice to the still unfrozen lake. They are among the most beautiful places to ski imaginable. The spring snowmelt comes earlier here, because of the lake's warming effect, than farther inland. The trailhead is at the entrance by the gazebo on the lakeside.

The park's most developed part is to the west, where a shallow, protected bay makes Lake Superior tolerable for **swimming**. Here too are **tennis courts, shuffleboard,** a **playground,** a **concession stand,** and another **picnic area.** (Marquette's huge **Shiras Pool** and a **water slide,** open to the general public, are a little outside the park entrance.) Summer **band concerts** are held on Thursday and Sunday evenings in the bandshell right across from the picnic area and playground. A 1/4-mile paved **Bog Walk Nature Trail** is off the first parking lot past the entrance. Presque Isle Park is at the end of Lakeshore Drive, about three miles from downtown. Presque Isle

Wildflower walk: though the Northwoods Supper Club has expanded a lot since its beginnings in 1934 as a restaurant-gas station (pictured here), it retains its woodsy setting. A naturalist gives tours through garden and woods, June-October.

Park is a splendid setting for **Art in the Park**, an art fair with live music, held the last weekend in July. *(906) 228-0460. Open year-round. No fees except for pool admission and x-c ski trail fee.* &

◆ **Jilbert's Dairy** provides dairy products for much of the U.P. Adjoining the dairy is its popular ice cream shop. A local favorite is "Moosetracks," vanilla with Reese's peanut butter cups mixed in. At any time you can look through glass windows at ice cream being made and milk being processed. Also on hand: a nifty collection of old milk bottles and an assortment of U.P. specialty foods from Baroni's spaghetti sauce to "squeaky cheese" (juustua), sweetish and soft. Traditionally served to guests with pulla (sweet cardamom bread) and coffee, juustua also shows up at Finnish smorgasbords, where it's eaten with rye bread and salmon. The "squeaky cheese" at Jilbert's is made from pasteurized milk which gives it a different flavor than that made by the many U. P. farmers who make it the traditional way from unpasteurized milk. *(906) 225-1363. Corner of W. Ridge & Meeske Ave. Take U.S. 41 to Business 41 (by the Holiday Inn); then take Business 41 to Meeske. You can see the large fiberglass cow and red barn from U.S. 41. Open daily 9a.m.-10 p.m. in the summer, close one hour earlier in the winter.* &

GUIDED TOURS OF THE AREA . . . . . Marquette native **Fred Huffman**, owner/operator of **Marquette Country Tours**, takes visitors on informative tours of the city and surrounding natural areas. Sunrise and sunset tours of the city are given regularly. Other tours include scenic waterfalls, the historic Marquette Iron Range, and Marquette's rugged north country, Big Bay, and vicinity. *For an appointment and price information, call Fred at (906) 226-6167.*

LUNCH AND A NATURE WALK THROUGH A NORTHWOODS GARDEN . . . . . In Marquette, the premiere destination restaurant for decades has been the **Northwoods Supper Club**, west outside town off U.S. 41. It has been expanded many times from a still-visible Art Deco-influenced log cabin of sorts. As with a good many Upper Michigan businesses, its owners were avid naturalists. They developed extensive terraced flower gardens viewed from the restaurant. Now gardener-naturalists have restored the gardens. From mid-June through October they lead a **Woods Walk** through gardens, woodlands, and wetlands, past a waterfall pool and by founder Fred Klumb's log cabin back in the woods. *3 1/2 miles west of Marquette, south off U.S. 41/M-28. Turn at large sign. Walk is at 10 a.m. Tues, Wed & Fri. $8 fee includes coffee & rolls, lunch. Reservations advised, especially for large groups. Kids' Day ($5 includes sack lunch) is Mon at 10 a.m. (906) 228-4343. &: yes for restaurant; call for walk.*

MORE HIKING AND SKI TRAILS . . . . . are on wild, beautiful Mead Paper land and state land along and near Lake Superior just 5 or so miles northwest of Marquette. If this gorgeous, rocky shore were a state park, it would be far more visited. It's treasured by locals today and a good area for bird-watching during spring and fall migration. We list them in order of distance of their parking areas from town off CR 550. See Sugarloaf Mt., the first trail, p. 769, for general directions out of town. . . . . The 18-mile hiking trail system of the **Little Presque Isle Tract** (rated easy to moderate, 4 loops from 3 to 7 miles) starts at the same parking area used by the **Mead/Wetmore Pond Interpretive Trail** (12 miles in 3 loops, rated easy to moderate for hiking and x-c skiing). A rough, uneven trail goes through old-growth forest, past rugged rock outcrops, to an overlook built onto a sphagnum bog. . . . . The **North Country Trail** crosses 550 a little west of the pond parking lot. The 21-mile segment between the Garlic River Bridge and Marquette is rated moderate to difficult for hikers, advanced for skiers. Parts of it follow the Lake Superior shore. . . . . The 5.6 mile **Harlow Lake Pathway** for hiking, skiing, and mountain biking has two loops. It's easy to moderate for hikers and bikers, moderate for skiers. . . . . . For trail maps call the DNR U.P. field headquarters in Marquette (906-228-6561), the Escanaba DNR office at 6833 Highway 2 (41/M-35) in Gladstone (906-786-2351), or the DNR office at 1985 U.S. 41 West in Ishpeming (906-485-1031). The **North Country Trail Association** is at 12 Middle Island Point, Marquette 49855 (906-225-1704). . . . Accurate, helpful maps and notes to all these trails are in Dennis Hansen's massive, monumental, authoritative *Trail Atlas of Michigan.* It covers over 520 trails for hiking, mountain biking, and cross-country skiing in 594 large-format pages. Get it from the author, 1801 Birchwood Dr., Okemos, MI 48864 for $26.95 plus tax if shipped within Michigan. Make checks to Hansen Publishing.

BIG BAY, A LUMBER TOWN AT THE END OF THE ROAD. . . . . is a favorite destination for people who like to feel away from it all. The company-built lumber town is tucked between the Huron Mountains and Lake Superior. Access from the west is cut off by the **Huron Mountain Club**, the summer retreat of extremely wealthy old families who raised local ire in 1995 by getting a conservation tax break while still refusing public admittance to hunt on their extensive land holdings. (In the U.P. the public has access rights not only to vast amounts of state and federal but to mining and paper company lands as well.) . . . . . In Big Bay are the **Lumberjack Tavern** restaurant (906-345-9912) and two of the

U.P.'s best-known lodgings: the wonderfully isolated **Big Bay Point Lighthouse** (906-345-9957), where you can watch awesome Lake Superior storms from the top of the tower, and the historic **Thunder Bay Inn** (906-345-9376), once the company store for the lumber company that built the village. Henry Ford bought the building in 1943 to use as a hotel for guests. Just down the hill was the lumber mill used to make panels for the famous Ford "woody" station wagons. In 1959 the popular bar here was the setting for parts of the movie *Anatomy of a Murder*. Locals still talk about it. Located in the Thunder Bay Inn, is the **Juniper Shop** selling northwoods gifts by local artisans. Open from noon-8 daily. & For more info, call the well-informed Marquette Country Tourism Council, (800) 544-4321. . . . . A remarkable portrait of the isolation of milltown life at the end of the lumber mill days around 1930 is Mildred Walker's fine novel **Fireweed** (p. 851), written from first-hand observation as the company doctor's wife in Big Bay and now republished by the University of Nebraska Press. A good read about the bright, energetic, Hollywood-infatuated daughter of a mill hand.

A SPECTACULAR FALL COLOR TRIP from Marquette to the remote village of **Big Bay** is a circle tour along county roads 510 and 550. You'll drive through thick forests and past **waterfalls** on the 35-mile dirt road out to Big Bay. Colors are usually at their peak from late September to mid-October.

WINTER SPORTS IN AND AROUND MARQUETTE . . . . . have much to recommend them. The season is from mid-December or earlier through March. The settings are unusually attractive and varied. On the simple, rustic side are the backwoods former mining lands of the **Lucy Hill luge run** in Negaunee, and the quiet and remote **cross-country ski trails** (one flat, two challenging) near **Suicide Hill**, a **ski-flying hill** in the woods outside Ishpeming. In contrast, there's the rock-and-roll intensity of **Marquette Mountain** (800-944-SNOW), where incredibly adept ski addicts are out in force even on weekdays in mid-March. Marquette Mountain's 600-foot drop is the third highest vertical drop in the Midwest, and the Lake Superior view from the top is stunning. (See p. 769.)

The **cross-country loops at Presque Isle Park** (page 000) can't be beat for scenery. **Al Quaal**, a wild and natural 300-acre Ishpeming city park on the north edge of town, overlooks Teal Lake. It hearkens back to the earlier, folksier, simpler style of winter sports brought by Scandinavians. Its 1200-foot iced **toboggan run** is great fun ($3 an hour if you use the park's rentals; open weeknights 4-8, weekends 1-8:30). Adjacent **downhill ski runs** and a **slalom run** with rope tows are also lighted. The five kilometers of cross-country **ski loops** (some easy, some intermediate) are gorgeous. In the winter of 1996-97, the park will add a new snowshoe trail. (No snowshoe rentals.) *Go north at the intersection of US 41 and Hickory, the corner where you'll see the Chamber of Commerce office. Best number to call for information: (906) 486-6181.*

Outstanding **snowmobiling** through many miles of off-road trails between Marquette, Ishpeming, and Big Bay is a magnet. **For information on winter sports**, call (800) 544-4321.

Michigan Iron Industry Museum

Overlooking a picturesque river valley near Negaunee, this superb museum shows how the region's iron was central to America's industrialization.

THIS IMPRESSIVE MUSEUM uses dramatic displays to illuminate the great historical importance of iron mining here in the Marquette Range. It's located in the rugged, wooded hills just outside the old iron-mining center of Negaunee. Red outcrops of conglomerate rock in this area are a stunning foil for the dark green of conifers. The delightful setting, fragrant with pine and meadow grasses in summer, makes this a nice place to linger and a handy rest and exercise stop for travelers heading across the Upper Peninsula.

The museum is at the place overlooking the Carp River where an iron forge was built just four years after surveyor William Burt's famous 1844 discovery of nearly pure iron deposits at the surface. That happened at Teal Lake, which can be seen from U.S. 41 in Negaunee, just a few miles west of here. Burt's magnetic compass fluctuated so suspiciously that he sent his men out to investigate. They returned with iron ore from rock outcrops. The next year prospectors from Jackson, Michigan, were guided by native Ojibway to a place where iron ore was right at the surface, visible in the roots of a fallen tree. In 1847 that site became the Jackson Mine on the south side of Negaunee. It was the first of the enormously important Lake Superior mines that launched great manufacturing industries and helped create the wealth of Great Lakes cities from Milwaukee to Buffalo.

The forge here converted ore directly into wrought iron used in things like nails, wire, and bolts. It took an acre of hardwoods to make five tons of iron. Little remains of the long-abandoned forge, but a pleasant **nature trail** leads from the museum past the 19th-century site. From this modest beginning blossomed 40 mines in the Marquette Range by 1872. They extracted a million tons a year of the richest iron ore in the world. But by the end of the 1870s the range's rich surface deposits were becoming exhausted and the Upper Peninsula's Menominee and Gogebic Ranges to the west were coming on strong.

An excellent, insightful **tape-slide show** on **"Life on Michigan's**

Mine shafts and horizontal drifts lie under large areas of Ishpeming and Negaunee, sometimes requiring weakened streets to be abandoned. This view of Ishpeming shows a March snowbank. To the left, the skyline is punctuated by three monumental Cleveland-Cliffs headframes that housed the hoist ropes which carried miners and ore up from the mines. Cliffs' president hired Prairie School architect George Maher to design monumental, Egyptian-inspired obelisks to house two headframes (1919). They were replaced by the tall, boxy headframe between them.

Iron Ranges" show how hard the mostly immigrant work force labored — for 60-hour work weeks — and how much work the women did, gardening, taking in boarders and their wash. Upper Peninsula mining began *before* settlement by farmers and town developers, so mining companies had to be community builders, too. They successfully developed a stable work force through low-cost housing rentals and various subsidies to churches, schools, community centers.

The museum does a good job of showing just how important the U.P.'s iron has been. Almost half of the nation's iron from 1850 to 1900 was mined from here. In the 150 years since 1833, the California gold rush produced less than a billion dollars of minerals. Michigan lumber has produced almost $4.5 billion of wood alone. The Keweenaw copper ranges generated about twice that amount. But the riches from iron dwarf these, worth some *$48 billion.*

Today none of the miles of U.P. underground iron mine shafts are producing ore. The only two mines operating today are the Tilden and the Empire, both open-pit operations. They are within a few miles of each other, off County Road 35 right across from the community of Palmer, southeast of Ishpeming. See page 781 for the memorable Tilden Mine tour.

Museum directions: *from U.S. 41, 3 miles east of Negaunee and 5 or 6 miles west of the outskirts of Marquette, turn south onto M-35 for*

*1 mile, turn west onto CR 492 for 2 miles, then turn north onto Forge Road. Signs are clear. For information about **special events** at the museum, call (906) 475-7857. Open daily May thru October, 9:30-4:30. ♿ Free.*

BLACK FLIES, RUSTY CARS, DEER-HUNTING, SEX, SAUNAS, BEER . . . . and other important aspects of U.P. life have been immortalized in the sympathetically satirical songs of **Da Yoopers** of Ishpeming. The group's "The Second Week of Deer Camp" got nationwide air play. Simple pleasures are extolled in songs like "Fishin' wit Fred": "It's a perfect day for fishin', drinking beer and telling lies. It's a little bit like Heaven when you're fishin' wit da guys." Da Yoopers have authentic North Country accents and a variety of musical styles to suit each topic, from Finnish accordion polkas to heavy metal. Pick up their tapes at Holiday gas stations or at **Da Yooper Shop** in Ishpeming. A beer can holster or beer gut T-shirt can be had and variations on outhouse yard art can be seen. Be advised: many listeners consider some of Da Yoopers' songs "too gross." They're earthy and far from tasteful, but not mean and not sexist, either. A big theme of late is various embarrassments of the digestive tract. Da Yoopers are in top form on their "Culture Shock" tape. *On U.S. 41 just west of Ishpeming. Look for bill board. Mail-order available. (906) 485-5595. Summer hours: Mon-Fri 9-9, Sat 9-8, Sun 10-7. Winter hours: Mon-Fri 9-5. ♿*

THE RISE OF DOWNHILL SKIING IN THE U.S. . . . . . is told at the **National Ski Hall of Fame** in Ishpeming. The museum shows how downhill skiing has developed since World War II from a minor sport brought by Scandinavian miners into a major economic force in many northern areas. The **American ski assault team** in WWII attracted national attention. Many Upper Michigan men were on it. Many returning soldier-skiers became resort managers when recreational skiing took off. Hollywood stars at the glamorous ski resort of Sun Valley, Idaho, popularized skiing in the 1940s and 1950s. A key to growth: Michigander Everett Kirchner's artificial snowmaking machine, first used at his Boyne Mountain resort. . . . . A skier could easily spend two hours at this museum. The local ski club started the hall years ago to draw attention to Ishpeming as the birthplace of U.S. ski-jumping. *On U.S. 41 between 2nd and 3rd about a mile west of Teal Lake. Look for the new building with a roof shaped like a ski jump. (906) 485-6323. Open daily: Mon-Fri 10-6, Sat 10-5, Sun 12-5. Closed major winter holidays. ♿ Adults $3, senior 55 and older $2.50, students $1, children under 10 free.*

EXPLORING ISHPEMING AND NEGAUNEE . . . . . is fun for people who like distinctive places. These towns are at once plain and stately, the results of booms and busts endured through a large measure of simple living. The depressed downtowns have many ornate sandstone-trimmed buildings. Near outlying mine headframes more houses cluster, some in amazingly picturesque spots. . . . . Don't miss **Jasper Hill** on Ishpeming's southeast side, on Jasper one block south of its intersection with Bluff. The dramatic park, punctuated with piles of red rock from mining, has a splendid view from its summit; across the way is the 1891 Swiss-style guest cottage owned by Cleveland-Cliffs Iron Mining, the dominant iron mining force on the Marquette Range. . . . . Another striking site: the vaguely Egyptian **headframes** of the Cliff Shafts Mine. From U.S. 41 on Ishpeming's west side, take Lakeshore Drive south to Lake Bancroft. . . . . Potter Marilyn Mutch has turned Negaunee's freight depot into the **Depot Gallery and Studio** (906-475-4067), where she works and exhibits some noteworthy area artists. It's on Rail at Gold, a block south of downtown. &: *no.*

IMMIGRANT LABOR FOR THE IRON MINES . . . . . came largely from **Italy** and **Finland.** Conditions in those countries caused large-scale emigration in the very years of iron mining's greatest boom, from the 1890s into the early 1920s. 1919 was iron's peak production year; by 1929 large-scale production was over. A lasting result of iron mining is an unusual blend of genes (a Finn and an Italian may produce dark-haired, pale-complected offspring), cultures, accents, and cuisines. **Cudighi** (COULD-uh-gi) is a spicy, fried pork sausage unique to the Ishpeming area, served in a sandwich with pizza fixings. Try it at **Ralph's Italian Delicatessen**, (906-485-4557), on U.S. 41 right across from the U.S. National Ski Hall of Fame. & Italian craftsmen made possible the area's outstanding stone architecture. Scandinavians developed winter sports and paid homage to Heikki Luunta (HEY-kee LOON-tuh), the Finnish snow god.

THE CULTURAL ICON OF THE U.P. . . . . is the late **John Voelker**, former Michigan Supreme Court justice, who quit to come home to Ishpeming and devote himself to fishing after his *Anatomy of a Murder* novel struck Hollywood paydirt. ***Trout Madness*** and ***Trout Magic*** reflect his passion for fishing. The crusty, completely unpretentious author lived in an old house up the hill from Ishpeming's library and drank down the street at the Rainbow Bar on East Canada at the intersection with First Street. His papers are at Northern Michigan University in Marquette.

Tilden Mine Tour

A dramatic look at a vast iron ore pit and the huge plant that turns ore into taconite pellets

NOT ONLY does this popular tour provide an insightful look at a vast and dramatic mining operation, it's a memorable aesthetic experience, even it it wasn't intended to be one. Artists of industry like Diego Rivera and Charles Sheeler would have loved this place.

The U.P. iron industry today excavates greatly diluted ore in huge, 300-ton blasts. Now that the more accessible veins of richer ore have been mined out, Lake Superior iron mining remains competitive only because of a process that concentrates the ore into 64% pure iron pellets called taconite. These can then be shipped economically from the Michigan ports of Marquette (see page 772) and Escanaba to steelmakers around the Great Lakes.

A bus takes tourgoers from Marquette (at noon) and Ishpeming (at 12:30) to the mine, where the tour lasts two hours. There's only one tour a day, so space is limited to the number the bus can hold. Sign up in advance. This tour is nearly always full.

Your tour guide is a summer employee at Cleveland Cliffs Iron who has a parent working at the firm. He or she has grown up around mining and is in all probability quite well informed and able to handle questions. The tour, designed by CCI public relations chief Dale Hemmela, gives outsiders a good overview of the precarious economics of U.S. iron mining today. CCI has owned these iron ore reserves since 1865. In the partnership operating the mine, it has joined with two Canadian steel companies, Algoma and Steelco, wishing to control costs of their basic material.

Oddly, the huge pit is less dramatic than the plant interior. The pit activity is far away. Blasts occur three times a week, in the morning, never at tour time. It's immediately apparent how enormously capital-intensive this operation is. Truck tires are 12 feet high, and they cost $12,000 to $20,000 each. A shovel costs $6.5 million. Mine operations never stop. The Tilden Mine employs 850 skilled workers, from metallurgists, engineers, and computer operators to heavy equipment operators. Today the hematite pit is some 500 feet below the surface. There's enough ore to go 800 feet more.

Inside the plant, the noise of crushers and huge rotating mills make it hard to hear. Signs explain steps in processing. A clearly written free souvenir booklet with color photos lets you review

Competent guides like Jennifer Matson are part of what makes the dramatic, educational Tilden Mine tour so successful.

everything: business rationale, operations, environmental impact. The plant experience involves almost all your senses. It is quite warm — briefly — by the kilns. Occasionally the angled geometry of the chutes and towers frame outside views of the massive piles of rugged red waste rock and the precisely angled piles of pellets. Even in this monumentally unnatural environment, weeds and pine trees are taking hold, attesting to the ultimate power of living things.

The tour ends in the quiet control room, where experienced employees invite visitors' questions. Tourgoers leave with a free plastic goody bag with souvenir taconite pellets. It bears the mining motto, "If it can't be grown, it has to be mined."

One tour per day mid-June thru late August, Tues-Sat. Bus leaves the Marquette Chamber of Commerce (906-226-6591) at noon, the Ishpeming Chamber of Commerce (906-486-4841) at 12:30. Bus seating is limited; call either Chamber of Commerce for reservations and for tips on appropriate dress (for example, no sandals allowed). Restricted to adults and children age 10 and up. &: no. Cost per person: $6.

IXL Museum

At a remote site where hardwood flooring
was first perfected, this striking mill
headquarters building takes you back in time.

FEW HISTORIC sites are preserved so splendidly well as this remote old office of a U.P. hardwood lumber mill. It was here in the 1880s that the machinery to produce hard-wood flooring was first perfected. Until then American homes used softer pine for wooden floors. Hardwoods like maple and oak were too difficult to work and tended to warp. Lumber mill manager George Earle perfected a kiln process here to remove the right amount of moisture from hardwood. He also created machinery to make tongue and groove hardwood sections, still the method for laying hardwood floors.

Located just south of the village of Hermansville, the Wisconsin Land & Lumber company grounds are in pristine condition. Except for the absence of a few original structures, things are little changed from decades ago. The kiln still operates, although the original company is defunct. The museum building was the business office, built in 1882. Earle's office was here. A medical doctor by training, he used the big table in the middle of his office for amputations and other emergency operations. This building is also where the 600 to 800 IXL workers came to receive their weekly scrip for pay, to spend in the company town. (The IXL name is a punning abbreviation for "I excel." IXL also developed the town of Blaney. See page 754.)

The interior has not been reconstructed to look like an historic office; it simply has changed little in recent decades. Old Burroughs adding machines and inkwells adorn big oak desks. Dumbwaiters sent messages between the first and second floors. The original old mechanical clocks and crank telephones remain in place, as if the place had suddenly been vacated 75 years ago and left untouched.

Hermansville is on U.S. 2 26 miles west of Escanaba and 15 miles east of Norway. Turn at the sign for the IXL Museum and go 4 blocks south. (906) 498-2498 or (906) 498-7724. Open Memorial Day thru Labor Day, 12:30-4 daily. Adults $1, students 50¢. &: no.

Piers Gorge

Along the Wisconsin border south of Norway, the big Menominee River cuts deep in a spectacular rush.

ERE the Menominee River has cut a dramatic, deep gorge and created powerful rapids of foaming water as it rushes towards Green Bay at Menominee and Marinette. The Michigan-Wisconsin border between Iron River and Green Bay is formed by the Menominee River and, from Iron River to Iron Mountain, by its smaller tributary, the Brule. At Piers Gorge the river has created an extraordinarily beautiful place where steep-sided bedrock walls up to 70 feet high contain the rushing river for a mile and a half as it roars over a series of stone shelves in four quite distinctive waterfalls.

Piers Gorge is a much subtler experience than the typical tourist waterfall. It's not at all a direct, well-trod path to a single overlook. Here the perspectives and views are constantly unfolding as you walk. You look down at steep rock walls, rushing water undercutting islands below and tearing at loose rock. Water tumbles over and smooths smaller chunks of rock lodged in the riverbed. The changing sounds of rushing water and smells of the forest envelop you. The power of water — and of natural forces — is everywhere evident. If a wild and lonely forest spectacle like Piers Gorge were in Germany, it would have been the subject of many romantic-era poems of contemplation and spiritual yearning.

Despite the drama, this isn't a big tourist spot. There are no cross-country ski trails or nearby camping sites. The road to the Piers Gorge parking lot is not plowed in the wintertime. Signs are few. The landowner does nothing to promote or discourage interest in this beautiful place.

A relatively easy, relatively level path lets you look down at the river from the bluff's rim. It starts at the parking area, briefly passing through a fragrant cedar swamp. For part of the way wood chips are being added by a volunteer group to smooth over the small rock shelves and roots that can trip careless hikers. Farther on, roots and footing is again occasionally uneven, not difficult for the reasonably healthy, but not for shufflers. Short side trails branch off to the gorge's rim. The more adventurous can take trails that descend tortuously along the canyon walls to the river itself. In places it's possible to frolic in the gentler rapids – at your own risk, of course – or step across half the wide river on the many stones and boulders lying in the riverbed. The river banks are loaded with stones of all shapes and sizes, providing plenty of ammunition for stone-skippers.

A surprising crescent of quiet beach appears after the third pier. Shortly you emerge into a clearing by a power line. Follow the red ribbons to the fourth pier, avoiding the better-worn trail made by mountain bikes and ATVs. You might prefer to skip the less spectacular fourth pier altogether. It's really more a rapids, with many fallen trees.

Argosy Adventures (715-251-3886) organizes Piers Gorge **raft expeditions** daily from April into September. It's located across the river in Niagara, Wisconsin, at the intersection of Highways 8 and 141. The three to four-hour trip involves more direct participation than raft trips down the Colorado, for instance. Passengers decide for themselves how to run the rapids, and half of them paddle. (It's four miles between put-in and takeout, both on the Wisconsin side.

The Menominee has a remote, wild look, yet the dams of Wisconsin Power and Light control the flow, so water level is consistent. Because the trip is short, weather vagaries are less of a factor.

From U.S. 2 at Norway (that's 8 miles east of Iron Mountain) turn south onto U.S. 8 and drive 2 miles. Look for Piers Gorge Road on your right. Drive 1/2 mile to parking lot. If you cross the bridge and get to Wisconsin, you have gone too far. Go back 1/4 mile and look for Piers Gorge Road on your left. ♿: no.

FOR LOCAL INFORMATION . . . . . about more things to do in and around the pretty town of **Norway**, stop in at **Northern Expressions** gift shop on the main downtown street just south of U.S. 2.

Iron Mountain Iron Mine

Travel far beneath the earth to see
how difficult and dangerous iron mining really was.

ON THIS INTERESTING and dramatic mine tour, visitors go through 2,600 feet of underground drifts and tunnels and learn what iron mining was really like. Led by a knowledgeable guide, visitors don raincoats and hard hats and ride the same railway system that took miners to their jobs until the mine closed down in 1945. Visitors experience the gloomy, drippy, difficult working conditions in a typical iron mine and see some pretty things, like a fault of rose quartz, along the way. There are also spectacular views of large manmade chambers called stopes on the 35-minute trip. **Drilling demonstrations** show how loud, dirty, and dangerous the work was in earlier years miners typically started at the age of 11 and died of black lung disease, **caused by breathing rock dust,** between 50 and 60.

The drama of going underground is what visitors remember about this efficient, 35-minute tour. It's short, and the tight schedule doesn't really invite questions and detailed explanations after the guide quickly goes over increasingly efficient drills and the tradeoffs they brought. Dangerous working conditions are detailed so frequently that visitors will walk away with a refreshed view of the importance of government occupational safety regulations. Also, it's a definite plus that guides are local adults (not young, quickly trained summer help) who grew up around miners. When listening to people from mining areas, it's always striking to realize the strong emotions bound up in this difficult, dangerous work: love and appreciation for parents' sacrifice, a good dose of realistic bitterness at the economic forces that determined the miners' lot, and an immense amount of pride.

When the first tunnel here was dug in 1870, the incredibly rich ore was 85% iron. But it took three men 10 hours to dig just four feet by hand. The highest-paid miner was the blaster, who got 25¢ an hour. Each of the Iron Range's many ethnic groups had its own job in the mines. The Finnish specialty was the timbering – constructing the tamarack supports that held up the horizontal drifts. Deep shaft mines like this finally became obsolete when huge power shovels made open-pit mining much more economical.

Wear a sweater; far underground it stays a constant 43° F. year around. In addition to the train ride, the tour also involves some easy optional walking along pathways made smooth for visitors by concrete. Electric lights make the portion of the mine on tour far brighter than miners ever experienced. Briefly you can see just how dark it was when the only illumination was with the candles or headlights on miners' lamps.

Kids and fans of roadside Americana will probably enjoy the tour's commercial trappings, beginning with the 12-foot wooden statue of Big John, the parking-lot repetition of Johnny Cash's ode to the heroic miner, "Big John," and the free form sculpture made of pick axes and shovels assembled on a telephone pole. If you want a more leisurely overview of mining strategy and techniques, combined with an engineer's detailed perspective, tour the Quincy Hoist and Arcadia copper mine in Hancock, where Michigan Tech mining students are your guides. If you enjoy mining lore, take both tours.

On U.S. 2 in Vulcan, 10 miles east of Iron Mountain and 2 miles east of Norway. (906) 563-8077. 35-40 minute tours late May to mid-Oct, daily 9-6 (tours begin at 8 in July & Aug.). ♿ Adults $5.50, children 6-12 $4.50, under 6 free.

A GOOD MUSEUM IN CASPIAN . . . . . just south of Iron River is the notable **Iron County Museum**. Lots of mining exhibits are in the old engine house of the famous Caspian Mine (1903-1937). Over 6 million tons of iron ore were lifted by the **giant hoist** just east of the engine house. This was among the most productive of the Menominee Range mines. Miniature **models of mines** show how shafts in the region were as long as one mile and how huge buckets called "skips" hauled the ore up. Logging had also been important in the area. An 80-foot **diorama of a lumber camp** shows such things as the dining hall, where "the cook made sure that everyone ate and only ate, by standing with a butcher knife and threatening anyone who talked." There are also three authentic Indian **dugout canoes**. Among the 20 outbuildings is a **1930s Finnish sauna**. *100 Museum Rd. Follow signs off U.S. 2. (906) 265-2617. Open June 1 thru Sept. 9-5 Mon-Sat, 1-5 Sun (close 1 hour earlier in Sept.); all other times by appointment. ♿ Adults $3, children 5-18 $2, under 5 free.*

IN NEARBY IRON MOUNTAIN . . . . . The **Cornish Pump and Mining Museum** has a 725-ton water pump, the nation's largest when built in 1890. It lifted 200 tons a minute from the shaft of the Chapin Iron Mine, the largest producer in the Menominee Range. Seeping water is a big problem for deep mines, which have to continuously pump out water to keep operating. It took 11,000 tons of coal a year just to operate the pump. Here as in many U.S. mining districts, experienced Cornish miners from Cornwall in the southwest of England took the lead in developing improved mining technologies. There are also lots of local mining artifacts and photos here, as well as a **World War II glider display**. The gliders were made in Kingsford, just south of Iron Mountain. *2 blocks west of U.S. 2 on Kent St. in Iron Mountain. (906) 774-1086. Open May to mid-October, Mon-Sat 9-5 and Sun 12-4.* &: *$4 adults, $2 students, children under 10 (with parents) free.* . . . . The **Menominee Range Museum**, located in an old Carnegie library building, has many local historical items, including reconstructions of a dentist's office, trapper's cabin, and a 19th-century kitchen and bedroom. *300 E. Ludington, 1 block east of U.S. 2. (906) 774-4276. Open May thru September, Mon-Sat 10-4.* &: *no. $4 adults, $2 students, children under 10 (with parents) free. Special rate available when you visit both the Cornish Pump and Mining and Menominee Range Museums.* . . . . . **Lake Antoine Park** is a delightful county park on Lake Antoine, just northeast of Iron Mountain. (Locals pronounce it, "an-TWINE," not the French way.) There's a spacious, wooded **picnic area**, a wonderful swimming **beach** with a swimmers' dock well out in the lake, and a **boat launch**. A **concession stand** sells hot dogs, ice cream, popcorn, and camping supplies. No reservations for the 90 **campsites**. *Open Memorial thru Labor Day. (906) 774-8875.* &: *toilets.*

Porcupine Mountain Wilderness State Park

Vast old-growth forests, rugged hiking trails, wonderful waterfalls and views, and wild rivers in a 60,000-acre park overlooking Lake Superior

THIS VAST and rugged place at the remote northwestern edge of the U.P. is one of the Midwest's few great remaining wilderness tracts. Here long, high ridges made the interior forests away from Lake Superior too inaccessible and too expensive to log. Actually the ridges are worn-out stubs of mountains formed when ancient, hard volcanic basalt was uplifted. Once exposed, the "edges" of the layers of uplifted volcanic rock and sediment eventually eroded, forming the ridges. The tree-covered ridges' shapes led local Ojibwa to call the area *Kaugabissing* — the place of the porcupines.

The 35,000 acres at the heart of the 60,000-acre park have never been logged. (That's the definition of a virgin forest.) What's even more unusual is that much of it is old-growth forest, where a favorable combination of rainfall, soil, and circumstances enable trees to grow very large. Catastrophic natural windstorms and fires can make a virgin forest little different from a logged forest. Dominant tree types here in the Porkies are hardwoods, mostly sugar maple, which makes for spectacular fall color, and eastern hemlock.

Park ranger/naturalist Bob Sprague points out that virgin forests of eastern hemlock are very special. They "capture the essence of what people expect to see in old-growth forests." Dark and mysterious, free of underbrush because of the dense canopy, hemlocks are the Midwestern forests most like the old-growth rain forests of the West Coast. They were the "forests primeval" described in Longfellow's "Evangeline," where "the murmuring pines and the hemlocks stood like Druids of eld." The trunks of hemlocks here are up to three feet across. A large sugar maple is two feet across. Virgin forests of white pine or hardwood have an irregular, shaggy look in contrast to the hemlocks' thick, dark canopy. Here the north-facing slope combines with the large water body of Lake Superior to create a moist, shady microclimate with more uniform temperatures than nearby areas. Eastern hemlocks flourish in damp climates from Nova Scotia west to Lake Superior and south to Georgia. Because their wood splinters easily, they were often passed over by loggers.

By the 1930s conservationists had recognized the Porcupine

The forest primeval: old-growth hemlocks (here) and hardwoods escaped logging because of the Porkies' rugged terrain. This scene by beautiful Overlooked Falls is easily reached.

Mountains' rarity and value as a wilderness area. Plans to make the area a national park were stymied by lack of funds during World War II. It became a state park in 1945. However, mining and timber interests successfully continued to eat away at their natural resources. Led by then-state senator Joe Mack of Ironwood, politicians proposed building a disruptive through road along Lake Superior. (Road beds and traffic upset wildlife and their feeding and reproduction patterns by carving up habitats into increasingly small fragments. Presently the lakeshore road ends seven miles into the park from the eastern entrance. Only the 25-mile South Boundary Road connects the eastern end near Ontonogan with the western end around the Presque Isle River, reached from Wakefield near Ironwood. Some legislators even advocated a dog track to bring in tourist dollars.) Development controversies were resolved in the Wilderness Natural Areas Act of 1972 and have remained dormant ever since.

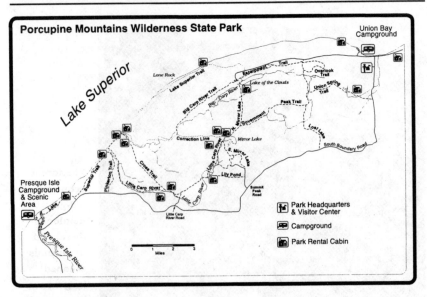

TODAY'S MULTIFACETED WILDERNESS PARK

The park offers visitors a huge variety of experiences, from short hikes and scenic overlooks (such as its signature sight, the much-visited Lake of the Clouds overlook), to dozens of beautiful waterfalls and 85 miles of hiking trails, to Lake Superior beaches, to 26 miles of groomed cross-country ski trails, to budget-priced downhill skiing on slopes with 640' vertical drops and super-scenic views.

The park's true highlights are the hiking trails leading into the old-growth forests, especially when they also lead to one of the over 30 waterfalls formed when rivers tumble down the ridges. The Porkies are one of the Midwest's premiere places to backpack. To really experience the Porkies, try to plan spending a day — or better yet, at least two days and a night — hiking and camping in the wilderness, away from the busy visitor spots and modern campground. Campers must be prepared to deal with hungry, clever black bears. (A detailed pamphlet, "How to Live with Black Bears," is given out at the Visitor Center or headquarters. It makes fascinating reading.) Some two dozen or more live in the park. The park has 16 frontier cabins, one wheelchair-accessible and the others on trails at least a mile from parking. They are arranged so they can be used for a three- or four-day backpack trip. Their popularity means they must be reserved well ahead in peak seasons.

In fact, this huge park can seem crowded due to clustering of visitors at certain times (summer, color season, winter weekends and Christmas week in the ski areas) and in certain places like scenic overlooks. To experience wilderness solitude, consider coming in attractive off seasons like mid- to late May when wildflowers are out (warblers fly through in mid-May, just when black flies are getting bad), or early October, when most leaves have fallen but some are left. Mid-May through mid-June are generally worst for black flies; they remain longer when there's been a lot of moisture from heavy snows.

PLANNING YOUR TRIP

For advance planning, there are two recommended **book-length guides** to the Porkies, each excellent in its way. (See note on p. 797.) Free **telephone planning help** is available year-round from the park's extremely helpful staff. For a **visitor packet** including camping at the park, area lodgings, and handouts customized to your interests, call (906) 885-5275 or write Porcupine Mts. State Park, 599 M-107, Ontonogan, MI 49953.

Serious backpackers can plan many different several-day adventures along the Porkies' 85 miles of trails. In this rugged wilderness, steep grades and unbridged stream crossings are common. For more complicated day trips and for overnights, it's a good idea to have a compass and be sure you understand and have planned for all the precautions mentioned in the "Backcountry information" handout (campfires permitted in metal rings only; take firestarter, high-energy food, first-aid; boil drinking water 5 minutes or filter or chemically treat it).

Backcountry camping is permitted anywhere in the park provided it's not within 1/4 mile of a cabin or road, but fires are permitted only in permanent campsites with fire rings. Currently there are about 100 such campsites on all sections of trail, readily apparent to hikers. More are being added all the time. **Registration** is required so park personnel know who's out there in case of emergencies; the fee is $6/night/group of 4. Registering in person is especially advised for first-time back-country campers because it makes sure they get the best advice on trail conditions, etc.

The **Visitor Center** should be visitors' first stop when it's open. That's from the May weekend before Memorial Day through October. It offers diverse informative free handouts, detailed hiking and topo maps for sale, an excellent **bookstore**, and interesting background exhibits. The short interpretive **nature trail** here is a good introduction to area plants and animals. Helpful park rangers at the Visitor

tion to area plants and animals. Helpful park rangers at the Visitor
Center can give information about trails, backpacking, canoeing,
fishing (for steelhead, salmon, and trout), and more. A big, detailed
relief map of the huge park helps orient visitors. An excellent 15-
minute multi-image **slide show**, held upon request, informs visitors
about the area's history, wildlife and natural features, and recreational possibilities. Many outstanding images are from Dan
Urbanski of the nearby Silver Image Studio. He's among the occasional outside summer speakers at the topical **evening programs**
held Monday through Thursday in July and August. (Usually they're
at 7 p.m.; call for details.) The year-round **activity schedule**
includes interesting **hikes** on many topics, held from June through
late September. *See page 796 for Visitor Center directions and hours.*

SEEING THE OLD-GROWTH FOREST

The essence of the Porcupine Mountains consists not of seeing the
celebrated scenic views but rather experiencing on foot the heart of
the magnificent, old-growth forests. For first-time visitors with varying amounts of time and energy, here are some choices. Each trail
includes a waterfall, river, or lake.

♦ *1-hour hike near a road.* Beautiful **Overlooked Falls** is in old-
growth hemlocks at the base of a gorge. It's reached by a fairly level,
1/4 mile trail from the end of the dead-end Little Carp River Road off
the west end of South Boundary Road. **Greenstone Falls** is a mile
farther down the picturesque Little Carp River Trail.

♦ *3 to 4-hour hike.* From **Government Peak Trailhead** to **Trap
Falls** and back. 2 1/2 miles each way. Goes through hemlocks, hardwoods, and a few big pine along the Big Carp River valley and uphill
to falls. A good, short hike despite some mud, hills, and obstacles.

♦ *All-day hike or easy overnight.* Parts of three trails combine to
make a 10-mile triangle. Take **Lily Pond Trail** from trailhead off the
Summit Peak Road. Hike 3 miles to Little Carp River Trail junction.
Hike 3 miles on Little Carp Trail to **Mirror Lake**. Take Mirror Lake
Trail back to Summit Peak Road and down to Lily Pond Trail trailhead. Trails are clearly marked, but hikers need to pay attention and
use the trail map. Or you can camp off the trail. To do this 9 1/2-mile
hike, your feet should be broken in and you should already be accustomed to a light pack if you're overnighting. A nice, short detour,
especially for bird-watchers, is to take Beaver Creek Trail, an 1/8
mile dead-end boardwalk midway between Lily Pond and Mirror Lake.

near the end of M-107, take either the Lake Superior Trail (lake views) or Big Carp River Trail (cliff-top hiking) to the mouth of the Big Carp River. Follow the Lake Superior Trail one mile to the Little Carp River mouth, then take the Little Carp River Trail deep into the park, past lots of waterfalls. On your way to Lake of the Clouds (just off M-107 and close to both starting points) you'll pass **Greenstone Falls**, Lily Pond, and Mirror Lake.

OTHER FAVORITE DESTINATIONS

♦ Many people enjoy the **waterfalls** along the **Presque Isle River**, on the park's far western edge, more than anything else they experience on an Upper Peninsula vacation. (Locals tend to say "Presk AISLE.") In their highly recommended *Guide to 199 Michigan Waterfalls*, the Penrose family, who seldom indulge in superlatives, say, "This is one of the most beautiful stretches of river in the entire Upper Peninsula. The pristine silence of the forest here is interrupted only by the water, a sound that is never far away." These falls, close to CR 519, are some 30 minutes southwest of the Visitor Center off South Boundary Road. In this book they are grouped in a chapter with other Ironwood-area waterfalls on page 800.

♦ **Lake Superior's Union Bay.** One of the park's few sandy beaches, and the only one accessible by car. Water temperatures vary in summer, depending on wind direction, and can be quite pleasant in late July, August, and September, disproving the myth that Lake Superior is too cold for swimming. See page 797 about kayaking and canoeing along the lake. *Along M-107 for 2 1/2 miles west from the main park entrance by Silver City to the Union Bay Campground.*

♦ **Lake of the Clouds Overlook,** at the end of M-107, is one of the state's most famous views. It looks down from a dramatic rocky ridge onto the Big Carp River Valley. From here the old-growth forests below seem like a distant green carpet. Scenic overlooks are near a parking lot, but not wheelchair-accessible. Expect a crowd of visitors in summer. Or you can earn the drama by approaching it on foot along the scenic, popular **Escarpment Trail** along the high ridge. It reveals interesting rock formations along the dramatic escarpment. You can start at either the Government Peak trailhead 4 miles east of the Lake of the Clouds main overlook or the Escarpment Trail, two miles east on the south side of M-107. A shorter trail connecting a number of high scenic viewpoints is the **Overlook Trail**, a 3 1/2-mile loop that also starts at the Government Peak trailhead off M-107 five miles west of the main park entrance.

If you're driving along M-107 to or from Lake of the Clouds, take time to stop at **Mead Mine** along M-107. Here you can enter about 100 feet of an old copper mineshaft. It's on the road's south side, just opposite the pleasant **picnic area** and historical marker on a hill overlooking Lake Superior. There's a good sunset view of Lake Superior from here. The closest picnic supplies are at the Silver City general store.

◆ **Summit Peak Observation Tower.** From the 35-foot tower at the park's highest point (1,958 feet above sea level, you're so high above the treetops of the forest here in the park's interior that you feel you're floating above an undulating sea of green. Come on a clear day (many are slightly hazy) and you can see all the way to the Apostle Islands. A panoramic sign points you to landmarks like the Copper Peak Ski Flying Hill and White Pine stacks. The shady half-mile trail up to the tower is pretty; the view towards sunset is especially striking. If you haven't exercised, you could huff and puff. The area just west of here suffered from the big windstorm of 1954. Wayside benches invite you to sit and enjoy the woods. It's a half mile from parking area to the seven-story tower. For a little more of a hike, you can go out and back along the Beaver Creek Trail from the Summit Peak parking lot (about a mile each way), or take the South Mirror Lake Trail from near the tower left to Mirror Lake (a mile each way) or back 1 1/2 miles to the Summit Peak Road (this is about 3/4 miles to the parking area). *Midway on the South Boundary Road, 20 minutes from either end, the asphalt Summit Peak Rd. penetrates two miles north to the parking area.*

Porcupine logistics: The 20-mile-long park is in a little-developed area between Ontonogan and Ironwood. The park's visitor center and main facilities are off M-107, about three miles west of Silver City, where M-64 turns inland from Lake Superior to the mining town of White Pine. Silver City is more a collection of resorts than a town. Its general store can fill many visitor needs. Visitors to the park's western end are closer to lodgings in Wakefield, Bessemer, and Ironwood. **Park phone:** *(906) 885-5275. TDD: (906) 885-5278. Fax: (906) 885-5798.* **Visitor Center** *open from weekend before Mem. Day through Oct. Hours: 10 to 6 at least. State park sticker required: $4/day, $20/year. ᕁ: Visitor center, some campgrounds, some overlooks. Call.*

TWO HELPFUL GUIDES TO THE PORKIES . . . . . A vast knowledge of all aspects of the Porcupine Mountains is presented in the fascinating if somewhat unwieldy *Porcupine Mountains Companion* (300+ pp., around $15), available at the visitor center or from Nequaket Natural History Assn., Box 103, White Pine, MI 49971. It details with trails, cabins, waterfalls, local history of Ojibwa (18 pp.), mining (22 pp.), geology (22 pp.), botany, wildlife, nearby day trips, and even a quick constellation guide. Richly illustrated, it's the perfect book for a long backpacking trip. . . . . Veteran Michigan outdoor writer Jim Du Fresne's *Michigan's Porcupine Mountains Wilderness State Park* (Thunder Bay Press, 159 pp., $11.95) provides a quicker, more convenient overview from someone with a lot of hands-on visitor experience. . . . . Both books can also be conveniently ordered from our *Michigan Catalog* mail-order service: (517) 629-4494.

CANOEING AND SEA KAYAKING ALONG LAKE SUPERIOR . . . . . is increasing in popularity. Rentals are available from the park concessionaire on M-107 just before the Union Bay campground. Local enthusiasts like to find a quiet place to pull in and set up camp on park land or national forest land west of the park. They advise taking along a weather radio; south of Union Bay the shore is often so rocky it's hard to beach a canoe. In some places it's a 30-foot clay bank.

THE CHARMS OF SKIING IN THE PORKIES . . . . It's a lot easier to get here from the Twin Cities than for those who live in lower Michigan, but there are lots of good reasons to plan for a ski week here — just not between Christmas and New Year's, when it's packed and snow can be iffy due to the lake effect's moderating temperature. Later the lake works in skiers' favor, creating lots of white powder that's skiable into April. Come in spring for the fewest weekend crowds. The **641- foot drop** is one of highest in Midwest. There are 11 miles of trails at all levels. Lift capacity is 3,600 skiers an hour. 42 km of groomed **cross-country trails** ($6-$8 adult trail fee) can be quickly accessed with a one-ride tow ticket on the downhill lift. Lake Superior views from both trail systems can be spectacular. Tow rates are low ($20 adults weekdays, $25 weekends, 12 and under free). The atmosphere is unglitzy and family-friendly. Where else, Jim Du Fresne points out, would the **ski lodge** have families' personal crock pots cooking dinner while they're out skiing? Rentals of snowboards and both kinds of skis are available, as are lessons. *Call the park for basic info; call 1 (800) BSC-7000 for snow reports. No parking fee to ski.*

WORTH A VISIT IN SILVER CITY. . . . . At his **Silver Image Studio** perched on the hillside in "downtown" Silver City, photographer Dan Urbanski sells posters, notecards, and photographs of his beautiful wilderness images of natural phenomena and wildlife in the Porcupines. He's a good information source, too. Open year round, daily in summer from 10-5 at least, evenings by chance. (906) 885-5895. . . . . Down the road toward the park, in a rustic cottage, the **Great Lakes Trading Company** hones in on the North Country look with pottery, folk art and a tastefully interesting range of other souvenirs and gifts.

A PLEASANT BEACH IN SILVER CITY . . . . . is at the mouth of the Iron River, just east of M-64 and the Holiday Inn. The cedars and stones between sandy beach and road make this a popular place to pull over, park the car along the road, and get out.

A GOOD U.P. LOCAL HISTORY MUSEUM . . . . . Ruth Ristola and her amazing index of local people past and present gets way beyond the usual mining and logging implements at U.P. museums into the sphere of the families and social interactions that are the web of life. The **Ontonogan County Historical Museum** is on the town's main street (it's both M-38 and U.S. 45), a couple blocks inland from Syl's, the consummate small-town bakery-cafe. Thanks to a new coat of lavender paint, you can't miss it. *Usually open daily except Sunday, year-round, 9-5:30. (906) 884-6165.* &

DINE WELL AND SEE A BEAR, TOO . . . . . Some of the Upper Peninsula's best food (not fancy, but made from scratch and consistently good) is served at the **Konteka Supper Club** at the back of the shopping center on M-64 in White Pine. **White Pine** is a company copper-mining town built in the 1950s. (In 1995 the mine closed, but the town isn't visibly affected. People up here are used to booms and busts.) The well-known Michigan architect Alden Dow designed the Konteka restaurant and motel. . . . . Food is put out at dinner on the rear lawn that backs up to a woods, and neighboring bears are showing up by July and August. (This is not done so much a visitor attraction as a bear management technique so bears don't rummage through the dumpster day and night, alarming patrons and townspeople. U.P. towns have been required to close their garbage dumps, and disappointed bears have become resourceful nuisances in many places.) The bears' movements are surprisingly graceful. . . . . Call (906) 885-5215 to order Konteka's box lunches and picnic takeout.

A DELIGHTFUL SIDE TRIP TO ROCKLAND AND OLD VICTORIA . . . . . If you're in the mood to explore and chat, take the 12-mile drive east from Ontonogan to Rockland along U.S. 45, past picturesque old farms and beautiful rocky hills. . . . The remote Victorian mining village of **Rockland** boomed after the **Ontonogan Boulder**, a huge mass of pure copper now in the Smithsonian Museum, was discovered south of here in 1856. Rockland, once the epitome of frontier modernity, had Michigan's first telephone system. Today's Rockland has shriveled. You need to stop, walk, and get oriented to be able to see the interesting but scattered things that remain. . . . . Stop first at **Henry's Never Inn** (906-886-9910), a bar on the west side of main street. Its furnishings reflect many layers of history reaching back to the original Brunswick back bar from 1900. From 5 to 9 Wednesdays through Saturdays, Henry's and its pleasant outdoor deck is packed with people from as far as L'Anse, Houghton and even Rhinelander, who

come for the terrific homemade smorgasbord. But by day, the old miners' bar is
quiet, and Henry's outspoken wife, Sally, will fill you in on Rockland history,
alluding to how Ontonogan stole everything, including the boulder and the county
seat. Property in this near-ghost town "has no value," she says, which is how her
daughter could buy up a vacant city block and turn it into a big flower garden, a
striking sight from the highway because of the fanciful white archways and neo-
rococo fencing. Henry Gagnon welded it of steel reinforcing rods in his free time. .
. . . Two miles south of town is the **Old Victoria Restoration,** a participating site
of the Keweenaw National Historic Park. It is a cluster of eight log houses built in
1899 around the shaft of the Victoria Mine. Restoring and furnishing the houses
is yet another Rockland example of artfully improvised bootstrap historic preservation, supported by visitor fees, a crafts fair the third Sunday in August, and
thimbleberry jam made by caretaker/guide Chris Dolton. He gives long, somewhat philosophical tours about the hard life here, especially for women. A picnic
table across the road invites visitors to linger at this now-pleasant spot. Groups
can arrange to stay here, *if* they're willing to chop wood and haul water. *From
Rockland, turn south just east of Henry's, go 2 miles south on the Victoria Dam
Road. Open Mem. Day weekend thru color season, 11:30-5:30 or by chance or by
appointment. (906) 886-2617.* **&:** *not officially, but wheelchairs can get into first
floors of most buildings. Donations appreciated.* . . . . At the end of the road is the
big **Victoria Dam and Reservoir,** built in 1931 in part to power a copper mine.
There a boat launch gives access to this remote and scenic artificial lake,

TWO INTERESTING ROCKLAND CRAFTSPEOPLE . . . . . welcome visitors to
their working studios. Brent Thorgren makes custom millwork and wainscoting
on beautiful old Victorian machinery at **Greenstone** (906) 886-2832. It's in a very
old, slab-sided log house on U.S. 45 at Maple on the east side of town. . . . . Call
Jessica Speer to arrange a visit to **One of a Kind Weaving** (906-886-2672), where
she makes contemporary woven rugs, woven lace, and throws, sold retail and
wholesale nationwide. She teaches classes and workshops here, too.

Gogebic Waterfalls & More

A region worth exploring, among attractive falls

FOR MANY FAMILIES in the Upper Peninsula, the perfect summer day is built around a walk to a waterfall and the picnic that goes with it. "No matter how enjoyable walking through the wilderness was, it was always better if you had a destination in mind," writes Laurie Penrose, co-author of the helpful *Guide to 199 Michigan Waterfalls.* (See page 808.)

Gogebic County at Michigan's far western tip is one of the nicest areas for summer waterfall-watching. (It's pronounced "go-GIBB-ick.") The Ojibwa word applies to the Gogebic Iron Range which extends from Wakefield to Ironwood and into Wisconsin past Hurley to Montreal. On the Michigan side, a belt of four dozen waterfalls on nine streams extends from Ironwood and Bessemer through the Porcupine Mountains. Here falls tumble quickly down from the highlands (ancient, eroded mountains, actually) to Lake Superior. The best-known waterfalls are on the Presque Isle and Black Rivers within half a mile of Lake Superior. Another nearby series is along the Ontonogan River, which empties into Lake Superior at Ontonogan. Here as elsewhere in the Upper Peninsula, water often has a golden tinge that comes from the tannin of hemlock roots.

Gogebic County has 22 easily visitable falls. Ten more waterfalls worth visiting are across the Montreal River in neighboring Iron County, Wisconsin. (See page 806.) With so many spots to choose from, visitors aren't as concentrated as in the Munising/Pictured Rocks area, also known for waterfalls. Fewer crowds make for a more enjoyable experience.

As always, early risers are rewarded by the morning freshness, rosy sunrises, and solitude. Being on the scene near dawn and dusk is especially worthwhile when visiting waterfalls, because the slanting light then illuminates the falls' mists and cascades most dramatically. When conditions are right, rainbows aren't rare.

On the other hand, it's also a sensuous experience to visit a waterfall in a cool, shady glade on a hot summer day, especially when the spray and stream can cool you off.

Their changeability — with the time of day and season of the year — is part of the charm of visiting waterfalls. This is one pastime well suited for all seasons. Spring snowmelt shows them at their most powerful, of course, though muddy roads can be a problem. Remember to be prepared for the U.P.'s famously annoying

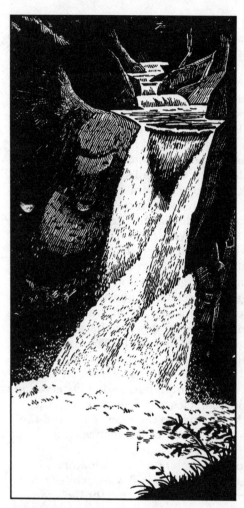

Gorge Falls on the Black River.

bugs, from mid-May through the July 4 holiday especially. By August some falls are reduced to a thin trickle, which can show off rock formations to better effect. Autumn's color and falling water is a fabulous combination. In winter, frozen waterfall formations can be dramatic in the snowy woods, though they are little visited. Snowshoes are a good way to get around. (See page 765 for the U. P.'s own snowshoe factory.)

The unfortunate temptation for energetic vacationers from afar is to take the checklist approach to waterfalls and pack in too many in too few days. See too many waterfalls and they blur together. The contemplative mood of these expeditions is destroyed, and a jaded, tired disappointment is the result.

Pretty pictures of waterfalls and easy roadside views don't begin to suggest the fascinating variety of waterfalls. Nor do they evoke the water's power, or the potent dimension of the water's sound, changing as you approach the falls.

Different falls reveal themselves to viewers in very different ways. Seen from the bottom of a gorge, a waterfall can create its own world that completely surrounds you, sometimes with mossy rocks and a ferny floor, other times with looming, dark crags of rock and a few struggling trees. Foaming water gives way to ripples and, sometimes, to placid pools. Viewed from above, the same fall can seem quite different. When you walk along a stream to reach a waterfall, it almost always reveals itself more dramatically than if you go directly from a parking lot to the waterfall. Some waterfalls take you completely by surprise. You can be walking through a rolling upland meadow and have a chasm open up before you with little warning. Waterfalls often are not fenced. Visiting them can be a very dangerous pastime for curious, adventurous children.

Sometimes a gush of water emerges suddenly from a forested hillside — the sort of rain forest image recollected from movies. More distinctive to the Upper Peninsula are the waterfalls where the motion of rushing water plays off against solid rock — or, more accurately, against rock that is solid for the time being but is revealed to be quite changeable by the waterfall's obvious dynamism and power to break off and sculpt the bedrock itself.

Some falls spread out in a leisurely fashion over a wide series of rocky shelves (for instance, Manido Falls on the Black River and Bonanza Falls between Silver City and White Pine). Some are tranquil woodland spots accented by a small silver stream trickling around rocks down a gentle hillside. Massive rock outcrops constrict others, like the Black River's Gorge Falls and those at Piers Gorge on the Menominee (page 784). Veils of water are quite a different phenomenon, often involving a lot of mist and rainbow effects. The red sandstones and conglomerates are characteristic of the mining ranges of the western Upper Peninsula. The conglomerates incorporate the underlying basalt of the Canadian Shield, that ancient volcanic rock formed before any organisms lived on Earth.

Waterfalls lend themselves to contemplation and to observations about how water moves around obstacles and how it shapes the earth. Then for some there's the analogy to the river of life and the obstacles along its course. It's no accident that Japanese and Chinese art cultivates an appreciation of waterfalls.

With all these hints in mind, here's a quick introductory overview of Gogebic Range waterfalls. Additional worthwhile waterfalls are described in the Penrose family's *Guide to 199 Michigan Waterfalls*. (See page 808.)

Three additional cautions before setting out on explorations. *First,* even improved paths have occasional tree roots that could trip walkers who shuffle. Mud can make paths slippery. Dangerous dropoffs can be just off a path. People with impaired walking (or with small children) should proceed with caution. *Second,* some of those placid pools have dangerous undertows. Swimming in unfamiliar pools is not advised. *Third,* if you're thinking of visiting waterfalls where trails are unmarked, consider investing in easily removable wire surveyors' flags (page 811).

Presque Isle River Waterfalls
in the Porcupine Mountains State Park

Waterfall enthusiasts point to these as the most compelling falls to visit if time is limited. The Penroses' waterfall guide (see page 808), which seldom elevates one waterfall above another, says "this is one of the most beautiful stretches of river we have found in the entire Upper Peninsula." Within a mile's hike of the parking areas are four waterfalls that stand out for their beauty and variety. The beautiful, easily accessible **Overlooked Falls** (p. 794) are a short drive away.

A new boardwalk along the river's west bank now makes the walk safer for anyone concerned about unsure, possibly slippery footing. Many people say the boardwalk is almost an attraction in its own right, akin to the environmental landscape art projects like Christo's *Running Fence* through the northern California hills. Every state park ranger knows that laying out trails is not just a job but an unheralded genre of landscape architecture. It combines practical concerns about construction, gradients, drainage, etc. with sensitivity to the hiker's aesthetic experience. Here the walks, stairways, and viewing platforms snake their way through an old-growth forest of hemlock and yellow birch that's typical of the Porcupines. Longtime park maintenance mechanics Carl Groitzsch and Roland Clisch built it a section at a time over a 10-year period, observing the lay of the land as they went along — a far cry from jobs designed from topo maps in a distant headquarters.

A picnic area is at the very end of County Road 519. Across a swinging bridge at the river mouth is Lake Superior. This is a busy place during spring steelhead and fall salmon runs. From the parking area, say the Penroses,

"a short walk leads to a network of stairs which drops to a trail. Just before the trail reaches the river, a boardwalk branches off to the right. [Return here later, but first] continue on the stairs to a suspension bridge. Just above it [is] a fascinating **unnamed falls**. . . . There the force of the powerful river. . . creates miniature whirlpools along the banks. The spinning action of the water has carved perfect half-circles into the stones which line the bank and polished them to a glossy black. . . . The best views of this effect come from the bridge."

Now go back and take the boardwalk upstream about 200 or 250 yards to the first overlook to **Manabezho Falls.** To reach the second overlook at the brink of the falls, go upstream 150 yards more, up one stairway and down another. At the falls, the Penroses say, "a thick band of white, rushing water, which spans the 150-foot-wide river, drops about 20 feet over a rock shelf. The largest section is tinged with gold, and its heavy flow creates a blanket of foam which trails downstream." In another 100 yards, **Manido Falls** is "a mass of white water" as it "descends over a network of gradually declining rock steps, then drops over a ledge of stone." Look up and down the river to see traces of the adjoining falls. The boardwalk ends at Manido Falls. Then rugged East/West River Trail goes another 1/4 mile to reach **Nawadaha Falls**, a 15-foot tumble across many rock steps that creates "a blanket of white foaming lace." To see the falls best, you need to take a side spur down to the river. The *Porcupine Mountains Companion* (page797) reports that the pool below Nawadaha Falls is "a good place to try for rainbow trout and brookies."

Here you are almost at South Boundary Road. If you want to hike a **2-mile loop** and revisit all the falls from the more difficult trail on the river's east bank, cross on the bridge here. The trail, occasionally rough and hilly, passes some very large virgin pine, hemlock, and cedar. It ends at the parking lots by the swinging bridge at the river mouth. &: *none of these falls.*

WATERFALLS ON THE BLACK RIVER, OTTAWA NATIONAL FOREST

The Black River and County Road 513 parallel each other for some 15 miles to Lake Superior from U.S. 2 in Bessemer. Turn at the car dealership and school in town. Five beautiful and distinctive waterfalls are clustered within the two miles before the river's mouth. They are among the most visited in the western Upper Peninsula. CR 513 winds through a rolling countryside of old farms and forests and passes the Copper Peak Ski Flying Hill. Adventurous sightseers might want to consult the Penroses' waterfall guide (page 808) for good directions to the beautiful **Chippewa Falls**, near Copper Peak but in an extremely rugged locale with no marked trail.

A good way for first-time visitors to experience these falls meaningfully is to plan two outings, separated perhaps by a picnic near the beach at Black River Harbor (page 805). Begin at the shared parking lot near Gorge and Potawatomi falls, about 13 miles from U.S. 2. The National Forest's **wheelchair-accessible path** permits quick, easy access to a **picnic area**, chemical toilet, and to the unusually beautiful **Potawatomi Falls**. Seen in August, the falls' beauty relies on pattern and complexity rather than volume, drop, or force. To defer to Laurie Penrose's subtle description in *A Guide to 199 Michigan Waterfalls*, "The water passed over the rock in small tendrils of white angel hair, which separated and joined in complicated patterns before reaching the base of the gorge. The delicate picture of this falls — nestled in the gorge and surrounded by the deep greens of high summer — is extraordinary."

A quarter mile downstream, the very different **Gorge Falls** can be reached either by a striking series of platforms and stairs along the river (this is the more scenic path) or by going back to the parking area and taking the path and stairs to the falls. (Neither way takes more than a few minutes.) Here the water, constricted in a narrow gorge, has pounded on stone to create a deep, smooth slide that ends in a mass of foam. The massive, rounded stone, unsoftened by vegetation of any kind, is striking testimony to the power of water. This wall of red stone confronts you as you descend to the final platform.

Great Conglomerate Falls is some half a mile *up*stream from Potawatomi Falls. (It's the first of this waterfall cluster on CR 513.) Here, over an extended stretch of river, water rushes around huge boulders and tears at trunks, felling several trees. It's an unsettling, wild landscape. The falls can be reached from a wide, smooth 3/4 mile trail from its own parking area. Or chose to take the west riverbank path from Potawatomi Falls. In 1995 this path was slippery, often steep with roots in the path, and sometimes not well marked. It was a 45-minute trek from Potawatomi Falls to the very beginning of Great Conglomerate Falls and back. *First-time visitors might want to postpone this waterfall to a later trip, and save their time and energy to enjoy fewer falls in a more leisurely way.*

Visiting **Rainbow Falls,** the last of the five falls, seems more like a physical challenge than an invitation to pleasure if you look at the 200-step stairway that leads from the parking area just off CR 513. (That's a quarter of a mile down and then back *up*, with no landings for a rest!) Fortunately the east bank offers a much more enjoyable way to reach this beautiful falls, named for the rainbows often seen in its mist. It allows you to conveniently see the nearby Sandstone Falls, too. Oddly, the elaborate national forest sign doesn't mention this route. Here it is.

Park at the lot at the very end of CR 513. Here at **Black River Harbor**, once the site of a fishing village, the national forest has made a pleasant **park** and shady **picnic area**. (The 40-site campground, with flush toilets but no showers or electricity, is a short way back from the lake on CR 513.) A wheelchair-accessible **foot bridge** leads across the river mouth up to a popular, sandy Lake Superior beach. Crossing the bridge, turn left to reach the beach. Kids love to jiggle and sway on the suspension bridge. To get to Rainbow Falls, look for the North Country Trail's triple blue diamonds in about 50 feet and turn immediately right, following the river upstream and up along the river wall on an earthen embankment made by the forest service. This trail reaches a plateau, then goes south past some massive old-growth hemlocks in the mixed virgin stand on the way to the **Rainbow Falls.** Here, in early afternoon before the sun sinks too low, the light effects can be memorable as light on the mist rising above the pool, creating a rainbow. Nearby the river has exposed layered sandstone, alternating gold and rose, for another colorful effect.

Another quarter mile along the North Country Trail takes you to **Sandstone Falls**, where the river makes leaps, first of five feet and then, passing between huge conglomerate rocks, dropping 20 feet.

Falls along the Montreal River

Three other unusual falls are outside Hurley along the river separating Michigan from Wisconsin. Here most of the water has been diverted by a power dam upstream, so the towering, dark rocks are more prominent than the water. The plunges here are taller and more dramatic than on the Presque Isle or Black rivers. The Penroses found the reduced water flow disappointing, but C.J. and Edna Elfont, who created the spectacular photograph book *Roar of Thunder, Whisper of Wind*, enjoyed the towering, dark cliffs of **Saxon Falls** immensely. At nearby **Superior Falls** the cliffs are golden sandstone. These falls are best viewed from the Wisconsin side. For **Wisconsin waterfall maps** and much more, stop by the 24-hour Wisconsin Travel Information Center in Hurley where U.S. 2 joins U.S. 51.

On the Michigan side of the Montreal, **Interstate Falls** (also known as **Peterson Falls** and **Montreal Falls**) is on private property belonging to River Falls Outdoors, a pleasant, rustic small resort for outdoors lovers. Guests staying at one of the cabins can enjoy a terrace view of the falls. Call (906) 932-5638 to ask permission and get directions for a falls visit.

Beyond waterfalls

The 1910s and 1920s were boom times for the Gogebic Iron Range, around the twin county seats of Ironwood, Michigan, and its sister city across the Montreal River, the once-notorious Hurley, Wisconsin. The last mine closed in 1951. Today the mining scars are mostly covered over by vegetation. Though Iron and Gogebic counties are heavily promoted as **Big Snow Country** during the ski season and thousands of ski chalet units are around the four ski resorts, the trappings of tourism with its hype and pretense do not dominate. Today the rugged landscape seems beguilingly scenic in an unmannered, unpretentious way.

The Gogebic is an interesting place to vacation because it's *not* just a tourist area. As in much of the Upper Peninsula, the mix of people and cultures adds much to a visitor's experience. The population is composed largely of Finns and Italians who came to work in the iron mines, and Croatians, Poles, and other Slavs from coal-mining regions of Eastern Europe. They had come earlier to mine what little coal was here.

Hurley's rough, crude past was the subject of Edna Ferber's novel *Come and Get It* (1934). It's set during the Prohibition years when nearly 200 saloons, disguised as soda shoppes, lined downtown's streets, and when Chicago gangsters established resorts and gambling rackets in northern Wisconsin mining and lumber towns.

"a sordid enough town. . . , with all its vices and crudeness of the mining camps of an earlier day, but with few of their romantic qualities. Lumber and iron were hard masters to serve. A cold, hard country of timber and ore. . . . A rich and wildly beautiful country, already seared and ravaged. . . . Encircling the town were the hills and ridges that had once been green velvety slopes, tree shades. Now the rigs and shafts of the iron mines stalked upon them with never a tree or blade of grass to be seen. . . . The timber lands — hundreds of thousands of acres of timber — went unsought until Jed Hewitt and the other paper-mill men from the New England coast came along and saw that their gold lay beneath the bark of the century-old pine forests."

Today, in contrast, the Gogebic Range is a pretty mellow place. People are friendly here even when they take you for a despised environmentalist from down below. It's a pleasure to chat with the folks sitting next to you at cafes. And the food is quite a surprise! Italian restaurants that still make lasagna and ravioli by hand because their customers expect it — and expect low prices, too. The beautifully renovated 1924 **Ironwood Theatre** in downtown Ironwood hosts a successful arts series of chamber music, plays, and more. (Call 906-932-0618 for details.)

It's interesting to note how mining towns like Ironwood and Iron Mountain — unpromising places that began as artificial company towns where ethnic groups with no common culture were thrown together — have become enduring communities that keep drawing their progeny back. (Great natural beauty and cheap real estate help, no doubt.) In these gritty towns, wealth was extracted and quickly exported without staying around and paying for fine buildings and cultural institutions beyond churches. In contrast, in Houghton and Marquette, some mining magnates lived in impressive homes and supported libraries, colleges, and the arts. Here mining families experienced booms and busts, and saw legions of their children forced to move away. To be in Wakefield or Bessemer at homecoming is to witness a sense of community that few upscale suburbs could match.

One small but telling sight here. On Aurora Street in downtown Ironwood, still lined with remnants of taverns from the wild and wooly boom times, people who have bicycled downtown lean their bicycles, unlocked, by the entrances of stores, confident that the bikes will still be there when they come out. That's the kind of civilized lifestyle you can still find up here.

HANDMADE PASTA THAT'S NOT FOR GOURMETS . . . . . Two casual spots, popular with locals and visitors alike, are both open daily. **Manny's** is in Ironwood, at the Norrie Location mineshaft neighborhood south of town. (From U.S. 2 take Bus. U.S. 2 to the main street, but stay straight up the hill, heading for the giant Paul Bunyan statue at the Norrie Location; Manny's is past the ball field.) **Fontecchio's Liberty Bell Chalet** is on Fifth at Division, a block north of Hurley's main street and the train tracks.

TWO RECOMMENDED BOOKS ON WATERFALLS . . . . . The Penrose family's *Guide to 199 Michigan Waterfalls* ($14.95) is indispensable because it gives such good directions to so many waterfalls, rapids, and dam sites. Every location has a clear area map. Many falls appear in black-and-white photos. (No directions are given to a few dozen falls that are not conveniently accessible, either because they're on private property without public permission or are too remote.) Bonuses are excellent introductions to each county, a complete index of all known names of waterfalls, and a locator map. *Roar of Thunder, Whisper of Wind: A Portrait of Michigan Waterfalls* (127 pp; Thunder Bay Press, $24.95 paper, $40 hardcover) offers C. J. Elfont's stunning, beautifully reproduced black-and-white photographs of waterfalls and the rocks, plants, and landscapes around them. The large-format camera work and occasional two-page spreads give this a you-are-there immediacy that the black-and-white photography somehow enhances. Unfortunately, the irritating text sounds as if the authors think they personally discovered many of the waterfalls depicted.

FREE RECREATION HANDOUTS . . . . . deal with hiking, mountain biking, hunting, fishing, canoeing, snowmobiling,camping, and more for the vast **Ottawa National Forest** that covers almost a million acres in Gogebic County and the far western Upper Peninsula. Stop by the supervisor's office in Ironwood on the north side of U.S. 2 at the east side of town, or call (906) 932-1330.

MOUNTAIN BIKING ALONG OLD LOGGING ROADS . . . . . Extensive networks of trails are in Iron County, Wisconsin, and neighboring parts of the Ottawa National Forest. Check out the **Pines and Mines Trail System** maps at either state travel information center. The maps include interesting info on history as well as natural features.

HELPFUL VISITOR INFO FOR TWO STATES . . . . . At the **Michigan Welcome Center** on the south side of U.S. 2 at the west edge of Ironwood, almost in Wisconsin, the staff goes way past the extra mile in advising visitors. They know a lot about the U.P.'s back roads and beaches, in addition to the visitor sights and accommodations promoted in their masses of brochures. Open 8 to 4 daily except holidays. (906) 932-3330. . . . . Across the Wisconsin border at the intersection of U.S. 2 and U.S. 51, the friendly **Wisconsin Travel Information Center** is open around the clock and staffed from 8 a.m. to 4 p.m. Mining displays and rock samples make it like a mini-museum. Free Wisconsin publications of special note: the fat, well-organized, unpuffy Wisconsin Auto Tours and the statewide bicycle maps highlighting Wisconsin's many rail-trails and low-traffic paved roads. . . . . . With almost a million acres in the far western Upper Peninsula, the **Ottawa National Forest** abounds in recreational opportunities: hunting, fishing, canoeing, waterfalls, hiking, camping, and more. The full range of free handouts, plus personal advice, can be had at the **Supervisor's Office** in Ironwood, on the north side of Cloverland/U.S. 2, 3 miles east of the Welcome Center and a half a mile east of K Mart. Open weekdays. (906) 932-1330.

BIG SNOW COUNTRY. . . . . Vertical drops of over 600' plus dependable snow thanks to proximity to Lake Superior make for the best skiing in the Middle West. (Searchmont near Sault Ste. Marie, Canada, is in the same league.) . . . . . **Big Snow Country** visitor bureau serves the area with its **snow reports** (800-272-7000) and **lodging referral service** (906) 932-4850. . . . . Ski resorts offer some most attractive summer deals and have lots of extras for family vacations. **Indian Head** (906-229-5181) is by far the most attractive. It has on-site golf, too. . . . . . For cross-country skiing, **Johnson's Nordic Trails** (906-224-4711) near Wakefield win raves for scenic beauty and grooming. 30k of trails are groomed for traditional and ski-skating. Rentals and lessons available.

TUCKED-AWAY BEACHES NEAR IRONWOOD . . . . . Take CR 505 as it twists and turns northwest from U.S. 2 in Ironwood at the middle of the three traffic lights. It goes out to **Little Girls' Point** on Lake Superior, a drive of 12 minutes or so. At the point, steps go down from a park to the beach, with a view of the distant Porcupine Mountains. The **park** has a **picnic area**, changing house, and grassy, shady **campground**. Oman's Agate Shop by the park should be open again. . . . . . West along the shore, the sandy beach comes right up to the road, where you can park. . . . . At **Black River Harbor** (page 805) a swinging footbridge leads from a shady park to the sandy **beach** and to waterfalls along the **North Country Trail**. It's at the end of CR 513. Turn onto it from U.S. 2 at the auto dealership in and school near downtown Bessemer. . . . . . For warmer swimming, there's the beach on the Black River in **Ramsay**, just south of U.S. 2 between Bessemer and Wakefield, and the **park in Wakefield** on the north side of Sunday Lake. (Look for the sign as M-28 heads away from the lake going northeast out of town.) It has a picnic area, playground, and campground.

FOR RAINY-DAY TIME TRAVELS. . . . . there are three area historical museums to visit, plus the history-filled ice cream shop at the interesting **Regal Country Inn** motel in Wakefield. (It's on U.S. 2 a mile east of downtown.) . . . . . The **Wakefield Museum** is in a former doctor's office and home at 306 Sunday Lake St. (That's the main street, which extends south at the intersection of M-28 and U.S. 2). It's open from mid-June through Labor Day, Monday-Saturday from 1 to 4. New furnaces may allow a longer season; call (906) 224-8151. . . . . **Ironwood's historical museum** is in the handsome 1885 Romanesque depot on Ayer at Lowell, clearly visible to your right from Bus. Rte. 2 just before you reach the center of town from U.S. 2. One highlight: a startlingly life-like chainsaw sculpture of local hero and longtime former State Senator Joe Mack, complete with his signature blue plaid sport coat painted on. (906) 932-0287. . . . . Except for a big wine vat and a few other items, Hurley's rough, raw past seems remote and subdued amid the three floors of the **Iron County Historical Museum**, in the splendid original Romanesque courthouse with its tall clock tower. Rag rugs made here (on speculation or to order) on three large, handcrafted looms are sold to benefit the museum. Open year-round from 10 to 2 Monday, Wednesday, Friday, and Saturday except for holidays. (715) 561-2244.

THE BIGGEST FARMERS' MARKET IN THE REGION . . . . . is the **Iron County Farmers' Market** in Hurley. Produce, maple syrup, and crafts are all from the area. It's across from the Wisconsin Travel Information Center on U.S. 51, to your left as you enter Wisconsin on U.S. 2. Depending on the growing season, it opens in mid-July and closes in late October. Market days: Wednesdays from 2 p.m., Saturdays from 10 a.m.

SHOPS OF NOTE IN IRONWOOD . . . . . Hardly a shopper's paradise, Ironwood does have a few stores worth searching out. . . . . Downtown at 105-107 Suffolk (Bus. U.S. 2.) across from DNN Bank, **Albert's** is a vintage dry goods store known far and wide for its classic Yooper clothes — tough, functional wool clothing made to keep you warm and last for years. The store hasn't been remodeled since before WWII. The open shelves are piled with stacks of wool Malones (bib overalls that are ideal hunting pants) and lots of Carhartt work clothes. Kromer hats — those wool hats with ear flaps and a string bow above the bill — are $13. John Albert, whose father started the store in 1906, also carries men's and women's shoes for outdoors, dress, and work. . . . . In the historic Ironwood Theatre building at 111 E. Aurora, downtown's main street, **WilderNest** has a tasteful array of North Country gifts and books. . . . . Since 1975 the **Pine Tree Gallery**

has displayed maps and art of the Upper Great Lakes, from some antique maps to pottery to paintings and prints of regional artists, including a number of Native Americans. It also functions as a cultural center, with **concerts** and **lectures** (call 906-932-5120), and as an impromptu visitor information center. Backroads adventures here and in the Porkies are a specialty. *On the north side of U.S. 2/Cloverland, a block east of the main central light at CR 505.*

A HOMEY CENTER OF FINNISH-AMERICAN CULTURE. . . . . is just outside Hurley on U. S. 2, a little west of U.S. 51. **Little Finland** is one of those charming, completely unprofessional museums where the people (exceptionally friendly people, in fact) are the history more than any artifacts. At the **log house** moved onto the site and furnished from the donor's memory, the tour guide may share how her grandmother arrived at Ellis Island with a bunch of adventurous girlfriends who had all saved to emigrate and was recruited to be a maid in Wisconsin. . . . . The big, new hall hosts six special events a year and has a library and a fine **gift shop** of Finnish imports — with famous contemporary glassware, folk-inspired table linens, candles, enamelware, books, language tapes, sauna items, Lapland dolls, and more. Delicious baked goods are served with Cool Whip and plenty of coffee. . . . . *Open Wednesdays and Saturdays 10 to 2 from April through December. (715) 561-4360.*

AN ESCORTED, DAY-LONG MOUNTAIN BIKE TOUR . . . . . Over 25 miles of scenic logging roads north of Ironwood starts at one friendly, comfortable complex of rental cottages and ends at another. Cost: about $100-$135/person including two nights' lodging and three meals. Lower rates for kids. Starts at **River Falls Outdoors** (it overlooks a waterfall), ends at **Bear Track Inn** near Black River Harbor and more waterfalls. Call (906) 932-5638 or (906)   932-2144.

EASY, TIDY TEMPORARY TRAIL MARKERS . . . . . are **surveyors' flags** on stiff, thin wires. Unlike the more widely available surveyor's tape, they're quickly picked up on your way back out. They cost about $4 per 100. Along with other hard-to-find supplies for agriculture & forestry, they can be ordered from Forestry Suppliers (800-647-5368) or Ben Meadows (800-241-6401).

THE FINNISH SPORT OF SKI-FLYING . . . . . seems to have been developed to test the ultimate Finnish value of **sisu**, that untranslatable quality of guts, strength, endurance, and sometimes a measure of bravery to the point of foolhardiness. Today it's more or less a dying sport. Contests were held only every few years at the **Copper Peak Ski Flying Hill** on Black River Road going out toward the falls. Now, the facility can't afford to operate and let summer visitors take the chair lift and elevator up to the landmark slide, 241 feel above the summit of Copper Peak.

Hanka Homestead

On a beautiful, remote hillside, take a trip back in time to a self-sufficient Finnish farm.

IN THE WESTERN Upper Peninsula, the Finnish-American heartland, Finns are the dominant ethnic group. Because of their numbers, and because they have intermarried for generations, Finns have so colored the regional culture and accent that you can meet Yoopers without a drop of Finnish blood who speak with a strong Finnish-influenced accent. Some Finnish descendants whose families have been in this country for four generations sound as if they learned English as a second language. Saunas are still commonly seen in back yards from Marquette to Copper Country on the Keweenaw Peninsula to the Gogebic Range at Michigan's western tip, around Ironwood, Michigan, and Hurley, Wisconsin. The world's only Finnish-American college, Suomi College, is in Hancock. Dozens of co-op stores, a feature of many Finnish agricultural communities, survive in small places. Unfussy Scandinavian cleanliness sets the norm up here. It's hard to find a Copper Country motel, no matter how old or primitive, that isn't clean. And Finns are hard to beat for being direct and unpretentious. One little ma-and-pa resort near Houghton bears this motto on it business card: "Come rest you weary butt/in our simple little hut."

Many aspects of Finnish culture have been incorporated into the distinctive Yooper culture: that down-to-earth, no-nonsense attitude and complete lack of pretension, plus a thrifty do-it-yourself resourcefulness. (No self-respecting Finn hires work out, observes Dennis Sotala, Copper Harbor park ranger and basketweaver, and a longtime observer of various permutations of Finnish-American culture.) Then there's that streak of bravery verging on foolhardiness that's an indication of the fabled quality of *sisu* (guts, endurance, inner strength, a blend of psychological and physical qualities), and a do-it-yourself self-reliance.

Pure Finnish survivals from their early days around 1900 are rare, however. Probably the most remarkable is the Hanka Homestead, a self-sufficient pioneer farmstead at the base of the Keweenaw Peninsula. Its farmhouse and nine outbuildings are carefully crafted Scandinavian log construction. The Hanka farm has been restored to the way it was in its prime in 1920, when it was the home of Herman Hanka, a disabled miner, his wife, and their four adult children. On the farm they continued the Old World ways they had brought with them to the U.S.

By the time you get to the Hankas' place, you've gone down five miles of country road off U.S. 41; turned at a fire tower near the top of a long, high hill and driven down a rugged gravel road through a mile of forest. It's quite remote from the outside world, just as the Finns were who homesteaded in this neighborhood in the 1890s. The log house (now a century old), two-story log barn, and smaller outbuildings sit in an 18-acre clearing, surrounded by forest. The Huron Mountains are blue in the distance across nearby Keweenaw Bay. The scene looks like something you'd expect to find in a remote hollow of the Smokey Mountains.

The Hanka place in its prime, summer 1920. Never modernized, it has been restored to then. This drawing is from a satisfying book sold at the homestead that tells about the farm and the lives of the people who lived there.

The Hanka Farm
· SUMMER 1920 ·
· Askel Hill, Pelkie, Michigan ·

One mainstay of self-sufficient local economies like these was that neighbors traded and shared harvest work and other skills and products. The disabled father, Herman Hanka, tanned hides and made shoes for neighbors. His son Jalmar tinkered and fixed things. The family boarded logging horses, which needed intermittent rest between periods of strenuous work. Jalmar and his brother Nik, the farm manager, worked in logging camps in the winter, where their sister, Mary, cooked. One neighbor went to town every Saturday to shop for the neighborhood. People raised their own grains and vegetables, kept chickens and sometimes a pig. They depended on the Jersey cow and her rich milk for butter and cheese. And they hunted rabbits, partridges, and deer. Such a short growing season (an average of 85 frost-free days) made farmers focus on cold-resistant root crops like turnips, rutabagas, and potatoes. Preserving and preparing food took up an immense amount of time. Social life consisted of visiting, playing instruments (Nik played the kantele, a homemade Finnish guitar), and the weekly Saturday sauna. Occasional dances were held at a pavilion that stood near where the fire tower is.

Finland's shifting 19th-century economy had transformed many independent farmers into a class of industrial workers and landless tenants without opportunities. Only the oldest son could hope to farm his own land. Finns emigrated to the northern U.S., largely to work in mines. Inexperienced as miners, they did the lower-paying timber work. Between the peak emigration years of 1899 and 1914, over 200,000 Finns came to the U.S., largely from two rural counties, Vaasa and Oulu. On the edges of U.P. mining towns, miners farmed smaller plots to support their large families. It was a big step up from working in the dangerous mines to buy a 40-acre farm under the Homestead Act and become a full-time farmer.

Everything changed in the 1920s for farms like the Hankas'. New sanitation policies allowed the sale only of Grade A milk, which had to be produced and cooled under super-sanitary, refrigerated conditions. Grade B milk produced at farms like these could be sold only as cheese. Phone service in this remote neighborhood, unreliable to begin with, became so expensive that customers dropped it and lines were removed. Forests reclaimed many fields. Sons went into the army, saw a bigger world, and often ended up working in Detroit's auto factories, like Mary's son, Arvo. Detroit even had a Finnish neighborhood around Livernois and Six Mile. The emigrant children returned to the U. P. only to retire.

The Hanka farm stopped being improved in 1923, when Nik, its energetic manager, died. Gradually most of the Hankas died off, but easy-going Jalmar lived on until 1966. His needs were simple and he didn't have the ambition to modernize. The farm pretty much remained a time capsule of old Finnish folkways.

Scouts from Old World Wisconsin, an outdoor museum of pioneer ethnic farm buildings in southeastern Wisconsin, came up here to buy the barn and move it. But they were so impressed with the unaltered condition of the classic Finnish farm that they encouraged a local group to preserve it as a museum. (Call 414-594-2116 for details on visiting Old World Wisconsin.) Recently the Hanka Homestead has become a cooperating site of the Keweenaw National Historic Park.

The **tour** is strong on explaining the how-tos of a subsistence lifestyle: how fish were smoked in the sauna, which was then prepared for the family's bath; how rag rugs were woven on looms passed around the neighborhood; how grain and food were stored. A satisfying amount of information on the people who lived here is available to the patient reader in a somewhat tedious $6 book.

Here as everywhere, volunteers are in short supply. If you're lucky, your guide may be descended from nearby Finnish farmers, and thus able to talk about the farm from personal experience. If you're *not* lucky, you may get a politically correct lecture on the virtues of simplicity and cooperation from an outsider who won't admit that a good many people who grew up on farms like these rejected the hard life for the perceived advantages of modern living.

Demonstrations and **music** are featured on special days each year: on opening day, on Juhannus (St. John's Day, June 24, when Finns celebrate with bonfires), on Log Cabin Day the 4th Sunday in June, on the last Sunday in July, and on Ancestors Day, the 2nd Sunday in September, when people who grew up on Askel Hill come back.

On U.S. 41 about 10 miles north of Baraga, turn west onto Arnheim Road. As you pass the fire tower, continue straight onto the gravel

*(the blacktop turns west). Follow the gravel road left (east) to the
farm. Open from Memorial Day thru the 2nd weekend of October on
Tues, Thurs, Sat, and Sun from 12-4. Call (906) 353-7116 for tours
by appointment if scheduled times don't fit your travel plans. &: call.
$2/adults, $1/children.*

TO EXPERIENCE A WORKING FINNISH-AMERICAN DAIRY FARM TODAY . . .
. . stay at **Palosaari's Rolling Acres** (906-523-4947), a bed and breakfast on a
third-generation farm not far from the Hanka Homestead. The 1940s Cape Cod
farmhouse is a trim, efficient headquarters of the 200-acre farm. Cliff and Evy
Palosaari are no part-time hobby farmers but the real thing. They're also warm,
unpretentious hosts who enjoy sharing stories and philosophizing with their
guests. They have seven grown children. One helps run the farm and intends to
buy it from his father. The heavily mechanized operation milks three dozen cows;
a farm tour explains the equipment, from plows to combines and large round
balers. Evy, active in many farm organizations, is also an expert baker well
versed in the old Finnish ways.

PREPARE YOURSELF TO SLOW DOWN AND ENTER THE NATURAL WORLD
. . . . . by stopping at the **Sturgeon River Slough Natural Area** alongside U.S.
41 about 18 miles north of Baraga. The grueling drive to get to the Keweenaw
Peninsula can leave you spinning. This is a good spot to start unwinding on the
last leg of your trip. There's a **lookout tower** and **picnic tables** by the roadside
parking area. You could pick up a pasty and fresh fruit at the Keweenaw Berry
farm just south of here and have a picnic. The **De Vriendt Nature Trail,** with
interesting interpretive signs, makes a 1.75-mile loop through the slough, now a
nesting site for Canada geese, mallards, wood ducks, black ducks, and blue-
winged teal. The view of sweeping marshland and sky is relaxing. The slough
had been pastureland so wet it could only be farmed by horses. Now channeliza-
tion and flood control structures regulate the Sturgeon River to avoid spring
flooding. The slough of onetime farms is managed as a stopover spot for migrating waterfowl and a nesting spot. The aim is to increase the Upper Peninsula's
resident goose population for hunting.

AN EXCEPTIONAL GIFT SHOP AND HERB GREENHOUSE . . . . . where the
accent is on nature and regional crafts is **Einerlei** on Route 41 in Chassell. This
restful, resourceful place makes you want to slow down, enjoy your home, and
watch birds. It has grown into a handsome, rambling series of spaces that feature natural-fiber sweaters that look handknit ($35 and up), books on decorating
and gardening, a tabletop shop, and a kitchen shop with fancy foods The tightly
planned rear **garden** of herbs, perennials, and scented geraniums (all for sale)
centers on a **greenhouse** disguised as a summer house. Tea, coffee, and snacks
may be enjoyed inside or on the deck. *(906) 523-4612. Look for the green
awnings on the west side of U.S. 41 in the center of Chassell. Open year-round.
May-Dec: mon-Sat 9-6, Sun 11-5. Jan-April: Mon-Sat 10-5. &: no.*

Quincy Mine Hoist, Underground Mine, Tram

A Keweenaw landmark outside Hancock shows how far mining companies went to extract copper.

THIS HUGE hoist is the centerpiece for the U.P.'s best all-around underground mine tour. The entire tour lasts two hours. First it shows the giant hoist, a spool 60 feet high serving a huge pulley. It held 13,200 feet of 1 5/8" cable. Here visitors get an interesting overview of mining at this famous site. There's a surprising aesthetic power to mining machinery and structures like this hoist and the adjacent shafthouse.

Then tourgoers take the new visitor **tramway** down the steep Quincy hill to to the mine entrance in east Hancock. In the 1880s four such tramways transported copper ore from area mines to stamping mills on the Portage Canal in Ripley. The tram offers a **panoramic view** across the canal to Houghton, the Michigan Tech campus, and the surrounding countryside. The optional underground tour takes visitors into the seventh level of Shaft No. 5.

Articulate Michigan Tech engineering students are able to field all kinds of mining-related questions on many levels. Engineering buffs of all ages are likely to enjoy this tour immensely.

The tour shows what a big-time operation Keweenaw copper mining once was. The hoist was designed to haul a five-ton skip loaded with ten tons of ore at a speed of 36 mph from a depth of almost two miles. At the beginning and end of each shift, 30-person man cars replaced the rock skips, to take miners down into and out of the mines. An informative six-minute newsreel-type film shows poignant glimpses of the men as they take their seats to be plunged to a dark, hot, and dangerous place of work. Skips and man cars were lowered at the shafthouses. Their tall headframes held the pulley ropes and counterweights. Each shafthouse was served by its own hoist in an adjacent hoist house. Here at the headframe copper ore — millions of tons — was pulled up and dumped, then taken downhill by rail car to be purified in a stamping plant at Ripley on the Portage Canal.

The hoist only operated from 1920 to 1931, near the end of the Copper Country's heyday. The Quincy Mining Company had the resources to build this largest-ever steam-powered hoist because it had mined one billion pounds of copper since opening in 1856. The firm was nicknamed "Old Reliable" because it always paid dividends to stockholders. The Quincy No. 5 mine had already extracted copper down to over a mile beneath the surface when the giant hoist was installed. Mine managers hoped that a much deeper shaft would be dug. But worldwide competition finally made the mile-deep increasingly low-grade copper in this part of the Keweenaw too expensive to extract, though only 10% of it has been removed. Much cheaper open-pit mining today supplies worldwide demand. The once-booming peninsula began its decline in the early 1920s. This mine closed in 1931. Of its over 80 levels, groundwater has flooded them up through the teens.

Tourgoers walk into the mine's seventh level, 500 feet below the hilltop surface, through an adit in the hillside. Adits are horizontal tunnels used to drain water. Coasts and hard hats are provided in this drippy environment, a chilly 40°. Loose rock has been bolted to be safe. The area used to lose a miner a week due to rockfalls and cave-ins. Visitors pass a Michigan Tech underground classroom, little used now that only a few students a year study mining. Then they enter a stope, a high, scaffolded "room" dug out of the rock where copper deposits were found.

Be sure to allow time before or after the tour to see the interesting videos and exhibits in the hoist house, where the tour begins. Worthwhile displays in the hoist house include a sampling of beautiful minerals from the Seaman Museum (page 821), an exhibit on Native American use of Keweenaw Copper 7,000 years ago, a video on Keweenaw mining, and models of a copper mine and equipment. The Quincy Mine Hoist Association, a volunteer group of mining enthusiasts, has restored the hoist, hoist house, and No. 2 shafthouse.

Located 1 mile north of Hancock on U.S. 41. (906) 482-3101. Mid-May thru mid-Oct. Summer hours: 9:30-6, with last tour at 5:30. Call for limited spring & fall hours. &: call. Hoist & underground mine tour with tram ride: $12.50 adults, $7 ages 12 and under, infants free. Surface tour & tram ride: $6 adults, $3 children. Tram ride only: $3.50.

ANOTHER COPPER MINE FARTHER NORTH . . . . . near Copper Harbor, is the **Delaware Copper Mine**, in operation from 1847 to 1887. You descend just 110-feet into the main shaft during the 40-minute tour. You can also see evidence of prehistoric mining pits and the ruins of 19th-century mining buildings. The new Rustic Lantern Tour takes you still deeper into the mine (into the 3rd shaft) and lasts from 1 to 1 1/2 hours. For the Rustic Lantern tour, which is available only from mid-July thru Labor Day, you have to be in good shape — you descend 1,800 feet at a 24° angle without the aid of stairs. The regular tour of the 1st and 2nd shaft has 100 feet of stairs to descend/climb. *Take U.S. 41 to Delaware, 38 miles north of the Houghton-Hancock bridge. It's 12 miles south of Copper Harbor. (906) 289-4688. Self-guided tours only from Memorial Day to mid-June and Labor Day thru Oct.; open 10-5. Guided tours from mid-June thru Labor Day; open 10-6 with last tour at 5:15. &: call. Adults $7, children 6-12 $4, children under 6 free.*

STOCK UP ON PICNIC SUPPLIES . . . . . at the **Keweenaw Co-op** in Hancock. It's definitely the best specialty grocery on the peninsula, with good produce, cheese, local specialties (see below), Asian and Middle Eastern ingredients, even wine and a deli section with meat, in addition to the expected natural and bulk foods and gourmet specialty items. Stop by for trail mixes and quality deli items before heading out to Copper Harbor, and you'll be prepared for impromptu picnics. *As you drive north out of Hancock, U.S. 41 swings hard right at Santori's Tire. To get to the co-op, don't go right, go straight up onto Ethel. Co-op is in 2 blocks at Ethel and Ingot. (906) 482-2030. Mon-Sat 9-9, Sun 10-6. Close earlier sometimes in the winter. &*

DISTINCTIVE YOOPER FOODS . . . . . are a mark of strong regional identity, self-sufficient isolation, and the great distance from normal distribution channels. Some groceries and big supermarkets like Fraki's in Calumet (one street north of Fifth) have **"squeaky cheese"** (*juustoa*, a pleasantly sweetish, somewhat Jello-y fresh cheese), **saffron rolls** (light dinner rolls, a Cornish introduction, flavored and colored with brilliant yellow saffron with raisins added), and local Vollwerth's sausage. **Thimbleberry jam** is sold at houses along main tourist routes, and **pasties**, that famous Cornish meat-potato-rutabaga pie eaten by miners for lunch, are everywhere. **Trenary toast** is a twice-baked cinnamon toast made in Trenary, south of Marquette, and dunked in coffee. Great for camping — it keeps forever.

"KEWEENAW" IS OJIBWAY FOR . . . . . "place of the crossing," referring to a much-used shortcut bypassing the rocks and reefs at the peninsula's tip. Traveling west, Ojibway canoes went up the Portage River and across Portage Lake, then made a short portage near present-day McLain State Park. The Portage Canal was dug in the mid 19th-century for shipping from mines. The Houghton Lift Bridge between Houghton and Hancock was built in 1959.

DOWNTOWN HOUGHTON . . . . . along **Shelden Avenue** is distinctive and architecturally rich, a college town full of surprises to reward the perceptive pedestrian. Lavishly ornamented buildings from the mining boom climb a steep hillside; interconnecting walkways make it easy to go from store to store in winter. The balanced retail mix is unusual for the 1990s: more galleries and coffeehouses, but still a hardware store and clothing stores, even the old movies, at **The Lode Theater** (906-482-0280). ♿: *except toilets.* There's plenty of parking on decks entered north (toward the waterway) off Shelden or from the street below it. . . . . Here are some noteworthy businesses, arranged from west (the lift bridge) to east (Tech campus). **Motherlode** coffeehouse at 314 Shelden (906-487-JAVA) pulls a lot together: pastries and sandwiches from 7:30 a.m. (9 a.m. Sun) to 11 p.m. or later; Internet access; estate-grown, hand-selected coffees and drinks from 75¢ a cup; eclectic live music most nights (strong on alternative folk & blues) beginning at 8:30, and Keweenaw-based art from $50. Singer-songwriter Joe Lannom., a local favorite, plays Thursdays. ♿: *no.* . . . . Across at 315 Shelden, sculptor Peter Ex started **TOSH Gallery** (906-482-2287) two years ago after the art world temporarily hit the skids in the early 90s and his own nationwide gallery sales dwindled for a time. Its emphasis: upper-end art, inspired by the North Country, often spiritual, that "speaks to humankind's origins and destinies . . . and to our relationships with the environment." Expect variety, from nature images in wood engravings by internationally known Ladislav Hanka to local resident Ken Leino's whimsical, weird cedar ducks. Open Mon-Sat 10-6. ♿: *one step.* . . . . . At 417 Shelden is another coffeehouse, **Sub Urban Exchange**, with live music, a younger, more alternative focus, and its own recording studio. Call (906) 482-7162 for hours and music. ♿: *no.* . . . . Down Shelden at 503, **The Windigo** (906-482-9700) offers an ethereal mix of jewelry, gifts, children's books, textiles, pottery, engraved datolite and copper, and more. ♿ . . . . . At 515 Shelden, the expanded **Book World** (906-482-8192) is a general book shop with a good regional section. *Mon-Sat 9:30-9, Sun 10-4.* ♿. . . . . At **Marie's Deli** (906-482-8650), 519 Shelden, Marie Catrib chats as she makes delicious meat and spinach pies and salads of her native Lebanon, plus cheesecakes, other baked goods, and entrees, to eat in or take out. A rear dining area overlooks the Portage Waterway. *Mon-Fri 7 a.m.-8 p.m., Sat 8-5.* ♿ . . . . . Next door at 520, **Einerlei Up North** is a new offshoot of the popular Chassel store (p. 816). "Clean North Woods contemporary" is the look, in jewelry, apparel like Distant Drum Designs, blown glass, peeled cedar shelving, and other home and office accessories. *(906) 482-9911. Mon-Sat 10-6, Sun 11-5.* ♿ . . . . . **The Isle Royale National Park Visitor Center** is by the dock at 800 E. Lakeshore below the tall Franklin Square Inn east of downtown. (906) 482-0984. In the same building the Isle Royale Natural History Association has a small shop with books, maps, a few posters, etc., either about the park or about subjects pertaining to it, such as wolves, moose, field guides, and Indian culture. The shop donates to the park a welcome $18,000 a year. Open Mon-Sat 8-4:30, closed Sat in off-season. (906) 482-7860. . . . . Houghton's discount stores and mall are southwest of downtown up the hill on M-26. Here too are found **Down Wind Sports** (906-482-2500), with Patagonia and other backpacking and camping lines. *In New Sharon Center, 1/2 mile past bridge, on left. Open Mon-Sat 9:30 to 5 at least, Sun 12-4.* ♿ . . . . . In a stone-based barn .6 mile west of the bridge, **Shades of the Past** (906-482-

In a stone-based barn .6 mile west of the bridge, **Shades of the Past** (906-482-2765) is where Tech geology grad Karl Stubenvoll makes gold jewelry, simple or high-fashion, often with local stones. . . . . About one mile south of the Copper Country Mall in Atlantic Mine, **New World Books** (906-482-1243) has a wide range of books about women and about Native American spirituality in addition to tarot decks, crystals, and such. The shop is part of owner Glen Belkola's home. *656 Fire Lane. Look for the red mail box that says New World Books on the left side of M-26 about 2 mile south of Houghton, turn left, and continue for 1/4 mile. Open daily year-round from 11-9. ৬: no..*

ROCKHOUNDS WILL BE DAZZLED . . . . . by the gorgeous displays at the **A.E. Seaman Mineral Museum** at Michigan Technological University, founded as Michigan's mining college. In 1990 an act of the state legislature made this the official mineralogical museum of Michigan. Highlights of its extensive collection include a complete collection of specimens from the mineral-rich Upper Peninsula, a cave of iron ores, and dramatic fluorescent minerals displayed under black light. Recent additions to the museum are the exhibit of unusual crystallized silver and gold, and the Lake Superior gemstones exhibit including datolites, Thompsonites, agates, and greenstones (Michigan's official gemstone, usually found on Isle Royale). *The campus is a mile east of downtown. 1400 Townsend Dr., on the 5th floor of the EERC building (adjacent to the university library and to parking Lot 5) on the Michigan Tech campus. (906) 487-2572. Metered parking available within 1 block of museum; on Sat you may park in Lot 5. Open year-round Mon-Fri 9-4:30; May 1 to Nov. 1, also open Sat. 12-4. ৬ 13 and over, $3, seniors 55 and over $2, 12 and under free.*

HANCOCK, JUST NORTH OF THE LIFT BRIDGE . . . . . once had an important shopping district in the center of the large Finnish community. The beautiful houses just east of the lift bridge were largely built by Cornish mining captains. . . . . Eclipsed by Houghton, lately downtown Hancock is coming back some. It's the home of the **Copper Country Community Arts Council** (906-482-2333) with its large gallery and studios. Stop by at 126 Quincy for the busy arts calendar. ৬ . . . . . Next block over at 208 Quincy is the classy **FinPro** Finnish imports shop, showcasing beautiful textiles, jewelry, and glassware. Its new **eat-in bakery** offers Finnish specialty breads, breakfast treats, tarts, and cookies. *(906) 482-9202. Open Mon-Fri 10-5:30, Sat to 4, and somesummer Sundays. ৬ . . . . .* **Suomi College**, the only Finnish-American college, has a beautiful new **Finnish Heritage Center** (906-487-7367) at 601 Quincy with an extensive historical archive. **Changing exhibits** of Finnish, Finnish-American, and regional artists, and occasional special events, are worth checking out. Open 9-4 weekdays. ৬ . . . . . In 1995 a Hancock laundromat made national news with a widely reported story about the arrest of a naked accordionist playing with friends in the wee hours. It sounded like a variant on Finnish *sisu*, but in fact the accordionist was a Tech student from a Mediterranean country. His friends danced in their underwear. It was just more natural to play accordion with no clothes, he explained. Later he gave clothed performances to raise money to pay his court fine.

Calumet and Laurium

*The past lives on in multi-ethnic Copper Country —
once a rollicking boom region bustling night and day.*

DURING THE COPPER BOOM in the early 1900s, the scene on Calumet's main street was more like a leading metropolis than a remote mining town. It had brick streets, movie theaters, a grand opera house, frequent trollies, electric lights, and impressive four-story buildings of brick and sandstone. Evenings were as bright and busy as daytime, because miners worked round-the-clock shifts and there was so much money to be spent.

The Keweenaw's booming copper mines had recruited workers from most parts of Europe. Many languages could be heard on the streets: Finnish, Italian, Croatian, Slovenian, French, Polish, Yiddish, German, Swedish, Norwegian, Greek, English (spoken in Cornish, Irish, and Scottish accents), Gaelic, and Welsh. Each major ethnic group had its saloons, over 70 in all, where outsiders dared not venture as the evening wore on. And virtually every nationality had its church, many of them magnificent, paid for in part by the Boston-based Calumet and Hecla mining company.

Starting in the 1870s, the copper mines around Calumet (then known as Red Jacket) proved the most profitable the world has known. Copper was an increasingly vital component used in the booming electrical and plumbing industries of a rapidly modernizing world. In those days the Keweenaw had the biggest copper mines anywhere.

The **Calumet and Hecla Mining Company** was the richest and biggest mining company of them all. Its striking Victorian **office building** (1898) also incorporated a library for community use. Contrasting irregular stones of red and gray face the large office, designed by a Boston architect related to the mine's principal investor, Quincy Adams Shaw. It is on Red Jacket Road, just west of U.S. 41 by the turnoff to Calumet. Today the office is home to the **Lake Superior Land Company** (906-337-0202), now part of Champion Paper, which owns the mining company's land. This is not a tourist spot. But it *is* interesting, and it's open to the public during business hours.

Despite the changes in ownership, the interior of these once nationally famous offices remains very much as it must have looked when Calumet and Hecla reigned supreme in these parts.

The varnished interior trim has never been painted or refinished. There are classic oak desks and map cases, cases of mineral specimens, and a big oil **portrait of Alexander Agassiz**, son of the famed Harvard botanist. Though he would rather have devoted himself full-time to the study of botany, Agassiz was persuaded to spend his most productive decades managing Calumet and Hecla in absentia. The company's Bostonian paternalism was widely resented here as controlling and condescending.

East of the office building is a big piece of "**float copper**," pure copper formed in pockets created by volcanic bubbles. Outside is a seated bronze **statue of Agassiz.** He has a cold, analytical gaze that changes unsettlingly as you shift your point of view.

Calumet and Hecla sold its mines and land to Universal Oil Products. A 1968 strike closed the long-declining mines altogether. Later Universal sold its property, which includes most of Keweenaw County, to Lake Superior Land. Champion Paper bought Lake Superior Land in 1996. The firm leases land for mineral rights, logging, and recreation; develops it, and sells it, sometimes in small lakefront lots. The Upper Peninsula's vast mining and timber lands are open to the public for hiking, hunting, and other forms of recreation, in exchange for favorable tax rates.

Today Calumet and its more genteel sister community of Laurium are shadows of what they were in the decade after 1910, when 40,000 people

Finns, Italians, Poles, Swedes, Norwegians, Croatians, French-Canadians, Russian Jews, Greeks — substantial numbers of most major American immigrant groups circa 1900 found their way to the Keweenaw Peninsula, either as mine workers or as small businesspeople catering to miners. Traces of mining are everywhere, from rusted headframes that dot the landscape to the stories of miners and their descendants.

lived in the area. Calumet now numbers 800, Laurium 2,200. After decades of decline, the population is now increasing.

The glorious, boisterous past is felt everywhere, but muted by the years, and by the simple lifestyle of local residents. They're a special breed. They include people who have hung on after the mines finally shut down in 1968; old-timers who have come back to retire; grown-up kids who came to love the area from visiting grandparents or attending Michigan Tech; and the nature-lovers, old hippies, New Agers, and Michigan Tech faculty who have moved to these towns 12 miles north of Houghton. As the heartland for hundreds of far-flung Finnish-Americans, Copper Country attracts quite a variety of Finns, from nature-loving urbanites to fundamentalist adherents of the Finnish Apostolic Church. Ask about where summer vacationers are from, and you'll discover over half of them have Copper Country roots two or three generations back.

There is an island atmosphere about this isolated place, akin to the gentle, faded mood of declining mining boom towns of the West, which are also populated by old hippies, artists, and retired miners. There remain many splendid red brick and red sandstone buildings of the boom years at the turn of the last century. Many have been preserved by local pride and by the complete absence of development pressure since Keweenaw copper mining first began to sour after World War I.

The people remain, too, hanging on to memories and to occasional lingering dreams that some day, when the world price of copper rises high enough, the mining companies will pump and drain off the water that has filled up the mines, reopen them, and tunnel farther south along the Keweenaw vein where much copper still lies deeply buried and untapped. (The Centennial Mine in nearby Kearsarge did reopen in 1990, but more as an adjunct to the timber industry. Its copper is used in a nearby facility that makes Wolmanized lumber.)

In 1992 the **Keweenaw National Historical Park** was established, modeled after the historic urban industrial park in Lowell, Massachusetts. Interim boundaries include historic landmarks in Calumet, plus the Quincy Hoist and the Quincy Smelter in Ripley. National Parks signs mark various park components, but nothing else has been funded. Development will take place over the next 15 years or so.

In the meantime, Copper Country is a proud backwater. "Living up here is like living in the 1950s," says Lake Linden's dentist, who likes to boast that he has the lowest income and best lifestyle of anyone in his University of Michigan dental school class. "The old

Splendid architecture, beautifully
detailed and still earthy in red
Jacobsville sandstone, is the
legacy of mining wealth of the
Keweenaw Peninsula and nearby
Marquette. The 1900 Calumet
Theater (here) can be toured in
July and August.

values are important. Most
people are honest. But you
have to make your own activities — there's not much
entertainment here. A lot of
newcomers don't understand
that." Michigan Tech has
trouble keeping faculty
whose wives love to shop.

It especially helps to have
a local map in looking around
Calumet and Laurium
because they are really collections of smaller communities, known as
"locations," consisting of miners' houses clustered around onetime
mine shafts: Tamarack, Centennial, Osceola, Red Jacket. Here miners (especially Scandinavians) kept milk cows and chickens and big
gardens out back, to help feed their large families and make ends
meet. The mining companies built these standard, six-room houses;
today they sell for around $20,000. Laurium has neighborhoods of
more substantial houses for managers and white-collar workers.

THINGS TO SEE IN CALUMET

◆ The handsome red sandstone **Calumet Theater**, was built in
1900 and paid for by taxes on Calumet's busy saloons. **Tours** are
held in the summer and fall. The interior has been faithfully
restored to its original rich colors of gilt, red, green, and cream. The
old theater still creaks enough to seem truly historic. You get to
visit the dizzying upper balcony and antiquated lights still in place.
When you get to the backstage dressing room used by Sarah
Bernhardt, among others, it's not hard to imagine the grueling life
of train travel that took the likes of John Philip Sousa and Douglas
Fairbanks to such remote corners of the country. Today many
kinds of events are held here, including local theater; visiting foreign bands and dance troupes; a country music series sponsored

by a local radio station; and the Detroit Symphony Orchestra. *Elm and Sixth. Call (906) 337-2610 for information. The 40-minute tours, beginning in early summer and running through color season, are from 10-4 on weekdays and 1-4 on weekend. Box office is open Tues-Sat, from 10-4 in the summer and 2-6 in the winter. &: main floor is barrier free but half the tour is not. $3 adults, $1.50 kids under 12, discounts for large groups .*

◆ Next to the theater at 322 Sixth, the landmark **Shute's 1890 Bar** has reopened and become a popular gathering spot. It still has the magnificent original back bar and all the trappings of boom-town saloons. The bar itself has a splendid stained-glass canopy with vines. Elaborate plaster caryatids frame the raised dance floor. The new owner's restoration has won high praise.

◆ **The Upper peninsula Firefighters' Memorial Museum** has filled the historic Red Jacket fire station with exhibits and memorabilia. *Sixth St. across from the Calumet Theater. No phone. Approximate season: early June into early October. Mon-Sat 10-2:30. &: ground level only. $2 adults, $1 ages 13-18, 12 and under free.*

◆ Near Seventh and Elm, a memorial park marks the site of the 1913 **Italian hall disaster**. At the Italian social hall's Christmas party, during the fifth month of a bitter mining strike, someone yelled, "Fire," and 73 people, mostly children, died, trampled and smothered, in a stairwell whose doors opened inward. Woody Guthrie's moving song blamed mining bosses for the unsolved deed. The hall was used for decades until it was demolished in 1964.

◆ Two blocks south, on Sixth at Portland, the **post office** has a dramatic W.P.A. mural of broad-backed miners at work deep within the earth.

◆ Retailing in Calumet isn't much any more. There's just not much money or enough visitors here, and it's too easy for local people to go to Houghton. Two visitor-oriented stores are neighbors on Fifth at Portland, as you enter downtown from Red Jacket Road. The selection of copper items here is tremendous, and prices are lower on similar things than in Copper Harbor. Items range from copper teapots, plates, and molds to burnished sailboats and copper jewelry. At **Copper World**, 101 Fifth (906-337-4016) second-generation owner Tony Bausano has added an excellent selection of videos and books about the region and about mining; a video monitor lets you preview videos. & Fifth-generation **Herman Jewelers** at 220 Fifth (906-337-2703) has more native agate and gemstone jewelry along with copper giftware. &: *no.*

◆ **Cross Country Sports** is run by Rick Oikarinen and a crew of avid mountain hikers and cross-country skiers who helped develop the Swedetown Trails. They are happy to give visitors specifics on the area's fabulous mountain biking and skiing. *Down town at 506 Oak between 5th and 6th. (906) 337-4520. Open Mon-Fri 9:30-6, Sat to 5. &: no.*

◆ **St. Anne's Roman Catholic Church,** a 1900 Gothic church built for French-Canadian immigrants, is the future home of the **Ethnic Embassy Religious Heritage Center** and **Children's Embassy for Peaceful Living**, a local council of churches project. It's in a cluster of impressive churches at the entrance to Calumet. Visitors are welcome to look in at renovations through plexiglass. Interior furnishings were removed years ago when the archdiocese first sold the church. *SW corner of Scott and Fifth Streets at Red Jacket Road.*

◆ Summer tours of the unusually elaborate **St. Paul the Apostle** church let you see the beautiful stained glass windows, altar, and paintings. Slovenian Catholics built it between 1903 and 1908. In her monumental *Buildings of Michigan,* architectural historian Kathryn Eckert calls it "a double-spired Richardsonian red sandstone extravaganza. . . . which rises authoritatively over the village like a cathedral of medieval Europe." Go north on Eighth from here and you'll be in Calumet's most attractive residential district. *Eighth and Oak. (906) 337-2044. The church is generally open as early as 7 a.m.; during summer, parishioners serve as guides from noon-3. &: no. No charge; donations appreciated.*

◆ **Coppertown**. This museum doesn't currently begin to approach the quality of the State of Michigan's iron-mining museum near Negaunee, but it does focus on copper mining and show how Calumet and Hecla produced usable copper from copper-bearing rock. Lots of mining equipment, old and new: drills, lamps, carts, and much more. *On Red Jacket Rd. between U.S. 41 and Calumet. (906) 337-4354. Open mid-June through Sept. Mon-Sat 10-4. Adults $3, children 12 & under free. Coppertown offers* **Calumet historic trolley rides**, *a 1-hour narrated tour along Fifth Street, Calumet's main street. Daily July through September, trolleys may leave Coppertown on the hour; adults $4, children $2. &: museum yes, trolley no.*

◆ The beautiful **Swedetown Ski Trails**, six miles of cross-country trails, wind through small, rolling hills. They're groomed for traditional cross-country and ski-skating, and they're skiable well into April, after the snow cover has melted on south-facing slopes up here.

LAURIUM

◆ Neighboring Laurium shows off Copper Country's more gracious side. Time has not been kind to the historic downtown along Hecla. But just east of it, along Tamarack, Pewabic, and Iroquois between Second and Fourth, is a lovely, settled, neighborhood of turn-of-the-century homes, built with style and comfort to compensate mine managers for the hardships of having to live in this remote place. Some houses are quite grand, with rear carriage houses, sweeping stairways, stained-glass windows, and low red sandstone walls along the street; some are merely pleasant. Yards feature flower gardens, very long wood piles, and occasional shrines to the Blessed Virgin. Deep maple shade sets this part of Laurium apart from the sparse streetscapes of miners' homes. *To get to Laurium from U.S. 41, turn southeast onto Lake Linden Rd. (M-26) at the visitor center, or at Third St. or School St.*

Laurium Manor, a bed and breakfast inn occupies a mining magnate's 41-room neoclassical revival mansion, now being restored to its original magnificence after being stripped of its fixtures by an earlier owner. Its enthusiastic young innkeeper-owners, Tech alums, raise extra funds with worthwhile tours. *320 Tamarack. (906) 337-2549. Guided tours daily June through October at noon, 1, 2, and 3; $4 adults, $2 children. Self-guided tours November through May; $3 adults, $2 children. Call first for self-guided tours to make sure someone is there. &: no.*

At Third and Pewabic, there's a corner **park** with a **band shell**, where Thursday-evening summer concerts take place at 7 o'clock. You can get a good Jilbert's ice cream cone for your walk through historic Laurium at the **Honey Cone**, 224 Hecla at Depot. For a takeout picnic in the park, you can pick up pasties at **Toni's Country Kitchen**, nearby on Third at Kearsarge. It's reputed to have the best pasties around.

◆ **Jukuri's Sauna** is one of three public saunas left in the U.P. (Lots of homes have saunas out back, or inside the main house.) This plain tile building has 12 private, gas-fired saunas. They're fired up three days a week. For many families, a relaxing visit to Jukuri's is a Saturday-night tradition, especially in mid-winter. (No one wears swimsuits, but men and women usually bathe separately.) Eating and unwinding is part of the event, and a big selection of junk food is sold in the pine-paneled foyer along with Jukuri's sweatshirts and T-shirts. *Wed & Fri 2-10 p.m., Sat noon-10. 600 Lake Linden Rd. (M-26). (906) 337-4145. &: no. $4 per person for private unit (45 minutes), under 12 free with parents.*

THE BEST DISPLAY OF COPPER-MINING HISTORY TODAY . . . . . is in
Lansing in the **State Historical Museum** (see page 426). Its **mining exhibits**
include a life-size recreated passage within a copper mine. Currently it covers
copper-mining far better than anything you'll find on location, although the
establishment of the **Keweenaw National Historical Park** may change that.

GOING DOWN TO LAKE LINDEN . . . . . from Laurium on M-26 is a spectacularly steep and scenic drive, because you're descending along the flat but tilted
top of the of volcanic crust along the fault line that carries the vein of copper. . . .
The **Douglass Houghton Falls** drop over the sheer cliffs of this edge. From M-26
about 1 1/2 miles southeast of the outskirts of Laurium, look for a flat dirt parking area to the left (northeast) side of the road. A path along the hilltop offers
splendid views and the pleasant sound of Hammell Creek plashing between
grassy banks. Then the creek disappears. Suddenly, without warning signs, a
canyon opens up before you, dangerous and dramatic, and you see the creek
rushing over rocks, then down to the canyon floor far below. There's no railing at
all; this worthwhile adventure is no jaunt for rambunctious children. . . . . **Lake
Linden** is a French-Canadian town built alongside the Calumet and Hecla
stamping mills. C&H's great innovation was to develop a process that utilized
small amounts of copper deposits carried by much of the area's rock, and not
just the pure pockets of "float copper" formed in volcanic gas bubbles. C & H
carried quantities of copper-bearing rock by narrow-gauge railway down to Lake
Linden on Torch Lake. There the rocks were crushed and the metal smelted out
of the rock. The onetime C&H office and medical dispensary now houses the collections of the **Houghton County Historical Museum**. *On M-26 south of downtown. (906) 296-4121. Open early June thru mid October, Mon-Sat 10-4:30, Sun
12-4.* &: *1st floor only. Adults $3, ages 12-21 $2, children 6 to 12 $1, children
under 6 free.* . . . . . The **Lindell Chocolate Shoppe** in downtown Lake Linden is
an elaborate sweet shoppe from the 1920s, the glory days of that restaurant
genre. Quick lunch counters and soda fountains like this thrived in newly industrialized areas, where workers had cash for inexpensive treats. Italian and especially Greek immigrants latched onto the sweet shoppe as a business opportunity where the whole family could work, making hand-dipped chocolates and
ice cream, and where it didn't matter if their English was rudimentary. Here the
Greek owners' names, Grammas and Pallis, are proudly spelled out in tiles on
the entryway. Inside, the marble counter on the soda fountain has given way to
Formica, but the back booths and paneling are perfectly preserved. The interior
is all aglow with golden oak, accented with little fringed lamps. The food is ordinary lunch-counter fare. *300 Calumet. (906) 296-0793. Hours are Mon-Sat from
6:30 a.m. to 7 p.m.* &: *no.*

M-26 from Phoenix
to Copper Harbor

Something like Maine, something like Scandinavia —
great natural beauty without any pretensions

ABOUT 15 MILES north of Calumet begins one of the most idyllic and undeveloped landscapes in the United States. From Eagle River to Copper Harbor, the Lake Superior shoreline looks a lot like Maine — only without the summer crowds. Rocky shores and islets are interrupted by occasional crescent bays and beaches — some sandy, some rocky. Few summer houses block the shoreline view from M-26. Frequent roadside parks have benches, picnic tables, and occasional gazebos. Tidy rustic signs hanging from brown cedar posts point out historic and scenic highlights. On the opposite side of the road, trails climb into ferny-floored forests of pine, balsam, and hardwoods. Here, and on cutover sunny areas of birch and aspen, the landscape looks amazingly like Scandinavia. Thimbleberry bushes with velvety, maple-like leaves and bright red berries border many roads and cover open woods; occasional houses advertise "THIMBLEBERRY JAM FOR SALE." The intensely-flavored spread is locally prized.

Every few miles a sign points out the path to a waterfall, formed as short creeks and rivers come cascading down to Lake Superior from the peninsula's high spine. Past Eagle Harbor, you can choose to drive along the lovely shore. Or you can take the famous Brockway Mountain Drive (page 838) up to a spectacular panoramic view of the shoreline and inland lakes that leaves you feeling you're floating above Earth's surface in a balloon.

Driving out from Calumet on U.S. 41, you follow a high ridge and fault line that forms the spine of the Keweenaw Peninsula. The ridge is marked by a string of spare, plain mining settlements — Kearsarge, Allouez, Ahmeek, Mohawk, Phoenix, Delaware — that stretch much of the way to Copper Harbor. Here the ancient, mineral-rich volcanic crust, part of the Canadian Shield, tilts northwest down into Lake Superior. The ridge is the crust's edge. At the hamlet of Cliff, it becomes a dramatic, sheer rocky precipice. The ridge looms over the Eagle River, which cuts through the Cliff Range at Phoenix and tumbles down to Lake Superior. At Phoenix M-26 turns northwest off U.S. 41 and takes the scenic route along the Eagle River and Lake Superior shore to Copper Harbor.

Waves crash against the rocks below the lighthouse at Eagle Harbor. Its museum and picnic area are a fine place to linger.

From here to the Keweenaw's tip at Copper Harbor, copper deposits were closer to the surface, and in smaller amounts. Mining boomed early, in the 1840s, and played out soon. All of Keweenaw County, from Allouez and Mohawk to Copper Harbor, numbers under 2,000 year-round residents.

In 1844, the Cliff Mine became the Keweenaw's first mine to strike it rich and earn big profits. It and nearby mining villages and shipping ports toward the Keweenaw's tip are the oldest European settlements in the western Upper Peninsula. Many houses and churches date from well before the Civil War and the ensuing industrial boom. They're simple frame buildings — sometimes you even see log houses — without any of the opulence of late 19th-century buildings in Calumet or Laurium, Houghton, or Marquette, with their sandstone ornament and stained glass.

Plan on stopping for a picnic along the way, perhaps in a secluded spot on the beach or in the woods, or in one of the two delightful little parks overlooking Lake Superior between Eagle Harbor and Copper Harbor. For best selection of fresh fruit and deli salads, you might want to plan ahead and stop at the food co-op in Hancock (page819) or the big supermarket in Calumet. Otherwise, there's a decent little grocery in Mohawk, simple general stores in Phoenix, Eagle Harbor, and Copper Harbor, and bakeries in and near Copper Harbor.

Here are some interesting stops along M-26 between Calumet and Copper Harbor:

♦ **Superior Crafts** in Mohawk. Resourceful locals make cedar rus-

tics, classic outdoor furniture and lawn swings, in a former mine
building, the "dry" where 300 to 400 miners used to clean up and
change clothes. Signs about mine safety precautions are still on the
walls. Furniture is boxed partly-assembled for convenient transportation. *On U.S. 41 just before you reach town. (906) 337-0875.
Mon-Fri 8-5, Sat 8-1.* ᕒ: *no.*

◆ **The Keweenaw Handcrafts Shop** and the **snow gauge** just north
of Ahmeek mark the entrance to Keweenaw County. The county is
full of charming W.P.A. relief projects from the 1930s like these.
Relief projects were widespread because of Keweenaw County's 85%
unemployment rate during the Depression. The shop, now run by
the Community Action Agency, sells things made by 181 craftspeople, from children to seniors, in three counties. Among the ordinary
dolls and kit crafts are some attractive, reasonably priced traditional crafts like rag rugs ($23 for a 55" rug) and handmade children's
sweaters under $20. *(906) 337-5737. Open daily Memorial Day thru
mid-October. Hours are 12-5 to July 1 and 11-5 thereafter.* ᕒ: *one
step.* The much-photographed **snow gauge** records annual cumulative snowfall, often 250 inches. Because the accumulated snow
continually compacts and melts, there's rarely more than five feet at
a time, except in drifts. (Snow removal is a major priority of local
government. Residents don't usually have to wait long for the snow
plow to come, but it's understood that all winter engagements are
tentative, depending on the weather.)

◆ In **Phoenix**, stop at the **picnic
table** by the **Church of the
Assumption** and take in the view of
river valley and rocky cliffs, the most
dramatic evidence of the Keweenaw
fault. The simple wood church was
built in 1858 to serve miners at the
Cliff mines. *On U.S. 41 near M-26
junction. Viewable by visitors from
mid-June through Sept, daily 12-5.
Donations welcome.*

◆ **Eagle River**, founded as a copper-shipping port in 1843, was
named after the many eagles soaring overhead. Now a summer
place with a tiny year-round population, it has several interesting
sights the hurried motorist might miss. On M-26 south of the village, the worn monuments in the rustic **Eagle River Cemetery**
attest to the many dangers and accidents that cut short miners'
lives. As you pass over the bridge across the **Eagle River gorge**,
pull over to the right, go over onto the old iron bridge, and look

upstream for a view of rushing rapids, the ruined dam of the Lake Superior Fuse Company, and the dramatic wood arches supporting the new bridge.

Turning left just past the river leads down to the sandy beach, passing the simple frame **Eagle River Store** near M-26. It has changed little since it was built to serve miners in 1867. New Owners Jack and Carol Treganowan share their Cornish heritage by offering books, tapes, souvenirs, and homemade saffron bread and tea biscuits in addition to ice cream cones, groceries, and sundries. *(906) 337-1392. Open Mem. Day-color season, daily 10-9.* &: *no.* On the beach, **Fitzgerald's** is a lively restaurant in a motel.

Douglas Houghton, Michigan's state geologist, first drew attention to the Upper Peninsula's mineral riches. He drowned off the shore of Eagle River after he ignored the recommendations of his French and Indian guides and continued their canoe expedition in a storm. The **Houghton monument** by M-26 is boring. Much more interesting is a visit to the **Keweenaw County courthouse**, on the upper road that branches off to the right as you cross the bridge. It looks like a frame Southern mansion, with massive columns and portico. Inside, you can get a good **map** of county highways and byways. Government in this tiny county is an exercise in small-scale thrift and ingenuity. The jail next door, behind the sheriff's pleasant frame house, was temporarily closed for remodeling to bring it up to code so that the tiny county will no longer be urged to pay for transporting prisoners considerable distances and jailing them at approved facilities. One thing that hasn't changed is that prisoners still eat good food prepared by the sheriff's wife for family and staff.

◆ **Sand Dunes Drive** is the name of the beautiful eight-mile stretch of M-26 between Eagle River and Eagle Harbor. It parallels the sandy beach of the **Great Sand Bay**. Frequent pullovers encourage motorists to get out and take a swim or walk down the beach. The tilted shelf of volcanic crust drops off so rapidly under water, that the bay is 1,300 feet deep. On the opposite side of the road is the steep, dark, rocky forest, carpeted in pine needles.

Delightful **Jacob's Falls** cascades right near the road, 2 1/2 miles east of Eagle River. Next to the scenic pullout, tucked away in the piney hillside, is **The Jam Pot**. This memorably quaint little spot has the sweet simplicity of an earlier, gentler, more personal era of tourism. To this idyllic spot three monks (yes, monks — complete with hooded brown robes) have withdrawn from the world and their native city of far-away Detroit, to establish the Society of St. John, recently affiliated with the Eastern Orthodox church. They

Brother Peter in front of The Jampot bakery by Jacob's Falls. Just one of its muffin makes a satisfying lunch.

bake very good muffins, breads, cookies, brownies, and giant chocolate chip cookies, along with rich rum cakes, largely sold mail-order. And they make jams and butters from a big variety of local berries — apple-plum butter, wild bilberry, strawberry, and more. (A continuing stream of publicity has, alas, necessitated a large new parking lot which does spoil the tucked-away mystique.)

The pumpkin muffin, full of raisins and nuts and iced with lemon frosting, wins raves for its flavor and texture. Just one makes a good lunch. The cakes — things like walnut ginger cake, lemon pound cake, the Abbey Cake, rich with walnuts, raisins, molasses, and bourbon — are quite elaborate and costly. Order forms are sent in back of a newsletter filled with prayers, scripture, meditations, and reflections. An excerpt: "When we hear the comment at The Jampot, 'Well, you certainly do live in God's country,' we are likely to respond, 'Everywhere is God's country.' If we are feeling talkative, we may also add, 'But it is easier to see Him in some places than in others.'" *Open Mon-Sat 10-6 May through fall color season in early Oct. No phone. Mailing address: The Society of St. John, Star Route 1, Box 226, Eagle Harbor, MI 49950.*

◆ **Eagle Harbor** is a quaint collection of ancient frame houses and newish cottages. They surround a shallow, protected harbor and **beach** that's one of Lake Superior's most reliably warm places to swim. It's the prettiest village in the northern Keweenaw, with just enough attractions to make it a lazily interesting place to stay: two good, homey restaurants with pie and takeout sandwiches for a picnic, easy access to Brockway Mountain Drive and other excursions, and two delightful local museums run by the Keweenaw Historical

Society, an energetic group of old-timers and summer people. The protected, shallow **beach** at the harbor is pleasantly warm for Lake Superior. Unfortunately jet-skis belonging to some summer people are a noisy intrusion. (Jet-skis generally haven't caught on here where summer is so short and the big lake so cold.)

The **Eagle Harbor Lighthouse and Museums** survey the harbor entrance. The picturesque brick lighthouse, built in 1871, is realistically furnished circa 1910-1920. Outside are **picnic tables** on a sunny, rocky promontory. An **overlook platform** has a grand view of the rocks. You could spend rainy hours looking at all the stuff in the museum next door: a mineral collection, paintings of local scenes, and a fine exhibit on the Keweenaw's prehistoric copper culture.

A separate **maritime museum** building covers shipwrecks and fishing in great detail. Another building deals with surveying, smelting, and mining. Many exhibits are dense reading, too much for casual visitors. But the museum is the best single place on the Keweenaw to assemble an overview of the area's history. *Follow signs from M-26 to lighthouse/museum. Open daily, mid-June thru Sept, 12-5. $1/person. &: no.*

The simple, one-room Rathbone School House has been preserved as the birthplace of the **Knights of Pythias** secret fraternal society. Eagle Harbor's schoolteacher, Justus Rathbone, dreamed up the rituals here and founded the order in 1864. The Knights' elaborate ritual costumes are in the **Rathbone School House** on a side street southeast of M-26 on the village's west side. The order's ceremonies, based on the Roman story of the friendship of Damon and Pythias, celebrate the virtues of brotherly friendship and self-sacrifice. Displays include some fabulous fake jewels and embroidered satin robes.The Knights' mock-Roman tunics are decorated with hundreds of metal discs. *Two blocks west of the harbor on Center, or one block south of St. Peter's-by-the Sea on M-26. Open daily 12-5, mid-June through September. &: no. Donations welcome.*

Leaving Eagle Harbor on M-26, look for the sign to North Wind Books out on Marina Road. A charming stucco cottage from 1912 is now a personal bookshop focusing on literature, history, and nature of the Great Lakes and upper Midwest, along with some well-chosen vacation reading, antique copper, and collectibles — chiefly Staffordshire transfer ware transferred off copper etchings. Saturdays in July and August various **authors** talk about their work from 10:30 to noon, and children's **storytimes** are Tuesdays at 10:30. *(906) 289-4911. Open May thru Xmas. Weekends in May. Mem. Day thru Oct: Tues-Sat 10-5, Sun & Mon 1-5. Nov & Dec: Tues-Sat 11-4, Sun & Mon 1-4. &: no.*

Rustic-style mileposts and directional signs are deployed throughout Keweenaw County. A Keweenaw County Road Commission employee cuts down replacement cedar posts in frozen swamps. In winter the signs are taken in and repainted. The picturesque signs, the lack of billboards, and the vast stretches of undeveloped land make much of the county seem like a vast park.

◆ From **Eagle Harbor to Copper Harbor**, the view along 14 miles of lakeshore drive is the Keweenaw's rockiest and most dramatic stretch of shoreline. Four and a half miles east of Eagle Harbor, a roadside sign indicates **Silver River Falls**. By all means take the easy path through an overarching woods, both leafy and pleasantly piney. You'll hear and soon see the sparkling little river descending from a stone-arched bridge. Alternately it spreads out over rocky terraces and rests in a series of pools.

Across the river, **Brockway Mountain Drive** (page 838) climbs 600 feet to one of the most spectacular views you're likely to see. Save it for an excursion from Copper Harbor, and stay on M-26. Soon you'll come to **Esrey Park**, with picnic tables and grills, where stone steps go up to a rocky perch and a rustic gazebo. Just west of the park is a Michigan Nature Association preserve. Look for the small signs that say "protected area." Across the road is a posted **hiking trail** through a magically mossy forest.

In a few miles, the road runs right beside a place where big, bare slabs of ancient volcanic crust tilt right into Lake Superior. A wide shoulder lets you get out and explore the rocks and the tiny lichen, tough little flowers and stunted trees that find sustenance in cracks in these rocks. Six miles east of here, **Hebard Park** is another simple little park with picnic tables, grills, outhouses, and wonderful view.

Three more miles and you come to the village of **Copper Harbor**, Keweenaw County's tourism hub.

"ONE CANNOT FEEL HISTORY FROM THE AUTOMOBILE," . . . . . advises a fine little free historical guide put out by the Keweenaw Historical Society, "so take leisurely walks through our old and abandoned villages, around mine sites and historic landmarks, allowing time to reflect upon those who have gone before. Your visit will be greatly enriched at no cost."

THE LOW-KEY CHARMS OF THE KEWEENAW'S EAST SHORE . . . . . Often when the scenic rugged, west-facing side of the peninsula is cloudy, the lower east side, protected by the high central ridge, is sunny. It's completely flat, and once you get away from the towns along Dollar Bay, there's virtually no traffic, which makes for wonderful, easy **bicycling**. People from Keweenaw towns and cities have their "camps" for fishing and hunting up here ("cottage" is too sedate a term) but there's little resort activity. . . . . From Mohawk, turn east from M-26 toward the town of Gay. At the **Gay Bar**, a typical Yooper bar, you can get a Gay Bar T-shirt, subtitled "Gay, Mich." . . . . . The scenic **shoreline drive** beginning at Gay passes many marshes, and shore birds are frequently seen. Wild blueberries can be picked from the road during most of August. . . . . There's a **roadside park** at Betsy Bay 7 miles northeast of Gay. Way across Keweenaw Bay, the Huron Mountains (the highest elevations in Michigan) beckon blue in the distance. . . . . The best swimming is almost 20 miles farther, at **Bete Grise** (locals say "BAY duh GREE"), east of Lac La Belle. Shallow depth makes for tolerably warm water for swimming. Eagles nest at Bear Bluff across Bete Grise Bay and are frequently seen.

For an even less traveled trip, go south from Lake Linden on Bootjack Road and Dreamland Road to get to **Jacobsville**, at the entry to the Portage Channel. Big red sandstone cliffs were quarried for many of the area's finest buildings. From the old lighthouse and breakwater, there's a fine view across the Keweenaw Bay to the Huron Mountains.

A GUIDE TO 9 UNMARKED KEWEENAW NATURE SANCTUARIES . . . . . gets you focusing on the plants and rocks and natural areas near some much-visited places (Great Sand Bay, the shore near Esrey Park, Brockway Mountain, the Estivant Pines). Look for **Walking Paths in Keweenaw** ($6.95) at Laughing Loon Handcrafts (p. 844) in Copper Harbor and some other area shops. . . . . The Michigan Nature Association has focused much effort on acquiring significant Keweenaw sites, sometimes paid for with bequests of suburban Detroit real estate. Most of these have trails. An interesting, large-format guide to all MNA sanctuaries (many prairie remnants and much in southeast Michigan) is available through Michigan Nature Association (810-324-2626) for $25. Ask for the **MNA Nature Sanctuary Guidebook, 7th Edition.**

Brockway Mountain Drive

See glorious sunsets, soaring hawks, and a splendid view of the Keweenaw's rocky shore on the highest highway between the Rockies and the Alleghenies.

MOST SPECTACULAR of all Keweenaw County's Depression-era relief projects is this nine-mile road that twists and climbs to one of the peninsula's highest peaks, a thousand feet above Lake Superior. At the windswept **Brockway Mountain Lookout**, you're so high above the Keweenaw Peninsula's rocky shore and the islands stretched out below you that the view seems almost like a living map, occasionally punctuated by freighters rounding Keweenaw Point. You can look down on soaring hawks and occasional eagles.

The mountain's western slope goes down to Lake Superior. It's the surface of the Keweenaw's uptilted, copper-bearing volcanic crust. Inland to the east, the broken edge along the north-south fault line becomes an almost vertical rocky cliff that drops down to the river valley below. Each spring, peaking in mid-April, hawks migrate northeast along the entire Keweenaw Peninsula. They gather by these cliffs to ride the updrafts out to the peninsula's end — a final boost before their long flight across Lake Superior. Look down for them coming from the direction of Eagle Harbor. They concentrate at the west end of Brockway Mountain, away from its Lake Superior face.

The view from the lookout is so riveting, it's easy to forget about all the other remarkable features of this unusual road, the highest between the Alleghenies and the Rockies. Isle Royale, over 40 miles away, can be seen on clear days. The habitat toward the top is actually semi-alpine and the trees are stunted by the strong winds. (A windproof jacket is a good idea even in summer.) The most elaborate of all the memorable rustic signs written and built by the KRC's talented signmakers interprets the site.

The mountain's many varied ecosystems are home to many **wildflowers and berries** as well as trillium, orchids, wild strawberries, and thimbleberries — over 700 flowers in all, including many rare and endangered species, some found nowhere else in Michigan. Blooms peak in the month of June. Incidentally, the proprietress of the summit gift shop is a knowledgeable naturalist, happy to answer question.

Here and all over the northern Keweenaw, the land seems like a vast park. Actually, most of it is onetime mining land now owned by Champion Paper (page 822). In return for favorable commercial forest taxes, this land is legally open to the public for recreational use, including rock-gathering, mountain-biking, and berry-picking. The Michigan Nature Association owns 200 prime acres. The drive's stone walls — and the drive itself — are part of a Depression-era make-work project.

Plan to get out and walk at several places along the drive. There are many wildflowers along the road throughout the summer and in the woods in spring. A half mile or so east of the summit, the Michigan Nature Association's **Klipfel Memorial Nature Sanctuary** is a popular overlook for its grand views and its covering of Alpine grasses, ground cover, and sedge. "From the point . . . one can watch the mist disappear from the valley shortly after sunrise. Soon the ravens rise from their overnight roost in the lowlands. Up and up they climb until they are soaring level with the mountain top." Another moving experience is to see the rise of the first evening stars. An interesting overlook over Copper Harbor and Lake Fanny Hooe is 3 1/2 miles east of the summit.

For maximum enjoyment, devote an hour or two to the drive and stop frequently. Bring binoculars, bug spray, walking shoes, and a compass if you want to hike in the forest. Take a trip at dusk, and you'll witness a **sunset view** that's hard to match. **Fall color season** is even more glorious. It usually begins the second week of September and lasts into mid-October.

Drive entrances are off M-26, 5 miles northeast of Eagle Harbor and half a mile west of Copper Harbor. The drive is not plowed in winter. It's open from the first snow-free days of spring (that's usually in late May) up to the first snowfall. No admission fee.

GUIDED ECO-TRIPS NEAR COPPER HARBOR . . . . . may be arranged through Jim Rooks' **Keweenaw Bear Track Tours**. He was instrumental in saving the **Estivant Pines**, one of the Upper Peninsula's last stands of virgin white pines. (Another is near Pinnacle Falls and yellow Dog Plains outside Marquette.) The pines are one of his popular tour destinations, along with old mine sites, bird-watching expeditions, geology or wildlife walks, cross-country skiing, and more. Not for the impatient — Rooks has lots to say — but a good way to focus on the details of the natural world around you. Fees are around $20/person/half day, $40/person/10-hour full day (includes lunch), kids 6-12 half price. Call in advance (906-289-4813) to arrange a trip tailored to your interests, or sign up for a regular 9 a.m. or 1 p.m. walk beginning at his wife's **Laughing Loon Hand-**

crafts. It's located at the northern tail end of Highway 41 (Old Military Trail) that begins in Miami, Florida. Get information about the Estivant Pines there or at Fort Wilkins. Look for *Walking Paths in Keweenaw*, a guide to the Michigan Nature Association's 11 preserves on the peninsula.

FOR A REWARDING HIKE TO A REMARKABLE BEACH . . . . . start at the west end of the parking lot at the Copper Harbor marina and look for the trail-head to beautiful **Agate Beach**. The trail heads west through an evergreen forest close to Lake Superior's shore. In about 3/4 of a mile it forks. Right takes you out along a peninsula that forms the harbor, to Hunter's Point. Left, and you cut across the peninsula's narrow base to come to Agate Beach, covered by pebbles and stones that sometimes include beautiful agates. They're hard to distinguish from other translucent, quartz-rich rocks because all are covered with little scratches that obscure the distinctive banding that becomes apparent when agates are cut and polished.

A NATURE TRAIL UP THE NORTH SIDE OF BROCKWAY MOUNTAIN . . . . . starts on U.S. 41 a little west of the westernmost of two places where the road crosses hemlock-lined Garden Brook. A 1.6 mile trail (not a loop) leads up to some fine views not seen from Brockway Mountain Drive itself. Most of the trail is in the Michigan Nature Association's Brockway Mt. Sanctuary. It comes out on U.S. 41 between the old Copper Harbor cemetery and a new roadside park.

WHEN TO COME . . . . . The bugs aren't as bad after the Fourth of July or so, and the northern Keweenaw is a wonderful hot-weather escape after that. But Don Kilpela, the knowledgeable evening cruise narrator of the Isle Royale Queen III, says, "It's *really* beautiful here at the end of August and September. The lake is at its warmest, which keeps the air warmer. In the last week of September, when the fall colors peak, this is one of the most beautiful places in our country. Then a storm in the first week of October blows down every leaf we have. Our color season ends quite abruptly."

Fort Wilkins
Historic Complex and Park

*A remote Army outpost from the 1840s comes alive
as the centerpiece of a delightful park.*

THE 1843 KEWEENAW copper rush in this remote area,
way beyond the frontier of settlement, led to building this
small fort. From 1843 to 1846 it was the area's only source
of law and order. The government's greatest concern was friction
between native Indians and unruly newcomers, but little hostility
actually broke out. By 1846 most of the small-time prospectors had
left. Large mining companies had stabilized the region, so the fort
was abandoned. It reopened after the Civil War, from 1867 to 1870,
to house excess troops the army was still obliged to keep on.

This was a typical 19th-century frontier garrison, the most
northern in the U.S., 600 miles from Detroit. The old fort became a
favorite picnic spot after the army abandoned it in the 1870s. The
thickly forested site is uncommonly picturesque. It's on beautiful
Lake Fanny Hooe, named after a pretty young lady who early visited
the fort and pronounced "hoe" like the tool. When the old fort
became a state park in 1923, less than half the structures
remained. Some buildings were rebuilt, starting as Depression
make-work projects.

What you see today is a stockade surrounding 19 buildings:
kitchen and mess room, hospital, bakery, company quarters, etc.
Some have been restored and authentically furnished as they might
have been by the state's first-rate Bureau of History. Other buildings have brief, to-the-point displays about military life and the
fort's archaeology and natural history.

Of the soldiers garrisoned here between 1844 and 1870, we
learn that 8% died while in the army, half of natural causes, and
11% deserted. The officers' quarters have fancy lamps and furniture
befitting their higher status. Their resident wives were supposed to
bring civilization to the frontier.

It's worth beginning your visit by seeing the well-written **tape-
slide show,** shown on demand in the visitor center in the second
building as you enter the fort. It provides a fine introduction to the
early history of Keweenaw copper-mining. (Just outside the fort is
an abandoned mine shaft from the 1840s.) **Living history** can be a
real highlight of a visit. You may come upon a soldier's wife doing

Costumed interpreters give convincing performances as soldiers' wives (here doing the wash) and as the schoolteacher. They answer questions about everyday life with the accents and vocabularies of the real-life people they represent.

the post's laundry, or the schoolteacher, or an officer and his wife. Reenactors have been trained to act as if it is the summer of 1870, and to stay in character (as developed through historical research), using the language and accents of that time. The park advises visitors to ask them about their life: where they're from, why they're in the army, what they eat, how long they work, how they spend free time. It's well worth overcoming any shyness and starting a conversation. Kids really enjoy this.

Don't miss the good, small **natural history bookstore** and a display of fresh wildflowers currently blooming. It's in the building closest to the path to the parking area. The larger **gift shop** outside the fort is also a camp store. It has nifty activity toys, books, and games for children. Check here for a schedule of **summer evening programs and events**, and for information on **boat tours** to the **Copper Harbor lighthouse/museum**, managed by the park.

2 1/2 miles east of Copper Harbor on U.S. 41. (906) 289-4215. TDD: (800) 827-7007. Park open year-round. Fort open mid-May thru mid-Oct, 8 a.m.-dusk. Park interpreters and living history on site 10-5:30 daily from mid-June to Labor Day. &: *ramp and paths to and within fort. Otherwise: inquire. State park sticker required; $4/day, $20/year.*

A DELIGHTFUL MIX OF NATURE AND PEOPLE . . . . . is to be found at **Fort Wilkins State Park**. . . . . The **evening lecture series** (at 7:30 nearly every night in summer) attracts local people as well as campers. Talks are indoors inside the fort barracks room across the parade grounds. Speakers are specialists in subjects from copper mining to moose and wolves. . . . . Summer people who belong to the **Fort Wilkins Natural History Association** operate the excellent **bookshop** just inside the fort. Proceeds help pay for the association's publications and for park interpretive programs. . . . . The two wooded **campgrounds** above Lake Fanny Hooe, with 165 modern sites, attract many repeat visitors each year who achieve the status of Copper Harbor summer regulars. Love of nature is the common bond that knits together area businesspeople, visitors, and summer residents. The park's permanent staff, **campground host**, and night ranger Dennis Sotala, a botanist by training, are excellent information sources. . . . . Though the park is not large (200 acres), you could spend many happy hours exploring its features. Alluring spots that might be missed are across U.S. 41 from the main park area: the **picnic area** where Fanny Hooe Creek empties into the harbor, and the nearby **red rocks** with their grand view of the lighthouse. The rocks are a fine place to read or sketch. . . . . A pretty two-mile **trail** through the woods along Lake Fanny Hooe connects the fort parking area, cemetery, and picnic area to the fort and campgrounds. . . . . Four miles of trail within the park and another 10 miles on the other side of Lake Fanny Hooe are groomed for **cross-country skiing**.

GETTING TO THE COPPER HARBOR LIGHTHOUSE . . . . . must be done by boat, even though the lighthouse and surrounding property is part of the state park. The abutting cottage association has denied right-of-way by land. A boat takes visitors on the unnarrated, 15-minute trip. A Bureau of History guide meets visitors and takes them through the 1866 lighthouse. It's charming on the outside but with unremarkable maritime displays and furnishings inside. Interpreted nature trails to the lighthouse and beyond pass artifacts from shipwrecks. A very simple 1840s keeper's house is by the boat dock. It's a pleasant enough trip. But the experience isn't any better than visits to the nearby Eagle Harbor lighthouse (p.835), and it is surpassed by visits to lighthouses whose towers can be climbed. Thrifty families might prefer to invest their travel dollars elsewhere. *Leaves from Copper Harbor's municipal marina (on the west edge of town opposite the Brockway Mountain Drive entrance) (906) 289-4966. Season: from Mem. Day through Sept. Leaves at 10, 12, 2, and 4. In July & August leaves hourly from 10 to 5.* &: *for very motivated. Call. $10 adults, $5 12 and under.*

HEAVEN FOR ROCKHOUNDS . . . . . The public is permitted to visit and gather rocks and berries on the vast land holdings of Champion Paper (p. 839), which includes most of the northern Keweenaw Peninsula. Maps of agate beaches and old mines with rock piles can be purchased at the **New Keweenaw Agate Shop** on U.S. 41 in Copper Harbor. Mineralogist-owner Les Tolen has a splendid collection of mineral specimens (datolite, greenstone, and malachite are native to the area), lots of books on area geology, and rockhounds' tools. *From Memorial Day through mid-October. open daily about 9-9. He may be away at shows other times; call first. (906) 289-4491.* ♿ . . . . . **Swede's Gift Shop** (906-289-4596) also carries Keweenaw minerals and jewelry. It's on U.S. 41across from the community buildings and restrooms. ♿

SHOPS IN COPPER HARBOR . . . . . especially for people interested in nature, are among the most interesting in the Upper Peninsula, an area unashamedly out of sync with trends and fashions. Almost every shop owner is quite familiar with the area's flora and fauna, its walks and beauty spots. They're happy to advise visitors when time permits. . . . . **Laughing Loon Handcrafts**, is run by dedicated naturalists Laurel and Jim Rooks. It has many nature-related gifts, comical and serious, jewelry, T shirts, and a fine selection of books on regional history and nature, including *Walking Paths in Keweenaw*. *On First and Bernard a block north of U.S. 41 at the east end of town. Open year-round, 9-9 in summer. (906-289-4813)* . . . . . Right on U.S. 41, the **Thunderbird Gift Center** at the Minnetonka Resort (906-289-4449) is a rambling, old-fashioned souvenir shop with all the classics (rubber tomahawks, etc.), plus new and used books, antiques, and a fun, old-timey museum full of antique dolls and Indian artifacts. The owner sells prints of her attractive drawings of local landmarks. . . . . Carl Kazak, proprietor of **The Copper Goose**, is another artist who knows the area well. . . . . . More good regional and nature books plus T shirts are at **The Harbor Side**. It doubles as the Isle Royale Queen ticket office. To reach the ferry dock from U.S. 41, turn north just east of the Minnetonka Resort. (906) 289-4437. Open 12-5 and for about an hour around the ferry's departure and arrival at 8 a.m. and 6:30 p.m. Other interesting shops are at the dock: Jamsen's Fish Market (smoked and fresh fish), the Fisherman's Daughter handcrafts, and Elizabeth's gifts and jewelry. . . . . Dennis Sotala and his wife, Shule Rayberg, make and sell their pottery (raku and salt-glazed) and baskets — sometimes to order —on the porch outside their tiny shop. Its current name is **Sataman Ruukku** (Finnish for "harbor pottery"). His interest in handcrafts and his exceptionally self-sufficient lifestyle is inspired by his hard-working Finnish forbears from this area. *On U.S. 41 across the side road from Johnson's Bakery Restaurant. (906) 289-4636.*

CULINARY HIGHLIGHTS. . . . . Cinnamon-pecan rolls at **Johnson's Bakery Restaurant**. . . . . Smoked fish at Jamsen's Fishery by the Isle Royale ferry. . . . . Most anything at the **Harbor Haus**, which overlooks the harbor on the east end of town. The food's German but not heavy. The coffee is European. The scrambled eggs with smoked whitefish and scallions is a terrific breakfast. And the view's great. . . . . Thimbleberry ice cream is among the flavors served at **The Berry Patch**, next to the post office on M-26 near Brockway Mountain Drive. . . . The year-round diner/bar is **The Pines**, with an unassuming northwoods atmosphere. Local people come for the Sunday turkey dinner. . . . . The food's nothing remarkable, but the **Keweenaw Mountain Lodge** (906-289-4403), a massive place of hand-hewn logs, is worth a visit. It was built (and is still operated) by the Keweenaw County Road Commission with WPA funds to create Depression jobs. The attractive log cottages are in great demand. No vistas here (too many trees), but you can play golf.

WHERE TO SWIM . . . . . The local favorite is **Lake Manganese,** a little over a mile south of Copper Harbor. It has a long, sandy beach, a gradual dropoff, and water that's warm enough to swim. From U.S. 41, take the road by the community building and The Pines, and turn right to the lake when the main road veers left. . . . . On the same road, .7 miles from the Pines corner in town, look for a pullover that marks the trail to the overlook for beautiful **Manganese Falls.** Go a a little beyond where the road turns sharply right. The pullover is on the left.

THE ILL-FATED BUOY-TENDER *MESQUITE* . . . . . hung up on the reef off Keweenaw Point in 1989 after the Coast Guard officer on duty made a navigational error, is now the star diving attraction of the **Keweenaw Underwater Preserve**. The *Mesquite* was lifting the buoy that marked the reef. Its commander's efforts to get off the reef only stuck the ship more. That night wind and waves from the southeast gave the ship such a pounding that it was decided to sink it. . . . . The waters here are unusually clear, and the underwater rocks and minerals are most unusual, but it's so cold a dry suit is usually required. For **diving charters** call Jim Jackman, (906) 337-3156.

SEA KAYAKING ADVENTURES, MOUNTAIN BIKE RENTALS, AND DOG SLEDDING . . . . . can be arranged through the well-regarded **Keweenaw Adventure Company** (906-289-4303). They're just outside town on the road to Lake Manganese that goes south at The Pines. The 2 1/2 hour paddle to a harbor island ($20) is a fine introduction to sea kayaking.

SUNSET CRUISES ON THE ISLE ROYALE QUEEN III . . . . . Enthusiastic, voluble narrator-skippers Don and Ben Kilpela are longtime residents who know so much — about Great Lakes shipping, local history, ecology — they can extemporize effectively. . . . . They begin the regular, 1 1/2 hour **sunset cruise** by scanning their radar to see what freighters are nearby, then choose one to chase. Drawing up close to a big ocean-going vessel with its six-story superstructure picked out in lights is spectacularly memorable, like something from a Fellini movie, one passenger commented. Its cargo (learned from a radio chat): sunflower seeds from Superior, Wisconsin. *Leaves Mon, Wed, Fri, Sun at 8 p.m. $10. Ages 12 & under: $5.* . . . . New in 1996: a 2 1/2 hour **lighthouse cruise** to **Manitou Island** and **Gull Rock**, two hard-to-reach lighthouses well off

Keweenaw Point. *Leaves Tues, Thurs & Sat at 8. $16. 12 & under $8.* . . . . Line up early to get a seat on the deck. Otherwise you'll be inside around a formica table (not a bad option on windy days). *Reservations advised: (906) 289-4437. The ferry dock is two blocks north of the town center.* &: *call.*

BRING BIKES . . . . . for a most relaxing stay in Copper Harbor. They're perfect transportation to anything around town, from Agate Beach by the marina (p. 840 to the state park to Manganese Falls (p. 845). In the early morning, traffic is very light along beautiful M-26 to Eagle Harbor, and its modest hills won't challenge out-of-shape cyclists. . . . . Bike thefts have presented no problem here. Local people leave bikes unlocked as they do errands.

Isle Royale

*Over 50 miles from the Michigan mainland,
this remote island is a superb place
to confront true wilderness.*

FOR the person seeking the ultimate Midwestern wilderness experience, this 44-mile-long island is the leading candidate. The largest and most remote of all Great Lakes islands is a four-hour or six-hour boat ride from Michigan's Upper Peninsula.

This least-visited National Park gets as many visitors in a season (about 16,000) as Yosemite and Yellowstone get in a day. It's a place where you can stay in a lodge with meals provided and attend evening programs on natural history, or where you can camp in the backcountry and go for days without seeing anyone – it's your choice. Away from the park's hub at Rock Harbor, the only sounds you hear are natural sounds, except for an infrequent boat whistle or a daily airplane flight. You might well see a moose up close, or find fresh wolf tracks in the mud, or canoe up to a rare gull in an inlet. You'll certainly hear the unforgettable laugh of the loon. Hikers will glimpse red foxes, which have become accustomed to people here and taken to hanging around campgrounds. (They should *not* be fed!) And canoeists can easily enjoy watching beavers for hours.

For the most part this has remained a pristine natural area. A few commercial fishermen have lived here in the past. The only known villages were short-lived, set up briefly by copper-mining companies in the late 19th century. Hundreds of years ago, Indians dug copper from hundreds of pits that can still be seen today.

The rock formations of Isle Royale (here) mirror those of the Keweenaw Peninsula's west-facing slope.

The narrow island, only three to nine miles wide, is a series of long ridges that are really uplifted lava shelves – the mirror image of the Keweenaw's dramatic geology. The highest points are the edges of the upthrust, broken crust. This is the rocky, subarctic landscape of the Laurentian Shield, Precambrian formations that are from the earth's oldest geological age. A much-studied timber wolf population which crossed on an ice bridge in 1948 has dwindled to 12. A moose herd which crossed frozen Lake Superior in 1912 now numbers 1,300, the greatest density of moose in the lower 48 states.

Hikers have 166 miles of paths to follow, including the 42-mile **Greenstone Trail** following the island's central ridge. This five- to six-day trek is the most popular. Some hikers start out after taking a seaplane to the southeastern end. The trip's first part is through thickly forested terrain affording few views. **Mount Ojibway** (elevation 1,183 feet) is one of several peaks along the trail that provides splendid views to the Canadian mainland 15 miles away. Small **campgrounds** are along the trail three to 12 miles apart. There are 36 campgrounds in all, with 253 campsites, but only a few allow fires. Other campers bring their own portable stoves. A water filter is also needed, except in the two campgrounds by the ferries on either end of the island. They have water, fire pits, and showers. Backpacking novices are advised to get in shape, try out equipment beforehand, and plan carefully before embarking on a trip where they may be several days' hike from help. Camping is free. Campers should obtain backcountry permits on the island; sites aren't reservable.

Many come for the **fishing**. Pike are plentiful in lakes such as Lake Richie. Lake Whittlesey is known for walleye, and huge Siskiwit Lake for brook trout. Because the island's 42 lakes have to be reached by foot, and boats have to be carried, none is heavily fished. Boats and canoes can be brought over from Houghton on the Ranger III. Some campgrounds are on islands reachable only by water.

For those who aren't into backpacking, a concessionaire runs **Rock Harbor Lodge**. Its 60 rooms cost $91.50 per person, double occupancy, including meals. It is the headquarters for **boat and canoe rentals**, **fishing charters**, **sightseeing tours** (including a two-hour evening cruise/nature hike), a **restaurant**, a **snack bar**, and a **store** with camping supplies. Free **nature walks** and nightly **auditorium programs** are held here, too. Twenty nearby **housekeeping cabins** (maximum occupancy of six) rent for $105.50 for one person (add $5 if you're staying only one day). Meals are not included, though cabin guests are welcome to eat at the lodge restaurant and snack bar. Make reservations well in advance.

Introductory information about Isle Royale may be obtained by calling or writing the park at (906) 482-0984; 87 N. Ripley, Hancock, MI 49931. Anyone investing the time and money in a trip to Isle Royale should also buy ahead of time a little book by ardent outdoorsman Jim Du Fresne to read on the boat. *Isle Royale National Park: Foot Trails & Water Routes* (The Mountaineers, ISBN 0-89886-082-2, $10.95) has interesting introductions to the island's history, flora and fauna, fish, and general logistical information. Detailed descriptions of hikes and trails, lakes and paddles will prove invaluable to anyone doing any walking or canoeing at all.

Late August and early September is the best time to visit Isle Royale. By then the sometimes irritating black fly population has dwindled, and so have the number of visitors. But the island is never crowded. Typically fewer than 300 people share the 134,000 acres.

The nation's most remote national park, Isle Royale is an improbable part of the state of Michigan. It's just 15 miles from Canada and far closer to Minnesota than Michigan. Legend has it that Benjamin Franklin secured it for the U.S. in negotiations with the British because he thought its copper would be useful in electrical experiments.

Open for visitors mid-April through October. Full services mid-June to Labor Day. Boat service from Copper Harbor (4 1/2 hours one-way), Grand Portage, Minnesota (7 1/2 hours), or Houghton (6 hours). Float plane from Houghton. For more details, write Isle Royale National Park, 87 N. Ripley, Houghton, MI 49931. (906) 482-0984. Reservations for Rock Harbor Lodge during off season (502) 773-2191; in season (906) 337-4993.

GET A REAL LOOK AT A FAMILY FISHERY . . . . . by visiting the **Edisen Fishery**, a short, memorable walk from the picturesque **Rock Harbor Light** and museum. In the 1930s Isle Royale had many small gill net fisheries like this. All but this were removed by the National Park Service. Few others survive anywhere on Lake Superior. Les and Donna Mattson live here all summer and enjoy sharing their experience and perspective about U.P. life (they're from the Keweenaw) and Lake Superior fishing. Les, a former commercial fisherman, now fishes for DNR research and for dinners served at the Rock Harbor Lodge. He attributes the decline of the Lake Superior fishery to the introduction of monofilament line. It enabled fishermen like himself to spend less time mending their nets and more time out fishing. . . . . The fishery and lighthouse are reachable only by water. The *M.V. Sandy*, based in Rock Harbor, makes half-day trips from Rock Harbor on Thursdays and Saturdays for $9.25, half price for children.

Top public Michigan golf courses

Michigan is well known as one of the top golfing states in the country, so it's tough to choose the best of a remarkable group of courses. But here are 17 that will challenge the most experienced golfer. Prices quoted are for 18 holes with a cart.

Hampshire Country Club—*Dowagiac.*
Gently rolling fairways and lots of trees make this long (7,000 yards from the blue tees) course a worthy challenge. It's a prequalifying site for the Western Am. The two toughest holes are on the original 18: the dogleg hole number 4, 460 yards bounded by woods and water, and the tight 475-yard 14th, with woods on both sides. $15 weekdays. $18 weekends. *(616) 782-7476.*

Lake Doster Golf Club—*Plainwell.*
This course north of Kalamazoo is one of the best in the state. It's a challenging, championship course, with water on eight of the holes and only two holes that run together, creating lots of opportunities for landing out of bounds. But what makes Lake Doster most difficult are the undulating greens. The third, a short par three, is one of the most beautiful and difficult in Michigan. From an elevated tee, you shoot to a green surrounded by water and sand. $22 weekdays. $25 weekends. *(616) 685-5308.*

Bedford Valley Golf Course—*Battle Creek.*
A traditional course with lots of big sand traps and sizable greens. It's 6876 yards from the blue tees. The front nine is lined with giant pines. The back nine is cut through a mature hardwood forest. $26 weekdays. $30 weekends. *(616) 965-3384.*

Salem Hills Golf Club—*Northville*
Voted the 6th most enjoyable course in Michigan, Salem Hills allows fairly wide-open tee shots but its approach shots are demanding and its par threes long. Toughest hole is the 11th, a 430-yard dogleg with a creek in front of the green. $20 weekdays without cart. $31 with cart. Weekends $38 with cart. *(810) 437-2152.*

Pine Trace Golf Club—*Rochester Hills.*
This Arthur Hills course was built in 1989. Its severe elevation changes remind many of the resort courses up north. Lots of woods, too. Perhaps your best bet for a public course in the Detroit area. 6600 yards. $48 weekends. $35 weekdays. *(810) 852-7100.*

Greystone—*Romeo.*
Famed for its final three holes, widely regarded as the toughest finish-

ing holes in the state. The 16th is a par three to an island green, the 17th has a tortuously narrow fairway, and the 18th entices you to risk a potentially disastrous shot across the lake. The second hole won a Golf Digest award for best designed hole: you tee off from a hill looking down at a long narrow green with a pond on the right and a huge sand-trap on the left. $43 weekdays. $48 weekends. Twilight (after 3 p.m.): $30 weekdays $35 weekends. *(810) 752-7030.*

The Fortress—*Frankenmuth.*
This Scottish links course has over 75 bunkers, with bent grass tees, fairways, and greens. Greens average a massive 3,000 square feet. Monday-Thursday $55. Friday-Sundays $59. *(517) 652-9229.*

Bay Valley Golf Club—*Bay City*
The rolling hills make this Jack Nicklaus-Desmond Muirhead-designed course an attractive one to play. Bay Valley has 13 water holes plus the famous 14th Heather Hole. It's a par three, and you have to shoot a good 170 yards over a field of heather to reach the green par. If you miss by as much as ten yards, you'll probably have to take another shot. Weekdays $54. Weekends $56. *(517) 686-5400.*

Timber Ridge Golf Course—*East Lansing.*
Highly respected, this course was built in 1988 on hilly terrain where a 1940s tree nursery was planted but never harvested. Some 60 variety of trees are now mature, adding to the allure of the setting, where slopes plunge as much as 80 feet. Golf Digest rated this one of the top 75 public courses in the country. Number 18 is the signature hole, a long par 4 whose second shot is over a big pond onto a two-tiered green. 6060 yards. $45 Monday-Thursday. $50 Friday-Sunday. *(517) 339-8000.*

The Pines at Lake Isabella—*Weidman, west of Mt. Pleasant.*
Located in a quiet, isolated region on 875-acre Lake Isabella, The Pines features rolling terrain, pine-lined fairways, and big, undulating greens. Number 9 is one of the hardest page 4s in the state—an uphill dogleg to the right. Number 15 is the signature hole: from the elevated tee you get a nice view of the lake. Resorters can make this a busy course on weekends, but before 1 p.m. on weekdays it's likely not to be crowded at all. Weekday $30; weekend is $35. *(517) 644-2300*

Saskatoon Golf Club—*Alto*
One of the most popular West Michigan courses, the Saskatoon hosts more group outings than any other course in the state. The four 9-hole courses are named by colors, and the newest, the Gold, is the most popular. The Gold's first three holes wind through woods, then open up for the final Scottish holes. One of the greens is an island. Two of the other nine-hole courses go down by the lake and through the woods, making this a wonderfully scenic location. $19 weekend. $17 weekdays.

(616) 891-9229.

L. E. Kaufman Golf Course—*Wyoming.*
The best public course in the Grand Rapids area, in part because it's so well maintained. Designed by Bruce Matthews. Buck Creek adds difficulty. On hole ten, the creek cuts diagonally across the fairway and catches lots of balls. The 407-yard 14th is as challenging as it is pretty—pines line both sides of the fairway. $18 weekends. M-F to noon is $12.50. *(616) 538-5050.*

Old Channel Trail Golf Course—*Montague*
The back nine of this impressive Lake Michigan shoreline course was designed by talented golf architect Robert Bruce Harris in 1926. The front nine was created in 1966 by another noted designer, Bruce Matthews. This original 18 has large rolling greens and Scottish bunkers among big, old maples. Now there's a third nine, designed by Matthews' son, Jerry, last year. It may be the most spectacular yet, with a dramatic, beautiful ravine. Old Channel Trail gives golfers the secluded, feel of many fine northern Michigan courses. Weekdays $15-$18. Weekends $16-$20. *(616) 894-5076.*

Grand Traverse Resort Golf Course—*north of Acme.*
Every serious golfer visiting Michigan should play The Bear at least once. It's a beautifully laid out course. Some of the holes have an open-link-style Scottish flavor with sand hills, hummocks, and waist-high grass in the deep rough. Other holes wind through cherry orchards and woods. It's not as long or as difficult as Treetops, but it remains a very challenging course with 75 bunkers and many tiered greens. 7000 yards. Weekdays $90. Weekends $100. Twilight $50. *(616) 938-1620.*

Belvedere Golf Club—*Charlevoix.*
This legendary course was built in 1927. It has hosted the Michigan Amateur 38 times. It features old-fashioned small greens. The emphasis is on short play, with very challenging three- and four-par holes. 6700 yards. $50 Sunday-Wednesday. $55 Thursday-Saturday. *(616) 547-2611.*

Treetops—*Gaylord.*
Arguably the most spectacular and difficult public courses in Michigan. The name "Treetops" comes from legendary designer Robert Trent Jones, whose sixth hole provides a breathtaking panorama of forested lands. His 7000+ yard course is the most difficult of the three. Its mounded fairways and greens allow few even lies. The Smith Signature course is the most natural and playable. Treetops has the only Fazio-designed course in the state. All three courses have great views. $84 for Fazio Premier and $74 on the Jones Masterpiece or Smith Signature. *(800) 444-6711.*

Greg Wilcox's Top Antiquing Areas

1. **Royal Oak—Birmingham**. *Metro Detroit*. More than 20 shops in the immediate Royal Oak area with several more quality shops in Birmingham. For more info about Royal Oak, see Lulu's, 405 N. Main. (810) 542-6464. In Birmingham, Watch Hill (810) 644-4775.

2. **Allen**. *Southern Michigan*. Billed as the antique capitol of Michigan. Over 26 shops in the area, more along U.S. 12. For more info, call (517) 869-2719.

3. **Schoolcraft, Galesburg, Mattawan, Lawton**. *Southwest Michigan*. Several quality shops around Kalamazoo. For more info: (616) 347-9672,

4. **Williamston, Okemos, Mason**. *Mid-Michigan*. Known as the heart of antiques country. Williamston has over 110 antique dealers with many other colllectible special interest shops in the area. Quality shops in Okemos; three large malls in Mason. For more info: (517) 655-5621.

5. **Petoskey-Harbor Springs**. *Northern Michigan*. A hot bed of antiques in the summer. Several shops open all year. For more info: (616) 347-9672.

6. **Traverse City**. *Northern Michigan*. The region's antique capitol. Most shops open summer & winter. For more info: call Antique Emporium, (616) 943-3685.

7. **Tri-City Area**. *Bay City, Saginaw, & Flint*. Bay City Antiques Center and Saginaw Antique Mall are twho of Michigan's top malls. For more info: (517) 893-1116.

8. **Marshall**. *Central Michigan*. Several quality shops and malls. More malls to east along I-94, in downtown Jackson. For more info: J.H. Cronin Antiques (616) 789-0077.

9. **Grand Rapids**. *West Michigan*. The center of west Michigan antiquing. For more info: Antiques by the Bridge (616) 451-3430.

10. **Pontiac Area Shops**. *Metro Detroit*. Many quality shops scattered along I-75 North. For more info: Water Tower Antiques Mall in Holly. (313) 634-3500.

11. **Southeastern Michigan**. *Ann Arbor-Saline-Ypsilanti-Wayne*. Several of Michigans best shops are included in this area. For more info: Hickory Hill Antiques, Farmington (313) 477-6630.

(12. **Harbor Country**. New Buffalo area. See pages 12-15.)

Greg Wilcox is publisher of **Michigan Antiques Trading Post,** *132 S. Putnam, Williamston MI 48895. (517) 655-5621. A free copy is available upon request.*

INDEX of PLACES

Each entry in this index of places and destinations is followed by an abbreviation for the region it's in.

SW=Southwest pp. 8-113
M-M=Marshall to Monroe
pp 114-193
MET=Metro Detroit
pp 194-357
SV=Flint, Saginaw Valley &
the Thumb pp 358-419
MID=Mid-Michigan
pp 420-450
W=West Michigan
pp 451-545
N Northern Michigan
pp 546-699
UP Upper Peninsula
pp 700-850

Regions are mapped on the contents page at the front of the book.

The SUBJECT INDEX is on page 863.

A

Abrams Planetarium MID 441
U.S.S. Acacia N 627
Acme N *Golf:* 851
Adrian M-M 115, 116, 136-9
Adrian College M-M 115
Adventist History Tour SW 113
Ahmeek UP 830
Air Zoo SW 83-5
Alamo SW 73
Albion M-M 102-3, 114-6, 124, 125, 129
Albion College M-M 115,123
Alcamo's Market MET 338
Alger Underwater Pres.UP 765
Algonac SV 359
Allegan W 453
Allen M-M 114, 130-5,140
Allendale W 452
Allouez UP 830, 831
Alma MID 420
Alpena N 546, 548, 688-692

Alto *Golf:* 851
American Museum of Magic M-M 125-8
Amon Orchards N 51, 610-1
Amtrak 101-4
Amway Grand Plaza W 454
Andrews University SW 46
Ann Arbor M-M 47, 102,115-6, 149-182
Ann Arbor Hands-On Museum M-M 160
Ann Arbor Street Art Fair M-M 159
Arcadia N 548
Archives of Michigan MID 425
Athens M-M 128
Atlanta N 548
Atwater Block Brewery MET 211
Au Sable State Forest N 698
Au Train UP 702
Awa Saginaw An SV 388-392

B

Bad Axe SV 358
S.S. Badger N 556-560
Baldwin N 546, 564-7
John Ball Zoo W 454, 464-6
Baraga Co. Tourism 701
Baroda SW 43
Battle Creek SW 85, 102-3, 110-113, 115-6. *Golf:* 851
Battle Creek Sanitarium SW113
Bay City SV 358-9, 398. *Golf:* 851. *Antiques:* 854.
Bay Mills/Brimley Historical Research Society UP 737
Bay Port SV 358
Bay View N 629, 638-640
Beal Botanical Garden MID 445-8
Bear Cave SW 36
Bear Lake N 548
Beaver Island N 546, 614-22
Beaver Island Maritime Museum N 618
Beaver Island Tours N 616
Beaver Island Toy Museum & Store N 619
Bellaire N 548
Bell's Ales SW 97-8
Belle Isle MET 194, 205, 278-87
Belle Isle Aquarium MET 283-4
Belle Isle Zoo MET 280
Bellwether Herbs N 584-5
Bentley Historical Library, U-M M-M 167

Benton Harbor SW 49, 51-52, 69, 71-2, 79, 115-6
Benton Harbor Fruit Market SW 52\
Benzie Area Museum N 570
Benzonia N 548, 568. 570
Bergland UP 702
Berrien Springs SW 34, 38, 45-6, 51
Bessemer UP 702, 807
Jesse Besser Museum N 688, 690
Beulah N 548
Big Bay UP 775-6
Big Island Lake Wilderness Area UP 761, 762
Big Rapids N 546, 548, 453
Big Spring (Kitch-iti-kipi) UP 722-3
Bill's Farm Market N 642
Binder Park Zoo SW 111-3
Bingham N 584
Birch Run SV 358, 387
Birmingham MET 102, 103, 194, 311-4\. *Antiques:* 854.
U.S.S. Biscayne Bay UP 712, 721
Black R. Harbor UP 805-6, 809
Andrew Blackbird Museum (Harbor Springs) N 649
Blaney Park UP 754
Bloomfield Hills MET 194, 315-20
Bloomingdale SW 73-6
Blue Star Highway SW 75
Boskydel Vineyard N 585
Bowers Harbor N 605
Bowers Harbor Vineyards N 605
Boyne City N 548
Braeloch Farms SW 106
Brethren N 548
Brevort UP 719
Bricktown MET 223
Bridgeport SV 104
Bridgman SW 11, 29
Brimley UP 736-7
Brimley State Park UP 737
Brockway Mt. Dr. UP 834, 836, 838-9
Bronner's CHRISTmas Wonderland SV 375-80
Bronson Park SW 93
Brooklyn M-M 114, 140
Buchanan SW 36
Busha's Brae Herb Farm N 588-9

C

SUBJECT INDEX

Each entry in this subject index is followed by an abbreviation for the region it's in.

SW =Southwest pp. 8-113

M-M=Marshall to Monroe pp 114-193

MET=Metro Detroit pp 194-357

SV=Flint, Saginaw Valley & the Thumb pp 358-419

MID=Mid-Michigan pp 420-450

WEST=West Michigan pp 451-545

NORTH=Northern Michigan pp 546-699

UPPER PENINSULA pp 700-850

Overview of subjects
Airplanes & Aviation
Antiques
Archaeology & Egyptology
Art Galleries & Exhibit Spaces
Art Museums
Art in Public Places
Beaches
Bicycling
Canoeing
Car Museums
Cross-Country Skiing
Children's Destinations
Engineering-related Sights
Ethnic Groups & Cultures
  including American Indian
Farms & Agricultural Tours
Fish & Hatcheries
Folk Art & Outsider Art
Environments/Folk/Outsider Art
Fruit
Gardens & Gardening
Geology
Great Lakes Maritime
Herbs
Hiking
Historic Interiors
Historic Neighborhoods
Industrial & Labor History
Industrial Tours & Demos

Lighthouses
Logging & Lumber Barons
Military History
Mining
Live Music
Nature Trails
Planetariums
Railroading & Amtrak
Rockhounds
Specialty Shopping & Food
Theater, Comedy & Drama
Picture Palaces
Waterfalls
Wheelchair-friendly outdoor
  places
Wine
Zoos

AIRPLANES & AVIATION
SW: Kalamazoo Air Zoo/Aviation History Museum 83-5. **M-M:** Michigan Space & Science Center 144-5, Yankee Air Museum/ Willow Run Airport 186-7. **MET:** Wright Bros. Cycle Shop, Greenfield Village 352. **NORTH:** gliders in Benzie Hist. Museum 520, Woolsey Airport, Northport 593, Island Airways 620. **UPPER PENINSULA:** WWII gliders from Kingsford 789.

ANTIQUES *See also "historic interiors," "archaeology" in subject index, individual historical museums listed in regular index.*
Perspective on manufacturing what are now antiques: 347, 352-3, 350.
SW: 12-6, 35, 97. **M-M:** 120-1, 129-33, 139, 151, 154, 156, 184, 185. 192. **MET:** 215, 223,298, 306-9, 331. **SV:** 392, 398. **MID:** 439. **WEST:** 454, 466, 476, 487. 499, 501 **NORTH:** 634, 648, 685, 854.

ARCHAEOLOGY
Refers to local digs unless otherwise noted.
SW: Ft. St. Joseph, Niles 34, Horn Archaeological Museum (Biblical), Berrien Springs 46, Kalamazoo Valley Museum (mummy how-to) 90-1. **M-M:** Kelsey Museum of Archaeology, U-M 162-3. **MET:**

Detroit Institute of Arts 247, Shrine of Black Madonna 267, Donna Jacobs Gallery 312. **SV:** Edison homesite 416, Chippewa Nature Center 405-6. **NORTH:** Colonial Michilimackinac 660.

ART GALLERIES & EXHIB-IT SPACES. *See also "art museums," which also have permanent collections. See also "archaeology." Crafts shops, cooperative galleries, and studio galleries not included for brevity. See "shopping."* **SW** Judith Racht 12, Lakeside 14, Krasl Art Center 67, Kalamazoo Institute of Arts 93. **M-M:** Ella Sharp Museum 146. **MET:** *In Detroit* AC,T 219, Dell Pryor 215, Detroit Artists' Market 211, Detroit Focus 218, International Artists 219, DuMouchelle Art Gallery & Auction 223, Gallery Biegas 218, National Conference of Artists 255, People Mover :"Art in the Stations" 225-6, Swords into Plowshares 217, Urban Park 221, Sherry Washington 218, Pewabic Pottery exhibit gallery 289. *In the Pointes* Edsel & E. Ford Home gallery 302. *In Birmingham* Halsted 312, Susanne Hilberry 311, Hill 312, Robert Kidd 301, David Klein 301, Lemberg 312, Donald Morris 312, G. R. N'Namdi 301-2, Elizabeth Stone 313. *In West Bloomfield* Jewish Community Center 329 *In Pontiac* Habatat 313, Revolution 314, Riki Schaeffer 314, Shaw Guido 314. **SV:** *In Flint* Mott Community College Fine Arts Gallery 366, Buckham Gallery 367. *In Midland* Midland Center for the Arts 403. **MID:** *In Lansing* Otherwise Gallery 439, Creole Gallery 439, Bare Bones Studio 439, Real World Emporium 439. *In East Lansing* Saper Galleries 443,

Thomas & Sons 443. **WEST:** *In Saugatuck* Joyce Petter Gallery 486, 492, Good Goods 489, Cain Gallery 490, Animalia 490, Water St. Gallery 490, De Graaf Fine Arts 490-1, Button Gallery 495, The Ark 495-6. *In Holland* Holland Arts Council 505, De Pree Art Center (Hope College) 508. **NORTH:** Joppich's Bay St. Gallery 592-3, Beech Tree Gallery 591, Tamarack Craftsman Gallery 589-90, Coyote Woman 647. **UPPER PENINSULA:** Depot Gallery, Negaunee 780. TOSH Gallery Houghton 820. Copper Country Comm. Arts Council, Hancock 821.

ART MUSEUMS
with permanent collections on display and (usually) changing exhibits. **M-M:** Brueckner Museum 124, Univ. of Mich. Museum of Art 163-4. **MET:** Cranbrook Academy of Art Museum 319. Detroit Institute of Arts 246-9. **SV:** *In Saginaw* 405, Awa Saginaw An teahouse incorporates the Japanese aesthetic 388. **MID:** Kresge Art Museum MSU 441. **WEST:** Muskegon Museum of Art 527, 533. **NORTH:** Dennos Museum Center 608.

PUBLIC ART
The best-known public art mentioned in this book.
Vito Acconci "Land of Boats" MET 210
Cranbrook MET 315-20
Marshall Fredericks MET 317, 325. SV 394. W 477.
Tyree Guyton "Heidelberg Project: MET 274-8
Maya Lin "Wave Field" M-M 166
Meijer Gardens & Sculpture Park W 477-8
Carl Milles MET 317, 319. "Sunday Morning" M-M 168
Louise Nevelson "Summer Night Tree" M-M 143
People Mover Art in the Stations MET 197, 225-6

AUTOMOTIVE HISTORY. *See also "car museums." In general index, see "Fords," "General Motors."* **SW:** Checker exhibit in Kalamazoo Valley Museum 90. **M-M:** Miller Motors (Hudsons) 182. **MET:** Detroit 194, Detroit Historical Museum 252-3, National Automotive Historical Collection, Detroit Public Library 256. Berry Gordy as autoworker 261-5. John Dodge 323. Henry Ford Museum "Automobile & American Life" 345-6. Greenfield Village Ford Mack Ave. factory 353. **SV:** Sloan Museum "Flint & the American Dream" 360, Labor Museum & Learning Center 363. **MID:** R. E. Olds Museum 435-6. **NORTH:** Taghon's Corner replica 1920s gas station & gasoline memorabilia 602.

BEACHES
All beaches are on one of the Great Lakes unless otherwise notes.
SW: New Buffalo 18, Warren Dunes S.P. 27, St. Joseph Silver Beach 65 & Tiscornia Park 68-9, South Haven 76. **M-M:** Sterling S.P. 191. **SV:** *In Flint* Bluebell Beach, Mott Lake 373, *Near Midland* Sanford Lake Co. Park 403. *Near Port Austin* Lighthouse Co. Park 413. *In Port Huron* Lighthouse Park 416, Lakeside Park 416. **WEST:** *In Saugatuck* Oval Beach 486, 496, Saugatuck Dunes S. P. 497. *Holland:* Holland S.P. 509, Tunnel Park 509. *Grand Haven area:* Kirk Park 499, 509, North Beach Park 514, 518, Grand Haven S.P & City Beach 514, 516, 517. *Muskegon area* Hoffmaster S.P. 524, Pleasure Island 525, Muskegon S.P. 527, 541. Whitehall/Montague Duck Lake S. P. (beaches on Duck Lake and Lake Michigan) 544, Medbury Park 543. **NORTH:** Stoney Lake & Lake Michigan (biking to) 551; Pentwater & Mears S. P. 552, 555, 560. Silver Lake 551, 552,

560. Little Point Sable 555. Ludington S. P. (Lake Michigan & Hamlin Lake) 561. Nordhouse Dunes & Lake Michigan Rec. Area 563. Frankfort town beach 570. *In Sleeping Bear Nat. Lakeshore area:* Platte R. Point beach 573, Esch Rd. beach 573, Empire beach 573, Glen Haven beach 574, Good Harbor Bay beach 574, Good Harbor beach 574, Glen Lake beach 574, S. Manitou Island 576, North Manitou Island 577. *North Leelanau Co:* Suttons Bay town beach 586. Bay Front Park (Northport) 591. Leelanau S.P. Cathead Bay 593. Peterson Park 594. Leland town beach 595. *On Old Mission Peninsula:* Haserot Beach 608, Old Mission Point 608. *Near Charlevoix:* Fisherman's Island S.P. 612-3, Mt. McSauba 624, Lake Mich. Beach 626. *On Beaver Island:* West Side Beach 621, Bill Wagner Beach 622, public beach (south end of island) 622, Iron Ore Bay 622. *Near Petoskey:* Petoskey S.P. 641. *Near Harbor Springs:* Thorne Swift 652. *Near Cross Village:* Bliss Twp. Beach 658, Sturgeon Bay 657-8. *Near Mackinaw City:* Wilderness S. P. 657, town beach 658. *Near Rogers City:* town beach 679, Seagull Point Park 682. Presque Isle Co. Lighthouse Park 682. *Near Alpena:* Besser Bell Natural Area 687, Negwegon S.P. 691. **UPPER PENINSULA:** DeTour State Forest 710. Big Shoal Beach, Drummond Island 712. Kiwanis Beach, St. Ignace 715. U.S. 2 near Brevort 719. Lake Mich. campground beach, Huron N.F. 719. Beach below Cut R. bridge 719. *Near Naubinway:* Hog Island Point, Prinski Park, Scott's Point 719-20. *Manistique area:* Roger's Beach & Manistique Twp. Park 723, Mueller Twp. Park by Seul Choix Point 724. *Garden Peninsula:* Fayette S. P. 728,

Sports Park complex with luge 527, 539. **NORTH:** Hart-Montague Trail 552. Ludington S.P. 562. Sleeping Bear Nat. Lakeshore 573, 579. Leelanau Trail 584. Leelanau S. P. 593. Mt. McSauba 624. Ski rentals in Petoskey 640. Wilderness S. P. 658. Rogers City Vogler Nature Preserve 682. Hoeft S.P. 682. Alpena area 692. Hartwick Pines 696. **UPPER PENINSULA:** Sand Dunes Trails near Brevort 718. Tahquamenon S. P. 747. Seney Refuge 753, Pictured Rocks 762. *Marquette area:* Presque Isle Park 773. Little Presque Isle/Harlow Lake area 775. Near Suicide Hill 776. Argosy rafting on Menominee R. Iron Mountain 785. Porkies 797. *Near Wakefield:* Johnson's Nordic Trails 809. *Northern Keweenaw:* Cross-Country Sports rentals 827. Swedetown Trails 827. Fort Wilkins 843.

CHILDREN'S DESTINATIONS. *See also "science museums." Does not include nature centers, art museums, historical museums, farm destinations, book shops, etc. which usually have things to interest children.*
SW. *In St. Joseph:* Curious Kids' Museum 66-7. Once Upon a Time 67. Toy Company 67. Everybody's Everything 68. Lions Park 68. *In Dowagiac:* Southwestern Michigan College Museum 62. *In Kalamazoo:* Kalamazoo Valley Museum 90-1. *Gull Lake area:* Cheff Center 110. *Battle Creek:* Binder Park children's zoo 111. **M-M** *Irish Hills* miscellany: 138. *In Jackson:* Michigan Space & Science Center 144-5. Ella Sharp Museum 146. *In Ann Arbor:* AA Hands-On Museum 160, U-M Exhibit Museum 161, Generations children's store 151, Not Just for Kids entertainment 159. **MET:** Belle Isle Zoo 281, Detroit Historical

Museum National Toy Gallery 254, Cranbrook Institute of Science 319-20, Detroit Science Center & Omnimax Theater 250, Detroit Zoo 303-5, Edsel Ford play house & kids' events 302, Henry Ford Museum Innovation Station 347, Meadow Brook play house 325, Muriel's Doll House 331, Elizabeth Stone Gallery (children's book illustrations) 313. **SV:** *In Flint* Sloan Museum anatomy & reproductive health 362, science & discovery center 362-03, Crossroads Village Toy Barn 370, Penny Whistle Place 372. *In Frankenmuth* Bavarian Inn Doll & Toy Factory 382, Kite Kraft 386, Memory Lane Arcade 386. *In Saginaw* Children's Zoo 392. In Midland Dow Gardens playful spirit 401, Hall of Ideas 403, Chippewa Nature Center weekend programs 407. **MID:** *Lansing area* Michigan Historical Museum "Growing Up in Michigan" 426, Impressions 5 science museum 434, MSU animal barns 442, MSU 4-H Children's Garden 450. **WEST:** *In Grand Rapids* Public Museum streets, carousel, and environment dioramas 458-62, Children's Theater, John Ball Park 466, animal sculptures at Meijer Gardens & Sculpture Park 477-8. *In Holland* Dutch Village 499, 510-2, Sand Castle toy shop 505. *In Grand Haven* Mackinaw Kite Co. 518. *Muskegon area* Pleasure Island water park 525, Michigan Adventure water park & amusement park 526, Muskegon Co. Museum "Body Works" 536, Muskegon Winter Sports Park luge lessons 539-41. **NORTH:** Shelby Pavilion rollerskating 557. S.S. Badger carferry puppet theater, storytime 556-8. Empire beach playground 574. Discovery Gallery, Dennos Museum Center 608. Amon Orchard Petting Zoo 611. Beaver

Island Toy Museum & Store 619. Children's movie matinee, Petoskey 637. Mackinaw Kite 662. Ft. Mackinac children's tour & discovery room 669. Old Presque Isle Lighthouse hands-on museum 685. **UPPER PENINSULA:** Kitch-iti-kipi (Big Spring) 722. Children's Embassy for Peaceful Living 827. Storytime at North Winds Books 835.

ENGINEERING-RELATED SIGHTS
SW: Cook [Nuclear] Energy Information Center 29-30. **M-M:** Michigan Space & Science Center 144-5. U-M Integrated Tech. Instr. Center/"Media Union" 165. U-M Phoenix nuclear lab 166. Fermi 2 nuclear power plant 191-2. **MET:** Ford Rouge Complex 334, Henry Ford Museum power & steam exhibits 347, Greenfield Village Edison's Menlo Park Complex 353, Henry Ford's Fair Lane power plant 356. **SV:** *In Flint* G.M. Truck & Bus plant tour 368-9. *In Midland* H. H. Dow Museum 397-8. **MID:** *In Lansing* Michigan Museum of Surveying 436. **WEST:** *In Grand Rapids* Public Museum "Furniture City" with Corliss engine, section of factory with line shaft 458-62. **UPPER PENINSULA:** Tilden Mine tour 781. Cornish Pump & Mining Museum 788-9. Quincy Hoist & underground copper mine 817.

ETHNIC GROUPS & CULTURES. *Because so many peoples have immigrated to Michigan, it's possible to make a world tour right here.*

Detroit Institute of Arts (DIA): MET 246-51. Encyclopedic collection touches all major world cultures.
Elderly Instruments MET 437-9 has music and acoustic instruments from most of the world.

331. **SV:** *In Flint* Crossroads Village cider mill 372, Atlas Mill 371. *In Frankenmuth* Zeilinger Wool Co. 382, Star of the West Milling 385. *In Midland* maple sugar making at Chippewa Nature Center 407. **MID:** *Lansing area* Michigan Historical Museum 426, Potter Park Zoo farm animals 433, MSU animal barns 442, MSU dairy store 442. **NORTH:** Port Oneida 1940s rural landscape 572, Leelanau Cheese Co. cheesemaking 590. Kilcherman's Christmas Cove antique apples 594. Amon's Orchards tours & petting zoo 610. Bill's Farm Market 642. **UPPER PENINSULA.:** Hanka Homestead 1920 log farm 812-5. Palosaari's Rolling Acres farm B&B 816.

FISH AND HATCHERIES
SW: Michigan Fish Interpretive Center at Wolf Lake 77-8. **METRO:** Belle Isle Aquarium 283. **WEST:** Northwoods stream & Pacific Northwest habitat aquarium, John Ball Zoo 464. **NORTH:** Sport fishing origins in Northport 591-2. John Cross Fishery 626. Carlson's Fishery 595. Oden State Fish Hatchery 653. Gautheir & Spaulding Fishery 679-80. **UPPER PENINSULA.:** fishing history display at St. Ignace McDonald's 717. Thompson State Hatchery, Manistiquye 729. Pendills Creek National Fish Hatchery 739. Thill's Fish Market, Marquette 771.

FOLK ART/OUTSIDER ART.
Stores & exhibits.
SW: Judith Racht Gallery 12. Woodrose 92. **M-M:** Peaceable Kingdom 153. Selo-Shevel Gallery 152. **MET.** Polish Art Center 270. Dos Manos 308. Lotus Imports 308. Hill Gallery 312. **MID:** MSU Museum 440. W: Good Goods 489, The Ark 495-6, "Little Netherlands" at Windmill Island 501, Shaker

Messenger 505, The Bridge 505, Tikal 506, Tin Ceiling 506, Lewis Cross passenger pigeon painting 516. **NORTH:** Benzie Co. Museum folk art sawmill 570. Inter-Arts Studio 588. Tamarack Craftsman Gallery 589-90. Grand Traverse Lighthouse lawn ornaments 593. Tampico 596. Mercade Imports 647. Fort Michilimackinac museum shop 662. Maeve's, Island Scrimshander on Mackinac Island 676. Fort Mackinac museum shop 661. **UPPER PENINSULA:** Luce Co. Inter Tribal Center for the Arts 749.

FOLK ART/OUTSIDER ART ENVIRONMENTS
M-M: St. Joseph's Shrine 138. McCourtie Park 139. Slayton Arboretum 134. **MET:** Tyree Guyton's Heidelberg Project 274-7, Redford Italian Bakery 277. **NORTH:** Shrine of the Pines 564-5. Beaver Island Toy Museum & Store 619. Legs Inn 654-6. Dinosaur Gardens 691. **UPPER PENINSULA:** Indian Village 715. Curio Fair 717.

FRUIT
Fruit in general: **SW** 18, 39, 48-58, 75, 79. **N** 579, 604, 610-611
Apples: 18, 51, 549, 594.
Blueberries: 18, 48, 50, 75, 76.
Cherries: 48, 57-58, 549, 579, 580, 586, 600. 604, 607, 608, 611.
Grapes: SW 37-44, N 604-7.
Peaches: SW 18, 48-50.

FURNITURE
See also "historic interiors" and "antiques" and look under local museums.
MET: Cranbrook Museum of Art 317, Arkitektura 313, "Made in America" at Henry Ford Museum 345-50. **W:** 500, "Furniture City" at Public Museum 458-62, Good Goods 489, 3 Chairs 504.

GARDENS & GARDENING
includes noteworthy grounds of estates. See also "herbs."
Events calendar includes several garden shows.
SW: *Near Niles* Fernwood 32-36. *Berrien Springs* Green Wellies shop 45. *Kalamazoo* Flowerfest 82, bedding plant capital 82, Bartlett-Upjohn House & Garden 99. *Gull Lake area* Kellogg Biological Station Manor House 110. **M-M:** *In Allen* Green Top 132-3. *In Hillsdale* Hidden Lake Garden 135-7,Slayton Arboretum 134. **MET:** *In Detroit* Detroit Garden Center (Moross House) 209, Eastern Market Flower Day 241, Whitcomb Conservatory & Gardens 280, *In the Pointes:* Edsel Ford House 301. *Northern suburbs* Cranbrook House 319, Meadow Brook Hall 325-6, Meadow Brook Landscape & Garden Show 326. *Dearborn* various period farm and household gardens at Greenfield Village 351-5, Fair Lane 356-7. **SV:** Japanese gardens 389-90, Rust Park rose gardens 392, Dow Gardens 399-402. **MID:** Potter Park Zoo Center for Backyard Gardeners 433, Beal Botanical Gardens 445-7, Botany Teaching Greenhouses (desert, tropical, butterfly) 447, Old Horticultural Gardens 447, MSU Horticultural Demo. Gardens with annual trial gardens, perennial gardens, idea gardens, children's gardens 448-50, Lewis Landscape Arboretum 450. **WEST:** *In Grand Rapids* Meijer Gardens & Sculpture Park 477-8. *In Saugatuck* Saugatuck town common 487, Ralph's Garden shop 488-9.Button Gallery gardens 494. *In Holland* Veldheer Tulip Gardens 499, 502, Tulip Lane 509, Centennial Park 499, 507. **NORTH:** In Manitowoc, WI West of the Lake Gardens 560. Loda Lake Wildflower Sanctuary 567. Legs Inn 654-6 **U.P.:** Shula Giddens Mem. Gardens 711.

on Detroit historic architecture) 224, Guardian Bldg. 227, Buhl Bldg. 229, Penobscot Bldg. 229, Detroit Historical Society 255, Fisher Bldg. 257-9, Hitsville USA (Motown Museum) 261-2, Fisher Mansion 291-3, Grosse Pointe War Memorial (Alger house) 295-6, Grosse Pointe Public Library 297, E. & E. Ford House 300-2, Meadow Brook Hall 322-6, Greenfield Village 351-5, Fair Lane 356-7. **SV:** *In Flint* Crossroads Village 370-3. *In Frankenmuth* St. Lorenz Church & Log Cabin Cjurch 383. *In Midland* Alden Dow Studio 401, 403, 1870s log homestead at Chippewa Nature Center 407. **MID:** *Lansing* Michigan State Capitol 422-5. Michigan Historical Museum 426-8. **WEST:** *In Grand Rapids* 1970s Oval Office, Gerald Ford Museum 456, Public Museum recreation of museum c. 1880, furniture factory c. 1910, showroom c. 1920 page 462-5, T. Stewart White House 471, Sanford House 473, Voigt House 474, Meyer May House 467, Vioctorian Garden Parlor, Meijer Sculpture Gardens 478. In Rockford Rosie's Diner 480. *In Holland* Holland Museum 18th c. Dutch cottage sitting room 499, 501, Dutch Village 499, 510. *In Grand Haven* Tri-Cities Historical Museum 516. *In Muskegon* Hackley & Hume Houses 528-30, Hackley Public Library 535. **NORTH:** White Pine Village, Ludington 563. Gwen Frostic Studio 568-70. Shrine of the Pines 564-5. Legs Inn 654-6. Colonial Michilimackinac 659-61. Fort Mackinac 669-70. Market St. houses, shops & churches on Mackinac Island 670-3. **U.P.:** IXL Museum (office c. 1880) 783. Old Victoria Restoration 799. Hanka Homestead Finnish log farm 812-5. Laurium Manor 828. Lindell Chocolate Shop 829. Ft. Wilkins restored to 1870 841-3.

NOTEWORTHY HISTORIC NEIGHBORHOODS & CEMETERIES
For guided walking tours, see Preservation Wayne 256 and Detroit Historical Society 255. **SW:** *Dowagiac* 62, House of David 70, in Kalamazoo South St. 95-6, Vine Neighborhood 96, Stuart Ave. 99. **M-M:** Marshall 117-9, Riverside Cemetery (Albion) 124, Depot Town & vicinity (Ypsilanti) 184-5, Monroe's Loranger Sq. 190, old Monroe 192. **MET:** Elmwood Cemetery 212, "Streets of Detroit" in Detroit Historical Museum 254, Indian Village 290, Grosse Pointe 295-7. **SV:** *In Saginaw* Old Town 392. *In Bay City* Center St. 398. *In Midland* Alden Dow designs (1930s-60s) 402-3. **MID:** North Lansing/Old Town 428, 433, 439. **WEST:** *In Grand Rapids* "Streets of Grand Rapids" in Public Museum 460, Heritage Hill 470-6. *In Holland* Dutch Village 499, 510, Eighth St. 499, 504, 507-8, Twelfth St. 507-8, 498. *In Grand Haven* Highland Park 514, 520-1, Lake Forest Cemetery 514, 521. **NORTH:** St. Wenceslas Church, Leelanau 589. Boulder Park Earl Young homes 625-6. Bay View 638-40. Weque-tonsing 650, 644. Belvedere & Chicago clubs, Charlevoix 623, 624, 626. *On Mackinac Island:* East Bluff cottages 673. Market St. & Huron St. 671-3. *In Alpena* buildings of Besser con-crete block 688-9. **U.P.:** Ridge-Arch Historic District, Marquette 722.

INDUSTRIAL & LABOR HISTORY
SV: 358-9. *In Flint* Sloan Museum Flint Sit-Down Strike 360-2, Labor & Learning Center 363, Sit-Down Strike Monument 364. *In Harbor Beach* Frank Murphy birthplace 412. **MID:** In Lansing Michigan Historical Museum 427. **WEST:**

Muskegon 529. **U.P.** Fayette Townsite 725-6. Michigan Iron Industry Museum 777-9.

INDUSTRIAL TOURS & DEMONSTRATIONS
SW: Cook Energy Info. Center (nuclear power) 29, Pears Mill (1840s gristmill) 36, Simplicity Patterns 36. **M-M:** Fermi II (nuclear power) 191. **MET:** auto plant videos, real body drop at Detroit Historical Museum 252-6, Armington & Sims Machine Shop with steam engines at Greenfield Village 351-5. **SV:** GM Truck & Bus Assembly Plant 368-9, Crossroads Village gristmill & lumber mill 370-3, Dow Chemical tour 395-7. **WEST:** Grand Rapids Public Museum to have furituremak-ing demos on 1910 equipment 461. Hush Puppy factory tour 483. Windmill Island windmill grinds grain 501. Wooden shoemaking on vintage Dutch equipment 499. **NORTH:** Mill Creek 18th c. sawmill 663.

LIGHTHOUSES
SW: St. Joseph 68, South Haven 76. **MET:** Windmill Point 205, 296, Coast Guard Lighthouse Operations Center 212, Livingstone Memorial Light 281-2, Windmill Point Lighthouse 296. **SV:** Point aux Barques light 413, Port Sanilac light 413, Fort Gratiot light 415, 4167-7, Huron Lightship 417-8. **WEST:** Holland "Big Red" 509, Grand Haven South Pier Light 514, 517, White River Lighthouse & Museum 542-3. **NORTH:** Little Sable Point 555. Big Point Sable 561. Manning Mem. Light, Empire 574. Grand Traverse Lighthouse & Museum, Leelanau S. P. 593-4. South Manitou Island 576 St. James (Beaver Island) 620. Beaver Head Light 622. Waugoshance Point lights 656. Old Mackinac Point Lighthouse 662. Presque Isle County Lighthouse Park 682. Old Presque Isle Lighthouse & hands-on museum 684-6. New

Arbutus Bog Boardwalk 404, Chippewa Nature Center 405-7. **WEST:** *Grand Haven* Duncan Park 521, dune stair trail Gillette Visitor Center at Hoffmaster S. P. 422. **NORTH:** Skyline Loop, Ludington S.P. 562. Shrine of Pines 564. Loda Lake Wildflower Sanctuary 567. Empire Bluff Trail 572. Pierce Stocking Scenic Drive 572. More Sleeping Bear Trails 578. Walks with Leelanau Conservancy 603. Little Sand Bay Preserve, Beaver Island 621-2. Fischer & Thorne Swift Preserves in Harbor Springs 651-2. Mill Creek State Historic Park 663-4. Seagull Point 680-1. Hoeft S.P. 683. Besser Bell Natural Area 687. New Presque Isle Lighthouse Park 686. Alpena Sportsman's Island 690. Big Pines at Hartwick Pines 694. Mertz Grade Nature Trail 697. **UPPER PENINSULA:** Interpretive trail on 17th & 18th c. Straits environment 716. Chippewa Trail, Indian Lake S. P. (native foods) 723. Seul Choix Point 724. Ninga Aki Pathway (plants used in traditional Ojibwa life) Garden Peninsul1 728. Whitefish Point Bird Observatory trails 744. Upper Tahquamenon Falls 746. Tahquamenon R. Logging Museum & Nature Study Area, Newberry 748. Seney Refuge 753. *Pictured Rocks:* Grand Sable Dunes 757. White Birch Forest Trail 748. Pictured Rocks nature trail 762. *Near Marquette:* Mead-Wetmore Pond nature trail 769. Bog trail, Presque Isle 773. Woods Walk, Northwoods Supper Club 775. Michigan Iron Museum trails 779. Sturgeon R. Slough Natural Area (Chassell) 816. Brockway Mt. & Klipfel nature sanctuaries 838-9. Isle Royale 849.

NATURE CENTERS. *A nature center has a building with interpretive exhibits and interpretive trails. Often there's a book-* *store/nature store too.* **SW:** Fernwood 32-6. Love Creek Co. Park 45, Sarett 71, Kellogg Bird Sanctuary 107-10. **M-M:** Hidden Lake Gardens 134. **MET:** Belle Isle 281. **SV:** Harley Outdoor Ed. Center 393. Chippewa Nature Center 405. **WEST:** Grand Rapids Public Museum Habitat exhibits 460, Gillette Visitor Center (sand dunes) 522. **NORTH:** Great Lakes Visitor Center, Ludington S. P. 562. Sleeping Bear Visitor Center 571-2.Thorne Swift Nature Preserve 652. Mackinac Island Butterfly House 671-2. Britisn Landing nature Center, Mackinac Island 675. **UPPER PENINSULA:** Whitefish Point Bird Observatory 743-4. Seney Refuge Visitor Center 752. Porcupine Mountains S.P. Visitor Center 793-4.

PLANETARIUMS
SW: Kalamazoo Valley Museum 91. **M-M:** University of Michigan Exhibit Museum 162. **MET:** Cranbrook 315-20. **SV:** Longway Planetarium, Flint 367. **MID:** Abrams Planetarium, East Lansing 441.**WEST:** Chaffee Planetarium, Grand Rapids 451. **NORTH:** Sky Theater, Alpena 690.

RAILROADING & AMTRAK
See also local historical museums.
Amtrak 101-4 (focuses on Detroit to Chicago route) **SW:** New Buffalo Railroad Museum 18, Niles depot 35, **SV:** Huckleberry RR 370. **WEST:** Grand Haven steam locomotive & coaling tower 515, Tri-Cities Historical Museum 516. **NORTH:** 546, 550, 570, 630, 631, 6455, 673. **UPPER PENINSULA:** Wheels of History Museum, Brimley 737.

ROCKHOUNDS
See also "Geology."
NORTH: Shelby Gemstones

551. Nature's Gifts 585. Nature Gems 592. Leelanau S. P. 593. Becky Thatcher Designs 601. Fisherman's Island S. P. 612, 624. Petoskey S. P. 641. Limestone & fossils in north-eastern Michigan 683, 684. **UPPER PENINSULA:** Fossils in Les Cheneaux/St. Ignace area 712. Agate beach, Grand Marais 757. Mineral exhibit at Quincy Hoist 818. Seaman Mineral Museum 820. Copper Harbor agate beach 840. Keweenaw Agate Shop 844.

SPECIALTY SHOPPING AND FOOD SHOPPING
See also: "antiques," "galleries", "books" and individual art museums, history museums, and nature centers.
SW: Harbor Country 12-7, St. Joseph 65-8, Kalamazoo 90-3. **M-M:** Marshall 120-2.. Ann Arbor 146-58, 170-4 (books), 176-7 (records). **MET:** Detroit 215, 216-9, 221-3, 236-41, 259. Hamtramck 269-72. Grosse Pointes 297-8. Royal Oak 306-310. Somerset Collection 321. Jewish bakeries & more 329. Plymouth & Northville 330-3. Arab Dearborn 341-4. **SV:** Frankenmuth 379-82, 385-6. Outlets at Birch Run 387. Bay City 398. **MID:** East Lansing & Williamston 442-3. **WEST:** Grand Rapids Eastown 454, 476. Rockford 482. Saugatuck 487-94. Holland 503-7, 511-2. Grand Haven 518. **NORTH:** Suttons Bay 587-8. Omena & Northport 589-92. Leland 595-7. Glen Arbor 599-601. Charlevoix 626-7. Petoskey 633-7. Harbor Springs 646-8. Mackinaw City 662. Mackinac Island 676-78. **UPPER PENINSULA:** Marquette 769-71. Ironwood 810. Houghton 819-21. Copper Harbor 844-5.

THEATER, COMEDY & DRAMA
Again, this list is by no means comprehensive. Consult local publications for more.